The Geometry of Multiple Images

The Geometry of Multiple Images

The Laws That Govern the Formation of Multiple Images of a Scene and Some of Their Applications

Olivier Faugeras

Quang-Tuan Luong

with contributions from

Théo Papadopoulo

The MIT Press
Cambridge, Massachusetts
London, England

Library of Congress Cataloging-in-Publication Data

Faugeras, Olivier, 1949- .
  The geometry of multiple images : the laws that govern the formation
  of multiple images of a scene and some of their applications /
  Olivier Faugeras, Quang-Tuan Luong ; with contributions from
  T. Papadopoulo.
    p. cm.
  Includes bibliographical references and index.
  ISBN 0-262-06220-8 (he. : alk. paper)
  1. Image processing-Digital techniques. 2. Geometry. 3. Computer
vision. I. Luong, Quang-Tuan. II. Papadopoulo, T. III. Title.

TA1637 .F39 2001
621.36'7-dc21   00-048970

Contents

Preface

This book is about mathematics and vision. Researchers and practitioners of machine and biological vision have been working hard over the last forty years or so to understand the laws of image formation, processing and understanding by machines, animals and humans. Although it is clear that this research agenda is far from having been completed, we think that the time has come to provide a more or less complete description of the state of knowledge in one of the subareas of vision, namely the description of the geometric laws that relate different views of a scene.

There are two reasons that makes us believe this; one is theoretical and the other application-motivated. The first reason is that geometry is one of the oldest and most developed parts of mathematics and is at the heart of the process of image formation, object modeling and recognition. Therefore it should not come as a surprise if we state that the framework for studying geometric problems in vision is available and ready for use. The second reason is that in our era of forceful communications through computers, images play a prominent role and will continue to do so in the foreseeable future. There is clearly a need to provide the community of producers and users of images, and in particular of images with a three-dimensional content, with a framework in which their problems can be clearly stated and, one hopes, solved.

This book is thus mostly about geometry because geometry is the natural language to describe 3D shapes and spatial relations. A camera can be thought of as a particular geometric engine, which constructs planar images of the three-dimensional world, through a projection. Although the ancient Greeks already knew several properties of projection, among them the conservation of the cross-ratio, the geometry of the image formation process was first understood by Renaissance painters (see figure 4.1) who made large use of vanishing points and derived geometric constructions for their practical use. At the time photography was discovered, people studied how to make measurements from perspective views of scenes, and this led to photogrammetry, which has had a wide range of successful applications. During the same century, mathematicians developed *projective geometry*, which was intended to deal with points at infinity and perspective projections. It is the reference framework which will be used all the way through this book, because it deals elegantly with the types of projections that most cameras perform.

Although the natural geometry which we use in most applications is the Euclidean geometry, one of the tenets of this book is that it is simpler and more efficient for vision to consider the Euclidean and affine geometries as special cases of the projective geometry. It is simpler because projective geometry is the geometry of image formation and provides a unified framework for thinking about all geometric problems that are relevant to vision. It is more efficient because the unified framework reduces the need for dealing with special cases and, more importantly, helps the designer of machine vision applications to clearly identify the type of geometric information that is relevant to her/his particular application, e.g. projective, affine or Euclidean, and therefore the type of processing that needs to be applied to the data in order to recover this information from the images. In this sense we are followers of Felix Klein and Herman Weyl, who stated in their Erlangen program of 1872 that the only important geometric properties are those which are invariant to the action of some group of transformations and conversely that every quantity that is invariant to the action of such a group must have an "interesting" geometric interpretation.

Chapter 1 is an introductory chapter which serves to present in a simple way, without much formalization, several of the main ideas of the book.

In order to achieve our goal of enumerating the geometric laws that govern the formation of the images of a scene we have first to collect the relevant mathematical tools. Since those are scattered through the mathematical literature the book has two chapters that develop the geometric and algebraic background that will be needed in the remaining. These chapters might be considered as reference material, and therefore skipped in a first reading. Chapter 2 is an exposition of projective, affine and Euclidean geometry from the Erlangen program viewpoint; that is to say the affine and Euclidean geometries are presented as special cases of the projective geometry. We will find this approach invaluable in almost all the other chapters of the book. The next chapter exposes a complementary viewpoint: whereas chapter 2 is basically geometric, this chapter is mostly algebraic and introduces the Grassman-Cayley algebra of a vector space. The reason this is relevant to vision is that this algebra is to geometry what the Boolean algebra is to logic: it is a tool for computing unions and intersections of linear geometric subspaces. As such it will provide us with another indispensable device for representing and computing with the geometry of multiple cameras or views.

Having laid this groundwork, we can start applying these ideas to systems of cameras. Chapter 4 is about the simplest of all such systems, one that has only one camera! But besides its pedagogical interest it serves as a testbed for our paradigm: starting from the observation that a camera is a projective engine, we provide a projective description of this engine. This description allows us to speak only about such projective invariant properties as the intersections of planes and lines or projective invariant quantities such as cross-ratios. If we then start wondering about affine invariant properties such as parallelism or certain ratios of lengths, the affine framework enters naturally through the plane at infinity. Finally, if we start pondering about Euclidean invariant properties such as angles and distances, the Euclidean framework becomes a natural thing to use. The power of our stratified approach is that you do not need to throw away everything that you have done so far to work your way through the computation of projective and affine properties; on the contrary, just add a little bit of information, i.e. the image of the absolute conic, and the miracle happens – you can now do Euclidean geometry with your camera.

Having described the simplest of all situations, we next turn in chapter 5 toward a (stratified) study of the systems of two cameras. The key concept in these systems is that of epipolar geometry which is used in all projects dealing with binocular stereo. We show that the epipolar geometry is a projective concept and that it can be described geometrically and algebraically quite simply and efficiently in that framework. No notions of affine or Euclidean geometry are necessary. From the algebraic viewpoint, a single 3×3 matrix, called the Fundamental matrix, summarizes everything you need to know about the epipolar geometry. Keeping in mind that some applications will require more knowledge than just projective, we also analyze how affine and Euclidean information is buried into the Fundamental matrix preparing the ground for their recovery in future chapters.

Because of its conceptual and practical importance chapter 6 is devoted to the methods that allow us to recover the Fundamental matrix from pairs of point correspondences between the views. This will confront us with the problem of parametrizing this matrix in a way that allows practical estimation techniques to be used while guaranteeing that the result of the estimation satisfies the constraint that all Fundamental matrixes must satisfy. It will also take us through the very important issues of deciding which pairs of correspondences are valid pairs and which should be considered as outliers and of characterizing the uncertainty of the estimated matrix, information that is quite important in applications.

Chapter 7 builds on the previous three chapters and achieves two main goals. It first spells out in detail the three levels of representation of the geometry of two views, projective, affine, and Euclidean, together with the amount of information that needs to be recovered either from the images themselves or from some external demon in order to reach a given level. In particular we introduce the idea of the canonical representation of a set of two cameras. The representation is attached to a given level and compactly represents all you have to know about the two cameras in order to analyze the geometry of the scene. Second, it describes a number of interesting vision tasks that can be achieved at each of the three levels of description.

In chapter 8 we address the problem of three views. Just like in the case of two views where the major concept was that of epipolar geometry and the corresponding Fundamental matrix, the relevant idea in the case of three views is that of trifocal geometry and the corresponding Trifocal tensors. We show that these tensors contain all the information about the geometry of three views. The Grassman-Cayley algebra is really useful here in providing simple and elegant descriptions of the relevant geometry and algebra. Of special importance for the next chapter is the analysis of the constraints that are satisfied by the coefficients of these tensors: they will play a prominent role in the estimation methods that will be presented. The Trifocal tensors are, like the Fundamental matrixes, purely projective entities but also contain affine and Euclidean information. The affine and Euclidean forms of the tensors are presented at the end of the chapter.

If estimating the Fundamental matrix of a pair of views is important it is no surprise that estimating the Trifocal tensors is vital in the case of three views. Chapter 9 is dedicated to this problem, which we solve in pretty much the same way as we solved the corresponding problem for the Fundamental matrix. The complexity is higher for several reasons. First we must use triples of correspondences rather than pairs, and second the constraints that must be satisfied by the coefficients of the Tensors are significantly more complicated than the one satisfied by those of the Fundamental matrixes. These algebraic constraints described in chapter 8 are used to parametrize the tensors so as to guarantee that the results of the estimation procedures will indeed be valid Trifocal tensors.

We went from the analysis of one view to two views, then to three views; is there an end to this? Surprisingly enough, and to the reader's relief, the answer to this question is yes. There are such things as Quadrifocal tensors and so on that describe the correspondences between four views but they are all algebraically dependent upon the Trifocal tensors and the Fundamental matrixes of the sub-triples and sub-pairs of views of the four views. Chapter 10 is therefore a brave leap into the world of N-views geometry for N arbitrary and greater than three. Because of this, the best way to represent the geometry of N cameras is through their projection matrices and the notion of the canonical representation of such matrices introduced in chapter 7 becomes even more useful. As usual we consider three such representations, one for each of the three levels of description. We spend quite some time describing various methods for computing the projective canonical representation from the Fundamental matrixes or the Trifocal tensors because this is the basic representation we start from even in the cases where affine and Euclidean descriptions are required. We indicate how it can be refined by Bundle Adjustment, a technique borrowed from photogrammeters and adapted to the projective framework.

Chapter 11 begins with the theoretical analysis of a very practical problem, that of recovering the Euclidean structure of the environment from a pair of views. In general this is achieved by adding to the environment a calibration object, i.e. an object with known Euclidean properties. This is very cumbersome if not impossible for many applications thereby motivating our interest in a solution that does not require this addition. It turns out that the connection between projective, affine and Euclidean geometry offers a natural set of solutions to the initial problem through the use of the images of the plane at infinity and the absolute conic. We call these techniques "self-calibration" since they do not require the use of any calibration objects other than the previous two mathematical entities. We conclude with examples of applications to the construction of 3D Euclidean models from an arbitrary number of uncalibrated views and to the insertion of synthetic 3D objects in image sequences, video or film.

Most chapters end with two sections, one that summarizes and discusses the main results in the chapter and another that provides more references and some further reading.

A comment on the style of this book. We have deliberately adopted the style of a book in mathematics with definitions, lemmas, propositions and theorems at the risk of losing the interest of some readers. We have also provided most of the proofs or given pointers to references where these proofs could be found. The reason is that we believe that vision has to establish itself as a science and that it will not do so if it does not ground itself in mathematics. A theorem is a theorem and an algorithm that makes use of it may or may not work. But if it does not work the cause will not have to be searched for in the theorem but elsewhere, thereby making the task of the designer of the algorithm, if not easier, at least better defined.

Of course we do not claim that our book solves the vision problem, if such a thing exists. We are very much aware of the fact that vision is much richer and intricate than geometry and that this book covers only a very small part of the material relevant to the field. Nonetheless we believe that our book offers the reader a number of conceptual tools and a number of theoretical results that are likely to find their way into many machine vision algorithms.

Acknowledgments   This book took seven years to write while the authors were working in different places in Europe (INRIA Sophia-Antipolis) and the US (MIT, Berkeley and SRI). During the course of the writing, Olivier Faugeras has benefited from many stimulating discussions with colleagues, collaborators and students at INRIA and MIT, in particular Didier Bondyfalat, Sylvain Bougnoux, Gabriela Csurka, Rachid Deriche, Frédéric Devernay, Eric Grimson, Radu Horaud, Stéphane Laveau, Liana Lorigo, Leonard Mcmillan, Eric Miller, Roger Mohr, Bernard Mourrain, Luc Robert, Seth Teller, Thierry Viéville, Cyril Zeller, Zhengyou Zhang and Imad Zoghlami. Special thanks go to Liana Lorigo and Eric Miller for their careful proof reading of the final manuscript. He is also very grateful to Luc Robert and Imad Zoghlami for taking a brave leap into the thriving world of industry and turning many of the ideas contained in this book into products. Thanks also to Dominique Pouliquen for telling them how to sell these products.

Last but not least he is extremely grateful to his wife, Agnès, and their sons Blaise, Clément, Cyrille and Quentin for their love, patience and support.

Quang-Tuan Luong wrote a first draft of what was to become eventually this book while he was a visiting scientist at the University of California at Berkeley. He would like to acknowledge the support and guidance he received from Jitendra Malik during that time. Discussions with David Forsyth, and the initial proof-reading of Joe Weber were also much appreciated. While colleagues at SRI International were all supportive, Marty Fischler deserves special thanks for showing constant interest for this work, and suggesting several clarifications which made the material more accessible. Carlo Tomasi gave Quang-Tuan Luong the opportunity to teach the material at Stanford. Frank Dellaert provided detailed comments on the introductory chapter.

He would like to extend thanks to old and new members of the Robotvis group, who were as welcoming and helpful during his short stays at INRIA, as when he was a graduate student there. His last thought goes to his parents, who encouraged him to become a scientist, and provided great love and support. In particular, he would like to dedicate this book to his mother Luong Ngoc Thu who inquired about the progress almost weekly, and to his father Luong The Vinh, who would have been pleased with the completion of this work.

The authors have also enjoyed interacting over the years with such colleagues as Richard Hartley, Amnon Shashua, Gunnar Sparr and Andrew Zisserman.

The final word of thanks is for Bernhard Geiger who drew the pictures that come before each chapter and tell us the adventures of Euclide in the world of Computer Vision.

Notation

Unless otherwise stated, vectors, matrices and tensors are represented in boldface. We use the following notations (the page numbers refer to the first appearance of the symbol in the text):

Sets

$\complement X$:   the complement of the set X.

$X \backslash Y$:   the set $X \cap \complement Y$, where X is a set and Y a subset of X.

$\emptyset$:   the empty set.

Σ_n: the set of permutations of the set of integers $\{1, \cdots, n\}$ (page 129).

$\varepsilon(\sigma)$:   the signature, equal to ± 1, of the permutation σ (page 129).

Vector spaces

E: a vector space defined on a field $\mathbb{K}$ ($\mathbb{K} = \mathbb{R}$, the set of real numbers or $\mathbb{K} = \mathbb{C}$, the set of complex numbers). E_n indicates that E_n is a vector space of dimension n.

$E^{\mathbb{C}}$:   the complexified vector space of the real vector space E (page 76).

$(\varepsilon_1, \cdots, \varepsilon_n)$:   the canonical basis of $\mathbb{K}^n$.
$\varepsilon_1 = [1, 0, \cdots, 0]^T, \ldots, \varepsilon_n = [0, \cdots, 0, 1]^T$.

$span(F)$:   the vector space generated by the subset F of the vector space E.

$\mathcal{L}(E; E')$:   the set of linear mappings from the vector space E in the vector space E'.

$\mathcal{IL}(E; E')$:   the set of invertible linear transforms from E to E', when $dim(E) = dim(E')$.

$\mathcal{LG}(E)$:   the group of linear invertible transformations from E into E (same as $\mathcal{IL}(E; E)$).

$\mathcal{OG}(E)$:   the group of the similarities, a subgroup of $\mathcal{LG}(E)$ (page 75).

$\mathcal{O}(E)$:   the orthogonal subgroup of $\mathcal{LG}(E)$ (page 74).

$\|\mathbf{x}\|$:   the norm of the vector $\mathbf{x}$ of an Euclidean vector space (page 74).

E^*:   the dual of the vector space E, i.e. the set $\mathcal{L}(E; K)$ of linear forms of E.

$H(E)$:   the set of hyperplanes of E. If E is of dimension $n > 1$, it is the set of vector subspaces of dimension $n - 1$.

$\mathbf{I}_n$:   the $n \times n$ identity matrix.

$\mathbf{A}^*$:   the adjoint matrix of the $n \times n$ matrix $\mathbf{A}$. It is the transpose of the cofactor matrix $cof\,\mathbf{A}$ of $\mathbf{A}$ whose (i, j)th entry is $(-1)^{i+j}det(\mathbf{A})_{ij})$, where $det(\mathbf{A})_{ij}) =$ determinant of the $(n-1) \times (n-1)$ matrix obtained by deleting the ith row and the jth column from $\mathbf{A}$:

$$\mathbf{A}^* = (cof\,\mathbf{A})^T.$$

The adjoint matrix satisfies the following relation:

$$\mathbf{A}^*\mathbf{A} = det(\mathbf{A})\mathbf{I}_n.$$

When $\mathbf{A}$ is invertible, this is equivalent to:

$$\mathbf{A}^* = det(\mathbf{A})\mathbf{A}^{-1}.$$

Affine spaces

X: an affine space, its associated vector space is noted $\overrightarrow{X}$.

$\mathcal{A}(X;X')$: the set of affine morphisms from the affine space X to the affine space X' (page 71).

$\overrightarrow{f}$: the element of $\mathcal{L}(\overrightarrow{X};\overrightarrow{X'})$ corresponding to an element f of $\mathcal{A}(X;X')$.

$\mathcal{AG}(X)$: the affine group of X, i.e. the set of invertible affine morphisms from X into itself (page 71).

$\mathcal{S}(X)$: the group of affine similarities, a subgroup of $\mathcal{AG}(X)$ (page 75).

$\mathcal{E}(X)$: the group of affine rigid displacements, a subgroup of $\mathcal{AG}(X)$ and of $\mathcal{S}(X)$ (page 75).

$\mathcal{B}$: an affine basis (page 70).

$\mathbf{m}_{/\mathcal{B}}$: the vector of affine coordinates of the point m in the affine basis $\mathcal{B}$.

$\mathbf{Q}_{\mathcal{B}}^{\mathcal{B}'}$: the matrix defining the change of coordinates between the affine basis $\mathcal{B}$ and the affine basis $\mathcal{B}'$ (page 72).

Projective spaces

$P(E)$: the projective space associated to the vector space E (page 78).

$\mathbb{P}^n$: $P(E_{n+1})$, the n-dimensional projective space attached to E_{n+1} (page 78).

$\langle S \rangle$: the smallest projective subspace of $P(E)$ containing the subset S or the projective subspace of $P(E)$ generated by S (page 89).

$\mathcal{M}(P(E);P(E'))$: the set of projective morphisms from the projective space $P(E)$ to the projective space $P(E')$ (page 83).

$\overrightarrow{f}$: the element of $\mathcal{L}(E;E')$ corresponding to an element f of $\mathcal{M}(P(E);P(E'))$.

$\mathcal{C}(P(E);P(E'))$: the set of invertible projective morphisms from the projective space $P(E)$ to the projective space $P(E')$ of same dimension (page 83).

$\mathcal{PLG}(E)$:   the group $\mathcal{C}(P(E); P(E))$ (page 86).

$H(P(E))$:   the set of hyperplanes of $P(E)$.

$\tilde{X}$:   the projective completion of the affine space X.

∞_X: the hyperplane at infinity of the affine space X (page 93).

$\mathcal{B}$:   a projective basis (page 80).

$\mathbf{m}_{/\mathcal{B}}$:   a coordinate vector of the point m in the projective basis $\mathcal{B}$.

$\mathbf{Q}_{\mathcal{B}}^{\mathcal{B}'}$:   the matrix defining the change of coordinates between the projective basis $\mathcal{B}$ and the projective basis $\mathcal{B}'$ (page 87).

$\{a, b; c, d\}$:   the cross-ratio of the four points a, b, c and d of a projective line (page 101).

$\mathbb{P}^{n*}$:   the dual of $\mathbb{P}^n$ (page 106).

$\mathcal{Q}$:   the matrix of a quadric (page 112).

Ω: the absolute conic (page 117).

Grassmann-Cayley algebra

$| \mathbf{x}_1, \cdots, \mathbf{x}_n |$:   the determinant of the n vectors $\mathbf{x}_1, \ldots, \mathbf{x}_n$ of E_n (page 129).

∇:   the join operator (page 129).

$G_k(E)$:   the vector space generated by all the extensors of step k (page 131).

$G(E)$:   the direct sum $G_0(E) \oplus G_1(E) \oplus \cdots \oplus G_n(E)$ (page 132).

$[\mathbf{L} \mid \mathbf{L}']$:   the Plücker product of the two lines L and L' (page 139).

$\triangle$:   the meet operator (page 142).

$\mathbf{I}$:   the integral (page 155).

$\langle \mathbf{y}, \mathbf{x} \rangle$:   the cap-product of the vector x and the covector y (page 148).

$\mathbf{a}(S)$:   the extensor $\mathbf{a}_{i_1} \nabla \cdots \nabla \mathbf{a}_{i_k}$ of $G_k(E_n)$ where S is the ordered set $i_1, \cdots, i_k$ of k elements of $\{1, \cdots, n\}$ (page 150).

$\boldsymbol{\eta}(S)$:   the cobasis associated to $\mathbf{a}(S)$ (page 150).

$*$:   the Hodge star operator (page 155).

$[\mathbf{x}]_\times$:   the matrix representation of the cross-product with the vector $\mathbf{x}$ of E_3 (page 9).

$\langle \mathbf{C}, \mathbf{C}' \rangle_\times$:   the cross-product operator defined by two points of $\mathbb{P}^3$ (page 164).

One camera

$\mathcal{P}$:   a 3×4 perspective projection matrix.

U, V, W: the three row vectors of the perspective projection matrix $\mathcal{P}$.

$\mathcal{R}$:   the retinal plane of a camera (page 178)

C: the optical center of a camera (page 180).

$\tilde{\mathcal{P}}$:   the 3×6 perspective projection matrix for lines (page 194).

$\mathcal{P}^+$:   an inverse perspective projection matrix (page 185).

$\mathcal{P}_\Pi^+$:   the inverse perspective projection matrix associated with the plane Π (page 186).

ω: the image of the absolute conic Ω (page 211).

ω^*:   the conic dual to ω (page 215).

$\mathbf{A}$:   the 3×3 matrix of the intrinsic parameters (page 209).

$\mathbf{K}$:   the Kruppa matrix proportional to $\mathbf{A}\mathbf{A}^T$ (page 215).

Two cameras

$\mathbf{F}$:   the Fundamental matrix or F-matrix of two views (page 261).

$\mathbf{E}$:   the Essential matrix or E-matrix of two views (page 282).

$\mathbf{e}, \mathbf{e}'$:   the two epipoles (page 260).

$\mathbf{S}$:   the special matrix or S-matrix of two views (page 275).

H_∞:   the morphism induced by the plane at infinity between two retinal planes (page 381).

Three cameras and more

$\mathcal{T}$:   a Trifocal tensor of three views (page 420).

$\mathbf{G}^n$:   the nth Trifocal matrix of a Trifocal tensor (page 420).

$\mathcal{R}^n$:   a vector in the right nullspace of matrix $\mathbf{G}^n$ (page 429).

$\mathcal{L}^n$:   a vector in the left nullspace of matrix $\mathbf{G}^n$ (page 430).

Uncertainty

$E(\mathbf{y})$:   the expected value of the random vector $\mathbf{y}$ (page 341).

$\Lambda_{\mathbf{y}}$:   the covariance matrix of the random vector $\mathbf{y}$ (page 341).

1 A tour into multiple image geometry

This Chapter provides a conceptual overview of the book by introducing in a simple and intuitive way some of its main ideas.

1.1   Multiple image geometry and three-dimensional vision

The purpose of vision is to infer descriptions of the world from images. We will concentrate on a limited but crucial type of description, that of geometry in space, and will investigate how it can be recovered using only geometric constraints and excluding semantic ones. As it will be explained soon, based on geometry alone, it is not possible to infer the 3-D positions of points in a scene from a single image of this scene. As humans, we rely on our semantic knowledge of the world to perform such an inference, but this capability can be easily fooled, as illustrated in Figure 1.1.

The central problem which we wish to address is therefore concerned with multiple images: given two (or more) images of a scene, a partially instantiated camera model, and points in these images which correspond to the same point in the world, construct a description of the 3-D spatial relations between the points in the world. In addition, one would like to complete the instantiation of the camera models and describe the 3-D spatial relations between the cameras which were used to create the images. Indeed, from the difference in position of image points, it is possible to infer spatial relations by taking advantage of the geometric rules which govern the formation of images. The theoretical focus of the book is on the rigorous exposition of these rules, using geometric and algebraic tools. Unlike standard texts on projective geometry, we concentrate on the relation between 3-D space and 2-D space, between points and their projection.

To give the reader an idea of the applications that we have in mind, we give two examples. Throughout this Chapter, we will pause to see which progress we will have made towards being able to process them. In the first example, we are handed ten images of a scene taken by an unknown and possibly zooming camera, three of which are shown in Figure 1.2 (the others are in Figure 10.8). Our goal is to be able to make accurate length measurements in space. From these images, we construct a 3-D geometric model of the buildings and illustrate the correctness of the recovered geometry by showing two rotated views of the reconstruction in Figure 1.3. The model can be used to generate a synthetic view, obtained from a higher viewpoint than the original images, as shown in Figure 1.4 (see also Figure 1.26). Figure 1.5 illustrate that the cameras positions and orientations can also be estimated as part of the reconstruction process.

The second example demonstrates the capacity of the techniques described in this book to deal with continuous streams of images for applications to augmented reality. The sequence (from which images in Figure 1.6 are extracted) is taken with an unknown camera from a helicopter flying over a site where a power plant is to

Figure 1.1: A few examples illustrating the difficulty, even for humans, of inferring the geometry of a scene from a single image. Viewers tend to assume that the angles formed by the grey card are right angles (top left). A bird's eye view (top right) reveals that only one of the four angles is a right angle. Relative size judgment can be easily misled by particular spatial configurations which defeat common assumptions (middle and bottom images).

Figure 1.2: A few images of the Arcades square in Valbonne, taken with a digital camera. Courtesy **Sylvain Bougnoux**, INRIA.

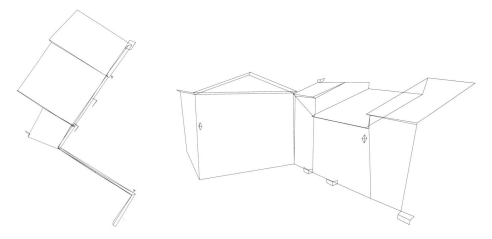

Figure 1.3: Top and front view of the reconstruction of the Arcades square in Valbonne, illustrating the metric correctness of the recovered 3-D model. Courtesy **Sylvain Bougnoux**, INRIA.

be constructed. We wish to add to the scene an artificial object, consisting of a model of the new power plant shown in Figure 1.7 while respecting the geometry of the scene and the movements of the camera. We show in Figure 1.8 three images of the modified sequence. It can be verified that the synthetic objects appear, as they should, to be static with respect to the environment.

1.2   Projective geometry [Chapters 2 and 3]

Euclidean geometry describes our world well: the measurements we make in terms of lengths, angles, parallelism, and orthogonality are meaningful because they are preserved by a change of coordinates which is a *displacement* (rotation and translation), a *Euclidean transformation*. Because of that, Euclidean geometry has also

Figure 1.4: Textured view of the reconstruction, illustrating that synthetic images can be generated from a novel viewpoint. Courtesy **Sylvain Bougnoux**, INRIA.

traditionally been used by vision scientists to describe the geometry of projection.

However, we believe that for the purpose of describing projections, projective geometry is a more adequate framework. As illustrated by Figure 1.2, the railroad tracks are parallel lines in 3-D space, but in the image they are no longer parallel, and appear to converge as they recede towards the horizon, towards a *vanishing point*. Any set of parallel, horizontal lines, whether they lie on the ground or not, appears to meet at a single point on the horizon line. In addition, all the points at infinity in 3-D have the same projection as the observer moves. The rails always seem to disappear at the same point, and as you move in the night, the moon and stars seem to follow you. Since parallelism is not preserved by projection, clearly neither are distances nor angles. Projective geometry is an extension of Euclidean geometry, which describes a larger class of transformations than just rotations and translations, including in particular the perspective projection performed by a camera. It makes it possible to describe naturally the phenomena at infinity that we just noticed. Between projective geometry and Euclidean geometry there are two other geometries, similarity[1] and affine, as illustrated in Table 1.2 (See also Table 1.4).

Let's start with a point of Euclidean[2] coordinates $[u, v]^T$ in the plane. Its projective coordinates are obtained by just adding 1 at the end: $[u, v, 1]^T$. Having now three coordinates, in order to obtain a "one-to-one" correspondence between

---

[1]The only difference between displacements and similarities is that the latter ones allow for a global scale factor. Since in the context of reconstruction from images, such an ambiguity is always present, we will designate by abuse of language *Euclidean.* transformations the similarity transformations.

[2]Technically speaking, the term "affine" would be more appropriate, but in the context of this section we use by abuse of language the more familiar term "Euclidean". See Chapter 2 for an explanation.

Figure 1.5: Another textured view of the reconstruction, showing also the estimated positions and orientations of some of the cameras: Courtesy **Sylvain Bougnoux**, INRIA.

Euclidean coordinates and projective coordinates, we have the rule that scaling by a nonzero factor is not significant, so that the two triples of coordinates $[u, v, 1]^T$ and $[\lambda u, \lambda v, \lambda]^T$ represent the same point.

More generally, the space of $(n + 1)$-tuples of coordinates, with the rule that proportional $(n + 1)$-tuples represent the same point, is called the *projective space* of dimension n and denoted $\mathbb{P}^n$. The object space will be considered as $\mathbb{P}^3$ and the image space as $\mathbb{P}^2$, called the *projective plane*. We will see in Section 1.3 that projective coordinates represent naturally the operation performed by a camera. Given coordinates in $\mathbb{R}^n$ we can build projective coordinates by the correspondence

$$[x_1, \ldots, x_n]^T \rightarrow [x_1, \ldots, x_n, 1]^T.$$

To transform a point in the projective coordinates back into Euclidean coordinates, we just divide by the last coordinate and then drop it:

$$[x_1, \ldots, x_n, x_{n+1}]^T \rightarrow [\frac{x_1}{x_{n+1}}, \ldots, \frac{x_n}{x_{n+1}}]^T.$$

We see that the projective space contains more points than the Euclidean space. Points with coordinates $[x_1, \ldots, x_n, x_{n+1}]^T$ with $x_{n+1} \neq 0$ can be viewed as the usual points, whereas the points with coordinates $[x_1, \ldots, x_n, 0]^T$ have no Euclidean equivalent. If we consider them as the limit of $[x_1, \ldots, x_n, \lambda]^T$, when $\lambda \rightarrow 0$ i.e. the limit of $[x_1/\lambda, \ldots, x_n/\lambda, 1]^T$, then we see that they are the limit of a point of $\mathbb{R}^n$ going to infinity in the direction $[x_1, \ldots, x_n]^T$, hence the appellation *point at infinity*. The projective space $\mathbb{P}^n$ can be viewed as the union of the usual space $\mathbb{R}^n$ (points $[x_1, \ldots, x_n, 1]^T$) and the set of points at infinity $[x_1, \ldots, x_n, 0]^T$. The neat thing about this formalism is that points at infinity are not special and are treated just like any other point.

Figure 1.6: Three images of a sequence taken from a helicopter: Courtesy **Luc Robert**, INRIA.

Let's go back to the projective plane. There is one point at infinity for each direction in the plane: $[1, 0, 0]^T$ is associated with the horizontal direction, $[0, 1, 0]^T$ is associated with the vertical direction, and so on.

To represent a line in the projective plane, we begin with the standard equation $au + bv + c = 0$. Since it is independent of scaling, we can write it using projective coordinates $\mathbf{m} = [x, y, z]^T$ of the point m:

$$\mathbf{l}^T \mathbf{m} = \mathbf{m}^T \mathbf{l} = ax + by + cz = 0,$$

where the line l is represented by a vector with three coordinates defined up to a scale factor, exactly like a 2-D point: $\mathbf{l} = [a, b, c]^T$ is the projective representation of the line. Since the representation of points is the same as the representation of lines, several results concerning points can be transposed to lines: this is the notion of *duality*. Please note that we use throughout the book the convention that bold

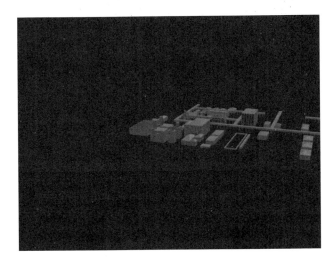

Figure 1.7: Model to insert in the sequence of Figure 1.6. Courtesy **Luc Robert**, INRIA.

type is used to represent the coordinate vector of the geometric object which is in corresponding normal type, such as $\mathbf{m}, m, \mathbf{l}$, and l in this example.

It can be verified with elementary algebra that the line containing the two points m and m' (their *join*) is expressed very simply as the cross-product of their representations:

$$\mathbf{l} \simeq \mathbf{m} \times \mathbf{m}' = \begin{bmatrix} yz' - zy' \\ zx' - xz' \\ xy' - yx' \end{bmatrix}.$$

Note that the three coordinates are just the determinants of the three 2×2 submatrices of $[\mathbf{m}\,\mathbf{m}']$. The points on the line are described by $\mathbf{m}'' = \alpha\mathbf{m} + \beta\mathbf{m}'$. The three points m, m', m'' are aligned if and only if

$$(\mathbf{m} \times \mathbf{m}')^T \mathbf{m}'' = \mid \mathbf{m}, \mathbf{m}', \mathbf{m}'' \mid = 0.$$

By duality, the point at the intersection (their *meet*) of lines l and l' is $\mathbf{m} \simeq \mathbf{l} \times \mathbf{l}'$. The other properties of lines in 2-D space are summarized in Table 1.2.

Therefore, in the projective plane, points and lines have the same representation, and the cross-product describes both meet and join. An important advantage of the representation is that the cross-product is a linear operator, while the description of the meet and join with usual coordinates involves divisions. Being a linear operator, the cross-product can be written as a matrix product $\mathbf{v} \times \mathbf{x} = [\mathbf{v}]_\times \mathbf{x}$ where $[\mathbf{v}]_\times$ is

Figure 1.8: Result obtained from Images 1.6 and 1.7. Courtesy **Luc Robert**, INRIA.

the skew-symmetric matrix whose left and right nullspaces are the vector **v**:

$$[\mathbf{v}]_\times = \begin{bmatrix} 0 & -v_3 & v_2 \\ v_3 & 0 & -v_1 \\ -v_2 & v_1 & 0 \end{bmatrix}. \tag{1.1}$$

Therefore we can use a simple matrix operator to represent the geometric operation of union of two points to form a line or intersection of two lines to form a point.

If the lines l and l' are parallel, then the previous formula is still valid and gives a point m whose coordinates are found to be proportional to $[b, -a, 0]^T$, or, equivalently, to $[b', -a', 0]^T$. This is a point at infinity which represents the direction of l. We note that all the points at infinity belong in fact to the line of equation $[0, 0, 1]^T$, which is called the *line at infinity* of $\mathbb{P}^2$, and denoted l_∞. The intersection of the line l with the line at infinity l_∞ is, as expected, the point at infinity of l $[b, -a, 0]^T$. This is to be contrasted to Euclidean geometry, where the intersection of

Figure 1.9: Scene with converging lines.

two parallel lines is not defined, and where using the general formula for computing their intersection point leads to a division by zero. In projective geometry, we don't have this problem and therefore we don't need to handle particular cases. All this makes it possible to deal generally with the intersection and union of geometric objects very simply.

If we move to $\mathbb{P}^3$, a number of things are similar, although duality and the representation of lines are more complex [Chapter 3]. A plane is represented by a vector with four coordinates defined up to a scale factor, exactly like a 3-D point: $\mathbf{\Pi} = [\pi_1, \pi_2, \pi_3, \pi_4]^T$ represents the projective equation of the plane $\pi_1 X + \pi_2 Y + \pi_3 Z + \pi_4 = 0$, which means that a point $\mathbf{M} = [X, Y, Z, 1]^T$ belongs to a plane $\mathbf{\Pi}$ if and only if $\mathbf{\Pi}^T \mathbf{M} = 0$. In $\mathbb{P}^3$, the points $[X, Y, Z, 0]^T$ therefore form a plane of equation $[0, 0, 0, 1]^T$, called the *plane at infinity*, and denoted Π_∞. Intuitively, this plane represents directions of the usual planes, since the intersection of Π_∞ with a plane $\mathbf{\Pi} = [\pi_1, \pi_2, \pi_3, \pi_4]^T$ gives $[\pi_1, \pi_2, \pi_3]^T$ which corresponds to the normal of the plane Π, all parallel planes having the same normal. When a point in $\mathbb{R}^3$ tends to the point at infinity M_∞, for example a point on a line receding towards the horizon, its projection tends to the projection of M_∞ which is usually a finite point of $\mathbb{P}_2$ called a *vanishing point*, just as we had seen in Figure 1.2. Now we see another reason why projective geometry will be a useful tool to describe projection: projective transformations mix finite and infinite points, therefore there are less special cases since the points at infinity, which in fact represent directions, are handled just like ordinary points.

	Euclidean	similarity	affine	projective
Transformations				
rotation, translation	×	×	×	×
isotropic scaling		×	×	×
scaling along axes, shear			×	×
perspective projections				×
Invariants				
distance	×			
angles, ratios of distances	×	×		
parallelism, center of mass	×	×	×	
incidence, cross-ratio	×	×	×	×

Table 1.1: An ordering of geometries: particular transformations and properties left invariant by the transformations. Each geometry is a subset of the next. More general transformations mean weaker invariants.

points		lines	
coordinates of m	$\mathbf{m} = [x, y, z]^T$	coordinates of l	$\mathbf{l} = [a, b, c]^T$
incidence $m \in l$	$\mathbf{m}^T \mathbf{l} = 0$	incidence $l \ni m$	$\mathbf{l}^T \mathbf{m} = 0$
line obtained by join	$\mathbf{m} \times \mathbf{m}'$	point obtained by meet	$\mathbf{l} \times \mathbf{l}'$
points in join	$\alpha\mathbf{m} + \beta\mathbf{m}'$	pencil containing meet	$\alpha\mathbf{l} + \beta\mathbf{l}'$
collinearity	$\mid \mathbf{m}, \mathbf{m}', \mathbf{m}'' \mid = 0$	concurrence	$\mid \mathbf{l}, \mathbf{l}', \mathbf{l}'' \mid = 0$
points at infinity	$\mathbf{m}_\infty = [x, y, 0]^T$	line at infinity	$\mathbf{l}_\infty = [0, 0, 1]^T$

Table 1.2: Summary of the properties of points and lines in the projective plane.

1.3 2-D and 3-D [Section 4.1.1]

It is quite easy to describe the geometric aspects of image formation for a single image, which is inferring positions of points in one image from positions in the world. In fact, these laws were already understood by the Italian painters of the Renaissance, who studied geometry in order to reproduce correctly the perspective effects in the images of the world that they where observing. Following them, the transformation from the three-dimensional space to the two-dimensional plane performed by a camera can be described using the *pinhole model* (Figure 1.3):

- a plane $\mathcal{R}$, called the *retinal plane*, or *image plane*,

- a point C which does not belong to $\mathcal{R}$: the *optical center*,

The projection m of a point of the space M is the intersection of the *optical ray* (C, M) with the retinal plane. The *optical axis* is the line going through C and

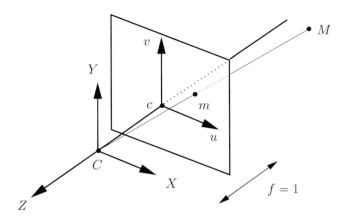

Figure 1.10: The pinhole model expressed in the *camera coordinate system* where the world coordinate system is aligned with the camera and the image coordinate system.

perpendicular to the retinal plane. It pierces that plane at the *principal point c*. If we consider an orthonormal system of coordinates in the retinal plane, centered at c, we can define a three-dimensional orthonormal system of coordinates, called the *camera coordinate system*, centered at the optical center C with two axes of coordinates parallel to the retinal ones and the third one parallel to the optical axis. The *focal length* is the distance between the point C and the plane $\mathcal{R}$. We choose here as unit in the world coordinate system the focal length. Changing this unit corresponds to a simple scaling of the image.

In these two systems of coordinates, the relationship between the coordinates of M, $[X, Y, Z]^T$, and those of its projection m, $[u, v]^T$, is given by Thales theorem:

$$u = \frac{X}{Z} \qquad v = \frac{Y}{Z}. \tag{1.2}$$

Vision is about inferring properties of the world from its images. A central problem of 3-D vision is therefore to invert the projection, which is quite difficult, since one tries to go from a poorer representation (2-D) to a richer representation (3-D). A point m in an image represents a whole incoming light ray, called the *optical ray* of m. By definition, the optical ray contains the optical center, therefore to define its position in 3-D in the camera coordinate system, we just need to specify another point along the ray, say of coordinates $[X, Y, Z]^T$. However, any point of coordinates $[\lambda X, \lambda Y, \lambda Z]^T$ represents the same ray, since both of them are projected to the same 2-D point m. There is an ambiguity along the optical ray, and the consequence of this observation is that using geometry alone we cannot infer the 3-D depth of a point from a single image using geometry alone. This essential ambiguity is best described by considering $[\lambda X, \lambda Y, \lambda Z]^T$ to be projective coordinates of the optical ray. Because of our choice of unit, $Z = 1$ on the image plane, and therefore the point m of usual coordinates $[u, v]$ has the 3-D coordinates $[u, v, 1]^T$. Projective coordinates of m are $[u, v, 1]^T$, so we see that these projective coordinates represent a point in 3-D on the optical ray of m. This property remains true if another triple of equivalent projective coordinates are used.

Using projective coordinates, the projection equation (1.2) can be written

$$
\mathbf{m} = \begin{bmatrix} x \\ y \\ z \end{bmatrix} = \underbrace{\begin{bmatrix} 1 & 0 & 0 & 0 \\ 0 & 1 & 0 & 0 \\ 0 & 0 & 1 & 0 \end{bmatrix}}_{\mathcal{P}_0} \begin{bmatrix} \mathcal{X} \\ \mathcal{Y} \\ \mathcal{Z} \\ \mathcal{T} \end{bmatrix} = \mathcal{P}_0 \mathbf{M}. \tag{1.3}
$$

The reward of using projective coordinates is that we have obtained a linear equation instead of a nonlinear one. The usual coordinates are related to projective coordinates by: $u = x/z, v = y/z$ and $X = \mathcal{X}/\mathcal{T}, Y = \mathcal{Y}/\mathcal{T}, Z = \mathcal{Z}/\mathcal{T}$.

Moreover, we can see that the description with projective coordinates is richer than the one with affine coordinates: the points for which $t = 0$ or $\mathcal{T} = 0$ do not have affine correspondents. The points $\mathcal{T} = 0$ are points at infinity (in space), which have been found to be of great utility by such artists-theorists as Piero Della Francesca, Leonardo, and Dürer, when they first formalized perspective projection. As explained in Section 1.2, they are obtained by the intersection of parallel lines and are treated like other points in projective geometry. In particular, they are mapped correctly by the projection matrix producing in general a real vanishing point.

Using projective geometry leads to a simpler, more unified expression of the problem. This make it possible to design more efficient multiple-view algorithms than before. However, the main reward is the ability to deal with a class of problems which couldn't be tackled before, because they depended on *camera calibration*, which we describe next.

The matrix $\mathcal{P}_0$ was particularly simple because of our particular choice of coordinate systems. In general the image coordinate system is defined by the pixels, and the world coordinate system is not aligned with the camera: The general form of the *projection matrix* is

$$
\mathcal{P} \simeq \underbrace{\begin{bmatrix} \alpha_u & \gamma & u_0 \\ 0 & \alpha_v & v_0 \\ 0 & 0 & 1 \end{bmatrix}}_{\mathbf{A}} \mathcal{P}_0 \underbrace{\begin{bmatrix} \mathbf{R} & \mathbf{t} \\ \mathbf{0}_3^T & 1 \end{bmatrix}}_{\mathcal{D}} = \mathbf{A}[\mathbf{R}\,\mathbf{t}], \tag{1.4}
$$

where

- **A** describes the characteristics of the camera or, more precisely, the imaging system. As a 3×3 matrix it represents a change of retinal coordinate system.

Its five entries are called the camera *intrinsic parameters*. α_u and α_v represent the focal length expressed in pixel units in each direction. They describe the total magnification of the imaging system resulting from both optics and image sampling. Their ratio, called the *aspect ratio*, is usually fixed, but is not always equal to 1 due to the digitalization phase. (u_0, v_0) represents the coordinates of the principal point, which usually are not $(0, 0)$ because we count pixels from a corner. The parameter γ, called the skew, is zero except for some very particular imaging situations: non-orthogonal pixels, images of images, and analysis of shadows[3].

- $\mathcal{D}$ describes the location and orientation of the camera with respect to the world coordinate system. It is a 4×4 displacement matrix describing the change of world coordinate system as a rotation $\mathbf{R}$ and a translation $\mathbf{t}$ (the pose of the camera), called the *extrinsic parameters*.

A general projection matrix, being 3×4, depends on eleven parameters (twelve minus a scale factor), which is the number of the intrinsic and extrinsic parameters combined. The decomposition $\mathcal{P} \simeq \mathbf{A}[\mathbf{R}\,\mathbf{t}]$ is unique because of the QR theorem, which states that a non-singular matrix can be factored uniquely as the product of a triangular matrix $\mathbf{A}$ and an orthogonal matrix $\mathbf{R}$.

1.4   Calibrated and uncalibrated capabilities

In the camera coordinate system (the particular coordinate system defined at the beginning of Section 1.3), the projective coordinates of a pixel represent a 3D point on its optical ray, and therefore give us the position of this optical ray in space in the coordinate system of the camera. In general it is not sufficient to measure pixels in order to infer from a pixel m the position of the optical ray in space. The matrix $\mathbf{A}$ is used to transform pixel coordinates into camera coordinates. A camera for which $\mathbf{A}$ is known is said to be *calibrated*. It then acts as a metric measurement device, able to measure the angle between optical rays. Furthermore, if $\mathcal{D}$ is known, then it is possible to relate the camera coordinate system to the world's or other camera's coordinate systems.

The classical (model-based) way to calibrate a camera is by determining its projection matrix using known control points in 3D. Let $\mathbf{U}$, $\mathbf{V}$, $\mathbf{W}$ represent the three row vectors of $\mathcal{P}$. For each correspondence $m \leftrightarrow M$ from 2-D to 3-D, we

---

[3]The two latter situations are adequately described by the full projection matrix because the product of two perspective projections, although not always a perspective transformation, is always a projective transformation. Similarly, the product of two perspective projections with a particular change of retinal coordinates (for example an orthogonal one) is not necessarily a perspective transformation with the same particular change of coordinates, but is always a projective transformation.

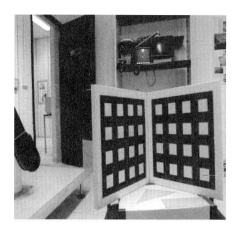 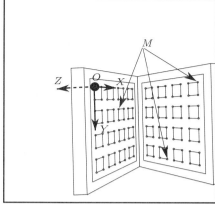

Figure 1.11: The calibration grid used at INRIA and the associated model.

obtain two linear equations in the entries of $\mathcal{P}$:

$$
\begin{bmatrix} u \\ v \\ 1 \end{bmatrix} = \mathbf{m} \simeq \mathcal{P}\mathbf{M} = \begin{bmatrix} \mathbf{U}^T\mathbf{M} \\ \mathbf{V}^T\mathbf{M} \\ \mathbf{W}^T\mathbf{M} \end{bmatrix} ; \quad \text{therefore} \quad \begin{cases} u\mathbf{W}^T\mathbf{M} - \mathbf{U}^T\mathbf{M} = 0, \\ v\mathbf{W}^T\mathbf{M} - \mathbf{V}^T\mathbf{M} = 0. \end{cases}
$$

The reference points M are measured in some 3-D coordinate frame, and their projections m detected. Usually a special object, like the one shown in Figure 1.11, is engineered so that both operations can be done with a good accuracy [Section 4.6]. Because $\mathcal{P}$ has 11 independent entries, from at least six 2-D to 3-D correspondences in general position it is possible to determine the projection matrix. Once $\mathcal{P}$ is known, it can be decomposed back into $\mathbf{A}$ and $\mathcal{D}$, which are the basis for 3-D measurements from images.

Model-based calibration is not always possible. First, many images such as those available in image libraries or from hand-held video come without calibration data at all or with calibration data which is imprecise (such as the reading of the focal length on the barrel of a zoom lens). Second, even if we have calibrated a system, the calibration data might change either because of involuntary reasons such as mechanical or thermal variations, or because of active controls such as focus or vergence, which add greatly to the flexibility and adaptivity of a vision system. While the first computer vision applications used robotic systems which could be pre-calibrated off-line, the trend today is towards the use of massive and ubiquitous imagery from all kinds of sources.

Because the usual world is Euclidean, a projective framework might seem at first unnecessarily abstract and complicated, but besides allowing us to understand and express the geometry of the problem in a much simpler way, it makes it possible to consider the world as a redundant superposition of projective, affine, and Euclidean structures, and to deal with these three structures simultaneously. This better understanding of the problem makes it possible:

- To propose linear or analytical approaches, using minimal data if necessary, to problems (such as the bundle adjustment, [Section 10.2]) which have in the past been dealt with only by large-scale minimization, with all the associated global convergence problems. In particular, the previous methods require a precise initialization point which the projective methods can provide.

- To characterize those configurations of points and of cameras which cause degeneracy and instability in the estimation process, and more generally, to improve the stability, robustness and precision of the estimation.

Thanks to the projective approach, we will be able to achieve the same metric results as model-based calibration in many circumstances without the need to use a calibration object or known reference points. For example, we can perform the following photogrammetric tasks.

- Using only constraints such as instances of parallelism and orthogonality in the scene, we obtain a metrically correct reconstruction of a scene (up to a global scale factor) from an arbitrary number of images taken by arbitrarily different cameras [Section 7.3 and 7.4].

- Using only simple constraints about a moving camera (such as zero-skew or constant aspect ratio), we track the 3-D motion and recover the internal parameters of this camera even when they vary over time [Section 11.4 and 11.5].

In a complementary way, we will see that for many applications such as

- the navigation and obstacle avoidance for an autonomous robot or vehicle [Section 7.2.6] and the detection of independent motion, and

- the synthesis of novel images from existing images [Section 7.2.7 and Section 8.1.1],

there is not even a need for metric representations or 3-D reconstruction. Instead, a non-metric description is more general, easier to obtain, and can capture more precisely the properties which are relevant to a given task.

1.5   The plane-to-image homography as a projective transformation [Section 4.1.4]

We begin by introducing an important example of projective transformation, the *homography* between a plane Π in space and the retinal plane.

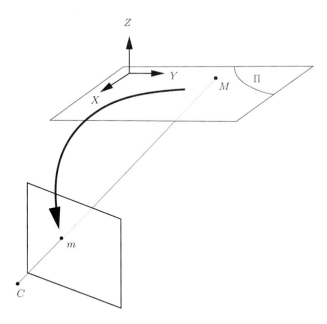

Figure 1.12: The homography between a plane in space and the retinal plane. The world coordinate system is aligned with plane Π.

If we choose the world coordinate system so that the first two axes define the plane, as illustrated in Figure 1.5, the projection of points of Π can be viewed as a transformation between two spaces $\mathbb{P}^2$, since for those points

$$\underbrace{\begin{bmatrix} x \\ y \\ z \end{bmatrix}}_{\mathbf{m}} \simeq \mathcal{P} \begin{bmatrix} \mathcal{X} \\ \mathcal{Y} \\ 0 \\ \mathcal{T} \end{bmatrix} = \underbrace{\begin{bmatrix} \mathcal{P}_{11} & \mathcal{P}_{12} & \mathcal{P}_{14} \\ \mathcal{P}_{21} & \mathcal{P}_{22} & \mathcal{P}_{24} \\ \mathcal{P}_{31} & \mathcal{P}_{32} & \mathcal{P}_{34} \end{bmatrix}}_{\mathbf{H}} \underbrace{\begin{bmatrix} \mathcal{X} \\ \mathcal{Y} \\ \mathcal{T} \end{bmatrix}}_{\mathbf{p}}.$$

Each point correspondence (m, p) yields two independent proportionality equations:

$$\frac{x}{z} = \frac{h_{11}\mathcal{X} + h_{12}\mathcal{Y} + h_{13}\mathcal{T}}{h_{31}\mathcal{X} + h_{32}\mathcal{Y} + h_{33}\mathcal{T}} , \quad \frac{y}{z} = \frac{h_{21}\mathcal{X} + h_{22}\mathcal{Y} + h_{23}\mathcal{T}}{h_{31}\mathcal{X} + h_{32}\mathcal{Y} + h_{33}\mathcal{T}},$$

which can be linearized in the entries of $\mathbf{H}$:

$$\begin{cases} h_{11}z\mathcal{X} + h_{12}z\mathcal{Y} + h_{13}z\mathcal{T} - h_{31}x\mathcal{X} - h_{32}x\mathcal{Y} - h_{33}x\mathcal{T} = 0, \\ h_{21}z\mathcal{X} + h_{22}z\mathcal{Y} + h_{23}z\mathcal{T} - h_{31}y\mathcal{X} - h_{32}y\mathcal{Y} - h_{33}y\mathcal{T} = 0. \end{cases}$$

$\mathbf{H}$ has eight entries (nine minus a scale factor), therefore from four correspondences $\mathbf{m}, \mathbf{p}$ in general position, $\mathbf{H}$ is determined uniquely by solving a linear system of equations. Here "general position" means that no three points are collinear, because if that was the case the equations would not be linearly independent. Once **H** is computed, we can use it to determine positions of points on Π from a *single* image. This simple example illustrates the power of projective geometry: the mapping between the two planes is done using just linear operations and four reference points, without the need to refer to more complicated representations like rotations, translations and camera parameters.

The transformation **H** is called a *homography*, or *projective transformation*[4] of $\mathbb{P}^2$. Generally speaking, a homography is any transformation H of $\mathbb{P}^n$ which is linear in projective coordinates (hence the terminology *linear projective*) and invertible (thus it conserves globally the space, a fact we denote: $H(\mathbb{P}^n) = \mathbb{P}^n$). It can be shown that these properties are equivalent to the fact that collinearity is preserved and subspaces mapped into subspaces of the same dimension. A homography can be described by an $(n+1) \times (n+1)$ non-singular matrix **H**, such that the image of **x** is **x'**:

$$\mathbf{x'} \simeq \mathbf{Hx}.$$

Like in $\mathbb{P}^2$ we needed four corresponding points in general position to define a homography, in $\mathbb{P}^n$ we need two sets of $n+2$ points such that no $n+1$ of them are linearly dependent to define a homography. Each such set is called a *projective basis*, and it corresponds to the choice of a projective coordinate system.

1.6   Affine description of the projection [Section 4.2]

The projection matrix $\mathcal{P}$ has to be of rank 3, otherwise its image would be a projective line instead of a projective plane. Since it has 4 columns, its nullspace is thus of dimension 1; any vector **C** of this nullspace defines a projective point C for which the projection is not defined; this point is the optical center.

Let us now partition the projection matrix $\mathcal{P}$ into the concatenation of a 3×3 sub-matrix **P** and a 3×1 vector **p**. The origin of the world coordinate system, the point $[0, 0, 0, 1]$, is projected onto **p**.

The optical center is also decomposed by separating its last coordinate from the first three:

$$\mathcal{P} = [\mathbf{P\,p}], \qquad \tilde{C} = \left[\begin{array}{c} \mathbf{C} \\ c \end{array} \right]. \tag{1.5}$$

The equation determining the optical center is $\mathcal{P}\tilde{C} = \mathbf{0}$. Using the decomposition just introduced, $\mathcal{P}\tilde{C} = \mathbf{PC} + \mathbf{p}c$, thus $\mathbf{PC} = -c\mathbf{p}$. Therefore, if $\det(\mathbf{P}) \neq 0$,

---

[4]A *perspective* transformation of $\mathbb{P}^2$ is obtained by using a projection matrix in camera coordinates, or in other words, such that its first 3×3 sub-matrix is orthogonal. Unlike projective transformations, perspective transformations do not form a group: the product of two perspective transformations is not necessary a perspective transformation.

then the solution is given by

$$\tilde{\mathbf{C}} \simeq \begin{bmatrix} -\mathbf{P}^{-1}\mathbf{p} \\ 1 \end{bmatrix} \tag{1.6}$$

so the optical center is finite. When $\det(\mathbf{P}) = 0$, it can be verified, using the fact that $\mathcal{P}$ has rank 3, that the optical center lies in the plane at infinity (i.e. $c = 0$).

Any projection matrix arising from a physical system has to satisfy $\det(\mathbf{P}) \neq 0$, since the optical center has to lie in the affine space (we refer to that as *perspective projection*). For simplicity, we will assume that this is the case in this introductory Chapter. The alternative class of models (*parallel projection*) can be considered as approximations to the pinhole model in some particular viewing situations. These include orthographic, weak perspective, and the affine camera [Section 4.4]. They yield a simpler geometry which is affine instead of being projective. The beauty of the projective model is that it handles perspective cameras and parallel cameras equally well. There is no need to distinguish between the two cases. However, it leaves open the possibility to specialize the analysis, which we do now.

At this affine level of description, we can introduce *directions* of optical rays. Since the projection of each point at infinity $[\mathbf{d}^T, 0]^T$ is the vanishing point $\mathbf{v} = \mathbf{P}\mathbf{d}$, $\mathbf{P}$ can be considered as the homography between the plane at infinity Π_∞ and the retinal plane $\mathcal{R}$. Note that parallel lines have the same direction, hence the same point at infinity, thus their projection is a set of lines of $\mathcal{R}$ which contains the vanishing point projection of this point at infinity. The optical ray corresponding to the pixel $\mathbf{m}$ thus has the direction $\mathbf{P}^{-1}\mathbf{m}$. This is illustrated in Figure 1.6.

From the decomposition Equation 1.4, it can be noticed that $\mathbf{P}$ depends only on the orientation of the camera and its intrinsic parameters, not on its position. Therefore we obtain the fact that we had pointed to at the beginning of this Chapter, that the projection of points at infinity is invariant under translation. The dependence of the finite points on the translation is embodied in the vector $\mathbf{p}$, which represents the projection of the origin of the world coordinate system.

Table 1.3 summarizes the descriptions of the projection matrix in the perspective projection case.

1.7   Structure and motion

Let us now add a second image. Two points, m in the first image, and m' in the second image, are said to be *corresponding* if they are the projections of the same 3-D point M in space. Having more than one image opens new possibilities and raises the following questions:

- Given a point m in the first image, where is its corresponding point m' in the second image?

- What is the 3-D geometry of the scene?

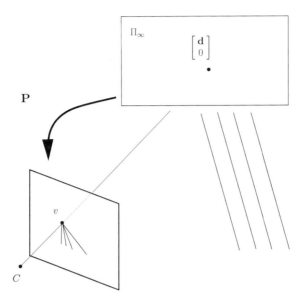

Figure 1.13: The first submatrix **P** of the projection matrix represents a homography between the plane at infinity and the retinal plane. It projects intersections of parallel lines in space to a vanishing point in the image. Its inverse gives the direction of the optical ray.

- What is the relative position of the two cameras?

Note there are several ways of representing the 3-D geometry of a scene. We could recover the depth of a point which is its distance to the image plane, we could recover the 3-D coordinates of a point, or we could recover the relative depths of two points.

We have seen that from a single image, even if we know the parameters of the camera model, we can infer only the position of the optical ray of m, not the position of the 3-D point M. With two images, given the correspondence (m, m'), we can intersect the optical rays of m and m', and so determine M. This is the principle of binocular stereopsis: when two images are taken from different positions, the difference in position of corresponding image points is related to the 3-D position of the object point. To actually infer that 3-D position requires that we can infer the position of the two optical rays in a common coordinate system. We need to know the relative position of the second camera with respect to the first one, which we call its *motion*. Algebraically, if we knew the projection matrices $\mathcal{P}$ and $\mathcal{P}'$, then we could compute M from m and m' by solving the system of four equations (each

level	decomposition	interpretation		
projective	$\mathcal{P}$	$\mathcal{P}$:	projection from object space $\mathbb{P}^3$ to retinal plane $\mathcal{R}$.	
affine	$[\mathbf{P}\,\mathbf{p}]$	$\mathbf{P}$:	homography between plane at infinity Π_∞ and $\mathcal{R}$.	
		$\mathbf{p}$:	projection of the origin of the world coordinate system.	
Euclidean	$\mathbf{A}[\mathbf{R}\,\mathbf{t}]$	$\mathbf{A}$:	change of coordinates in $\mathcal{R}$ (5 intrinsic parameters).	
		$(\mathbf{R},\mathbf{t})$:	camera pose in world coordinates.	

Table 1.3: Descriptions of the projection matrix.

proportionality vector equation gives two independent equations):

$$\begin{cases} \mathcal{P}\mathbf{M} & \simeq & \mathbf{m}, \\ \mathcal{P}'\mathbf{M} & \simeq & \mathbf{m}'. \end{cases} \qquad (1.7)$$

Therefore, in order to be able to determine the 3-D *structure* of the scene, we also need to be able to determine the projection matrices $\mathcal{P}$ and $\mathcal{P}'$ which encode the geometry of the cameras. The two problems of motion determination and structure determination are inter-related, and we will designate them collectively as the *reconstruction problem*.

In the system of equations (1.7), we notice that we have three unknowns (the coordinates of M) and four equations. For a solution to exist, the coordinates of m and m' must satisfy a constraint; in other words, given m, the point m' cannot be an arbitrary point of the second image. In fact, in some particular cases that we are going to examine in Section 1.8 and Section 1.9, it is possible to predict the position of the point m' from the position of the point m.

1.8   The homography between two images of a plane [Section 5.1.1]

We first examine the particular situation when the 3-D points lie on a plane Π. Planes are important entities: in practice because they appear naturally in many scenes and in theory because they are subspaces which have the same dimension as the images. As we have seen in Section 1.5, there is a homography between the retinal plane of the first camera and the plane Π and also a homography between the retinal plane of the second camera and the plane Π; therefore by composition there is a homography H between the two retinal planes called a *planar homography*, because it is induced by the plane Π and described by a 3×3 matrix $\mathbf{H}$. This homography is illustrated in Figure 1.8. If m and m' are projections of a point M which belongs to Π, then

$$\mathbf{m}' \simeq \mathbf{H}\mathbf{m}.$$

Reversing the roles of the two images transforms $\mathbf{H}$ into its inverse. As in Section 1.5, $\mathbf{H}$ can be determined in general from 4 correspondences. Once $\mathbf{H}$ is known, for any projection m of a point of Π, it is possible to predict the position of its correspondent in the other image. Some care must be taken if Π goes through either of the two optical centers [Section 5.1.1].

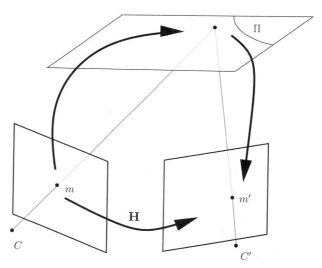

Figure 1.14: The planar homography between two images is obtained by composition of single view homographies.

An important special case occurs when Π is the plane at infinity Π_∞. Then, $\mathbf{H}_\infty$ has a particularly simple expression in terms of the two projection matrices $\mathcal{P}$ and $\mathcal{P}'$, obtained using the decomposition in Section 1.6:

$$\mathbf{H}_\infty \simeq \mathbf{P}'\mathbf{P}^{-1}. \tag{1.8}$$

1.9   Stationary cameras [Section 5.1.2]

A related situation occurs when the two optical centers are identical, i.e. when the two images are taken from the same viewpoint with the camera rotated. Let m and m' be arbitrary corresponding points, i.e. the images of a point in the scene. For any plane Π, not going through the optical center, they are also the images of the point of intersection of their common optical ray with the plane. They are therefore related by **H**, which in this case is independent of the plane Π. The homography **H** can be used to merge the images and to build image mosaics, as illustrated in Figure 1.15. By applying it to the whole first image, we transform it into a new image which, when overlaid on the second image, forms a larger image representing the scene as it would have appeared from the point of view of the second image but with a larger field of view. If we have several images taken from the same viewpoint, we can iterate the process of choosing one of the images as the reference image and warping all of the other images onto it by applying the corresponding homographies. Note that in this process, we have begun to address the problem of generating new views from existing images: by applying a homography to a single image, we can generate a new view obtained from the same viewpoint but with a rotation of the camera. This process does not handle translation of the camera to a new viewpoint.

Two images taken from the same viewpoint cannot be used to recover the 3-D structure: since the optical ray of two corresponding points is the same, the ambiguity along this ray remains, just like when we have a single image. Therefore, there must be a non-null translational component of the motion for us to be able to recover structure from two images. In the reminder of this section, we assume that the points do not lie on a plane and that the optical centers are distinct.

1.10 The epipolar constraint between corresponding points [Section 5.2.1]

When the points in space and the two cameras are in general position, it is not possible to predict the position of the correspondent m' of a point m, because this position depends on the depth of the 3-D point M along the optical ray. However, geometrically, this position is not arbitrary: M has to lie along the optical ray of m, and therefore m' is necessarily located on the projection of that optical ray in the second camera. This line is called the *epipolar line* of the point m in the second image. See Figure 1.10. If we are able to compute this line, then when looking for the correspondent of m, we need not search the whole second image, but only this line, hence reducing the search space from 2-D to 1-D.

There is another way to view the same construction, by considering it as a way to constrain the cameras rather than the correspondence. Assuming that we know a valid correspondence, $m \leftrightarrow m'$, the relative position of the cameras must be such that optical rays L_m and $L_{m'}$ intersect. Another way to formulate this is to say that the two optical rays and the line between the optical centers (called the *baseline*) are coplanar. The common plane is called the *epipolar plane*.

Algebraically, because the point M depends on three coordinates, and the correspondence $m \leftrightarrow m'$ depends on a total of four parameters, there must be an

Figure 1.15: Two images taken from the same viewpoint, and the composite image obtained by applying a homography to the second image and superimposing it to the first image.

algebraic constraint linking the coordinates of m and m'. We will see next that this constraint is remarkably simple.

1.11   The Fundamental matrix [Section 5.2.1]

The relationship between the point m and its epipolar line l'_m in the second image is projective linear, since the optical ray of m is a linear function of m, and projection is also linear. Therefore, there is a 3×3 matrix which describes this correspondence, called the *Fundamental matrix*, giving the epipolar line of the point m: $\mathbf{l}'_m = \mathbf{Fm}$. If two points m and m' are in correspondence, then the point m' belongs to the

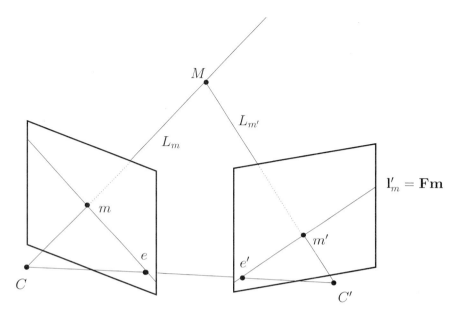

Figure 1.16: Epipolar geometry. Given m, the point m' has to lie on its the epipolar line l'_m. Given a valid correspondence $m \leftrightarrow m'$, the intersection of the optical rays L_m and $L_{m'}$ is not empty, and they are coplanar with the baseline CC'.

epipolar line of m, therefore they satisfy the *epipolar constraint*:

$$\mathbf{m}'^{T}\mathbf{F}\mathbf{m} = 0, \tag{1.9}$$

which is bilinear in the coordinates of the image points. Reversing the roles of the two images transforms $\mathbf{F}$ into its transpose. Figure 1.11 shows two images and a few epipolar lines.

The Fundamental matrix depends only on the configuration of the cameras (intrinsic parameters, position and orientation) and not on the 3-D points in the scene. In the generic case where we do not assume any spatial relationship between the points in space, the only information available comes from *projective correspondences*, the correspondence of points undergoing linear projection. The epipolar constraint fully describes the correspondence of a pair of generic corresponding points in each image, the ambiguity along the epipolar line being caused by the ambiguity along the optical ray of the projection operation. Since the fundamental matrix depends only on camera geometry, it describes all the epipolar constraints, so it encodes all the information available from projective correspondences. Therefore, no other general constraint is available. This will be confirmed later, with a parameter counting argument, when we will see that it is sufficient to build a 3-D

Figure 1.17: Two images with a few corresponding points and epipolar lines.

reconstruction of points and cameras compatible with projective correspondence.

Since all the optical rays contain the optical center C of the first camera, all the epipolar lines contain the projection of C in the second image (the point where the first camera is seen by the second camera), called the *epipole*. See Figure 1.10. The fact that the epipole in the second image belongs to all the epipolar lines implies $\mathbf{e}'^T \mathbf{F} \mathbf{m} = 0$ for any m, and therefore $\mathbf{e}'^T \mathbf{F} = \mathbf{0}$, or equivalently, $\mathbf{F}^T \mathbf{e}' = 0$. By reversing the role of the two images, $\mathbf{F} \mathbf{e} = 0$. We conclude that $\mathbf{F}$ is a matrix of rank two:

$$\det(\mathbf{F}) = 0.$$

Since it satisfies this algebraic constraint and is only defined up to a scale factor (like all the projective quantities), $\mathbf{F}$ depends on seven parameters.

1.12   Computing the Fundamental matrix [Chapter 6]

Each point correspondence (m, m') yields one equation (1.9), therefore with a sufficient number of point correspondences in general position we can determine $\mathbf{F}$. No knowledge about the cameras or scene structure is necessary. The first step for all the algorithms that we discuss in the book is almost always the computation of the Fundamental matrix, which is of utmost theoretical and practical importance.

Equation 1.9 is linear in the entries of $\mathbf{F}$. It can be rewritten as

$$\mathbf{U}^T \mathbf{f} = 0,$$

where $\mathbf{m} = [u, v, 1]^T$ and $\mathbf{m}' = [u', v', 1]^T$ so

$$\mathbf{U} = [uu', vu', u', uv', vv', v', u, v, 1]^T,$$
$$\mathbf{f} = [F_{11}, F_{12}, F_{13}, F_{21}, F_{22}, F_{23}, F_{31}, F_{32}, F_{33}]^T.$$

Combining the rows $\mathbf{U}$ for each correspondence provides a linear system of the form $\tilde{\mathbf{U}} \mathbf{f} = 0$. Using seven points, it is possible to compute $\mathbf{F}$ using the rank constraint

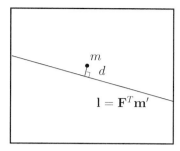 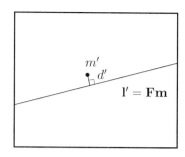

Figure 1.18: Error function used for the computation of the Fundamental matrix: sum of epipolar distances $d^2 + d'^2$.

$\det(\mathbf{F}) = 0$, however because this constraint is cubic there can be three solutions. With eight correspondences in general position, there is a unique solution which is obtained linearly. In practice, we have more than eight correspondences, but they are not exact, so we can seek a least-squares solution:

$$\min_{\mathbf{f}} \|\tilde{\mathbf{U}}\mathbf{f}\| \quad \text{subject to} \quad \|\mathbf{f}\| = 1. \tag{1.10}$$

The constraint $\|\mathbf{f}\| = 1$ is necessary because $\mathbf{F}$ is defined up to a scale factor.

This approach suffers from two difficulties. First, unlike the case of seven points, we notice that the rank constraint is no longer satisfied. Second, the error function in Equation 1.10 was obtained algebraically but has no geometric relevance. However, this approach can give acceptable results if care is taken in renormalizing the pixel coordinates to the interval $[-1, 1]$ to improve the numerical conditioning of matrix $\tilde{\mathbf{U}}$. It has the advantage of simplicity. Practice has shown that the most precise results with noisy data are obtained by using nonlinear minimization techniques which rely on a symmetrized geometric error criterion and enforce the rank constraint by an adequate parameterization. A proven such approach is to minimize the error function illustrated in Figure 1.12:

$$\sum_i \{d(\mathbf{m}'_i, \mathbf{F}\mathbf{m}_i)^2 + d(\mathbf{m}_i, \mathbf{F}^T\mathbf{m}'_i)^2\},$$

where $d(.,.)$ is the perpendicular distance of a point to a line. In practice, it is also important to use robust techniques to reject false correspondences. All these algorithmic refinements are the subject of Chapter 6.

Although eight correspondences are in general sufficient to determine the Fundamental matrix, there are some configuration of 3-D points, called *critical surfaces* for which even with an arbitrarily large number of correspondences, the Fundamental matrix is not uniquely determined. These configurations are important in practice because if the scene is close to such a configuration, the determination of the Fundamental matrix is quite unstable. Planes are a particular case of critical surfaces, which are quadrics examined in more detail in Section 5.5.

1.13   Planar homographies and the Fundamental matrix [Section 5.2.4]

We have seen in Section 1.8 that for a given plane Π, the correspondence is entirely determined by a planar homography $\mathbf{H}$; in other words, $\mathbf{H}$ can be used to compute corresponding points in the second image from points in the first image. We have just seen that for points in general 3-D position, the Fundamental matrix can be used to constrain correspondences along one direction, that of the epipolar line. There is an important relation between these two matrices, the planar homography H and the Fundamental matrix. As will be seen later, this relation is at the heart of techniques for positioning 3-D points in space from their projections.

Given the two cameras, and therefore the Fundamental matrix, a planar homography is defined by its associated plane. Since a plane depends on three parameters, and a homography on eight parameters, not all 3×3 invertible matrices define a planar homography, so $\mathbf{H}$ must satisfy six constraints, given $\mathbf{F}$. On the other hand, the planar homography constrains the Fundamental matrix because it can be used to generate a point on the epipolar line of any point: if m is a point of the first image, then its optical ray intersects the plane Π at M_Π. $\mathbf{H}m$ represents the projection of M_Π into the second image. Since by construction the point M_Π belongs to the optical ray of m, the point $\mathbf{H}m$ belongs to the epipolar line of m. Therefore, given $\mathbf{H}$, it is sufficient to know the epipole e' to determine the Fundamental matrix: the epipolar line l'_m contains $\mathbf{H}m$ and the epipole e', therefore, $l'_m = e' \times \mathbf{H}m$. Since by definition of $\mathbf{F}$, $l'_m = \mathbf{F}m$, we conclude that

$$\mathbf{F} \simeq [\mathbf{e}']_\times \mathbf{H} \tag{1.11}$$

This is illustrated in Figure 1.13. Conversely, it can be shown that any matrix $\mathbf{H}$ which satisfies this constraint is a planar homography generated by some plane.

Applying both sides of Equation (1.11) to the vector $\mathbf{e}$, and using the fact that $\mathbf{F}e = 0$ and $[\mathbf{e}']_\times \mathbf{e}' = 0$ shows that

$$\mathbf{H}\mathbf{e} \simeq \mathbf{e}';$$

therefore, once the Fundamental matrix is known, the correspondence of three points is sufficient to define a planar homography[5] since the correspondence (e, e') provides the needed fourth point.

The decomposition (1.11) of the Fundamental matrix is not unique, since it is obtained for any planar homography. Considering two planar homographies $\mathbf{H}_1$ and $\mathbf{H}_2$, Equation 1.11 implies that there exist scalars λ_1 and λ_2 such that $[\mathbf{e}']_\times (\lambda_1 \mathbf{H}_1 +$

---

[5]Again, the case where the plane goes through either optical center is special; see Chapter 5.

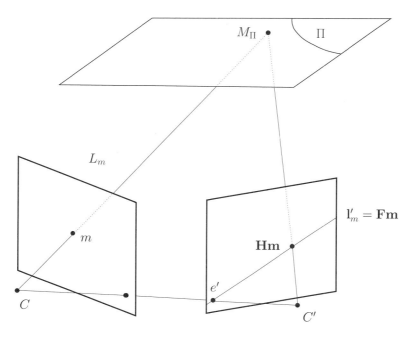

Figure 1.19: Relation between the Fundamental matrix and a planar homography. The points $\mathbf{Hm}$ and e' define the epipolar line of m.

$\lambda_2 \mathbf{H}_2) = 0$. It can be shown by inspection that if a matrix $\mathbf{H}$ is such that $[\mathbf{e}']_\times \mathbf{H} = 0$, then there exists a vector $\mathbf{r}$ such that $\mathbf{H} = \mathbf{e}' \mathbf{r}^T$. We therefore conclude that

$$\mathbf{H}_2 \simeq \mathbf{H}_1 + \mathbf{e}' \mathbf{r}^T. \tag{1.12}$$

This equation can be understood geometrically by applying both of its terms to the point m of the first image. Because $\mathbf{r}^T \mathbf{m}$ is a scalar, it says that the point of coordinates $\mathbf{H}_2 \mathbf{m}$ in the second image belongs to the line defined by e' and the point of coordinates $\mathbf{H}_1 \mathbf{m}$. This is true because, as discussed in the derivation of Equation 1.11, it is the epipolar line of m. In fact, the direction of the vector $\mathbf{r}$ represents the projection in the first image of the intersection of the planes corresponding respectively to $\mathbf{H}_1$ and to $\mathbf{H}_2$. To see that, note that a point belongs to both planes if and only if $\mathbf{H}_2 \mathbf{m} \simeq \mathbf{H}_1 \mathbf{m}$, and therefore $\mathbf{r}^T \mathbf{m} = 0$. This is illustrated in Figure 1.13. The consequence of this equation is that the family of planar homographies is parameterized by a vector of dimension three, which is expected since the family of planes of $\mathbb{P}^3$ has this dimension. Knowing any of these homographies make it possible to generate all of them.

At this point, one could wonder how to obtain a planar transformation without relying on some prior knowledge of the scene to identify a plane. The trick is that

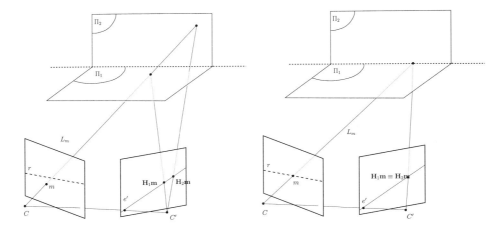

Figure 1.20: Relation between two planar homographies. Left: generic point. The points e', $\mathbf{H}_1\mathbf{m}$, and $\mathbf{H}_2\mathbf{m}$ are aligned. Right: L_m intersect the line $\Pi_1 \cap \Pi_2$. $\mathbf{H}_1\mathbf{m}$, and $\mathbf{H}_2\mathbf{m}$ are identical. m lies on the line r, projection of $\Pi_1 \cap \Pi_2$.

from just $\mathbf{F}$, we can always obtain one by using the *special matrix* defined as

$$\mathbf{S} = [\mathbf{e}']_\times \mathbf{F}. \qquad (1.13)$$

It can be verified that $\mathbf{S}$ satisfies $\mathbf{F} \simeq [\mathbf{e}']_\times \mathbf{S}$, using the identity $\mathbf{I} \simeq \mathbf{v}\mathbf{v}^T - [\mathbf{v}]_\times[\mathbf{v}]_\times$; therefore it is equivalent to know $\mathbf{F}$ or $\mathbf{S}$. The small price to pay for this "free" planar transformation is that it is singular, since the two matrices which appear in Equation 1.13 are singular. It can be shown that the plane generating $\mathbf{S}$ is through the optical center C' (hence the singularity) and projects to the line of equation $\mathbf{e}'$ in the second image. Because it is attached to the system of two cameras, it is called the *intrinsic plane* Π_S.

We end this section by giving an expression of the Fundamental matrix as a function of the projection matrices, which can can be used on a calibrated stereo rig to guide the correspondence process by limiting it to epipolar lines. We write the two projection matrices $\mathcal{P} = [\mathbf{P}\ \mathbf{p}]$ and $\mathcal{P}' = [\mathbf{P}'\ \mathbf{p}']$. We place ourselves in the perspective case (as opposed to the parallel case, see Section 1.6) by assuming $\det(\mathbf{P}) \neq 0$. The epipole $\mathbf{e}'$ is the projection $\mathcal{P}'\tilde{\mathbf{C}}$ of the optical center $\tilde{\mathbf{C}}$ given by Equation 1.6; therefore

$$\mathbf{e}' \simeq \mathcal{P}'\tilde{\mathbf{C}} \simeq [\mathbf{P}'\ \mathbf{p}'] \begin{bmatrix} -\mathbf{P}^{-1}\mathbf{p} \\ 1 \end{bmatrix} \simeq \mathbf{p}' - \mathbf{P}'\mathbf{P}^{-1}\mathbf{p}.$$

Now that we know the epipole, to apply Equation 1.11 in order to determine $\mathbf{F}$, we need only a planar homography between the two images. One such homography is the one induced by the plane at infinity, given in Equation 1.8. Using this, we obtain an expression of the Fundamental matrix as a function of the projection matrices:

$$\mathbf{F} = [\mathbf{p}' - \mathbf{P}'\mathbf{P}^{-1}\mathbf{p}]_\times \mathbf{P}'\mathbf{P}^{-1}$$

1.14 A stratified approach to reconstruction

The reconstruction problem can be stated as that of determining the projection matrices $\mathcal{P}$ and $\mathcal{P}'$, as well as the 3-D points M_i, given a set of N correspondences (m_i, m_i'). The solution is not unique because it depends on the choice of a coordinate system, expressed by the 4×4 matrix $\mathcal{H}$. If $(\mathcal{P}, \mathcal{P}', \mathbf{M}_1, \cdots, \mathbf{M}_N)$ is a solution to the reconstruction problem, then $(\mathcal{P}\mathcal{H}^{-1}, \mathcal{P}'\mathcal{H}^{-1}, \mathcal{H}\mathbf{M}_1, \cdots, \mathcal{H}\mathbf{M}_N)$ is also a solution, since

$$\begin{cases} \mathbf{m} & \simeq & \mathcal{P}\mathbf{M} & = (\mathcal{P}\mathcal{H}^{-1})(\mathcal{H}\mathbf{M}), \\ \mathbf{m}' & \simeq & \mathcal{P}'\mathbf{M} & = (\mathcal{P}'\mathcal{H}^{-1})(\mathcal{H}\mathbf{M}). \end{cases} \tag{1.14}$$

In other words, all the pairs of projection matrices of the form $(\mathcal{P}\mathcal{H}, \mathcal{P}'\mathcal{H})$, where $\mathcal{H}$ is an arbitrary projective transformation, are potentially equivalent. However, if we have some constraints about the correspondences, then we can hope to limit the ambiguity $\mathcal{H}$ by enforcing that these constraints have to be satisfied by the pair $(\mathcal{P}\mathcal{H}, \mathcal{P}'\mathcal{H})$.

We will see in Section 1.15 that from uncalibrated images, there are no further restrictions. We can recover only a *projective reconstruction*, which means reconstruction of points up to a general projective transformation $\mathcal{H}$ of space. To obtain an *Euclidean reconstruction* (i.e. up to a Euclidean transformation plus scale), we need to use either some *a priori* information about the world, which makes it possible to determine in succession the plane at infinity (Section 1.17) and the intrinsic parameters of a camera (Section 1.18), or either some *a priori* information about the camera, which makes it possible to perform self-calibration (Section 1.23). The flow chart of the approach to recover Euclidean reconstruction from uncalibrated images is summarized in Figure 1.21.

1.15 Projective reconstruction [Section 7.2]

Point correspondences (m_i, m_i') are the only information that we have in this section. The projective correspondence information can be summarized by the Fundamental matrix $\mathbf{F}$ of the pairs of images, that we compute from the correspondences. Any pair of projection matrices $(\mathcal{P}, \mathcal{P}')$ is a valid solution to the reconstruction problem if and only if its Fundamental matrix is compatible with the point correspondences (m_i, m_i'), or in other words if its Fundamental matrix is $\mathbf{F}$.

It can be shown [Section 7.2] that any pair $(\mathcal{P}, \mathcal{P}')$ has Fundamental matrix $\mathbf{F}$

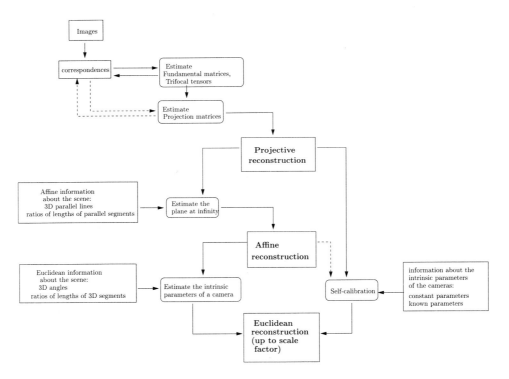

Figure 1.21: Euclidean reconstruction from images can be achieved using information either about the world or about the cameras.

if, and only if it is of the form

$$\begin{cases} \mathcal{P} & \simeq & [\mathbf{I}_3\,\mathbf{0}_3]\mathcal{H}, \\ \mathcal{P}' & \simeq & [\mathbf{H}\,\mu\mathbf{e}']\mathcal{H}, \end{cases} \quad \text{with } \mathcal{H} = \begin{bmatrix} \mathcal{P} \\ \mathbf{\Pi}^T \end{bmatrix}, \qquad (1.15)$$

where

- $\mathcal{P}$ is an arbitrary projection matrix (11 parameters) $\mathbf{\Pi}$ is the projective equation of an arbitrary plane (3 parameters), μ is an arbitrary constant (1 parameter), which is in fact the common scale of $\mathcal{P}$ and $\mathbf{\Pi}$ in the matrix $\mathcal{H}$. Together, these 15 parameters represent the projective ambiguity in reconstruction: the arbitrary choice of the projective basis in 3-D, or, equivalently, of the matrix $\mathcal{H}$.

- The remaining elements in $\mathcal{P}'$ are: the epipole $\mathbf{e}'$ of $\mathbf{F}$ in the second image and the homography $\mathbf{H}$, compatible with $\mathbf{F}$ and generated by the plane Π. These entities are uniquely determined by $\mathbf{F}$ and Π. This shows that given the Fundamental matrix $\mathbf{F}$, once a projective basis in $\mathbb{P}^3$ is chosen by fixing the 15 previous parameters, $\mathcal{P}'$ is uniquely determined.

So we have partitioned the $22 = 11 \times 2$ parameters of a pair of projection matrices into two types of parameters: the projective correspondence of the pair of cameras embedded in the Fundamental matrix (7 parameters), and a projective transformation (15 parameters), which represents the ambiguity in reconstruction. The Fundamental matrix is invariant to the choice of the projective basis in $\mathbb{P}^3$. From the decomposition in Equation 1.15, it is easy to verify that

$(\mathcal{P}_1, \mathcal{P}'_1)$ and $(\mathcal{P}_2, \mathcal{P}'_2)$ have the same Fundamental matrix
$$\Leftrightarrow$$
$\mathcal{P}_1 = \mathcal{P}_2\mathcal{H}$ and $\mathcal{P}'_1 = \mathcal{P}'_2\mathcal{H}$, where $\mathcal{H}$ is a projective transformation of $\mathbb{P}^3$

which shows that when the only constraints on the matches come from the Fundamental matrix, all of the reconstructions up to a projective transformations are acceptable. The basic steps of the projective reconstruction are as follows:

- Obtain pairs of correspondences m_i, m'_i.

- Solve for the Fundamental matrix with Equation 1.9

- Compute the special matrix $\mathbf{S} = [\mathbf{e}']_\times \mathbf{F}$ ($\mathbf{e}'$ is given by $\mathbf{F}^T\mathbf{e}' = 0$).

- Compute a particular pair of projection matrices, called the *projective canonical representation*, obtained by choosing the "simplest" pairs among those in Equation 1.15 using $\mathbf{S}$ as a particular instance of $\mathbf{H}$:

$$\begin{cases} \mathcal{P} & \simeq & [\mathbf{I}_3\,\mathbf{0}_3], \\ \mathcal{P}' & \simeq & [\mathbf{S}\,\mu\mathbf{e}']. \end{cases} \qquad (1.16)$$

This pair is an invariant representation in the sense that its elements do not depend on the choice of projective coordinates in $\mathbb{P}^3$.

- Solve for M_i with Equation 1.7.

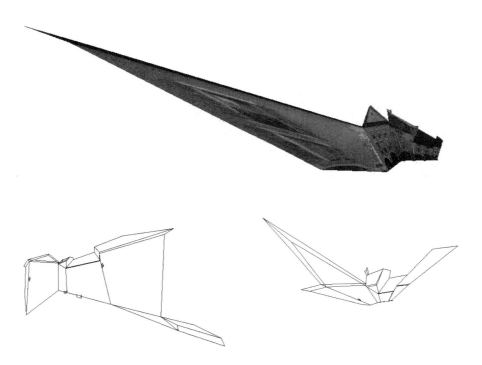

Figure 1.22: Three projective reconstructions, seen from a similar viewpoint. Each reconstruction can be transformed into another by a projective transformation of $\mathbb{P}^3$. Although the deformation can be large, incidence (coplanarity, alignment, and intersection) is preserved.

The previous algorithm will often yield a reconstruction with a very significant projective distortion because a projective transformation does not even preserve depth ordering, let alone relative distances. This means in particular that we cannot make meaningful measurements in such a reconstruction.

1.16 Reconstruction is not always necessary [Section 7.2]

There are applications for which the projective distortion is not a problem because we are not interested in reconstructing the 3-D shape.

A first example is the detection of obstacles for the navigation of a robot or the generation of alarms in a surveillance system, for which we need only qualitative measurements. This can often be achieved by positioning points with respect to a reference plane, assuming that we can identify three correspondences of points lying on this plane so that we can compute its planar homography $\mathbf{H}$. Points above the ground plane or points closer to the robot than a predefined frontal plane can be identified as obstacles. Using the projective canonical form, we can write the reconstructions equations as

$$\mathbf{m} \simeq [\mathbf{I}_3\, \mathbf{0}_3]\mathbf{M}, \qquad \mathbf{m}' \simeq [\mathbf{H}\, \mu\mathbf{e}']\mathbf{M}.$$

The first equation implies $\mathbf{M} = \begin{bmatrix} \mathbf{m} \\ \rho \end{bmatrix}$ where ρ is an unknown related to the position of the point M in a certain projective coordinate system. The substitution into the second equation yields the relation

$$\mathbf{m}' \simeq \mathbf{H}\mathbf{m} + \mu\rho\mathbf{e}', \tag{1.17}$$

where $\kappa = \mu\rho$ is a quantity called *projective parallax*. This quantity can be computed from the correspondence (m, m'), knowing $\mathbf{H}$ and $\mathbf{e}'$, for example by taking the cross-product of both terms with $\mathbf{m}'$. See Figure 1.16. The projective planar parallax turns out [Section 7.2.4] to be proportional to the distance of the point M to the plane Π and inversely proportional to the depth of the point M, which is its distance to the optical center C. This double dependency is illustrated in Figure 1.16. Although projective transformations do not preserve depth ordering, it can be sufficient to know that κ changes sign when M crosses the plane, being zero if M belongs to Π. This observation makes it possible to position a set of points on one side of a reference plane, once again without the need for reconstruction.

A second example is the synthesis of new images from two reference images. Here, the end result is a new image, so the intermediary representation of shape is not important. Once the point M is reconstructed in a projective frame, we could reproject it with any projection matrix $\mathcal{P}''$, generating a new image. In fact, no actual reconstruction is necessary. If $\mathbf{F}_{12}$ is the Fundamental matrix from image 1 to the new image, and $\mathbf{F}_{23}$ is the Fundamental matrix from image 2 to the new image, then given a point m in image 1 and a point m' in image 2, the point in image 3 is obtained in general as the intersection of the epipolar lines $\mathbf{F}_{12}\mathbf{m}$ and $\mathbf{F}_{23}\mathbf{m}'$. This operation is called *transfer*: points m and m' are transferred to the third image using the knowledge of the epipolar geometry. This idea makes it

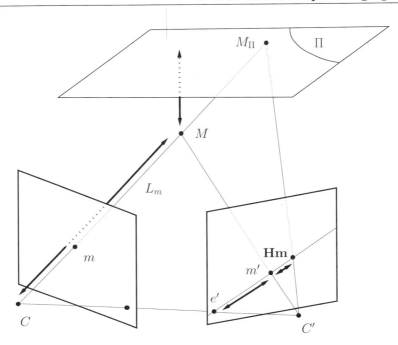

Figure 1.23: Projective parallax. The points **Hm**, e', and m' are aligned. The ratio of their distances is the projective parallax, proportional to the distance of M to Π and inversely proportional to the depth of M.

possible to represent a scene as a collection of images rather than as a 3-D model. We have made some progress towards our goal of generating synthetic views, but to insert a Euclidean model and follow a given camera trajectory we need to recover further information.

1.17   Affine reconstruction [Section 7.3]

Projective reconstruction depends only on the Fundamental matrix, which can be computed from point correspondences. We have just seen that in the general case, from two images we are able to reconstruct points and projection matrices which are obtained from the "true" points by a projective transformation. If, in addition, we have some affine information, we can reduce the ambiguity in reconstruction from a general projective transformation of $\mathbb{P}^3$ to an affine transformation of $\mathbb{P}^3$, which means that we are able to reconstruct points and projection matrices which are obtained from the "true" points by a transformation which is more constrained, and therefore induces less deformations and preserves more properties. However, the affine information has to come from some additional knowledge about the world or

Figure 1.24: Planar parallax. The third image is obtained by warping the second image by the homography of the ground plane, so that points on this plane are mapped to their position in the first image, and superimposing with the first image. The projective parallax is the length of the vector between original and warped points. It is zero for points of the reference plane, increases with height above this plane, and decreases with depth. Remark that the vectors all point towards the epipole in the image, which is near infinity in the direction X.

the system of cameras. Correspondences alone can not provide affine information.

An affine transformation is a particular projective transformation which preserves the plane at infinity Π_∞. It is easy to see that a transformation $\mathcal{A}$ conserves Π_∞ if, and only if, the last row of the matrix of $\mathcal{A}$ is of the form $[0, 0, 0, \mu]$, with $\mu \neq 0$. Since this matrix is defined only up to a scale factor, we can take $\mu = 1$, then the transformation $\mathcal{A}$ is fully described by its first 3×3 sub-matrix $\mathbf{A}$ and the 3 first coordinates of the last column vector $\mathbf{b}$:

$$\mathcal{A} = \begin{bmatrix} \mathbf{A} & \mathbf{b} \\ \mathbf{0}_3^T & 1 \end{bmatrix},$$

which yields the classical description of a transformation of the affine space $\mathbb{R}^3$: $\mathbf{x}' = \mathbf{A}\mathbf{x} + \mathbf{b}$. We have seen that points at infinity represent directions. An affine transformation therefore preserves parallelism: parallel subspaces are transformed in subspaces which are still parallel. Other properties [Chapter 2] are that depth ordering and the ratios of distances of three aligned points are also preserved. This limits the amount of distortion introduced in the reconstruction.

The affine space is characterized by the plane at infinity Π_∞ in $\mathbb{P}^3$, which has three parameters. Affine information between two images is encoded as the correspondence of projections of points of Π_∞. The correspondence of points of Π_∞, like the correspondence of points of any plane, is described by a planar homography matrix called the *infinity homography* $\mathbf{H}_\infty$ whose expression as a function of the projection matrices was given in Equation 1.8. Once $\mathbf{F}$ is known, the three additional parameters necessary to describe $\mathbf{H}_\infty$ are in the vector $\mathbf{r}_\infty$:

$$\mathbf{H}_\infty \simeq \mathbf{S} + \mathbf{e}'\mathbf{r}_\infty^T.$$

As a particular case of Equation 1.12, in this equation the vector $\mathbf{r}_\infty$ represents the projection in the first image of the intersection of the intrinsic plane Π_S with the plane at infinity, which is the *vanishing line* of Π_S, containing the vanishing points of all sets of parallel lines of Π_S.

Once $\mathbf{F}$ is known, three correspondences of points at infinity are necessary to determine $\mathbf{H}_\infty$. One way to obtain them is to consider three corresponding vanishing points. Since parallel lines in $\mathbb{P}^3$ intersect on the plane at infinity, a vanishing point, which is the intersection of projections of parallel lines, is the projection of one point of Π_∞. Other ways to obtain one constraint on the plane at infinity include using the correspondence of one horizon point which lies at a large distance from the cameras and using knowledge of the ratio of distances for three aligned points.

When affine correspondence is known, we can restrict further the pairs $(\mathcal{P}, \mathcal{P}')$ of possible projection matrices. We require, in addition to the fact that it has $\mathbf{F}$ as its Fundamental matrix, the fact that $\mathbf{H}_\infty$ is its infinity homography. In fact, this requirement is redundant: if $\mathbf{H}_\infty$ is known, then using Equation 1.11, it is sufficient to specify one epipole to define $\mathbf{F}$ and to complete the description of affine correspondence. It can be verified that the pairs of projection matrices which have infinity homography $\mathbf{H}_\infty$ and epipole $\mathbf{e}'$ are of the form

$$\left\{ \begin{array}{ccc} \mathcal{P} & \simeq & [\mathbf{I}_3\ \mathbf{0}_3]\mathcal{A}, \\ \mathcal{P}' & \simeq & [\mathbf{H}_\infty\ \mu\mathbf{e}']\mathcal{A}, \end{array} \right. \quad \text{with } \mathcal{A} = \left[\begin{array}{c} \mathcal{P} \\ \mathbf{0}_3^T\ 1 \end{array} \right]. \qquad (1.18)$$

This decomposition is a particular case of Equation 1.16, obtained with $\Pi = [0, 0, 0, 1]^T$. The crucial remark is that the transformation of space is an affine transformation rather than a projective one. This decomposition separates the total 22 parameters into two types of parameters:

- 12 correspond to the affine ambiguity in reconstruction: the arbitrary choice of the affine basis (11 obtained by fixing $\mathcal{P}$, 1 is μ)

- 10 describe the affine correspondence: 8 as the infinity homography $\mathbf{H}_\infty$ and 2 as the epipole $\mathbf{e}'$. That is, given affine correspondence as an infinity homography and an epipole, once an affine basis is chosen by fixing the 12 previous parameters, $\mathcal{P}'$ is uniquely defined.

From the decomposition in Equation 1.18 it is easy to verify that

$$(\mathcal{P}_1, \mathcal{P}'_1) \text{ and } (\mathcal{P}_2, \mathcal{P}'_2) \text{ have the same infinity homography}$$
$$\text{and Fundamental matrix}$$
$$\Leftrightarrow$$
$$\mathcal{P}_1 = \mathcal{P}_2 \mathcal{A} \text{ and } \mathcal{P}'_1 = \mathcal{P}'_2 \mathcal{A}, \ \mathcal{A} \text{ being an affine transformation of } \mathbb{P}^3.$$

To summarize, when we have identified the plane at infinity Π_∞, a pair of images with epipole $\mathbf{e}'$ and infinity homography $\mathbf{H}_\infty$ determines a reconstruction up to an affine transformation of $\mathbb{P}^3$ (see Figure 1.25 for an example). The reconstruction can be performed using one particular pair of projection matrices, the *affine canonical representation*, whose elements do not depend on the choice of the affine basis in $\mathbb{P}^3$. We remark that it can be obtained from the projective representation described in Equation 1.16 by multiplication by the matrix $\mathbf{Q}_A^{-1}$:

$$\begin{cases} \mathcal{P} &= [\mathbf{I}_3\,\mathbf{0}_3] &= [\mathbf{I}_3\,\mathbf{0}_3]\mathbf{Q}_A^{-1} \\ \mathcal{P}' &= [\mathbf{H}_\infty\,\mu\mathbf{e}'] &= [\mathbf{S}\,\mu\mathbf{e}']\mathbf{Q}_A^{-1} \end{cases} \quad \text{with } \mathbf{Q}_A^{-1} = \begin{bmatrix} \mathbf{I}_3 & \mathbf{0}_3 \\ \mathbf{r}_\infty^T & \mu \end{bmatrix}.$$

According to Equation 1.14, to upgrade the projective reconstruction of the points to an affine reconstruction, we need only to apply the transformation $\mathbf{Q}_A$. Because affine transformations include shear and different scalings along axes, the relative distances of points are not preserved. However, the relative distances of *aligned* points are preserved, so we can begin to make quantitative measurements, such as locating the middle of a segment.

1.18   Euclidean reconstruction [Section 7.4]

We now go one step further and reach more familiar ground by examining the case when in addition to the affine correspondence, we have Euclidean information. This information makes it possible to reduce the ambiguity to a *similarity transformation* (displacement plus scale) and to obtain the reconstructions illustrated in Figure 1.26, in which we can measure angles and relative distances. Just like affine transformations are particular projective transformations, similarity transformations are particular affine transformations for which the first 3×3 sub-matrix satisfies $\mathbf{A}\mathbf{A}^T = s\mathbf{I}_3$. It will be seen in Section 1.23 that this algebraic condition corresponds to the invariance to transformation of a geometric object which is a subset of the plane at infinity, the absolute conic Ω, just as the affine transformations are characterized by the invariance of Π_∞. Therefore there is a hierarchy

Figure 1.25: Three affine reconstructions, seen from a similar viewpoint. Each reconstruction can be transformed into another by an affine transformation of $\mathbb{P}^3$. There are shear and different scalings along axes, but parallelism is preserved.

of transformations: similarity is a subset of affine, which is a subset of projective. Each time we restrain the transformation, we further constrain the reconstruction, but to do so, we need more information.

Figure 1.26: A Euclidean reconstruction, seen from a viewpoint similar to the projective and affine reconstructions. Other reconstructions would be transformed into this one by a Euclidean transformation, which is equivalent to a change of viewpoint and a global scaling. Angles and relatives distances are correct (the slight convergence is due to projection).

Euclidean information in an image is encoded as the projection of Ω, or more concretely, as the matrix of intrinsic parameters of the camera which we will call $\mathbf{A}$. In general, this matrix represents five parameters which are known when the camera is calibrated. They can be determined from a combination of knowledge about the camera (for example most real cameras have a zero skew and known aspect ratio, which reduces the number of parameters to three) and of knowledge about the world (such as angles and ratios of distances).

When $\mathbf{A}$ is known, we can restrict further the pairs $(\mathcal{P}, \mathcal{P}')$ of admissible reconstructions. We first note that if we decompose each projection matrix into intrinsic and extrinsic parameters, we have the classical decomposition for any pair of projection matrices:

$$\begin{cases} \mathcal{P} & \simeq & \mathbf{A}[\mathbf{R}_1\,\mathbf{t}_1] & = & [\mathbf{A}\,\mathbf{0}_3]\mathcal{S} \\ \mathcal{P}' & \simeq & \mathbf{A}'[\mathbf{R}_2\,\mathbf{t}_2] & = & \mathbf{A}'[\mathbf{R}\,\mu\mathbf{t}]\mathcal{S} \end{cases} \quad \text{with} \quad \mathcal{S} = \begin{bmatrix} \mathbf{R}_1 & \mathbf{t}_1 \\ \mathbf{0}_3^T & 1/\mu \end{bmatrix},$$

where $\mathbf{R} = \mathbf{R}_2\mathbf{R}_1^T$ and $\mathbf{t} = \mathbf{t}_2 - \mathbf{R}_2\mathbf{R}_1^T\mathbf{t}_1$ represents the relative displacement between the two camera coordinate systems. Let's count again: of the total 22 parameters:

- 7 correspond to a similarity transformation representing the arbitrary choice of the Euclidean basis (6 obtained by fixing the coordinate system of the first camera through $\mathbf{R}_1$ and $\mathbf{t}_1$, and 1 being μ which represents the scale),

- 15 describe the intrinsic parameters (5 for each camera) and the relative Euclidean transformation $\mathbf{R}, \mathbf{t}$ (position and orientation) of the two cameras.

The direction of the translation is determined, but its norm is not because of the depth-speed ambiguity: one cannot distinguish between a close point moving slowly and a distant point moving proportionally faster.

Computing from the projection matrix, we obtain with easy algebra

$$\mathbf{e}' = \mathbf{A}\mathbf{t} \ , \ \mathbf{H}_\infty = \mathbf{A}'\mathbf{R}\mathbf{A}^{-1}.$$

From that result, we conclude that we can characterize the Euclidean correspondence by either one of the two sets of fifteen parameters:

- the affine correspondence plus intrinsic parameters of one camera: $\mathbf{H}_\infty, \mathbf{e}', \mathbf{A}$

- the intrinsic parameters of both cameras and the displacement between two cameras: $\mathbf{A}, \mathbf{A}', \mathbf{R}, \mathbf{t}$.

Similarly to the previous situations:

$$(\boldsymbol{\mathcal{P}}_1, \boldsymbol{\mathcal{P}}_1') \text{ and } (\boldsymbol{\mathcal{P}}_2, \boldsymbol{\mathcal{P}}_2') \text{ have the same Euclidean correspondence}$$
$$\Leftrightarrow$$
$$\boldsymbol{\mathcal{P}}_1 = \boldsymbol{\mathcal{P}}_2\boldsymbol{\mathcal{S}} \text{ and } \boldsymbol{\mathcal{P}}_1' = \boldsymbol{\mathcal{P}}_2'\boldsymbol{\mathcal{S}},$$

where $\boldsymbol{\mathcal{S}}$ is a Euclidean (similarity) transformation of $\mathbb{P}^3$.

We can now obtain a *Euclidean canonic representation* as a specialization of affine and projective strata. In this case, this particular pair of projection matrices are obtained just by using as 3-D coordinate system the first camera's coordinate system.

$$\begin{cases} \boldsymbol{\mathcal{P}} & \simeq & [\mathbf{A}\,\mathbf{0}_3] & = & [\mathbf{I}_3\,\mathbf{0}_3]\mathbf{Q}_A^{-1}\mathbf{Q}_E^{-1} \\ \boldsymbol{\mathcal{P}}' & \simeq & \mathbf{A}'[\mathbf{R}\,\mu\mathbf{t}] & = & [\mathbf{S}\,\mu\mathbf{e}']\mathbf{Q}_A^{-1}\mathbf{Q}_E^{-1} \end{cases} \tag{1.19}$$

with

$$\mathbf{Q}_A^{-1} = \begin{bmatrix} \mathbf{I}_3 & \mathbf{0}_3 \\ \mathbf{r}_\infty^T & \mu \end{bmatrix} \quad \text{and} \quad \mathbf{Q}_E^{-1} = \begin{bmatrix} \mathbf{A} & \mathbf{0}_3 \\ \mathbf{0}^T & 1 \end{bmatrix}. \tag{1.20}$$

Starting from a projective reconstruction, which requires only point correspondences, we can upgrade to an affine reconstruction when $\mathbf{r}_\infty$ is known (3 degrees of freedom) by applying $\mathbf{Q}_A$ to the points M_i, and to a Euclidean reconstruction

PROJECTIVE	**homography** (incidence, $\mathbb{P}^3$)		
reconstruction ambiguity	$\mathcal{H} = \begin{bmatrix} \mathcal{P} \\ \mathbf{\Pi}^T \end{bmatrix}$	$\mathcal{H}$ non-singular	15
invariant description	$\mathbf{S}$: special matrix $\mathbf{e}'$: epipole		7
canonical form	$\begin{cases} \mathcal{P} & \simeq & [\mathbf{I}_3\,\mathbf{0}_3]\mathcal{H} \\ \mathcal{P}' & \simeq & [\mathbf{S} + \mathbf{e}'\mathbf{r}_{\Pi}^T\,\mu\mathbf{e}']\mathcal{H} \end{cases}$		22
AFFINE	**affine transformation** (parallelism, Π_∞)		
reconstruction ambiguity	$\mathcal{A} = \begin{bmatrix} \mathbf{P} & \mathbf{p} \\ \mathbf{0}_3^T & 1/\mu \end{bmatrix}$	$\mathbf{P}$ non-singular	12
invariant description	$\mathbf{H}_\infty$: infinity homography		8
	$\mathbf{e}'$: epipole		2
canonical form	$\begin{cases} \mathcal{P} & \simeq & [\mathbf{I}_3\,\mathbf{0}_3]\mathcal{A} \\ \mathcal{P}' & \simeq & [\mathbf{H}_\infty\,\mu\mathbf{e}']\mathcal{A} \end{cases}$		22
EUCLIDEAN	**similarity** (angles, Ω)		
reconstruction ambiguity	$\mathcal{S} = \begin{bmatrix} \mathbf{R}_1 & \mathbf{t}_1 \\ \mathbf{0}_3^T & 1/\mu \end{bmatrix}$	$\mathbf{R}_1$ orthogonal	7
invariant description	$\mathbf{A},\mathbf{A}'$: intrinsic parameters		5+5
	$\mathbf{R}$: rotation between cameras		3
	$\mathbf{t}$: direction of translation between cameras		2
canonical form	$\begin{cases} \mathcal{P} & \simeq & [\mathbf{A}\,\mathbf{0}_3]\mathcal{S} \\ \mathcal{P}' & \simeq & \mathbf{A}'[\mathbf{R}\,\mu\mathbf{t}]\mathcal{S} \end{cases}$		22

Table 1.4: Canonical forms for the geometries of two images: for each level of description, we have a partition of the 22 parameters describing two projective images into an invariant representation, which represent the correspondence, and the ambiguity in reconstruction. The last column indicates the number of degrees of freedom.

when $\mathbf{A}$ is known (5 DOF) by applying $\mathbf{Q}_E$. $\mathbf{Q}_A$ is a projective transformation which moves the plane at infinity, and $\mathbf{Q}_E$ is an affine transformation which moves the absolute conic in the plane at infinity. Each upgrade reduces the reconstruction ambiguity, first from a general homography (15 DOF) to affine (12 DOF), then from affine to similarity (7 DOF). The representations and ambiguities in reconstruction are summarized in Table 1.4.

We have come a bit closer to our goal of building metric models and generating synthetic augmented images, provided that some information about the scene is available. However, from a practical point of view, using only two images does not afford a lot of robustness towards image noise and imprecision. Moreover, for complex objects, it is necessary to integrate several viewpoints to cover all of the parts which would be occluded from just two views.

1.19   The geometry of three images [Section 8.1]

Although two images make it possible to perform a reconstruction of the scene from point correspondences, adding a third image has two significant geometrical benefits.

First, the point correspondence problem becomes entirely constrained, because, as remarked in Section 1.16, the point in the third image can be transferred from the correspondence in the first two images $m \leftrightarrow m'$, and the fundamental matrices, as

$$\mathbf{m}'' \simeq \mathbf{F}_{12}\mathbf{m} \times \mathbf{F}_{23}\mathbf{m}', \qquad (1.21)$$

where $\mathbf{F}_{12}$ (respectively $\mathbf{F}_{23}$) is the Fundamental matrix between view 1 and view 2 (respectively 3). While the epipolar constraint is bilinear in the coordinates of the two image points, this equation is *trilinear* in the coordinates of the three image points.

We note that this method of transfer fails if the two lines represented by $\mathbf{F}_{13}\mathbf{m}$ and $\mathbf{F}_{23}\mathbf{m}'$ are identical. This can happen if the 3-D point M of which m, m', m'' are projections belongs to the plane containing the three optical centers (called *Trifocal plane*) or if the three optical centers are aligned. We are going to see that the three Fundamental matrices $\mathbf{F}_{12}$, $\mathbf{F}_{23}$, and $\mathbf{F}_{13}$ are not independent but are linked by three constraints which express that all the epipoles belong to the Trifocal plane. $\mathbf{F}_{31}\mathbf{e}_{32}$, the epipolar line of $\mathbf{e}_{32}$ in the first image, is the intersection of the trifocal plane with the first retinal plane. The epipoles $\mathbf{e}_{12}$ and $\mathbf{e}_{13}$ also belong to this plane and to the first retinal plane, thus: $\mathbf{e}_{12} \times \mathbf{e}_{13} \simeq \mathbf{F}_{31}\mathbf{e}_{32}$. The two other equations follow by a circular permutation of indices. This is illustrated in Figure 1.19. Therefore the system of Fundamental matrices depends on at most $18 = 7 \times 3 - 3$ parameters. It can be shown [Section 8.1] that this number is exact. The degeneracy of transfer and the non-independence of the Fundamental matrices suggest that they might not be the best way to represent the geometry of three images.

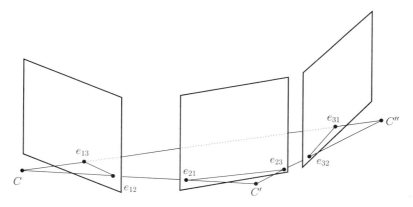

Figure 1.27: The six epipoles of three images lie on the *trifocal plane* defined by the three optical centers.

Second, it is possible to use line correspondences, unlike in the case of two images. As we have discussed in Section 1.10 in general two optical rays L_m and $L_{m'}$ do not intersect. Therefore the correspondence of two points yields one constraint which we described in the image as the epipolar constraint, and is formulated in space as the concurrency of L_m and $L_{m'}$. Knowing the projection l of a line L in space constrains L to lie on a plane Π_l going through the optical center. For any two lines l in the first image and l' in the second image, the planes Π_l and Π'_l will always intersect on a certain line $L_{ll'}$ which projects back to l and l'. Contrast Figure 1.10 and Figure 1.19. Therefore the correspondence of two lines in just two images does not yield any constraint. Let assume we have three images, and the correspondence $l \leftrightarrow l' \leftrightarrow l''$ of a line in each image. We can construct as before a line $L_{l'l''}$ which projects into l' in the second image and l'' in the third image. We can pick any point m on the line l and consider its optical ray L_m. Now that we have two lines, L_m and $L_{l'l''}$, we can obtain a constraint on the cameras called the *Trifocal constraint* by writing that they are concurrent, generalizing the construction we did with points in two images. See Figure 1.19. Note that unlike the case of two images, this construction is not symmetric. One image, the one where we have picked the point, plays a special role, while the two others play symmetric roles.

1.20   The Trifocal tensor [Chapter 8]

Let's put some algebra behind this geometric intuition. In two images, the correspondence of points is described by the 3×3 Fundamental matrix. We will see in this section that in three images, the correspondence of points and lines is described by a $3 \times 3 \times 3$ tensor $\mathcal{T}$, of entries T_i^{jk}, called the *Trifocal tensor*.

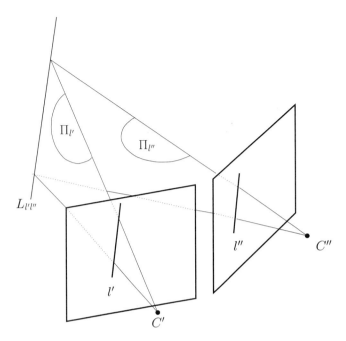

Figure 1.28: A line-line correspondence in two images. For any l' and l'', there is always a valid reconstruction $L_{l'l''}$, obtained by intersecting the planes $\Pi_{l'}$ and $\Pi_{l''}$.

We adopt the usual summation convention for tensors (*Einstein convention*), that any index repeated as subscript and superscript implies a summation over the range value, which in this section will always be 1..3. Any formula involving indices holds for any choice of values of the indices which are not repeated. Because of that, the order in which the terms are listed is unimportant. For instance, the correspondence of points through a homography matrix $\mathbf{H} = (H)_{ij}$ is written as $(m')^i = H^i_j m^j$. Superscripts designate *contravariant* indices (coordinates of points, row index of matrices), subscripts designate *covariant* indices (coordinates of lines, column index of matrices). These transform inversely under changes of basis, so that the contraction (dot product, or sum over all values) of a covariant-contravariant pair is invariant.

It can be shown [Section 8.2] that given the lines l' in the second image and l'' in the third image, the line l, which is the projection in the first image of their reconstruction, is given by

$$l_i = l'_j l''_k \mathcal{T}^{jk}_i. \tag{1.22}$$

The Trifocal tensor lets us predict the position of a line in a third image from its position in two images.

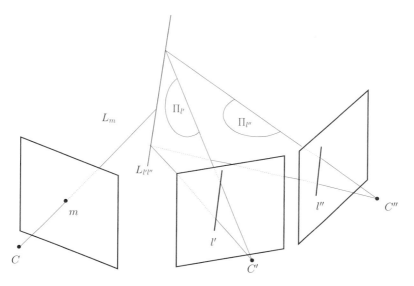

Figure 1.29: A point-line-line correspondence in three images. The optical ray L_m must intersect the line $\Pi_{l'} \cap \Pi_{l''}$.

The basic Trifocal constraint, obtained with a correspondence $m \leftrightarrow l' \leftrightarrow l''$ of a point in the first image and lines in the other images, is obtained by considering a point m on the the line l:

$$m^i l'_j l''_k \mathcal{T}_i^{jk} = 0. \tag{1.23}$$

It expresses the concurrency of the optical ray of m and the 3-D line projected to l' and l''. This constraint is the analogue for three images of the epipolar constraint for two images. While the epipolar constraint was bilinear in image coordinates, the Trifocal constraint is trilinear. It yields a considerably richer and more complex geometry. In the case of two images, the only geometric operation we could do with the Fundamental matrix was to apply it to a point and obtain the epipolar line. There are more possibilities with the Trifocal tensor, which we detail next and summarize in Table 1.5.

If we apply $\mathcal{T}$ only to the line l', i.e. fix it, we obtain a 3×3 matrix $\mathbf{H}'$ which maps a point from the first image to a point in the third image. Equation 1.23 can be read

$$l''_k \overbrace{m^i \underbrace{l'_j \mathcal{T}_i^{jk}}_{H'^k_i}}^{m''^k} = 0.$$

This equation is true for any line l'' containing the projection in the third image of the intersection of the optical ray L_m of m with the plane $\Pi_{l'}$ defined by the line

1	2	3	resulting object
m			**G**, correlation from image 2 to image 3
	l'		**H''**, homography from image 1 to image 3
		l''	**H'**, homography from image 1 to image 2
m	l'		m'', point in image 3
m		l''	m', point in image 2
	l'	l''	l, line in image 1
m	l'	l''	scalar

Table 1.5: Contractions of the Trifocal tensor. This table shows the geometric objects resulting from applying the Trifocal tensor in different ways.

l'. See Figure 1.20. Therefore, the matrix **H'** is a planar homography from the first image to the third image, generated by the plane $\Pi_{l'}$. The Trifocal tensor lets us predict the position of a point in a third image from a point in the first image and a line in the second image. A similar result is obtained by exchanging images 2 and 3. In the more frequent case when we have two points $m \leftrightarrow m'$, the projections of M, we can choose a line through one of the points and do the transfer. We notice that this construction always works provided that the point M does not lie on the line joining the optical centers of the two first cameras, whereas the transfer based on the Fundamental matrices described by Equation 1.21 suffered from several other degeneracies.

Last, if we apply $\mathcal{T}$ only to the point m, i.e. fix it, we obtain a 3×3 matrix **G** which maps a line l' from the second image to a point m'' in the third image. Such a mapping is called a *correlation*. Equation 1.23 can be read

$$l''_k \, l'^j \, \underbrace{\overbrace{m^i \mathcal{T}_i^{jk}}^{m''^k}}_{G^{jk}} = 0.$$

All the points m'' are projections of a point of the optical ray L_m, therefore as l' varies, its mapping by **G** describes the epipolar line of m in the third image. Remark that no other points of the third image than this line are reached by **G**, therefore the range of **G** has dimension 1, and we conclude that **G** has rank 2. See Figure 1.20. This result indicates that there is a connexion between the Trifocal tensor and the Fundamental matrices. In fact, the three Fundamental matrices can be computed from the Trifocal tensor [Section 8.2.4].

As a particular case of those results, the entries $\mathcal{T}_i^{jk}$ of the Trifocal tensor can themselves be interpreted as homographies or correlations by remarking that those entries are obtained by applying the tensor to the three entities $[1,0,0]^T$, $[0,1,0]^T$, $[0,0,1]^T$. Considering them as lines in the second image yields the three *intrinsic*

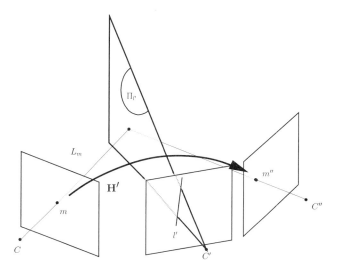

Figure 1.30: The line l' defines the plane Π'_l, which generates an homography $\mathbf{H}'$ between the first image and the third image.

homographies $\mathbf{H}'^k$, of entries $(H'^k)^j_i = \mathcal{T}^{jk}_i$. The tensor can be viewed as a stack of these three homographies. Considering them as points in the first image yields three matrices, the *Trifocal matrices* $\mathbf{G}^i$ of entries $(G^i)^{jk} = \mathcal{T}^{jk}_i$.

As discussed in Section 1.19, the Trifocal tensor depends on 18 independent parameters. $\mathcal{T}$ has $27 = 3 \times 3 \times 3$ entries defined up to a scale factor. Therefore, like the Fundamental matrix had to satisfy one constraint $\det(\mathbf{F}) = 0$, the Trifocal tensor has to satisfy eight algebraic constraints [Section 8.4]. We have seen three of them: the matrices $\mathbf{G}^i$ have zero determinant. Like the Fundamental matrix could be expressed as a function of the epipole and a homography, we have the relation [Section 8.2]

$$\mathcal{T}^{jk}_i = (e')^j (H'')^k_i - (e'')^k (H')^j_i,$$

where e' (respectively e'') is the epipole in the second (respectively third) image with respect to the first image, $\mathbf{H}'$ is a planar homography of a plane Π between the first and the second image, and $\mathbf{H}''$ is the planar homography of the same plane Π between the first and the third images.

1.21 Computing the Trifocal tensor [Chapter 9]

If we have the correspondence of one point m in the first image and two lines l' and l'' respectively in the second and third images, then the basic Trifocal constraint of Equation 1.23 gives one equation which is linear in the entries of $\mathcal{T}$. In practice,

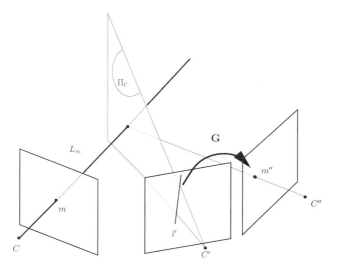

Figure 1.31: The point m defines the optical ray L_m, which generates a correlation G between the second image and the second image.

however, we are more often given the correspondence of three lines or of three points.

The first case, $l \leftrightarrow l' \leftrightarrow l''$ is quite simple: we write that the first line l_i and the line $l'_j l''_k \mathcal{T}_i^{jk}$ transferred from l' and l'' are identical, which can be expressed by the fact that their cross-product is zero. This gives three equations, two of which are independent.

In the second case, we notice that the Trifocal constraint holds for any line l' going through the point m' in the second image, and also for any line l'' going through the point m'' in the third image. Since lines through a point form a projective space of dimension one, there are two independent choices for l', as well as for l'', which yield a total of four independent equations. One possible choice is to consider the horizontal and vertical lines going through the points m' and m'', as illustrated in Figure 1.21

$\mathcal{T}$ has $27 = 3 \times 3 \times 3$ entries defined up to a scale factor. Since each correspondence of lines (respectively points) gives 2 (respectively 4) linear equations in the entries $\mathcal{T}_i^{jk}$, provided that $2\,n_{lines} + 4\,n_{points} \geq 26$ (n_{lines} and n_{points} represent the numbers of lines and points respectively), we can solve linearly for the entries of $\mathcal{T}_i^{jk}$ by constraining them to have sum 1.

Even more than for the Fundamental matrix, data normalization is crucial for the linear method to yield correct results. However, the best methods are obtained by minimizing a symmetrized geometric error function while enforcing algebraic constraints. The problem of correctly parameterizing the Tensor to enforce those constraints is quite tricky, and the symmetrization of the error function is also more

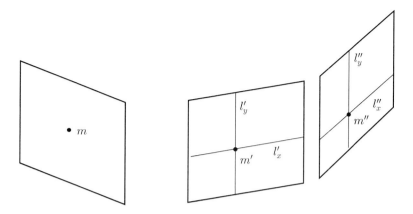

Figure 1.32: A point-point-point correspondence gives four point-line-line correspondences using the cross-hair directions.

difficult to express than for the Fundamental matrix.

1.22 Reconstruction from N images [Chapter 10]

We have seen in Section 1.15 that from two images, with no more information than point correspondences, it is possible to obtain only a projective reconstruction. This situation does not change when more views are added. The reasoning in Section 1.14 still holds, and the new views do not help obtain more constraints. Going from two views to three views, the number of parameters describing the correspondence goes from 7 for the Fundamental matrix to 18 for the Trifocal tensor, while the number of unknown camera parameters grows from $22 = 2 \times 11$ to $33 = 3 \times 11$. The remaining ambiguity is just the same 15 parameters for the projective transformation.

With a fourth view, one might consider quadrilinear constraints as a generalization of the trilinear constraints (Trifocal tensor) and bilinear constraints (Fundamental matrix). However, it turns out [Section 10.2] that the quadrilinear constraints can always be expressed as an algebraic combination of trilinear and bilinear constraints, so they wouldn't help. Moreover, beyond four views there are no further entities.

The projective geometry of N views can be represented using a canonical representation which extends the one introduced for two views in Section 1.15:

$$
\begin{cases}
\mathcal{P}_1 = [\mathbf{I}_3\,\mathbf{0}_3], \\
\mathcal{P}_2 = [\mathbf{P}_2\,\mathbf{p}_2], \\
\mathcal{P}_3 = [\mathbf{P}_3\,\mathbf{p}_3], \\
\vdots \\
\mathcal{P}_N = [\mathbf{P}_N\,\mathbf{p}_N],
\end{cases}
\tag{1.24}
$$

where $\mathbf{P}_2$ is the homography between views 1 and 2 associated with a plane Π, which is determined by the projective basis chosen, and $\mathbf{p}_2$ is the second epipole. As we have just discussed at the beginning of this section, while the first two matrices depend on a total of seven parameters to describe the geometry of the cameras (four additional parameters, the relative scale of $\mathbf{P}_2$ and $\mathbf{p}_2$, and Π are part of the projective ambiguity), all of the remaining matrices $\mathcal{P}_3 \ldots \mathcal{P}_n$ depend on 11 parameters each and therefore do not require a particular parameterization other than by their entries, hence our notation. However, there is a simple geometric interpretation of those entries, illustrated by Figure 1.22. $\mathbf{p}_i$ represents the coordinates of the epipole in the image i with respect to the first image, and $\mathbf{P}_i$ is the homography generated by Π between image one and image i. To see this, let us consider the point $\mathbf{m}$ in the first image, projection of a point M of Π. Because its planar parallax (see Equation 1.17) is zero, we have $\mathbf{M} = \begin{bmatrix} \mathbf{m} \\ 0 \end{bmatrix}$. Therefore, $\mathcal{P}_i\mathbf{M} = \mathbf{P}_i\mathbf{m}$.

The affine case is obtained as the particular case when the plane Π is the plane at infinity Π_∞, and the Euclidean case is obtained by replacing the homographies by rotations and the epipoles by translations, and using camera coordinates in the images.

We now use the more familiar Euclidean case to illustrate that the *local* representations (based on pairs of views) 1-2 and 2-3 are not sufficient to determine the representation 1-3, and therefore the global representation for three views 1-2-3, but that on the other hand, this global representation can be recovered from the three local representations, 1-2,1-3,2-3. Since a similarity has 7 degrees of freedom (see Table 1.4), the representation 1-2-3 has $33 - 7 = 26$ parameters, consisting of 3×5 intrinsic camera parameters, 2×3 rotation parameters, 3×3 translation parameters, minus the global scale μ:

$$
\begin{cases}
\mathcal{P}_1 = \mathbf{A}_1[\mathbf{I}_3\,\mathbf{0}_3], \\
\mathcal{P}_2 = \mathbf{A}_2[\mathbf{R}_{12}\,\mu\mathbf{t}_{12}], \\
\mathcal{P}_3 = \mathbf{A}_3[\mathbf{R}_{13}\,\mu\mathbf{t}_{13}].
\end{cases}
\tag{1.25}
$$

This scale factor μ must be the same for $\mathcal{P}_2$ and $\mathcal{P}_3$ because when we have three views, there is only a global scale indetermination, but the ratio of the local scale factors is completely determined, as we shall see soon. Each local (two-view) rep-

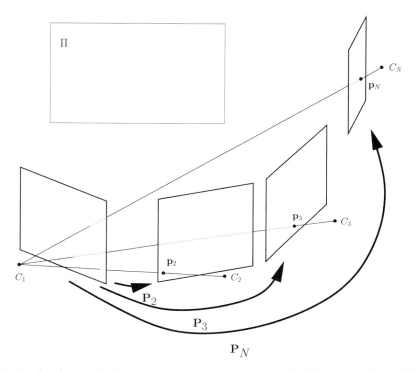

Figure 1.33: In the projective canonical representation for N views, $\mathcal{P}_1 = [\mathbf{I}_3\,\mathbf{0}_3]$, $\mathcal{P}_i = [\mathbf{P}_i\,\mathbf{p}_i]$, $\mathbf{P}_i$ is the homography generated by Π, and $\mathbf{p}_i$ is the epipole in the image.

resentation $i - j$ is written as

$$\left\{ \begin{array}{l} \mathcal{P}_{Li} = \mathbf{A}_i[\mathbf{I}_3\,\mathbf{0}_3], \\ \mathcal{P}_{Lj} = \mathbf{A}_j[\mathbf{R}_{ij}\,\mu_{ij}\mathbf{t}_{ij}], \end{array} \right.$$

where $\mathbf{t}_{ij}$ is the translation from the camera coordinate system of image i to the camera coordinate system of image j, and μ_{ij} is an unknown scale factor which arises from the fact that from correspondences, one cannot determine the absolute translation between two views, but only its direction. Let's try to obtain the direction of $\mathbf{t}_{13}$ from the representations 1-2 and 2-3. The relation between the translations is

$$\mu_{13}\mathbf{t}_{13} = \mu_{12}\mathbf{R}_{23}\mathbf{t}_{12} + \mu_{23}\mathbf{t}_{23}. \tag{1.26}$$

Because the scale factors μ_{12} and μ_{23} are unknown, it is not possible to determine the direction of $\mathbf{t}_{13}$ and therefore to build the representation 1-2-3. This is not surprising because we have here 3×5 intrinsic camera parameters, 2×3 rotation

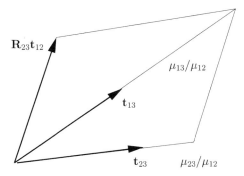

Figure 1.34: From the directions of $\mathbf{R}_{23}\mathbf{t}_{12}$ and $\mathbf{t}_{23}$ alone, it is not possible to recover the direction of $\mathbf{t}_3$. Their relative scale is necessary and sufficient. Reciprocally this relative scale can be recovered if the three directions are known.

parameters, 3×3 translation parameters, minus the two local scales μ_{ij} which totals only 25! However, if we know also the representation 1-3, i.e. $\mathbf{t}_{13}$, then the ratios μ_{23}/μ_{12} and μ_{13}/μ_{12} can be computed by expressing the coplanarity of the three vectors involved, which recovers the translations up to a global scale factor. This is illustrated in Figure 1.22.

The affine case is very similar. In the projective case, the reasoning is just the same, but instead of one unknown scale, four parameters are implied (remember that the system of three fundamental matrices depend on 18 parameters, while two independent fundamental matrices have 14 parameters). It is found [Section 10.2] that from the three Fundamental matrices or from the Trifocal tensor, one can recover a representation of the form (1.24). From that result, one can devise an incremental method which starts from a canonical representation of an $N - 1$-tuple of projection matrices and incorporates an Nth view, yielding a representation for N views.

Adding more views in general does not make it possible to upgrade from a projective to an affine or Euclidean representation without specific knowledge (such as for instance the fact that the cameras are identical, as discussed in the next section); however, it improves the robustness of the estimation and makes it possible to deal with more complex scenes. Several algorithms for reconstruction from N views are examined in Chapter 10.

1.23 Self-calibration of a moving camera using the absolute conic [Sections 2.3, 4.3.2]

We have explained how using some knowledge about the world made it possible to upgrade a projective reconstruction to affine and Euclidean. This knowledge has to be supplied to the system interactively by the user. An alternative, and more automatic, way to supply this information is to use constraints about the camera's intrinsic parameters, such that the fact that they are partially known (for instance for most cameras the skew is zero since the pixel grid is orthogonal, and the aspect ratio is known) or constant across images.

In order to use these constraints for this purpose, we now give a projective encoding of Euclidean structure, using the absolute conic. Let us consider the projective plane $\mathbb{P}^2$. When we move from an affine to a Euclidean representation, we gain the notion of angles and distances, and can define geometric entities such as circles. In projective geometry all the second order loci (ellipses, parabolas, hyperbolas) lose their distinction and are called *conics*, with an equation of the form $\mathbf{m}^T \mathbf{Q} \mathbf{m} = 0$, where $\mathbf{Q}$ is a square matrix. Their projective equivalence is illustrated by the fact that any form can be projected into any other form. Using the duality of points and lines, a conic can be considered not only as a locus of points, but also as a locus of lines, the set of lines which are tangent to the conic. For a given conic of matrix $\mathbf{Q}$, its *dual conic* (the set of its tangents) has matrix the adjoint matrix of $\mathbf{Q}$:

$$\mathbf{Q}^* = \det(\mathbf{Q})\mathbf{Q}^{-1} \qquad (1.27)$$

In the projective plane $\mathbb{P}^2$, just like two lines always intersect provided that we add to the affine points the line at infinity, so do two circles, provided that we add to the affine points two complex points in the line at infinity. Indeed, we encourage the reader to verify by simple algebra the surprising fact that all the circles contain the two particular points $I = [1, i, 0]$ and $J = [1, -i, 0]$, called *circular points*, which satisfy $x^2 + y^2 = z = 0$. Similarly, the Euclidean space $\mathbb{P}^3$ is characterized by the *absolute conic* Ω, which is the set of points $[X, Y, Z, T]^T$ satisfying $X^2 + Y^2 + Z^2 = 0$ and $T = 0$. In other words Ω is the conic in Π_∞ of matrix $\mathbf{I}_3$. Like the plane at infinity was used to characterize affine transformations, the absolute conic can be used to characterize similarity transformations. It can be verified that a projective transformation is a similarity transformation if and only if it leaves the absolute conic invariant.

Because the change of pose corresponds to a Euclidean transformation, which, as a particular case of a similarity transformation, leaves the absolute conic invariant, we conclude that its projection ω which is also a conic with only complex points, does not depend on the pose of the camera. Therefore, its equation in the retinal coordinate system does not depend on the extrinsic parameters and depends only on the intrinsic parameters. Computing in the camera coordinate system, it is easy to see that its matrix is $\mathbf{B} = \mathbf{A}^{-T}\mathbf{A}^{-1}$, whereas its dual conic has matrix, using Equation 1.27,

$$\mathbf{K} = \mathbf{B}^* = \det(\mathbf{B})\mathbf{B}^{-1} \simeq \mathbf{A}\mathbf{A}^T.$$

When the camera is calibrated, in the camera coordinate system, the projection of the absolute conic is just an imaginary circle of radius one. The general uncalibrated case is illustrated in Fig. 1.23. The matrix $\mathbf{K}$ is called the *Kruppa matrix*. It

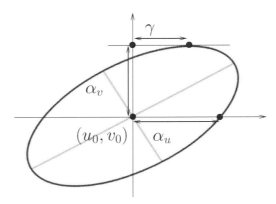

Figure 1.35: The way the five intrinsic parameters of Equation 1.4 affect the image of the absolute conic in the imaginary plane.

is symmetric and defined up to a scale factor, and therefore it depends on five independent parameters which can be recovered uniquely from $\mathbf{K}$.

The principle of self-calibration is to use the absolute conic as a calibration object. It has the advantage of being always available for free, however since it is a rather inaccessible object, all we can do with it is to write constraints across images. The knowledge of the infinity homography or of the Fundamental matrix makes it possible to write equations relating the intrinsic parameters of the two images. When we move a camera, we can obtain several such equations. Combining enough of them with the constraints on intrinsic parameters make it possible to recover the intrinsic parameters. Therefore just by moving a camera, observing its environment, and establishing point correspondences, we are able to calibrate the camera and eventually perform a Euclidean reconstruction of the environment, without ever needing a calibration object.

1.24   From affine to Euclidean [Section 11.1]

We first start with the simpler case when the infinity homography is known. A practically important situation when this occurs is the case of a stationary camera which rotates and zooms while staying at a fixed position. While this situation does not make it possible to recover structure, it is the most favorable to recover the calibration because, as we shall see soon, in this case the constraints take a particularly simple form.

We remark that in $\mathbf{H}_\infty \simeq \mathbf{A}'\mathbf{R}\mathbf{A}^{-1}$, $\mathbf{H}_\infty$ depends on eight parameters, and the rotation on three parameters, so we should be able to write five constraints on the intrinsic parameters. To express them, we eliminate the motion using the fact that a rotation matrix is orthogonal: $\mathbf{R}\mathbf{R}^T = \mathbf{I}_3$. This step yields a linear relation between the infinity homography and the intrinsic parameters:

$$\mathbf{H}_\infty \mathbf{K} \mathbf{H}_\infty^T \simeq \mathbf{K}', \tag{1.28}$$

where $\mathbf{K}$ and $\mathbf{K}'$ are the two Kruppa matrices. One could think that this is sufficient to solve for the five intrinsic parameters when they are constant ($\mathbf{K} = \mathbf{K}'$), but it turns out that one of the equations in this case is redundant because the infinity homography satisfies the additional constraint $\det(\mathbf{H}_\infty) = 1$. More precisely, it can be verified that there is a two dimensional space of solutions, spanned by the expected solution $\mathbf{K} = \mathbf{A}\mathbf{A}^T$ and the spurious solution $\mathbf{K} = \mathbf{A}\mathbf{U}(\mathbf{A}\mathbf{U})^T$, where $\mathbf{U}$ is the axis of the rotation. Two rotations along different axis are therefore necessary to solve for all of the intrinsic parameters.

We can remark that self-calibration depends only on the rotational component of the motion: it relies on the absolute conic, which being an object at infinity, has an projection not affected by translations but only by rotations. In particular, if there is no rotation, then Equation 1.28 becomes a tautology. In order to recover camera calibration from $\mathbf{H}_\infty$ it is therefore necessary to have a motion with a non-null rotational component. We will see that these conclusions extend to the recovery of camera calibration from $\mathbf{F}$, since it uses equations which are derived from Equation 1.28.

1.25 From projective to Euclidean [Section 11.2]

We now consider the general case when only a projective representation is available.

We note that the representation of Euclidean correspondence consisting of $\mathbf{A}$, $\mathbf{A}'$, $\mathbf{F}$ is redundant since it contains seventeen parameters, while a minimal representation has only fifteen parameters, so there must be two constraints between the Fundamental matrix and the intrinsic parameters. Another way to see it is to remark that the Fundamental matrix can be expressed as

$$\mathbf{F} = \mathbf{A}'^{-T}[\mathbf{t}]_\times \mathbf{R} \mathbf{A}^{-1}.$$

$\mathbf{F}$ depends on seven parameters and the motion on five parameters (the scale of the translation is not determined), so there must be two constraints, obtained again by eliminating the displacement. They can be obtained algebraically by multiplying Equation 1.28 by $[\mathbf{e}']_\times$ left and right,

$$[\mathbf{e}']_\times \mathbf{K}'[\mathbf{e}']_\times \simeq [\mathbf{e}']_\times \mathbf{H}_\infty \mathbf{K} \mathbf{H}_\infty^T [\mathbf{e}']_\times,$$

and using Equation 1.11:

$$\mathbf{F}\mathbf{K}\mathbf{F}^T \simeq [\mathbf{e}']_\times \mathbf{K}'[\mathbf{e}']_\times,$$

which is equivalent to two polynomial equations of degree 2 in the coefficients of $\mathbf{K}$ and $\mathbf{K}'$. These equations are called the *Kruppa equations*. Examples of applications of these equations are:

- Computing the focal lengths of the two cameras from the Fundamental matrix of a pair of images, assuming that the other intrinsic parameters are known.

- Computing all of the intrinsic parameters of a moving camera with constant intrinsic parameters from three images.

The Kruppa equations make it possible to perform self-calibration from the Fundamental matrices by solving only for the intrinsic parameters using polynomial methods. While this is interesting when we have few images, when we have a large number of images, it is advantageous to start from the projective canonical representation, because being global, it is numerically a more stable representation. We recover affine and Euclidean information at the same time by solving for the eight parameters of the projective transformation of Equation 1.20:

$$\mathcal{H} = \mathbf{Q}_A^{-1} \mathbf{Q}_E^{-1} = \begin{bmatrix} \mathbf{A} & \mathbf{0}_3 \\ \mathbf{r}_\infty^T \mathbf{A} & \mu \end{bmatrix}.$$

According to Equation 1.19, this transformation maps the set of canonical perspective projection matrices $\mathcal{P}_i$ into canonical Euclidean projection matrices:

$$\mathcal{P}_i \mathcal{H} \simeq \mathbf{A}_i [\mathbf{R}_i \, \mathbf{t}_i], \quad 2 \leq i \leq n.$$

We use the same trick as we did in the affine case: we multiply the first 3×3 submatrix (remember that only the rotational motion is relevant for self-calibration) by its transpose, eliminating the unknown rotation matrices $\mathbf{R}_i$:

$$\mathcal{P}_i \begin{bmatrix} \mathbf{K} & \mathbf{K}\mathbf{r}_\infty \\ \mathbf{r}_\infty^T \mathbf{K} & \mathbf{r}_\infty^T \mathbf{K}\mathbf{r}_\infty \end{bmatrix} \mathcal{P}_i^T \simeq \mathbf{K}_i, \quad 2 \leq i \leq n.$$

These equations make it possible to generalize self-calibration to the case of variable intrinsic parameters. Any constraints on the intrinsic parameters $\mathbf{A}_i$ translates into constraints on the Kruppa matrices $\mathbf{K}_i$. For instance, it can be verified with easy algebra that when the pixels are orthogonal, $K_{13}K_{23} - K_{33}K_{12} = 0$. If enough constraints are available, we can solve for $\mathbf{K}$ and $\mathbf{r}_\infty$ by nonlinear minimization. Since there are 8 unknowns, it is crucial to have a good starting point, which can be obtained with the Kruppa equations. This approach was used to self-calibrate the cameras and obtain the results presented at the beginning of the Chapter.

Like there are critical configurations of points which do not allow us to obtain a unique solution for the estimation of the Fundamental matrix, there are critical sequences of motions which do not allow us to obtain a unique solution for the estimation of the camera parameters. We have seen one of them, motions with parallel rotation axis and arbitrary translations. Other configurations are examined in Section 11.6.

1.26   References and further reading

Three dimensional problems involving several images have traditionally been studied under the assumption that the cameras are calibrated, with a few exceptions (the first use of projective geometry to analyze two-view geometry seems to be an unnoticed paper by Thompson (Thompson, 1968)). In the early 90's, Forsyth, Mundy *et al.* (Forsyth et al., 1990) in the context of object recognition, Koenderink and Van Doorn (Koenderink and van Doorn, 1991) in the context of structure from motion, and Barrett *et al.* (Barrett et al., 1992) in the context of image transfer, discovered that useful tasks could be performed using non-metric representations. Following the results of Faugeras (Faugeras, 1992) and Hartley *et al.* (Hartley et al., 1992) on projective reconstruction, an enormous burst of research was launched.

A decade later, there are so many papers that it has not been possible to cover all the important topics. In this book, we concentrate on the geometry of reconstruction and positioning from finite correspondences.

Invariants and object recognition   The approach developed in this book relies on the fact that the appearance of an object changes as the viewpoint changes in order to reconstruct the object and the camera motion. On the other hand this variation is one of the fundamental difficulties in recognizing objects from images. Another approach, which one might call the invariance program, seeks to overcome the problem that the appearance of an object depends on viewpoint by using geometric descriptions which are unaffected by the imaging transformation. These invariant measures can be used to index a library of object models for recognition. Many papers representative of this line of research can be found in the book edited by Mundy and Zisserman (Mundy and Zisserman, 1992). The follow-up of this book (Mundy et al., 1994) also has several papers which deal with the reconstruction approach. The two approaches are complementary in the sense that one of them concentrates on relations within the system of cameras while the other concentrates on relations within configurations of 3-D points.

There are numerous invariant descriptions which can be measured from images without any prior knowledge of the position, orientation and calibration of the camera. However, a fundamental limitation of the approach is that no *general* invariants of point sets can be measured from a single image (Burns et al., 1993; Barrett et al., 1991; Clemens and Jacobs, 1991). This means that we need either additional knowledge about the object (such as symmetry (Rothwell et al., 1993), which is the same as having two mirrored images of the same object, or planarity (Forsyth et al., 1990)) or multiple views. A significant part of the survey paper on object recognition using invariance of Zisserman *et al.* (Zisserman et al., 1995b) is a summary of results on the construction of invariants for 3-D objects from a single perspective view. Using continuous invariant descriptors can yield other difficulties. For example, all curves map arbitrarily close to a circle by projective transformations (Astrom, 1995).

If multiple views are used, the approach that we describe in the book can be applied. An important unifying result of Carlsson and Weinshall (Carlsson and Weinshall, 1998; Carlsson, 1995; Weinshall et al., 1996) is the fundamental duality of the 3-D motion estimation and structure estimation problem. They show that for points and cameras in general position, the problem of computing camera geometry from N points in M views is equivalent to the problem of reconstructing $M + 4$ points in $N - 4$ views.

Infinitesimal displacements   In this book, we concentrate on the general case when the displacements are finite. The appropriate data is discrete point correspondences. When the displacements are small, the cameras are closely spaced and some of the image projections are nearly the same. Then some quantities become infinitesimal so that the approximation by a differential analysis is appropriate. Verri and Trucco (Verri and Trucco, 1999) propose a differential technique based on optical flow for estimating the location of the epipole. The method requires a minimum of six points. It is based on a new rewrite of the optical flow equations in terms of a generalization of the time-to-impact, and without decoupling rotation and translation.

The relationship between optical flow and 3-D structure is well understood in the calibrated case (Koenderink and van Doorn, 1975; Longuet-Higgins and Prazdny, 1980; Maybank, 1987). The uncalibrated case was first investigated by Viéville and Faugeras (Viéville and Faugeras, 1996), who used the first-order expansion of the motion equation between two views and analyzed the observability of the infinitesimal quantities. A more ambitious approach was taken by Astrom and Heyden (Astrom and Heyden, 1998). They consider the N-views case and take a Taylor expansion of the projection equations By gathering the projection equations by the powers of Δt using a principle similar to the one described in Section 10.2, they obtain multi-linear constraints which link corresponding points and their derivatives. Recently, Triggs (Triggs, 1999a) proposed a more tractable approach to the N-views case, which bridges the gap between the differential and the discrete formulation, using finite difference expansions.

Brooks *et al.* (Brooks et al., 1997) derived, similarly to Viéville and Faugeras, a differential epipolar equation for uncalibrated optical flow. This equation incorporates two matrices which encode information about the ego-motion and intrinsic parameters of the camera. Given enough points, the composite ratio of some entries of these matrices are determined and, under some conditions, a closed form formula is obtained from these ratios. In (Brooks et al., 1998), a method is presented for the robust determination of the two matrices. The problem of self-calibration from image derivatives was also addressed by Brodsky et al (Brodsky et al., 1998).

Illumination and photometry   In this book, we concentrate on geometry, which is only one of the attributes of the 3-D world. Some researchers have begun to combine geometry and photometry. For example, Belhumeur and Kriegman show that from perspective images of a scene where the camera is in fixed viewpoint, but where point light sources vary in each image, one can only reconstruct the surface up to a family of projective transformations from shadows (Kriegman and Belhumeur, 1998), whereas from orthographic images and light sources at infinity, the family of transformation is restricted to affine transformation, and that for Lambertian surfaces one can only reconstruct the surface up to this family of affine transformations (Belhumeur et al., 1997).

2 Projective, affine and Euclidean geometries

This chapter describes the fundamental tools of projective, affine and Euclidean geometry that will be used later in the book. It is organized as follows.

In Section 2.1 we explain the advantages of an approach to the problems of multiple views geometry based on projective geometry and give a quick tour of projective, affine, and Euclidean geometries, which should be sufficient to grasp the main results of this book.

The next two sections, Sections 2.2 and 2.3, introduce the basic notions of affine and Euclidean geometries that are used in the rest of the book. The presentation is probably somewhat different from what people in computer vision, graphics or robotics are used to, but it is in agreement with the way we will introduce and use projective geometry. The idea is that, since we are used to reasoning in affine or Euclidean spaces, the reader will easily integrate this rather theoretical presentation with his current representation of geometry, his geometric "Weltanschauung". The mathematically inclined reader will have no difficulty. The most important notions introduced in Section 2.3 are those of a real Euclidean vector space and two sub-groups of its group of invertible linear transformations, the orthogonal group and the group of similarities. The elements of the first subgroup preserve the vector norm whereas those of the second subgroup multiply it by a fixed number, one for each element of the subgroup. It turns out that the second subgroup is very important in computer vision where there is usually no natural scale. Another very important but somewhat difficult notion is that of the isotropic cone which is at the heart of the connection, described in Section 2.7, between projective and Euclidean geometries. It requires to consider the underlying vector space as complex, the corresponding operation is called complexification. In this context, the isotropic cone appears as a cone traced out by complex lines. It offers a beautiful and very useful characterization of the group of similarities as the group of invertible linear transformations that leave the isotropic cone globally invariant.

This discussion of affine and Euclidean geometries is meant to pave the ground for Section 2.4 where we introduce the fundamental notions of projective spaces, morphisms, and bases which are used many times in the book. We illustrate some of these notions with the example of the pinhole camera that is discussed in greater details in Chapter 4. A key theorem in this section is Theorem 2.1 which is at the heart of the representation of two and three views described in Chapters 5 and 8 as well as of many applications described in Chapters 7 and 10.

Section 2.5 ties together Sections 2.2 and 2.4 and shows how affine geometry can be considered as a special case of projective geometry. This step is a first step in achieving our goal of describing the affine and Euclidean geometries as special cases of projective geometry. The key notions are those of the projective completion of an affine space by the addition of a special hyperplane called the hyperplane at infinity, and of the part at infinity of an affine subspace. Parallelism between two affine subspaces appears simply as an inclusion relation between their parts at infinity. The projective group of the projective completion of an affine space appears naturally in this setting as containing as a subgroup the group of affine transformations. This subgroup is characterized by the fact that it leaves the hyperplane at infinity globally invariant.

Section 2.6 introduces more useful tools from projective geometry. The key concept in that section is that of the cross-ratio, a basic quantity that is invariant to the action of projective morphisms. It is at the heart of the second key theorem, Theorem 2.2, which is fundamental in the characterization of the epipolar geometry of two views in Chapter 5. Another important component of this section is the introduction of duality which is again useful in describing the geometry of two views: the notions of epipolar pencils and epipolar planes that are described at great length in Chapter 5 are most conveniently described by duality. A final important point in this section is the proof that ratios of projective coordinates, the basic invariants of projective geometry, are in fact cross-ratios. Combined with the results of the previous section, this proof allows us to describe all invariants of the affine groups, e.g. ratios of the lengths of the segments determined by three aligned points, as projective invariants, i.e. cross-ratios. Because they are used in several places in the book, we discuss a little bit the conics of $\mathbb{P}^2$, the quadrics of $\mathbb{P}^3$ and their duals.

Section 2.7 ties the projective, affine and Euclidean geometries together through the notion of complexification introduced in Section 2.3. Given an affine space, we have seen in Section 2.5 that it can be naturally considered as a subspace of its projective completion and that its affine group can be considered as the subgroup of the group of the homographies of its projective completion that leaves the hyperplane at infinity globally invariant. If the affine space is a Euclidean affine space, then the isotropic cone introduced in Section 2.3 defines a surface called the absolute quadric which lies in the hyperplane at infinity. The group of similarities appears naturally as the subgroup of the group of the homographies of the projective completion of the original affine space that leaves the absolute quadric invariant. This allows us to describe all invariants of the group of similarities, e.g. angles and ratios of lengths, as projective invariants, i.e. cross-ratios. The special cases of $\mathbb{P}^2$ and $\mathbb{P}^3$ are particularly important: we discuss the absolute points in $\mathbb{P}^2$ and the absolute conic of $\mathbb{P}^3$ whose dual cone of planes is important for self-calibration.

2.1   Motivations for the approach and overview

This chapter is the first in a series of two in which we will develop the necessary tools from geometry and algebra to unfold the theory and tackle some applications of the reconstruction of 3D structure from multiple views.

This chapter describes the three kinds of geometries that are relevant to this problem, i.e. the projective, affine and Euclidean geometries. As explained in Chapter , the tenet of this book is that we gain immensely in simplicity and therefore in comprehension if we adopt from the very beginning the correct point of view, namely that of projective geometry, and consider the affine and Euclidean geometries as special cases. There are four main advantages in using a projective framework for computer vision:

- As we will see in this chapter and later in Chapter 4, a camera is a projective engine. Therefore, projective geometry is the correct modeling tool. As a consequence of this,

- the algebra is simpler than in the usual (affine or Euclidean) framework,

- there are less special cases since, for example, the points at infinity are handled in a natural way, and

- the projective framework unifies different geometric concepts in a single framework and clarifies their relations. Affine and Euclidean geometries are defined as particular instances of a more general concept. This allows us to understand which level of description is relevant for a given vision task.

Before delving into a more complete and rigorous approach, we give a quick and informal tour of projective, affine, and Euclidean geometries.

2.1.1   Projective spaces: basic definitions

The *projective space* of dimension n, $\mathbb{P}^n$, is the quotient space of $\mathbb{R}^{n+1} \setminus \{\mathbf{0}_{n+1}\}$ by the equivalence relation:

$$[x_1, \ldots, x_{n+1}]^T \sim [x'_1, \ldots, x'_{n+1}]^T \quad \Leftrightarrow$$
$$\exists \lambda \neq 0 , \ [x_1, \ldots, x_{n+1}]^T = \lambda [x'_1, \ldots, x'_{n+1}]^T$$

This means that proportional $(n+1)$-tuples of coordinates $\mathbf{x} = [x_1, \ldots, x_{n+1}]^T$ and $\mathbf{x}' = [x'_1, \ldots, x'_{n+1}]^T$ represent the same point in projective space. The object space will be considered as $\mathbb{P}^3$ and the image space as $\mathbb{P}^2$.

Any point $\mathbf{h}$ of $\mathbb{P}^n$ defines a *hyperplane*, which is the set of points $\mathbf{x}$ of $\mathbb{P}^n$ whose coordinates satisy

$$\sum_{1 \leq i \leq n+1} h_i x_i = \mathbf{h}^T \mathbf{x} = 0.$$

In $\mathbb{P}^3$, the hyperplanes are planes; in $\mathbb{P}^2$, they are lines. A hyperplane of $\mathbb{P}^n$ can be considered as a projective subspace of dimension $n - 1$. A first important remark which can be made from the definition is that $\mathbf{h}$ and $\mathbf{x}$ play symmetrical roles, and this symmetry is the *duality* between points and hyperplanes. A second important remark is that since the system of two equations $\{\mathbf{h}_1^T \mathbf{x} = 0, \mathbf{h}_2^T \mathbf{x} = 0\}$ is homogeneous, it always has a non-null solution provided that $n \geq 2$; therefore, the intersection of two hyperplanes is always a (non-empty) projective subspace V of dimension $n - 2$. This result is easily generalized to the intersection of any two projective subspaces of dimension $n \geq 1$, which is one of the reasons for the greater simplicity of projective spaces, whereas in the usual affine geometry there are exceptions due to parallelism. Moreover, observe that all of the hyperplanes containing V form a projective space of dimension 1, called a *pencil of hyperplanes*.

A *projective basis* is any set of $n + 2$ points of $\mathbb{P}^n$ such that no $n + 1$ of them are linearly dependent. Any point of $\mathbb{P}^n$ can be expressed as a linear combination of points of the basis. The *canonical projective basis* is the one formed by the points $\varepsilon_i = [0, \ldots, 1, \ldots 0]^T$, $1 \leq i \leq n + 1$, where 1 is in the ith position and $\varepsilon_{n+2} = [1, \ldots, 1]^T$.

Any symmetric $(n + 1) \times (n + 1)$ matrix $\mathcal{Q}$ defines a *quadric*, which is the set of points $\mathbf{x}$ of $\mathbb{P}^n$ whose coordinates satisfy

$$\sum_{1 \leq i, j \leq n+1} \mathcal{Q}_{ij} x_i x_j = \mathbf{x}^T \mathcal{Q} \mathbf{x} = 0.$$

In $\mathbb{P}^3$, the quadrics are quadric surfaces, in $\mathbb{P}^2$, they are conics, and in $\mathbb{P}^1$ they reduce to two points. The intersection of a hyperplane of $\mathbb{P}^n$ and a quadric of $\mathbb{P}^n$ yields a quadric of $\mathbb{P}^{n-1}$.

Felix Klein introduced in 1872 the idea that the basis for a geometry is the set of properties which remain invariant under a given transformation group. We are going to consider some of these groups now and discuss their invariants.

2.1.2 Projective geometry

A *homography*, is any transformation H of $\mathbb{P}^n$ which is linear in projective coordinates (hence the terminology *linear projective*) and invertible (thus $H(\mathbb{P}^n) = \mathbb{P}^n$). It can be described by an $(n + 1) \times (n + 1)$ non-singular matrix $\mathbf{H}$, such that the image of $\mathbf{x}$ is $\mathbf{x}'$:

$$\mathbf{x}' = \mathbf{H}\mathbf{x}.$$

The basic consequence of the linearity is that homographies map hyperplanes to hyperplanes. More generally, they map any projective subspace to a subspace of the same dimension, a property which is called *conservation of incidence*. Homographies form a group $\mathcal{PLG}_n$ which is called the *projective group*. Given two projective bases, there is a unique homography which maps the first basis to points of the second one, and thus homographies can be thought of as transformations that perform changes of projective coordinates.

Let A, B, C, D be four collinear points, which can be considered as points of a $\mathbb{P}^1$. The basic projective invariant by any homography is the *cross-ratio* (ratio of ratios of lengths):

$$\{A, B; C, D\} = \frac{\overline{AC}}{\overline{AD}} : \frac{\overline{BC}}{\overline{BD}}. \tag{2.1}$$

The points at infinity are handled with the obvious conventions:

$$\frac{\infty}{\infty} = 1 \ , \ \frac{a}{\infty} = 0 \ , \ \frac{\infty}{a} = \infty \qquad a \in \mathbb{R}$$

The cross-ratio of four hyperplanes in a pencil that intersect at a projective subspace V of dimension $n-2$ is defined as the cross-ratio of the four intersection points of the hyperplanes with any line not containing or contained in V. It can be shown that this quantity does not depend on the line considered.

2.1.3 Affine geometry

Let us choose a hyperplane Π_∞ in $\mathbb{P}^n$ and call it the *hyperplane at infinity*. The *affine transformations* form the subgroup $\mathcal{AG}_n$ of $\mathcal{PLG}_n$ defined by the transformations $\mathcal{A}$ which conserve the hyperplane at infinity, which means that $\mathcal{A}(\Pi_\infty) = \Pi_\infty$. There is a one-to-one correspondence between $\mathbb{R}^n$ and $\mathbb{P}^n \backslash \Pi_\infty$, called the *affine space*. Two subspaces of $\mathbb{P}^n$ not contained in Π_∞ are said to be *parallel* if their intersection is in Π_∞. This implies that affine transformations are those which preserve parallelism.

A classical convention, which will be used throughout this book, is to take the hyperplane $[0, \ldots, 0, 1]^T$ (i.e. $x_{n+1} = 0$) as Π_∞. The usual n-dimensional affine space $\mathbb{R}^n$ is then mapped to $\mathbb{P}^n \backslash \Pi_\infty$ by the bijective correspondence

$$[x_1, \ldots, x_n]^T \to [x_1, \ldots, x_n, 1]^T.$$

Points $[x_1, \ldots, x_n, 1]^T$ can thus be viewed as the usual points, whereas the points $[x_1, \ldots, x_n, 0]^T$ cannot be reached by this map. If we consider them as the limit of $[x_1, \ldots, x_n, \lambda]^T$, when $\lambda \to 0$ i.e. the limit of $[x_1/\lambda, \ldots, x_n/\lambda, 1]^T$, then we see that they are the limit of a point of $\mathbb{R}^n$ going to infinity in the direction $[x_1, \ldots, x_n]^T$, hence the appellation *point at infinity*. For this reason, the *direction* $[x_1, \ldots, x_n]^T$ of any hyperplane of the form $[x_1, \ldots, x_n, x_{n+1}]^T$ is defined by its intersection with the hyperplane at infinity Π_∞. It is easy to see that a homography H conserves Π_∞ if and only if the last row of the matrix $\mathbf{H}$ of H is of the form $[0, \ldots, 0, \mu]$, with $\mu \neq 0$. Since this matrix is defined only up to a scale factor, we can take $\mu = 1$, and then the transformation H is fully described by its first $n \times n$ submatrix $\mathbf{A}$ and the n first coordinates of the last column vector $\mathbf{b}$:

$$\mathbf{H} = \begin{bmatrix} \mathbf{A} & \mathbf{b} \\ \mathbf{0}_n^T & 1 \end{bmatrix}, \tag{2.2}$$

which yields the classical description of a transformation of the affine space $\mathbb{R}^n$: $\mathbf{x}' = \mathbf{A}\mathbf{x} + \mathbf{b}$.

Let A, B, C be three collinear points, and let the fourth point be the point at infinity of the line defined by these three points. Since the image of this point by any affine transformation remains at infinity, from (2.1), we conclude that the *ratio of distances of three collinear points*

$$\{A, B; C, \infty\} = \frac{\overline{AC}}{\overline{BC}}$$

is invariant by an affine transformation. A consequence of this property is the fact that affine transformations leave invariant centers of mass and convex hulls.

2.1.4   Euclidean geometry

Let us choose a quadric Ω of Π_∞ and call it the *absolute quadric*. In $\mathbb{P}^3$, this quadric is called the *absolute conic* and in $\mathbb{P}^2$, the *circular points*. The *similarity transformations* define the subgroup $\mathcal{S}_n$ of $\mathcal{PLG}_n$ defined by the transformations $\mathcal{S}$ which conserve the absolute quadric, which means that $\mathcal{S}(\Omega) = \Omega$. Note that this invariant implies that $\mathcal{S}(\Pi_\infty) = \Pi_\infty$, and therefore the similarity transformations form a subgroup of the affine group. Much the same way as Π_∞ can be used to define directions of hyperplanes, Ω can be used to define angles between two hyperplanes h_1 and h_2 by the Laguerre formula: $\alpha = \frac{1}{2i} \log(\{h_1, h_2; h_a, h_b\})$ where h_i and h_j are the two hyperplanes of the pencil defined by h_1 and h_2, which are tangent to the absolute quadric. This observation implies that Euclidean transformations are those which preserve angles.

A classic convention is to choose the equation of the absolute quadric Ω to be $\sum_1^n x_i^2 = 0$. The transformations which preserve Ω can be shown to be the affine transformations (2.2) for which we have the additional constraint $\mathbf{A}\mathbf{A}^T = s\mathbf{I}_n$, which means that the first $n \times n$ submatrix is proportional to an orthogonal matrix. They are called *similarities* and preserve the *relative distance*, which is the ratio of the distances of *any* three points.

2.2   Affine spaces and affine geometry

2.2.1   Definition of an affine space and an affine basis

We begin with the definition of an affine space:

Definition 2.1 *An **affine space** is a set X of points, a vector space E and an application $\Theta : X \times X \to E$ which satisfies the two properties:*

> *1. $\forall a \in X$, the application $\Theta_a : b \to \Theta(a, b)$ is one-to-one from X into E.*

> *2. $\forall a, b, c \in X$ one has $\Theta(a, b) + \Theta(b, c) = \Theta(a, c)$.*

We can think of $\Theta(a, b)$ as the vector $\overrightarrow{ab}$ which we also write as

$$\overrightarrow{ab} = b - a.$$

It is convenient to write $E = \overrightarrow{X}$. An affine space is a triplet $(X, \overrightarrow{X}, \Theta)$ that satisfies the above two conditions.

An affine space is therefore very close to a vector space, and it will not surprise the reader that the definition of an affine basis is very similar to that of a basis in a vector space. Let us assume that the dimension of $\overrightarrow{X}$ is n, which we denote $\overrightarrow{X}_n$, X_n being the corresponding n-dimensional affine space.

Definition 2.2 *An* **affine basis** *of the affine space* X_n *is a set* $\mathcal{B}$ *of* $n+1$ *points* $m_1, \ldots, m_{n+1}$ *of* X_n *such that the* n *vectors* $\overrightarrow{m_1 m_i}$, $i = 2, \ldots, n+1$, *form a basis of* $\overrightarrow{X}_n$.

m_1 is the origin of the basis. Given a point m of X_n, its affine coordinates in the basis are the n values x_i, $i = 1, \ldots, n$, such that

$$\overrightarrow{m_1 m} = \sum_{i=1}^{n} x_i \overrightarrow{m_1 m_{i+1}},$$

i.e. they are the coordinates of the vector $\overrightarrow{m_1 m}$ in the basis $\overrightarrow{m_1 m_{i+1}}, i = 1, \ldots, n$, of $\overrightarrow{X}_n$. We write $\mathbf{m}$ for the vector $[x_1, \ldots, x_n]^T$. Examples are shown in Figure 2.1 in the cases $n = 2$ and $n = 3$.

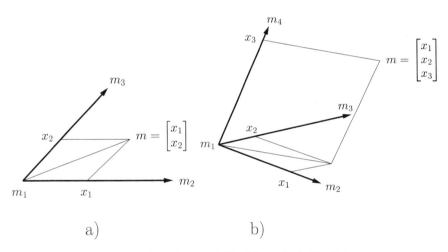

Figure 2.1: An affine basis of X_2 (a) and of X_3, (b).

2.2.2 Affine morphisms, affine group

We are interested in extending to affine spaces the notion of linear application defined for vector spaces. This can be done fairly simply as follows.

Definition 2.3 *Given two affine spaces* $(X, \overrightarrow{X}, \Theta)$ *and* $(X', \overrightarrow{X'}, \Theta')$, *consider a linear application* $\overrightarrow{f}$ *from* $\overrightarrow{X}$ *to* $\overrightarrow{X'}$, $\overrightarrow{f} \in \mathcal{L}(\overrightarrow{X}, \overrightarrow{X'})$. *For each pair* (a, a') *in* $X \times X'$

there exists a unique application f from X to X' such that the diagram

$$
\begin{array}{ccc}
X \times X & \xrightarrow{\; f \times f \;} & X' \times X' \\
\downarrow{\scriptstyle \Theta} & & \downarrow{\scriptstyle \Theta'} \\
\overrightarrow{X} & \xrightarrow{\; \overrightarrow{f} \;} & \overrightarrow{X'}
\end{array}
$$

is commutative and $f(a) = a'$. Such an application is called an **affine morphism** *from X to X'. The set of morphisms is denoted $\mathcal{A}(X; X')$.*

We can say this differently in a perhaps more pictorial way:

$$\overrightarrow{f(b)f(c)} = \overrightarrow{f}(\overrightarrow{bc}),$$

which can also be written as

$$f(c) = f(b) + \overrightarrow{f}(\overrightarrow{bc}).$$

The reader may convince himself of the truth of this assertion as follows. First, by definition of Θ', $\Theta'(f(b), f(c)) = \overrightarrow{f(b)f(c)}$. Second, because of the commutativity of the above diagram, $\Theta'(f(b), f(c)) = \overrightarrow{f}(\Theta(b, c))$, and third, $\Theta(b, c) = \overrightarrow{bc}$, again by definition of Θ. In words, an affine transformation is a translation followed by a linear application.

Also note that the condition $f(a) = a'$ is essential to guarantee uniqueness. Had we not added this condition, the morphism f would have been defined up to the addition of an arbitrary vector of $\overrightarrow{X'}$, i.e. if f were a solution, $f + \overrightarrow{y'}$ would also be one for all vectors $\overrightarrow{y'}$ of $\overrightarrow{X'}$.

Definition 2.4 *When $X = X'$ the set of invertible affine morphisms forms a group called the* **affine group** $\mathcal{AG}(X)$ *of X.*

It is easy to express a morphism f in matrix form using affine bases. Let $(m_1, \ldots, m_{n+1})$ be an affine basis of X_n and $(m'_1, \ldots, m'_{p+1})$ be an affine basis of X'_p. Let $\varepsilon_i = \overrightarrow{m_1 m_{i+1}}, i = 1, \ldots, n$, be the corresponding basis of $\overrightarrow{X}_n$ and $\varepsilon'_i = \overrightarrow{m'_1 m'_{i+1}}, i = 1, \ldots, p$, be the corresponding basis of $\overrightarrow{X'}_p$. Let m be a point of X_n, so we have

$$f(m) = f(m_1) + \overrightarrow{f}(\overrightarrow{m_1 m}),$$

which implies

$$\overrightarrow{m'_1 f(m)} = \overrightarrow{m'_1 f(m_1)} + \overrightarrow{f}(\overrightarrow{m_1 m}),$$

for all points m of X_n. If we consider the $p \times n$ matrix $\mathbf{A}$ of $\overrightarrow{f}$ in those two bases and denote by $\mathbf{b}$ the n-dimensional vector $\overrightarrow{m'_1 f(m_1)}$, by $\mathbf{m}$ the vector $\overrightarrow{m_1 m}$ and by $\mathbf{m'}$ the vector $\overrightarrow{m'_1 f(m)}$, we can rewrite the previous equation as

$$\mathbf{m}' = \mathbf{A}\mathbf{m} + \mathbf{b}$$

or

$$\begin{bmatrix} \mathbf{m}' \\ 1 \end{bmatrix} = \begin{bmatrix} \mathbf{A} & \mathbf{b} \\ \mathbf{0}_n^T & 1 \end{bmatrix} \begin{bmatrix} \mathbf{m} \\ 1 \end{bmatrix}, \tag{2.3}$$

where $\mathbf{0}_n$ is the n-dimensional null vector.

Equation 2.3 shows that

Proposition 2.1 *The number of degrees of freedom of the affine group $\mathcal{AG}(X_n)$ of an n-dimensional affine space X_n is $n(n+1)$.*

2.2.3 Change of affine basis

Let $\mathcal{B} = (m_1, \ldots, m_{n+1})$ and $\mathcal{B}' = (m_1', \ldots, m_{n+1}')$ be two affine bases of an affine space X_n of dimension n. Let $\mathbf{m}_{/\mathcal{B}} \equiv \overrightarrow{m_1 m}_{/\mathcal{B}} = [x_1, \ldots, x_n]^T$ the vector of affine coordinates of a point in the basis $\mathcal{B}$ and $\mathbf{m}_{/\mathcal{B}'} \equiv \overrightarrow{m_1' m}_{/\mathcal{B}'} = [x_1', \ldots, x_n']^T$ its vector of affine coordinates in the basis $\mathcal{B}'$. Let $\mathbf{Q}_{\mathcal{B}}^{\mathcal{B}'} = [q_{ij}]$, $i, j = 1, \ldots, n$, be the $n \times n$ matrix whose kth column vector is the vector $\overrightarrow{m_1 m_{k+1}}$ expressed in the vector basis $(\overrightarrow{m_1' m_2'}, \ldots, \overrightarrow{m_1' m_{n+1}'})$. We write

$$\mathbf{m}_{/\mathcal{B}} = \sum_{i=1}^{n} x_i \overrightarrow{m_1 m_{i+1}},$$

express the vectors $\overrightarrow{m_1 m_{i+1}}$ in the basis $(\overrightarrow{m_1' m_2'}, \ldots, \overrightarrow{m_1' m_{n+1}'})$ using the matrix $\mathbf{Q}_{\mathcal{B}}^{\mathcal{B}'}$:

$$\overrightarrow{m_1 m_{i+1}} = \sum_{j=1}^{n} q_{ji} \overrightarrow{m_1' m_{j+1}'},$$

and obtain an expression which is equal to the vector $\overrightarrow{m_1 m}$ expressed in the basis $\mathcal{B}'$, denoted $\overrightarrow{m_1 m}_{/\mathcal{B}'}$:

$$\overrightarrow{m_1 m}_{/\mathcal{B}'} = \sum_{j=1}^{n} (\sum_{i=1}^{n} q_{ji} x_i) \overrightarrow{m_1' m_{j+1}'} = \mathbf{Q}_{\mathcal{B}}^{\mathcal{B}'} \overrightarrow{m_1 m}_{/\mathcal{B}}.$$

In order to obtain the full expression giving the change of affine basis, we write

$$\overrightarrow{m_1' m}_{/\mathcal{B}'} = \overrightarrow{m_1' m_1}_{/\mathcal{B}'} + \overrightarrow{m_1 m}_{/\mathcal{B}'}$$

or

$$\mathbf{m}_{/\mathcal{B}'} = \overrightarrow{m_1 m}_{/\mathcal{B}'} - \overrightarrow{m_1 m_1'}_{/\mathcal{B}'}.$$

Therefore we conclude that the relation between the affine coordinates of m in the two affine bases $\mathcal{B}$ and $\mathcal{B}'$ is

$$\mathbf{m}_{/\mathcal{B}'} = \mathbf{Q}_{\mathcal{B}}^{\mathcal{B}'} (\mathbf{m}_{/\mathcal{B}} - \mathbf{m}_1'_{/\mathcal{B}}). \tag{2.4}$$

2.2.4   Affine subspaces, parallelism

We start with a definition:

Definition 2.5 *Let X be an affine space and Y a subset of X. Y is called an* **affine subspace** *of X if and only if there exists a point a of X and a vector subspace $\overrightarrow{Y}$ of $\overrightarrow{X}$ such that $Y = a + \overrightarrow{Y}$ (see Figure 2.2). The dimension of the affine subspace is the dimension of the corresponding vector subspace.*

Note that the choice of the point a is not important: any other point b will do. To see why, first note that if x and y are two points of $\overrightarrow{Y}$, then the vector $\overrightarrow{x-y}$ is clearly in $\overrightarrow{Y}$. Next, let b be another point of Y. We have

$$a + \overrightarrow{Y} = b + \overrightarrow{a-b} + \overrightarrow{Y}$$

and, according to the previous remark, $\overrightarrow{a-b} + \overrightarrow{Y} = \overrightarrow{Y}$.

For example, a point is an affine subspace of dimension 0, a line an affine subspace of dimension 1, and a hyperplane an affine subspace of dimension $n-1$.

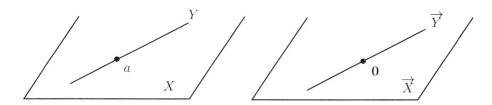

Figure 2.2: Definition of an affine subspace Y of an affine space X and relation with the associated vector spaces.

Definition 2.6 *Two affine subspaces S and T of X are said to be* **parallel**, *denoted $S \,//\, T$, if and only if the corresponding vector subspaces are such that $\overrightarrow{S} \subseteq \overrightarrow{T}$ or $\overrightarrow{T} \subseteq \overrightarrow{S}$.*

This definition implies that if $S \,//\, T$, then either $S \subseteq T$ or $T \subseteq S$ or $S \cap T = \emptyset$. This consequence is because if $S \cap T \neq \emptyset$, then they have a point in common, say a. We then have $S = a + \overrightarrow{S}$ which is either included in or contains $a + \overrightarrow{T}$. However, $a + \overrightarrow{T} = T$, hence the conclusion. Two examples of parallel affine subspaces are shown in Figure 2.3. Note that in both cases $\overrightarrow{Y} \subseteq \overrightarrow{X}$.

2.3   Euclidean spaces and Euclidean geometry

There is an elegant and simple way to introduce the Euclidean geometry as a specialization of the affine and projective geometries. This allows us to do all of our

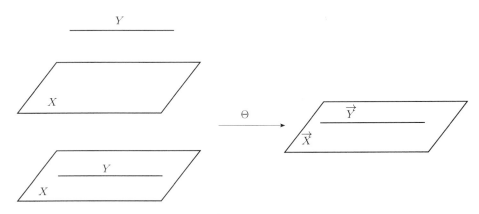

Figure 2.3: Two examples of parallel affine subspaces: in the first case $Y \cap X = \emptyset$, in the second $Y \subseteq X$.

thinking and computations in projective space, thereby gaining in simplicity, while still allowing us to have access to its affine and Euclidean specializations. This will be done in Section 2.7.

2.3.1 Euclidean spaces, rigid displacements, similarities

We first remind the reader of a few definitions and properties of the Euclidean vector spaces.

Definition 2.7 *A Euclidean vector space is a real (i.e. $\mathbb{K} = \mathbb{R}$) vector space E where we have defined a bilinear symmetric definite positive form, i.e. a function $\varphi : E \times E \longrightarrow \mathbb{R}$ such that $\varphi(\mathbf{x}, \mathbf{y})$ is linear with respect to $\mathbf{x}$ and $\mathbf{y}$, $\varphi(\mathbf{x}, \mathbf{y}) = \varphi(\mathbf{y}, \mathbf{x})$, and $\varphi(\mathbf{x}, \mathbf{x}) > 0$ for all $\mathbf{x} \neq \mathbf{0}$. The inner product of two vectors $\mathbf{x}$ and $\mathbf{y}$ is equal to $\varphi(\mathbf{x}, \mathbf{y})$, the norm of a vector $\mathbf{x}$, denoted $\|\mathbf{x}\|$, is equal to $\sqrt{\varphi(\mathbf{x}, \mathbf{x})}$. If $\varphi(\mathbf{x}, \mathbf{y}) = 0$, then the vectors $\mathbf{x}$ and $\mathbf{y}$ are said to be orthogonal.*

Remark: The standard example is the case in which $E = \mathbb{R}^n$ and $\varphi(\mathbf{x}, \mathbf{y}) = \sum_{i=1}^{n} x_i y_i$.

An orthonormal basis of the Euclidean vector space E is a basis $\mathbf{a}_i \, i = 1, \cdots, n$, such that $\varphi(\mathbf{a}_i, \mathbf{a}_j) = \delta_{ij}$. The Gram-Schmidt orthonormalization process is an algorithm for building an orthonormal basis from any basis.

The orthogonal group, denoted $\mathcal{O}(E)$, of E is the subgroup of the elements f of $\mathcal{LG}(E)$ such that their matrices $\mathbf{A}$ in an orthonormal basis of E are orthogonal, i.e. satisfy $\mathbf{A}\mathbf{A}^T = \mathbf{A}^T\mathbf{A} = \mathbf{I}$. Rotations and symmetries with respect to hyperplanes, are elements of $\mathcal{O}(E)$. The characteristic property of the elements of $\mathcal{O}(E)$ is that they preserve the norm: $f \in \mathcal{O}(E)$ if and only if $\|f(\mathbf{x})\| = \|\mathbf{x}\|$ for all $\mathbf{x}$. The number of degrees of freedom of the orthogonal group $\mathcal{O}(E_n)$ is therefore $n(n-1)/2$.

Besides the orthogonal group, there is another subgroup of $\mathcal{LG}(E)$ which does not preserve the norm of the elements of E and plays an important role in computer vision; it is called the group of similarities, denoted $\mathcal{OG}(E)$. Here is the definition:

Definition 2.8 *A similarity of ratio $\mu > 0$ is an element f of $\mathcal{LG}(E)$ such that $\|f(\mathbf{x})\| = \mu\|\mathbf{x}\|$ for all $\mathbf{x}$. The set of similarities form a subgroup of $\mathcal{LG}(E)$, denoted $\mathcal{OG}(E)$.*

This is the natural group to use in vision where we usually do not have an absolute unit of length. We see that a similarity, unlike an orthogonal transformation, does not preserve lengths, but ratios of lengths.

It is readily seen that $\mathcal{OG}(E)$ is the subgroup of the elements f of $\mathcal{LG}(E)$ such that their matrices $\mathbf{A}$ in an orthonormal basis of E are proportional to an orthonormal matrix, $\mathbf{A}\mathbf{A}^T = \mathbf{A}^T\mathbf{A} = \mu\mathbf{I}$, $\mu > 0$. The number of degrees of freedom of the orthogonal group $\mathcal{OG}(E_n)$ is therefore $n(n-1)/2 + 1$.

Having defined a Euclidean vector space, we can use it to define a Euclidean affine space:

Definition 2.9 *An n-dimensional Euclidean affine space is an affine space $(X_n, \overrightarrow{X}_n)$ such that $\overrightarrow{X}_n$ is a Euclidean vector space. An affine basis $(m_1, m_2, \ldots, m_{n+1})$ of X_n is said to be orthonormal if $(\overrightarrow{m_1 m_2}, \ldots, \overrightarrow{m_1 m_{n+1}})$ is an orthonormal basis of $\overrightarrow{X}_n$.*

We can also define two interesting groups of $\mathcal{AG}(X)$:

Definition 2.10

1. *The group $\mathcal{E}(X)$ of affine Rigid Displacements is the subgroup of the affine group $\mathcal{AG}(X)$ defined as the affine morphisms f such that $\overrightarrow{f}$ is in $\mathcal{O}(\overrightarrow{X})$. The number of degrees of freedom of the group of affine Rigid Displacements $\mathcal{E}(X_n)$ is therefore $n(n-1)/2 + n = n(n+1)/2$.*

2. *The group $\mathcal{S}(X)$ of affine similarities is the subgroup of the affine group $\mathcal{AG}(X)$ defined as the affine morphisms f such that $\overrightarrow{f}$ is in $\mathcal{OG}(\overrightarrow{X})$. The number of degrees of freedom of the group of affine similarities $\mathcal{S}(X_n)$ is therefore $n(n-1)/2 + n + 1 = n(n+1)/2 + 1$.*

2.3.2   The isotropic cone

We are now going to take a step outside the field of real numbers. So far we have assumed that all vector spaces that we considered, and therefore the affine spaces that we built on top of them, were defined over the field $\mathbb{R}$ of the real numbers. In order to give a projective interpretation of a Euclidean affine space, we need to consider vector spaces defined over the field of complex numbers.

More precisely, if E_n is a real vector space of dimension n, it can naturally be considered as a complex vector space of the same dimension simply by choosing a basis in E_n: a vector $\mathbf{x}$ of E_n with coordinates $(x_1, \ldots, x_n)$ is considered a vector of $\mathbb{R}^n$ and therefore a vector of $\mathbb{C}^n$. We denote by $E_n^{\mathbb{C}}$ the *complexified* vector space attached to E_n. We proceed similarly for an n-dimensional affine space X_n, by considering the vector space $\overrightarrow{X}_n$ and its complexified space $\overrightarrow{X}_n^{\mathbb{C}}$.

Definition 2.11 *This operation is called* **complexification** *(of a vector space or an affine space).*

We now consider a real vector space E_n of dimension n and its complexified space $E_n^{\mathbb{C}}$. Let L be the quadratic form such that $L(\mathbf{x}) = \|\mathbf{x}\|^2$ is positive definite on E_n but not on $E_n^{\mathbb{C}}$. Let us denote by $L^{\mathbb{C}}$ the extension of L to $E_n^{\mathbb{C}}$. We have the following proposition:

Proposition 2.2 *The set of vectors $\mathbf{x}$ of $E_n^{\mathbb{C}}$ such that $L^{\mathbb{C}}(\mathbf{x}) = 0$ is called the* **isotropic cone** *of E_n. For $n = 2$ it is composed of two one-dimensional vector spaces generated by two complex conjugate vectors.*

Proof :   The name of *cone* is justified by the fact that $\mathbf{0}$ belongs to the set and that if $\mathbf{x}$ is in it, then $\lambda\mathbf{x}$ is also in it for all complex numbers λ (think of $\mathbf{0}$ as the vertex of the cone). When $n = 2$, if $\mathbf{x} = [z_1, z_2]^T$, we have $L^{\mathbb{C}}(\mathbf{x}) = z_1^2 + z_2^2$, and therefore $L^{\mathbb{C}}(\mathbf{x}) = 0$ is equivalent to $z_2 = \pm i z_1$. We thus obtain the two vector spaces generated by the vectors $\mathbf{I} = [1, i]^T$ and $\mathbf{J} = [1, -i]^T$; see Figure 2.4. $\square$

When $n = 3$, if $\mathbf{x} = [z_1, z_2, z_3]^T$, $L^{\mathbb{C}}(\mathbf{x}) = z_1^2 + z_2^2 + z_3^2$. Let us look at what happens

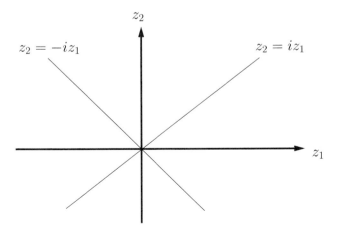

Figure 2.4: In two dimensions, the isotropic cone is the two complex lines of equations $z_2 = \pm i z_1$.

in the plane $z_3 = 1$: $L^{\mathbb{C}}(\mathbf{x}) = z_1^2 + z_2^2 + 1 = z_1^2 + z_2^2 - (i)^2$. The intersection of the isotropic cone with the previous plane appears to be a circle of radius i! Each point on that circle defines a vector space of dimension 1 and the isotropic cone is the union of all of those vector spaces; see Figure 2.5. In the case where $z_3 = 0$, we find the two one-dimensional vector spaces generated by the vectors $[1, i, 0]^T$ and $[1, -i, 0]^T$. Note that all vectors of the isotropic cone have complex coordinates.

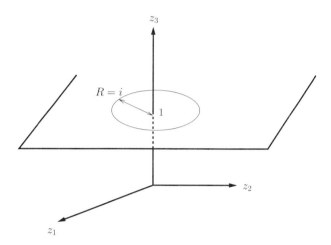

Figure 2.5: In three dimensions, the isotropic cone is the union of circles with imaginary radii.

The two lines I and J are called the *isotropic* lines of E.

The isotropic cone is closely related to the group of similarities $\mathcal{OG}(E)$:

Proposition 2.3 *An element f of $\mathcal{LG}(E)$ is in $\mathcal{OG}(E)$ if and only if it leaves the isotropic cone of E globally invariant.*

Proof : Let us choose an orthonormal basis of E and let $\mathbf{A}$ be the matrix of f in that basis. We know that $\mathbf{A}$ is proportional to an orthogonal matrix: $\mathbf{A}\mathbf{A}^T = \mu\mathbf{I}$. Let $\mathbf{x}$ be a vector of $E^{\mathbb{C}}$ belonging to the isotropic cone: $\mathbf{x}^T\mathbf{x} = 0$. Because of the orthogonality (up to scale) of $\mathbf{A}$, the vector $\mathbf{A}\mathbf{x}$ is also on the isotropic cone since $\mathbf{x}^T\mathbf{A}^T\mathbf{A}\mathbf{x} = \mu\mathbf{x}^T\mathbf{x} = 0$. Conversely, if $\mathbf{x}^T\mathbf{A}^T\mathbf{A}\mathbf{x} = 0$ for all vectors $\mathbf{x}$ on the isotropic cone, then we choose the vectors $\mathbf{x}_{kl} = [0 \ldots 1 \ldots i \ldots 0]^T$ where the 1 is in the kth position and the i in the lth. Let $\mathbf{c}_k$ be the columns of matrix $\mathbf{A}$. Since $\mathbf{A}\mathbf{x}_{kl} = \mathbf{c}_k + i\mathbf{c}_l$, we have

$$\mathbf{x}_{kl}^T\mathbf{A}^T\mathbf{A}\mathbf{x}_{kl} = \|\mathbf{c}_k\|^2 - \|\mathbf{c}_l\|^2 + 2i\mathbf{c}_k \cdot \mathbf{c}_l = 0, \quad \forall k, l.$$

Therefore the norm $\|\mathbf{c}_k\|$ of the column vectors of $\mathbf{A}$ is constant and they are all orthogonal to each other. Hence $\mathbf{A}$ is proportional to an orthogonal matrix and thus f is in $\mathcal{OG}(E)$. $\square$

2.4   Projective spaces and projective geometry

2.4.1   Basic definitions

We begin with a formal definition of a projective space and then provide some intuition.

Definition 2.12 *The **projective space** of dimension n, denoted $\mathbb{P}^n$ or $P(E_{n+1})$ is obtained by taking the quotient of an $n + 1$-dimensional vector space E_{n+1} (real or complex), minus the null vector $\mathbf{0}_{n+1}$, with respect to the equivalence relation*

$$\mathbf{x} \simeq \mathbf{x}' \quad \Leftrightarrow \quad \exists \lambda \neq 0 \ , \ \mathbf{x} = \lambda \mathbf{x}'.$$

It is clear that the binary relation $\simeq$ is an equivalence relation (reflexive, symmetric and transitive); therefore one can talk about the quotient of $E_{n+1} \backslash \{\mathbf{0}_{n+1}\}$ with respect to $\simeq$, sometimes denoted

$$\mathbb{P}^n = P(E_{n+1}) = (E_{n+1} \backslash \{\mathbf{0}_{n+1}\})/ \simeq \ .$$

For intuition, it is useful to think of a nonzero vector as defining a line through the origin in E_{n+1} (the null vector $\mathbf{0}_{n+1}$). Two such vectors are equivalent for the equivalence relation $\simeq$ if and only if they define the same line. The equivalence class of a vector is the set of all nonzero vectors which are parallel to it (it can be thought of as the line defined by this vector). The set of all equivalence classes is the projective space $\mathbb{P}^n$. A point in that space is called a *projective point*. It is an equivalence class of vectors, called *coordinate vectors*, and can be represented by any vector in the class. If $\mathbf{x}$ is such a vector, then $\lambda \mathbf{x}$, $\lambda \neq 0$, is also in the class and represents the same projective point. Therefore they are not equal to $\mathbf{0}_{n+1}$ (we have excluded the zero vector from the beginning) and are defined up to a scale factor. It is sometimes useful to differentiate between the projective point, denoted x, and one of its coordinate vectors, denoted $\mathbf{x}$. This distinction can be stated mathematically by considering the mapping

$$p: \quad E_{n+1} \backslash \mathbf{0}_{n+1} \rightarrow P(E_{n+1}),$$

which to every vector $\mathbf{x}$ of $E_{n+1} \backslash \mathbf{0}_{n+1}$ associates the corresponding projective point x. This mapping is called the *canonical projection*. An example is shown in Figure 2.6 which shows null vector of E, a vector $\mathbf{x}$ of $E \backslash \{\mathbf{0}\}$ and the line $(\mathbf{0}, \mathbf{x})$ which is the projective point $x = p(\mathbf{x})$.

An illustration from computer vision   The Figure 2.6 suggests an interesting interpretation of the canonical projection in terms of the operation performed by the pinhole camera. The pinhole camera which will be studied in great detail in the next chapter associates to each point M of the 3D world different from the optical center C the optical ray (C, M), i.e. the line going through the C

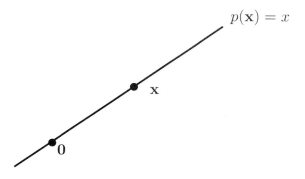

Figure 2.6: $P(E)$ is the set of lines through the origin $\mathbf{0}$ of E.

and M. The correspondence $M \rightarrow (C, M)$ can be considered a metaphor for the canonical projection (see Section 2.4.2 for another useful example built from the pinhole camera). The fact that two distinct points M_1 and M_2 can define the same optical ray is one way of saying that the canonical projection is not one-to-one.

If we choose a basis $\mathbf{a}_i$, $i = 1, \cdots, n+1$, of E_{n+1}, we see that a projective point x of $\mathbb{P}^n$ is represented by an $n + 1$ coordinate vector $\mathbf{x} = [x_1, \ldots, x_{n+1}]^T$ where at least one of the x_i's is nonzero. The x_i's are the *projective* or *homogeneous coordinates* of x, denoted $x_1 : \ldots : x_{n+1}$. Two $n + 1$ vectors $\mathbf{x} = [x_1, \ldots, x_{n+1}]^T$ and $\mathbf{x}' = [x'_1, \ldots, x'_{n+1}]^T$ represent the same point in projective space if and only if there exists a nonzero scalar λ such that $x_i = \lambda x'_i$ for $1 \leq i \leq n + 1$ (they satisfy $p(\mathbf{x}) = p(\mathbf{x}')$). This is another way to see that the correspondence p between coordinate vectors and points is not one-to-one, which makes the application of linear algebra to projective geometry a little more complicated.

We introduce now the notion of projective independence of points which is the analog for projective spaces of the notion of linear independence for vector spaces.

Definition 2.13 *p points $m_1, \ldots, m_p$ of $P(E)$ are said to be projectively independent (respectively dependent) if and only if for some choice of coordinate vectors $\mathbf{m}_1, \ldots, \mathbf{m}_p$, the vectors are linearly independent (respectively dependent) in E.*

It is readily proven that this definition is in effect independent of the choice of the coordinate vectors.

2.4.2   Projective bases, projective morphisms, homographies

An important notion is that of a *projective basis*. This concept is the extension to projective spaces of the idea of a basis in a vector space. There is a small difficulty here which is due to the fact that the canonical projection p is not one-to-one. Indeed, a vector space of dimension n can be represented with n basis vectors, and an affine space of dimension n can be represented with an affine basis, i.e. $n+1$ points (see Section 2.2), but it turns out that a projective space of dimension n needs $n+2$ points for a basis.

To understand this, consider a basis $\mathbf{a}_i, i = 1, \cdots, n+1$, of E_{n+1}. The $n+1$ projective points $a_i = p(\mathbf{a}_i)$ do not determine the projective coordinates of a point x: there is no way, given the projective points $a_i = p(\mathbf{a}_i)$, to recover a coordinate vector $\mathbf{x}$ of the projective point x since any vectors $\lambda_i \mathbf{a}_i$, $\lambda_i \neq 0$, satisfy $p(\lambda_i \mathbf{a}_i) = a_i$, and there is of course no reason why the λ_i's should be equal! That is, given the $n+1$ points a_i, the choice of the coordinate vectors $\mathbf{a}_i$ depends upon $n+1$ free parameters (instead of 1) and hence, so does the coordinate vector of $\mathbf{x}$ in this basis. Adding an $n+2$nd point will do the trick.

Definition 2.14 *A* **projective basis** *is any set $\mathcal{B}$ of $n+2$ points $m_1, \cdots, m_{n+2}$ of $\mathbb{P}^n$ such that there exists a basis $\mathbf{a}_i, i = 1, \cdots, n+1$, of E_{n+1} such that*

$$p(\mathbf{a}_i) = m_i, i = 1, \cdots, n+1, \text{ and } m_{n+2} = p(\mathbf{a}_1 + \cdots + \mathbf{a}_{n+1}). \tag{2.5}$$

An example of a projective basis in $\mathbb{P}^1$ is given in Figure 2.7. The crucial observation

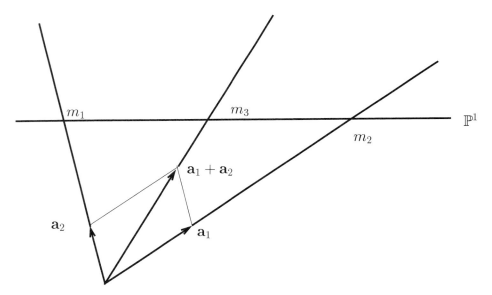

Figure 2.7: The projective basis (m_1, m_2, m_3) of $\mathbb{P}^1$ and one of the corresponding bases of E_2, $(\mathbf{a}_1, \mathbf{a}_2)$.

is that, given a projective basis, two bases $\mathbf{a}_i$ and $\mathbf{a}'_i$ of E_{n+1} satisfying the previous condition are proportional:

Proposition 2.4 *Let $m_1, \cdots, m_{n+2}$ be a projective basis of $\mathbb{P}^n$, and let $\mathbf{a}_i$ and $\mathbf{a}_i'$, $i = 1, \cdots, n+1$, be two bases of E_{n+1} such that for each of them the conditions (2.5) are true. Then there exists $\lambda \neq 0$ such that $\mathbf{a}_i' = \lambda \mathbf{a}_i, i = 1, \cdots, n+1$, i.e. the two bases are proportional.*

Proof :   We can either use Figure 2.8 or do some algebra. Because of (2.5), one has $\mathbf{a}_i' = \lambda_i \mathbf{a}_i$, $i = 1, \cdots, n+1$ and $\mathbf{a}_1' + \cdots + \mathbf{a}_{n+1}' = \lambda(\mathbf{a}_1 + \cdots + \mathbf{a}_{n+1})$. Therefore $\lambda(\mathbf{a}_1 + \cdots + \mathbf{a}_{n+1}) = \lambda_1 \mathbf{a}_1 + \cdots + \lambda_{n+1}\mathbf{a}_{n+1}$ and, because the vectors $\mathbf{a}_1, \cdots, \mathbf{a}_{n+1}$ are a basis of E_{n+1}, $\lambda_1 = \cdots = \lambda_{n+1} = \lambda$. $\square$

Therefore, given a projective basis $m_1, \cdots, m_{n+2}$ of $\mathbb{P}^n$, there exists an infinity of bases of E_{n+1} such that (2.5) holds and all of those bases are proportional. As advertised, we have reduced the number of degrees of freedom in the choice of the coordinate vectors $\mathbf{a}_i$ of the points m_i, $i = 1, \cdots, n+1$, from $n+1$ to 1 by choosing an $n + 2$nd point m_{n+2}.

Hence we can talk unambiguously of the projective coordinates of a point m in that projective basis as being its projective or homogeneous coordinates in any basis of E_{n+1} such that (2.5) holds.

Note that the vector $[1, \cdots, 1]^T$ is a coordinate vector of the point m_{n+2} in the projective basis $m_1, \cdots, m_{n+2}$. Note also that any subset of $n+1$ points chosen among the $n+2$ points $m_1, \cdots, m_{n+2}$ are projectively independent.

A natural question is that of the influence of the point m_{n+2}. Let $\mathbf{a}_1, \cdots, \mathbf{a}_{n+1}$ be a set of coordinate vectors of $(m_1, \cdots, m_{n+1})$ satisfying (2.5). If we fix $m_1, \cdots, m_{n+1}$ and change m_{n+2}, then how does the basis $\mathbf{a}_1, \cdots, \mathbf{a}_{n+1}$ change? Let m_{n+2}' be another point of projective coordinates $x_1' : \cdots : x_{n+1}'$ in the projective basis $(m_1, \cdots, m_{n+2})$, and consider the projective basis $(m_1, \cdots, m_{n+1}, m_{n+2}')$. We want to find a set of vectors $\mathbf{a}_1', \cdots, \mathbf{a}_{n+1}'$ such that $\mathbf{a}_i' = \lambda_i \mathbf{a}_i$, $i = 1, \cdots, n+1$ (so that $p(\mathbf{a}_i') = m_i$, $i = 1, \cdots, n+1$) and such that $p(\mathbf{a}_1' + \cdots + \mathbf{a}_{n+1}') = m_{n+2}'$. This last equality is equivalent to $\lambda_1 \mathbf{a}_1 + \cdots + \lambda_{n+1}\mathbf{a}_{n+1} = \lambda(x_1' \mathbf{a}_1 + \cdots + x_{n+1}' \mathbf{a}_{n+1})$ for some nonzero λ, implying $\lambda_i = \lambda x_i'$, $i = 1, \cdots, n+1$. The new scale factors on the vectors $\mathbf{a}_i$ are proportional to a set of projective coordinates of the point m_{n+2}' in the projective basis $(m_1, \cdots, m_{n+2})$. This situation is shown for $\mathbb{P}^1$ in Figure 2.9.

We are now interested in generalizing to projective spaces the notion of linear application defined for vector spaces. Given two vector spaces E and E', we denote $\mathcal{L}(E; E')$ the set of linear applications from E to E'. Given $\overrightarrow{f} \in \mathcal{L}(E; E')$, the basic idea for extending $\overrightarrow{f}$ to an application f from $P(E)$ to $P(E')$ is to define f by the condition $f \circ p = p' \circ \overrightarrow{f}$ to make the diagram

$$
\begin{array}{ccc}
E & \xrightarrow{\;\overrightarrow{f}\;} & E' \\
\downarrow{\scriptstyle p} & & \downarrow{\scriptstyle p'} \\
P(E) & \xrightarrow{\;f\;} & P(E')
\end{array}
$$

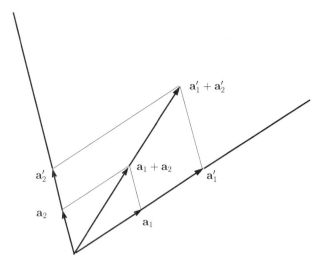

Figure 2.8: A geometric proof that two bases satisfying the conditions of the text are proportional: because of Thales' theorem, $\dfrac{a'_1 + a'_2}{a_1 + a_2} = \dfrac{a'_1}{a_1}$ and $\dfrac{a'_1 + a'_2}{a_1 + a_2} = \dfrac{a'_2}{a_2}$, therefore $\dfrac{a'_1}{a_1} = \dfrac{a'_2}{a_2}$.

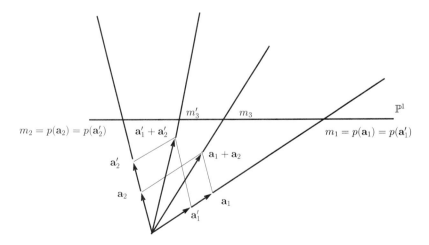

Figure 2.9: Changing the last point of a projective basis is equivalent to choosing different scale factors on the vectors of the original basis of E_{n+1}.

commutative. p and p' are the canonical projections from E to $P(E)$ and from E' to $P(E')$, respectively. This strategy looks as if it would work well since the relation $\overrightarrow{f}(\lambda\mathbf{x}) = \lambda\overrightarrow{f}(\mathbf{x})$ implies that the linear application $\overrightarrow{f}$ is compatible with the two equivalence relations defining $P(E)$ and $P(E')$.

In effect since $f \circ p(\lambda\mathbf{x}) = f \circ p(\mathbf{x})$ by definition of p, one must have $p' \circ \overrightarrow{f}(\lambda\mathbf{x}) = p' \circ \overrightarrow{f}(\mathbf{x})$. This last equality is true if $\overrightarrow{f}$ is linear, by definition of p'.

There is a hidden problem though, namely the fact that since the nullspace, or kernel, of $\overrightarrow{f}$ is in general not reduced to $\mathbf{0}$, there is no guarantee that the image $\overrightarrow{f}(E\backslash\{\mathbf{0}\})$ is contained in $E'\backslash\{\mathbf{0}\}$. In general one can only define an application $P(E)\backslash p(\overrightarrow{f}^{-1}(\mathbf{0})) \longrightarrow P(E')$ and *not* an application $P(E) \longrightarrow P(E')$. Such applications are called *projective morphisms*. Here is the definition.

Definition 2.15 *An application* $f : P(E) \longrightarrow P(E')$ *is called a* **projective morphism** *if and only if there exists an* $\overrightarrow{f} \in \mathcal{L}(E;E')$ *such that f is obtained by* $f \circ p = p' \circ \overrightarrow{f}$ *on* $P(E)\backslash p(\overrightarrow{f}^{-1}(\mathbf{0}))$. *The set of those projective morphisms is denoted* $\mathcal{M}(P(E);P(E'))$. *When* $\overrightarrow{f}$ *is an isomorphism (is one-to-one, which implies that the dimensions of E and E' are the same), f is a real application* $P(E) \longrightarrow P(E')$, *called a* **homography**. *The set of homographies is denoted* $\mathcal{C}(P(E);P(E'))$.

We can easily represent the projective morphisms (and therefore the homographies) in terms of matrices. Let g be a projective morphism, $\mathbf{a}_j, j = 1, \cdots, n+1$, and $\mathbf{a}'_i, i = 1, \cdots, m+1$, be two bases of E and E' and $\mathbf{A} = \{a_{ij}\}$ be the matrix of an $\overrightarrow{f}$ in $\mathcal{L}(E;E')$ such that $f = g$ in those two bases. We attach projective coordinates in $P(E)$ and $P(E')$ to those two bases according to the previous discussion. Let $q \in P(E)\backslash p(\overrightarrow{f}^{-1}(\mathbf{0}))$ have projective coordinates $x_1 : \ldots : x_{n+1}$ and $g(q) \in P(E')$ be its image by g. Let $\mathbf{x}$ be a vector of E such that $p(\mathbf{x}) = q$ and consider the vector $\mathbf{y} = \mathbf{A}\mathbf{x}$ of E'. One has $g \circ p(\mathbf{x}) = p' \circ \overrightarrow{f}(\mathbf{x}) = p'(\mathbf{A}\mathbf{x})$, and since $g \circ p(\mathbf{x}) = g(q)$, $\mathbf{A}\mathbf{x}$ is a coordinate vector of the projective point $g(q)$. Hence, the projective coordinates of $g(q)$ are $\sum_{j=1}^{n+1} a_{1j}x_j : \ldots : \sum_{j=1}^{n+1} a_{m+1j}x_j$, which can be rewritten compactly in matrix form:

$$\mathbf{g(q)} \simeq \mathbf{A}\mathbf{q}.$$

This equality shows that the matrix representation of a projective morphism or a homography is defined up to a nonzero scale factor.

Examples of the actual computation of matrices representing projective morphisms are given in the next section and in Section 2.6.1.

2.4.2.1   An illustration from computer vision: perspective projection

As an example of this situation, consider the Figure 2.10 in which we have made the process of image formation by the pinhole camera slightly more precise than in Figure 2.6 by adding the retinal plane: the image of the 3D point M is the intersection m of the optical ray (C, M) with the plane in the figure.

This defines a projective morphism $\mathcal{P}$ from $\mathbb{P}^3$ to $\mathbb{P}^2$, called a *perspective projection*. A mapping $\overrightarrow{\mathcal{P}}$ from $\mathbb{R}^4$ to $\mathbb{R}^3$ such that $\mathcal{P} \circ p = p' \circ \overrightarrow{\mathcal{P}}$ is represented by a 3×4 matrix $\boldsymbol{\mathcal{P}}$. It should be clear from the figure that the point C does not have an image through this projective morphism. This means that $\boldsymbol{\mathcal{P}}\mathbf{C} = \mathbf{0}$, i.e. that all coordinate vectors of the optical center C are in the kernel $\boldsymbol{\mathcal{P}}^{-1}(\mathbf{0})$ of $\boldsymbol{\mathcal{P}}$. The projective point C is a projective subspace (see the next section for the definition of projective subspaces) of dimension 0 arising from a vector space of dimension 1. This vector space is simply the nullspace of matrix $\boldsymbol{\mathcal{P}}$ which indeed has dimension 1 since we will see in the next chapter that its rank is 3.

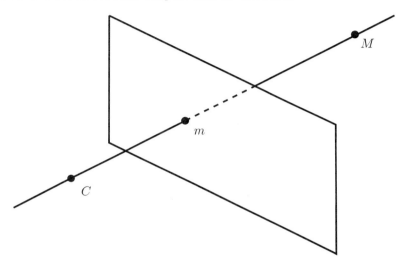

Figure 2.10: The perspective projection from $\mathbb{P}^3$ to $\mathbb{P}^2$ with center C defines a projective morphism which is not defined at the center C.

Let us compute a matrix $\boldsymbol{\mathcal{P}}$ representing this projective morphism. In order to do this, we choose two particular projective bases of $\mathbb{P}^3$ and $\mathbb{P}^2$. Consider Figure 2.11. The point m_4 (of coordinate vector $[0, 0, 0, 1]^T$) of the first projective basis is chosen at the optical center of the camera, the three points m_1, m_2 and m_3 (of coordinate vectors $\mathbf{m}_1 = [1, 0, 0, 0]^T$, $\mathbf{m}_2 = [0, 1, 0, 0]^T$ and $\mathbf{m}_3 = [0, 0, 1, 0]^T$) are chosen in the retinal plane of the camera. The point denoted m_{123} has coordinate vector $\mathbf{m}_{123} = [1, 1, 1, 0]^T$. Note that the four points (m_1, m_2, m_3, m_{123}) form a projective basis of $\mathbb{P}^2$. The point m_5 of coordinate vector $[1, 1, 1, 1]^T$ is on the line (m_4, m_{123}). We choose $(m_1, m_2, m_3, m_4, m_5)$ as the projective basis of $\mathbb{P}^3$ and (m_1, m_2, m_3, m_{123}) as the projective basis of $\mathbb{P}^2$. In order to distinguish between the vectors representing

(m_1, m_2, m_3, m_{123}) as points of $\mathbb{P}^3$ and as points of $\mathbb{P}^2$, we denote the second by $\mathbf{m}_1', \mathbf{m}_2', \mathbf{m}_3'$ and $\mathbf{m}_{123}'$. Note that $\mathbf{m}_1' = [1,0,0]^T$, $\mathbf{m}_2' = [0,1,0]^T$, $\mathbf{m}_3' = [0,0,1]^T$, $\mathbf{m}_{123}' = [1,1,1]^T$.

With that choice of projective bases, we are now ready to compute the matrix $\mathcal{P}$. We use the definition of $\mathcal{P}$. Since $\mathcal{P}(m_i) = m_i$, $i = 1,2,3$, $\boldsymbol{\mathcal{P}}$ satisfies $\boldsymbol{\mathcal{P}}\mathbf{m}_i = \lambda_i \mathbf{m}_i'$, $i = 1,2,3$. Similarly, since $\mathcal{P}(m_5) = m_{123}$, we must have $\boldsymbol{\mathcal{P}}(\sum_{i=1}^4 \mathbf{m}_i) = \lambda_5 \mathbf{m}_{123}'$. Finally, since $\mathcal{P}(m_4)$ is undefined, $\boldsymbol{\mathcal{P}}\mathbf{m}_4 = \mathbf{0}$. Putting all of this together we find that $\lambda_1 = \lambda_2 = \lambda_3 = \lambda_5$ and

$$\boldsymbol{\mathcal{P}} \simeq [\mathbf{I}_3 \ \mathbf{0}_3] \stackrel{\text{def}}{\equiv} \boldsymbol{\mathcal{P}}_0,$$

where $\mathbf{I}_3$ is the 3×3 identity matrix.

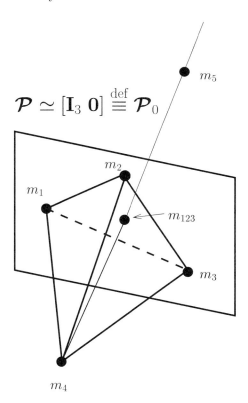

Figure 2.11: For a specific choice of the projective basis, the projective morphism $\mathcal{P}$ is represented by the matrix $\boldsymbol{\mathcal{P}}$ of the figure.

2.4.2.2   The projective group $\mathcal{PLG}(E)$

According to the above presentation, a homography $P(E) \to P(E)$ is represented by an invertible matrix. Therefore we conclude that the set of homographies $\mathcal{C}(P(E); P(E))$ (see Definition 2.15) form a group, denoted $\mathcal{PLG}(E)$ and called the projective group of $P(E)$. Therefore we have the following definition, an echo of Definition 2.4.

Definition 2.16 *The set of homographies of a projective space $P(E)$ forms a group called the projective group $\mathcal{PLG}(E)$ of $P(E)$.*

Since the matrices representing the elements of $\mathcal{PLG}(E_{n+1}) \stackrel{\text{def}}{=} \mathcal{PLG}_n$ are $(n+1) \times (n+1)$ matrices defined up to a scale factor, we have an echo to Proposition 2.1:

Proposition 2.5 *The number of degrees of freedom of the projective group $\mathcal{PLG}(E_{n+1})$ is $n(n+2)$.*

A related notion that we will find useful when we study the cross-ratio in Section 2.6.1 is that of an *orbit* of a configuration of points for $\mathcal{PLG}(E)$. For a given configuration $\mathcal{C}$ of points, we can apply any element f of $\mathcal{PLG}(E)$ to all points of $\mathcal{C}$, thereby obtaining in general a new configuration $\mathcal{D} = f(\mathcal{C})$. We have the following definition.

Definition 2.17 *The orbit of $\mathcal{C}$ is the set of configurations $\mathcal{D}$ such that there exists an element f of $\mathcal{PLG}(E)$ such that $\mathcal{D} = f(\mathcal{C})$.*

2.4.2.3   The First fundamental theorem of projective geometry

We can then prove the so-called *First fundamental theorem of projective geometry*:

Theorem 2.1 (First fundamental theorem of projective geometry)
Let $P(E_n)$ and $P(E'_n)$ be two projective spaces of same (finite) dimension n, $m_i, i = 1, \cdots, n+2$, and $m'_i, i = 1, \cdots, n+2$, two projective bases of $P(E_n)$ and $P(E'_n)$, respectively. Then there exists a unique homography $g : P(E_n) \longrightarrow P(E'_n)$ such that $g(m_i) = m'_i, i = 1, \cdots, n+2$.

Proof : Let $\mathbf{a}_i$ and $\mathbf{a}'_i$ be two bases of E_n and E'_n attached to the two projective bases. We can define $\overrightarrow{f} \in \mathcal{L}(E_n; E'_n)$ by $\mathbf{a}'_i = \overrightarrow{f}(\mathbf{a}_i), i = 1, \cdots, n+1$, and $g = f$ is certainly a solution. Let us show it is unique. If g and g' are two solutions, then the homography $g'^{-1} \circ g : P(E_n) \longrightarrow P(E_n)$ leaves the projective basis m_i invariant. According to Proposition 2.4, this implies that $g'^{-1} \circ g$ is represented by $\lambda \mathbf{I}_n$. $\square$

Let us notice in passing that if we consider the set $\mathcal{B}$ of all configurations of $n+2$ points of $P(E_{n+1})$ that are projective bases, this theorem tells us that the orbit (see Definition 2.17) of any projective basis is the whole set $\mathcal{B}$. In that sense, all projective bases of $P(E_{n+1})$ are equivalent.

The projective line   As an important special case, let us consider the situation where $E = \mathbb{K}^2$, $\mathbb{K}$ being the set of real numbers $\mathbb{R}$ or the set of complex numbers $\mathbb{C}$. In the case of $\mathbb{R}$, the set $\mathbb{K}$ is the usual real line, in the case of $\mathbb{C}$, it is the usual real plane. The projective space $P(\mathbb{K}^2)$ is called the projective line $\mathbb{P}^1(\mathbb{K})$. We show that there is a one-to-one correspondence between $\mathbb{K}$ and the projective line $\mathbb{P}^1(\mathbb{K})$ minus a point.

Let $\varepsilon_1 = [1,0]^T$, $\varepsilon_2 = [0,1]^T$ be the canonical basis of $\mathbb{K}^2$ (see Figure 2.12). Each coordinate vector $\mathbf{x}$ is equal to $x_1 \varepsilon_1 + x_2 \varepsilon_2$ and we note $p(\mathbf{x}) = p(x_1, x_2)$. The mapping $\theta \to p(\theta, 1)$ is one-to-one from $\mathbb{K}$ onto $P(\mathbb{K}) \backslash \{p(1,0)\}$, the last set being the projective line minus the point ε_1. It is represented in Figure 2.12 by the affine line of equation $x_2 = 1$. We note that $\theta = x_1 : x_2$ and therefore if $\theta \neq \theta'$ the two points $p(\theta, 1)$ and $p(\theta', 1)$ are distinct: the mapping is injective. Conversely, let m be a point of $P(\mathbb{K}) \backslash \{p(1,0)\}$ and $[x_1, x_2]^T$ a coordinate vector of m. Since $x_2 \neq 0$ the ratio $\theta = x_1 : x_2$ is well-defined and the vector $[\theta, 1]^T$ is also a coordinate vector of m: the mapping is surjective.

This shows that $P(\mathbb{K})$ can be considered as $\mathbb{K}$ plus a single point which, for reasons that will appear later, is called the point at infinity of $\mathbb{K}$, and denoted ∞.

More precisely, the mapping $\theta \longrightarrow p(\theta, 1)$ from $\mathbb{K} \cup \{\infty\} \to P(\mathbb{K})$ is one-to-one if we agree to map the special "number" ∞ onto $p(1,0)$. The parameter $\theta = x_1 : x_2$ is sometimes called the *projective parameter* of the point x. Therefore we have the interesting formula, $\infty = \dfrac{1}{0}$. We note $\tilde{\mathbb{K}}$ the augmented set $\mathbb{K} \cup \{\infty\}$. We identify $\tilde{\mathbb{K}}$ with $P(\mathbb{K})$ through the previous mapping.

When $\mathbb{K} = \mathbb{R}$, it is important to distinguish between $P(\mathbb{R}) = \mathbb{R} \cup \infty$ and the completed real line $\mathbb{R} \cup \{+\infty\} \cup \{-\infty\}$ which is often used in analysis. In projective geometry there is no difference between "going to $+\infty$" and "going to $-\infty$".

Returning to Figure 2.12, we see that the x_1-axis, defined by the vector ε_1 is parallel to the line of equation $x_2 = 1$. Therefore, in order to obtain the projective point ε_1 corresponding to the coordinate vector ε_1, the projective parameter θ has to go to infinity.

2.4.2.4   Change of projective basis

Let $\mathcal{B} = (m_1, \ldots, m_{n+2})$ and $\mathcal{B}' = (m'_1, \ldots, m'_{n+2})$ be two projective bases of $P(E_{n+1})$ and m be a point. Let $\mathbf{m}_{/\mathcal{B}}$ be a coordinate vector of m in the projective basis $\mathcal{B}$ and $\mathbf{m}_{/\mathcal{B}'}$ a coordinate vector of the same point in the basis $\mathcal{B}'$. Let $f_{\mathcal{B}}^{\mathcal{B}'}$ be the unique homography such that $f_{\mathcal{B}}^{\mathcal{B}'}(m'_i) = m_i$, $i = 1, \ldots, n+2$, and $\mathbf{Q}_{\mathcal{B}}^{\mathcal{B}'} = [q_{ij}]$, $i, j = 1, \ldots, n+1$, an $(n+1) \times (n+1)$ matrix representing $f_{\mathcal{B}}^{\mathcal{B}'}$ in the projective basis $\mathcal{B}'$. That is, the column vectors of $\mathbf{Q}_{\mathcal{B}}^{\mathcal{B}'}$ are proportional to the coordinate vectors of the points m_i expressed in the projective basis $\mathcal{B}'$.

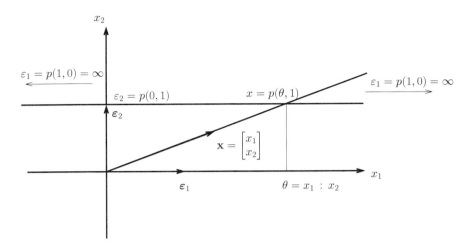

Figure 2.12: The projective line (see text).

We write

$$\mathbf{m}_{/\mathcal{B}} = \sum_{i=1}^{n+1} x_i \mathbf{m}_i,$$

express the coordinate vectors $\mathbf{m}_i$ in the vector basis $(\mathbf{m}'_1, \ldots, \mathbf{m}'_{n+1})$ using the matrix $\mathbf{Q}_{\mathcal{B}}^{\mathcal{B}'}$:

$$\mathbf{m}_i = \sum_{j=1}^{n+1} q_{ji} \mathbf{m}'_j,$$

replace the vectors $\mathbf{m}_i$ in the previous equation and obtain a vector that is proportional to $\mathbf{m}_{/\mathcal{B}'}$:

$$\sum_{j=1}^{n+1} (\sum_{i=1}^{n+1} q_{ji} x_i) \mathbf{m}'_j.$$

Therefore, the relation between the coordinate vectors $\mathbf{m}_{/\mathcal{B}}$ and $\mathbf{m}_{/\mathcal{B}'}$ is

$$\mathbf{m}_{/\mathcal{B}'} \simeq \mathbf{Q}_{\mathcal{B}}^{\mathcal{B}'} \mathbf{m}_{/\mathcal{B}}. \tag{2.6}$$

Note that this equation is very similar to Equation 2.4 that describes a change of affine basis.

2.4.3   Projective subspaces

Let V be a subset of $P(E_{n+1})$ such that it is itself a projective space associated with a proper vector subspace F of E (i.e. $p(F) = V$). V is called a *projective subspace* of $P(E)$. Its dimension is $dim(F) - 1$ and is strictly less than n. We will find many useful instances of projective subspaces.

For example, let $m_1, \cdots, m_p$, $p < n + 1$, be projectively independent points of $P(E_{n+1})$, and let us consider the set V of all points m such that $m_1, \cdots, m_p, m$ are projectively dependent. It is clear that V is a projective subspace of $P(E)$ associated with the vector subspace $span(\mathbf{m}_1, \ldots, \mathbf{m}_p)$ of dimension p of $P(E)$ generated by the linearly independent vectors $\mathbf{m}_1, \cdots, \mathbf{m}_p$. It is therefore of projective dimension $p - 1$. Simple examples of projective subspaces are

- the empty subspace ($p = 0$, projective dimension -1!),

- the projective point ($p = 1$, projective dimension 0),

- the projective line ($p = 2$, projective dimension 1),

- the projective plane ($p = 3$, projective dimension 2),

- and the projective hyperplane ($p = n$, projective dimension $n - 1$).

This shows that the homographies $\mathcal{C}(E; E')$ or $\mathcal{C}(E)$ transform a projective subspace into a projective subspace of the same dimension. Similarly the projective morphisms transform a projective subspace into a projective subspace of dimension less than or equal to its original dimension. A good example is the perspective projection from $\mathbb{P}^3$ to $\mathbb{P}^2$ given in Section 2.4.2.1: it transforms a line of $\mathbb{P}^3$ into a line of $\mathbb{P}^2$ unless the original line goes through the center of projection. In that case the projection of the line is a point.

This discussion shows that there is a one-to-one correspondence between the set $H(E_{n+1})$ of the vector hyperplanes (vector subspaces of dimension n) and the set $H(P(E_{n+1}))$ of the projective hyperplanes (projective subspaces of dimension $n - 1$). We will return to those in a future section (Section 2.6.2) because of their importance in the definition of the principle of duality.

2.4.3.1 Why is projective geometry simpler than affine or Euclidean geometry?

Because the intersection of any number of vector subspaces of the same vector space is a vector space, we conclude that the intersection of any number of projective subspaces is a projective subspace (possibly the empty one, think of two skew lines of $\mathbb{P}^3$).

One can therefore define the projective subspace defined by any subset S of a projective space $P(E)$ as the intersection, denoted $\langle S \rangle$, of all projective subspaces of $P(E)$ containing S.

Consider now two projective subspaces V and W of $P(E)$. Although their union $V \cup W$ is usually not a projective subspace (think of two projective lines of $\mathbb{P}^2$ or $\mathbb{P}^3$), we can talk about $\langle V \cup W \rangle$, the projective subspace defined by $V \cup W$. If V

and W are attached to the vector subspaces F and G of E, then there is a simple relation between $\langle V \cup W \rangle$ and the vector spaces F and G:

Proposition 2.6 $\langle V \cup W \rangle$, *the projective subspace defined by* $V \cup W$, *is associated with the vector space* $F + G$.

Proof : This proposition holds because the vector space $F + G$ is the intersection of all vector spaces containing F and G. □

The well-known formula of linear algebra

$$dim(F + G) + dim(F \cap G) = dim(F) + dim(G)$$

can be rewritten in terms of projective subspaces as

$$dim(\langle V \cup W \rangle) + dim(V \cap W) = dim(V) + dim(W). \qquad (2.7)$$

This equation shows the superiority of projective geometry with respect to affine geometry. Let us take a few examples.

$P(E) = \mathbb{P}^2$: Let us assume that V and W are two distinct lines, hence $dim(V) + dim(W) = 2 = dim(P(E))$. Let us look at $\langle V \cup W \rangle$. It is clearly equal to $\mathbb{P}^2$ if $V \neq W$ and to V if $V = W$. Hence $dim(\langle V \cup W \rangle) \leq 2$, the inequality being strict if and only if the two lines are identical; hence Formula 2.7 shows that $dim(V \cap W) = 0$ if the two lines are distinct. Figure 2.13 shows clearly that

$$\langle V \cup W \rangle = \left\{ \begin{array}{ll} \mathbb{P}^2 & \text{if} \quad V \neq W, \\ V = W & \text{otherwise.} \end{array} \right.$$

Hence two distinct lines of a projective plane always intersect at a point unlike in the affine and Euclidean cases.

$P(E) = \mathbb{P}^3$: Let us assume that V and W are two distinct planes, hence $dim(V) + dim(W) = 4 > dim(P(E))$. Let us look at $\langle V \cup W \rangle$. It is clearly equal to $\mathbb{P}^3$ if $V \neq W$ and to V if $V = W$. Hence, $dim(\langle V \cup W \rangle) \leq 3$, the inequality being strict if and only if the two planes are identical, and $dim(V \cap W) \geq 1$, the inequality being strict if and only if the two planes are identical. Similarly to the previous case

$$\langle V \cup W \rangle = \left\{ \begin{array}{ll} \mathbb{P}^3 & \text{if} \quad V \neq W, \\ V = W & \text{otherwise.} \end{array} \right.$$

Hence two distinct projective planes of the projective space $\mathbb{P}^3$ always intersect along a line unlike in the affine and Euclidean cases.

$P(E) = \mathbb{P}^3$: Let us assume that V is a plane, and let m be a point not in V. Let W be any line going through m. We have $dim(V) + dim(W) = 3$ and

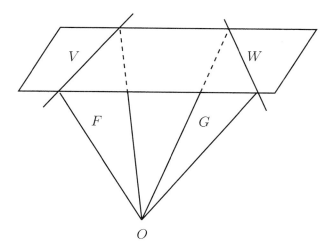

Figure 2.13: The figure shows the two lines V and W and the corresponding two-dimensional vector spaces F and G: $F + G = E_3$ unless $V = W$.

$dim(\langle V \cup W \rangle) = 3$ since the line W cannot be included in V which implies $\langle V \cup W \rangle = \mathbb{P}^3$. It follows that $dim(V \cap W) = 0$, and hence any line going through m intersects V at a point unlike in the affine and Euclidean cases. A similar reasoning, based on Equation 2.7, shows that a line always intersects a plane in $\mathbb{P}^3$, unlike in the affine and Euclidean cases.

Our discussion of the relationship between the affine and projective spaces in Section 2.5 will shed more light on those examples.

Let us consider now the case of hyperplanes in more detail. We defined in Section 2.4.3 a projective hyperplane H to be a projective subspace of $P(E_{n+1})$ generated by n projectively independent points m_i. Let $\mathbf{m}_i$, $i = 1, \cdots, n$, be coordinate vectors of the n points m_i and $\mathbf{x}$ a coordinate vector of a point in H. By definition of H, this statement is equivalent to the remark that the $(n+1) \times (n+1)$ determinant $\det(\mathbf{m}_1, \cdots, \mathbf{m}_n, \mathbf{x})$ is equal to 0. Expanding this determinant, we can rewrite it as

$$\sum_{1 \leq i \leq n+1} h_i x_i = \mathbf{h}^T \mathbf{x} = 0, \tag{2.8}$$

where the vector $\mathbf{h}$ is a function of the coordinates of the vectors $\mathbf{m}_i$, $i = 1, \cdots, n$. This vector is different from $\mathbf{0}$ since its coordinates are the $n + 1$ $n \times n$ minors constructed from the n coordinate vectors $\mathbf{m}_i$, $i = 1, \cdots, n$, which have been assumed to be linearly independent.

Considering Equation 2.8 and noticing that it is homogeneous in the coordinates of $\mathbf{h}$, we conclude that the set $H(P(E))$ of projective hyperplanes is in one-to-one correspondence with the projective space $P(E^*)$ since the vector $\mathbf{h}$ defines an element of E^*, i.e. a linear form on E, up to a nonzero scale factor. As we have seen previously that the set $H(P(E))$ of projective hyperplanes was also in one-to-one correspondence with the set $H(E)$ of hyperplanes, we have the following one-to-one correspondences:

$$H(E) \leftrightarrow H(P(E)) \leftrightarrow P(E^*). \qquad (2.9)$$

2.4.3.2 Incidence properties

The group of homographies $\mathcal{PLG}(E)$ of $P(E)$ preserves the so-called *incidence* properties in the following sense. Let V be a projective subspace of $P(E)$ and f be a homography. $f(V)$ is a projective subspace of $P(E)$ of the same dimension as V.

Examples are many; let us give a few. A set of collinear points of $\mathbb{P}^2$ or $\mathbb{P}^3$ is transformed to a set of collinear points. A set of coplanar points of $\mathbb{P}^3$ is transformed to a set of coplanar points. The point of intersection of a line and a plane of $\mathbb{P}^3$ is transformed to the point of intersection of the transformed line and the transformed plane.

When we move from the set of homographies to the set $\mathcal{M}(E; E')$ of projective morphisms from $P(E)$ to $P(E')$, the situation is similar: a projective subspace V of $P(E)$ is transformed into a projective subspace of $P(E')$ of dimension less than or equal to that of V. For example, in the case of the perspective projection from $\mathbb{P}^3$ to $\mathbb{P}^2$, a set of aligned points is transformed to a single point if the line containing the points goes through the center of projections or to a set of aligned points if it does not.

2.4.3.3 Lines of $\mathbb{P}^2$

According to our discussion, the hyperplanes of $\mathbb{P}^2$ are lines. They are projective subspaces that are generated by sets of two distinct points. The equation of a line in a projective basis is written

$$u_1 x_1 + u_2 x_2 + u_3 x_3 = 0.$$

The vector $\mathbf{u} = [u_1, u_2, u_3]^T$ is defined up to a scale factor and represents a point u of the projective space $P(E_3^*)$.

We saw that two distinct lines u and v of $\mathbb{P}^2$ always intersect at a point. A simple computation shows that this point is represented by the cross-product $\mathbf{u} \times \mathbf{v}$ of the coordinate vectors of the two lines. In Chapter 3 we will see an interpretation of this based on the Grassman-Cayley algebra.

2.4.3.4 Planes of $\mathbb{P}^3$

The hyperplanes of $\mathbb{P}^3$, the three-dimensional projective space, are called planes. They are projective subspaces that are generated by sets of three points in general position (i.e. distinct and not aligned). The equation of a plane is

$$u_1 x_1 + u_2 x_2 + u_3 x_3 + u_4 x_4 = 0.$$

The vector $\mathbf{u} = [u_1, u_2, u_3, u_4]^T$ is defined up to a scale factor and represents a point u of the projective space $P(E_4^*)$.

We saw that two distinct planes always intersect along a projective subspace which, according to Equation 2.7, is of dimension 1, i.e. is a line. Lines of $\mathbb{P}^3$ are studied in detail in Chapter 3.

It is now the right time to connect the affine and projective geometries.

2.5   Affine and projective geometry

In this section we connect the two notions of affine and projective spaces. The key idea is to consider an affine space as a projective space minus a hyperplane or, conversely, a projective space as the union of an affine space of the same dimension and a projective space of dimension one less.

2.5.1   Projective completion of an affine space

In order to be able to reason projectively in an affine space, it is convenient to embed the affine space into a projective space. The easiest way to do this embedding is to consider an affine basis $m_1, \ldots, m_{n+1}$ of an affine space X of dimension n. A point m of X is uniquely represented by the vector $\overrightarrow{m_1 m} = \mathbf{m} = [x_1, \ldots, x_n]^T$ of $\mathbb{R}^n$, so we can embed m into $P(\mathbb{R}^{n+1})$ by associating it with the projective point $\tilde{m}$ with projective coordinate vector $\tilde{\mathbf{m}} = [\mathbf{m}^T, 1]^T$. Using the canonical projection p (Section 2.4.1), we have

$$\tilde{m} = p([\mathbf{m}^T, 1]^T).$$

Using this identification of X as a subset of $P(\mathbb{R}^{n+1})$, we see that X can be seen as the complement in $P(\mathbb{R}^{n+1}) = \tilde{X}$ of the hyperplane of equation $x_{n+1} = 0$. We call this hyperplane the hyperplane at infinity or the part at infinity, ∞_X, of X. We note that $\infty_X = P(\overrightarrow{X})$ since a coordinate vector of $\tilde{m}$ in ∞_X is $[\mathbf{m}^T, 0]^T$. The relation between the affine basis $(m_1, \ldots, m_{n+1})$ of X and a corresponding basis of $\tilde{X}$ is studied in Section 2.5.2.

The question now is, what is the interpretation of ∞_X with respect to X? We have the following definition:

Definition 2.18 *Let $(X, \overrightarrow{X}, \Theta)$ be an affine space. The **projective completion** $\tilde{X}$ of X is equal to*

$$X \cup \infty_X = X \cup P(\overrightarrow{X}).$$

The dimension of the vector space corresponding to the projective space $\tilde{X}$, denoted $\overrightarrow{\tilde{X}}$, is one higher than the dimension of $\overrightarrow{X}$.

Consider an affine subspace S of X, which can be considered as a subset of $P(\mathbb{R}^{n+1})$ by the previous identification. As a consequence, the projective subspace $\langle S \rangle$ of $\tilde{X}$ is equal to the union of S and a subset ∞_S of ∞_X, namely $\infty_X \cap \langle S \rangle$, and is called its part at infinity. Furthermore, $\infty_S = P(\overrightarrow{S})$ since ∞_X is the set of points $\tilde{m}$ of coordinate vectors $[\mathbf{m}^T, 0]^T$.

It is now easy to prove the following proposition:

Proposition 2.7 *Two affine subspaces S and S' are parallel if and only if their parts at infinity are included in one another:*

$$S \; // \; S' \Leftrightarrow \infty_S \subseteq \infty_{S'} \quad or \quad \infty_{S'} \subseteq \infty_S.$$

Proof : Indeed, we know from Definition 2.6 that $S \; // \; S'$ if and only if $\overrightarrow{S} \subseteq \overrightarrow{S'}$ or $\overrightarrow{S'} \subseteq \overrightarrow{S}$ which is equivalent to $\infty_S \subseteq \infty_{S'}$ or $\infty_{S'} \subseteq \infty_S$ since $\infty_S = P(\overrightarrow{S})$ and $\infty_{S'} = P(\overrightarrow{S'})$. $\square$

Let us immediately draw some important useful consequences of this proposition.

2.5.1.1   Projective completion of the affine line

Let us first consider an affine space X_1 of dimension 1, i.e. an affine line. The corresponding vector space $\overrightarrow{X_1}$ is of dimension 1 and is isomorphic to $\mathbb{K}$, and ∞_{X_1} is a projective subspace of dimension 0, in effect $P(\overrightarrow{X_1})$, of the projective line $\tilde{X}_1$, which is the completion of the affine line X_1. Hence, ∞_{X_1} is a point called the *point at infinity* of the affine line X_1 (see Section 2.4.2.3).

2.5.1.2   Projective completion of the affine plane

Let us consider now the case of the affine plane, i.e. of an affine space X_2 of dimension 2. The corresponding vector space $\overrightarrow{X_2}$ is of dimension 2 and ∞_{X_2} is a projective subspace of dimension 1, in effect $P(\overrightarrow{X_2})$, of the projective plane $\tilde{X}_2$, which is the completion of the affine plane X_2. Hence ∞_{X_2} is a projective line called the *line at infinity* of the affine plane X_2.

Consider now two parallel affine lines l_1 and l_2 of X_2. According to Proposition 2.7, their points at infinity ∞_{l_1} and ∞_{l_2} are identical. That is, two parallel affine lines of an affine plane intersect at a point of the line at infinity of the projective completion of the affine plane; see Figure 2.14. The line at infinity ∞_{X_2}, sometimes also denoted l_∞, can thus be thought of as the set of directions of lines of the affine plane X_2. We return to this topic in Section 2.5.2.1.

2.5.1.3   Projective completion of the affine space

Finally, let us consider the case of the affine space, i.e. of an affine space X_3 of dimension 3. The previous discussion shows that the part at infinity ∞_{X_3} is in this

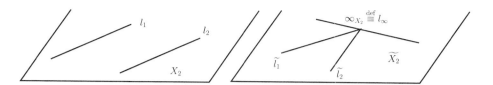

Figure 2.14: Two parallel affine lines of an affine plane (left) intersect at a point of the line at infinity of the projective completion of the affine plane (right).

case a projective plane, i.e. a projective subspace of dimension 2 of the projective completion $\tilde{X}_3$ of X_3. This plane is called the *plane at infinity* of X_3 and is usually denoted Π_∞. The same reasoning as in the previous paragraph shows that two parallel affine lines of X_3 intersect at a point of the plane at infinity which appears as the set of directions of lines of the affine space X_3.

Similarly, two parallel affine planes of X_3 intersect at a line of the plane at infinity called their direction (see Sections 2.5.2.2 and 2.5.3).

2.5.2 Affine and projective bases

Another important item is the relation between an affine basis $m_1, \ldots, m_{n+1}$ of an affine space X of dimension n and the corresponding projective basis of its projective completion $\tilde{X}$.

Assuming that $(\overrightarrow{m_1 m_2}, \ldots, \overrightarrow{m_1 m_{n+1}})$ is the canonical basis of $\overrightarrow{X}$, a vector space of dimension n, we can think of these n vectors as representing the n points $\tilde{p}_1 = p\left(\begin{bmatrix} \overrightarrow{m_1 m_2} \\ 0 \end{bmatrix} \right), \ldots, \tilde{p}_n = p\left(\begin{bmatrix} \overrightarrow{m_1 m_{n+1}} \\ 0 \end{bmatrix} \right)$ of ∞_X. Equivalently, we can say that the equation of ∞_X in the projective basis that we are building is in effect $x_{n+1} = 0$ (see also Section 2.5.3).

The $n + 1$st point $\tilde{p}_{n+1}$ is the projective point $p\left(\begin{bmatrix} \mathbf{0}_n \\ 1 \end{bmatrix} \right)$. Since its last projective coordinate is not equal to 0 this point is not in ∞_X and is therefore a point of X. Since its affine coordinates are $\mathbf{0}_n$, it is the origin m_1 of the affine basis. Figure 2.15 provides an example in X_2. With reference to that figure, the vectors $\overrightarrow{m_1 m_2}$ and $\overrightarrow{m_1 m_3}$ define two points on the line at infinity ∞_{X_2}, and the origin m_1 defines a third point not in ∞_{X_2}. The fourth point is $m_1 + \overrightarrow{m_1 m_2} + \overrightarrow{m_1 m_3}$.

Returning to the general case, the $n + 2$nd point is $\tilde{p}_{n+2} = p([1, \ldots, 1])^T$, i.e. the point $m_1 + \sum_{i=1}^{n} \overrightarrow{m_1 m_{i+1}}$ which is also not in ∞_X since its last projective coordinate is nonzero.

The set of $n + 2$ points $(\tilde{p}_1, \cdots, \tilde{p}_{n+2})$ is clearly a projective basis which is attached to the affine basis $(m_1, m_2, \ldots, m_{n+1})$. It is now easy to verify that a point m of X with affine coordinates $[X_1, \cdots, X_n]^T$ in the affine basis $(m_1, m_2, \ldots, m_{n+1})$, is a point of $\tilde{X}$, with projective coordinates $[X_1, \cdots, X_n, 1]^T$ in the projective basis

$(\tilde{p}_1, \cdots, \tilde{p}_{n+2})$.

Conversely, a point $\tilde{m}$ of $\tilde{X}$ of projective coordinates $[x_1, \cdots, x_{n+1}]^T$ in the projective basis $(\tilde{p}_1, \cdots, \tilde{p}_{n+2})$ is either an affine point of affine coordinates $[x_1/x_{n+1}, \cdots, x_n/x_{n+1}]^T$ in the affine basis $(m_1, m_2, \ldots, m_{n+1})$ if $x_{n+1} \neq 0$ or a point at infinity, in ∞_X, if $x_{n+1} = 0$. Let us now work out some details in the cases,

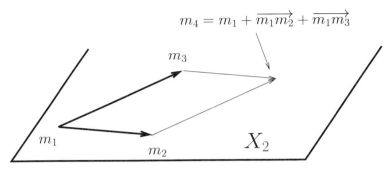

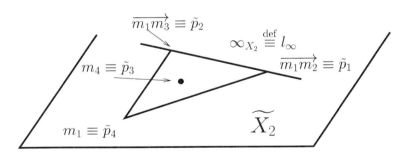

Figure 2.15: The relation between an affine basis (m_1, m_2, m_3) of the affine plane X_2 and the corresponding projective basis $(\tilde{p}_1, \tilde{p}_2, \tilde{p}_3, \tilde{p}_4)$ of its projective completion $\tilde{X}_2$ (see text).

important in practice, where $n = 2, 3$.

2.5.2.1   Affine and projective lines of the plane

We consider an affine basis (m_1, m_2, m_3) of the affine plane and the corresponding projective basis $(\tilde{p}_1, \tilde{p}_2, \tilde{p}_3, \tilde{p}_4)$ of the projective plane. We denote by $[X_1, X_2]^T$ the affine coordinates in the affine basis (m_1, m_2, m_3) and by $[x_1, x_2, x_3]^T$ the projective coordinates in the projective basis $(\tilde{p}_1, \tilde{p}_2, \tilde{p}_3, \tilde{p}_4)$.

The equation of an affine line l in the basis (m_1, m_2, m_3) is, as usual, $u_1 X_1 + u_2 X_2 + u_3 = 0$. Since the affine point m of affine coordinates (X_1, X_2) is also the projective point $\tilde{m}$ of projective coordinates $(X_1, X_2, 1)$, it is seen that the equation of the projective line $\tilde{l}$, the projective completion of the affine line l, is simply $u_1 x_1 + u_2 x_2 + u_3 x_3 = 0$. This line is represented by the vector $\mathbf{l} \simeq [u_1, u_2, u_3]^T$.

The equation of the line at infinity l_∞ is $x_3 = 0$ and is represented by the vector $\mathbf{l}_\infty \simeq [0, 0, 1]^T$. The point of intersection d of $\tilde{l}$ and l_∞, i.e. the point at infinity of the affine line l, is represented by the cross-product $\mathbf{l} \times \mathbf{l}_\infty = [-u_2, u_1, 0]^T$. We note that the vector $[-u_2, u_1]^T$ is parallel to the affine line l.

This was to be expected since, according to the discussion of Section 2.5.1, this point at infinity is what we denoted ∞_l which is equal to $P(\overrightarrow{l})$. $\overrightarrow{l}$ is a vector space of dimension 1 associated with the affine subspace l of dimension 1 of the affine plane. This vector space is generated by the vector $[-u_2, u_1]^T$.

A consequence of this analysis is that two parallel lines in the affine plane have the same point at infinity and therefore intersect on the line at infinity as was shown in Section 2.5.1.2.

Conversely, given a projective line $\tilde{l}$ of equation $u_1 x_1 + u_2 x_2 + u_3 x_3 = 0$, its affine part corresponds to points not on l_∞, i.e. for which $x_3 \neq 0$. Dividing by x_3 in the equation of the line, we find that the equation of the affine line l is $u_1 X_1 + u_2 X_2 + u_3 = 0$ with $X_1 = x_1/x_3$ and $X_2 = x_2/x_3$.

2.5.2.2 Affine and projective planes in space

The discussion about planes in $\mathbb{P}^3$ is very similar to that of lines in $\mathbb{P}^2$.

We consider an affine basis (m_1, m_2, m_3, m_4) of the affine space and the corresponding projective basis $(\tilde{p}_1, \tilde{p}_2, \tilde{p}_3, \tilde{p}_4, \tilde{p}_5)$ of the projective space. We denote by $[X_1, X_2, X_3]^T$ the affine coordinates in the affine basis (m_1, m_2, m_3, m_4) and by $[x_1, x_2, x_3, x_4]^T$ the projective coordinates in the projective basis $(\tilde{p}_1, \tilde{p}_2, \tilde{p}_3, \tilde{p}_4, \tilde{p}_5)$.

The equation of an affine plane Π in the basis (m_1, m_2, m_3, m_4) is, as usual, $u_1 X_1 + u_2 X_2 + u_3 X_3 + u_4 = 0$. Since the affine point m of affine coordinates $[X_1, X_2, X_3]^T$ is also the projective point $\tilde{m}$ of projective coordinates $[X_1, X_2, X_3, 1]^T$, it is seen that the equation of the projective plane $\tilde{\Pi}$, projective completion of the affine plane Π, is simply $u_1 x_1 + u_2 x_2 + u_3 x_3 + u_4 x_4 = 0$. This plane is represented by the vector $\tilde{\mathbf{\Pi}} \simeq [u_1, u_2, u_3, u_4]^T$.

The equation of the plane at infinity Π_∞ is $x_4 = 0$. The intersection of Π with Π_∞ is the system of equations $x_4 = 0$, $u_1 x_1 + u_2 x_2 + u_3 x_3 = 0$. The vector $\mathbf{u} \simeq [u_1, u_2, u_3]^T$ is called the direction of the plane. Two affine planes which are parallel have the same line at infinity and therefore have the same direction.

Conversely, given a projective plane $\tilde{\Pi}$ of equation $u_1 x_1 + u_2 x_2 + u_3 x_3 + u_4 x_4 = 0$, its affine part corresponds to points not on Π_∞, i.e. for which $x_4 \neq 0$. Dividing by

x_4 in the equation of the plane, we find that the equation of the affine plane Π is $u_1 X_1 + u_2 X_2 + u_3 X_3 + u_4 = 0$ with $X_1 = x_1/x_4$, $X_2 = x_2/x_4$ and $X_3 = x_3/x_4$.

2.5.2.3   Affine and projective lines in space

In affine geometry, a 3D line L is usually represented by a point m and a vector $\mathbf{u}$, its direction. Its projective completion $\tilde{L}$ is represented by the point $\tilde{m}$ of projective coordinates $\tilde{\mathbf{m}} \simeq [\mathbf{m}^T, 1]^T$ which is not in Π_∞ and the projective point L_∞ in Π_∞ of projective coordinates $\mathbf{L}_\infty \simeq [\mathbf{u}^T, 0]^T$. Since two parallel affine lines have the same direction, they intersect at a point in Π_∞.

Similarly, the projective completion of an affine line parallel to an affine plane intersects its projective completion at a point on the line at infinity of the affine plane; see Figure 2.16 (remember that this is a pictorial representation of a projective situation, therefore, L does not look parallel to Π in the figure).

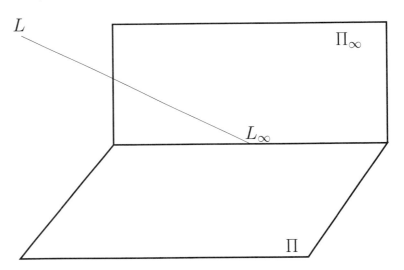

Figure 2.16: The affine line L is parallel to the affine plane Π: their point of intersection, L_∞, is in the plane at infinity Π_∞.

2.5.3   Affine subspace X_n of a projective space $\mathbb{P}^n$

Inversely, given a projective space of dimension n, it is easy to see that the complement of any hyperplane can be considered "naturally" as an affine space of the same dimension. Let Π_∞ be a hyperplane of $\mathbb{P}^n$, and consider the set $\mathbb{P}^n \backslash \Pi_\infty$. Possibly after a change of projective basis, we can assume that Π_∞ is represented by the vector $[0, \ldots, 0, 1]^T$ (its equation is $x_{n+1} = 0$). If we choose the point $m_1 = p([0, \ldots, 0, 1]^T)$

which is not in Π_∞ as the origin, then the set $\mathbb{P}^n \backslash \Pi_\infty$ can be naturally considered as an n-dimensional affine space X_n through the one-to-one correspondence

$$m = m_1 + [x_1, \ldots, x_n]^T \leftrightarrow \tilde{m} \text{ represented by } [x_1, \ldots, x_n, 1]^T.$$

The point of $\mathbb{P}^n \backslash \Pi_\infty$ represented by $[x_1, \ldots, x_n, 1]^T$ can thus be viewed as the point of X_n given by $m_1 + [x_1, \ldots, x_n]^T$.

The points of Π_∞ are represented by vectors of the type $[x_1, \ldots, x_n, 0]^T$ and cannot be reached by this map. If we consider them as the limit of $[x_1, \ldots, x_n, \lambda]^T$, when $\lambda \to 0$ i.e. as the limit of $[x_1/\lambda, \ldots, x_n/\lambda, 1]^T$, then we see that they are the limit of a point of X_n, i.e. the point $m_1 + [x_1/\lambda, \ldots, x_n/\lambda]^T$, going to infinity in the direction $[x_1, \ldots, x_n]^T$, hence the appellation *points at infinity*.

For this reason, the vector $[u_1, \ldots, u_n]^T$ defined by a hyperplane represented by the vector $[u_1, \ldots, u_n, u_{n+1}]^T$, i.e. of equation $u_1 x_1 + \cdots + u_{n+1} x_{n+1} = 0$, is called the *direction* of the hyperplane. It represents the hyperplane's intersection with the hyperplane at infinity Π_∞.

2.5.4 Relation between $\mathcal{PLG}(\vec{\tilde{X}})$ and $\mathcal{AG}(X)$

Let $\tilde{X}$ be the projective completion of X. We assume that ∞_X is defined by the equation $x_{n+1} = 0$. We saw in Section 2.2.1 that every affine morphism f could be written in matrix form as Equation 2.3. This equation shows that f can be considered as a projective morphism $\tilde{f}$ of $\tilde{X}$, in effect as a homography of $\tilde{X}$, which is an element of $\mathcal{C}(\tilde{X})$ such that $\tilde{f}(\infty_X) = \infty_X$. Conversely, let $\tilde{f}$ be a projective morphism of $\tilde{X}$ such that $\tilde{f}(\infty_X) = \infty_X$. A matrix $\tilde{\mathbf{A}}$ representing $\tilde{f}$ is of the form

$$\tilde{\mathbf{A}} = \begin{bmatrix} \mathbf{A} & \mathbf{b} \\ \mathbf{0} & 1 \end{bmatrix}, \tag{2.10}$$

with $\det(\mathbf{A}) \neq 0$.

This equation shows that the restriction f of $\tilde{f}$ to X can be written as (2.3). In conclusion, we have the proposition:

Proposition 2.8 *The affine group $\mathcal{AG}(X)$ can be identified with the subgroup of $\mathcal{PLG}(\vec{\tilde{X}})$ which leaves ∞_X globally invariant.*

In particular, the elements of $\mathcal{AG}(X)$ preserve parallelism. We have seen that two parallel affine subspaces had their parts at infinity included in one another. Applying an affine transformation, the parts at infinity of the transformed affine subspaces which are the images by the affine transformation of the parts at infinity of the original subspaces bear the same relationship. For example, a line and a plane of X_3 which are parallel intersect in Π_∞ and so do the line and the plane transformed by any affine transformation; see Figure 2.17. Note that in general

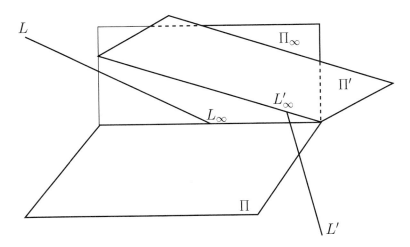

Figure 2.17: The affine line L and the affine plane Π are parallel because their point of intersection L_∞ is in the plane at infinity, Π_∞, as are the transformed line L' and the transformed plane Π' by an affine transformation.

the transformed lines are not parallel to the original lines except when the affine transformation is the composition of a scaling with a translation, i.e. when the matrix $\mathbf{A}$ that appears in (2.3) is a multiple of the identity matrix.

Let us consider some special cases of interest.

Relation between $\mathcal{PLG}(\vec{\tilde{X}}_1)$ **and** $\mathcal{AG}(X_1)$ A homography H of the projective line $\mathbb{P}^1(\mathbb{K})$ is defined by a 2×2 matrix $\mathbf{A}$ defined up to a scale factor. A point m' with projective coordinates $\mathbf{m}' = [x_1', x_2']^T$ is the image of a point m represented by $\mathbf{m} = [x_1, x_2]^T$ if

$$\mathbf{m}' \simeq \mathbf{A}\mathbf{m}.$$

Let us write

$$\mathbf{A} = \begin{bmatrix} a & b \\ c & d \end{bmatrix},$$

so we have $x_1' : x_2' = ax_1 + bx_2 : cx_1 + dx_2$ in projective coordinates. In affine coordinates, $X_1' = x_1'/x_2'$ and $X_1 = x_1/x_2$, hence

$$X_1' = \frac{aX_1 + b}{cX_1 + d}.$$

If H is a homography, then $\det(\mathbf{A}) = ad - bc$ is nonzero.

The projective notation $x_1' : x_2' = ax_1 + bx_2 : cx_1 + dx_2$ better guides our understanding of how the homography "works" than does the affine notation. For example, suppose that $x_2 = 0$, i.e. that m is the point at infinity of the projective line. We then have $x'_1 : x'_2 = a : c$ which means that the image $H(\infty)$ of the point at infinity is either the same point if $c = 0$ or the point of affine coordinate a/c if $c \neq 0$.

If $c = 0$, then d must be nonzero in order for H to be a homography. Hence $X'_1 = \frac{a}{d} X_1 + \frac{b}{d}$ and we recognize an affine transformation of the affine line! Another way of seeing this is to note that $\mathbf{A}$ is proportional to the matrix

$$\begin{bmatrix} \frac{a}{d} & \frac{b}{d} \\ 0 & 1 \end{bmatrix},$$

which is indeed of the form (2.10). This transformation preserves the point at infinity of the affine line, as found in the previous paragraph.

We have seen that if $c \neq 0$ then $H(\infty) = a/c$. Conversely if $cx_1 + dx_2 = 0$, i.e. $x_1 : x_2 = -d : c$, then $x'_2 = 0$. Therefore $H(-d/c) = \infty$. This situation is usually expressed by the sentence, "if $X_1 \to -d/c$ then $X'_1 \to \infty$" and "if $X_1 \to \infty$ then $X'_1 \to \infty$ if $c = 0$ and $X'_1 \to a/c$ otherwise. This example shows quite vividly the simplicity that is sometimes gained by thinking projectively even in an affine framework.

2.6 More projective geometry

We now return to our study of projective geometry armed with our new intuition that allows us to relate concepts in affine and projective geometries.

2.6.1 Cross-ratios

Because of the First fundamental theorem of projective geometry (Theorem 2.1), all triples of distinct points of $\mathbb{P}^1(\mathbb{K})$ are projectively equivalent: there is always a homography that transforms the first triple into the second. This is not true of quadruples of points. But it is possible to classify the orbits (see Definition 2.17) of four-tuples of points under the action of $\mathcal{PLG}(\mathbb{K}^2)$ with a single number in $\tilde{\mathbb{K}}$.

This number is called the cross-ratio of the four points and has innumerable applications. We start with a formal definition of the cross-ratio then show how to compute it and prove some of its properties.

Definition 2.19 *Let a, b, c, d be four points of $\mathbb{P}^1(\mathbb{K})$ such that the first three points are distinct, and let us denote by $h_{a,b,c}$ the unique homography from $\mathbb{P}^1(\mathbb{K})$ onto $\tilde{\mathbb{K}}$ such that $h_{a,b,c}(a) = \infty$, $h_{a,b,c}(b) = 0$, $h_{a,b,c}(c) = 1$. The* **cross-ratio** *of those four points, denoted $\{a, b; c, d\}$, is the element $h_{a,b,c}(d)$ of $\tilde{\mathbb{K}}$.*

Because the homography $h_{a,b,c}$ is by definition one-to-one we have immediately the important property

$$\{a,\, b;\, c,\, d\} = \left\{ \begin{array}{c} \infty \\ 0 \\ 1 \end{array} \right. \iff d = \left\{ \begin{array}{c} a \\ b \\ c \end{array} \right. .$$

In practice, one often has to work with projective coordinates. We have the following proposition:

Proposition 2.9 *Let a_i, $i = 1, \cdots, 4$, be four points of $\mathbb{P}^1(\mathbb{K})$ such that the first three points are distinct. Let us denote (λ_i, μ_i) their homogeneous coordinates. The cross-ratio of the four points a_i can be shown to be equal to the function*

$$\{a_1,\, a_2;\, a_3,\, a_4\} = \left. \begin{vmatrix} \lambda_1 & \lambda_3 \\ \mu_1 & \mu_3 \\ \lambda_1 & \lambda_4 \\ \mu_1 & \mu_4 \end{vmatrix} \middle/ \begin{vmatrix} \lambda_2 & \lambda_3 \\ \mu_2 & \mu_3 \\ \lambda_2 & \lambda_4 \\ \mu_2 & \mu_4 \end{vmatrix} \right. \tag{2.11}$$

of their homogeneous coordinates.

Proof : We write down a matrix representing the homography $h_{a,b,c}$. As a matter of fact it is easier to derive a matrix of the inverse homography $h_{a,b,c}^{-1}$. Let $\mathbf{A}$ be such a matrix. According to the Definition 2.19 we have $\mathbf{A}\varepsilon_i = \alpha_i \mathbf{a}_i$, $i = 1, 2, 3$, and hence $\mathbf{A} = [\alpha_1 \mathbf{a}_1\ \alpha_2 \mathbf{a}_2]$. Let $\mathbf{B}$ be the 2×2 matrix $[\mathbf{a}_1\ \mathbf{a}_2]$. Those three conditions are equivalent to

$$\mathbf{B} \begin{bmatrix} \alpha_1 \\ \alpha_2 \end{bmatrix} = \alpha_3 \mathbf{a}_3,$$

which yields

$$\begin{bmatrix} \alpha_1 \\ \alpha_2 \end{bmatrix} = \alpha_3 \mathbf{B}^{-1} \mathbf{a}_3,$$

and therefore the matrix $\mathbf{A}$ is defined up to the scale factor α_3.

A matrix proportional to $\mathbf{B}^{-1}$ is readily computed as the adjoint $\mathbf{B}^* = \det(\mathbf{B})\mathbf{B}^{-1}$ of $\mathbf{B}$:

$$\mathbf{B}^* = \begin{bmatrix} \mu_2 & -\lambda_2 \\ -\mu_1 & \lambda_1 \end{bmatrix},$$

which yields

$$\begin{bmatrix} \alpha_1 \\ \alpha_2 \end{bmatrix} \simeq \begin{bmatrix} \begin{vmatrix} \lambda_3 & \lambda_2 \\ \mu_3 & \mu_2 \end{vmatrix} \\ \begin{vmatrix} \lambda_1 & \lambda_3 \\ \mu_1 & \mu_3 \end{vmatrix} \end{bmatrix} .$$

Since

$$\mathbf{A} = [\alpha_1 \mathbf{a}_1 \; \alpha_2 \mathbf{a}_2] = \mathbf{B} \begin{bmatrix} \alpha_1 & 0 \\ 0 & \alpha_2 \end{bmatrix},$$

$$\mathbf{A}^{-1} \simeq \begin{bmatrix} 1/\alpha_1 & 0 \\ 0 & 1/\alpha_2 \end{bmatrix} \mathbf{B}^*,$$

and therefore,

$$\mathbf{A}^{-1}\mathbf{a}_4 \simeq \begin{bmatrix} 1/\alpha_1 & 0 \\ 0 & 1/\alpha_2 \end{bmatrix} \mathbf{B}^*\mathbf{a}_4.$$

Putting all of this together, we find that

$$\mathbf{A}^{-1}\mathbf{a}_4 \simeq \left[\frac{\begin{vmatrix} \lambda_2 & \lambda_4 \\ \mu_2 & \mu_4 \end{vmatrix}}{\begin{vmatrix} \lambda_2 & \lambda_3 \\ \mu_2 & \mu_3 \end{vmatrix}}, \; \frac{\begin{vmatrix} \lambda_1 & \lambda_4 \\ \mu_1 & \mu_4 \end{vmatrix}}{\begin{vmatrix} \lambda_1 & \lambda_3 \\ \mu_1 & \mu_3 \end{vmatrix}} \right]^T$$

from which (2.11) follows. $\square$

If we introduce the projective parameters (see Section 2.4.2) $\theta_i = \dfrac{\lambda_i}{\mu_i}$ of the four points with the usual convention that $\theta_i = \infty$ if $\mu_i = 0$, then we find another useful expression:

$$\{a_1, \, a_2; \, a_3, \, a_4\} = \frac{\theta_1 - \theta_3}{\theta_1 - \theta_4} \Bigg/ \frac{\theta_2 - \theta_3}{\theta_2 - \theta_4}. \tag{2.12}$$

Properties of the cross-ratio related to the effect of permutations can be read off this formula:

Proposition 2.10 *The cross-ratio $\{a_1, \, a_2; \, a_3, \, a_4\}$ satisfies the relations*

$$\{a_1, \, a_2; \, a_3, \, a_4\} = \{a_2, \, a_1; \, a_3, \, a_4\}^{-1} = \{a_1, \, a_2; \, a_4, \, a_3\}^{-1}, \tag{2.13}$$

$$\{a_1, \, a_2; \, a_3, \, a_4\} + \{a_1, \, a_3; \, a_2, \, a_4\} = 1. \tag{2.14}$$

Since all permutations of four numbers can be generated from those three transpositions, we can generate all possible values of the cross-ratio when one permutes the four numbers $(a_1, \, a_2, \, a_3, \, a_4)$. One finds only six different values:

Proposition 2.11 *If $\{a_1, \, a_2; \, a_3, \, a_4\} = k$, then the 24 permutations of $(a_1, \, a_2, \, a_3, \, a_4)$ generate only six values of the cross-ratio:*

$$k, \, \frac{1}{k}, \, 1 - k, \, 1 - \frac{1}{k}, \, \frac{1}{1-k}, \, \frac{k}{k-1}.$$

The cross-ratio possesses the following important property:

Proposition 2.12 *The cross-ratio is a projective invariant, i.e. it is invariant under the action of* $\mathcal{PLG}(\mathbb{K})$.

Proof : We have to prove that if k is a homography, and $a' = k(a)$, $b' = k(b)$, $c' = k(c)$ and $d' = k(d)$, then $\{a, b; c, d\} = \{a', b'; c', d'\}$. We give two proofs.

The first is to note that $h_{a',b',c'} \circ k = h_{a,b,c}$. Therefore, since $\{a', b'; c', d'\} = h_{a',b',c'}(d')$ and $d' = k(d)$, we have also $\{a', b'; c', d'\} = h_{a',b',c'}(k(d))$ which is equal to $h_{a,b,c}(d)$, i.e. to $\{a, b; c, d\}$.

The second is to note as $\mathbf{A}$ a matrix representing the homography k. Then by using Equation 2.11 to compute $\{a', b'; c', d'\}$, we see that the determinant

$$\begin{vmatrix} \lambda_a & \lambda_c \\ \mu_a & \mu_c \end{vmatrix} = |\,\mathbf{a},\,\mathbf{c}\,|$$

that appears in the expression of $\{a, b; c, d\}$ must be replaced by $|\,\mathbf{Aa},\,\mathbf{Ac}\,| = \det(\mathbf{A})\,|\,\mathbf{a},\,\mathbf{c}\,|$, and the terms $det^2(\mathbf{A})$ cancel out. $\square$

This proposition can in fact be extended to the general case of four aligned points of $\mathbb{P}^n$: if we apply a projective morphism to those four points, we obtain four points belonging to a projective space of dimension less than or equal to 1 (see Section 2.4.3.2). If the dimension is equal to 1, then the images of the four points are still on a line and their cross-ratio is equal to the cross-ratio of the original points since the restriction of the projective morphism to the line containing the four points is a homography from that line to its image. An interesting example can be found with perspective projection:

Proposition 2.13 *The cross-ratio of the images by a perspective projection of four points aligned on a line which is not an optical ray is equal to the cross-ratio of the original four point; see Figure 2.18.*

The cross-ratio completely characterizes the set $\mathcal{C}(P(E_2), P(E_2'))$ of homographies between one-dimensional projective spaces and therefore also the set $\mathcal{PLG}(E_2)$ because of the *Second fundamental theorem of projective geometry*:

Theorem 2.2 (Second fundamental theorem of projective geometry)
Let $P(E_2)$ and $P(E_2')$ be two one-dimensional projective spaces. The two following statements are equivalent:

1. f is in $\mathcal{C}(P(E_2); P(E_2'))$.

2. f is one-to-one and preserves the cross-ratio.

Proof : We will admit the theorem, the proof being in fact quite complicated and outside the scope of this book. The interested reader is referred to (Berger, 1987). $\square$

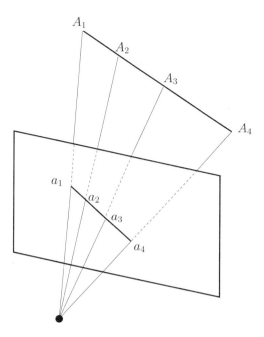

Figure 2.18: The cross-ratio $\{A_1, A_2; A_3, A_4\}$ is equal to the cross-ratio $\{a_1, a_2; a_3, a_4\}$.

Cross-ratios have a simple interpretation in affine geometry. Let A, B, C, D be four collinear points of $\mathbb{P}^n \backslash \Pi_\infty$ such that A, B, C are distinct. Considering that $\mathbb{P}^n \backslash \Pi_\infty$ is an affine space of dimension n, there exist two numbers α and β such that $\overrightarrow{AC} = \alpha \overrightarrow{AB}$ and $\overrightarrow{AD} = \beta \overrightarrow{AB}$. Let ∞ be the point at infinity of the affine line determined by the four points. Since neither A nor B is at infinity, the points A, B, C, D have projective parameters 0, 1, α, β in the projective basis (A, B, ∞). Therefore, according to (2.12), their cross-ratio $\{A, B; C, D\}$ is equal to

$$\frac{\alpha}{\beta} \bigg/ \frac{1-\alpha}{1-\beta} = \frac{\overline{AC}}{\overline{AD}} : \frac{\overline{BC}}{\overline{BD}}. \tag{2.15}$$

The points at infinity are handled with the obvious conventions:

$$\frac{\infty}{\infty} = 1 \ , \quad \frac{a}{\infty} = 0 \ , \quad \frac{\infty}{a} = \infty, \qquad a \in \mathbb{R}.$$

In the case where one of the points, say D, is in Π_∞, so $D = D_\infty$, we immediately find that

$$\{A, B; C, D_\infty\} = \frac{\overline{AC}}{\overline{BC}}. \tag{2.16}$$

Therefore,

Proposition 2.14 *The ratio of the distances of three aligned points of an affine space is the cross-ratio of the three points and the point at infinity of the line they define.*

Since the image of this point by any affine transformation remains at infinity, from (2.15), we can conclude that the *ratio of the distances of three collinear points is invariant by an affine transformation*: it is an affine invariant.

2.6.2 Duality

In the previous sections we have several times met the notion that points and hyperplanes of an n-dimensional projective space are made of the same components: both are represented by homogeneous $(n + 1)$-dimensional nonzero vectors. More precisely we have seen that the set $H(E)$ of hyperplanes of the vector space is in one-to-one correspondence with the set $H(P(E))$ of hyperplanes of the projective space $P(E)$ which itself is in one-to-one correspondence with the projective space $P(E^*)$ built on the dual E^* of the vector space E (Equation 2.9).

Let us now recall a useful result from linear algebra which will be used to study projective lines in $P(E^*)$ which can be interpreted, as we will see later, as pencils of hyperplanes, e.g. pencils of lines in $\mathbb{P}^2$ and pencils of planes in $\mathbb{P}^3$. Examples of these notions are the pencil of epipolar planes and the two pencils of epipolar lines which play an important role in stereo vision (see Chapter 5). When E is of dimension $n + 1$, $P(E_{n+1})$ is denoted $\mathbb{P}^n$ (Definition 2.12). $P(E_{n+1}^*)$, the dual of $P(E_{n+1})$, is denoted $\mathbb{P}^{n*}$.

Theorem 2.3 *Let E be a vector space of dimension n; its dual E^* is also of dimension n. Let F be a subset of E and $span(F)$ the vector subspace of E that it generates. Let us denote*

$$F^\perp = \{f \in E^* \ : \ f(F) = 0\}$$

the orthogonal of F in E^*; it is a vector subspace of E^* and satisfies the conditions

$$F^\perp = span(F)^\perp, \quad dim(span(F)) + dim \, F^\perp = n.$$

Similarly, given a subset S of E^*, we denote

$$S^\perp = \{x \in E \ : \ f(x) = 0 \ \forall f \in S\}$$

its orthogonal set in E. It is a vector subspace of E and satisfies the conditions

$$span(S)^\perp = S^\perp, \quad dim \, S^\perp + dim(span(S)) = n.$$

Proof :   The proof is outside the scope of this book and requires nothing but elementary linear algebra.   □

Let us now consider a projective line of $P(E_{n+1}^*)$, i.e. a "line of hyperplanes". Thanks to the previous theorem, this line has a very simple interpretation in $P(E_{n+1})$: it defines a pencil of hyperplanes. Here is the proposition.

Proposition 2.15 *Let Δ be a projective line of $P(E_{n+1}^*)$. There exists a projective subspace V of $P(E_{n+1})$ of dimension $n-2$ such that $\Delta = \{H \in H(P(E_{n+1})) : H \supset V\}$. Conversely, for any such V, the set $\{H \in H(P(E_{n+1})) : H \supset V\} \subset P(E_{n+1}^*)$ is a projective line. Moreover, $\forall x \in P(E_{n+1}) \backslash V$ there exists a unique $H \in \Delta$ containing x.*

Proof :   Because Δ is a projective line of $P(E_{n+1}^*)$ there exists a vector subspace F^* of E_{n+1}^* of dimension 2 such that $\Delta = P(F^*)$. Let us consider the orthogonal F in E_{n+1} of F^*, i.e. the set of $\mathbf{x} \in E_{n+1}$ such that $f(\mathbf{x}) = 0$ for all $f \in F^*$. According Theorem 2.3, F is of dimension $n-1$ and the associated projective subspace $P(F) = V$ is of dimension $n-2$. By definition Δ is the set of hyperplanes that contain V since for all f in F^*, i.e. for all hyperplanes of the line of hyperplanes, $f(\mathbf{x}) = 0$ for all vectors $\mathbf{x}$ in F.

Conversely, given such a $V = P(F)$ of dimension $n-2$ one constructs the orthogonal F^* in $P(E_{n+1}^*)$ of F which, according to Theorem 2.3, is of dimension 2; hence $\Delta = P(F^*)$ is a projective line, i.e. a line of hyperplanes.

Finally, given a point x in $P(E)$ not in V, we can consider the projective subspace $\langle x, V \rangle$ which is of dimension $n-1$, hence a hyperplane. It contains V by construction, therefore it belongs to Δ. It is unique since there is only one projective subspace of dimension $n-1$ containing x and V as soon as x is not in V.   □

Let us take two examples of great practical importance.

$n = 2$ This is the case of the projective plane $\mathbb{P}^2$. Hyperplanes are lines and Δ is a pencil of lines. The set V is of dimension 0; it is the point of intersection of the pencil of lines; see Figure 2.19.

$n = 3$ This is the case of the projective space $\mathbb{P}^3$. Hyperplanes are planes and Δ is a pencil of planes. The set V is of dimension 1; it is the line of intersection of the pencil of planes; see Figure 2.20.

Since a pencil of hyperplanes is a projective line of $P(E^*)$, one is tempted to consider the cross-ratio of four points on this line, i.e. of four hyperplanes in the pencil. This notion will turn out to be important in Chapter 5. The computation of this cross-ratio is often made easier thanks to the following lemma and the resulting propositions.

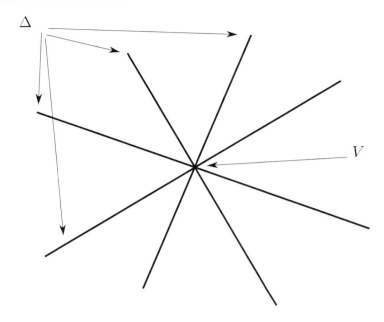

Figure 2.19: A pencil of lines.

Lemma 2.1 *Let Δ be a pencil of hyperplanes, V the associated projective subspace and D a line not intersecting V. The application $\Delta \longrightarrow D$ defined by $H \longrightarrow H \cap D$, where H is a hyperplane of Δ, is a homography.*

Proof : Let H and H' be two distinct hyperplanes of Δ defined by the two linear forms φ and ψ in E^*, i.e. $H = p(\varphi^{-1}(0))$ and $H' = p(\psi^{-1}(0))$. Let $a = D \cap H$ and $b = D \cap H'$ be the points of intersection of D with H and H' respectively. Since φ and ψ are defined up to a scale factor, one can arrange those scale factors in such a way that for two coordinate vectors $\mathbf{x}$ and $\mathbf{y}$ of a and b, i.e. such as $p(\mathbf{x}) = a$ and $p(\mathbf{y}) = b$, one has $\varphi(\mathbf{y}) = -\psi(\mathbf{x}) = 1$ (as well as, of course, $\varphi(\mathbf{x}) = \psi(\mathbf{y}) = 0$).

Having done this normalization we simply write that D is the set of points $p(\lambda\mathbf{x}+\mu\mathbf{y})$ with $(\lambda, \mu) \in \mathbb{K}^2 \backslash (0,0)$ and Δ is the set of hyperplanes $p((\xi\varphi+\eta\psi)^{-1}(0))$ with $(\xi, \eta) \in \mathbb{K}^2 \backslash (0,0)$. In order to find the relationship between (λ, μ) and (ξ, η), we write that the point of projective coordinates (λ, μ) which is the intersection of the line D with the hyperplane of Δ of projective coordinates (ξ, η) is defined by the relation

$$(\xi\varphi + \eta\psi)(\lambda\mathbf{x} + \mu\mathbf{y}) = 0$$

which can be rewritten as $\xi\mu - \eta\lambda = 0$ which means $\xi : \eta = \lambda : \mu$. The correspondence between D and Δ is the identity, therefore a homography. $\square$

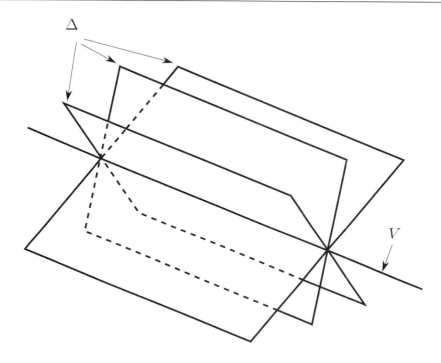

Figure 2.20: A pencil of planes.

Note that the homography that we have built in the proof is a homography from a line in $P(E^*)$, a line of hyperplanes, to a line in $P(E)$, a usual line.

This lemma allows us to talk about the cross-ratio of four hyperplanes in a pencil, e.g. four lines in a pencil of lines of $\mathbb{P}^2$ or four planes in a pencil of planes of $\mathbb{P}^3$. In detail, we have the following proposition.

Proposition 2.16 *Let H_i, $i = 1, \cdots, 4$, be four hyperplanes in the same pencil Δ of $P(E)$ such that the first three are distinct, V the associated projective subspace, and D a line not intersecting V, i.e. such that $D \cap V = \emptyset$ as in Lemma 2.1. Then for all $i = 1, \cdots, 4$ the intersection $D \cap H_i$ is a single point h_i and the cross-ratios $\{h_1, h_2; h_3, h_4\}$ and $\{H_1, H_2; H_3, H_4\}$ taken in D and Δ, respectively, are equal; see Figure 2.21.*

Proof : The fact that the line intersects each hyperplane at a single point arises from the facts that each line always intersects a hyperplane and that the intersection is either a single point or the line if the line is included in the hyperplane. The second case cannot occur because otherwise the line would intersect V which is a hyperplane (i.e. a projective subspace of dimension $n - 2$) of the hyperplane seen as a projective space of dimension $n - 1$. The equality of the cross-ratios is a direct consequence of the previous lemma and the fact that homographies preserve cross-ratios (see Proposition 2.12). □

In particular, the cross-ratio of the four points of intersection of D with the H_i's

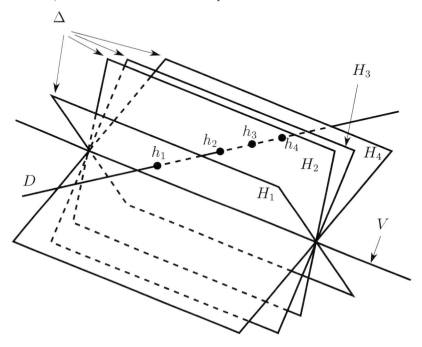

Figure 2.21: The cross-ratio of four planes of a pencil.

is independent of D.

Let us take two examples, one in dimension 2 and the other in dimension 3.

Consider in $\mathbb{P}^2$ the pencil of lines generated by the two lines l and l' represented by the vectors $\mathbf{l}$ and $\mathbf{l'}$ which can be regarded as two points in the dual $\mathbb{P}^{*2}$. Any line $\mathcal{L}$ of the pencil is a point on the line generated by the two points l and l' of $\mathbb{P}^{*2}$ and is therefore represented by the vector $\mathcal{L} = \alpha\mathbf{l} + \beta\mathbf{l'}$. Let r be a line not in the pencil, i.e. not going through the point of intersection of l and l' represented by the cross-product $\mathbf{l} \times \mathbf{l'}$. The ratio $\theta_{\mathcal{L}} = \alpha/\beta$ is a projective parameter for the pencil of lines generated by l and l': $\theta_l = \infty$, $\theta_{l'} = 0$. Hence the cross-ratio of four lines l_1, l_2, l_3, l_4 in the pencil is given by Equation 2.12.

Consider now the point of intersection of the line $\mathcal{L}$ with the line r. It is represented by the vector $\mathcal{L} \times \mathbf{r} = \alpha\mathbf{l} \times \mathbf{r} + \beta\mathbf{l'} \times \mathbf{r}$. Since the two points represented by $\mathbf{l} \times \mathbf{r}$ and $\mathbf{l'} \times \mathbf{r}$ are on r, the parameter $\theta_{\mathcal{L}}$ is also seen as the projective parameter of the point of intersection of $\mathcal{L}$ with r. Hence the cross-ratio of the four points of intersection of four lines of the pencil with the line r is also equal to the cross-ratio of the four lines which is seen to be independent of the choice of the line r as long as this line does not go through the point of intersection of the lines of the pencil.

The case in dimension 3 is shown in Figure 2.21. Note that if we choose any plane going through the line D, this plane intersects the four planes of the pencil along four lines which intersect at a point on V and, according to the previous discussion, the cross-ratio of those four lines is equal to the cross-ratio of the four points h_i, $i = 1, 2, 3, 4$:

Proposition 2.17 *The cross-ratio of four planes of a pencil is equal to the cross-ratio of their four lines of intersection with any plane not going through V.*

A useful application of Proposition 2.16 is an interpretation of the ratios of the projective coordinates as cross-ratios which we study now. Let m_i, $i = 1, \cdots, n+2$, be a projective basis, $\mathbf{m}_i$, $i = 1, \cdots, n+1$, the corresponding vector basis, and x a projective point with projective coordinates $[x_1, \cdots, x_{n+1}]^T$. We know that these projective coordinates are determined by their ratios x_i/x_j which can be interpreted as cross-ratios as follows (see Figure 2.22 for the dimension 2).

Proposition 2.18 *Given the two indices i, j, $i \neq j$, consider the two hyperplanes*

$$
\begin{aligned}
H_0 &= \langle m_1, \cdots, m_{i-1}, \hat{m}_i, m_{i+1}, \cdots, m_{j-1}, \hat{m}_j, m_{j+1}, \cdots, m_{n+2}\rangle, \\
H &= \langle m_1, \cdots, m_{i-1}, \hat{m}_i, m_{i+1}, \cdots, m_{j-1}, \hat{m}_j, m_{j+1}, \cdots, m_{n+1}, x\rangle.
\end{aligned}
$$

The notation $\hat{m}_i$ indicates that the point m_i has been deleted. One has the relation

$$
\frac{x_i}{x_j} = \{m_i, m_j; (m_i, m_j) \cap H_0, (m_i, m_j) \cap H\}.
$$

Proof : We consider the pencil of hyperplanes generated by H_0 and H (the corresponding set V is $\langle m_1, \cdots, \hat{m}_i, \cdots, \hat{m}_j, \cdots, m_{n+1}\rangle$). The line (m_i, m_j) does not intersect V by construction, so we can talk about the cross-ratio of the four hyperplanes $\langle m_i, V\rangle$, $\langle m_j, V\rangle$, H_0, H. In order to compute this cross-ratio we build a homography between $\mathbb{P}^1 = \tilde{\mathbb{K}}$ and the line (m_i, m_j), or the previous pencil, by $p(\lambda, \mu) \longrightarrow p(\lambda \mathbf{m}_i + \mu \mathbf{m}_j)$.

We define this correspondence by $\infty = p(1, 0) \longrightarrow m_i$, $0 = p(0, 1) \longrightarrow m_j$, $1 = p(1, 1) \longrightarrow p(\mathbf{m}_i + \mathbf{m}_j) = (m_i, m_j) \cap H_0$, and $x_i/x_j = p(x_i, x_j) \longrightarrow p(x_i \mathbf{m}_i + x_j \mathbf{m}_j) = (m_i, m_j) \cap H$.

We have to verify that $p(\mathbf{m}_i + \mathbf{m}_j) = (m_i, m_j) \cap H_0$ and $p(x_i \mathbf{m}_i + x_j \mathbf{m}_j) = (m_i, m_j) \cap H$. We do it for the first case. Because of Definition 2.14, the vector $\mathbf{m}_i + \mathbf{m}_j$ is equal to $\mathbf{m}_{n+2} - \mathbf{m}_1 - \ldots - \hat{\mathbf{m}}_i - \ldots - \hat{\mathbf{m}}_j - \ldots - \mathbf{m}_{n+1}$. Therefore $\mathbf{m}_i + \mathbf{m}_j$ is a linear combination of $(\mathbf{m}_1, \ldots, \hat{\mathbf{m}}_i, \ldots, \hat{\mathbf{m}}_j, \ldots, \mathbf{m}_{n+2})$ and defines a point in H_0. A similar reasoning applies to $x_i \mathbf{m}_i + x_j \mathbf{m}_j$ and H.

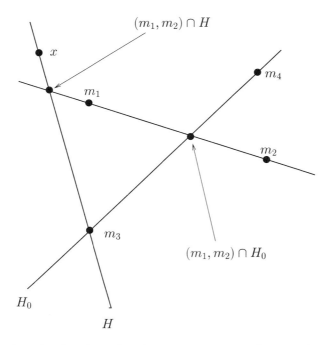

Figure 2.22: The ratio $\frac{x_1}{x_2}$ of the first two projective coordinates of x is equal to the cross-ratio $\{m_1, m_2; (m_1, m_2) \cap H_0, (m_1, m_2) \cap H\}$.

Since homographies preserve the cross-ratio (Proposition 2.12), the cross-ratio of the four points is equal to the cross-ratio of the corresponding points in $\mathbb{P}^1$, i.e. to $\{\infty, 0; 1, \frac{x_i}{x_j}\} = \frac{x_i}{x_j}$. $\square$

2.6.3   Conics, quadrics and their duals

We use in several places of this book conics and quadrics as well as their duals. We start with a general presentation in $P(E_{n+1})$. Let $\boldsymbol{\mathcal{Q}}$ be a symmetric $(n+1) \times (n+1)$ matrix in some basis of E_{n+1}. We have the following definition.

Definition 2.20 *Let $\boldsymbol{\mathcal{Q}}$ be a symmetric $(n + 1) \times (n + 1)$ matrix. The quadric $\mathcal{Q}$ of $P(E_{n+1})$ defined by $\boldsymbol{\mathcal{Q}}$ is the set of projective points m such that their coordinate vectors $\mathbf{m}$ in the projective basis associated with the basis of E_{n+1} where $\mathcal{L}$ is defined satisfy the quadratic equation*

$$\mathbf{m}^T \boldsymbol{\mathcal{Q}} \mathbf{m} \equiv S(\mathbf{m}) = 0. \tag{2.17}$$

We note that this definition is independent of the particular choice of projective coordinates for m since Equation 2.17 is homogeneous of degree 2 in the coordinates of $\mathbf{m}$. We also note that the matrix $\boldsymbol{\mathcal{Q}}$ is only defined up to a nonzero scale factor.

In the case where $n = 2$, quadrics are usually called *conics*.

Let us introduce another notation. Given two points m and n, we define

$$S(\mathbf{m}, \mathbf{n}) = S(\mathbf{n}, \mathbf{m}) = \mathbf{m}^T \boldsymbol{\mathcal{Q}} \mathbf{n} = \mathbf{n}^T \boldsymbol{\mathcal{Q}} \mathbf{m} \qquad (2.18)$$

since $\boldsymbol{\mathcal{Q}}$ is symmetric and study the intersection of the line (m, n) with $\mathcal{Q}$. Any point p on (m, n) is described by $\mathbf{p} = \lambda \mathbf{m} + \mu \mathbf{n}$. This point is on $\mathcal{Q}$ if and only if $S(\mathbf{p}) = 0$, yielding the quadratic equation in λ, μ

$$\lambda^2 S(\mathbf{m}) + 2\lambda\mu S(\mathbf{m}, \mathbf{n}) + \mu^2 S(\mathbf{n}) = 0, \qquad (2.19)$$

which shows that a general line intersects a general quadric in at most two points, real or complex.

We now introduce the notion of a dual quadric. Let $\mathcal{Q}$ be a quadric defined by the matrix $\boldsymbol{\mathcal{Q}}$ and m be a point of $\mathcal{Q}$ which we consider to be fixed for the moment. Consider the set of points n such that

$$S(\mathbf{m}, \mathbf{n}) = S(\mathbf{n}, \mathbf{m}) = 0.$$

Two cases can happen. First, the vector $\boldsymbol{\mathcal{Q}}\mathbf{m}$ can be $\mathbf{0}$. This is only possible if the matrix $\boldsymbol{\mathcal{Q}}$ is not full rank. The quadric $\mathcal{Q}$ is said to be *degenerate*. We will return to this case later and assume for the moment that the matrix $\boldsymbol{\mathcal{Q}}$ is full rank, i.e. that $\boldsymbol{\mathcal{Q}}\mathbf{m}$ is nonzero. The corresponding quadric $\mathcal{Q}$ is said to be *nondegenerate*. The vector $\boldsymbol{\mathcal{Q}}\mathbf{m}$ defines a hyperplane of $P(E_{n+1})$ (and therefore a point of $P(E_{n+1}^*)$). This hyperplane is tangent to $\mathcal{Q}$, as shown in the next proposition:

Proposition 2.19 *Let m be a point of the non-degenerate quadric $\mathcal{Q}$. The hyperplane Π_m defined by the vector $\boldsymbol{\mathcal{Q}}\mathbf{m}$ is tangent to $\mathcal{Q}$ at m; see Figure 2.23.*

Proof :   Let us consider a point n of Π_m: this point is such that $\mathbf{n}^T \boldsymbol{\mathcal{Q}}\mathbf{m} = S(\mathbf{m}, \mathbf{n}) = 0$. The points of intersection of the line (m, n) with $\mathcal{Q}$ are given by Equation 2.19 which reduces to $\mu^2 S(\mathbf{n}) = 0$. If n is on the quadric, then $S(\mathbf{n}) = 0$ and the line (m, n) is entirely contained in $\mathcal{Q}$; otherwise the intersection is defined by $\mu = 0$, i.e. is the point m counted twice: (m, n) is tangent to $\mathcal{Q}$. In conclusion, all the lines of Π_m going through m are either contained in $\mathcal{Q}$ or tangent to $\mathcal{Q}$ at m: Π_m is tangent to $\mathcal{Q}$ at m. $\square$

We now show that all hyperplanes tangent to $\mathcal{Q}$ considered as points of $P(E_{n+1}^*)$ fall on a quadric of $P(E_{n+1}^*)$, called the quadric dual to $\mathcal{Q}$ and denoted $\mathcal{Q}^*$.

Proposition 2.20 *The hyperplanes Π tangent to a non-degenerate quadric $\mathcal{Q}$ of $P(E_{n+1})$ are the points of a non-degenerate quadric $\mathcal{Q}^*$ of $P(E_{n+1}^*)$. This quadric is defined by the matrix $\boldsymbol{\mathcal{Q}}^*$, the adjoint matrix of $\boldsymbol{\mathcal{Q}}$. The equation of the dual quadric is therefore*

$$\boldsymbol{\Pi}^T \boldsymbol{\mathcal{Q}}^* \boldsymbol{\Pi} = 0. \qquad (2.20)$$

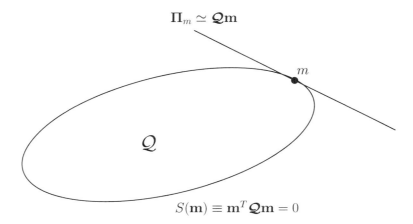

Figure 2.23: The hyperplane represented by the coordinate vector $\boldsymbol{\mathcal{Q}}\mathbf{m}$ is tangent to the quadric $\mathcal{Q}$ of equation $\mathbf{m}^T\boldsymbol{\mathcal{Q}}\mathbf{m} = 0$ at the point m.

Proof :   Let Π_m be a hyperplane tangent to $\mathcal{Q}$ at a point m. According to Proposition 2.19, $\Pi_m \simeq \boldsymbol{\mathcal{Q}}\mathbf{m} \neq \mathbf{0}$. We show that Π_m satisfies (2.20). Let $\boldsymbol{\mathcal{Q}}^*$ be the adjoint matrix of $\boldsymbol{\mathcal{Q}}$, i.e. the transpose of the matrix of cofactors of $\boldsymbol{\mathcal{Q}}$. This matrix is symmetric and satisfies $\boldsymbol{\mathcal{Q}}\boldsymbol{\mathcal{Q}}^* = \det(\boldsymbol{\mathcal{Q}})\mathbf{I}_{n+1}$. Therefore $\Pi_m^T\boldsymbol{\mathcal{Q}}^*\Pi_m = \mathbf{m}^T\boldsymbol{\mathcal{Q}}^T\boldsymbol{\mathcal{Q}}^*\Pi_m = \mathbf{m}^T\boldsymbol{\mathcal{Q}}\boldsymbol{\mathcal{Q}}^*\Pi_m \simeq \mathbf{m}^T\Pi_m = S(\mathbf{m}) = 0$. Conversely, let Π be a point of $\mathcal{Q}^*$ defined by (2.20), i.e. a hyperplane. Consider the point m defined by $\mathbf{m} \simeq \boldsymbol{\mathcal{Q}}^*\Pi$. Note that this implies that $\Pi \simeq \boldsymbol{\mathcal{Q}}\mathbf{m}$. We verify that m is a point of Π:

$$\mathbf{m}^T\Pi \simeq \Pi^T\boldsymbol{\mathcal{Q}}^{*T}\Pi = \Pi^T\boldsymbol{\mathcal{Q}}^*\Pi = 0$$

by definition of $\mathcal{Q}^*$. We then verify that m is on $\mathcal{Q}$:

$$\mathbf{m}^T\boldsymbol{\mathcal{Q}}\mathbf{m} \simeq \Pi^T\mathbf{m} = 0$$

since m is in Π. We next verify that all the lines (m, n) of Π are either contained in $\mathcal{Q}$ or tangent to it at m. The same algebra as in the previous proposition shows that

$$S(\lambda\mathbf{m} + \mu\mathbf{n}) = \lambda^2 S(\mathbf{m}) + 2\lambda\mu S(\mathbf{m}, \mathbf{n}) + \mu^2 S(\mathbf{n}).$$

We just saw that $S(\mathbf{m}) = 0$. $S(\mathbf{m}, \mathbf{n})$ is also equal to 0 because it is equal to $\mathbf{m}^T\boldsymbol{\mathcal{Q}}\mathbf{n} \simeq \Pi^T\mathbf{n} = 0$ since n is in Π. Therefore, either n is on $\mathcal{Q}$ and the whole line (m, n) belongs to the quadric, or this line is tangent to it at m. Hence Π is tangent to $\mathcal{Q}$ at m. □

Let us take an example with $n = 2$. We are in the projective plane $\mathbb{P}^2$, and the previous propositions show that, given a non-degenerate conic $\mathcal{C}$, its tangent lines l fall on a conic $\mathcal{C}^*$ in the dual space $\mathbb{P}^{2*}$. Conversely, given a non-degenerate conic $\mathcal{C}^*$ in $\mathbb{P}^{2*}$, its points l represent a one parameter family of lines in $\mathbb{P}^2$ whose envelope is a non-degenerate conic $\mathcal{C}$; see Figure 2.24. We make good use of this result in Section 6.7. The study of quadrics and their duals is a very large body of

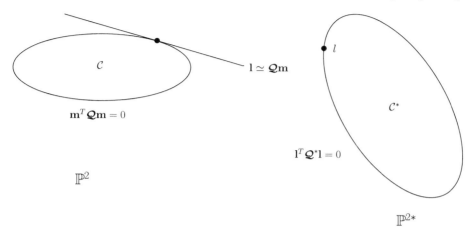

Figure 2.24: The duality between the conics $\mathcal{C}$ and $\mathcal{C}^*$: $\mathcal{C}^*$ is the set of points in $\mathbb{P}^{2*}$ representing the tangents to $\mathcal{C}$; $\mathcal{C}$ is the envelope in $\mathbb{P}^2$ of the lines represented by the points of $\mathcal{C}^*$.

mathematics, and we will not pursue it here. The interested reader is referred to (Berger, 1987) or (Semple and Kneebone, 1952). We will concentrate on one case that we will require in Chapter 11 where we will use the absolute quadric, the dual of the absolute conic. Therefore we choose $n = 3$ and consider some of the possible types of quadrics. This can be achieved through the following proposition.

Proposition 2.21 *The Equation 2.17 of a quadric $\mathcal{Q}$ of $\mathbb{P}^3$ can always be transformed, by a change of projective basis, into*

$$\sum_{i=1}^{r} \lambda_i x_i^2 = 0,$$

where $r \leq 4$ is the rank of the matrix $\mathcal{Q}$ and the λ_i are equal to ± 1.

Proof : $\mathcal{Q}$ being a symmetric matrix, there exists an orthogonal matrix $\mathbf{U}$ such that

$$\mathcal{Q} = \mathbf{U}^T diag(\mu_i) \mathbf{U},$$

where the $\mu_i, i = 1, 4$, are the real eigenvalues of $\mathcal{Q}$. If the rank of $\mathcal{Q}$ is r, then there are r nonzero eigenvalues. Assume that the nonzero eigenvalues are $\mu_1, \ldots, \mu_r$, and let $\mathbf{V} = \left[\sqrt{|\mu_1|} \mathbf{U}_1, \cdots \sqrt{|\mu_r|} \mathbf{U}_r, \mathbf{U}_{r+1}, \cdots, \mathbf{U}_4 \right]$, where the vectors $\mathbf{U}_i, i =$

$1, \cdots, 4$, are the column vectors of $\mathbf{U}$. The matrix $\mathbf{V}$ defines a change of projective basis of $\mathbb{P}^3$. In this basis, the equation of $\mathcal{Q}$ is of the announced type.   □

This result allows us to consider the case of interest in this book, i.e. $r = 3$:

Proposition 2.22 *Let $\mathcal{Q}$ be a quadric defined by the matrix $\mathbf{Q}$. When the rank r of $\mathbf{Q}$ is equal to 3, the quadric is a cone with vertex ε_4.*

Proof :   Because of Proposition 2.21, the equation of the quadric can be written after a change of projective basis as

$$\lambda_1 x_1^2 + \lambda_2 x_2^2 + \lambda_3 x_3^2 = 0.$$

Therefore, the point ε_4 is on $\mathcal{Q}$. It is also easy to verify that for every point m of $\mathcal{Q}$, the line (m, ε_4) is on $\mathcal{Q}$; hence, it is a cone.   □

We now interpret this proposition in the dual space:

Proposition 2.23 *Let $\mathcal{Q}^*$ be a quadric in $\mathbb{P}^{3*}$ defined by the matrix $\mathbf{Q}^*$. When the rank r of $\mathbf{Q}^*$ is equal to 3, the quadric is a cone of planes. These planes are tangent to a planar conic $\mathcal{C}$. $\mathcal{C}$ is in the plane of the "vertex" plane of the cone. $\mathcal{Q}^*$ is called the quadric dual to the conic $\mathcal{C}$.*

Proof :   The first part of the proposition is a direct consequence of Proposition 2.22. We now look at its geometric interpretation. Applying the same change of projective coordinates in $\mathbb{P}^{3*}$ as in $\mathbb{P}^3$ in Proposition 2.22, the equation of $\mathcal{Q}^*$ is

$$\lambda_1 u_1^2 + \lambda_2 u_2^2 + \lambda_3 u_3^2 = 0. \tag{2.21}$$

The plane ε_4, the vertex of the cone is such that for each plane Π of $\mathcal{Q}^*$, the line (Π, ε_4), i.e. the pencil of planes defined by Π and ε_4, is on $\mathcal{Q}^*$. The planes in $\mathcal{Q}^*$ form a system of pencils of planes with axes in the plane ε_4. Let us consider the axes of these pencils. If Π in $\mathcal{Q}^*$ has coordinates $[u_1, u_2, u_3, u_4]^T$, then the coordinates of the line $l = \Pi \cap \varepsilon_4$ are $[u_1, u_2, u_3]^T$ and satisfy (2.21). The lines l therefore envelop the non-degenerate conic $\mathcal{C}$ whose dual equation is (2.21).   □

The Figure 2.25 shows this situation: the plane ε_4 is the vertex of $\mathcal{Q}^*$. Two of the pencils of planes with axes l and l' are shown. The lines l and l' are tangent to the conic $\mathcal{C}$ in the plane ε_4. We will make good use of this situation in the next section and in Section 11.4.2.3 of Chapter 11.

2.7   Projective, affine and Euclidean geometry

We now tie together the three geometric structures that have been studied so far, the projective, affine and Euclidean geometries.

We have seen in Section 2.3.2 the definitions of the complexification of a real vector space E and of an affine space X, Definition 2.11. We proceed in a similar way for a projective space $P(E)$ by considering E and its complexified space $E^{\mathbb{C}}$.

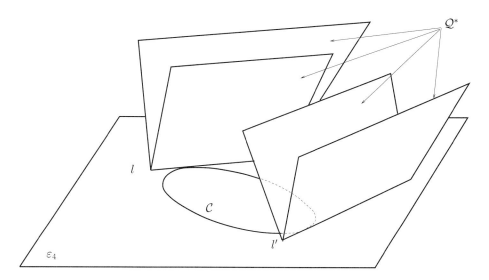

Figure 2.25: The degenerate dual quadric $\mathcal{Q}^*$ of rank 3 is the set of planes tangent to the conic $\mathcal{C}$. This conic is in the plane ε_4. This plane is the vertex of the cone $\mathcal{Q}^*$ (see text).

Definition 2.21 *We define the* **complexified projective space**, $P(E)^{\mathbb{C}}$, *to be equal to the projective space*, $P(E^{\mathbb{C}})$ *built from the complexified vector space* $E^{\mathbb{C}}$.

We have also seen in Section 2.5 how to associate with an affine space X its projective completion $\tilde{X}$. It can be verified, by choosing an affine basis of X, that when we complexify X to $X^{\mathbb{C}}$ and its projective completion $\tilde{X}$ to $\tilde{X}^{\mathbb{C}}$, the result is as we might expect: the projective completion $\widetilde{X^{\mathbb{C}}}$ of the complexified affine space $X^{\mathbb{C}}$ is the complexified of its projective completion $\tilde{X}^{\mathbb{C}}$. See Figures 2.26 and 2.27 for examples in dimensions 2 and 3.

2.7.1 Relation between $\mathcal{PLG}(\vec{\tilde{X}})$ and $\mathcal{S}(X)$

Proposition 2.3 can be extended to the group $\mathcal{S}(X)$ of affine similarities as follows. Using the previous notation, we denote by $\tilde{X}^{\mathbb{C}}$ the complexified projective space of the projective completion $\tilde{X}$ of X. We know that $\tilde{X}^{\mathbb{C}} = X^{\mathbb{C}} \cup \infty_{X^{\mathbb{C}}}$ and that the part at infinity of $\infty_{X^{\mathbb{C}}}$ of $X^{\mathbb{C}}$ is the projective space $P(\vec{X}^{\mathbb{C}})$. The quadratic form $L^{\mathbb{C}}$ defines in $P(\vec{X}^{\mathbb{C}})$ two points called the circular points if $n = 2$ (see Figure 2.26), a conic Ω called the absolute conic or the umbilic if $n = 3$ (see Figure 2.27) and a general quadric if $n > 3$. Note that all points on the umbilic have complex coordinate vectors. To be consistent with the vector space situation, we denote

I and J the two circular points in the case $n = 2$. Following the discussion in Section 2.6.3, especially Proposition 2.23, the absolute conic can also be seen as the dual of a quadric cone $\mathcal{Q}^*$, called the absolute quadric in (Triggs, 1997a), in dual space. This cone is the set of planes tangent to Ω plus the plane at infinity. The

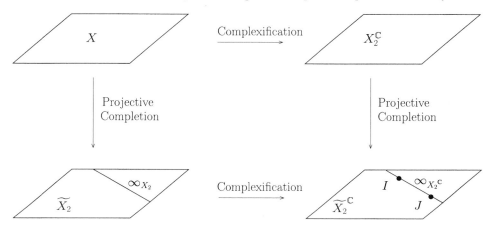

Figure 2.26: The circular points I and J are in the complexified projective completion of the affine plane X_2.

analog of Proposition 2.3 is thus the following.

Proposition 2.24 *An element f of $\mathcal{AG}(X_n)$ is in $\mathcal{S}(X_n)$ if and only if it leaves the absolute quadric globally invariant. The two special cases of interest for us are:*

$n = 2$ *The similarities leave the circular points invariant.*

$n = 3$ *The similarities leave the absolute conic invariant.*

Proof :   The proof is by definition. We note that $f \in \mathcal{S}(X_n)$ is equivalent to $\overrightarrow{f} \in \mathcal{OG}(\overrightarrow{X_n})$. The proposition is thus a direct consequence of Proposition 2.3. $\square$

Let us specify coordinates and use the results of Sections 2.5.2.1 and 2.5.2.2. In the case $n = 2$, a point of $\tilde{X}_2$ has projective coordinates $[x_1, x_2, x_3]^T$. The line at infinity, l_∞, of X_2 is the line of equation $x_3 = 0$. The coordinates of the circular points I and J satisfy the equations $x_1^2 + x_2^2 = x_3 = 0$. Hence one can choose

$$\mathbf{I} \simeq [1, -i, 0]^T, \quad \mathbf{J} \simeq [1, i, 0]^T. \tag{2.22}$$

In the case $n = 3$, a point of $\tilde{X}_3$ has projective coordinates $[x_1, x_2, x_3, x_4]^T$. The equation of the plane at infinity, Π_∞, is $x_4 = 0$. The absolute conic Ω is defined by the equations $x_1^2 + x_2^2 + x_3^2 = x_4 = 0$. Its dual quadric, $\mathcal{Q}^*$, is defined by the equation

$$u_1^2 + u_2^2 + u_3^2 = 0.$$

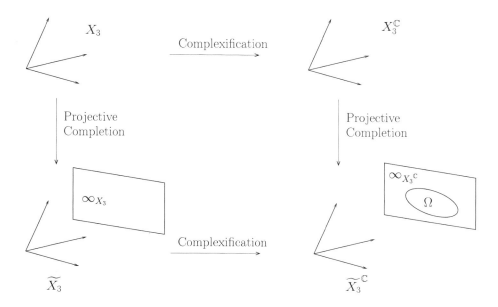

Figure 2.27: The absolute conic, also called the umbilic, is in the complexified projective completion of the affine space X_3.

Its matrix is given by

$$\mathcal{Q}^* \simeq \begin{bmatrix} \mathbf{I}_3 & \mathbf{0}_3 \\ \mathbf{0}_3^T & 0 \end{bmatrix}. \tag{2.23}$$

It is a cone whose vertex is ε_4, i.e. Π_∞. Besides Π_∞, this cone contains all the planes tangent to Ω. The equation of such a plane is

$$X_1 x_1 + X_2 x_2 + X_3 x_3 + \lambda x_4 = 0,$$

where the point of coordinates $[X_1, X_2, X_3, 0]^T$ is on Ω.

2.7.2 Angles as cross-ratios

In much the same way as we have used Π_∞ to define directions of lines and hyperplanes, Ω can be used to define angles between two lines or two hyperplanes. The interesting feature is that angles are thereby introduced as projective invariants. We detail the two cases of interest, $n = 2$ and $n = 3$.

2.7.2.1 Angle of two lines of $\mathbb{P}^2$

Let us consider two affine lines l_1 and l_2 of X_2. We embed X_2 in its projective completion $\tilde{X}_2 = \mathbb{P}^2$ by completing it with the line at infinity l_∞. On l_∞ we consider the circular points I and J and the points at infinity $l_{1\infty}$ and $l_{2\infty}$ of l_1 and l_2.

The cross-ratio $\{l_{1\infty} \, l_{2\infty}; \, I, \, J\}$ is invariant under the action of any homography of $\mathbb{P}^2$, i.e. any element of the group $\mathcal{PLG}(\overrightarrow{X}_2)$ (Proposition 2.12), and therefore under the action of any element of the group of affine transformations $\mathcal{AG}(X_2)$ and under the action of any element of the group of similarities, $\mathcal{S}(X_2)$.

Proposition 2.8 tells us that every affine transformation leaves l_∞ globally invariant; therefore the images of $l_{1\infty}$ and $l_{2\infty}$ are the points at infinity of the transformed lines. Similarly, Proposition 2.24 tells us that the circular points are globally invariant under the action of the similarities.

To summarize, let s be a similarity, and let $l_1' = s(l_1)$ and $l_2' = s(l_2)$ be the two lines that are the images of l_1 and l_2 under s. $s(l_{1\infty})$ and $s(l_{2\infty})$ are the points at infinity $l_{1\infty}'$ and $l_{2\infty}'$ of $s(l_1)$ and $s(l_2)$. Moreover, $s(I) = I$ or $s(I) = J$. Therefore $\{l_{1\infty}, \, l_{2\infty}; \, I, \, J\} = \{l_{1\infty}', \, l_{2\infty}'; \, I, \, J\}$ or $\{l_{1\infty}, \, l_{2\infty}; \, I, \, J\} = \{l_{1\infty}', \, l_{2\infty}'; \, J, \, I\}$.

Modulo this difference which we will soon explain, the cross-ratio of the four points $l_{1\infty}$, $l_{2\infty}$ and I, J is an invariant of the two lines under the action of the group of similarities. Note that, according to Proposition 2.16, this cross-ratio is that of the four lines l_1, l_2 and the two lines going through the point of intersection of l_1 and l_2 and the circular points (I, J); see Figure 2.28.

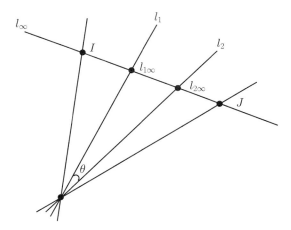

Figure 2.28: The angle θ between the two planar lines is given by Laguerre's formula.

We now show that this cross-ratio is closely related to the angle of the two lines l_1 and l_2:

Proposition 2.25 (Laguerre) *The angle θ between the two lines l_1 and l_2 is given by Laguerre's formula*

$$\theta = \frac{1}{2i} \log(\{l_{1\infty}, \, l_{2\infty}; \, I, \, J\}). \tag{2.24}$$

Proof : Let us choose an orthonormal affine basis (m_1, m_2, m_3) in which the equations of l_1 and l_2 can be written $X_2 = 0$ and $X_2 = X_1 \tan(\theta)$: it suffices to choose m_1 to be the point of intersection of l_1 and l_2 and m_2 on l_1 at a distance of 1 of m_1; m_3 is on the line orthogonal to l_1 at a distance of 1 to m_1. The projective equation of l_1 in the projective basis associated with the affine basis (m_1, m_2, m_3) (see Section 2.5.2) is $x_2 = 0$. The projective equation of l_1 in the same basis is $x_1 \tan(\theta) - x_2 = 0$. The points at infinity $l_{1\infty}$ and $l_{2\infty}$ have projective coordinates $(1,0,0)$ and $(1, \tan(\theta), 0)$. Since I and J have projective coordinates $(1, -i, 0)$ and $(1, i, 0)$, respectively, we can choose the four numbers $0, \tan(\theta), -i, i$ as the projective parameters of the four points $l_{1\infty}, l_{2\infty}, I, J$. Their cross-ratio, computed using Formula 2.12, is found to be equal to $e^{2i\theta}$. $\square$

Note that if we exchange the roles of I and J in the previous computation, we simply change $e^{2i\theta}$ to $e^{-2i\theta}$. Thus, for the similarities that exchange the circular points I and J, the angle between two lines is not preserved but its sign is changed. The difference lies in the sign of the determinant of the matrix $\mathbf{A}$ that defines the similarity. If it is positive, the circular points are preserved and so are the angles; if it is negative, the circular points are swapped and the angles see their sign changed.

Note that two lines are perpendicular if and only if the cross-ratio $\{l_{1\infty}, l_{2\infty}; I, J\}$ is equal to -1 since $e^{i\pi} = -1$.

2.7.2.2 Angle of two lines of $\mathbb{P}^3$

The case of two lines in space is quite similar. Consider two space lines L_1 and L_2, with points at infinity $L_{1\infty}$ and $L_{2\infty}$. Their angle θ is defined as follows. We build the common perpendicular to the two lines and the parallel L_1' to L_1 going through A_2 (see Figure 2.29). It also goes through the point at infinity $L_{1\infty}$ of L_1. θ is the angle between the two planar lines L_1' and L_2. From the previous section, this angle is computed from the cross-ratio of the four points $L_{1\infty}, L_{2\infty}, I$ and J, where I and J are the circular points of the line $(L_{1\infty}, L_{2\infty})$. Note in passing that these circular points are the points of intersection of the line $(L_{1\infty}, L_{2\infty})$ with the absolute conic Ω. A reasoning very similar to that of the previous section shows that the angle of two lines is an invariant under the action of the group of similarities $\mathcal{S}(X_3)$.

2.7.2.3 Angle between two planes of $\mathbb{P}^3$

The angle between two planes can also computed as a projective invariant. Let us look at Figure 2.30. The planes are Π_1 and Π_2, and they intersect along the line L and intersect the plane at infinity Π_∞ along the two lines $\mathbf{L}_{1\infty}$ and $L_{2\infty}$ which go through the point L_∞ of intersection of L with Π_∞. Let us draw from L_∞ in Π_∞ the two complex conjugate lines L_I and L_J tangent to the absolute conic Ω. The reader will convince himself that the angle θ between Π_1 and Π_2 is given by Laguerre's formula $\frac{1}{2i} \log\{L_{1\infty}, L_{2\infty}; L_I, L_J\}$. Note that the cross-ratio that appears in this formula is also that of the four planes $\{\Pi_1, \Pi_2; \Pi_I, \Pi_J\}$, where Π_I and Π_J are

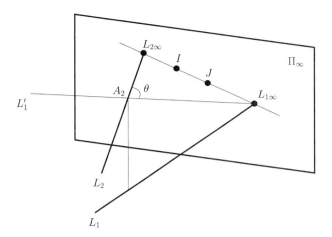

Figure 2.29: The angle θ between the two space lines is given by Laguerre's formula.

the two planes going through the line L and tangent to Ω. Another projective interpretation of the angle θ of two planes is provided by the absolute quadric $\mathcal{Q}^*$. In Euclidean coordinates, a plane Π is represented by a unit normal vector $\mathbf{n}$ and its signed distance to the origin, d. The corresponding projective representation is $[\mathbf{n}^T, -d]^T$. The matrix of the absolute quadric is given by Equation 2.23. Hence, given two planes Π_1 and Π_2 such that $\Pi_1 = [\mathbf{n}_1^T, -d_1]^T$ and $\Pi_2 = [\mathbf{n}_2^T, -d_2]^T$, we have

$$\Pi_2^T \mathcal{Q}^* \Pi_1 \simeq \mathbf{n}_2^T \mathbf{n}_1 = \cos\theta.$$

This relation remains true in any projective coordinate system. Note that because of the ambiguity on the scale factors on $\mathcal{Q}^*$, Π_1 and Π_2, we only obtain a quantity that is proportional to the cosine of the angles of the two planes. But we have the following proposition.

Proposition 2.26 *Two planes Π_1 and Π_2 are orthogonal if and only if*

$$\Pi_2^T \mathcal{Q}^* \Pi_1 = 0$$

in some arbitrary projective basis.

2.8   Summary

To summarize what we have seen in this chapter, we start from a real affine space X_n of dimension n, and define its projective completion $\tilde{X}_n$, a real projective space of dimension n. We also consider the real vector space $\overrightarrow{\tilde{X}_n}$ of dimension $n+1$ attached to the projective space $\tilde{X}_n$.

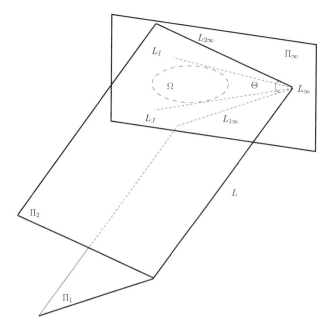

Figure 2.30: The angle θ between the two planes Π_1 and Π_2 is given by Laguerre's formula.

There are three important ideas that have been introduced.

The first idea is the relation between the two spaces $\tilde{X}_n$ and X_n: the affine space is considered as a subspace of the projective space. This allows us to think about affine properties as projective ones, thereby keeping a unified framework well-adapted to computer vision. Moreover, if we add some extra structure to the affine space X_n and turn it into a Euclidean affine space, we can still keep the same unifying viewpoint of the projective geometry. We therefore work with the hierarchy

$$\text{Projective Space} \quad \supset \quad \text{Affine Space} \quad \supset \quad \text{Euclidean Space.} \qquad (2.25)$$

The second idea is that to this hierarchy of spaces corresponds a hierarchy of groups of transformations: the group $\mathcal{PLG}(\overrightarrow{\tilde{X}_n})$ of homographies of $\tilde{X}_n$ contains as a subgroup the group $\mathcal{AG}(X_n)$ of affine transformations of X_n, and this subgroup has been characterized as leaving invariant the hyperplane at infinity. The group $\mathcal{AG}(X_n)$ contains as a subgroup the group $\mathcal{S}(X_n)$ of affine similarities, and this subgroup has been characterized as leaving invariant the absolute quadric. Finally the group $\mathcal{E}(X_n)$ of affine displacements is the subgroup of $\mathcal{S}(X_n)$ that preserves distances. Therefore, besides the hierarchy (2.25) of spaces, we have the hierarchy of groups of transformations

$$\mathcal{PLG}(\overrightarrow{\tilde{X}_n}) \supset \mathcal{AG}(X_n) \supset \mathcal{S}(X_n) \supset \mathcal{E}(X_n). \tag{2.26}$$

The third idea is that to each of the four groups corresponds a class of invariants, i.e. quantities attached to geometric configurations that do not change when one applies a transformation of the group to that configuration. The most important example of such an invariant for $\mathcal{PLG}(\overrightarrow{\tilde{X}_n})$ is the cross-ratio of four collinear points. For the affine group, the corresponding invariant is the ratio of the algebraic distances of three collinear points which we have shown to be the cross-ratio of the four points obtained by adding to the three given points the point at infinity of the line they define. We have also seen that the group of affine similarities preserves angles and ratios of distances that can be defined as cross-ratios, i.e. as projective quantities, such as Laguerre 's formula. Finally, the group of affine displacements is well-known to preserve distances.

The relations between the four groups $\mathcal{PLG}(\overrightarrow{X_n})$, $\mathcal{AG}(X_n)$, $\mathcal{S}(X_n)$ and $\mathcal{E}(X_n)$ as well as their main properties are summarized in Table 2.1.

2.9   References and further reading

Projective, affine and Euclidean geometries are very old and respectable subjects indeed. The reader interested in a somewhat basic introduction to these questions targeted toward the computer vision community is referred to Chapter 23 of (Mundy and Zisserman, 1992). A book that contains more mathematical developments but which is still quite easy to read and useful to build up intuition is (Semple and Kneebone, 1952). The reader interested in more advanced notions in particular from algebraic geometry is referred to (Semple and Roth, 1949) for a somewhat traditional but useful viewpoint and to the book by Abhyankar (Abhyankar, 1985) for a more modern and practical approach. The absolute reference for the material written in this chapter remains (Berger, 1987) that should be regularly reread.

There exists a specialization of projective geometry which is neither affine nor Euclidean and which has some use in computer vision and computer graphics. The idea is to take a fresh look at the definition of a projective space (Definition 2.12) and constrain the scalar λ that appears in the definition to be not only different from 0 but also strictly positive. It is easy to verify that we still have an equivalence relation. The corresponding spaces are called oriented projective spaces and their geometry the oriented projective geometry. This geometry is natural for computer vision and computer graphics in the sense that it can be used to distinguish the points which are *in front* of a camera from those which are *behind* the camera. It has not been widely used in mathematics but has been proposed by Stolfi (Stolfi, 1991) as a tool for expressing some computer synthesis problems. More recently

Table 2.1: Some important groups of transformations: form of the transformation matrix, number of degrees of freedom, characteristic invariants.

$\mathcal{PLG}(E_{n+1}) \equiv \mathcal{PLG}(\overrightarrow{\tilde{X}_n})$	**homography**
$\mathbf{H} \simeq \begin{bmatrix} \mathbf{A} & \mathbf{b} \\ \mathbf{c}^T & d \end{bmatrix}$ $\det(\mathbf{H}) \neq 0$	$n^2 + 2n$
incidence	cross-ratio of 4 points: $\frac{\overline{AC}}{\overline{AD}} : \frac{\overline{BC}}{\overline{BD}}$
$\mathcal{AG}(X_n)$	**affine transformation**
$\mathbf{H} = \begin{bmatrix} \mathbf{A} & \mathbf{b} \\ \mathbf{0}^T & 1 \end{bmatrix}$ $\det(\mathbf{A}) \neq 0$	$n^2 + n$
$\mathbf{H}(\Pi_\infty) = \Pi_\infty$ parallelism	ratio of distances of 3 collinear points: $\frac{\overline{AB}}{\overline{AC}}$
$\mathcal{S}(X_n)$	**similarity**
$\mathbf{H} = \begin{bmatrix} \mathbf{A} & \mathbf{b} \\ \mathbf{0}^T & 1 \end{bmatrix}$ $\mathbf{A}^T\mathbf{A} = s\mathbf{I}_n,\, s > 0$	$\frac{1}{2}(n^2 + n + 2)$
$\mathbf{H}(\Omega) = \Omega$ angles	ratio of distances of any 4 points: $\frac{AB}{CD}$
$\mathcal{E}(X_n)$	**rigid displacement**
$\mathbf{H} = \begin{bmatrix} \mathbf{A} & \mathbf{b} \\ \mathbf{0}^T & 1 \end{bmatrix}$ $\mathbf{A}^T\mathbf{A} = \mathbf{I}_n$	$\frac{1}{2}(n^2 + n)$
distances	distance of 2 points: AB

Laveau and Faugeras have used it for such applications as image based rendering (Laveau and Faugeras, 1996); Hartley's Chirality invariants (Hartley, 1998a) are also closely related to this geometry. Finally, the epipolar ordering used by Luong and Faugeras (Luong and Faugeras, 1994b) can also be thought of in the context of oriented projective geometry.

3 Exterior and double or Grassmann-Cayley algebras

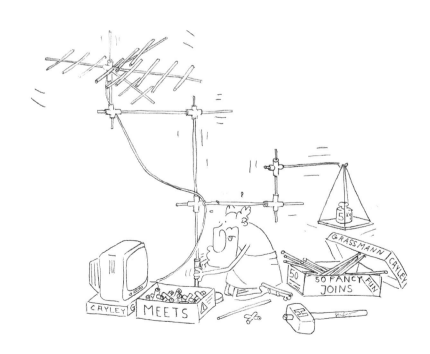

This chapter brings in a complementary viewpoint to the one that was put forward in Chapter 2.

We have learned about projective and affine subspaces and have seen that they are associated with vector subspaces. We have also discussed the ideas of incidence that are related to the notions of intersection and union of projective subspaces as well as the idea of duality. One problem with duality is that it requires the introduction of the dual space of the underlying vector space and that our geometric intuition is poor in the dual space.

The thrust of this chapter is to show that incidence and duality can be dealt with *algebraically* and within the *same* framework, i.e. without the need for the dual space. This is achieved through the introduction of the exterior and double (also called Grassmann-Cayley) algebras which are defined over the underlying vector space E which will be assumed to be of dimension n. To help guide the reader's intuition we will take many examples with $n = 3$ and 4, corresponding to planar and space projective geometry, respectively.

In Section 3.1, we introduce the join operator, describe its algebraic properties, and introduce the extensors of steps 0 to n. They correspond roughly to vector subspaces of dimensions 0 to n of E. We then show that each set of extensors of step k, $k = 0, \cdots, n$, denoted $G_k(E)$, can be considered naturally a vector space of dimension $\binom{n}{k}$. Their direct sum, $G(E)$, is also a vector space of dimension 2^n. In order to compute in these vector spaces we need to choose vector bases: we discuss a *canonical* way to do this. The join operator is next shown to act on $G(E)$ and to provide it with a first algebraic structure, called the exterior algebra of the join. The fundamental result of this section is the geometric interpretation of the join of two extensors: it corresponds in general to the union of the two vector spaces and, as advertised, can be computed algebraically using for example the *canonical* basis.

We then look a little closer at the various sets of extensors and show in Section 3.2 that their coordinates in the canonical basis satisfy a set of second degree algebraic relations called the Plücker coordinates. The standard example is that of the set of 3D lines.

Section 3.3 is dedicated to the study of a second operator, the meet, defined on $G(E)$. This operator provides $G(E)$ with another algebraic structure, called the exterior algebra of the meet, hence the name of double algebra. The fundamental result of this section is the geometric interpretation of the meet of two extensors: it corresponds in general to the intersection of the two vector spaces and, as in the case of the join, can be computed algebraically.

Section 3.4 explains an interesting connection between the join and the meet operators and duality. This connection is achieved through a third operator defined on $G(E)$, the Hodge operator, which turns joins into meets and vice versa. This operator maps $G_k(E)$ onto $G_{n-k}(E)$ and allows us to consider the two spaces as dual of each other. This approach has two advantages: it embeds the space, $G_k(E)$, and its dual, $G_{n-k}(E)$, in the same space, i.e. $G(E)$ and allows us to deal consistently with such operations as unions and intersections of subspaces of the space or its dual using the basic operations of join and meet.

3.1 Definition of the exterior algebra of the join

Given n vectors $\mathbf{x}_i$, $i = 1, \cdots, n$ of E we call their determinant their *bracket*, denoted $\mid \mathbf{x}_1, \cdots, \mathbf{x}_n \mid$. The basic idea of the exterior algebra is to allow us to work with vector subspaces of E *algebraically*. Since vector subspaces of dimension $k \leq n$ are generated by sets of k linearly independent vectors, it is natural to consider such sets.

We first remind the reader of some facts about permutations. Consider the set Σ_n of permutations of the set of integers $\{1, \ldots, n\}$. If σ is in Σ_n, we write $\{\sigma(1), \ldots, \sigma(n)\}$. Every permutation of Σ_n can be written (not uniquely) as a product of transpositions, each one exchanging two consecutive elements. The number of those transpositions is not unique but its parity (odd or even) is. The signature of the permutation σ, denoted $\varepsilon(\sigma)$, is equal to $+1$ if the parity is even and -1 otherwise.

3.1.1 First definitions: The join operator

We consider ordered sets of k, $k \leq n$, vectors of E. Such ordered sets are called k-sequences. We first define an equivalence relation over the set of k-sequences as follows. Given two k-sequences $\mathbf{a}_1, \cdots, \mathbf{a}_k$ and $\mathbf{b}_1, \cdots, \mathbf{b}_k$, we say that they are equivalent when for every choice of vectors $\mathbf{x}_{k+1}, \cdots, \mathbf{x}_n$ we have

$$\mid \mathbf{a}_1, \cdots, \mathbf{a}_k, \mathbf{x}_{k+1}, \cdots, \mathbf{x}_n \mid = \mid \mathbf{b}_1, \cdots, \mathbf{b}_k, \mathbf{x}_{k+1}, \cdots, \mathbf{x}_n \mid . \qquad (3.1)$$

That this defines an equivalence relation is immediate. We use this relation to define a new notion:

Definition 3.1 (Extensors) *An equivalence class under this relation is called an* **extensor** *of step k and is written as*[1]

$$\mathbf{a}_1 \nabla \mathbf{a}_2 \nabla \cdots \nabla \mathbf{a}_k . \qquad (3.2)$$

The product operator ∇ is called the *join* for reasons that will soon become clear.

Let us now give an intuitive interpretation of the equivalence relation (3.1). We have the following proposition.

Proposition 3.1 *Two k-sequences of vectors are equivalent if and only if either the vectors in each sequence are not linearly independent or if they generate the same vector subspace of dimension k and there exists a unimodal (i.e. of unit determinant) linear application that takes the first sequence onto the second.*

---

[1]It is sometimes also written as $\mathbf{a}_1 \wedge \mathbf{a}_2 \cdots \wedge \mathbf{a}_k$.

Proof :   The first part of the proposition is easy. If the two k-sequences do not contain linearly independent vectors, then the determinants that appear in (3.1) are always equal to 0 and the two k-sequences are equivalent. Conversely, if the two determinants in (3.1) are always equal to 0, then let us assume for example that the vectors $(\mathbf{a}_1, \ldots, \mathbf{a}_k)$ are linearly independent. We can find $n - k$ vectors $\mathbf{a}_{k+1}, \ldots, \mathbf{a}_n$ such that $(\mathbf{a}_1, \ldots, \mathbf{a}_n)$ is a basis of E. Therefore, the determinant $\mid \mathbf{a}_1, \ldots, \mathbf{a}_n \mid$ is non zero: a contradiction. The same reasoning applies to the vectors $(\mathbf{b}_1, \ldots, \mathbf{b}_k)$.

Let us now suppose that the vectors $\mathbf{a}_1, \ldots, \mathbf{a}_k$ and $\mathbf{b}_1, \ldots, \mathbf{b}_k$ are linearly independent. We can assume that, possibly after a change of coordinate system, $\mathbf{a}_1 = \varepsilon_1, \ldots, \mathbf{a}_k = \varepsilon_k$. Let us call A the vector space of dimension k generated by the vectors $\mathbf{a}_i$ and B the one generated by the vectors $\mathbf{b}_i$. Assume that $A \neq B$. It is then possible to complete the set of k linearly independent vectors $\mathbf{a}_i$ with $n - k$ vectors $\mathbf{a}'_{k+1}, \ldots, \mathbf{a}'_n$ to form a basis of E and to do so in such a way that some of the $\mathbf{a}'_j$ are in B. Therefore for $\mathbf{x}_{k+1} = \mathbf{a}'_{k+1}, \ldots, \mathbf{x}_n = \mathbf{a}'_n$, the relation (3.1) is not satisfied. We conclude that Equation 3.1 implies that $A = B$.

By expressing the vectors $\mathbf{b}_i$ in the basis of the $\mathbf{a}_i$, the right-hand side of (3.1) is equal to

$$\left| \begin{array}{cccc} \mathbf{Q}^A_B & \mathbf{x}_{k+1} & \cdots & \mathbf{x}_n \\ \mathbf{0}_{(n-k)\times(n-k)} & & & \end{array} \right|,$$

where, as in Chapter 2 Sections 2.2.3 and 2.4.2.4, the matrix $\mathbf{Q}^A_B$ is the $k \times k$ matrix whose ith column vector is the vector $\mathbf{b}_i$ expressed in the basis $(\mathbf{a}_1, \ldots, \mathbf{a}_k)$. This expression is equal to $det(\mathbf{Q}^A_B)D_{k+1,\ldots,n}(\mathbf{x}_{k+1}, \ldots, \mathbf{x}_n)$. The left-hand side of (3.1) is equal to $D_{k+1,\ldots,n}(\mathbf{x}_{k+1}, \ldots, \mathbf{x}_n)$. We have denoted by $D_{k+1,\ldots,n}(\mathbf{x}_{k+1}, \ldots, \mathbf{x}_n)$ the $(n-k) \times (n-k)$ determinant of the $n-k$ last coordinates of the x's. We conclude that $det(\mathbf{Q}^A_B) = 1$. Inversely, if $A = B$ and $det(\mathbf{Q}^A_B) = 1$, then Equation 3.1 is satisfied for all x's. □

We now show that it is possible to turn the set of extensors of step k into a vector space, i.e to define the addition of extensors of the same step and the multiplication of an extensor by a scalar. Because of the well-known properties of determinants, it is easy to derive the following properties of the ∇ operation.

Proposition 3.2 *For every $i = 1, \cdots, k$, $\mathbf{a}_1, \cdots, \mathbf{a}_{i-1}, \mathbf{a}_{i+1}, \cdots, \mathbf{a}_k, \mathbf{x}, \mathbf{y} \in E$ and $\alpha, \beta \in \mathbb{K}$, and for every permutation σ of $\{1, \cdots, k\}$, we define two operations:*

Linearity : $\mathbf{a}_1 \nabla \cdots \nabla \mathbf{a}_{i-1} \nabla (\alpha\mathbf{x} + \beta\mathbf{y}) \nabla \mathbf{a}_{i+1} \nabla \cdots \nabla \mathbf{a}_k =$
$$\alpha(\mathbf{a}_1 \nabla \cdots \nabla \mathbf{a}_{i-1} \nabla \mathbf{x} \nabla \mathbf{a}_{i+1} \nabla \cdots \nabla \mathbf{a}_k)$$
$$+ \beta(\mathbf{a}_1 \nabla \cdots \nabla \mathbf{a}_{i-1} \nabla \mathbf{y} \nabla \mathbf{a}_{i+1} \nabla \cdots \nabla \mathbf{a}_k),$$

and

Antisymmetry : $\mathbf{a}_{\sigma(1)} \nabla \mathbf{a}_{\sigma(2)} \nabla \cdots \nabla \mathbf{a}_{\sigma(k)} = sign(\sigma)\mathbf{a}_1 \nabla \mathbf{a}_2 \nabla \cdots \nabla \mathbf{a}_k.$

These two operations are compatible with the equivalence relation defined on k-sequences.

Proof : The first part of the proposition follows directly from the fact that

$$| \mathbf{a}_1, \ldots, \mathbf{a}_{i-1}, \alpha \mathbf{x} + \beta \mathbf{y}, \mathbf{a}_{i+1}, \ldots, \mathbf{a}_k, \mathbf{x}_{k+1}, \ldots, \mathbf{x}_n | =$$
$$\alpha \, | \, \mathbf{a}_1, \ldots, \mathbf{a}_{i-1}, \mathbf{x}, \mathbf{a}_{i+1}, \ldots, \mathbf{a}_k, \mathbf{x}_{k+1}, \ldots, \mathbf{x}_n \, | +$$
$$\beta \, | \, \mathbf{a}_1, \ldots, \mathbf{a}_{i-1}, \mathbf{y}, \mathbf{a}_{i+1}, \ldots, \mathbf{a}_k, \mathbf{x}_{k+1}, \ldots, \mathbf{x}_n \, | \; . \quad (3.3)$$

The second part of the proposition follows from the following property of determinants:

$$| \, \mathbf{a}_{\sigma(1)}, \ldots, \mathbf{a}_{\sigma(k)}, \mathbf{x}_{k+1}, \ldots, \mathbf{x}_n \, | = sign(\sigma) \, | \, \mathbf{a}_1, \ldots, \mathbf{a}_k, \mathbf{x}_{k+1}, \ldots, \mathbf{x}_n \, | \; .$$

$\square$

Because of the previous proposition, we can talk meaningfully of linear combinations of extensors of same steps. Let us denote by $G_k(E)$, $1 \le k \le n$, the vector space generated by all extensors of step k, i.e. by all linear combinations of terms like (3.2). It is clear from the definition that $G_1(E) = E$. To be complete one defines $G_0(E)$ to be equal to the field K.

From Proposition 3.2 follows the following extremely useful fact.

Proposition 3.3 *If* $\mathbf{e}_1, \cdots, \mathbf{e}_n$ *is a basis of* E, *then the* $\binom{n}{k}$ *extensors of step* k $\mathbf{e}_{i_1} \triangledown \mathbf{e}_{i_2} \triangledown \cdots \triangledown \mathbf{e}_{i_k}, 1 \le i_1 < i_2 < \cdots < i_k \le n$, *form a basis of* $G_k(E)$. *This basis is called the* **canonical basis** *of* $G_k(E)$ *associated with the basis* $(\mathbf{e}_1, \cdots, \mathbf{e}_n)$ *of* E.

In fact, what follows from Proposition 3.2 is the fact that these extensors generate $G_k(E)$. One can also show that they are linearly independent.

Let us take two simple examples, namely the two cases that will be used mostly in this book. In both cases we assume that $(\mathbf{e}_1, \cdots, \mathbf{e}_n)$ is the canonical basis $(\varepsilon_1, \cdots, \varepsilon_n)$ of E:

$n = 3$ The canonical basis of $G_2(E_3)$ is $\varepsilon_1 \triangledown \varepsilon_2$, $\varepsilon_2 \triangledown \varepsilon_3$, $\varepsilon_1 \triangledown \varepsilon_3$. The canonical basis of $G_3(E_3)$ is $\varepsilon_1 \triangledown \varepsilon_2 \triangledown \varepsilon_3$.

$n = 4$ The canonical basis of $G_2(E_4)$ is $\varepsilon_1 \triangledown \varepsilon_2$, $\varepsilon_2 \triangledown \varepsilon_3$, $\varepsilon_3 \triangledown \varepsilon_4$, $\varepsilon_1 \triangledown \varepsilon_4$, $\varepsilon_2 \triangledown \varepsilon_4$, $\varepsilon_1 \triangledown \varepsilon_3$. The canonical basis of $G_3(E_4)$ is $\varepsilon_1 \triangledown \varepsilon_2 \triangledown \varepsilon_3$, $\varepsilon_2 \triangledown \varepsilon_3 \triangledown \varepsilon_4$, $\varepsilon_1 \triangledown \varepsilon_3 \triangledown \varepsilon_4$. The canonical basis of $G_4(E_4)$ is $\varepsilon_1 \triangledown \varepsilon_2 \triangledown \varepsilon_3 \triangledown \varepsilon_4$.

Moreover, we have the important corollary:

Corollary 3.1 *The coordinates of an extensor of step* k $\mathbf{a}_1 \triangledown \mathbf{a}_2 \triangledown \cdots \triangledown \mathbf{a}_k$ *in the basis* $\varepsilon_{i_1} \triangledown \ldots \triangledown \varepsilon_{i_k}$ *are easily shown to be the* $\binom{n}{k}$ $k \times k$ *minors of the* $n \times k$ *matrix* $\mathbf{A}$ *whose* k *column vectors are the* k *vectors* $\mathbf{a}_i$ *built from the rows indexed by* $i_1, i_2, \cdots, i_k$ *and denoted* $a_{i_1 \cdots i_k}$:

$$\mathbf{a}_1 \triangledown \mathbf{a}_2 \triangledown \cdots \triangledown \mathbf{a}_k = \sum_{1 \le i_1 < \cdots < i_k \le n} a_{i_1 \cdots i_k} \, \varepsilon_{i_1} \triangledown \ldots \triangledown \varepsilon_{i_k}.$$

Those minors are called the *Plücker* coordinates of the extensor of step k $\mathbf{a}_1 \nabla \mathbf{a}_2 \nabla \cdots \nabla \mathbf{a}_k$. We will see in a coming section that they are not independent and that there exist quadratic relations between them called the Plücker relations. In Section 3.1.2.3 we work out in detail the case of straight lines in 3D space.

We alluded before to the fact that one of the features of the exterior algebra (still to be defined) was to allow us to treat subspaces of a vector space E algebraically. One of the reasons why this treatment is possible is that there exists a very simple relationship between extensors of step k and k-dimensional subspaces of E. The relation is as follows.

Proposition 3.4 *Let V be a k-dimensional subspace of E and $\mathbf{a}_1$, $\mathbf{a}_2 \cdots$, $\mathbf{a}_k$ and $\mathbf{b}_1$, $\mathbf{b}_2 \cdots$, $\mathbf{b}_k$ be two bases of V. Then there exists a non-zero scalar α such that:*

$$\alpha(\mathbf{a}_1 \nabla \mathbf{a}_2 \nabla \cdots \nabla \mathbf{a}_k) = \mathbf{b}_1 \nabla \mathbf{b}_2 \nabla \cdots \nabla \mathbf{b}_k.$$

Proof : Applying the definition and expressing the basis $\mathbf{b}_1$, $\mathbf{b}_2 \cdots$, $\mathbf{b}_k$ in the basis $\mathbf{a}_1$, $\mathbf{a}_2 \cdots$, $\mathbf{a}_k$ as we did in the proof of Proposition 3.1, we find that $\alpha = det(\mathbf{Q}^A_{\mathcal{B}})$, the determinant of the basis $\mathbf{b}_1$, $\mathbf{b}_2 \cdots$, $\mathbf{b}_k$ expressed in the basis $\mathbf{a}_1$, $\mathbf{a}_2 \cdots$, $\mathbf{a}_k$ □

In terms of projective spaces, this proposition means precisely the following.

Proposition 3.5 *There is a one to one correspondence between the $(k-1)$-dimensional projective subspaces of $P(E)$ or the k-dimensional vector subspaces of E and the elements of the projective space $P(G_k(E))$ built from the $\binom{n}{k}$-dimensional vector space $G_k(E)$ whose coordinate vectors are extensors of step k.*

Examples of this important proposition are provided later in this chapter but the reader should be aware of the fact that there are vectors in $G_k(E)$ which are not extensors of step k, e.g. $\varepsilon_1 \nabla \varepsilon_2 + \varepsilon_3 \nabla \varepsilon_4$.

We now recall the definition of an algebra.

Definition 3.2 *Let E be a vector space. By a bilinear map*

$$f : E \times E \longrightarrow E,$$

we mean a map such that given $\mathbf{x} \in E$, the map $\mathbf{y} \longrightarrow f(\mathbf{x}, \mathbf{y})$ is linear and given $\mathbf{y} \in E$, the map $\mathbf{x} \longrightarrow f(\mathbf{x}, \mathbf{y})$ is linear. By an algebra we mean a vector space E together with a bilinear map $f : E \times E \longrightarrow E$.

The exterior algebra $G(E)$ can now be defined:

Definition 3.3 (The exterior algebra of the join) *The exterior algebra of the join of an n-dimensional vector space E is the direct sum $G(E)$ of all the vector spaces $G_k(E)$, $k = 0, \cdots, n$:*

$$G(E) = G_0(E) \oplus G_1(E) \oplus \cdots \oplus G_n(E),$$

together with the bilinear map:

$$f_\nabla : G(E) \times G(E) \longrightarrow G(E),$$

such that $f_\nabla(\mathbf{x}, \mathbf{y}) = \mathbf{x} \nabla \mathbf{y}$.

Since each $G_k(E)$, $k = 0, \ldots, n$, is a vector space of dimension $\binom{n}{k}$, $G(E)$ is a vector space of dimension 2^n. The map f_∇ is well-defined since if $\mathbf{A} \in G_k(E)$ and $\mathbf{B} \in G_h(E)$, $k + h \le n$ are extensors of steps k and h, then their join is an extensor of step $k + h$, otherwise it is equal to 0: $(\mathbf{a}_1 \nabla \ldots \nabla \mathbf{a}_k) \nabla (\mathbf{b}_1 \nabla \ldots \nabla \mathbf{b}_h) = \mathbf{a}_1 \nabla \ldots \nabla \mathbf{a}_k \nabla \mathbf{b}_1 \nabla \ldots \nabla \mathbf{b}_h$. Using linearity (Proposition 3.2), if $\mathbf{A}$ and $\mathbf{B}$ are elements of $G_k(E)$ and $G_h(E)$, respectively, i.e. linear combinations of extensors, then their join is an element of $G_{k+h}(E)$. Note that to be coherent one defines $a\nabla\mathbf{B} = a\mathbf{B}$ for all a in $G_0(E)$, i.e. every scalar, and every extensor $\mathbf{B}$ of $G_k(E)$, $k \ge 0$.

3.1.2   Properties of the join operator

In this section we derive some important algebraic and geometric properties of the join operator and provide some simple examples. The geometric interpretation of the join of two extensors is based upon Proposition 3.5.

3.1.2.1   Algebraic properties

Applying the properties of determinants, one easily sees that the join operator is not commutative and satisfies the following proposition.

Proposition 3.6 *Let* $\mathbf{A} \in G_k(E)$ *and* $\mathbf{B} \in G_h(E)$; *then*

$$\mathbf{B} \nabla \mathbf{A} = (-1)^{kh} \mathbf{A} \nabla \mathbf{B},$$

where it is understood that if $h + k > n$, *then* $\mathbf{A} \nabla \mathbf{B} = \mathbf{B} \nabla \mathbf{A} = \mathbf{0}$.

It is also easy, using again properties of determinants, to verify that the join operator is associative:

Proposition 3.7 *Let* $\mathbf{A} \in G_k(E)$, $\mathbf{B} \in G_h(E)$ *and* $\mathbf{C} \in G_l(E)$; *then*

$$(\mathbf{A} \nabla \mathbf{B}) \nabla \mathbf{C} = \mathbf{A} \nabla (\mathbf{B} \nabla \mathbf{C}),$$

where it is understood that both sides of the equality are equal to $\mathbf{0}$ *whenever* $h + k + l > n$.

3.1.2.2   Geometric interpretation of the join operator

Let us now come to the geometric interpretation of the join operation. The idea is that two extensors **A** and **B** can be thought of as the coordinate vectors of two projective subspaces A and B of $P(E)$, and, under some mild conditions, their join $\mathbf{A} \triangledown \mathbf{B}$ is a coordinate vector of the projective subspace $\langle A \cup B \rangle$ generated by A and B. In detail,

Proposition 3.8 *Let* **A** *and* **B** *be two extensors and* A *and* B *the corresponding projective subspaces of* $P(E)$. *Then*

1. $\mathbf{A} \triangledown \mathbf{B} = 0$ *if and only if* $A \cap B \neq \emptyset$.

2. *If* $A \cap B = \emptyset$ *then the extensor* $\mathbf{A} \triangledown \mathbf{B}$ *is associated with the projective subspace generated by* A *and* B.

Proof :   Let $\mathbf{A} = \mathbf{a}_1 \triangledown \cdots \triangledown \mathbf{a}_k \neq \mathbf{0}$ and $\mathbf{B} = \mathbf{b}_1 \triangledown \cdots \triangledown \mathbf{b}_h \neq \mathbf{0}$. $\mathbf{A} \triangledown \mathbf{B} = \mathbf{0}$ if and only if the $k + h$ vectors are linearly dependent or, equivalently, two vector subspaces $span\{\mathbf{a}_1, \cdots, \mathbf{a}_k\}$ and $span\{\mathbf{b}_1, \cdots, \mathbf{b}_h\}$ have a non-zero intersection. Also equivalent is the property that the intersection $A \cap B$ of the corresponding projective subspaces is non-empty.

   If $A \cap B = \emptyset$, then $span\{\mathbf{a}_1, \cdots, \mathbf{a}_k\} \cap span\{\mathbf{b}_1, \cdots, \mathbf{b}_h\} = \{\mathbf{0}\}$, the $k + h$ vectors are linearly independent and generate $span\{\mathbf{a}_1, \cdots, \mathbf{a}_k, \mathbf{b}_1, \cdots, \mathbf{b}_h\} = span\{\mathbf{a}_1, \cdots, \mathbf{a}_k\} + span\{\mathbf{b}_1, \cdots, \mathbf{b}_h\}$ whose corresponding projective subspace is precisely $\langle A \cup B \rangle$, see Proposition 2.6. $\square$

3.1.2.3   The example of 3D lines: I

We assume that E is of dimension 4, therefore $P(E)$ is the projective space $\mathbb{P}^3$, and $G_2(E)$ is a vector space of dimension $\binom{4}{2} = 6$. The elements of $P(G_2(E))$ (a projective space of dimension 5) whose coordinate vectors are extensors of step 2 are, according to Proposition 3.5, in one to one correspondence with the projective subspaces of $\mathbb{P}^3$ of dimension 1, i.e. the lines!

   The Plücker coordinates of a line, a point L of $P(G_2(E_4))$, are therefore the coordinates of one of its coordinate vectors $\mathbf{L}$ in the canonical basis $\varepsilon_1 \triangledown \varepsilon_2$, $\varepsilon_1 \triangledown \varepsilon_3$, $\varepsilon_1 \triangledown \varepsilon_4$, $\varepsilon_2 \triangledown \varepsilon_3$, $\varepsilon_2 \triangledown \varepsilon_4$, $\varepsilon_3 \triangledown \varepsilon_4$ of $G_2(E_4)$. What are those coordinates? Since $\mathbf{L} \in G_2(E_4)$ is an extensor of step 2, we can write $\mathbf{L} = \mathbf{M} \triangledown \mathbf{M}'$ where $\mathbf{M}$ and $\mathbf{M}'$ are two vectors of E representing two projective points, see Figure 3.1. L is the line (M, M'). If we write $\mathbf{M} = \sum_{i=1}^{4} x_i \varepsilon_i$ and $\mathbf{M}' = \sum_{i=1}^{4} x'_i \varepsilon_i$, then we easily find that $\mathbf{L} = \sum_{1 \leq i_1 < i_2 \leq 4} (x_{i_1} x'_{i_2} - x_{i_2} x'_{i_1}) \varepsilon_{i_1} \triangledown \varepsilon_{i_2}$. The six Plücker coordinates of the line are the quantities $L_{i_1 i_2} = x_{i_1} x'_{i_2} - x_{i_2} x'_{i_1}$, $i_1 < i_2$, which are the 2×2 minors of the 4×2 matrix $[\mathbf{M} \ \mathbf{M}']$, see Corollary 3.1.

   A point P belongs to the line L if and only if the three vectors $\mathbf{P}, \mathbf{M}, \mathbf{M}'$ are linearly dependent or, equivalently, the join $\mathbf{P} \triangledown \mathbf{M} \triangledown \mathbf{M}'$ is equal to $\mathbf{0}$. Hence we have the following proposition.

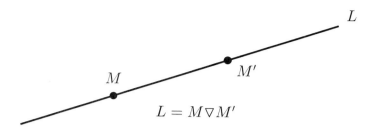

Figure 3.1: The line L defined by the two points M and M' is represented by their join $\mathbf{M} \triangledown \mathbf{M}'$.

Proposition 3.9 *Let L be a line defined by two points M and M' or its Plücker coordinates $\mathbf{L} = \mathbf{M} \triangledown \mathbf{M}'$. We then have the equivalence*

$$P \in L \Leftrightarrow \mathbf{P} \triangledown \mathbf{L} = \mathbf{P} \triangledown \mathbf{M} \triangledown \mathbf{M}' = \mathbf{0}.$$

Note that for a given $\mathbf{L}$, the equation $\mathbf{P} \triangledown \mathbf{L} = \mathbf{0}$ is linear in the coordinates of $\mathbf{P}$. More precisely, the mapping $\mathbf{P} \to \mathbf{P} \triangledown \mathbf{L}$ from $G_1(E)$ into $G_3(E)$ is linear. Its matrix $\mathbf{A}$ expressed in the bases $(\varepsilon_1, \dots, \varepsilon_4)$ of $G_1(E)$ and $(\varepsilon_1 \triangledown \varepsilon_2 \triangledown \varepsilon_3, \varepsilon_2 \triangledown \varepsilon_3 \triangledown \varepsilon_4, \varepsilon_1 \triangledown \varepsilon_3 \triangledown \varepsilon_4, \varepsilon_1 \triangledown \varepsilon_2 \triangledown \varepsilon_4)$ of $G_3(E)$ is readily obtained as a function of the Plücker coordinates of L:

$$\mathbf{A} = \begin{bmatrix} L_{23} & -L_{13} & L_{12} & 0 \\ 0 & L_{34} & -L_{24} & L_{23} \\ L_{34} & 0 & -L_{14} & L_{13} \\ L_{24} & -L_{14} & 0 & L_{12} \end{bmatrix}. \tag{3.4}$$

This matrix is of rank 2, and therefore its null space is of dimension 2, as expected.

Proof : The proof of (3.4) follows from the observation that the ith column of $\mathbf{A}$ is $\varepsilon_i \triangledown \mathbf{L}$. Concerning the rank of $\mathbf{A}$, as the two points M and M' are different, at least one of the the Plücker coordinates L_{ij} is nonzero, therefore at least one of the 2×2 minors of $\mathbf{A}$ is nonzero, and therefore the rank of $\mathbf{A}$ is larger than or equal to 2. Conversely, since $\mathbf{M} \triangledown \mathbf{M} \triangledown \mathbf{M}' = \mathbf{M}' \triangledown \mathbf{M} \triangledown \mathbf{M}' = \mathbf{0}$, we have $\mathbf{AM} = \mathbf{AM}' = \mathbf{0}$ and the dimension of the nullspace of $\mathbf{A}$ is larger than or equal to 2, hence its rank is less than or equal to 2. In conclusion, its rank must be equal to 2. $\square$

Note that Proposition 3.8 does not always "work" when we would expect it to. If we take the example of two coplanar 3D lines L and L', then we would expect their join $\mathbf{L} \triangledown \mathbf{L}'$ to represent the plane containing L and L'. Unfortunately this is not the case since, if M is the point of intersection of L and L', P another point of L and P' another point of L', then we have that L is represented by $\mathbf{M} \triangledown \mathbf{P}$ and L' by $\mathbf{M} \triangledown \mathbf{P}'$, and hence $\mathbf{L} \triangledown \mathbf{L}'$ is equal to $\mathbf{0}$!

3.1.2.4   The example of 3D planes: I

Let us consider again the case where E is of dimension 4. According to Proposition 3.5, there is a one to one correspondence between the elements of $G_3(E_4)$ which are extensors of size 3 and the 2-dimensional projective subspaces of $\mathbb{P}^3$, i.e. the planes. Given three vectors $\mathbf{M}$, $\mathbf{M}'$ and $\mathbf{M}''$ of $G_1(E_4)$, they represent three points of $\mathbb{P}^3$, and their join $\mathbf{M} \triangledown \mathbf{M}' \triangledown \mathbf{M}''$ therefore represents the plane generated by these three points unless it is zero.

To better understand this situation, let us use Proposition 3.7 and rewrite $\mathbf{M} \triangledown \mathbf{M}' \triangledown \mathbf{M}''$ as $\mathbf{M} \triangledown (\mathbf{M}' \triangledown \mathbf{M}'')$. According to the previous section, $\mathbf{M}' \triangledown \mathbf{M}''$ represents the line L determined by the points M' and M'' unless they are identical in which case $\mathbf{M}' \triangledown \mathbf{M}''$ is zero and so is $\mathbf{M} \triangledown \mathbf{M}' \triangledown \mathbf{M}''$. Let us assume that they are not and apply Proposition 3.8: the join $\mathbf{M} \triangledown L$ is zero if and only if M belongs to L, i.e. if the three points M, M' and M'' are distinct and aligned; if it is nonzero, then it represents the projective subspace generated by M and L, i.e. the plane determined by the three points, see Figure 3.2.

According to Corollary 3.1, the coordinates of $\mathbf{M} \triangledown \mathbf{M}' \triangledown \mathbf{M}''$ in the canonical basis $\varepsilon_1 \triangledown \varepsilon_2 \triangledown \varepsilon_3$, $\varepsilon_2 \triangledown \varepsilon_3 \triangledown \varepsilon_4$, $\varepsilon_1 \triangledown \varepsilon_3 \triangledown \varepsilon_4$, $\varepsilon_1 \triangledown \varepsilon_2 \triangledown \varepsilon_4$ of $G_3(E_4)$ are the four 3×3 minors of the 4×3 matrix $\left[\mathbf{M}\, \mathbf{M}'\, \mathbf{M}'' \right]$ corresponding to rows $(1, 2, 3)$, $(2, 3, 4)$, $(1, 3, 4)$, respectively (see Table 3.1). We will see in Section 3.4.5.1 another interpretation of

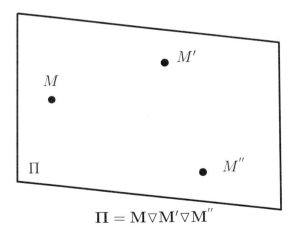

$$\mathbf{\Pi} = \mathbf{M} \triangledown \mathbf{M}' \triangledown \mathbf{M}''$$

Figure 3.2: The plane Π containing the three points M, M', M'' is represented by their join $\mathbf{M} \triangledown \mathbf{M}' \triangledown \mathbf{M}''$.

this fact based on the duality principle.

3.2 Plücker relations

It turns out that the previous statement that the points of $P(E)$ whose coordinate vectors are extensors of step k are in one to one correspondence with the projective subspaces of $P(E)$ is slightly inaccurate in the following sense. If we consider $\binom{n}{k}$ elements of K, then they are not in general the Plücker coordinates of an extensor of step k of $G_k(E)$. In order for them to be such coordinates, they must satisfy a number of polynomial constraints of degree 2 called the Plücker relations. This fact is relatively easy to see using simple relations between determinants.

3.2.1 Derivation of the Plücker relations

Let us consider an extensor $\mathbf{A} = \mathbf{a}_1 \nabla \mathbf{a}_2 \nabla \cdots \nabla \mathbf{a}_k$ of step k. We denote (a_i^j), $j = 1, \cdots, n$, $i = 1, \cdots, k$, the n coordinates of the vectors in some basis of E and $A_{i_1, i_2, \cdots, i_k}$, $1 \leq i_1 < i_2 < \cdots < i_k \leq n$, the Plücker coordinates of $\mathbf{A}$ in the corresponding basis of $G_k(E)$.

Let us now consider the $k-1$ indices $1 \leq i_1 < i_2 < \cdots < i_{k-1} \leq n$ and the $k+1$ indices $1 \leq j_1 < j_2 < \cdots < j_{k+1} \leq n$, and let us form the expression

$$F_{i_1 \cdots i_{k-1}, j_1 \cdots j_{k+1}} = \sum_{\lambda=1}^{k+1} (-1)^\lambda A_{s(i_1, \cdots i_{k-1}, j_\lambda)} A_{j_1 \cdots j_{\lambda-1} j_{\lambda+1} \cdots j_{k+1}}, \qquad (3.5)$$

where $s(i_1, \cdots i_{k-1}, j_\lambda)$ indicates that the index j_λ has been inserted in the right position in the sequence $i_1, \cdots i_{k-1}$ so that the resulting sequence is increasing. Note that if j_λ is equal to i_l ($1 \leq l \leq k-1$), then i_l appears twice in the sequence and the corresponding coefficient $A_{s(i_1, \cdots i_{k-1}, j_\lambda)}$ is 0.

Let us rewrite $F_{i_1 \cdots i_{k-1}, j_1 \cdots j_{k+1}}$ using the fact that the Plücker coordinates are minors:

$$F_{i_1 \cdots i_{k-1}, j_1 \cdots j_{k+1}} = \sum_{\lambda=1}^{k+1} (-1)^\lambda s \begin{pmatrix} \begin{vmatrix} a_1^{i_1} & a_2^{i_1} & \dots & a_k^{i_1} \\ a_1^{i_2} & a_2^{i_2} & \dots & a_k^{i_2} \\ \multicolumn{4}{c}{\dotfill} \\ a_1^{i_{k-1}} & a_2^{i_{k-1}} & \dots & a_k^{i_{k-1}} \\ a_1^{j_\lambda} & a_2^{j_\lambda} & \dots & a_k^{j_\lambda} \end{vmatrix} \end{pmatrix} \begin{vmatrix} a_1^{j_1} & a_2^{j_1} & \dots & a_k^{j_1} \\ \multicolumn{4}{c}{\dotfill} \\ a_1^{j_{\lambda-1}} & a_2^{j_{\lambda-1}} & \dots & a_k^{j_{\lambda-1}} \\ a_1^{j_{\lambda+1}} & a_2^{j_{\lambda+1}} & \dots & a_k^{j_{\lambda+1}} \\ \multicolumn{4}{c}{\dotfill} \\ a_1^{j_{k+1}} & a_2^{j_{k+1}} & \dots & a_k^{j_{k+1}} \end{vmatrix} ,$$

where the symbol s in front of the first determinant indicates that the last row is inserted in the correct place. Let us denote by A^μ the cofactor of $a_\mu^{j_\lambda}$, $\mu = 1, \ldots, k$.

By expanding this determinant with respect to the row j_λ, $F_{i_1 \cdots i_{k-1}, j_1 \cdots j_{k+1}}$ can be rewritten as

$$F_{i_1 \cdots i_{k-1}, j_1 \cdots j_{k+1}} = \sum_{\mu=1}^{k} \sum_{\lambda=1}^{k+1} (-1)^\lambda A^\mu a_\mu^{j_\lambda} \begin{vmatrix} a_1^{j_1} & a_2^{j_1} & \cdots & a_k^{j_1} \\ \cdots\cdots\cdots\cdots\cdots\cdots\cdots\cdots \\ a_1^{j_{\lambda-1}} & a_2^{j_{\lambda-1}} & \cdots & a_k^{j_{\lambda-1}} \\ a_1^{j_{\lambda+1}} & a_2^{j_{\lambda+1}} & \cdots & a_k^{j_{\lambda+1}} \\ \cdots\cdots\cdots\cdots\cdots\cdots\cdots\cdots \\ a_1^{j_{k+1}} & a_2^{j_{k+1}} & \cdots & a_k^{j_{k+1}} \end{vmatrix}.$$

The sum over λ is the expansion, with respect to its first column, of the $(k+1) \times (k+1)$ determinant

$$\begin{vmatrix} a_\mu^{j_1} & a_1^{j_1} & a_2^{j_1} & \cdots & a_k^{j_1} \\ \cdots\cdots\cdots\cdots\cdots\cdots\cdots\cdots\cdots \\ a_\mu^{j_{\lambda-1}} & a_1^{j_{\lambda-1}} & a_2^{j_{\lambda-1}} & \cdots & a_k^{j_{\lambda-1}} \\ a_\mu^{j_\lambda} & a_1^{j_\lambda} & a_2^{j_\lambda} & \cdots & a_k^{j_\lambda} \\ a_\mu^{j_{\lambda+1}} & a_1^{j_{\lambda+1}} & a_2^{j_{\lambda+1}} & \cdots & a_k^{j_{\lambda+1}} \\ \cdots\cdots\cdots\cdots\cdots\cdots\cdots\cdots\cdots \\ a_\mu^{j_{k+1}} & a_1^{j_{k+1}} & a_2^{j_{k+1}} & \cdots & a_k^{j_{k+1}} \end{vmatrix}.$$

Finally we obtain

$$F_{i_1 \cdots i_{k-1}, j_1 \cdots j_{k+1}} = \sum_{\mu=1}^{k} A^\mu \begin{vmatrix} a_\mu^{j_1} & a_1^{j_1} & a_2^{j_1} & \cdots & a_k^{j_1} \\ \cdots\cdots\cdots\cdots\cdots\cdots\cdots\cdots\cdots \\ a_\mu^{j_{\lambda-1}} & a_1^{j_{\lambda-1}} & a_2^{j_{\lambda-1}} & \cdots & a_k^{j_{\lambda-1}} \\ a_\mu^{j_\lambda} & a_1^{j_\lambda} & a_2^{j_\lambda} & \cdots & a_k^{j_\lambda} \\ a_\mu^{j_{\lambda+1}} & a_1^{j_{\lambda+1}} & a_2^{j_{\lambda+1}} & \cdots & a_k^{j_{\lambda+1}} \\ \cdots\cdots\cdots\cdots\cdots\cdots\cdots\cdots\cdots \\ a_\mu^{j_{k+1}} & a_1^{j_{k+1}} & a_2^{j_{k+1}} & \cdots & a_k^{j_{k+1}} \end{vmatrix},$$

but for each value of μ the corresponding determinant in the sum has two identical columns and is therefore equal to 0. It follows that

$$F_{i_1 \cdots i_{k-1}, j_1 \cdots j_{k+1}} = 0.$$

In general there are several Plücker relations, and the question arises of how many of those relations are algebraically independent. The answer can be found in the following proposition.

Proposition 3.10 *The number of algebraically independent Plücker relations satisfied by an extensor of step k is equal to:*

$$\binom{n}{k} - k(n-k) - 1.$$

Proof :   Consider the mapping f $E^k \rightarrow G_k(E)$ defined by $f(\mathbf{x}_1, \ldots, \mathbf{x}_k) = \mathbf{x}_1 \triangledown \ldots \triangledown \mathbf{x}_k$. Its image is the set of extensors of step k. It is not one to one since two k-sequences $(\mathbf{x}_1, \ldots, \mathbf{x}_k)$ and $(\mathbf{y}_1, \ldots, \mathbf{y}_k)$ differing by a unimodal linear transformation have the same image (Proposition 3.4). The dimension of the set of unimodal linear transformations of a k-dimensional vector space is $k^2 - 1$, the dimension of the set E^k is nk, hence the dimension of the set of extensors of step k is equal to $k(n - k) + 1$. Since it is embedded in a vector space of dimension $\binom{n}{k}$, we obtain the result. □

3.2.2   The example of 3D lines: II

Let us take the example of the lines. We have $k = 2$ and we choose $i_1 = 1$, $j_1 = 2$, $j_2 = 3$, $j_3 = 4$ in Equation 3.5. This yields immediately a Plücker relation between the Plücker coordinates $(L_{ij}, 1 \leq i < j \leq 4)$ of a line:

$$L_{12}L_{34} - L_{13}L_{24} + L_{14}L_{23} = 0. \tag{3.6}$$

Proposition 3.10 tells us that it is the only Plücker relation for lines.

We use Equation 3.6 to define a product between two elements $\mathbf{L}$ and $\mathbf{L}'$ of $G_2(\mathbb{R}^4)$ (not necessarily lines):

$$[\mathbf{L} \mid \mathbf{L}'] = L_{12}L'_{34} + L'_{12}L_{34} - L_{13}L'_{24} - L'_{13}L_{24} + L_{14}L'_{23} + L'_{14}L_{23}. \tag{3.7}$$

This product is called the Plücker product between two lines. From the definition of the Plücker product, it is clear that it is commutative, i.e.:

$$[\mathbf{L} \mid \mathbf{L}'] = [\mathbf{L}' \mid \mathbf{L}]. \tag{3.8}$$

We now have the important proposition:

Proposition 3.11 *An element $\mathbf{L}$ of $G_2(E)$ represents a line if and only if the Plücker product $[\mathbf{L} \mid \mathbf{L}]$ is equal to 0.*

Proof :   Indeed, we have seen that if L was a line, then (3.6) held true. Conversely if (3.6) holds, suppose without loss of generality that $L_{13} \neq 0$. The two vectors $\mathbf{M}_{13} = [0, L_{12}, L_{13}, L_{14}]^T$ and $\mathbf{M}_{31} = [L_{13}, L_{23}, 0, -L_{34}]^T$ are nonzero and linearly independent. By the Plücker relation (3.6) it is easily verified that $\mathbf{L} \simeq \mathbf{M}_{13}\triangledown\mathbf{M}_{31}$, in fact $\mathbf{L} = L_{13}(\mathbf{M}_{13}\triangledown\mathbf{M}_{31})$. □

The Plücker product (3.7) has an interesting interpretation in terms of the join $\mathbf{L}\triangledown\mathbf{L}'$:

Proposition 3.12 *We have the following relation:*

$$\mathbf{L}\triangledown\mathbf{L}' = [\mathbf{L} \mid \mathbf{L}']\, \varepsilon_1 \triangledown \varepsilon_2 \triangledown \varepsilon_3 \triangledown \varepsilon_4. \tag{3.9}$$

Proof : It is just a matter of applying the definitions:

$$\mathbf{L} = L_{12}\varepsilon_1 \nabla \varepsilon_2 + L_{13}\varepsilon_1 \nabla \varepsilon_3 + L_{14}\varepsilon_1 \nabla \varepsilon_4 + L_{23}\varepsilon_2 \nabla \varepsilon_3 + L_{24}\varepsilon_2 \nabla \varepsilon_4,$$

and:

$$\mathbf{L}' = L'_{12}\varepsilon_1 \nabla \varepsilon_2 + L'_{13}\varepsilon_1 \nabla \varepsilon_3 + L'_{14}\varepsilon_1 \nabla \varepsilon_4 + L'_{23}\varepsilon_2 \nabla \varepsilon_3 + L'_{24}\varepsilon_2 \nabla \varepsilon_4.$$

Because of Propositions 3.2 and 3.6, we find the announced result.   □

3.2.3   The example of 3D planes: II

$G_3(E)$ is a vector space of dimension $\binom{4}{3} = 4$ and Proposition 3.10 shows that there exist no Plücker relations between the coordinates of an extensor of step 3.

3.3   The meet operator: The Grassmann-Cayley algebra

To continue our program to define algebraic operations which can be interpreted as geometric operations on the projective subspaces of $P(E)$ we define a second operator, called the meet, on the exterior algebra $G(E)$ which, as we will see, corresponds to the geometric operation of intersection of projective subspaces.

3.3.1   Definition of the meet

In order to define the meet, we first have to define the notion of a split:

Definition 3.4 *Let $\mathbf{A}$ be an extensor of step k, $\mathbf{A} = \mathbf{a}_1 \nabla \cdots \nabla \mathbf{a}_k$. Let $(h_1, \ldots, h_r)$ be an r-tuple of integers such that $\sum_{i=1}^{r} h_i = k$, $h_j \geq 0$, $j = 1, \ldots, k$. A split of class $(h_1, \ldots, h_r)$ is a r-tuple of extensors $(\mathbf{A}_1, \cdots, \mathbf{A}_r)$ such that*

- $\mathbf{A}_i = \begin{cases} 1 \ if \ h_i = 0 \\ \mathbf{a}_{i_1} \nabla \ldots \nabla \mathbf{a}_{i_{h_i}} \ otherwise \end{cases}$ *where $1 \leq i_1 < \cdots < i_{h_i} \leq k$.*

- $\mathbf{A}_i \nabla \mathbf{A}_j \neq 0 \ \forall i \neq j$.

- $\mathbf{A}_1 \nabla \ldots \nabla \mathbf{A}_r = \pm \mathbf{A}$.

Note that the r extensors $\mathbf{A}_i$, $i = 1, \ldots, r$ form a partition of the extensor $\mathbf{A}$, they "split " $\mathbf{A}$ into subextensors, each of size h_i. Given $\mathbf{A}$ and $(h_1, \ldots, h_r)$, we denote by $\mathcal{S}(\mathbf{A}; h_1, \ldots, h_r)$ the finite set of splits of class $(h_1, \ldots, h_r)$ of the extensor $\mathbf{A}$ and define $sign(\mathbf{A}_1, \ldots, \mathbf{A}_r)$ to be equal to 1 if $\mathbf{A}_1 \nabla \ldots \nabla \mathbf{A}_r = \mathbf{A}$ and -1 otherwise.

Let us pause for a while and take an example. Let $\mathbf{A} = \mathbf{a}_1 \nabla \mathbf{a}_2 \nabla \mathbf{a}_3$, then $\mathcal{S}(\mathbf{A}; 1, 1, 1) = (\mathbf{a}_1, \mathbf{a}_2, \mathbf{a}_3)$, $\mathcal{S}(\mathbf{A}; 1, 2) = \{(\mathbf{a}_1, \mathbf{a}_2 \nabla \mathbf{a}_3), (\mathbf{a}_2, \mathbf{a}_1 \nabla \mathbf{a}_3), (\mathbf{a}_3, \mathbf{a}_1 \nabla \mathbf{a}_2)\}$, and $\mathcal{S}(\mathbf{A}; 0, 3) = \mathbf{a}_1 \nabla \mathbf{a}_2 \nabla \mathbf{a}_3$.

We also extend the notion of bracket to the case of extensors as follows. Let $\mathbf{A}_1 = \mathbf{a}_{11} \triangledown \ldots \triangledown \mathbf{a}_{1s_1}, \ldots, \mathbf{A}_h = \mathbf{a}_{h1} \triangledown \ldots \triangledown \mathbf{a}_{hs_h}$ be h extensors. We then define:

$$| \mathbf{A}_1, \ldots, \mathbf{A}_h | = \begin{cases} | \mathbf{a}_{11}, \ldots, \mathbf{a}_{hs_h} | & \text{if} \quad s_1 + \ldots s_h = n, \\ 0 & \text{otherwise.} \end{cases}$$

We can then state the following property that will be used to define the meet of two extensors:

Proposition 3.13 *Let* $\mathbf{A} = \mathbf{a}_1 \triangledown \ldots \triangledown \mathbf{a}_k$ *be an extensor of step* k *and* $\mathbf{B} = \mathbf{b}_1 \triangledown \ldots \triangledown \mathbf{b}_p$ *an extensor of step* p. *The following equality holds:*

$$\sum_{(\mathbf{A}_1, \mathbf{A}_2) \in \mathcal{S}(\mathbf{A}; n-p, k+p-n)} sign(\mathbf{A}_1, \mathbf{A}_2) \mid \mathbf{A}_1, \mathbf{B} \mid \mathbf{A}_2 =$$

$$\sum_{(\mathbf{B}_1, \mathbf{B}_2) \in \mathcal{S}(\mathbf{B}; k+p-n, n-k)} sign(\mathbf{B}_1, \mathbf{B}_2) \mid \mathbf{A}, \mathbf{B}_2 \mid \mathbf{B}_1. \quad (3.10)$$

Proof :   The proof of this equality is adapted from (Barnabei et al., 1985). The left-hand and the right-hand sides define two functions f and g from E^{k+p} into $G_{p+k-n}(E)$:

$$f, g : E^{k+p} \longrightarrow G_{p+k-n}(E),$$

such that

$$f(\mathbf{a}_1, \cdots, \mathbf{a}_k, \mathbf{b}_1, \cdots, \mathbf{b}_p) = \sum_{(\mathbf{A}_1, \mathbf{A}_2) \in \mathcal{S}(\mathbf{A}; n-p, k+p-n)} sign(\mathbf{A}_1, \mathbf{A}_2) \mid \mathbf{A}_1, \mathbf{B} \mid \mathbf{A}_2,$$

and

$$g(\mathbf{a}_1, \cdots, \mathbf{a}_k, \mathbf{b}_1, \cdots, \mathbf{b}_p) = \sum_{(\mathbf{B}_1, \mathbf{B}_2) \in \mathcal{S}(\mathbf{B}; k+p-n, n-k)} sign(\mathbf{B}_1, \mathbf{B}_2) \mid \mathbf{A}, \mathbf{B}_2 \mid \mathbf{B}_1.$$

f and g are $(k + p)$-multilinear. Therefore, they coincide if and only if they take the same values on any $(k + p)$-tuple of vectors taken from the basis $(\varepsilon_1, \cdots, \varepsilon_n)$ of E. Moreover, since they are alternating in the first k variables and in the last p variables, it is sufficient to prove that

$$f(\varepsilon_{i_1}, \cdots, \varepsilon_{i_k}; \varepsilon_{j_1}, \cdots, \varepsilon_{j_p}) = g(\varepsilon_{i_1}, \cdots, \varepsilon_{i_k}; \varepsilon_{j_1}, \cdots, \varepsilon_{j_p})$$

for $i_1 < \cdots < i_k$ and $j_1 < \cdots < j_p$.

Let us define the two sets of integers $I = \{i_1, \cdots, i_k\}$ and $J = \{j_1, \cdots, j_p\}$. They are such that $I \cup J = \{1, \cdots, n\}$ and $\mid I \cap J \mid = p + k - n = d$. Let us now consider the extensor $\mathbf{A}_1$ in the left-hand side of (3.10) and its set of indexes I_1. All $\mathbf{A}_1$'s such that $I_1 \cap (I \cap J)$ yield $\mid \mathbf{A}_1, \mathbf{B} \mid = 0$ because of the properties of determinants. Hence there is only one such I_1 namely $\complement J$ which indeed contains

$k - d = n - p$ elements. A similar reasoning for the right-hand side of (3.10) shows that there is only one possibility for the set J_2 of indexes of the extensor $\mathbf{B}_2$, i.e. $\complement I$.

We may thus as well change the indexes in such a way that $i_1 = j_1, \cdots, i_d = j_d$. This implies that $I_1 = \{i_{d+1}, \cdots, i_k\}$ and $J_2 = \{j_{d+1}, \cdots, j_p\}$. From there we obtain that

$$
\begin{aligned}
f(\varepsilon_{i_1}, \cdots, \varepsilon_{i_k}; \varepsilon_{j_1}, \cdots, \varepsilon_{j_p}) &= sign(\mathbf{A}_1, \mathbf{A}_2) \mid \mathbf{A}_1, \mathbf{B} \mid \mathbf{A}_2 = \\
sign(\varepsilon_{i_{d+1}}, \cdots, \varepsilon_{i_k}, \varepsilon_{i_1}, \cdots, \varepsilon_{i_d}) &\mid \varepsilon_{i_{d+1}}, \cdots, \varepsilon_{i_k}, \varepsilon_{i_1}, \cdots, \varepsilon_{i_d}, \varepsilon_{j_{d+1}}, \cdots, \varepsilon_{j_p} \mid \\
&\qquad \varepsilon_{i_1} \nabla \cdots \nabla \varepsilon_{i_d},
\end{aligned}
$$

with

$$
sign(\varepsilon_{i_{d+1}}, \cdots, \varepsilon_{i_k}, \varepsilon_{i_1}, \cdots, \varepsilon_{i_d}) = (-1)^{d(k-d)}.
$$

Similarly

$$
\begin{aligned}
g(\varepsilon_{i_1}, \cdots, \varepsilon_{i_k}; \varepsilon_{j_1}, \cdots, \varepsilon_{j_p}) &= sign(\mathbf{B}_1, \mathbf{B}_2) \mid \mathbf{A}, \mathbf{B}_2 \mid \mathbf{B}_1 = \\
sign(\varepsilon_{j_1}, \cdots, \varepsilon_{j_d} \varepsilon_{j_{d+1}}, \cdots, \varepsilon_{j_p}) &\mid \varepsilon_{i_1}, \cdots, \varepsilon_{i_k}, \varepsilon_{j_{d+1}}, \cdots, \varepsilon_{j_p} \mid \varepsilon_{j_1} \nabla \cdots \nabla \varepsilon_{j_d},
\end{aligned}
$$

with

$$
sign(\varepsilon_{j_1}, \cdots, \varepsilon_{j_d}, \varepsilon_{j_{d+1}}, \cdots, \varepsilon_{j_p}) = 1,
$$

and

$$
\begin{aligned}
\mid \varepsilon_{i_1}, \cdots, \varepsilon_{i_k}, \varepsilon_{j_{d+1}}, \cdots, \varepsilon_{j_p} \mid = \\
(-1)^{d(k-d)} \mid \varepsilon_{i_{d+1}}, \cdots, \varepsilon_{i_k}, \varepsilon_{i_1}, \cdots, \varepsilon_{i_d}, \varepsilon_{j_{d+1}}, \cdots, \varepsilon_{j_p} \mid .
\end{aligned}
$$

Therefore we have proved that
$f(\varepsilon_{i_1}, \cdots, \varepsilon_{i_k}; \varepsilon_{j_1}, \cdots, \varepsilon_{j_p}) = g(\varepsilon_{i_1}, \cdots, \varepsilon_{i_k}; \varepsilon_{j_1}, \cdots, \varepsilon_{j_p})$ and the proof is completed. □

This proposition allows us to define the meet of two extensors:

Definition 3.5 (The meet of two extensors) *Let $\mathbf{A}$ and $\mathbf{B}$ be two extensors of sizes k and p, respectively. Their meet, denoted $\mathbf{A} \bigtriangleup \mathbf{B}$, is given by either side of Equation 3.10 if $k \geq 1$, $p \geq 1$, $k + p \geq n$ and is equal to 0 if $k + p < n$. If $p = 0$, $\mathbf{B}$ is then a scalar b and we take $\mathbf{A} \bigtriangleup \mathbf{B} = 0$ if $k < n$ and $\mathbf{A} \bigtriangleup \mathbf{B} = b \mid \mathbf{A} \mid$ if $k = n$.*

It is important to note that if $k + p \geq n$, the meet is an element of $G_{k+p-n}(E)$. In particular, we have the following very useful property:

Proposition 3.14 *Let $\mathbf{A}$ and $\mathbf{B}$ be two extensors of sizes $1 \leq k \leq n-1$ and $p = n - k$:*

$$
\mathbf{A} \bigtriangleup \mathbf{B} = \mid \mathbf{A}, \mathbf{B} \mid . \tag{3.11}
$$

Proof :   In the case where $k + p = n$, there is only one term in the sum of the left-hand side or the right-hand side of (3.10) and that term is equal to $\mid \mathbf{A}, \mathbf{B} \mid$. $\square$

This defines the meet of two extensors. We extend it to arbitrary elements of $G_k(E)$ and $G_p(E)$ by linearity, i.e. if $\mathbf{A} = \sum \alpha_i \mathbf{A}_i$ and $\mathbf{B} = \sum \beta_j \mathbf{B}_j$ where the $\mathbf{A}_i$'s are extensors of step k, the $\mathbf{B}_j$'s are extensors of step p, and the α_i's and β_j's are elements of K, we define $\mathbf{A} \triangle \mathbf{B}$ to be $\sum \alpha_i \beta_j \mathbf{A}_i \triangle \mathbf{B}_j$.

Having done this, we see that the vector space $G(E)$ can be equipped with a second structure of algebra through the meet operator:

Definition 3.6 (The exterior algebra of the meet) *The meet operator defines a second structure of algebra on the vector space $G(E)$ through the bilinear map:*

$$f_\triangle : G(E) \times G(E) \longrightarrow G(E),$$

such that $f_\triangle(\mathbf{x}, \mathbf{y}) = \mathbf{x} \triangle \mathbf{y}$. This structure is called the exterior algebra of the meet.

The next proposition is a consequence of the definition of the meet that we state without proof. The meet operation is not commutative and satisfies the

Proposition 3.15 *Let $\mathbf{A} \in G_k(E)$ and $\mathbf{B} \in G_p(E)$; then*

$$\mathbf{A} \triangle \mathbf{B} = (-1)^{(n-k)(n-p)} \mathbf{B} \triangle \mathbf{A}.$$

It is also possible to verify the following important property:

Proposition 3.16 *The meet operation is associative, i.e. if $\mathbf{A}$, $\mathbf{B}$, $\mathbf{C}$ are extensors, the following holds:*

$$(\mathbf{A} \triangle \mathbf{B}) \triangle \mathbf{C} = \mathbf{A} \triangle (\mathbf{B} \triangle \mathbf{C}).$$

We can now define the double or Grassmann-Cayley algebra:

Definition 3.7 (The Grassmann-Cayley or double algebra)
The vector space $G(E)$, endowed with the two operations ∇ and $\triangle$, has two structures of algebra and is thus known as the double algebra or Grassmann-Cayley algebra of the vector space E.

There is a deep relation between the two algebras which can be discovered through duality. This is the topic of the next section.

Before studying this relation we come to the analog for the meet of Proposition 3.8:

Proposition 3.17 *Let $\mathbf{A}$ and $\mathbf{B}$ be two extensors of steps k and p, respectively, and let A and B be the corresponding projective subspaces of $P(E)$.*

1. *if* $\langle A \cup B \rangle \neq P(E)$ *then* $\mathbf{A} \triangle \mathbf{B} = \mathbf{0}$.

2. *If* $\langle A \cup B \rangle = P(E)$ *then*

    (a) *if* $A \cap B = \emptyset$, *then* $k + p = n$ *and* $\mathbf{A} \triangle \mathbf{B} \in G_0(E) = K$,

    (b) *if* $A \cap B \neq \emptyset$, *then* $\mathbf{A} \triangle \mathbf{B}$ *is the extensor associated with the projective subspace* $A \cap B$.

Proof :   Let us assume first that $\langle A \cup B \rangle \neq P(E)$. If $k + p < n$, the proposition is trivially true by definition of the $\triangle$. If $k + p \geq n$, none of the terms $\mid \mathbf{A}_1, \mathbf{B} \mid$ that appear in the definition of $\mathbf{A} \triangle \mathbf{B}$ can differ from 0, because otherwise we would have $\langle A \cup B \rangle = P(E)$.

    If $A \cup B$ spans the whole space $P(E)$ we must have $k + p \geq n$. By Equation 2.7, if $A \cap B = \emptyset$ this implies $k + p = n$. By Proposition 3.14 we get $\mathbf{A} \triangle \mathbf{B} = \mid \mathbf{A}, \mathbf{B} \mid \in K$. If $A \cap B \neq \emptyset$ then $k + p > n$, and let us take a basis $\{\mathbf{c}_1, \cdots, \mathbf{c}_d\}$ of the vector subspace of E corresponding to the intersection $A \cap B$ ($d = k + p - n > 0$) and complete it to a basis $\{\mathbf{c}_1, \cdots, \mathbf{c}_d, \mathbf{a}_1, \cdots, \mathbf{a}_{k-d}\}$ of the vector subspace associated with A and to a basis $\{\mathbf{c}_1, \cdots, \mathbf{c}_d, \mathbf{b}_1, \cdots, \mathbf{b}_{l-d}\}$ of the vector subspace associated with B. We can therefore write $\mathbf{A} = \alpha(\mathbf{c}_1 \nabla \cdots \nabla \mathbf{c}_d \nabla \mathbf{a}_1 \nabla \cdots \nabla \mathbf{a}_{k-d})$ and $\mathbf{B} = \beta(\mathbf{c}_1 \nabla \cdots \nabla \mathbf{c}_d \nabla \mathbf{b}_1 \nabla \cdots \nabla \mathbf{b}_{l-d})$. If we now compute $\mathbf{A} \triangle \mathbf{B}$ using (3.10) we find a single summand of the form

$$sign(\mathbf{a}_1 \nabla \ldots \nabla \mathbf{a}_{k-d}, \mathbf{c}_1 \nabla \ldots \nabla \mathbf{c}_d) \mid \mathbf{a}_1 \nabla \ldots \nabla \mathbf{a}_{k-d}, \mathbf{B} \mid \mathbf{c}_1 \nabla \ldots \nabla \mathbf{c}_d =$$
$$\gamma(\mathbf{c}_1 \nabla \ldots \nabla \mathbf{c}_d).$$

for some nonzero γ, and this extensor is associated with the intersection subspace $A \cap B$. $\square$

3.3.2   Some planar examples

We illustrate Proposition 3.17 with some familiar examples drawn from plane geometry. This is the case where $n = 3$, hence $P(E)$ is the projective plane $\mathbb{P}^2$. Let us consider an extensor of size 2, $\mathbf{l}$, representing a line l and an extensor of size 1, $\mathbf{a}$, representing a point a. If a belongs to the line l, $\langle l \cup a \rangle \neq \mathbb{P}^2$ and therefore, according to Proposition 3.17, $\mathbf{l} \triangle \mathbf{a} = \mathbf{0}$. If a does not belong to l, then $\langle l \cup a \rangle = \mathbb{P}^2$, $l \cap a = \emptyset$ and the meet $\mathbf{l} \triangle \mathbf{a}$ is a number (Proposition 3.17, part 2.a), see Figure 3.3.

    Let $\mathbf{a}, \mathbf{b}, \mathbf{c}, \mathbf{d}$ be four extensors of size 1 corresponding to four distinct points. The join $\mathbf{l} = \mathbf{a} \nabla \mathbf{b}$ of $\mathbf{a}$ and $\mathbf{b}$, an element of $G_2(E)$, represents the line $l = (a, b)$ and the join $\mathbf{m} = \mathbf{c} \nabla \mathbf{d}$ represents the line $m = (c, d)$. The meet $\mathbf{l} \triangle \mathbf{m}$ is an element of $G_{2+2-3}(E) = G_1(E)$ and represents in general a point: it is of course the point of intersection of l and m. Indeed, $\langle l \cup m \rangle = \mathbb{P}^2$ unless $l = m$, in which case, according

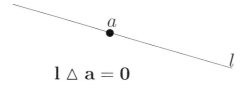

$$\mathbf{l} \triangle \mathbf{a} = \mathbf{0}$$

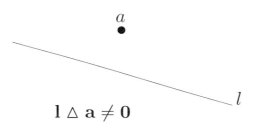

$$\mathbf{l} \triangle \mathbf{a} \neq \mathbf{0}$$

Figure 3.3: Proposition 3.17 at work (see text).

to Proposition 3.17, $\mathbf{l} \triangle \mathbf{m} = \mathbf{0}$. Otherwise, according to the same proposition, $\mathbf{l} \triangle \mathbf{m}$ is the extensor of size 1 associated with the point $l \cap m$, see Figure 3.4.

Let us compute $\mathbf{l} \triangle \mathbf{m}$. According to the left-hand side of Formula 3.10, we have:

$$\mathbf{l} \triangle \mathbf{m} = \mid \mathbf{acd} \mid \mathbf{b} - \mid \mathbf{bcd} \mid \mathbf{a},$$

and, according to the right-hand side, we have:

$$\mathbf{l} \triangle \mathbf{m} = \mid \mathbf{abd} \mid \mathbf{c} - \mid \mathbf{abc} \mid \mathbf{d}. \tag{3.12}$$

If we compute instead $\mathbf{m} \triangle \mathbf{l}$, we obtain with the left-hand side of (3.10) $\mid \mathbf{cab} \mid \mathbf{d} - \mid \mathbf{dab} \mid \mathbf{c}$. Using a standard property of determinants, this is equal to $\mid \mathbf{abc} \mid \mathbf{d} - \mid \mathbf{abd} \mid \mathbf{c}$ and, according to (3.12), is equal to $-(\mathbf{l} \triangle \mathbf{m})$, as forecast by Proposition 3.15 (see Figure 3.4).

3.3.3   Some 3D examples

We illustrate Proposition 3.17 with some familiar examples drawn from space geometry. This is the case where $n = 4$, hence $P(E)$ is the projective space $\mathbb{P}^3$. We consider first two extensors $\mathbf{L}$ and $\mathbf{L}'$ of size 2, i.e. representing two distinct lines L and L'. If the two lines are coplanar, $\langle L, L' \rangle = \mathbb{P}^2 \neq \mathbb{P}^3$ and therefore, according to Proposition 3.17, $\mathbf{L} \triangle \mathbf{L}' = 0$, which is somewhat unfortunate because one would

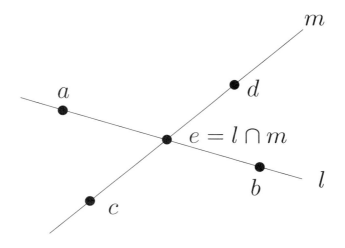

$$\mathbf{e} = \mathbf{l} \,\triangle\, \mathbf{m}$$

Figure 3.4: The point e is defined by the meet $\mathbf{l} \,\triangle\, \mathbf{m}$ of the the two lines $l = (a, b)$ and $m = (c, d)$.

have liked it to be an extensor of step 1 representing the point of intersection of L and L'. In the case where the two lines are not coplanar, $\langle L, L' \rangle = \mathbb{P}^3$ but $L \cap L' = \emptyset$ and hence $\mathbf{L} \,\triangle\, \mathbf{L}'$ is a number, see Figure 3.5.

Consider now an extensor of step 3, $\mathbf{\Pi}$, representing a plane Π, and let us interpret the meet $\mathbf{\Pi} \,\triangle\, \mathbf{L}$. If the line L is not in the plane Π, $\langle \Pi, L \rangle = \mathbb{P}^3$, $\Pi \cap L \neq \emptyset$ and therefore, according to Proposition 3.17, the meet $\mathbf{\Pi} \,\triangle\, \mathbf{L}$ is an extensor of size 1 representing the point of intersection of the plane and the line, see Figure 3.6. On the other hand, if L lies in Π we are in the case where $\langle \Pi, L \rangle \neq \mathbb{P}^3$ and thus $\mathbf{\Pi} \,\triangle\, \mathbf{L} = \mathbf{0}$.

3.4   Duality and the Hodge operator

We said that the Grassmann-Cayley algebra would allow us to come up with a convenient way of dealing with duality. Now comes the time that we will fulfill this promise. One of the powerful ideas contained in the Grassmann-Cayley formalism is that of unifying vector spaces and their duals. In the previous chapter, we saw several examples of the use of dual spaces when we dealt with 2D lines and points or 3D planes and points or with pencils of lines in the plane or with pencils of

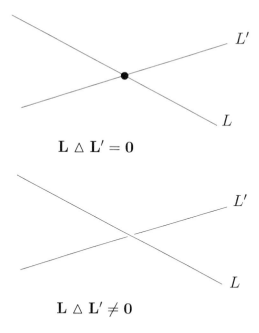

$$\mathbf{L} \bigtriangleup \mathbf{L'} = \mathbf{0}$$

$$\mathbf{L} \bigtriangleup \mathbf{L'} \neq \mathbf{0}$$

Figure 3.5: Proposition 3.17 at work (see text).

planes in 3D space. Each time we had to step back from the space of interest and think in a different space, the dual, where intuition is lacking. In the Grassmann-Cayley formalism, we are going to show that it is possible to consider the dual of the vector space $G_k(E)$ $k = 0, \ldots, n$ as being the vector space $G_{n-k}(E)$. This has the intellectual advantage of embedding the space and its dual in the same space, i.e. $G(E)$ and the practical advantage to be able to deal consistently with such operations as unions and intersections of subspaces of the space or its dual using the basic operations of join and meet. The key to this small miracle is an operator defined on the Grassmann-Cayley algebra and called the Hodge operator.

3.4.1 Duality

We now come to the definition of duality in the context of the Grassmann-Cayley algebra. In order to avoid bringing in the dual space E^* of E as we did in Section 2.4, we will show that $G_{n-1}(E)$ can be identified with E^*. This will allow to express the duality principle within the Grassmann-Cayley algebra as well as provide us with a very simple relationship between the operators ∇ and $\bigtriangleup$. We start with this case. It will turn out to be a special case of a general process that we will also describe.

In this section we denote $\mathcal{A}$ a basis $\{\mathbf{a}_1, \cdots, \mathbf{a}_n\}$ of E and $\mathcal{A}^*$ the corresponding

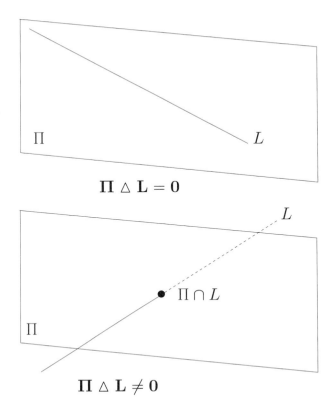

$$\mathbf{\Pi} \bigtriangleup \mathbf{L} = \mathbf{0}$$

$$\mathbf{\Pi} \bigtriangleup \mathbf{L} \neq \mathbf{0}$$

Figure 3.6: The point of intersection of the line L with the plane Π is represented by the extensor $\mathbf{\Pi} \bigtriangleup \mathbf{L}$.

basis $\{\mathbf{a}_1^*, \cdots, \mathbf{a}_n^*\}$ of its dual E^*, i.e. the set of linear forms such that $\mathbf{a}_i^*(\mathbf{a}_j) = \delta_{ij}$.

An extensor of step $n - 1$ is called a *covector*. In this book we are mainly concerned with the cases $n = 3$ and $n = 4$. Covectors in $G(E_3)$ are elements of $G_2(E_3)$, i.e. represent lines of $\mathbb{P}^2$. Covectors in $G(E_4)$ are elements of $G_3(E_4)$, i.e. represent planes of $\mathbb{P}^3$.

Given a vector $\mathbf{x}$ and a covector $\mathbf{y}$, we define their *cap-product* as

$$\langle \mathbf{y}, \mathbf{x} \rangle = \mathbf{x} \bigtriangleup \mathbf{y}. \tag{3.13}$$

It is an element of $G_0(E)$, i.e. a scalar. This allows us to establish an isomorphism of vector spaces between E^* and $G_{n-1}(E)$ that preserves the action of linear forms on vectors:

Proposition 3.18 *The dual E^* of E is in one to one linear correspondence with $G_{n-1}(E)$. If $\mathbf{f}$ is an element of E^*, i.e. a linear form, and $\tilde{\mathbf{f}}$ is its image through* *this correspondence, i.e. an element of $G_{n-1}(E)$, then*

$$\mathbf{f}(\mathbf{x}) = \langle \tilde{\mathbf{f}}, \mathbf{x} \rangle \quad \forall \mathbf{x} \in E.$$

Proof : The first part of the proposition is obvious since E^* and $G_{n-1}(E)$ have the same dimension. In order to prove the second part, let us consider the following basis of $G_{n-1}(E)$:

$$\boldsymbol{\eta}_i = \mid \mathbf{a}_i, \mathbf{a}_1, \ldots, \hat{\mathbf{a}}_i, \ldots \mathbf{a}_n \mid^{-1} \mathbf{a}_1 \nabla \ldots \nabla \hat{\mathbf{a}}_i \nabla \ldots \nabla \mathbf{a}_n \quad i = 1, \cdots, n.$$

Note that this is not the canonical basis of $G_{n-1}(E)$ associated with $\mathcal{A}$. The notation $\hat{\mathbf{a}}_i$ indicates that the vector $\mathbf{a}_i$ has been erased from the sequence it appears in. If $\mathbf{f}$ is an element of E^* of coordinates f_i in the basis $\mathcal{A}^*$ of E^*, the element $\tilde{\mathbf{f}}$ of $G_{n-1}(E)$ of coordinates f_i in the previous basis of $G_{n-1}(E)$ is such that for all $\mathbf{x}$ of E, $f(\mathbf{x}) = \langle \tilde{f}, \mathbf{x} \rangle$. Indeed, let us write

$$\tilde{\mathbf{f}} = \sum_j f_j \boldsymbol{\eta}_j \quad \text{and} \quad \mathbf{x} = \sum_i x_i \mathbf{a}_i,$$

we have

$$\langle \tilde{\mathbf{f}}, \mathbf{x} \rangle = \sum_{i,j} x_i f_j \mathbf{a}_i \vartriangle \boldsymbol{\eta}_j.$$

Because of Proposition 3.14

$$\mathbf{a}_i \vartriangle \boldsymbol{\eta}_j = \mid \mathbf{a}_i, \mathbf{a}_1 \nabla \ldots \nabla \hat{\mathbf{a}}_j \nabla \ldots \nabla \mathbf{a}_n \mid\mid \mathbf{a}_j, \mathbf{a}_1, \ldots, \hat{\mathbf{a}}_j, \ldots \mathbf{a}_n \mid^{-1} =$$

$$\begin{cases} 0 & \text{if } i \neq j, \\ 1 & \text{otherwise.} \end{cases}$$

This defines a linear one to one mapping between E^* and $G_{n-1}(E)$ which can thus be identified as vector spaces. $\square$

Note that the cap-product allows us to combine a line y of $\mathbb{P}^2$ (represented by a covector of $G(E_3)$) and a point x (represented by a vector of E_3). This is reminiscent, although different, of the traditional combination of lines and points described in Chapter 2 Section 2.4.3.3. In this chapter a line u is represented by a vector $\mathbf{u}$ and the inner product $\mathbf{u}^T \mathbf{x}$ is zero if and only if the point x is on the line u.

The cap-product allows us also to combine a plane y of $\mathbb{P}^3$ (represented by a covector of $G(E_4)$) and a point x (represented by a vector of E_4). This is reminiscent, although different, of the traditional combination of planes and points described in Chapter 2 Section 2.4.3.4. In this chapter a plane u is represented by a vector $\mathbf{u}$ and the inner product $\mathbf{u}^T \mathbf{x}$ is zero if and only if the point x is on the plane u.

The Hodge operator to be described soon is a way to reconcile the two viewpoints.

The above definition of the cap-product is a special case of a general process which we now describe, even though we will only need it for lines of $\mathbb{P}^3$. We begin with a general definition of the cap-product:

Definition 3.8 (Cap product) *Given a vector* $\mathbf{x}$ *of* $G_k(E)$ *and a vector* $\mathbf{y}$ *of* $G_{n-k}(E)$ *we define their cap-product as:*

$$\langle \mathbf{y}, \mathbf{x} \rangle = \mathbf{x} \vartriangle \mathbf{y}.$$

This is an element of $G_0(E)$, *therefore a scalar.*

We now proceed to establish a one to one linear relationship between the dual $G_k(E)^*$ of $G_k(E)$ and $G_{n-k}(E)$ that preserves the effect of linear forms in a sense to be made precise. Let $S = \{i_1, \cdots, i_k\}$ be an ordered subset of the ordered set $\{1, \cdots, n\}$, we define the extensor of step k $\mathbf{a}(S)$ as:

$$\mathbf{a}(S) = \mathbf{a}_{i_1} \nabla \cdots \nabla \mathbf{a}_{i_k}.$$

When S ranges over all ordered k-elements subsets of $\{1, \cdots, n\}$, we know from Proposition 3.3 that the set of extensors $\mathbf{a}(S)$ is the canonical basis of $G_k(E)$ associated with $\mathcal{A}$.

We now use this notation and definition to define an *associated cobasis* of $G_{n-k}(E)$.

Definition 3.9 (Associated cobasis) *Let*

$$\boldsymbol{\eta}(S) = \mid \mathbf{a}(S), \mathbf{a}(\complement S) \mid^{-1} \mathbf{a}(\complement S),$$

that is,

$$\boldsymbol{\eta}(S) = (-1)^{i_1 + \cdots + i_k - k(k+1)/2} \mid \mathbf{a}_1, \cdots, \mathbf{a}_n \mid^{-1} \mathbf{a}_{p_1} \nabla \cdots \nabla \mathbf{a}_{p_{n-k}}, \qquad (3.14)$$

where $\complement S = \{p_1, \cdots, p_{n-k}\}$ *is the* $(n-k)$-*elements ordered subset of* $\{1, \cdots, n\}$ *complementary to* S. *As* S *ranges over all* k-*elements subsets of* $\{1, \cdots, n\}$, *the set of extensors* $\boldsymbol{\eta}(S)$ *is a basis of* $G_{n-k}(E)$ *called the* **associated cobasis** *of the basis* $\mathbf{a}(S)$ *of* $G_k(E)$.

We are now ready to prove the following proposition which is a generalization of Proposition 3.18:

Proposition 3.19 *The dual* $G_k(E)^*$ *of* $G_k(E)$ *is in one to one linear correspondence with* $G_{n-k}(E)$. *If* $\mathbf{f}$ *is an element of* $G_k(E)^*$, *i.e. a linear form on* $G_k(E)$, *and* $\tilde{\mathbf{f}}$ *is its image through this correspondence, i.e. an element of* $G_{n-k}(E)$, *then*

$$\mathbf{f}(\mathbf{x}) = \langle \tilde{\mathbf{f}}, \mathbf{x} \rangle \quad \forall \mathbf{x} \in G_k(E).$$

Proof : Let $\mathbf{a}(S)$ be, as before, the basis of $G_k(E)$ and $\mathbf{a}(S)^*$ the corresponding basis of $G_k(E)^*$, i.e. such that $\mathbf{a}(S')^*(\mathbf{a}(S)) = \delta_{SS'}$ (S' varies among the ordered subsets of k elements of $\{1, \cdots, n\}$). We consider next the basis $\boldsymbol{\eta}(S)$ of $G_{n-k}(E)$. Let $\mathbf{f}$ be an element of $G_k(E)^*$ with coordinates f_S in the basis $\mathbf{a}(S)^*$:

$$f = \sum_S f_S \mathbf{a}(S)^*.$$

We associate with $\mathbf{f}$ the element $\tilde{\mathbf{f}}$ of $G_{n-k}(E)$ of coordinates f_S in the basis $\boldsymbol{\eta}(S)$

$$\tilde{\mathbf{f}} = \sum_S f_S \boldsymbol{\eta}(S).$$

We verify that $\mathbf{f}(\mathbf{x}) = \langle \tilde{\mathbf{f}}, \mathbf{x} \rangle$ for all elements $\mathbf{x}$ of $G_k(E)$. Indeed, let us write $\mathbf{x} = \sum_S x_S \mathbf{a}(S)$; we have $\langle \tilde{\mathbf{f}}, \mathbf{x} \rangle = \sum_{S,S'} x_S f_{S'} \mathbf{a}(S) \vartriangle \boldsymbol{\eta}(S')$. According to Definition 3.9 and to Proposition 3.14

$$\mathbf{a}(S) \vartriangle \boldsymbol{\eta}(S') = \mid \mathbf{a}(S), \, \boldsymbol{\eta}(S') \mid \, \mid \mathbf{a}(S'), \, \mathbf{a}(\complement S') \mid = \begin{cases} 0 & \text{if} \quad S \neq S', \\ 1 & \text{if} \quad S = S'. \end{cases}$$

This defines a linear one to one mapping between $G_k(E)^*$ and $G_{n-k}(E)$. $\square$

We saw a special case of this before: when $k = 1$, the basis $\boldsymbol{\eta}(S)$ is precisely the set of covectors

$$\boldsymbol{\eta}_i = \mid \mathbf{a}_i, \mathbf{a}_1, \cdots, \mathbf{a}_{i-1}, \hat{\mathbf{a}}_i, \mathbf{a}_{i+1}, \cdots, \mathbf{a}_n \mid^{-1} \mathbf{a}_1 \nabla \cdots \nabla \mathbf{a}_{i-1} \nabla \hat{\mathbf{a}}_i \nabla \mathbf{a}_{i+1} \nabla \cdots \nabla \mathbf{a}_n.$$
(3.15)

that we considered previously.

These covectors play an important role in the study of duality since we have the theorem:

Theorem 3.1 *Let $\{\mathbf{a}_1, \cdots, \mathbf{a}_n\}$ be a basis of E and $S = \{i_1, \cdots, i_k\}$, $k \leq n$, $i_1 < \cdots < i_k$. Then*

$$\boldsymbol{\eta}(S) = \boldsymbol{\eta}_{i_1} \vartriangle \cdots \vartriangle \boldsymbol{\eta}_{i_k}.$$

The proof of this theorem is outside the scope of this book but the interested reader is referred to, for example, (Barnabei et al., 1985). There is a useful consequence of this theorem:

Corollary 3.2

$$\boldsymbol{\eta}_1 \vartriangle \cdots \vartriangle \boldsymbol{\eta}_i = \mid \mathbf{a}_1, \cdots, \mathbf{a}_n \mid^{-1} \mathbf{a}_{i+1} \nabla \cdots \nabla \mathbf{a}_n \quad i = 1, \cdots, n.$$

In particular, when $i = n$:

$$\boldsymbol{\eta}_1 \vartriangle \cdots \vartriangle \boldsymbol{\eta}_n = \mid \mathbf{a}_1, \cdots, \mathbf{a}_n \mid^{-1}.$$

Proof : This is a straightforward consequence of Definition 3.9 and Theorem 3.1. $\square$

Covectors are very much alike vectors. For example

Proposition 3.20 *Any linear combination of covectors is a covector.*

Proof : Let $\mathbf{y}_1$ and $\mathbf{y}_2$ be two covectors. The intersection of the corresponding two projective subspaces of $P(E)$ y_1 and y_2 is either of dimension $n-1$ or $n-2$. If it is equal to $n-1$, the two projective spaces are identical and $\mathbf{y}_1 = k\mathbf{y}_2$ for some $k \in K$. Otherwise we can choose a basis $\mathbf{b}_1, \cdots, \mathbf{b}_{n-2}$ of the vector subspace associated with the intersection $y_1 \cap y_2$. We can write $\mathbf{y}_1 = (\mathbf{b}_1 \nabla \cdots \nabla \mathbf{b}_{n-2})\nabla \mathbf{c}_1$ and $\mathbf{y}_2 = (\mathbf{b}_1 \nabla \cdots \nabla \mathbf{b}_{n-2})\nabla \mathbf{c}_2$ for some vectors $\mathbf{c}_1$ and $\mathbf{c}_2$. Hence $\lambda_1 \mathbf{y}_1 + \lambda_2 \mathbf{y}_2 = (\mathbf{b}_1 \nabla \cdots \nabla \mathbf{b}_{n-2})\nabla(\lambda_1 \mathbf{c}_1 + \lambda_2 \mathbf{c}_2)$, a covector. $\square$

Extensors of arbitrary steps can be obtained by taking the meet of covectors, a property that is at the heart of our upcoming study of duality through the Hodge operator.

Proposition 3.21 *The meet of k covectors is either 0 or an extensor of step $n-k$. It is 0 if and only if the k covectors are linearly dependent.*

Proof : Let us prove the second part of the proposition. If the covectors are linearly dependent their meet is obviously 0 because of the properties of the meet. Suppose now that they are linearly independent and show that their meet is a non-zero extensor of size $n-k$ which will complete the proof of the whole proposition. To say that k covectors $\mathbf{y}_i$ are linearly independent is to say that the k vector spaces $V_i, i = 1, \cdots, k$ of dimension $n-1$ corresponding to the projective subspaces y_i are such that there exist k linearly independent vectors $\mathbf{b}_i, i = 1, \cdots, k$ such that E is generated by V_i and $\mathbf{b}_i$ for each i. Let us complete the set $\{\mathbf{b}_1, \cdots, \mathbf{b}_k\}$ to a basis $\{\mathbf{b}_1, \cdots, \mathbf{b}_k, \mathbf{c}_1, \cdots, \mathbf{c}_{n-k}\}$ of E. In this basis, each covector $\mathbf{y}_i, i = 1, \cdots, k$ can be written

$$\mathbf{y}_i = \mathbf{b}_1 \nabla \cdots \hat{\mathbf{b}}_i \cdots \nabla \mathbf{b}_k \nabla \mathbf{c}_1 \nabla \cdots \nabla \mathbf{c}_{n-k} \quad i = 1, \cdots, k.$$

The meet of the k covectors is found to be proportional to the extensor of size $n-k$ $\mathbf{c}_1 \nabla \cdots \nabla \mathbf{c}_{n-k}$ which is non-zero since the $n-k$ vectors $\mathbf{c}_1, \cdots, \mathbf{c}_{n-k}$ are linearly independent. $\square$

There is a whole set of useful relations that simplify the computation of expressions containing combinations of vectors, covectors, meets and joins. We will use the following proposition:

Proposition 3.22 *Let $\mathbf{a}_1, \cdots, \mathbf{a}_k$ be vectors of $G_1(E)$, $\boldsymbol{\gamma}_1, \cdots, \boldsymbol{\gamma}_s$ be covectors, i.e. elements of $G_{n-1}(E)$. Let A be the extensor of step k $\mathbf{a}_1 \nabla \cdots \nabla \mathbf{a}_k$. If $k \geq s$ we have the following relation:*

$$\mathbf{A} \vartriangle (\boldsymbol{\gamma}_1 \vartriangle \cdots \vartriangle \boldsymbol{\gamma}_s) =$$
$$\sum_{(\mathbf{A}_1, \cdots, \mathbf{A}_s, \mathbf{A}_{s+1}) \in \mathcal{S}(\mathbf{A}; \underbrace{1, \cdots, 1}_{s}, k-s)} sign(\mathbf{A}_1, \cdots, \mathbf{A}_{s+1}) \mid \mathbf{A}_1, \boldsymbol{\gamma}_1 \mid \cdots \mid \mathbf{A}_s, \boldsymbol{\gamma}_s \mid \mathbf{A}_{s+1}.$$

$$(3.16)$$

The proof of this equation is again outside the scope of this book but requires nothing more than the property of associativity of the meet. The interested reader is again referred to (Barnabei et al., 1985).

As a first example of the use of Equation 3.16, let us compute the point of intersection M of a plane Π defined by three points M_1, M_2, M_3 with a line L defined as the intersection of the two planes Π_1 and Π_2. We have:

$$\mathbf{M} = \mathbf{\Pi} \vartriangle \mathbf{L} = (\mathbf{M}_1 \triangledown \mathbf{M}_2 \triangledown \mathbf{M}_3) \vartriangle (\mathbf{\Pi}_1 \vartriangle \mathbf{\Pi}_2).$$

We now use Equation 3.16 in the special case $k = 3$, $s = 2$, with $\mathbf{A} = \mathbf{\Pi} = \mathbf{M}_1 \triangledown \mathbf{M}_2 \triangledown \mathbf{M}_3$:

$$\sum_{(\mathbf{A}_1, \mathbf{A}_2, \mathbf{A}_3) \in \mathcal{S}(\mathbf{A}; 1, 1, 1)} sign(\mathbf{A}_1, \mathbf{A}_2, \mathbf{A}_3) \mid \mathbf{A}_1, \mathbf{\Pi}_1 \parallel \mathbf{A}_2, \mathbf{\Pi}_2 \mid \mathbf{A}_3 =$$

$$(\mid \mathbf{M}_1, \mathbf{\Pi}_1 \parallel \mathbf{M}_2, \mathbf{\Pi}_2 \mid - \mid \mathbf{M}_2, \mathbf{\Pi}_1 \parallel \mathbf{M}_1, \mathbf{\Pi}_2 \mid) \mathbf{M}_3 +$$

$$(\mid \mathbf{M}_2, \mathbf{\Pi}_1 \parallel \mathbf{M}_3, \mathbf{\Pi}_2 \mid - \mid \mathbf{M}_3, \mathbf{\Pi}_1 \parallel \mathbf{M}_2, \mathbf{\Pi}_2 \mid) \mathbf{M}_2 +$$

$$(\mid \mathbf{M}_3, \mathbf{\Pi}_1 \parallel \mathbf{M}_1, \mathbf{\Pi}_2 \mid - \mid \mathbf{M}_1, \mathbf{\Pi}_1 \parallel \mathbf{M}_3, \mathbf{\Pi}_2 \mid) \mathbf{M}_1.$$

We now give another result that is often useful in practice and that will be needed in Chapter 10.

Proposition 3.23 (Cramer relation in $G_3(E_4)$) *Let $\mathbf{\Pi}_i$, $i = 1, \cdots, 5$ be five covectors, they satisfy the following relation, called the Cramer relation:*

$$\mid \mathbf{\Pi}_2, \mathbf{\Pi}_3, \mathbf{\Pi}_4, \mathbf{\Pi}_5 \mid \mathbf{\Pi}_1 - \mid \mathbf{\Pi}_1, \mathbf{\Pi}_3, \mathbf{\Pi}_4, \mathbf{\Pi}_5 \mid \mathbf{\Pi}_2 + \mid \mathbf{\Pi}_1, \mathbf{\Pi}_2, \mathbf{\Pi}_4, \mathbf{\Pi}_5 \mid \mathbf{\Pi}_3 -$$

$$\mid \mathbf{\Pi}_1, \mathbf{\Pi}_2, \mathbf{\Pi}_3, \mathbf{\Pi}_5 \mid \mathbf{\Pi}_4 + \mid \mathbf{\Pi}_1, \mathbf{\Pi}_2, \mathbf{\Pi}_3, \mathbf{\Pi}_4 \mid \mathbf{\Pi}_5 = \mathbf{0}. \quad (3.17)$$

Proof : Since $G_3(E_4)$ is a vector space of dimension 4, the five covectors $\mathbf{\Pi}_i$, $i = 1, \cdots, 5$ are linearly dependent, i.e. there exist five scalars λ_i, $i = 1, \cdots, 5$ not all equal to 0, such that

$$\sum_{i=1}^{5} \lambda_i \mathbf{\Pi}_i = \mathbf{0}.$$

we compute the ratios λ_i/λ_5, $i = 1, \cdots, 4$ by taking the meet of this equation with $\mathbf{\Pi}_2 \vartriangle \mathbf{\Pi}_3 \vartriangle \mathbf{\Pi}_4$, $\mathbf{\Pi}_1 \vartriangle \mathbf{\Pi}_3 \vartriangle \mathbf{\Pi}_4$, $\mathbf{\Pi}_1 \vartriangle \mathbf{\Pi}_2 \vartriangle \mathbf{\Pi}_4$ and $\mathbf{\Pi}_1 \vartriangle \mathbf{\Pi}_2 \vartriangle \mathbf{\Pi}_3$.   □

3.4.2   The example of 3D lines: III

Let us consider the question of duality in the case of 3D lines which are represented by the extensors of step 2 of $G_2(\mathbb{R}^4)$, according to Proposition 3.19. The dual of $G_2(\mathbb{R}^4)$ can be identified with $G_2(\mathbb{R}^4)$. What is the corresponding cap-product? Let $\mathbf{a}_1$, $\mathbf{a}_2$, $\mathbf{a}_3$, $\mathbf{a}_4$ be a basis of $\mathbb{R}^4$, $\mathbf{a}_1 \triangledown \mathbf{a}_2, \ldots, \mathbf{a}_3 \triangledown \mathbf{a}_4$, the corresponding canonical basis of $G_2(\mathbb{R}^4)$. If we set $D = | \mathbf{a}_1, \mathbf{a}_2, \mathbf{a}_3, \mathbf{a}_4 |^{-1}$, the associated cobasis is readily shown, using Equation 3.14, to be:

$$\begin{aligned} \boldsymbol{\eta}(1,2) &= D\mathbf{a}_3 \triangledown \mathbf{a}_4 \quad \boldsymbol{\eta}(1,3) = -D\mathbf{a}_2 \triangledown \mathbf{a}_4 \quad \boldsymbol{\eta}(1,4) = D\mathbf{a}_2 \triangledown \mathbf{a}_3, \\ \boldsymbol{\eta}(2,3) &= D\mathbf{a}_1 \triangledown \mathbf{a}_4 \quad \boldsymbol{\eta}(2,4) = -D\mathbf{a}_1 \triangledown \mathbf{a}_3 \quad \boldsymbol{\eta}(3,4) = D\mathbf{a}_1 \triangledown \mathbf{a}_2. \end{aligned} \tag{3.18}$$

We have defined in Equation 3.7 the Plücker product $[\mathbf{L}|\mathbf{L}']$ of two elements of $G_2(\mathbb{R}^4)$. L being fixed, the application $f_L : \mathbf{L}' \to [\mathbf{L}|\mathbf{L}']$ is a linear form on $G_2(\mathbb{R}^4)$ hence, according to Proposition 3.19, it can be written as a cap-product $\langle \mathbf{M}, \mathbf{L}' \rangle$ for some element $\mathbf{M}$ of $G_2(\mathbb{R}^4)$ considered as its own dual. Looking at Expression 3.7, we find that f_L can be written in the dual basis:

$$f_L = L_{34}(\mathbf{a}_1 \triangledown \mathbf{a}_2)^* + L_{12}(\mathbf{a}_3 \triangledown \mathbf{a}_4)^* - L_{24}(\mathbf{a}_1 \triangledown \mathbf{a}_3)^* - L_{13}(\mathbf{a}_2 \triangledown \mathbf{a}_4)^* + L_{23}(\mathbf{a}_1 \triangledown \mathbf{a}_4)^* + \\ L_{14}(\mathbf{a}_2 \triangledown \mathbf{a}_3)^*.$$

According to Equations 3.18, $f_L(L') = \langle \mathbf{M}, L' \rangle$, where

$$\mathbf{M} = \sum_{1 \le i_1 < i_2 \le 4} L_{i_1 i_2} \boldsymbol{\eta}(i_1, i_2) = *\mathbf{L}',$$

where we denote by $*\mathbf{L}'$ the vector of $G_2(\mathbb{R}^4)$ that has the same coordinates as $\mathbf{L}'$ but in the basis $\boldsymbol{\eta}(i_1, i_2)$ rather than in the canonical basis of $G_2(\mathbb{R}^4)$. This notation will become clearer in the next section when we discuss the Hodge operator.

Therefore, the relationship between the Plücker product that was defined on $G_2(\mathbb{R}^4)$ and the cap-product is extremely simple:

$$[\mathbf{L}|\mathbf{L}'] = \langle *\mathbf{L}', \mathbf{L} \rangle. \tag{3.19}$$

Of course, since we can exchange the roles of $\mathbf{L}$ and $\mathbf{L}'$ (Equation 3.8), we also have $[\mathbf{L}|\mathbf{L}'] = \langle *\mathbf{L}, \mathbf{L}' \rangle$.

This is a general phenomenon that we will encounter again in Sections 3.4.4.1 and 3.4.5.1.

We end this section with an important result concerning the linear mappings from one of the vector spaces $G_k(E_n)$, $k = 0, \cdots, n$ to one of the vector spaces $G_l(E_m)$, $l = 0, \cdots, m$. This result is used several times in later chapters, e.g. Propositions 4.5, 4.9 and 4.12.

Proposition 3.24 *Let E_n and E_m be two real vector spaces of dimensions n and m, respectively, and let $f : G_k(E_n) \longrightarrow G_l(E_m)$ be a linear mapping. If we choose a basis $(\mathbf{a}_1, \cdots, \mathbf{a}_n)$ of E_n and a basis $(\mathbf{b}_1, \cdots, \mathbf{b}_m)$ of E_m, f is defined by a $\binom{n}{k} \times \binom{m}{l}$ matrix $\mathbf{A}$ in the associated canonical bases of $G_k(E_n)$ and $G_l(E_m)$.*

The transposed matrix $\mathbf{A}^T$ represents a linear mapping f_t from $G_l(E_m)^* \equiv G_{m-l}(E_m)$ to $G_k(E_n)^* \equiv G_{n-k}(E_n)$ in the associated cobases of $G_{m-l}(E_m)$ and $G_{n-k}(E_n)$:

$$f_t : G_{m-l}(E_m) \longrightarrow G_{n-k}(E_n).$$

Proof : The proof is a direct consequence of our analysis of duality. $\square$

3.4.3 The Hodge operator

Let us do some more groundwork and define a special element of $G_n(E)$, called the integral. We assume that the basis $\mathcal{A}$ of E is now unimodal. The extensor $\mathbf{I} = \mathbf{a}_1 \triangledown \cdots \triangledown \mathbf{a}_n$ is called the integral. It is easily checked that the following properties of the integral are true:

Proposition 3.25 *For each extensor $\mathbf{A}$ of positive step:*

$$\mathbf{A} \triangledown \mathbf{I} = \mathbf{I} \triangledown \mathbf{A} = 0.$$

For each extensor k of step 0:

$$k \triangledown \mathbf{I} = k\mathbf{I}.$$

For each extensor $\mathbf{A}$:

$$\mathbf{A} \triangle \mathbf{I} = \mathbf{I} \triangle \mathbf{A} = \mathbf{A}.$$

For every n-tuple $(\mathbf{b}_1, \cdots, \mathbf{b}_n)$ of vectors of E, we have the identity:

$$\mathbf{b}_1 \triangledown \cdots \triangledown \mathbf{b}_n = \mid \mathbf{b}_1, \cdots, \mathbf{b}_n \mid \mathbf{I}.$$

Let $\mathbf{A}$ and $\mathbf{B}$ be two extensors such that $step(\mathbf{A}) + step(\mathbf{B}) = n$. Then

$$\mathbf{A} \triangledown \mathbf{B} = (\mathbf{A} \triangle \mathbf{B}) \triangledown \mathbf{I} = \mid \mathbf{A}, \mathbf{B} \mid \mathbf{I}.$$

Proof : The proof is obvious from the definitions. $\square$

We note that $\mathbf{I}$ is a unit for the meet operation and a 0 for the join.

We are now in a position to relate the two exterior algebras, defined by the join and meet operators, by a suitable operator, called the Hodge star operator.

Definition 3.10 (Hodge star operator) *We define the Hodge star operator relative to the unimodal basis $\mathcal{A}$ to be the unique linear operator $* : G(E) \to G(E)$ such that*

$$*1 = \mathbf{I},$$

and for each ordered subset S of $\{1, \cdots, n\}$

$$*\mathbf{a}(S) = \boldsymbol{\eta}(S).$$

According to Theorem 3.1, this means that for all ordered k-subset $S_k = \{i_1, \cdots, i_k\}$:

$$*(\mathbf{a}_{i_1} \triangledown \cdots \triangledown \mathbf{a}_{i_k}) = \boldsymbol{\eta}_{i_1} \triangle \cdots \triangle \boldsymbol{\eta}_{i_k}.$$

This operator is unique since it is defined on the basis of $G(E)$ associated with the basis $\mathcal{A}$ of E and has the following properties

Theorem 3.2 *A Hodge star operator is an algebra isomorphism between the exterior algebra of the join $(G(E), \nabla)$ and the exterior algebra of the meet $(G(E), \triangle)$, i.e.*

$$*(\mathbf{x} \nabla \mathbf{y}) = (*\mathbf{x}) \triangle (*\mathbf{y}) \; and \; *(\mathbf{x} \triangle \mathbf{y}) = (*\mathbf{x}) \nabla (*\mathbf{y}),$$

for every $\mathbf{x}, \mathbf{y}, \in G(E)$.

It maps the set of extensors of $G_k(E)$ onto the set of extensors of $G_{n-k}(E)$.

It satisfies the following properties

$$*\mathbf{I} = 1,$$

and

$$*(*\mathbf{x}) = (-1)^{k(n-k)} \mathbf{x} \; \forall \mathbf{x} \in G_k(E).$$

Proof :   Let us first prove the second assertion. Let $\mathbf{B} = \mathbf{b}_1 \nabla \cdots \nabla \mathbf{b}_k$ be an extensor of $G_k(E)$ and $b_{i_1, \cdots, i_k}$ its Plücker coordinates in the basis $\mathbf{a}_{i_1} \nabla \cdots \nabla \mathbf{a}_{i_k}$ of $G_k(E)$:

$$\mathbf{b}_1 \nabla \cdots \nabla \mathbf{b}_k = \sum_{i_1, \cdots, i_k} b_{i_1, \cdots, i_k} \mathbf{a}_{i_1} \nabla \cdots \nabla \mathbf{a}_{i_k}.$$

Because of the linearity of the $*$ operator and since $*(\mathbf{a}_{i_1} \nabla \cdots \nabla \mathbf{a}_{i_k}) = \boldsymbol{\eta}_{i_1} \triangle \cdots \triangle \boldsymbol{\eta}_{i_k}$:

$$*\mathbf{B} = \sum_{i_1, \cdots, i_k} b_{i_1, \cdots, i_k} * (\mathbf{a}_{i_1} \nabla \cdots \nabla \mathbf{a}_{i_k}) = \sum_{i_1, \cdots, i_k} b_{i_1, \cdots, i_k} \boldsymbol{\eta}_{i_1} \triangle \cdots \triangle \boldsymbol{\eta}_{i_k},$$

and the last term is equal to $\mathbf{c}_1 \triangle \cdots \triangle \mathbf{c}_k$, where each $\mathbf{c}_i$ is a covector with the same coordinates as the vector $\mathbf{b}_i$ but in the basis $\boldsymbol{\eta}_1, \cdots, \boldsymbol{\eta}_n$ of $G_{n-1}(E)$ (check it). Since the covectors $\mathbf{c}_i$ are linearly independent, Proposition 3.21 tells us that their meet is an extensor of step $n - k$.

Let us prove that $*$ is one to one. Since it maps $G_k(E)$ into $G_{n-k}(E)$, we consider successively the cases $k = 0$ and $k \neq 0$.

$k = 0$ Let $k \in K$. Because of the linearity of the $*$ operator, $*k = k\mathbf{I}$, hence $*$ is one to one from $G_0(E)$ into $G_n(E)$.

$k \neq 0$ Let $\mathbf{B}$ be an element of $G_k(E)$. We denote S_k the k-elements ordered subsets of $\{1, \cdots, n\}$. We have

$$\mathbf{B} = \sum_{S_k} b_{S_k} \mathbf{a}(S_k),$$

and

$$*\mathbf{B} = \sum_{S_k} b_{S_k} * \mathbf{a}(S_k) = \sum_{S_k} b_{S_k} \boldsymbol{\eta}(S_k).$$

Because of Definition 3.9, $\eta(S_k) = (-1)^{n_{S_k}} \mathbf{a}(S_{n-k})$, where $S_{n-k} = \complement S_k$ and n_{S_k} is given by Equation 3.14. Thus,

$$*\mathbf{B} = \sum_{S_{n-k}} (-1)^{n_{S_k}} b_{S_k} \mathbf{a}(S_{n-k}),$$

which shows that $*$ is again one to one.

Let us now look at the question of algebra isomorphism. Because of the second assertion, it is sufficient to consider extensors of the form $\mathbf{a}(S_k)$ and $\mathbf{a}(S_l)$.

Let us then prove that $*(\mathbf{a}(S_k)\nabla\mathbf{a}(S_l)) = *\mathbf{a}(S_k) \triangle *\mathbf{a}(S_l)$. By definition of the $*$ operator, $*\mathbf{a}(S_k) = \eta(S_k)$ and $*\mathbf{a}(S_l) = \eta(S_l)$. Since $\mathbf{a}(S_k)\nabla\mathbf{a}(S_l) = 0$ if $S_k \cap S_l \neq \emptyset$ and $(-1)^{\epsilon_{kl}}\mathbf{a}(S_{k+l})$ otherwise, where ϵ_{kl} equals 0 or 1, we have to consider the two cases.

$S_k \cap S_l \neq \emptyset$ In this case we have $\mathbf{a}(S_k)\nabla\mathbf{a}(S_l) = 0$, hence $*(\mathbf{a}(S_k)\nabla\mathbf{a}(S_l)) = 0$. $\eta(S_k) \triangle \eta(S_l)$ is also equal to 0 because, for example, of Proposition 3.21.

$S_k \cap S_l = \emptyset$ In this case we have

$$*(\mathbf{a}(S_k)\nabla\mathbf{a}(S_l)) = (-1)^{\epsilon_{kl}} \eta(S_{k+l}).$$

But $\eta(S_k) \triangle \eta(S_l)$ is proportional to the same quantity, the factor being equal to $(-1)^{\epsilon_{kl}}$ (check it), since $\mathbf{y} \triangle \mathbf{z} = -\mathbf{z} \triangle \mathbf{y}$ for two covectors $\mathbf{y}$ and $\mathbf{z}$ (Proposition 3.15).

Thus we have proved that $*(\mathbf{x}\nabla\mathbf{y}) = *\mathbf{x} \triangle *\mathbf{y}$ for all elements $\mathbf{x}, \mathbf{y}$ of $G(E)$.

Consider now the integral $\mathbf{I} = \mathbf{a}_1 \nabla \cdots \nabla \mathbf{a}_n$. By definition of the $*$ operator, $*\mathbf{I} = \eta_1 \triangle \cdots \triangle \eta_n$ which is equal to 1 according to Corollary 3.2 and the fact that the basis $\mathcal{A}$ is unimodal.

To prove the last property, it is sufficient to consider the extensors of step k $\mathbf{a}(S_k)$. By definition of the $*$ operator, $*\mathbf{a}(S_k) = \eta(S_k)$ which, by Definition 3.9, is equal to $(-1)^{n_{S_k}}\mathbf{a}(\complement S_k)$. Thus $* * \mathbf{a}(S_k) = (-1)^{n_{S_k}} * \mathbf{a}(\complement S_k) = (-1)^{n_{S_k}}\eta(\complement S_k)$. By Definition 3.9 $\eta(\complement S_k) = (-1)^{n_{\complement S_k}}\mathbf{a}(S_k)$. There remains to show that $n_{S_k} + n_{\complement S_k}$ has the same parity as $k(n-k)$. According to Equation 3.14 again, we have

$$n_{S_k} + n_{\complement S_k} = \frac{1}{2}(n(n+1) - k(k+1) - (n-k)(n-k+1)) = k(n-k).$$

To finish the proof, we show that $*(\mathbf{x} \triangle \mathbf{y}) = (*\mathbf{x})\nabla(*\mathbf{y})$ for all $\mathbf{x}$ and $\mathbf{y}$ in $G(E)$. Assume $x \in G_k(E)$ and $y \in G_l(E)$. Since $\mathbf{x} = (-1)^{k(n-k)} * *\mathbf{x}$ and $\mathbf{y} = (-1)^{l(n-l)} * *\mathbf{y}$, $\mathbf{x} \triangle \mathbf{y} = (-1)^{k(n-k)+l(n-l)}(* * \mathbf{x}) \triangle (* * \mathbf{y})$. We have already proved that the right-hand side is equal to $(-1)^{k(n-k)+l(n-l)} * ((*\mathbf{x})\nabla(*\mathbf{y}))$. Therefore, applying the $*$ operator once again, we obtain $*(\mathbf{x} \triangle \mathbf{y}) = (-1)^{k(n-k)+l(n-l)} * *((*\mathbf{x})\nabla(*\mathbf{y}))$. Because $*\mathbf{x} \in G_{n-k}(E)$ and $*\mathbf{y} \in G_{n-l}(E)$, $(*\mathbf{x})\nabla(*\mathbf{y})$ is in $G_{2n-k-l}(E)$ and $* * ((*\mathbf{x})\nabla(*\mathbf{y})) = (-1)^{(2n-k-l)(k+l-n)}((*\mathbf{x})\nabla(*\mathbf{y}))$. It is easy to verify that $k(n-k) + l(n-l) + (2n-k-l)(k+l-n)$ is an even number and the result follows. $\square$

3.4.4 The example of 2D lines: II

Let us now see in detail how the Hodge operator works when $dim\, E = 3$, i.e. when we work with $\mathbb{P}^2$. In this case we only have to worry about $G_1(E_3)$, i.e. E_3, and $G_2(E_3)$ which, according to the previous discussion can be identified with the dual E_3^* of E_3, i.e. with the lines of $\mathbb{P}^2$. Let us choose the canonical basis (hence unimodal) of E_3, $(\varepsilon_1, \varepsilon_2, \varepsilon_3)$.

3.4.4.1 Cap-products, points and lines

By applying Equation 3.14 or Equation 3.15, we obtain the following relations:

$$*\varepsilon_1 = \varepsilon_2 \nabla \varepsilon_3 \quad *\varepsilon_2 = -\varepsilon_1 \nabla \varepsilon_3 = \varepsilon_3 \nabla \varepsilon_1 \quad *\varepsilon_3 = \varepsilon_1 \nabla \varepsilon_2,$$

and also

$$*(\varepsilon_1 \nabla \varepsilon_2) = \varepsilon_3 \quad *(\varepsilon_2 \nabla \varepsilon_3) = \varepsilon_1 \quad *(\varepsilon_1 \nabla \varepsilon_3) = -*(\varepsilon_3 \nabla \varepsilon_1) = -\varepsilon_2.$$

In other words, the Hodge operator allows us to identify the basis $(\varepsilon_1, \varepsilon_2, \varepsilon_3)$ of E_3 with the basis $(\varepsilon_2 \nabla \varepsilon_3, \varepsilon_3 \nabla \varepsilon_1, \varepsilon_1 \nabla \varepsilon_2)$ of $G_2(E_3)$, its associated cobasis. This has several practical interesting consequences, one of them is stated in the following proposition

Proposition 3.26 *Let $\mathbf{y}$ be a covector, i.e. representing a line of $\mathbb{P}^2$, with coordinates expressed in the associated cobasis of the canonical basis of E_3. According to Proposition 3.19, we identify $\mathbf{y}$ with the vector which has the same coordinates as $\mathbf{y}$ in the canonical basis of E_3^*, the dual of E_3. Through this identification, the cap-product of $\mathbf{y}$ with any vector $\mathbf{x}$ of $G_1(E_3)$ with coordinates expressed in the canonical basis of E_3 is equal to the dot product of $\mathbf{y}$ with $\mathbf{x}$:*

$$\langle \mathbf{y}, \mathbf{x} \rangle = \mathbf{x} \,\Delta\, \mathbf{y} = \mathbf{y}^T \mathbf{x} = \mathbf{x}^T \mathbf{y}.$$

Proof : The proof is of course the same as in Proposition 3.18 or Proposition 3.19. Let $y_i, i = 1, 2, 3$ and x_i be the coordinates of $\mathbf{y}$ and $\mathbf{x}$ in their respective bases. We verify that the cap-product $\langle \mathbf{y}, \mathbf{x} \rangle$ is equal to $\sum_{i=1}^{3} x_i y_i \,(*\varepsilon_i) \,\Delta\, \varepsilon_i = \sum_{i=1}^{3} x_i y_i$. Therefore the cap-product $\langle \mathbf{y}, \mathbf{x} \rangle$ is equal to the usual inner or dot product $\mathbf{y}^T \mathbf{x}$ which is equal to $y(\mathbf{x})$ where y is considered as a linear form on E_3. $\square$

3.4.4.2 The line going through two points, the intersection of two lines

Using the definition (3.10) of the meet operation, we can build the multiplication table of $G_2(E_3)$ for the meet operation:

Δ	$\varepsilon_2 \nabla \varepsilon_3$	$\varepsilon_1 \nabla \varepsilon_3$	$\varepsilon_1 \nabla \varepsilon_2$
$\varepsilon_2 \nabla \varepsilon_3$	0	$-\varepsilon_3$	$-\varepsilon_2$
$\varepsilon_1 \nabla \varepsilon_3$	ε_3	0	$-\varepsilon_1$
$\varepsilon_1 \nabla \varepsilon_2$	ε_2	ε_1	0

Given two elements $\mathbf{x} = \sum_{i=1}^{3} x_i \varepsilon_i$ and $\mathbf{y} = \sum_{i=1}^{3} y_i \varepsilon_i$ of $G_1(E_3)$ we verify from the previous table that $*(\mathbf{x} \nabla \mathbf{y}) = (*\mathbf{x}) \triangle (*\mathbf{y})$. In effect we find that the coordinates of both terms in the associated cobasis $(*\varepsilon_1, *\varepsilon_2, *\varepsilon_3)$ are equal to the coordinates of the usual cross-product $\mathbf{x} \times \mathbf{y}$ of the two vectors $\mathbf{x}$ and $\mathbf{y}$ expressed in the basis $(\varepsilon_1, \varepsilon_2, \varepsilon_3)$. Hence we have found the interesting relation:

$$\mathbf{x} \times \mathbf{y} = *(\mathbf{x} \nabla \mathbf{y}). \tag{3.20}$$

The important geometric interpretation of this relation is that the line going through the points x and y, $\mathbf{x} \nabla \mathbf{y}$, can be represented by the cross-product $\mathbf{x} \times \mathbf{y}$ in the canonical basis of $G_1(E_3)$ by applying the Hodge operator to $\mathbf{x} \nabla \mathbf{y}$.

There is another geometric interpretation of this relation which we obtain by going to the dual. Let us now consider that $\mathbf{x}$ and $\mathbf{y}$ are two elements of $G_2(E_3)$, i.e. represent two lines. We write $\mathbf{x} = \sum_{i=1}^{3} x_i(*\varepsilon_i)$ and $\mathbf{y} = \sum_{i=1}^{3} y_i(*\varepsilon_i)$. Note that the basis which is used for $G_2(E_3)$ is not the canonical one $(\varepsilon_1 \nabla \varepsilon_2, \varepsilon_2 \nabla \varepsilon_3, \varepsilon_1 \nabla \varepsilon_3)$ but rather the dual through the Hodge operator of the canonical basis of $G_1(E_3)$, its associated cobasis.

$\mathbf{x} \triangle \mathbf{y}$ represents the point of intersection of the two lines and, according to the first property of the Theorem 3.2, $*(\mathbf{x} \triangle \mathbf{y}) = (*\mathbf{x}) \nabla (*\mathbf{y})$. According to the third property of Theorem 3.2, we have $*(*\mathbf{x}) = \mathbf{x}$ for all vectors of $G_1(E_3)$. For the same reason, $(\mathbf{x} \triangle \mathbf{y}) = *((*\mathbf{x}) \nabla (*\mathbf{y}))$ which is equal to $(*\mathbf{x}) \times (*\mathbf{y})$ according to the previous discussion. Hence we find the useful property that if two projective lines are represented by two vectors $\mathbf{x}$ and $\mathbf{y}$ expressed in the dual basis $(*\varepsilon_1, *\varepsilon_2, *\varepsilon_3)$ of the canonical basis of E_3 and if we identify those vectors with the vectors of E_3 with the same coordinates in the canonical basis $(\varepsilon_1, \varepsilon_2, \varepsilon_3)$, their point of intersection is represented in the same basis by the cross-product of those two vectors.

To summarize:

Proposition 3.27 *Let x and y be two distinct points of $\mathbb{P}^2$ represented by the vectors $\mathbf{x}$ and $\mathbf{y}$ in the canonical basis $(\varepsilon_1, \varepsilon_2, \varepsilon_3)$ of E_3. The line (x, y) is represented by the cross-product $\mathbf{x} \times \mathbf{y}$ in the associated cobasis $(*\varepsilon_1, *\varepsilon_2, *\varepsilon_3)$ of $G_2(E_3)$, see Figure 3.7.*

Let l and l' be two distinct lines of $\mathbb{P}^2$ represented by the vectors $\mathbf{l}$ and $\mathbf{l'}$ in the cobasis $(*\varepsilon_1, *\varepsilon_2, *\varepsilon_3)$ of $G_2(E_3)$. Their point of intersection is represented by the cross-product $\mathbf{l} \times \mathbf{l'}$ in the basis $(\varepsilon_1, \varepsilon_2, \varepsilon_3)$ of E_3, see Figure 3.8.

Given this geometric interpretation of the cross-product, we can state and prove the following useful proposition.

Proposition 3.28 *Let $\mathbf{H}$ be an invertible 3×3 matrix representing a homography of $\mathbb{P}^2$ and let $\mathbf{x}$ and $\mathbf{y}$ two vectors of $G_1(E_3)$. The cross-product $\mathbf{H}\mathbf{x} \times \mathbf{H}\mathbf{y}$ is equal to $\mathbf{H}^{*T}(\mathbf{x} \times \mathbf{y})$, where $\mathbf{H}^*$ is the adjoint matrix of $\mathbf{H}$.*

Proof : Proposition 3.24 tells us that the matrix $\mathbf{H}^{-T}$ represents the homography from $\mathbb{P}^{2*}$ to $\mathbb{P}^{2*}$ that corresponds to $\mathbf{H}$. In other words, when $\mathbf{H}$ acts on points,

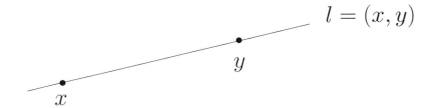

Figure 3.7: The points x and y are represented by the vectors $\mathbf{x}$ and $\mathbf{y}$ in the canonical basis of $G_1(E_3) = E_3$. The line $l = (x, y)$ is represented by the joint $\mathbf{x}\nabla\mathbf{y}$ in the canonical basis of $G_2(E_3)$ and by the cross-product $\mathbf{x} \times \mathbf{y}$ in the associated cobasis of $G_2(E_3)$.

$\mathbf{H}^{-T}$ acts on lines. Proposition 3.27 tells us that $\mathbf{H}\mathbf{x} \times \mathbf{H}\mathbf{y}$ represents the line going through the two points represented by $\mathbf{H}\mathbf{x}$ and $\mathbf{H}\mathbf{y}$. This line is therefore the line transformed by $\mathbf{H}^{-T}$ of the line going through the two points $\mathbf{x}$ and $\mathbf{y}$ and since $\mathbf{H}^{-T}$ is proportional to the transpose of the adjoint matrix of $\mathbf{H}$, the result follows, up to a scale factor. If we choose special values, e.g. $\mathbf{x} = \varepsilon_1$ and $\mathbf{y} = \varepsilon_2$, we obtain that the scale factor is equal to 1. □

3.4.4.3   The cross-product operation

Let us consider a vector $\mathbf{v}$ of $G_1(E) = E$. The mapping from $G_1(E)$ to $G_2(E)$ which with each vector $\mathbf{x}$ of $G_1(E)$ associates the join $\mathbf{v}\nabla\mathbf{x}$ of $\mathbf{v}$ and $\mathbf{x}$, an element of $G_2(E)$ is linear. If we concatenate it with the Hodge operator, we obtain a linear mapping from $G_1(E)$ to $G_1(E)$. Taking coordinates, we have:

$$\mathbf{v}\nabla\mathbf{x} = (v_1 x_2 - v_2 x_1)\varepsilon_1\nabla\varepsilon_2 + (v_2 x_3 - v_3 x_2)\varepsilon_2\nabla\varepsilon_3 + (v_1 x_3 - v_3 x_1)\varepsilon_1\nabla\varepsilon_3.$$

Taking the Hodge operator of both sides, we obtain:

$$*(\mathbf{v}\nabla\mathbf{x}) = (v_2 x_3 - v_3 x_2)\varepsilon_1 + (v_3 x_1 - v_1 x_3)\varepsilon_2 + (v_1 x_2 - v_2 x_1)\varepsilon_3,$$

which we write in matrix form:

$$*(\mathbf{v}\nabla\mathbf{x}) = [\mathbf{v}]_\times \mathbf{x}.$$

The matrix $[\mathbf{v}]_\times$ has the following remarkable form:

$$[\mathbf{v}]_\times = \begin{bmatrix} 0 & -v_3 & v_2 \\ v_3 & 0 & -v_1 \\ -v_2 & v_1 & 0 \end{bmatrix}.$$

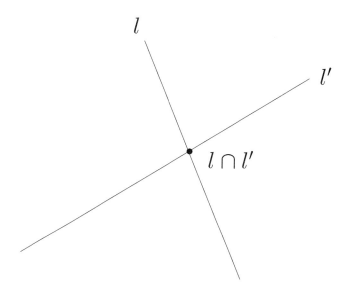

Figure 3.8: The lines l and l' are represented by the vectors $\mathbf{l}$ and $\mathbf{l}'$ in the associated cobasis of $G_2(E_3)$. Their point of intersection represented by the cross-product $\mathbf{l} \times \mathbf{l}'$ in the canonical basis of $G_1(E_3) = E_3$.

3.4.4.4 Tensor representation of the cross-product

In Chapter 9 we will need the following representation of the cross-product of two vectors. Let $\mathbf{x}$ and $\mathbf{y}$ be two vectors of $G_1(E_3)$. The mapping $(\mathbf{x}, \mathbf{y}) \longrightarrow \mathbf{x} \times \mathbf{y}$ from $G_1(E_3) \times G_1(E_3)$ into $G_1(E_3)$ is bilinear. It can therefore be represented by an operator, denoted ϵ, such that the ith component of $\mathbf{x} \times \mathbf{y}$ is given by

$$\sum_{j,k=1}^{3} \epsilon_{ijk} x_j y_k.$$

The relation (3.20) allows us to compute the values of the ϵ_{ijk}'s:

$$\mathbf{x} \times \mathbf{y} = *(\mathbf{x}\nabla\mathbf{y}) = \sum_{j,k=1}^{3} x_j y_k * (\varepsilon_j \nabla \varepsilon_k).$$

Some simple algebra shows that ϵ_{ijk} is precisely equal to 0 if any two of the indexes i, j, k are equal and to the signature $\epsilon(\{i, j, k\})$ of the permutation $\{i, j, k\}$ of $\{1, 2, 3\}$ otherwise. ϵ is known as the Eddington or Levi-Civita tensor. To summarize:

Proposition 3.29 *The ith coordinate of the cross product of two vectors* $\mathbf{x}$ *and* $\mathbf{y}$ *of $G_1(E_3)$ is given by the Eddington or Levi-Civita tensor:*

$$(\mathbf{x} \times \mathbf{y})_i = \sum_{j,k=1}^{3} \epsilon_{ijk} x_j y_k, \tag{3.21}$$

where

$$\epsilon_{ijk} = \begin{cases} 0 & if \quad i = j \quad or \quad j = k \quad or \quad k = i, \\ \varepsilon(\{i,j,k\}) & otherwise. \end{cases} \tag{3.22}$$

3.4.5   The example of 3D planes: III

What we have been doing in the previous paragraphs is to use the duality principle implemented as the Hodge operator to simplify our computations, e.g. compute in $G_1(E_3) = E_3$ instead of computing in $G_2(E_3)$ when dealing with lines. We can apply the same method in $\mathbb{P}^3$ to deal with planes. E_4 is now of dimension 4.

3.4.5.1   Cap-products, points and planes

The action of the Hodge operator on the basis $(\varepsilon_1, \varepsilon_2, \varepsilon_3, \varepsilon_4)$ is easily found to be, using again Equations 3.14 or 3.15:

$$*\varepsilon_1 = \varepsilon_2 \triangledown \varepsilon_3 \triangledown \varepsilon_4 \quad *\varepsilon_2 = -\varepsilon_1 \triangledown \varepsilon_3 \triangledown \varepsilon_4 \quad *\varepsilon_3 = \varepsilon_1 \triangledown \varepsilon_2 \triangledown \varepsilon_4 \quad *\varepsilon_4 = -\varepsilon_1 \triangledown \varepsilon_2 \triangledown \varepsilon_3. \tag{3.23}$$

The Hodge operator allows us to identify the basis $(\varepsilon_1, \varepsilon_2, \varepsilon_3, \varepsilon_4)$ of E_4 and the basis
$(\varepsilon_2 \triangledown \varepsilon_3 \triangledown \varepsilon_4, -\varepsilon_1 \triangledown \varepsilon_3 \triangledown \varepsilon_4, \varepsilon_1 \triangledown \varepsilon_2 \triangledown \varepsilon_4, -\varepsilon_1 \triangledown \varepsilon_2 \triangledown \varepsilon_3)$ of $G_3(E_4)$.

Just like in the previous 2D example, we use the cobasis $(*\varepsilon_1, *\varepsilon_2, *\varepsilon_3, *\varepsilon_4)$ of $G_3(E_4)$ instead of the canonical one. We have the following proposition, analog to Proposition 3.26.

Proposition 3.30 *Let $\mathbf{\Pi}$ be a covector, i.e. representing a plane of $\mathbb{P}^3$, with coordinates expressed in the associated cobasis of the canonical basis of E_4. According to Proposition 3.19, we identify $\mathbf{\Pi}$ with the vector which has the same coordinates as $\mathbf{\Pi}$ in the canonical basis of E_4^*, the dual of E_4. Through this identification, the cap-product of $\mathbf{\Pi}$ with any vector $\mathbf{M}$ of $G_1(E_4)$ with coordinates expressed in the canonical basis of E_4 is equal to the dot product of $\mathbf{\Pi}$ with $\mathbf{M}$:*

$$\langle \mathbf{\Pi}, \mathbf{M} \rangle = \mathbf{M} \vartriangle \mathbf{\Pi} = \mathbf{\Pi}^T \mathbf{M} = \mathbf{M}^T \mathbf{\Pi}.$$

Proof :   Let $y_i, i = 1, 2, 3, 4$ and x_i be the coordinates of $\mathbf{\Pi}$ and $\mathbf{M}$ in their respective bases. The proof consists, as in Proposition 3.19, in verifying that the cap-product $\langle \mathbf{\Pi}, \mathbf{M} \rangle$ is equal to $\sum_{i=1}^{4} x_i y_i \ (*\varepsilon_i) \vartriangle \varepsilon_i = \sum_{i=1}^{4} x_i y_i$. Therefore the cap-product $\langle \mathbf{\Pi}, \mathbf{M} \rangle$ is equal to the usual inner or dot product $\mathbf{\Pi}^T \mathbf{M}$ which is equal to $\Pi(\mathbf{M})$ where Π is considered as a linear form on E_4. $\square$

We will also need in future chapters the dual interpretation of the intersection of three planes. Let us thus consider three planes $\mathbf{\Pi}$, $\mathbf{\Pi}'$, $\mathbf{\Pi}''$ with coordinates expressed in the cobasis $*\varepsilon_j$, $j = 1, 2, 3, 4$, e.g $\Pi = \sum_i \pi_i \varepsilon_i$. Their point of intersection M is represented by their meet:

$$\mathbf{M} = \mathbf{\Pi} \vartriangle \mathbf{\Pi}' \vartriangle \mathbf{\Pi}''.$$

Let us apply the Hodge operator to both sides of this equality:

$$*\mathbf{M} = *(\mathbf{\Pi} \vartriangle \mathbf{\Pi}' \vartriangle \mathbf{\Pi}'') = (*\mathbf{\Pi})\triangledown(*\mathbf{\Pi}')\triangledown(*\mathbf{\Pi}'').$$

Let us denote by M_{ijk} the 3×3 minor built on the columns i, j, k, $1 \leq i < j < k \leq 4$ of the 3×4 matrix $\mathcal{P}$ whose rows are the three vectors Π^T, Π'^T, Π''^T, expressed in the basis $*\varepsilon_j$, $j = 1, \ldots, 4$. Note that those minors are the Plücker coordinates of $-(*\mathbf{\Pi})\triangledown(*\mathbf{\Pi}')\triangledown(*\mathbf{\Pi}'')$ in the canonical basis of $G_3(E_4)$:

$$*\mathbf{M} = - \sum_{1 \leq i < j < k \leq 4} M_{ijk}\varepsilon_i \triangledown \varepsilon_j \triangledown \varepsilon_k.$$

But, because of Equations 3.23, this can be rewritten as:

$$*\mathbf{M} = -(M_{234}(*\varepsilon_1) - M_{134}(*\varepsilon_2) + M_{124}(*\varepsilon_3) - M_{123}(*\varepsilon_4)).$$

Taking the Hodge operator of both sides, we obtain:

$$* * \mathbf{M} = -(M_{234} * *\varepsilon_1 - M_{134} * *\varepsilon_2 + M_{124} * *\varepsilon_3 - M_{123} * *\varepsilon_4),$$

and since $* * \mathbf{x} = -\mathbf{x}$ for all vectors $\mathbf{x}$ of $E_4 = G_1(E_4)$ (Theorem 3.2), we end up with:

$$\mathbf{M} = -M_{234}\varepsilon_1 + M_{134}\varepsilon_2 - M_{124}\varepsilon_3 + M_{123}\varepsilon_4. \tag{3.24}$$

This allows us to compute the coordinates of the point of intersection of three planes $\mathbf{\Pi}_i$, $\mathbf{\Pi}'$, $\mathbf{\Pi}''$ defined by their duals $*\mathbf{\Pi}$, $*\mathbf{\Pi}'$, $*\mathbf{\Pi}''$. In particular, these coordinates are proportional to the cofactors of $\mathcal{P}$, i.e. the 3×3 minors multiplied by -1 if the missing column has an odd index (see Table 3.2).

3.4.5.2 The cross-product operation

We can also extend the notion of the matrix $[v]_\times$ developed in the previous paragraph for the cross-product as follows. Consider two projective points C and C' represented by two vectors $\mathbf{C}$ and $\mathbf{C}'$ of $G_1(E_4)$. Consider the mapping from $G_1(E_4)$ to $G_3(E_4)$ which associates with a vector $\mathbf{M}$ the plane $\mathbf{C}\triangledown\mathbf{C}'\triangledown\mathbf{M}$. This application is linear. Let us write:

$$\mathbf{C}\triangledown\mathbf{C}' = \sum_{1 \leq i < j \leq 4} L_{ij}\varepsilon_i \triangledown \varepsilon_j,$$

where the coefficients L_{ij} are the Plücker coordinates of the line (C, C'). Taking the join with $\mathbf{M}$, we obtain:

$$\mathbf{C} \triangledown \mathbf{C'} \triangledown \mathbf{M} = (L_{34}M_2 - L_{24}M_3 + L_{23}M_4)\varepsilon_2 \triangledown \varepsilon_3 \triangledown \varepsilon_4 +$$
$$(L_{34}M_1 - L_{14}M_3 + L_{13}M_4)\varepsilon_1 \triangledown \varepsilon_3 \triangledown \varepsilon_4 +$$
$$(L_{24}M_1 - L_{14}M_2 + L_{12}M_4)\varepsilon_1 \triangledown \varepsilon_2 \triangledown \varepsilon_4 +$$
$$(L_{23}M_1 - L_{13}M_2 + L_{12}M_3)\varepsilon_1 \triangledown \varepsilon_2 \triangledown \varepsilon_3.$$

This gives the expression of $\mathbf{C} \triangledown \mathbf{C'} \triangledown \mathbf{M}$ in the canonical basis of $G_3(E)$. If we concatenate our mapping with the Hodge operator we obtain a linear mapping of $G_1(E)$ to $G_1(E)$ defined by:

$$* (\mathbf{C} \triangledown \mathbf{C'} \triangledown \mathbf{M}) = -(L_{34}M_2 - L_{24}M_3 + L_{23}M_4)\varepsilon_1 +$$
$$(L_{34}M_1 - L_{14}M_3 + L_{13}M_4)\varepsilon_2 - (L_{24}M_1 - L_{14}M_2 + L_{12}M_4)\varepsilon_3 +$$
$$(L_{23}M_1 - L_{13}M_2 + L_{12}M_3)\varepsilon_4.$$

We write this in matrix form as:

$$*(\mathbf{C} \triangledown \mathbf{C'} \triangledown \mathbf{M}) = \langle \mathbf{C}, \mathbf{C'} \rangle_\times \mathbf{M}.$$

We have proved the following proposition

Proposition 3.31 *Let C, C' and M be three projective points and L_{ij}, $1 \leq i < j \leq 4$ the Plücker coordinates of the line (C, C'). The antisymmetric matrix $\langle \mathbf{C}, \mathbf{C'} \rangle_\times$ given by the expression*

$$\langle \mathbf{C}, \mathbf{C'} \rangle_\times = \begin{bmatrix} 0 & -L_{34} & L_{24} & -L_{23} \\ L_{34} & 0 & -L_{14} & L_{13} \\ -L_{24} & L_{14} & 0 & -L_{12} \\ L_{23} & -L_{13} & L_{12} & 0 \end{bmatrix}, \tag{3.25}$$

is such that the vector $\langle \mathbf{C}, \mathbf{C'} \rangle_\times \mathbf{M}$ expressed in the canonical basis $(\varepsilon_1, \varepsilon_2, \varepsilon_3, \varepsilon_4)$ of E_4 is a representation of the plane $\mathbf{C} \triangledown \mathbf{C'} \triangledown \mathbf{M}$ in the associated cobasis $(*\varepsilon_1, *\varepsilon_2, *\varepsilon_3, *\varepsilon_4)$ of $G_3(E_4)$.

3.4.6   The example of 3D lines: IV

Let us consider a special case of the case studied in Section 3.1.2.3. Let us consider the affine subspace X_3 of the projective space $\mathbb{P}^3$, complement of the plane of equation $x_4 = 0$, see Section 2.5. Let L be a line defined by two points M and M'. In the special case where both M and M' are not in the plane at infinity, we can choose their last coordinates equal to 1: $x_4 = x'_4 = 1$. Replacing x_4 and $\overrightarrow{x'_4}$ by those values, we find that L_{14}, L_{24} and L_{34} are the coordinates of the vector $\overrightarrow{M'M}$

and that $L_{23}, -L_{13}$ and L_{12} are the coordinates of the cross-product $\overrightarrow{OM} \times \overrightarrow{OM'}$. The vector coordinates are computed in the three-dimensional affine subspace X_3 (see Section 2.5.3). The point O is the origin of the affine basis associated with the canonical projective basis of $\mathbb{P}^3$ with coordinate vectors $(\varepsilon_1, \varepsilon_2, \varepsilon_3, \varepsilon_4, \sum_i \varepsilon_i)$ (see Section 2.5.2). According to this section, O is the point represented in $\mathbb{P}^3$ by the vector ε_4. A picture, drawn in X_3, is shown in Figure 3.9. Note that this relation

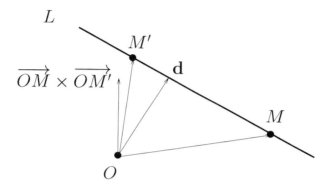

Figure 3.9: The line L is defined by the two affine points M and M': its six Plücker coordinates of the line L are obtained as explained in the text.

between the coordinates of $\overrightarrow{M'M}$ and $\overrightarrow{OM} \times \overrightarrow{OM'}$ and the Plücker coordinates of the line is best expressed in the basis $(\varepsilon_1 \nabla \varepsilon_4, \ \varepsilon_2 \nabla \varepsilon_4, \ \varepsilon_3 \nabla \varepsilon_4, \ \varepsilon_2 \nabla \varepsilon_3, \ \varepsilon_3 \nabla \varepsilon_1, \ \varepsilon_1 \nabla \varepsilon_2)$ of $G_2(E_4)$ which is neither the canonical basis nor its associated cobasis. Note that in this basis, the Plücker relation (3.6) is written

$$L_{12}L_{34} + L_{31}L_{24} + L_{14}L23 = 0,$$

which is exactly the (obvious) relation

$$\overrightarrow{M'M} \cdot (\overrightarrow{OM} \times \overrightarrow{OM'}) = 0.$$

We can also notice that L is in the plane at infinity if and only if M and M' are at infinity, i.e. $x_4 = x'_4 = 0$. This is equivalent to $L_{14} = L_{24} = L_{34} = 0$.

When the line L is not at infinity, we can compute the vector $\mathbf{d} = \overrightarrow{Oo}$, where o is the projection of the origin O onto the line (Figure 3.9). $\mathbf{d}$ is easily found to be given by

$$\mathbf{d} = \frac{1}{\|\overrightarrow{MM'}\|^2} \overrightarrow{MM'} \times (\overrightarrow{OM} \times \overrightarrow{OM'}).$$

Consider now the line $*L$ dual of L. Three of its Plücker coordinates are those of $\overrightarrow{OM} \times \overrightarrow{OM'}$ along the vectors $(*(\varepsilon_2 \nabla \varepsilon_3), *(\varepsilon_3 \nabla \varepsilon_1), *(\varepsilon_1 \nabla \varepsilon_2))$, i.e. (Equations 3.18)

$(\varepsilon_1 \nabla \varepsilon_4, \varepsilon_2 \nabla \varepsilon_4, \varepsilon_3 \nabla \varepsilon_4)$. The remaining three Plücker coordinates are those of $\overrightarrow{M'M}$ along the vectors $(*(\varepsilon_1 \nabla \varepsilon_4), *(\varepsilon_2 \nabla \varepsilon_4), *(\varepsilon_3 \nabla \varepsilon_4))$, i.e. (Equations 3.18) $(\varepsilon_2 \nabla \varepsilon_3, \varepsilon_3 \nabla \varepsilon_1, \varepsilon_1 \nabla \varepsilon_2)$. This shows that L^* is in the plane defined by O and the two vectors $\mathbf{d}$ and $\overrightarrow{OM} \times \overrightarrow{OM'}$. In that plane it is orthogonal to the vector $\mathbf{d}$. The projection o^* of the origin O onto L^* defines a vector $\mathbf{d}^*$ given by

$$\mathbf{d}^* = \frac{1}{\|\overrightarrow{OM_1} \times \overrightarrow{OM_2}\|^2} \overrightarrow{M_1 M_2} \times (\overrightarrow{OM_1} \times \overrightarrow{OM_2}),$$

see Figure 3.10. Note that $\mathbf{d}$ and $\mathbf{d}^*$ verify the relation $\mathbf{d} \cdot \mathbf{d}^* = 1$. Proposition 3.12

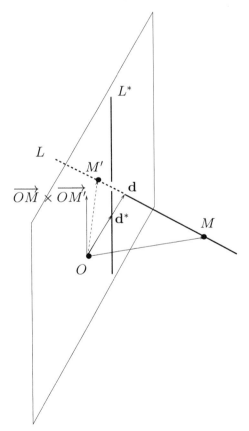

Figure 3.10: The line L^* dual of the line L is orthogonal to L and in the plane defined by the origin O and the two vectors indicated in the text.

allows us to find some useful expressions for the Plücker product. $[L \mid L']$ for different representations of L and L':

Proposition 3.32 *Let L and L' be two lines. If the two lines are represented as the joins of two points A and B and A' and B', respectively, then:*

$$[\mathbf{L} \mid \mathbf{L'}] = \mid \mathbf{A}, \mathbf{B}, \mathbf{A'}, \mathbf{B'} \mid .$$

If the two lines are represented as the meets of two planes P and Q and P' and Q', then:

$$[\mathbf{L} \mid \mathbf{L'}] = \mid \mathbf{P}, \mathbf{Q}, \mathbf{P'}, \mathbf{Q'} \mid . \tag{3.26}$$

If one line is represented as the meet of two planes P and Q and the other as the join of two points A' and B', then:

$$[\mathbf{L} \mid \mathbf{L'}] = \langle \mathbf{P}, \mathbf{A'} \rangle \langle \mathbf{Q}, \mathbf{B'} \rangle - \langle \mathbf{Q}, \mathbf{A'} \rangle \langle \mathbf{P}, \mathbf{B'} \rangle. \tag{3.27}$$

Proof : All properties are fairly direct consequences of Proposition 3.12. If $\mathbf{L} = \mathbf{A} \triangledown \mathbf{B}$ and $\mathbf{L'} = \mathbf{A'} \triangledown \mathbf{B'}$, we have $\mathbf{L} \triangledown \mathbf{L'} = \mathbf{A} \triangledown \mathbf{B} \triangledown \mathbf{A'} \triangledown \mathbf{B'} = \mid \mathbf{A}, \mathbf{B}, \mathbf{A'}, \mathbf{B'} \mid \mathbf{I}$ where $\mathbf{I} = \varepsilon_1 \triangledown \varepsilon_2 \triangledown \varepsilon_3 \triangledown \varepsilon_4$ and the result follows. If $\mathbf{L} = \mathbf{P} \triangle \mathbf{Q}$ and $\mathbf{L'} = \mathbf{P'} \triangle \mathbf{Q'}$, $\mathbf{L} \triangledown \mathbf{L'} = (\mathbf{P} \triangle \mathbf{Q}) \triangledown (\mathbf{P'} \triangle \mathbf{Q'})$. We thus have to compute $(\mathbf{P} \triangle \mathbf{Q}) \triangledown (\mathbf{P'} \triangle \mathbf{Q'})$. Taking the Hodge operator, this is equivalent to computing:

$$((*\mathbf{P}) \triangledown (*\mathbf{Q})) \triangle ((*\mathbf{P'}) \triangledown (*\mathbf{Q'})),$$

which, because of Definitions 3.10, is equal to $\mid (*\mathbf{P}), (*\mathbf{Q}), (*\mathbf{P'}), (*\mathbf{Q'}) \mid$. Since this determinant is also equal to the determinant $\mid \mathbf{P}, \mathbf{Q}, \mathbf{P'}, \mathbf{Q'} \mid$ and since, according to Theorem 3.2, $*1 = \mathbf{I} = \varepsilon_1 \triangledown \varepsilon_2 \triangledown \varepsilon_3 \triangledown \varepsilon_4$, we have:

$$\mathbf{L} \triangledown \mathbf{L'} = \mid \mathbf{P}, \mathbf{Q}, \mathbf{P'}, \mathbf{Q'} \mid \mathbf{I}.$$

Finally, let us consider the case where $\mathbf{L} = \mathbf{P} \triangle \mathbf{Q}$ and $\mathbf{L'} = \mathbf{A'} \triangledown \mathbf{B'}$. We have $\mathbf{L} \triangledown \mathbf{L'} = (\mathbf{P} \triangle \mathbf{Q}) \triangledown (\mathbf{A'} \triangledown \mathbf{B'})$. Let us take the Hodge operator of both sides:

$$*(\mathbf{L} \triangledown \mathbf{L'}) = ((*\mathbf{P}) \triangledown (*\mathbf{Q})) \triangle ((*\mathbf{A'}) \triangle (*\mathbf{B'})),$$

because of Equation 3.16 of Proposition 3.22 where we take $k = s = 2$, we have:

$$*(\mathbf{L} \triangledown \mathbf{L'}) = \mid *\mathbf{P}, *\mathbf{A'} \mid \mid *\mathbf{Q}, *\mathbf{B'} \mid - \mid *\mathbf{P}, *\mathbf{B'} \mid \mid *\mathbf{Q}, *\mathbf{A'} \mid .$$

Let us consider one of the brackets on the right-hand side, e.g. $\mid *\mathbf{P}, *\mathbf{A'} \mid$. By definition it is equal to $*\mathbf{P} \triangle *\mathbf{A'}$ which is equal to $*(\mathbf{P} \triangledown \mathbf{A'})$ which is itself equal to $*(\mid \mathbf{P}, \mathbf{A'} \mid \mathbf{I})$. By the linearity of the Hodge operator and the definition of the cap-product, this is equal to $\langle \mathbf{P}, \mathbf{A'} \rangle$. Hence the result. $\square$

An important consequence of this proposition is a characterization of coplanar 3D lines:

Proposition 3.33 *Let L and L' be two lines. The Plücker product* $[\mathbf{L} \mid \mathbf{L}']$ *is equal to 0 if and only if the two lines are coplanar.*

Proof : This follows directly from the first of the relations in the previous proposition. Indeed, $\mid \mathbf{A}, \mathbf{B}, \mathbf{A}', \mathbf{B}' \mid = 0$ is equivalent to the fact the four points are coplanar. $\square$

We finish this section by giving some properties of the dual line $*\mathbf{L}$ of a line $\mathbf{L}$.

3.5   Summary and conclusion

In this chapter we have covered a lot of ground. The thread that we have followed is the idea that unions and intersections of vector or projective spaces can be treated algebraically. This idea is conceptually and computationally powerful as will be shown in the next chapters.

There are four keys to the success of this endeavor.

1. The definition of a set of "large" vector spaces, the $G_k(E)$'s which contain elements, the extensors of step k, which are in one to one correspondence with the k-dimensional vector subspaces of the vector space E (Proposition 3.5). The direct sum $G(E)$ of these vector spaces allows us to encompass the set of all vector subspaces of E.

2. The definition of a first operator, the join, on $G(E)$ which we have shown in Proposition 3.8 to be closely related to the union of two vector or projective subspaces.

3. The definition of a second operator, the meet, on $G(E)$ which we have shown in Proposition 3.17 to be closely related to the intersection of two vector or projective subspaces.

4. The definition of a third operator, the Hodge star operator, which instantiates computationally the principle of duality introduced in Chapter 2.

Thanks to these four keys, we now have a complete view of the operations of unions and intersections of vector and projective spaces and of duality in a common algebraic/geometric framework, the Grassmann-Cayley algebra. The join, meet and Hodge star operators are the algebraic tools that will allow us to describe concisely and simply in the next chapters the intricate geometry of sets of cameras.

We summarize some of the results that will be used most often in the sequel for those who do not wish to study the details of the constructions of the Grassmann-Cayley algebra. These results are for the case $n = 4$. Points of $\mathbb{P}^3$ are represented by their coordinate vectors, elements of $E_4 \equiv G_1(E_4)$, in the canonical basis $(\varepsilon_1, \varepsilon_2, \varepsilon_3, \varepsilon_4)$, e.g $\mathbf{M} = \sum_i x_i \varepsilon_i$. Planes of $\mathbb{P}^3$ are also represented by their coordinate vectors, elements of $G_3(E_4)$ in the cobasis $(*\varepsilon_1, *\varepsilon_2, *\varepsilon_3, *\varepsilon_4)$

(see Section 3.4.5.1), e.g. $\mathbf{\Pi} = \sum_i \pi_i (*\varepsilon_i)$. Finally, lines of $\mathbb{P}^3$ are a bit special since $G_2(E_4)$ is its own dual (see Section 3.4.6). Therefore, lines can either be represented in the canonical basis $(\varepsilon_1 \nabla \varepsilon_2, \varepsilon_1 \nabla \varepsilon_3, \varepsilon_1 \nabla \varepsilon_4, \varepsilon_2 \nabla \varepsilon_3, \varepsilon_2 \nabla \varepsilon_4, \varepsilon_3 \nabla \varepsilon_4)$ of $G_2(E_4)$, e.g. $\mathbf{L} = \sum_{1 \leq i < j \leq 4} L_{ij} \, \varepsilon_i \nabla \varepsilon_j$ or in its associated cobasis $(*(\varepsilon_1 \nabla \varepsilon_2),$ $*(\varepsilon_1 \nabla \varepsilon_3), *(\varepsilon_1 \nabla \varepsilon_4), *(\varepsilon_2 \nabla \varepsilon_3), *(\varepsilon_2 \nabla \varepsilon_4), *(\varepsilon_3 \nabla \varepsilon_4))$ which is equal to $(\varepsilon_3 \nabla \varepsilon_4,$ $-\varepsilon_2 \nabla \varepsilon_4, \varepsilon_2 \nabla \varepsilon_3, \varepsilon_1 \nabla \varepsilon_4, -\varepsilon_1 \nabla \varepsilon_3, \varepsilon_1 \nabla \varepsilon_2)$, e.g. $\mathbf{L} = \sum_{1 \leq i < j \leq 4} L_{ij} * (\varepsilon_i \nabla \varepsilon_j)$. The results are presented in Tables 3.1 and 3.2.

We obtain similar descriptions by applying the Hodge operator. Note that we assume that the planes are represented in the associated cobasis of the the canonical basis of E_4 rather than in the canonical basis of $G_3(E_4)$.

3.6 References and further reading

The Grassmann-Cayley algebra was introduced to the computer vision community by Carlsson (Carlsson, 1994).The nice thing about it is that it combines the algebraic power of the tensor notation, as introduced by Triggs (Triggs, 1995), and further refined by Heyden (Heyden, 1998a) for dealing with multiple images, with the geometric intuition carried by the join and meet operators.

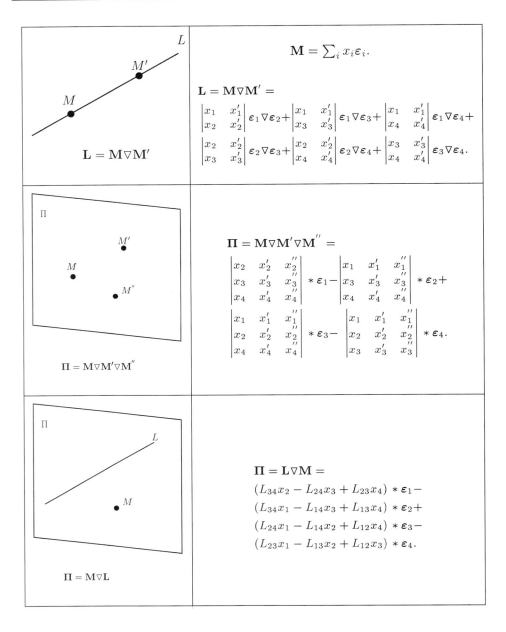

Table 3.1: The main results on the join (∇) operator that are used in this book: The first column shows the geometry and the Grassmann-Cayley notation, the second column shows how to compute the actual coordinates.

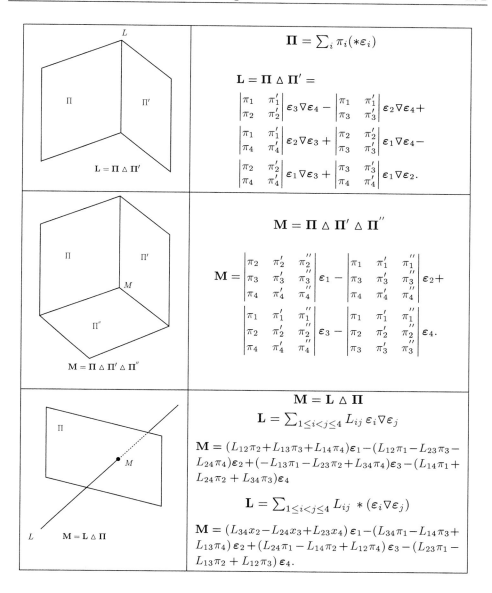

$$\mathbf{\Pi} = \sum_i \pi_i (*\varepsilon_i)$$

$$\mathbf{L} = \mathbf{\Pi} \,\triangle\, \mathbf{\Pi}' =$$

$$\begin{vmatrix} \pi_1 & \pi'_1 \\ \pi_2 & \pi'_2 \end{vmatrix} \varepsilon_3 \nabla \varepsilon_4 - \begin{vmatrix} \pi_1 & \pi'_1 \\ \pi_3 & \pi'_3 \end{vmatrix} \varepsilon_2 \nabla \varepsilon_4 +$$

$$\begin{vmatrix} \pi_1 & \pi'_1 \\ \pi_4 & \pi'_4 \end{vmatrix} \varepsilon_2 \nabla \varepsilon_3 + \begin{vmatrix} \pi_2 & \pi'_2 \\ \pi_3 & \pi'_3 \end{vmatrix} \varepsilon_1 \nabla \varepsilon_4 -$$

$$\begin{vmatrix} \pi_2 & \pi'_2 \\ \pi_4 & \pi'_4 \end{vmatrix} \varepsilon_1 \nabla \varepsilon_3 + \begin{vmatrix} \pi_3 & \pi'_3 \\ \pi_4 & \pi'_4 \end{vmatrix} \varepsilon_1 \nabla \varepsilon_2.$$

$$\mathbf{M} = \mathbf{\Pi} \,\triangle\, \mathbf{\Pi}' \,\triangle\, \mathbf{\Pi}''$$

$$\mathbf{M} = \begin{vmatrix} \pi_2 & \pi'_2 & \pi''_2 \\ \pi_3 & \pi'_3 & \pi''_3 \\ \pi_4 & \pi'_4 & \pi''_4 \end{vmatrix} \varepsilon_1 - \begin{vmatrix} \pi_1 & \pi'_1 & \pi''_1 \\ \pi_3 & \pi'_3 & \pi''_3 \\ \pi_4 & \pi'_4 & \pi''_4 \end{vmatrix} \varepsilon_2 +$$

$$\begin{vmatrix} \pi_1 & \pi'_1 & \pi''_1 \\ \pi_2 & \pi'_2 & \pi''_2 \\ \pi_4 & \pi'_4 & \pi''_4 \end{vmatrix} \varepsilon_3 - \begin{vmatrix} \pi_1 & \pi'_1 & \pi''_1 \\ \pi_2 & \pi'_2 & \pi''_2 \\ \pi_3 & \pi'_3 & \pi''_3 \end{vmatrix} \varepsilon_4.$$

$$\mathbf{M} = \mathbf{L} \,\triangle\, \mathbf{\Pi}$$

$$\mathbf{L} = \sum_{1 \le i < j \le 4} L_{ij} \, \varepsilon_i \nabla \varepsilon_j$$

$$\mathbf{M} = (L_{12}\pi_2 + L_{13}\pi_3 + L_{14}\pi_4)\varepsilon_1 - (L_{12}\pi_1 - L_{23}\pi_3 - L_{24}\pi_4)\varepsilon_2 + (-L_{13}\pi_1 - L_{23}\pi_2 + L_{34}\pi_4)\varepsilon_3 - (L_{14}\pi_1 + L_{24}\pi_2 + L_{34}\pi_3)\varepsilon_4$$

$$\mathbf{L} = \sum_{1 \le i < j \le 4} L_{ij} \, * (\varepsilon_i \nabla \varepsilon_j)$$

$$\mathbf{M} = (L_{34}x_2 - L_{24}x_3 + L_{23}x_4)\,\varepsilon_1 - (L_{34}\pi_1 - L_{14}\pi_3 + L_{13}\pi_4)\,\varepsilon_2 + (L_{24}\pi_1 - L_{14}\pi_2 + L_{12}\pi_4)\,\varepsilon_3 - (L_{23}\pi_1 - L_{13}\pi_2 + L_{12}\pi_3)\,\varepsilon_4.$$

Table 3.2: The main results on the meet ($\triangle$) operator that are used in this book. They are the duals of the results shown in the previous table. The first column shows the geometry and the second the Grassmann-Cayley notation, the second column shows how to compute the actual coordinates. In the third row, the line L is represented either in the canonical basis of $G_2(E_4)$ (top) or in the associated cobasis (bottom).

4 One camera

A camera is a particular geometric engine which constructs planar images of the three-dimensional world through a projection. The geometry of the image formation process was first understood by Renaissance painters who made large use of vanishing points and derived geometric constructions for their practical use. At the time photography was discovered, people studied how to make measurements from perspective views of scenes, and this lead to photogrammetry which has had a wide range of successful applications. During the same century, mathematicians developed *projective geometry* which was intended to deal with points at infinity and perspective projections. It is the reference framework which will be used throughout this book because it deals elegantly with the general case of the type of projection that a camera performs. Although the natural geometry which we use is Euclidean, it is much simpler to consider the Euclidean and affine geometries as special cases of the projective geometry than the reverse.

Although modeling the properties of light bouncing off surfaces is a complex problem, the geometry involved in Computer Graphics is relatively simple because understanding the geometry of a single camera is sufficient to generate images from three-dimensional specifications. However, our exposition of the geometry of a single camera is rather sophisticated because we have in mind the inverse problem of generating 3-D descriptions from images. In order to lay the ground for the next chapters, we will therefore address also the question of what 3-D (partial) descriptions are obtained from a single view.

In this chapter, the tools which have been introduced in the previous two chapters are used to describe a camera. Following the approach that was put forward in Chapter 2, we go from the most general setting, i.e. the projective one, to the most specific, i.e. the Euclidean one, to clearly identify the properties of the camera which are pertinent for a given level of description.

We therefore start in Section 4.1 with the projective level since a camera is really a "projective engine". Not surprisingly, perhaps, we find that this level of description is very rich. We first introduce the pinhole camera model which plays a central role in this book and analyze the corresponding perspective projection matrix in terms of projective geometry and the Grassman-Cayley algebra introduced in Chapter 3. We next discuss a sort of pseudo-inverse of that perspective projection matrix, called the inverse projection matrix, which we have found to be quite useful in theory and in practice. Since planes play a prominent role in many applications of computer vision, we also connect the perspective projection matrix to the images of planes. This section ends with a curious generalization of the perspective projection to the case of 3D lines which can be skipped during a first reading.

Section 4.2 goes on to an affine description of the pinhole camera. This description still assumes that the ambient space is a projective space of dimension 3 but this space is now considered as the projective completion of an affine space of dimension 3. In other words, the plane at infinity is assumed to be known. An interesting phenomenon occurs in that case: The class of pinhole cameras splits into two subclasses according to whether the optical center is in the plane at infinity or not. The first case corresponds to the class of affine cameras and is studied later in the chapter. The second case corresponds to the case of perspective projection cameras for which the optical center is at a finite distance. The remainder of this section is devoted to a study of this case. The most interesting new facts are those connected to the affine notions of parallelism, vanishing points and vanishing lines. They have played such an important role in the development of painting from the XV-th century on through the introduction of perspective effects that we present a short analysis of several paintings from that perspective, so to speak.

In Section 4.3, we continue to explore the perspective projection camera model in the Euclidean setting. The ambient space is still assumed to be an affine space of dimension 3 which has been completed to a projective space by adding a plane at infinity, but we now add to the plane at infinity the absolute conic that was introduced in Chapter 2. We describe the internal and external parameters that play a central role in the problems of calibration that are studied in Chapters 7, 10, and 11 and connect the internal parameters to the image of the absolute conic.

The next section, Section 4.4, is dedicated to the special case of the class of pinhole cameras with optical centers at infinity. This class is called the class of affine cameras, and the correct setting for their study is of course the affine or Euclidean one. In the affine setting, we introduce three classes of affine cameras which have been studied by several authors, classified according to the exact type of projection that they perform: The orthographic, scaled orthographic and para-perspective projections. We then discuss the Euclidean setting in all three cases and show various ways of adapting to these cases the decomposition of the projection matrix into internal and external parameters, introduced in the previous section for the perspective projection camera.

We end with some practical results. Section 4.5 discusses the practically important corrections to the pinhole model that must be introduced in order to take into account the nonlinear distortions due to non-perfect lenses. Section 4.6 discusses how to recover the projection matrix using a single view of a known object, a technique known as calibration.

4.1 The Projective model

The pinhole camera is given an historic and intuitive presentation in Section 4.1.1, which serves to introduce a particular form of the projection matrix. Generalizing this in Section 4.1.2, we study the general projection matrix mapping a point in space to a point in the image. Projective geometry appears to be the most natural framework to describe the type of projection performed by a camera. In Section 4.1.3, the *inverse projection matrix* is defined. This matrix is a mapping from points in the image to points in space is defined and also accounts for the projection of planes. In Section 4.1.4, it is shown that the previous mapping can be seen as a homography between two projective planes. In Section 4.1.5, the projection of lines is considered.

4.1.1   The pinhole camera

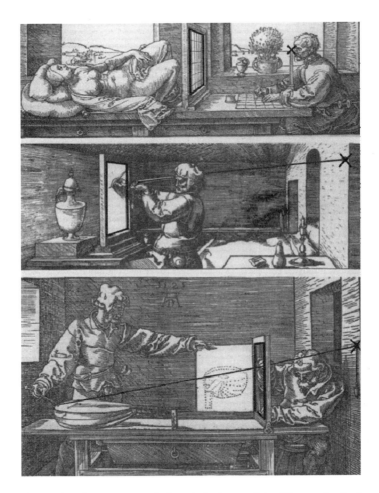

Figure 4.1: An early illustration of the pinhole model. The retinal plane and the optical center are both outlined.

A bit of history   A camera produces plane images of the physical world that we perceive as three-dimensional. Well before the invention of photography, there was a community that was concerned with representing images of the world on flat surfaces. Until the development of modern art, a central goal of occidental painting was imitation of nature. Many artists and theorists, believing that imitation must be based on scientific principles, made decisive contributions to the science of perspective. The ancient Greeks knew a lot of geometric properties of the projection, among them the conservation of the cross-ratio, and the notion of motion parallax. However, they thought of the eye as an "active" device projecting particles towards the world rather than a as passive device.

The Italian painters of the Renaissance were the first to understand image formation and to study geometry in order to correctly reproduce the perspective effects in the images of the world that they where observing. Perspective was invented by Filippo Brunelleschi around 1413. Such artists-theorists as Piero Della Francesca (della Francesca, 1984), Leonardo (de Vinci, 1998), and Dürer (Dürer, 1977) pushed the theory to a considerably sophisticated stage. By 1600, it had had a complete mathematical formulation, based mostly on the notion of vanishing points and lines. A fascinating account of the invention, further production of theoretical texts, and the interaction between theory and practice can be found in the book by the art historian Kemp (Kemp, 1990), who focuses on the technical aspects of perspective. Another interesting history of the mathematical techniques and discoveries made by Renaissance painters is the book by Field (Field, 1997). A more cultural approach is found in the classic work of Panofsky (Panofsky, 1991), who shows that perspective is a spatial system which is compatible with the modes of knowledge, belief, and exchange that characterized the cultures in which it arises. Our own modernity, Panofsky shows, is inseparable from its mathematical expression of the concept of infinity within continuous and homogeneous space. A recent very penetrating discussion of the issues raised by this work is presented by Damisch (Damisch, 1994). The mathematical developments in our book can be seen as an attempt to push as far as possible the concept of linear perspective.

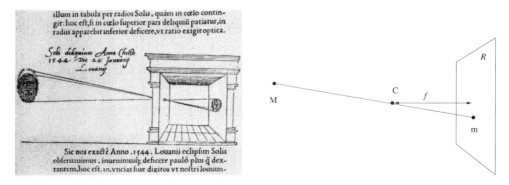

Figure 4.2: Pinhole cameras: an early picture of the camera obscura and its model.

During the XVI-th century, while the theory of perspective was being developed, *perspective machines* were introduced to help the painter accurately reproduce perspective without having to perform mathematical calculations. The perspective machines can be seen as the first instantiation of cameras, except that a human operator makes the final transcription. As it can be seen in the series of engraving by Dürer (Dürer, 1977) shown Figure 4.1, they all use a particular *image plane* $\mathcal{R}$ where the image forms, and a particular point C which does not belong to $\mathcal{R}$: The *optical center*. In those first perspective machines, the eye of the drawer is maintained fixed, and a device is used to materialize the intersection of a visual ray with the image plane. These machines served more as conceptual tools used to illustrate the geometry of central projection than as practical image-forming tools.

The first image-forming device was the *camera obscura* (literally, dark room) in which an operator sits inside a light-tight box of depth f whose front face is pierced by a pinhole C. Light rays enter the box at this point and form a perspective upside-down image on the rear face of the box, which can be observed directly. The image m of a point of the space M is the intersection of the *optical ray* (C, M) with the retinal plane. Although this phenomenon was known before, the first picture of a pinhole camera obscura could be a drawing in Gemma Frisius' *De Radio Astronomica et Geometrica* (1545), shown in Figure 4.2. Gemma Frisius, an astronomer, had used the pinhole in his darkened room to study the solar eclipse of 1544. The camera obscura underwent important developments in the XVIII-th century, and was used by painters (like Vermeer and other Dutch masters) as a portable device. When, at the beginning of the XIX-th century, Niepce and Daguerre put a photosensitive surface inside a camera obscura, the first photograph was created. By that time, the pinhole had been long replaced by a lens to increase light gathering power and sharpness. Modern cameras are nothing but enhanced versions of this design. Recently, pinhole photography has enjoyed a revival.

A simple model for the pinhole camera   The components of the transformation from the three-dimensional space to the two-dimensional plane performed by a pinhole camera can be described as

- a plane $\mathcal{R}$, called the *retinal plane* or *image plane*,

- a point C which does not belong to $\mathcal{R}$: The *optical center*, and

- the *focal length* f, the distance between the point C and the plane $\mathcal{R}$.

The image m of a point of the space M is the intersection of the *optical ray* (C, M) with the retinal plane. This is the *pinhole model*, named after the first image-forming devices. The components can be seen in the series of engraving by Dürer (Dürer, 1977) shown Figure 4.1.

The *optical axis* is the line going through C and perpendicular to the retinal plane. It pierces that plane at the *principal point* c. We consider a two-dimensional orthonormal system of coordinates which is in the retinal plane, centered at c and denoted $\mathcal{F}_c = (c, x_c, y_c)$, and we define a three-dimensional orthonormal system of coordinates which is called the *camera coordinate system* and is centered at the optical center C with two axes of coordinates parallel to the retinal ones and the third one parallel to the optical axis $\mathcal{F}_C = (C, X_C, Y_C, Z_C)$. In these two systems of coordinates, shown in Figure 4.3, the relationship between the coordinates of M and its image m is a simple consequence Thales' theorem:

$$x_c = f\frac{X_C}{Z_C}, \quad y_c = f\frac{Y_C}{Z_C}. \tag{4.1}$$

The choice of f corresponds just to a scaling in the image. If the unit in the camera coordinate system is chosen to be f, then the camera coordinate system is said to be *normalized*. By definition, in the normalized camera coordinate system the focal length is 1.

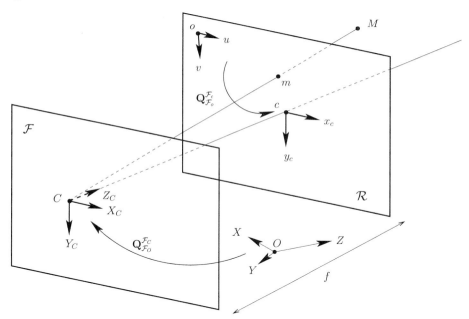

Figure 4.3: The general perspective or pinhole camera model.

The projection equations (4.1) are nonlinear but if we write them using the homogeneous coordinates of m and M, then they become linear:

$$\begin{bmatrix} Z_C x_c \\ Z_C y_c \\ Z_C \end{bmatrix} = \underbrace{\begin{bmatrix} f & 0 & 0 & 0 \\ 0 & f & 0 & 0 \\ 0 & 0 & 1 & 0 \end{bmatrix}}_{\mathcal{P}_C} \begin{bmatrix} X_C \\ Y_C \\ Z_C \\ 1 \end{bmatrix}. \tag{4.2}$$

In this equation $Z_C x_c$, $Z_C y_c$ and Z_C should be considered as the projective coordinates x, y, z of the pixel m and X_C, Y_C, Z_C, 1 as the projective coordinates $\mathcal{X}$, $\mathcal{Y}$, $\mathcal{Z}$, $\mathcal{T}$ of the point M. We verify with this equation that the projective coordinates are defined up to a scale factor since multiplying them by an arbitrary nonzero factor does not change the Euclidean coordinates of either m or M. The matrix $\boldsymbol{\mathcal{P}}_C$ is called the *perspective projection matrix*. It appears here in its simplest form, called *normalized*, since we have chosen a special coordinate system both for the world and for the image. The projection matrix was already present in the work of Roberts (Roberts, 1965) at MIT which is considered to be the first PhD thesis in computer vision.

The main property of this camera model is thus that *the relationship between the world coordinates and the pixel coordinates is linear projective*. This property is independent of the choice of the coordinate systems in the retinal plane or in the three-dimensional space. In particular we have indicated in Figure 4.3 another world coordinate system $\mathcal{F}_O = (O, X, Y, Z)$ and another retinal coordinate system $\mathcal{F}_o = (o, u, v)$. This property is the main reason for using the projective formalism to describe a camera. This camera model ignores nonlinear effects such as those caused by lens distortions, which are discussed in detail in Section 4.5.

4.1.2   The projection matrix

The general perspective projection matrix   Let us now consider two arbitrary systems of projective coordinates, one for the image and one for the object space. Using the terminology introduced in Chapter 2, we express the relationship between 2-D pixels and 3-D points as a morphism which maps points from $\mathbb{P}^3$ to $\mathbb{P}^2$. As was shown in the same chapter, this morphism can be described by a 3×4 matrix $\boldsymbol{\mathcal{P}}$, called the *perspective projection matrix* of the camera:

$$\mathbf{m} = \begin{bmatrix} x \\ y \\ z \end{bmatrix} \simeq \boldsymbol{\mathcal{P}} \begin{bmatrix} \mathcal{X} \\ \mathcal{Y} \\ \mathcal{Z} \\ \mathcal{T} \end{bmatrix} = \boldsymbol{\mathcal{P}}\mathbf{M}. \tag{4.3}$$

Since it has 3 rows, the projection matrix $\boldsymbol{\mathcal{P}}$ is of rank less than or equal to 3. If its rank were equal to 2, then the image of the world would be a projective line. If its rank were equal to 1, the image of the world would be a projective point. From this we conclude that for any reasonable camera, the rank of $\boldsymbol{\mathcal{P}}$ must be equal to 3. Its nullspace is therefore of dimension 1, corresponding to a unique point of $\mathbb{P}^3$, the optical center C, whose image is not defined since $\boldsymbol{\mathcal{P}}C = \mathbf{0}$ and $\mathbf{0}$ does not represent a projective point (remember Section 2.4.2 in Chapter 2). To summarize, we have proved the following proposition.

Proposition 4.1 *The* **perspective projection** *matrix of a camera is a 3×4 matrix of rank 3, defined up to a scale factor. The optical center is the unique* *projective point C satisfying*

$$\mathcal{P}\mathbf{C} = \mathbf{0}. \tag{4.4}$$

Geometric elements Let us first give a geometric interpretation of the rows of the projection matrix. We use the notation

$$\mathcal{P} = \begin{bmatrix} \boldsymbol{U}^T \\ \boldsymbol{V}^T \\ \boldsymbol{W}^T \end{bmatrix}, \tag{4.5}$$

where $\boldsymbol{U}^T$, $\boldsymbol{V}^T$, and $\boldsymbol{W}^T$ are the row vectors of $\mathcal{P}$. Each of the vectors $\boldsymbol{U}$, $\boldsymbol{V}$, $\boldsymbol{W}$ represents a plane in 3D, i.e. they are covectors, elements of $G_3(\mathbb{R}^4)$. These three planes are called the *projection planes* of the camera. The projection equation (4.3) can be rewritten as

$$x : y : z = \langle \boldsymbol{U}, \mathbf{M} \rangle : \langle \boldsymbol{V}, \mathbf{M} \rangle : \langle \boldsymbol{W}, \mathbf{M} \rangle,$$

where for example $\langle \boldsymbol{U}, \mathbf{M} \rangle$ is the cap-product of the plane represented by $\boldsymbol{U}$ with the point represented by $\mathbf{M}$ (see Equation 3.13 in Chapter 3). Alternatively, following the discussion in Section 3.4.5.1, it also represents the product with the column vector $\mathbf{M}$ of the row vector $\boldsymbol{U}^{*T}$ which has the same coordinates in the dual basis $(\varepsilon_1^*, \ldots, \varepsilon_4^*)$ as does $\boldsymbol{U}$ in the basis $(*\varepsilon_1, \ldots, *\varepsilon_4)$; see Proposition 3.30. The Hodge operator allows us to identify the vectors $\boldsymbol{U}$, $\boldsymbol{V}$, $\boldsymbol{W}$ with the vectors $\boldsymbol{U}^*$, $\boldsymbol{V}^*$, $\boldsymbol{W}^*$ whenever needed. This relation is equivalent to three scalar equations, two of which are independent:

$$\begin{array}{rcl} x\langle \boldsymbol{V}, \mathbf{M} \rangle - y\langle \boldsymbol{U}, \mathbf{M} \rangle &=& 0, \\ y\langle \boldsymbol{W}, \mathbf{M} \rangle - z\langle \boldsymbol{V}, \mathbf{M} \rangle &=& 0, \\ z\langle \boldsymbol{V}, \mathbf{M} \rangle - x\langle \boldsymbol{W}, \mathbf{M} \rangle &=& 0, \end{array} \tag{4.6}$$

where $\langle \boldsymbol{U}, \mathbf{M} \rangle = \boldsymbol{U}^T\mathbf{M}$, $\langle \boldsymbol{V}, \mathbf{M} \rangle = \boldsymbol{V}^T\mathbf{M}$, $\langle \boldsymbol{W}, \mathbf{M} \rangle = \boldsymbol{W}^T\mathbf{M}$.

The planes of equation $\langle \boldsymbol{U}, \mathbf{M} \rangle = 0$, $\langle \boldsymbol{V}, \mathbf{M} \rangle = 0$ and $\langle \boldsymbol{W}, \mathbf{M} \rangle = 0$ are mapped to the image lines of equations $x = 0$, $y = 0$, and $z = 0$, respectively. We have the proposition

Proposition 4.2 *The three* **projection planes** *of a perspective camera intersect the retinal plane along the three lines going through the first three points of the canonical projective basis.*

Proof : Indeed, the three lines of equations $x = 0$, $y = 0$, and $z = 0$ intersect at the three points ε_1, ε_2 and ε_3. □

If normalized coordinates are used in 2-D and in 3-D, then the projection planes of the camera are simply the three planes $X = 0$, $Y = 0$, and $Z = 0$, as illustrated in Figure 4.5.

The optical center is the unique point C which satisfies $\mathcal{P}\mathbf{C} = \mathbf{0}$. Therefore it is the intersection of the three planes represented by $\mathbf{U}, \mathbf{V}, \mathbf{W}$. In the Grassman-Cayley formalism, it is represented by the meet of those three planes $\mathbf{U} \vartriangle \mathbf{V} \vartriangle \mathbf{W}$ or, equivalently, by $*((*\mathbf{U})\triangledown(*\mathbf{V})\triangledown(*\mathbf{W}))$. This interpretation is illustrated in Figure 4.4 for a general projective camera frame and in Figure 4.5 for the camera coordinate system. Because of Equation 3.24, the projective coordinates of C are the four 3×3 cofactors of matrix $\mathcal{P}$:

Proposition 4.3 *The optical center C of the camera is the meet $\mathbf{U} \vartriangle \mathbf{V} \vartriangle \mathbf{W}$ of the three projection planes:*

$$\mathbf{C} \simeq \mathbf{U} \vartriangle \mathbf{V} \vartriangle \mathbf{W}.$$

Therefore, if we scale the perspective projection matrix $\mathcal{P}$ by λ, then the representation of C is scaled by λ^3.

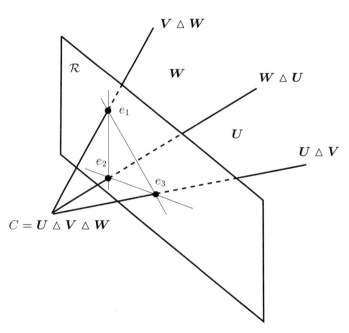

Figure 4.4: Geometrical interpretation of the three rows of the projection matrix as planes in the general case. The three projection planes $\mathbf{U}, \mathbf{V}$ and $\mathbf{W}$ are projected into the axes of the retinal coordinate system. The three projection rays intersect the retinal plane at the first three points of the retinal projective basis. The three projection planes meet at the optical center.

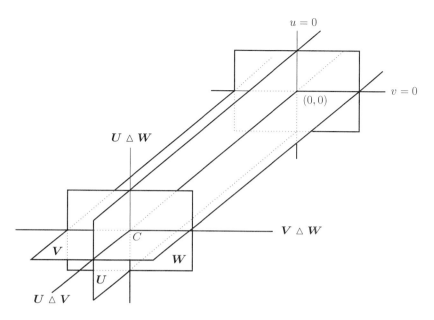

Figure 4.5: Geometrical interpretation of the three rows of the projection matrix as planes, pictured in the case of a normalized camera. The optical axis $\boldsymbol{U} \triangle \boldsymbol{V}$ is obtained as the intersection of the planes $\boldsymbol{U}$ and $\boldsymbol{V}$.

The three projection planes intersect along the three lines $\boldsymbol{U} \triangle \boldsymbol{V}$, $\boldsymbol{V} \triangle \boldsymbol{W}$ and $\boldsymbol{W} \triangle \boldsymbol{U}$ called the *projection rays*. These three lines meet at the optical center C and intersect the retinal plane at the first three points ε_1, ε_2 and ε_3 of the canonical projective basis. Given a pixel m, its optical ray (C, m) can be expressed very simply as a linear combination of the three projection rays:

Proposition 4.4 *The optical ray L_m of the pixel m of projective coordinates (x, y, z) is given by*

$$\mathbf{L}_m = x \boldsymbol{V} \triangle \boldsymbol{W} + y \boldsymbol{W} \triangle \boldsymbol{U} + z \boldsymbol{U} \triangle \boldsymbol{V}. \qquad (4.7)$$

Proof : Let us consider the plane $x\boldsymbol{V} - y\boldsymbol{U}$. This plane contains the optical center $\boldsymbol{U} \triangle \boldsymbol{V} \triangle \boldsymbol{W}$ since both $\boldsymbol{V}$ and $\boldsymbol{U}$ do. Moreover, it also contains the point M. To see this, let us take the cap-product (cap-products are defined in Section 3.4 of Chapter 3)

$$\langle x\boldsymbol{V} - y\boldsymbol{U}, \mathbf{M} \rangle = x \langle \boldsymbol{V}, \mathbf{M} \rangle - y \langle \boldsymbol{U}, \mathbf{M} \rangle,$$

but since $x : y = \langle \boldsymbol{U}, \mathbf{M} \rangle : \langle \boldsymbol{V}, \mathbf{M} \rangle$, this expression is equal to 0. Therefore, the plane $x\boldsymbol{V} - y\boldsymbol{U}$ contains the optical ray (C, m). Similarly, the planes $z\boldsymbol{U} - x\boldsymbol{W}$ and $y\boldsymbol{W} - z\boldsymbol{V}$ also contain the optical ray (C, m), which can therefore be found as the intersection of any of these two planes. Taking for instance the first two planes that we considered, we obtain

$$(x\boldsymbol{V} - y\boldsymbol{U}) \triangle (z\boldsymbol{U} - x\boldsymbol{W}) = -x(x\boldsymbol{V} \triangle \boldsymbol{W} + y\boldsymbol{W} \triangle \boldsymbol{U} + z\boldsymbol{U} \triangle \boldsymbol{V}).$$

The scale factor x is not significant, and if it is zero, another choice of two planes can be made for the calculation. We conclude that the optical ray $L_m = (C, m)$ is represented by the line $x\boldsymbol{V} \triangle \boldsymbol{W} + y\boldsymbol{W} \triangle \boldsymbol{U} + z\boldsymbol{U} \triangle \boldsymbol{V}$ (see Section 4.1.5 for another interesting interpretation of this formula). $\quad\square$

This construction is illustrated in Figure 4.6 for a normalized camera. Compare this figure with Figure 4.5.

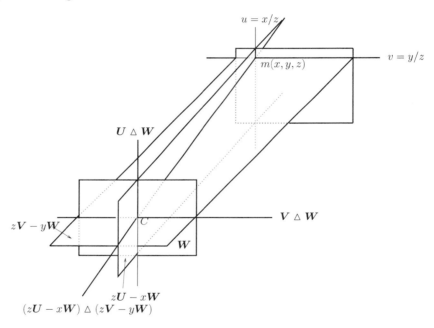

Figure 4.6: The optical ray (C, m) is obtained as the intersection of the two planes $(z\boldsymbol{U} - x\boldsymbol{W})$ and $(z\boldsymbol{V} - y\boldsymbol{W})$. Each of them is a plane of a pencil defined by the optical ray containing the point m.

We also have an interesting interpretation of the matrix $\boldsymbol{\mathcal{P}}^T$ which we give in the following proposition.

Proposition 4.5 *The transpose $\boldsymbol{\mathcal{P}}^T$ of the perspective projection matrix defines a mapping from the set of lines of the retinal plane to the set of planes going through* *the optical center. This mapping associates with the line l represented by the vector* $\mathbf{l} = [u, v, w]^T$ *the plane* $\boldsymbol{\mathcal{P}}^T \mathbf{l} = u\boldsymbol{U} + v\boldsymbol{V} + w\boldsymbol{W}$.

Proof : The fact that $\boldsymbol{\mathcal{P}}^T$ maps planar lines to planes is a consequence of duality and Proposition 3.24. The plane $u\boldsymbol{U} + v\boldsymbol{V} + w\boldsymbol{W}$ contains the optical center since each projection plane contains it. Why does it contain the line l? Take a point m on the line l. It is represented by $\mathbf{m} = [x, y, z]^T$ such that $\mathbf{m}^T \mathbf{l} = 0$. According to Proposition 4.4, the optical ray L_m of m is represented by $\mathbf{L}_m = x\boldsymbol{V} \vartriangle \boldsymbol{W} + y\boldsymbol{W} \vartriangle \boldsymbol{U} + z\boldsymbol{U} \vartriangle \boldsymbol{V}$. The meet $\mathbf{L}_m \vartriangle \boldsymbol{\mathcal{P}}^T \mathbf{l}$ is shown to be equal to $(ux + vy + wz)\boldsymbol{U} \vartriangle \boldsymbol{V} \vartriangle \boldsymbol{W}$, i.e. to $(\mathbf{m}^T\mathbf{l})\boldsymbol{U} \vartriangle \boldsymbol{V} \vartriangle \boldsymbol{W}$. It is therefore equal to 0 for all points m of the line l which therefore belongs to the plane $\boldsymbol{\mathcal{P}}^T \mathbf{l}$. □

4.1.3   The inverse projection matrix

In this section we investigate the relationships between the perspective projection performed by a pinhole camera and the set of 3D planes of $\mathbb{P}^3$. We begin with a definition:

Definition 4.1 *Given a projection matrix* $\boldsymbol{\mathcal{P}}$, *we call the* **inverse projection matrix** *of* $\boldsymbol{\mathcal{P}}$ *any* 4×3 *matrix* $\boldsymbol{\mathcal{P}}^+$ *such that*

$$\boldsymbol{\mathcal{P}}\boldsymbol{\mathcal{P}}^+ \simeq \mathbf{I}_3. \tag{4.8}$$

Note that since the rank of $\boldsymbol{\mathcal{P}}$ is 3, so is the rank of any matrix $\boldsymbol{\mathcal{P}}^+$ satisfying (4.8).

We are going to show that there is a natural one-to-one relationship between the planes of $\mathbb{P}^3$ not going through the optical center C of the camera and the matrices $\boldsymbol{\mathcal{P}}^+$:

Proposition 4.6 *There is a one-to-one correspondence between the planes of* $\mathbb{P}^3$ *not going through the optical center* C *of the camera and the set of inverse projection matrices given by*

$$\Pi \to \boldsymbol{\mathcal{P}}_\Pi^+ = [\boldsymbol{V} \vartriangle \boldsymbol{W} \vartriangle \boldsymbol{\Pi} \quad \boldsymbol{W} \vartriangle \boldsymbol{U} \vartriangle \boldsymbol{\Pi} \quad \boldsymbol{U} \vartriangle \boldsymbol{V} \vartriangle \boldsymbol{\Pi}]. \tag{4.9}$$

Therefore, if we scale the perspective projection matrix $\boldsymbol{\mathcal{P}}$ *by* λ, *and the representation of the plane* Π *by* μ, *then the inverse perspective projection matrix* $\boldsymbol{\mathcal{P}}_\Pi^+$ *is scaled by* $\lambda^2 \mu$.

Proof : Let $\boldsymbol{\mathcal{P}}^+$ be a matrix satisfying (4.8). Let us write $\boldsymbol{\mathcal{P}}^+ = [\mathbf{Q}_1 \, \mathbf{Q}_2 \, \mathbf{Q}_3]$ where $\mathbf{Q}_i$, $i = 1, 2, 3$, is a vector of $\mathbb{R}^4$ or $G_1(\mathbb{R}^4)$ representing a point of $\mathbb{P}^3$. The join $\mathbf{Q}_1 \triangledown \mathbf{Q}_2 \triangledown \mathbf{Q}_3$ of these three points is a nonzero element of $G_3(\mathbb{R}^4)$ representing a plane Π since the rank of $\boldsymbol{\mathcal{P}}^+$ is 3. This plane contains the three points Q_1, Q_2, Q_3. Because of the definition (4.8), the points Q_1, Q_2, Q_3 satisfy

$$\begin{aligned} \langle \boldsymbol{V}, \mathbf{Q}_1 \rangle &= \langle \boldsymbol{W}, \mathbf{Q}_1 \rangle &= 0, \\ \langle \boldsymbol{W}, \mathbf{Q}_2 \rangle &= \langle \boldsymbol{U}, \mathbf{Q}_2 \rangle &= 0, \\ \langle \boldsymbol{U}, \mathbf{Q}_3 \rangle &= \langle \boldsymbol{V}, \mathbf{Q}_3 \rangle &= 0, \\ \langle \boldsymbol{U}, \mathbf{Q}_1 \rangle &= \langle \boldsymbol{V}, \mathbf{Q}_2 \rangle &= \langle \boldsymbol{W}, \mathbf{Q}_3 \rangle. \end{aligned} \tag{4.10}$$

The first three lines indicate that Q_1 belongs to the line of intersection $\boldsymbol{V} \vartriangle \boldsymbol{W}$ of the two planes $\boldsymbol{V}$ and $\boldsymbol{W}$, Q_2 belongs to the line $\boldsymbol{W} \vartriangle \boldsymbol{U}$ and Q_3 belongs to $\boldsymbol{U} \vartriangle \boldsymbol{V}$. This scenario is equivalent to the existence of three nonzero scalars $\lambda_i, i = 1, 2, 3$, such that

$$\mathbf{Q}_1 = \lambda_1 \boldsymbol{V} \vartriangle \boldsymbol{W} \vartriangle \boldsymbol{\Pi} \quad \mathbf{Q}_2 = \lambda_2 \boldsymbol{W} \vartriangle \boldsymbol{U} \vartriangle \boldsymbol{\Pi} \quad \mathbf{Q}_3 = \lambda_3 \boldsymbol{U} \vartriangle \boldsymbol{V} \vartriangle \boldsymbol{\Pi}.$$

The fourth line of the previous relation shows that $\lambda_1 = \lambda_2 = \lambda_3$ since $\langle \boldsymbol{U}, \mathbf{Q}_1 \rangle = \lambda_1 \mid \boldsymbol{U}, \boldsymbol{V}, \boldsymbol{W}, \boldsymbol{\Pi} \mid$, $\langle \boldsymbol{V}, \mathbf{Q}_2 \rangle = \lambda_2 \mid \boldsymbol{U}, \boldsymbol{V}, \boldsymbol{W}, \boldsymbol{\Pi} \mid$, and $\langle \boldsymbol{W}, \mathbf{Q}_3 \rangle = \lambda_3 \mid \boldsymbol{U}, \boldsymbol{V}, \boldsymbol{W}, \boldsymbol{\Pi} \mid$. Hence we have

$$\boldsymbol{\mathcal{P}}^+ \simeq [\boldsymbol{V} \vartriangle \boldsymbol{W} \vartriangle \boldsymbol{\Pi} \quad \boldsymbol{W} \vartriangle \boldsymbol{U} \vartriangle \boldsymbol{\Pi} \quad \boldsymbol{U} \vartriangle \boldsymbol{V} \vartriangle \boldsymbol{\Pi}].$$

Inversely, any matrix $\boldsymbol{\mathcal{P}}_\Pi^+$ of the form (4.9) such that $\boldsymbol{\Pi}$ does not go through C is of rank 3 and clearly satisfies the equations (4.10). $\square$

Note that if we take $\boldsymbol{\mathcal{P}}_\Pi^+$ equal to (4.9) and $\mathbf{C} = \boldsymbol{U} \vartriangle \boldsymbol{V} \vartriangle \boldsymbol{W}$, then the scale factor in Equation 4.8 is exactly $-\langle \boldsymbol{\Pi}, \mathbf{C} \rangle$, i.e.

$$\boldsymbol{\mathcal{P}} \boldsymbol{\mathcal{P}}_\Pi^+ = -\langle \boldsymbol{\Pi}, \mathbf{C} \rangle \mathbf{I}_3. \tag{4.11}$$

Indeed, let us compute for example the elements $(1, 1)$ and $(1, 2)$ of this matrix. The element $(1, 1)$ is equal to $\langle \boldsymbol{U}, \boldsymbol{V} \vartriangle \boldsymbol{W} \vartriangle \boldsymbol{\Pi} \rangle$ which, by definition of the cap-product, is equal to $\boldsymbol{V} \vartriangle \boldsymbol{W} \vartriangle \boldsymbol{\Pi} \vartriangle \boldsymbol{U}$ which, by Proposition 3.14, is equal to the determinant $\mid \boldsymbol{V}, \boldsymbol{W}, \boldsymbol{\Pi}, \boldsymbol{U} \mid$ which is equal to $- \mid \boldsymbol{U}, \boldsymbol{V}, \boldsymbol{W}, \boldsymbol{\Pi} \mid$ which is equal to $-\langle \boldsymbol{\Pi}, \boldsymbol{U} \vartriangle \boldsymbol{V} \vartriangle \boldsymbol{W} \rangle$ which is equal to $-\langle \boldsymbol{\Pi}, \mathbf{C} \rangle$. Similarly the element $(1, 2)$ is equal to $\langle \boldsymbol{U}, \boldsymbol{W} \vartriangle \boldsymbol{U} \vartriangle \boldsymbol{\Pi} \rangle = \mid \boldsymbol{U}, \boldsymbol{W}, \boldsymbol{U}, \boldsymbol{\Pi} \mid = 0$.

Equation 4.8 which $\boldsymbol{\mathcal{P}}_\Pi^+$ satisfies allows us to interpret $\boldsymbol{\mathcal{P}}_\Pi^+$ as representing a morphism from $\mathbb{P}^2$ to $\mathbb{P}^3$ with the interesting following property

Proposition 4.7 *Given an image point* $\mathbf{m}$, *the point* $\boldsymbol{\mathcal{P}}_\Pi^+ \mathbf{m}$ *of* $\mathbb{P}^3$ *is the intersection of the optical ray* L_m *of* $\mathbf{m}$ *with the plane* Π.

Proof : The point M represented by $\boldsymbol{\mathcal{P}}_\Pi^+ \mathbf{m}$ is on L_m since $\boldsymbol{\mathcal{P}} \boldsymbol{\mathcal{P}}_\Pi^+ \mathbf{m} \simeq \mathbf{m}$. It is also in Π since $\langle \boldsymbol{\Pi}, \boldsymbol{\mathcal{P}}_\Pi^+ \mathbf{m} \rangle \simeq x \langle \boldsymbol{\Pi}, \boldsymbol{V} \vartriangle \boldsymbol{W} \vartriangle \boldsymbol{\Pi} \rangle + y \langle \boldsymbol{\Pi}, \boldsymbol{W} \vartriangle \boldsymbol{U} \vartriangle \boldsymbol{\Pi} \rangle + \langle \boldsymbol{\Pi}, \boldsymbol{U} \vartriangle \boldsymbol{V} \vartriangle \boldsymbol{\Pi} \rangle = 0$ $\square$

This proposition is illustrated in Figure 4.7.

Let us now compute a matrix $\boldsymbol{\mathcal{P}}_\Pi^+$ in a special case. We assume that the perspective projection matrix is

$$\boldsymbol{\mathcal{P}}_0 = \begin{bmatrix} 1 & 0 & 0 & 0 \\ 0 & 1 & 0 & 0 \\ 0 & 0 & 1 & 0 \end{bmatrix},$$

and that a representation of the plane Π is the vector $[a, b, c, d]^T$. This statement means that the vector $[a, b, c, d]^T$ is a coordinate vector of Π in the basis

$(*\varepsilon_1, *\varepsilon_2, *\varepsilon_3, *\varepsilon_4)$. Similarly, the row vectors of $\boldsymbol{\mathcal{P}}_0$ are representations of $\boldsymbol{U}, \boldsymbol{V}, \boldsymbol{W}$ in the same basis:

$$
\begin{array}{rcl}
\boldsymbol{U} & = & [1, 0, 0, 0]^T, \\
\boldsymbol{V} & = & [0, 1, 0, 0]^T, \\
\boldsymbol{W} & = & [0, 0, 1, 0]^T.
\end{array}
$$

In order to compute $\boldsymbol{\mathcal{P}}_{0\Pi}^+$ we need to compute the coordinates of the vectors $\boldsymbol{V} \triangle \boldsymbol{W} \triangle \boldsymbol{\Pi}$, $\boldsymbol{W} \triangle \boldsymbol{U} \triangle \boldsymbol{\Pi}$, $\boldsymbol{U} \triangle \boldsymbol{V} \triangle \boldsymbol{\Pi}$. To do this, we use Equation 3.24. Let us do it in detail for the first one. We form the 4×3 matrix of the three column vectors $\boldsymbol{V}, \boldsymbol{W}$ and $\boldsymbol{\Pi}$:

$$
\begin{bmatrix}
0 & 0 & a \\
1 & 0 & b \\
0 & 1 & c \\
0 & 0 & d
\end{bmatrix},
$$

and compute its cofactors, thereby obtaining the vector $[-d, 0, 0, a]^T$ expressed in the canonical basis $(\varepsilon_1, \varepsilon_2, \varepsilon_3, \varepsilon_4)$. Similarly we find that $\boldsymbol{W} \triangle \boldsymbol{U} \triangle \boldsymbol{\Pi} = [0, -d, 0, b]^T$ and $\boldsymbol{U} \triangle \boldsymbol{V} \triangle \boldsymbol{\Pi} = [0, 0, -d, c]^T$. We have therefore the sought for expression of matrix $\boldsymbol{\mathcal{P}}_{0\Pi}^+$:

$$
\begin{bmatrix}
-d & 0 & 0 \\
0 & -d & 0 \\
0 & 0 & -d \\
a & b & c
\end{bmatrix}. \tag{4.12}
$$

Let m be a pixel of projective coordinates (x, y, z). The projective coordinates of $\boldsymbol{\mathcal{P}}_{0\Pi}^+ \mathbf{m}$ are $(\mathcal{X} = -dx, \mathcal{Y} = -dy, \mathcal{Z} = -dz, \mathcal{T} = ax + by + cz)$ and verify $a\mathcal{X} + b\mathcal{Y} + c\mathcal{Z} + d\mathcal{T} = 0$ which shows that the point represented by $\boldsymbol{\mathcal{P}}_{0\Pi}^+ \mathbf{m}$ belongs to the plane Π, as expected.

The matrix $\boldsymbol{\mathcal{P}}_{\Pi}^+$ satisfies two more interesting properties:

Proposition 4.8

$$
\boldsymbol{\Pi}^T \boldsymbol{\mathcal{P}}_{\Pi}^+ = 0, \tag{4.13}
$$

$$
\langle \boldsymbol{\Pi}, \mathbf{C} \rangle \mathbf{I}_4 + \boldsymbol{\mathcal{P}}_{\Pi}^+ \boldsymbol{\mathcal{P}} = \mathbf{C} \boldsymbol{\Pi}^T, \tag{4.14}
$$

where we have identified, as explained in Section 3.4.5.1, $\boldsymbol{\Pi}$, an element of $G_3(\mathbb{R}^4)$, a covector, with $*\boldsymbol{\Pi}$, an element of $G_1(\mathbb{R}^4)$.

Proof : The first relation follows from the fact that $\boldsymbol{\Pi}^T(\boldsymbol{V} \triangle \boldsymbol{W} \triangle \boldsymbol{\Pi}) = \langle \boldsymbol{\Pi}, \boldsymbol{V} \triangle \boldsymbol{W} \triangle \boldsymbol{\Pi} \rangle$ because of Proposition 3.30. We then use the definition (3.13) of the cap-product and write it as $\boldsymbol{\Pi} \triangle \boldsymbol{V} \triangle \boldsymbol{W} \triangle \boldsymbol{\Pi} = | \boldsymbol{\Pi}, \boldsymbol{V}, \boldsymbol{W}, \boldsymbol{\Pi} |$ which is equal to 0 because of the properties of determinants. We obtain two other similar equations using the same reasoning. For the second relation, we proceed as follows. From the definition (4.8) of $\boldsymbol{\mathcal{P}}_{\Pi}^+$ and Equation 4.11 we deduce immediately that

$$
\boldsymbol{\mathcal{P}}(\langle \boldsymbol{\Pi}, \mathbf{C} \rangle \mathbf{I}_4 + \boldsymbol{\mathcal{P}}_{\Pi}^+ \boldsymbol{\mathcal{P}}) = \mathbf{0}
$$

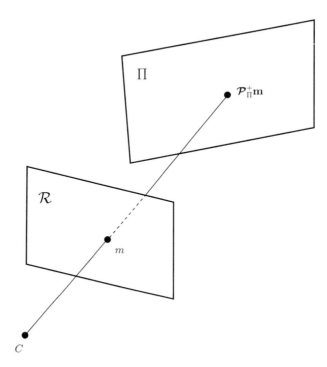

Figure 4.7: Inverse projection. $\boldsymbol{\mathcal{P}}_\Pi^+\mathbf{m}$ is the intersection of the optical ray of $\mathbf{m}$ and the plane Π.

and

$$((\langle\boldsymbol{\Pi},\mathbf{C}\rangle\mathbf{I}_4 + \boldsymbol{\mathcal{P}}_\Pi^+\boldsymbol{\mathcal{P}})\boldsymbol{\mathcal{P}}_\Pi^+ = \mathbf{0}.$$

The first equation shows that the rank of $\langle\boldsymbol{\Pi},\mathbf{C}\rangle\mathbf{I}_4 + \boldsymbol{\mathcal{P}}_\Pi^+\boldsymbol{\mathcal{P}}$ is 1 and, since $\boldsymbol{\mathcal{P}}\mathbf{C} = \mathbf{0}$, that

$$\langle\boldsymbol{\Pi},\mathbf{C}\rangle\mathbf{I}_4 + \boldsymbol{\mathcal{P}}_\Pi^+\boldsymbol{\mathcal{P}} \simeq \mathbf{C}\mathbf{X}^T,$$

where $\mathbf{X}$ is any vector. The second equation, together with (4.13) shows that

$$((\langle\boldsymbol{\Pi},\mathbf{C}\rangle\mathbf{I}_4 + \boldsymbol{\mathcal{P}}_\Pi^+\boldsymbol{\mathcal{P}}) \simeq \mathbf{Y}\boldsymbol{\Pi}^T,$$

where $\mathbf{Y}$ is any vector. Combining the two results we find that

$$\langle\boldsymbol{\Pi},\mathbf{C}\rangle\mathbf{I}_4 + \boldsymbol{\mathcal{P}}_\Pi^+\boldsymbol{\mathcal{P}} = \lambda\mathbf{C}\boldsymbol{\Pi}^T.$$

Multiplying both sides of this equation on the left by $\boldsymbol{\Pi}^T$ shows that $\lambda = 1$, since $\boldsymbol{\Pi}^T\mathbf{C} = \langle\boldsymbol{\Pi},\mathbf{C}\rangle$ and $\boldsymbol{\Pi}^T\boldsymbol{\mathcal{P}}_\Pi^+ = \mathbf{0}$. □

Note that Equation 4.14 is compatible with the scaling properties of $\mathbf{C}$ and $\boldsymbol{\mathcal{P}}_{\Pi}^{+}$ given in Propositions 4.3 and 4.6. There is also an interesting interpretation of matrix $\boldsymbol{\mathcal{P}}_{\Pi}^{+T}$ which we give in the following proposition (see Figure 4.8)

Proposition 4.9 *The transpose $\boldsymbol{\mathcal{P}}_{\Pi}^{+T}$ of the inverse perspective projection matrix associated with the plane Π defines a mapping from the set of planes to the set of image lines in the retinal plane. This mapping associates with the plane Π' (different from Π) represented by the vector $\boldsymbol{\Pi}'$ the line $\boldsymbol{\mathcal{P}}_{\Pi}^{+T}\boldsymbol{\Pi}'$, the image of the line of intersection of the planes Π and Π'.*

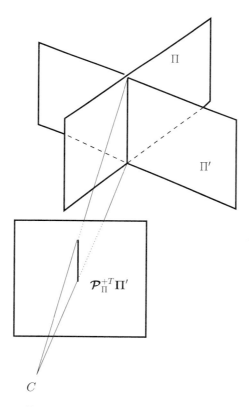

Figure 4.8: The line $\boldsymbol{\mathcal{P}}_{\Pi}^{+T}\boldsymbol{\Pi}'$ is the image of the line of intersection of the planes Π and Π'.

Proof : The fact that $\boldsymbol{\mathcal{P}}_{\Pi}^{+T}$ maps planes to lines is a consequence of duality and of Proposition 3.24. Let us take the transpose of Equation 4.14:

$$\langle \boldsymbol{\Pi}, \mathbf{C} \rangle \mathbf{I}_4 + \boldsymbol{\mathcal{P}}^T \boldsymbol{\mathcal{P}}_{\Pi}^{+T}. = \boldsymbol{\Pi}\mathbf{C}^T$$

Multiplying both sides on the right with $\mathbf{\Pi}'$ gives

$$\langle \mathbf{\Pi}, \mathbf{C} \rangle \mathbf{\Pi}' + \boldsymbol{\mathcal{P}}^T (\boldsymbol{\mathcal{P}}_{\Pi}^{+T} \mathbf{\Pi}') = \mathbf{\Pi} (\mathbf{C}^T \mathbf{\Pi}').$$

Because $\mathbf{C}^T \mathbf{\Pi}' = \langle \mathbf{\Pi}', \mathbf{C}^T \rangle$, we obtain

$$\boldsymbol{\mathcal{P}}^T (\boldsymbol{\mathcal{P}}_{\Pi}^{+T} \mathbf{\Pi}') = \langle \mathbf{\Pi}', \mathbf{C} \rangle \mathbf{\Pi} - \langle \mathbf{\Pi}, \mathbf{C} \rangle \mathbf{\Pi}'.$$

Let us interpret the right-hand side of this equation: it defines a plane which is a linear combination of the two planes Π and Π', therefore which goes through their line of intersection. Furthermore, because of the weighting factors $\langle \mathbf{\Pi}', \mathbf{C} \rangle$ for $\mathbf{\Pi}$ and $-\langle \mathbf{\Pi}, \mathbf{C} \rangle$ for $\mathbf{\Pi}'$, it is easy to verify that this plane contains the point C. Looking now at the left-hand side, we see that this plane is the image by $\boldsymbol{\mathcal{P}}^T$ of the line represented by $\boldsymbol{\mathcal{P}}_{\Pi}^{+T} \mathbf{\Pi}'$. Therefore this line is indeed the image of the line of intersection of Π and Π'. $\square$

Summary   Here are the properties of the different matrices that we derived from the projection $\boldsymbol{\mathcal{P}}$:

- $\boldsymbol{\mathcal{P}}$ maps a point M of $\mathbb{P}^3$ ($\neq C$) to a point m of $\mathbb{P}^2$

- $\boldsymbol{\mathcal{P}}^T$ maps a line l of $\mathbb{P}^2$ to a plane Π' of $\mathbb{P}^3$ containing C

- $\boldsymbol{\mathcal{P}}_{\Pi}^{+T}$ maps a plane Π' of $\mathbb{P}^3$ ($\neq \Pi$) to a line l of $\mathbb{P}^2$

- $\boldsymbol{\mathcal{P}}_{\Pi}^{+}$ maps a point m of $\mathbb{P}^2$ to a point M of $\mathbb{P}^3$ contained in Π

At this point, the reader might suspect that quantities that we have examined so far are in the following duality.

$$
\begin{array}{cc}
\boldsymbol{\mathcal{P}} & \boldsymbol{\mathcal{P}}_{\Pi}^{+T} \\
\boldsymbol{\mathcal{P}}^T & \boldsymbol{\mathcal{P}}_{\Pi}^{+} \\
C & \Pi \\
M & \Pi' \\
m & l
\end{array}
$$

This is indeed correct and illustrates even more the richness of the projective model, but in order not to appear as if we were elaborating *ad infinitum* on the different ways to view a projection matrix, we will leave it to the reader.

A particular inverse projection matrix is obtained with $\mathbf{\Pi} = *\mathbf{C}$. This plane is always a valid choice: it clearly never contains C since $\langle *\mathbf{C}, \mathbf{C} \rangle \neq 0$. The particular resulting inverse projection matrix is the *pseudo-inverse* $\boldsymbol{\mathcal{P}}^+ = \boldsymbol{\mathcal{P}}^T (\boldsymbol{\mathcal{P}} \boldsymbol{\mathcal{P}}^T)^{-1}$.

4.1.4   Viewing a plane in space: The single view homography

Equivalent projection matrices for a planar surface   In general, given a
sufficient numbers of 3-D points and their 2-D projections, the projection matrix
$\mathcal{P}$ is uniquely determined, as discussed in Section 4.6. However, if all of the 3-D
points M_i lie in a plane Π, then there is a family of projection matrices $\mathcal{P}_{c,\Pi}$ which
are equivalent to $\mathcal{P}$ in the sense that all the projections $\mathcal{P}M_i$ and $\mathcal{P}_{c,\Pi}M_i$ are
identical. This is summarized in the following proposition.

Proposition 4.10 *The perspective projection matrices*

$$\mathcal{P}_{c,\Pi} = \begin{bmatrix} (\boldsymbol{U} - c_1\boldsymbol{\Pi})^T \\ (\boldsymbol{V} - c_2\boldsymbol{\Pi})^T \\ (\boldsymbol{W} - c_3\boldsymbol{\Pi})^T \end{bmatrix},$$

where $\boldsymbol{U}^T, \boldsymbol{V}^T, \boldsymbol{W}^T$ are the rows of $\mathcal{P}$, $\boldsymbol{\Pi}$ represents a 3D plane Π, and $\mathbf{c} = [c_1, c_2, c_3]^T$ represents an arbitrary point of the retinal plane, are such that $\mathcal{P}M \simeq \mathcal{P}_{c,\Pi}M$ if and only if M belongs to Π, except for the optical ray L_c of c.

Proof :   If M is in Π then clearly $\mathcal{P}_{c,\Pi}M = \mathcal{P}M - \langle \boldsymbol{\Pi}, \mathbf{M} \rangle \mathbf{c} = \mathcal{P}M$. Conversely,
if $\mathcal{P}M \simeq \mathcal{P}_{c,\Pi}M$ then

$$\mathcal{P}M - \langle \boldsymbol{\Pi}, \mathbf{M} \rangle \mathbf{c} = \alpha \mathcal{P}M$$

for some value of α. There are two cases to distinguish. The first case is when the
two points represented by $\mathcal{P}M$ and $\mathbf{c}$ are distinct. The previous equation implies
that $\langle \boldsymbol{\Pi}, \mathbf{M} \rangle = 0$ and $\alpha = 1$, i.e. that M belongs to the plane Π. The second
case is when the two points are identical, i.e. when M is on the optical ray of the
point defined by $\mathbf{c}$. In that case, the condition $\langle \boldsymbol{\Pi}, \mathbf{M} \rangle = 0$ does not necessarily
hold. Except for this special case we can say that the condition $\mathcal{P}M \simeq \mathcal{P}_{c,\Pi}M$ is
equivalent to the fact that the point M is in the plane Π. $\square$

There are two particular cases where the equivalent matrix $\mathcal{P}_{c,\Pi}$ takes a simple
form. The second case is best discussed in the affine framework; see Section 4.4.2.
The other case is when the plane Π is one of the planes defined by the canonical
basis, for example $\boldsymbol{\Pi} = [0, 0, 1, 0]^T$. If we take $\mathbf{c} = [\mathcal{P}_{13}, \mathcal{P}_{23}, \mathcal{P}_{33}]^T$ (i.e. the third
column of $\mathcal{P}$), then

$$\mathcal{P}_{c,\Pi} = \begin{bmatrix} \mathcal{P}_{11} & \mathcal{P}_{12} & 0 & \mathcal{P}_{14} \\ \mathcal{P}_{21} & \mathcal{P}_{22} & 0 & \mathcal{P}_{24} \\ \mathcal{P}_{31} & \mathcal{P}_{32} & 0 & \mathcal{P}_{34} \end{bmatrix}.$$

The projection can be viewed as a transformation between two spaces $\mathbb{P}^2$ since

$$\mathbf{m} \simeq \mathcal{P}_{c,\Pi}M = \begin{bmatrix} \mathcal{P}_{11} & \mathcal{P}_{12} & \mathcal{P}_{14} \\ \mathcal{P}_{21} & \mathcal{P}_{22} & \mathcal{P}_{24} \\ \mathcal{P}_{31} & \mathcal{P}_{32} & \mathcal{P}_{34} \end{bmatrix} \begin{bmatrix} \mathcal{X} \\ \mathcal{Y} \\ \mathcal{T} \end{bmatrix}.$$

This transformation is discussed next.

The homography between the retinal plane and a plane in space

Using the previous observation, the projection of points which lie in a plane Π not going through C can be seen as the composition of two operations. First, a mapping from a projective coordinate system of Π represented as a $\mathbb{P}^2$ to the projective basis of $\mathbb{P}^3$ in which the projection matrix $\mathcal{P}$ is expressed. This is followed by the projection $\mathcal{P}$. The first mapping can be expressed as a general mapping from $\mathbb{P}^2$ to $\mathbb{P}^3$ whose range is Π; therefore, it can be written as a $\mathcal{P}'^{+}_{\Pi}$, where $\mathcal{P}'$ is a projection matrix (the corresponding optical center C' should not be in Π). The relationship between the points p of Π (expressed in some projective basis of Π) and the points m of $\mathcal{R}$ is therefore, in the most general case

$$\mathbf{m} \simeq \mathbf{H}\mathbf{p} \quad \text{where} \quad \mathbf{H} = \mathcal{P}\mathcal{P}'^{+}_{\Pi}.$$

The rank of $\mathbf{H}$ is seen to be three since Π does not contain C or C'. The inverse relationship can be written as

$$\mathbf{p} \simeq \mathbf{H}^{-1}\mathbf{m} \quad \text{where} \quad \mathbf{H}^{-1} = \mathcal{P}'\mathcal{P}^{+}_{\Pi}.$$

Indeed we have $\mathbf{H}\mathbf{H}^{-1} = \mathcal{P}\mathcal{P}'^{+}_{\Pi}\mathcal{P}'\mathcal{P}^{+}_{\Pi}$. Because of (4.14), we have

$$\mathcal{P}'^{+}_{\Pi}\mathcal{P}' = \mathbf{C}'\mathbf{\Pi}^{T} - \langle \mathbf{\Pi}, \mathbf{C}' \rangle \mathbf{I}_4,$$

and therefore

$$\mathcal{P}\mathcal{P}'^{+}_{\Pi}\mathcal{P}'\mathcal{P}^{+}_{\Pi} = \mathcal{P}\mathbf{C}'\mathbf{\Pi}^{T}\mathcal{P}^{+}_{\Pi} - \langle \mathbf{\Pi}, \mathbf{C}' \rangle \mathcal{P}\mathcal{P}^{+}_{\Pi}.$$

Because of (4.13) $\mathbf{\Pi}^{T}\mathcal{P}^{+}_{\Pi} = \mathbf{0}$, and using (4.11) we find the right-hand side to be equal to the product $\langle \mathbf{\Pi}, \mathbf{C} \rangle \langle \mathbf{\Pi}, \mathbf{C}' \rangle \mathbf{I}_3$, hence $\mathbf{H}\mathbf{H}^{-1} \simeq \mathbf{I}_3$.

This expression makes clear the difference between the inverse projection $\mathcal{P}^{+}_{\Pi}$ and the homography $\mathbf{H}^{-1}$: both map a point of the retina to a point of the plane Π, but in the first case, this point is expressed in the projective basis of $\mathbb{P}^3$ used to express $\mathcal{P}$, whereas in the second case, this point is expressed in a projective basis attached to Π, a $\mathbb{P}^2$. The most general form of $\mathcal{P}'$ is actually useful only to account for the case of two views, and will be developed in Section 5.1.1. In the case of a single view, which is addressed here, the matrix $\mathcal{P}'$ can be taken to be of a simple particular form.

If the world coordinate system is chosen such that the plane Π is represented by $\mathbf{\Pi}_{\mathcal{Z}} = [0, 0, 1, 0]^{T}$ (or $\mathcal{Z} = 0$), then a natural mapping from coordinates in $\mathbb{P}^3$ to coordinates in $\mathbb{P}^2$ for points of Π is the orthographic projection

$$\begin{bmatrix} \mathcal{X} \\ \mathcal{Y} \\ \mathcal{T} \end{bmatrix} \simeq \underbrace{\begin{bmatrix} 1 & 0 & 0 & 0 \\ 0 & 1 & 0 & 0 \\ 0 & 0 & 0 & 1 \end{bmatrix}}_{\mathcal{P}_o} \begin{bmatrix} \mathcal{X} \\ \mathcal{Y} \\ \mathcal{Z} \\ \mathcal{T} \end{bmatrix}. \tag{4.15}$$

It is found that

$$\mathbf{H} = \mathcal{P}\mathcal{P}^{+}_{o\Pi_{\mathscr{Z}}} = \left[\begin{array}{ccc} \mathcal{P}_{11} & \mathcal{P}_{12} & \mathcal{P}_{14} \\ \mathcal{P}_{21} & \mathcal{P}_{22} & \mathcal{P}_{24} \\ \mathcal{P}_{31} & \mathcal{P}_{32} & \mathcal{P}_{34} \end{array} \right],$$

which is the expression which has been previously found. In the general case, a displacement is applied to the world coordinate system so that Π has equation $\mathbf{\Pi}_Z$ and the matrix $\mathcal{P}'$ has the form $\mathcal{P}_o[\mathbf{R}\ \mathbf{t}]$, where $\mathbf{R}$ is an orthogonal matrix.

The homography discussed in this section (as well as the inverse projection matrix, which is another avatar of the same transformation) has several important practical applications. The first comes from the fact that when the 3D points lie in a plane, it is possible to determine their 3D positions from a *single* image. This fact has been used extensively for navigation, the reference plane being the ground; see Figure 4.9 for an example. The same idea can be used to warp an image to remove the perspective distortion, for example by identifying a rectangle in the scene and then applying a homography which maps the (convergent) image of this rectangle into a rectangle; see Figure 4.10. Another important consequence is the existence of invariants attached to planar objects, which can be computed from a single view; see for example many of the chapters in (Mundy and Zisserman, 1992).

Figure 4.9: Homography between the retinal plane and a plane in 3D. By applying an adequate homography to the boxes enclosing the cars (left), a bird's eye view (right) is obtained, where the cars are properly positioned.

Figure 4.10: Homography between the retinal plane and a virtual plane. By applying adequate homographies to the left images, synthetic rotated images are created, so that the perspective distortion is removed on the main subject's plane.

4.1.5   Projection of a line

Given two 3-D points M_1 and M_2, the line $\mathbf{L} \equiv \mathbf{M}_1 \triangledown \mathbf{M}_2$ is an element of $G_2(\mathbb{R}^4)$ represented by its Plücker coordinates (see Section 3.1.2.3). The image l of that line through a camera defined by the perspective projection matrix $\mathcal{P}$ is, according to Proposition 3.27, represented by the 3×1 vector

$$l = \mathcal{P}\mathbf{M}_1 \times \mathcal{P}\mathbf{M}_2 = [\langle \boldsymbol{V}, \mathbf{M}_1 \rangle \langle \boldsymbol{W}, \mathbf{M}_2 \rangle - \langle \boldsymbol{W}, \mathbf{M}_2 \rangle \langle \boldsymbol{V}, \mathbf{M}_1 \rangle,$$

$$\langle \boldsymbol{W}, \mathbf{M}_1 \rangle \langle \boldsymbol{U}, \mathbf{M}_2 \rangle - \langle \boldsymbol{U}, \mathbf{M}_2 \rangle \langle \boldsymbol{W}, \mathbf{M}_1 \rangle, \langle \boldsymbol{U}, \mathbf{M}_1 \rangle \langle \boldsymbol{V}, \mathbf{M}_2 \rangle - \langle \boldsymbol{V}, \mathbf{M}_2 \rangle \langle \boldsymbol{U}, \mathbf{M}_1 \rangle]^T .$$

Equation (3.27) of Proposition 3.32 allows us to recognize the Plücker products of the projection rays of the camera with the line L:

$$l \simeq [[\boldsymbol{V} \, \triangle \, \boldsymbol{W} \mid \mathbf{L}], [\boldsymbol{W} \, \triangle \, \boldsymbol{U} \mid \mathbf{L}], [\boldsymbol{U} \, \triangle \, \boldsymbol{V} \mid \mathbf{L}]]^T . \qquad (4.16)$$

We can rewrite this in matrix form:

$$l \simeq \tilde{\mathcal{P}}\mathbf{L}, \qquad (4.17)$$

where $\tilde{\mathcal{P}}$ is the 3×6 matrix

$$\begin{bmatrix} (\boldsymbol{V} \vartriangle \boldsymbol{W})^T \\ (\boldsymbol{W} \vartriangle \boldsymbol{U})^T \\ (\boldsymbol{U} \vartriangle \boldsymbol{V})^T \end{bmatrix}.$$

The matrix $\tilde{\mathcal{P}}$ plays for 3-D lines the same role that the matrix $\mathcal{P}$ plays for 3-D points. Equation 4.17 is thus equivalent to

$$l_1 : l_2 : l_3 = [\boldsymbol{V} \vartriangle \boldsymbol{W} \mid \mathbf{L}] : [\boldsymbol{W} \vartriangle \boldsymbol{U} \mid \mathbf{L}] : [\boldsymbol{U} \vartriangle \boldsymbol{V} \mid \mathbf{L}].$$

We have the following proposition.

Proposition 4.11 *The pinhole camera also defines a mapping from the set of lines of $\mathbb{P}^3$ to the set of lines of $\mathbb{P}^2$. This mapping is a morphism from $P(G_2(\mathbb{R}^4))$ to $P(G_2(\mathbb{R}^3))$. This morphism is represented by a 6×4 matrix, denoted $\tilde{\mathcal{P}}$, whose row vectors are the Plücker coordinates of the projection rays of the camera:*

$$\tilde{\mathcal{P}} = \begin{bmatrix} (\boldsymbol{V} \vartriangle \boldsymbol{W})^T \\ (\boldsymbol{W} \vartriangle \boldsymbol{U})^T \\ (\boldsymbol{U} \vartriangle \boldsymbol{V})^T \end{bmatrix}. \tag{4.18}$$

The image l of a 3D line L is given by

$$l_1 : l_2 : l_3 = [\boldsymbol{V} \vartriangle \boldsymbol{W} \mid \mathbf{L}] : [\boldsymbol{W} \vartriangle \boldsymbol{U} \mid \mathbf{L}] : [\boldsymbol{U} \vartriangle \boldsymbol{V} \mid \mathbf{L}].$$

The nullspace of this mapping contains the set of lines going through the optical center of the camera.

Proof :   We have already proved it. Let us just make it more precise. The rows of the matrix $\tilde{\mathcal{P}}$ are linear forms over the vector space $G_2(\mathbb{R}^4)$. We have seen in Chapter 3 that those linear forms could be identified with elements of $G_2(\mathbb{R}^4)$ and that, if the basis was unimodal, then the relationship between the Plücker product of two elements of $G_2(\mathbb{R}^4)$ was identical to the cap-product of those two elements (Equation 3.19). This is how Equation 4.17 should be interpreted. Regarding the nullspace, if L is a 3D line such that $\tilde{\mathcal{P}}\mathbf{L} = \mathbf{0}$, then L intersects all three projection rays of the camera and hence goes through the optical center. But note that there may be elements of $G_2(\mathbb{R}^4)$ which are not lines, i.e. extensors of step 2, and verify $\tilde{\mathcal{P}}\mathbf{L} = \mathbf{0}$.   □

The dual interpretation is also of interest:

Proposition 4.12 *The 3×6 matrix $\tilde{\mathcal{P}}^T$ represents a morphism from $\mathbb{P}^2$ to the set of 3D lines, subset of $P(G_2(\mathbb{R}^4))$, which associates with each pixel m its optical ray L_m.*

Proof : Since $\tilde{\mathcal{P}}$ represents a linear mapping from $G_2(\mathbb{R}^4)$ to $G_2(\mathbb{R}^3)$, $\tilde{\mathcal{P}}^T$ represents a linear mapping from the dual $G_2(\mathbb{R}^3)^*$ of $G_2(\mathbb{R}^3)$ which we can identify with $G_1(\mathbb{R}^3)$, to the dual $G_2(\mathbb{R}^4)^*$ which we can identify with $G_2(\mathbb{R}^4)$. Hence it corresponds to a morphism from $\mathbb{P}^2$ to $P(G_2(\mathbb{R}^4))$ (see also Proposition 3.24). If the pixel m has projective coordinates x, y and z, then we have

$$\tilde{\mathcal{P}}^T \mathbf{m} \simeq x\boldsymbol{V} \vartriangle \boldsymbol{W} + y\boldsymbol{W} \vartriangle \boldsymbol{U} + z\boldsymbol{U} \vartriangle \boldsymbol{V}$$

and we recognize the right-hand side to be a representation of the optical ray L_m (Proposition 4.4). $\square$

We finish this study with the case in which the line L is represented as the meet of two planes Π_1 and Π_2:

Proposition 4.13 *If* $\mathbf{L} = \boldsymbol{\Pi}_1 \vartriangle \boldsymbol{\Pi}_2$, *then its image* l *is obtained by the expressions*

$$l_1 : l_2 : l_3 = \mid \boldsymbol{V}, \boldsymbol{W}, \boldsymbol{\Pi}_1, \boldsymbol{\Pi}_2 \mid : \mid \boldsymbol{W}, \boldsymbol{U}, \boldsymbol{\Pi}_1, \boldsymbol{\Pi}_2 \mid : \mid \boldsymbol{U}, \boldsymbol{V}, \boldsymbol{\Pi}_1, \boldsymbol{\Pi}_2 \mid$$

or

$$l \simeq \mathcal{P}_{\Pi_2}^{+^T} \boldsymbol{\Pi}_1 \simeq \mathcal{P}_{\Pi_1}^{+^T} \boldsymbol{\Pi}_2.$$

Proof : The first expression is a direct consequence of Equation 4.16 and of Proposition 3.32. The other two expressions follow from the interpretation of the matrices $\mathcal{P}_{\Pi}^{+^T}$ given in Section 4.1.3, Proposition 4.9. $\square$

4.2 The affine model: The case of perspective projection

In the projective framework, we have seen that any pinhole camera has an optical center. Projective geometry does not distinguish between points at infinity and finite points of the (usual) affine space. However, in terms of affine space, this distinction is important. When the optical center is not at infinity, it represents a point in affine space. The optical rays all go through this point. This is the perspective model, which will be studied in this section. By contrast, when the optical center is at infinity, as will be studied in Section 4.4, it represents a direction in affine space. The optical rays are all parallel to this direction.

In Section 4.2.1 we give an affine interpretation of the projection matrix, and introduce the notion of perspective projection. In Section 4.3.1 we give a Euclidean interpretation of the projection matrix in terms of the classical intrinsic and extrinsic parameters. In Section 4.3.2 another representation for the intrinsic parameters is introduced.

Our representation of the world has now shifted from a general projective space $\mathbb{P}^3$ to an affine space X_3 which has been projectively completed as explained in

Section 2.5 by a plane at infinity, denoted Π_∞. We assume that we have chosen an affine basis (M_0, M_1, M_2, M_3), and we denote (X, Y, Z) the affine coordinates of a point in this basis. A point M of X_3 is also considered as a point $\tilde{M}$ of its projective completion with projective coordinates $(X, Y, Z, 1)$ in the projective basis attached to the affine basis (see Section 2.5.2). We denote $(\mathcal{X}, \mathcal{Y}, \mathcal{Z}, \mathcal{T})$ the projective coordinates of a point of the projective completion of X_3. The equation of the plane at infinity Π_∞ is $\mathcal{T} = 0$. The relations between the affine and projective coordinates of a point of X_3 are

$$X = \frac{\mathcal{X}}{\mathcal{T}}, \quad Y = \frac{\mathcal{Y}}{\mathcal{T}}, \quad Z = \frac{\mathcal{Z}}{\mathcal{T}}.$$

In terms of coordinate vectors, if $\mathbf{M}$ is the 3×1 vector of affine coordinates of M, then $\tilde{\mathbf{M}} \simeq \left[\mathbf{M}^T, 1\right]^T$ is a coordinate vector of the projective point $\tilde{M}$. Similarly, the coordinate vector $\tilde{\mathbf{M}}$ of a point in Π_∞ will be written $\tilde{\mathbf{M}} \simeq \left[\mathbf{M}^T, 0\right]^T$ where $\mathbf{M}$ is a coordinate vector of a point in Π_∞ considered as a two-dimensional projective space.

A similar notation will be applied to planes. A plane Π of X_3 of equation $uX + vY + wZ + r = 0$ will be considered as included in the projective plane $\tilde{\Pi} = \Pi \cup \infty_\Pi$ where, according to Section 2.5, ∞_Π is the line at infinity of the plane Π, its direction. In terms of coordinate vectors, the plane $\tilde{\Pi}$ is represented by $[u, v, w, r]^T$.

What we did to the ambient space we do also to the retinal plane of the camera. We now assume that it is a two-dimensional affine space X_2 which has been projectively completed by adding a line at infinity l_∞. We also assume that we have chosen an affine basis (m_0, m_1, m_2) and we denote (u, v) the pixel affine coordinates in that basis. A pixel m of X_2 is also considered as a point $\tilde{m}$ of its projective completion with projective coordinates $(u, v, 1)$ in the projective basis attached to the affine basis (see Section 2.5.2). We denote (x, y, z) the projective coordinates of a point of the projective completion of X_2. The equation of the line at infinity l_∞ is $z = 0$. The relations between the affine and projective coordinates of a point of X_2 are

$$u = \frac{x}{z}, \quad v = \frac{y}{z}.$$

Equation 4.3 is still valid in the projective completions of X_3 and X_2 but the plane and lines at infinity will now play a prominent role.

4.2.1 The projection matrix

The affine framework allows us to give an interesting interpretation of the third projection plane of the perspective projection matrix:

Proposition 4.14 *The third projection plane $\mathbf{W}$ of the perspective projection matrix $\mathcal{P}$ is the focal plane of the camera.*

Proof : The points of the plane of equation $\langle W, \tilde{\mathbf{M}} \rangle = 0$ are mapped to the points in the retinal plane such that $z = 0$. This is the equation of the line at infinity in the retinal plane. The plane represented by W is therefore the set of points in 3D space which do not project at finite distance in the retinal plane. These points form the *focal plane*, which is the plane containing the optical center and parallel to the retinal plane. $\square$

We now decompose the projection matrix $\mathcal{P}$ as a 3×3 sub-matrix $\mathbf{P}$ and a 3×1 vector $\mathbf{p}$:

$$\mathcal{P} = [\mathbf{P} \ \mathbf{p}]. \tag{4.19}$$

The operation of perspective projection can be described as the composition of an affine transformation of 3-space and a normalized perspective projection:

$$\begin{bmatrix} x \\ y \\ z \end{bmatrix} = \begin{bmatrix} 1 & 0 & 0 & 0 \\ 0 & 1 & 0 & 0 \\ 0 & 0 & 1 & 0 \end{bmatrix} \begin{bmatrix} \mathbf{P} & \mathbf{p} \\ \mathbf{0}_3^T & 1 \end{bmatrix} \begin{bmatrix} \mathcal{X} \\ \mathcal{Y} \\ \mathcal{Z} \\ \mathcal{T} \end{bmatrix}. \tag{4.20}$$

We investigate next the notion of the optical center of the camera and how we have to modify it to adjust to the affine setting.

Proposition 4.15 *The pinhole camera can be of two types:*

1. *The optical center is at a finite distance in which case the matrix $\mathbf{P}$ is of rank 3. In this case we talk about a **perspective projection** and a **perspective camera**. Its affine coordinates are*

$$\mathbf{C} = -\mathbf{P}^{-1}\mathbf{p}. \tag{4.21}$$

2. *The optical center is at infinity in which case the matrix $\mathbf{P}$ is of rank 2. We talk about a **parallel projection** and an **affine camera**. The direction of projection is represented by any vector in the nullspace of $\mathbf{P}$.*

Proof : Let us write a coordinate vector of the optical center as

$$\tilde{\mathbf{C}} = \begin{bmatrix} \mathbf{C} \\ c \end{bmatrix}.$$

The equation determining the optical center is thus $\mathbf{P}\mathbf{C} = -c\mathbf{p}$. There are two cases to consider:

$\det(\mathbf{P}) \neq 0$
   This situation yields

$$\mathbf{C} = -c\mathbf{P}^{-1}\mathbf{p},$$

which implies that $c \neq 0$.

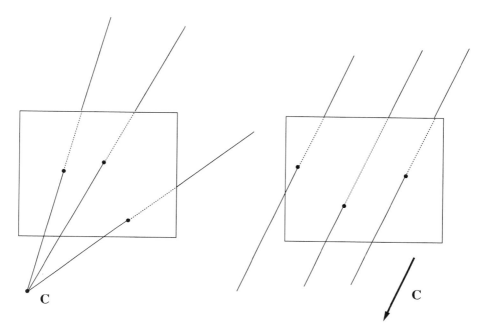

Figure 4.11: Perspective and parallel projections. In perspective projection, all of the optical rays pass through the optical center, a point of affine space. In parallel projection, all of the optical rays are parallel to the direction of projection (a point at infinity).

det$(\mathbf{P}) = 0$

Two cases can happen. The first is when the vector $\mathbf{p}$ belongs to the image of the linear mapping defined by the matrix $\mathbf{P}$. This situation implies that the rank of $\mathcal{P}$ is strictly less than 3 and is thus impossible. The second case is when $\mathbf{p}$ does not belong to this image. The equation $\mathbf{PC} = -c\mathbf{p}$ has no solution if $c \neq 0$, in contradiction of the fact that there exists an optical center. Hence $c = 0$ and the optical center is at infinity. The vector $\mathbf{C}$ is any vector in the nullspace of the matrix $\mathbf{P}$ which must be of dimension 1 because of the rank condition on $\mathcal{P}$.

Note that in the first case, as expected, there is no problem with scaling the perspective projection matrix $\mathcal{P}$ by λ since $\mathbf{p}$ is scaled by λ and $\mathbf{P}^{-1}$ by λ^{-1}. $\square$

Parallel projections will be studied in more detail in Section 4.4. We now assume that the optical center is at a finite distance and therefore that the camera is performing a perspective projection.

4.2.2   The inverse perspective projection matrix

The matrix $\mathbf{P}$ has an interesting interpretation in terms of the plane at infinity:

Proposition 4.16 *The matrix* $\mathbf{P}$ *represents the homography between the plane at infinity and the retinal plane. The inverse perspective projection matrix* $\mathcal{P}^+_{\Pi_\infty}$ *is given by*

$$\mathcal{P}^+_{\Pi_\infty} = \begin{bmatrix} \mathbf{P}^{-1} \\ \mathbf{0}_3^T \end{bmatrix}. \tag{4.22}$$

Proof :   According to Equation 4.19, the image of each point at infinity $[\mathbf{M}^T, 0]^T$ is $\mathbf{m} = \mathbf{PM}$. Hence, since $\det(\mathbf{P}) \neq 0$, $\mathbf{P}$ defines a homography between the plane at infinity Π_∞ and the retinal plane $\mathcal{R}$. The inverse perspective matrix is easily obtained from the inverse homography. $\square$

An immediate consequence of the previous proposition is that the direction of the optical ray L_m of the pixel m, i.e. its point at infinity, is represented by $[\mathbf{P}^{-1}\mathbf{m}, 0]^T$.

Although from a purely projective standpoint the two cases are equivalent, and can be exchanged by a change of coordinate system (used for instance in (Faugeras and Robert, 1996)), the constraint $\det(\mathbf{P}) \neq 0$ is important in practice, since from the standpoint of the usual affine space the two types of projection have quite different properties, as illustrated in Figure 4.11.

We specialize now the analysis of the inverse projection matrix which has been done so far in the purely projective framework (see Section 4.1.3). The plane at infinity will naturally play an important role in this new development. To simplify the derivations, we assume that $\mathcal{P}$ has been normalized in such a way that $\tilde{C}_4$ (the fourth coordinate of $\tilde{\mathbf{C}}$) is equal to 1.

Let us write an inverse projection matrix as

$$\mathcal{P}^+ \simeq \begin{bmatrix} \mathbf{Q} \\ \mathbf{q}^T \end{bmatrix}, \tag{4.23}$$

where $\mathbf{Q}$ is a 3×3 matrix and $\mathbf{q}$ a 3×1 vector. We know from Proposition 4.6 that there exists a unique plane $\tilde{\Pi}$ represented by the vector $[\mathbf{\Pi}^T, d]^T$ such that $\mathcal{P}^+ \simeq \mathcal{P}^+_{\tilde{\Pi}}$. The following proposition gives an interpretation of the vector $\mathbf{q}$.

Proposition 4.17 *The vector* $\mathbf{q}$ *is a representation of the image of the line at infinity of the plane* $\tilde{\Pi}$.

Proof :   Indeed, the plane at infinity is represented by the vector $\mathbf{\Pi}_\infty \simeq \varepsilon_4$ of the canonical basis of $\mathbb{R}^4$ and, according to Proposition 4.9, this line is represented by $\mathcal{P}^{+T}\mathbf{\Pi}_\infty \simeq \mathbf{q}$. $\square$

We now show that the family of inverse projection matrices is parameterized by the set of three-dimensional vectors $\mathbf{q}$. We begin with a proposition that describes the relation between the matrix $\mathbf{Q}$ and the plane $\tilde{\Pi}$:

Proposition 4.18 *The matrix* $\mathbf{Q}$ *of Equation 4.23 is given by*

$$\mathbf{Q} = \mathbf{C}\mathbf{q}^T - \langle \tilde{\mathbf{\Pi}}, \tilde{\mathbf{C}} \rangle \mathbf{P}^{-1}. \tag{4.24}$$

Proof : The equation $\mathcal{P}\mathcal{P}_{\tilde{\Pi}}^+ = -\langle \tilde{\mathbf{\Pi}}, \tilde{\mathbf{C}} \rangle \mathbf{I}_3$ defining the inverse projection matrices is equivalent to

$$\mathbf{P}\mathbf{Q} + \mathbf{p}\mathbf{q}^T = -\langle \tilde{\mathbf{\Pi}}, \tilde{\mathbf{C}} \rangle \mathbf{I}_3.$$

Since $\mathbf{C} = -\mathbf{P}^{-1}\mathbf{p}$, this equation is equivalent to

$$\mathbf{Q} = \mathbf{C}\mathbf{q}^T - \langle \tilde{\mathbf{\Pi}}, \tilde{\mathbf{C}} \rangle \mathbf{P}^{-1}.$$

$\square$

We continue by describing the relation between the plane $\tilde{\Pi}$ and the vector $\mathbf{q}$:

Proposition 4.19 *The vector* $\mathbf{q}$ *of Equation 4.23 is given by*

$$\mathbf{P}^T\mathbf{q} - \mathbf{\Pi} = \mathbf{0}. \tag{4.25}$$

Proof : We use Proposition 4.8 and write that $\tilde{\mathbf{\Pi}}^T \mathcal{P}_{\tilde{\Pi}}^+ = \mathbf{0}$. Since $\tilde{\mathbf{\Pi}}^T = \left[\mathbf{\Pi}^T, d \right]$ we first obtain

$$\tilde{\mathbf{\Pi}}^T \mathcal{P}_{\tilde{\Pi}}^+ = \mathbf{\Pi}^T \mathbf{Q} + d\mathbf{q}^T,$$

and, replacing $\mathbf{Q}$ by its value given by Equation 4.24,

$$-\langle \tilde{\mathbf{\Pi}}, \tilde{\mathbf{C}} \rangle \mathbf{\Pi}^T \mathbf{P}^{-1} + \mathbf{\Pi}^T \mathbf{C}\mathbf{q}^T + d\mathbf{q}^T = \mathbf{0},$$

which implies

$$(\mathbf{\Pi}^T \mathbf{C} + d)\mathbf{q} = \mathbf{P}^{-T} \mathbf{\Pi} \langle \tilde{\mathbf{\Pi}}, \tilde{\mathbf{C}} \rangle.$$

$\mathbf{\Pi}^T\mathbf{C} + d = \tilde{\mathbf{\Pi}}^T \tilde{\mathbf{C}} = \langle \tilde{\mathbf{\Pi}}, \tilde{\mathbf{C}} \rangle$ is different from 0 since the plane $\tilde{\Pi}$ does not go through C, so we can divide both sides by it to obtain

$$\mathbf{q} = \mathbf{P}^{-T}\mathbf{\Pi}.$$

$\square$

Putting all this together,

Proposition 4.20 *The one-to-one relationship between the set of planes* $\tilde{\Pi}$ *not going through the optical center* $\tilde{C}$ *of the camera and the set of inverse perspective projection matrices is:*

$$\mathcal{P}_{\tilde{\Pi}}^+ = \left[\begin{array}{c} (\mathbf{C}\mathbf{\Pi}^T - \langle \tilde{\mathbf{\Pi}}, \tilde{\mathbf{C}} \rangle \mathbf{I}_3)\mathbf{P}^{-1} \\ \mathbf{\Pi}^T \mathbf{P}^{-1} \end{array} \right]. \tag{4.26}$$

Proof : It is just a matter of putting together Equations 4.23, 4.24 and 4.25. □

Note that since the plane at infinity is represented by $\tilde{\mathbf{\Pi}}_\infty = [\mathbf{0}^T, 1]^T$, its corresponding vector $\mathbf{q} = \mathbf{P}^{-T}\mathbf{\Pi}_\infty$ is equal to $\mathbf{0}$. Moreover, since $\langle \tilde{\mathbf{\Pi}}_\infty, \tilde{\mathbf{C}} \rangle = 1$, we find

$$\mathcal{P}^+_{\tilde{\Pi}_\infty} \simeq \left[\begin{array}{c} \mathbf{P}^{-1} \\ \mathbf{0}^T \end{array} \right],$$

as in Proposition 4.16.

4.2.3 Vanishing points and lines

Let us now make good use of our fresh knowledge of projective geometry and its relation with affine geometry to give an interpretation of vanishing points and lines.

According to Chapter 2, all affine lines parallel to a given line L intersect at a single point M_∞ in the plane at infinity. If we form an image of these lines with a pinhole camera, then they all converge to the image m_∞ of M_∞. m_∞ is called the vanishing point of each of the 2D lines. We have the following definition; see Figure 4.12.

Definition 4.2 *The **vanishing point** of the image of a 3D line is the image of its point at infinity.*

Similarly, consider a plane Π. Its line at infinity L_∞ is its intersection with Π_∞. The image l_∞ of L_∞ is the *vanishing line* of the plane Π. In particular the vanishing point of a line l, image of a line L in Π, has its vanishing point on the vanishing line l_∞; see Figure 4.13.

We illustrate the use of vanishing points by analyzing two classical constructions from the XVII-th century, using detailed calculations with projective coordinates.

The fact that projections of a set of parallel lines converge to a vanishing point is illustrated in Figure 4.14. Note how in this figure, the convergence of lines gives a sense of depth. The lines of interest are those which are parallel to the optical axis of the camera. In the normalized camera coordinate system, since Z is the direction of the optical axis, such lines are defined by two points of projective coordinates $\mathbf{M}_1 = [X, Y, Z_1, 1]^T$ and $\mathbf{M}_2 = [X, Y, Z_2, 1]^T$. The line (M_1, M_2) is the set of points of the form $\lambda\mathbf{M}_1 + \mu\mathbf{M}_2$. The intersection of this line with the plane at infinity is the point M_∞ of this line which has a null fourth component, therefore for this point $\lambda + \mu = 0$, and $\mathbf{M}_\infty = [0, 0, \lambda(Z_1 - Z_2), 0] \simeq [0, 0, 1, 0]^T$, corresponding to the affine direction $[0, 0, 1]^T$. The vanishing point of this line is the projection of $\mathbf{M}_\infty$. In the camera coordinate system, the projection matrix is of the form given in Equation 4.2. The point at infinity $\mathbf{M}_\infty$ is projected to the point of projective coordinates $\mathbf{v} = [0, 0, 1]^T$, which represents the center of the image. The two points M_1 and M_2 are projected into the points of projective coordinates $\mathbf{m}_1 = [fX, fY, Z_1]^T$ and $\mathbf{m}_2 = [fX, fY, Z_2]^T$. They define a line which contains $\mathbf{v}$, since $(\mathbf{m}_1 \times \mathbf{m}_2)^T\mathbf{v} = 0$. In addition it can be seen that $\lim_{Z_1 \to \infty} \mathbf{m}_1 = \mathbf{v}$.

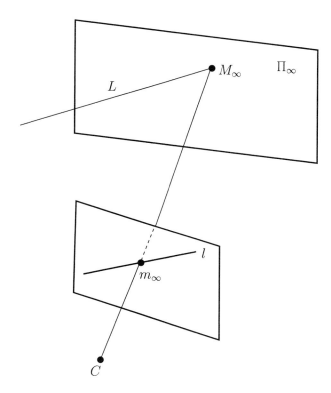

Figure 4.12: The vanishing point of the line l, image of L, is the point m_∞, image of M_∞.

The fact that all of the vanishing points of coplanar sets of lines are projected onto a line, called the vanishing line of the plane, is illustrated in Figure 4.15. It can be remarked that the use of two sets of converging lines is sufficient to create a strong sense of space. For this reason, paintings containing tiled floors were quite common during the Renaissance and also in Dutch painting. As illustrated by Kemp (Kemp, 1990) this construction is most fundamental in linear perspective, and can therefore be seen in many paintings.

We chose one painting which is not very well known, but uses a very wide angle of view, much wider than the natural angle of human vision, and therefore illustrates the virtuosity in the use of perspective which had been achieved at this time. There are three systems of converging lines, two associated respectively with the sides of the square tiles, and one passing along their diagonal axis.

Assuming that the plane of the floor is parallel to the plane X-Z of the normalized camera coordinate system (which means that the viewing direction is parallel to the floor and the picture is not tilted sideways), and that the latter lines are parallel to

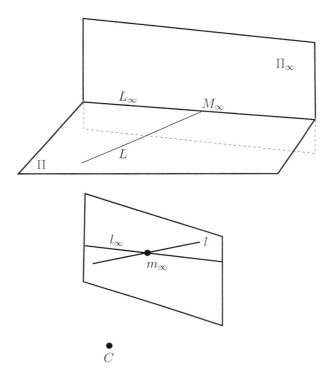

Figure 4.13: The vanishing line l_∞ of the plane Π is image l_∞ of the intersection L_∞ of Π and Π_∞.

the optical axis, their direction is, as previously, $[0,0,1]^T$, which yields the vanishing point $\mathbf{v}_2 = [0,0,1]^T$. Note that this information could be deduced from the analysis of the image. The direction of the sides of the tiles are $[-1,0,1]^T$ and $[1,0,1]^T$, which give respectively the vanishing points $\mathbf{v}_1 = [-f,0,1]^T$ and $\mathbf{v}_3 = [f,0,1]^T$. These three vanishing points therefore lie on the line of equation $y_c = 0$, which is the vanishing line of the plane representing the floor; see Figure 4.3. This line is called the *horizon line*.

It can also be verified that the point $\mathbf{v}_2$ lies at the middle of the segment $(\mathbf{v}_1, \mathbf{v}_3)$. Let us anticipate the next section a bit by presenting some metric considerations. For esthetic reasons, the painting has been decentered, so that the point $\mathbf{v}_2$ is not at the center of the frame. If we denote by x_0 and y_0 this amount of decentering, then the actual positions of the three vanishing points are determined by the affine coordinates

$$\mathbf{v}_1 = \begin{bmatrix} -f + x_0 \\ y_0 \end{bmatrix}, \qquad \mathbf{v}_2 = \begin{bmatrix} x_0 \\ y_0 \end{bmatrix}, \qquad \mathbf{v}_3 = \begin{bmatrix} f + x_0 \\ y_0 \end{bmatrix}.$$

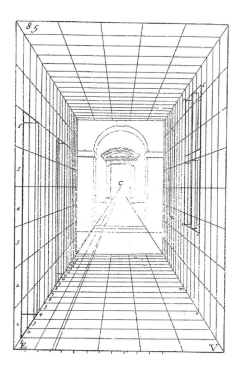

Figure 4.14: Illustration of the notion of vanishing point by Abraham Bosse. Left: scaled box of interior space from (Bosse, 1648). Right: study of architectural perspective with light and shade from (Bosse, 1664). The receding lines, parallel to the viewing direction, converge at the middle of the image.

Since the vanishing points of two systems of orthogonal lines lie within the image (almost within for $\mathbf{v}_1$), it can be concluded that the horizontal (asymmetrical) field of view θ is at least 90 degrees. More precisely, this field of view can be obtained by

$$\theta = 2\arctan\left(\frac{w}{2f}\right) \quad \text{with} \quad 2f = y_3 - y_2 = y_2 - y_1,$$

where we have denoted by y_i the horizontal coordinates of $\mathbf{v}_i$ in an arbitrary unit, and by w the width of the image, in the same unit. Measurements on the image give approximatively $\theta = 105^o$, which is indeed a very wide field of view. From a photographer's point of view, this would be obtained with a 14mm lens on a 35mm camera, or a 72mm lens on a 5 by 7 inches camera. However, a significant image shift in both directions is also necessary to produce the image. If we consider the circular field of view centered at the point (x_0, y_0) (which means that w now

Figure 4.15: Illustration of the notion of vanishing line. Top: Gerard Houckgeest, *Interior of the New Church at Delft with the Tomb of William the Silent*, 1651, Maurithuis. Bottom left: The basic underlying perspective construction, as illustrated by Vredeman de Vries (Vredeman de Vries, 1604). This construction was already known to Renaissance painters of the XVth century. Bottom right: The three systems of converging lines in Houckgeest's painting. v_1, v_3: perpendicular sides of the tiles, v_2: diagonal of the tiles. The three vanishing points lie on the horizon line, and v_2 is the midpoint of the segment (v_1, v_3).

is the distance between the point v_2 and the upper right corner) then this angle comes close to $135°$. Regardless of the format which is used, current lenses[1] offer a considerably smaller angle of coverage (for an explanation; see (Stroebel, 1999)). With modern optics, it is impossible to make a photograph match the painting!

4.3 The Euclidean model: The case of perspective projection

We now enrich our representation of the world which has so far been that of a general affine space X_3, projectively completed to a general projective space $\mathbb{P}^3$. We now assume the existence of a Euclidean structure in that affine space. Besides projective and affine bases, we will also use Euclidean bases but to be consistent with our approach, we will always consider changes of coordinate systems as *projective* changes of coordinate systems, i.e. they will be represented by 4×4 (respectively 3×3) matrices for the 3D space (respectively for the retina). These changes of coordinates correspond to the *extrinsic* and *intrinsic* camera parameters, which are introduced in Section 4.3.1. The Euclidean structure can be defined projectively, as explained in Section 2.3, by the absolute conic Ω in the plane at infinity Π_∞. This leads in Section 4.3.2 to an alternative description of the camera parameters in terms of image or dual image of the absolute conic, which will play in important role in the remainder of this book.

4.3.1 Intrinsic and Extrinsic parameters

As shown in Figure 4.3, we consider the general Euclidean world coordinate system $\mathcal{F}_O = (O, X, Y, Z)$ which is related to the camera normalized coordinate system $\mathcal{F}_C = (C, X_C, Y_C, Z_C)$ by a rigid displacement described by the rotation matrix $\mathbf{R}$ and the translation vector $\mathbf{t}$. This rigid displacement is a change of Euclidean coordinates and therefore also a change of projective coordinates represented by the 4×4 matrix

$$\mathbf{Q}_{\mathcal{F}_O}^{\mathcal{F}_C} = \begin{bmatrix} \mathbf{R} & \mathbf{t} \\ \mathbf{0}^T & 1 \end{bmatrix}.$$

If we think of $\mathcal{F}_O$ as the laboratory coordinate system, the displacement describes the pose of the camera in the laboratory. The parameters describing the displacement are called the *extrinsic camera parameters*.

The coordinate system $\mathcal{F}_o = (o, u, v)$ is related to the coordinate system $\mathcal{F}_c = (c, x_c, y_c)$ by a change of scale of magnitude k_u and k_v along the u- and v-axes, respectively, followed by a translation $[u_0, v_0]^T$. The change of coordinate system between $\mathcal{F}_c$ and $\mathcal{F}_o$ is described by a 3×3 matrix $\mathbf{Q}_{\mathcal{F}_c}^{\mathcal{F}_o}$ which, as we will see in a

---

[1] As of 1999, the widest angle of coverage available is the $120°$ of the Schneider Super-Angulon-XL 47mm.

moment, is an affine transformation of the retinal plane. In general, the principal point $[u_0, v_0]^T$ is relatively close to the image center and almost always lies in the image. However, for images which are cropped or which are taken with cameras with shifting capacities, this is not necessarily the case. In addition, the second coordinate axis is rotated by θ around o. The parameters relating the two retinal coordinate systems do not depend on the pose of the camera and are called the *intrinsic camera parameters*. The coordinate system $\mathcal{F}_o$ is the coordinate system that we use when we address the pixels in an image. It is usually centered at the upper left-hand corner of the image which is usually not the point c. The pixels are usually not square and have aspect ratios depending on the actual size of the photosensitive cells of the camera as well as on the idiosyncrasies of the acquisition system. The matrix $\mathbf{Q}_{\mathcal{F}_c}^{\mathcal{F}_o}$ can easily be shown to be equal to

$$
\mathbf{Q}_{\mathcal{F}_c}^{\mathcal{F}_o} = \begin{bmatrix} k_u & -k_u \cot\theta & u_0 \\ 0 & \dfrac{k_v}{\sin\theta} & v_0 \\ 0 & 0 & 1 \end{bmatrix}. \tag{4.27}
$$

In effect, with respect to Figure 4.16, we have $\overrightarrow{x}_c = k_u \overrightarrow{u}$ and $k_v \overrightarrow{v} = \overrightarrow{x}_c \cos\theta + \overrightarrow{y}_c \sin\theta$. Therefore, $\overrightarrow{y}_c = -k_u \cot\theta \overrightarrow{u} + \dfrac{k_v}{\sin\theta} \overrightarrow{v}$.

For most of the imaging situations which are commonly encountered, the retinal axes are orthogonal, and therefore the angle θ is $\pi/2$. However, in order to be totally general this angle has to be considered for several reasons. First, the projection matrices, being 3×4 matrices defined up to a scale factor, depend on 11 free parameters. Since a displacement is described by 6 parameters (3 for the rotation, 3 for the translation), there are 5 intrinsic parameters, and therefore, in addition to the scale factors and the coordinates of the principal point, one additional intrinsic parameter is needed to ensure the existence of the decomposition of any projection matrix into extrinsic and intrinsic parameters. Second, from a practical standpoint, there are some special imaging situations which cannot be properly described without considering θ. These situations include the case of pixel grids which have a non-orthogonal arrangement, the case where the optical axis may not be orthogonal to the image plane, which can happen when a bellows camera is used, the case when images are enlarged with a tilted easel, and the case when pictures of pictures are considered. The two first interpretations will be made clearer in Section 4.4. Even if the value of θ is known, if we include its recovery into the computation scheme, then we obtain an easy quality check on the results.

Using Equation 4.2 and the basic properties of changes of coordinate systems, we can express the relation between the image coordinates in the $\mathcal{F}_o$ coordinate system and the three-dimensional coordinates in the $\mathcal{F}_O$ coordinate system. The projection giving 2-D pixel coordinates from 3-D world coordinates can be described as a composition of a rigid displacement, the projection expressed in the camera normalized

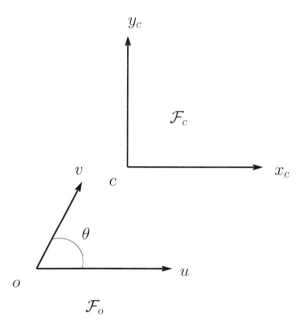

Figure 4.16: The relation between the systems of coordinates $\mathcal{F}_c$ and $\mathcal{F}_o$; see text.

coordinate system, as defined in (4.2) and a change of retinal coordinates:

$$\tilde{\mathbf{m}}_{/\mathcal{F}_o} = \mathbf{Q}_{\mathcal{F}_c}^{\mathcal{F}_o} \boldsymbol{\mathcal{P}}_C \mathbf{Q}_{\mathcal{F}_O}^{\mathcal{F}_C} \tilde{\mathbf{M}}_{/\mathcal{F}_O}.$$

We take the focal length parameter out of $\boldsymbol{\mathcal{P}}_C$ and write

$$\tilde{\mathbf{m}}_{/\mathcal{F}_o} = \mathbf{A} \underbrace{\begin{bmatrix} 1 & 0 & 0 & 0 \\ 0 & 1 & 0 & 0 \\ 0 & 0 & 1 & 0 \end{bmatrix}}_{\boldsymbol{\mathcal{P}}_0} \mathbf{Q}_{\mathcal{F}_O}^{\mathcal{F}_C} \tilde{\mathbf{M}}_{/\mathcal{F}_O}. \qquad (4.28)$$

The 3×3 matrix $\mathbf{A}$ is easily deduced from $\mathbf{Q}_{\mathcal{F}_c}^{\mathcal{F}_o}$:

$$\mathbf{A} = \begin{bmatrix} fk_u & -fk_u \cot \theta & u_0 \\ 0 & \dfrac{fk_v}{\sin \theta} & v_0 \\ 0 & 0 & 1 \end{bmatrix}. \qquad (4.29)$$

Note that it depends on the products fk_u, fk_v which means that we cannot discriminate between a change of focal length and a change of units on the pixel axes. For this reason, we introduce the parameters $\alpha_u = fk_u$ and $\alpha_v = fk_v$. The five intrinsic parameters are thus

- the scale factors α_u, α_v,

- the orthogonality correction angle θ, or *skew*, and

- the coordinates of the principal point u_0, v_0.

Two points are worth noting. First, the matrix $\mathbf{A}$ has to be invertible, which is equivalent to $\alpha_u \alpha_v \neq 0$. Second, $\mathbf{A}$, being upper triangular, defines an affine transformation of the projective plane rather than a general projective transformation of this plane.

In practice, the pixel grid is aligned well enough that $\theta = \pi/2$, so that the model (4.29) takes the simpler form

$$\mathbf{A} = \begin{bmatrix} \alpha_u & 0 & u_0 \\ 0 & \alpha_v & v_0 \\ 0 & 0 & 1 \end{bmatrix}.$$

Since α_u and α_v are expressed as focal length in pixel units, one may also think of α_u as a focal length f' and $\alpha_v = kf'$ as the product of the focal length by the *aspect ratio k*. For a camera with an isotropic scale (or equivalently aspect ratio 1), we have $\alpha_u = \alpha_v$. Departures from this convention were common during the digitalization phase[2], but the aspect ratio could usually be pre-calibrated, and therefore assumed to be known. The case of known aspect ratio can easily be transformed into aspect ratio 1. This problem seems less common nowadays. Last, in several cases, the principal point can be assumed to coincide with the image center. We have a hierarchy of practical models for the intrinsic parameters:

- Full model (5 parameters)

- Zero skew: $\theta = \pi/2$ (4 parameters)

- Zero skew and unit aspect ratio (3 parameters)

- Zero skew, unit aspect ratio, principal point known (1 parameter)

It should be noted that the particular form of the matrix $\mathbf{A}$ results from an arbitrary choice. The one which is used in this book is natural, but other ones are possible, as long as they satisfy the key property that the decomposition (4.3) exists and is unique for any matrix $\mathcal{P}$ such that the left 3×3 sub-matrix $\mathbf{P}$ is invertible, a condition which is necessary from the previous decomposition since it is the product of an invertible matrix, $\mathbf{A}$, and a rotation matrix. Matrix $\mathbf{Q}_{\mathcal{F}_O}^{\mathcal{F}_C}$ depends on 6 extrinsic parameters, three defining the rotation and three defining the translation. It can thus be seen that we have a total of 11 independent parameters. This number is the number of parameters of a 3×4 projection matrix, since it is

---

[2]Lots of images used at INRIA in the past for instance had an aspect ratio which was not 1, as will be seen in some examples of this book.

defined only up to a scale factor. The proof of decomposability for the form of $\mathbf{A}$ used here can be found in (Faugeras, 1995). A similar model, but with a slightly different definition of the angle θ which is less symmetric, is studied in great detail in (Toscani, 1987). Another possible choice for $\mathbf{A}$, which yields a simpler algebra at the expense of a less straightforward geometric interpretation, is to consider as intrinsic parameters the elements of an upper triangular matrix whose last diagonal element is set to 1:

$$\mathbf{A} = \begin{bmatrix} \alpha & \gamma & u_0 \\ 0 & \beta & v_0 \\ 0 & 0 & 1 \end{bmatrix}. \tag{4.30}$$

In this model, the parameter γ, called skew factor, also accounts for the non-orthogonality of camera axis. The fact that a unique decomposition (4.3) is possible is found by applying the QR theorem (Atkinson, 1989): provided that it is invertible, the left sub-matrix 3×3 of $\mathcal{P}$ can be decomposed as $\mathbf{P} = \mathbf{A}\mathbf{R}$, where $\mathbf{A}$ is upper triangular and $\mathbf{R}$ is a rotation matrix. An easy way to obtain the decomposition is to write

$$\mathbf{P}\mathbf{P}^T = \mathbf{A}\mathbf{R}\mathbf{R}^T\mathbf{A}^T = \mathbf{A}\mathbf{A}^T$$

and to apply the formulae in Equation 4.35 to get $\mathbf{A}$ from $\mathbf{K} = \mathbf{P}\mathbf{P}^T$. Then, we obtain the decomposition

$$[\mathbf{P}\ \mathbf{p}] = \left(\frac{\det(\mathbf{P})}{\alpha\beta}\right)^{\frac{1}{3}} [\mathbf{A}\mathbf{R}\ \mathbf{A}\mathbf{T}].$$

It can be easily verified that the two representations for the intrinsic parameters are in one-to-one correspondence with each other:

$$\alpha_u = \alpha, \qquad \theta = -\operatorname{arccot}\left(\frac{\gamma}{\alpha}\right), \qquad \alpha_v = \frac{\alpha\beta}{\sqrt{\alpha^2 + \gamma^2}}.$$

A way to avoid this problem of multiple interpretations of the 5 coefficients is to parameterize the change of retinal coordinate system via the coefficients of the image of the absolute conic. This approach is the subject of the next section.

4.3.2   The absolute conic and the intrinsic parameters

The image of the absolute conic   We now study the relations between the coefficients of the equation of the image ω of the absolute conic Ω, introduced in Section 2.7.1, and the intrinsic parameters. We start with a proposition:

Proposition 4.21 *The image ω of the absolute conic does not depend on the position and orientation of the camera. Its matrix $\mathbf{B}$ is given by the expression*

$$\mathbf{B} = \mathbf{A}^{-T}\mathbf{A}^{-1}. \tag{4.31}$$

Proof : Let us choose a Euclidean coordinate system $\mathcal{F}_O$ and a retinal coordinate system $\mathcal{F}_o$ which will remain fixed in the following. Let $\mathcal{P}^+_{\Pi_\infty / \mathcal{F}_O}$ be the inverse perspective projection matrix of Π_∞ expressed in $\mathcal{F}_O$. Given a pixel m, its inverse image M in Π_∞ is represented by $\mathbf{M}_{/\mathcal{F}_O} = \mathcal{P}^+_{\Pi_\infty / \mathcal{F}_O} \mathbf{m}$. Since M belongs to Ω if and only if $\mathbf{M}^T_{/\mathcal{F}_O} \mathbf{M}_{/\mathcal{F}_O} = 0$, we have the equation of ω

$$\mathbf{m}^T \mathcal{P}^{+T}_{\Pi_\infty / \mathcal{F}_O} \mathcal{P}^+_{\Pi_\infty / \mathcal{F}_O} \mathbf{m} = 0.$$

According to Equation 4.22, this equation is eqivalent to

$$\mathbf{m}^T \mathbf{P}^{-T} \mathbf{P}^{-1} \mathbf{m} = 0.$$

According to Equation 4.28, the matrix $\mathbf{P}$ is equal to $\mathbf{AR}$, therefore we have $\mathbf{P}^{-T}\mathbf{P}^{-1} = \mathbf{A}^{-T}\mathbf{A}^{-1}$, as claimed. Itremains to show that this matrix remains the same when we move the camera.

Moving the camera to a different position and orientation is equivalent to changing the Euclidean coordinate system $\mathcal{F}_O$ to another one $\mathcal{F}_{O'}$. The inverse perspective projection matrix $\mathcal{P}^+_{\Pi_\infty / \mathcal{F}_{O'}}$ expressed in this coordinate system is equal to $\mathbf{Q}^{\mathcal{F}_{O'}}_{\mathcal{F}_O} \mathcal{P}^+_{\Pi_\infty / \mathcal{F}_O}$. Therefore, the equation of ω becomes

$$\mathbf{m}^T \mathcal{P}^{+T}_{\Pi_\infty / \mathcal{F}_O} \mathbf{Q}^{\mathcal{F}_{O'} \, T}_{\mathcal{F}_O} \mathbf{Q}^{\mathcal{F}_{O'}}_{\mathcal{F}_O} \mathcal{P}^+_{\Pi_\infty / \mathcal{F}_O} \mathbf{m} = 0.$$

Using again Equation 4.22 and the fact that

$$\mathbf{Q}^{\mathcal{F}_{O'}}_{\mathcal{F}_O} = \left[\begin{array}{cc} \mathbf{R} & \mathbf{t} \\ \mathbf{0} & 1 \end{array} \right],$$

where $\mathbf{R}$ is orthogonal, we find that the equation of ω is the same. $\square$

Equation 4.31 shows that the knowledge of ω is equivalent to the knowledge of the intrinsic parameters. If the camera is normalized with focal length 1, then ω is just a circle of radius $i = \sqrt{-1}$. More generally, using the first formulation that we introduced, the equation of ω is found to be

$$\frac{(u - u_0)^2}{\alpha_u^2} + \frac{(v - v_0)^2}{\alpha_v^2} + 2\frac{(u - u_0)(v - v_0)\cos\theta}{\alpha_u \alpha_v} + 1 = 0.$$

From that equation, it is easy to picture the effect of each intrinsic parameter on the shape of ω. For instance, the center of ω corresponds to the principal point.

By construction, the matrix $\mathbf{B}$ is positive definite, which is equivalent to the fact that the conic ω has no real point. This fact, in turn, is equivalent to the fact that the absolute conic Ω has no real point. Conversely, any plane conic with no real point is defined by a positive definite matrix $\mathbf{B}$.

For a positive definite matrix $\mathbf{B}$, there is a unique matrix $\mathbf{A}$ which satisfies (4.31). How do we recover this matrix of intrinsic parameters $\mathbf{A}$? Hartley (Hartley, 1997b) explains how to use the Cholesky decomposition (Atkinson, 1989) of $\mathbf{B}$, a general method for solving the equation $\mathbf{X}\mathbf{X}^T = \mathbf{Y}$. Using an SVD, $\mathbf{Y} = \mathbf{U}\mathbf{D}\mathbf{V}^T$. Since $\mathbf{D}$ is diagonal, real and positive, consider its square root $\mathbf{E}$ and apply the QR decomposition to it. This solution is general, however, and for the 3×3 matrices involved in this problem, it is easy to find a closed-form formula, which will be made explicit next through the Kruppa matrix.

Application to the measurement of angles As an application of the previous paragraph, we now expand on the idea that if the image of the absolute conic is known in a camera, it becomes a metric measurement device that can compute angles between optical rays (Faugeras, 1993). We will use this analysis in Chapter 7.

We use the notations of Section 2.6.3. Let us rewrite the equation of ω as

$$S(\mathbf{m}) = \mathbf{m}^T \mathbf{B} \mathbf{m} = 0.$$

Similarly, we denote $S(\mathbf{m}, \mathbf{n})$ the expression $\mathbf{m}^T \mathbf{B} \mathbf{n}$. Because $\mathbf{B}$ is symmetric this expression is also equal to $S(\mathbf{n}, \mathbf{m})$.

We use Laguerre's formula (2.24) given in Chapter 2 as follows. Let m and n be two image points and consider the two optical rays (C, m) and (C, n). Let us call α the angle (between 0 and π) that they form, let M and N be their intersections with the plane at infinity, and let A and B be the two intersections of the line (M, N) with the absolute conic Ω. The angle α between (C, m) and (C, n) is given by Laguerre's formula $\frac{1}{2i} \log(\{M, N; A, B\})$. The reason is that the line at infinity of the plane defined by the three points C, m, n is the intersection of that plane with the plane at infinity, i.e. the line (M, N). The absolute points of that plane are the intersections A and B of that line with the absolute conic Ω.

The cross-ratio $\{M, N; A, B\}$ is preserved under the projection to the retinal plane, and thus the angle between (C, m) and (C, n) is given by $\frac{1}{2i} \log(\{m, n; a, b\})$, where the points a and b are the "images" of the points A and B.

Since a and b are the two intersections of the line (m, n) with ω, we see that the angle can be computed from the image ω of the absolute conic only This situation is depicted in Figure 4.17. In detail, the line (m, n) is represented by $\mathbf{m} + \theta \mathbf{n}$. The variable θ is a projective parameter of that line. Point m has projective parameter 0, and point n has projective parameter ∞. The reader should not worry about this situation, since the magic of the cross-ratio will take care of it!

In order to compute the projective parameters of a and b we perform the following simple computation. A point of the line (m, n) is represented by $\mathbf{m} + \theta \mathbf{n}$. Hence the projective parameters of a and b are the roots of the quadratic equation

$$S(\mathbf{m}) + 2\theta S(\mathbf{m}, \mathbf{n}) + S(\mathbf{n})\theta^2 = 0.$$

Let θ_0 and $\overline{\theta_0}$ be the two roots, which are complex conjugate. According to Equa-

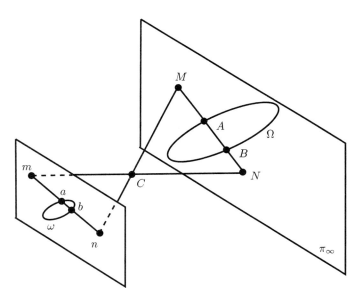

Figure 4.17: How to compute the angle between the optical rays (C, m) and (C, n) using the image of the absolute conic.

tion 2.12, we have

$$\{m, n; a, b\} = \frac{0 - \theta_0}{0 - \bar{\theta}_0} : \frac{\infty - \theta_0}{\infty - \bar{\theta}_0}.$$

The ratio containing ∞ is equal to 1, and therefore

$$\{m, n; a, b\} = \frac{\theta_0}{\bar{\theta}_0} = e^{2i\,Arg(\theta_0)},$$

where $Arg(\theta_0)$ is the argument of the complex number θ_0. In particular, we have $\alpha = Arg(\theta_0)\ (\pi)$. A straightforward computation shows that the two roots are equal to

$$\frac{-S(\mathbf{m}, \mathbf{n}) \pm i\sqrt{S(\mathbf{m})S(\mathbf{n}) - S(\mathbf{m}, \mathbf{n})^2}}{S(\mathbf{n})}. \tag{4.32}$$

Simple considerations show that the equation

$$\cos \alpha = -\frac{S(\mathbf{m}, \mathbf{n})}{\sqrt{S(\mathbf{m})S(\mathbf{n})}} \tag{4.33}$$

uniquely defines α between 0 and π. The sine is therefore positive and given by $\sqrt{1 - \cos^2 \alpha}$.

The Kruppa matrix Another matrix which will play an important role in the rest of this book is the matrix of ω^*, the conic dual to ω. The elements of the dual conic are lines which are tangent to ω. If m is a point on ω, the line l tangent to ω at m is represented by the vector $\mathbf{l} = \mathbf{B}m$ (Proposition 2.19). Since m is such that $\mathbf{m}^T\mathbf{B}m = 0$, l is such that

$$\mathbf{l}^T\mathbf{B}^{-T}\mathbf{l} = 0,$$

since the matrix $\mathbf{B}$ is invertible. We use this remark and Proposition 2.20 to define the Kruppa matrix:

Definition 4.3 *The lines tangent to ω, considered as points in the dual $\mathbb{P}^{2*}$ of $\mathbb{P}^2$, lie on another conic ω^* whose matrix $\mathbf{K}$, according to Equation 4.31, is given by*

$$\mathbf{K} \simeq \mathbf{A}\mathbf{A}^T. \tag{4.34}$$

We call this matrix the Kruppa *matrix.*

Equation 4.34 shows that $\mathbf{K}$ is definite.

The explicit formulae giving the entries of $\mathbf{A}$ as a function of the entries of $\mathbf{K}$ can be found very simply, as shown in the next proposition.

Proposition 4.22 *The intrinsic parameters $u_0, v_0, \alpha, \beta, \gamma$ are functions of the Kruppa coefficients:*

$$
\begin{aligned}
K_{11} &= \alpha^2 + \gamma^2 + u_0^2 \qquad & \alpha &= \sqrt{K_{11} - u_0^2 - \gamma^2} \\
K_{12} &= u_0 v_0 + \beta\gamma & \gamma &= \frac{K_{12} - u_0 v_0}{\beta} \\
K_{22} &= \beta^2 + v_0^2 & \beta &= \sqrt{K_{22} - v_0^2} \\
K_{13} &= u_0 \\
K_{23} &= v_0
\end{aligned}
\tag{4.35}
$$

In particular,

$$
\begin{aligned}
\beta &= \frac{\sqrt{K_{22}K_{33} - K_{23}^2}}{K_{33}}, \\
\gamma &= \frac{K_{13}K_{23} - K_{33}K_{12}}{K_{33}\sqrt{K_{22}K_{33} - K_{23}^2}}.
\end{aligned}
\tag{4.36}
$$

Proof : The proof is just a matter of combining Equations 4.30 and 4.34. □

Some constraints on the intrinsic parameters can easily be transposed to constraints on matrices $\mathbf{B}$ or $\mathbf{K}$. When the pixel grid is orthogonal ($\theta = \frac{\pi}{2}$),

$$K_{13}K_{23} - K_{33}K_{12} = 0 \tag{4.37}$$

and $S([1,0,0]^T, [0,1,0]^T) = 0$. When the pixel grid is orthogonal and the aspect ratio one, the two circular points $\mathbf{I} = [1, -i, 0]^T$ and $\mathbf{J} = [1, i, 0]^T$ lie on ω, therefore

$S(\mathbf{I}, \mathbf{I}) = S(\mathbf{J}, \mathbf{J}) = 0$, Section 2.7.1. These constraints can be linearly combined with the constraints described in Section 7.4.4 (Liebowitz and Zisserman, 1999).

We have now at our disposal three different representations for the intrinsic parameters of a camera. The reader might at this point wonder why it is useful to have that many. The answer is that some constraints are better expressed with some representations than with others. For example, the zero-skew constraint is linear in $\mathbf{B}$ and quadratic in $\mathbf{K}$.

4.4   The affine and Euclidean models: The case of parallel projection

In this section, we consider the case where the affine structure of the world and the retina is known and discuss a class of camera models which correspond to the case $\det(\mathbf{P}) = 0$. As seen in Section 4.2, this property implies that the center of projection C is at infinity and the projection is parallel to the direction $\mathbf{C}$. No real camera performs an exact parallel projection but it turns out that, in some cases that we will discuss, the parallel model is a good approximation.

Parallel projection has been widely used by architects and military strategists starting from the end of the XVI-th century to draw views of cities, gardens, and palaces, as illustrated by Figure 4.18. It helped the XVII-th century architects to emphasize regularity (there is no convergence of parallel lines), while the architects of the beginning of the XX-th century (Bauhaus in Germany, De Stijl in the Netherlands, etc.) liked the idea of an abstract and theoretical viewpoint. Because parallel projection has the practical advantage to make it is possible to use the image as a map to directly measure distances along certain directions in space, it has also been used for industrial drawing, as illustrated by Figure 4.19. The techniques necessary to relate two parallel views in order to represent all of the spatial parameters of an object were systematically developed by Monge as the "descriptive geometry" that he taught at Ecole Polytechnique at the end of the XVIII-th century.

In Section 4.4.1 we introduce the parallel cameras by examining different flavors of parallel models as an approximation to the perspective model. In Section 4.4.2 we study the most general model which has the property to preserve parallelism; it is the *affine camera*. This model is *linear* instead of being merely *linear projective*. In Section 4.4.3, a Euclidean interpretation of the affine model is given.

4.4.1   Orthographic, weak perspective, para-perspective projections

Before turning to the general model, we illustrate the basic ideas behind the parallel models using the camera coordinate system, like we did in the perspective case.

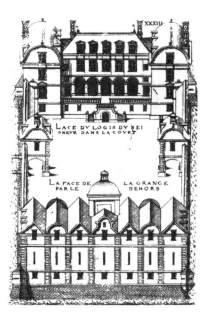

Figure 4.18: Examples of parallel projection in architecture.

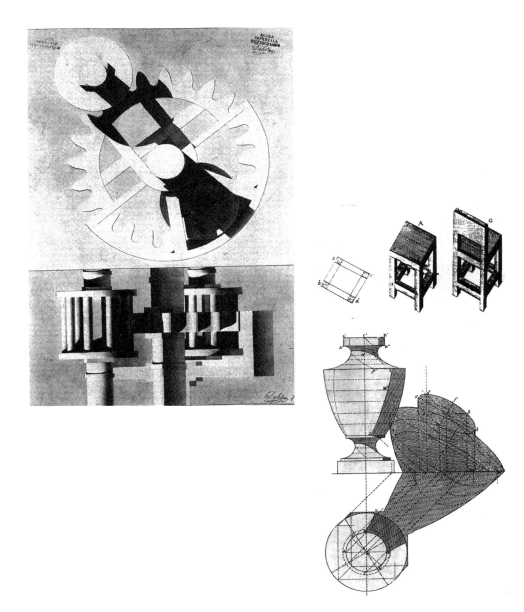

Figure 4.19: Examples of parallel projection in industrial drawing.

The orthographic projection   Let us start from the perspective model in the camera coordinate system, and refer it to the retinal plane instead of to the focal plane, which amounts to translating the camera along the Z-axis by f; the perspective projection matrix can be written as

$$
\mathcal{P} = \begin{bmatrix} f & 0 & 0 & 0 \\ 0 & f & 0 & 0 \\ 0 & 0 & 1 & 0 \end{bmatrix} \begin{bmatrix} 1 & 0 & 0 & 0 \\ 0 & 1 & 0 & 0 \\ 0 & 0 & 1 & f \\ 0 & 0 & 0 & 1 \end{bmatrix} \simeq \begin{bmatrix} 1 & 0 & 0 & 0 \\ 0 & 1 & 0 & 0 \\ 0 & 0 & \frac{1}{f} & 1 \end{bmatrix}.
$$

If we let f go to infinity, which is to say that the optical center goes towards infinity, then we find the *orthographic projection* defined by the projection matrix $\mathcal{P}_o$ of Equation 4.15.

The orthographic projection ignores depth: two identical objects with the same orientation have the same projection, regardless of their position in space. Therefore this model does not attempt to model the most fundamental effect of linear perspective, the fact that the size of the projections of objects decrease as their distance to the camera increases.

By contrast, the weak perspective or scaled orthographic approximation that we describe next takes into account the global depth of the scene with a scale factor. Within each weak perspective view, there is still no variation of reprojection size with distance; however, the scale can change with each view, making it possible to account for a displacement of the camera towards or away from the scene.

Weak perspective, or scaled orthographic projection   The projection of certain special configurations of points in space can be accounted for by a simpler model than the pinhole model. In the camera coordinate system, if we observe with a camera of focal length f a plane of equation $Z = Z_G$ which is parallel to the retinal plane (*fronto-parallel*), then for all the points of that plane the projection equations become

$$
x = f\frac{X}{Z_G}, \quad y = f\frac{Y}{Z_G}.
$$

A first consequence is that we cannot differentiate a change in focal length f from a change in distance Z_G. We will see more precisely in Section 4.4.3 that this situation implies that the focal length cannot be considered to be an "intrinsic" parameter, but rather that there is a global scale factor for each view. With that ambiguity in mind, for the rest of the section we assume $f = 1$ without loss of generality.

A second consequence is that we can incorporate the *structure* parameter Z_G in the *projection*. This approach is a general method to obtain simpler (more constrained) projections. However, the projection will be valid only if the 3D points are close to the structural distributions which allowed us to define the specific projection model. The idea to incorporate specific constraints into projection models has been extended to the case of particular motions as well (Wiles and Brady, 1996a).

Thus the projection *of this particular configuration* can be described by the projection matrix

$$\mathcal{P} = \begin{bmatrix} 1 & 0 & 0 & 0 \\ 0 & 1 & 0 & 0 \\ 0 & 0 & 0 & Z_G \end{bmatrix}. \tag{4.38}$$

This type of projection is called *weak perspective* or *scaled orthographic*. It adds to the *orthographic* projection the scale factor Z_G (supposed constant and equal to 1 in the latter model) which accounts for changes in image size when the distance between the object and the camera is varied.

The reader can easily verify that *the relation between world coordinates and pixel coordinates is affine*. Thus the projection preserves parallelism.

It remains to be seen how good an approximation this approximation is to the actual perspective projection. This investigation is our next task. Let us consider a generic 3-D scene, with points at depths Z_i. Let Z_G be the average value of the depths. If the relative depth variations in the scene $\Delta Z_i / Z_G = Z_i / Z_G - 1$ are small, then we might approximate the individual depths Z_i by Z_G, which leads to the weak perspective model, as an approximation of the perspective model. To be more precise, for a point M_i of depth $Z_i = Z_G + \Delta Z_i$, the perspective projection is expanded as a Taylor series:

$$\mathbf{m}_{persp} = \frac{1}{Z_G + \Delta Z_i} \begin{bmatrix} X_i \\ Y_i \end{bmatrix} = \frac{1}{Z_G} \left(1 - \frac{\Delta Z_i}{Z_G} + \text{ Higher order terms} \right) \begin{bmatrix} X_i \\ Y_i \end{bmatrix}.$$

The weak perspective can be therefore seen as a zero-order approximation of the perspective projection. The difference between the perspective and the weak perspective projections is

$$\mathbf{m}_{persp} - \mathbf{m}_{wp} = -\frac{\Delta Z_i}{Z_G} \frac{1}{Z_i} \begin{bmatrix} X_i \\ Y_i \end{bmatrix} + \text{ Higher order terms.}$$

This equation shows that a small field of view (X/Z and Y/Z small) as well as a small departure from the average plane contributes to the validity of the approximation.

Geometrically, in the weak perspective model, points are first projected orthographically onto the fronto-parallel plane $Z = Z_G$ and then perspectively onto the image.

Para-perspective projection For a large field of view, the fact that the points are first projected orthographically in the weak perspective model creates a large approximation error. In the *para-perspective projection*, the first phase, the projection onto the average plane, is done using a parallel projection which is oblique. The direction is chosen to be defined by the line (C, G), where G is the centroid of the points, of coordinates $[X_G, Y_G, Z_G]^T$. The image coordinates of the projected point can be found to be equal to

$$\left[X + X_G - \frac{X_G}{Z_G}Z, Y + Y_G - \frac{Y_G}{Z_G}Z, Z_G \right]^T .$$

The para-perspective projection matrix is therefore

$$\mathcal{P} = \begin{bmatrix} 1 & 0 & -X_G/Z_G & X_G \\ 0 & 1 & -Y_G/Z_G & Y_G \\ 0 & 0 & 0 & Z_G \end{bmatrix} . \tag{4.39}$$

This equation is a generalization of Equation 4.38 which is obtained by setting $X_G = Y_G = 0$, meaning that the direction of the parallel projection is the optical axis, and a special case of the general affine camera model. The weak perspective projection model made it possible to differentiate objects which are close to the camera from objects which are far thanks to the parameter Z_G. In addition, the para-perspective projection model takes into account the distance of the object to the optical axis, thanks to the two parameters X_G and Y_G.

The para-perspective projection matrix can alternatively be written

$$\mathcal{P} = \begin{bmatrix} 1 & 0 & -\cot\theta_x & Z_G\cot\theta_x \\ 0 & 1 & -\cot\theta_y & Z_G\cot\theta_y \\ 0 & 0 & 0 & Z_G \end{bmatrix} ,$$

where the direction of projection is given by the angles θ_x in the X-Z plane and θ_y in the Y-Z plane, and the average depth Z_G.

For a point M_i of coordinates $[X_G + \Delta X_i, Y_G + \Delta Y_i, Z_G + \Delta Z_i]$, the perspective projection can be expanded as a Taylor series:

$$\begin{aligned} \mathbf{m}_{persp} &= \frac{1}{Z_G+\Delta Z_i} \begin{bmatrix} X_G + \Delta X_i \\ Y_G + \Delta Y_i \end{bmatrix} \\ &= \frac{1}{Z_G}\left(1 - \frac{\Delta Z_i}{Z_G} + \text{ Higher order terms}\right) \begin{bmatrix} X_G + \Delta X_i \\ Y_G + \Delta Y_i \end{bmatrix} \\ &= \mathbf{m}_{para} - \begin{bmatrix} \frac{\Delta X_i \Delta Z_i}{Z_G^2} + \text{ Higher order terms} \\ \frac{\Delta Y_i \Delta Z_i}{Z_G^2} + \text{ Higher order terms} \end{bmatrix} . \end{aligned}$$

The para-perspective projection can therefore be also seen as a first order approximation to the perspective model. The primary factor which contributes to the quality of the approximation is still a small relative depth variation. Other factors are a small field of view and a small spatial extension of the object. It can be denoted that in the examples used in (Poelman and Kanade, 1997), where the para-perspective model was applied to recover 3D structure from a set of images, an object was reconstructed, rather than a whole scene.

Figure 4.20: Parallelism is better preserved by perspective projection for a shallow objects and a small fields of view. Left: The facade of the building is more parallelogram-like than the side, since it has a smaller depth variation. Right: parallelism is better preserved for the central line markings than for the sides of the road, which are seen with a wider angle of view.

The parallel models are well-suited for the imaging situation where pictures are taken with a telephoto lens. In this case, first, the field of view is small, and second, the distance of the camera to the objects is large. A lot of the earlier applications of computer vision were concerned with military imagery, where it is often the case that one cannot get close and has therefore to use powerful telephotos. For this class of imagery, the orthographic and scaled orthographic models were appropriate.

Generally speaking, a characteristic property of the family of parallel projection models that we have examined is that they preserve parallelism, as opposed to perspective projection, which causes images of parallel lines to converge at vanishing points. Therefore, intuitively, the more parallel lines tend to remain parallel, the more the approximation is valid. Intuitive examples are given in Figure 4.20. In Figure 4.21, we show a sequence of images of the same object, where the camera simultaneously zooms in and zooms out so that the size of the image of the object remains constant. There is a gradual transition from strong perspective to weak perspective.

The difference between the models presented in this section is illustrated in Figure 4.22, where we have taken a slice along a plane $Y = Y_0$. A summary of these models is presented in Table 4.1.

4.4.2   The general model: The affine projection matrix

The general case which is examined in this section is that of cameras for which the first 3×3 submatrix of the projection matrix is singular. We saw in Section 4.2.1 that this situation implies that the optical center is at infinity. In this case we know

Figure 4.21: The camera moves back while zooming in, with the size of the object image kept constant in the left sequence, as in Hitchcock's Vertigo. For reference, the field of view is kept constant in the right sequence. There is a gradual transition from strong perspective to weak perspective. In the first image, the sides of the sign are strongly converging, in the last image, they are almost parallel.

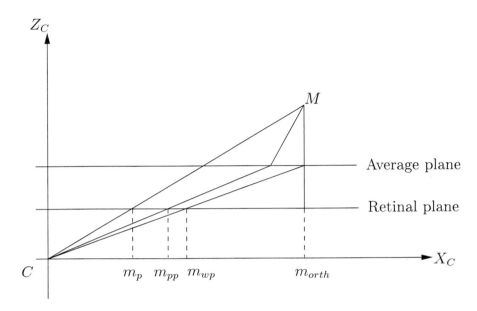

Figure 4.22: One dimensional image formation: four different models. The figure shows the images of the point M in the full perspective model (m_p), the para-perspective model (m_{pp}), the weak perspective model (m_{wp}) and the orthographic model (m_{orth}).

Orthographic	$\begin{bmatrix} 1 & 0 & 0 & 0 \\ 0 & 1 & 0 & 0 \\ 0 & 0 & 0 & 1 \end{bmatrix}$	ignores distance and position
Weak perspective	$\begin{bmatrix} 1 & 0 & 0 & 0 \\ 0 & 1 & 0 & 0 \\ 0 & 0 & 0 & Z_G \end{bmatrix}$	takes into account distance
Para-perspective	$\begin{bmatrix} 1 & 0 & -X_G/Z_G & X_G \\ 0 & 1 & -Y_G/Z_G & Y_G \\ 0 & 0 & 0 & Z_G \end{bmatrix}$	takes into account distance and position

Table 4.1: The parallel approximations in the camera coordinate system, ordered by increasing generality.

from Section 2.5 that the point represents a direction of the affine space. Hence, the optical center can be thought of in this case as a direction of projection, the direction of all optical rays. . However, by parallel projection, one generally means something more precise, namely the fact that parallel lines in 3-D are projected into parallel lines in the image. The three models which we examined had this property. The last row of the projection matrix was proportional to $[0,0,0,1]^T$. We generalize this observation with the following definition and proposition.

Proposition 4.23 *An **affine camera** is defined by the fact that its focal plane is the plane at infinity* Π_∞. *The perspective projection matrix, called the **affine projection matrix** takes the simpler form*

$$\mathcal{P} \simeq \left[\begin{array}{ccc|c} & \mathbf{P}_A & & \mathbf{p}_A \\ 0 & 0 & 0 & 1 \end{array} \right],$$

where $\mathbf{P}_A$ *is a* 2×3 *matrix of rank 2 and* $\mathbf{p}_A$ *a* 2×1 *vector. The matrix* $\mathbf{P}_A$ *is called the **reduced projection matrix**. A camera preserves parallelism if and only if it is affine.*

Proof : Since Π_∞ is represented by the vector $[0,0,0,1]^T$ we obtain the announced form for the matrix $\mathcal{P}$ as a consequence of Proposition 4.14. The matrix $\mathbf{P}_A$ is of rank two since $\mathcal{P}$ is of rank 3.

If $\mathcal{P}$ is affine, it can be seen by inspection that the points at infinity in 3D space are mapped to the points at infinity in the retina, which means that the images of two 3D lines that meet at a point in Π_∞ meet at a point on l_∞ and therefore are parallel. Reciprocally, let assume that any pair of parallel lines of $\mathbb{P}^3$, L_1 and L_2, is projected into a pair of parallel lines of $\mathbb{P}^2$. Parallelism means that $L_1 \cap L_2$ is a point at infinity M_∞, and so is $m_\infty = l_1 \cap l_2$. Because of the conservation of incidence, M_∞ is projected into m_∞. Since the relation holds for any pair of lines, we conclude that the plane Π_∞ of $\mathbb{P}^3$ is projected into the line at infinity l_∞ of $\mathbb{P}^2$. Therefore the plane Π_∞ is the focal plane.
□

A consequence of this proposition is that $\mathcal{P}$ induces a projective morphism from $\mathbb{P}^2$ to $\mathbb{P}^1$: A point in Π_∞ representing a direction of line $[d_X, d_Y, d_Z]^T$ is mapped to a point of l_∞ in the retinal plane $\mathcal{R}$ representing a direction of line $[d_u, d_v]^T$ and the relation between the two is given by the matrix $\mathbf{P}_A$:

$$\left[\begin{array}{c} d_u \\ d_v \end{array} \right] = \mathbf{P}_A \left[\begin{array}{c} d_X \\ d_Y \\ d_Z \end{array} \right]. \tag{4.40}$$

Formally, all of the machinery which has been used for the full projective projection matrix can be transposed to $\mathbf{P}_A$ in the case of lines, with a reduction of one dimension (Quan and Kanade, 1996).

When considering the points which are not at infinity, the projective morphism $\mathcal{P}$ from $\mathbb{P}^3$ to $\mathbb{P}^2$ can be expressed as an affine morphism from X_3 to X_2 (see Definition 2.3):

$$\left[\begin{array}{c} u \\ v \end{array} \right] = \mathbf{P}_A \left[\begin{array}{c} X \\ Y \\ Z \end{array} \right] + \mathbf{p}_A. \tag{4.41}$$

Because of the linearity of the projection, the ratios of distances along aligned points are preserved. It is also easy to verify that:

Proposition 4.24 *The affine camera projects any center of mass (and in particular the centroid) of a set of 3D points into the center of mass of the projections of the points.*

This remark makes it possible to simplify further the projection equations in the affine case by canceling the vector $\mathbf{p}_A$. Let $\mathbf{m}_0$ and $\mathbf{m}$ be images of 3D points $\mathbf{M}_0$ and $\mathbf{M}$, then the projection equation for points can be written

$$\Delta\mathbf{m} = \mathbf{P}_A \Delta\mathbf{M}, \tag{4.42}$$

where $\Delta\mathbf{m} = \mathbf{m} - \mathbf{m}_0$ and $\Delta\mathbf{M} = \mathbf{M} - \mathbf{M}_0$ are relative coordinates. In particular, since the centroid of the 3D points, $\mathbf{M}_0 = \frac{1}{n}\sum_{i=1}^{n}\mathbf{M}_i$, is projected onto the centroid of the 2D points, $\mathbf{m}_0 = \frac{1}{n}\sum_{i=1}^{n}\mathbf{m}_i$, if we express all of the 3D points with respect to their centroids and all of the 2D points with respect to their centroids, then the projection can be described by just the 2×3 matrix $\mathbf{P}_A$.

Although in one case it is an inhomogeneous quantity and in the other case it is significant only up to a scale factor, the same reduced projection matrix $\mathbf{P}_A$ describes the projection of points (Equation 4.42) and of lines (Equation 4.40). This case is noticeably simpler than the perspective case where two distinct matrices were necessary.

Since the matrix $\mathbf{P}_\mathbf{A}$ is of rank 2, there is a unique direction $\mathbf{C}$ (defined up to a scale factor) such that $\mathbf{P}_A\mathbf{C} = 0$. $\mathbf{C}$ is the direction of projection. Two points of affine coordinates $\mathbf{M}_1$ and $\mathbf{M}_2$ have the same projection if and only if $\mathbf{M}_1 - \mathbf{M}_2 = \lambda\mathbf{C}$.

A special case of interest which is related to the previous discussion in Section 4.1.4 and to the upcoming one in Paragraph 5.4.2.2 of Chapter 5 is the following. Suppose that a perspective projection camera with focal plane represented by $\boldsymbol{W}$ is pointed to a plane parallel to the focal plane (fronto-parallel) represented by $\mathbf{\Pi}$. This situation is equivalent to $\tilde{\boldsymbol{W}} = \alpha\tilde{\mathbf{\Pi}}$ for some α. Consider the vector $\mathbf{c} = [0, 0, \alpha]^T$. Then, according to Proposition 4.10, the projection matrix $\mathcal{P}_{c,\Pi}$ is equivalent to $\mathcal{P}$ in the sense that $\mathcal{P}_{c,\Pi}\mathbf{M} \simeq \mathcal{P}\mathbf{M}$ for all points in Π. Because of our choice of $\mathbf{c}$, however, the matrix $\mathcal{P}_{c,\Pi}$ represents an affine camera even if $\mathcal{P}$ does not.

The curious reader might at this point be left wondering which kind of projection takes place when the optical center is at infinity but the focal plane is not the plane at infinity or, in algebraic terms, when the first 3×3 submatrix of the projection matrix is singular without the last row being null. The interpretation for this case is given for completeness. However we will not be using this class of projections in the reminder of the book.

Proposition 4.25 *When the optical center is at infinity but the focal plane is not the plane at infinity, the projection can be described as the composition of an orthographic projection with a homography of the retinal plane which is not affine.*

Proof : Let us write $\mathcal{P} = [\mathbf{P}\,\mathbf{p}]$, and let $\mathbf{u}$ be a unit vector of the kernel of $\mathbf{P}$ and $\mathbf{v}$ any vector which is not parallel to $\mathbf{u}$. Then it can be verified that by defining $\mathbf{H}$ and $\mathbf{R}$ as

$$\mathbf{H} = \mathbf{P}\,[\underbrace{\frac{(\mathbf{u} \times \mathbf{v}) \times \mathbf{u}}{\|(\mathbf{u} \times \mathbf{v}) \times \mathbf{u}\|}, \frac{\mathbf{u} \times \mathbf{v}}{\|\mathbf{u} \times \mathbf{v}\|}, \mathbf{u}]}_{\mathbf{R}^T} + [\mathbf{0}_3\,\mathbf{0}_3\,\mathbf{p}],$$

the projection can be decomposed under the form

$$\mathcal{P} = \mathbf{H}\mathcal{P}_o \begin{bmatrix} \mathbf{R} & \mathbf{0}_3 \\ \mathbf{0}_3^T & 1 \end{bmatrix},$$

where $\mathcal{P}_o$ is defined in Equation 4.15. Denote that the decomposition has one degree of freedom in the choice of the vector $\mathbf{v}$, which was to be expected since we have 8 parameters in the homography and 3 in the rotations, but only 10 in the projection matrix, due to the constraint $\det(\mathbf{P}) = 0$. □

4.4.3 Euclidean interpretation of the parallel projection

We now discuss the intrinsic and extrinsic parameters of an affine camera. If we consider a change of retinal coordinate system and a change of world coordinate system such as those presented for the perspective case, we have many more parameters than needed to account for the general affine matrix. Therefore there is no "natural" Euclidean interpretation of an affine projection matrix, and in the literature several different decompositions (for example (Shapiro et al., 1995), (Quan, 1996), (Basri, 1996)) have been presented.

Interpretation as an orthographic projection A decomposition in intrinsic and extrinsic parameters similar to the one used for the perspective projection is

$$\mathcal{P} = \begin{bmatrix} \alpha & \gamma & u_0 \\ 0 & \beta & v_0 \\ 0 & 0 & 1 \end{bmatrix} \begin{bmatrix} 1 & 0 & 0 & 0 \\ 0 & 1 & 0 & 0 \\ 0 & 0 & 0 & 1 \end{bmatrix} \begin{bmatrix} \mathbf{R} & \mathbf{t} \\ \mathbf{0}_3^T & 1 \end{bmatrix}$$

$$\begin{bmatrix} \mathbf{p}_1^T & p_1 \\ \mathbf{p}_2^T & p_2 \\ \mathbf{0}^T & 1 \end{bmatrix} = \begin{bmatrix} \alpha\mathbf{r}_1^T + \gamma\mathbf{r}_2^T & \alpha t_X + \gamma t_Y + u_0 \\ \beta\mathbf{r}_2^T & \beta t_Y + v_0 \\ \mathbf{0} & 1 \end{bmatrix},$$

where $\mathbf{R} = [\mathbf{r}_1, \mathbf{r}_2, \mathbf{r}_3]^T$ is a rotation matrix. The decomposition is clearly not unique, since there are eleven Euclidean parameters. We notice that:

- There is a coupling between the principal point u_0, v_0 and the two first components of the translation. Shifting the image with the affine model is equivalent to just applying a translation in the world. For any values of u_0 and v_0, there are valid values of t_X and t_Y. This situation was to be expected since there is no principal point in the orthographic projection. In the following, we choose $u_0 = v_0 = 0$.

- Translating the image along Z does not produce any change in the projection since it is parallel to this axis; thus, t_Z cancels and can be set to an arbitrary value without affecting the other parameters.

These remarks have some implications for the perspective model as well. Since the position of the principal point is arbitrary for an affine model, for a perspective model where the focal length is large, we can expect some instability in the estimation of its principal point.

Once these choices are made, we are left with eight parameters: the scale factors α, β, the skew γ, the rotation, and the first two components of the translation t_X, t_Y. The solution is uniquely determined (up to a sign) by

$$\beta = \|\mathbf{p}_2\| \qquad \mathbf{r}_2 = \frac{1}{\beta}\mathbf{p}_2 \qquad \gamma = \mathbf{p}_1^T \mathbf{r}_2$$

$$\alpha = \|\mathbf{p}_1 - \gamma \mathbf{r}_2\| \qquad \mathbf{r}_1 = \frac{1}{\alpha}(\mathbf{p}_1 - \gamma \mathbf{r}_2) \qquad t_Y = \frac{p_2}{\beta}$$

$$t_X \qquad = \frac{1}{\alpha}(p_1 - \gamma t_Y) \qquad \mathbf{r}_3 \qquad = \mathbf{r}_1 \times \mathbf{r}_2$$

The decomposition for the reduced matrix is

$$\mathbf{P}_A = \mathbf{A}_A \begin{bmatrix} 1 & 0 & 0 \\ 0 & 1 & 0 \end{bmatrix} \mathbf{R} = \underbrace{\begin{bmatrix} \alpha & \gamma \\ 0 & \beta \end{bmatrix}}_{\mathbf{A}_A} \begin{bmatrix} \mathbf{r}_1^T \\ \mathbf{r}_2^T \end{bmatrix}.$$

The six parameters which appear in the decomposition of the reduced matrix are unambiguous in this formulation, unlike the eleven parameters which appear in the decomposition of the full matrix, for which we had to put three additional constraints. This decomposition can also be found by applying a QR decomposition to the matrix $\mathbf{P}_A$, as suggested by Quan (Quan, 1996), by writing

$$\mathbf{P}_A \mathbf{P}_A^T = \mathbf{A}_A \mathbf{A}_A^T = \begin{bmatrix} \alpha^2 + \gamma^2 & \beta\gamma \\ \beta\gamma & \beta^2 \end{bmatrix}. \tag{4.43}$$

The reduced intrinsic parameter matrix can alternatively be written as

$$\mathbf{A}_A = \lambda \begin{bmatrix} k & \gamma' \\ 0 & 1 \end{bmatrix}, \tag{4.44}$$

where λ is a scaling factor that depends not only on the camera, but also on the structure, k is an aspect ratio, and γ' is a skew factor. This formulation makes it clear that for most practical purposes, the affine camera is calibrated up to a scale factor since those two parameters are very likely to be known. The scale factor varies at each view and depends on the distance between the object and the camera, which is in contrast with the case of the perspective camera where the intrinsic parameters do not depend on the 3D structure.

Interpretation as weak perspective Using the more general weak perspective as the core model yields a somewhat similar decomposition of the projection matrix. The previous discussion can be summarized in the following proposition.

Proposition 4.26 *An affine projection matrix can be decomposed uniquely (up to a sign), using eight parameters, as*

$$\mathcal{P} = \frac{1}{Z_G} \begin{bmatrix} k & \gamma' & 0 \\ 0 & 1 & 0 \\ 0 & 0 & 1 \end{bmatrix} \begin{bmatrix} 1 & 0 & 0 & 0 \\ 0 & 1 & 0 & 0 \\ 0 & 0 & 0 & Z_G \end{bmatrix} \begin{bmatrix} \mathbf{R} & \mathbf{t} \\ \mathbf{0}_3^T & 1 \end{bmatrix},$$

$$\begin{bmatrix} \mathbf{p}_1^T & p_1 \\ \mathbf{p}_2^T & p_2 \\ \mathbf{0}^T & 1 \end{bmatrix} = \frac{1}{Z_G} \begin{bmatrix} k\mathbf{r}_1^T + \gamma'\mathbf{r}_2^T & kt_X + \gamma't_Y \\ \mathbf{r}_2^T & t_Y \\ \mathbf{0} & Z_G \end{bmatrix},$$

where $\mathbf{R} = [\mathbf{r}_1, \mathbf{r}_2, \mathbf{r}_3]^T$ *is a rotation matrix, k an aspect ratio, γ' a skew, and Z_G the distance to the object.*

The difference between this decomposition and the one based on the orthographic model is only how we account for the magnification. Since the orthographic model does not include a scale factor to account for the distance of the object, we needed to consider different intrinsic parameters to account for different magnifications. On the other hand, with the weak perspective model, the two intrinsic parameters representing the aspect ratio and skew are maintained constant, while the scale depends on the distance to the object. The scale is inversely proportional to Z_G: The further away the object, the smaller the magnification.

Interpretation as para-perspective We have just seen that there are three intrinsic parameters in the interpretation of an affine projection matrix as an orthographic projection or weak perspective projection. A general para-perspective projection also has three parameters: The three coordinates X_G, Y_G, Z_G of the reference point. Therefore, we do not need to introduce new intrinsic parameters.

Proposition 4.27 *An affine projection matrix can be decomposed as the product of a para-perspective projection matrix and a change of world coordinate system:*

$$\mathcal{P} = \frac{1}{Z_G} \begin{bmatrix} 1 & 0 & -\frac{X_G}{Z_G} & X_G \\ 0 & 1 & -\frac{Y_G}{Z_G} & Y_G \\ 0 & 0 & 0 & Z_G \end{bmatrix} \begin{bmatrix} \mathbf{R} & \mathbf{t} \\ \mathbf{0}_3^T & 1 \end{bmatrix},$$

$$\begin{bmatrix} \mathbf{p}_1^T & p_1 \\ \mathbf{p}_2^T & p_2 \\ \mathbf{0}^T & 1 \end{bmatrix} = \frac{1}{Z_G} \begin{bmatrix} \mathbf{r}_1^T - \frac{X_G}{Z_G}\mathbf{r}_3^T & t_X + X_G(1 - \frac{t_Z}{Z_G}) \\ \mathbf{r}_2^T - \frac{Y_G}{Z_G}\mathbf{r}_3^T & t_Y + Y_G(1 - \frac{t_Z}{Z_G}) \\ \mathbf{0}_3^T & Z_G \end{bmatrix},$$

where $\mathbf{R} = [\mathbf{r}_1, \mathbf{r}_2, \mathbf{r}_3]^T$ *is a rotation matrix. This decomposition is up to one degree of freedom, which can be fixed by fixing for instance one component of the translation.*

Proof : Since we have used nine parameters for eight degrees of freedom, we expect some ambiguity, and, indeed, the ambiguity along the projection axis is visible on the last column of the matrix since there is a coupling between the coordinates of the reference point and those of the translation. Once X_G, Y_G, Z_G have been recovered, the ambiguity can be resolved by taking for instance $t_Z = Z_G$, and then X_G and Y_G can be obtained uniquely.

We concentrate now on the reduced part. We have to solve the system of equations

$$\begin{cases} a_0\mathbf{r}_1 + a_1\mathbf{r}_3 = \|\mathbf{p}_1\|\mathbf{u}_1, \\ a_0\mathbf{r}_2 + a_2\mathbf{r}_3 = \|\mathbf{p}_2\|\mathbf{u}_2, \end{cases} \tag{4.45}$$

where the vectors $\mathbf{u}_i = \mathbf{p}_i/\|\mathbf{p}_i\|$, $i = 1, 2$, are unit vectors, and $a_0 = 1/Z_G$, $a_1 = -X_G/Z_G^2$, and $a_2 = -Y_G/Z_G^2$. The unknowns are a_0, a_1, a_2, and the vectors $\mathbf{r}_1$, $\mathbf{r}_2$, $\mathbf{r}_3$. The constraint is that the matrix $[\mathbf{r}_1, \mathbf{r}_2, \mathbf{r}_3]$ is a rotation matrix.

We assume for simplicity that the vectors $\mathbf{u}_1$ and $\mathbf{u}_2$ are neither parallel nor orthogonal. The interested reader will have no difficulty in solving the system (4.45) in either of those two special cases. The three vectors $\mathbf{u}_1$, $\mathbf{u}_2$ and $\mathbf{u}_3 = (\mathbf{u}_1 \times \mathbf{u}_2)/\|\mathbf{u}_1 \times \mathbf{u}_2)\|$ form a basis of $\mathbb{R}^3$, and we express the vectors $\mathbf{r}_1$ and $\mathbf{r}_2$ in this basis, taking into account (4.45)

$$\begin{cases} \mathbf{r}_1 = \alpha_1\mathbf{u}_1 + \gamma_1\mathbf{u}_3, \\ \mathbf{r}_2 = \alpha_2\mathbf{u}_2 + \gamma_2\mathbf{u}_3. \end{cases} \tag{4.46}$$

The three conditions $\|\mathbf{r}_1\|^2 = \|\mathbf{r}_2\|^2 = 1$ and $\mathbf{r}_1 \cdot \mathbf{r}_2 = 0$ are equivalent to

$$\begin{cases} \alpha_1^2 + \gamma_1^2 = 1, \\ \alpha_2^2 + \gamma_2^2 = 1, \\ c\alpha_1\alpha_2 + \gamma_1\gamma_2 = 0, \end{cases} \tag{4.47}$$

where $c = \mathbf{u}_1 \cdot \mathbf{u}_2$ is different from 0 by hypothesis. We then write the condition $\mathbf{p}_1 \cdot \mathbf{r}_1 = \mathbf{p}_2 \cdot \mathbf{r}_2$ which is a consequence of (4.45)

$$\alpha_1\|\mathbf{p}_1\| = \alpha_2\|\mathbf{p}_2\|.$$

We denote by r the ratio $\|\mathbf{p}_1\|/\|\mathbf{p}_2\|$. The last condition implies that $\alpha_1\alpha_2 = \alpha_2^2 r = \alpha_1^2/r$. We use these relations together with the last equations of (4.47) to eliminate α_1 and α_2 between the first two equations of (4.47):

$$\begin{cases} -\gamma_1\gamma_2\dfrac{r}{c} + \gamma_1^2 = 1, \\ -\dfrac{\gamma_1\gamma_2}{rc} + \gamma_2^2 = 1. \end{cases} \tag{4.48}$$

We then eliminate for example γ_2 between these two equations. Letting $x = 1 - \gamma_1^2$, we obtain

$$c^2 x^2 + x(1 + r^2) - r^2 = 0.$$

This quadratic equation in the unknown x is readily seen to have two real roots of opposite sign. Only the positive root is of interest to us. We easily verify that it is also less than or equal to 1, as required.

This process yields in general four distinct solutions for the pair $(\alpha_1\,\gamma_1)$, i.e. for $\mathbf{r}_1$, and to each of these solutions corresponds a unique solution for the pair $(\alpha_2,\,\gamma_2)$, i.e. for $\mathbf{r}_2$. The vector $\mathbf{r}_3$ is then obtained as $\mathbf{r}_1 \times \mathbf{r}_2$. Once the matrix $\mathbf{R}$ has been obtained, it is an easy matter to compute the coefficients a_i:

$$a_0 = \mathbf{p}_1^T\mathbf{r}_1 = \mathbf{p}_2^T\mathbf{r}_2, \qquad a_1 = \mathbf{p}_1^T\mathbf{r}_3, \qquad a_2 = \mathbf{p}_2^T\mathbf{r}_3.$$

$\square$

The reduced affine projection matrix is given by

$$\mathbf{P}_A = \begin{bmatrix} f & 0 & u_0 \\ 0 & f & v_0 \end{bmatrix}, \mathbf{R}$$

with $f = 1/Z_G$, $u_0 = -X_G/Z_G^2$, and $v_0 = -Y_G/Z_G^2$. This remark shows that varying the reference point X_G, Y_G, Z_G is equivalent to varying intrinsic parameters. As remarked in (Basri, 1996), if the reference point is specified by a centroid (the usual case with affine projection), then there are constraints on the form of the projection matrix with this decomposition.

The coordinates X_G, Y_G are equivalent to a principal point, which in turn is equivalent to a translation in world coordinates. The depth Z_G is equivalent to a focal length, which in turn is equivalent to translation of the reference plane. However, the intrinsic parameters in the two types of decomposition are different. Using again the fact that $\mathbf{R}$ is orthogonal, we obtain

$$\mathbf{P}_A\mathbf{P}_A^T = \begin{bmatrix} f^2 + u_0^2 & u_0 v_0 \\ u_0 v_0 & f^2 + v_0^2 \end{bmatrix}.$$

These equations are equivalent to those used by Basri (Basri, 1996), who solves them for the unknowns f, u_0, v_0 to prove the existence of the decomposition. This solution for this problem is more complicated than the solution obtained with Equation 4.43, therefore in practice it is more convenient to use the decomposition based on the weak perspective and intrinsic parameters than to use the decomposition based on para-perspective. It is possible to relate the para-perspective decomposition to the weak perspective:

$$\mathbf{A}_A = \sqrt{f^2 + v_0^2} \begin{bmatrix} \dfrac{f\sqrt{f^2 + u_0^2 + v_0^2}}{f^2 + v_0^2} & \dfrac{u_0 v_0}{f^2 + v_0^2} \\ 0 & 1 \end{bmatrix}.$$

We can conclude that, provided that a change of world coordinates is allowed, every affine projection can be described alternatively as an orthographic projection with scale factors and skew factor, or alternatively as a para-perspective projection with an arbitrary reference point. In particular, no skew factor is needed in this case.

4.5   Departures from the pinhole model: Nonlinear distortion

The pinhole camera is a *linear* model (in projective coordinates for the case of perspective projection, in affine coordinates for the case of parallel projection) which has very nice geometric properties that we have studied in detail in this chapter. We now take a closer look at the validity of this model and describe ways of extending it to incorporate a broader class of cameras and lenses by taking into account nonlinear distortion.

This distortion is in contrast with linear distortion, which results simply from perspective. When a wide angle of view is used, the resulting image sometimes appears distorted. For example, it was observed by Leonardo (who found this rather strange) that under perspective projection with a wide field of view, spheres are projected as ellipses and not circles. Indeed, a sphere is projected on a circle only when the center of the sphere is located on the optical axis. Generally speaking, three-dimensional objects appear to be stretched out of shape in directions radiating from the image center.

We describe nonlinear distortion in Section 4.5.1 and a method to correct it within a projective approach in Section 4.5.2.

4.5.1   Nonlinear distortion of the pinhole model

For the projection to be linear, three implicit hypotheses are made in the pinhole model:

1. the image is formed on a surface which is actually planar,

2. the pixels are regularly spaced in the image plane, and

3. the lens does not have optical distortion.

It is generally acknowledged that the two first hypotheses are satisfied with a sufficient degree of precision: The position of the CCD photo-sensors is controlled with a high degree of accuracy. Image plane distortions in a CCD camera are mainly caused by synchronization imprecision in the A/D conversion step (which results in a shift between two successive pixel lines) and by signal perturbation on the transmitted video signal. Recent photogrammetric investigations (Dahler, 1987; Beyer, 1990; Beyer, 1992; Lenz, 1987) have shown that these distortions are small (0.1 pixel). They can even be neglected if a synchronous A/D conversion is used. Problems could appear when using low quality cameras (such as in (Toscani, 1987)) which show an important and irregular tangential distortion. When using film-based cameras (as opposed to CCD cameras), there might be problems due to the lack of film flatness. For such cameras, a correction has to be done on the whole image plane. One technique to perform this task is to use local mappings defined by the observation of a regular pattern such as a grid made of lines (Toscani, 1987; Peuchot, 1992; Brand et al., 1993). It allows one to obtain a very good precision, and does not require an explicit model of the distortion. Since every transformation which maps lines into lines is projective linear, the correction results in an exact perspective transformation over the image plane (Brand et al., 1993).

An actual pinhole camera has no optical distortion, since light travels in a straight light through the pinhole. By contrast, the path of light in a lens is quite complex because of the number of elements involved and the physical phenomena involved. There are many factors to be optimized in lens design, including sharpness, ability to focus on a wide range of distances, color rendition, and uniformity of illumination. Image shape (absence of distortion) is only one of those factors, so it is not surprising that it is not always corrected. Distortion is particularly important on low-cost wide-angle and zoom lenses. On the other hand, narrow-field lenses (telephotos) are easier to correct. For an introduction to photographic optics, the reader is referred to the books of Kingslake (Kingslake, 1992) and Stroebel (Stroebel et al., 1990; Stroebel, 1999).

We model nonlinear distortion of lenses by adding a special term. It transforms the ideal normalized image coordinates x and y into the coordinates

$$\begin{cases} x' = x + \delta_x(x, y), \\ y' = y + \delta_y(x, y). \end{cases}$$

The distortion elements which are the most often considered are:

• The radial distortion (symmetrical with respect to the center of distortion), which is represented by a polynomial:

$$\begin{cases} \delta_x^r = x(K_1 r^2 + K_2 r^4 + K_3 r^6 + \dots \\ \delta_y^r = y(K_1 r^2 + K_2 r^4 + K_3 r^6 + \dots \end{cases}$$

- The decentering distortion (Brown, 1966):

$$\begin{cases} \delta_x^c = P_1(r^2 + 2x^2) + 2P_2xy \\ \delta_y^c = P_2(r^2 + 2y^2) + 2P_1xy \end{cases}$$

with $r = \sqrt{x^2 + y^2}$. The center of distortion is usually taken to be the principal point. This approximation is carefully examined by Wilson (Willson, 1994; Willson and Shafer, 1993) who gives a comprehensive taxonomy for the property of "image center".

Most of the authors (Tsai, 1987; Hung and Shieh, 1990; Beyer, 1992; Fraser, 1992) find that a reprojection precision from 0.1 to 0.5 pixels is reached by only considering the first radial distortion term. Such a precision is sufficient to allow for metric three-dimensional applications using CCD cameras. Considering that the decentering distortion is taken into account by a shift of the principal point (or vice-versa) is also a good approximation (Stein, 1993).

The radial distortion grows with the angle of view. It is quite small in the center of the image even for cameras which are affected by distortion. It has been noticed (Shortis et al., 1991) that in practice, in the center of the image, this distortion can be modeled by a linear function $\delta^r = K_0 r$, so that considering that the radial distortion is taken into account by a change of focal length is a satisfying approximation for the central portion of the image. This fact was used for instance by (Hung and Shieh, 1990; Weng et al., 1992a). However, depending on the lenses which are used, on the borders, the radial distortion can be negligible or it can also reach such large values as ten pixels. In the last case, a correction step is necessary. Beyer(Beyer, 1992), using photogrammetric techniques, finds an improvement of a factor of 6 by the introduction of K_1, and another factor of 6 with K_2, K_3, P_1, P_2 together. Weng et al (Weng et al., 1992a) find an improvement of a factor of 4 using K_1, and then only a factor of 1.2 with four tangential distortion terms. The difference could come from the use of the computer vision methodology which does not allow them to obtain localizations which are sufficiently precise and redundant. One has to keep in mind that we are not only limited by the precision of calibration, but also by the precision of measurement for the coordinates of image points. If no sub-pixel detection operator is used systematically, then there is no need to correct the distortion if the errors remain approximatively of the size of the pixel.

4.5.2   Distortion correction within a projective model

The classical calibration methods which take into account camera distortion do that by estimating all of the parameters, intrinsic and extrinsic, at the same time. The result is therefore a completely calibrated camera. However, all these methods, reviewed in Section 4.6, require the use of a calibration object with known 3D coordinates. In this section, we describe a method which requires only the presence of straight lines in the scene. This knowledge is necessary since we are considering a single view.

If more than one view is available, then using the multi-image constraints which will be presented in Chapters 5 and 8, a sufficient number of point correspondences are in theory enough to recover the distortion. One simply adds the distortion terms to the motion parameters to be recovered by nonlinear optimization. In practice, the epipolar constraint used with two views gave mixed results in experiments by Zhang (Zhang, 1996), whereas Stein (Stein, 1997) obtained more convincing results with three views thanks to the trifocal tensor, which makes it possible to completely predict the coordinates of a point in the third view.

To find the distortion from a single image, it is possible to use a fundamental property: A camera follows the pinhole model if and only if the projection of every line in space onto the camera is a line. Consequently, to remove the distortion it is sufficient to apply a transformation in the image which "straightens" all of the observed lines. Therefore it is not necessary to perform a complete calibration of the camera in order to correct the distortion. Rather, the distortion can be corrected independently of the calibration of any parameter, by only applying a transformation in the image plane.

A first application of this idea has been described by Brand *et al.* (Brand et al., 1993; Mohr et al., 1993a), using a plane calibration grid composed of straight lines whose intersections can be detected very precisely. Each point on the image of the grid is mapped (nonlinearly) to a virtual coordinate frame with arbitrary pixel coordinates which is distortion free, using the knowledge of a functional model of the calibration grid. This transformation is then extended for all the pixels in the image, using local bilinear interpolation functions for the coordinates. Therefore no analytical model of the distortion is necessary. The new points, which now form a distortion free image, are then backprojected to the original pixel coordinate system by a homography defined by four points chosen next to the corners of the image. The comparison with the original pixel coordinates gives a distortion map. It can be noted that this operation introduces a "hidden" projective transformation in the image. However, this transformation does not matter since it is contained in the pinhole model.

Devernay (Devernay and Faugeras, 1995) has proposed another method, which has the advantage of not requiring a calibration object. Rather, it is assumed that the environment contains a certain number of straight lines. Edges are detected. The following procedure is performed until convergence. A polygonal approximation with a large tolerance is used to extract potential straight segments. For each of the segments, the measure of distortion error is computed as the sum of squares of the distances from the points to the segment. The camera distortion is modeled analytically using the first order radial distortion K_1, and a center of distortion $[c_x, c_y]$ different from the principal point. The difference accounts for decentering distortion, whereas the fact that an aspect ratio s_x is used prior to compensating for distortion amounts to a tangential distortion. The undistorted coordinates are given by

$$x_u = x_d + (x_d - c_x)K_1 r_d^2, \qquad y_u = y_d + (y_d - c_y)K_1 r_d^2,$$

where $r_d = \sqrt{\left(\dfrac{x_d - c_x}{s_x}\right)^2 + (y_d - c_y)^2}$ is the distorted radius. The reverse relations are obtained by solving a polynomial of degree 3:

$$r_u = r_d \left(1 + K_1 r_d^2\right),$$

where $r_u = \sqrt{\left(\dfrac{x_u - c_x}{s_x}\right)^2 + (y_u - c_y)^2}$ is the undistorted radius and r_d the distorted radius. A nonlinear minimization of the sum of all of the distortion errors is performed by optimizing over the camera distortion parameters. Two results of applying this procedure are shown Figure 4.23 and Figure 4.24. In Table 4.2, the radial distortion parameter is compared with the one recovered by the Tsai method.

Figure 4.23: A distorted image with the detected segments (left) and the same image at the end of the distortion calibration with segments extracted from undistorted edges (right): Some outliers were removed and longer segments are detected. This image was affected by pin-cushion distortion, corresponding to a positive value of K_1.

4.6   Calibration techniques

Classical calibration methods use *a priori* knowledge of the environment to compute the projection matrix from a single view.

Figure 4.24: The calibration grid used for Tsai calibration: Original distorted image (left) and image undistorted using the parameters computed by our method (right).

camera/lens	IndyCam	Sony 8mm	Sony 12.5mm	Sony 16mm
Tsai	0.135	0.0358	0.00772	0.00375
Devernay	0.154	0.0412	0.0164	0.0117

Table 4.2: The distortion parameter K_1 obtained by different methods. This parameter does not have exactly the same meaning across the different methods since the Devernay method allows a variation in the center of distortion. Note that with the zoom lens, the shorter the focal length, the higher the distortion.

4.6.1   Coordinates-based methods

These methods are based on the observation of an object for which the three-dimensional coordinates of n reference points M_j are known. The projections m_j of these points are measured in the image and yield pixel coordinates (u_j, v_j). The reference objects which are used are generally calibration grids composed of repeated patterns (circles or rectangles) chosen to define points of interest which can be measured with a very good precision. Such a grid was shown in Figure 4.24.

The basic idea is that since the coordinates of both the points M_j and m_j are available, it is possible to compute the parameters of the projection using the n projection equations $\mathbf{m}_j \simeq \mathcal{P}\mathbf{M}_j$, provided we have a sufficient number of points. Let us write the projection matrix

$$\mathcal{P} = \left[\begin{array}{c} \boldsymbol{U}^T \\ \boldsymbol{V}^T \\ \boldsymbol{W}^T \end{array} \right].$$

The classical approaches used in photogrammetry were based on multiple views. See Section 7.4.5 for a short description. Interestingly, satisfactory methods based on a single view were available only in the mid 80's. We next describe the two best known of them.

Tsai's radial alignment method The basic idea is to use a physical constraint (radial alignment) to separate two groups of parameters. The constraint depends on only one of these two groups, and the values of its elements can be obtained easily. Most of the extrinsic parameters are in one-to-one correspondence with solutions of linear equations which are not affected by radial distortion. An iterative computation gives then the z component of the translation, the effective focal distance, and the radial distortion components. Whereas in the original formulation (Tsai, 1986; Tsai, 1987) the coordinates of the principal points were assumed to be known, they are computed as well in (Lenz and Tsai, 1987). The advantage of the method is that it avoids large scale nonlinear minimizations, whereas the modelization remains quite accurate, since two radial distortion parameters are taken into account. It is also very efficient and allows for the use of plane calibration grids. However, several authors (Faugeras and Toscani, 1986; Hung and Shieh, 1990; Weng et al., 1992a) have found that the results can be less precise than those obtained with a linear method in the case where the radial distortion remains small. The explanation is that the radial component, a part of the information provided by the reference points, is discarded.

Methods based on linear estimation The idea of this family of methods is to first obtain an initial estimate of the parameters using the linear model, then to start from this initial estimate to obtain the distortion parameters by a nonlinear minimization. The perspective projection matrix $\mathcal{P}$ is first estimated using the linear least-squares criterion

$$\sum_i \{(u_i(\boldsymbol{W}^T\mathbf{M}_i) - (\boldsymbol{U}^T\mathbf{M}_i))^2 + (v_i(\boldsymbol{W}^T\mathbf{M}_i) - (\boldsymbol{V}^T\mathbf{M}_i))^2\}. \tag{4.49}$$

In the approach of Faugeras and Toscani (Faugeras and Toscani, 1986), which exemplifies this family of methods, the constraint $\|[W_1, W_2, W_3]^T\| = 1$ ensures the invariance of the intrinsic parameters with respect to arbitrary Euclidean transformations. Since the angle θ (see Section 4.3.1) is introduced, there is a one-to-one correspondence between the intrinsic and extrinsic parameters and the entries of the matrix $\mathcal{P}$. An estimate of the uncertainty on the calibration parameters is obtained by using a Kalman filter. The calibration of the nonlinear distortion is done using a local method which relies on the partition of the image plane into rectangles. In each rectangle, a bilinear deformation is applied:

$$u = a + bu_d + cv_d + du_dv_d, \qquad v = e + fu_d + gv_d + hu_dv_d,$$

where (u, v) are corrected from the measured coordinates (x_d, y_d), and the coefficients a, b, c, d, e, f, g and h are computed for each rectangle.

Using a subsequent nonlinear minimization

$$\sum_{i=1}^{n}\left(\left(u_i - \frac{\boldsymbol{U}^T\mathbf{M}_i}{\boldsymbol{W}^T\mathbf{M}_i}\right)^2 + \left(v_i - \frac{\boldsymbol{V}^T\mathbf{M}_i}{\boldsymbol{W}^T\mathbf{M}_i}\right)^2\right),$$

which is similar to the bundle adjustment error function, gives a result which is more robust to noise (see (Vaillant, 1990; Faugeras, 1993) for example).

4.6.2   Using single view homographies

The calibration object which is the easiest to build consists of a plane. It is easy to ensure planarity with high precision and to print a precise pattern. However, one of the problems with the linear calibration methods is that it is degenerate if all of the points lie in a plane, since, as we have seen in Section 4.1.4, the solution is not unique. Therefore to use such a method it is necessary to build a calibration object which has two or more planes (see Figure 4.24), which is not easy to do if high precision is required.

The method that we present in this section, due to Sturm and Maybank (Sturm and Maybank, 1999) and Zhang (Zhang, 1999) that we follow, uses multiple images of a plane. We assume that we are in the situation of Section 4.1.4 where we observe a plane, which we assume without loss of generality to be represented by $\mathbf{\Pi} = [0, 0, 1, 0]^T$ (its equation is $Z = 0$). Using the Euclidean decomposition of the projection matrix

$$\mathcal{P} = \mathbf{A}[\mathbf{r}_1 \ \mathbf{r}_2 \ \mathbf{r}_3 \ \mathbf{t}],$$

where the vector $\mathbf{r}_i$ is the i-th column of the rotation vector $\mathbf{R}$, the homography between the plane Π and the retinal plane is

$$\mathbf{H} = [\mathbf{h}_1 \ \mathbf{h}_2 \ \mathbf{h}_3] \simeq \mathbf{A}[\mathbf{r}_1 \ \mathbf{r}_2 \ \mathbf{t}].$$

We note that $\mathbf{H}$ has eight parameters, while the displacement $\mathbf{R}, \mathbf{t}$ has only two, so there must be two constraints on the intrinsic parameters. Indeed, we have

Proposition 4.28 *If* $\mathbf{H} = [\mathbf{h}_1 \ \mathbf{h}_2 \ \mathbf{h}_3]$ *is a homography between the retinal plane and a plane* Π, *then the image of the absolute conic of matrix* $\mathbf{B}$ *satisfies the two equations*

$$\begin{aligned}\mathbf{h}_1^T\mathbf{B}\mathbf{h}_2 &= 0, \\ \mathbf{h}_1^T\mathbf{B}\mathbf{h}_1 &= \mathbf{h}_2^T\mathbf{B}\mathbf{h}_2.\end{aligned} \qquad (4.50)$$

These equations depend only on the direction of the plane, not on its distance to the origin.

Proof :   The two equations are obtained by using the fact that the vectors $\mathbf{r}_i$ are orthonormal and the expression in Equation 4.31 for the image of the absolute conic.

These two equations can be obtained geometrically as follows. In the world coordinate system $\mathcal{F}_O$, the direction of the plane Π has coordinates $\mathbf{l} = [\mathbf{r}_1 \times \mathbf{r}_2]$ (see Section 2.5.2.2); therefore its intersection with the absolute conic is the two circular points $[\mathbf{r}_1 \pm i\mathbf{r}_2]$ which are projected into the image points $\mathbf{m}_\infty = \mathbf{A}(\mathbf{r}_1 \pm i\mathbf{r}_2) = \mathbf{h}_1 \pm i\mathbf{h}_2$. Writing that these two points belong to the image of the absolute conic using Equation 4.31, we obtain

$$(\mathbf{h}_1 \pm i\mathbf{h}_2)\mathbf{A}^{-T}\mathbf{A}^{-1}(\mathbf{h}_1 \pm i\mathbf{h}_2) = 0,$$

which is equivalent (by separating the real and imaginary parts) to Equation 4.51. Therefore, by observing one plane, we obtain two linear constraints on the image of the absolute conic. Since the circular points depend only on the direction of the plane Π, all of the parallel planes yield the two same constraints. $\square$

Therefore, to solve for the five intrinsic parameters, we need three views of the plane at different orientations. There is no need to compute the displacement of the plane.

4.7   Summary and discussion

We have used the three levels (projective, affine, Euclidean) to analyze the pinhole model, whose main property, which justifies our use of projective geometry, is that it is linear projective. The most general projection is represented by a 3×4 projection matrix between $\mathbb{P}^3$ and $\mathbb{P}^2$, whose rows $\boldsymbol{U}, \boldsymbol{V}, \boldsymbol{W}$ define three planes of $\mathbb{P}^3$. The essential operations of determining the optical center, the unique point $\mathbf{C}$ such that $\mathcal{P}\mathbf{C} = 0$, the optical ray of a point m of $\mathcal{R}$, and the backprojection of m onto a plane Π, can be done using the three reference planes using only projective operations. An affine description makes it possible to distinguish between two types of projection while the camera remains uncalibrated, whereas a Euclidean description relates the projection matrix to calibration parameters and the displacement from the world coordinate system to the camera coordinate system.

In the general case, the optical center is a point of affine space. The camera, in this case, is described

- affinely as $\mathbf{P}$, a homography between the plane at infinity Π_∞ and $\mathcal{R}$, and $\mathbf{p}$, a projection of the origin of the world coordinate system,

- from a Euclidean point of view as an affine transformation of the plane $\mathbf{A}$ parameterized by the 5 intrinsic parameters, a normalized perspective projection, and a displacement between the world coordinate system and the camera coordinate system $(\mathbf{R}, \mathbf{T})$ corresponding to the 6 extrinsic parameters.

In some particular viewing situations, an alternative model can be used, based on parallel projection. This model corresponds to the case when the optical center $\mathbf{C}$ is at infinity. The optical center therefore represents the direction of projection. The affine camera is obtained when the retinal plane is the plane at infinity. It is described

- affinely as $\mathbf{P}_A$, a linear mapping between directions of $\mathbb{P}^3$ and $\mathbb{P}^2$, and $\mathbf{p}_A$, a translation which can be canceled without losing the model's generality.

- from a Euclidean point of view, alternatively as an affine transformation of the plane $\mathbf{A}_A$ parameterized by 3 intrinsic parameters followed by an orthographic or weak perspective projection, or a para-perspective projection, both of which are followed by a displacement where the component of translation parallel to the direction of projection is arbitrary.

These interpretations are summarized in Table 4.3.

Projective		$\begin{bmatrix} \boldsymbol{U}^T \\ \boldsymbol{V}^T \\ \boldsymbol{W}^T \end{bmatrix}$
Affine	$\begin{bmatrix} \mathbf{P} & \mathbf{p} \end{bmatrix}$	$\begin{bmatrix} \mathbf{P}_A & \mathbf{p}_A \\ \mathbf{0}_3^T & 1 \end{bmatrix}$
Euclidean	$\begin{bmatrix} \alpha & \gamma & u_0 \\ 0 & \beta & v_0 \\ 0 & 0 & 1 \end{bmatrix} \begin{bmatrix} \mathbf{R} & \mathbf{t} \end{bmatrix}$	$\left[\begin{array}{cc} \begin{bmatrix} \alpha & \gamma \\ 0 & \beta \end{bmatrix} \begin{bmatrix} \mathbf{r}_1^T \\ \mathbf{r}_2^T \end{bmatrix} & \begin{bmatrix} \alpha & \gamma \\ 0 & \beta \end{bmatrix} \begin{bmatrix} t_X \\ t_Y \end{bmatrix} \\ \mathbf{0}_3^T & 1 \end{array} \right]$ Orthographic $\left[\begin{array}{cc} \begin{bmatrix} f & 0 & u_0 \\ 0 & f & v_0 \end{bmatrix} \begin{bmatrix} \mathbf{R} \end{bmatrix} & \begin{bmatrix} f t_X \\ f t_Y \end{bmatrix} \\ \mathbf{0}_3^T & 1 \end{array} \right]$ Para-perspective
	Perspective projection models	Parallel projection models

Table 4.3: Interpretations of the general projection matrix.

Affine models are interesting for several reasons. First, they expose the ambiguities which arise when perspective effects are small and allow one to avoid degeneracies and the computation of ill-conditioned parameters, resulting in more stable and more efficient algorithms. Second, the linearity of the relation between object space and image space allows for several recovery techniques, among them direct estimation of some Euclidean parameters as will be seen in Section 5.4.1 and the elegant *factorization method* discussed in Section 10.2.3.2 of Chapter 10. Last, the affine camera has few intrinsic parameters, and they can usually be assumed safely to be known; therefore it is in general possible to deal easily with uncalibrated images using this formalism.

However, no real camera is affine. All cameras perform a perspective projection. The affine model provides a good approximation to the perspective model when the field of view is small and when the relative variation of depth is small compared with the distance to the camera. The affine camera remains an approximation to physical imaging systems, and it mixes the projection and the structure. A camera might be considered as affine when looking at some scenes, and that assumption might not hold a few frames later. Another related problem is that some motions cannot be described by this model, as will be seen in Chapter 5. These difficulties are why we will emphasize the most general model, the perspective projection, and we will generally suppose, unless mentioned otherwise, that the camera optical center is in the affine space.

4.8   References and further reading

Calibration from a single view by linear determination of the perspective transformation matrix followed by a decomposition of this matrix has been known for a while (Yakimovsky and Cunningham, 1978; Sutherland, 1974; Ganapathy, 1984; Abdel-Aziz and Karara, 1971), but in the earlier formulations, the simplification of the model could in some cases yield an insufficient precision. The intermediate variables are also overdetermined, since they have to satisfy some constraints. Starting from 1986, two-stage methods have become available. They do not suffer from these difficulties. A review of the state-of-the-art for camera calibration up to 1989 can be found in (Tsai, 1989).

There have been several techniques proposed to improve on the linear estimation of the projection matrix. Puget and Skordas (Puget and Skordas, 1990) propose to apply the linear part of the previous method at different camera positions and to average the intrinsic parameters. Robert (Robert, 1996) notes that the precision of the feature detection is crucial, and therefore optimizes the coefficients of the perspective projection matrix directly from the values of the gradient in the image and the 3D model, using a snake-like algorithm. Weng *et al.* (Weng et al., 1992a) introduce an iterative coupling between the two stages of linear estimation and nonlinear distortion estimation. Grotsky and Tamburino (Grotsky and Tamburino, 1990) propose a more general framework to solve the calibration problem for a pinhole camera without distortion. This method is based on linear projection equations and makes it easier to take into account additional constraints on intrinsic and extrinsic parameters. In particular, it allows one to use a planar calibration object, unlike the Faugeras and Toscani method and the derived methods.

Measurements and reconstruction from one view are possible if we have some knowledge about the scene. Although this topic is old (Kanade, 1981), the projective approach has brought new results. Rothwell *et al.* (Rothwell et al., 1993) takes advantage of repeating structures (including symmetry) to compute projective invariants of point sets from a single view. Van Gool *et al.* (Van Gool et al., 1998) discuss a specific class of planar projective transformations, planar homologies, which arise when considering multiple instances of a plane in 3D. Criminisi *et al.*, using only the vanishing line of a reference plane and a vanishing point for another direction (Criminisi et al., 1999b), show how to determine the ratio of distances of planes parallel to the reference plane and affine measurement within those planes. In (Criminisi et al., 1999a) they show how to compute the covariance matrix of the single plane homography and use that matrix to characterize the uncertainty of their measurements. Huynh (Huynh, 1999) uses symmetry to obtain an affine reconstruction. If the projection is affine, then symmetry makes it is possible to determine image backprojection up to a similarity transformation ambiguity and the object plane orientation (Mukherjee et al., 1995). Caprile and Torre (Caprile and Torre, 1990) find the principal point and focal length of a camera, using the vanishing points of three orthogonal directions. In particular, the orthocenter of these three points gives the principal point. This technique, which seems to have been known for a while in the photogrammetric literature (for instance (Gracie, 1968)), is discussed in more detail in Section 7.4.4. Liebowitz and Zisserman show how to remove perspective distortion (an operation they call *rectification*) in a plane by determining a homography. This homography is determined by using metric information such as known angles, equality of angles, or ratios of lengths in that plane (Liebowitz and Zisserman, 1998). They next express a combination of constraints on the camera intrinsic parameters (such as zero-skew, known aspect ratio) and of constraints arising from knowledge of the world in order to recover a Euclidean reconstruction, (Liebowitz and Zisserman, 1999; Liebowitz et al., 1999) thereby generalizing (Caprile and Torre, 1990). Using the image of the absolute conic yields linear relations. Jelinek and Taylor (Jelinek and Taylor, 1999) recover an unknown focal length by using linearly parameterized models. While the linear calibration technique needs six points and recovers all the five intrinsic parameters, Triggs (Triggs, 1999b) uses constraints on the dual image of the absolute conic to propose polynomial solutions to the problem of recovering only the focal length (respectively focal length and principal point) from four (respectively five) known points. Kim *et al.* (Kim et al., 1998) recover the position of a point from its shadow on a plane.

Orthographic and weak perspective models have been known since the beginning of computer vision, and a lot of earlier work used them because of their simplicity. The para-perspective model was introduced by (Ohta et al., 1981) and named in

(Aloimonos, 1990). The affine camera, as a general form of uncalibrated parallel projection, was introduced by Mundy and Zisserman (Mundy and Zisserman, 1992). A precise examination of the relations between the weak perspective, paraperspective, and perspective models is done by Horaud, Christy *et al.* (Christy and Horaud, 1996; Horaud et al., 97). Based on that analysis, they propose iterative algorithms for pose estimation and structure from motion which start from the more approximate model and end up with the more precise one. Methods for selecting the most appropriate camera model based only on the observed projections have been recently studied by Wiles and Brady (Wiles and Brady, 1996b). The idea is to use the simplest model which accurately models the data, by maximizing measures of efficiency, clarity, and accuracy.

An abundant literature deals with various distortion models and tries to address the problem of their practical utility. The conclusions seem to depend on the experimental set-up and on the optics used. A systematic investigation using high quality optics is presented by Lavest (Lavest, 1992), based on the distortion curves provided by the constructor Angénieux. These curves show that the distortion is a complex, non-monotonic function of the distance to the principal point, the focal distance, and the focusing distance. This author gives an example to show that if the distortion is not taken into account, then the 3D reconstruction errors can increase by an order of magnitude.

Several authors (Horn, 1986; Krotkov, 1989; Lavest et al., 1993; Tarabanis and Tsai, 1991; Tarabanis et al., 1992) have found that the pinhole model is not adequate for a precise description of a complex optical system such as a zoom lens. In consequence, they have used a more general model of a thick lens, for which the optical center is replaced by two nodal points. One of the most detailed presentations of this model is given by Lavest, Rives and Dhome (Lavest et al., 1993), who show, using an optical analysis of the approximations leading to the pinhole model, as well as numerous experimentations, that in the case of a variable focal length lens, the virtual displacement of the optical center is not proportional to the variation of focal distance. It is proportional to the variation of the object principal plane, and is much larger. However, in spite of these negative conclusions, the approximation by the pinhole model remains valid if one no longer considers the distance between the object and the image to be constant. This means that, according to these authors, if we do not assume that the position of the camera remains fixed during a change of focal length, then we can still use the pinhole model. Similar conclusions are obtained by Willson (Willson, 1994) who proposes to calibrate a zoom lens by using a different pinhole model (with distortion) for each lens setting and then characterizing the relationship between lens setting and each of the pinhole model parameters. Simpler models have been proposed. Enciso *et al.* model the zoom and focus by a three parameter affine transformation in the image (Enciso et al., 1994). Sturm (Sturm, 1997b) uses a one-parameter model for a zooming camera, which is obtained by an off-line process and is then used to self-calibrate using low degree polynomials.

Another approach to overcoming the limitations of the pinhole model is to use a two-plane model (Martins et al., 1981; Gremban et al., 1988; Wei and Ma, 1991; Wei and Ma, 1993): The idea is to start from a certain number of correspondences between image points and three-dimensional points lying on two planes. Then the three-dimensional coordinates of any point of the two planes can be obtained by interpolation from the coordinates of its image. The optical ray is obtained by joining the two points lying in the two reference planes. The model differs from the pinhole model mainly by the fact that the optical rays are no longer constrained to meet at a single point. It has been generalized to the case of N planes (Champleboux et al., 1992). This model takes into account distortions.

The projective machinery that we used in this chapter can be partially extended to deal with other image-forming devices which do not follow the pinhole model at all. Gupta and Hartley (Gupta and Hartley, 1997) study the linear pushbroom camera which consists of a linear area of sensors moving to scan an image. This camera is shown to approximate a SPOT satellite pushbroom sensor. The linear pushbroom camera and the pinhole camera are both instances of the cubic rational polynomial camera described by Hartley and Saxena (Hartley and Saxena, 1997). Although the Synthetic Aperture Radar (SAR) sensor models the projection as complicated radical functions, the cubic rational polynomial camera provides a relatively good model.

5 Two views: The Fundamental matrix

If we observe the same scene from different points of view, then we expect the different images to be related in some way, even if the position, orientation, and nature of the cameras differ a lot. This chapter is devoted to the study of the relations between two images of points in the scene. The remarkable thing is that for the general pinhole camera model which was presented in the previous chapter, point correspondences, i.e. images of the same 3D point, satisfy a simple geometric constraint, called the epipolar constraint, if the optical centers of the two cameras are different. The algebraic formulation of this constraint is bilinear in the projective coordinates of the corresponding points and gives rise to an important projective invariant of a pair of views called the Fundamental matrix. As shown in Chapter 7, this constraint allows us to recover a projectively invariant description of the geometry of two views, i.e. a pair of perspective projection matrices, using only image measurements. The reader will have guessed that since the epipolar constraint is a projective entity, the appropriate setting for its analysis is projective geometry. Indeed, we will take very few excursions into affine and Euclidean geometry in this chapter.

Section 5.1 considers the special cases when it is possible to compute the position of a corresponding point just by applying a projective linear transformation. We first analyze the conceptually and practically important situation in which the 3D points lie in a plane. We show that the images of such points are related by a projective morphism (a notion introduced in Chapter 2) which can be described nicely using the inverse projection matrix attached to that plane. We next study the case in which the optical centers are identical, where all corresponding points are related by a morphism. This case is the basis for the construction of panoramic views, or mosaics.

In the general case, when the optical centers are distinct and the 3D points in general configuration, although it is not possible to compute the position of a corresponding point, this position is linearly constrained by the epipolar geometry, to which Section 5.2 is devoted. The analysis is done from two viewpoints, geometric and algebraic. The geometric analysis uncovers the epipolar geometry, the epipoles, the two pencils of epipolar lines, the pencil of epipolar planes and the epipolar homography. This is the occasion to put to good use a lot of the material on projective geometry that was exposed in Chapter 2. We also introduce the Fundamental matrix that describes the epipolar geometry and provide several equivalent expressions based on the perspective and inverse projection matrices of the two cameras. We show that it depends in general upon seven independent parameters, which can be described as the four coordinates of the two epipoles and the three parameters of the epipolar homography. We complete the geometric analysis with an algebraic one based on the Grassman-Cayley algebra introduced in Chapter 3.

In section 5.2.4, we investigate the class of projective morphisms between the two views that arise from a 3D plane. The central result is that not all projective morphisms between the two views are induced by a 3D plane. Those which are must satisfy some relations with the Fundamental matrix which are made explicit in theorem 5.1 and corollary 5.1. By choosing a special plane attached to the second view and going through its optical center we then introduce a remarkable planar morphism that will be used in Chapters 7 and 10 to define a canonical form of the perspective projection matrices.

So far the analysis was done on the projective level and was totally general. We now specialize the analysis by entering the realm of affine geometry. This realm makes it possible to distinguish, as in the previous chapter, between the case of perspective projection, which is discussed in section 5.3, and the case of parallel projection, which is discussed in section 5.4.

In section 5.3.1, we stay at the affine level, to analyze the special morphism, called the infinity morphism, that is induced by the plane at infinity between the two images of a pair of pinhole cameras. This morphism provides us in particular with an interesting alternative representation of the Fundamental matrix.

In section 5.3.2 we push a little further and enter the Euclidean kingdom to describe the relation between the Fundamental matrix, a projective entity, and the Essential matrix introduced by Longuet-Higgins (Longuet-Higgins, 1981), a Euclidean entity. The relation is through the internal parameters of the two cameras and will play an important role in our future study of the calibration problems. We then study some special, but practically important, cases.

In section 5.4, we consider the case of parallel projection. In section 5.4.1, it is shown that when the two cameras are affine cameras, the Fundamental matrix takes a simpler form that depends only upon four parameters. Section 5.4.2 is devoted to the analysis of the fact that this condition is not a necessary and sufficient condition for the two cameras to be affine and that there are other cases in which the affine form of the Fundamental matrix can and should be used.

As we did with perspective cameras, we then relate in section 5.4.3 the affine Fundamental matrix to rigid motion. Unlike in the perspective case, it is not possible to recover all of the parameters of the motion (and therefore the structure) using only two views.

Section 5.5 ends the chapter with a discussion of the problem of degeneracy for the Fundamental matrix. It is important to understand degeneracy because near the degenerate configurations the algorithms to estimate the Fundamental matrix become unstable. In general, a sufficiently large number of point correspondences determines the Fundamental matrix. However, if the points lie on certain special spatial configurations, called critical surfaces, then there are several possible Fundamental matrices even with an arbitrarily large number of correspondences. Critical surfaces are particular quadrics. Interestingly, the degenerate configurations are also no-parallax configurations, since the position of a corresponding point can be predicted by a quadratic transformation. A particular case of practical importance is that of planes.

5.1   Configurations with no parallax

In general, it is not possible to account for the difference between two views just by an analytical transformation because the visibility, as well as the difference in projection, in the two images of a three dimensional point depends on its position in space. Multiple points M_1 and M_2 which project to a common image point m in a first view can project to different locations m'_1 and m'_2 in a second view, as illustrated in Fig. 5.1.

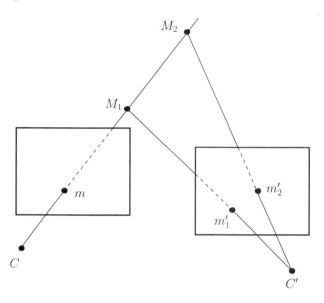

Figure 5.1: The parallax effect: Depending on its depth, two points with a common projection in the first view have different projections in the second view.

This effect is the *parallax effect*. However, the location of the point m', although not unique, is quite constrained, and this idea will be developed in the next section. In this section, we concentrate on two important special cases where the location of the point m' can actually be computed analytically from the location m. Note that in these situations, the visibility also remains invariant from view to view. The difference between a pair of images with no parallax (rotated around the optical center) and a pair of image with parallax (translated) is illustrated in Fig. 5.2.

In Section 5.1.1, it is shown that the observation of a plane in space generates a projective morphism between the two images, which in general, i.e. when the plane does not go through either of the two optical centers, is a homography $\mathbf{H}$. These morphisms are extremely important in theory and in practice.

In particular, the matrix $\mathbf{H}$ plays a crucial role in the case when these optical

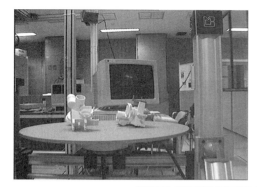 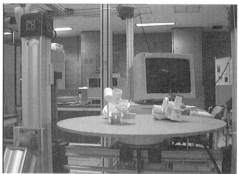

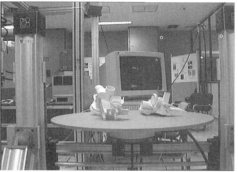

Figure 5.2: Between the left and right image, the camera rotates, but does not translate. There is no parallax: The relative positions of foreground and background are preserved. Between the right and bottom image the camera rotates and translates. Notice the parallax. For example the relative position of the white parts and the computer screen have changed.

centers are identical since, as discussed in Section 5.1.2, it completely describes the relation between two views taken at the same position.

5.1.1 The correspondence between the two images of a plane

Derivation of the homography Let Π be a plane not going through either of the two optical centers C and C'. Let $\mathcal{P}$ be the first projection matrix, with optical center C, and $\mathcal{P}'$ be the second projection matrix, with optical center C', and let Π be a plane not going through either of the two optical centers. Note that we *do not* assume that the two optical centers are distinct.

The plane Π induces a correspondence between the two images which is, not surprisingly, a homography.

Proposition 5.1 *A plane* Π *not going through the optical centers of a pair of cameras induces a homography* H_Π *between the two retinal planes. This homography is represented by the* 3×3 *matrix* $\mathbf{H}_\Pi$:

$$\mathbf{H}_\Pi \simeq \boldsymbol{\mathcal{P}}' \boldsymbol{\mathcal{P}}_\Pi^+. \tag{5.1}$$

The inverse homography H_Π^{-1} *is represented by*

$$\mathbf{H}_\Pi^{-1} \simeq \boldsymbol{\mathcal{P}} \boldsymbol{\mathcal{P}}_\Pi^{'+}.$$

The corresponding homographies for lines are represented by the matrices of cofactors $\mathbf{H}_\Pi^*$ *and* $\mathbf{H}_\Pi^T$, *respectively.*

Proof : According to proposition 4.6, there is a one-to-one correspondence between the set of planes not going through C and the set of inverse projection matrices $\boldsymbol{\mathcal{P}}^+$ of the first camera. Let $\boldsymbol{\mathcal{P}}_\Pi^+$ be the matrix attached to the plane Π. According to proposition 4.7, the matrix $\boldsymbol{\mathcal{P}}_\Pi^+$ defines a morphism from the first retinal plane to Π which, to each image point m, associates the intersection M of its optical ray L_m with Π. This point is projected back onto the second retina by the second camera, defining morphism H_Π from the first retina to the second which is represented by the matrix $\boldsymbol{\mathcal{P}}' \boldsymbol{\mathcal{P}}_\Pi^+$. The fact that this morphism is one-to-one and is therefore a homography is obvious geometrically; see Fig. 5.3. In order to find the inverse of $\mathbf{H}_\Pi$ we can use proposition 4.8. We multiply both sides of equation (5.1) with $\boldsymbol{\mathcal{P}}$ and, using equation (4.14), obtain

$$\mathbf{H}_\Pi \boldsymbol{\mathcal{P}} \simeq \boldsymbol{\mathcal{P}}'(\mathbf{C}\boldsymbol{\Pi}^T - \langle \boldsymbol{\Pi}, \mathbf{C} \rangle \mathbf{I}_4) = (\boldsymbol{\mathcal{P}}'\mathbf{C})\boldsymbol{\Pi}^T - \langle \boldsymbol{\Pi}, \mathbf{C} \rangle \boldsymbol{\mathcal{P}}'.$$

We now multiply both sides with $\boldsymbol{\mathcal{P}}_\Pi^{'+}$ on the right and note that, because of proposition 4.8 again, $\boldsymbol{\Pi}^T \boldsymbol{\mathcal{P}}_\Pi^{'+} = \mathbf{0}$. We obtain

$$\mathbf{H}_\Pi \boldsymbol{\mathcal{P}} \boldsymbol{\mathcal{P}}_\Pi^{'+} = -\langle \boldsymbol{\Pi}, \mathbf{C} \rangle \boldsymbol{\mathcal{P}}' \boldsymbol{\mathcal{P}}_\Pi^{'+}.$$

The product $\boldsymbol{\mathcal{P}}' \boldsymbol{\mathcal{P}}_\Pi^{'+}$ is proportional to $\mathbf{I}_3$ because of definition 4.1 and we finally obtain

$$\mathbf{H}_\Pi \boldsymbol{\mathcal{P}} \boldsymbol{\mathcal{P}}_\Pi^{'+} \simeq \mathbf{I}_3,$$

which shows that H_Π is invertible and that

$$\mathbf{H}_\Pi^{-1} \simeq \boldsymbol{\mathcal{P}} \boldsymbol{\mathcal{P}}_\Pi^{'+}.$$

The result for lines follows directly from duality (proposition 3.24). $\square$

If the plane Π goes through the second (respectively the first) optical center C' (respectively C), the first (respectively the second) part of the proposition still

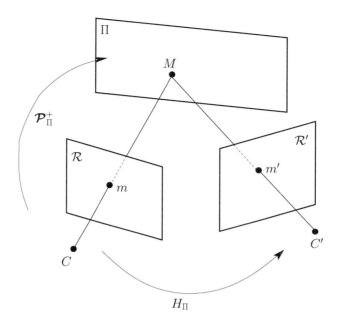

Figure 5.3: The homography between two images of a plane.

holds. We simply have to change the word homography into the word morphism. In the first case, the plane Π induces a mapping for which all points of the first retinal plane are mapped to the line of intersection of Π and the second retinal plane. This mapping is not one-to-one but it is still represented by the matrix $\mathcal{P}'\mathcal{P}_\Pi^+$; see figure 5.4. In the second case, the plane Π induces a mapping for which all points of the second retinal plane are mapped to the line of intersection of Π and the first retinal plane. This mapping is obviously not one-to-one but it is still represented by the matrix $\mathcal{P}\mathcal{P}_\Pi'^+$.

Proposition 4.6 allows us to write down very simple expressions for $\mathbf{H}_\Pi$ and $\mathbf{H}_\Pi^{-1}$, as functions of the projection matrices and the equation of the plane. The advantage of these expressions is that each entry is only a sum of terms of degree 3 in the entries of the projection matrices and linear in the plane coordinates.

Proposition 5.2 *The set of matrices $\mathbf{H}_\Pi$ ($\mathbf{H}_\Pi^{-1}$) representing the morphisms induced by a plane Π not going through the optical center C (respectively C') between the first and the second image planes (respectively between the second and the first image planes) is described as*

$$\mathbf{H}_\Pi \simeq \begin{bmatrix} |\boldsymbol{U'},\boldsymbol{V},\boldsymbol{W},\boldsymbol{\Pi}| & |\boldsymbol{U'},\boldsymbol{W},\boldsymbol{U},\boldsymbol{\Pi}| & |\boldsymbol{U'},\boldsymbol{U},\boldsymbol{V},\boldsymbol{\Pi}| \\ |\boldsymbol{V'},\boldsymbol{V},\boldsymbol{W},\boldsymbol{\Pi}| & |\boldsymbol{V'},\boldsymbol{W},\boldsymbol{U},\boldsymbol{\Pi}| & |\boldsymbol{V'},\boldsymbol{U},\boldsymbol{V},\boldsymbol{\Pi}| \\ |\boldsymbol{W'},\boldsymbol{V},\boldsymbol{W},\boldsymbol{\Pi}| & |\boldsymbol{W'},\boldsymbol{W},\boldsymbol{U},\boldsymbol{\Pi}| & |\boldsymbol{W'},\boldsymbol{U},\boldsymbol{V},\boldsymbol{\Pi}| \end{bmatrix}, \qquad (5.2)$$

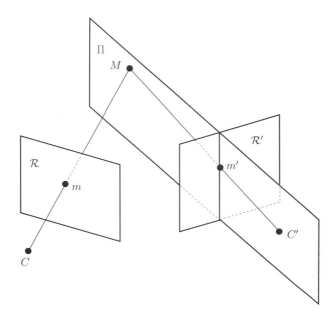

Figure 5.4: The morphism between two images of a plane when the plane goes through the second optical center.

$$\mathbf{H}_{\Pi}^{-1} \simeq \left[\begin{array}{ccc} |\,U, V', W', \Pi\,| & |\,U, W', U', \Pi\,| & |\,U, U', V', \Pi\,| \\ |\,V, V', W', \Pi\,| & |\,V, W', U', \Pi\,| & |\,V, U', V', \Pi\,| \\ |\,W, V', W', \Pi\,| & |\,W, W', U', \Pi\,| & |\,W, U', V', \Pi\,| \end{array} \right].$$

Proof :   In order to obtain the expression for $\mathbf{H}_{\Pi}$ we use equation (4.9) which gives the expression of $\mathcal{P}_{\Pi}^{+}$. We obtain

$$\mathbf{H}_{\Pi} \simeq \left[\begin{array}{c} U'^{T} \\ V'^{T} \\ W'^{T} \end{array} \right] [V \vartriangle W \vartriangle \Pi\, W \vartriangle U \vartriangle \Pi\, U \vartriangle V \vartriangle \Pi].$$

We then use the identification of a vector in $G_3(\mathbb{R}^4)$ with its image in $G_1(\mathbb{R}^4)$ by the Hodge operator:

$$U'^{T}(V \vartriangle W \vartriangle \Pi) = \langle U', V \vartriangle W \vartriangle \Pi \rangle = (V \vartriangle W \vartriangle \Pi) \vartriangle U' =$$
$$- U' \vartriangle V \vartriangle W \vartriangle \Pi \simeq U' \vartriangle V \vartriangle W \vartriangle \Pi.$$

The proof for $\mathbf{H}_{\Pi}^{-1}$ is identical. Note that these expressions show that the correspondences $\Pi \longrightarrow \mathbf{H}_{\Pi}$ and $\Pi \longrightarrow \mathbf{H}_{\Pi}^{-1}$ are linear. $\square$

It is important to note that not all homographies between the two images arise from a plane in 3-space. The reader can convince himself of this fact by a simple counting argument. The set of homographies from $\mathbb{P}^2$ to $\mathbb{P}^2$ is 8-dimensional but the set of 3D planes is 3-dimensional.

5.1.2 Identical optical centers: Application to mosaicing

If the two optical centers are identical (finite or infinite), then we have the following important result.

Proposition 5.3 *When the two optical centers are identical, all pairs of corresponding points are related by a morphism.*

Proof : Indeed, let us consider an arbitrary plane Π, not containing the optical centers C and C'. If m and m' are corresponding pixels, then they are both the image of the point of intersection of the common optical ray $L_m \equiv L_{m'}$ with Π, and therefore

$$\mathbf{m}' \simeq \mathbf{H}_\Pi \mathbf{m}. \tag{5.3}$$

For details see figure 5.5. $\square$

Note that the previous reasoning shows that the image morphism is independent of the plane Π. All the planes generate the same morphism. In particular, in the case of perspective cameras, this morphism is the same as the infinity morphism.

In the case of a perspective camera, this situation occurs when the camera rotates around its optical center. We say that the camera is stationary. It should be clear that from the two images that we can recover the direction of the optical rays but not the position of the point M along this direction. Depth recovery is not possible with stationary cameras. However, if the goal is not to reconstruct space, but rather to gain knowledge of the camera's internal parameters or to create images, then this motion is particularly interesting, precisely because the motion is described by an analytical relation between the views. Applications of the first kind will be discussed in Section 11.1, where it will be seen that self-calibration is easier for stationary cameras than in the general case. Applications of the second kind deal with combining multiple views to create a mosaic view, a panorama, or a higher resolution view. We discuss them now.

The idea behind image mosaicing is simple and follows immediately from proposition 5.3. Equation 5.3 applies to all matches (m, m') between the two images. If we have at least four such correspondences, then we can estimate the matrix $\mathbf{H}_\infty$. By applying it to the whole image 1, we transform it into a new image which, when overlaid on the image 2, forms a bigger image representing the scene as it would have appeared from the point of view of image 2 but with a bigger field. An extension of this idea which makes it possible to build panoramic views is presented in Section 11.1.4.

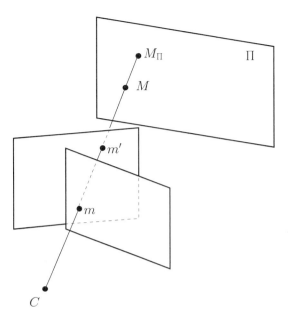

Figure 5.5: m and m' correspond to each other by the morphism induced by Π.

This idea is the theory. From a practical point of view, if the shift of the optical center is negligible relative to the distances of the scene points, then the images match approximately by the homography induced by the plane at infinity.

If we have several views, then we can iterate the same reasoning: Each pair of images matches according to the homography induced by the plane at infinity. If we choose one of the views as the reference image, then we can match all of the other images with it by applying the corresponding homography.

As an example, Figure 5.6 shows five images of a building taken from approximately the same viewpoint and noted one to five from top to bottom and from left to right. Four homographies have been estimated from point correspondences: $\mathbf{H}_{12}$, $\mathbf{H}_{23}$, $\mathbf{H}_{34}$, and $\mathbf{H}_{45}$. Figure 5.7 shows an associated mosaic in which all of the images have been warped by homographies to the central image, image 3 of rectangular shape in the figure. 1 has been warped to 3 by $\mathbf{H}_{23}\mathbf{H}_{12}$, and 5 has been warped to 3 by $\mathbf{H}_{34}^{-1}\mathbf{H}_{45}^{-1}$.

Figure 5.8 shows a slightly different example: All of the images have also been warped to the central image but the infinity homographies have been approximated by affine transformations, simply by setting the first two elements of their last row to zero. Because affine transformations preserve parallelism, the transformed images still have parallel edges in contrast with figure 5.7. But the quality of the resulting mosaic is much lower: We must use the full power of homographies. We see why the common practice of stitching together snapshots by trying to align them does not work very well: in that case, the transformations which are implicitly used are Euclidean, which is even more restrictive than affine!

Figure 5.6: Five images taken from approximately the same viewpoint (Courtesy **Luc Robert**, INRIA).

The situation is slightly different in the case of affine cameras. Remember that in this case, C represents the direction of projection rather than the position of the optical center. Therefore this situation occurs when the camera does not undergo a rotation out of the image plane so that it is "pointed in the same direction". The typical application there is to stitch together views taken of the earth's surface by

Figure 5.7: The five images are warped to the middle one through estimated homographies (note that the transformed regions are not parallelograms): Courtesy **Imad Zoghlami**, INRIA.

a high-flying plane or satellite. In this case, unlike the one previously described, using an affine transformation for mosaicing would produce satisfying results.

The inverse application of the idea of mosaicing is to compute synthetic rotations, which is, given an image of a scene, to synthesize a new image which corresponds to the camera staying at the same position but looking at a different angle. To synthesize such a new image it is sufficient to transform the reference view with the appropriate homography, as was illustrated in Section 4.1.4. If the original image is a mosaic (like in the Quicktime VR system (Chen, 1995)), then one can generate any view that an observer stationed at the point where the camera was located could see in any direction.

5.2   The Fundamental matrix

From now on, we generally assume that the two optical centers are distinct.

This section introduces the Fundamental matrix at a projective level. In Section 5.2.1, we take a geometric viewpoint, and introduce the Fundamental matrix as a way to express the epipolar constraint. Starting from this geometrical interpretation, we derive several expressions for the Fundamental matrix.

A complementary approach is then taken in Section 5.2.2 where we focus on the

Figure 5.8: The five original images are warped to the middle one through approximations of the previous homographies by affine transformations (note that the transformed regions are parallelograms): Courtesy **Imad Zoghlami**, INRIA.

bilinear constraint between corresponding pixels. This approach provides us with an alternative derivation of the Fundamental matrix using the Grassman-Cayley algebra.

In Section 5.2.3, the Fundamental matrix is related to the epipolar homography, which gives a geometric interpretation of its seven degrees of freedom.

In Section 5.2.4, we show that there is a very simple relationship between the Fundamental matrix and the projective morphisms induced by a plane, as well as between two such morphisms. In Section 5.2.5, a special morphism is introduced, the epipolar projection **S**, which is shown to depend only on **F**. It provides us a with a new decomposition of the Fundamental matrix. This decomposition is important to define the canonical representations of sets of cameras that will be studied in Chapters 7 and 10.

5.2.1   Geometry: The epipolar constraint

Epipolar geometry   The epipolar geometry is the basic constraint which arises from the existence of two viewpoints. These two viewpoints can be obtained either by observing the scene with two different cameras at the same time (stereovision) or with a moving camera at two different instants (structure from motion). In the latter case, we will suppose in this chapter that the scene does not contain moving objects, so that all of the points which are observed undergo the same rigid displacement with respect to the camera. In the case where several rigid objects are observed, the considerations in this chapter are valid for each object taken separately. The case of non-rigid motion is not considered in this book.

Let us consider two images taken by two pinhole cameras with distinct optical centers, as shown in Figure 5.9. Please note that the considerations in this section hold in the general projective case and are thus valid using pixel coordinates and uncalibrated cameras. Let C and C' be the two optical centers. The line (C, C') intersects the two retinal planes $\mathcal{R}$ and $\mathcal{R}'$ at points e and e', respectively. They are called the *epipoles*. The lines through e in the first image and through e' in the second image are the *epipolar lines*. Let us consider a point M in space and its images m and m'. The point m' has to lie on the image, in the second camera, of the optical ray (C, M) of the first camera. This constraint is the *epipolar constraint*, well-known in stereovision: For each point m in the first image, its corresponding point m' in the second image lies on its epipolar line l'_m. Similarly, for a given point m' in the second image, its corresponding point m in the first image lies on its epipolar line $l_{m'}$. l'_m and $l_{m'}$ are called corresponding epipolar lines. The two epipolar lines are the intersection of the retinal planes with the *epipolar plane*, noted Π in figure 5.9, containing the two optical centers C, C' and the point M.

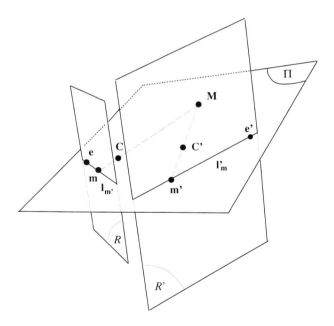

Figure 5.9: The epipolar geometry.

The Fundamental matrix   An extremely important consequence of the projective linearity of the camera model is that the relationship between $\mathbf{m}$, a projective coordinate vector of a point m and $\mathbf{l}'_m$, a projective coordinate vector of its corresponding epipolar line l'_m (see section 2.4.3.3), is projective linear. In effect, it is a morphism between the projective plane $\mathbb{P}^2$ and its dual $\mathbb{P}^{2*}$. This is because it is the composition of the relations between $\mathbf{m}$ and its optical ray (C, M), and between the optical ray (C, M) and its projection $\mathbf{l}'_m$, which are both projective linear. We thus have the following definition.

Definition 5.1 *The 3×3 matrix $\mathbf{F}$ which describes the correspondence between a point and its epipolar line is called the* Fundamental matrix, *or* F-matrix. *It corresponds to a projective morphism between the first retinal plane, considered as a projective plane $\mathbb{P}^2$, and the dual of the second retinal plane, considered as the dual $\mathbb{P}^{2*}$ of a projective plane. A pair of views for which the F-matrix is known is said to be* weakly calibrated.

Note that the existence of this matrix is a direct consequence of the pinhole camera model.

The epipolar constraint   Let us now express the epipolar constraint using the Fundamental matrix. For a given point of projective coordinates $\mathbf{m}$ in the first image, the projective representation $\mathbf{l}'_m$ of its the epipolar line in the second image is given by

$$\mathbf{l}'_m \simeq \mathbf{F}\mathbf{m}.$$

Since the point m' corresponding to m belongs to the line l'_m by definition, it follows that

$$\mathbf{m}'^T \mathbf{F}\mathbf{m} = 0. \tag{5.4}$$

Note that by reversing the role of the two images, the Fundamental matrix is changed to its transpose. Indeed, transposing equation (5.4), we obtain

$$\mathbf{m}^T \mathbf{F}^T \mathbf{m}' = 0.$$

This equation shows that the epipolar line $l_{m'}$ of m' is $\mathbf{F}^T \mathbf{m}'$. We have therefore proved the following proposition.

Proposition 5.4 *The epipolar line l'_m of m is represented by $\mathbf{F}\mathbf{m}$, the epipolar line $l_{m'}$ of m' is represented by $\mathbf{F}^T \mathbf{m}'$ and the epipolar constraint is expressed as*

$$\mathbf{m}'^T \mathbf{F}\mathbf{m} = \mathbf{m}^T \mathbf{F}^T \mathbf{m}' = 0.$$

To see examples of Fundamental matrices in simple cases, the reader is referred to Section 5.3.5.

Geometric derivations for the Fundamental matrix We first give the algebraic formulation of the geometric reasoning. Let $\mathcal{P}$ and $\mathcal{P}'$ be the perspective projection matrices of the two cameras. According to proposition 4.1, the two optical centers C and C' are the unique projective points satisfying

$$\mathcal{P}\mathbf{C} = \mathbf{0} \quad \mathcal{P}'\mathbf{C}' = \mathbf{0}.$$

We assume in what follows that the two optical centers are different. Let $\mathcal{P}_\Pi^+$ be an inverse projection of $\mathcal{P}$ (definition 4.1); according to proposition 4.6 there exists a unique plane Π not going through C such that $\mathbf{\Pi}^T\mathcal{P}_\Pi^+ = \mathbf{0}_4^T$.

Two points of the optical ray of the pixel m are the optical center C and the point M_Π, intersection of the optical ray with the plane Π. Since by construction the plane Π does not contain the optical center, the optical ray is always well-defined by C and M_Π.

This construction gives us a first interesting expression for the Fundamental matrix:

Proposition 5.5 *The Fundamental matrix can be expressed as a function of the perspective projection matrix of the second camera and any inverse perspective projection matrix of the first camera as*

$$\mathbf{F} \simeq [\mathbf{e}']_\times \mathcal{P}'\mathcal{P}^+. \tag{5.5}$$

Proof : The projection of C in the second image is precisely the epipole in the second image:

$$\mathbf{e}' \simeq \mathcal{P}'\mathbf{C}.$$

e' is well-defined since C' is different from C. The projection of M_Π in the second image is $\mathcal{P}'\mathcal{P}^+\mathbf{m}$.

The projective representation of the epipolar line l'_m is obtained by taking the cross-product of these two points, and it is seen that this expression is linear in $\mathbf{m}$:

$$\mathbf{l}' \simeq \underbrace{[\mathcal{P}'\mathbf{C}]_\times \mathcal{P}'\mathcal{P}^+}_{\mathbf{F}}\mathbf{m}$$

Since $[\mathcal{P}'\mathbf{C}] \simeq \mathbf{e}'$, this step completes the proof. $\square$

Note that we have dropped the subscript Π in the expression of the inverse projection. The previous reasoning does not depend on the choice of Π (or, in other words, on the point on the optical ray used to define the optical ray). Therefore, the matrix $\mathbf{F}$ does not depend on the choice of Π, and we can take $\mathbf{\Pi} = (*\mathbf{C})$ ($*$ is the Hodge operator defined in Chapter 2, section 3.4), i.e. the plane which has the same projective coordinates as the optical center C, which has the advantage of being intrinsic to the camera.

The expression previously given for the Fundamental matrix is entirely general, valid for perspective projections as well as parallel projections. If we know that the projection falls specifically into one of those two cases, then there are simpler expressions, which are described respectively in Section 5.3.1 and in Section 5.4.

Alternatively, the epipolar line $l_{m'}$ is obtained as $\mathbf{l}_{m'} \simeq (\boldsymbol{\mathcal{P}}\mathbf{C}') \times \mathbf{m}$. It is mapped to the epipolar plane by applying $\boldsymbol{\mathcal{P}}^T$. This plane is then mapped to the epipolar line l'_m by applying $\boldsymbol{\mathcal{P}}'^{+T}$. It can be noted that this last result does not depend on the choice of the plane Π' because the epipolar plane contains the second optical center. Combining all these operations, we obtain

Proposition 5.6 *The Fundamental matrix can be expressed as a function of the perspective projection matrix of the first camera and any inverse perspective projection matrix of the second camera as*

$$\mathbf{F} \simeq \boldsymbol{\mathcal{P}}'^{+T}\boldsymbol{\mathcal{P}}^T[\boldsymbol{\mathcal{P}}\mathbf{C}']_\times \simeq \boldsymbol{\mathcal{P}}'^{+T}\boldsymbol{\mathcal{P}}^T[\mathbf{e}]_\times . \tag{5.6}$$

It can be noted that this expression could be found directly by reversing the roles of the two images and transposing the previous result.

Let us derive geometrically a third, more symmetrical expression for $\mathbf{F}$. By substitution of $\mathbf{m} \simeq \boldsymbol{\mathcal{P}}\mathbf{M}$, $\mathbf{m}' \simeq \boldsymbol{\mathcal{P}}'\mathbf{M}$ in the epipolar constraint $\mathbf{m}'^T\mathbf{F}\mathbf{m} = 0$, we obtain

$$\mathbf{M}^T\boldsymbol{\mathcal{P}}'^T\mathbf{F}\boldsymbol{\mathcal{P}}\mathbf{M} = 0.$$

Since this relation must hold for any point $\mathbf{M}$, we conclude that the matrix $\boldsymbol{\mathcal{P}}'^T\mathbf{F}\boldsymbol{\mathcal{P}}$ must be skew-symmetric. The geometric interpretation of the matrix $\boldsymbol{\mathcal{P}}'^T\mathbf{F}\boldsymbol{\mathcal{P}}$ is that it associates to a point M which does not lie on the line (C, C') the plane $\langle C, C', M \rangle$, i.e. its epipolar plane. We have seen this operator in section 3.4 of Chapter 2, equation (3.25), and therefore

$$\boldsymbol{\mathcal{P}}'^T\mathbf{F}\boldsymbol{\mathcal{P}} \simeq \langle \mathbf{C}, \mathbf{C}' \rangle_\times$$

We multiply this equation on the right by an inverse projection matrix of $\boldsymbol{\mathcal{P}}$ and on the left by the transpose of an inverse projection matrix of $\boldsymbol{\mathcal{P}}'$ (definition 4.1). Because of equation (4.8), we obtain the following proposition.

Proposition 5.7 *The Fundamental matrix can be expressed as a function of the two perspective projection matrices $\boldsymbol{\mathcal{P}}$ and $\boldsymbol{\mathcal{P}}'$:*

$$\mathbf{F} \simeq \boldsymbol{\mathcal{P}}'^{+T}\langle \mathbf{C}, \mathbf{C}' \rangle_\times \boldsymbol{\mathcal{P}}^+ . \tag{5.7}$$

The 4×4 matrix $\langle \mathbf{C}, \mathbf{C}' \rangle_\times$ has been defined in Chapter 2, equation (3.25). The matrices $\boldsymbol{\mathcal{P}}^+$ and $\boldsymbol{\mathcal{P}}'^+$ are any inverse projection matrices.

The Fundamental matrix is not any 3×3 matrix. Its rank is 2 as shown in the next proposition.

Proposition 5.8 *The Fundamental matrix is of rank two. Its nullspace is $\mathbf{e}$. The nullspace of $\mathbf{F}^T$ is $\mathbf{e}'$:*

$$\mathbf{F}\mathbf{e} = \mathbf{F}^T\mathbf{e}' = \mathbf{0}.$$

Proof : Indeed, the epipolar line of the epipole e is represented by $\mathbf{Fe}$. Geometrically, this line l'_e is the image of the optical ray (C, e) in the second image. By construction this line is reduced to a point, e', implying that $l'_e \simeq \mathbf{Fe} = \mathbf{0}$. The same argument applies to the second epipole. The rank of $\mathbf{F}$ is therefore less than or equal to 2. For it to be strictly less than 2 would require the existence of at least two distinct points e_1 and e_2 in the first image such that the two optical rays $(C, e_i), i = 1, 2$, would go through C'. But then they would be identical to (C, C') and the two points e_i would be the same, a contradiction. Hence the rank of $\mathbf{F}$ is equal to 2. □

The reader should note that the formulae given in this section for the Fundamental matrix are the most general possible. However, simpler formulae are available when it is known that the projection is perspective, and are given in section 5.3.1.

5.2.2 Algebra: The bilinear constraint

In the previous section, we have derived geometrically an expression for the Fundamental matrix, as well as for the epipolar constraint. In this section, we perform an algebraic derivation of the bilinear constraint, which gives an alternative expression for the Fundamental matrix.

There is a very simple and natural way of deriving the Fundamental matrix in the Grassman-Cayley formalism. It gives an expression whose advantage is that each entry is only a sum of terms of degree 4 in the entries of the projection matrices. No matrix operations (in particular inversions) are required. We use the simple idea that two pixels m and m' are in correspondence if and only if their optical rays (C, m) and (C', m') intersect. We then write down this condition using proposition 3.33 and obtain the Fundamental matrix using the properties of the Grassman-Cayley algebra.

We denote the rows of $\boldsymbol{\mathcal{P}}$ by $\boldsymbol{U}^T$, $\boldsymbol{V}^T$, $\boldsymbol{W}^T$, and the rows of $\boldsymbol{\mathcal{P}}'$ by $\boldsymbol{U'}^T$, $\boldsymbol{V'}^T$, $\boldsymbol{W'}^T$. We have the following proposition.

Proposition 5.9 *The expression of the Fundamental matrix* $\mathbf{F}$ *as a function of the row vectors of the matrices* $\boldsymbol{\mathcal{P}}$ *and* $\boldsymbol{\mathcal{P}}'$ *is*

$$\mathbf{F} \simeq \begin{bmatrix} |\boldsymbol{V},\boldsymbol{W},\boldsymbol{V'},\boldsymbol{W'}| & |\boldsymbol{W},\boldsymbol{U},\boldsymbol{V'},\boldsymbol{W'}| & |\boldsymbol{U},\boldsymbol{V},\boldsymbol{V'},\boldsymbol{W'}| \\ |\boldsymbol{V},\boldsymbol{W},\boldsymbol{W'},\boldsymbol{U'}| & |\boldsymbol{W},\boldsymbol{U},\boldsymbol{W'},\boldsymbol{U'}| & |\boldsymbol{U},\boldsymbol{V},\boldsymbol{W'},\boldsymbol{U'}| \\ |\boldsymbol{V},\boldsymbol{W},\boldsymbol{U'},\boldsymbol{V'}| & |\boldsymbol{W},\boldsymbol{U},\boldsymbol{U'},\boldsymbol{V'}| & |\boldsymbol{U},\boldsymbol{V},\boldsymbol{U'},\boldsymbol{V'}| \end{bmatrix}. \quad (5.8)$$

Proof : Let m and m' be two pixels. They are in correspondence if and only if their optical rays $(C, m) = L_m$ and $(C', m') = L'_{m'}$ intersect. According to proposition 3.33, this fact is equivalent to the fact that the Plücker product $[\mathbf{L}_m | \mathbf{L}'_{m'}]$ of the two optical rays is equal to 0. Let us translate this statement algebraically. Let (x, y, z) (respectively (x', y', z')) be the projective coordinates of m (respectively m'). Using proposition 4.4, we write

$$\mathbf{L}_m \simeq \tilde{\boldsymbol{\mathcal{P}}}^T \mathbf{m} = x\boldsymbol{V} \vartriangle \boldsymbol{W} + y\boldsymbol{W} \vartriangle \boldsymbol{U} + z\boldsymbol{U} \vartriangle \boldsymbol{V}$$

and

$$\mathbf{L}'_{m'} \simeq \tilde{\boldsymbol{\mathcal{P}}}'^T \mathbf{m}' = x'\boldsymbol{V}' \vartriangle \boldsymbol{W}' + y'\boldsymbol{W}' \vartriangle \boldsymbol{U}' + z'\boldsymbol{U}' \vartriangle \boldsymbol{V}'.$$

We now want to compute $[\mathbf{L}_m | \mathbf{L}'_{m'}]$. In order to do this, we use proposition 3.12 and compute $\mathbf{L}_m \triangledown \mathbf{L}'_{m'}$:

$$\mathbf{L}_m \triangledown \mathbf{L}'_{m'} \simeq (x\boldsymbol{V} \vartriangle \boldsymbol{W} + y\boldsymbol{W} \vartriangle \boldsymbol{U} + z\boldsymbol{U} \vartriangle \boldsymbol{V}) \triangledown (x'\boldsymbol{V}' \vartriangle \boldsymbol{W}' + y'\boldsymbol{W}' \vartriangle \boldsymbol{U}' + z'\boldsymbol{U}' \vartriangle \boldsymbol{V}')$$

Using the linearity of the join operator, we obtain an expression which is bilinear in the coordinates of m and m' and contains terms such as

$$(\boldsymbol{V} \vartriangle \boldsymbol{W}) \triangledown (\boldsymbol{V}' \vartriangle \boldsymbol{W}').$$

Since $\boldsymbol{V} \vartriangle \boldsymbol{W}$ and $\boldsymbol{V}' \vartriangle \boldsymbol{W}'$ are extensors of step 2, we can apply proposition 3.25 and write

$$(\boldsymbol{V} \vartriangle \boldsymbol{W}) \triangledown (\boldsymbol{V}' \vartriangle \boldsymbol{W}') = | \boldsymbol{V}, \boldsymbol{W}, \boldsymbol{V}', \boldsymbol{W}' | \, \mathbf{I},$$

where $\mathbf{I}$ is the integral defined in section 3.4. We have similar expressions for all terms in $\mathbf{L}_m \triangledown \mathbf{L}'_{m'}$. We thus obtain

$$\mathbf{L}_m \triangledown \mathbf{L}'_{m'} = (\mathbf{m}'^T \mathbf{F} \mathbf{m}) \mathbf{I},$$

where the 3×3 matrix $\mathbf{F}$ is defined by equation (5.8). Since $\mathbf{L}_m \triangledown \mathbf{L}'_{m'} = [\mathbf{L}_m \mid \mathbf{L}'_{m'}] \, \mathbf{I}$, the conclusion follows. $\square$

Let us determine the epipoles in this formalism. We have the following simple proposition.

Proposition 5.10 *The expression of the epipoles e and e' as a function of the row vectors of the matrices $\boldsymbol{\mathcal{P}}$ and $\boldsymbol{\mathcal{P}}'$ is*

$$\mathbf{e} \simeq \begin{bmatrix} | \boldsymbol{U}, \boldsymbol{U}', \boldsymbol{V}', \boldsymbol{W}' | \\ | \boldsymbol{V}, \boldsymbol{U}', \boldsymbol{V}', \boldsymbol{W}' | \\ | \boldsymbol{W}, \boldsymbol{U}', \boldsymbol{V}', \boldsymbol{W}' | \end{bmatrix}, \quad \mathbf{e}' \simeq \begin{bmatrix} | \boldsymbol{U}', \boldsymbol{U}, \boldsymbol{V}, \boldsymbol{W} | \\ | \boldsymbol{V}', \boldsymbol{U}, \boldsymbol{V}, \boldsymbol{W} | \\ | \boldsymbol{W}', \boldsymbol{U}, \boldsymbol{V}, \boldsymbol{W} | \end{bmatrix}. \qquad (5.9)$$

Proof : We have seen previously that e (respectively e') is the image of C' (respectively C) by the first (respectively the second) camera. According to proposition 4.3, these optical centers are represented by the vectors of $G_1(\mathbb{R}^4)$ $\boldsymbol{U} \vartriangle \boldsymbol{V} \vartriangle \boldsymbol{W}$ and $\boldsymbol{U}' \vartriangle \boldsymbol{V}' \vartriangle \boldsymbol{W}'$. Therefore, for example, the first coordinate of e is

$$\langle \boldsymbol{U}, \boldsymbol{U}' \vartriangle \boldsymbol{V}' \vartriangle \boldsymbol{W}' \rangle,$$

which, according to equation (3.13) is equal to
$(\boldsymbol{U}' \vartriangle \boldsymbol{V}' \vartriangle \boldsymbol{W}') \vartriangle \boldsymbol{U} = - | \boldsymbol{U}, \boldsymbol{U}', \boldsymbol{V}', \boldsymbol{W}' |.$ $\square$

5.2.3   The epipolar homography

Geometric observation   Let us enrich the idea of epipolar geometry and consider the one parameter family of planes going through (C, C') as shown in Fig. 5.10. This family is a pencil of planes (see Chapter 2, section 2.6.2) called the *pencil of epipolar planes*. Let Π be any plane of the pencil, it intersects the two retinal planes along two corresponding epipolar lines l and l', respectively.

When Π rotates around (C, C'), l and l' rotate around the epipoles e and e', respectively. The two pencils of lines are called the *epipolar pencils*. An important property of these two pencils is described in the following proposition:

Proposition 5.11 *The two pencils of epipolar lines are related by a homography.*

Proof :   We have to show that there is a one-to-one correspondence between the two pencils of epipolar lines that preserves the cross-ratio (theorem 2.2). Let l be an epipolar line, i.e. a line in the first image going through the epipole e. It determines a unique epipolar plane $\Pi = (C, l)$ which intersects the second retinal plane along the corresponding epipolar line l'. Exchanging the roles of l and l', we find that the mapping $l \longleftrightarrow l'$ between two corresponding epipolar lines is one-to-one. Given now four pairs of corresponding epipolar lines, they determine four epipolar planes. The cross-ratio of the four lines in the first image is obtained (see proposition 2.16) as the cross-ratio of the four points of intersection with any line not going through e. But, according to the same theorem, this cross-ratio is also the cross-ratio of the four epipolar planes which, for the same reason is also the cross-ratio of the four corresponding epipolar lines is the second image. $\square$

Definition 5.2 *The homography that we just constructed between the two pencils of epipolar lines is called the **epipolar homography**.*

We now show how to parameterize the Fundamental matrix as a function of the two epipoles e and e' and the epipolar homography. The result is described in the following proposition:

Proposition 5.12 *Let (p_1, p_2) (respectively (p'_1, p'_2)) be a line in the first image (respectively second) which does not contain the epipole e (respectively e'). We then have the decomposition of the Fundamental matrix*

$$\mathbf{F} \simeq [\mathbf{e}']_\times [\mathbf{p}'_1, \mathbf{p}'_2] \underbrace{\begin{bmatrix} a & b \\ c & d \end{bmatrix}}_{h} \begin{bmatrix} \mathbf{p}_2^T \\ -\mathbf{p}_1^T \end{bmatrix} [\mathbf{e}]_\times, \tag{5.10}$$

where h is the epipolar homography; the two pencils of epipolar lines in each image are respectively parameterized by the lines (p_1, p_2) and (p'_1, p'_2).

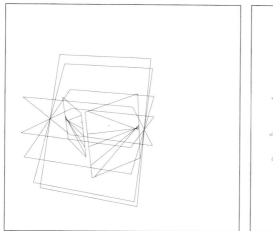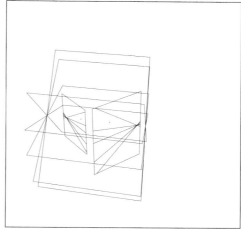

Figure 5.10: The epipolar pencils (stereogram for cross-fusion).

Proof : The idea is to parameterize the two epipolar pencils with the points of intersection of the epipolar lines with the lines (p_1, p_2) and (p_1', p_2'), respectively. Let m be a point in the first image different from e. The epipolar line l of m is, according to proposition 3.27, represented by $\mathbf{l} \simeq \mathbf{e} \times \mathbf{m}$; similarly, the line (p_1, p_2) is represented by $\mathbf{p}_1 \times \mathbf{p}_2$, and the point of intersection of l and (p_1, p_2) is represented by $\mathbf{l} \times (\mathbf{p}_1 \times \mathbf{p}_2)$. Expanding this double cross-product, we find

$$\lambda \mathbf{p}_1 + \mu \mathbf{p}_2,$$

where $\lambda = \mathbf{l}^T \mathbf{p}_2$ and $\mu = -\mathbf{l}^T \mathbf{p}_1$. As in section 2.4.2.3, we define the projective parameter $\tau = \frac{\lambda}{\mu}$:

$$\tau = -\frac{(\mathbf{e} \times \mathbf{m})^T \mathbf{p}_2}{(\mathbf{e} \times \mathbf{m})^T \mathbf{p}_1}. \tag{5.11}$$

We have parameterized the first epipolar pencil with the parameter τ. We proceed similarly in the second image and parameterize the second epipolar pencil with the projective parameter τ':

$$\tau' = -\frac{(\mathbf{e}' \times \mathbf{m}')^T \mathbf{p}_2'}{(\mathbf{e}' \times \mathbf{m}')^T \mathbf{p}_1'} \tag{5.12}$$

Let $\mathbf{h} = \begin{bmatrix} a & b \\ c & d \end{bmatrix}$ be a representation of the epipolar homography. Two epipolar lines are in correspondence if and only if

$$\tau' = \frac{a\tau + b}{c\tau + d}.$$

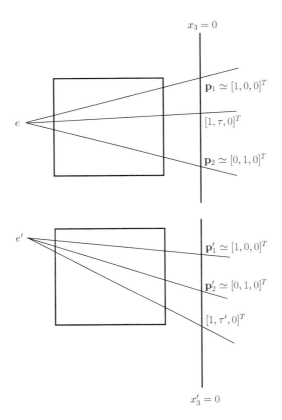

Figure 5.11: Parameterization of the epipolar homography.

Replacing τ and τ' by their values (5.11) and (5.12) and identifying the resulting expression with equation (5.4), we find

$$F_{ij} = (\mathbf{p}'_1 \times \mathbf{e}')_i (\mathbf{p}_2 \times \mathbf{e})_j a - (\mathbf{p}'_1 \times \mathbf{e}')_i (\mathbf{p}_1 \times \mathbf{e})_j b$$
$$+ (\mathbf{p}'_2 \times \mathbf{e}')_i (\mathbf{p}_2 \times \mathbf{e})_j c - (\mathbf{p}'_2 \times \mathbf{e}')_i (\mathbf{p}_1 \times \mathbf{e})_j d, \qquad (5.13)$$

from which we deduce (5.10). □

Looking at this decomposition, we see that $\mathbf{F}$ can be decomposed as a product of several transformations:

- the mapping represented by $[\mathbf{e}]_\times$, which maps a point of $\mathcal{R}$ to its epipolar line,

- the mapping represented by the matrix $\begin{bmatrix} \mathbf{p}_2^T \\ -\mathbf{p}_1^T \end{bmatrix}$ from an epipolar line l to the projective coordinates $[\mathbf{p}_2^T l, -\mathbf{p}_1^T l]$ of its point of intersection with the line

(p_1, p_2),

- h, the homography between the two pencils of epipolar lines parameterized by their points of intersection with (p_1, p_2) and (p_1', p_2'), respectively,

- the mapping represented by the matrix $\begin{bmatrix} \mathbf{p}_2' \\ -\mathbf{p}_1' \end{bmatrix}$ from the projective coordinates $[\lambda', \mu']$ to the point $\lambda \mathbf{p}_1' + \mu \mathbf{p}_2'$, and

- the mapping represented by $[\mathbf{e}']_\times$, which maps a point of $\mathcal{R}'$ to its epipolar line.

In the affine case where we know the lines at infinity l_∞ and l_∞' of the two retinal planes and if the epipoles e and e' are not at infinity, we can choose $(p_1, p_2) = l_\infty$ and $(p_1', p_2') = l_\infty'$. Assuming, as in section 2.5, that those lines have the equation $x_3 = 0$ (respectively $x_3' = 0$), we can choose $\mathbf{p}_1 = \mathbf{p}_1' \simeq [1, 0, 0]^T$ and $\mathbf{p}_2 = \mathbf{p}_2' \simeq [0, 1, 0]^T$. The previous decomposition of the matrix $\mathbf{F}$ has the simple form

$$\mathbf{F} = [\mathbf{e}']_\times \begin{bmatrix} -b & a & 0 \\ -d & c & 0 \\ 0 & 0 & 0 \end{bmatrix} [\mathbf{e}]_\times, \tag{5.14}$$

which is shown in figure 5.11.

We can now characterize the number of degrees of freedom of the Fundamental matrix. This characterization is important if we want to know what is the minimum number of point correspondences necessary to estimate the Fundamental matrix. We have the following proposition.

Proposition 5.13 *The Fundamental matrix has 7 degrees of freedom: The two coordinates of the epipoles and the three parameters of the epipolar homography. Another proof is to notice that the F-matrix is defined up to scale, defining a projective morphism, and it has to satisfy the constraint $det(\mathbf{F}) = 0$ since its rank is two, leaving us with $9 - 2 = 7$ independent degrees of freedom.*

Proof :   The result follows directly from proposition 5.12 since it provides an analytic expression of the Fundamental matrix as a function of those 7 parameters. □

This proposition also says that the minimum number of point correspondences required to obtain a finite number of solutions for the Fundamental matrix is 7. The number of solutions in that case is in general 3, as stated in the following proposition.

Proposition 5.14 *Given 7 point correspondences (m_i, m_i'), $i = 1, \ldots, 7$, the number of Fundamental matrices satisfying the epipolar constraint (5.4) for all of those pairs is in general 3.*

Proof :   The epipolar constraint (5.4) is linear in the entries of $\mathbf{F}$. Since $\mathbf{F}$ is defined only up to a scale factor, provided that there are eight point correspondences in generic position $\mathbf{m}_i \leftrightarrow \mathbf{m}'_i$, the homogeneous system of equations $\mathbf{m}'^T_i \mathbf{F} \mathbf{m}_i = 0$ has a unique nonzero solution. Indeed, the corresponding matrix is 8×9 and of rank 8 in general. Therefore its nullspace is of dimension 1 which defines, up to a scale factor, a unique Fundamental matrix. Note that it may not satisfy the rank 2 constraint. This approach will be studied in great detail in Chapter 6. If we have only 7 point correspondences, then the previous system of equations has in general a nullspace of dimension 2 and every solution can be expressed as a linear combination of two solutions $\mathbf{F}_1$ and $\mathbf{F}_2$:

$$\lambda_1 \mathbf{F}_1 + \lambda_2 \mathbf{F}_2$$

Enforcing the constraint $\det(\mathbf{F}) = 0$ leads to the expression $\det(\lambda_1 \mathbf{F}_1 + \lambda_2 \mathbf{F}_2) = 0$, which is homogeneous of degree 3 in λ_1 and λ_2. We thus obtain either one or three real solutions for $\mathbf{F}$.

$\square$

5.2.4   Relations between the Fundamental matrix and planar homographies

We now study the relation between the F-matrix of a pair of cameras and the matrix representation of the homography induced by a plane not going through any of the two optical centers of the stereo rig. It should be clear that there must exist some relation between the two since we have seen that not any homography between the two image planes is induced by a 3D plane.

We begin with a definition:

Definition 5.3 *Let H be a homography from image 1 to image 2. We say that this homography is a **planar homography** if and only if there exists a plane Π such that $H = H_\Pi$.*

The main result is that the characterization of planar homographies is quite simple:

Theorem 5.1 *Given a pair of images and the corresponding Fundamental matrix $\mathbf{F}$, let H be a homography from the first to the second image plane represented by the matrix $\mathbf{H}$. The four following conditions are equivalent.*

  1. The homography H is a planar homography.

  2.

$$\mathbf{H}^T \mathbf{F} + \mathbf{F}^T \mathbf{H} = \mathbf{0} \tag{5.15}$$

  3.

$$\mathbf{H}^T \mathbf{F} \simeq [\mathbf{e}]_\times$$

4.

$$\mathbf{F} \simeq [\mathbf{e}']_\times \mathbf{H} \qquad (5.16)$$

Proof : Note that condition 2 is equivalent to the fact that matrix $\mathbf{H}^T\mathbf{F}$ is antisymmetric. Let us show first that $2 \Leftrightarrow 3$. If 2 is true, then the matrix $\mathbf{H}^T\mathbf{F}$ is antisymmetric. Since it is of rank 2 because $\mathbf{H}$ is of rank 3, it is proportional to $[\mathbf{x}]_\times$ where $\mathbf{x}$ is any nonzero vector in its nullspace. Because of proposition 5.8, $\mathbf{e}$ is in the nullspace of $\mathbf{F}$ and hence in the nullspace of $\mathbf{H}^T\mathbf{F}$; therefore 3 is true. Conversely, if 3 holds, the matrix $\mathbf{H}^T\mathbf{F}$ is antisymmetric and 2 is true. The geometry is shown in figure 5.12.

By multiplying the two sides of (5.15) by $\mathbf{H}^{-1}$ to the right and by $\mathbf{H}^{-T}$ to the left we obtain the equivalent relation

$$\mathbf{F}\mathbf{H}^{-1} + \mathbf{H}^{-T}\mathbf{F}^T = \mathbf{0}.$$

We see that 2 is equivalent to the condition obtained from 3 by changing $\mathbf{F}$ in $\mathbf{F}^T$ and $\mathbf{H}$ into $\mathbf{H}^{-1}$. Using proposition again 5.8, we write

$$\mathbf{H}^{-T}\mathbf{F}^T \simeq [\mathbf{e}']_\times \,,$$

from which 4 follows. We have therefore proved the equivalences $2 \Leftrightarrow 3 \Leftrightarrow 4$.

We prove now that 1 implies 4. If H is a planar homography, corresponding to the plane Π, we know from proposition 5.1 that $\mathbf{H}_\Pi \simeq \mathcal{P}'\mathcal{P}_\Pi^+$. But equation (5.5) can be written $\mathbf{F} \simeq [\mathbf{e}']_\times \mathbf{H}_\Pi$ from which the result follows.

To finish the proof, we show that 4 implies 1. Assuming that 4 is true, we show that we can uniquely compute a representation of a plane Π not going through C and such that $H = H_\Pi$. In order to do this we use proposition 5.2 that gives the expression of $\mathbf{H}_\Pi$ as a function of $\mathbf{\Pi}$ and the rows of the matrices $\mathcal{P}$ and $\mathcal{P}'$. We write $\mathbf{\Pi}$ as a linear combination of U, V, W and one of the projection planes of the second camera. This interpretation is always possible since we have assumed that there existed a Fundamental matrix between the two views. This step implies that the two optical centers are distinct and therefore that at least one of the three planes U', V', W', say U', does not go through C and is therefore linearly independent of U, V, W. We write

$$\mathbf{\Pi} = \alpha U + \beta V + \gamma W + \delta U'.$$

Replacing $\mathbf{\Pi}$ by this expression in the equation giving $\mathbf{H}_\Pi$ in proposition 5.2, we find that the coefficients $h_{ij}, i, j = 1, 2, 3$, of $\mathbf{H}$ must satisfy the following system of linear equations.

$$h_{11} = \alpha \mid U', V, W, U \mid \qquad h_{12} = \beta \mid U', W, U, V \mid \qquad h_{13} = \gamma \mid U', U, V, W \mid$$

$$\begin{aligned} h_{21} &= \alpha \mid V', V, W, U \mid + & h_{22} &= \beta \mid V', W, U, V \mid + & h_{23} &= \gamma \mid V', U, V, W \mid + \\ & \delta \mid V', V, W, U' \mid & & \delta \mid V', W, U, U' \mid & & \delta \mid V', U, V, U' \mid \end{aligned}$$

$$\begin{aligned} h_{31} &= \alpha \mid W', V, W, U \mid + & h_{32} &= \beta \mid W', W, U, V \mid + & h_{33} &= \gamma \mid W', U, V, W \mid + \\ & \delta \mid W', V, W, U' \mid & & \delta \mid W', W, U, U' \mid & & \delta \mid W', U, V, U' \mid \end{aligned}$$

Let $\mathbf{e}' \simeq [e'_1, e'_2, e'_3]^T$. We notice that because of our assumptions, the plane $\boldsymbol{U}'$ does not go through the optical center $\boldsymbol{U} \bigtriangleup \boldsymbol{V} \bigtriangleup \boldsymbol{W}$ and that, therefore, the bracket $\mid \boldsymbol{U}', \boldsymbol{V}, \boldsymbol{W}, \boldsymbol{U} \mid \simeq e'_1$ is nonzero. This reasoning yields $\alpha = h_{11}/e'_1$, $\beta = h_{12}/e'_1$, $\gamma = h_{13}/e'_1$. In order to show existence and uniqueness we only have to show that the last six equations yield a unique value for δ.

Replacing α, β and γ by their values in those six equations, noticing that $[\mid \boldsymbol{U}', \boldsymbol{W}, \boldsymbol{U}, \boldsymbol{V} \mid, \mid \boldsymbol{V}', \boldsymbol{V}, \boldsymbol{W}, \boldsymbol{U}' \mid, \mid \boldsymbol{W}', \boldsymbol{W}, \boldsymbol{U}, \boldsymbol{U}' \mid]^T \simeq \mathbf{e}'$ (proposition 5.10), and identifying the coefficients of α and β with the coefficients of the Fundamental matrix (equation (5.8)) we obtain

$$-h_{11}e'_2 + h_{21}e'_1 = -\delta F_{31}e'_1, \quad -h_{12}e'_2 + h_{22}e'_1 = -\delta F_{32}e'_1,$$
$$-h_{13}e'_2 + h_{23}e'_1 = -\delta F_{33}e'_1, \quad h_{11}e'^{(3)} - h_{31}e'_1 = -\delta F_{21}e'_1,$$
$$h_{12}e'^{(3)} - h_{32}e'_1 = -\delta F_{22}e'_1, \quad h_{13}e'^{(3)} - h_{33}e'_1 = -\delta F_{23}e'_1.$$

We recognize the left-hand sides to be the last two rows of $[\mathbf{e}']_\times \mathbf{H}$ and the right-hand sides to be the product by $-\delta e'_1$ of the last two rows of matrix $\mathbf{F}$. Because we have assumed that condition 4 was true, we can compute a unique value for δ which completes the proof that $4 \Rightarrow 1$. $\square$

An examination of the proof of the previous proposition shows that we can extend our analysis to the case where the plane considered goes through one of the two optical centers. We restrict ourselves to the case where it goes through the second optical center, the other case being easily deduced from this one.

When the plane goes through C', it induces a morphism between the two images which can be represented by a 3×3 matrix of rank 2: The image of the first retinal plane by this morphism is the line of intersection of the plane and the second retinal plane. Not all such morphisms between the two image planes are induced by a plane going through the second optical center. In order to characterize them we need a definition analogous to definition 5.3:

Definition 5.4 *Let H be a morphism of rank two from image 1 to 2. We say that this morphism is a* **planar morphism** *if and only if there exists a plane Π going through the second optical center such that $H = H_\Pi$.*

The Proof of theorem 5.1 shows that the following corollary is true.

Corollary 5.1 *Given a pair of images and the corresponding Fundamental matrix $\mathbf{F}$, let H be a morphism of rank 2 from the first to the second image plane represented by the matrix $\mathbf{H}$. The following conditions are equivalent*

   1. The morphism H is a planar morphism.

   2.

$$\mathbf{F} \simeq [\mathbf{e}']_\times \mathbf{H}$$

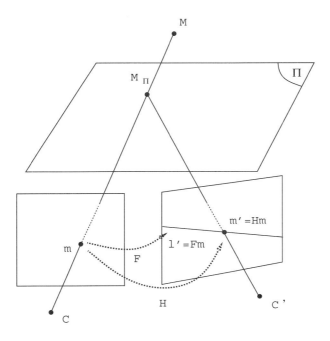

Figure 5.12: Relation between the Fundamental matrix and a planar homography.

An analogy can be noted with the decomposition of the Essential matrix $\mathbf{E} = [\mathbf{t}]_\times \mathbf{R}$ in equation (5.32) as the product of an antisymmetric matrix and a rotation matrix $\mathbf{R}$, since the Fundamental matrix is decomposed as the product of an antisymmetric matrix and a non-singular matrix (in the general case) $\mathbf{H}$. It is obvious that this decomposition is not unique, since $\mathbf{H}$ can be any matrix defining a correspondence compatible with $\mathbf{F}$. More precisely, since the matrix equation (5.15) includes six homogeneous equations, the family of compatible matrices has three degrees of freedom, which correspond to the choice of a plane in $\mathbb{P}^3$. Once the Fundamental matrix is known, a compatible homography matrix is uniquely determined by *three* point correspondences, the fourth correspondence being $e \leftrightarrow e'$. Each point correspondence gives two equations, but because of the epipolar constraint, these two equations provide only one additional constraint for a compatible matrix.

From this theorem follows the following useful proposition.

Proposition 5.15 *Any planar homography satisfies the condition*

$$\mathbf{H}e \simeq \mathbf{e}'. \qquad (5.17)$$

Any planar morphism of rank 2 satisfies the condition

$$\mathbf{H}e = \mathbf{0}.$$

Proof : This proposition is a consequence of condition 4 of theorem 5.1: Since $\mathbf{Fe} = \mathbf{0}$ and $\mathbf{F} \simeq [\mathbf{e}']_\times \mathbf{H}$, one has necessarily $\mathbf{He} \simeq \mathbf{e}'$ or $\mathbf{He} = \mathbf{0}$. The first case corresponds to a planar homography and the second to a planar morphism of rank 2. Indeed, if the plane goes through C', then the image of the epipole e is, according to figure 5.4, the image of C' through the second camera. □

The relation between planar homographies is also quite simple but requires some care. It is described in the following proposition.

Proposition 5.16 *Let H_1 and H_2 be two planar homographies or morphisms corresponding to the two planes Π_1 and Π_2. There exist two matrices $\mathbf{H}_1$ and $\mathbf{H}_2$ representing H_1 and H_2 such that*

$$\mathbf{H}_2 = \mathbf{H}_1 + \mathbf{e}'\mathbf{l}_{12}^T, \tag{5.18}$$

where $\mathbf{e}'$ is a coordinate vector of e' and $\mathbf{l}_{12}$ is a coordinate vector of the image in the first camera of the line of intersection of the two planes Π_1 and Π_2.

The matrices $\mathbf{H}_1$ and $\mathbf{H}_2$ do not depend upon the choice of the coordinate vector $\mathbf{e}'$. The vector $\mathbf{l}_{12}$ does depend upon this choice and if $\mathbf{e}' \to \lambda\mathbf{e}'$ for $\lambda \neq 0$, then $\mathbf{l}_{12} \to \frac{1}{\lambda}\mathbf{l}_{12}$

Proof : Since neither Π_1 nor Π_2 goes through C, the inverse perspective matrices $\mathcal{P}_{\Pi_1}^+$ and $\mathcal{P}_{\Pi_2}^+$ are well-defined. Therefore, according to proposition 4.8, we have

$$\langle \Pi_1, \mathbf{C} \rangle \mathbf{I}_4 + \mathcal{P}_{\Pi_1}^+ \mathcal{P} = \mathbf{C}\Pi_1^T.$$

Multiplying both sides of this equation to the left by $\mathcal{P}'$ and to the right by $\mathcal{P}_{\Pi_2}^+$, we find

$$\langle \Pi_1, \mathbf{C} \rangle \mathcal{P}'\mathcal{P}_{\Pi_2}^+ + \mathcal{P}'\mathcal{P}_{\Pi_1}^+ \mathcal{P}\mathcal{P}_{\Pi_2}^+ = \mathcal{P}'\mathbf{C}(\mathcal{P}_{\Pi_2}^{+T}\tilde{\Pi}_1)^T.$$

The conclusion follows from the fact that $\mathcal{P}'\mathcal{P}_{\Pi_2}^+ \simeq \mathbf{H}_2$, $\mathcal{P}'\mathcal{P}_{\Pi_1}^+ \simeq \mathbf{H}_1$, and $\mathcal{P}\mathcal{P}_{\Pi_2}^+ \simeq \mathbf{I}_3$ (definition 4.1) and the fact that $\mathcal{P}_{\Pi_2}^{+T}\Pi_1$ represents the image in the first camera of the line of intersection of the two planes Π_1 and Π_2 (proposition 4.13).

Let us interpret this result. What we have proved is that, given representations $\hat{\mathbf{H}}_1$, $\hat{\mathbf{H}}_2$ and $\hat{\mathbf{e}}'$ of the planar morphisms H_1 and H_2 and of the epipole e', there exist three scalars α_1, α_2 and β such that

$$\alpha_1\hat{\mathbf{H}}_1 + \alpha_2\hat{\mathbf{H}}_2 + \beta\hat{\mathbf{e}}'\mathbf{l}_{12}^T = \mathbf{0}. \tag{5.19}$$

Multiplying both sides of this equation on the left with $[\hat{\mathbf{e}}']_\times$ we obtain an equation that fixes the ratio $\frac{\alpha_1}{\alpha_2}$:

$$\alpha_1 [\hat{\mathbf{e}}']_\times \hat{\mathbf{H}}_1 + \alpha_2 [\hat{\mathbf{e}}']_\times \hat{\mathbf{H}}_2 = \mathbf{0}.$$

Each matrix that appears is in effect proportional to $\mathbf{F}$ (theorem 5.1 and corollary 5.1).

We define $\mathbf{H}_1 = \frac{\alpha_1}{\alpha_2}\hat{\mathbf{H}}_1$ and $\mathbf{H}_2 = -\hat{\mathbf{H}}_2$.

Multiplying both sides of (5.19) on the left with $\hat{\mathbf{e}}'^T$ and transposing, we obtain

$$\beta\|\hat{\mathbf{e}}'\|^2 \mathbf{l}_{12} = -\alpha_1\hat{\mathbf{H}}_1^T\hat{\mathbf{e}}' - \alpha_2\hat{\mathbf{H}}_2^T\hat{\mathbf{e}}'.$$

This equation can be rewritten as

$$\frac{\beta}{\alpha_2}\|\hat{\mathbf{e}}'\|\mathbf{l}_{12} = -\mathbf{H}_1\frac{\hat{\mathbf{e}}'}{\|\hat{\mathbf{e}}'\|} + \mathbf{H}_2\frac{\hat{\mathbf{e}}'}{\|\hat{\mathbf{e}}'\|}. \tag{5.20}$$

We now choose an *arbitrary* value for the ratio $\frac{\beta}{\alpha_2}$ and let $\mathbf{e}' = \frac{\beta}{\alpha_2}\hat{\mathbf{e}}'$. According to equation (5.20) this determines $\mathbf{l}_{12}$. We have obtained equation (5.18).

Multiplying $\mathbf{e}'$ by λ is equivalent, according to the previous discussion, to multiplying the ratio $\frac{\beta}{\alpha_2}$ by the same amount and hence, according to (5.20), to dividing $\mathbf{l}_{12}$ by λ. $\square$

We hope that this proof has drawn the reader's attention to the fact that equation (5.18) requires some care in its interpretation. This xcare is sometimes the price you have to pay for pictorial simplicity!

Proposition 5.17 *Conversely, given a planar homography or morphism H_1, one of its representations $\mathbf{H}_1$, and a coordinate vector $\mathbf{e}'$ of the epipole e', the mapping from $\mathbb{R}^3$ to the set of planar morphisms*

$$\mathbf{l}_{12} \longrightarrow \mathbf{H}_2 = \mathbf{H}_1 + \mathbf{e}'\mathbf{l}_{12}^T,$$

defined by equation (5.18) is one-to-one.

Proof : The mapping defines a planar morphism since $[\mathbf{e}']_\times \mathbf{H}_2 = [\mathbf{e}']_\times \mathbf{H}_1$ and the right-hand side is proportional to $\mathbf{F}$ according to corollary 5.1. Therefore, according to the same corollary, H_2 is a planar morphism. We know from proposition 5.16 that the mapping is surjective since any planar morphism can be written as (5.18). Consider now two vectors $\mathbf{l}_{12}$ and $\mathbf{l}'_{12}$ corresponding to the planar morphisms H_2 and H'_2. According to (5.18), we have $\mathbf{H}_2 - \mathbf{H}'_2 = \mathbf{e}'(\mathbf{l}_{12} - \mathbf{l}'_{12})^T$. The matrix $\mathbf{e}'(\mathbf{l}_{12} - \mathbf{m}_{12})^T$ is nonzero as soon as the vectors l_{12} and m_{12} are different; hence the mapping is injective. $\square$

The zero vector corresponds to the plane Π_1. A consequence of this proposition is that for a given nonzero vector $\mathbf{l}_{12}$, corresponding to the plane Π_2, the one parameter family of planes represented by the the vectors $\lambda\mathbf{l}_{12}$ is the pencil of planes whose axis is the line of intersection of Π_1 and Π_2.

5.2.5 The S-matrix and the intrinsic planes

We now introduce the matrix of a special planar morphism which is intrinsic to the pair of cameras. This morphism turns out to be quite useful.

We will use an algebraic trick, and will then give a geometric interpretation. Using the relation

$$(\mathbf{v}^T\mathbf{w})\mathbf{I}_3 = \mathbf{v}\mathbf{w}^T - [\mathbf{w}]_\times[\mathbf{v}]_\times \tag{5.21}$$

in which we choose $\mathbf{v} = \mathbf{w} = \mathbf{e}'$, we obtain, by multiplying both sides to the right by the matrix $\mathbf{F}$,

$$\mathbf{F} = \underbrace{\frac{\mathbf{e}'}{\|\mathbf{e}'\|^2}\mathbf{e}'^T\mathbf{F}}_{\mathbf{0}} + [\mathbf{e}']_\times \underbrace{(-\frac{[\mathbf{e}']_\times}{\|\mathbf{e}'\|^2}\mathbf{F})}_{\simeq\mathbf{S}} \tag{5.22}$$

According to equation (5.22), we define $\mathbf{S} \simeq [\mathbf{e}']_\times\mathbf{F}$. We call this matrix the *special matrix* of the two views. We verify that $\mathbf{F} \simeq [\mathbf{e}']_\times\mathbf{S}$. Furthermore, the special matrix $\mathbf{S}$ has the following property (see figure 5.13).

Proposition 5.18 *The special matrix defines a planar morphism between the two image planes. This morphism is called the* epipolar projection. *The corresponding plane, noted Π_0' and called the second intrinsic plane, goes through the second optical center C' and intersects the second retinal plane along the line, noted $\langle e'\rangle$ and called the second intrinsic line, represented by the vector $\mathbf{e}'$. The image of a point m is the point of intersection of its epipolar line l_m' with $\langle e'\rangle$.*

Proof :   Since the second condition of corollary 5.1 is satisfied, we only have to show that the rank of $\mathbf{S}$ is 2. This rank is clearly less than or equal to 2 since $\mathbf{F}$ is of rank 2. $\mathbf{e}$ is in the nullspace. In order for $\mathbf{m}$ different from $\mathbf{e}$ to be in the nullspace, it is necessary that the epipolar line represented by $\mathbf{Fm}$ be identical to the line represented by $\mathbf{e}'$. But this condition is impossible since all epipolar lines go through the epipole e' whereas the line represented by $\mathbf{e}'$ does not. Therefore $rank(\mathbf{S}) = 2$.

The second part of the proposition follows from the fact that for every pixel m in the first image, one has $\mathbf{e}'^T\mathbf{Sm} = 0$ as is easily verified from the definition of $\mathbf{S}$. $\square$

The transpose $\mathbf{S}^T$ of $\mathbf{S}$ defines a planar morphism from the set of lines of the second view to the set of lines of the first view:

Proposition 5.19 *The image of a line l' in the second view by $\mathbf{S}^T$ is the epipolar line of its point of intersection with the line represented by $\mathbf{e}'$.*

Proof :   Algebraically we have $\mathbf{S}^Tl' \simeq \mathbf{F}^T[\mathbf{e}']_\times l'$. Since $[\mathbf{e}']_\times l'$ represents the point of intersection of l' with the line represented by $\mathbf{e}'$, the conclusion follows.

Geometrically, we consider the optical ray of the second camera defined as the intersection of the two planes going through C' and intersecting the second retinal plane along l' and and the line represented by $\mathbf{e}'$. Its image in the first view is the epipolar line described in the proposition. $\square$

If we exchange the two images we are led to consider the plane going through the first optical center and whose intersection with the first retinal plane is represented by the vector $\mathbf{e}$. It is therefore natural to propose the following

Definition 5.5 *The first intrinsic plane of the pair of images is the plane going through the first optical center whose line of intersection with the first (respectively second) retinal plane is called the first intrinsic line and is represented by the vector* $\mathbf{e}$. *This line is noted* $\langle e \rangle$. *This plane is noted* Π_0.

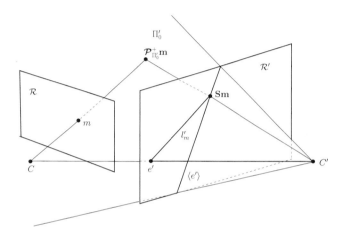

Figure 5.13: The epipolar projection.

As has been mentioned, this mechanism is important because it allows us to define a planar morphism compatible with $\mathbf{F}$ without identifying an actual plane in the scene. The price we pay is that the resulting morphism is of rank 2, and the plane depends on the second projection matrix. The same mechanism could be in fact used to define another singular matrix $\mathbf{S}_{l'}$, starting from an arbitrary line of l' of $\mathcal{R}'$, as the unique compatible matrix which satisfies $\mathbf{l'}^T \mathbf{S}_{l'} = \mathbf{0}$. We would have found that $\mathbf{S}_{l'}$ was the correspondence generated by the plane (C', l') and the relations $\mathbf{F} \simeq [\mathbf{e'}]_\times \mathbf{S}_{l'}$, and $\mathbf{S}_{l'} \simeq [\mathbf{l'}]_\times \mathbf{F}$. However, there is one advantage in considering the line $\langle e' \rangle$: this line never contains the point e', which ensures that the construction is always non-degenerate.

Note that if a plane Π goes through C and C' (an epipolar plane), it defines a morphism H_Π of rank 1 between the retinal planes $\mathcal{R}$ and $\mathcal{R}'$ such that

$$\mathbf{H}_\Pi \mathbf{m} \simeq \mathbf{e'} \quad \forall \mathbf{m} \qquad \mathbf{H}_\Pi \mathbf{e} = \mathbf{0}.$$

The second intrinsic plane and the corresponding morphism can be used to represent all other planar morphisms through equation (5.18) of proposition 5.16:

Definition 5.6 *The* **intrinsic representation** *of a plane* Π *not going through* C *is the vector* $\mathbf{r}_\Pi$ *such that*

$$\mathbf{H}_\Pi = \mathbf{S} + \mathbf{e}'\mathbf{r}_\Pi^T. \tag{5.23}$$

Let us note that just as in proposition 5.16, the practical interpretation of equation (5.23) is a bit subtle. Given a representation $\hat{\mathbf{H}}_\Pi$, $\hat{\mathbf{S}}$ and $\hat{\mathbf{e}}'$ of the planar morphisms H_Π, of the special matrix and of the epipole e', there exist three scalars α, β and γ such that

$$\alpha\hat{\mathbf{H}}_\Pi + \beta\hat{\mathbf{S}} + \gamma\hat{\mathbf{e}}'\mathbf{r}_\Pi^T = \mathbf{0}. \tag{5.24}$$

The ratio $\frac{\alpha}{\beta}$ is determined by the equation $\alpha\left[\hat{\mathbf{e}}'\right]_\times \hat{\mathbf{H}}_\Pi + \beta\left[\hat{\mathbf{e}}'\right]_\times \hat{\mathbf{S}} = \mathbf{0}$, which leads us to define $\mathbf{H}_\Pi = \frac{\alpha}{\beta}\hat{\mathbf{H}}_\Pi$ and $\mathbf{S} = -\hat{\mathbf{S}}$. The ratio $\frac{\gamma}{\beta}$ is determined, together with the vector $\mathbf{r}_\Pi$, by an equation similar to (5.20): We multiply both sides of (5.24) by $\hat{\mathbf{e}}'^T$ on the left and transpose the result:

$$\frac{\gamma}{\beta}\|\hat{\mathbf{e}}'\|\mathbf{r}_\Pi = -\mathbf{H}_\Pi^T \frac{\hat{\mathbf{e}}'}{\|\hat{\mathbf{e}}'\|}.$$

We choose an arbitrary value for the ratio $\frac{\gamma}{\beta}$ and define $\mathbf{e}' = \frac{\gamma}{\beta}\hat{\mathbf{e}}'$. This choice determines the vector $\mathbf{r}_\Pi$. The choice of the ratio $\frac{\gamma}{\beta}$ corresponds to choosing the norm of $\mathbf{e}'$. Just like in proposition 5.16, if $\mathbf{e}' \to \lambda\mathbf{e}'$ for $\lambda \neq 0$, then $\mathbf{r}_\Pi \to \frac{1}{\lambda}\mathbf{r}_\Pi$.

5.3   Perspective projection

We assume in this section that the affine structure of the world is known, and that at least one of the two cameras performs a perspective projection, i.e. that at least one of the two optical centers is at a finite distance. Without loss of generality we assume that it is the first optical center.

5.3.1   The affine case

The fact that the affine structure of the world is known means that we know the plane at infinity. In contrast to the previous case where we only had projective planes and used the intrinsic planes as a reference to characterize all the planar homographies and morphisms, it is natural now to use the plane at infinity as a reference. This is the thread that we follow. The case where both cameras perform a parallel projection is degenerate in this context since the plane at infinity goes through both optical centers and does not define a planar morphism of rank 2. This case will be examined in Section 5.4.

We write the two projection matrices using their affine decomposition:

$$\mathcal{P} = [\mathbf{P}\ \mathbf{p}] \quad , \quad \mathcal{P}' = [\mathbf{P}'\ \mathbf{p}']$$

and assume that $\det(\mathbf{P}) \neq 0$.

We can easily characterize the epipoles:

Proposition 5.20 *The epipole in the second camera is represented by*

$$\mathbf{e}' \simeq -\mathbf{P}'\mathbf{P}^{-1}\mathbf{p} + \mathbf{p}'.$$

In the case that the second camera performs a perspective projection, the epipole in the first camera is represented by

$$\mathbf{e} \simeq -\mathbf{P}\mathbf{P}'^{-1}\mathbf{p}' + \mathbf{p}.$$

Proof : The proof is a direct consequence of equation (4.21) of proposition 4.15. □

We can now turn ourselves toward the characterization of the morphism induced by the plane at infinity: using proposition 4.16 and equation (4.22) we immediatly obtain

Proposition 5.21 *The planar morphism induced by the plane at infinity between the two image planes is represented by the matrix*

$$\mathbf{H}_\infty = \mathbf{P}'\mathbf{P}^{-1}. \tag{5.25}$$

This matrix is called the *infinity morphism*. In the case where the second camera also performs a perspective projection, it is a homography. It allows us to determine whether two 3D lines in the scene are parallel or not, just by checking if their intersection in the first image is mapped to their intersection in the second image by $\mathbf{H}_\infty$ since this is equivalent to whether the intersection of the two 3D lines belongs to Π_∞.

We can immediately relate the F-matrix and the infinity morphism by applying Corollary 5.1:

Proposition 5.22 *The F-matrix is related to the infinity morphism by*

$$\mathbf{F} \simeq [\mathbf{e}']_\times \mathbf{H}_\infty \tag{5.26}$$

We can also apply proposition 5.16 to characterize planar morphisms relatively to the infinity morphism:

Proposition 5.23 *Any planar morphism H_Π corresponding to the plane Π not going through the first optical center can be represented as*

$$\mathbf{H}_\Pi \simeq \mathbf{H}_\infty + \mathbf{e}'\mathbf{q}^T, \tag{5.27}$$

where $\mathbf{q}$ is a representation of the image of the line at infinity of Π in the first camera.

The same warning as proposition 5.16 and definition 5.6 should be made about the interpretation of this proposition.

This formulation separates two types of parameters: $\mathbf{q}$ correspond to the *affine* description of the structure of Π, whereas $\mathbf{H}_\infty$ and the epipole $\mathbf{e}'$ can be considered as *affine* descriptions of the motion of the camera.

Looking at equation (5.26) it might be tempting to say that the affine structure of the scene, $\mathbf{H}_\infty$, can be recovered from its projective structure, given by $\mathbf{F}$. This idea is of course not true since there are as many ways of writing $\mathbf{F}$ as equation (5.26) as there are planes not going through the optical center C. A way to see this fact is to use the intrinsic representation (5.23) of the plane at infinity

$$\mathbf{H}_\infty = \mathbf{S} + \mathbf{e}'\mathbf{r}_\infty^T, \tag{5.28}$$

which shows that in order to define H_∞ from $\mathbf{F}$ we need the three extra parameters of the vector $\mathbf{r}_\infty$.

The vector $\mathbf{r}_\infty$ is a complete characterization of the plane at infinity, once the Fundamental matrix is known. It is seen that three parameters are needed indeed. Conversely, it is not possible to determine $\mathbf{F}$ from $\mathbf{H}_\infty$ alone. The additional information which is needed is $\mathbf{e}'$. Therefore, two alternative ways to represent the affine information between the views are $(\mathbf{H}_\infty, \mathbf{e}')$, and $(\mathbf{S}, \mathbf{e}', \mathbf{r}_\infty)$.

At this point, the careful reader should wonder how the vector $\mathbf{r}_\infty$, apparently defined up to a scale factor, determines in effect three parameters. We gave the answer previously in our comments to propositions 5.16, 5.23 and to definition 5.6: Once the scale of $\mathbf{e}'$, $\mathbf{F}$ (and therefore of $\mathbf{S}$) and of $\mathbf{H}_\infty$ is chosen, the scale of $\mathbf{r}_\infty$ is totally determined, up to sign.

5.3.2   The Euclidean case: Epipolar geometry

We assume in this section that the Euclidean structure of the images and of the world is known. We note $\mathbf{A}$ and $\mathbf{A}'$ the matrices of the intrinsic parameters of each camera. We denote by $\mathcal{F}_C$ and $\mathcal{F}_{C'}$ the normalized coordinate systems (orthonormal) attached to each camera, by $\mathcal{F}_O$ a general orthonormal affine coordinate system, by $\mathcal{F}_c$ and $\mathcal{F}_{c'}$ the normalized pixel coordinate systems, and by $\mathcal{F}_o$ and $\mathcal{F}_{o'}$ the regular (affine) pixel coordinate systems.

We first assume that the space coordinates are expressed in $\mathcal{F}_O$ and the image coordinates in $\mathcal{F}_o$ and $\mathcal{F}_{o'}$. According to equation (4.28), the two perspective projection matrices are given by the expressions

$$\mathcal{P} \simeq \mathbf{A}\mathcal{P}_0 \mathbf{Q}_{\mathcal{F}_O}^{\mathcal{F}_C} \tag{5.29}$$

and

$$\mathcal{P}' \simeq \mathbf{A}'\mathcal{P}_0 \mathbf{Q}_{\mathcal{F}_O}^{\mathcal{F}_{C'}}. \tag{5.30}$$

Epipolar geometry   We now choose the world coordinate system $\mathcal{F}_O$ equal to the normalized coordinate system of the first camera $\mathcal{F}_C$ and write

$$\mathbf{Q}_{\mathcal{F}_C}^{\mathcal{F}_{C'}} = \left[\begin{array}{cc} \mathbf{R} & \mathbf{t} \\ \mathbf{0}^T & 1 \end{array} \right],$$

where $\mathbf{R}$ is the 3×3 rotation matrix between $\mathcal{F}_C$ and $\mathcal{F}_{C'}$ and $\mathbf{t}$ is the vector $\overrightarrow{\mathbf{C'C}}$ expressed in $\mathcal{F}_{C'}$. In this coordinate system, equation (5.29) becomes

$$\mathcal{P} \simeq \left[\begin{array}{cc} \mathbf{A} & \mathbf{0} \end{array} \right],$$

while equation (5.30) becomes

$$\mathcal{P}' \simeq \left[\begin{array}{cc} \mathbf{A'R} & \mathbf{A't} \end{array} \right].$$

As an immediate consequence of proposition 5.20, we have

Proposition 5.24 *When the world coordinate system is the canonical coordinate system of the first camera, the two epipoles are obtained as*

$$\mathbf{e} \simeq \mathbf{AR}^T\mathbf{t}, \qquad \mathbf{e}' \simeq \mathbf{A't}.$$

We can also express the infinity morphism:

Proposition 5.25 *The planar morphism induced by the plane at infinity between the two image planes is represented by the matrix*

$$\mathbf{H}_\infty \simeq \mathbf{A'RA}^{-1}.$$

In the case where the two views have the same intrinsic parameters, the planar morphism induced by the plane at infinity possesses an interesting property:

Proposition 5.26 (Module constraint) *When the intrinsic parameters are equal in the two views $(\mathbf{A} = \mathbf{A}')$ any matrix representing the planar morphism induced by the plane at infinity has eigenvalues which have the same magnitude.*

Proof :   Because of proposition 5.25, $\mathbf{H}_\infty$ is proportional to a matrix that is similar to a rotation matrix. Since the eigenvalues of a rotation matrix all have a magnitude of 1, the result follows.   □

This constraint is used in Chapter 11.

The final piece of the puzzle is the Fundamental matrix which can also be expressed as a function of the intrinsic and the extrinsic parameters of the pair of cameras:

Proposition 5.27 *The Fundamental matrix between the two views is given by*

$$\mathbf{F} \simeq \mathbf{A}'^{-T}[\mathbf{t}]_\times \mathbf{RA}^{-1}. \tag{5.31}$$

Proof :   According to proposition 5.22, we have

$$\mathbf{F} \simeq [\mathbf{e'}]_\times \mathbf{H}_\infty.$$

Using propositions 5.24 and 5.25, we obtain

$$\mathbf{F} \simeq [\mathbf{A't}]_\times \mathbf{A'RA}^{-1}.$$

Using the fact, proved in appendix A.1, that $[\mathbf{A't}]_\times \simeq \mathbf{A}'^{-T}[\mathbf{t}]_\times \mathbf{A}'^{-1}$, the result follows.   □

Definition 5.7 *The matrix* $[\mathbf{t}]_\times \mathbf{R}$ *is called the* Essential matrix *or* E-matrix *and noted* $\mathbf{E}$*:*

$$\mathbf{E} = [\mathbf{t}]_\times \mathbf{R}. \tag{5.32}$$

Its rank is either 2 or 0 if there is no translation. Because of the depth/speed ambiguity, it depends on five parameters only, the three parameters of the 3-D rotation and the two parameters defining the direction of translation.

The relation (5.31) between the Fundamental and Essential matrices can be written

$$\mathbf{F} \simeq \mathbf{A}'^{-T} \mathbf{E} \mathbf{A}^{-1}. \tag{5.33}$$

5.3.3   The Essential matrix

The Essential matrix is important in motion analysis with a calibrated camera. We review some of its main properties.

The Longuet-Higgins equation   Let us now express the pixel coordinates in the normalized pixel coordinate systems $\mathcal{F}_c$ and $\mathcal{F}_{c'}$. According to equation (5.31), the F-matrix is proportional to the E-matrix and the epipolar constraint can be written

$$\mathbf{m}'^T \mathbf{E} \mathbf{m} = 0.$$

This equation is known in the motion literature as the Longuet-Higgins equation (Longuet-Higgins, 1981), and has also been found by Tsai and Huang (Tsai and Huang, 1984). As shown in figure 5.14, its geometric interpretation is simply that the three vectors $\overrightarrow{Cm'}$, $\mathbf{t}$, and $\overrightarrow{Cm}$ are coplanar.

Constraints satisfied by the Essential matrix   In addition to the constraint $\det(\mathbf{E}) = 0$ and the fact that they are defined up to a scale factor, the Essential matrices have to satisfy an additional algebraic constraint. Huang and Faugeras (Huang and Faugeras, 1989; Faugeras, 1993) have shown that the three following

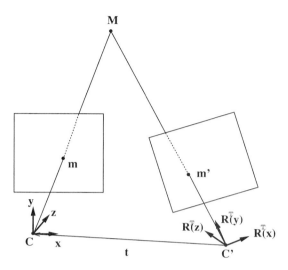

Figure 5.14: A geometric interpretation of the Longuet-Higgins equation.

properties are equivalent and, together with the rank constraint, are sufficient to ensure that a matrix $\mathbf{E}$ is an Essential matrix.

$$
\begin{aligned}
(i) & \quad \text{The two non-null singular values of } \mathbf{E} \text{ are equal,} \\
(ii) & \quad (\mathbf{l}_1^2 + \mathbf{l}_2^2 + \mathbf{l}_3^2)^2 = 4(\|\mathbf{l}_1 \times \mathbf{l}_2\|^2 + \|\mathbf{l}_1 \times \mathbf{l}_2\|^2 + \|\mathbf{l}_1 \times \mathbf{l}_2\|^2), \text{ and} \\
(iii) & \quad \text{trace}^2(\mathbf{E}\mathbf{E}^T) = 2\,\text{trace}((\mathbf{E}\mathbf{E}^T)^2),
\end{aligned}
\tag{5.34}
$$

where $\mathbf{l}_i$ are the row vectors of $\mathbf{E}$. It can be noted that the conditions of Huang and Faugeras define only one algebraic constraint. Counting also the rank constraint, it is seen that an essential matrix is thus defined by two algebraic constraints. A 3×3 matrix defined up to a scale factor has 8 parameters and thus seems to leave us with 6 parameters, whereas we know that there are only 5 parameters. The explanation for this apparent paradox is that any of the Huang-Faugeras constraints is in fact equivalent to *two* independent algebraic constraints, a fact which will be proved in Section 11.2.2 by an explicit decomposition. Another characterization of the Essential matrices, due to Maybank (Maybank, 1990), is obtained in terms of their symmetric and antisymmetric parts:

$$
\text{sym}(\mathbf{E}) = \frac{1}{2}(\mathbf{E} + \mathbf{E}^T) \ , \ \text{asy}(\mathbf{E}) = \frac{1}{2}(\mathbf{E} - \mathbf{E}^T),
$$

and so yields indeed two constraints. A 3×3 matrix satisfying $\det(\mathbf{E}) = 0$ is an essential matrix if and only if both of the following two conditions are satisfied.

$$\left\{\begin{array}{l} \text{If } \lambda_1, \lambda_2, \lambda_3 \text{ are the eigenvalues of sym}(\mathbf{E}), \text{ numbered such that} \\ \lambda_1\lambda_2 < 0, \text{ then: } \lambda_1 + \lambda_2 = \lambda_3. \\ \text{If asy}(\mathbf{E}) = [\mathbf{c}]_\times, \text{ and } \mathbf{b} \text{ is the eigenvector of sym}(\mathbf{E}) \text{ associated with } \lambda_3, \\ \text{then } \mathbf{b}^T\mathbf{c} = 0. \end{array}\right.$$

(5.35)

These conditions mean that the Essential matrix in the coordinate system associated with the eigenvectors of $\mathbf{E} + \mathbf{E}^T$ is of the form

$$\mathbf{E} = \left[\begin{array}{ccc} \lambda_1 & 0 & y \\ 0 & \lambda_2 & -x \\ -y & x & \lambda_1 + \lambda_2 \end{array}\right].$$

In addition $\mathbf{b} = \mathbf{t} - \mathbf{R}^T\mathbf{t}$, where $\mathbf{E} = [\mathbf{t}]_\times\mathbf{R}$.

Recovering the rotation and the direction of translation from the Essential matrix Given a matrix $\mathbf{E}$ which exactly satisfies the constraints (5.34), it is of the form $[\mathbf{t}]_\times\mathbf{R}$. In order to recover the direction of translation, we solve $\mathbf{E}^T\mathbf{t} = 0$. Since we can only recover the direction of the translation, we choose a solution $\mathbf{t}$ such that $\|\mathbf{t}\| = 1$. Note that another solution, also of unit norm, is $-\mathbf{t}$. Then it can be shown (see for example (Faugeras, 1993)) that there are two solutions for $\mathbf{R}$, $\mathbf{E}^{*T} \pm [\mathbf{t}]_\times\mathbf{E}$. The two solutions are related by the rotation $\mathbf{R}_{\mathbf{t},\pi}$ of axis $\mathbf{t}$ and angle π. Since $\mathbf{R}_{\mathbf{t},\pi} = \mathbf{I}_3 + 2[\mathbf{t}]_\times^2$, it can be verified that $[\mathbf{t}]_\times\mathbf{R}_{\mathbf{t},\pi}\mathbf{R} = -[\mathbf{t}]_\times\mathbf{R}$. As noted by Longuet-Higgins (Longuet-Higgins, 1981), there are four possible rotation/translation pairs based on the two possible choices for $\mathbf{R}$ and two possible signs for $\mathbf{t}$. The correct one should be chosen based on the requirement that the visible points be in front of both cameras.

If the matrix $\mathbf{E}$ has been obtained by some estimation procedure, for example the eight-point algorithm (see section 6.1.2 in Chapter 6), it will not in general satisfy the constraints (5.34) and therefore will not exactly be of the form $[\mathbf{t}]_\times\mathbf{R}$. It is shown in (Hartley et al., 1992) that the matrix $\hat{\mathbf{E}}$ (*the closest essential matrix*) which is of this form and which minimizes the Frobenius norm $\|\hat{\mathbf{E}} - \mathbf{E}\|$ can be obtained as follows. If $\mathbf{E}$'s SVD decomposition is $\mathbf{E} = \mathbf{U}\text{diag}(\sigma_1, \sigma_2, \sigma_3)\mathbf{V}^T$, with $\sigma_1 \geq \sigma_2 \geq \sigma_3$, then $\hat{\mathbf{E}} = \mathbf{U}\text{diag}(\sigma, \sigma, 0)\mathbf{V}^T$, with $\sigma = \frac{\sigma_1 + \sigma_2}{2}$.

Since $\mathbf{U}$ and $\mathbf{V}$ are orthogonal matrices, we have a decomposition into the product of a skew-symmetric matrix and an orthogonal matrix:

$$\mathbf{E} = \sigma \underbrace{(\mathbf{U}[\mathbf{t}_0]_\times\mathbf{U}^T)}_{[\mathbf{t}]_\times}\underbrace{(\mathbf{U}\mathbf{R}_0\mathbf{V}^T)}_{\mathbf{R}},$$

with

$$
\mathrm{diag}(\sigma, \sigma, 0) = \sigma \underbrace{\begin{bmatrix} 0 & -1 & 0 \\ 1 & 0 & 0 \\ 0 & 0 & 0 \end{bmatrix}}_{[\mathbf{t}_0]_\times} \underbrace{\begin{bmatrix} 0 & 1 & 0 \\ -1 & 0 & 0 \\ 0 & 0 & 1 \end{bmatrix}}_{\mathbf{R}_0}.
$$

The signs of $\mathbf{t}$ and $\mathbf{R}$ are determined by noting that since $\mathbf{R}$ is a rotation matrix, $\det(\mathbf{R}) = +1$. The second decomposition is obtained by replacing the matrices $\mathbf{t}_0$ and $\mathbf{R}_0$ by their transposes. It can be shown that the solution just described is equivalent to the method described in (Faugeras et al., 1987; Toscani and Faugeras, 1987): first determine $\mathbf{t}$ as the solution of $\min_{\|\mathbf{t}\|=1} \|\mathbf{E}^T \mathbf{t}\|^2$ by solving an eigenvalue problem, and then determine $\mathbf{R}$ as the solution of $\min_{\mathbf{R}} \|\mathbf{E} - [\mathbf{t}]_\times \mathbf{R}\|$ by using quaternions.

Fundamental and Essential matrices   Note that the decomposition of a general perspective projection matrix into intrinsic and extrinsic parameters (see section 4.3.1 in Chapter 4), implies that any Fundamental matrix can be written as in equation (5.31). This equation expresses the relation between the weak calibration (known Fundamental matrix) and the strong calibration (known intrinsic parameters, known Essential matrix). The consequences will be explored in great detail in Chapter 11. One thing which is obvious from this relation is that in the general case it is not possible to recover the intrinsic parameters and the motion parameters from a Fundamental matrix, since the total number of the former is 10, whereas there are only 7 in the latter.

Unlike the Essential matrix, which is characterized by the algebraic constraints presented in the previous section, the only constraint on the Fundamental matrix is that it is of rank two, a fact that is also found from equation (5.33), the rank of $\mathbf{E}$ being two. Thus it is incorrect to consider the Fundamental matrix as an Essential matrix written in a different coordinate system, since it does not satisfy all of the algebraic constraints that must be satisfied by an Essential matrix.

Let us emphasize the main difference between these two matrices: One, $\mathbf{E}$, is a Euclidean entity and can be decomposed into displacements parameters, translation and rotation, whereas the other, $\mathbf{F}$, is a projective entity, and can be decomposed into the parameters of the epipolar homography. The similarities are that both matrices express the epipolar constraint, in two different coordinate systems, and that both can be factored as the product of an antisymmetric matrix and another matrix. However, by definition of $\mathbf{E}$, the other matrix is a rotation matrix (equation 5.32), whereas the other matrix in the case of $\mathbf{F}$ is not uniquely determined; see Section 5.2.4.

5.3.4   Structure and motion parameters for a plane

The matrix of the homography or morphism induced by a plane can be decomposed in an interesting manner in the case where the intrinsic parameters are known:

Proposition 5.28 *Let* Π *be a plane not going through the optical center* C *of the first camera and represented by the vector* $\tilde{\Pi} = \left[\mathbf{n}^T, -d\right]^T$ *in the first camera canonical coordinate system, where* $\mathbf{n}$ *is of unit norm. The homography (morphism) induced by* Π *between the two image planes is given by*

$$\mathbf{H}_{\Pi} \simeq \mathbf{A}' \left(\mathbf{R} + \frac{1}{d}\mathbf{t}\mathbf{n}^T\right) \mathbf{A}^{-1}. \tag{5.36}$$

Proof :   We apply propositions 5.23, 5.24 and 5.25 to express $\mathbf{H}_{\Pi}$ in the pixel coordinate systems:

$$\mathbf{H}_{\Pi} \simeq \mathbf{A}'\mathbf{R}\mathbf{A}^{-1} + \mathbf{A}'\mathbf{t}\mathbf{q}^T,$$

where $\mathbf{q}$ is a representation of the image in the first camera of the line at infinity of Π. The image of the line at infinity of the plane Π in the first camera is represented by $\mathbf{n}$ in the normalized pixel coordinate system, and therefore it is represented by $\mathbf{A}^{-T}\mathbf{n}$ in the pixel coordinate system. Therefore, there exists a λ such that

$$\mathbf{H}_{\Pi} \simeq \mathbf{A}' \left(\mathbf{R} + \lambda\mathbf{t}\mathbf{n}^T\right) \mathbf{A}^{-1}.$$

The value of λ can be obtained by choosing a special point in Π, for example the point represented by $\left[d\mathbf{n}^T, 1\right]^T$. Its image in the first image is represented by $\mathbf{m} \simeq d\mathbf{A}\mathbf{n}$, its image in the second image is represented by $\mathbf{m}' \simeq d\mathbf{A}'\mathbf{R}\mathbf{n} + \mathbf{A}'\mathbf{t}$ and λ is chosen in such a way that $\mathbf{H}_{\Pi}\mathbf{m} \simeq \mathbf{m}'$. An easy computation shows that this process yields $\lambda = \frac{1}{d}$. $\square$

In equation (5.36), two types of parameters appear. The structure parameters, related to the plane, are $\mathbf{n}$ and d. The motion parameters $\mathbf{R}$ and $\mathbf{t}$ describe the displacement between the two cameras in the first camera normalized coordinate system. It has been shown (Tsai and Huang, 1982; Faugeras and Lustman, 1986) that, in the case of calibrated cameras, equation (5.36) allows to recover both types parameters from a homography matrix. However, the structure parameters which are recovered is the vector $\mathbf{n}/d$. Therefore, if the scale for $\mathbf{t}$ is known, then we can also recover the exact distance of the plane to the origin, which is the inverse of the norm of the vector $\mathbf{n}/d$. In the case of two-view analysis, this scale is not known, and therefore $\|\mathbf{t}\|$ and d are recovered only up to a common scale factor, which precisely expresses the depth-speed ambiguity.

The special homography matrix $\mathbf{H}_{\infty} \simeq \mathbf{A}'\mathbf{R}\mathbf{A}^{-1}$, is obtained for $d \to \infty$. We have seen before that this matrix is indeed the infinity morphism. It is seen that this matrix is obtained as a limit of the homography matrix of any plane when the distance of this plane to the origin goes to ∞. Similarly, this matrix $\mathbf{H}_{\infty}$ is also obtained for $\mathbf{t} = 0$: When the two optical centers are identical, any homography is identical to the infinity morphism.

5.3.5   Some particular cases

There are a number of imaging situations where the Fundamental matrix takes a special form and therefore depends on a smaller number of parameters than in the general case. In this section, we examine those resulting from special displacements such as pure translation or axis rotation. In Section 5.4, we will also consider the affine approximation, which is more subtle, because it which is valid for certain 3D structures viewed under certain conditions. The special forms for a Fundamental matrix with constant intrinsic parameters are summarized in table 5.1.

Displacement	Fundamental matrix	DOF
Rectified cameras	$\mathbf{F} = \begin{bmatrix} 0 & 0 & 0 \\ 0 & 0 & a \\ 0 & -a & 0 \end{bmatrix}$	0
Pure translation	$\mathbf{F} = \begin{bmatrix} 0 & c & a \\ -c & 0 & b \\ -a & -b & 0 \end{bmatrix}$	2
Axis rotation	$\mathbf{F} = [\mathbf{e}']_\times [\mathbf{u}]_\times [\mathbf{e}]_\times$	6
Retinal displacement	$\mathbf{F} = \begin{bmatrix} 0 & 0 & a \\ 0 & 0 & b \\ c & d & e \end{bmatrix}$	4

Table 5.1: Forms of the Fundamental matrix for a moving camera with constant intrinsic parameters undergoing specific displacements.

No parallax   If the two optical centers are identical (finite or infinite), then there is no epipolar constraint at all since the Fundamental matrix reduces to the null matrix; see section 5.1.2.

We will see in Section 5.5 that if all of the points are planar, so that the two views are related by a homography, then the Fundamental matrix is not uniquely defined.

Pure translations   In the case where there is no rotational component of the displacement, equation (5.31) becomes: $\mathbf{F} \simeq \mathbf{A}'^{-T}[\mathbf{t}]_\times \mathbf{A}^{-1}$. If, in addition, the intrinsic parameters are the same for both views, then $\mathbf{F}$ is an antisymmetric matrix, the two epipoles are identical, and we have: $\mathbf{F} \simeq [\mathbf{e}]_\times \simeq [\mathbf{e}']_\times$. If the camera is calibrated, then we have simply $\mathbf{F} \simeq [\mathbf{t}]_\times$, where $\mathbf{t}$ is the translation between the two cameras. Conversely, if $\mathbf{F}$ is an antisymmetric matrix, then, because of (5.33), $\mathbf{E}$ is also an antisymmetric matrix, which implies that $\mathbf{R}$ is the identity matrix. We note that, in this particular case, $\mathbf{F}$ depends only on two independent parameters that determine the position of the epipole in the image plane.

A point m lies on its corresponding epipolar line drawn in the same image, or, in other words, two corresponding epipolar lines are identical, since $\mathbf{l}'_m = [\mathbf{e}']_\times \mathbf{m}$, and therefore $\mathbf{l}'^T_m \mathbf{m} = 0$. Points move along lines radiating from the epipole, which coincides in this case with the Focus of Expansion (FOE), which is also the vanishing point of the translation direction. This concept can be seen in Fig. 5.15.

 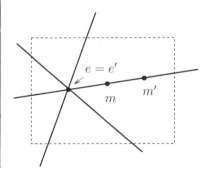

Figure 5.15: Example of epipolar geometry in the case of pure translation. Two corresponding epipolar lines are identical. Corresponding points "radiate" from the epipole.The epipole is the vanishing point of the direction of translation. Here the epipole is in the image because the translation is predominantly in the optical axis direction.

A case of special interest is when the translation is parallel to the x-axis in the first image. This case results in a configuration called "rectified" which is often favored for stereo rigs of video or still cameras as illustrated in Fig. 5.16 because the corresponding epipolar lines then turn out to be the same as corresponding horizontal scanlines, as illustrated in Fig. 5.17. The Fundamental matrix is simply

$$\mathbf{F}_{\mathrm{rec}} = \begin{bmatrix} 0 & 0 & 0 \\ 0 & 0 & 1 \\ 0 & -1 & 0 \end{bmatrix}. \tag{5.37}$$

As an illustration, let us consider a pixel of coordinates (x_1, y_1) in the first image. The projective representation of its epipolar line in the second image is given by

$$\mathbf{l}' = \mathbf{F}_{\mathrm{rec}} \begin{bmatrix} x_1 \\ y_1 \\ 1 \end{bmatrix} = \begin{bmatrix} 0 \\ 1 \\ -y_1 \end{bmatrix},$$

which is indeed the line of equation $y = y_1$. In practice, it is often difficult to align the two cameras of the rig with extreme precision, so there will be an offset and the two pencils will not be exactly parallel. Converging cameras yield epipolar lines such as those shown in Fig. 5.18. However, as we will see in Section 7.2.5, if we are able to compute the Fundamental matrix, then we can bring the two images to a rectified configuration even if the two cameras were not originally in such a configuration.

Figure 5.16: Two small stereo rigs with on-board processing developed at SRI International. The cameras are in the "rectified" configuration.

Generally speaking, translations in the image plane $t_z = 0$ result in parallel epipolar lines since the epipole will be at infinity. On the other hand, if the camera translates mostly along its optical axis (in a forward or backwards motion), then the epipoles will be near the center of the image, as was the case in Fig. 5.15.

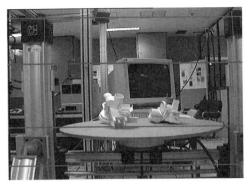

Figure 5.17: Example of epipolar geometry in the case of pure translation parallel to the image plane ("rectified" configuration). Epipolar lines are corresponding horizontal scanlines. The epipole is the point at infinity in the x-direction.

Axis rotations and planar motions A fixed axis rotation is characterized by the fact that there is no translational component along the rotation axis (screw-motion component) or, in other words, that the rotation axis $\mathbf{U}$ and the translation vector $\mathbf{t}$ are orthogonal. This type of displacement is quite important in practice because there are several situations where it occurs. A pure translation is a particular case of planar motion. A motion of this type can be performed with good accuracy by a robotic head. It also occurs for a vehicle which is moving on a plane. Last, it describes exactly the geometry of a catadioptric system where stereo is captured with a single camera by using two mirrors (Gluckman and Nayar, 1999).

Viéville (Viéville, 1994) has shown that the condition $\mathbf{U} \perp \mathbf{t}$ is satisfied if and only if one of two equivalent conditions is satisfied by the Essential matrix:

- $\text{trace}(\mathbf{E}) = 0$, and

- $\det(\mathbf{E} + \mathbf{E}^T) = 0$

The key to the proof is to note that the Essential matrix in the coordinate system associated with the eigenvectors of $\mathbf{E} + \mathbf{E}^T$ is of the form

$$\mathbf{E} = \begin{bmatrix} a & 0 & -b \\ 0 & -a & b \\ b & -b & 0 \end{bmatrix}, \quad \text{where} \quad \begin{cases} \|\mathbf{t}\|a = \sqrt{\dfrac{1 - \cos\theta}{2}} \\ \|\mathbf{t}\|b = \sqrt{\dfrac{1 + \cos\theta}{2}} \end{cases} \quad \theta\text{: Angle of the rotation.}$$

Such a form is obtained by combining either of Viéville's conditions with the Maybank's constraints (5.35).

The condition on the trace does not transpose easily to the Fundamental matrix, but it is clear that the condition on the symmetric part does when the intrinsic parameters of the first and the second cameras are equal since $\det(\mathbf{E} + \mathbf{E}^T) = \det(\mathbf{A})^2\det(\mathbf{F} + \mathbf{F}^T)$. We summarize this discussion:

Proposition 5.29 *A Fundamental matrix arising from a fixed axis rotation with constant intrinsic parameters satisfies the additional algebraic constraint*

$$det(\mathbf{F} + \mathbf{F}^T) = 0.$$

Note that the result does not hold if the two cameras have different intrinsic parameters.

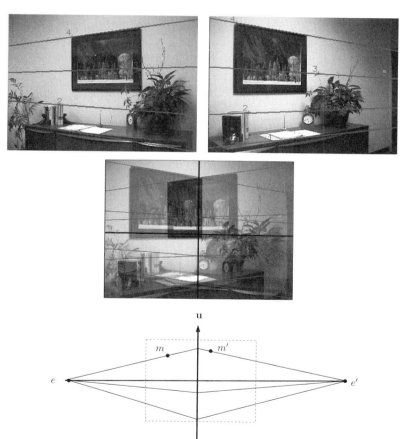

Figure 5.18: Example of epipolar geometry in the case of planar motion. Epipolar lines intersect on **u**, projection of the screw axis. The vanishing line of the plane of motion is the line joining the two epipoles.

As showed by Gluckman and Nayar (Gluckman and Nayar, 1999), since the screw axis $\mathbf{U}$ remains fixed with respect to the coordinate system of the two cameras, its image $\mathbf{u}$ is identical in both views, and therefore corresponding epipolar lines intersect in $\mathbf{u}$, as illustrated in Fig. 5.18. Let us consider two corresponding points m and m'. The epipolar line of a point m is the line through e' containing the point of intersection of $\mathbf{u}$ and (e, m): $\mathbf{l}'_m = \mathbf{e}' \times (\mathbf{u} \times (\mathbf{e} \times \mathbf{m}))$, and therefore the Fundamental matrix can be written

$$\mathbf{F} = [\mathbf{e}']_\times [\mathbf{u}]_\times [\mathbf{e}]_\times,$$

which depends only on six parameters, as expected. From such a matrix $\mathbf{F}$, the projection of the screw axis $\mathbf{u}$ can be recovered from $\lambda_i, \mathbf{v}_i$, the non-null eigenvalues and eigenvectors of $\mathbf{F} + \mathbf{F}^T$, by $\mathbf{u} = \sqrt{|\lambda_1|}\mathbf{v}_1 \pm \sqrt{|\lambda_2|}\mathbf{v}_2$, the ambiguity being resolved by the fact that the wrong expression is equal to $\mathbf{e}' \times \mathbf{e}$. It can also be noted that the plane of motion contains the two optical centers, and therefore the vanishing line of this plane is the line containing the two epipoles.

Retinal motion   In this type of motion, the retinal plane remains invariant. This situation occurs if the translation is parallel to the retinal plane and there is no rotation out of this plane. We will see in Section 5.4.2 that in this case the Fundamental matrix is affine (even if the projection matrices are not), so that the epipolar geometry takes a particularly simple form.

5.4   Parallel projection

In this section, we study the Fundamental matrix obtained with parallel (or affine) cameras. This study is done at the affine (uncalibrated) level in Section 5.4.1 and at the Euclidean (calibrated) level in Section 5.4.3. In Section 5.4.2 we examine the conditions in which the Fundamental matrix takes an affine form, which turns out *not* to be equivalent to the fact that the cameras are affine.

5.4.1   Affine epipolar geometry

We consider in this section the case where both of the cameras perform a parallel projection. We have seen in Proposition 4.23 that, using the notations of Section 5.2.2, we have $\boldsymbol{W} \simeq \boldsymbol{W}' \simeq [0, 0, 0, 1]^T$.

Let us first consider a planar morphism, induced by some plane. Since both cameras are affine instead of projective, the planar morphism is also an affine transformation. Another way to see that idea is to remark that since the brackets are alternate forms, it can be concluded by inspection of Equation 5.2 that $H_{31} = H_{32} = 0$, so that the planar morphism is

$$
\mathbf{H}_A \simeq
\begin{bmatrix}
h_{11} & h_{12} & h_{13} \\
h_{21} & h_{22} & h_{23} \\
0 & 0 & 1
\end{bmatrix}.
\tag{5.38}
$$

The epipoles are the intersections of the line joining the optical centers with the retinal planes. Since both optical centers are at infinity, so is the line joining them, and therefore so are the epipoles, a fact which can also be seen by inspecting Equation 5.9.

Let now turn to the Fundamental matrix. With the special forms of the matrix **H** and of the epipoles, Theorem 5.1 and Corollary 5.1 show that the first 2×2 submatrix of **F** is null:

$$
\mathbf{F}_A =
\begin{bmatrix}
0 & 0 & a \\
0 & 0 & b \\
c & d & e
\end{bmatrix}.
\tag{5.39}
$$

This result can also be found by direct inspection of equation (5.8). With this particular form of the Fundamental matrix, called the **affine Fundamental matrix**, we obtain a much simpler form for the epipolar constraint. If (u, v) and (u', v') are affine coordinates of corresponding points m and m', then we have $\mathbf{m} \simeq [u, v, 1]^T$ and $\mathbf{m}' \simeq [u', v', 1]^T$. The epipolar constraint (5.4) is a linear function of these coordinates, instead of being quadratic in the general case:

$$
\mathbf{m}'^T \mathbf{F}_A \mathbf{m} = au' + bv' + cu + dv + e = 0.
$$

If the reduced projection matrices are decomposed as

$$
\mathbf{P}_A = \begin{bmatrix} \mathbf{P}_u^T \\ \mathbf{P}_v^T \end{bmatrix} , \quad
\mathbf{P}'_A = \begin{bmatrix} \mathbf{P}_u'^T \\ \mathbf{P}_v'^T \end{bmatrix} ,
$$

then the epipolar equation can be rewritten under the reduced form

$$
\begin{bmatrix} a & b & c & d \end{bmatrix}
\begin{bmatrix} u' \\ v' \\ u \\ v \end{bmatrix} = 0 \quad \text{with:} \quad
\begin{cases}
a &= -\,|\mathbf{P}_v, \mathbf{P}'_u, \mathbf{P}'_v|, \\
b &= |\mathbf{P}_u, \mathbf{P}'_u, \mathbf{P}'_v|, \\
c &= -\,|\mathbf{P}_u, \mathbf{P}_v, \mathbf{P}'_v|, \\
d &= |\mathbf{P}_u, \mathbf{P}_v, \mathbf{P}'_u|.
\end{cases}
\tag{5.40}
$$

With a Fundamental matrix of the form (5.39), the epipolar lines are all parallel to each other, and so are the epipolar planes, as illustrated in Fig. 5.19. The geometrical reason is that the optical rays are parallel, and that parallelism is preserved by projection. The reverse property is not true, since a Fundamental matrix with both epipoles $\mathbf{e} = [x, y, 0]^T$ and $\mathbf{e}' = [x', y', 0]^T$ at infinity takes the more general form

$$
\mathbf{F} =
\begin{bmatrix}
\alpha y y' & -\alpha x y' & -\beta x y' \\
-\alpha y x' & \alpha x x' & \beta x x' \\
\gamma y x' & -\gamma x x' & \delta
\end{bmatrix},
$$

where α, β, γ and δ are arbitrary.

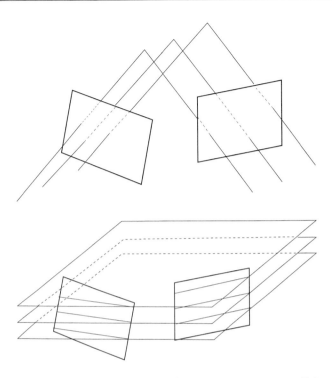

Figure 5.19: Affine epipolar geometry: Optical rays are parallel, and therefore pencils of epipolar lines and epipolar planes are parallel.

5.4.2   Cyclopean and affine viewing

5.4.2.1   Cyclopean viewing

It is clear that equation (5.39) holds even if the two projection matrices are not affine, since we have only used the fact that $\boldsymbol{W} \simeq \boldsymbol{W}'$ to deduce that the four brackets forming the the first 2×2 submatrix of $\mathbf{F}$ were null. That is, when the two focal planes are identical, a situation called "cyclopean viewing", the form of the Fundamental matrix is that of equation (5.39). In terms of relative displacement, the translation is in the image plane, and there is no rotation out of the image plane. In fact, this case is the only one in which the Fundamental matrix takes the form (5.39):

Proposition 5.30 *The Fundamental matrix takes the form (5.39), where a, b, c, d, e are not all zero, if and only if*

$$\boldsymbol{W} \simeq \boldsymbol{W}'.$$

Proof : We just saw the necessary part. Conversely, let us suppose that $\mathbf{F}$ takes the form (5.39). Using the expression (5.8), we have

$$| \, \boldsymbol{V}, \boldsymbol{W}, \boldsymbol{V}', \boldsymbol{W}' \, | = 0, \quad | \, \boldsymbol{U}, \boldsymbol{W}, \boldsymbol{V}', \boldsymbol{W}' \, | = 0, \quad | \, \boldsymbol{V}, \boldsymbol{W}, \boldsymbol{U}', \boldsymbol{W}' \, | = 0,$$
$$| \, \boldsymbol{U}, \boldsymbol{W}, \boldsymbol{U}', \boldsymbol{W}' \, | = 0.$$

Let us introduce the line $\mathbf{L} = \boldsymbol{W} \vartriangle \boldsymbol{W}'$ and the four lines $\mathbf{L}_1 = \boldsymbol{U} \vartriangle \boldsymbol{U}'$, $\mathbf{L}_2 = \boldsymbol{U} \vartriangle \boldsymbol{V}'$, $\mathbf{L}_3 = \boldsymbol{V} \vartriangle \boldsymbol{U}'$ and $\mathbf{L}_4 = \boldsymbol{V} \vartriangle \boldsymbol{V}'$. Proposition 3.33 and the previous equations tell us that L intersects those four lines. Now, the fact that L_1 and L_2 are in the plane $\boldsymbol{U}$ implies that *if they are distinct*, then L is also in $\boldsymbol{U}$. Similarly, the fact that L_3 and L_4 are in the plane $\boldsymbol{V}$ implies that *if they are distinct*, then L is also in $\boldsymbol{V}$. Let us consider this generic case first. If L is in $\boldsymbol{U}$ and $\boldsymbol{V}$, which have to be distinct because of the rank condition on $\mathcal{P}$, then L must be equal to their intersection. But this situation implies that $\boldsymbol{W}$ also contains this line and therefore is a linear combination of $\boldsymbol{U}$ and $\boldsymbol{V}$, contradicting the rank condition on $\mathcal{P}$. Therefore one must have $\boldsymbol{W} \vartriangle \boldsymbol{W}' = \mathbf{0}$ which means that $\boldsymbol{W} \simeq \boldsymbol{W}'$.

Let us consider the special cases now. If we assume that L_3 and L_4 are identical, then the line of intersection of the two planes $\boldsymbol{U}'$ and $\boldsymbol{V}'$ is in $\boldsymbol{V}$ and L has to intersect this line. Let us now consider the two lines L_1 and L_2 which are in the planes $\boldsymbol{U}'$ and $\boldsymbol{V}'$, respectively. The line L must go through the point of intersection of the three lines L_1, L_2 and $L_3 \equiv L_4$ which is therefore also the optical center for the two cameras. Since the two cameras have the same optical center, the Fundamental matrix is equal to $\mathbf{0}$ which is not permitted by the hypothesis on a, b, c, d, e. The case where L_1 and L_2 are identical is similar to the previous one, as is the case where $L_1 \equiv L_2$ and $L_3 \equiv L_4$. $\square$

An alternative proof can be found in (Torr, 1995). We have a similar result for the planar homographies: it is clear that equation (5.38) holds in the "cyclopean" conditions, and as an echo of prop. 5.30, we have

Proposition 5.31 *All the planar morphisms take the form (5.38) if and only if*

$$\boldsymbol{W} \simeq \boldsymbol{W}'.$$

Proof : We just saw the necessary part. The converse part is a matter of proving that if for any $\boldsymbol{\Pi}$, we have $| \, \boldsymbol{W}', \boldsymbol{V}, \boldsymbol{W}, \boldsymbol{\Pi} \, | = 0$ and $| \, \boldsymbol{W}', \boldsymbol{W}, \boldsymbol{U}, \boldsymbol{\Pi} \, | = 0$, then $\boldsymbol{W} \simeq \boldsymbol{W}'$. In particular, we can take $\boldsymbol{\Pi} = \boldsymbol{U}'$ and $\boldsymbol{\Pi} = \boldsymbol{V}'$ and apply the proof of Prop. 5.30. $\square$

5.4.2.2   Affine viewing situations

We now give the slightly counterintuitive result that it is possible to describe the epipolar geometry with an affine Fundamental matrix not only when the projections are not affine (which was the subject of the previous paragraph), but even in some situations in which the epipoles are actually not at infinity.

We remember from Chapter 4, section 4.4.2, that the presence of a dominant planar structure implies that a perspective projection matrix may appear as a parallel projection one. The affine approximation is exact if all of the points lie in a plane Π fronto-parallel with respect to the camera. If two cameras are considered, then Π has to be fronto-parallel with respect to the two cameras. This fact is equivalent to the fact that the rotation between the two cameras has an axis parallel to the optical axis (the two retinal planes have to remain parallel), and that the normal to Π is parallel to the optical axis. It follows that -the two retinal planes are parallel, not necessarily equal. We call this situation the *affine viewing situation:*

Definition 5.8 *When the two focal planes are parallel and the imaged points lie in a common fronto-parallel plane, the two cameras are said to be in the affine viewing situation.*

It is easily seen that the homography between the two views in normalized coordinates is affine:

$$\mathbf{R} + \frac{1}{d}\mathbf{t}\mathbf{N}^T = \begin{bmatrix} \cos\theta & -\sin\theta & t_x/d \\ \sin\theta & \cos\theta & t_y/d \\ 0 & 0 & t_z/d \end{bmatrix}.$$

The fact that the matrices $\mathbf{A}$ and $\mathbf{A}'$ are affine is equivalent to the fact that the homography (5.36) $\mathbf{H}$ relating the two views of the plane is affine. We have proved the following proposition.

Proposition 5.32 *In the affine viewing situation all planar morphisms are described by an affine correspondence and, in normalized coordinates, by a similarity transform.*

The converse is not true, i.e. the fact that the planar homography induced by a plane between the two retinal plane is affine does not imply that the two cameras are in the affine viewing situation, since the converse problem of computing the Fundamental matrix between the two views is under-constrained. However, since all of the points lie on a plane, there is an ambiguity on the Fundamental matrix and it is in general possible to find an affine Fundamental matrix compatible with the affine morphism:

Proposition 5.33 *In the case where a planar morphism is described by an affine matrix $\mathbf{H}$, there is a one parameter linear family of affine Fundamental matrices compatible with that planar morphism.*

Proof : The compatibility equations (5.15) with an affine Fundamental matrix of the form (5.39), are equivalent to the three equations

$$
\begin{aligned}
H_{11}a + H_{21}b + H_{33}c &= 0, \\
H_{12}a + H_{22}b + H_{33}d &= 0, \\
H_{13}a + H_{23}b + H_{33}e &= 0.
\end{aligned}
$$

Since H_{33} is not zero, the family of compatible Fundamental matrices can be parametrized linearly by the two parameters a and b. $\square$

We can conclude that *projectively* the situation is equivalent to a configuration where the affine hypothesis is verified. The equivalence is, of course, not affine.

We also note that

Proposition 5.34 *If the Fundamental matrix is affine and the coefficients c and d in (5.39) are nonzero, then all planar morphisms are affine transformations.*

Proof : By inspection of (5.15), we see that two of the equations are $cH_{31} = 0$ and $dH_{32} = 0$. Hence H is affine. $\square$

The previous considerations explain why the affine model may be used even if the camera performs a perspective projection, for example in the case of a motion such as a translation along the optical axis if the image points lie approximately in a fronto-parallel plane. The word approximately refers to two things: 1) the plane can be approximately fronto-parallel and still induce a morphism very close to an affine transformation and 2) the 3D points lie approximately in that plane. In this case, the epipoles obtained from the motion are at the image center, and it may seem strange that a model which places them at infinity can be used. The "true" Fundamental matrix computed from the projection matrices is *not* affine. However, because of the ambiguity due to the fact that the points lie in (near) a plane, other epipolar geometries exist, and at least one of them is affine.

5.4.3 The Euclidean case

We now assume that the intrinsic parameters are known and relate the affine Fundamental matrix (which becomes an affine analog of the Essential matrix) to Euclidean motion. In the perspective case, we were able to extract all five motion parameters from the Essential matrix. In fact, the problem was overconstrained since the Essential matrix has eight linearly independent entries. In the parallel case, we expect the situation to be quite different since the Fundamental matrix has only four linearly independent entries, visibly not enough to constrain the problem.

We will follow the exposition of (Shapiro et al., 1995; Shapiro, 1995) and consider in this section the reduced projection matrices. In order to be able to use normalized coordinates, we need only to know the parameters k and γ' of Equation 4.44. In normalized coordinates, the reduced projection matrices are

$$\mathbf{P}_A = \frac{1}{Z_{av}} \begin{bmatrix} 1 & 0 & 0 \\ 0 & 1 & 0 \end{bmatrix}, \quad \mathbf{P}'_A = \frac{1}{Z'_{av}} \begin{bmatrix} r_{11} & r_{12} & r_{13} \\ r_{21} & r_{22} & r_{23} \end{bmatrix}, \tag{5.41}$$

where $\mathbf{R}$ is the rotation between the normalized coordinate system of the first camera and the normalized coordinate system of the second camera, and Z_{av} and Z'_{av} are the unknown scales associated with each of the cameras.

The reduced epipolar equation is obtained from Equation 5.40:

$$\begin{bmatrix} r_{23} & -r_{13} & sr_{32} & -sr_{31} \end{bmatrix} \begin{bmatrix} u' \\ v' \\ u \\ v \end{bmatrix} = 0.$$

In this equation, the scale factor $s = Z_{av}/Z'_{av}$ indicates the degree of looming or receding of the object. If $s > 1$, then the object is looming (getting closer to the camera).

There are four Euclidean parameters to describe the motion: Three for the rotation, and one for the scale factor. Since the reduced epipolar equation contains only three independent parameters, the Euclidean parameters contain one degree of freedom. Of the several possible ways to parameterize the rotation, Koenderink and Van Doorn's representation (Koenderink and van Doorn, 1991), that we will designate by KvD for brevity, is the most appropriate because it makes this degree of freedom an explicit parameter and therefore distinguishes clearly between the three entities which can be recovered and the one which is ambiguous.

Koenderink and Van Doorn decompose a rotation $\mathbf{R}$ as the product of a rotation $\mathbf{R}_\theta$ of axis Z and angle θ (cyclotorsion) followed by a rotation $\mathbf{R}_\rho$ with a fronto-parallel axis I_ϕ angled at ϕ to the X-axis and of angle ρ (rotation out of the image plane). Note that the projection in the first image of the axis I_ϕ is angled at $(\phi - \theta)$ and the projection in the second image of I_ϕ is angled at ϕ. This situation is illustrated in Fig. 5.20. The effect of the variation of the parameters on the epipolar geometry is quite intuitive, as seen in Fig. 5.21: The cyclotorsion $\mathbf{R}_\theta$ rotates the epipolar lines, the rotation $\mathbf{R}_\rho$ causes foreshortening along the epipolar lines (orthogonal to ϕ), and a change in the scale factor s alters the epipolar line spacing uniformly. The value of ρ has no effect on the epipolar geometry, as illustrated by Fig. 5.22, so it cannot be recovered from two views, which gives rise to the *bas-relief ambiguity* on a direction perpendicular to the epipolar planes, as illustrated in Fig. 5.23. However, this parameter can be recovered from three views, as will be discussed in Sec 8.8.2.

Let us now confirm this geometrical analysis with algebra. Let μ be the angle

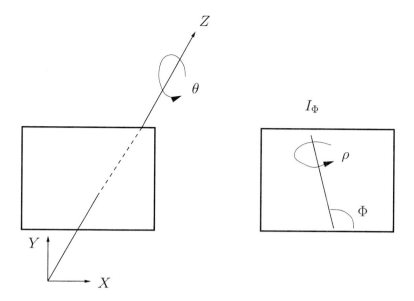

Figure 5.20: The Koenderink and Van Doorn (KvD) representation of rotations.

$\phi - \theta$. The KvD parameterization of a rotation is matrix is, in the case when $\rho \neq 0$,

$$
\begin{bmatrix}
(1 - \cos\rho)\cos\phi\cos\mu + \cos\rho\cos\theta & (1 - \cos\rho)\cos\phi\cos\mu - \cos\rho\sin\theta & \sin\theta\sin\rho \\
(1 - \cos\rho)\cos\phi\cos\mu + \cos\rho\sin\theta & (1 - \cos\rho)\cos\phi\cos\mu + \cos\rho\cos\theta & -\cos\theta\sin\rho \\
-\sin\rho\sin\mu & \sin\rho\cos\mu & \cos\rho
\end{bmatrix}.
$$
(5.42)

It is a variant of the Euler-angle form, as discussed in (Shapiro et al., 1995). Using the KvD representation, the reduced epipolar equation takes the form

$$
\begin{bmatrix} \sin\rho\cos\phi & \sin\rho\sin\phi & -s\cos(\phi - \theta) & -s\sin(\phi - \theta) \end{bmatrix}
\begin{bmatrix} u' \\ v' \\ u \\ v \end{bmatrix} = 0.
$$

In that case, the parameters s, θ, and ϕ totally describe the affine Fundamental matrix in the calibrated case. Those parameters can easily be recovered up to an ambiguity of π for the angles from the entries of the affine normalized Fundamental matrix by

$$
\tan\phi = \frac{b}{a}, \tan(\phi - \theta) = \frac{d}{c}, s^2 = \frac{c^2 + d^2}{a^2 + b^2}.
$$
(5.43)

In the case when $\rho = 0$, the previous parameterization is degenerate. This case occurs when the rotation is entirely in the image plane. The direction of projection

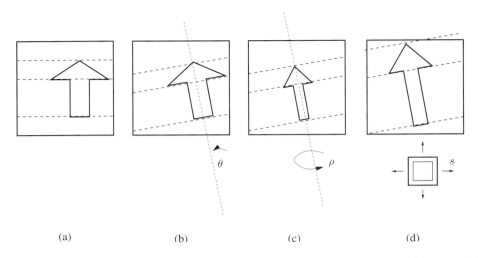

(a)   (b)   (c)   (d)

Figure 5.21: Effect of scale and KvD rotations on the epipolar lines: (a) initial (b) cyclotorsion (c) rotation out of the image plane (d) scale.

for the two cameras is the same. Remember that in the parallel case the direction of projection represents the more general projective optical center. We conclude that the two cameras have the same optical center, which is a configuration with no parallax examined in Section 5.1.2. This configuration has no epipolar geometry.

5.5   Ambiguity and the critical surface

Although in general the Fundamental matrix is uniquely determined from eight point correspondences, if the points happen to belong to certain special spatial configurations, then there are several possible Fundamental matrices even with an arbitrarily large number of correspondences. The goal of this section is to study the most general case when such a situation occurs. In Section 5.5.1 we show that the points in space have to lie on a particular hyperboloid of one sheet, called a *critical surface*, of which we study some properties. In Section 5.5.2, we examine the analytic relation which exists between image coordinates when the points lie in a critical surface. This makes it possible to characterize the possible Fundamental matrices from the image data. In addition, this provides a practical means to quantify the proximity of the 3D points which have given rise to the point correspondences to such a critical surface. In Section 5.5.3, we examine a particular case which is of practical importance: The case of a planar critical surface.

In practice, it is important to understand the ambiguous configurations, because near those configurations, the estimation of the Fundamental matrix becomes

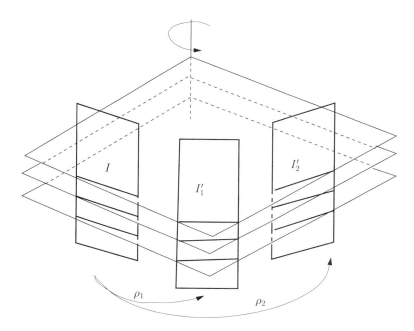

Figure 5.22: The value of ρ has no effect on the epipolar geometry. Since the epipolar planes are parallel, a rotation by ρ_1 and a rotation by ρ_2 yield the same epipolar lines in the images I_1' and I_2'.

unstable, as investigated theoretically and experimentally in (Luong and Faugeras, 1996), in which it is found that many viewing situations generate a "critical volume".

5.5.1 The critical surfaces

Sometimes the problem of obtaining Fundamental matrices from point correspondences does not have a unique solution, even with an arbitrarily large number of such correspondences. It is clear that this situation cannot happen for points in general configuration, but only for some special configurations of points in space. We characterize those configurations. We begin with a definition:

Definition 5.9 *A set of point correspondences is ambiguous if it satisfies the epipolar constraint for two distinct (i.e. linearly independent) Fundamental matrices.*

Another way to express the ambiguity is to say that there are at least two pairs of projection matrices that yield the same images:

$$\begin{cases} \mathcal{P} &= [\mathbf{I}\ \mathbf{0}] \\ \mathcal{P}_1' &= [\mathbf{H}_1\ \mathbf{e}_1'] \end{cases} \qquad \begin{cases} \mathcal{P} &= [\mathbf{I}\ \mathbf{0}] \\ \mathcal{P}_2' &= [\mathbf{H}_2\ \mathbf{e}_2'] \end{cases} \qquad (5.44)$$

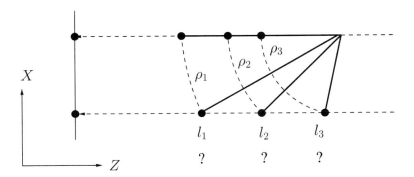

Figure 5.23: The bas-relief or depth-turn ambiguity. Under parallel projection on two views, it is not possible to distinguish the amount of rotation of the cameras from the depth. This ambiguity is illustrated in this figure in the equivalent case of moving points and a fixed camera.

with $\mathbf{F}_1 = [\mathbf{e}'_1]_\times \mathbf{H}_1$ and $\mathbf{F}_2 = [\mathbf{e}'_2]_\times \mathbf{H}_2$. We assume for simplicity that $\mathbf{H}_i, i = 1, 2$, defines a homography, i.e. is invertible.

These perspective projection matrices are defined in a common projective frame in which the three optical centers C, C_1 and C_2 are represented by the vectors

$$\mathbf{C} = [\mathbf{0}_3^T, 1]^T, \quad \mathbf{C}_1 = \begin{bmatrix} -\mathbf{H}_1^{-1}\mathbf{e}'_1 \\ 1 \end{bmatrix}, \quad \mathbf{C}_2 = \begin{bmatrix} -\mathbf{H}_2^{-1}\mathbf{e}'_2 \\ 1 \end{bmatrix}.$$

Proposition 5.35 *Let us consider an ambiguous set of correspondences* $m_i \leftrightarrow m'_i$, *images of the 3D points* M_i. *If two Fundamental matrices for this set are* $\mathbf{F}_1 = [\mathbf{e}'_1]_\times \mathbf{H}_1$ *and* $\mathbf{F}_2 = [\mathbf{e}'_2]_\times \mathbf{H}_2$, *then the points* M_i *lie on a quadratic surface of equation* $(\mathbf{H}_1\mathbf{M} + \mathbf{e}'_1)^T \mathbf{F}_2 \mathbf{M} = 0$ *or* $(\mathbf{H}_2\mathbf{M} + \mathbf{e}'_2)^T \mathbf{F}_1 \mathbf{M} = 0$ *called a* critical surface. *This surface is a hyperboloid of one sheet.*

Proof : We drop the index i in order to simplify the notations. If we denote by $\mathbf{m}$ the projection of M in the first view, and by $\mathbf{m}'_1$ and $\mathbf{m}'_2$ its projections in the second view, then there exists a λ such that

$$\mathbf{m}'_i \simeq \mathbf{H}_i\mathbf{m} + \lambda\mathbf{e}'_i, \tag{5.45}$$

where, by definition of ambiguity, $\mathbf{m}'_1 \simeq \mathbf{m}'_2$. The point M is represented by the vector $\mathbf{M} \simeq [\mathbf{m}^T, \lambda]^T$ in the projective basis corresponding to the equations (5.44). Using equations (5.44) we can write

$$\mathbf{H}_2\mathbf{m} + \lambda\mathbf{e}'_2 \simeq \mathbf{H}_1\mathbf{m} + \lambda\mathbf{e}'_1,$$

and thus the three vectors $\mathbf{H}_2\mathbf{m} + \lambda\mathbf{e}'_2$, $\mathbf{e}'_1$, and $\mathbf{H}_1\mathbf{m}$ are coplanar. We multiply both sides of the previous equation with $[\mathbf{e}'_1]_\times$, use the Fundamental matrix $\mathbf{F}_1 =$

$[\mathbf{e}_1']_\times \mathbf{H}_1$, and obtain

$$(\mathbf{H}_2\mathbf{m} + \lambda\mathbf{e}_2')^T \mathbf{F}_1\mathbf{m} = 0 \tag{5.46}$$

This equation is that of a quadric $\mathcal{Q}_1$ with matrix

$$\mathcal{Q}_1 = \begin{bmatrix} \mathbf{H}_2^T\mathbf{F}_1 + \mathbf{F}_1^T\mathbf{H}_2 & \mathbf{F}_1^T\mathbf{e}_2' \\ \mathbf{e}_2'^T\mathbf{F}_1 & 0 \end{bmatrix}$$

It should be clear that this quadric contains the three optical centers C, C_1 (because $\mathbf{H}_1^{-1}\mathbf{F}_1 \simeq [\mathbf{e}_1']_\times$) and C_2 of the three cameras. It also contains the line (C, C_1) defined by the vectors $\alpha\mathbf{C} + \beta\mathbf{C}_1$. Indeed, $(\alpha\mathbf{C} + \beta\mathbf{C}_1)^T\mathcal{Q}_1(\alpha\mathbf{C} + \beta\mathbf{C}_1) = 2\alpha\beta\mathbf{C}_1^T\mathcal{Q}_1\mathbf{C} = 0$ for all α and β.

Permuting the subscripts 1 and 2, we see that the points M belonging to a second quadric $\mathcal{Q}_2$ of matrix

$$\mathcal{Q}_2 = \begin{bmatrix} \mathbf{H}_1^T\mathbf{F}_2 + \mathbf{F}_2^T\mathbf{H}_1 & \mathbf{F}_2^T\mathbf{e}_1' \\ \mathbf{e}_1'^T\mathbf{F}_2 & 0 \end{bmatrix}$$

project to the points m_2' such that $\mathbf{m}_1' \simeq \mathbf{m}_2'$. This quadric also contains the three optical centers C, C_1 and C_2 as well as the line (C, C_2), which is a real line.

The intersection of $\mathcal{Q}_1$ (respectively $\mathcal{Q}_2$) with the plane $[\mathbf{0}_3^T, 1]^T$ is the conic of matrix $\mathbf{H}_2^T\mathbf{F}_1 + \mathbf{F}_1^T\mathbf{H}_2$ (respectively $\mathbf{H}_1^T\mathbf{F}_2 + \mathbf{F}_2^T\mathbf{H}_1$) which has an infinity of real points. Quadrics which contain a real line and an infinity of real points at infinity are hyperboloids of one sheet. $\square$

These quadrics are *critical surface pairs* meaning that it is not possible to distinguish between the image of the set of 3D points on $\mathcal{Q}_1$ observed with the pair of projection matrices $(\mathcal{P}, \mathcal{P}_1')$ and the image of a set of 3D points on $\mathcal{Q}_2$ observed with the pair of projection matrices $(\mathcal{P}, \mathcal{P}_2')$ as illustrated in figure 5.24. One notes that the image of $\mathbf{M}_2$ (respectively $\mathbf{M}_1$) after the camera displacement is on the same epipolar line as $\mathbf{m}_1$ (respectively $\mathbf{m}_2$). Degenerate cases include elliptic (and normal), parabolic, and hyperbolic cylinders, elliptic (and normal) cones, hyperbolic paraboloid, and pairs of planes, as illustrated in Fig. 5.25. Critical surfaces cannot be ellipsoids (having no real points at infinity) or hyperboloids of two sheets (not containing a real line). Many more properties of the critical surfaces, in particular in the Euclidean case, are studied by Maybank (Maybank, 1992).

5.5.2 The quadratic transformation between two ambiguous images

The previous section characterized ambiguity in terms of 3D space: The 3D points lie on particular surfaces. In this section, we characterize ambiguity in terms of image coordinates.

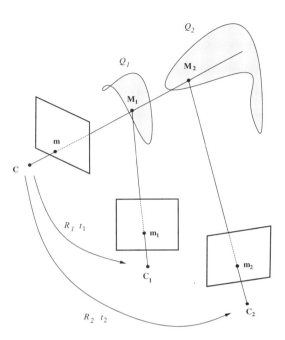

Figure 5.24: Critical surfaces: It is not possible to distinguish between the image of the set of 3D points Q_1 observed during displacement $\mathbf{R}_1$, $\mathbf{t}_1$, and the image of a set of points set of 3D points Q_2 observed during displacement $\mathbf{R}_2$, $\mathbf{t}_2$. Differences in intrinsic parameters are omitted.

Definition 5.10 *Quadratic transformations are invertible mappings (except possibly at special points) of $\mathbb{P}^2$ into $\mathbb{P}^2$, whose coordinates are homogeneous polynomials of degree 2. The corresponding inverse transformations must also be homogeneous polynomials of degree 2.*

The simplest example of a quadratic transformation is the *reciprocal transformation*, defined by

$$\Phi_0(\mathbf{x}) = [x_2 x_3, x_3 x_1, x_1 x_2]^T.$$

From this definition, we can see that Φ_0 is defined in each point of $\mathbb{P}^2$ except for the points $\varepsilon_1 = [1, 0, 0]^T$, $\varepsilon_2 = [0, 1, 0]^T$ and $\varepsilon_3 = [0, 0, 1]^T$, which are called *Fundamental points* of Φ_0. We also notice that Φ_0 is invertible, since it is it own inverse.

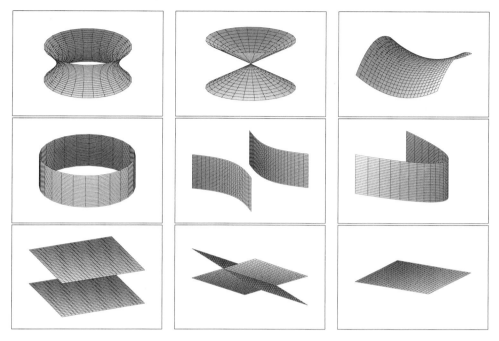

Figure 5.25: Varieties of critical surfaces. The general case is the hyperboloid of one sheet. Degenerate cases includes cones, hyperbolic paraboloids, cylinders (elliptic, hyperbolic, parabolic), and pairs of planes (parallel, intersecting, coincident).

In the general case, a quadratic transformation Φ has three Fundamental points $\mathbf{g}_1$, $\mathbf{g}_2$, $\mathbf{g}_3$ which are distinct from those of Φ^{-1}, $\mathbf{g}_1'$, $\mathbf{g}_2'$, $\mathbf{g}_3'$. and we have

$$\Phi = \mathbf{A}\Phi_0\mathbf{B}, \tag{5.47}$$

where $\mathbf{A}$ and $\mathbf{B}$ are two homographies which can interpreted as changes of retinal coordinates:

$$\begin{aligned} \mathbf{A}\varepsilon_1 = \mathbf{g}_1', \quad \mathbf{A}\varepsilon_2 = \mathbf{g}_2', \quad \mathbf{A}\varepsilon_3 = \mathbf{g}_3', \quad \mathbf{A}\varepsilon_4 = \mathbf{g}_4', \\ \mathbf{B}\mathbf{g}_1 = \varepsilon_1, \quad \mathbf{B}\mathbf{g}_2 = \varepsilon_2, \quad \mathbf{B}\mathbf{g}_3 = \varepsilon_3, \quad \mathbf{B}\mathbf{g}_4 = \varepsilon_4, \end{aligned} \tag{5.48}$$

where $\varepsilon_4 = [1, 1, 1]^T$. The inverse of Φ is $\Phi^{-1} = \mathbf{B}^{-1}\Phi_0\mathbf{A}^{-1}$. The point $\mathbf{g}_4$ can be chosen arbitrarily, whereas the point $\mathbf{g}_4'$ is determined by Φ (Semple and Kneebone, 1952). Thus $\mathbf{A}$ depends on 8 parameters (the projective coordinates of the points $\mathbf{g}_i'$, $i = 1, 2, 3, 4$) and $\mathbf{B}$ depends on 6 parameters (the projective coordinates of the points $\mathbf{g}_i$, $i = 1, 2, 3$). Thus Φ depends on 14 parameters.

Proposition 5.36 *Let us consider an ambiguous set of correspondences $m_i \leftrightarrow m_i'$.*

Then there exists a quadratic transformation between the points m_i and the points m'_i.

Proof :   Given two ambiguous images there exist two Fundamental matrices $\mathbf{F}_1$ and $\mathbf{F}_2$ such that for each pair $(\mathbf{m}, \mathbf{m}')$ of corresponding points,

$$\mathbf{m}'^T \mathbf{F}_1 \mathbf{m} = 0 \quad \text{and} \quad \mathbf{m}'^T \mathbf{F}_2 \mathbf{m} = 0.$$

We conclude from these two equations that

$$\mathbf{m}' \simeq \mathbf{F}_1 \mathbf{m} \times \mathbf{F}_2 \mathbf{m}. \tag{5.49}$$

This equation defines in general a quadratic transformation between the coordinates of the points in the two images. Indeed, the inverse is

$$\mathbf{m} = \mathbf{F}_1^T \mathbf{m}' \times \mathbf{F}_2^T \mathbf{m}',$$

which is clearly also of degree two.

$\square$

The correspondence defined in Equation 5.49 can be obtained geometrically as follows. The optical ray (C, m) (like any other line) intersects the quadric $\mathcal{Q}_1$ at two points in general. Since one of the points of intersection is C, the other one, M_1, is uniquely defined. The point m' is obtained as a projection of M_1. An expression, which is also clearly quadratic, is obtained using Equations 5.45 and 5.46:

$$\mathbf{m}' \simeq \left(\mathbf{e}_1'^T \mathbf{F}_2 \mathbf{m} \right) \mathbf{H}_1 \mathbf{m} + \left(\mathbf{m}^T \mathbf{H}_1^T \mathbf{F}_2 \mathbf{m} \right) \mathbf{e}_1' \tag{5.50}$$

This expression is alternatively obtained by the substitution of $\mathbf{F}_1 = [\mathbf{e}_1']_\times \mathbf{H}_1$ and $\mathbf{F}_2 = [\mathbf{e}_2']_\times \mathbf{H}_2$ into Equation 5.49.

In some degenerate cases Equation 5.49 can define a transformation which is *linear* in the coordinates of $\mathbf{m}$. The critical surface is then just a plane, and yields an infinite number of ambiguous image pairs, as examined in Section 5.5.3. The expression in Equation 5.50 reduces to the planar morphism $\mathbf{H}_1$ if and only if $\mathbf{F}_2$ is compatible with $\mathbf{H}_1$. This can happen only if the critical surface is a plane *and* if $\mathbf{H}_1$ is chosen to be the planar morphism of this plane.

In the general case, the quadratic transformation allows us to check if image points are close to the projection of a critical surface, much the same way as the planar morphism allowed us to check if they were close to the projection of a plane.

Proposition 5.37 *If the points in the two images are related by a quadratic transformation, then there are exactly three possible Fundamental matrices. The epipoles of these Fundamental matrices are the Fundamental points of the quadratic transformation.*

Proof : By making a change of coordinate systems in both retinal planes as described previously, we can simplify the problem by assuming that the quadratic transformation is Φ_0. By expanding the epipolar constraint, which says that the point m and its image by Φ_0 are in correspondence:

$$\Phi_0(\mathbf{m})^T \mathbf{F m} = 0$$

for the generic point $\mathbf{m} = [x_1, x_2, x_3]^T$, we obtain a condition which must be satisfied for any values of x_1, x_2, x_3:

$$(F_{11} + F_{22} + F_{33})x_1 x_2 x_3$$
$$+ x_2^2 x_3 F_{12} + x_2 x_3^2 F_{13} + x_3^2 x_1 F_{23} + x_3 x_1^2 F_{21} + x_1^2 x_2 F_{31} + x_1 x_2^2 F_{32} = 0$$

This condition implies that $\mathbf{F}$ is diagonal and that its trace is null. Since $\mathbf{F}$ has to be of rank 2, one and only one of the three diagonal terms is zero. We therefore conclude that there are three solutions:

$$\mathbf{F}_1 = \mathrm{diag}(0, 1, -1) \quad \mathbf{F}_2 = \mathrm{diag}(1, 0, -1) \quad \mathbf{F}_3 = \mathrm{diag}(1, -1, 0)$$

whose corresponding epipoles are the pairs $(\varepsilon_1, \varepsilon_1)$, $(\varepsilon_2, \varepsilon_2)$, $(\varepsilon_3, \varepsilon_3)$, which are the Fundamental points of the reciprocal transformation.

By going back to the original coordinate system in the retinas, we obtain the announced result.

$\square$

In the case of the Fundamental matrices, there are always three solutions. So, if we can find two compatible Fundamental matrices, then there exists a third one. This situation is unlike the case of Essential matrices, studied by Hu and Ahuja (Hu and Ahuja, 1993), where there are actually two solutions.

5.5.3 The planar case

A plane is a particular critical surface, which is very important. Although in the general case, there were only three solutions for the Fundamental matrix (which is analogous to the case where there are only seven correspondences), in the planar case, there is a two-parameter family of solutions (which is analogous to the case where there are only six correspondences). In Section 5.2.4 we studied the planar morphisms compatible with a Fundamental matrix. Here, the dual viewpoint is taken. We first characterize all of the Fundamental matrices compatible with a given planar morphism:

Proposition 5.38 *Given a planar morphism* $\mathbf{H}$*, the set of Fundamental matrices compatible with* $\mathbf{H}$ *is the two-parameter family* $\mathbf{F} = [\mathbf{e}']_\times \mathbf{H}$*, where* $\mathbf{e}'$ *is arbitrary.*

Proof : This proposition is a direct consequence of theorem 5.1. □

We then consider the quadratic transformation; it turns out that it reduces to the planar morphism: if two Fundamental matrices $\mathbf{F}_1$ and $\mathbf{F}_2$ are compatible with the same planar morphism $\mathbf{H}$, then Equation 5.49 becomes

$$\mathbf{m}' = \mathbf{F}_1 \mathbf{m} \times \mathbf{F}_2 \mathbf{m} = ([\mathbf{e}'_1]_\times \mathbf{H} \mathbf{m}) \times ([\mathbf{e}'_2]_\times \mathbf{H} \mathbf{m}) = \mid \mathbf{e}'_1, \mathbf{e}'_2, \mathbf{H} \mathbf{m} \mid \mathbf{H} \mathbf{m}.$$

Finally, we characterize the relationship between two compatible Fundamental matrices:

Proposition 5.39 *Two Fundamental matrices $\mathbf{F}_1$ and $\mathbf{F}_2$ are compatible with the same planar morphism $\mathbf{H}$ if and only if the pair of epipoles of each matrix satisfies the epipolar constraint with the other matrix.*

Proof : If $\mathbf{F}_2$ is compatible with the planar morphism $\mathbf{H}$, then the epipoles are related by $\mathbf{H}\mathbf{e}_2 \simeq \mathbf{e}'_2$ if $\mathbf{H}$ is a homography or $\mathbf{H}\mathbf{e}_2 = \mathbf{0}$ if it is a morphism of rank 2 (proposition 5.15), therefore in the first case

$$\mathbf{e}'_2{}^T \mathbf{F}_1 \mathbf{e}_2 = \mathbf{e}_2^T \mathbf{H}^T \mathbf{F}_1 \mathbf{e}_2.$$

Since the Fundamental matrix $\mathbf{F}_1$ is compatible with the same planar morphism $\mathbf{H}$, the matrix $\mathbf{H}^T \mathbf{F}_1$ is skew-symmetric and therefore the last term is equal to zero.

In the second case we use the fact that $\mathbf{F}_1 \simeq [\mathbf{e}'_1]_\times \mathbf{H}$ to express $\mathbf{e}'_2{}^T \mathbf{F}_1 \mathbf{e}_2$ as $\mathbf{e}'_2{}^T [\mathbf{e}'_1]_\times \mathbf{H} \mathbf{e}_2$ which is equal to 0.

A similar reasoning proves that $\mathbf{e}'_1{}^T \mathbf{F}_2 \mathbf{e}_1 = 0$.

Let us now prove the converse. We suppose that

$$\mathbf{e}'_1{}^T \mathbf{F}_2 \mathbf{e}_1 = 0, \quad \mathbf{e}'_2{}^T \mathbf{F}_1 \mathbf{e}_2 = 0, \tag{5.51}$$

and seek a matrix $\mathbf{H}$ compatible with both $\mathbf{F}_1$ and $\mathbf{F}_2$. Let $\mathbf{H}_1$ and $\mathbf{H}_2$ be two planar homographies compatible with $\mathbf{F}_1$ and $\mathbf{F}_2$, respectively. According to Equation 5.18 such a matrix satisfies

$$\mathbf{H} \simeq \mathbf{H}_1 + \mathbf{e}'_1 \mathbf{r}_1^T \simeq \mathbf{H}_2 + \mathbf{e}'_2 \mathbf{r}_2^T,$$

for some vectors $\mathbf{r}_1$ and $\mathbf{r}_2$. This can be written as a system of three equations:

$$\mathbf{h}_{1i} + r_{1i} \mathbf{e}'_1 = \lambda (\mathbf{h}_{2i} + r_{2i} \mathbf{e}'_2) \quad i = 1, 2, 3,$$

where $\mathbf{h}_{1i}$ (respectively $\mathbf{h}_{2i}$) are the column vectors of $\mathbf{H}_1$ (respectively $\mathbf{H}_2$), and r_{1i} (respectively r_{2i}) is the i-th component of $\mathbf{r}_1$ (respectively $\mathbf{r}_2$). Each equation yields

$$r_{1i} = \frac{\mid \mathbf{h}_{1i}, \mathbf{h}_{2i}, \mathbf{e}'_2 \mid}{\mid \mathbf{h}_{2i}, \mathbf{e}'_1, \mathbf{e}'_2 \mid}, \quad r_{2i} = \frac{\mid \mathbf{h}_{1i}, \mathbf{h}_{2i}, \mathbf{e}'_1 \mid}{\mid \mathbf{h}_{1i}, \mathbf{e}'_1, \mathbf{e}'_2 \mid}, \quad \lambda = \frac{\mid \mathbf{h}_{1i}, \mathbf{e}'_1, \mathbf{e}'_2 \mid}{\mid \mathbf{h}_{2i}, \mathbf{e}'_1, \mathbf{e}'_2 \mid}. \tag{5.52}$$

The system has a solution if and only if the three equations yield the same value for λ:

$$\frac{\mid \mathbf{h}_{11}, \mathbf{e}_1', \mathbf{e}_2' \mid}{\mid \mathbf{h}_{21}, \mathbf{e}_1', \mathbf{e}_2' \mid} = \frac{\mid \mathbf{h}_{12}, \mathbf{e}_1', \mathbf{e}_2' \mid}{\mid \mathbf{h}_{22}, \mathbf{e}_1', \mathbf{e}_2' \mid} = \frac{\mid \mathbf{h}_{13}, \mathbf{e}_1', \mathbf{e}_2' \mid}{\mid \mathbf{h}_{23}, \mathbf{e}_1', \mathbf{e}_2' \mid},$$

which can be rewritten in the form

$$\mathbf{H}_1^T(\mathbf{e}_1' \times \mathbf{e}_2') \simeq \mathbf{H}_2^T(\mathbf{e}_1' \times \mathbf{e}_2').$$

This last condition is transformed using proposition 3.28 and $\mathbf{H}_i^{-1}\mathbf{e}_i' \simeq \mathbf{e}_i$:

$$\mathbf{e}_1 \times \mathbf{H}_1^{-1}\mathbf{e}_2' \simeq \mathbf{e}_2 \times \mathbf{H}_2^{-1}\mathbf{e}_1'.$$

This relation is satisfied if

$$\mid \mathbf{e}_1, \mathbf{H}_1^{-1}\mathbf{e}_2', \mathbf{e}_2 \mid = 0 \quad \text{and} \quad \mid \mathbf{e}_2, \mathbf{H}_2^{-1}\mathbf{e}_1', \mathbf{e}_1 \mid = 0,$$

which we recognize to be the two conditions in Equation 5.51.

To obtain an expression which involves only the Fundamental matrices, we can use the S-matrices as homographies. The expression for the planar morphism $\mathbf{H}$ is, according to Equation 5.52,

$$\mathbf{H} = [\mathbf{e}_1']_\times \mathbf{F}_1 + \mathbf{e}_1'[\mathbf{r}_1, \mathbf{r}_2, \mathbf{r}_3] \quad \text{with} \quad \mathbf{r}_i = \frac{((\mathbf{e}_1' \times \mathbf{f}_{1i}) \times (\mathbf{e}_2' \times \mathbf{f}_{2i}))^T \mathbf{e}_2'}{(\mathbf{e}_2' \times \mathbf{f}_{2i})^T(\mathbf{e}_1' \times \mathbf{e}_2')},$$

where $\mathbf{f}_{1i}$ (respectively $\mathbf{f}_{2i}$) are the column vectors of $\mathbf{F}_1$ (respectively $\mathbf{F}_2$). $\square$

5.6 Summary

In this chapter, we have studied in detail the laws that govern the formation of two images of the same scene. The key geometric concepts from which those laws can be derived are those of epipolar geometry when the optical centers are different and planar morphism when they are identical. We have shown that the epipolar geometry could be concisely and elegantly summarized by a 3×3 matrix of rank 2 defined up to scale, the *Fundamental matrix*. This matrix, which contains all of the geometric information relating two uncalibrated cameras, can be recovered from image measurements only. No other information beyond point correspondences is necessary as we will show in Chapter 6. There is an important link between the Fundamental matrix and planar morphisms.

The reader is now familiar with our way of viewing geometric entities within the three contexts of the projective, affine and Euclidean geometries. The Fundamental matrix is no exception and we propose to consider it successively in those three settings:

1. In the projective framework, it is naturally decomposed into the elements of the epipolar homography. As such, we will see in Chapter 7 that it can be used to perform a certain number of three-dimensional tasks, without the need for a stronger calibration, e.g. the determination of the internal parameters of the cameras or their relative position and orientation. These tasks will be said to be done under *weak calibration*.

2. In the affine framework, it is related to the infinity morphism. It will be seen in Chapter 7 that this relation can be exploited to perform some useful tasks provided that some extra information about the structure of the world, e.g. it contains parallel lines, or about the camera motion, e.g. it is a pure translation, is available.

3. In the Euclidean framework, it is related to the internal and motion parameters, hence to the Essential matrix. This relation is the basis of a method for recovering the calibration and motion parameters without a calibration grid. This method, called *self-calibration*, is described in Chapter 11.

The elements used to describe the correspondence (motion parameters) and the plane (structure parameters) at the three levels of description are summarized in table 5.2. The Fundamental matrix is obtained using motion parameters alone, while by combining motion and structure parameters we obtain the planar morphisms. These concepts are summarized in table 5.3, which references the equations where the corresponding quantities were defined in this section.

	motion parameters (DOF)			planar structure parameters
projective	$\mathbf{S}$	Special matrix	5	$\mathbf{r}$ intrinsic representation
	$\mathbf{e}'$	epipole	2	
affine	$\mathbf{H}_\infty$	Infinity homography	8	$\mathbf{q}$ vanishing line
	$\mathbf{e}'$	epipole	2	
Euclidean	$\mathbf{A}, \mathbf{A}'$	intrinsic parameters	5+5	$\mathbf{n}, d$ normal, distance to origin
	$\mathbf{R}, \mathbf{t}$	rotation, translation	3+2	

Table 5.2: Summary of correspondence and planar structure descriptions.

5.7 References and further reading

The Essential matrix has been used in the context of displacement analysis by people who thought conceptually in the three-dimensional Euclidean space. For these people (Longuet-Higgins (Longuet-Higgins, 1981), Tsai and Huang (Tsai and Huang,

	F	Eq.	**H**	Eq.	$\mathbf{\Pi} = [\mathbf{n}^T \; -d]^T$
projective	$[\mathbf{e}']_\times \mathbf{S}$	(5.22)	$\mathbf{S} + \mathbf{e}'\mathbf{r}^T$	(5.23)	$\mathbf{r}$
affine	$[\mathbf{e}']_\times \mathbf{H}_\infty$	(5.26)	$\mathbf{H}_\infty + \mathbf{e}'\mathbf{q}^T$	(5.27)	$\mathbf{q} = \mathbf{r} - \mathbf{r}_\infty$
Euclidean	$\mathbf{A}'^{-T}[\mathbf{t}]_\times \mathbf{R}\mathbf{A}^{-1}$	(5.31)	$\mathbf{A}'(\mathbf{R} + \mathbf{t}\mathbf{n}^T/d)\mathbf{A}^{-1}$	(5.36)	$\mathbf{n}/d = \mathbf{A}^T\mathbf{q}$

Table 5.3: Stratified descriptions for the Fundamental matrix, planar morphisms, and planes.

1984)), the Essential matrix was a mechanism for expressing a constraint between three-dimensional metric entities, the two optical rays, the translation and the rotation between the two cameras. Although implicitly present, the idea of the epipolar constraint even (what the so-called Longuet-Higgins equation expresses) was not explicitly articulated. This situation is also true of subsequent work by Demazure (Demazure, 1988) and Faugeras and Maybank (Faugeras and Maybank, 1990b) who studied the algebraic properties of Essential matrices in the same conceptual framework and the number of solutions to the displacement estimation problem with the minimum number (five) of correspondences.

The idea that a generalization of this matrix summarizes the information about a projective correspondence between the two retinal planes or a homography between two pencils of lines, i.e. two $\mathcal{P}^1$'s, casts a fundamentally different light on the problem. The term "Fundamental matrix" was introduced in Luong's PhD thesis (Luong, 1992), where it was shown that it directly provides the two epipoles (i.e. the vertices of the two pencils of epipolar lines) and the 3 parameters of the homography between these two pencils. The links with the planar morphism (also uncovered in (Hartley and Gupta, 1993)) and with the Essential matrix were also established. The infinity homography was proposed as a representation of affine motion by Quan and Mohr (Quan and Mohr, 1992). The pseudo-inverse matrix was used independently in (Zhang and Xu, 1998), although with no geometric interpretation.

Image mosaicing has become a popular research area, with applications to video compression and indexing, increasing the field of view and resolution of a camera, construction of virtual environments, and virtual travel. Recent work includes (Mann and Picard, 1994; Chen, 1995; Irani et al., 1995; Szeliski, 1996; Peleg and Herman, 1997; Zoglami et al., 1997; Sawhney et al., 1998; Davis, 1998; Sawhney and Kumar, 1999; Shum and Szeliski, 1999). The last paper contains many references to the literature.

A plane is the simplest surface which generates an analytical correspondence between two images. The next simplest surface is a particular quadric, which is studied

by Shashua and Toelg (Shashua and Toelg, 1997). This quadric is applied to the
infinitesimal case in (Wexler and Shashua, 1999). It generates quadratic transformations between images which are different from those described in Section 5.5.2.
Critical surfaces were known to photogrammeters at the beginning of the century
(Krames, 1940; Wunderlich, 1941; Hofmann, 1950) who called them "*gefährliche
Flächen*". They were then rediscovered and studied theoretically by computer
vision scientists in the case of reconstruction from optical flow (Maybank, 1985;
Horn, 1987; Negahdaripour, 1989) and point correspondences (Longuet-Higgins,
1988; Maybank, 1990; Horn, 1990; Maybank, 1992). All of this work was in the
context of calibrated cameras, with the exception of (Maybank, 1992). It was first
proved by Longuet-Higgins (Longuet-Higgins, 1988) that the *maximum* number of
ambiguous *Essential* matrices is three. These solutions are studied extensively by
Maybank (Maybank, 1992). If one looks for solutions which are Essential matrices,
only two exist, as shown recently by Hu and Ahuja (Hu and Ahuja, 1993). Using MDL theory to describe image disparity, Maybank and Sturm (Maybank and
Sturm, 1999) experimentally find a curious result which is somewhat related to the
conclusion of (Luong and Faugeras, 1996) regarding the practical existence of critical volumes: Even for non-coplanar scenes, a model consisting of a homography plus
a 2-D deviation is always more compact than is a model consisting of an F-matrix
plus a deviation along the epipolar line.

By far, the most complete study of the special form of F and H matrices arising from special displacements is due to Viéville and Lingrand (Viéville and Lingrand, 1999). They developed a unified hierarchical formalism for models already
developed in the literature and for some novel models. Particular forms for intrinsic parameters, translation, rotation, and relations between the rotation axis and
translation are enumerated, and all of their combinations considered. A special form
which we have not detailed in this chapter occurs often with a stereo rig. Brooks
et al. (Brooks et al., 1996; de Agapito et al., 1998) and Li *et al.* (Li et al., 1996)
consider a particular kind of stereo head, with vergence and coplanar optical axes.
The translation between the two cameras has no component in Y, while the rotation
is around the Y axis. The Fundamental matrix satisfies $F_{11} = F_{22} = 0$ and depends
only on five parameters which can be determined using specific algorithms and parameterization. A particular case, when all but two degrees of freedom are known,
is used in a real time system (Bjorkman and Eklundh, 1999). We have discussed
only ego-motion. The complementary viewpoint to the problem is to consider object motions. An example of special motions are those generated by articulations,
studied by Sinclair *et al.* (Sinclair and Zesar, 1996; Sinclair, 1996; Sinclair et al.,
1997).

Lee and Huang introduced the orthographic (Huang and Lee, 1989), and later
weak perspective (Lee and Huang, 1990), epipolar geometry equation. This equation
was generalized to the affine case by Shapiro *et al.* (Shapiro et al., 1995). Shimshoni
et al. (Shimshoni et al., 1999) give a different geometric interpretation of the one-

parameter ambiguity in terms of the viewing sphere. More details about the epipolar geometry of parallel cameras can be found in the book by Shapiro (Shapiro, 1995), as well as in the book by Xu and Zhang (Xu and Zhang, 1996). The idea to combine one parallel view with perspective views has been explored for the uncalibrated case by Marugame *et al.* (Marugame et al., 1999), who also uses self-calibration of some intrinsic parameters to recover Euclidean structure, and for the calibrated case by Zhang *et al.* (Zhang et al., 1999).

6 Estimating the Fundamental matrix

We have seen in Chapter 5 that the Fundamental matrix was the basic description of the projective geometry of two views. We will see in Chapter 11 that it is at the heart of a method for computing the internal parameters of a moving camera if those parameters are not changing, a so-called self-calibration method. We will also see in Chapters 7 and 10 that it is central to methods that recover the 3D projective geometry of the observed scene.

It is therefore important to have robust and reliable methods for estimating the Fundamental matrix of two views from image measurements, i.e. from point correspondences.

To set the stage for this chapter, we will assume that we have two views of a scene taken by two cameras. Those two cameras will be assumed to be perspective projective cameras unless otherwise specified. n (respectively n') points of interest have been detected in image 1 (respectively in image 2) by methods which will not be described here (see for example (Zhang et al., 1995)). We wish to establish a set of correspondences (m_i, m'_i), $i = 1, \ldots, p$, with p less than or equal to $min(n, n')$, between the points of interest in the two views such that the two pixels of each pair are likely to be the images of the same 3D point. We also wish to compute the estimate of the Fundamental matrix $\mathbf{F}$ that best explains those correspondences. What we mean by explain and by best will hopefully be made clear in the following.

We will assume that the correspondences (m_i, m'_i), $i = 1, \ldots, p$, are *given*, a usually somewhat unrealistic situation. This assumption will allow us to concentrate on the estimation algorithms themselves.

We describe in Section 6.1 a number of methods for estimating the F-matrix from the p epipolar constraints (5.4) without taking into account the fact that the F-matrix must have rank 2. All of those methods treat the estimation problem as linear in $\mathbf{F}$ and either ignore the rank constraint or reintroduce it after the linear estimation process is completed.

In Section 6.2 we tackle this problem of rank directly and prepare the ground for more powerful algorithms that will force the estimated matrix to have rank 2. This constraint will be achieved through parameterization by the epipolar homography (see Section 5.2.3). In the process, we will lose the simplicity of the linear methods of the previous section but will gain something important: The result of our estimation will be an admissible Fundamental matrix.

The following section proposes another improvement to the original linear methods. Not only should the output of our estimation procedure be an admissible Fundamental matrix but it should also be optimal in a meaningful sense. The problem is that the epipolar constraint does not immediately yield a meaningful error function. Section 6.3 proposes a number of such functions, including the distance to the epipolar lines which is the most important in practice.

In Section 6.4, we deal with the problem of the robustness of the estimators of the F-matrix. We have assumed thus far a list of *perfect* correspondences between the two views. In practice, those correspondences are often far from perfect due to noisy data and imperfect detection algorithms. We discuss methods such as the M-estimators, the random sampling consensus and the least-median-of-squares that provide ways to reduce or even eliminate poor correspondences.

Section 6.5 is dedicated to a study of most of the methods presented so far on a pair of images for which the ground truth Fundamental matrix is available.

In Section 6.6 we address the problem of evaluating the confidence of our final estimation. We show how this evalutation can be done by computing first order derivatives of our error criteria and modeling the uncertainty of the point correspondences.

We use those results in Section 6.7.2 to derive the uncertainty of the recovered epipoles, information that is often useful in applications, and to introduce the notion of epipolar band: if the Fundamental matrix has some uncertainty attached to it, then it has an impact on the epipolar lines. This impact can be summarized in the idea of an epipolar band, a fattening of the epipolar line that should be taken into account when searching for new correspondences, e.g. in stereo.

6.1 Linear methods

The key idea in these methods is to notice that, given a pair of corresponding pixels (m, m'), Equation 5.4 of Chapter 5 is linear in the coefficients of the Fundamental matrix $\mathbf{F}$. It follows directly that, given sufficiently many of those equations one should be able to compute the coefficients of $\mathbf{F}$ if the system is well-conditioned. This idea was used by Longuet-Higgins (Longuet-Higgins, 1981) to solve for the coefficients of the Essential matrix (see Chapter 5 Section 5.3.3 and (Faugeras, 1993)).

6.1.1 An important normalization procedure

In all of the linear estimation techniques that will be described in this section, we deal with projective coordinates of the pixels. In a typical image of dimensions 512×512, a typical image point will have projective coordinates whose orders of magnitude are given componentwise by the triple $(250, 250, 1)$. The fact that the first two coordinates are more than one order of magnitude larger than the third one has the effect of causing poor numerical conditioning.

This effect was analyzed by Hartley (Hartley, 1997c) who wisely advocated normalizing the points in the two images so that their three projective coordinates are of roughly the same order. This normalization is achieved by making two affine changes of coordinates, one in each image. The estimation of the Fundamental matrix takes place in these new coordinate systems, thereby buying greater numerical stability. The result can then be expressed in the original coordinate systems by performing two inverse affine transformations.

In detail, the two affine transformations, represented by the two 3×3 matrices $\mathbf{T}$ and $\mathbf{T}'$, are computed in such a way that

- the centroid of the transformed point is at the origin $[0, 0, 1]^T$, and

- the averaged distance of the transformed points to the origin is $\sqrt{2}$.

The reader will easily verify that these two conditions uniquely determine the two affine transformations $\mathbf{H}$ and $\mathbf{H}'$.

As stated, the estimation will be performed on the pair of corresponding pixels $(\hat{m}_i, \hat{m}'_i)$ where $\hat{\mathbf{m}}_i = \mathbf{H}\mathbf{m}_i$ and $\hat{\mathbf{m}}'_i = \mathbf{H}'\mathbf{m}'_i$, resulting in a Fundamental matrix $\hat{\mathbf{F}}$. The corresponding Fundamental matrix expressed in the original coordinates is simply

$$\mathbf{H}'^T \hat{\mathbf{F}} \mathbf{H}.$$

6.1.2   The basic algorithm

Principle   Let $\mathbf{m} = [u, v, 1]^T$ and $\mathbf{m}' = [u', v', 1]^T$ be two corresponding points. If the Fundamental matrix is $\mathbf{F} = (F_{ij})_{1 \leq i,j \leq 3}$, then the epipolar constraint $\mathbf{m}'^T \mathbf{F} \mathbf{m} = 0$ can be rearranged as

$$\mathbf{U}^T \mathbf{f} = 0, \tag{6.1}$$

where

$$\begin{aligned} \mathbf{U} &= [uu', vu', u', uv', vv', v', u, v, 1]^T, \text{and} \\ \mathbf{f} &= [F_{11}, F_{12}, F_{13}, F_{21}, F_{22}, F_{23}, F_{31}, F_{32}, F_{33}]^T. \end{aligned}$$

Equation 6.1 is linear and homogeneous in the 9 unknown coefficients of matrix $\mathbf{F}$. Thus if we are given 8 matches, then we will be able, in general, to determine a unique solution for $\mathbf{F}$, defined up to a scale factor. This approach is known as the eight-point algorithm.

Least-squares solution   A straightforward possibility for increasing the robustness of the eight-point algorithm is the use of more than 8 points. In this case, we have more linear equations than unknowns, and, in the presence of noise, we look for the minimum of the error criterion

$$C(\mathbf{F}) = \sum_{i=1}^{p} (\mathbf{m}_i'^T \mathbf{F} \mathbf{m}_i)^2, \tag{6.2}$$

which is equivalent to finding the minimum of

$$C(\mathbf{f}) = \|\tilde{\mathbf{U}}\mathbf{f}\|^2, \tag{6.3}$$

where

$$\tilde{\mathbf{U}} = \begin{bmatrix} \mathbf{U}_1^T \\ \vdots \\ \mathbf{U}_p^T \end{bmatrix}. \tag{6.4}$$

Since $\mathbf{F}$ is defined only up to a scale factor, there are two ways to solve the least-squares problem. The first uses a closed-form solution via the linear equations. In detail, one of the coefficients of $\mathbf{F}$ is set to 1, yielding a parameterization of $\mathbf{F}$ by eight values, which are the ratios of the eight other coefficients to the normalizing one. The question of the best choice of the coefficient for the normalization is addressed in a more general context in Section 6.2. Let us assume for the sake of discussion that the normalizing coefficient is F_{33}. We can rewrite (6.3) as

$$\min_{\mathbf{g}} \|\tilde{\mathbf{V}}\mathbf{g} + \mathbf{b}\|^2$$

where $\tilde{\mathbf{V}}$ is formed with the first 8 columns of $\tilde{\mathbf{U}}$,
$\mathbf{g} = [F_{11}, F_{12}, F_{13}, F_{21}, F_{22}, F_{23}, F_{31}, F_{32}]^T$ and $\mathbf{b}$ is the ninth column of $\tilde{\mathbf{U}}$. The solution is known to be

$$\mathbf{g} = -(\tilde{\mathbf{V}}^T\tilde{\mathbf{V}})^{-1}\tilde{\mathbf{V}}^T\mathbf{b}$$

if the matrix $(\tilde{\mathbf{V}}^T\tilde{\mathbf{V}})$ is invertible.

The second method solves the classical problem

$$\min_{\mathbf{f}} \|\tilde{\mathbf{U}}\mathbf{f}\| \quad \text{with} \quad \|\mathbf{f}\| = 1. \tag{6.5}$$

The solution is the eigenvector associated with the smallest eigenvalue of $\tilde{\mathbf{U}}^T\tilde{\mathbf{U}}$. More details on this linear algebra problem can be found in Appendix A.1. The advantage of this second approach is that all of the coefficients of $\mathbf{F}$ play the same role.

Discussion The advantage of the eight-point algorithm is that it leads to a non-iterative computation method which is easy to implement using any linear algebra numerical package; however, we have found that it is quite sensitive to noise, even with numerous data points. There are two main problems, which have been identified in (Luong, 1992):

- The constraint $\det(\mathbf{F}) = 0$ is not satisfied. Several means to enforce this constraint are examined in Sections 6.1.3 and 6.2.

- The quantity that is minimized in (6.2) does not have a good geometric interpretation. One could say that one might be trying to minimize an irrelevant quantity. This observation leads directly to the distance minimization algorithm presented in Section 6.3.

6.1.3   Enforcing the rank constraint by approximation

The linear methods fundamentally cannot take into account the rank constraint directly and easily. Therefore, all methods that do so while staying in the linear realm appear slightly awkward. We examine three of them.

Two-step approximate linear determination of parameters   The idea is to note that in Equation 5.10 of Proposition 5.12, if the epipoles are known, then the Fundamental matrix is a linear function of the coefficients (a, b, c, d) of the epipolar homography.

In the linear algorithms, there is no reason for the estimated Fundamental matrix to satisfy the rank constraint. We determine the epipole $\mathbf{e}$ by solving the constrained minimization problem

$$\min_{\mathbf{e}} \|\mathbf{Fe}\|^2 \quad \text{subject to} \quad \|\mathbf{e}\|^2 = 1, \tag{6.6}$$

which yields $\mathbf{e}$ as the unit norm eigenvector of matrix $\mathbf{F}^T\mathbf{F}$ corresponding to the smallest eigenvalue. The same processing applies in reverse to the computation of the epipole e'.

Once the epipoles are known, we can use Equation 5.10 or, if the epipoles are not at infinity, Equation 5.14, and write the expression $\mathbf{m}_i'^T\mathbf{Fm}_i$ as a linear expression of the coefficients of the epipolar homography:

$$\mathbf{m}_i'^T\mathbf{Fm}_i = (e_y e_x' - e_y u_i' + v_i u_i' - v_i e_x')a + (u_i u_i' - u_i e_x' - e_x u_i' + e_x e_x')b$$
$$+ (e_y v_i' + v_i e_y' - e_y e_y' - v_i v_i')c + (e_x v_i' + u_i e_y' - u_i v_i' - e_x e_y')d = 0,$$

where (u_i, v_i) (respectively (u_i', v_i')) are the affine coordinates of m_i (respectively m_i'). This equation can be used to solve for the coefficients of the epipolar homography in a least-squares formulation, thereby completing the determination of the parameters of $\mathbf{F}$.

Using the closest rank 2 matrix   Another approach to enforce the rank constraint, proposed originally by Tsai and Huang (Tsai and Huang, 1984), is to replace the matrix $\mathbf{F}$ found by the eight-point algorithm by the singular matrix $\mathbf{F}'$ which minimizes the Frobenius norm $\|\mathbf{F} - \mathbf{F}'\|$. This step can be done using a singular value decomposition. If $\mathbf{F} = \mathbf{U}\text{diag}(\lambda_1, \lambda_2, \lambda_3)\mathbf{V}^T$, with $\lambda_1 \geq \lambda_2 \geq \lambda_3 \geq 0$, then $\mathbf{F}' = \mathbf{U}\text{diag}(\lambda_1, \lambda_2, 0)\mathbf{V}^T$. Details on this linear algebra technique are given in Appendix A.1.

This approach gives epipoles which are identical to those obtained by the previous method, but an epipolar homography which is different. Experiments conducted by Ponce and Genc (Ponce and Genc, 1998) suggest that the two-step method is slightly superior.

Solving a cubic equation This approach can be seen as an extension of the method described in Proposition 5.14. One selects two components of $\mathbf{F}$, say, without loss of generality, F_{32} and F_{33} and rewrites (6.3) as

$$\min_{\mathbf{h}} \|\tilde{\mathbf{W}}\mathbf{h} + F_{32}\mathbf{W}_8 + F_{33}\mathbf{W}_9\|^2. \tag{6.7}$$

The vector $\mathbf{h}$ is made of the first 7 components of the vector $\mathbf{f}$, the matrix $\tilde{\mathbf{W}}$ is made of the first 7 columns of matrix $\tilde{\mathbf{U}}$, and the vectors $\mathbf{W}_8$ and $\mathbf{W}_9$ are the eighth and ninth column vectors of that matrix, respectively. The solution $\hat{\mathbf{h}}$ of (6.7) is

$$\hat{\mathbf{h}} = -\left(\tilde{\mathbf{W}}^T \tilde{\mathbf{W}}\right)^{-1} \tilde{\mathbf{W}}^T (F_{32}\mathbf{W}_8 + F_{33}\mathbf{W}_9)$$

and is seen to be a linear function of F_{32} and F_{33}: We have a linear family of solutions parametrized by F_{32} and F_{33}. In that family of solutions, there are some that satisfy the condition $\det(\mathbf{F}) = 0$. They are obtained by expressing the determinant of the solutions as a function of F_{32} and F_{33}. One obtains a homogeneous polynomial of degree 3 which must be zero. Solving for one of the two ratios $F_{32} : F_{33}$ or $F_{33} : F_{32}$ one obtains at least one real solution for the ratio and therefore at least one solution for the Fundamental matrix.

This approach raises several questions:

- In the case where there are more than one real root to the cubic polynomial, how does one choose among the corresponding solutions for $\mathbf{F}$? A possible answer is that one keeps the one that minimizes the criterion (6.3).

- How does one choose the two coefficients of $\mathbf{F}$ that are left free? a possible answer is that one does not initially but tries all $\binom{9}{2} = 36$ possible choices and selects the pair that yields the best solution as described in the previous item.

6.2 Enforcing the rank constraint by parameterization

We have just seen that the linear methods were plagued by the fact that it was difficult to enforce the rank 2 constraint and that this constraint could be incorporated only at the end of the process. This raises the question of whether or not one could obtain a better solution (for the moment in the sense of criterion (6.3)).

In this section we study a parametrization of the Fundamental matrix with exactly seven parameters such that the corresponding matrices are all of rank 2. Such a parameterization will turn the Fundamental matrix estimation into a nonlinear problem, which is not problematic, however, since we will change the error function (6.3) into another one, more geometrically significant, which is not quadratic in the coefficients of $\mathbf{F}$ and cannot be minimized anyway using linear least-squares.

6.2.1   Parameterizing by the epipolar homography

The basic idea is to use as parameters for $\mathbf{F}$ the seven scalars which represent the epipolar homography: Two coordinates for each epipole and three coefficients for the epipolar homography. A straightforward approach, based on Equation 5.10, would be to use the affine coordinates of the epipoles and set arbitrarily one of the four coefficients a, b, c, d of the epipolar homography to 1. In addition to enforce the rank constraint and to ensure a minimal parameterization, another advantage of this approach is that it directly yields the geometrically relevant parameters.

However, as has been seen, this parameterization assumes that the epipoles are finite. In theory, it becomes degenerate if the epipoles are at infinity. In practice, it becomes unstable. To tackle this problem, we define different maps by normalizing the projective coordinates of the epipoles by one of them, not necessarily the last.

Denoting the columns of $\mathbf{F}$ by the vectors $\mathbf{c}_1$, $\mathbf{c}_2$ and $\mathbf{c}_3$, we have

$$Rank(\mathbf{F}) = 2 \iff \exists (j_1, j_2, j_3) \in [1,3], \ \exists (\lambda_{j_2}, \lambda_{j_3}) \in \mathbb{R}^2 \quad \mathbf{c}_{j_1} + \lambda_{j_2}\mathbf{c}_{j_2} + \lambda_{j_3}\mathbf{c}_{j_3} = 0.$$

This equivalence represents a subset of all of the 3×3 matrices of rank strictly less than 3, i.e. it also includes matrices of rank 1. $\mathbf{F}$ is then parametrized by λ_{j_2}, λ_{j_3}, $\mathbf{c}_{j_2}$ and $\mathbf{c}_{j_3}$.

This parametrization implies a division of the set of F-matrices into three overlapping subsets corresponding to the three maps defined by $j_1 = 1$, $j_1 = 2$ and $j_1 = 3$. Each of these maps amounts to choosing the normalizing component for the epipole $\mathbf{e}$. Indeed, the matrices of rank 2 having the forms

$$[\mathbf{c}_1, \mathbf{c}_2, \lambda \mathbf{c}_2] \ [\mathbf{c}_1, \mathbf{0}_3, \lambda \mathbf{c}_3] \ [\mathbf{c}_1, \mathbf{c}_2, \mathbf{0}_3]$$

have no parametrization if we take $j_1 = 1$.

Note that the choice of j_1 is equivalent to choosing a component of the coordinate vectors of the epipole $\mathbf{e}$, namely the j_1th, and dividing the remaining two components by this one. In particular, one excludes the case where that component is equal to zero. Indeed, if we denote the 3-vector of j_1th coordinate equal to u, j_2th coordinate equal to v, and j_3th coordinate equal to w by $\{x_{j_1} = u, x_{j_2} = v, x_{j_3} = w\}$, then the vector $\{x_{j_1} = 1, x_{j_2} = \lambda_{j_2}, x_{j_3} = \lambda_{j_3}\}$ is clearly in the nullspace of $\mathbf{F}$ and is therefore a coordinate vector of the epipole $\mathbf{e}$.

To make the problem symmetrical, the same decomposition for the column vectors is used for the row vectors, denoted $\mathbf{r}_1^T$, $\mathbf{r}_2^T$, $\mathbf{r}_3^T$:

$$Rank(\mathbf{F}) = 2 \iff \exists (i_1, i_2, i_3) \in [1,3], \ \exists (\mu_{i_2}, \mu_{i_3}) \in \mathbb{R}^2 \quad \mathbf{r}_{i_1} + \mu_{i_2}\mathbf{r}_{i_2} + \mu_{i_3}\mathbf{r}_{i_3} = 0.$$

This statement has the effect of dividing the set of F-matrices into nine subsets corresponding to the choice of a column j_1 and a row i_1; see Figure 6.1. $\mathbf{F}$ is then parametrized by the 8-vector

$$\mathbf{f}_8 = [\lambda_{j_2}, \lambda_{j_3}, \mu_{i_2}, \mu_{i_3}, F_{i_2 j_2}, F_{i_2 j_3}, F_{i_3 j_2}, F_{i_3 j_3}]^T,$$

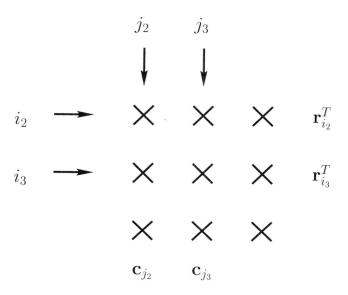

Figure 6.1: The matrix $\mathbf{F}$ is represented by the four numbers at the intersection of the columns j_2, j_3 and the rows i_2, i_3 and by the four numbers λ_{j_2}, λ_{j_3} and μ_{i_2}, μ_{i_3}.

where the two coordinates μ_{i_2} and μ_{i_3} are such that $\mathbf{e}' = \{x_{i_1} = 1, x_{i_2} = \mu_{i_2}, x_{i_3} = \mu_{i_3}\}$, and the four elements $F_{i_2 j_2}$, $F_{i_2 j_3}$, $F_{i_3 j_2}$ and $F_{i_3 j_3}$ are the coefficients of $\mathbf{F}$ appearing in $\mathbf{c}_{j_2}$, $\mathbf{c}_{j_3}$, $\mathbf{r}_{i_2}$ and $\mathbf{r}_{i_3}$. These four coefficients parameterize the epipolar homography which maps an epipolar line in the first image to its corresponding epipolar line in the second (see Section 5.2.3).

The function that computes $\mathbf{F}$ from a given 8-vector $\mathbf{f}_8$ is written $\mathbf{F}_{i_1 j_1}(\mathbf{f}_8)$. For example with $i_1 = 3$ and $j_1 = 3$, we obtain

$$\mathbf{F} = \mathbf{F}_{i_1 j_1}(\mathbf{f}_8) =$$
$$\begin{bmatrix} F_{i_2 j_2} & F_{i_2 j_3} & -\lambda_{j_2} F_{i_2 j_2} - \lambda_{j_3} F_{i_2 j_3} \\ F_{i_3 j_2} & F_{i_3 j_3} & -\lambda_{j_2} F_{i_3 j_2} - \lambda_{j_3} F_{i_3 j_3} \\ -\mu_{i_2} F_{i_2 j_2} - \mu_{i_3} F_{i_3 j_2} & -\mu_{i_2} F_{i_2 j_3} - \mu_{i_3} F_{i_3 j_3} & \mu_{i_2}(\lambda_{j_2} F_{i_2 j_2} + \lambda_{j_3} F_{i_2 j_3}) + \\ & & \mu_{i_3}(\lambda_{j_2} F_{i_3 j_2} + \lambda_{j_3} F_{i_3 j_3}) \end{bmatrix}.$$

At last, to take into account the fact that the Fundamental matrix is defined only up to a scale factor, only three of the four elements defining the epipolar homography are kept in the representation of $\mathbf{F}$. Let $i_{2,3} \in \{i_2, i_3\}$ and $j_{2,3} \in \{j_2, j_3\}$ be such that $F_{i_{2,3} j_{2,3}} \neq 0$. If k is the position of $F_{i_{2,3} j_{2,3}}$ in $\mathbf{f}_8$, then $\mathbf{F}$ is parametrized by the 7-vector obtained from the 8-vector

$$[\lambda_{j_2}, \lambda_{j_3}, \mu_{i_2}, \mu_{i_3}, \frac{F_{i_2 j_2}}{F_{i_{2,3} j_{2,3}}}, \frac{F_{i_2 j_3}}{F_{i_{2,3} j_{2,3}}}, \frac{F_{i_3 j_2}}{F_{i_{2,3} j_{2,3}}}, \frac{F_{i_3 j_3}}{F_{i_{2,3} j_{2,3}}}]^T$$

by removing its kth coordinate which is equal to 1.

Conversely, given a set of four indices i_1, j_1, $i_{2,3}$, $j_{2,3}$ and seven numbers arranged in a vector $\mathbf{f}_7 = [\lambda_{j_2}, \lambda_{j_3}, \mu_{i_2}, \mu_{i_3}, a, b, c]^T$, the function that computes $\mathbf{F}$ from $\mathbf{f}_7$ is denoted $\mathbf{F}_{i_1 j_1 i_{2,3} j_{2,3}}(\mathbf{f}_7)$. For $i_1 = 3$, $j_1 = 3$, $i_{2,3} = i_2 = 1$ and $j_{2,3} = j_3 = 2$, for example, we have

$$\mathbf{F} = \mathbf{F}_{i_1 j_1 i_{2,3} j_{2,3}}(\mathbf{f}_7) =$$

$$\begin{bmatrix} F_{i_2 j_2} & 1 & -\lambda_{j_2} F_{i_2 j_2} - \lambda_{j_3} \\ F_{i_3 j_2} & F_{i_3 j_3} & -\lambda_{j_2} F_{i_3 j_2} - \lambda_{j_3} F_{i_3 j_3} \\ -\mu_{i_2} F_{i_2 j_2} - \mu_{i_3} F_{i_3 j_2} & -\mu_{i_2} - \mu_{i_3} F_{i_3 j_3} & \begin{matrix} \mu_{i_2}(\lambda_{j_2} F_{i_2 j_2} + \lambda_{j_3}) + \\ \mu_{i_3}(\lambda_{j_2} F_{i_3 j_2} + \lambda_{j_3} F_{i_3 j_3}) \end{matrix} \end{bmatrix}. \quad (6.8)$$

Our discussion shows that there is a total of $3 \times 3 \times 4 = 36$ different maps corresponding to the three choices for i_1, the three choices for j_1 and the four choices for $(i_{2,3}, j_{2,3})$. In Section 6.2.3, we examine one way to choose the "best" map for a given F-matrix.

6.2.2 Computing the Jacobian of the parameterization

The Jacobian matrix $\frac{d\mathbf{F}_{i_1 j_1 i_{2,3} j_{2,3}}(\mathbf{f}_7)}{d\mathbf{f}_7}$ of the parametrization is used in the following section and in the computation of the covariance matrix of $\mathbf{F}$ in Section 6.6. Using the chain rule we have

$$\frac{d\mathbf{F}_{i_1 j_1 i_{2,3} j_{2,3}}(\mathbf{f}_7)}{d\mathbf{f}_7} = \frac{d\mathbf{F}_{i_1 j_1}(\mathbf{f}_8)}{d\mathbf{f}_8} \frac{d\mathbf{f}_8(\mathbf{f}_7)}{d\mathbf{f}_7}(\mathbf{f}_7),$$

where $\mathbf{f}_8(\mathbf{f}_7)$ is the function that computes $\mathbf{f}_8$ from a given $\mathbf{f}_7$. For $i_{2,3} = i_2 = 1$ and $j_{2,3} = j_3 = 2$, for example, we have

$$\mathbf{f}_8(\mathbf{f}_7) = [\lambda_{j_2}, \lambda_{j_3}, \mu_{i_2}, \mu_{i_3}, F_{i_2 j_2}, 1, F_{i_3 j_2}, F_{i_3 j_3}]^T.$$

For $i_1 = 3$ and $j_1 = 3$, for example, we have

$$\frac{d\mathbf{F}_{i_1 j_1}(\mathbf{f}_8)}{d\mathbf{f}_8} =$$

$$\begin{bmatrix} 0 & 0 & -F_{i_2 j_2} & 0 & 0 & -F_{i_3 j_2} & 0 & 0 & F_{i_2 j_2}\mu_{i_2} + F_{i_3 j_2}\mu_{i_3} \\ 0 & 0 & -F_{i_2 j_3} & 0 & 0 & -F_{i_3 j_3} & 0 & 0 & F_{i_2 j_3}\mu_{i_2} + F_{i_3 j_3}\mu_{i_3} \\ 0 & 0 & 0 & 0 & 0 & 0 & -F_{i_2 j_2} & -F_{i_2 j_3} & F_{i_2 j_2}\lambda_{j_2} + F_{i_2 j_3}\lambda_{j_3} \\ 0 & 0 & 0 & 0 & 0 & 0 & -F_{i_3 j_2} & -F_{i_3 j_3} & F_{i_3 j_2}\lambda_{j_2} + F_{i_3 j_3}\lambda_{j_3} \\ 1 & 0 & -\lambda_{j_2} & 0 & 0 & 0 & -\mu_{i_2} & 0 & \lambda_{j_2}\mu_{i_2} \\ 0 & 1 & -\lambda_{j_3} & 0 & 0 & 0 & 0 & -\mu_{i_2} & \lambda_{j_3}\mu_{i_2} \\ 0 & 0 & 0 & 1 & 0 & -\lambda_{j_2} & -\mu_{i_3} & 0 & \lambda_{j_2}\mu_{i_3} \\ 0 & 0 & 0 & 0 & 1 & -\lambda_{j_3} & 0 & -\mu_{i_3} & \lambda_{j_3}\mu_{i_3} \end{bmatrix}^T.$$

$$(6.9)$$

All of the other expressions of $\frac{d\mathbf{F}_{i_1 j_1}(\mathbf{f}_8)}{d\mathbf{f}_8}$ corresponding to different values of $(i_1, i_2, i_{2,3}, j_1, j_2, j_{2,3})$ are obtained from the matrix (6.9) after permutations of some of its rows and some of its columns.

Furthermore, $\frac{d\mathbf{f}_8(\mathbf{f}_7)}{d\mathbf{f}_7}$ is equal to the 8×8 identity matrix from which we remove the kth column. Thus, $\frac{d\mathbf{F}_{i_1 j_1 i_{2,3} j_{2,3}}(\mathbf{f}_7)}{d\mathbf{f}_7}$ is finally obtained from $\frac{d\mathbf{F}_{i_1 j_1}(\mathbf{f}_8)}{d\mathbf{f}_8}$ by removing the kth column and taking $F_{i_{2,3} j_{2,3}}$ equal to 1.

6.2.3   Choosing the best map

Given a matrix $\mathbf{F}$ and the epipoles, or an approximation of them, $\mathbf{F}$ can in general be represented by several of the 36 possible maps. The possibilities raise an important question: Is there a well-founded way of choosing one among the 36 possible representations of $\mathbf{F}$?

One possible ground for answering this question is to look at the Jacobian matrix $\mathbf{J}_{i_1 j_1 i_{2,3} j_{2,3}} = \frac{d\mathbf{F}_{i_1 j_1 i_{2,3} j_{2,3}}(\mathbf{f}_7)}{d\mathbf{f}_7}$ for each of the possible maps and to choose the map(s) for which this Jacobian matrix has the highest rank. Since $\mathbf{J}_{i_1 j_1 i_{2,3} j_{2,3}}$ is a 7×9 matrix, this rank is less than or equal to 7. It is therefore natural to choose i_1, j_1, $i_{2,3}$ and $j_{2,3}$ in order to "maximize" the rank of $\mathbf{J}_{i_1 j_1 i_{2,3} j_{2,3}}$. This objective can be achieved by maximizing the norm of the vector $\mathbf{d}_{i_1 j_1 i_{2,3} j_{2,3}}$ whose coordinates are the nonzero determinants of the 7×7 submatrices of $\frac{d\mathbf{F}_{i_1 j_1 i_{2,3} j_{2,3}}(\mathbf{f}_7)}{d\mathbf{f}_7}$, so that the Jacobian would be as "far" as possible from a singular matrix.

According to the previous paragraph and after some calculations, $\mathbf{d}_{i_1 j_1 i_{2,3} j_{2,3}}$ is obtained from the 8-vector

$$(F_{i_2 j_2} F_{i_3 j_3} - F_{i_2 j_3} F_{i_3 j_2})^2 [-\lambda_{j_2}, \lambda_{j_3}, -\mu_{i_2}, \mu_{i_3}, -\mu_{i_2}\lambda_{j_2}, \mu_{i_2}\lambda_{j_3}, \mu_{i_3}\lambda_{j_2}, -\mu_{i_3}\lambda_{j_3}]^T$$

by removing its kth coordinate so that

$$\|\mathbf{d}_{i_1 j_1 i_{2,3} j_{2,3}}\| = (F_{i_2 j_2} F_{i_3 j_3} - F_{i_2 j_3} F_{i_3 j_2})^2$$
$$\sqrt{(\lambda_{j_2}^2 + \lambda_{j_3}^2 + 1)(\mu_{i_2}^2 + \mu_{i_3}^2 + 1) - \mu_{i_{2,3}}^2 \lambda_{j_{2,3}}^2}$$

with $F_{i_{2,3} j_{2,3}} = 1$.

6.3   The distance minimization approach

As a tentative strategy for improving on the eight-point algorithm at the expense of more computation time, we examine a family of methods based on the nonlinear minimization of a distance. The choice of this distance takes care of the difficulties due to the normalization, while the parameterization of the Fundamental matrix ensures that the rank constraint is satisfied. Using the p point correspondences $\mathbf{m}_i \leftrightarrow \mathbf{m}'_i$, $1 \le i \le p$, the principle of these methods is as follows.

1. Apply a linear method to obtain a Fundamental matrix $\mathbf{F}_L$.

2. Compute the seven parameters $\mathbf{f}_I$ such that the matrix $\mathbf{F}(\mathbf{f}_I)$ minimizes $\|\mathbf{F}_L - \mathbf{F}(\mathbf{f}_I)\|$.

3. Using $\mathbf{F}(\mathbf{f}_I)$ as a starting point, minimize the nonlinear error function with respect to the vector $\mathbf{f}$ of parameters:

$$\min_{\mathbf{f}} \sum_{i=1}^{p} d^2 \left(\mathbf{F}(\mathbf{f}), \mathbf{m}_i, \mathbf{m}'_i\right),$$

where d is a distance in measurement space.

Parameterizations were discussed in Section 6.2.

The distance minimization approach was introduced in (Luong, 1992; Luong and Faugeras, 1996). It has proven to be one of the most reliable algorithms for the estimation of the Fundamental matrix.

6.3.1   The distance to epipolar lines

We now introduce a new error function that is based on the idea that we would like to minimize a geometrically meaningful quantity. The idea is to use a non-quadratic error function and to minimize

$$\sum_{i} d^2 \left(\mathbf{m}'_i, \mathbf{F}\mathbf{m}_i\right).$$

However, unlike in the case of the linear criterion, the two images do not play symmetric roles since this function deals only with the epipolar lines in the second image. It is therefore necessary (and natural) to use the error function

$$\sum_{i} \left(d^2 \left(\mathbf{m}'_i, \mathbf{F}\mathbf{m}_i\right) + d^2 \left(\mathbf{m}_i, \mathbf{F}^T \mathbf{m}'_i\right)\right) \tag{6.10}$$

in which the two images play the same role and which can be written

$$\sum_{i} \left(\frac{1}{(\mathbf{F}\mathbf{m}_i)_1^2 + (\mathbf{F}\mathbf{m}_i)_2^2} + \frac{1}{(\mathbf{F}^T\mathbf{m}'_i)_1^2 + (\mathbf{F}^T\mathbf{m}'_i)_2^2}\right) \left(\mathbf{m}'^T_i \mathbf{F}\mathbf{m}_i\right)^2, \tag{6.11}$$

using the fact that $\mathbf{m}'^T_i \mathbf{F}\mathbf{m}_i = \mathbf{m}^T_i \mathbf{F}^T \mathbf{m}'_i$. It can be observed that this criterion does not depend on the scale factor used to compute $\mathbf{F}$.

6.3.2 The Gradient criterion and an interpretation as a distance

Taking into account pixel uncertainty Pixels are measured with some uncertainty. When minimizing the expression in (6.2), we have a sum of terms $C_i = \mathbf{m}_i'^T \mathbf{F} \mathbf{m}_i$ which have different variances. It is natural to weight them so that the contribution of each of these terms to the total criterion will be inversely proportional to its variance. The variance of C_i is given as a function of the variance of the points $\mathbf{m}_i$ and $\mathbf{m}_i'$ by

$$\sigma^2_{C_i} = \left[\begin{array}{cc} \frac{\partial C_i^T}{\partial \mathbf{m}_i} & \frac{\partial C_i^T}{\partial \mathbf{m}_i'} \end{array} \right] \left[\begin{array}{cc} \Lambda_{\mathbf{m}_i} & \mathbf{0} \\ \mathbf{0} & \Lambda_{\mathbf{m}_i'} \end{array} \right] \left[\begin{array}{c} \frac{\partial C_i}{\partial \mathbf{m}_i} \\ \frac{\partial C_i}{\partial \mathbf{m}_i'} \end{array} \right], \tag{6.12}$$

where $\Lambda_{\mathbf{m}_i}$ and $\Lambda_{\mathbf{m}_i'}$ are the covariance matrices of the points $\mathbf{m}$ and $\mathbf{m}'$, respectively. These points are uncorrelated as they are measured in different images. We make the classical assumption that their covariance is isotropic and uniform, that is,

$$\Lambda_{\mathbf{m}_i} = \Lambda_{\mathbf{m}_i'} = \left[\begin{array}{cc} \sigma & 0 \\ 0 & \sigma \end{array} \right].$$

Equation 6.12 reduces to

$$\sigma^2_{C_i} = \sigma^2 \|\nabla C_i\|^2$$

, where ∇C_i denotes the gradient of C_i with respect to the four-dimensional vector $(u_i, v_i, u_i', v_i')^T$ built from the affine coordinates of the points $\mathbf{m}_i$ and $\mathbf{m}_i'$. Thus,

$$\nabla C_i = \left(\left(\mathbf{F}^T \mathbf{m}_i'\right)_1, \left(\mathbf{F}^T \mathbf{m}_i'\right)_2, \left(\mathbf{F} \mathbf{m}_i\right)_1, \left(\mathbf{F} \mathbf{m}_i\right)_2 \right)^T.$$

We obtain the criterion

$$\sum_i \frac{(\mathbf{m}_i'^T \mathbf{F} \mathbf{m}_i)^2}{(\mathbf{F}\mathbf{m}_i)_1^2 + (\mathbf{F}\mathbf{m}_i)_2^2 + (\mathbf{F}^T\mathbf{m}_i')_1^2 + (\mathbf{F}^T\mathbf{m}_i')_2^2}, \tag{6.13}$$

which is also independent of the scale factor chosen for $\mathbf{F}$. We can note that there is a similarity between this criterion and the distance criterion (6.11). Each of its terms has the form $\frac{1}{k^2+k'^2}C$, whereas the first one has terms $(\frac{1}{k^2} + \frac{1}{k'^2})C$.

Interpretation as a distance We can also consider the problem of computing the Fundamental matrix from the definition (5.4) in the general framework of surface fitting. The surface $\mathcal{S}$ is modeled by the implicit equation $g(\mathbf{x}, \mathbf{f}) = 0$, where $\mathbf{f}$ is the sought parameter vector describing the surface which best fits the data points $\mathbf{x}_i$. The goal is to minimize a quantity $\sum_i d(\mathbf{x}_i, \mathcal{S})^2$, where d is a distance. In our case, the data points are the vectors $\mathbf{x}_i = (u_i, v_i, u_i', v_i')$, $\mathbf{f}$ is one of the 7 dimensional parameterizations introduced in the previous section, and g is given by (5.4). The linear criterion can be considered as a generalization of the Bookstein distance (Bookstein, 1979) for conic fitting. The idea is to approximate the true distance of the point $\mathbf{x}$ to the surface by the number $g(\mathbf{x}, \mathbf{f})$ in order to obtain a closed-form solution. A more precise approximation has been introduced by Sampson (Sampson, 1982). It is based on the first-order approximation

$$g(\mathbf{x}) \approx g(\mathbf{x}_0) + (\mathbf{x} - \mathbf{x}_0) \cdot \nabla g(\mathbf{x}) = g(\mathbf{x}_0) + \|\mathbf{x} - \mathbf{x}_0\| \, \|\nabla g(\mathbf{x})\| \cos(\mathbf{x} - \mathbf{x}_0, \nabla g(\mathbf{x})).$$

If $\mathbf{x}_0$ is the point of $\mathcal{S}$ which is the nearest to $\mathbf{x}$, we have the two properties $g(\mathbf{x}_0) = 0$ and $\cos(\mathbf{x} - \mathbf{x}_0, \nabla g(\mathbf{x}_0)) = 1$. If we make the further first-order approximation that the gradient has the same direction at $\mathbf{x}$ and at $\mathbf{x}_0$: $\cos(\mathbf{x} - \mathbf{x}_0, \nabla g(\mathbf{x}_0)) \approx \cos(\mathbf{x} - \mathbf{x}_0, \nabla g(\mathbf{x}))$, we obtain

$$d(\mathbf{x}, \mathcal{S}) = \|\mathbf{x} - \mathbf{x}_0\| \approx \frac{g(\mathbf{x})}{\|\nabla g(\mathbf{x})\|}.$$

It is now obvious that the criterion (6.13) can be written $\sum_i d(\mathbf{x}_i, \mathcal{S})^2$.

It would be possible to use a second-order approximation such as the one introduced by Nalwa and Pauchon (Nalwa and Pauchon, 1987); however, the experimental results presented later show that it would not be very useful practically.

6.3.3 The "optimal" method

Optimal methods, in the statistical sense of "maximal likelihood", are known in the literature of structure from motion analysis (Weng et al., 1993). They are closely related to photogrammetric reprojection methods or bundle adjustment (Slama, 1980), where the structure is estimated along with the relative displacement of the cameras. We will return to these methods in Chapter 10.

Given the point correspondences $\mathbf{m}_i \leftrightarrow \mathbf{m}_i'$, $1 \le i \le p$, under the assumption that errors on $\mathbf{m}_i$ and $\mathbf{m}_i'$ are independent but equal Gaussian perturbations, the maximum likelihood estimate of the Fundamental matrix is obtained as the rank two matrix $\mathbf{F}$ with *exactly* satisfies the epipolar constraints $\hat{\mathbf{m}}_i'^T \mathbf{F} \hat{\mathbf{m}}_i = 0$ while minimizing the sum of squared distances $\sum_i \{d^2(\mathbf{m}_i, \hat{\mathbf{m}}_i) + d^2(\mathbf{m}_i', \hat{\mathbf{m}}_i')\}$ of the "true" points $\hat{\mathbf{m}}_i, \hat{\mathbf{m}}_i'$ to the observed points. That is, we estimate not only $\mathbf{F}$, but also the most likely true positions $\hat{\mathbf{m}}_i, \hat{\mathbf{m}}_i'$. Because of the epipolar constraint, there are $4 - 1$ degrees of freedom for each point correspondence, so the total number of parameters is $3p + 7$.

Despite this very large number of parameters, the particular structure of the problem allows for a tractable solution, thanks to techniques already used in (Slama, 1980). In detail, the problem can be alternatively formulated as

$$\min_{\mathbf{f}, \mathbf{M}_1, \ldots, \mathbf{M}_p} \sum_i \{d^2(\mathbf{m}_i, \mathcal{P}(\mathbf{f})\mathbf{M}_i) + d^2(\mathbf{m}_i', \mathcal{P}'(\mathbf{f})\mathbf{M}_i)\}, \qquad (6.14)$$

where $\mathbf{f}$ is a vector of parameters for $\mathbf{F}$, $\{\mathbf{M}_i\}$ are the 3D coordinates of the points in space, and $\mathcal{P}(\mathbf{f}), \mathcal{P}'(\mathbf{f})$ are the perspective projection matrices in the first and second images, given the Fundamental matrix $\mathbf{F}(\mathbf{f})$. These matrices, as well as the 3D coordinates $\{\mathbf{M}_i\}$ are determined only up to a projective transformation of space, as discussed in Chapter 7. Note that each term of the sum depends only on the point $\mathbf{M}_i$. Given the "motion" parameters $\mathbf{f}$, the "structure" parameters $\mathbf{M}_i$ that minimize the criterion in Equation 6.14 can be estimated by performing a projective reconstruction. As explained in Chapter 7, there are several methods for performing this task, which involve relatively fast computations involving at most 3 parameters. Therefore, the method remains tractable because the estimation of the Fundamental matrix parameters $\mathbf{f}$ can be decoupled from the estimation of the parameters $\mathbf{M}_i$: Since the optimal parameters $\mathbf{M}_i$ can be determined from the parameters $\mathbf{f}$, we have to minimize only over $\mathbf{f}$. At each iteration, we have to perform the projective reconstruction of p points. The problem can be rewritten as

$$\min_{\mathbf{f}} \left\{ \sum_i \min_{\mathbf{M}_i} \left(d^2(\mathbf{m}_i, \mathcal{P}(\mathbf{f})\mathbf{M}_i) + d^2(\mathbf{m}'_i, \mathcal{P}'(\mathbf{f})\mathbf{M}_i) \right) \right\}.$$

This formulation makes it clear that the criterion which is minimized is a distance between measured points and *reprojected points*, a classical error measure in Computer Vision. It is mentioned in (Hartley, 1997c) that this method gives very good results. However, despite the simplification that we mention, it is considerably more computationally expensive than the other methods described in this chapter.

6.4   Robust Methods

Until now, we assumed that point matches were given. They can be obtained by techniques such as correlation and relaxation (Zhang et al., 1995). Such techniques exploit some *heuristics* in one form or another, for example, intensity similarity or rigid/affine transformation in image plane, which are not applicable to all cases. Among the matches established, we may find two types of *outliers* due to

Bad locations In the estimation of the Fundamental matrix, the location error of a point of interest is assumed to exhibit Gaussian behavior. This assumption is reasonable since the error in localization for most points of interest is small (within one or two pixels), but a few points are possibly incorrectly localized (more than three pixels away). The latter points will severely degrade the accuracy of the estimation.

False matches In the establishment of correspondences, only heuristics have been used. Because the only geometric constraint, i.e. the epipolar constraint, in terms of the *Fundamental matrix*, is not yet available, many matches are possibly false. These errors will ruin the estimation process and the final estimate of the Fundamental matrix.

The outliers will severely hurt the precision of the Fundamental matrix if we directly apply the methods described above, which are all least-squares techniques.

Least-squares estimators assume that the noise corrupting the data has zero mean, which yields an *unbiased* parameter estimate. If the noise variance is known, a *minimum-variance* parameter estimate can be obtained by choosing appropriate weights on the data. Furthermore, least-squares estimators implicitly assume that the entire set of data can be interpreted by *only one parameter vector* of a given model. Numerous studies have been conducted which clearly show that least-squares estimators are vulnerable to the violation of these assumptions. Sometimes even when the data contains only one bad datum, least-squares estimates may be completely perturbed. During the last three decades, many robust techniques have been proposed which are not very sensitive to departure from the assumptions on which they depend.

Recently, computer vision researchers have paid much attention to the robustness of vision algorithms because the data are unavoidably error prone (Haralick, 1986; Zhuang et al., 1992). Many so-called *robust regression* methods have been proposed that are not so easily affected by outliers (Huber, 1981; Rousseeuw and Leroy, 1987). The reader is referred to (Rousseeuw and Leroy, 1987, chapter 1) for a review of different robust methods. The two most important robust methods are the *M-estimators* and the *least-median-of-squares* (LMedS) method, which will be presented below. More details together with a description of other parameter estimation techniques commonly used in computer vision are provided in (Zhang, 1998a).

6.4.1   M-Estimators

Let r_i be the *residual* of the ith datum, i.e. the difference between the ith observation and its fitted value. For example, in the case of the linear methods described in Section 6.1, $r_i = \mathbf{m}_i^{'T}\mathbf{F}\mathbf{m}_i$. In the case of the nonlinear methods described in Section 6.3 $r_i^2 = d^2(\mathbf{m}_i', \mathbf{F}\mathbf{m}_i) + d^2(\mathbf{m}_i, \mathbf{F}^T\mathbf{m}_i')$.

The standard least-squares method tries to minimize $\sum_i r_i^2$, which is unstable if there are outliers present in the data. Outlying data give an effect so strong in the minimization that the parameters thus estimated are distorted. The M-estimators try to reduce the effect of outliers by replacing the squared residuals r_i^2 by another function of the residuals, yielding the error function

$$\min_{\mathbf{f}} \sum_i \rho(r_i) \,, \tag{6.15}$$

where ρ is a symmetric, positive function with a unique minimum at zero and is chosen to be growing slower than the square function. $\mathbf{f} = [f_1, \ldots, f_q]^T$ is the parameter vector to be estimated (in the case of the Fundamental matrix, $q = 7$). Instead of solving problem (6.15) directly, it is more efficient in practice to solve a sequence of reweighted least-squares problems.

The M-estimator of $\mathbf{f}$ based on the function $\rho(r_i)$ is a vector $\mathbf{f}$ which is a solution of the system of q equations

$$\sum_i \psi(r_i) \frac{\partial r_i}{\partial f_j} = 0 , \quad \text{for } j = 1, \ldots, q, \tag{6.16}$$

where the derivative $\psi(x) = \mathrm{d}\rho(x)/\mathrm{d}x$ is called the *influence function*. If we now define a *weight function*

$$w(x) = \frac{\psi(x)}{x} , \tag{6.17}$$

then Equation 6.16 becomes

$$\sum_i w(r_i) r_i \frac{\partial r_i}{\partial f_j} = 0 , \quad \text{for } j = 1, \ldots, q. \tag{6.18}$$

This system of equations is exactly what we obtain if we solve the iterated reweighted least-squares problem

$$\min_{\mathbf{f}} \sum_i w\left(r_i^{k-1}\right) r_i^2 \quad k \geq 1 , \tag{6.19}$$

where the superscript $^{(k)}$ indicates the iteration number. The weight $w(r_i^{(k-1)})$ should be recomputed after each iteration in order to be used in the next iteration.

The influence function $\psi(x)$ measures the influence of a datum on the value of the parameter estimate. For example, for the least-squares with $\rho(x) = x^2/2$, the influence function is $\psi(x) = x$, that is, the influence of a datum on the estimate increases linearly with the size of its error, which confirms the non-robustness of the least-squares estimate. When an estimator is robust, it may be inferred that the influence of any single observation (datum) is insufficient to yield any significant offset (Rey, 1983).

There have been a number of different M-estimators proposed in the literature. The reader is referred to (Zhang, 1998a) for a comprehensive review.

It seems difficult to select a ρ-function for general use without being rather arbitrary. The results reported in Section 6.5 use the Tukey function:

$$\rho(r_i) = \begin{cases} \dfrac{(c\sigma)^2}{6} \left(1 - \left[1 - \left(\dfrac{r_i}{c\sigma}\right)^2\right]^3\right) & \text{if } |r_i| \leq c\sigma \\ (c\sigma)^2/6 & \text{otherwise,} \end{cases}$$

where σ is some estimated standard deviation of errors and $c = 4.6851$ is the tuning constant. The corresponding weight function is

$$w_i = \begin{cases} \left[1 - \left(\dfrac{r_i}{c\sigma}\right)^2\right]^2 & \text{if } |r_i| \leq c\sigma \\ 0 & \text{otherwise.} \end{cases}$$

Another commonly used function is the tri-weight function

$$w_i = \begin{cases} 1 & |r_i| \leq \sigma \\ \sigma/|r_i| & \sigma < |r_i| \leq 3\sigma \\ 0 & 3\sigma < |r_i| . \end{cases}$$

In (Olsen, 1992; Luong, 1992), this weight function was used for the estimation of the epipolar geometry.

Inherent in the different M-estimators is the simultaneous estimation of σ, the standard deviation of the residual errors. If we can adequately estimate the standard deviation of the errors of good data (inliers), then data whose error is larger than a certain number of standard deviations can be considered as outliers. Thus, the estimation of σ itself should be robust.

The results of the M-estimators will depend on the method used to compute them. The *robust standard deviation* estimate is related to the median of the absolute values of the residuals, and is given by

$$\hat{\sigma} = 1.4826[1 + 5/(p - q)] \; \underset{i}{\text{median}} \, |r_i| . \tag{6.20}$$

The constant 1.4826 is a coefficient used to achieve the same efficiency as a least-squares in the presence of only Gaussian noise: The median of the absolute values of random numbers sampled from the Gaussian normal distribution $N(0, 1)$ is equal to $\Phi^{-1}(\frac{3}{4}) \approx 1/1.4826$. $5/(p - q)$, where p is the size of the data set and q is the dimension of the parameter vector, compensates for the effect of a small set of data. The reader is referred to (Rousseeuw and Leroy, 1987, page 202) for the details of these magic numbers.

Our experience shows that M-estimators are robust to outliers due to bad localization. They are, however, not robust to false matches because they depend heavily on the initial guess, which is usually obtained by least-squares. This attribute leads us to use other more robust techniques.

6.4.2   Monte-Carlo methods

The random sampling consensus (RANSAC), introduced in the field of image understanding by Fischler and Bolles (Fischler and Bolles, 1981), is an early robust method designed to eliminate outliers. In the usual methods, the largest data set is used to obtain an initial solution by computing the unknown parameters with an averaging operator. By contrast, the RANSAC method uses initial minimal data sets of size large enough to allow for the computation of the parameters and then enlarges these sets by incorporating data consistent with the parameters computed from the initial data set. A number of m initial sets are obtained by random sampling. The best solution is the one which generates the biggest consensus set.

One difficulty with this algorithm is that a compatibility threshold σ has to be preset. By contrast, the least-median-of-squares (LMedS) method (Rousseeuw and Leroy, 1987), introduced in the field of estimation, although very related to the previous one, does not require such a threshold. It estimates the parameters by solving the nonlinear minimization problem

$$\min_{\mathbf{f}} \ \operatorname*{median}_{i} \ r_i^2 \ .$$

That is, the estimates must yield the smallest value for the median of squared residuals computed for the entire data set. The median is a more robust estimator than the mean, which is classically used. Unlike the M-estimators, the LMedS problem cannot be reduced to a weighted least-squares problem because there is no analytical way to compute the median. It must be solved by a search in the space of possible estimates generated from the data. Since this space is too large, only a randomly chosen subset of data can be analyzed.

The two algorithms are rather computationally expensive because a relatively large sampling (typically more than 100 samples) must be performed to have a large probability to obtain a subset of data with no outliers. They have the rather similar structure described next.

Given p point correspondences: $\{(\mathbf{m}_i, \mathbf{m}_i')|i = 1, \ldots, p\}$, we proceed through the following steps.

1. A Monte Carlo type technique is used to draw m random subsamples of $q = 7$ different point correspondences (recall that 7 is the minimum number required to determine the epipolar geometry).

2. For each subsample, indexed by J, we use the technique described in Proposition 5.14 to compute the Fundamental matrix $\mathbf{F}_J$. We may have at most 3 solutions.

3. For each $\mathbf{F}_J$, compute the residual distances r_i for each of the p correspondences. If we use the LMedS method, then we compute the median, denoted by M_J, of the squared residuals:

$$M_J = \operatorname*{median}_{i=1,\ldots,p} \left[d^2(\mathbf{m}_i', \mathbf{F}_J \mathbf{m}_i) + d^2(\mathbf{m}_i, \mathbf{F}_J^T \mathbf{m}_i') \right] \ .$$

If we use RANSAC, then we compute the consistent correspondences, i.e. those for which $r_i^2 < \sigma^2$.

4. If we use the LMedS method, then we retain the estimate $\mathbf{F}_J$ for which M_J is minimal among all m M_J's. If we use RANSAC, then we keep the sample J that yields the largest consistent set.

An important question in relation to these method is the determination of the number m of random samples.

A subsample is "good" if it consists of q correct correspondences. Assuming that the whole set of correspondences may contain up to a fraction ε of outliers, the probability that at least one of the m subsamples is good is given by

$$P = 1 - [1 - (1-\varepsilon)^q]^m . \tag{6.21}$$

Indeed, $(1-\varepsilon)^q$ is the probability that a sample of q correspondences does not contain any outlier, and $[1 - (1-\varepsilon)^q]^m$ is the probability that all m samples contain at least one outlier. By requiring that P be near 1, one can determine m for given values of q and ε:

$$m = \frac{\log(1-P)}{\log[1 - (1-\varepsilon)^q]} .$$

In the results shown in Section 6.5, we take $\varepsilon = 40\%$ and require that $P = 0.99$; thus $m = 163$. Note that the algorithm can be sped up considerably by means of parallel computing because the processing for each subsample can be done independently.

Experiments in (Torr and Murray, 1997) have shown that the two methods give comparable results, with RANSAC having a slight edge when an estimate of the standard deviation is available. Compared to the M-estimators, the improvement is considerable, as also noted by (Zhang et al., 1995). However, further improvements are obtained by rerunning a weighted least-squares procedure.

The *robust standard deviation* estimate is given by (6.20); that is,

$$\hat{\sigma} = 1.4826[1 + 5/(p-q)]\sqrt{M_J} ,$$

where M_J is the minimal median estimated by the LMedS. Based on $\hat{\sigma}$, we can assign a weight for each correspondence:

$$w_i = \begin{cases} 1 & \text{if } r_i^2 \le (2.5\hat{\sigma})^2 \\ 0 & \text{otherwise. ,} \end{cases}$$

The correspondences having $w_i = 0$ are outliers and should not be further taken into account. We thus conduct an additional step:

5. Refine the Fundamental matrix **F** by solving the weighted least-squares problem

$$\min_{\mathbf{f}} \sum_i w_i r_i^2 .$$

The Fundamental matrix is now robustly and accurately estimated because outliers have been detected and discarded by the RANSAC or LMedS method.

In order for the Monte-Carlo technique to work, the seven points in each random sample should be well-scattered over the whole images. However, the seven points of a subsample thus generated may be very close to each other. Such a situation should be avoided because the estimation of the epipolar geometry from such points is highly instable and the result is useless. It is a waste of time to evaluate such a subsample. In order to achieve higher stability and efficiency, a *regularly random selection method* based on bucketing techniques can be used (Zhang et al., 1995).

6.5   An example of Fundamental matrix estimation with comparison

We show an example of the results obtained by some of the previously described methods on a stereo pair. The implementation was done by Zhang for a review of Fundamental matrix estimation methods (Zhang, 1998a). The pair of images is a pair of calibrated stereo images (see Figure 6.2). By "calibrated" we mean that the intrinsic parameters of both cameras and the displacement between them have been computed off-line through standard stereo calibration (see for example (Faugeras, 1993)).

There are 241 point matches which are established automatically by the technique described in (Zhang et al., 1995). Outliers have been discarded. The calibrated parameters of the cameras are of course not used, but the Fundamental matrix computed from these parameters serves as a ground truth. Figure 6.3 shows four pairs of epipolar lines, corresponding, from left to right, to the point matches labelled 1, 220, 0 and 183, respectively. The intersections of these lines are the two epipoles, which are clearly very far from the images since the two retinal planes are almost the same.

Figure 6.2: Image pair used for comparing different estimation techniques of the Fundamental matrix

The epipolar geometry estimated with the linear method is shown in Figure 6.4 for the same set of point matches. The epipoles are now in the images, which is a completely different result than the ground truth result. If we perform a data normalization before applying the linear method, then the result is considerably improved, as shown in Figure 6.5. This result is visually very close to the ground

Figure 6.3: Epipolar geometry estimated through classical stereo calibration, which serves as the ground truth.

truth one.

The nonlinear method gives an even better result, as shown in Figure 6.6. A comparison with the "true" epipolar geometry is shown in Figure 6.7. There is only a small difference in the orientation of the epipolar lines.

Table 6.1: Comparison of different methods for estimating the fundamental matrix.

Method	$\Delta \mathbf{F}$	$\mathbf{e}$		$\mathbf{e}'$		RMS	CPU
Calib.		5138.18	-8875.85	1642.02	-2528.91	0.99	
linear	5.85%	304.018	124.039	256.219	230.306	3.40	0.13s
normal.	7.20%	-3920.6	7678.71	8489.07	-15393.5	0.89	0.15s
nonlinear	0.92%	8135.03	-14048.3	1896.19	-2917.11	0.87	0.38s
gradient	0.92%	8166.05	-14104.1	1897.80	-2920.12	0.87	0.40s
M-estim.	0.12%	4528.94	-7516.3	1581.19	-2313.72	0.87	1.05s
reproj.	0.92%	8165.05	-14102.3	1897.74	-2920.01	0.87	19.1s
LMedS	0.13%	3919.12	-6413.1	1500.21	-2159.65	0.75	2.40s

Quantitative results are provided in Table 6.1. The estimated Fundamental matrices are normalized by their Frobenius norm. The elements in the first column indicate the methods used in estimating the Fundamental matrix: The classical stereo calibration (**Calib.**), the linear method described in Section 6.1 (**linear**), the linear method with the prior data normalization described in Section 6.1.1

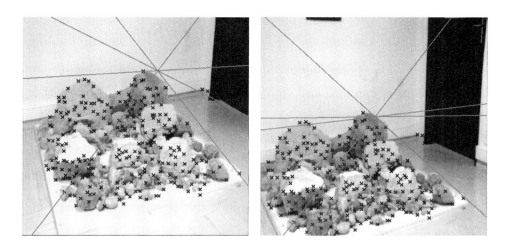

Figure 6.4: Epipolar geometry estimated with the linear method.

(**normal.**), the nonlinear method described in Section 6.3 based on the minimization of the distances between points and epipolar lines (**nonlinear**), the nonlinear method described in Section 6.3.2 based on the minimization of gradient-weighted epipolar errors (**gradient**), the M-estimator with the Tukey function described in Section 6.4.1 (**M-estim.**), the nonlinear method based on the minimization of distances between observed points and reprojected ones described in Section 6.3.3 (**reproj.**), and the LMedS technique described in Section 6.4.2 (**LMedS**). The Fundamental matrix of **Calib.** is used as a reference.

The second column shows the difference between the Fundamental matrix estimated by each method and that estimated by **Calib**. The difference is measured as the Frobenius norm $\Delta \mathbf{F} = \|\mathbf{F} - \mathbf{F_{Calib}}\| \times 100\%$. Since each $\mathbf{F}$ is normalized by its Frobenius norm, $\Delta \mathbf{F}$ is directly related to the angle between two unit vectors. It can be seen that although we have observed that method **normal** has considerably improved the result of the linear method, its $\Delta \mathbf{F}$ is the largest. It seems that $\Delta \mathbf{F}$ is not appropriate to measure the difference between two Fundamental matrices. We will describe another measure in the next section.

The third and fourth columns show the positions of the two epipoles. The fifth column gives the root of the mean of squared distances between points and their epipolar lines. We can see that even with **Calib.**, the RMS is as high as 1 pixel. There are two possibilities: either the stereo system is not very well calibrated, or the points are not well localized; we believe the latter is the major reason because the corner detector we use only extracts points within pixel precision. The last column shows the approximate CPU time in seconds when the program is run on a Sparc 20 workstation. **Nonlinear**, **gradient** and **reproj** give essentially the

Figure 6.5: Epipolar geometry estimated with the linear method with prior data normalization.

same result, although **reproj** is much more time consuming. The M-estimator and LMedS techniques give the best results since the influence of poorly localized points has been reduced in M-estimator and such points are simply discarded in LMedS. Actually, LMedS has detected five outliers. Of course, these two methods are more time consuming than the nonlinear method.

From the above discussion, it appears that the Frobenius norm of the difference between two normalized Fundamental matrices is clearly not an appropriate measure of comparison. In the following, we describe a measure which characterizes well the difference between two Fundamental matrices. Let the two fundamental matrices be $\mathbf{F}_1$ and $\mathbf{F}_2$. The measure is computed as follows (see Figure 6.8).

Step 1: Choose *randomly* a point $\mathbf{m}$ in the first image.

Step 2: Draw the epipolar line of $\mathbf{m}$ in the second image using $\mathbf{F}_1$. The line is shown as a dashed line and is defined by $\mathbf{F}_1\mathbf{m}$.

Step 3: If the epipolar line does not intersect the second image, then go to **Step 1**.

Step 4: Choose *randomly* a point $\mathbf{m}'$ on the epipolar line. Note that $\mathbf{m}$ and $\mathbf{m}'$ correspond to each other exactly with respect to $\mathbf{F}_1$.

Step 5: Draw the epipolar line of $\mathbf{m}$ in the second image using $\mathbf{F}_2$, i.e. $\mathbf{F}_2\mathbf{m}$, and compute the distance, denoted by d_1', between point $\mathbf{m}'$ and line $\mathbf{F}_2\mathbf{m}$.

Step 6: Draw the epipolar line of $\mathbf{m}'$ in the first image using $\mathbf{F}_2$, i.e. $\mathbf{F}_2^T\mathbf{m}'$, and compute the distance, denoted by d_1, between point $\mathbf{m}$ and line $\mathbf{F}_2^T\mathbf{m}'$.

Figure 6.6: Epipolar geometry estimated with the nonlinear method.

Step 7: Conduct the same procedure from **Step 2** through **Step 6**, but reversing the roles of $\mathbf{F}_1$ and $\mathbf{F}_2$, and compute d_2 and d'_2.

Step 8: Repeat **Step 1** through **Step 7** N times.

Step 9: Compute the average distance of d's, which is the measure of difference between the two Fundamental matrices.

In this procedure, a random number generator based on the uniform distribution is used. The two Fundamental matrices and the two images play symmetric roles.

Clearly, the measure computed as above, *in pixels*, is physically meaningful because it is defined in the image space in which we observe the surrounding environment. Furthermore, when N tends to infinity, we uniformly sample the whole 3D space visible from the given epipolar geometry. If the image resolution is 512×512 and if we consider a pixel resolution, then the visible 3D space can be approximately sampled by 512^3 points. In our experiment, we set $N = 50000$. Using this method, we can compute the distance between each pair of Fundamental matrices, and we obtain a symmetric matrix. The result is shown in Table 6.2, where only the upper triangle is displayed (because of symmetry). We arrive at the following conclusions.

- The linear method is very bad.

- The linear method with prior data normalization gives quite a reasonable result.

- The nonlinear method based on point-line distances and that based on gradient-weighted epipolar errors give very similar results to those obtained based on

Figure 6.7: Comparison between the epipolar geometry estimated through classical stereo calibration (shown in dark lines) and that estimated with the nonlinear method (shown in grey lines).

minimization of distances between observed points and reprojected ones. The latter should be avoided because it is too time consuming.

- M-estimators or the LMedS method give still better results because they try to limit or eliminate the effect of poorly localized points. The epipolar geometry estimated by LMedS is closer to the one computed through stereo calibration.

The LMedS method should definitely be used if the given set of matches contains false matches.

Table 6.2: Distances between the Fundamental matrices estimated by different techniques.

	linear	normal.	nonlinear	gradient	M-estim.	reproj.	LMedS
Calib.	**116.4**	**5.97**	**2.66**	**2.66**	**2.27**	**2.66**	**1.33**
linear		117.29	115.97	116.40	115.51	116.25	115.91
normal.			4.13	4.12	5.27	4.11	5.89
nonlinear				0.01	1.19	0.01	1.86
gradient					1.19	0.00	1.86
M-estim.						1.20	1.03
reproj.							1.88

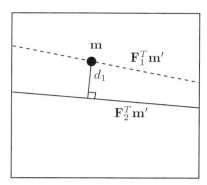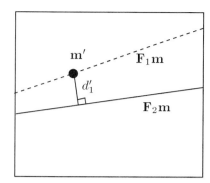

Figure 6.8: Definition of the difference between two Fundamental matrices in terms of image distances.

6.6 Computing the uncertainty of the Fundamental matrix

In this section we investigate the computation of the uncertainty of the Fundamental matrix from an estimate of the uncertainty of the pixels.

We start with a fairly general discussion of the problem of computing the mean and covariance matrix of a random vector $\mathbf{y}$ that is a function of a random vector $\mathbf{x}$ with known mean and covariance. This discussion is similar to the one given in (Faugeras, 1993).

The covariance matrix of $\mathbf{y}$ is defined by the positive symmetric matrix

$$\Lambda_{\mathbf{y}} = E\left[(\mathbf{y} - E[\mathbf{y}])(\mathbf{y} - E[\mathbf{y}])^T\right],\tag{6.22}$$

where $E[\mathbf{y}]$ denotes the mean of the random vector $\mathbf{y}$. We now consider two situations of practical interest regarding the relation between $\mathbf{x}$ and $\mathbf{y}$.

6.6.1 The case of an explicit function

The simplest situation is when $\mathbf{y}$ is an explicit function φ of $\mathbf{x}$. We assume that φ is C^1:

$$\mathbf{y} = \varphi(\mathbf{x}).$$

Writing the first order Taylor expansion of φ in the neighborhood of the mean $E[\mathbf{x}]$ of $\mathbf{x}$ yields

$$\varphi(\mathbf{x}) = \varphi(E[\mathbf{x}]) + D\varphi(E[\mathbf{x}]) \cdot (\mathbf{x} - E[\mathbf{x}]) + \mathcal{O}(x),\tag{6.23}$$

where $D\varphi(E[\mathbf{x}])$ is the Jacobian matrix of φ evaluated at $(E[\mathbf{x}])$. The function $\mathcal{O}(x) = \varphi(\mathbf{x}) - \varphi(E[\mathbf{x}]) - D\varphi(E[\mathbf{x}]) \cdot (\mathbf{x} - E[\mathbf{x}])$ is bounded in each coordinate by $\varepsilon(\|\mathbf{x} - E[\mathbf{x}]\|^2)$ where the function $t \to \varepsilon(t)$ from $\mathbb{R}$ into $\mathbb{R}$ is such that $\lim_{t \to 0} \varepsilon(t) = 0$. By considering now that any realization of $\mathbf{x}$ is sufficiently close to $E[\mathbf{x}]$, we can approximate φ by the first order terms of (6.23) which yields

$$
\begin{aligned}
E[\mathbf{y}] &\approx \varphi(E[\mathbf{x}]) \\
\varphi(\mathbf{x}) - \varphi(E[\mathbf{x}]) &\approx D\varphi(E[\mathbf{x}]) \cdot (\mathbf{x} - E[\mathbf{x}]).
\end{aligned}
$$

We then have

$$
\begin{aligned}
E\left[(\varphi(\mathbf{x}) - \varphi(E[\mathbf{x}]))(\varphi(\mathbf{x}) - \varphi(E[\mathbf{x}]))^T\right] &\approx \\
E\left[D\varphi(E[\mathbf{x}])(\mathbf{x} - E[\mathbf{x}])(\mathbf{x} - E[\mathbf{x}])^T D\varphi(E[\mathbf{x}])^T\right] &= \\
D\varphi(E[\mathbf{x}])E[(\mathbf{x} - E[\mathbf{x}])(\mathbf{x} - E[\mathbf{x}])^T]D\varphi(E[\mathbf{x}])^T,
\end{aligned}
$$

which gives us a first order approximation of the covariance matrix of $\mathbf{y}$ as a simple function of the covariance matrix of $\mathbf{x}$:

$$
\Lambda_{\mathbf{y}} = D\varphi(E[\mathbf{x}])\Lambda_{\mathbf{x}}D\varphi(E[\mathbf{x}])^T. \tag{6.24}
$$

6.6.2   The case of an implicit function

In the cases of interest for this chapter, the relation between $\mathbf{x}$ and $\mathbf{y}$ is implicit, i.e. they are such that $\varphi(\mathbf{x}, \mathbf{y}) = \mathbf{0}$. This situation happens precisely, as shown in the next theorem, when $\mathbf{y}$ is obtained as the minimum with respect to $\mathbf{z}$ of some error function $C(\mathbf{x}, \mathbf{z})$.

We use the well-known implicit functions theorem (see (Spivak, 1979; Faugeras, 1993)).

Proposition 6.1 *Let an error function* $C : \mathbb{R}^m \times \mathbb{R}^q \to \mathbb{R}$ *be a function of class* C^∞, $\mathbf{x}_0 \in \mathbb{R}^m$ *be the measurement vector and* $\mathbf{y}_0 \in \mathbb{R}^q$ *be a local extremum of* $C(\mathbf{x}_0, \mathbf{z})$. *If the Hessian* $\mathbf{H}$ *of* C *with respect to* $\mathbf{z}$ *is invertible at* $(\mathbf{x}, \mathbf{z}) = (\mathbf{x}_0, \mathbf{y}_0)$ *then there exists an open set* U' *of* $\mathbb{R}^m$ *containing* $\mathbf{x}_0$ *and an open set* U'' *of* $\mathbb{R}^q$ *containing* $\mathbf{y}_0$ *and a* C^∞ *mapping* $\varphi : \mathbb{R}^m \to \mathbb{R}^q$ *such that for* $(\mathbf{x}, \mathbf{y})$ *in* $U' \times U''$ *the two relations "$\mathbf{y}$ is a local extremum of* $C(\mathbf{x}, \mathbf{z})$ *with respect to* $\mathbf{z}$ " *and* $\mathbf{y} = \varphi(\mathbf{x})$ *are equivalent. Furthermore, we have the equation*

$$
D\varphi(\mathbf{x}) = -\mathbf{H}^{-1}\frac{\partial \mathbf{\Phi}}{\partial \mathbf{x}}, \tag{6.25}
$$

where $\mathbf{\Phi} = \left(\frac{\partial C}{\partial \mathbf{z}}\right)^T$ *and* $\mathbf{H} = \frac{\partial \mathbf{\Phi}}{\partial \mathbf{z}}$.

Taking $\mathbf{x}_0 = E[\mathbf{x}]$ and $\mathbf{y}_0 = E[\mathbf{y}]$, (6.24) then becomes

$$
\Lambda_{\mathbf{y}} = \mathbf{H}^{-1}\frac{\partial \mathbf{\Phi}}{\partial \mathbf{x}}\Lambda_{\mathbf{x}}\frac{\partial \mathbf{\Phi}}{\partial \mathbf{x}}^T\mathbf{H}^{-T}. \tag{6.26}
$$

As in the previous case, we have obtained a first order approximation of the covariance matrix of $\mathbf{y}$ as a simple function of the covariance matrix of $\mathbf{x}$.

6.6.3   The error function is a sum of squares

In order to get closer to the case of the Fundamental matrix, we study the case where C is of the form

$$\sum_{i=1}^{p} C_i^2(\mathbf{x}_i, \mathbf{z}), \tag{6.27}$$

with $\mathbf{x} = [\mathbf{x}_1^T, \ldots, \mathbf{x}_p^T]^T$. In this case, we have

$$\boldsymbol{\Phi} = 2 \sum_i C_i \frac{\partial C_i}{\partial \mathbf{z}}^T$$

$$\mathbf{H} = \frac{\partial \boldsymbol{\Phi}}{\partial \mathbf{z}} = 2 \sum_i \frac{\partial C_i}{\partial \mathbf{z}}^T \frac{\partial C_i}{\partial \mathbf{z}} + 2 \sum_i C_i \frac{\partial^2 C_i}{\partial \mathbf{z}^2}.$$

It is often possible to neglect the terms $C_i \frac{\partial^2 C_i}{\partial \mathbf{z}^2}$ with respect to the terms $\frac{\partial C_i}{\partial \mathbf{z}}^T \frac{\partial C_i}{\partial \mathbf{z}}$ (see classical books on numerical analysis (Press et al., 1988)). We assume this to be the case and write

$$\mathbf{H} = \frac{\partial \boldsymbol{\Phi}}{\partial \mathbf{z}} \approx 2 \sum_i \frac{\partial C_i}{\partial \mathbf{z}}^T \frac{\partial C_i}{\partial \mathbf{z}}.$$

In the same way we have

$$\frac{\partial \boldsymbol{\Phi}}{\partial \mathbf{x}} \approx 2 \sum_i \frac{\partial C_i}{\partial \mathbf{z}}^T \frac{\partial C_i}{\partial \mathbf{x}},$$

and Equation 6.26 becomes

$$\Lambda_{\mathbf{y}} = 4\mathbf{H}^{-1} \left(\sum_{i,j} \frac{\partial C_i}{\partial \mathbf{z}}^T \frac{\partial C_i}{\partial \mathbf{x}} \Lambda_{\mathbf{x}} \frac{\partial C_j}{\partial \mathbf{x}}^T \frac{\partial C_j}{\partial \mathbf{z}} \right) \mathbf{H}^{-T}. \tag{6.28}$$

We now suppose that the $\mathbf{x}_i$ are independent variables so that $\Lambda_{\mathbf{x}}$ is of the form

$$\begin{bmatrix} \Lambda_{\mathbf{x}_1} & & & \\ & \Lambda_{\mathbf{x}_2} & & \mathbf{0} \\ & & \ddots & \\ \mathbf{0} & & & \Lambda_{\mathbf{x}_p} \end{bmatrix},$$

and Equation 6.28 can be written

$$\Lambda_{\mathbf{y}} = 4\mathbf{H}^{-1} \left(\sum_{i,j,k} \frac{\partial C_i}{\partial \mathbf{z}}^T \frac{\partial C_i}{\partial \mathbf{x}_k} \Lambda_{\mathbf{x}_k} \frac{\partial C_j}{\partial \mathbf{x}_k}^T \frac{\partial C_j}{\partial \mathbf{z}} \right) \mathbf{H}^{-T}$$

$$= 4\mathbf{H}^{-1} \left(\sum_{i} \frac{\partial C_i}{\partial \mathbf{z}}^T \frac{\partial C_i}{\partial \mathbf{x}_i} \Lambda_{\mathbf{x}_i} \frac{\partial C_i}{\partial \mathbf{x}_i}^T \frac{\partial C_i}{\partial \mathbf{z}} \right) \mathbf{H}^{-T}$$

since C_i depends only upon $\mathbf{x}_i$.

By definition, $\sigma_{C_i} = \frac{\partial C_i}{\partial \mathbf{x}_i} \Lambda_{\mathbf{x}_i} \frac{\partial C_i}{\partial \mathbf{x}_i}^T$, and the previous equation becomes

$$\Lambda_{\mathbf{y}} = 4\mathbf{H}^{-1} \left(\sum_{i} \sigma_{C_i} \frac{\partial C_i}{\partial \mathbf{z}}^T \frac{\partial C_i}{\partial \mathbf{z}} \right) \mathbf{H}^{-T}. \tag{6.29}$$

Considering that the mean of C_i at the minimum is zero and under the somewhat strong assumption that the C_i's are independent and identically distributed[1], we can approximate σ_{C_i} by the well known formula (see (Bard, 1974))

$$\frac{C_{min}}{p-q},$$

where $C_{min} = \sum_i C_i(\mathbf{x}_i, \mathbf{y})$. Although it has little influence when p is big, the inclusion of q in the formula above aims to correct the effect of a small sample set. Indeed, for $p = q$, we can usually find an estimate of $\mathbf{y}$ such that $C_i = 0$ for all i, which makes the estimation of the variance using this formula, senseless.

We summarize this discussion in the following proposition.

Proposition 6.2 *Assume that the error function C is of the form (6.27) and that the following four hypotheses are satisfied.*

1. *The terms $C_i \frac{\partial^2 C_i}{\partial \mathbf{z}^2}$ are negligible with respect to the terms $\frac{\partial C_i}{\partial \mathbf{z}}^T \frac{\partial C_i}{\partial \mathbf{z}}$,*

2. *the $\mathbf{x}_i$ are independent random variables,*

3. *the C_i's are independent and identically distributed, and*

4. *the means of the C_i's at the minimum are zero.*

Equation 6.26 can then be simplified as

$$\Lambda_{\mathbf{y}} = \frac{2C_{min}}{p-q} \mathbf{H}^{-1} \mathbf{H} \mathbf{H}^{-T} = \frac{2C_{min}}{p-q} \mathbf{H}^{-T}. \tag{6.30}$$

---

[1]It is under this assumption that the solution given by the least-squares technique is optimal.

6.6.4 The hyper-ellipsoid of uncertainty

Let us see how we can use the previous analyses to represent the uncertainty on $\mathbf{y}$. The idea is to perform a change of variable. We define the random vector χ by

$$\chi = \Lambda_{\mathbf{y}}^{-\frac{1}{2}}(\mathbf{y} - E[\mathbf{y}]).$$

Since we have characterized (up to first order) the random variable $\mathbf{y}$ by its first (the mean) and second order (the covariance matrix) moments, we may as well assume (as an approximation) that it follows a Gaussian distribution. As a consequence, χ also follows a Gaussian distribution with zero mean and covariance:

$$E\left[\chi\chi^T\right] = E\left[\Lambda_{\mathbf{y}}^{-\frac{1}{2}}(\mathbf{y} - E[\mathbf{y}])(\mathbf{y} - E[\mathbf{y}])^T\Lambda_{\mathbf{y}}^{-\frac{1}{2}}\right] = \Lambda_{\mathbf{y}}^{-\frac{1}{2}}\Lambda_{\mathbf{y}}\Lambda_{\mathbf{y}}^{-\frac{1}{2}} = I_r.$$

Consequently, the random variable $\delta_{\mathbf{y}}$ defined by

$$\delta_{\mathbf{y}} = \chi^T\chi = (\mathbf{y} - E[\mathbf{y}])^T\Lambda_{\mathbf{y}}^{-1}(\mathbf{y} - E[\mathbf{y}])$$

follows a χ^2 distribution of r degrees of freedom, where r is the rank of $\Lambda_{\mathbf{y}}$. Given a scalar k, we thus know the probability, equal to $P_{\chi^2}(k, r)$, that $\delta_{\mathbf{y}}$ appears between 0 and k^2. In other words, we have the following proposition.

Proposition 6.3 *If we consider that* $\mathbf{y}$ *follows a Gaussian distribution, then the probability that* $\mathbf{y}$ *lies inside the k-hyper-ellipsoid defined by the equation*

$$(\mathbf{y} - E[\mathbf{y}])^T\Lambda_{\mathbf{y}}^{-1}(\mathbf{y} - E[\mathbf{y}]) = k^2, \tag{6.31}$$

where k is any scalar, is equal to

$$P_{\chi^2}(k, r),$$

where r is the rank of $\Lambda_{\mathbf{y}}$.

The k-hyper-ellipsoid makes it possible to graphically represent the uncertainty related to $\Lambda_{\mathbf{y}}$. We usually restrict ourselves to the two- or three-dimensional case by choosing two or three coordinates of $\mathbf{y}$ and extracting from $\Lambda_{\mathbf{y}}$ the corresponding submatrix in order to draw an ellipse or an ellipsoid.

6.6.5 The case of the Fundamental matrix

As explained in Sections 6.1 and 6.3, $\mathbf{F}$ is computed using a sum of squares of implicit functions of p point correspondences. Thus, referring to the previous paragraph, we have $q = 7$, $m = 4p$ and the error function is $C(\hat{\mathbf{m}}, \mathbf{f}_7)$, where $\hat{\mathbf{m}} = (\mathbf{m}_1, \mathbf{m}'_1, \cdots, \mathbf{m}_p, \mathbf{m}'_p)^T$ and $\mathbf{f}_7$ is the vector described in Section 6.2.1. $\Lambda_{\mathbf{f}_7}$ is thus computed with Equation 6.30 using the Hessian given as a by-product of the minimization of $C(\hat{\mathbf{m}}, \mathbf{f}_7)$.

According to Equation 6.24, $\Lambda_{\mathbf{F}}$ is then deduced from $\Lambda_{\mathbf{f}_7}$:

$$\Lambda_{\mathbf{F}} = \frac{d\mathbf{F}_{i_1 j_1 i_{2,3} j_{2,3}}(\mathbf{f}_7)}{d\mathbf{f}_7} \Lambda_{\mathbf{f}_7} \frac{d\mathbf{F}_{i_1 j_1 i_{2,3} j_{2,3}}(\mathbf{f}_7)}{d\mathbf{f}_7}^T , \qquad (6.32)$$

where $\frac{d\mathbf{F}_{i_1 j_1 i_{2,3} j_{2,3}}(\mathbf{f}_7)}{d\mathbf{f}_7}$ is computing as explained in Section 6.2.

6.7   Some applications of the computation of $\Lambda_{\mathbf{F}}$

Now that we know how to compute $\Lambda_{\mathbf{F}}$ from the measurement uncertainties, we can make good use of it to compute the uncertainty of the epipoles, or of the coefficients of the epipolar homography, or of the tolerance that must be introduced in the process of finding corresponding pixels using the epipolar geometry. We give two examples. Two other examples will be given in Chapter 7 where we will characterize the uncertainty of the projective reconstruction obtained from two views and in Chapter 11 where we will use our estimate of the uncertainty on $\mathbf{F}$ to weight Kruppa's equations.

6.7.1   Uncertainty of the epipoles

Suppose that, according to the notations of Section 6.2.1, we have $j_1 = 1$, $j_2 = 2$, and $j_3 = 3$. The vector $[1, \lambda_{j_2}, \lambda_{j_3}]^T$ is a coordinate vector of the epipole e whose image coordinates form the vector $\mathbf{e} = [1/\lambda_{j_3}, \lambda_{j_2}/\lambda_{j_3}]^T$. Let $\boldsymbol{\lambda} = [\lambda_{j_2}, \lambda_{j_3}]^T$. The covariance matrix $\Lambda_{\boldsymbol{\lambda}}$ of $\boldsymbol{\lambda}$ is a 2×2 submatrix of $\Lambda_{\mathbf{f}_7}$ and the covariance matrix $\Lambda_{\mathbf{e}}$ follows directly from the analysis of Section 6.6.1. Up to first order, we have

$$\Lambda_{\mathbf{e}} = \frac{\partial g(\mathbf{e})}{\partial \mathbf{e}} \Lambda_{\boldsymbol{\lambda}} \frac{\partial g(\mathbf{e})}{\partial \mathbf{e}}^T ,$$

where g is the function $(\lambda_{j_2}, \lambda_{j_3}) \longrightarrow \mathbf{e}$.

To illustrate this computation, Figure 6.9 is a stereo pair for which the camera's displacement is roughly in the direction of the optical axis. Point correspondences have been established between the two views and the matrix $\mathbf{F}$ estimated from those correspondences together with its covariance matrix. Figure 6.10 shows the ellipses of uncertainty of the two epipoles. According to the analysis of Section 6.6.4, we have chosen the value of k in Equation 6.31 in such a way that the probability $P_{\chi^2}(k, 2)$ that the epipole is inside the corresponding ellipse is 75%.

Another example is shown in Figures 6.11 and 6.12. The first one shows two images of Death Valley in California taken from two viewpoints roughly on the same vertical with roughly parallel view directions. The Fundamental matrix has been estimated as in the previous example as well as its covariance matrix. It can be seen in Figure 6.11, which also shows a few corresponding epipolar lines, that the epipoles are far from the images. Figure 6.12 shows their ellipses of uncertainty: The small squares represent the images.

Figure 6.9: A stereo pair with matched points, some epipolar lines, and the epipoles in the middle of the images.

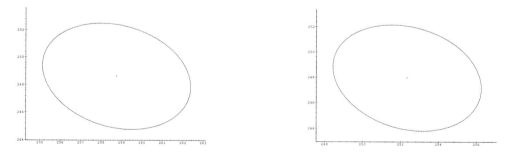

Figure 6.10: The ellipses of uncertainty of the two epipoles in Figure 6.9.

Figure 6.11: Another stereo pair with matched points, some epipolar lines, and the epipoles which, in this case, are way outside the images.

Figure 6.12: The ellipses of uncertainty of the two epipoles in Figure 6.11.

6.7.2 Epipolar Band

Let us consider as a second example the case where we want to exploit the epipolar structure of a pair of images to simplify the correspondence process. Given a pixel in the first image, we know that its corresponding pixel lies on the epipolar line defined by the pixel. The search for that corresponding pixel can therefore be reduced to a search along that line. This situation is the ideal noise-free case. In practice, the given pixel has often been detected through some corner or edge detector and its position is not known exactly. Moreover, the epipolar line is computed by applying the Fundamental matrix to a coordinate vector of the pixel (see Chapter 5) and that Fundamental matrix itself is noisy. A natural question to ask is how should the knowledge of the uncertainty of the pixel and the Fundamental matrix influence the search of the corresponding pixel. We will see that the search should take place in an area of the second image, called the epipolar band, that is delimited by the two branches of a hyperbola.

Let us denote by $\mathbf{m}_0 = [u_0, v_0]^T$ the vector of image coordinates of the given pixel m_0, by $\tilde{\mathbf{m}}_0 = [u_0, v_0, 1]^T$ a coordinate vector of the corresponding projective point. A coordinate vector of the epipolar line l_0 of m_0 is the vector $\tilde{\mathbf{l}}_0 = \mathbf{F}\tilde{\mathbf{m}}_0$. We denote by l_{01}, l_{02}, l_{03} its coordinates. Assuming without loss of generality that $l_{03} \neq 0$, we consider the two-dimensional vector $\mathbf{l}_0 = \left[\frac{l_{01}}{l_{03}}, \frac{l_{02}}{l_{03}} \right]^T$.

We are given the covariance matrices $\Lambda_{\mathbf{m}_0}$ of $\mathbf{m}_0$ and $\Lambda_{\mathbf{F}}$ of $\mathbf{F}$. A repeated application of the result of Section 6.6.1 allows us to compute

$$\Lambda_{\tilde{\mathbf{l}}_0} = \frac{\partial \tilde{\mathbf{l}}_0}{\partial \mathbf{F}} \Lambda_{\mathbf{F}} \frac{\partial \tilde{\mathbf{l}}_0}{\partial \mathbf{F}}^T + \mathbf{F} \Lambda_{\tilde{\mathbf{m}}_0} \mathbf{F}^T,$$

because $\frac{\partial \tilde{\mathbf{l}}_0}{\partial \tilde{\mathbf{m}}_0} = \mathbf{F}$ and

$$\Lambda_{\mathbf{l}_0} = \frac{\partial \mathbf{l}_0}{\partial \tilde{\mathbf{l}}_0} \Lambda_{\tilde{\mathbf{l}}_0} \frac{\partial \mathbf{l}_0}{\partial \tilde{\mathbf{l}}_0}^T.$$

Let us now consider the ellipse of uncertainty $\mathcal{C}$ defined by

$$(\mathbf{l} - \mathbf{l}_0)^T \Lambda_{\mathbf{l}_0}^{-1} (\mathbf{l} - \mathbf{l}_0) = k^2. \tag{6.33}$$

We know from Section 6.6.4 that the interpretation of this ellipse is that the point l has a probability $P_{\chi^2}(k, 2)$ of falling inside that ellipse. That is, the epipolar line of m_0 represented by l has a probability $P_{\chi^2}(k, 2)$ of falling inside the ellipse of uncertainty. This statement is not directly interpretable in the image plane since it is made about a point in the dual plane (see Chapter 2). In order to obtain such an interpretation we will have to call upon the dual conic $\mathcal{C}^*$ of $\mathcal{C}$. This dual conic will allow us to answer the question: Where are in the image plane the lines corresponding to the points in the dual plane inside $\mathcal{C}$?

We first rewrite Equation 6.33 projectively as

$$\tilde{\mathbf{l}}^T \mathbf{A} \tilde{\mathbf{l}} = 0,$$

with

$$\mathbf{A} = \begin{bmatrix} \Lambda_{l_0}^{-1} & -\Lambda_{l_0}^{-1}\mathbf{l}_0 \\ -\mathbf{l}_0^T\Lambda_{l_0}^{-T} & \mathbf{l}_0^T\Lambda_{l_0}^{-1}\mathbf{l}_0 - k^2 \end{bmatrix}. \tag{6.34}$$

Because $\mathcal{C}$ is an ellipse, the determinant of $\Lambda_{l_0}^{-1}$ is positive.

The dual conic $\mathcal{C}^*$ of $\mathcal{C}$ is defined by the adjoint $\mathbf{A}^*$ of matrix $\mathbf{A}$. The following lemma is needed in the proof of Proposition 6.4.

Lemma 6.1 *Let* $\mathbf{A}$ *be a symmetric* 3×3 *matrix of rank 3 which we write*

$$\mathbf{A} = \begin{bmatrix} \mathbf{B} & \mathbf{b} \\ \mathbf{b}^T & c \end{bmatrix},$$

where $\mathbf{B}$ *is a symmetric* 2×2 *matrix of rank 2,* $\mathbf{b}$ *a* 2×1 *vector and* c *a scalar. Then the relation*

$$c - \mathbf{b}^T\mathbf{B}^{-1}\mathbf{b} = \frac{det(\mathbf{A})}{det(\mathbf{B})}$$

is true.

Proof : The proof is left to the reader. The only slight difficulty is the use of the formula $\mathbf{B}\mathbf{B}^* = \det(\mathbf{B})\mathbf{I}_2$. □

We are now ready to prove the following proposition.

Proposition 6.4 *Let* $\mathcal{C}$ *be the ellipse defined by the matrix* $\mathbf{A}$ *of Equation 6.34 and* $\mathcal{C}^*$ *its dual conic defined by the adjoint matrix* $\mathbf{A}^*$. *A line* l^* *intersects* $\mathcal{C}^*$ *in two real points, one real point, and two imaginary points if and only if its dual* l *is respectively outside, on, or inside* $\mathcal{C}$.

Proof : Let l^* be defined by the two points m_1 and m_2. The points of intersection of the line $l^* = (m_1, m_2)$ with the conic $\mathcal{C}^*$ are obtained by solving the quadratic equation in θ

$$(\mathbf{m}_1 + \theta\mathbf{m}_2)^T\mathbf{A}^*(\mathbf{m}_1 + \theta\mathbf{m}_2) = 0.$$

The discriminant of this equation is proportional to

$$\Delta = \left(\mathbf{m}_1^T\mathbf{A}^*\mathbf{m}_2\right)^2 - \left(\mathbf{m}_1^T\mathbf{A}^*\mathbf{m}_1\right)\left(\mathbf{m}_2^T\mathbf{A}^*\mathbf{m}_2\right). \tag{6.35}$$

We now look for the condition that a point l in the dual plane represented by $\tilde{\mathbf{l}} = [l_1, l_2, 1]^T$ is inside $\mathcal{C}$. Since $\mathcal{C}$ separates the plane into two regions, one for which $\tilde{\mathbf{l}}^T\mathbf{A}\tilde{\mathbf{l}} > 0$ and one for which $\tilde{\mathbf{l}}^T\mathbf{A}\tilde{\mathbf{l}} < 0$, it suffices to compare the signs of $\tilde{\mathbf{l}}^T\mathbf{A}\tilde{\mathbf{l}}$ and $\tilde{\mathbf{l}}_0^T\mathbf{A}\tilde{\mathbf{l}}_0$: l is inside, on, and outside $\mathcal{C}$, respectively, if and only if $\left(\tilde{\mathbf{l}}^T\mathbf{A}\tilde{\mathbf{l}}\right)\left(\tilde{\mathbf{l}}_0^T\mathbf{A}\tilde{\mathbf{l}}_0\right)$ is positive, null, or negative, respectively.

We use Lemma 6.1 to prove that

$$-k^2 = \tilde{\mathbf{l}}_0^T\mathbf{A}\tilde{\mathbf{l}}_0 = \frac{\det(\mathbf{A})}{\det\left(\Lambda_{l_0}^{-1}\right)}.$$

Indeed, using the notations of that lemma,

$$\mathbf{l}_0^T \Lambda_{\mathbf{l}_0}^{-1} \mathbf{l}_0 - k^2 - \mathbf{l}_0^T \Lambda_{\mathbf{l}_0}^{-T} \Lambda_{\mathbf{l}_0} \Lambda_{\mathbf{l}_0}^{-1} \mathbf{l}_0 = \frac{\det(\mathbf{A})}{\det\left(\Lambda_{\mathbf{l}_0}^{-1}\right)},$$

and the left-hand side is equal to $-k^2$.

Since $\mathcal{C}$ is an ellipse, $\det(\mathbf{B}) = \det\left(\Lambda_{\mathbf{l}_0}^{-1}\right)$ is positive and we are therefore interested in the sign of

$$\det(\mathbf{A}) \left(\tilde{\mathbf{l}}^T \mathbf{A}\tilde{\mathbf{l}}\right).$$

We now take into account the fact that $\tilde{\mathbf{l}} \simeq \mathbf{m}_1 \times \mathbf{m}_2$ and use the relation

$$\mathbf{A}(\mathbf{m}_1 \times \mathbf{m}_2) = \frac{1}{\det(\mathbf{A})} \left(\mathbf{A}^{*T}\mathbf{m}_1 \times \mathbf{A}^{*T}\mathbf{m}_2\right),$$

which allows us to write

$$\det(\mathbf{A}) \left(\tilde{\mathbf{l}}^T \mathbf{A}\tilde{\mathbf{l}}\right) = \mid \mathbf{m}_1 \times \mathbf{m}_2, \ \mathbf{A}^{*T}\mathbf{m}_1, \ \mathbf{A}^{*T}\mathbf{m}_2 \mid.$$

Expanding the right-hand side of this equality and taking into account the fact that $\mathbf{A}^*$ is symmetric we obtain

$$\det(\mathbf{A}) \left(\tilde{\mathbf{l}}^T \mathbf{A}\tilde{\mathbf{l}}\right) = -\Delta.$$

Hence if l^* intersects $\mathcal{C}^*$ in two distinct real points, then Δ is positive (Equation 6.35), so $\tilde{\mathbf{l}}^T \mathbf{A}\tilde{\mathbf{l}}$ and $\tilde{\mathbf{l}}_0^T \mathbf{A}\tilde{\mathbf{l}}_0$ have opposite signs and l is outside the ellipse $\mathcal{C}$. Similarly, if l^* intersects $\mathcal{C}^*$ in two identical real points, i.e. is tangent to $\mathcal{C}^*$, then Δ is zero and l is also tangent to $\mathcal{C}$. Finally if l^* intersects $\mathcal{C}^*$ in two imaginary point, Δ is negative and l is inside $\mathcal{C}$. This situation is shown in Figure 6.13. $\square$

We will use Proposition 6.4 in two ways, the first of which is to determine the type of $\mathcal{C}^*$. We have the following proposition.

Proposition 6.5 *The conic $\mathcal{C}^*$ dual to the ellipse of uncertainty $\mathcal{C}$ is respectively a hyperbola, a parabola, or an ellipse according to the fact that the point l^∞ of coordinate vector $[0, 0, 1]^T$ representing the dual of the line at infinity is outside, on, or inside $\mathcal{C}$.*

Proof : According to Proposition 6.4 the line at infinity $l^{\infty *}$, defined by the two points ε_1 and ε_2 of the canonical projective basis of coordinate vectors $[1, 0, 0]^T$ and $[0, 1, 0]^T$, intersects the dual conic $\mathcal{C}^*$ of the ellipse $\mathcal{C}$ in two real points, one real point, or two complex points if and only if the point l^∞ represented by $\varepsilon_1 \times \varepsilon_2 = \varepsilon_3$ is inside, on, or outside $\mathcal{C}$. And we know that a conic that intersects the line at infinity in two real points, one real point, or two complex points is, respectively, a hyperbola, a parabola, or an ellipse. $\square$

The situation is shown in Figure 6.14. The second application we make of Proposition 6.4 is in the definition of the epipolar band.

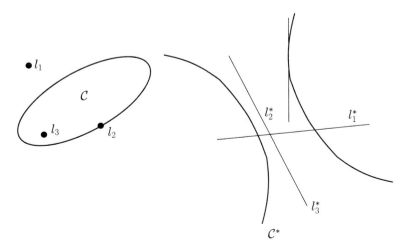

Figure 6.13: Relationship between an ellipse and its dual conic.

Definition 6.1 *The* **epipolar band** *is the set of lines in the image that correspond to the points in the dual plane inside the ellipse of uncertainty C. According to Proposition 6.4, it is the set of lines that do not intersect the dual C^* of that ellipse.*

According to Proposition 6.5, the type of C^*, i.e. ellipse, parabola, or hyperbola, depends upon the position of the origin of affine coordinates, the point represented by $[0, 0, 1]^T$ with respect to C. In our experience, this point has always been outside C; therefore, the epipolar band is the region between the two branches of the hyperbola C^*; see Figure 6.15.

We have used the estimated covariance matrix of the Fundamental matrix of the image pair shown in Figure 6.9 to compute the epipolar bands of a few point correspondences. They are drawn in Figure 6.16 for an ellipse of uncertainty corresponding to a value of k such that $P_{\chi^2}(k, 2) = 95\%$ We also show in the same figure the epipolar lines drawn in dashed lines and the matched points indicated by a +. Note that the matched points are located in the area where the two sections of hyperbolas are closest to each other. This observation suggests that the covariance matrix of the Fundamental matrix actually captures, to some extent, the matching information (disparity in stereo terminology). Such areas could be first examined when searching for point matches. Figure 6.17 shows the same results for the image pair in Figure 6.11.

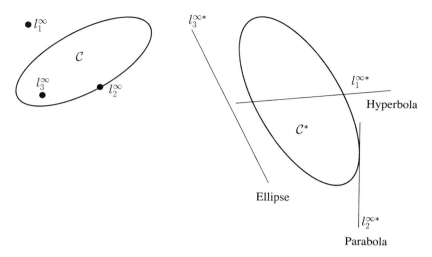

Figure 6.14: The type of the conic $\mathcal{C}^*$ in the image plane (hyperbola, parabola, ellipse) depends on the position of the point ε_3 with respect to the conic $\mathcal{C}$.

6.8 References and further reading

Estimation of a homography   The problem of computing the parameters of a homography turns out to be easier than the computation of the Fundamental matrix since (i) the homography matrices are not singular and therefore are not subject to a rank constraint, and (ii) the homography matrices describe a correspondence between two points.

The fact that there is such an analytic relation between the coordinates of matched points implies that we are able to identify planes using only measurements in the image. Predict-and-verify algorithms have been developed by (Faugeras and Lustman, 1988) and more recently by Sinclair *et al.* (Sinclair and Blake, 1996; Sinclair et al., 1993) and (Robert and Faugeras, 1995), using uncalibrated cameras.

A homography is uniquely specified from two projective bases, which are two sets of four points such that any three of these points do not lie on a line. Let $\mathbf{m} = [u, v, 1]^T \leftrightarrow \mathbf{m}' = [u', v', 1]^T$ be a point correspondence. By writing that the two proportionality constraints obtained from $\mathbf{m}' \simeq \mathbf{Hm}$ are satisfied, we obtain two linear equations in the entries of $\mathbf{H}$. The simplest approach is to solve the resulting system using a linear least-squares procedure, however it was found (Luong, 1992) that better results are obtained by nonlinear minimization of error functions comparable to the ones we presented for the estimation of the Fundamental matrix. Kanatani and Ohta (Kanatani and Ohta, 1999) address the problem of optimal computation of the homography in the presence of noise using the renormalization technique. They derive a theoretical accuracy bound and show that it is reached

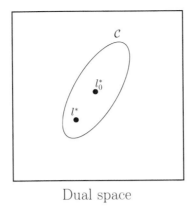 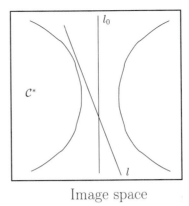

Figure 6.15: Duality between the image plane and the parameter space of the epipolar lines.

by their algorithm.

Viéville *et al.* (Viéville et al., 1996b) study the case of a moving camera, where the change of intrinsic parameters between two consecutive frames and the amplitude of the displacement are small, and the observed objects are relatively distant. In this case the homography matrix of a plane is close to the identity, and specific optimal results are obtained.

The fact that the homography is an analytical relation between two corresponding points makes it possible to estimate the parameters using the image intensities rather than correspondences. In order to deal with the correspondence problem, a pyramid of images at different resolutions is built (3 or 4 levels), and the parameters of the homography are iteratively estimated in a coarse to fine manner. After each iteration, the transformation based on the current set of parameters for the homography is applied to the second image to reduce the residual displacement. A first approach is based on nonlinear minimization of a sum of squared differences (SSD) of image intensities using a Laplacian pyramid (Bergen et al., 1992; Kumar et al., 1995) or multi-resolution splines (Szeliski and Coughland, 1994). A second approach (Mann and Picard, 1997) uses the brightness constancy constraint, which yields linear equations.

Estimation of the Fundamental matrix   As traced in (Faugeras and Maybank, 1990b), the problem of recovering epipolar geometry from seven point correspondences was first given by the French mathematician Chasles (Chasles, 1855). It has been solved by Hesse (Hesse, 1863) and nicely summarized by Sturm (Sturm, 1869).

The original eight-point algorithm was introduced by Longuet-Higgins (Longuet-Higgins, 1981) and has been extensively studied in the literature (Longuet-Higgins,

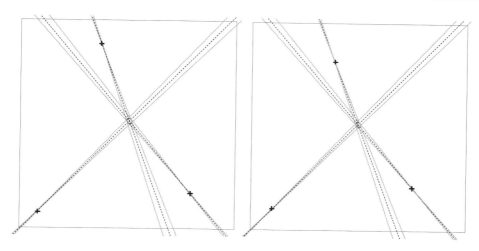

Figure 6.16: A few correspondences from the image pair shown in Figure 6.9 and the epipolar bands. The borders are hyperbolas.

1984; Tsai and Huang, 1984; Fang and Huang, 1984; Weng et al., 1989; Lee, 1991) for the computation of the Essential matrix. It has been shown to be very sensitive to noise. Several researchers (Faugeras et al., 1992; Olsen, 1992; Hartley, 1992) subsequently remarked that the eight-point algorithm could also be used to compute the Fundamental matrix.

Weng, Ahuja and Huang (Weng et al., 1993) described nonlinear minimization approaches to estimate the Essential matrix. The distance minimization approach to compute the Fundamental was independently introduced by Luong (Luong, 1992; Luong and Faugeras, 1996) using a geometric justification. Zhang (Zhang, 1998b) studied the conditions when the three nonlinear cost functions that we presented ((1) distance to epipolar line, (2) gradient weight, (3) distance to reprojections) are theoretically and empirically equivalent. It was found that (2) and (3) are equivalent for epipoles at infinity and that (1) and (2) are equivalent for epipoles at infinity and identical scales. These findings are consistent with what was found by Shapiro, Zisserman and Brady (Shapiro et al., 1995) in the affine case where the cost functions are quite similar, and equivalent when the scale does not change. It can be noted that there is no rank problem in the estimation of the affine fundamental matrix and that the linear cost function (algebraic distance) is very close to the nonlinear cost functions. This situation makes the accurate estimation of affine epipolar geometry much simpler than in the general case.

Practice has confirmed the reliability of the geometric minimization approach. However, since this method involves nonlinear minimization, it is somewhat computationally expensive. Several researchers have tried to find an improvement over

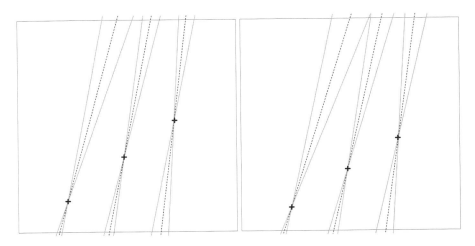

Figure 6.17: A few correspondences from the image pair shown in Figure 6.11 and the epipolar bands. The borders are hyperbolas.

the linear method and have obtained almost the performance of the geometric minimization approach with faster algorithms.

Leedan and Meer (Leedan and Meer, 1998) carefully considered the algebraic error function and concluded that during the linearization of the bilinear form the errors are transformed so that each data point will have a different covariance matrix. They tackled this problem with the errors-in-variables model and generalized singular value decomposition.

On the other hand, Hartley (Hartley, 1998c) claimed that the main problem resides not in minimizing the algebraic error function, but in the fact that the linear method does not take into account the constraints which should be imposed over the estimated quantities. He gave an efficient method to do so.

These two papers described general methods which could be applied to other problems as well. A discussion of broad categories of problems in computer vision which involve bilinear estimation can be found in Koenderink and Van Doorn (Koenderink and vanDoorn, 1997).

We turn to work aimed specifically towards estimation of the Fundamental matrix. Considering the parallax with respect to a plane makes it possible to decouple the rotational part of the retinal motion (as represented by the homography of the plane) and the translational part. This decoupling allows one to compute the epipole directly if at least one plane has been identified (Beardsley, 1992; Luong and Faugeras, 1996), which, of course, is not always possible.

Lawn and Cipolla (Lawn and Cipolla, 1994) propose a variant of this idea using affine motion parallax, where no actual identification of a plane is required. Instead a heuristic about the world is used: Within a triangle defined by three close points, the structure can be approximated by a plane. They consider *locally* an affine model, so that the local transformation between two images of a plane can be described by an affine relation obtained by picking three correspondences. This model is valid when the depth variation spanned by the three points remain small with respect to the distance to the camera.

Another way to cancel the rotational part of the motion has been introduced by Heeger and Jepson (Heeger and Jepson, 1992). By making an algebraic manipulation, the choice of appropriate linear combinations of optical flow equations gives linear constraints on the translational component. Transposing the idea to the discrete uncalibrated case provides a linear algorithm which yields the epipole without introducing an additional variable, unlike the eight point algorithm. Lawn and Cipolla (Lawn and Cipolla, 1996) formulate the idea using again the local affine hypothesis. Ponce and Genc's linear subspace method (Ponce and Genc, 1998) computes one epipole based on the construction of two linear constraints obtained by combining the classical epipolar constraints. Their method is general, since they do not rely on a local affine hypothesis. Indeed a particular choice of projective basis is used to reduce the problem. Boufama and Mohr's virtual parallax method (Boufama and Mohr, 1995) relies on the same particular choice of projective basis and uses the parallax equations to obtain an algebraic equation constraining the epipole. The results obtained with these two last general methods appear good, but one might be concerned about their dependence on the correspondences chosen as basis points. A modern formulation of Sturm's (Sturm, 1869) method due to Maybank and Faugeras (Maybank and Faugeras, 1992), is in the same spirit. Despite several improvements, the results reported in (Luong and Faugeras, 1994b) were not very satisfying.

General references for robust techniques are (Huber, 1981; Rousseeuw and Leroy, 1987; Meer et al., 1991). Applications of those techniques for the Fundamental matrix determination problem can be found in (Shapiro and Brady, 1995; Torr and Murray, 1997; Zhang, 1998a), the two latter papers having a good comparative study. Torr and Zisserman (Torr and Zisserman, 1998) describe a new robust technique for the computation and parameterization of multiple view relations. As shown by the work of Torr and colleagues (Torr, 1995; Torr and Murray, 1994; Torr et al., 1998; Torr, 1998), the problems of robust estimation, model selection, degeneracy detection, and motion segmentation are intricately related. The presence of outliers can make a degenerate configuration appear non-degenerate. Motion segmentation can be based on the epipolar constraint since the points in each rigid object will have a distinct fundamental matrix. However, once the dominant motion is found, one has to distinguish between independently moving objects and outliers. Other applications of the epipolar geometry for motion segmentation are (Xu and Tsuji, 1996; Xu and Zhang, 1996; Weber and Malik, 1997).

Other robust methods applied to the Fundamental matrix estimation problem include genetic algorithms (Chai and Ma, 1998), reactive tabu search, and tensor voting. Reactive tabu search (Ke et al., 1998) is a meta-heuristic search technique which optimizes a cost function while avoiding local minima. Two sets of points are matched, outliers are detected, and the F-matrix is computed, all in one step. Tensor voting, proposed by Tang and Medioni (Tang et al., 1999), is a highly robust method which works even in situations where the outliers outnumber the inliers. A voting method in the spirit of the Hough transform identifies a hyperplane in 8-D space. It uses locality and efficient data structures in order to prevent the complexity from growing with dimensionality, unlike the Hough methods.

The implicit function theorem was used to estimate the uncertainty of the Fundamental matrix in (Luong, 1992); however, the implementation had a global scaling problem which was later fixed in (Csurka et al., 1997). Torr and Zisserman (Torr and Zisserman, 1997a) propose another method to assess the quality of the Fundamental matrix estimation based on self-consistency across image resolutions.

In this chapter, we focussed on the estimation of the Fundamental matrix from point correspondences. It is not possible to estimate the Fundamental matrix from line correspondences using only two views; however, it is possible from three views as will be seen in Chapter 9. However Zhang (Zhang, 1995) has shown that the Essential matrix can be estimated from the correspondence of line segments which are such that two matched segments contain the projection of a common part of the line in space. Other primitives which can be used to estimate the Fundamental matrix include conics (Kahl and Heyden, 1998; Kahl and Heyden, 1999) and apparent contours. Porrill and Pollard (Porrill and Pollard, 1991) used epipolar tangent points to refine the epipolar geometry obtained from point correspondences. At points at which the epipolar plane is tangent to a surface, the occluding contour is tangent to the corresponding epipolar lines. Conversely, corresponding image epipolar tangent points backproject to a 3D point on the surface; therefore image epipolar tangent point are equivalent to a point correspondence. Cipolla et al. (Cipolla et al., 1995) (Mendonçca. and Cipolla, 1999) estimated epipolar geometry from epipolar tangencies alone. The solution involves an iterative search. In (Astrom et al., 1999a) epipolar constraints were generalized for curved surfaces. Schmid and Zisserman (Schmid and Zisserman, 1998) showed that the homography between the images induced by the plane of the curve can be computed from two views given only the epipolar geometry.

7 Stratification of binocular stereo and applications

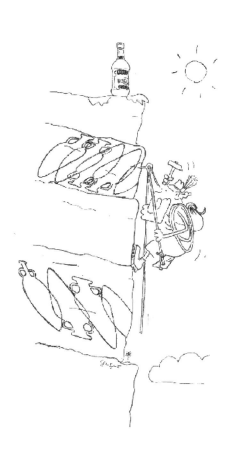

This chapter is devoted to the investigation of exactly what kind of information about the structure of the environment and the cameras can be recovered as a function of the amount of knowledge that is available, e.g. the Fundamental matrix. We limit ourselves to the case of two cameras because this example is of great practical interest and because it clearly shows the importance of a clear distinction between the three geometric worlds in which we now roam, the projective, affine and Euclidean geometries. In Chapter 10 we tackle the full problem of recovering the structure of the scene and the geometry of the cameras from an arbitrary number of views.

Section 7.1 starts with some groundwork. In order to define the kind of information that can be recovered from the scene from two cameras for a given amount and type of prior knowledge, we first note that this information must be invariant under the action of the group corresponding to the available knowledge, in practice the projective group of $\mathbb{P}^3$, the affine group and the group of similitudes. These groups of transformations act on the perspective projection matrices of the cameras and define a set of orbits (see Chapter 2 for a definition) on the set of all possible pairs of projection matrices that can be attached to the cameras given the available knowledge. We propose to characterize each orbit by a set of special pairs of projection matrices which we call the canonical pairs of the orbit. We apply these ideas to the three groups mentioned previously.

We start this agenda in Section 7.2 with the study of the Fundamental matrix and show that in this case the measurements that we can make in the environment are projective invariants, i.e. quantities that will not change if we apply an arbitrary projective transformation to the world, modeled as a three-dimensional projective space $\mathbb{P}^3$. We call this representation of the environment the *projective stratum*: We can recover the structure of the world up to an arbitrary projective transformation. We give the expression of the canonical pairs of projection matrices and provide a simple interpretation of the projective basis in which they are obtained. We then discuss in detail the notion of planar parallax that is important in many applications involving planar structures and describe two such applications: The detection of objects crossing a user-defined virtual plane and the rendering of virtual views of the scene from viewpoints other than those corresponding to the two acquired views.

We continue in Section 7.3 with the analysis of the affine situation where we assume that the infinity morphism, i.e. the morphism induced by the plane at infinity between the two views, is known. In this case we show that we can measure affine invariants, i.e. quantities that will not change if we apply an arbitrary affine transformation to the environment, modeled as a three-dimensional affine space. We call this representation of the environment the *affine stratum*: We can recover the structure of the world up to an arbitrary affine transformation. Following the same track as in the previous section, we give the expression of the canonical pairs of projection matrices and describe the affine basis in which they are obtained. We also discuss the notion of planar parallax in the affine setting and spend some time investigating some ways of recovering the infinity morphism either from *a priori* information about parts of the scene or from active motion of the stereo rig. We end this section, like the previous one, with an application to the measurement of 3D affine quantities directly from the images allowing, for example, the control of a robot vehicle.

We finish with Section 7.4 which is devoted the study of the Euclidean case. In the cases where we also know the two images of the absolute conic (or any equivalent information such as the internal parameters) we show that we can measure Euclidean invariants, i.e. quantities that will not change if we apply an arbitrary three-dimensional similitude to the environment, modeled as a three-dimensional Euclidean space. We call this representation of the environment the *Euclidean stratum*: We can recover the structure of the world up to an arbitrary similitude. As the reader should now expect, we provide the expression of the canonical pair of projection matrices and discuss the notion of planar parallax in the Euclidean setting. We then discuss a number of methods that allow the recovery of this Euclidean stratum from the affine stratum from *a priori* information about the scene, i.e. from known 3D angles of lines or from known ratios of lengths. We finish with a brief description of the standard calibration techniques which make use of calibration grids.

7.1 Canonical representations of two views

Given a pair of pinhole cameras represented by their perspective projection matrices $(\mathcal{P}, \mathcal{P}')$ in some image and space coordinate systems, we know from Chapter 4 how $\mathcal{P}$ and $\mathcal{P}'$ will change if we change the space coordinate system: If $\mathcal{H}$ is the corresponding homography, then they will become $\mathcal{P}\mathcal{H}$ and $\mathcal{P}'\mathcal{H}$, respectively. The images themselves will of course not be affected by this change of coordinate system. It is therefore natural to consider the pair $(\mathcal{P}, \mathcal{P}')$ as equivalent to the pair $(\mathcal{P}\mathcal{H}, \mathcal{P}'\mathcal{H})$.

In practice we are interested in projective, affine and Euclidean changes of coordinates, and, therefore, the homography $\mathcal{H}$ belongs to the three groups $\mathcal{PLG}$, $\mathcal{AG}$ and $\mathcal{E}$, respectively (see Chapter 2). Each of these three groups acts on pairs of projection matrices by multiplication to the right. This situation is reminiscent of the discussion in Section 2.4.2.2. In effect, for a given pair of projection matrices, we can consider its orbit, i.e. all pairs obtained by multiplying each one on the right by an element of the group. All pairs in the same orbit are equivalent in the intuitive sense that they all correspond to the same images and in the mathematical sense that the relation defined by

$$(\mathcal{P}_1, \mathcal{P}'_1) \equiv (\mathcal{P}_2, \mathcal{P}'_2) \iff \exists\, \mathcal{H} \in \mathcal{G} \text{ such that } \mathcal{P}_1 = \mathcal{P}_2\mathcal{H} \text{ and } \mathcal{P}'_1 = \mathcal{P}'_2\mathbf{H}$$

is an equivalence relation ($\mathcal{G}$ is one of the three groups mentioned above). The equivalence classes are the orbits.

The next step is to identify within each orbit a pair which is particularly simple and to use it to represent the orbit. This choice is somewhat arbitrary but we will follow the custom and choose $\mathcal{P} \simeq \mathcal{P}_0$ when $\mathcal{G} = \mathcal{PLG}$ or $\mathcal{G} = \mathcal{AG}$ and $\mathcal{P} \simeq \mathbf{A}\mathcal{P}_0$ when $\mathcal{G} = \mathcal{E}$. Note that this choice is *a priori* possible since $\mathcal{P}$ depends upon 11 parameters, $\mathcal{PLG}$ upon 15 parameters, $\mathcal{AG}$ upon 12, $\mathcal{E}$ upon 6 parameters, and $\mathbf{A}$ upon 5 parameters. An element of a given orbit of the form $(\mathcal{P}_0, \mathcal{P}')$ for $\mathcal{G} = \mathcal{PLG}$ or $\mathcal{G} = \mathcal{AG}$ or of the form $(\mathbf{A}\mathcal{P}_0, \mathcal{P}')$ for $\mathcal{G} = \mathcal{E}$ is called a *canonical* element of the orbit.

Note that this element is not unique in the case of $\mathcal{PLG}$ where we would expect a 4-parameter family of canonical elements for each orbit and in the case of $\mathcal{AG}$ where we would expect a 1-parameter family of elements. This observation will be confirmed by Propositions 7.1 and 7.9.

7.2 Projective stratum

7.2.1 The projection matrices

We consider the situation where we have estimated the Fundamental matrix $\mathbf{F}$ between two views using for example the techniques described in Chapter 6, and we address the problem of determining what kind of 3D information can be extracted about the world. According to the analysis done in Section 7.1 we know that this information can only be projective and we confirm this observation in this section by explicitly computing the canonical representation of the pair $(\mathcal{P}, \mathcal{P}')$ of the projection matrices. It turns out that this canonical representation is not unique and that there is a four-parameter family of matrices $\mathcal{P}'$ such that $\mathcal{P} \simeq \mathcal{P}_0$ and the Fundamental matrix between the two views is proportional to $\mathbf{F}$:

Proposition 7.1 *For a given Fundamental matrix* $\mathbf{F}$*, it is always possible to choose a projective basis of* $\mathbb{P}^3$ *such that* $\mathcal{P} \simeq \mathcal{P}_0$*.* $\mathcal{P}'$ *then takes the simple form*

$$\mathcal{P}' = [\mathbf{H}_\Pi \; \mu\mathbf{e}'] = [\mathbf{S} + \mathbf{e}'\mathbf{r}^T \; \mu\mathbf{e}'] = [\mathbf{S} \; \mathbf{e}'] \mathbf{Q}_\mathcal{B}^{\mathcal{B}_0}, \tag{7.1}$$

where

$$\mathbf{Q}_\mathcal{B}^{\mathcal{B}_0} = \begin{bmatrix} \mathbf{I}_3 & \mathbf{0}_3 \\ \mathbf{r}^T & \mu \end{bmatrix} \tag{7.2}$$

describes a change of projective coordinates. This change of coordinates is interpreted after Proposition 7.2.

$\mathbf{H}_\Pi$ *represents a planar morphism induced by an arbitrary plane* Π *not going through the optical center* C *of the first view.* $\mathbf{r}$ *is the intrinsic representation of* Π *(see Section 5.2.5), and* μ *is a scalar.*

When the two projection matrices take this form we talk about a **projective canonical form**.

Proof : The analysis done in Section 2.4.2.1 of Chapter 2 shows that it is always possible to choose a projective basis $(E_1, \ldots, E_5)$ such that $\mathcal{P} \simeq \mathcal{P}_0$. This basis is further analyzed in Proposition 7.2. For the moment we need only the fact that $C = E_4$. Let us write the usual decomposition $\mathcal{P}' = [\mathbf{P}'\mathbf{p}']$. Since $C = E_4$, $\mathbf{e}' \simeq \mathcal{P}'C \simeq \mathcal{P}'E_4 = \mathbf{p}'$.

Let us choose a plane Θ not going through C. Equation 4.12 gives us the form of the inverse perspective projection matrix $\mathcal{P}_\Theta^+$ of the first camera with respect to Θ, namely,

$$\mathcal{P}_{0\Theta}^+ \simeq \left[\begin{array}{c} d\mathbf{I}_3 \\ \boldsymbol{\theta}^T \end{array} \right].$$

d is nonzero since Θ does not go through C, and $\boldsymbol{\theta}$ is an arbitrary vector of dimension 3.

Proposition 5.5 gives an expression for the Fundamental matrix $\mathbf{F}$:

$$\mathbf{F} \simeq [\mathbf{e}']_\times \mathcal{P}'\mathcal{P}_{0\Theta}^+.$$

The right-hand side is equal to $[\mathbf{e}']_\times \left[d\mathbf{P}' + \mathbf{p}'\boldsymbol{\theta}^T \right]$ and, since $\mathbf{p}' \simeq \mathbf{e}'$, we have $\mathbf{F} \simeq [\mathbf{e}']_\times \mathbf{P}'$.

According to Theorem 5.1 and to Corollary 5.1, it follows that the matrix $\mathbf{P}'$ represents a planar morphism (of rank 2 or 3) between the two views. Therefore, according to Equation 5.23, there exists a plane Π, not going through C, with intrinsic representation (Definition 5.6) $\mathbf{r}$ such that $\mathbf{P}' \simeq \mathbf{S} + \mathbf{e}'\mathbf{r}^T$. $\square$

The proposition singles out the projection matrices $\mathcal{P}'_0 \simeq \left[[\mathbf{e}']_\times \mathbf{F} \, \mu\mathbf{e}' \right]$, corresponding to the choice $\mathbf{r} = \mathbf{0}$ in Equations 7.1 and 7.2, as the simplest in the four-parameter family of projection matrices compatible with the Fundamental matrix $\mathbf{F}$. The plane Π is the second intrinsic plane Π'_0 of the pair of views (see Definition 5.5). The other members in the class can be written

$$\mathcal{P}'_{\Pi,\mu} = [\mathbf{H}_\Pi \, \mu\mathbf{e}'], \tag{7.3}$$

where Π is an arbitrary plane not going through the first optical center and μ is an arbitrary number.

Note that the special form (7.1) for $\mathcal{P}$ and $\mathcal{P}'$ corresponds to a particular choice of a projective basis. We use capital letters for the 3D projective canonical basis, i.e. $(E_1, E_2, E_3, E_4, E_5)$, and lower-case letters for the 2D canonical basis, i.e. $(\varepsilon_1, \varepsilon_2, \varepsilon_3, \varepsilon_4)$.

Proposition 7.2 *The projective canonical form corresponds to choosing $E_4 = C$, the optical center of the first camera, and E_1, E_2, E_3 three non-aligned points in the reference plane Π. The fifth point, E_5, is such that its image in the first camera is ε_4 and its image in the second camera is represented by*

$$\mathbf{s} = \sum_{i=1}^{3} {}^i\mathbf{H}_\Pi + \mu\mathbf{e}', \tag{7.4}$$

where $^{i}\mathbf{H}_{\Pi}$ is the ith column of matrix $\mathbf{H}_{\Pi}$ appearing in Equation 7.3. We call this frame a **projective canonical frame** *for the pair of cameras, and we denote it by* (Π, μ). *Moreover, if we assume that we use the original pixel coordinates in the first image, i.e. that it has not undergone a homography, then the plane* (E_1, E_2, E_4) *is the focal plane of the first camera.*

Proof : Refer to Figure 7.1. The optical center of a camera with projection matrix $\mathcal{P}_0$ is the point E_4 of the canonical projective basis. The images of the points E_i, $i = 1, 2, 3$, in the first camera are the points ε_i, $i = 1, 2, 3$, and their images in the second camera are represented by the first three columns of the matrix $\mathbf{H}_{\Pi}$. By definition of H_{Π}, the three points E_i are in the plane Π and since they are part of a projective basis, they must be in general position, i.e. not aligned. If we are using the original pixel coordinates in the first camera, then the points ε_1 and ε_2 are at infinity which means that E_1 and E_2 are in the focal plane of the camera. $\square$

The interpretation of the real number μ that appears in the equations (7.1) of the projective canonical representation of two views is that it controls the fifth point of the canonical frame, i.e. the global scale of the reconstructed scene. Denoting by h the point of the second image represented by $\mathbf{h} = \sum_{i=1}^{3} {}^{i}\mathbf{H}_{\Pi}$, we see that when μ varies, the point s varies on the line (e', h) but for the point h which corresponds to $\mu = 0$ and the point e' which corresponds to $\mu = \infty$. This observation corresponds to moving the point E_5 of the canonical frame on the optical ray of the point ε_4 with the exception of the point C and its point of intersection with $\Pi = (E_1, E_2, E_3)$. Therefore, varying μ corresponds to a change of projective coordinates; we will use this remark later. We now understand the notation $\mathbf{Q}_{\mathcal{B}}^{\mathcal{B}_0}$ used in Proposition 7.1. It

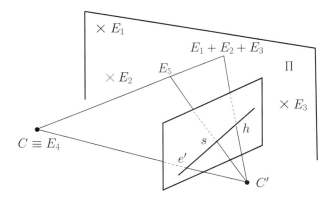

Figure 7.1: The projective canonical frame (see text).

describes the change of projective coordinates from the projective canonical frame $\mathcal{B} \equiv (\Pi, \mu)$ to the projective canonical frame $\mathcal{B}_0 \equiv (\Pi_0', 1)$. Because of duality, the matrix $\mathbf{Q}_{\mathcal{B}_0}^{\mathcal{B}\,T}$ describes how the representations for planes change when we go from

(Π, μ) to $(\Pi'_0, 1)$. A simple computation shows that

$$\mathbf{Q}_{\mathcal{B}_0}^{\mathcal{B}\,T} = \begin{bmatrix} \mathbf{I}_3 & -\mathbf{r}/\mu \\ \mathbf{0}_3^T & 1/\mu \end{bmatrix}.$$

Therefore, the plane Π, represented by ε_4 in (Π, μ), is represented by $\begin{bmatrix} -\mathbf{r}^T, 1 \end{bmatrix}^T$ in $(\Pi'_0, 1)$. It can be verified that the image of the line of intersection of Π and Π'_0 in the first view is, as expected, represented by the vector $\mathbf{r}$ (Proposition 5.16).

7.2.2 Projective reconstruction

In the previous section, we chose a particular canonical element. We showed that fixing the first projection matrix imposes a special form for the second matrix, which turned out to contain some of our most familiar friends, the planar homography and epipole. We now extend this result to all of the projection matrices which have the same Fundamental matrix.

Proposition 7.3 *The pairs $(\mathcal{P}, \mathcal{P}')$ with Fundamental matrix $\mathbf{F}$ are of the form:*

$$\begin{cases} \mathcal{P} & \simeq & [\mathbf{I}_3 \; \mathbf{0}_3]\mathcal{H} \\ \mathcal{P}' & \simeq & [\mathbf{H}_\Pi \; \mu\mathbf{e}']\mathcal{H} \end{cases} \text{ with } \mathcal{H} \simeq \begin{bmatrix} \mathcal{P} \\ \Pi^T \end{bmatrix},$$

where $\mathbf{H}_\Pi$ is a planar homography compatible with $\mathbf{F}$, and Π is the projective representation of the associated plane Π.

Proof : The first matrix equality is trivial. Let us assume that $\mathbf{H}_\Pi$ is a planar homography compatible with $\mathbf{F}$. Equation 4.14 can be rewritten as $\mathbf{I}_4 \simeq -\mathcal{P}_\Pi^+ \mathcal{P} + \mathbf{C}\Pi^T$. By multiplying to the left by $\mathcal{P}'$ and using the expression in Equation 5.1 for the homography and $\mathbf{e}' \simeq \mathcal{P}'\mathbf{C}$, we obtain the second matrix equality. Conversely, let us assume that $\mathcal{P}' = \mathbf{H}_\Pi \mathcal{P} + \mu\mathbf{e}'\Pi^T$ and that $\mathbf{F} = [\mathbf{e}']_\times \mathbf{H}_\Pi$. The Fundamental matrix of $\mathcal{P}, \mathcal{P}'$ is given by Equation 5.5:

$$\mathbf{F}' = \left[\left(\mathbf{H}_\Pi \mathcal{P} + \mu\mathbf{e}'\Pi^T \right) \mathbf{C} \right]_\times \left(\mathbf{H}_\Pi \mathcal{P} + \mu\mathbf{e}'\Pi^T \right) \mathcal{P}^+.$$

Since $\mathbf{C}$ is the optical center of $\mathcal{P}$, we have $\mathcal{P}\mathbf{C} = 0$, so the term between brackets is proportional to $\mathbf{e}'$. Since $[\mathbf{e}']_\times \mathbf{e}' = 0$, $\mathbf{F}' \simeq \mathbf{F}$ is equivalent to $\mathbf{H}_\Pi \mathcal{P}\mathcal{P}^+ \simeq \mathbf{H}_\Pi$, which is clearly true since by definition $\mathcal{P}\mathcal{P}^+ \simeq \mathbf{I}_3$. $\square$

This decomposition separates two types of parameters: The projective correspondence of the pair of cameras, and a projective transformation, which represents an arbitrary choice of projective coordinates. From this decomposition, it is an easy matter to prove the following proposition, which shows that a Fundamental matrix determines a reconstruction up to a projective transformation.

Proposition 7.4 *$(\mathcal{P}_1, \mathcal{P}'_1)$ and $(\mathcal{P}_2, \mathcal{P}'_2)$ have the same Fundamental matrix if and only if there exists $\mathcal{H}$, a homography of $\mathbb{P}^3$, such that $\mathcal{P}_1 = \mathcal{P}_2\mathcal{H}$ and $\mathcal{P}'_1 = \mathcal{P}'_2\mathcal{H}$.*

Proof : Using the previous proposition, if $(\mathcal{P}_1, \mathcal{P}'_1)$ and $(\mathcal{P}_2, \mathcal{P}'_2)$ have the same Fundamental matrix, then they can be written

$$\begin{cases} \mathcal{P}_1 &= [\mathbf{I}_3 \, \mathbf{0}_3] \, \mathcal{H}_1, \\ \mathcal{P}'_1 &= [\mathbf{H} \, \mathbf{e}'] \, \mathcal{H}_1, \end{cases}$$

and

$$\begin{cases} \mathcal{P}_2 &= [\mathbf{I}_3 \, \mathbf{0}_3] \, \mathcal{H}_2, \\ \mathcal{P}'_2 &= [\mathbf{H} \, \mathbf{e}'] \, \mathcal{H}_2. \end{cases}$$

We can therefore take $\mathcal{H} = \mathcal{H}_2^{-1} \mathcal{H}_1$. Conversely, if

$$\begin{cases} \mathcal{P}_1 &= [\mathbf{I}_3 \, \mathbf{0}_3] \, \mathcal{H}_1, \\ \mathcal{P}'_1 &= [\mathbf{H}_1 \, \mathbf{e}'_1] \, \mathcal{H}_1, \end{cases}$$

and

$$\begin{cases} \mathcal{P}_2 &= [\mathbf{I}_3 \, \mathbf{0}_3] \, \mathcal{H}_2, \\ \mathcal{P}'_2 &= [\mathbf{H}_2 \, \mathbf{e}'_2] \, \mathcal{H}_2, \end{cases}$$

then from $\mathcal{P}_1 = \mathcal{P}_2 \mathcal{H}$ and $\mathcal{P}'_1 = \mathcal{P}'_2 \mathcal{H}$ we get

$$\begin{cases} [\mathbf{I}_3 \, \mathbf{0}_3] &= [\mathbf{I}_3 \, \mathbf{0}_3] \mathcal{H}' \\ [\mathbf{H}_1 \, \mathbf{e}'_1] &= [\mathbf{H}_2 \, \mathbf{e}'_2] \mathcal{H}' \end{cases},$$

with $\mathcal{H}' = \mathcal{H}_2 \mathcal{H} \mathcal{H}_1^{-1}$. This entails $\mathcal{H}' = \begin{bmatrix} \mathbf{I}_3 & \mathbf{0}_3 \\ \mathbf{r}^T & \lambda \end{bmatrix}$, from which we conclude $\mathbf{e}'_1 = \mathbf{e}'_2$ and $\mathbf{H}_2 = \mathbf{H}_1 + \mathbf{e}'_2 \mathbf{r}^T$, from which follows $\mathbf{F}_1 = [\mathbf{e}'_1]_\times \mathbf{H}_1 = [\mathbf{e}'_2]_\times \mathbf{H}_2 = \mathbf{F}_2$. □

To summarize, in the most general case, a pair of views $(\mathcal{P}, \mathcal{P}')$ with Fundamental matrix $\mathbf{F}$ determines a reconstruction up to a general projective transformation of $\mathbb{P}^3$ (see Figure 1.22 for an example), which can be computed using

$$\begin{cases} \mathcal{P} &= [\mathbf{I} \, \mathbf{0}], \\ \mathcal{P}' &= [\mathbf{S} + \mathbf{e}' \mathbf{r}^T \; \mu \mathbf{e}']. \end{cases} \tag{7.5}$$

In terms of degrees of freedom, a pair of projection matrices has $22 = 11 \times 2$ parameters.

- 15 represent the projective ambiguity in reconstruction: The arbitrary choice of the projective basis (11 obtained by fixing $\mathcal{P}$, 4 are $\mathbf{r}, \mu$).

- 7 describe the projective correspondence encoded by the Fundamental matrix.

7.2.3 Dealing with real correspondences

We now tackle the practical problem that some of the correspondences (m, m') may not exactly satisfy the epipolar constraint $\mathbf{m}'^T\mathbf{F}\mathbf{m} = 0$, as seen for example in Chapter 6. Hence these correspondences do not define a 3D point M since the optical rays of m and m' do not intersect. In order to obtain such a point unambiguously, one may wish to "slightly" modify the positions of the points m and m' in such a way that the modified points $\hat{m}$ and $\hat{m}'$ are as close as possible to the measured points m and m' and exactly satisfy the epipolar constraint.

We can achieve this goal by using the epipolar homography (Section 5.2.3). Let us consider two points p_1 and p_2 in the first image (respectively p_1' and p_2' in the second image) such that the line $l \equiv (p_1, p_2)$ does not go through the epipole e (respectively the line $l' \equiv (p_1', p_2')$ does not go through e'). The epipolar pencil in the first view can be parametrized by λ, where the parameter λ defines the point p_λ of the line (p_1, p_2) such that $\mathbf{p}_\lambda \simeq \mathbf{p}_1 + \lambda\mathbf{p}_2$. When λ varies, the line $l_\lambda \equiv (e, p_\lambda)$ is an epipolar line and all epipolar lines are of the form (e, p_λ) for some value of λ. The corresponding epipolar line is readily obtained in the second image as the line $l_\lambda' \equiv (e', p_\lambda')$ where the point p_λ' is the intersection of the line (p_1', p_2') with the epipolar line of the point p_λ:

$$\mathbf{p}_\lambda' \simeq \mathbf{l}' \times \mathbf{F}\mathbf{p}_\lambda.$$

The problem of correcting a given correspondence (m, m') can now be cast as the one of finding the value of λ that minimizes the sum of the squares of the distances of the points m and m' to the pair (l_λ, l_λ') of corresponding epipolar lines. Let $\hat{\lambda}$ be defined as

$$\hat{\lambda} = argmin_\lambda \left(d^2(m, l_\lambda) + d^2(m', l_\lambda') \right).$$

$\hat{m}$ (respectively $\hat{m}'$) is the projection of m onto $l_{\hat{\lambda}}$ (respectively of m' onto $l_{\hat{\lambda}}'$); see Figure 7.2).

Let us now see how $\hat{\lambda}$ can be computed. The line l_λ (respectively l_λ') is represented by the vector $\mathbf{e} \times \mathbf{p}_\lambda$ (respectively by the vector $\mathbf{e}' \times \mathbf{p}_\lambda'$). The coordinates of these vectors are affine functions of λ. Therefore, the squared distance of m (respectively m') to l_λ (respectively l_λ') is a rational function of λ whose numerator and denominator are polynomials of degree 2 in λ:

$$d^2(m, l_\lambda) = \frac{N(\lambda)}{D(\lambda)}, \qquad d^2(m', l_\lambda') = \frac{N'(\lambda)}{D'(\lambda)}$$

The error criterion is thus the rational function

$$\frac{N(\lambda)}{D(\lambda)} + \frac{N'(\lambda)}{D'(\lambda)} = \frac{N(\lambda)D'(\lambda) + N'(\lambda)D(\lambda)}{D(\lambda)D'(\lambda)},$$

whose numerator and denominator are polynomials in λ of degree 4.

In order to minimize this error criterion, we compute its derivative which is also a rational fraction whose numerator is readily found to be a polynomial of degree 7 in λ. The real roots of this polynomial are candidate values for $\hat{\lambda}$. By computing the values of the error criterion for these at most 7 candidates, the value of $\hat{\lambda}$ is readily found and therefore the points $\hat{m}$ and $\hat{m}'$ are also found.

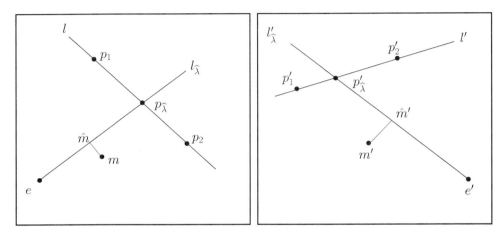

Figure 7.2: The parametrization of the pencils of epipolar lines by λ allows us to construct the pair $(\hat{m}, \hat{m}')$ from the measured pair (m, m'); see text.

7.2.4 Planar parallax

We now put together the canonical representation that has been derived in the previous section with some of the results of Chapter 5 on the relations between between the F-matrix and planar morphisms or homographies. In particular, we show how to compute the 3D projective coordinates in any projective canonical frame of the 3D point M associated with a pair (m, m') of corresponding pixels.

We start with the following proposition which implies that the 3D projective coordinates in any of the projective canonical frames of a point M in the scene with images (m, m') can be computed once the F-matrix between the two views is known.

Proposition 7.5 *In a projective canonical frame, the relation between two corresponding pixels m and m' can be written*

$$\mathbf{m}' \simeq \mathbf{H}_\Pi \mathbf{m} + \kappa_{\Pi,\mu} \mathbf{e}'. \tag{7.6}$$

*The number $\kappa_{\Pi,\mu}$ is called the **projective parallax** of the corresponding 3D point M with respect to the plane Π. In particular, $\kappa_{\Pi,\mu} = 0$ if and only if the point*

M is in Π*. The ratio of* $\kappa_{\Pi,\mu}/\mu$ *and any nonzero coordinate of* $\mathbf{m}$ *is a projective invariant, i.e. does not depend upon the choice of* μ *in (7.1). These ratios define the projective coordinates of M in the projective canonical frame.*

Proof : Because $\mathcal{P} \simeq \mathcal{P}_0$ in a projective canonical frame, if $\mathbf{m}$ is a coordinate vector of the pixel m, then $\mathbf{M}_{\Pi,\mu} = \left[\mathbf{m}^T, \rho_{\Pi,\mu}\right]^T$ must be a coordinate vector of the corresponding 3D point M since $\mathcal{P}_0 \mathbf{M}_{\Pi,\mu} = \mathbf{m}$. This coordinate vector is expressed in the canonical frame (Π, μ). Applying $\mathcal{P}'_{\Pi,\mu}$ to this vector we obtain $\mathbf{m}' \simeq \mathbf{H}_\Pi \mathbf{m} + \mu \rho_{\Pi,\mu} \mathbf{e}'$. Let us define $\kappa_{\Pi,\mu} = \mu \rho_{\Pi,\mu}$. Since $\mu \neq 0$ we have $\kappa_{\Pi,\mu} = 0$ if and only if M is in Π.

Dividing by μ yields $\rho_{\Pi,\mu}$ and hence the projective coordinates $m_1 : m_2 : m_3 : \rho_{\Pi,\mu}$ of M in the canonical frame (Π, μ) which are by definition invariant to changes in μ since, as we saw, those changes correspond to a change of projective coordinate system. $\square$

The previous proposition shows that the ratios $\kappa_{\Pi,\mu}/(\mu m_i)$, $i = 1, 2, 3$, define the projective coordinates of the 3D point M in the projective canonical frame. Therefore the computation of these ratios is of great practical importance. Let us show for example how we can compute the ratio $\kappa_{\Pi,\mu}/(\mu m_3)$. We have seen in Chapter 2, Proposition 2.18 that it is equal to the cross-ratio of the four points $\{E_4, E_3; (E_4, E_3) \cap H_0, (E_4, E_3) \cap H\}$, where the plane H_0 is the plane (E_1, E_2, E_5) and the plane H is the plane (E_1, E_2, M). Because of Proposition 2.16, this cross-ratio is equal to the cross-ratio of the four planes (E_1, E_2, E_4), (E_1, E_2, E_3), (E_1, E_2, E_5) and (E_1, E_2, M). According to the same proposition, this cross-ratio is equal to the cross-ratio of the four points (P_3, Q, E_5, M), where P_3 and Q are the points of intersection of the line (E_5, M) with the planes (E_1, E_2, E_4) and (E_1, E_2, E_3), respectively; see Figure 7.3. This cross-ratio can be computed directly from the two views as follows.

The planes (E_1, E_2, E_3) and (E_1, E_2, E_4) induce planar morphisms between the two views. Because $C = E_4$, we consider the morphisms induced by these planes from the second view to the first. Let h_i, $i = 1, 2, 3$, be the three points in the second view represented by the columns of the matrix $\mathbf{H}_\Pi$.

The first planar morphism, denoted H_{123}, is determined by the four correspondences (h_1, ε_1), (h_2, ε_2), (h_3, ε_3) and (e', e). The second morphism, denoted H_{124}, is partly determined by the two correspondences (h_1, ε_1), (h_2, ε_2) and the fact that $\mathbf{H}_{124}\mathbf{e}' = \mathbf{0}$. To complete its determination, we must also find the image of h_3: By definition, it is the intersection of its epipolar line l_{h_3} in the first image with the line $(\varepsilon_1, \varepsilon_2)$, the trace of the plane (E_1, E_2, E_4) on the retinal plane of the first view.

Note that $\mathbf{H}_{123}$ cannot be of rank 2, or equivalently the plane (E_1, E_2, E_3) cannot go through C since $C = E_4$. Hence H_{123} is a homography. For another way of determining H_{123} and H_{124}, see the proof of Proposition 7.6.

The matrix $\mathbf{H}_{123}^T$ (respectively $\mathbf{H}_{124}^T$) maps the lines of the first image to the lines of the second image. Two lines that correspond to each other under this morphism

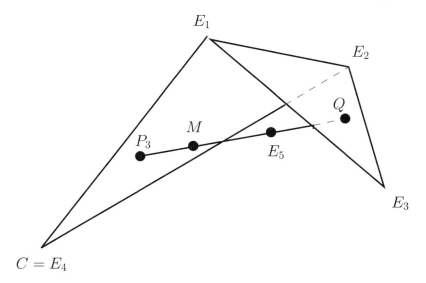

Figure 7.3: The cross-ratio $\{P_3, Q; E_5, M\}$ is equal to the ratio $\kappa_{\Pi,\mu}/(\mu m_3)$ (see text).

are images of the same 3D line in the plane (E_1, E_2, E_3) (respectively in the plane (E_1, E_2, E_4)). If we apply $\mathbf{H}^T_{123}$ (respectively $\mathbf{H}^T_{124}$) to the line (ε_4, m), the image in the first view of the 3D line (E_5, M), and intersect it with the line (s, m'), the image in the second view of the same 3D line, then we obtain the image q' of Q (respectively the image p'_3 of P_3); see Figure 7.4. Since the cross-ratio is invariant under perspective projection, the cross-ratio of the four image points (p'_3, q', s, m') is equal to the cross-ratio of the four 3D points (P_3, Q, E_5, M). This process fails when either one of the transformed lines is identical to the line (s, m') since in those cases the point of intersection is not defined.

This situation occurs when the line (E_5, M) is in the plane (E_1, E_2, E_3) or in the plane (E_1, E_2, E_4). Since E_5 is not in either plane, it never happens.

We have the following proposition.

Proposition 7.6 *Given a correspondence* (m, m'), *a matrix* $\mathbf{H}_\Pi$ *of the planar morphism determined by the plane* Π, *the Fundamental matrix* $\mathbf{F}$ *between the two views, and the scale* μ, *the ratio* $\kappa_{\Pi,\mu}/(\mu m_i)$, $i = 1, 2, 3$, *i.e. the ratio of the fourth and the ith projective coordinates of the 3D point* M *in the corresponding projective canonical frame, is equal to the cross-ratio of the points* p'_i, q', s, m'. *The points* p'_1 *and* p'_2 *are defined in the proof.*

Proof :   We have already proved this statement for $i = 3$. To make the proof more constructive, we provide analytical expressions for the matrices $\mathbf{H}_{123}$ and

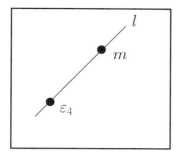 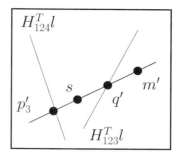

Figure 7.4: The cross-ratio $\{P_3, Q; E_5, M\}$ is equal to the cross-ratio $\{p'_3, q'; s, m'\}$ (see text).

$\mathbf{H}_{124}$ that are necessary to construct the points p'_i and q'. The first matrix is easy to determine: The plane (E_1, E_2, E_3) is the plane Π and hence $\mathbf{H}_{123} \simeq \mathbf{H}_\Pi^{-1}$. By analogy to the definition of the matrix $\mathbf{S}$, the matrix $\mathbf{H}_{124}$ is proportional to $[\varepsilon_3]_\times \mathbf{F}^T$. Indeed, the vector ε_3 represents the line $(\varepsilon_1, \varepsilon_2)$ which is the intersection of the plane (E_1, E_2, E_4) with the first retinal plane.

The cases $i = 1, 2$ are similar. They both involve the homography H_{123} induced by Π and the morphism H_{234} induced by the plane (E_2, E_3, E_4) for $i = 1$ and the morphism H_{134} induced by the plane (E_1, E_3, E_4) for $i = 2$. The corresponding matrices are proportional to $[\varepsilon_i]_\times \mathbf{F}^T$, $i = 1, 2$, respectively. The points p'_1 and p'_2 are obtained as the intersections of the lines represented by $\mathbf{H}_{234}^T\mathbf{l}$ and $\mathbf{H}_{134}^T\mathbf{l}$ with the line (s, m'). Note that the three lines $\mathbf{H}_{123}^T\mathbf{l}$, $\mathbf{H}_{234}^T\mathbf{l}$ and $\mathbf{H}_{134}^T\mathbf{l}$ intersect at the epipole e'; see Figure 7.5. $\square$

Let us now give a simple "Euclidean" interpretation of the projective parallax.

Proposition 7.7 *If the pixel coordinates are used in the first image, then the projective parallax is given by the formula*

$$\kappa_{\Pi,\mu} = \mu \, \frac{d(E_5, \Pi_f)}{d(E_5, \Pi)} \, \frac{d(M, \Pi)}{d(M, \Pi_f)}. \tag{7.7}$$

Proof : Consider Figure 7.6. We have seen previously that when pixel coordinates were used for the first camera, the plane (E_1, E_2, E_4) was its focal plane, Π_f. The proof is then to write $\{P, Q; E_5, M\} = \frac{\overline{PE_5}}{\overline{PM}} : \frac{\overline{QE_5}}{\overline{QM}}$, to project the two points M and E_5 orthogonally onto the two planes Π and Π_f and to apply Thales' theorem twice. $\square$

This result is important since it allows us to relate a "projective" quantity $k_{\Pi,\mu}$ to four Euclidean quantities and the scale μ. We will soon see an application. For now, we can observe this relation in the example given in Figure 7.7.

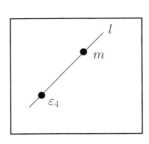 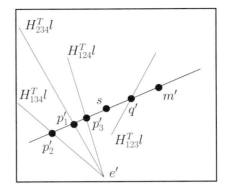

Figure 7.5: The cross-ratios $\{p_i', q'; s, m'\}$, $i = 1, 2, 3$, yield the projective coordinates of the point M of images m and m' in the projective canonical frame (see text).

7.2.5 Image rectification

We explore a technique for transforming a stereo pair by applying homographies H and H' to the two image planes to make the epipolar geometry simpler in the sense that the Fundamental matrix of the transformed images is

$$[\varepsilon_1]_\times = \begin{bmatrix} 0 & 0 & 0 \\ 0 & 0 & -1 \\ 0 & 1 & 0 \end{bmatrix}.$$

If $\mathbf{F}$ is the estimated matrix we have

$$\mathbf{F} \simeq \mathbf{H}'^T [\varepsilon_1]_\times \mathbf{H}. \tag{7.8}$$

Let (m, m') be a pair of corresponding points in the original images. The transformed points $\hat{m} = Hm$ and $\hat{m}' = H'm'$ satisfy the simpler epipolar constraint

$$\hat{\mathbf{m}}'^T [\varepsilon_1]_\times \hat{\mathbf{m}} = 0,$$

which is equivalent to saying that they have the same "vertical" coordinates.

Given a Fundamental matrix $\mathbf{F}$, there are clearly many ways of choosing H and H' to satisfy (7.8); in effect the problem depends upon 16 parameters (8 for each of the rectifying homographies) minus 7 for the F-matrix, i.e. 9. We will provide a geometric interpretation of these parameters in a moment.

We begin by displaying a pair of *canonical* rectifying homographies that depend only upon the F-matrix. We consider its SVD decomposition

$$\mathbf{F} = \mathbf{U}' diag(0, \sigma_1, \sigma_2) \mathbf{U}^T, \tag{7.9}$$

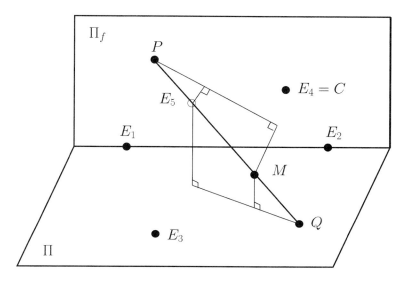

Figure 7.6: The cross-ratio $\{P,\,Q;\,E_5,\,M\}$ is equal to $\frac{d(E_5,\Pi_f)}{d(E_5,\Pi)}\,\frac{d(M,\Pi)}{d(M,\Pi_f)}$ (see text).

where $\mathbf{U}'$ and $\mathbf{U}$ are orthogonal matrices which we write

$$\mathbf{U}' = [\mathbf{e}'\,\mathbf{u}_1'\,\mathbf{u}_2'], \quad \mathbf{U} = [\mathbf{e}\,\mathbf{u}_1\,\mathbf{u}_2].$$

Since $\mathbf{F}$ is defined up to a scale factor, we introduce the ratio $\sigma = \sigma_2/\sigma_1 > 0$ and rewrite (7.9) as

$$\mathbf{F} = \left[\mathbf{e}'\,\mathbf{u}_1'\,\sqrt{\sigma}\mathbf{u}_2'\right][\varepsilon_1]_\times\left[\mathbf{e}\,\sqrt{\sigma}\mathbf{u}_2\,-\,\mathbf{u}_1\right]^T.$$

We have thus obtained the pair of rectifying homographies

$$\mathbf{H}_0 \simeq \left[\mathbf{e}\,\sqrt{\sigma}\mathbf{u}_2\,-\,\mathbf{u}_1\right]^T, \quad \mathbf{H}_0' \simeq \left[\mathbf{e}'\,\mathbf{u}_1'\,\sqrt{\sigma}\mathbf{u}_2'\right]^T. \tag{7.10}$$

Let us now characterize the set of pairs of rectifying homographies. The result is given in the following proposition.

Proposition 7.8 *The set of pairs of rectifying homographies depends upon 9 free parameters. This set is described in terms of the canonical pair (H_0, H_0') by the equations*

$$\mathbf{H} \simeq \mathbf{M}\mathbf{H}_0, \quad \mathbf{H}' \simeq \mathbf{M}'\mathbf{H}_0',$$

where the matrices $\mathbf{M}$ and $\mathbf{M}'$ are given by

$$\mathbf{M} = \begin{bmatrix} a & b & c \\ 0 & e & f \\ 0 & h & i \end{bmatrix}, \quad \mathbf{M}' = \begin{bmatrix} a' & b' & c' \\ 0 & e & f \\ 0 & h & i \end{bmatrix},$$

Figure 7.7: Planar parallax. The third image is obtained by warping the second image by the homography of the ground plane, so that points on this plane are mapped to their position in the first image, and superimposing with the first image. The planar parallax is the length of the vector between original and warped points. It is zero for points of the reference plane, and is proportional to the height above this plane and inversely proportional to the depth. These vectors all point towards the epipole in the image.

with

$$\begin{vmatrix} e & f \\ h & i \end{vmatrix} \neq 0.$$

Proof : If $(\mathbf{H}, \mathbf{H}')$ is such a pair, then one must have

$$\mathbf{H} \simeq \mathbf{M}\mathbf{H}_0, \quad \mathbf{H}' \simeq \mathbf{M}'\mathbf{H}_0',$$

for a pair $(\mathbf{M}, \mathbf{M}')$ of homographies that satisfy the equation

$$\mathbf{M}'^T[\varepsilon_1]_\times \mathbf{M} \simeq [\varepsilon_1]_\times. \tag{7.11}$$

If we define

$$\mathbf{M} = \begin{bmatrix} a & b & c \\ d & e & f \\ g & h & i \end{bmatrix}, \quad \mathbf{M'} = \begin{bmatrix} a' & b' & c' \\ d' & e' & f' \\ g' & h' & i' \end{bmatrix},$$

then the matrix equation (7.11) easily yields the results of the proposition. Since the 10 parameters $(a, b, c, a', b', c', e, f, h, i)$ are defined up to scale, there are 9 degrees of freedom. □

The geometric interpretation of these parameters is shown in Figure 7.8.

- a (respectively a') is a scale factor along the x-axis.

- b (respectively b') controls the inclination of the rectified image.

- b (respectively c') is the abscissa of the origin of the rectified image.

- e is a common scale factor along the y-axis in both images (because of the epipolar constraint).

- f is the common vertical coordinate of the origin of coordinates.

- h controls the "perspective" distortion of the rectified images.

- i is a global scale factor.

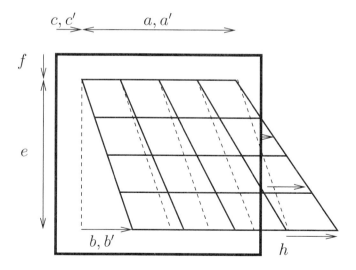

Figure 7.8: Geometric interpretation of the parameters of the rectifying homographies.

3-D	α_u	θ	u_0	α'_u	θ'	u'_0	α_v	v_0	Φ
algebraic	a	b	c	a'	b'	c'	e	f	h

Table 7.1: Correspondence between some of the intrinsic parameters of the two views and the parameters of the rectifying homographies.

These parameters correspond to some of the intrinsic parameters of the two views (except for h), as shown in Table 7.1. We can also give a purely projective, image-based, interpretation of the rectification process. Consider Figure 7.9. In each image we use the projective bases (e, v, o, h) and (e', v', o', h'), respectively. Notice that (v, v'), (o, o') and (h, h') are corresponding pairs of points. We denote by (x_1, x_2, x_3) the projective coordinates of m in the first basis. According to Proposition 2.18, the ratio x_1/x_3 is equal to the cross-ratio $\{e, o; c', c\}$ which, according to the same figure, is equal to the cross-ratio $\{e, a; b, m\}$. Similarly, the ratio x_2/x_3 is equal to the cross-ratio $\{v, o; d', a\}$ which, according to the same figure, is equal to the cross-ratio $\{v, c; d, m\}$. These cross-ratios are preserved by the rectifying homography H which maps e to the point at infinity of the x-axis, v to the point at infinity of the y-axis, o to the upper left-hand corner of the rectified image and h to the lower right-hand corner. Hence, the first one is equal to the x affine coordinate of $\hat{m}$ and the second to the y affine coordinate of $\hat{m}'$.

An example of rectification is shown in Figure 7.10. We have applied the method described above to the pair of images in Figure 5.18.

7.2.6 Application to obstacle detection

This section describes how to use the previous results to provide a robot with the ability to detect obstacles. The only requirement is that the robot be equipped with a stereo rig which can be very simply calibrated, as explained next.

- As described in Chapter 6, some correspondences between two views taken by the cameras are obtained and used to compute the Fundamental matrix.

- Three particular correspondences are given to the system; they define a virtual plane Π in front of the robot (see Figure 7.11).

- The H-matrix of Π is computed as described in Chapter 5.

The Fundamental matrix, as well as the plane H-matrix, remains the same for any other pair of views taken by the system, as long as the intrinsic parameters of both cameras and the relative attitudes of the cameras do not change. According to the previous section, the images can be rectified so that $\mathbf{H}_\Pi \simeq \mathbf{I}_3$ and the epipolar lines are the image rows. Correlation based stereo can then be run on the pair of rectified images (see Figure 7.12). For each pair (m, m') of correspondences,

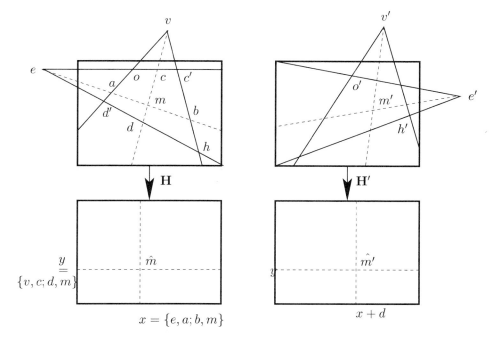

Figure 7.9: Rectification of a stereo pair from four pairs of corresponding points: The epipoles e, e', two vanishing points (v, v'), the origins of coordinates (o, o'), and the lower right-hand corners (h, h'). The coordinates in the rectified images are cross-ratios in the original images.

the disparity (i.e. the difference in horizontal coordinates of the two pixels) is the projective parallax. If we look again at Equation 7.7, we see that its sign changes only when the 3D point M crosses Π: $d(E_5, \Pi_f)$ and $d(E_5, \Pi)$ are independent of the position of M and $d(M, \Pi_f)$ has a constant sign since M is always (except for possible false matches) "in front of" Π_f.

Therefore, the sign of the disparity indicates which parts of the scene are beyond the plane Π and which are between the plane and the cameras. Figure 7.13 shows the disparity map obtained by correlation. The intensity encodes closeness to the camera. Figure 7.14 shows the segmentation of the disparity map in two parts corresponding to the positive and negative values. On the left-hand side, points with negative disparities, that is points in front of the reference plane, are shown: Those points represent potential obstacles or intruders. Similarly, the right-hand side of the figure shows the points with positive disparities, that is, the points which are beyond the reference plane.

Figure 7.10: Example of rectification of epipolar geometry. The pair of images in Figure 5.18 has been warped so that convergent epipolar lines are now parallel and aligned.

7.2.7   Application to image based rendering from two views

Image synthesis from images is a fairly recent concept which originated in the statement that in fact a scene can be represented by its set of views, and that it may be possible to avoid the explicit reconstruction of a three-dimensional model of the scene in order to synthesize new views.

Let us take a simple example: Given two views, written 1 and 2, of a single object for which the Fundamental matrix is known, we imagine a virtual camera that we wish to move in the scene in order to simulate camera motion. From the two real images, which are the data of the problem, can we synthesize what the camera would see if we really moved it? Several remarks must be made. The first one is common sense: We will not be able to invent the parts of the scene which are not seen in the initial views. The second one is more technical since we saw that the Fundamental matrix contained only projective information and when we talk about moving a camera, even though virtual, in the scene, we do n0t have all the necessary information.

We will for now ignore this second point and get to the problem of synthesizing a third view from two others. We may suppose that this virtual view, written 3, is linked to the real views by the two Fundamental matrices which get added to the Fundamental matrix of the two real views. We call these matrices $\mathbf{F}_{31}$ and $\mathbf{F}_{32}$.

Let m_1 and m_2 be two matching pixels from views 1 and 2, i.e. the images of a single 3D point of the scene. How do we construct the point m_3, the image of this same 3D point in the third view? The answer is in general very simple: We plot the epipolar lines of m_1 and m_2 in the third image (which is possible since we know the epipolar geometries), and the point m_3 is in general the intersection point of these two lines, when it exists (for more detail, see Section 8.1.1).

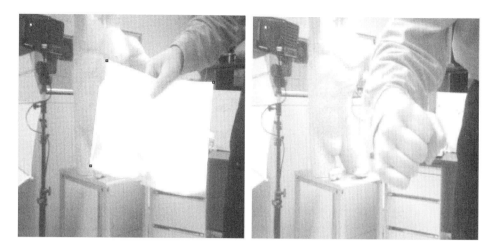

Figure 7.11: The paper used to define the plane and the left image of the fist taken as an example.

Let us be more specific. The point m_3 does not exist when the 3D point considered lies in the Trifocal plane defined by the three optical centers (see Section 8.1). In this case the previous construction fails, but we show in Chapter 8 that we can get away with this construction by using the Trifocal tensor. However the point m_3 thus constructed is not the image of the 3D point when the latter is not visible from the third view because of occlusion; see Figure 7.15. However we can proceed slightly differently.

Instead of constructing the virtual image from pairs (m_1, m_2), we will start from the virtual image and for each of its pixels m_3 we look for the matching pair (m_1, m_2). We plot the epipolar lines $\mathbf{F}_{31}\mathbf{m}_3$ and $\mathbf{F}_{32}\mathbf{m}_3$ of m_3 in images 1 and 2 and we orient them from the epipole so that the epipolar line and the optic ray (C_3, m_3) of C_3 both run towards the scene. We also suppose that each pixel of image 1 matches a pixel of image 2 (e.g. with the help of a stereo algorithm based on correlation similar to that used in the examples of Figures 7.11 to 7.14), in practice this step is not necessary. We can thus plot in image 2 the curve of the points corresponding to the points of image 1 located on the epipolar line of m_3. This curve intersects in general the epipolar line of m_3 in image 2 at one or more points. The relevant point is the first one encountered when we run down this epipolar line oriented as described above from the epipole; see Figure 7.16.

From the stereo pair of Figure 7.17, we can then synthesize the image of Figure 7.18 where we can see that the left part of the torso which is not visible in real images is not visible in the synthesized image. The latter reconstructs well the three-dimensional geometry of the object present in the scene with this geometry

Figure 7.12: The left and right rectified images of the fist in figure 7.11 .

represented only by matching points between images 1 and 2.

Returning to the second remark at the beginning of this section, more information than the Fundamental matrix between the two real views is needed, and in particular the intrinsic parameters of the first camera are needed. In practice, we can compute the internal parameters of the real views by self-calibration (see Chapter 11) and thus position the virtual camera with respect to the real cameras.

We will show in Chapter 10 an example of the application of these ideas to film synthesis from a set of images.

7.3   Affine stratum

In the previous case of the projective stratum, the only information we had at our disposal was the Fundamental matrix. We saw that it allowed us to reconstruct the scene up to a 3D homography. We now explore the situation where we have more knowledge about the scene.

We saw in Chapter 2 that an affine structure can be defined on a projective space by singling out a specific plane. The complement of that plane has a natural affine structure and the plane itself can be interpreted as the plane of infinity of this affine space. Our situation is somewhat similar: Knowledge of the Fundamental matrix allows us to represent the real world as a projective space but we know from experience that it is in fact an affine space (and even a Euclidean space, but this will come later). In order to retrieve the affine structure, we need to somehow "identify" its plane at infinity which is one of the planes of our so far projective environment. But in a projective space, the plane at infinity is just a plane and therefore induces

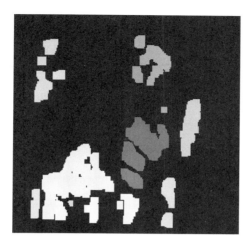

Figure 7.13: The disparity map obtained from the rectified images of Figure 7.12.

a planar morphism between our two views. This morphism, denoted H_∞, is a homography (the corresponding matrix is of rank 3) if and only if the plane does not go through any of the optical center: This situation occurs when both cameras perform a perspective projection. A planar morphism of rank 2 is obtained when one camera performs a parallel projection. We assume without loss of generality that it is the second camera. When both cameras are affine, the morphism is of rank 1. This case if of no interest here.

7.3.1 The projection matrices

If the infinity morphism is known, we can choose $\mathbf{r} = \mathbf{r}_\infty$ in Equation 7.1. It turns out that there is a one parameter family of matrices $\mathcal{P}'$ such that $\mathcal{P} \simeq \mathcal{P}_0$ and $\mathbf{H}_\Pi \simeq \mathbf{H}_{\Pi_\infty}$. We thereby obtain a characterization of the *affine canonical form*:

Proposition 7.9 *For a given Fundamental matrix* $\mathbf{F}$ *and infinity morphism, the condition* $\mathcal{P} \simeq \mathcal{P}_0$ *implies that* $\mathcal{P}'$ *takes the simple form*

$$\mathcal{P}' \simeq [\mathbf{H}_\infty \; \mu\mathbf{e}'] = [\mathbf{S}, \mathbf{e}'] \, \mathbf{Q}^{\mathcal{B}_0}_{\mathcal{B}_\infty}, \tag{7.12}$$

where

$$\mathbf{Q}^{\mathcal{B}_0}_{\mathcal{B}_\infty} = \left[\begin{array}{cc} \mathbf{I}_3 & \mathbf{0}_3 \\ \mathbf{r}^T_\infty & \mu \end{array} \right] \tag{7.13}$$

describes a change of projective coordinates from an affine frame to the projective canonical frame $\mathcal{B}_0 \equiv (\Pi'_0, 1)$. *This affine frame is interpreted after Proposition 7.10.*

 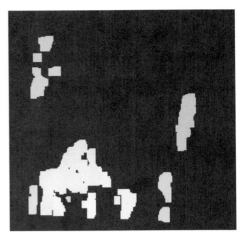

Figure 7.14: The absolute value of the negative disparities on the left, showing that the fist and a portion of the arm are between the robot and the plane of rectification, and the positive disparities on the right, corresponding to the points located beyond the plane.

When the projection matrices take this form we talk about the **affine canonical form**.

Proof : We have to prove that, for a given pair $(\mathcal{P} = [\mathbf{P}\ \mathbf{p}], \mathcal{P}')$ of projection matrices, the first one being such that the matrix $\mathbf{P}$ is of rank 3, there exists an *affine* change of coordinates such that $\mathcal{P} \simeq \mathcal{P}_0$ and $\mathcal{P}'$ takes the form (7.12). Let $\mathcal{A}$ be a 4×4 matrix describing an affine change of coordinates:

$$\mathcal{A} = \begin{bmatrix} \mathbf{X} & \mathbf{x} \\ \mathbf{0} & \mu \end{bmatrix}.$$

μ is an arbitrary nonzero number, $\mathbf{X}$ is a 3×3 matrix of rank 3, and $\mathbf{x}$ is a 3×1 vector. The condition $\mathcal{P} \simeq \mathcal{P}_0$ implies that $\mathbf{PX} \simeq \mathbf{I}_3$ and $\mathbf{Px} + \mu\mathbf{p} = \mathbf{0}$. The first relation yields $\mathbf{X} = \lambda\mathbf{P}^{-1}$ for some nonzero λ, and the second yields $\mathbf{x} = -\mu\mathbf{P}^{-1}\mathbf{p}$. The matrix $\mathcal{A}$ therefore takes the form:

$$\begin{bmatrix} \lambda\mathbf{P}^{-1} & -\mu\mathbf{P}^{-1}\mathbf{p} \\ \mathbf{0} & \mu \end{bmatrix}.$$

Since the vector $\mathbf{P}^{-1}\mathbf{p}$ does not depend on the scale of $\mathcal{P}$, we can absorb the factor λ in $\mathcal{P}$ and deduce that the form for $\mathcal{P}'$ is

$$\mathcal{P}' \simeq \begin{bmatrix} \mathbf{P}'\mathbf{P}^{-1} & \mu(-\mathbf{P}'\mathbf{P}^{-1}\mathbf{p} + \mathbf{p}') \end{bmatrix}.$$

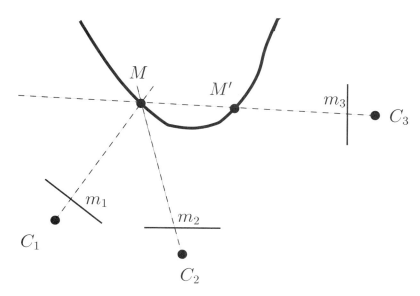

Figure 7.15: The occlusion problem: Camera C_3 sees M' but not M. On the other hand m_3 is at the intersection of the epipolar lines with respect to the third view of m_1 and m_2 (assuming that M is not in the trifocal plane). How can we decide that the geometric construction fails because of occlusion?

According to Propositions 5.20 and 5.21 this statement can be rewritten

$$\mathcal{P}' \simeq \left[\begin{array}{cc} \mathbf{H}_\infty & \mu \mathbf{e}' \end{array} \right].$$

□

We can adapt Proposition 7.2 to the affine setting. In this case we have a one-parameter family of projection matrices compatible with $\mathbf{F}$ and $\mathbf{H}_\infty$:

Proposition 7.10 *The affine canonical frame corresponds to choosing an affine frame centered at the optical center of the first camera. We call this frame an* **affine canonical frame** *for the pair of cameras and denote it by* $\mathcal{B}_\infty \equiv (\Pi_\infty, \mu)$. *The number μ controls the global scale of the scene.*

Proof : The proof follows from that of Proposition 7.2 by specializing the projective canonical frame and using the results of Section 2.5.2 where we related an affine basis to a projective basis of its projective completion. An affine basis (O, A_1, A_2, A_3) corresponds to the projective basis $(E_1, E_2, E_3, E_4, E_5)$ such that $E_4 = O$, E_1, E_2, E_3 are the points in Π_∞ in the directions of the vectors $\overrightarrow{OA_1}$, $\overrightarrow{OA_2}$ and $\overrightarrow{OA_3}$, and E_5 is represented by $\mathbf{E}_{1234} = \mathbf{E}_1 + \mathbf{E}_2 + \mathbf{E}_3 + \mathbf{E}_4 =$

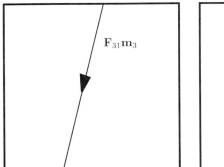 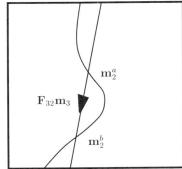

Figure 7.16: The epipolar path: The relevant point is m_2^a.

$O + \overrightarrow{OA_1} + \overrightarrow{OA_2} + \overrightarrow{OA_3}$. Since the affine canonical frame is a projective canonical frame, we have $O = C$ and we verify that the three points E_1, E_2, E_3 are in Π_∞. We also saw in Proposition 7.2 that changing the value of μ was equivalent to having E_5 move along the line (C, E_{1234}) minus the point C and the point at infinity of the optical ray (C, ε_4). Writing $\mathbf{E}_5 = \mu \mathbf{E}_4 + \mathbf{E}_{1234}$, a straightforward computation shows that the corresponding change of projective coordinates is described by a 4×4 matrix proportional to

$$\begin{bmatrix} 1 & 0 & 0 & 0 \\ 0 & 1 & 0 & 0 \\ 0 & 0 & 1 & 0 \\ 0 & 0 & 0 & \mu + 1 \end{bmatrix}.$$

The case $\mu = -1$ corresponds to a point E_5 in Π_∞ and is therefore not allowed. Hence the previous matrix is proportional to the matrix

$$\begin{bmatrix} \frac{1}{\mu+1} & 0 & 0 & 0 \\ 0 & \frac{1}{\mu+1} & 0 & 0 \\ 0 & 0 & \frac{1}{\mu+1} & 0 \\ 0 & 0 & 0 & 1 \end{bmatrix},$$

which is an *affine* transformation which simply changes the lengths of the vectors $\overrightarrow{CA_1}$, $\overrightarrow{CA_2}$ and $\overrightarrow{CA_3}$ by the same factor. $\square$

We can now interpret the change of projective coordinates described by the matrix $\mathbf{Q}_{\mathcal{B}_\infty}^{\mathcal{B}_0}$ as a change from an affine coordinate system, denoted $\mathcal{B}_\infty$, of origin C (in effect its corresponding projective frame, as discussed in Section 2.5.2) to the projective canonical frame $\mathcal{B}_0 \equiv (\Pi_0', 1)$.

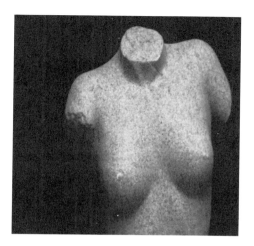

Figure 7.17: Stereo pair of a torso.

7.3.2 Affine reconstruction

We first decompose a pair of projection matrix into two types of parameters: The affine correspondence of the pair of cameras (represented by the infinity homography and the epipole), and an affine transformation, which represents an arbitrary choice of affine coordinates. This is done by fixing $\mathbf{r} = \mathbf{r}_\infty$ in Proposition 7.3:

Proposition 7.11 *The pairs* $(\mathcal{P}, \mathcal{P}')$ *with epipole* $\mathbf{e}'$ *and infinity homography* $\mathbf{H}_\infty$ *are of the form*

$$\begin{cases} \mathcal{P} & \simeq & [\mathbf{I}_3\,\mathbf{0}]\mathcal{H}, \\ \mathcal{P}' & \simeq & [\mathbf{H}_\infty\,\mu\mathbf{e}']\mathcal{H}, \end{cases} \quad with\ \mathcal{H} = \left[\begin{array}{c} \mathcal{P} \\ \mathbf{0}_3^T\ 1 \end{array}\right].$$

The crucial remark is that the transformation of space is an affine transformation rather than a projective one. From that, it is an easy matter to verify the following proposition.

Proposition 7.12 $(\mathcal{P}_1, \mathcal{P}'_1)$ *and* $(\mathcal{P}_2, \mathcal{P}'_2)$ *have the same infinity homography and epipole if and only if* $\mathcal{P}_1 = \mathcal{P}_2\mathcal{A}$ *and* $\mathcal{P}'_1 = \mathcal{P}'_2\mathcal{A}$, $\mathcal{A}$ *being an affine transformation of* $\mathbb{P}^3$.

When we have identified the plane at infinity Π_∞, a pair of views $(\mathcal{P}, \mathcal{P}')$ with epipole $\mathbf{e}'$ and infinity homography $\mathbf{H}_\infty$ determines a reconstruction up to an affine transformation of $\mathbb{P}^3$ (see Figure 1.25 for an example) which can be computed using the affine canonical representation

$$\begin{cases} \mathcal{P} & = & [\mathbf{I}_3\,\mathbf{0}]\mathbf{Q}^{\mathcal{B}_0}_{\mathcal{B}_\infty}, \\ \mathcal{P}' & = & [\mathbf{H}_\infty\,\mu\mathbf{e}'] = [\mathbf{S}\,\mathbf{e}']\,\mathbf{Q}^{\mathcal{B}_0}_{\mathcal{B}_\infty}. \end{cases} \tag{7.14}$$

Figure 7.18: Synthesis of a side view from the previous images.

Let us count again the number of degrees of freedom. Of the total 22 parameters,

- 12 correspond to the affine ambiguity in reconstruction: The arbitrary choice of the affine basis (11 obtained by fixing $\mathcal{P}$, 1 is μ), and

- 10 describe the affine correspondence: 8 as the infinity homography $\mathbf{H}_\infty$, and 2 as the epipole $\mathbf{e}'$.

The projective reconstruction is upgraded to the affine reconstruction by applying the projective transformation $\mathbf{Q}_{\mathcal{B}_0}^{\mathcal{B}_\infty}$ to the 3D points. Because of duality, the matrix $\mathbf{Q}_{\mathcal{B}_0}^{\mathcal{B}_\infty\,T}$ describes how the representations for planes change when we go from $\mathcal{B}_\infty \equiv (\Pi_\infty, \mu)$ to $\mathcal{B}_0 \equiv (\Pi_0', 1)$. A simple computation shows that

$$\mathbf{Q}_{\mathcal{B}_0}^{\mathcal{B}_\infty\,T} = \begin{bmatrix} \mathbf{I}_3 & -\mathbf{r}_\infty/\mu \\ \mathbf{0}_3^T & 1/\mu \end{bmatrix}.$$

Therefore, the plane Π_∞, represented by ε_4 in (Π_∞, μ), is represented by $[-\mathbf{r}_\infty^T, 1]^T$ in $(\Pi_0', 1)$. It can be verified that the image of the line of intersection of Π_∞ and Π_0' in the first view is, as expected, represented by the vector $\mathbf{r}_\infty$ (Proposition 5.16).

7.3.3   Affine parallax

We have an echo of Proposition 7.5:

Proposition 7.13 *In the affine canonical frame, the relation between two corresponding pixels m and m' can be written*

$$\mathbf{m}' \simeq \mathbf{H}_{\Pi_\infty}\mathbf{m} + \kappa_{\Pi_\infty,\mu}\mathbf{e}'. \tag{7.15}$$

The number $\kappa_{\Pi_\infty,\mu}$ is called the **affine parallax** *of the corresponding 3D point M. In particular, $\kappa_{\Pi_\infty,\mu} = 0$ if and only if the point M is at infinity. The ratio of $\kappa_{\Pi_\infty,\mu}/\mu$ and any nonzero coordinate of m is an affine invariant, i.e. does not depend upon the choice of μ in (7.12).*

Proof : We simply adapt the proof of Proposition 7.5 to this case. Equation 7.15 is an immediate consequence of our choice of Π as Π_∞. The rest of the proposition follows from Proposition 7.10. □

We gave a geometric interpretation and a way to compute the projective planar parallax. We now do the same for the affine planar parallax. Let us reinterpret in the affine framework the fact that the ratio $\kappa_{\Pi,\mu}/(\mu m_3)$ is equal to the cross-ratio (P, Q, E_5, M). We have $\Pi = \Pi_\infty$, and $m_3 = 1$. Let us denote by θ_P, θ_Q, θ_{E_5} and θ_M the projective parameters of the four points (P, Q, E_5, M) on the *affine* line (E_5, M). The point Q is in the plane (E_1, E_2, E_3), i.e. Π_∞; hence $\theta_Q = \infty$ and the cross-ratio is equal to the ratio of the algebraic lengths $\overline{E_5 P}/\overline{MP}$. Let (X, Y, Z) be the affine coordinates of M in the affine canonical frame. The affine coordinates of the point E_5 are $(\lambda, \lambda, \lambda)$ (where $\lambda = 1/(1 + \mu)$), the equation of the plane (E_1, E_2, E_4) is $Z = 0$, and we readily find that the value of the ratio $\overline{E_5 P}/\overline{MP}$ is simply λ/Z. Therefore the affine planar parallax is given by the simple formula

$$\kappa_{\Pi_\infty,\mu} = \frac{\mu}{1+\mu} \cdot \frac{1}{Z}.$$

For a given global scale μ, the affine parallax is inversely proportional to Z. Z is the third coordinate of the point M in the canonical affine frame (Π_∞, μ) and can be interpreted as a depth as follows. Because in the canonical affine frame we have $\mathcal{P} \simeq \mathcal{P}_0$, the focal plane of the first camera is the plane of equation $Z = 0$. The Z-axis of the affine canonical frame, which is not necessarily the optical axis of the first camera, is nonetheless not parallel to the retinal plane and therefore Z is proportional to the depth. i.e. the Euclidean distance to the optical center C of the first camera.

7.3.4 Estimating $\mathbf{H}_\infty$

We now review some of the techniques for evaluating the infinity morphism. They fall broadly in two categories. In the first category we find the methods that use some *a priori* knowledge about the scene. In the second category we find the methods that use active motion.

7.3.4.1 Using *a priori* knowledge about the world

These methods are based on the knowledge of some affine invariants, i.e. of quantities which do not change when the scene undergoes to an arbitrary affine transformation, i.e. an arbitrary member of $\mathcal{AG}$ (see Chapter 2, Section 2.2). Let us take two examples.

Parallel lines   Parallelism is the basic affine property. Let us suppose that we have been able to identify in two images a set of lines which are images of parallel lines in 3D space. This task has been addressed by many researchers (Magee and Aggarwal, 1984; Quan and Mohr, 1989; Collins and Weiss, 1990; Brillault-O'Mahony, 1991; Straforini et al., 1993; Tai et al., 1993; Lutton et al., 1994; Mclean and Kotturi, 1995; Shufelt, 1999). It can be performed with good results when the scene contains man-made objects such as buildings. In Figure 7.19 we show a set of parallel lines on an image which will be used to illustrate this section.

Figure 7.19: An image of a series of aerial views of houses, showing line segments used for the computation of Π_∞.

Let (l_i, l'_i), $i = 1, 2$, be two pairs of line correspondences. Each of these correspondences determines a 3D line L_i. These two 3D lines happen to be parallel in the "real" space. That is, considered as lines in the ambient projective space, they meet at the point V_{12} in Π_∞. The images v_{12} and v'_{12} of V_{12} are nothing but the points of intersection of the lines l_1 and l_2 in the first image and of the lines l'_1 and l'_2 in the second image, respectively (in effect their vanishing points). In terms of

H_∞, this yields one pair of points, i.e. (v_{12}, v'_{12}), that correspond to each other:

$$\mathbf{H}_\infty \mathbf{v}_{12} \simeq \mathbf{v}'_{12}.$$

Since the pair (e, e') is already known from the Fundamental matrix, in theory we only need three pairs of 3D parallel lines to determine H_∞. This technique works only if the four points at infinity form a real quadrangle, i.e. are projectively independent. This property can easily be checked in the images.

The previous scheme does not enforce the fact that corresponding vanishing points have to satisfy the epipolar constraint. A way to do so with multiple views is described in (Faugeras et al., 1998b). We describe it here for the case of two. The idea is to directly estimate the plane at infinity in the canonical projective frame of the pair of cameras.

Let L_j be the parallel lines in space, and (l_j, l'_j) their images in the two views. Let also v (respectively v') be the vanishing point of the lines l_j (respectively of the lines l'_j) in the image. We have

$$\mathbf{v} \simeq \boldsymbol{\mathcal{P}}\mathbf{V}, \qquad \mathbf{v}' \simeq \boldsymbol{\mathcal{P}}'\mathbf{V},$$

where V is the point of intersection in space of the lines L_j. This point, which represents their direction, belongs to the plane at infinity Π_∞. Since v (respectively v') belongs to all of the lines l_j (respectively all of the lines l'_j), the 3D point V can be found by minimizing the error function

$$\min_{\mathbf{V}} \sum_j d^2(l_j, \boldsymbol{\mathcal{P}}\mathbf{V}) + d^2(l'_j, \boldsymbol{\mathcal{P}}'\mathbf{V}), \qquad \text{subject to} \qquad \|\mathbf{V}\| = 1.$$

This method yields one point V_k per set of parallel lines. Each of the points V_k belongs to Π_∞. Once three non-collinear such points are obtained, a coordinate vector of Π_∞ (in fact of $*\Pi_\infty$ as discussed in Section 3.4.5) is obtained as $*(\mathbf{V}_1 \triangledown \mathbf{V}_2 \triangledown \mathbf{V}_3)$ or equivalently by expanding the 4×4 determinant $|\mathbf{V}_1, \mathbf{V}_2, \mathbf{V}_3, \mathbf{\Pi}_\infty|$. In case one has more than three points, Π_∞ can be obtained by solving the linear least-squares problem

$$\min_{\mathbf{\Pi}_\infty} \sum_k \|\mathbf{V}_k^T \mathbf{\Pi}_\infty\|^2, \qquad \text{subject to} \quad \|\mathbf{\Pi}_\infty\| = 1.$$

Let us now see how we can recover the affine canonical form for the pair of cameras. According to Equation 7.12 we need to determine the vector $\mathbf{r}_\infty$. Let us denote by $\boldsymbol{\mathcal{H}}_{AP}$ the matrix

$$\begin{bmatrix} \mathbf{I}_3 & \mathbf{0}_3 \\ \mathbf{r}_\infty^T & \mu \end{bmatrix}.$$

If a 3D point M is represented by the coordinate vector $\mathbf{M}$ in the affine canonical frame, then it is represented by $\boldsymbol{\mathcal{H}}_{AP}^{-1}$ in the projective canonical frame. Similarly, if a plane is represented by the coordinate vector $\mathbf{\Pi}$ in the affine canonical frame, then it is represented by $\mathcal{H}_{AP}^T \Pi$ in the projective canonical frame. Therefore, since Π_∞ is represented by ε_4 in the affine canonical frame, it is represented by $\mathcal{H}_{AP}^T e_4$ in the projective canonical frame. Thus $[\mathbf{r}_\infty^T, \mu]^T \simeq \Pi_\infty$, which yields $\mathbf{r}_\infty$ up to scale. The scale can be resolved by enforcing $\mathbf{H}_\infty \mathbf{v}_k \simeq \mathbf{v}_k'$. Note that $\mu \neq 0$ forces the last coordinate of Π_∞ to be nonzero but this constraint is a consequence of the fact that the first camera performs a perspective projection: Its optical center is represented by ε_4 and does not belong to Π_∞.

An alternative solution to the affine canonical frame is the use of an object-centered coordinate system. A homography $\mathcal{H}$ of $\mathbb{P}^3$ is defined by the following change of projective basis.

- A point M_0 of the scene is chosen as the new origin $[0, 0, 0, 1]^T$.

- Three directions, i.e. three points in Π_∞, $\mathbf{V}_1, \mathbf{V}_2, \mathbf{V}_3$ are chosen for the points $[1, 0, 0, 0]^T, [0, 1, 0, 0]^T, [0, 0, 1, 0]^T$.

- A point M_S, not in Π_∞, is chosen and assigned arbitrary affine coordinates $[\alpha, \beta, \gamma, 1]^T$, with $\alpha, \beta, \gamma \neq 0$. Hence M_S should not be in any of the three affine coordinate planes $(M_S, \mathbf{V}_i, \mathbf{V}_j)$, $i, j = 1, 2, 3, i \neq 3$.

The parameters α, β, γ simply represent the scale factors along the coordinate axes. For instance, changing the value of α will just stretch the reconstructed scene along the $\mathbf{V}_1$ axis, as shown in Figure 7.20.

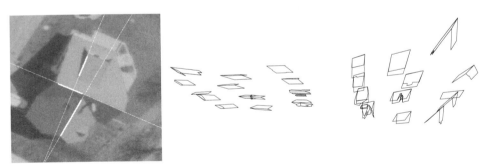

Figure 7.20: Line segments and directions used for defining the coordinate axes (left), top-view (middle) and side-view (right) of the affine reconstruction. They differ only by one scale factor along the direction of the top edge of the roof.

An interesting fact about this approach is that if the directions $\mathbf{V}_1, \mathbf{V}_2$ and $\mathbf{V}_3$ are chosen so that they are mutually orthogonal, then one obtains an affine orthogonal frame. To obtain an orthonormal affine frame only the scale factors α, β, γ remain to be computed. This idea is discussed in the Section 7.4.4.

Ratios of distances   The ratio of distances of aligned points is the basic affine invariant. The second example is concerned with the case of three aligned points, say (A, B, C), in three-space with a known ratio k of oriented lengths $\overline{AC}/\overline{BC}$. We saw in Chapter 2, Equation 2.16, that this ratio is equal to the cross-ratio $\{A, B; C, L_\infty\}$ where L_∞ is the point of intersection of the line (A, B, C) with Π_∞. Consider now what happens in the first image, the situation in the second being identical. Let (a, b, c) be the images of (A, B, C) and l_∞ be the image of L_∞. The first three points are known; the fourth one is not. But, because the cross-ratio is invariant with respect to perspective projection, we have $\{A, B; C, L_\infty\} = k = \{a, b; c, l_\infty\}$. If we go back to the definition (2.12) of the cross-ratio, we find one linear equation for the projective parameter of l_∞. The point l_∞ is therefore uniquely determined. Applying the same procedure in the second image, we determine the image l'_∞ of L_∞. The final result is a pair (l_∞, l'_∞) of corresponding points for the infinity morphism, H_∞. Just like in the previous case of parallel lines, three sets of three aligned points with known ratios of oriented lengths are in theory sufficient to determine H_∞ provided that the points at infinity of each of the three sets are not aligned, which can be checked in the images.

7.3.4.2   Using a stereo rig

Another way of estimating the infinity morphism is to perform pure translations with a stereo rig while tracking such features as points and lines. Let us consider the case of a 3D line L that is seen as l_1 and l'_1 in the first position of the rig. After translation, the line is seen as l_2 and l'_2. Since translating the rig is equivalent to translating the line, this motion is equivalent to keeping the rig fixed and forming the images of two parallel lines L_1, seen as (l_1, l'_1), and L_2 seen as (l_2, l'_2). Therefore this case is exactly the same as in the previous section: The vanishing points v_{12} and v'_{12}, intersections of the lines l_1 and l_2 and l'_1 and l'_2, respectively, are the images of the point at infinity V_{12} of the two parallel lines L_1 and L_2. In fact, we will see in Section 10.4 that when using a moving stereo rig, there is no need to restrict ourselves to translations

7.3.5   Application to affine measurements

We present a few more examples of the use of affine information. The first example demonstrates that one can make affine measurements directly in the images. Suppose that we are given two pairs (m_i, m'_i), $i = 1, 2$, of corresponding points. The midpoints q and q' of the two image segments (m_1, m_2) and (m'_1, m'_2) do not in general correspond to each other and are not the images of the midpoint P of the 3D line segment (M_1, M_2). The question is whether or not we can build the images p and p' of P without actually reconstructing M_1 and M_2.

The answer is a straightforward application of the discussion in the previous section: Construct the vanishing points v and v' of the two lines $l = (m_1, m_2)$ and

$l' = (m'_1, m'_2)$ from H_∞; p (respectively p') is then the point of l (respectively of l') such that the cross-ratio $\{m_1, m_2; p, v\}$ (respectively $\{m'_1, m'_2; p', v'\}$) is equal to -1. An example is shown in Figure 7.21.

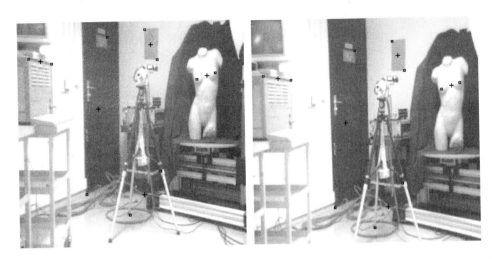

Figure 7.21: The images of the midpoints of some 3D segments: The endpoints of the segments are shown as squares, the midpoints as crosses. No 3D reconstruction was performed.

The second example is similar but shows a potential application to robot navigation. Suppose that a robot equipped with a stereo rig that has been affinely calibrated is navigating down a straight hallway such as the one shown in Figure 7.22. A possible and certainly simple strategy for its navigation would be "to stay in the middle". This strategy can be translated into something like "keep the images of the midline of the hallway in some predefined part of the two views". The problem is that the midline does not exist physically in the environment but since it is an affine concept and we have assumed that the rig was affinely calibrated, we should be able to compute it from the edges of the hallway. This approach is explained in Figure 7.23. Let l_1, l_2 (respectively l'_1, l'_2) be the images of the edges of the hallway; we want to compute the image l (respectively l') of its midline. Pick a point m_1 on l_1, m_2 on l_2, and the corresponding points m'_1 and m'_2 in the second image are at the intersection of the epipolar lines l'_{m_1} and l'_{m_2} of m_1 and m_2 with l'_1 and l'_2, respectively. We have thus constructed two pairs (m_1, m'_1) and (m_2, m'_2) of corresponding points, and we have just seen how to construct the points m and m' which are the images of the midpoint M of the 3D points M_1 and M_2. M is by definition on the midline of the hallway. If we iterate this construction once more, then we have found our lines l and l'.

Figure 7.22: Result of the computation in the images, i.e. without a 3D reconstruction, of the midline of the corridor. The stereo rig is affinely calibrated.

7.4 Euclidean stratum

According to Section 7.1, the Euclidean canonical representation is obtained when $\mathcal{P} \simeq \mathbf{A}\mathcal{P}_0$ where $\mathbf{A}$ is the matrix of the internal parameters, defined in Section 4.3.1, of the first camera.

7.4.1 The projection matrices

We assume that the Fundamental matrix $\mathbf{F}$ between the two views, the infinity morphism H_∞, and the internal parameters of the two cameras, represented by the two upper-triangular matrices $\mathbf{A}$ and $\mathbf{A}'$, are known. We obtain a characterization of the *Euclidean canonical form*

Proposition 7.14 *For a given Fundamental matrix $\mathbf{F}$, infinity morphism, and internal parameters, the condition $\mathcal{P} \simeq \mathbf{A}\mathcal{P}_0$ implies that $\mathcal{P}'$ takes the simple form:*

$$\mathcal{P}' \simeq \mathbf{A}'\,[\mathbf{R}\ \mathbf{t}] = [\mathbf{S}\ \mathbf{e}']\,\mathbf{Q}_{\mathcal{B}_\infty}^{\mathcal{B}_0}\mathbf{Q}_{\mathcal{E}}^{\mathcal{B}_\infty}, \tag{7.16}$$

where $\mathbf{Q}_{\mathcal{B}_\infty}^{\mathcal{B}_0}$ is given by Equation 7.13 and

$$\mathbf{Q}_{\mathcal{E}}^{\mathcal{B}_\infty} = \begin{bmatrix} \mathbf{A} & \mathbf{0}_3 \\ \mathbf{0}_3^T & 1 \end{bmatrix} \tag{7.17}$$

describes a change of affine coordinates from an orthonormal affine basis of origin C to a general affine basis also centered at C.

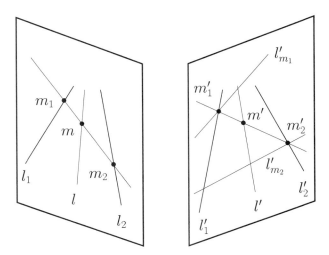

Figure 7.23: How to compute the images l and l' of the midline of the corridor from the images l_1, l_2, l_1' and l_2' of its left and right sides.

The matrix $\mathbf{R}$ is the rotation matrix that describes the rotation from the normalized coordinate system $\mathcal{F}_C$ of the first camera to that, $\mathcal{F}_{C'}$, of the second. The vector $\mathbf{t}$ is the vector $\overrightarrow{C'C}$ expressed in the second camera normalized coordinate system.

Proof :   Proposition 5.24 gives us $\mathbf{e}' \simeq \mathbf{A}'\mathbf{t}$. Proposition 5.25 gives us $\mathbf{H}_\infty \simeq \mathbf{A}'\mathbf{R}\mathbf{A}^{-1}$. Thus if we multiply the affine canonical form of Proposition 7.14 on the right by the matrix

$$\begin{bmatrix} \mathbf{A} & \mathbf{0}_3 \\ \mathbf{0}_3^T & 1 \end{bmatrix},$$

which represents an affine change of coordinate system, then we obtain Equation 7.16. □

We can also adapt Propositions 7.2 and 7.10 to the Euclidean setting:

Proposition 7.15 *The Euclidean canonical frame corresponds to choosing an affine frame which is the canonical coordinate system $\mathcal{F}_C$ of the first camera (see Chapter 4). We call this frame the **Euclidean canonical frame**.*

Proof :   The proof is simply a reading of the beginning of Section 5.3.2. □

7.4.2 Euclidean reconstruction

We note that if we decompose each projection matrix into intrinsic and extrinsic parameters, we have the classical decomposition

$$\begin{cases} \mathcal{P} & \simeq & \mathbf{A}[\mathbf{R}_1\,\mathbf{t}_1] & = & [\mathbf{A}\,\mathbf{0}]\mathcal{D}, \\ \mathcal{P}' & \simeq & \mathbf{A}'[\mathbf{R}_2\,\mathbf{t}_2] & = & \mathbf{A}'[\mathbf{R}\,\mu\mathbf{t}]\mathcal{D}, \end{cases} \quad \text{with} \quad \mathcal{D} = \begin{bmatrix} \mathbf{R}_1 & \mathbf{t}_1 \\ \mathbf{0}_3^T & 1/\mu \end{bmatrix},$$

where $\mathbf{R} = \mathbf{R}_2\mathbf{R}_1^T$ and $\mathbf{t} = \mathbf{t}_2 - \mathbf{R}_2\mathbf{R}_1^T\mathbf{t}_1$ represents the relative displacement between the two camera normalized coordinate systems. Let us count again the degrees of freedom: Of the total 22 parameters,

- 7 correspond to a similarity transformation representing the arbitrary choice of the Euclidean basis (6 obtained by fixing the coordinate system of the first camera $\mathbf{R}_1,\mathbf{t}_1$, 1 is μ which represents the scale), and

- 15 describe the intrinsic parameters (5 for each camera) and the relative Euclidean motion $\mathbf{R}$, $\mathbf{t}$ (position and orientation) of the two cameras.

The direction of the translation is determined, but not its norm because of the depth-speed ambiguity: One cannot distinguish between a close point moving slowly and a distant point moving proportionally faster. We can characterize the Euclidean reconstruction by either one of the two sets of fifteen parameters:

- the affine reconstruction plus the intrinsic parameters of one camera: $\mathbf{H}_\infty, \mathbf{e}', \mathbf{A}$, or

- the intrinsic parameters of both cameras and the displacement between two cameras: $\mathbf{A}$, $\mathbf{A}'$, $\mathbf{R}$, $\mathbf{t}$.

Using this definition it is easy to see that

Proposition 7.16 $(\mathcal{P}_1, \mathcal{P}_1')$ and $(\mathcal{P}_2, \mathcal{P}_2')$ *have the same Euclidean reconstruction if and only if* $\mathcal{P}_1 = \mathcal{P}_2\mathcal{S}$ *and* $\mathcal{P}_1' = \mathcal{P}_2'\mathcal{S}$, $\mathcal{S}$ *being a similarity transformation of* $\mathbb{P}^3$.

We can now write a Euclidean reconstruction as a specialization of affine strata and projective strata:

$$\begin{cases} \mathcal{P} & \simeq & [\mathbf{A}\,\mathbf{0}] & = & [\mathbf{I}\,\mathbf{0}]\mathbf{Q}_{\mathcal{B}_\infty}^{\mathcal{B}_0}\,\mathbf{Q}_{\mathcal{E}}^{\mathcal{B}_\infty}, \\ \mathcal{P}' & \simeq & \mathbf{A}'[\mathbf{R}\,\mu\mathbf{t}] & = & [\mathbf{S}\,\mu\mathbf{e}']\mathbf{Q}_{\mathcal{B}_\infty}^{\mathcal{B}_0}\,\mathbf{Q}_{\mathcal{E}}^{\mathcal{B}_\infty}. \end{cases}$$

Starting from a projective reconstruction, which requires only point correspondences, we can upgrade to an affine reconstruction when $\mathbf{r}_\infty$ is known (3 DOF), by applying $\mathbf{Q}_{\mathcal{B}_0}^{\mathcal{B}_\infty}$ to the points M_i, and to a Euclidean reconstruction when $\mathbf{A}$ is known (5 DOF), by applying $\mathbf{Q}_{\mathcal{B}_\infty}^{\mathcal{E}}$. Each upgrade reduces the reconstruction ambiguity, first from a general homography (15 DOF) to an affine transformation (12 DOF), then to a similarity (7 DOF).

We have already seen that $\mathbf{Q}^{\mathcal{B}\infty}_{\mathcal{B}_0}$ is a projective transformation which moves the plane at infinity. $\mathbf{Q}^{\mathcal{E}}_{\mathcal{B}\infty}$ is an affine transformation which corresponds to a change of the absolute conic or, equivalently, of the absolute quadric. The matrix of Ω in the plane at infinity in a Euclidean frame is simply $\mathbf{I}_3$. When we apply the change of affine coordinates defined by $\mathbf{Q}^{\mathcal{B}\infty}_{\mathcal{E}}$, this matrix becomes $\mathbf{A}^{-T}\mathbf{A}$ which is indeed the matrix of the absolute conic (Proposition 4.21).

Similarly for the absolute quadric, because of duality, the change of coordinates is describes for planes by $\mathbf{Q}^{\mathcal{B}\infty}_{\mathcal{E}}{}^{T}$. Hence, if $\mathcal{Q}^*$ is the matrix of the absolute quadric in a Euclidean frame, then its matrix in an affine frame is $\mathbf{Q}^{\mathcal{B}\infty}_{\mathcal{E}}{}^{T}\mathcal{Q}^*\mathbf{Q}^{\mathcal{B}\infty}_{\mathcal{E}}{}^{-T}$. Because of Equation 2.23, the equation of the absolute quadric is found to be

$$\begin{bmatrix} \mathbf{K} & \mathbf{0}_3 \\ \mathbf{0}_3^T & 1 \end{bmatrix},$$

where $\mathbf{K}$ is the Kruppa matrix (Definition 4.3) giving the equation of the conic dual to the image of the absolute conic.

The transformation from the Euclidean representation to the projective representation is given by

$$\mathbf{Q}^{\mathcal{B}_0}_{\mathcal{E}} = \mathbf{Q}^{\mathcal{B}_0}_{\mathcal{B}\infty}\mathbf{Q}^{\mathcal{B}\infty}_{\mathcal{E}} = \begin{bmatrix} \mathbf{A} & \mathbf{0}_3 \\ \mathbf{r}_\infty^T\mathbf{A} & \mu \end{bmatrix}. \tag{7.18}$$

7.4.3 Euclidean parallax

Propositions 7.5 and 7.13 extend to the Euclidean case where they can be interpreted very simply.

Proposition 7.17 *In the Euclidean canonical frame, the relation between two corresponding pixels m and m' can be written*

$$Z'\tilde{\mathbf{m}}' = Z\mathbf{R}\tilde{\mathbf{m}} + \mathbf{t}. \tag{7.19}$$

Z (respectively Z') is the depth of the 3D point M whose image is m (respectively m') in the camera normalized coordinate system of the first view (respectively, the second).

$\tilde{\mathbf{m}} = [x, y, 1]^T$ (respectively $\tilde{\mathbf{m}}' = [x', y', 1]^T$) is the vector of coordinates of pixel m (respectively m') in the normalized pixel coordinate system $\mathcal{F}_c$ of the first camera (respectively $\mathcal{F}_{c'}$ of the second); see Chapter 4.

If M is at infinity, then the relation reduces to

$$\tilde{\mathbf{m}}' \simeq \mathbf{R}\tilde{\mathbf{m}}. \tag{7.20}$$

Proof : Assume first that M is not at infinity.

Let $\tilde{\mathbf{M}}_{/\mathcal{F}_C} = [X, Y, Z, 1]^T$ be the vector of coordinates of M in the first camera normalized coordinate system, $\mathcal{F}_C$. Since $\tilde{\mathbf{m}} = \mathbf{A}^{-1}\tilde{\mathbf{m}}_{/\mathcal{F}_o}$, we have (Equation 4.28) $Z\tilde{\mathbf{m}} = \mathbf{M}_{/\mathcal{F}_C} = [X, Y, Z]^T$. Let $\tilde{\mathbf{M}}_{/\mathcal{F}_{C'}} = [X', Y', Z', 1]^T$ be the vector of coordinates of M in the second camera normalized coordinate system, $\mathcal{F}_{C'}$. We have $Z'\tilde{\mathbf{m}}' = \mathbf{M}_{/\mathcal{F}_{C'}} = [X', Y', Z']^T$. Since $\mathbf{M}_{/\mathcal{F}_{C'}} = \mathbf{R}\mathbf{M}_{/\mathcal{F}_C} + \mathbf{t}$, Equation 7.19 follows.

If M is at infinity, then we have $\tilde{\mathbf{M}}_{/\mathcal{F}_C} \simeq [X, Y, Z, 0]^T$, $\tilde{\mathbf{M}}_{/\mathcal{F}_{C'}} = [X', Y', Z', 0]^T$, $\tilde{\mathbf{m}} \simeq \mathbf{M}_{/\mathcal{F}_C} = [X, Y, Z]^T$, $\tilde{\mathbf{m}}' \simeq \mathbf{M}_{/\mathcal{F}_{C'}} = [X', Y', Z']^T$, and $\mathbf{M}_{/\mathcal{F}_{C'}} \simeq \mathbf{R}\mathbf{M}_{/\mathcal{F}_C}$. Equation 7.20 follows. $\square$

7.4.4 Recovery of the intrinsic parameters

To convert the affine representation to a Euclidean representation, it is necessary and sufficient to identify the images of the absolute conic. As has been seen in Chapter 4, five parameters are needed. We consider several approaches that use *a priori* information about the scene. Methods that do not require such information will be described in Chapter 11.

7.4.4.1 Upgrading from affine with known angles

The first basic similarity invariant is the angle of two lines. The angle α between two 3D lines L_1 and L_2 in the world yields a constraint on the coefficients of ω. Refer to Section 2.7.2.2 where we show that the angle of two lines in 3D is equal to the cross-ratio of their points at infinity and the two points of intersection of the line defined by these points with the absolute conic Ω. This cross-ratio is unchanged by perspective projection and is therefore equal to the cross-ratio of the vanishing points v_1 and v_2 (respectively v'_1 and v'_2) of the images l_1 and l_2 (respectively l'_1 and l'_2) of the two lines with the two points of intersection of the line (v_1, v_2) (respectively (v'_1, v'_2)) with ω (respectively ω'). We have computed this cross-ratio in Section 4.3.2. Equation 4.33 yields the following relation

$$S(\mathbf{v}_1, \mathbf{v}_2)^2 = S(\mathbf{v}_1, \mathbf{v}_1)S(\mathbf{v}_2, \mathbf{v}_2)\cos^2\alpha.$$

We have a similar expression in the second view.

The vanishing points can be obtained from the infinity morphism H_∞. This equation is a quadratic constraint on the coefficients of the equation of ω.

Let us give another approach and interpretation. According to the proof of Proposition 7.14, the transformation which maps the affine representation to the Euclidean representation is given by $\mathbf{H}_e$ such that its inverse $\mathbf{H}_e^{-1}$ is equal to:

$$\mathbf{H}_e^{-1} = \begin{bmatrix} \mathbf{A} & \mathbf{0}_3 \\ \mathbf{0} & 1 \end{bmatrix}, \tag{7.21}$$

where the matrix $\mathbf{A}$ represents the intrinsic parameters of the first camera, provided that the first projection matrix $\mathcal{P}$ is in affine canonical form. Starting from the affine representation consisting of the projection matrices $\mathcal{P}$, $\mathcal{P}'$ suppose that we have identified a pair of orthogonal lines in the scene (the extension to the case where the angle of the two lines is not 90 degrees is left to the reader). The points at infinity of these lines can be computed from their images, the infinity morphism and the projection matrices. We denote by $\mathbf{V}$, $\mathbf{V}^{\perp}$ their *affine* coordinates, i.e. the first three coordinates of their projective coordinates (the last one is zero since they belong to Π_{∞}). Since the transformation $\mathbf{H}_e$ maps the points to a Euclidean frame, we must have $(\mathbf{A}^{-1}\mathbf{V})^T(\mathbf{A}^{-1}\mathbf{V}^{\perp}) = 0$. Note that this equation can be rewritten as $\mathbf{V}^T\mathbf{B}\mathbf{V}^{\perp} = 0$ where $\mathbf{B} = \mathbf{A}^{-T}\mathbf{A}^{-1}$ is the matrix of the image ω of the absolute conic in the first image. Thus, each pair of orthogonal line yields one *linear* constraint between the coefficients of the equation of ω (the constraint becomes quadratic if the angle is not equal to 90 degrees). In general if one has several pairs of orthogonal lines, then one finds the coefficients of $\mathbf{B}$ by minimizing the quadratic error function

$$\min_{\mathbf{B}} \sum_i \|\mathbf{V}_i^T\mathbf{B}\mathbf{V}_i^{\perp}\|^2.$$

Note that even if the initial representation is not in canonic form, the matrix $\mathbf{A}$ can still be taken as upper triangular. Let us see why. If the three axes assigned to the affine coordinate system were orthogonal, then all we would have to recover to obtain an orthonormal frame would be the three scale factors on each axis, so that in this case $\mathbf{A}$ would have the form $\text{diag}(\alpha, \beta, \gamma)$. But in general, this is not the case, and therefore we have to introduce the parameters λ, μ, ν which account for the "skew" of the coordinate system, mapping $\mathbf{V}_1$ to $[1, 0, 0, 0]^T$ (as before), $\mathbf{V}_2$ to $[\lambda, 1, 0, 0]^T$, and $\mathbf{V}_3$ to $[\mu, \nu, 1, 0]^T$ (see Section 7.3.4.1). The expression for the matrix $\mathbf{A}$ is therefore a general upper triangular matrix:

$$\mathbf{A} = \begin{bmatrix} \alpha & \beta\lambda & \gamma\mu \\ 0 & \beta & \gamma\nu \\ 0 & 0 & \gamma \end{bmatrix}.$$

Only two of the scale factors can be recovered, and we can fix $\gamma = 1$. Therefore five unknowns remain, as expected, and it is necessary in general to find five pairs of perpendicular lines in the scene.

When only three intrinsic parameters (the focal length and the coordinates of the principal point) are considered in the matrix $\mathbf{A}$, the knowledge of three mutually orthogonal directions is sufficient to recover the intrinsic parameters as well as the rotation between the camera coordinate system and the coordinate system defined by the three orthogonal directions.

Figure 7.24 shows a reconstruction obtained in an affine frame with orthogonal axes, and different values of the scale factors. Two edges aligned with two orthogonal coordinate axes remain orthogonal in the final affine reconstruction, for any value of the scale parameters α, β, γ (see Section 7.3.4.1). This is the case of the roof which has been used to define the two horizontal directions (left). The relative values of the scale factors used for the two displayed affine reconstructions (middle, right) are very different. This difference drastically modifies the aspect of the reconstructed roof (at the bottom-right in each view), but the principal directions remain orthogonal in both reconstructions. Figure 7.25 shows the final Euclidean reconstruction after computation of these scale factors.

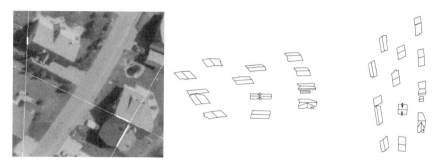

Figure 7.24: Line segments and directions used for defining the coordinate axes (left); two top-views (left) and (right) of the scene reconstructed with two different values of the scale-factor along one of the horizontal axes (see text).

7.4.4.2 Upgrading from affine with known ratios of lengths

The second basic similarity invariant is the ratio of the lengths of two line segments. It is easy to see that angles can be used to compute ratios of lengths. Let us consider four points A, B, C and D and suppose we want to compute the ratio $\frac{AB}{CD}$. Considering the two triangles ABC and BCD, as shown in Figure 7.26, we can write, for the first triangle,

$$\frac{AB}{\sin \gamma} = \frac{BC}{\sin \alpha}$$

and, for the second,

$$\frac{BC}{\sin \delta} = \frac{CD}{\sin \beta},$$

from which we obtain the ratio $\frac{AB}{CD}$ as a function of the four angles α, β, γ and δ:

$$\frac{AB}{CD} = \frac{\sin \gamma \cdot \sin \delta}{\sin \alpha \cdot \sin \beta}. \tag{7.22}$$

Figure 7.27 shows the computation in the first image plane. Using H_∞, we construct the four vanishing points v_{ab}, v_{ac}, v_{bc}, v_{bd}, and v_{cd} of the image lines

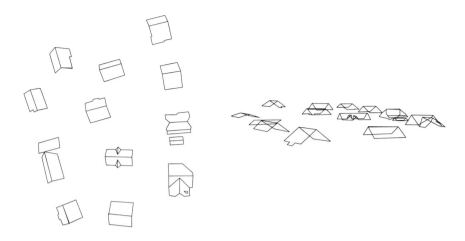

Figure 7.25: Top-view (left) and side-view (right) of the scene reconstructed after adjustment of the scale factors in order to preserve orthogonality. The frame of reference is the same as in Figure 7.24.

(a, b), (a, c), (b, c), (b, d) and (c, d). The sines which appear in Equation 7.22 are then obtained through Equation 4.33. More specifically, we obtain a neat formula (7.23) for the ratio $\frac{AB}{CD}$ computed in the first image in which appears only the equation of ω:

$$\frac{AB}{CD} = \sqrt{\frac{S(\mathbf{v}_{ab})}{S(\mathbf{v}_{cd})} \cdot \frac{S(\mathbf{v}_{ac})S(\mathbf{v}_{bc}) - S(\mathbf{v}_{ac}, \mathbf{v}_{bc})^2}{S(\mathbf{v}_{ab})S(\mathbf{v}_{ac}) - S(\mathbf{v}_{ab}, \mathbf{v}_{ac})^2} \cdot \frac{S(\mathbf{v}_{bd})S(\mathbf{v}_{cd}) - S(\mathbf{v}_{bd}, \mathbf{v}_{cd})^2}{S(\mathbf{v}_{bc})S(\mathbf{v}_{bd}) - S(\mathbf{v}_{bc}, \mathbf{v}_{bd})^2}}$$

$$(7.23)$$

The geometry is shown is Figure 7.27.

Conversely, if we know the ratio of the lengths of two non-coplanar segments AB and CD, then we can use Equation 7.23 to derive another constraint on the coefficients of the equation of ω. Let us call r the (known) ratio $\frac{AB}{CD}$ and define

$$D(\mathbf{v}_{pq}, \mathbf{v}_{st}) = S(\mathbf{v}_{pq}, \mathbf{v}_{st})^2 - S(\mathbf{v}_{pq}, \mathbf{v}_{pq})S(\mathbf{v}_{st}, \mathbf{v}_{st}),$$

where v_{pq} is the vanishing point of the line (p, q). Using Equation 7.23 we obtain the constraint

$$D(\mathbf{v}_{ac}, \mathbf{v}_{bc})D(\mathbf{v}_{cd}, \mathbf{v}_{bd})S(\mathbf{v}_{ab}, \mathbf{v}_{ab}) = r^2 D(\mathbf{v}_{ac}, \mathbf{v}_{ab})D(\mathbf{v}_{bc}, \mathbf{v}_{bd})S(\mathbf{v}_{cd}, \mathbf{v}_{cd}) \quad (7.24)$$

on the coefficients of the equation of ω, which is seen to be a polynomial of degree 8 in the coefficients of the equation of ω.

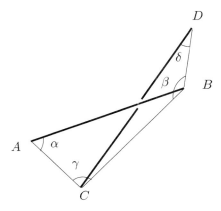

Figure 7.26: Computing the ratio of the lengths of the two segments AB and CD from the angles α, β, γ and δ.

7.4.5 Using knowledge about the world: Point coordinates

Upgrading from a projective representation   A projective representation can be upgraded to a Euclidean representation using point coordinates. To determine the projective transformation $\mathcal{H}$ which transforms the projective reconstruction to the Euclidean reconstruction, it is sufficient to know the Euclidean coordinates of five points. One advantage of this approach is that if the projective (or affine) reconstruction has been done with high precision, then the projective (or affine) properties (such as epipolar geometry) will be well preserved even if the coordinates of the reference points are not known with extreme precision. For instance in (Zhang et al., 1997) it was shown that using point correspondences to compute the epipolar geometry and then upgrading to Euclidean using a calibration object yields superior precision in epipolar geometry.

Another advantage of this approach is that it can be applied with more general constraints than points coordinates. The transformation $\mathcal{H}$ contains an arbitrary similitude transform, which is fixed by making a choice of an arbitrary Euclidean coordinate system and frame. This choice can be made so as to facilitate the expression of the constraints. For example, a natural choice in a scene which contains the ground and walls is to take the ground as the plane $Z = 0$, and two orthogonal walls as the two other planes defining the Euclidean coordinate system. Given

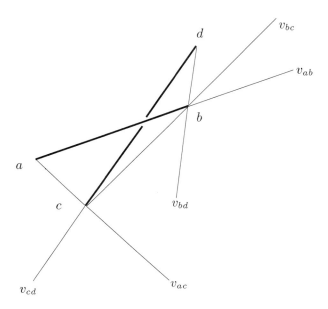

Figure 7.27: Computing the ratio of the lengths of the two segments AB and CD from the vanishing points v_{ab}, v_{ac}, v_{bc}, v_{bd}, and v_{cd} of the image lines (a, b), (a, c), (b, c), (b, d) and (c, d).

the projective representation defined by the projection matrices $\boldsymbol{\mathcal{P}}_i$ and the points $\mathbf{M}_j$, the Euclidean representation is given by the projection matrices $\boldsymbol{\mathcal{P}}_i\boldsymbol{\mathcal{H}}$ and the points $\boldsymbol{\mathcal{H}}^{-1}\mathbf{M}_j$. Any Euclidean information on the scene can then be expressed as a function of $\boldsymbol{\mathcal{H}}^{-1}\mathbf{M}_j$, yielding constraints on $\boldsymbol{\mathcal{H}}^{-1}$. These constraints are in general at least quadratic in the entries of $\boldsymbol{\mathcal{H}}^{-1}$, since the Euclidean coordinates are obtained by

$$X = (\boldsymbol{\mathcal{H}}^{-1}\mathbf{M}_j)_1/(\boldsymbol{\mathcal{H}}^{-1}\mathbf{M}_j)_4,$$
$$Y = (\boldsymbol{\mathcal{H}}^{-1}\mathbf{M}_j)_2/(\boldsymbol{\mathcal{H}}^{-1}\mathbf{M}_j)_4,$$
$$Z = (\boldsymbol{\mathcal{H}}^{-1}\mathbf{M}_j)_3/(\boldsymbol{\mathcal{H}}^{-1}\mathbf{M}_j)_4.$$

Examples of such constraints which are easily expressed are (Boufama et al., 1993)

- known coordinates of a 3D point,

- knowledge of the fact that a point belongs to one of the coordinate system's plane,

- knowledge that two points define a line parallel to one of the coordinate system axes, and

- a known distance between two points.

Classical calibration   The last sections have brought us closer to classical calibration methods which extensively use *a priori* knowledge of the environment to compute a canonical Euclidean representation. These methods are based on the observation of an object for which the three-dimensional coordinates of n reference points M_j are known. The projections m_j of these points are measured in the image and yield pixel coordinates (u_j, v_j). The reference objects which are used are generally calibration grids composed of repeated patterns (circles or rectangles) chosen to define points of interest which can be measured with very good precision. The basic idea is that since the coordinates of both the points M_j and m_j are available, it is possible to compute the parameters of the projection using the n projection equations $\mathbf{m}_j \simeq \mathcal{P}(\mathbf{M}_j)$, provided we have a sufficient number of points. Let us write the projection matrix

$$\mathcal{P} = \left[\begin{array}{c} \boldsymbol{U}^T \\ \boldsymbol{V}^T \\ \boldsymbol{W}^T \end{array} \right].$$

The classical approaches used in photogrammetry are based on the *bundle adjustment* method (see Chapter 10 for a detailed description and more references). This method requires m views and n points M_i, of which only some control points need to be known. It is based on the minimization of the error function

$$\sum_{i=1}^{m} \sum_{j=1}^{n} \left(\left(u_{ij} - \frac{\boldsymbol{U}_i^T \mathbf{M}_j}{\boldsymbol{W}_i^T \mathbf{M}_j} - \Delta_u(u_{ij}, v_{ij}) \right)^2 + \left(v_{ij} - \frac{\boldsymbol{V}_i^T \mathbf{M}_j}{\boldsymbol{W}_i^T \mathbf{M}_j} - \Delta_v(u_{ij}, v_{ij}) \right)^2 \right).$$

The minimization is done with espect to

- all of the projection matrices $\mathcal{P}_i$,

- many distortion parameters contained in the functions Δ_u and Δ_v which account for the deviation from the pinhole model, and

- all of the 3D points M_j except the control points.

This approach yields extremely high precision but requires many carefully positioned control points. The nonlinear optimization has to be performed over a very large parameter space, and in spite of the use of sparse techniques, remains computationally very expensive.

7.5   Summary

For each level of description, we have a partition of the 22 parameters describing two projective views into a set of invariant descriptors, which represent the correspondences, and into the ambiguity in reconstruction, as detailed in Table 7.2.

PROJECTIVE	**homography** (incidence, $\mathbb{P}^3$)		
reconstruction ambiguity	$\mathcal{H} = \begin{bmatrix} \boldsymbol{\mathcal{P}} \\ \boldsymbol{\Pi}^T \end{bmatrix}$	$\mathcal{H}$ non-singular	15
invariant description	$\mathbf{S}$: special matrix		5
	$\mathbf{e}'$: epipole		2
canonical form	$\begin{cases} \boldsymbol{\mathcal{P}} & \simeq & [\mathbf{I}_3\, \mathbf{0}_3]\mathcal{H} \\ \boldsymbol{\mathcal{P}}' & \simeq & [\mathbf{S} + \mathbf{e}'\mathbf{r}_\Pi^T \; \mu\mathbf{e}']\mathcal{H} \end{cases}$		22
AFFINE	**affine transformation** (parallelism, Π_∞)		
reconstruction ambiguity	$\mathcal{A} = \begin{bmatrix} \mathbf{P} & \mathbf{p} \\ \mathbf{0}_3^T & 1/\mu \end{bmatrix}$	$\mathbf{P}$ non-singular	12
invariant description	$\mathbf{H}_\infty$: infinity homography		8
	$\mathbf{e}'$: epipole		2
canonical form	$\begin{cases} \boldsymbol{\mathcal{P}} & \simeq & [\mathbf{I}_3\, \mathbf{0}_3]\mathcal{A} \\ \boldsymbol{\mathcal{P}}' & \simeq & [\mathbf{H}_\infty\, \mu\mathbf{e}']\mathcal{A} \end{cases}$		22
EUCLIDEAN	**similarity** (angles, Ω)		
reconstruction ambiguity	$\mathcal{S} = \begin{bmatrix} \mathbf{R}_1 & \mathbf{t}_1 \\ \mathbf{0}_3^T & 1/\mu \end{bmatrix}$	$\mathbf{R}_1$ orthogonal	7
invariant description	$\mathbf{A}, \mathbf{A}'$: intrinsic parameters		5+5
	$\mathbf{R}$: rotation between cameras		3
	$\mathbf{t}$: direction of translation between cameras		2
canonical form	$\begin{cases} \boldsymbol{\mathcal{P}} & \simeq & [\mathbf{A}\, \mathbf{0}_3]\mathcal{S} \\ \boldsymbol{\mathcal{P}}' & \simeq & \mathbf{A}'[\mathbf{R}\, \mu\mathbf{t}]\mathcal{S} \end{cases}$		22

Table 7.2: Canonical forms for the geometries of two images: For each level of description, we have a partition of the 22 parameters describing two projective images into an invariant representation, which represent the correspondence, and the ambiguity in reconstruction. The last column indicates the number of degrees of freedom.

Starting from a projective reconstruction, which requires only point correspondences, we can upgrade to an affine reconstruction when $\mathbf{r}_\infty$ is known (3 DOF), by applying $\mathbf{Q}_\mathcal{B}^{\mathcal{B}\infty}$ to the points, and to a Euclidean reconstruction when $\mathbf{A}$ is known (5 DOF), by applying $\mathbf{Q}_{\mathcal{B}_\infty}^{\mathcal{E}}$:

$$\left\{ \begin{array}{rcl} \mathcal{P} & = & [\mathbf{I}_3\,\mathbf{0}]\,\mathbf{Q}_{\mathcal{B}\infty}^{\mathcal{B}_0}\,\mathbf{Q}_{\mathcal{E}}^{\mathcal{B}\infty}, \\ \mathcal{P}' & = & [\mathbf{S}\,\mathbf{e}']\,\mathbf{Q}_{\mathcal{B}\infty}^{\mathcal{B}_0}\,\mathbf{Q}_{\mathcal{E}}^{\mathcal{B}\infty}. \end{array} \right.$$

where $\mathbf{Q}_{\mathcal{B}\infty}^{\mathcal{B}_0}$ is given by Equation 7.13 and $\mathbf{Q}_{\mathcal{E}}^{\mathcal{B}\infty}$ is given by Equation 7.17.

In any one of the projective canonical coordinate systems, a point M which is projected into m in the first camera can be written under the form $\begin{bmatrix} \mathbf{m} \\ \kappa \end{bmatrix}$. If the second projection matrix is $[\mathbf{H}, \mathbf{e}']$, then κ can be recovered from the disparity equation

$$\mathbf{m}' \simeq \mathbf{Hm} + \kappa \mathbf{e}'.$$

The scalar κ is an invariant for its level of representation. In the Euclidean and affine cases, κ is inversely proportional to the depth of M. In the projective case, κ is inversely proportional to the depth of M and proportional to the orthogonal distance from M to the plane defined by $\mathbf{H}$.

7.6 References and further reading

The idea that the determination of the projection matrices and reconstruction are not required, but that measures of projective invariants in the images are sufficient for positioning was formulated by Mohr *et al.* (Mohr and Arbogast, 1990; Mohr and Morin, 1991), and also in (Sparr and Nielsen, 1990). One of the benefits of studying in depth the relations between points and projections is that we find that, for a number of tasks, actual reconstruction is not necessary. One such task is the creation of new images. For references on transfer in a third view and image synthesis, see Chapter 8.

Projective reconstruction, planar parallax, and stereo rectification The possibility of projective reconstruction from uncalibrated images up to a projective transformation was first discovered by Faugeras (Faugeras, 1992) and Hartley *et al.* (Hartley et al., 1992). A formulation of projective depth as an invariant using two planes was also given by Shashua (Shashua, 1994). Analytical methods for projective reconstruction based on elimination in systems of linear equations were proposed by Ponce *et al.* (Ponce et al., 1994). Several methods for triangulation from a pair of point correspondences were studied by Hartley and Sturm (Hartley and Sturm, 1997). In a similar spirit, Rothwell *et al.* (Rothwell et al., 1997) compared several methods for projective reconstruction from two views.

The decomposition of image motion into a planar homographic transfer plus a residual image parallax vector was suggested by several authors, including (Sawhney, 1994; Anandan et al., 1994; Viéville et al., 1996b; Shashua and Navab, 1996). Irani and Anandan (Irani and Anandan, 1996), considering pairs of points, showed that the relative structure of points, and the rigidity of a scene, can be determined directly from the parallax vectors without the need for computing the epipolar geometry. Crimisini *et al.* (Criminisi et al., 1998) extended the result on positioning-reconstruction duality of (Carlsson and Weinshall, 1998) to parallax. They pointed to the duality of the geometry of two views of seven points, four of which are coplanar, and the geometry of the three views of six points, four of which are coplanar. Cross *et al.* (Cross et al., 1999) investigated the geometry of bitangents to a smooth surface when a reference plane is available. The Fundamental matrix, Trifocal tensor, and projection matrices of N views can be recovered. Unlike the general methods on epipolar tangency, theirs does not require iterative search. Irani, Anandan and Weishall (Irani et al., 1998) developed an alternative way to view parallax an applied it to the problem of novel view synthesis. They decomposed the projection into a perspective projection onto the reference plane (which depends only on points and camera position), and a homography from the reference plane to the retinal plane (which depends on orientations and intrinsic parameters). In (Weinshall et al., 1998), they applied this framework to stratified reconstruction. Relative ordering from the plane can be obtained from only the knowledge of two parallel lines on the plane, and more information, given in terms of distances of points from the plane, leads to affine and Euclidean reconstructions. Closely related are work on fixation and dominant plane stabilization such as (Irani et al., 1997; Zelnik-Manor and Irani, 1999a).

Projective rectification by reprojection onto a common plane has many degrees of freedom. The problem is to find a rectification which minimizes the distortion of the rectified images. The differences between the approaches presented in the literature reside in the way the authors interpret what a minimal distortion is.

Chen and Medioni (Chen and Medioni, 1999b) used a simple method which works well when the initial misalignment is small. They picked two pairs of corresponding epipolar lines, and directly computed the transformation to map them to two pairs of horizontal and aligned epipolar lines. Hartley (Hartley, 1999) defined a transformation which is at the first order the closest to Euclidean near a certain point. The method is essentially linear, however the fact that it does not use an image-based criterion results in a lack of precision, and the distortion criterion lacks a clear interpretation over the images. More principled approaches are available: Robert *et al.* (Robert et al., 1996) minimized the deviation from orthogonality of the angles of the rectified images. Zeller (Zeller, 1996) maximized the area ratio of the rectified image by its bounding box. Loop and Zhang (Loop and Zhang, 1999) considered a stratified decomposition of the rectification matrices, and aimed to minimize the projective part of the distortion. Isgro and Trucco (Isgro and Trucco,

1999) proposed to rectify without prior determination of the Fundamental matrix.

The rectification methods described previously, based on a reprojection on a common plane, fail if the epipoles are inside the images, since they would result in infinitely large images. If the epipole is close to an image, then the resulting rectified image can be very large or distorted in one of its dimensions. Polleyfeys *et al.* (Pollefeys et al., 1999) presented a nonlinear approach. The image is reparameterized using polar coordinates around the epipoles, and corresponding half-epipolar lines are determined using the *oriented* fundamental matrix. Starting from one of the extreme epipolar lines, the rectified image is built up row by row in a nonlinear way (each row corresponds to an angular sector, and within it, epipolar distances are preserved), the distance between two consecutive epipolar lines being adjusted locally to avoid pixel compression. A look-up table is used to get back to the original images.

Affine and Euclidean strata While Luong and Viéville (Luong and Viéville, 1993; Luong and Viéville, 1996) introduced the idea of projective, affine, and Euclidean stratification through projection matrices, Faugeras (Faugeras, 1995) introduced it through the properties of three dimensional space. The canonical representation framework is used by Beardsley *et al.* (Beardsley et al., 1997), where they introduce a "Quasi-Euclidean" representation meant to minimize projective distortion using guesses about the intrinsic parameters and motion. Starting from the initial reconstruction in a canonical frame, the 3-D reconstruction is updated using Kalman filtering.

From two projections (l, l') of a line L, one can use the homography $\mathbf{H}$ of a plane Π to determine the projection of the intersection of L with Π in the first image: $\mathbf{l} \times \mathbf{H}^T \mathbf{l}'$. Robert and Faugeras (Robert and Faugeras, 1995) use this idea to compute the convex hull. Reid and Zisserman (Reid and Zisserman, 1996) determined the "plumb-line" projection of the a 3-D point onto the ground plane, assuming that the vertical vanishing point in two images and the homography induced by the ground plane are known. Robert *et al.* (Robert et al., 1995) used this construction to determine the relative height of a point above the ground plane. They remarked that if one camera is affine, then the relative height is metrically correct, and that experimentally it is accurate enough for navigation. Robert and Hebert (Robert and Hebert, 1994) found the homography which best warps the first image into the second one, and then obtained slope from that homography under various calibration assumptions. The idea to upgrade a projective representation directly to a Euclidean representation using some *a priori* knowledge of the scene is due to Boufama and Mohr (Boufama et al., 1993; Mohr et al., 1995). In its stratified variation, it has been explored in the context of reconstruction of buildings (Faugeras et al., 1998b; Liebowitz et al., 1999), but also of faces (Zhang et al., 1998) using a fuzzy model.

Viéville and Lingrand (Viéville and Lingrand, 1999) showed that using motions which are unknown, but of a known special form, one can sometimes recover the affine or Euclidean strata, and they give closed-form formulae for doing so. Before, the kind of special motion investigated the most was pure translational motion (Beardsley et al., 1994; Moons et al., 1996). In that context, Garding *et al.* (Garding et al., 1996) remarked that for viewpoints related by a pure translation, the ambiguity in space is in the general case a *relief transformation*, which is more general than affine, but less than projective, in that it preserves in particular the ordering. A general framework for finding the most general ambiguity in reconstruction according to the knowledge available about the cameras was developed by Mundy and Zisserman (Mundy and Zissermann, 1994). Another line of attack is to calibrate a camera using known motion (Basu, 1993; Dron, 1993; Du and Brady, 1993; Dema, 1996; Collins and Tsin, 1999).

8 Three views: The trifocal geometry

In Chapter 5 we studied in detail the algebraic-geometric constraint that relates the images of a three-dimensional point in two views. This study led us to introduce the Fundamental matrix as the means to describe the laws of epipolar geometry that are basic for understanding any stereo algorithm.

In this chapter we consider the case of three views and show that there are several algebraic-geometric constraints that relate the three images of a three-dimensional point. It turns out that it is simpler to first study the constraints that relate the three images of a three-dimensional line rather than those that relate the images of a three-dimensional point. This observation naturally leads us to introduce a new entity, the Trifocal tensor, that more or less plays for three views the role played by the Fundamental matrix for two. Because of the larger complexity of the geometry of three views compared to that of two views, the properties of the Trifocal tensor are richer than those of the Fundamental matrix and are perhaps more demanding for the reader. Despite this conceptual difficulty, the persevering reader will be rewarded by the sheer beauty of the structure of the Trifocal tensor and an increase in the power of prediction between views which eventually will lead to a simplification in the design of computer vision algorithms, e.g. in stereo and motion analysis.

The first part, Section 8.1, of this chapter is devoted to studying the geometry of three views from the perspective of the geometry of two, i.e. with the help of the Fundamental matrices. This perspective is only natural since we are now fluent in the use of the Fundamental matrices. We will seize this opportunity to study the problem of transfer: Given a point correspondence between two of the three views satisfying the relevant epipolar constraint, can we find a point in the third view that satisfies the other two epipolar constraints? We will discover that the answer to this question is in general yes except in two important cases. The investigation of this question will provide us with the opportunity to introduce a new geometric entity, the Trifocal plane, and to discover that the three Fundamental matrices are not independent but are related in an interesting and meaningful way.

The second part, Section 8.2, takes a fresh look at the geometry of three views by considering line correspondences. The Grassman-Cayley algebra plays a prominent role in allowing us to gracefully introduce the Trifocal tensors which govern those line correspondences. There are three such tensors, each one corresponding to the choice of a particular reference view among the three. The remaining part of the section is devoted to a first description of the structure of these tensors. Since each tensor is described by a $3 \times 3 \times 3$ cube of coefficients, there are various ways of splitting it into three 3×3 matrices. The most natural way, almost imposed by the definition, leads to the notion of Trifocal matrices. The remaining two ways provide even more insight in the intricate structure of the Trifocal tensor, yielding two sets of three planar morphisms that are induced between two of the three views by the three projection planes of the third one. Armed with these new tools we tackle the problem of changing the reference view, i.e. of computing the other two

Trifocal tensors given one of them. We end this long section with a detailed analysis of the geometric properties of the Trifocal matrices which we find to be somewhat analogous to Fundamental matrices and with a study of the relations between the Trifocal tensor and planar homographies that echoes the one done in Chapter 5 between the Fundamental matrix and planar homographies.

The third part, Section 8.3, returns to the problem of transfer which was one of the starting points of this chapter to show that the problems that we had encountered with the use of the three Fundamental matrices evaporate if we use the Trifocal tensors.

In the fourth part, Section 8.4, we make a first attempt at answering the question of the constraints that must be satisfied by the 27 coefficients of a Trifocal tensor. The reader will remember from Chapter 5 that a Fundamental matrix satisfies one algebraic constraint. A Trifocal tensor has to satisfy many more constraints. In this section we identify three sets of such constraints, the epipolar constraints provided by the Trifocal matrices, the axes constraints, and the extended rank constraints. This discussion is in preparation for the next chapter on the estimation of the Trifocal tensor from point and line correspondences where these constraints will be needed.

The constraints that have been identified so far are not independent. Section 8.5 goes further than the previous one in identifying smaller subsets of those constraints that are sufficient to force a tensor to be a Trifocal tensor. Besides the theoretical interest of these results, there is a practical interest for the design of estimation algorithms. This practical interest will be important in Chapter 9.

So far we have been considering the most general situation, the projective case. The remaining of the chapter is dedicated to the specialization of the analysis first to the affine case in Section 8.6 and next to the Euclidean case in Section 8.7. Because of its practical importance we spend some time explaining how, given a Euclidean Trifocal tensor, we can recover the relative extrinsic parameters of two of the views with respect to the other views.

Section 8.8 is a short analysis of the special case where all three cameras are affine. We describe the simpler form of the the Trifocal tensor and show that, when the intrinsic parameters of the cameras are known, the Trifocal tensor yields the remaining two unknown parameters that were not attainable using the methods described in Section 5.4.3.

8.1   The geometry of three views from the viewpoint of two

We denote by 1, 2 and 3 the three views. In order to avoid some degenerate cases, we make the following assumption.

Hypothesis 8.1 *The three optical centers C_1, C_2 and C_3 are distinct. We call this* *assumption* the **general viewpoint** *assumption.*

The correspondences between each pair (i, j) of views can therefore be described by the Fundamental matrices $\mathbf{F}_{ij}$ and we have

$$\mathbf{F}_{ij} = \mathbf{F}_{ji}^{T}.$$

The three Fundamental matrices seem to be a good way to represent the geometry of three views. Let us look at this representation a little closer.

8.1.1   Transfer

We start with an example. Given two corresponding points m_1 in the first view and m_2 in the second view, i.e. such that

$$\mathbf{m}_2^T \mathbf{F}_{12} \mathbf{m}_1 = 0,$$

we consider the epipolar line, represented by $\mathbf{F}_{13}\mathbf{m}_1$, of m_1 and the one, represented by $\mathbf{F}_{23}\mathbf{m}_2$, of m_2 in the third image. If those two vectors are nonzero, i.e. if they do represent lines, and if they are not proportional, i.e. if they do not represent the same line, we can construct their point of intersection m_3 which is the image of the point of intersection M of the two optical rays of m_1 and m_2; see Figure 8.1.

This process fails in the following cases.

- If $\mathbf{F}_{13}\mathbf{m}_1 = \mathbf{0}$, i.e. if and only if $m_1 = e_{13}$ the epipole in the first view of the third.

- If $\mathbf{F}_{23}\mathbf{m}_2 = \mathbf{0}$, i.e. if and only if $m_2 = e_{23}$ the epipole in the first view of the third.

- If the two lines represented by $\mathbf{F}_{13}\mathbf{m}_1$ and $\mathbf{F}_{23}\mathbf{m}_2$ are identical. Since the first line goes through the epipole e_{31} in the third view of the first and the second line goes through the epipole e_{32} in the third view of the second, we must consider two more cases:

  - If the two epipoles e_{31} and e_{32} are distinct, i.e. if the three optical centers are not aligned, then the two lines represented by $\mathbf{F}_{13}\mathbf{m}_1$ and $\mathbf{F}_{23}\mathbf{m}_2$ are identical if and only if either e_{32} belongs to the first one or e_{31} belongs to the second line. We will see next that this case corresponds to the fact that the point M is in the plane formed by the three optical centers C_1, C_2 and C_3; see Figure 8.2.

  - If the two epipoles e_{31} and e_{32} are identical, i.e. if the three optical centers are aligned, then the epipolar planes $(C_1 C_3, m_1)$ and $(C_2 C_3, m_2)$ are identical and therefore the two epipolar lines represented by $\mathbf{F}_{13}\mathbf{m}_1$ and $\mathbf{F}_{23}\mathbf{m}_2$ are identical; see Figure 8.3.

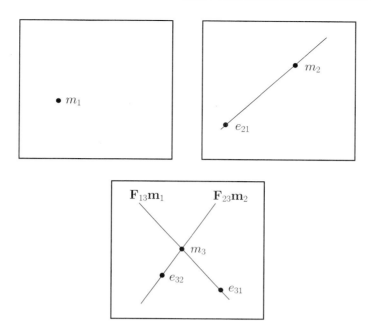

Figure 8.1: When the three optical centers are not aligned, and the 3-D point not in the Trifocal plane defined by the optical centers, the position of m_3 can be inferred from a pair (m_1, m_2) of corresponding points in the first two views with the Fundamental matrices.

This analysis clearly points to the fact that even though the three Fundamental matrices are *a priori* sufficient to describe the geometry of three views the number of special cases to consider can grow rapidly. We summarize this in a proposition:

Proposition 8.1 *Given two corresponding points m_1 and m_2 in views 1 and 2, the point m_3 image in the third view of the point M of intersection of the optical rays of m_1 and m_2 is obtained as*

$$\mathbf{m}_3 \simeq \mathbf{F}_{13}\mathbf{m}_1 \times \mathbf{F}_{23}\mathbf{m}_2,$$

*except if $m_1 = e_{13}$, or $m_2 = e_{23}$, or if the three optical centers are aligned or, if they are not aligned, if M is in the plane formed by the three optical centers C_1, C_2 and C_3. This plane is called the **Trifocal plane**.*

There is nothing special in the role played by the pair (1, 2) of views and exactly the same proposition holds if we consider the pair (2, 3) or the pair (3, 1).

The process of *predicting* a point in a third view from two corresponding points in two other views is known as *transfer*. One main consequence of our analysis is

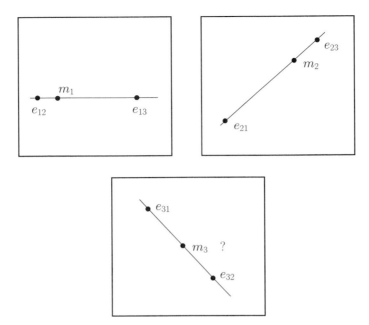

Figure 8.2: When the three optical centers are not aligned, but the 3-D point is in the Trifocal plane defined by the optical centers, the position of m_3 cannot be inferred from a pair (m_1, m_2) of corresponding points in the first two views with the Fundamental matrices.

that the transfer fails each time the three optical centers are aligned. In practice, the problem is more serious since each time the three optical centers are close to being aligned the two epipolar lines represented by $\mathbf{F}_{13}\mathbf{m}_1$ and $\mathbf{F}_{23}\mathbf{m}_2$ are very close and their intersection is poorly defined. This situation causes problems in some applications; see Chapter 10.

Note that we also have proved the following important proposition.

Proposition 8.2 *Given a 3D point M, its three images m_1, m_2 and m_3 satisfy the three relations*

$$\mid \mathbf{F}_{13}\mathbf{m}_1, \mathbf{F}_{23}\mathbf{m}_2, \mathbf{m}_3 \mid = \mid \mathbf{m}_1, \mathbf{F}_{21}\mathbf{m}_2, \mathbf{F}_{31}\mathbf{m}_3 \mid = \mid \mathbf{F}_{12}\mathbf{m}_1, \mathbf{m}_2, \mathbf{F}_{32}\mathbf{m}_3 \mid = 0. \quad (8.1)$$

The converse is *almost* true:

Proposition 8.3 *Given three points m_1, m_2 and m_3 in three views that satisfy the equations (8.1), they are in general the images of a 3D point M except in two cases:*

    1. the optical centers are aligned, or

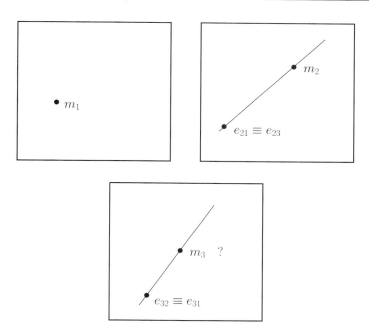

Figure 8.3: When the three optical centers are aligned, the position of m_3 cannot be inferred from a pair (m_1, m_2) of corresponding points in the first two views with the Fundamental matrices.

   2. the optical centers are not aligned and each point m_i belongs to the line defined by the two epipoles e_{ij} and e_{ik} of the other two views.

Proof :   The proof consists of showing examples in the two main cases of interest, optical centers aligned and optical centers not aligned. In the first case, Figure 8.4 shows an example of three points m_1, m_2 and m_3 that satisfy each of the three equations (8.1) but are not the images of a single 3D point. This situation is because if, for example, $\mathbf{m}_2^T \mathbf{F}_{12} \mathbf{m}_1 = 0$, i.e. if m_1 and m_2 satisfy the epipolar constraint, then we have $\mathbf{F}_{13} \mathbf{m}_1 \simeq \mathbf{F}_{23} \mathbf{m}_2$, $\mathbf{F}_{21} \mathbf{m}_2 \simeq \mathbf{F}_{31} \mathbf{m}_3$ and $\mathbf{F}_{12} \mathbf{m}_1 \simeq \mathbf{F}_{32} \mathbf{m}_3$ for all pixels m_3 on the epipolar line defined by $\mathbf{F}_{13} \mathbf{m}_1 \simeq \mathbf{F}_{23} \mathbf{m}_2$.

   In the case where the optical centers are not aligned, Figure 8.5 shows an example of three points m_1, m_2 and m_3 that are in the plane defined by the three optical centers C_1, C_2, C_3 and that satisfy all equations (8.1) but are not the images of a single 3D point. This situation occurs because for all pixels m_1, m_2, m_3 on the three lines (e_{12}, e_{13}), (e_{23}, e_{21}), (e_{31}, e_{32}) we also have $\mathbf{F}_{13} \mathbf{m}_1 \simeq \mathbf{F}_{23} \mathbf{m}_2$, $\mathbf{F}_{21} \mathbf{m}_2 \simeq \mathbf{F}_{31} \mathbf{m}_3$ and $\mathbf{F}_{12} \mathbf{m}_1 \simeq \mathbf{F}_{32} \mathbf{m}_3$.   □

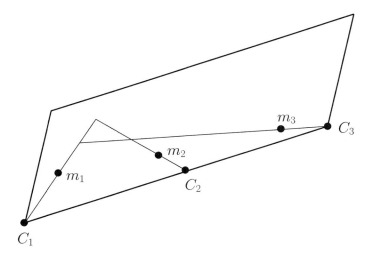

Figure 8.4: The three optical centers are aligned: The three points m_1, m_2 and m_3 satisfy the equations (8.1) but are not the images of a single 3D point.

8.1.2 Trifocal geometry

We first consider the case where C_1, C_2, C_3 are not aligned. The line $\mathbf{F}_{32}\mathbf{e}_{31}$, epipolar line of e_{31} in the second image, is the image of the line (C_1, C_3) in the second retina. Thus it is the intersection of the *Trifocal plane* (C_1, C_2, C_3) with the second retina. The epipoles e_{21} and e_{23} also belong to this plane and to the second retina, thus the epipolar line $\mathbf{t}_2 = \mathbf{e}_{21} \times \mathbf{e}_{23}$ is identical to $\mathbf{F}_{32}\mathbf{e}_{31}$. The same is true when we permute the indices 1,2,3. This situation yields six vector equations but only three of them are independent, for instance,

$$\mathbf{F}_{32}\mathbf{e}_{31} \simeq \mathbf{e}_{21} \times \mathbf{e}_{23} \simeq \mathbf{t}_2, \quad \mathbf{F}_{13}\mathbf{e}_{12} \simeq \mathbf{e}_{32} \times \mathbf{e}_{31} \simeq \mathbf{t}_3, \quad \mathbf{F}_{21}\mathbf{e}_{23} \simeq \mathbf{e}_{13} \times \mathbf{e}_{12} \simeq \mathbf{t}_1$$

or

$$\mathbf{F}_{23}\mathbf{e}_{21} \simeq \mathbf{e}_{31} \times \mathbf{e}_{32} \simeq \mathbf{t}_3, \quad \mathbf{F}_{31}\mathbf{e}_{32} \simeq \mathbf{e}_{12} \times \mathbf{e}_{13} \simeq \mathbf{t}_1, \quad \mathbf{F}_{12}\mathbf{e}_{13} \simeq \mathbf{e}_{23} \times \mathbf{e}_{21} \simeq \mathbf{t}_2. \tag{8.2}$$

The three lines t_1, t_2, t_3 defined by the corresponding vectors are called the *Trifocal lines*.

Each of these vector equations yields only *one* equation since, in addition, the epipolar constraint must be satisfied: Taking the dot product of the first equation with $\mathbf{e}_{31}$ produces one scalar equation, but taking the dot product with $\mathbf{e}_{32}$ does not produce a new equation since $\mathbf{e}_{32}^T\mathbf{F}_{23} = \mathbf{0}$. Another way to obtain these relations is to note that, for instance, the points e_{21} and e_{31} are in correspondence since they are both images of the point C_1, respectively in views 2 and 3; see Figure 8.6. As

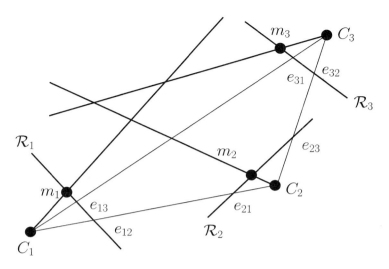

Figure 8.5: The three points m_1, m_2 and m_3 belong to the three Trifocal lines (e_{12}, e_{13}), (e_{23}, e_{21}), (e_{31}, e_{32}): They satisfy the equations (8.1) but are not the images of a single 3D point.

previously, other indices play a similar role, which yields the set of scalar relations

$$\mathbf{e}_{31}^T \mathbf{F}_{23} \mathbf{e}_{21} = 0, \qquad \mathbf{e}_{12}^T \mathbf{F}_{31} \mathbf{e}_{32} = 0, \qquad \mathbf{e}_{23}^T \mathbf{F}_{12} \mathbf{e}_{13} = 0. \qquad (8.3)$$

In fact it can be shown that, with the values of the $\mathbf{F}_{ij}$ and $\mathbf{e}_{ij}$ given in Chapter 5, Equations 5.8 and 5.9, the previous relations are

$$\mathbf{F}_{32} \mathbf{e}_{31} = -\mathbf{e}_{21} \times \mathbf{e}_{23}, \qquad \mathbf{F}_{13} \mathbf{e}_{12} = -\mathbf{e}_{32} \times \mathbf{e}_{31}, \qquad \mathbf{F}_{21} \mathbf{e}_{23} = -\mathbf{e}_{13} \times \mathbf{e}_{12}, \quad (8.4)$$

$$\mathbf{F}_{23} \mathbf{e}_{21} = -\mathbf{e}_{31} \times \mathbf{e}_{32}, \qquad \mathbf{F}_{31} \mathbf{e}_{32} = -\mathbf{e}_{12} \times \mathbf{e}_{13}, \qquad \mathbf{F}_{12} \mathbf{e}_{13} = -\mathbf{e}_{23} \times \mathbf{e}_{21}. \quad (8.5)$$

We use these remarks to formulate a definition.

Definition 8.1 *Three Fundamental matrices that satisfy Equations 8.2 or 8.3 are said to be* compatible.

This discussion proves that the three Fundamental matrices are not independent. The algebraic argument presented above and illustrated Figure 8.6 proves that the triple of Fundamental matrices depends upon *at most* 18 parameters: Three Fundamental matrices depend upon 21 parameters and the three algebraic relations (8.3) leave only 18 parameters since they are algebraically independent.

If $\mathcal{P}_1$, $\mathcal{P}_2$, $\mathcal{P}_3$ are the projection matrices of the first, second, and third views, then the equation of the Trifocal plane is

$$\mathbf{\Pi}_T \simeq \mathcal{P}_1^T (\mathbf{e}_{12} \times \mathbf{e}_{13}) \simeq \mathcal{P}_2^T (\mathbf{e}_{23} \times \mathbf{e}_{21}) \simeq \mathcal{P}_3^T (\mathbf{e}_{31} \times \mathbf{e}_{32}).$$

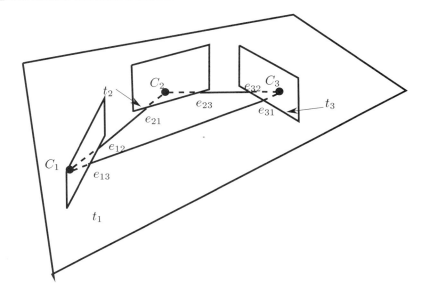

Figure 8.6: The Trifocal geometry.

To prove that there are exactly 18 parameters one can proceed geometrically in several ways, e.g. (Viéville et al., 1996a), or as follows. As it was said in Section 5.2.3, the epipolar geometry of two cameras is determined by the positions of each epipole and the three coefficients of the homography between epipolar lines. It is clear that the 14 parameters of $\mathbf{F}_{12}$ and $\mathbf{F}_{23}$ are independent. Let us suppose that these two matrices are given and figure out the parameters necessary to represent $\mathbf{F}_{13}$. Because of the trifocal construction detailed previously, the Trifocal lines $\mathbf{t}_1 = \mathbf{F}_{12}^T \mathbf{e}_{23}$ and $\mathbf{t}_3 = \mathbf{F}_{23} \mathbf{e}_{21}$ are corresponding epipolar lines. That is, the following constraints hold.

- The epipole e_{13} is constrained to lie on t_1. The degree of freedom left is the position on this line.

- The epipole e_{31} is constrained to lie on t_3. The degree of freedom left is the position on this line.

- t_1 and t_3 are in correspondence through the homography. The two degrees of freedom left are the choice of two other pairs of corresponding epipolar lines.

Therefore, we find that four additional parameters are needed to account for the epipolar geometry of three views. We will obtain the same result following a different route in Chapter 10, Propositions 10.4 and 10.5.

8.1.3   Optical centers aligned

If the optical centers are aligned, then there is no Trifocal plane. The system of cameras has to satisfy two additional constraints, which describe the fact that C_3 lies on the line (C_1, C_2), and therefore there remain only 16 free parameters. Looking at Figure 8.6, it is clear that in this particular case, the epipoles satisfy the relations

$$\mathbf{e}_{12} \simeq \mathbf{e}_{13}, \qquad \mathbf{e}_{21} \simeq \mathbf{e}_{23}, \qquad \mathbf{e}_{31} \simeq \mathbf{e}_{32}. \qquad (8.6)$$

Each of these equations is equivalent to two scalar equations, unlike in the general case. The system of three Fundamental matrices therefore depends only on 15 parameters at most. Therefore, the three Fundamental matrices in this case do not contain enough information to recover the global geometry of the system of three cameras. We will see in Section 8.3 that the Trifocal tensor, to be described next, allows us to recover that geometry.

8.2   The Trifocal tensors

The richness of the geometry of three cameras can only be captured by considering triples of primitives. As opposed to the case of two cameras, the most natural and simple way to derive constraints of order three between primitives is to consider line correspondences. It is also the way it has appeared originally in the literature (Spetsakis and Aloimonos, 1990a). Other triples of correspondences can easily be dealt with from the analysis of line correspondences. We describe some aspects in Section 8.9 and use all possible combinations of points and lines in correspondence in Chapter 9.

8.2.1   Geometric derivation of the Trifocal tensors

Let us consider three views with projection matrices $\mathcal{P}_i, i = 1, 2, 3$, and a 3D line L with images l_i. Given two images l_j and l_k of L, L can be defined as the intersection (the meet) of the two planes $\mathcal{P}_j^T \mathbf{l}_j$ and $\mathcal{P}_k^T \mathbf{l}_k$ (see Figure 8.7):

$$\mathbf{L} = \mathcal{P}_j^T \mathbf{l}_j \,\vartriangle\, \mathcal{P}_k^T \mathbf{l}_k.$$

Keep in mind that the vector $\mathbf{L}$ is the 6×1 vector of Plücker coordinates of the line L.

Let us write the right-hand side of this equation explicitly in terms of the row vectors of the matrices $\mathcal{P}_j$ and $\mathcal{P}_k$ and the coordinates of $\mathbf{l}_j$ and $\mathbf{l}_k$:

$$\mathbf{L} = \left(l_j^1 \boldsymbol{U}_j + l_j^2 \boldsymbol{V}_j + l_j^3 \boldsymbol{W}_j \right) \,\vartriangle\, \left(l_k^1 \boldsymbol{U}_k + l_k^2 \boldsymbol{V}_k + l_k^3 \boldsymbol{W}_k \right).$$

By expanding the meet operator in the previous equation, it can be rewritten in a less compact form with the advantage of making the dependency on the projection planes of the matrices $\mathcal{P}_j$ and $\mathcal{P}_k$ explicit:

$$\mathbf{L} = \mathbf{l}_j^T \begin{bmatrix} U_j \triangle U_k & U_j \triangle V_k & U_j \triangle W_k \\ V_j \triangle U_k & V_j \triangle V_k & V_j \triangle W_k \\ W_j \triangle V_k & W_j \triangle V_k & W_j \triangle W_k \end{bmatrix} \mathbf{l}_k. \tag{8.7}$$

This equation should be interpreted as giving the Plücker coordinates of L as a linear combination of the lines defined by the meets of the projection planes of the perspective matrices $\mathcal{P}_j$ and $\mathcal{P}_k$, the coefficients being the products of the projective coordinates of the lines l_j and l_k.

The image l_i of L is therefore obtained by applying the matrix $\tilde{\mathcal{P}}_i$ defined in Section 4.1.5 of Chapter 4 to the Plücker coordinates of L, hence the equation

$$\mathbf{l}_i = \tilde{\mathcal{P}}_i \left(\mathcal{P}_j^T \mathbf{l}_j \triangle \mathcal{P}_k^T \mathbf{l}_k \right), \tag{8.8}$$

which is valid for $i \neq j \neq k$. Note that if we exchange view j and view k, because of proposition 9 in chapter 1, we just change the sign of $\mathbf{l}_i$ and therefore we do not change l_i. For future reference, we rewrite Equation 8.8 in a more compact form:

$$\mathbf{l}_i = \mathcal{T}_i(\mathbf{l}_j, \mathbf{l}_k). \tag{8.9}$$

$\mathcal{T}_i$ represents a mapping $\mathcal{T}_i$ from the set of lines in views j and k to the set of lines in view i. In order to study its properties, we write the coordinates of $\mathbf{l}_i$ as

$$\mathbf{l}_i = \begin{bmatrix} \mathbf{l}_j^T \mathbf{G}_i^1 \mathbf{l}_k \\ \mathbf{l}_j^T \mathbf{G}_i^2 \mathbf{l}_k \\ \mathbf{l}_j^T \mathbf{G}_i^3 \mathbf{l}_k \end{bmatrix}. \tag{8.10}$$

The three 3×3 matrices $\mathbf{G}_i^n, n = 1, 2, 3$, are obtained from Equations 8.7 and 8.8; using the notations of Chapter 3 where we defined the Plücker product of two 3D lines (Equation 3.7) we find

$$\mathbf{G}_i^1 =$$
$$\begin{bmatrix} [V_i \triangle W_i | U_j \triangle U_k] & [V_i \triangle W_i | U_j \triangle V_k] & [V_i \triangle W_i | U_j \triangle W_k] \\ [V_i \triangle W_i | V_j \triangle U_k] & [V_i \triangle W_i | V_j \triangle V_k] & [V_i \triangle W_i | V_j \triangle W_k] \\ [V_i \triangle W_i | W_j \triangle U_k] & [V_i \triangle W_i | W_j \triangle V_k] & [V_i \triangle W_i | W_j \triangle W_k] \end{bmatrix}. \tag{8.11}$$

The matrices $\mathbf{G}_i^2$ and $\mathbf{G}_i^3$ are obtained by changing the terms $V_i \triangle W_i$ into $W_i \triangle U_i$ and $U_i \triangle V_i$, respectively. Those three matrices are so important in studying the Trifocal tensors that we give them names:

Definition 8.2 *The three matrices* $\mathbf{G}_i^n$, *n = 1, 2, 3, are called the* **Trifocal matrices** *for view i.*

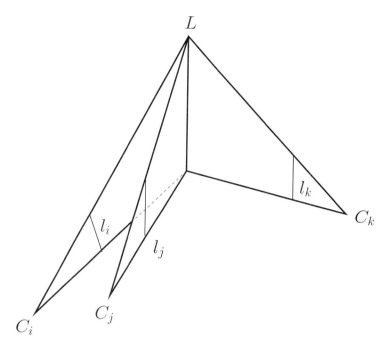

Figure 8.7: The line l_i is the image by camera i of the 3D line L intersection of the planes defined by the optical centers of the cameras j and k and the lines l_j and l_k, respectively.

We will denote by $\mathbf{G}_i^{n(m)}$, $m = 1, 2, 3$, the mth column vector of the Trifocal matrix $\mathbf{G}_i^n$.

Using Equation 3.26, we can also rewrite this expression in terms of 4×4 determinants. For completeness we include the results for $\mathbf{G}_i^2$ and $\mathbf{G}_i^3$ in the following proposition which describes the computation of the Trifocal tensor $\boldsymbol{\mathcal{T}}_i$ from the three perspective projection matrices $\boldsymbol{\mathcal{P}}_i$, $\boldsymbol{\mathcal{P}}_j$ and $\boldsymbol{\mathcal{P}}_k$:

Proposition 8.4 *Given the three perspective projection matrices*

$$\boldsymbol{\mathcal{P}}_i \simeq \left[\begin{array}{c} \boldsymbol{U}_i^T \\ \boldsymbol{V}_i^T \\ \boldsymbol{W}_i^T \end{array} \right], \quad \boldsymbol{\mathcal{P}}_j \simeq \left[\begin{array}{c} \boldsymbol{U}_j^T \\ \boldsymbol{V}_j^T \\ \boldsymbol{W}_j^T \end{array} \right], \quad \boldsymbol{\mathcal{P}}_k \simeq \left[\begin{array}{c} \boldsymbol{U}_k^T \\ \boldsymbol{V}_k^T \\ \boldsymbol{W}_k^T \end{array} \right],$$

the three Trifocal matrices that define the Trifocal tensor $\boldsymbol{\mathcal{T}}_i$ are given by the for-

mulae

$$\mathbf{G}_i^1 = \begin{bmatrix} |\boldsymbol{V}_i,\boldsymbol{W}_i,\boldsymbol{U}_j,\boldsymbol{U}_k| & |\boldsymbol{V}_i,\boldsymbol{W}_i,\boldsymbol{U}_j,\boldsymbol{V}_k| & |\boldsymbol{V}_i,\boldsymbol{W}_i,\boldsymbol{U}_j,\boldsymbol{W}_k| \\ |\boldsymbol{V}_i,\boldsymbol{W}_i,\boldsymbol{V}_j,\boldsymbol{U}_k| & |\boldsymbol{V}_i,\boldsymbol{W}_i,\boldsymbol{V}_j,\boldsymbol{V}_k| & |\boldsymbol{V}_i,\boldsymbol{W}_i,\boldsymbol{V}_j,\boldsymbol{W}_k| \\ |\boldsymbol{V}_i,\boldsymbol{W}_i,\boldsymbol{W}_j,\boldsymbol{U}_k| & |\boldsymbol{V}_i,\boldsymbol{W}_i,\boldsymbol{W}_j,\boldsymbol{V}_k| & |\boldsymbol{V}_i,\boldsymbol{W}_i,\boldsymbol{W}_j,\boldsymbol{W}_k| \end{bmatrix}, \quad (8.12)$$

$$\mathbf{G}_i^2 = \begin{bmatrix} |\boldsymbol{W}_i,\boldsymbol{U}_i,\boldsymbol{U}_j,\boldsymbol{U}_k| & |\boldsymbol{W}_i,\boldsymbol{U}_i,\boldsymbol{U}_j,\boldsymbol{V}_k| & |\boldsymbol{W}_i,\boldsymbol{U}_i,\boldsymbol{U}_j,\boldsymbol{W}_k| \\ |\boldsymbol{W}_i,\boldsymbol{U}_i,\boldsymbol{V}_j,\boldsymbol{U}_k| & |\boldsymbol{W}_i,\boldsymbol{U}_i,\boldsymbol{V}_j,\boldsymbol{V}_k| & |\boldsymbol{W}_i,\boldsymbol{U}_i,\boldsymbol{V}_j,\boldsymbol{W}_k| \\ |\boldsymbol{W}_i,\boldsymbol{U}_i,\boldsymbol{W}_j,\boldsymbol{U}_k| & |\boldsymbol{W}_i,\boldsymbol{U}_i,\boldsymbol{W}_j,\boldsymbol{V}_k| & |\boldsymbol{W}_i,\boldsymbol{U}_i,\boldsymbol{W}_j,\boldsymbol{W}_k| \end{bmatrix}, \quad (8.13)$$

$$\mathbf{G}_i^3 = \begin{bmatrix} |\boldsymbol{U}_i,\boldsymbol{V}_i,\boldsymbol{U}_j,\boldsymbol{U}_k| & |\boldsymbol{U}_i,\boldsymbol{V}_i,\boldsymbol{U}_j,\boldsymbol{V}_k| & |\boldsymbol{U}_i,\boldsymbol{V}_i,\boldsymbol{U}_j,\boldsymbol{W}_k| \\ |\boldsymbol{U}_i,\boldsymbol{V}_i,\boldsymbol{V}_j,\boldsymbol{U}_k| & |\boldsymbol{U}_i,\boldsymbol{V}_i,\boldsymbol{V}_j,\boldsymbol{V}_k| & |\boldsymbol{U}_i,\boldsymbol{V}_i,\boldsymbol{V}_j,\boldsymbol{W}_k| \\ |\boldsymbol{U}_i,\boldsymbol{V}_i,\boldsymbol{W}_j,\boldsymbol{U}_k| & |\boldsymbol{U}_i,\boldsymbol{V}_i,\boldsymbol{W}_j,\boldsymbol{V}_k| & |\boldsymbol{U}_i,\boldsymbol{V}_i,\boldsymbol{W}_j,\boldsymbol{W}_k| \end{bmatrix}. \quad (8.14)$$

A more pictorial view is shown in Figure 8.8: The mapping $\mathcal{T}_i$ is represented as a 3×3 cube, the three horizontal planes representing the Trifocal matrices $\mathbf{G}_i^n, n = 1, 2, 3$. It can be thought of as a black box which takes as its input two lines l_j and l_k and outputs a third one, l_i.

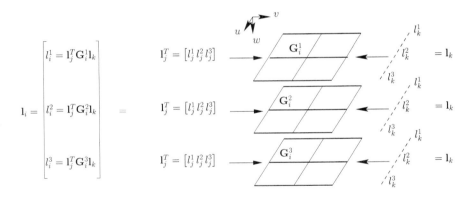

Figure 8.8: A three-dimensional representation of the Trifocal tensor $\boldsymbol{\mathcal{T}}_i$.

Is this mapping always well-defined? Equivalently, when can one not use Equation 8.8 to compute the coordinates of l_i given l_j and l_k? The answer is in the following two cases.

1. One cannot use this equation when the two planes determined by (C_j, l_j) and (C_k, l_k) are identical, i.e. when l_j and l_k are corresponding epipolar lines between views j and k, or, equivalently, when the 3D line L is in an epipolar plane of the camera pair (j, k). The meet that appears in Equation 8.8 is then 0 and the line l_i is undefined; see Figure 8.9. If L is also in an epipolar plane of the camera pair (i, j), then it is in the Trifocal plane of the three cameras and prediction is not possible by any of the formulae such as (8.8).

2. Also, one cannot use this equation when l_j and l_k are epipolar lines between views i and j and i and k, respectively, or, equivalently, when they are the images of the same optical ray in view i so l_i is reduced to a point (see Figure 8.10).

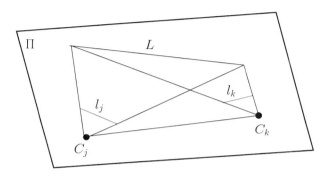

Figure 8.9: When l_j and l_k are corresponding epipolar lines, the two planes $\mathcal{P}_j^T l_j$ and $\mathcal{P}_k^T l_k$ are identical to the epipolar plane Π and therefore $\mathcal{T}_i(\mathbf{l}_j, \mathbf{l}_k) = \mathbf{0}$.

Except in those two cases, Equation 8.9 defines an application $\mathcal{T}_i$ from $\mathbb{P}^{*2} \times \mathbb{P}^{*2}$, the Cartesian product of two duals of the projective plane, into $\mathbb{P}^{*2}$. As seen in Chapters 2 and 3, this application is represented by an application $\boldsymbol{\mathcal{T}}_i$ from $G_2(\mathbb{R}^3) \times G_2(\mathbb{R}^3)$ into $G_2(\mathbb{R}^3)$. This application is bilinear and antisymmetric and is represented by the Trifocal matrices $\mathbf{G}_i^n, n = 1, 2, 3$. It is called the *Trifocal tensor* for view i. One can obviously define two other mappings $\mathcal{T}_j$ and $\mathcal{T}_k$ and the corresponding tensors $\boldsymbol{\mathcal{T}}_j$ and $\boldsymbol{\mathcal{T}}_k$ for views j and k.

Definition 8.3 $\boldsymbol{\mathcal{T}}_1$, $\boldsymbol{\mathcal{T}}_2$ and $\boldsymbol{\mathcal{T}}_3$ are called the Trifocal tensors of the three views.

The properties of $\mathcal{T}_i$ can be summarized in the following theorem.

Theorem 8.1 *The application* $\mathcal{T}_i : \mathbb{P}^{2*} \times \mathbb{P}^{2*} \longrightarrow \mathbb{P}^{2*}$ *is represented by the application* $\boldsymbol{\mathcal{T}}_i : G_2(\mathbb{R}^3) \times G_2(\mathbb{R}^3) \longrightarrow G_2(\mathbb{R}^3)$ *such that*

$$\boldsymbol{\mathcal{T}}_i(\mathbf{l}_j, \mathbf{l}_k) = \tilde{\boldsymbol{\mathcal{P}}}_i \left(\boldsymbol{\mathcal{P}}_j^T \mathbf{l}_j \,\triangle\, \boldsymbol{\mathcal{P}}_k^T \mathbf{l}_k \right).$$

$\boldsymbol{\mathcal{T}}_i$ *is called the* **Trifocal tensor** *for view i and has the following properties*

1. It is bilinear and antisymmetric.

2. It is equal to **0** *if and only if*

   (a) l_j and l_k are epipolar lines with respect to the ith view, or

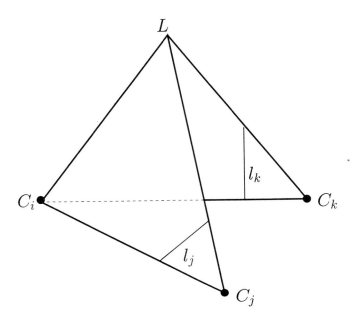

Figure 8.10: When l_j and l_k are epipolar lines with respect to view i, the line l_i is reduced to a point; hence $\boldsymbol{\mathcal{T}}_i(\mathbf{l}_j, \mathbf{l}_k) = \mathbf{0}$.

   (b) l_j and l_k are corresponding epipolar lines with respect to the pair (j, k) of cameras.

3. Let l_k be an epipolar line in view k with respect to view i and l_i the corresponding epipolar line in view i, Then for all lines l_j in view j that are not epipolar lines with respect to view i,

$$\boldsymbol{\mathcal{T}}_i(\mathbf{l}_j, \mathbf{l}_k) = \mathbf{l}_i.$$

4. Similarly, let l_j be an epipolar line in view j with respect to view i and l_i the corresponding epipolar line in view i. Then for all lines l_k in view k that are not epipolar lines with respect to view i,

$$\boldsymbol{\mathcal{T}}_i(\mathbf{l}_j, \mathbf{l}_k) = \mathbf{l}_i.$$

5. If l_j and l_k are non-corresponding epipolar lines with respect to the pair (j, k) of views, then $\boldsymbol{\mathcal{T}}_i(\mathbf{l}_j, \mathbf{l}_k) \simeq \mathbf{t}_i$, the Trifocal line of the ith view, if the optical centers are not aligned and $\boldsymbol{\mathcal{T}}_i(\mathbf{l}_j, \mathbf{l}_k) = \mathbf{0}$ otherwise.

Proof :   We have already proved items 1 and 2 of this theorem.

In order to prove item 2, we note that if l_k is an epipolar line with respect to view i, then the line L is contained in an epipolar plane for the pair (i, k) of views. Two cases can happen. If L goes through C_i, i.e. if l_j is an epipolar line with respect to view i, then l_i is reduced to a point: This case is item 1.a of the theorem and it is excluded here.

If L does not go through C_i, then its image in view i is in effect independent of its position in the plane (C_i, C_k, l_k) as long as it does not go through C_i or C_k. Precisely, for each line l_j in view j which is not an epipolar line with respect to view i (the case we just considered and excluded), $\boldsymbol{T}_i(\mathbf{l}_j, \mathbf{l}_k) = \mathbf{l}_i$. This reasoning proves item 2.

Item 3 follows by symmetry, exchanging the roles of views j and k.

Finally, if l_j and l_k are non-corresponding epipolar lines with respect to the pair (j, k) of views, then the two planes (C_j, l_j) and (C_k, l_k) intersect along the line (C_j, C_k). Thus, if C_i is not on that line, then its image l_i in the ith view is the Trifocal line t_i; see Figure 8.6. If C_i is on that line, i.e. if the three optical centers are aligned, then the line (C_j, C_k) is an optical ray of the ith view and $\boldsymbol{T}_i(\mathbf{l}_j, \mathbf{l}_k) = \mathbf{0}$. $\square$

8.2.2 The six intrinsic planar morphisms

Our presentation so far has been to look at the three horizontal planes of the cube representing the Trifocal tensor $\boldsymbol{T}_i$ in Figure 8.8, i.e. those corresponding to constant values of w. To get a fuller picture of the structure of the Trifocal tensor we consider now the three vertical slices corresponding to constant values of u and the three vertical slices corresponding to constant values of v. We are going to discover that each of these slices, a 3×3 matrix, represents a morphism between the retinal plane $\mathcal{R}_j$ for the first series of slices, the retinal plane $\mathcal{R}_k$ for the second series, and the retinal plane $\mathcal{R}_i$. We call these morphisms the *intrinsic* planar morphisms of $\boldsymbol{T}_i$.

We state the results as two propositions.

Proposition 8.5 *Each 3×3 vertical slice parallel to the (u, w) plane of Figure 8.8 defines a planar morphism denoted H_{ji}^v, $v = 1, 2, 3$, between the retinal plane $\mathcal{R}_j$ and the retinal plane $\mathcal{R}_i$; see Figure 8.11. These planar morphisms are induced by the three projection planes $\boldsymbol{U}_k, \boldsymbol{V}_k, \boldsymbol{W}_k$ of the kth view. They are called the* **intrinsic planar morphisms** *of $\boldsymbol{T}_i$ associated with view j. Their matrices are given by*

$$\mathbf{H}_{ji}^v \simeq \left[\mathbf{G}_i^{1(v)} \, \mathbf{G}_i^{2(v)} \, \mathbf{G}_i^{3(v)} \right], \quad v = 1, 2, 3. \tag{8.15}$$

Proof :   Let us prove it for $v = 1$. The corresponding 3×3 matrix is equal to

$$\mathbf{H}_{ji}^1 = \left[\mathbf{G}_i^{1(1)} \; \mathbf{G}_i^{2(1)} \; \mathbf{G}_i^{3(1)} \right] =$$

$$\begin{bmatrix} |\, \boldsymbol{V}_i, \boldsymbol{W}_i, \boldsymbol{U}_j, \boldsymbol{U}_k \,| & |\, \boldsymbol{W}_i, \boldsymbol{U}_i, \boldsymbol{U}_j, \boldsymbol{U}_k \,| & |\, \boldsymbol{U}_i, \boldsymbol{V}_i, \boldsymbol{U}_j, \boldsymbol{U}_k \,| \\ |\, \boldsymbol{V}_i, \boldsymbol{W}_i, \boldsymbol{V}_j, \boldsymbol{U}_k \,| & |\, \boldsymbol{W}_i, \boldsymbol{U}_i, \boldsymbol{V}_j, \boldsymbol{U}_k \,| & |\, \boldsymbol{U}_i, \boldsymbol{V}_i, \boldsymbol{V}_j, \boldsymbol{U}_k \,| \\ |\, \boldsymbol{V}_i, \boldsymbol{W}_i, \boldsymbol{W}_j, \boldsymbol{U}_k \,| & |\, \boldsymbol{W}_i, \boldsymbol{U}_i, \boldsymbol{W}_j, \boldsymbol{U}_k \,| & |\, \boldsymbol{U}_i, \boldsymbol{V}_i, \boldsymbol{W}_j, \boldsymbol{U}_k \,| \end{bmatrix} .$$

According to Proposition 5.2, this matrix is that of the morphism induced by the plane $\boldsymbol{U}_k$ between the retinal planes $\mathcal{R}_j$ and $\mathcal{R}_i$. $\square$

We have a similar proposition for the three other vertical slices parallel to the plane

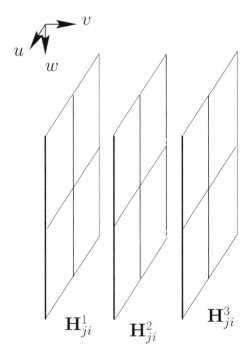

Figure 8.11: The first set of three intrinsic planar morphisms of $\mathcal{T}_i$.

(v, w).

Proposition 8.6 *Each 3×3 vertical slice parallel to the (v, w) plane of Figure 8.8 defines a planar morphism denoted H_{ki}^u, $u = 1, 2, 3$, between the retinal plane $\mathcal{R}_k$ and the retinal plane $\mathcal{R}_i$; see Figure 8.12. These planar morphisms are induced by the three projection planes $\boldsymbol{U}_k, \boldsymbol{V}_k, \boldsymbol{W}_k$ of the jth view. They are called the*

intrinsic planar morphisms *of $\boldsymbol{T}_i$ associated with view k. Their matrices are*

$$\mathbf{H}_{ki}^u \simeq \left[\mathbf{G}_i^{1T(u)} \; \mathbf{G}_i^{2T(u)} \; \mathbf{G}_i^{3T(u)} \right], \quad u = 1, 2, 3,$$

where $\mathbf{G}_i^{nT(u)}$ is the uth column vector of the transpose of the Trifocal matrix $\mathbf{G}_i^n$.

Proof : Let us prove it for $u = 1$. The corresponding 3×3 matrix is equal to

$$\mathbf{H}_{ki}^1 = \left[\mathbf{G}_i^{1T(1)} \; \mathbf{G}_i^{2T(1)} \; \mathbf{G}_i^{3T(1)} \right] =$$

$$\begin{bmatrix} |\boldsymbol{V}_i, \boldsymbol{W}_i, \boldsymbol{U}_j, \boldsymbol{U}_k| & |\boldsymbol{W}_i, \boldsymbol{U}_i, \boldsymbol{U}_j, \boldsymbol{U}_k| & |\boldsymbol{U}_i, \boldsymbol{V}_i, \boldsymbol{U}_j, \boldsymbol{U}_k| \\ |\boldsymbol{V}_i, \boldsymbol{W}_i, \boldsymbol{U}_j, \boldsymbol{V}_k| & |\boldsymbol{W}_i, \boldsymbol{U}_i, \boldsymbol{U}_j, \boldsymbol{V}_k| & |\boldsymbol{U}_i, \boldsymbol{V}_i, \boldsymbol{U}_j, \boldsymbol{V}_k| \\ |\boldsymbol{V}_i, \boldsymbol{W}_i, \boldsymbol{U}_j, \boldsymbol{W}_k| & |\boldsymbol{W}_i, \boldsymbol{U}_i, \boldsymbol{U}_j, \boldsymbol{W}_k| & |\boldsymbol{U}_i, \boldsymbol{V}_i, \boldsymbol{U}_j, \boldsymbol{W}_k| \end{bmatrix}.$$

According to Proposition 5.2, this matrix is that of the morphism induced by the plane $\boldsymbol{U}_j$ between the retinal planes $\mathcal{R}_k$ and $\mathcal{R}_i$. □

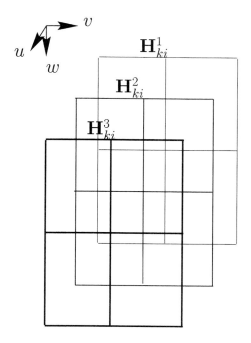

Figure 8.12: The second set of three intrinsic planar morphisms of $\mathcal{T}_i$.

8.2.3   Changing the reference view

The question we address here is that of computing $\mathcal{T}_j$ from $\mathcal{T}_i$, $j \neq i$. This computation is useful in practice since one often estimates only one of the three tensors of three views (see Chapter 9).

The important result is that, given $\mathcal{T}_i$, the other two tensors are easily computed through some very simple algebraic expressions on the coefficients of $\boldsymbol{\mathcal{T}}_i$ as explained in the following theorem

Theorem 8.2 *The relation $\mathcal{T}_j$ such that*

$$\boldsymbol{\mathcal{T}}_j(\mathbf{l}_k, \mathbf{l}_i) = \tilde{\boldsymbol{\mathcal{P}}}_j \left(\boldsymbol{\mathcal{P}}_k^T \mathbf{l}_k \vartriangle \boldsymbol{\mathcal{P}}_i^T \mathbf{l}_i \right)$$

is obtained from $\mathcal{T}_i, i \neq j$, from the relations

$$\left[\mathbf{G}_j^{1T(m)} \ \mathbf{G}_j^{2T(m)} \ \mathbf{G}_j^{3T(m)} \right] = \lambda_m \left[\mathbf{G}_i^{2(m)} \times \mathbf{G}_i^{3(m)} \ \mathbf{G}_i^{3(m)} \times \mathbf{G}_i^{1(m)} \ \mathbf{G}_i^{1(m)} \times \mathbf{G}_i^{2(m)} \right]^T.$$

The λ_m, $m = 1, 2, 3$, can in general be obtained linearly from a pair (l_j, l_k) of lines through the expression (see proof)

$$\mathbf{l}_j \simeq \boldsymbol{\mathcal{T}}_j(\mathbf{l}_k, \boldsymbol{\mathcal{T}}_i(\mathbf{l}_j, \mathbf{l}_k)).$$

Proof :   Consider Figure 8.13. According to Propositions 8.5 and 8.6, the intrinsic planar morphisms H_{ij}^u of $\boldsymbol{\mathcal{T}}_j$ are in general the inverses of the intrinsic planar morphisms H_{ji}^v of $\boldsymbol{\mathcal{T}}_i$. When these are homographies, i.e. one-to-one, one has in terms of matrices

$$\mathbf{H}_{ij}^u \simeq \left(\mathbf{H}_{ji}^u \right)^{-1}, \quad u = 1, 2, 3.$$

When they are not homographies, i.e. not one-to-one, one has

$$\mathbf{H}_{ij}^u \simeq \left(\mathbf{H}_{ji}^u \right)^*, \quad u = 1, 2, 3.$$

where $\mathbf{A}^*$ denotes the adjoint of the matrix $\mathbf{A}$. Since one has $\mathbf{A}^* \simeq \mathbf{A}^{-1}$ when $\mathbf{A}$ is invertible, we can choose in all cases $\mathbf{H}_{ij}^u \simeq \left(\mathbf{H}_{ji}^u \right)^*, u = 1, 2, 3$. According to Propositions 8.5 and 8.6, we have thus determinesd $\boldsymbol{\mathcal{T}}_j$ up to two parameters:

$$\mathbf{H}_{ij}^u = \left[\mathbf{G}_j^{1T(u)} \ \mathbf{G}_j^{2T(u)} \ \mathbf{G}_j^{3T(u)} \right] \simeq \left[\mathbf{G}_i^{1(u)} \ \mathbf{G}_i^{2(u)} \ \mathbf{G}_i^{3(u)} \right]^*,$$

and hence

$$\mathbf{H}_{ij}^u = \lambda_u \left[\mathbf{G}_i^{2(u)} \times \mathbf{G}_i^{3(u)} \ \mathbf{G}_i^{3(u)} \times \mathbf{G}_i^{1(u)} \ \mathbf{G}_i^{1(u)} \times \mathbf{G}_i^{2(u)} \right]^T.$$

The ratios of the λ_u's are determined as follows. Let l_j and l_k be two lines such that $\boldsymbol{\mathcal{T}}_i(\mathbf{l}_j, \mathbf{l}_k) \neq \mathbf{0}$ and let us denote l_i the line $\mathcal{T}_i(l_j, l_k)$: $\mathbf{l}_i \simeq \boldsymbol{\mathcal{T}}_i(\mathbf{l}_j, \mathbf{l}_k)$. If $\boldsymbol{\mathcal{T}}_j(\mathbf{l}_k, \mathbf{l}_i)$ is not equal to $\mathbf{0}$ (see Theorem 8.1), then one must have $\mathbf{l}_j \simeq \boldsymbol{\mathcal{T}}_j(\mathbf{l}_k, \mathbf{l}_i)$. The coordinates of $\boldsymbol{\mathcal{T}}_j(\mathbf{l}_k, \mathbf{l}_i)$ are linear homogeneous functions of the three λ_u's and we can therefore compute the ratios $\lambda_1 : \lambda_2 : \lambda_3$. $\square$

A similar result can be obtained for changing from $\mathcal{T}_i$ to $\mathcal{T}_k$.

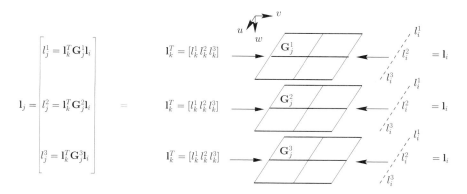

Figure 8.13: A three-dimensional representation of the Trifocal tensor $\mathcal{T}_j$: Compare with Figure 8.8.

8.2.4 Properties of the Trifocal matrices $\mathbf{G}_i^n$

In this section, we detail the algebraic and geometric properties of the matrices $\mathbf{G}_i^n, n = 1, 2, 3$, that appear in the definition of $\mathcal{T}_i$. These matrices have interesting properties which are closely related to the epipolar geometry of the views j and k. We start with a characterization of their right and left nullspaces.

Proposition 8.7 *The matrices* $\mathbf{G}_i^n$ *are of rank 2 exactly under the hypothesis (8.1) and their nullspaces are the three images, denoted* $\mathcal{R}_k^n, n = 1, 2, 3$, *in the k-th retinal plane of the three projection rays of camera i. These three lines intersect at the epipole* e_{ki}.

Proof : The nullspace of $\mathbf{G}_i^n$ is the set of lines $\mathcal{R}_k^n$ such that $\mathcal{T}_i(\mathbf{l}_j, \mathcal{R}_k^n)$ has a zero in the n-th coordinate for all lines l_j. The corresponding lines l_i such that $\mathbf{l}_i = \mathcal{T}_i(\mathbf{l}_j, \mathcal{R}_k^n)$ all go through the point represented by $\varepsilon_n, n = 1, 2, 3$, in the i-th retinal plane. This statement is true if and only if $\mathcal{R}_k^n$ is the image in the k-th retinal plane of the projection ray $\boldsymbol{V}_i \, \triangle \, \boldsymbol{W}_i \, (n = 1)$, $\boldsymbol{W}_i \, \triangle \, \boldsymbol{U}_i \, (n = 2)$ and $\boldsymbol{U}_i \, \triangle \, \boldsymbol{V}_i \, (n = 3)$. Theorem 8.1 shows that l_i is independent of the choice of l_j and represented by $\varepsilon_n \times \mathbf{e}_{ik}$.

Let us show that the rank of $\mathbf{G}_i^n$ cannot be less than two. Consider for example the case $n = 1$. We have just seen that the nullspace of $\mathbf{G}_i^1$ is the image of the projection ray $\boldsymbol{V}_i \, \triangle \, \boldsymbol{W}_i$ in view k. Under our general viewpoint assumption, this projection ray and the optical center C_k define a unique plane unless the projection ray goes through C_k, a situation that can be avoided by a change of coordinates in the retinal plane of the ith camera if C_k is distinct from C_i. Therefore there is a unique line in the right nullspace of $\mathbf{G}_i^1$ and its rank is equal to 2. Similar reasonings apply to $\mathbf{G}_i^2$ and $\mathbf{G}_i^3$. $\square$

A similar reasoning applies to the matrices $\mathbf{G}_i^{nT}$:

Proposition 8.8 *The matrices* $\mathbf{G}_i^{nT}$ *are of rank 2 exactly under the hypothesis (8.1) and their nullspaces are the three images, denoted* $\mathcal{L}_j^n, n = 1, 2, 3$, *in the j-th retinal plane of the three projection rays of camera i. These three lines intersect at the epipole* e_{ji}.

The situation is represented pictorially in Figure 8.14.
As a byproduct of Propositions 8.7 and 8.8, we have a way to recover the epipoles e_{ij} and e_{ik} in view i.

Proposition 8.9 *The epipole* e_{ij} *can be recovered from the three epipolar lines* $\mathcal{L}_j^n, n = 1, 2, 3$. *Similarly, the epipole* e_{ik} *can be recovered from the three epipolar lines* $\mathcal{R}_k^n, n = 1, 2, 3$.

Proof :   The three epipolar lines corresponding to $\mathcal{R}_k^n$, $n = 1, 2, 3$, in view i are obtained as $\mathcal{T}_i(\mathbf{l}_j, \mathcal{R}_k^n), n = 1, 2, 3$, for any l_j which is not an epipolar line for the pair (i, j) (see Theorem 8.1). They intersect at the epipole e_{ik}. Similarly, the three epipolar lines corresponding to $\mathcal{L}_j^n$, $n = 1, 2, 3$, in view i are obtained as $\mathcal{T}_i(\boldsymbol{\mathcal{L}}_j^n, \mathbf{l}_k), n = 1, 2, 3$, for any l_k which is not an epipolar line for the pair (i, k). They intersect at the epipole e_{ij}. $\square$

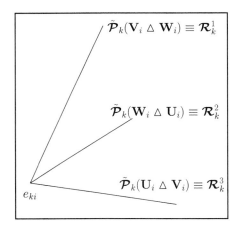 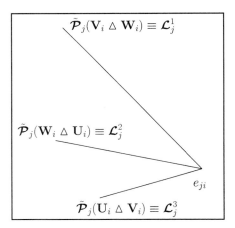

Figure 8.14: The lines $\mathcal{L}_j^n$ (respectively $\mathcal{R}_k^n$), $n = 1, 2, 3$, in the nullspaces of the matrices $\mathbf{G}_i^{nT}$ (respectively $\mathbf{G}_i^n$) are the images of the three projection rays of camera i. Hence, they intersect at the epipole e_{ji} (respectively e_{ki}). The corresponding epipolar lines in camera i are obtained as $\mathcal{T}_i(\mathcal{L}_j^n, l_k)$ (respectively $\mathcal{T}_i(l_j, \mathcal{R}_k^n)$) for $l_k \neq \mathcal{R}_k^n$ (respectively $l_j \neq \mathcal{L}_j^n$).

Before we further explore the properties of the matrices $\mathbf{G}_i^n$, we characterize more precisely the rank of the two sets of three vectors in their nullspaces.

Proposition 8.10 *Under the hypothesis (8.1), the rank of each of the matrices* $\left[\mathcal{R}_k^1\,\mathcal{R}_k^2\,\mathcal{R}_k^3\right]$ *and* $\left[\mathcal{L}_j^1\,\mathcal{L}_j^2\,\mathcal{L}_j^3\right]$ *is exactly 2.*

Proof : We know from Propositions 8.7 and 8.8 that the the ranks are less than or equal to 2 because each triplet of lines intersect at an epipole. In order for the ranks to be equal to 1, we would need to have only one line in either retinal plane. But this situation would mean that the three planes defined by C_k (respectively C_j) and the three projection rays of the ith camera are identical which is impossible since $C_i \neq C_k$ (respectively $C_j \neq C_k$) and the three projection rays of the ith camera are not coplanar. $\square$

We can then show that the epipolar geometry between the three views, i.e. the Fundamental matrices, can be recovered from the $\mathcal{T}_i, i = 1, 2, 3$.

Proposition 8.11 *The two Fundamental matrices* $\mathbf{F}_{ij}$ *and* $\mathbf{F}_{ik}$ *can be recovered uniquely from* $\mathcal{T}_i$.

Proof : By combining Propositions 5.1, 8.5 and 8.6 with the fact that the two epipoles e_{ij} and e_{ik} can be determined from $\mathcal{T}_i$ (Proposition 8.9) we can write

$$\mathbf{F}_{ji} = [\mathbf{e}_{ij}]_\times \mathbf{H}_{ji}^v, \quad v = 1, 2, 3,$$

and

$$\mathbf{F}_{ki} = [\mathbf{e}_{ik}]_\times \mathbf{H}_{ki}^u, \quad u = 1, 2, 3.$$

$\square$

The simplest way to recover $\mathbf{F}_{jk}$ is to compute $\mathcal{T}_j$ as explained in Proposition 8.2 and to apply the same technique as described in Proposition 8.11.

We can now characterize further the matrices $\mathbf{G}_i^n$, as summarized in the following proposition.

Proposition 8.12 *The matrices* $\mathbf{G}_i^n$ *can be expressed simply, but not uniquely, as functions of the epipoles* e_{ji} *and* e_{ki}:

$$\mathbf{G}_i^n = \mathbf{e}_{ji}\mathbf{h}_k^{(n)T} + \mathbf{h}_j^{(n)}\mathbf{e}_{ki}^T, \tag{8.16}$$

where the points $h_k^{(n)}$ *and* $h_j^{(n)}$ *belong to the epipolar lines* $\mathcal{R}_k^n$ *and* $\mathcal{L}_j^n$, *respectively.*

Proof : Because of Proposition 8.7 or 8.8, the matrices $\mathbf{G}_i^n$ can be expressed as the sum of two matrices of rank 1:

$$\mathbf{G}_i^n = \mathbf{r}_j^{(n)}\mathbf{s}_k^{(n)T} + \mathbf{s}_j^{(n)}\mathbf{r}_k^{(n)T}.$$

Moreover, a vector in the nullspace of $\mathbf{G}_i^n$ is represented by the cross-product $\mathbf{s}_k^{(n)} \times \mathbf{r}_k^{(n)}$ since its rank is two. Hence, according to Proposition 3.27, the points $s_k^{(n)}$ and

$r_k^{(n)}$ belong to the line $\mathcal{R}_k^n$. A similar reasoning shows that the points $s_j^{(n)}$ and $r_j^{(n)}$ belong to the line $\mathcal{L}_j^n$.

Let us now use Theorem 8.1. Part 1.a states that if l_j and l_k are epipolar lines with respect to the ith view, then $\boldsymbol{T}_i(\mathbf{l}_j, \mathbf{l}_k) = \mathbf{0}$. Equivalently, for all lines l_j going through e_{ji} and all lines l_k going through e_{ki}, we must have

$$\mathbf{l}_j^T \mathbf{G}_i^n \mathbf{l}_k = \left(\mathbf{l}_j^T \mathbf{r}_j^{(n)}\right)\left(\mathbf{s}_k^{(n)T}\mathbf{l}_k\right) + \left(\mathbf{l}_j^T \mathbf{s}_j^{(n)}\right)\left(\mathbf{r}_k^{(n)T}\mathbf{l}_k\right) = 0. \qquad (8.17)$$

Let us now use the facts that l_j and l_k are epipolar lines:

$$\mathbf{l}_j = \mathbf{e}_{ji} \times \mathbf{m}_j \quad \mathbf{l}_k = \mathbf{e}_{ki} \times \mathbf{m}_k,$$

where m_j and m_k are arbitrary points. Furthermore, we know that $s_j^{(n)}$ and $r_j^{(n)}$ (respectively $s_k^{(n)}$ and $r_k^{(n)}$) are aligned with the epipole e_{ji} (respectively the epipole e_{ki}); hence, for example,

$$\mathbf{r}_j^{(n)} = \alpha_j \mathbf{s}_j^{(n)} + \beta_j \mathbf{e}_{ji},$$
$$\mathbf{r}_k^{(n)} = \alpha_k \mathbf{s}_k^{(n)} + \beta_k \mathbf{e}_{ki},$$

for some constants $\alpha_j, \beta_j, \alpha_k, \beta_k$. We plug all of these values into Equation 8.17 and obtain

$$\left|\mathbf{e}_{ji}, \mathbf{m}_j, \mathbf{s}_j^{(n)}\right| \left|\mathbf{e}_{ki}, \mathbf{m}_k, \mathbf{s}_k^{(n)}\right| (\alpha_j + \alpha_k) = 0.$$

This equation must be true for all points m_j and m_k. There are three possibilities: $s_j^{(n)} = e_{ji}$, $s_k^{(n)} = e_{ki}$, or $\alpha_j + \alpha_k = 0$. The first two cases are prohibited by the fact that the points $s_j^{(n)}$ and $r_j^{(n)}$ (respectively $s_k^{(n)}$ and $r_k^{(n)}$) must be distinct for the rank of $\mathbf{G}^n$ to be equal to 2. In effect, if $\mathbf{s}_j^{(n)} \simeq \mathbf{e}_{ji}$, then we have also $\mathbf{r}_j^{(n)} \simeq \mathbf{e}_{ji}$. Thus, $\mathbf{G}^n \simeq \mathbf{e}_{ji}\left(\mathbf{s}_k^{(n)T} + \mathbf{r}_k^{(n)T}\right)$ and is therefore of rank less than 2. Since we have assumed that the rank of $\mathbf{G}^n$ is equal to 2, we must have $\alpha_j + \alpha_k = 0$.

If we replace $r_j^{(n)}$ and $r_k^{(n)}$ by their expressions in terms of $s_j^{(n)}$ and $s_k^{(n)}$, respectively, and take into account the fact that $\alpha_j + \alpha_k = 0$, then we obtain the expression for $\mathbf{G}_i^n$

$$\mathbf{G}_i^n = \beta_j \mathbf{e}_{ji}\mathbf{s}_k^{(n)T} + \beta_k \mathbf{s}_j^{(n)}\mathbf{e}_{ki}^T,$$

which is indeed of the form (8.16). $\square$

We give in the next section an interpretation of the points $h_k^{(n)}$ and $h_j^{(n)}$ (Proposition 8.16).

We now give a nice geometric interpretation of the Trifocal matrices $\mathbf{G}_i^n$ and $\mathbf{G}_i^{nT}, n = 1, 2, 3$, in terms of morphisms from $\mathbb{P}^{*2}$, the set of projective planar lines to $\mathbb{P}^2$. Let us start with the $\mathbf{G}_i^n, n = 1, 2, 3$:

Proposition 8.13 *The matrix* $\mathbf{G}_i^n, n = 1, 2, 3,$ *defines a morphism from the set of lines of the kth retinal plane considered as a* $\mathbb{P}^2$ *to the jth retinal plane. The image of this morphism is the epipolar line* $\mathcal{L}_j^n$, *i.e. the image by the jth camera of one of the projection rays of the ith camera, which is also the left kernel of* $\mathbf{G}_i^n$. *Geometrically, given a line l in the kth image, we consider the plane* (C_k, l) *and its intersection M with the corresponding projection ray of the ith camera. The image m of l through* $\mathbf{G}_i^n$ *is the image of M by the jth camera. M, and hence m, is not defined when the plane* (C_k, l) *contains the corresponding projection ray, i.e. when l is equal to* $\mathcal{R}_k^n$, *the right kernel of* $\mathbf{G}_i^n$.

Proof : This proposition is a direct consequence of Proposition 8.12. Let us consider Equation 8.16 and apply $\mathbf{G}_i^n$ to a line represented by $\mathbf{l}$:

$$\mathbf{G}_i^n \mathbf{l} = \left(\mathbf{h}_k^{(n)T} \mathbf{l} \right) \mathbf{e}_{ji} + \left(\mathbf{e}_{ki}^T \mathbf{l} \right) \mathbf{h}_j^{(n)T}.$$

Since, according to Proposition 8.12, the point $h_j^{(n)}$ is on the epipolar line $\mathcal{L}_j^n$, the image m of l is a point of the jth retinal plane on $\mathcal{L}_j^n$. Since the rank of $\mathbf{G}_i^n$ is known to be two, the image is a projective line; therefore it is $\mathcal{L}_j^n$. The geometric interpretation follows from the definition of the Trifocal tensor $\mathcal{T}_i$ and the definition of $\mathcal{L}_j^n$ as the image of the corresponding projection ray of the ith camera (see Figure 8.15). $\square$

A completely analogous analysis can be done for the matrices $\mathbf{G}_i^{nT}, n = 1, 2, 3.$ We will just state the proposition since the proof is identical:

Proposition 8.14 *The matrix* $\mathbf{G}_i^{nT}, n = 1, 2, 3,$ *defines a morphism from the set of lines of the jth retinal plane considered as a* $\mathbb{P}^2$ *to the kth retinal plane. The image of this morphism is the epipolar line* $\mathcal{R}_k^n$, *i.e. the image by the kth camera of one of the projection rays of the ith camera, which is also the right kernel of* $\mathbf{G}_i^n$. *Geometrically, given a line l in the jth image, we consider the plane* (C_j, l) *and its intersection M with the corresponding projection ray of the ith camera. The image m of l through* $\mathbf{G}_i^{nT}$ *is the image of M by the kth camera. M, and hence m, is not defined when the plane* (C_j, l) *contains the corresponding projection ray, i.e. when l is equal to* $\mathcal{L}_j^n$, *the left kernel of* $\mathbf{G}_i^n$.

We now investigate a property of the matrices $\mathbf{G}_i^n$ that draws a strong parallel between those matrices and the Fundamental matrices. We have seen that each matrix $\mathbf{G}_i^n$ represents a morphism that maps lines to points (Proposition 8.13). This observation is in contrast to the fact that, as seen in Chapter 5, a Fundamental matrix is a morphism that maps points to lines. We recall also that a Fundamental matrix defines a homography between the two pencils of epipolar lines in the two images. If we draw the analogy between the Fundamental matrices and the Trifocal matrices even further, we should be able to find a homography between two sets of points, each set being on a line. That this is indeed the case is shown in the following proposition.

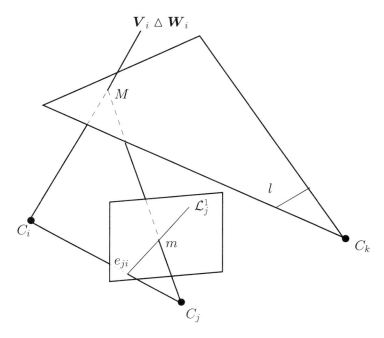

Figure 8.15: The matrix $\mathbf{G}_i^n$ defines a morphism from the set of lines of the kth image to the points on the epipolar line $\mathcal{L}_j^n$.

Proposition 8.15 *The matrix $\mathbf{G}_i^n$ defines a homography between the points of the line $\mathcal{R}_k^n$ and those of the line $\mathcal{L}_j^n$. This homography is geometrically defined as follows. Given a point a on $\mathcal{R}_k^n$, consider any line l going through a. The image b of l by $\mathbf{G}_i^n$ is on $\mathcal{L}_j^n$ and is independent of the choice of l. The correspondence $a \to b$ is a homography g_i^n from the points of $\mathcal{R}_k^n$ to the points of $\mathcal{L}_j^n$. Furthermore,*

$$g_i^n(e_{ki}) = e_{ji}.$$

Proof : Note that, because of Proposition 8.13 and Figure 8.15, the construction described in the proposition is equivalent to noting that, given a point a on $\mathcal{R}_k^n$, the optical ray (C_k, a) intersects the projection ray of view i corresponding to $\mathcal{R}_k^n$ in a point A and b is the image of A in view j. It follows that a) the correspondence $a \to b$ is one-to-one, b) it preserves the cross-ratio (this proves that g_i^n is a homography; see Theorem 2.2) and c) b does not depend upon the choice of the line l going through a. Furthermore, if $a = e_{ki}$, then the line (C_k, e_{ki}) is the line (C_k, C_i). It intersects any optical ray of the ith view in C_i whose image in view j is e_{ji}. Hence $g_i^n(e_{ki}) = e_{ji}$. □

8.2.5 Relation with planar homographies

Just like there are some very simple relations between planar homographies and the Fundamental matrix of a stereo pair, there also exist interesting and simple relations between the Trifocal tensors and planar homographies.

In detail, we have the following proposition.

Proposition 8.16 *The matrices* $\mathbf{G}_i^n, n = 1, 2, 3,$ *can be written, for any plane* Π *not going through the optical center* $C_i,$

$$\mathbf{G}_i^n = \mathbf{e}_{ji} \mathbf{H}_{ik}^{\Pi(n)T} + \mathbf{H}_{ij}^{\Pi(n)} \mathbf{e}_{ki}^T,$$

where $\mathbf{H}_{ij}^{\Pi(n)}$ *(respectively* $\mathbf{H}_{ik}^{\Pi(n)}$*) is the nth column vector of a matrix of the planar morphism induced by* Π *between the retinal planes* i *and* j *(respectively* j *and* k*).*

Proof :   According to Proposition 5.10, we have

$$\mathbf{e}_{ji} \simeq \begin{bmatrix} |\boldsymbol{U}_j, \boldsymbol{U}_i, \boldsymbol{V}_i, \boldsymbol{W}_i| \\ |\boldsymbol{V}_j, \boldsymbol{U}_i, \boldsymbol{V}_i, \boldsymbol{W}_i| \\ |\boldsymbol{W}_j, \boldsymbol{U}_i, \boldsymbol{V}_i, \boldsymbol{W}_i| \end{bmatrix} \quad \mathbf{e}_{ki} \simeq \begin{bmatrix} |\boldsymbol{U}_k, \boldsymbol{U}_i, \boldsymbol{V}_i, \boldsymbol{W}_i| \\ |\boldsymbol{V}_k, \boldsymbol{U}_i, \boldsymbol{V}_i, \boldsymbol{W}_i| \\ |\boldsymbol{W}_k, \boldsymbol{U}_i, \boldsymbol{V}_i, \boldsymbol{W}_i| \end{bmatrix}.$$

According to Proposition 5.2, the planar morphisms H_{ij}^{Π} and H_{ik}^{Π} induced by a plane Π between the retinal planes (i, j) and (i, k) are given by

$$\mathbf{H}_{ij}^{\Pi} \simeq \begin{bmatrix} |\boldsymbol{U}_j, \boldsymbol{V}_i, \boldsymbol{W}_i, \boldsymbol{\Pi}| & |\boldsymbol{U}_j, \boldsymbol{W}_i, \boldsymbol{U}_i, \boldsymbol{\Pi}| & |\boldsymbol{U}_j, \boldsymbol{U}_i, \boldsymbol{V}_i, \boldsymbol{\Pi}| \\ |\boldsymbol{V}_j, \boldsymbol{V}_i, \boldsymbol{W}_i, \boldsymbol{\Pi}| & |\boldsymbol{V}_j, \boldsymbol{W}_i, \boldsymbol{U}_i, \boldsymbol{\Pi}| & |\boldsymbol{V}_j, \boldsymbol{U}_i, \boldsymbol{V}_i, \boldsymbol{\Pi}| \\ |\boldsymbol{W}_j, \boldsymbol{V}_i, \boldsymbol{W}_i, \boldsymbol{\Pi}| & |\boldsymbol{W}_j, \boldsymbol{W}_i, \boldsymbol{U}_i, \boldsymbol{\Pi}| & |\boldsymbol{W}_j, \boldsymbol{U}_i, \boldsymbol{V}_i, \boldsymbol{\Pi}| \end{bmatrix}$$

and

$$\mathbf{H}_{ik}^{\Pi} \simeq \begin{bmatrix} |\boldsymbol{U}_k, \boldsymbol{V}_i, \boldsymbol{W}_i, \boldsymbol{\Pi}| & |\boldsymbol{U}_k, \boldsymbol{W}_i, \boldsymbol{U}_i, \boldsymbol{\Pi}| & |\boldsymbol{U}_k, \boldsymbol{U}_i, \boldsymbol{V}_i, \boldsymbol{\Pi}| \\ |\boldsymbol{V}_k, \boldsymbol{V}_i, \boldsymbol{W}_i, \boldsymbol{\Pi}| & |\boldsymbol{V}_k, \boldsymbol{W}_i, \boldsymbol{U}_i, \boldsymbol{\Pi}| & |\boldsymbol{V}_k, \boldsymbol{U}_i, \boldsymbol{V}_i, \boldsymbol{\Pi}| \\ |\boldsymbol{W}_k, \boldsymbol{V}_i, \boldsymbol{W}_i, \boldsymbol{\Pi}| & |\boldsymbol{W}_k, \boldsymbol{W}_i, \boldsymbol{U}_i, \boldsymbol{\Pi}| & |\boldsymbol{W}_k, \boldsymbol{U}_i, \boldsymbol{V}_i, \boldsymbol{\Pi}| \end{bmatrix}.$$

For the proof we choose $\mathbf{H}_{ik}^{\Pi}$ equal to the right-hand side and $\mathbf{H}_{ij}^{\Pi}$ equal to the negative of the right-hand side. We consider the three matrices $\mathbf{e}_{ji} \mathbf{H}_{ik}^{\Pi(n)T} + \mathbf{H}_{ij}^{\Pi(n)} \mathbf{e}_{ki}^T, n = 1, 2, 3,$ and show that they are proportional to the matrices $\mathbf{G}_i^n$ given in Equations 8.12, 8.13 and 8.14. Let us prove it for one of them. The element $(1, 1)$ of matrix $\mathbf{e}_{ji} \mathbf{H}_{ik}^{\Pi(1)T} + \mathbf{H}_{ij}^{\Pi(1)} \mathbf{e}_{ki}^T$ is equal to

$$|\boldsymbol{U}_j, \boldsymbol{U}_i, \boldsymbol{V}_i, \boldsymbol{W}_i| \, |\boldsymbol{U}_k, \boldsymbol{V}_i, \boldsymbol{W}_i, \boldsymbol{\Pi}| - |\boldsymbol{U}_j, \boldsymbol{V}_i, \boldsymbol{W}_i, \boldsymbol{\Pi}| \, |\boldsymbol{U}_k, \boldsymbol{U}_i, \boldsymbol{V}_i, \boldsymbol{W}_i|.$$

Using the properties of the $\triangle$ operator, we rewrite this expression

$$(|\boldsymbol{U}_j, \boldsymbol{U}_i, \boldsymbol{V}_i, \boldsymbol{W}_i| \, \boldsymbol{U}_k - |\boldsymbol{U}_k, \boldsymbol{U}_i, \boldsymbol{V}_i, \boldsymbol{W}_i| \, \boldsymbol{U}_k) \triangle (\boldsymbol{V}_i \triangle \boldsymbol{W}_i \triangle \boldsymbol{\Pi}). \qquad (8.18)$$

Let us use Cramer's rule on the five vectors $\boldsymbol{U}_i, \boldsymbol{V}_i, \boldsymbol{W}_i, \boldsymbol{U}_j$ and $\boldsymbol{U}_k$:

$$| \boldsymbol{V}_i, \boldsymbol{W}_i, \boldsymbol{U}_j, \boldsymbol{U}_k | \boldsymbol{U}_i - | \boldsymbol{U}_i, \boldsymbol{W}_i, \boldsymbol{U}_j, \boldsymbol{U}_k | \boldsymbol{V}_i + | \boldsymbol{U}_i, \boldsymbol{V}_i, \boldsymbol{U}_j, \boldsymbol{U}_k | \boldsymbol{W}_i -$$
$$| \boldsymbol{U}_i, \boldsymbol{V}_i, \boldsymbol{W}_i, \boldsymbol{U}_k | \boldsymbol{U}_j + | \boldsymbol{U}_i, \boldsymbol{V}_i, \boldsymbol{W}_i, \boldsymbol{U}_j | \boldsymbol{U}_k = \boldsymbol{0}.$$

Therefore

$$| \boldsymbol{U}_i, \boldsymbol{V}_i, \boldsymbol{W}_i, \boldsymbol{U}_j | \boldsymbol{U}_k - | \boldsymbol{U}_i, \boldsymbol{V}_i, \boldsymbol{W}_i, \boldsymbol{U}_k | \boldsymbol{U}_j =$$
$$| \boldsymbol{U}_i, \boldsymbol{W}_i, \boldsymbol{U}_j, \boldsymbol{U}_k | \boldsymbol{V}_i - | \boldsymbol{V}_i, \boldsymbol{W}_i, \boldsymbol{U}_j, \boldsymbol{U}_k | \boldsymbol{U}_i - | \boldsymbol{U}_i, \boldsymbol{V}_i, \boldsymbol{U}_j, \boldsymbol{U}_k | \boldsymbol{W}_i.$$

We replace $| \boldsymbol{U}_i, \boldsymbol{V}_i, \boldsymbol{W}_i, \boldsymbol{U}_j | \boldsymbol{U}_k - | \boldsymbol{U}_i, \boldsymbol{V}_i, \boldsymbol{W}_i, \boldsymbol{U}_k | \boldsymbol{U}_j$ by its value in (8.18) and use the fact that $\boldsymbol{V}_i \vartriangle \boldsymbol{V}_i \vartriangle \boldsymbol{W}_i \vartriangle \boldsymbol{\Pi} = \boldsymbol{W}_i \vartriangle \boldsymbol{V}_i \vartriangle \boldsymbol{W}_i \vartriangle \boldsymbol{\Pi} = 0$ to obtain

$$| \boldsymbol{U}_j, \boldsymbol{U}_i, \boldsymbol{V}_i, \boldsymbol{W}_i || \boldsymbol{U}_k, \boldsymbol{V}_i, \boldsymbol{W}_i, \boldsymbol{\Pi} | - | \boldsymbol{U}_j, \boldsymbol{V}_i, \boldsymbol{W}_i, \boldsymbol{\Pi} || \boldsymbol{U}_k, \boldsymbol{U}_i, \boldsymbol{V}_i, \boldsymbol{W}_i | =$$
$$- | \boldsymbol{V}_i, \boldsymbol{W}_i, \boldsymbol{U}_j, \boldsymbol{U}_k || \boldsymbol{U}_i, \boldsymbol{V}_i, \boldsymbol{W}_i, \boldsymbol{\Pi} | .$$

The reader can check that in general

$$\mathbf{e}_{ji} \mathbf{H}_{ik}^{\Pi(n)T} + \mathbf{H}_{ij}^{\Pi(n)} \mathbf{e}_{ki}^T = - | \boldsymbol{U}_i, \boldsymbol{V}_i, \boldsymbol{W}_i, \boldsymbol{\Pi} | \, \mathbf{G}_i^n \simeq \mathbf{G}_i^n, \quad n = 1, 2, 3.$$

$\square$

The situation is shown in Figure 8.16.

We now prove a lemma that will be used in Section 8.7.

Lemma 8.1 *For any tensor $\boldsymbol{\mathcal{T}}_i$ such as in Proposition 8.16, the three lines represented by $\boldsymbol{\mathcal{T}}_i(\mathbf{e}_{ji}, \mathbf{e}_{ki})$, $\mathbf{H}_{ik}^{\Pi\,T}\mathbf{e}_{ki}$ and $\mathbf{H}_{ij}^{\Pi\,T}\mathbf{e}_{ji}$ intersect at a point.*

Proof : Let us look at Figure 8.17 which represents the case $i = 1$, $j = 2$, $k = 3$. Consider the plane Π_2 (respectively Π_3) defined by the optical center C_2 (respectively C_3) and the line e_{21} (respectively e_{31}) represented by the vector $\mathbf{e}_{21}$ (respectively $\mathbf{e}_{31}$). Π_2 (respectively Π_3) is the second intrinsic plane of the pair $(1, 2)$ (respectively of the pair $(1, 3)$) of views (Definition 5.5). They intersect along a 3D line denoted E_{23} in the figure whose image by camera 1 is by definition $\boldsymbol{\mathcal{T}}_1(\mathbf{e}_{21}, \mathbf{e}_{31})$; see Figure 8.7.

Π_2 (respectively Π_3) intersects Π along a line E_2 (respectively E_3) whose image by camera 1 is represented by $\mathbf{H}_{12}^{\Pi\,T}\mathbf{e}_{21}$ (respectively $\mathbf{H}_{13}^{\Pi\,T}\mathbf{e}_{31}$).

The point A of intersection of the three planes Π, Π_2 and Π_3 is at the intersection of the three 3D lines E_{23}, E_2 and E_3. The three images by camera 1 of those three lines therefore intersect at a single point. $\square$

Another question that is related to the analysis done in Section 5.2.4 and worth asking is the following. Let Π be a plane. It induces homographies H_{ji}^{Π} and H_{ki}^{Π} between the retinal pairs (j, i) and (k, i). Conversely, given two homographies H_{ji} and H_{ki} between the retinal pairs (j, i) and (k, i), what are the conditions so that they are planar homographies (Definition 5.3) corresponding to the same plane Π?

The conditions are summarized in the following proposition.

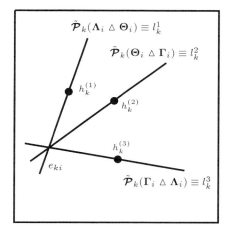
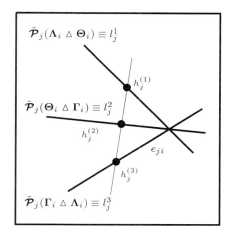

Figure 8.16: Illustration of Proposition 8.16. Note that the points $h_j^{(n)}, n = 1, 2, 3$, can be aligned, which corresponds to the case where the plane Π goes through the optical center C_j. The same is true of the points $h_k^{(n)}, n = 1, 2, 3$, if Π goes through C_k. Finally, if Π goes through C_j and C_k, i.e. if it is an epipolar plane for the pair (j, k), then both sets of points are aligned.

Proposition 8.17 *Given a triple of images and a Trifocal tensor $\boldsymbol{\mathcal{T}}_i$, let H_{ji} and H_{ki} be two homographies between the retinal pairs (j, i) and (k, i). The following two conditions are equivalent.*

1. *The pair (H_{ji}, H_{ki}) is a pair of planar homographies corresponding to the same plane.*

2. *Let $\mathbf{K}_i^n$ be the matrix $\mathbf{H}_{ji}\mathbf{G}_i^n\mathbf{H}_{ki}$, and let $\mathbf{I}_n$ be the 2×3 matrix obtained by removing the nth row of the 3×3 identity matrix. 15 relations hold:*

$$\mathbf{I}_n\mathbf{K}_i^n\mathbf{I}_n^T + \mathbf{I}_n\mathbf{K}_i^{nT}\mathbf{I}_n^T = \mathbf{0}, \quad n = 1, 2, 3. \tag{8.19}$$

They are equivalent to the nine equations

$$K_{i\,22}^1 = K_{i\,33}^1 = K_{i\,23}^1 + K_{i\,32}^1 = 0, \tag{8.20}$$

$$K_{i\,33}^2 = K_{i\,11}^2 = K_{i\,31}^2 + K_{i\,13}^2 = 0, \tag{8.21}$$

$$K_{i\,11}^3 = K_{i\,22}^3 = K_{i\,12}^3 + K_{i\,21}^3 = 0. \tag{8.22}$$

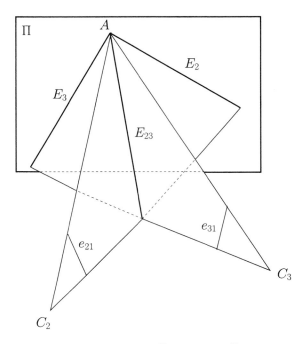

Figure 8.17: The three lines $\boldsymbol{\mathcal{T}}(\mathbf{e}_{21}, \mathbf{e}_{31})$, $\mathbf{H}_{12}^T\mathbf{e}_{21}$ and $\mathbf{H}_{13}^T\mathbf{e}_{31}$ intersect at the point image of A in the first retinal plane.

To those nine equations, we have to add six equations:

$$
\begin{aligned}
K_{i\,11}^1 &= K_{i\,31}^3 + K_{i\,13}^3 = K_{i\,21}^2 + K_{i\,12}^2, \\
K_{i\,22}^2 &= K_{i\,21}^1 + K_{i\,12}^1 = K_{i\,32}^3 + K_{i\,23}^3, \\
K_{i\,33}^3 &= K_{i\,23}^2 + K_{i\,32}^2 = K_{i\,31}^1 + K_{i\,13}^1.
\end{aligned}
\tag{8.23}
$$

Proof :   Let us prove that 1) implies 2).

Consider a 3D line L in the plane Π, and its images l_i, l_j and l_k satisfy

$$
\mathbf{l}_j = \mathbf{H}_{ji}^T\mathbf{l}_i, \quad \mathbf{l}_k = \mathbf{H}_{ki}^T\mathbf{l}_i.
\tag{8.24}
$$

Let us replace $\mathbf{l}_j$ and $\mathbf{l}_k$ by the values in the expressions (8.10) and look at the nth coordinate $l_i^{(n)}$ of $\mathbf{l}_i$. We must have

$$
l_i^{(n)} \simeq \mathbf{l}_i^T\mathbf{H}_{ji}\mathbf{G}_i^n\mathbf{H}_{ki}^T\mathbf{l}_i
\tag{8.25}
$$

for all vectors $\mathbf{l}_i$. Let $\mathbf{K}_i^n = \mathbf{H}_{ji}\mathbf{G}_i^n\mathbf{H}_{ki}^T$.

Let us consider the case $n = 1$ and choose l_i such that $l_i^{(1)} = 0$ (the line l_i goes through the point ε_1). Since the first coordinate of $\mathbf{l}_i$ is zero, we write $\mathbf{l}_i = [0, \mathbf{p}_i^T]^T$, and Equation 8.25 can be rewritten as

$$\mathbf{p}_i^T \mathbf{I}_1 \mathbf{K}_i^1 \mathbf{I}_1^T \mathbf{p}_i = 0, \quad \forall \mathbf{p}_i,$$

where $\mathbf{I}_1$ is the 2×3 matrix obtained by crossing out the first row of the 3×3 identity matrix. It follows that the matrix $\mathbf{I}_1 \mathbf{K}_i^1 \mathbf{I}_1^T$ is antisymmetric which is Equation 8.19 for $n = 1$ and Equation 8.20. The cases $n = 2$ and $n = 3$ are similar.

We must now ensure that the scale factors which are hidden in Equation 8.25 are all equal. If we compute the right-hand sides of this equation for $n = 1, 2, 3$, we find

$$l_i^{(1)} \left(K_{i\,11}^1 l_i^{(1)} + \left(K_{i\,21}^1 + K_{i\,12}^1 \right) l_i^{(2)} + \left(K_{i\,31}^1 + K_{i\,13}^1 \right) l_i^{(3)} \right)$$

$$l_i^{(2)} \left(\left(K_{i\,21}^2 + K_{i\,12}^2 \right) l_i^{(1)} + K_{i\,22}^2 l_i^{(2)} + \left(K_{i\,23}^2 + K_{i\,32}^2 \right) l_i^{(3)} \right)$$

$$l_i^{(3)} \left(\left(K_{i\,31}^3 + K_{i\,13}^3 \right) l_i^{(1)} + \left(K_{i\,32}^3 + K_{i\,23}^3 \right) l_i^{(2)} + K_{i\,33}^3 l_i^{(3)} \right)$$

It follows that the three linear forms $\mathbf{l}_i \longrightarrow K_{11}^1 l_i^{(1)} + (K_{21}^1 + K_{12}^1) l_i^{(2)} + (K_{31}^1 + K_{13}^1) l_i^{(3)}$, $\mathbf{l}_i \longrightarrow (K_{21}^1 + K_{12}^1) l_i^{(1)} + K_{22}^2 l_i^{(2)} + (K_{23}^3 + K_{32}^3) l_i^{(3)}$ and $\mathbf{l}_i \longrightarrow (K_{31}^1 + K_{13}^1) l_i^{(1)} + (K_{32}^2 + K_{23}^2) l_i^{(2)} + K_{33}^3 l_i^{(3)}$ are equal and this equality is equivalent to the equations (8.23).

The proof of the converse, i.e. that 2) implies 1) is left to the reader. $\square$

8.3 Prediction revisited

We have seen in Section 8.1 that the prediction with the Fundamental matrices $\mathbf{F}_{13}$ and $\mathbf{F}_{23}$ of a third point m_3 in image 3 from two corresponding points m_1 and m_2 in images 1 and 2 failed in two cases: when the two points m_1 and m_2 were on the Trifocal lines t_1 and t_2 and when the three optical centers were aligned. We now show that the Trifocal tensor allows us to perform that prediction, that transfer, in both cases.

8.3.1 Prediction in the Trifocal plane

In the case where the optical centers are not aligned and the points m_2 and m_3 belong to the Trifocal lines t_2 and t_3, we can use the Trifocal tensor $\mathcal{T}_1$ to predict m_1 from m_2 and m_3. The idea is as follows. Consider a line l_2 (respectively l_3) going through m_2 (respectively m_3) and different from t_2 (respectively from t_3). The line $\mathcal{T}_1(l_2, l_3)$ is different from t_3 because of our choice of l_2 and l_3 and intersects t_3 at m_3; see Figure 8.18.

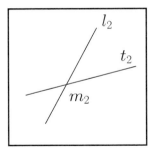
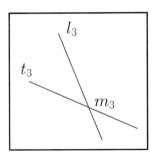

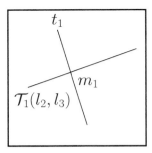

Figure 8.18: The line $\boldsymbol{\mathcal{T}}_1(\mathbf{l}_2, \mathbf{l}_3)$ intersects the Trifocal line t_3 at m_3, the point corresponding to m_1 and m_2.

8.3.2   Optical centers aligned

We saw in Section 8.1.2 that if the optical centers of the three cameras were aligned, then it was not possible to transfer a point, say from views 2 and 3 to view 1, because the two epipolar lines were identical. This problem does not occur if we use the Trifocal tensor $\boldsymbol{\mathcal{T}}_1$.

Indeed, let m_2 and m_3 be two pixels in images 2 and 3 satisfying the epipolar constraint. Let l_2 and l_3 be two lines going through the points m_2 and m_3, respectively. Then, under the condition of the next proposition, the line $\boldsymbol{\mathcal{T}}(\mathbf{l}_2, \mathbf{l}_3)$ intersects the epipolar line of m_2 in image 1, which is identical to the epipolar line of m_3, at the point m_1 corresponding to (m_2, m_3).

Proposition 8.18 *Let m_2 and m_3 be two points in images 2 and 3 such that m_2 and m_3 satisfy the epipolar constraint for the pair (2,3) of views. Let l_2, l_3 be two lines going through the points m_2 and m_3, respectively, and such that l_k, $k = 2, 3$, does not go through the epipole e_{k1}. Then, the point of intersection m_1 of the line $\boldsymbol{\mathcal{T}}(\mathbf{l}_2, \mathbf{l}_3)$ with the epipolar line in image 1 of m_2 (which is identical to the epipolar line of m_3) is well-defined and is the point in image 1 corresponding to the pair*

(m_2, m_3).

Proof : The condition on (l_2, l_3) ensures that, according to Theorem 8.1, the line $\mathcal{T}(\mathbf{l}_2, \mathbf{l}_3)$ is well-defined and different from the epipolar line of m_2 in image 1. Since the 3D line L defined by $\mathcal{P}_2^T \mathbf{l}_2 \,\triangle\, \mathcal{P}_3^T \mathbf{l}_3$ goes through the point M whose images in images 2 and 3 are m_2 and m_3, the conclusion follows. $\square$

8.4 Constraints satisfied by the tensors

The question of precisely characterizing the constraints satisfied by the tensors is of great practical importance as we will see in the next chapter where we discuss the problem of estimating the tensors from triplets of line correspondences. More specifically, we know that the tensor is equivalent to the knowledge of the three perspective projection matrices and that they depend upon 18 parameters. On the other hand a Trifocal tensor depends upon 27 parameters up to scale, i.e. 26 parameters. There must therefore exist constraints between the coefficients that define the tensor. As a matter of fact, we have already seen several such constraints when we studied the matrices $\mathbf{G}^n$ in Section 8.2.4. In the next section we recall those constraints and determine the form of the Trifocal tensor that they imply.

But let us start with a definition of the set of Trifocal tensors with which we are interested in working. We saw in Section 8.2.4 that any Trifocal tensor could be written as in Equation 8.16. Conversely, let us assume that a tensor $\mathcal{T}_i$ can be written as (8.16), and consider the two matrices

$$\mathbf{H}_{ik} = \left[\mathbf{h}_k^{(1)} \, \mathbf{h}_k^{(2)} \, \mathbf{h}_k^{(3)} \right], \quad \mathbf{H}_{ij} = \left[\mathbf{h}_j^{(1)} \, \mathbf{h}_j^{(2)} \, \mathbf{h}_j^{(3)} \right].$$

Then, using the Equations 8.12 to 8.14, it is easy to check that $\mathcal{T}_i$ arises from the three perspective projection matrices

$$\mathcal{P}_i = [\mathbf{I}_3 \, \mathbf{0}], \quad \mathcal{P}_j = [\mathbf{H}_{ij} \, \mathbf{e}_{ji}], \quad \mathcal{P}_k = [-\mathbf{H}_{ik} \, \mathbf{e}_{ki}].$$

It is therefore coherent to use this equation as the definition of the set of Trifocal tensors:

Definition 8.4 *Any tensor of the form (8.16) is a Trifocal tensor.*

To simplify the notations, we will assume in the following that $i = 1$ and will ignore the ith index everywhere, i.e. denote $\mathcal{T}_1$ by $\mathcal{T}$. Referring to Figure 8.8, we will be using several notations: $\mathcal{T}^{uv}$ represents the vector formed with the column of index (u, v) in the cube, $\mathcal{T}_w^{\cdot v}$ the vth column vector of the matrix $\mathbf{G}^w$, $\mathcal{T}_w^{u \cdot}$ its uth row vector. Similarly, $\mathcal{T}_w^{\cdot \cdot}$ is the matrix $\mathbf{G}^w$.

8.4.1   Rank and epipolar constraints

We recall the constraints on the matrices $\mathbf{G}^n$ in the following proposition.

Proposition 8.19 *The Trifocal tensor $\mathcal{T}$ satisfies the three constraints, called the* **Trifocal rank** *constraints,*

$$det(\mathbf{G}^n) = det(\mathcal{T}_{\,n}^{\,\cdot\,\cdot}) = 0, \quad n = 1, 2, 3.$$

The Trifocal tensor $\mathcal{T}$ satisfies the two constraints, called the **Trifocal epipolar** *constraints,*

$$\left| \mathcal{R}_3^1, \, \mathcal{R}_3^2, \, \mathcal{R}_3^3 \right| = \left| \mathcal{L}_2^1, \, \mathcal{L}_2^2, \, \mathcal{L}_2^3 \right| = 0.$$

Those five relations are clearly algebraically independent since the rank constraints say nothing about the way the kernels are related. We will see in Section 8.5 that they constrain the form of the matrices $\mathbf{G}^n$ in a way that is reminiscent of Proposition 8.12; see Proposition 8.22.

8.4.2   The 27 axes constraints

We now show that the coefficients of $\mathcal{T}$ satisfy nine more algebraic constraints of degree 6 which are defined as follows. Let $\varepsilon_n, n = 1, 2, 3$, be the canonical basis of $\mathbb{R}^3$ and let us consider the four lines $\lambda_1 = \mathcal{T}(\varepsilon_{k_2}, \varepsilon_{k_3}) = \mathcal{T}_{\cdot}^{k_2 \, k_3}$, $\lambda_2 = \mathcal{T}_{\cdot}^{l_2 \, k_3}$, $\lambda_3 = \mathcal{T}_{\cdot}^{k_2 \, l_3}$ and $\lambda_4 = \mathcal{T}_{\cdot}^{l_2 \, l_3}$ where the indices k_2 and l_2 (respectively k_3 and l_3) are different and vary between 1 and 3. For example, if $k_2 = k_3 = 1$ and $l_2 = l_3 = 2$, then the four lines are the images in camera 1 of the four 3D lines $\boldsymbol{U}_2 \wedge \boldsymbol{U}_3$, $\boldsymbol{V}_2 \wedge \boldsymbol{U}_3$, $\boldsymbol{U}_2 \wedge \boldsymbol{V}_3$ and $\boldsymbol{V}_2 \wedge \boldsymbol{V}_3$.

These four lines which can be chosen in nine different ways satisfy an algebraic constraint which is detailed in the following theorem.

Theorem 8.3 *The bilinear mapping $\mathcal{T}$ satisfies the 9 algebraic constraints*

$$\left| \mathcal{T}_{\cdot}^{k_2 \, k_3}, \, \mathcal{T}_{\cdot}^{k_2 \, l_3}, \, \mathcal{T}_{\cdot}^{l_2 \, l_3} \right| \left| \mathcal{T}_{\cdot}^{k_2 \, k_3}, \, \mathcal{T}_{\cdot}^{l_2 \, k_3}, \, \mathcal{T}_{\cdot}^{l_2 \, l_3} \right| -$$

$$\left| \mathcal{T}_{\cdot}^{l_2 \, k_3}, \, \mathcal{T}_{\cdot}^{k_2 \, l_3}, \, \mathcal{T}_{\cdot}^{l_2 \, l_3} \right| \left| \mathcal{T}_{\cdot}^{k_2 \, k_3}, \, \mathcal{T}_{\cdot}^{l_2 \, k_3}, \, \mathcal{T}_{\cdot}^{k_2 \, l_3} \right| = 0, \quad (8.26)$$

where $k_2, l_2, k_3, l_3 = 1, 2, 3$ and $k_2 \neq l_2$, $k_3 \neq l_3$. They are called the **Trifocal vertical** *constraints in reference to Figure 8.8.*

Proof : We consider the two pencils of lines (see Section 2.6.2) defined by $a_2 \lambda_1 + b_2 \lambda_2$ and $a_2 \lambda_3 + b_2 \lambda_4$ where a_2 and b_2 are two arbitrary numbers which are not both zero. Those two pencils are in projective correspondence, the homography being the identity. It is known (see for example (Semple and Kneebone, 1952)) that the point of intersection of two corresponding lines of two pencils in projective correspondence lies on a conic. The equation of that conic is very easily obtained.

Let m_1 be a point on the conic. m_1 is on the line of the first pencil defined by $a_2\boldsymbol{\lambda}_1 + b_2\boldsymbol{\lambda}_2$; hence $a_2(\mathbf{m}_1^T\boldsymbol{\lambda}_1) + b_2(\mathbf{m}_1^T\boldsymbol{\lambda}_2) = 0$. Similarly, m_1 is on the corresponding line of the second pencil defined by $a_2\boldsymbol{\lambda}_3 + b_2\boldsymbol{\lambda}_4$ and hence $a_2(\mathbf{m}_1^T\boldsymbol{\lambda}_3) + b_2(\mathbf{m}_1^T\boldsymbol{\lambda}_4) = 0$. Since for each point m_1 on the conic there exists a value of $a_2 : b_2$, we must have $(\mathbf{m}_1^T\boldsymbol{\lambda}_1)(\mathbf{m}_1^T\boldsymbol{\lambda}_4) - (\mathbf{m}_1^T\boldsymbol{\lambda}_2)(\mathbf{m}_1^T\boldsymbol{\lambda}_3) = 0$ which can be rewritten

$$\mathbf{m}_1^T \left(\boldsymbol{\lambda}_1\boldsymbol{\lambda}_4^T - \boldsymbol{\lambda}_2\boldsymbol{\lambda}_3^T \right) \mathbf{m}_1 = 0. \tag{8.27}$$

The matrix defining the conic is the even part of the matrix $\boldsymbol{\lambda}_1\boldsymbol{\lambda}_4^T - \boldsymbol{\lambda}_2\boldsymbol{\lambda}_3^T$, i.e.

$$\frac{1}{2} \left(\boldsymbol{\lambda}_1\boldsymbol{\lambda}_4^T + \boldsymbol{\lambda}_4\boldsymbol{\lambda}_1^T - \boldsymbol{\lambda}_2\boldsymbol{\lambda}_3^T - \boldsymbol{\lambda}_3\boldsymbol{\lambda}_2^T \right),$$

whose determinant can be shown to be equal to

$$| \boldsymbol{\lambda}_1, \boldsymbol{\lambda}_3, \boldsymbol{\lambda}_4 \,|\, | \boldsymbol{\lambda}_1, \boldsymbol{\lambda}_2, \boldsymbol{\lambda}_4 | - | \boldsymbol{\lambda}_2, \boldsymbol{\lambda}_3, \boldsymbol{\lambda}_4 \,|\, | \boldsymbol{\lambda}_1, \boldsymbol{\lambda}_2, \boldsymbol{\lambda}_3 | \,.$$

This expression is the left-hand side of Equation 8.26.

It remains to show that this expression is equal to 0. We do it by showing that the above conic is in effect degenerate, being reduced to the two lines (a_{12}, a_{34}) and (a_{13}, a_{24}), where the point a_{ij} is the intersection of the two lines λ_i and λ_j represented by the cross-product $\boldsymbol{\lambda}_i \times \boldsymbol{\lambda}_j$. Using the same example as before, i.e. $k_2 = k_3 = 1$ and $l_2 = l_3 = 2$, those two lines are the images in the first camera of the lines $\boldsymbol{U}_3 \vartriangle \boldsymbol{V}_3$ and $\boldsymbol{U}_2 \vartriangle \boldsymbol{V}_2$. In general, those two lines are the images in the first camera of the m_3th ($m_3 \neq k_3$ and $m_3 \neq l_3$) projection ray of the third camera and of the m_2th ($m_2 \neq k_2$ and $m_2 \neq l_2$) projection ray of the second camera, respectively.

The proof is very simple since a point m_1 on the line (a_{12}, a_{34}) is represented by $\mathbf{m}_1 = \alpha_1\boldsymbol{\lambda}_1 \times \boldsymbol{\lambda}_2 + \beta_1\boldsymbol{\lambda}_3 \times \boldsymbol{\lambda}_4$ and a point m_1 on the line (a_{13}, a_{24}) is represented by $\mathbf{m}_1 = \alpha_1\boldsymbol{\lambda}_1 \times \boldsymbol{\lambda}_3 + \beta_1\boldsymbol{\lambda}_2 \times \boldsymbol{\lambda}_4$. In both cases one verifies that Equation 8.27 is satisfied for all values of α_1 and β_1. $\square$

The reader can convince himself that if he takes any general set of lines, then Equation 8.26 is in general *not* satisfied. For instance, let $\boldsymbol{\lambda}_i = \boldsymbol{\varepsilon}_i, i = 1, 2, 3, 4$. It is readily verified that the left-hand side of (8.26) is equal to -2.

Referring to Figure 8.8, what Theorem 8.3 says is that if we take four vertical columns of the Trifocal cube (shown as dashed lines in the figure) arranged in such a way that they form a prism with a square basis, then the expression (8.26) is equal to 0. It turns out that the same kind of relations hold for the other two principal directions of the cube (shown as solid lines of different widths in the same figure):

Theorem 8.4 *The bilinear mapping* $\boldsymbol{T}$ *also satisfies the 18 algebraic constraints of degree 6*

$$\left| \boldsymbol{T}_{k_1}^{.k_3}, \boldsymbol{T}_{k_1}^{.l_3}, \boldsymbol{T}_{l_1}^{.l_3} \right| \left| \boldsymbol{T}_{k_1}^{.k_3}, \boldsymbol{T}_{l_1}^{.k_3}, \boldsymbol{T}_{l_1}^{.l_3} \right| -$$
$$\left| \boldsymbol{T}_{l_1}^{.k_3}, \boldsymbol{T}_{k_1}^{.l_3}, \boldsymbol{T}_{l_1}^{.l_3} \right| \left| \boldsymbol{T}_{k_1}^{.k_3}, \boldsymbol{T}_{l_1}^{.k_3}, \boldsymbol{T}_{k_1}^{.l_3} \right| = 0 \tag{8.28}$$

and

$$\left|\mathcal{T}_{k_1}^{k_2\cdot},\ \mathcal{T}_{k_1}^{l_2\cdot},\ \mathcal{T}_{l_1}^{l_2\cdot}\right|\left|\mathcal{T}_{k_1}^{k_2\cdot},\ \mathcal{T}_{l_1}^{k_2\cdot},\ \mathcal{T}_{l_1}^{l_2\cdot}\right|-$$

$$\left|\mathcal{T}_{l_1}^{k_2\cdot},\ \mathcal{T}_{k_1}^{l_2\cdot},\ \mathcal{T}_{l_1}^{l_2\cdot}\right|\left|\mathcal{T}_{k_1}^{k_2\cdot},\ \mathcal{T}_{l_1}^{k_2\cdot},\ \mathcal{T}_{k_1}^{l_2\cdot}\right|=0. \quad (8.29)$$

They are called the **Trifocal horizontal** *constraints in reference to Figure 8.8.*

Proof : We give the proof for the first set of constraints which concern the columns of the matrices $\mathbf{G}^n$. The proof is analogous for the other set concerning the rows.

The three columns of $\mathbf{G}^n$ represent three points $G_k^n, k = 1, 2, 3$, of the epipolar line $\mathcal{L}_2^n$ (see Proposition 8.13). To be concrete, let us consider the first two columns $\mathcal{T}_1^{\cdot 1}$ and $\mathcal{T}_1^{\cdot 2}$ of $\mathbf{G}^1$ and $\mathcal{T}_2^{\cdot 1}$ and $\mathcal{T}_2^{\cdot 2}$ of $\mathbf{G}^2$; the proof is similar for the other combinations. Following the proof of Theorem 8.3, we consider the two sets of points defined by $a_2\mathcal{T}_1^{\cdot 1} + b_2\mathcal{T}_1^{\cdot 2}$ and $a_2\mathcal{T}_2^{\cdot 1} + b_2\mathcal{T}_2^{\cdot 2}$. These two sets are in projective correspondence, the homography being the identity. It is known (it is the dual of the situation in Theorem 8.3) that the line joining two corresponding points envelops a conic. It is easily shown that the equation of this conic is

$$\boldsymbol{\lambda}_2^T\left(\mathcal{T}_1^{\cdot 1}\mathcal{T}_2^{\cdot 2T} - \mathcal{T}_1^{\cdot 2}\mathcal{T}_2^{\cdot 1T}\right)\boldsymbol{\lambda}_2 = 0. \quad (8.30)$$

The determinant of the matrix defining this conic is equal to

$$\left|\mathcal{T}_1^{\cdot 1},\ \mathcal{T}_1^{\cdot 2},\ \mathcal{T}_2^{\cdot 2}\right|\left|\mathcal{T}_1^{\cdot 1},\ \mathcal{T}_2^{\cdot 1},\ \mathcal{T}_2^{\cdot 2}\right| - \left|\mathcal{T}_2^{\cdot 1},\ \mathcal{T}_1^{\cdot 2},\ \mathcal{T}_2^{\cdot 2}\right|\left|\mathcal{T}_1^{\cdot 1},\ \mathcal{T}_2^{\cdot 1},\ \mathcal{T}_1^{\cdot 2}\right|.$$

This expression is the left-hand side of Equation 8.28 in the special case $k_1 = k_3 = 1$, $l_1 = l_3 = 2$. In order to show that this expression is equal to 0, we show that the conic is degenerate, containing two lines of lines, i.e. two pencils of lines (see Section 2.6.2). The envelope of those two pencils are the two points of intersection of the lines in each pencil. This result is readily obtained from a geometric interpretation.

Let us consider the two lines, denoted $\mathcal{L}_2^1$ and $\mathcal{L}_2^2$ in Section 8.2.4, and represented by the cross-products $\mathcal{T}_1^{\cdot 1} \times \mathcal{T}_1^{\cdot 2}$ and $\mathcal{T}_2^{\cdot 1} \times \mathcal{T}_2^{\cdot 2}$. All lines l_2 in the pencil defined by those two lines are represented by $\alpha_2\mathcal{T}_1^{\cdot 1} \times \mathcal{T}_1^{\cdot 2} + \beta_2\mathcal{T}_2^{\cdot 1} \times \mathcal{T}_2^{\cdot 2}$ and satisfy Equation 8.30. The corresponding conic hence contains that pencil of lines which goes through the epipole e_{21} (see Figure 8.14).

Similarly, let us consider the two lines $(\mathcal{T}_1^{\cdot 1}, \mathcal{T}_2^{\cdot 1})$ and $(\mathcal{T}_1^{\cdot 2}, \mathcal{T}_2^{\cdot 2})$ represented by the cross-products $\mathcal{T}_1^{\cdot 1} \times \mathcal{T}_2^{\cdot 1}$ and $\mathcal{T}_1^{\cdot 2} \times \mathcal{T}_2^{\cdot 2}$. All lines l_2 in the pencil defined by those two lines are represented by $\alpha_2\mathcal{T}_1^{\cdot 1} \times \mathcal{T}_2^{\cdot 1} + \beta_2\mathcal{T}_1^{\cdot 2} \times \mathcal{T}_2^{\cdot 2}$ and satisfy Equation 8.30. The corresponding conic hence contains that pencil of lines which goes through the point of intersection of the two lines $(\mathcal{T}_1^{\cdot 1}, \mathcal{T}_2^{\cdot 1})$ and $(\mathcal{T}_1^{\cdot 2}, \mathcal{T}_2^{\cdot 2})$. $\square$

Definition 8.5 *The 27 constraints described in Theorems 8.3 and 8.4 are called the* **Trifocal axes** *constraints.*

8.4.3   The extended rank constraints

We show that the Trifocal tensor also satisfies a set of ten algebraic constraints that are of a lesser degree, i.e. three, than the twenty seven vertical, row and column constraints described in the previous section.

Proposition 8.20 *The Trifocal tensor $\mathcal{T}$ satisfies the ten algebraic constraints, called the* **Trifocal extended rank** *constraints,*

$$rank\left(\sum_{n=1}^{3} \lambda_n \mathbf{G}^n\right) \leq 2, \quad \forall \lambda_n, \; n = 1, 2, 3.$$

Proof :   The proof can be done either algebraically or geometrically. The algebraic proof simply uses the parameterization (8.16) and verifies that the constraints described in Proposition 8.21 are satisfied. In the geometric proof one uses Proposition 8.13 and Figure 8.15 and notices that for fixed values (not all zero) of the λ_n's, and for a given line l_3 in view 3, the point which is the image in view 2 of line l_3 by $\sum_{n=1}^{3} \lambda_n \mathbf{G}^n$ is the image of the point defined by

$$\lambda_1 \boldsymbol{\mathcal{P}}_3^T l_3 \; \triangle \; (\boldsymbol{V}_1 \; \triangle \; \boldsymbol{W}_1) + \lambda_2 \boldsymbol{\mathcal{P}}_3^T l_3 \; \triangle \; (\boldsymbol{W}_1 \; \triangle \; \boldsymbol{U}_1) + \lambda_3 \boldsymbol{\mathcal{P}}_3^T l_3 \; \triangle \; (\boldsymbol{U}_1 \; \triangle \; \boldsymbol{V}_1).$$

This expression can be rewritten as

$$\boldsymbol{\mathcal{P}}_3^T l_3 \; \triangle \; (\lambda_1 \boldsymbol{V}_1 \; \triangle \; \boldsymbol{W}_1 + \lambda_2 \boldsymbol{W}_1 \; \triangle \; \boldsymbol{U}_1 + \lambda_3 \boldsymbol{U}_1 \; \triangle \; \boldsymbol{V}_1). \tag{8.31}$$

The line $\lambda_1 \boldsymbol{V}_1 \; \triangle \; \boldsymbol{W}_1 + \lambda_2 \boldsymbol{W}_1 \; \triangle \; \boldsymbol{U}_1 + \lambda_3 \boldsymbol{U}_1 \; \triangle \; \boldsymbol{V}_1$ is an optical ray of the first camera (Proposition 4.4), and when l_3 varies in view 3, the point defined by (8.31) is well-defined except when l_3 is the image of that line in view 3. In that case the meet in (8.31) is zero and the image of that line is in the nullspace of $\sum_{n=1}^{3} \lambda_n \mathbf{G}^n$ which is therefore of rank less than or equal to 2.   □

Note that the Proposition 8.20 is equivalent to the vanishing of the 10 coefficients of the homogeneous polynomial of degree 3 in the three variables $\lambda_n, n = 1, 2, 3$ equal to $\det(\sum_{n=1}^{3} \lambda_n \mathbf{G}^n)$. The coefficients of the terms $\lambda_n^3, \; n = 1, 2, 3$ are the determinants $\det(\mathbf{G}^n), \; n = 1, 2, 3$. Therefore the extended rank constraints contain the rank constraints.

To be complete, we give the expressions of the seven Trifocal extended rank constraints which are different from the three rank constraints:

Proposition 8.21 *The seven extended Trifocal rank constraints different from the* *three rank constraints are given by*

$$\lambda_1^2 \lambda_2 \quad \left| \boldsymbol{\mathcal{T}}_1^{\cdot 1}, \boldsymbol{\mathcal{T}}_1^{\cdot 2}, \boldsymbol{\mathcal{T}}_2^{\cdot 3} \right| + \left| \boldsymbol{\mathcal{T}}_1^{\cdot 1}, \boldsymbol{\mathcal{T}}_2^{\cdot 2}, \boldsymbol{\mathcal{T}}_1^{\cdot 3} \right| + \left| \boldsymbol{\mathcal{T}}_2^{\cdot 1}, \boldsymbol{\mathcal{T}}_1^{\cdot 2}, \boldsymbol{\mathcal{T}}_1^{\cdot 3} \right| = 0, \quad (8.32)$$

$$\lambda_1^2 \lambda_3 \quad \left| \boldsymbol{\mathcal{T}}_1^{\cdot 1}, \boldsymbol{\mathcal{T}}_1^{\cdot 2}, \boldsymbol{\mathcal{T}}_3^{\cdot 3} \right| + \left| \boldsymbol{\mathcal{T}}_1^{\cdot 1}, \boldsymbol{\mathcal{T}}_3^{\cdot 2}, \boldsymbol{\mathcal{T}}_1^{\cdot 3} \right| + \left| \boldsymbol{\mathcal{T}}_3^{\cdot 1}, \boldsymbol{\mathcal{T}}_1^{\cdot 2}, \boldsymbol{\mathcal{T}}_1^{\cdot 3} \right| = 0, \quad (8.33)$$

$$\lambda_2^2 \lambda_1 \quad \left| \boldsymbol{\mathcal{T}}_2^{\cdot 1}, \boldsymbol{\mathcal{T}}_2^{\cdot 2}, \boldsymbol{\mathcal{T}}_1^{\cdot 3} \right| + \left| \boldsymbol{\mathcal{T}}_2^{\cdot 1}, \boldsymbol{\mathcal{T}}_1^{\cdot 2}, \boldsymbol{\mathcal{T}}_2^{\cdot 3} \right| + \left| \boldsymbol{\mathcal{T}}_1^{\cdot 1}, \boldsymbol{\mathcal{T}}_2^{\cdot 2}, \boldsymbol{\mathcal{T}}_2^{\cdot 3} \right| = 0, \quad (8.34)$$

$$\lambda_2^2 \lambda_3 \quad \left| \boldsymbol{\mathcal{T}}_2^{\cdot 1}, \boldsymbol{\mathcal{T}}_2^{\cdot 2}, \boldsymbol{\mathcal{T}}_3^{\cdot 3} \right| + \left| \boldsymbol{\mathcal{T}}_2^{\cdot 1}, \boldsymbol{\mathcal{T}}_3^{\cdot 2}, \boldsymbol{\mathcal{T}}_2^{\cdot 3} \right| + \left| \boldsymbol{\mathcal{T}}_3^{\cdot 1}, \boldsymbol{\mathcal{T}}_2^{\cdot 2}, \boldsymbol{\mathcal{T}}_2^{\cdot 3} \right| = 0, \quad (8.35)$$

$$\lambda_3^2 \lambda_1 \quad \left| \boldsymbol{\mathcal{T}}_3^{\cdot 1}, \boldsymbol{\mathcal{T}}_3^{\cdot 2}, \boldsymbol{\mathcal{T}}_1^{\cdot 3} \right| + \left| \boldsymbol{\mathcal{T}}_3^{\cdot 1}, \boldsymbol{\mathcal{T}}_1^{\cdot 2}, \boldsymbol{\mathcal{T}}_3^{\cdot 3} \right| + \left| \boldsymbol{\mathcal{T}}_1^{\cdot 1}, \boldsymbol{\mathcal{T}}_3^{\cdot 2}, \boldsymbol{\mathcal{T}}_3^{\cdot 3} \right| = 0, \quad (8.36)$$

$$\lambda_3^2 \lambda_2 \quad \left| \boldsymbol{\mathcal{T}}_3^{\cdot 1}, \boldsymbol{\mathcal{T}}_3^{\cdot 2}, \boldsymbol{\mathcal{T}}_2^{\cdot 3} \right| + \left| \boldsymbol{\mathcal{T}}_3^{\cdot 1}, \boldsymbol{\mathcal{T}}_2^{\cdot 2}, \boldsymbol{\mathcal{T}}_3^{\cdot 3} \right| + \left| \boldsymbol{\mathcal{T}}_2^{\cdot 1}, \boldsymbol{\mathcal{T}}_3^{\cdot 2}, \boldsymbol{\mathcal{T}}_3^{\cdot 3} \right| = 0, \quad (8.37)$$

$$\lambda_1 \lambda_2 \lambda_3 \quad \left| \boldsymbol{\mathcal{T}}_1^{\cdot 1}, \boldsymbol{\mathcal{T}}_2^{\cdot 2}, \boldsymbol{\mathcal{T}}_3^{\cdot 3} \right| + \left| \boldsymbol{\mathcal{T}}_1^{\cdot 1}, \boldsymbol{\mathcal{T}}_3^{\cdot 2}, \boldsymbol{\mathcal{T}}_2^{\cdot 3} \right| + \left| \boldsymbol{\mathcal{T}}_2^{\cdot 1}, \boldsymbol{\mathcal{T}}_1^{\cdot 2}, \boldsymbol{\mathcal{T}}_3^{\cdot 3} \right| +$$

$$\left| \boldsymbol{\mathcal{T}}_2^{\cdot 1}, \boldsymbol{\mathcal{T}}_3^{\cdot 2}, \boldsymbol{\mathcal{T}}_1^{\cdot 3} \right| + \left| \boldsymbol{\mathcal{T}}_3^{\cdot 1}, \boldsymbol{\mathcal{T}}_1^{\cdot 2}, \boldsymbol{\mathcal{T}}_2^{\cdot 3} \right| + \left| \boldsymbol{\mathcal{T}}_3^{\cdot 1}, \boldsymbol{\mathcal{T}}_2^{\cdot 2}, \boldsymbol{\mathcal{T}}_1^{\cdot 3} \right| = 0. \quad (8.38)$$

8.5 Constraints that characterize the Trifocal tensor

We now show two results which are related to the question of finding subsets of constraints which are sufficient to characterize the Trifocal tensors. These subsets are the implicit equations of the manifold of the Trifocal tensors. The first result is given in the following theorem.

Theorem 8.5 *Let $\boldsymbol{\mathcal{T}}$ be a bilinear mapping from $\mathbb{P}^{2*} \times \mathbb{P}^{2*}$ to $\mathbb{P}^{2*}$ which satisfies the fourteen Trifocal rank, epipolar and vertical constraints. Then this mapping is a Trifocal tensor, i.e. it satisfies Definition 8.4. Those fourteen algebraic equations are a set of implicit equations of the manifold of Trifocal tensors.*

The second result is that the ten extended constraints and the epipolar constraints also characterize the Trifocal tensors.

Theorem 8.6 *Let $\boldsymbol{\mathcal{T}}$ be a bilinear mapping from $\mathbb{P}^{2*} \times \mathbb{P}^{2*}$ to $\mathbb{P}^{2*}$ which satisfies the twelve Trifocal extended rank and epipolar constraints. Then this mapping is a Trifocal tensor, i.e. it satisfies Definition 8.4. Those twelve algebraic equations are another set of implicit equations of the manifold of Trifocal tensors.*

The proof of these theorems will take us some time. We start with a proposition that we will use to prove that the three rank constraints and the two epipolar constraints are not sufficient to characterize the set of Trifocal tensors.

Proposition 8.22 *If a tensor $\boldsymbol{\mathcal{T}}$ satisfies the three Trifocal rank constraints and the two Trifocal epipolar constraints, then its matrices $\mathbf{G}^n, n = 1, 2, 3$, can be written*

$$\mathbf{G}^n = a_n \mathbf{X}^{(n)} \mathbf{Y}^{(n)T} + \mathbf{e}_{21} \mathbf{Y}^{(n)T} + \mathbf{X}^{(n)} \mathbf{e}_{31}^T, \quad (8.39)$$

where e_{21} (respectively e_{31}) is a fixed point of image 2 (respectively of image 3), the three vectors $\mathbf{X}^{(n)}$ represent three points of image 2, and the three vectors $\mathbf{Y}^{(n)}$ represent three points of image 3.

Proof : The rank constraints allow us to write

$$\mathbf{G}^n = \mathbf{X}_1^{(n)}\mathbf{Y}_1^{(n)T} + \mathbf{X}_2^{(n)}\mathbf{Y}_2^{(n)T},$$ (8.40)

where the six vectors $\mathbf{X}_1^{(n)}$, $\mathbf{X}_2^{(n)}$ $n = 1, 2, 3$, represent six points of the second image and the six vectors $\mathbf{Y}_1^{(n)}$, $\mathbf{Y}_2^{(n)}$ $n = 1, 2, 3$, represent six points of the third image.

The right nullspace of $\mathbf{G}^n$ is simply the cross-product $\mathbf{X}_1^{(n)} \times \mathbf{X}_2^{(n)}$, the left nullspace being $\mathbf{Y}_1^{(n)} \times \mathbf{Y}_2^{(n)}$. These two sets of three nullspaces are of rank 2 (Proposition 8.19). Let us consider the first set. We can write the corresponding matrix as

$$\left[\mathbf{X}_1^{(1)} \times \mathbf{X}_2^{(1)}\ \mathbf{X}_1^{(2)} \times \mathbf{X}_2^{(2)}\ \mathbf{X}_1^{(3)} \times \mathbf{X}_2^{(3)}\right] = \mathbf{Z}_1 \mathbf{T}_1^T + \mathbf{Z}_2 \mathbf{T}_2^T.$$

With obvious notations, we have in particular

$$\mathbf{X}_1^{(1)} \times \mathbf{X}_2^{(1)} = T_{11}\mathbf{Z}_1 + T_{21}\mathbf{Z}_2.$$

Geometrically, the line represented by the vector $\mathbf{X}_1^{(1)} \times \mathbf{X}_2^{(1)}$, i.e. the line going through the points $X_1^{(1)}$ and $X_2^{(1)}$, belongs to the pencil of lines defined by the two lines represented by the vectors $\mathbf{Z}_1$ and $\mathbf{Z}_2$. Therefore it goes through their point of intersection represented by the cross-product $\mathbf{Z}_1 \times \mathbf{Z}_2$ and we write $\mathbf{X}_2^{(1)}$ as a linear combination of $\mathbf{X}_1^{(1)}$ and $\mathbf{Z}_1 \times \mathbf{Z}_2$:

$$\mathbf{X}_2^{(1)} = \alpha_1\mathbf{X}_1^{(1)} + \beta_1\mathbf{Z}_1 \times \mathbf{Z}_2.$$

We write $\mathbf{e}_{21}$ for $\mathbf{Z}_1 \times \mathbf{Z}_2$ and note that our reasoning is valid for $X_1^{(n)}$ and $X_2^{(n)}$:

$$\mathbf{X}_2^{(n)} = \alpha_n\mathbf{X}_1^{(n)} + \beta_n\mathbf{e}_{21}, \quad n = 1, 2, 3.$$

The same reasoning can be applied to the pairs $\mathbf{Y}_1^{(n)}$, $\mathbf{Y}_2^{(n)}$, $n = 1, 2, 3$ yielding the expression

$$\mathbf{Y}_1^{(n)} = \gamma_n\mathbf{Y}_2^{(n)} + \delta_n\mathbf{e}_{31}.$$

We have exchanged the roles of $\mathbf{Y}_1^{(n)}$ and $\mathbf{Y}_2^{(n)}$ for reasons of symmetry in the final expression of $\mathbf{G}_n$. Replacing $\mathbf{X}_2^{(n)}$ and $\mathbf{Y}_1^{(n)}$ by their values in the definition (8.40) of the matrix $\mathbf{G}_n$, we obtain

$$\mathbf{G}^n = (\alpha_n + \gamma_n)\mathbf{X}_1^{(n)}\mathbf{Y}_2^{(n)T} + \delta_n\mathbf{X}_1^{(n)}\mathbf{e}_{31}^T + \beta_n\mathbf{e}_{21}\mathbf{Y}_2^{(n)T}.$$

We can absorb the coefficients δ_n in $\mathbf{X}_1^{(n)}$ and the coefficients β_n in $\mathbf{Y}_2^{(n)}$, and we obtain the announced relation. □

The next proposition is a proof of Theorem 8.5 that the fourteen rank and epipolar constraints characterize the set of Trifocal tensors.

Proposition 8.23 *Let* $\mathcal{T}$ *be a bilinear mapping from* $\mathbb{P}^{2*} \times \mathbb{P}^{2*}$ *to* $\mathbb{P}^{2*}$ *which satisfies the fourteen Trifocal rank, epipolar and vertical constraints. Then its matrices* $\mathbf{G}^n$ *take the form*

$$\mathbf{G}^n = \mathbf{e}_{21}\mathbf{Y}^{(n)T} + \mathbf{X}^{(n)}\mathbf{e}_{31}^T. \tag{8.41}$$

Proof :   We show that the nine vertical constraints imply that $\mathcal{T}(\mathbf{l}_{21}, \mathbf{l}_{31}) = \mathbf{0}$ for all pairs of epipolar lines (l_{21}, l_{31}), i.e. for all pairs of lines such that l_{21} contains the point e_{21} and l_{31} contains the point e_{31} defined in (8.26). It follows that $a_n(\mathbf{l}_{21}^T\mathbf{X}^{(n)}) \cdot (\mathbf{Y}^{(n)T}\mathbf{l}_{31}) = 0$ for all pairs of epipolar lines (l_{21}, l_{31}) which implies $a_n = 0$ unless either $X^{(n)}$ is identical to e_{21} or $Y^{(n)}$ is identical to e_{31} which contradicts the hypothesis that the rank of $\mathbf{G}^n$ is two.

It is sufficient to show that each of the nine constraints implies that $\mathcal{T}(\mathbf{l}_{21i}, \mathbf{l}_{31j}) = \mathbf{0}$, $i, j = 1, 2, 3$ where l_{21i} (respectively l_{31j}) is an epipolar line for the pair $(1, 2)$ (respectively the pair $(1, 3)$) of cameras, going through the ith (respectively the jth) point of the projective canonical basis. This result is sufficient because we can assume that, for example, e_{21} does not belong to the line represented by ε_3. In that case, any epipolar line l_{21} can be represented as a linear combination of $\mathbf{l}_{211}$ and $\mathbf{l}_{212}$:

$$\mathbf{l}_{21} = \alpha_2\mathbf{l}_{211} + \beta_2\mathbf{l}_{212}.$$

Similarly, any epipolar line l_{31} can be represented as a linear combination of $\mathbf{l}_{311}$ and $\mathbf{l}_{312}$, given that e_{31} does not belong to the line represented by ε_3:

$$\mathbf{l}_{31} = \alpha_3\mathbf{l}_{311} + \beta_3\mathbf{l}_{312}.$$

The bilinearity of $\mathcal{T}$ allows us to conclude that $\mathcal{T}(\mathbf{l}_{21}, \mathbf{l}_{31}) = \mathbf{0}$.

We now construct the six lines l_{21i} and l_{31j}. The three lines $l_{21i}, i = 1, 2, 3$, correspond to the three possible choices of (k_2, l_2), $k_2 \neq l_2$, $k_2, l_2 = 1, 2, 3$. Similarly, the three lines $l_{31j}, j = 1, 2, 3$, correspond to the three possible choices of (k_3, l_3), $k_3 \neq l_3$, $k_3, l_3 = 1, 2, 3$. To help the reader follow the proof, we encourage him or her to take the example $k_2 = k_3 = 1$ and $l_2 = l_3 = 2$. If the tensor $\mathcal{T}$ were a Trifocal tensor, then the four lines $\lambda_1, \lambda_2, \lambda_3, \lambda_4$ would be the images of the 3D lines $\boldsymbol{U}_2 \triangle \boldsymbol{U}_3$, $\boldsymbol{W}_2 \triangle \boldsymbol{U}_3$, $\boldsymbol{U}_2 \triangle \boldsymbol{W}_3$, $\boldsymbol{W}_2 \triangle \boldsymbol{W}_3$, respectively.

We now consider the two lines d_1 and d_2 in image 1 which are defined as follows. d_1 goes through the point of intersection of λ_1 and λ_2 (the image of the point $\boldsymbol{U}_2 \triangle \boldsymbol{W}_2 \triangle \boldsymbol{U}_3$) and the point of intersection of the lines λ_3 and λ_4 (the image of the point $\boldsymbol{U}_2 \triangle \boldsymbol{W}_2 \triangle \boldsymbol{W}_3$). In our example, d_1 is the image of the projection ray $\boldsymbol{U}_2 \triangle \boldsymbol{W}_2$; therefore it goes through the epipole $e12$. d_2, on the other hand, goes through the point of intersection of λ_2 and λ_4 (the image of the point $\boldsymbol{W}_2 \triangle \boldsymbol{U}_3 \triangle \boldsymbol{W}_3$) and the point of intersection of λ_1 and λ_3 (the image of the point $\boldsymbol{U}_2 \triangle \boldsymbol{U}_3 \triangle \boldsymbol{W}_3$). In our example, d_2 is the image of the projection ray $\boldsymbol{U}_3 \triangle \boldsymbol{W}_3$; therefore it goes through the epipole e_{13}. Using elementary geometry, it is easy to find

$$\mathbf{d}_1 = \mid \lambda_2, \lambda_3, \lambda_4 \mid \lambda_1 - \mid \lambda_1, \lambda_3, \lambda_4 \mid \lambda_2,$$
$$\mathbf{d}_2 = \mid \lambda_1, \lambda_3, \lambda_4 \mid \lambda_2 + \mid \lambda_1, \lambda_2, \lambda_3 \mid \lambda_4.$$

According to the definition of the lines $\lambda_1, \lambda_2, \lambda_3, \lambda_4$, $\mathbf{d}_1$ is the image by $\boldsymbol{T}$ of the two lines $(\mid \lambda_2, \lambda_3, \lambda_4 \mid \varepsilon_{k_2} - \mid \lambda_1, \lambda_3, \lambda_4 \mid \varepsilon_{l_2}, \varepsilon_{k_3})$ and $\mathbf{d}_2$ the image by $\boldsymbol{T}$ of the two lines $(\varepsilon_{l_2}, \mid \lambda_1, \lambda_3, \lambda_4 \mid \varepsilon_{k_3} + \mid \lambda_1, \lambda_2, \lambda_3 \mid \varepsilon_{l_3})$. One of the lines l_{21i} is represented by $\mid \lambda_2, \lambda_3, \lambda_4 \mid \varepsilon_{k_2} - \mid \lambda_1, \lambda_3, \lambda_4 \mid \varepsilon_{l_2}$, and one of the lines l_{31j} is represented by $\mid \lambda_1, \lambda_3, \lambda_4 \mid \varepsilon_{k_3} + \mid \lambda_1, \lambda_2, \lambda_3 \mid \varepsilon_{l_3}$.

We now proceed to show that $\boldsymbol{T}(l_{21i}, l_{31j}) = \mathbf{0}$. Using the bilinearity of $\boldsymbol{T}$, we have

$$\boldsymbol{T}(l_{21i}, l_{31j}) =$$
$$\mid \lambda_2, \lambda_3, \lambda_4 \mid\mid \lambda_1, \lambda_3, \lambda_4 \mid \boldsymbol{T}(\varepsilon_{k_2}, \varepsilon_{k_3}) + \mid \lambda_2, \lambda_3, \lambda_4 \mid\mid \lambda_1, \lambda_2, \lambda_3 \mid \boldsymbol{T}(\varepsilon_{k_2}, \varepsilon_{l_3}) -$$
$$\mid \lambda_1, \lambda_3, \lambda_4 \mid\mid \lambda_1, \lambda_3, \lambda_4 \mid \boldsymbol{T}(\varepsilon_{l_2}, \varepsilon_{k_3}) - \mid \lambda_1, \lambda_3, \lambda_4 \mid\mid \lambda_1, \lambda_2, \lambda_3 \mid \boldsymbol{T}(\varepsilon_{l_2}, \varepsilon_{l_3}).$$

We now use the constraint (8.26)

$$\mid \lambda_1, \lambda_3, \lambda_4 \mid\mid \lambda_1, \lambda_2, \lambda_4 \mid - \mid \lambda_2, \lambda_3, \lambda_4 \mid\mid \lambda_1, \lambda_2, \lambda_3 \mid = 0$$

to replace the coefficient of the second term by $\mid \lambda_1, \lambda_3, \lambda_4 \mid\mid \lambda_1, \lambda_2, \lambda_4 \mid$. The coefficient $\mid \lambda_1, \lambda_3, \lambda_4 \mid$ is a factor and we have

$$\boldsymbol{T}(l_{21i}, l_{31j}) = \mid \lambda_1, \lambda_3, \lambda_4 \mid (\mid \lambda_2, \lambda_3, \lambda_4 \mid \lambda_1 - \mid \lambda_1, \lambda_3, \lambda_4 \mid \lambda_2 +$$
$$\mid \lambda_1, \lambda_2, \lambda_4 \mid \lambda_3 - \mid \lambda_1, \lambda_2, \lambda_3 \mid \lambda_4).$$

The second factor is seen to be equal to 0 because of Cramer's relation. Thus, each of the nine constraints in Theorem 8.3 yields a relation $\boldsymbol{T}(l_{21i}, l_{31j}) = 0$ for $i, j = 1, 2, 3$.

Let us see what this argument means in terms of the linear applications defined by the matrices $\mathbf{G}^n$. Consider the first line in image 3, l_{311}; its image by $\mathbf{G}^n$, $n = 1, 2, 3$, is a point on the line $\mathcal{L}_2^n = (X^{(n)}, e_{21})$, $n = 1, 2, 3$. Because of the epipolar constraint, those lines intersect at e_{21}. According to what we have just proved, those three points are also on the three lines l_{21i}, $i = 1, 2, 3$. This situation is only possible if a) the three lines l_{21i}, $i = 1, 2, 3$, are identical (see Figure 8.19), which they are not in general, or if b) the three points are identical and the three lines go through that point (see Figure 8.20). The second possibility is the correct one and implies that a) the three points are identical with the point of intersection, e_{21}, of the three lines $\mathcal{L}_2^n$, $n = 1, 2, 3$, and b) the three lines l_{21i}, $i = 1, 2, 3$, go through e_{21}. A similar reasoning shows that the three lines l_{31j}, $j = 1, 2, 3$, go through the epipole e_{31}.

This step completes the proof of the proposition and of Theorem 8.5. $\square$

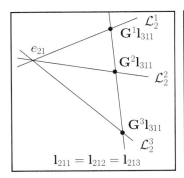 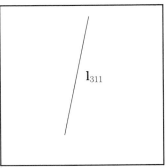

Figure 8.19: If the three lines l_{21i}, $i = 1, 2, 3$ are identical, then the conditions for the point represented $\mathbf{G}^n l_{311}$ to be on the four lines $\mathcal{L}_2^n$ and l_{21i}, $i = 1, 2, 3$, for each $n = 1, 2, 3$, are satisfied; see the proof of Proposition 8.23.

An intriguing question is whether there are other sets of constraints that imply this parametrization. In other words does there exist simpler implicit parametrization of the manifold of Trifocal tensors? One answer is contained in Theorem 8.6. Before we prove it we prove two interesting results, the first one is unrelated, and the second is

Proposition 8.24 *Any bilinear mapping* $\mathcal{T}$ *which satisfies the 14 Trifocal rank, epipolar and vertical constraints also satisfies the 18 row and columns constraints.*

Proof : The proof consists of noticing that if $\mathcal{T}$ satisfies the rank, epipolar and vertical constraints, according to Proposition 8.23, then it satisfies Definition 8.4 and therefore, according to Theorem 8.4, it satisfies the row and column constraints. □

The reader may wonder about the ten extended rank constraints: Are they sufficient to characterize the trilinear tensor? The following proposition answers this question negatively.

Proposition 8.25 *The ten Trifocal extended rank constraints do not imply the Trifocal epipolar constraints.*

Proof : The proof consists of exhibiting a counterexample. The reader can verify that the tensor $\mathcal{T}$ defined by

$$\mathbf{G}^1 = \begin{bmatrix} 0 & 0 & 0 \\ -1 & -1 & 0 \\ 1 & 0 & 1 \end{bmatrix}, \quad \mathbf{G}^2 = \begin{bmatrix} -1 & -1 & 0 \\ 0 & 0 & 0 \\ 0 & 1 & 0 \end{bmatrix},$$

$$\mathbf{G}^3 = \begin{bmatrix} -1 & 0 & -1 \\ 0 & 1 & 0 \\ 0 & 0 & 0 \end{bmatrix}$$

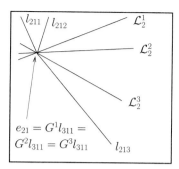 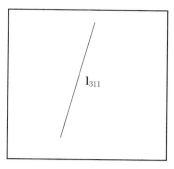

Figure 8.20: If the three lines l_{21i}, $i = 1, 2, 3$ all go through e_{21}, then the conditions for the point represented $\mathbf{G}^n l_{311}$ to be on the four lines $\mathcal{L}_2^n$ and on $l_{21i}, i = 1, 2, 3$, for each $n = 1, 2, 3$, are satisfied; see the proof of Proposition 8.23.

satisfies the ten extended rank constraints and that the corresponding three left nullspaces are the canonic lines represented by ε_n, $n = 1, 2, 3$, which do not satisfy one of the epipolar constraints. $\square$

Before we prove Theorem 8.6 we prove the following proposition.

Proposition 8.26 *The three Trifocal rank constraints and the two Trifocal epipolar constraints do not characterize the set of Trifocal tensors.*

Proof : Proposition 8.22 gives us a parametrization of the matrices $\mathbf{G}^n$ in that case. It can be verified that for such a parametrization, the vertical constraints are not satisfied. Assume now that the rank and epipolar constraints imply that the tensor is a Trifocal tensor. Then, according to Proposition 8.3, it satisfies the vertical constraints, a contradiction. $\square$

We are now ready to prove Theorem 8.6.
Proof : The proof consists of showing that any bilinear application $\mathcal{T}$ that satisfies the five rank and epipolar constraints, i.e. whose matrices $\mathbf{G}^n$ can be written as in (8.39), and the remaining seven extended rank constraints (8.32-8.38) can be written as in (8.41), i.e. is such that $a_n = 0$, $n = 1, 2, 3$.

If we use the parametrization (8.39) and evaluate the constraints (8.32-8.37), we find

$$-a_2 \ \left| \mathbf{e}_{21}, \mathbf{X}^{(1)}, \mathbf{X}^{(2)} \right| \ \left| \mathbf{e}_{31}, \mathbf{Y}^{(1)}, \mathbf{Y}^{(2)} \right|, \tag{8.42}$$

$$-a_3 \ \left| \mathbf{e}_{21}, \mathbf{X}^{(1)}, \mathbf{X}^{(3)} \right| \ \left| \mathbf{e}_{31}, \mathbf{Y}^{(1)}, \mathbf{Y}^{(3)} \right|, \tag{8.43}$$

$$-a_1 \ \left| \mathbf{e}_{21}, \mathbf{X}^{(1)}, \mathbf{X}^{(2)} \right| \ \left| \mathbf{e}_{31}, \mathbf{Y}^{(1)}, \mathbf{Y}^{(2)} \right|, \tag{8.44}$$

$$-a_3 \ \left| \mathbf{e}_{21}, \mathbf{X}^{(2)}, \mathbf{X}^{(3)} \right| \ \left| \mathbf{e}_{31}, \mathbf{Y}^{(2)}, \mathbf{Y}^{(3)} \right|, \tag{8.45}$$

$$-a_1 \ \left| \mathbf{e}_{21}, \mathbf{X}^{(1)}, \mathbf{X}^{(3)} \right| \ \left| \mathbf{e}_{31}, \mathbf{Y}^{(1)}, \mathbf{Y}^{(3)} \right|, \tag{8.46}$$

$$-a_2 \ \left| \mathbf{e}_{21}, \mathbf{X}^{(2)}, \mathbf{X}^{(3)} \right| \ \left| \mathbf{e}_{31}, \mathbf{Y}^{(2)}, \mathbf{Y}^{(3)} \right|. \tag{8.47}$$

In those formulae, our attention is drawn to determinants of the form $\left| \mathbf{e}_{21}, \mathbf{X}^{(i)}, \mathbf{X}^{(j)} \right|, i \neq j$ (type 2, because of $\mathbf{e}_{21}$), and $\left| \mathbf{e}_{31}, \mathbf{Y}^{(i)}, \mathbf{Y}^{(j)} \right|, i \neq j$ (type 3, because of $\mathbf{e}_{31}$). The nullity of a determinant of type 2 (respectively of type 3) implies that the epipole e_{21} (respectively e_{31}) is on the line defined by the two points $X^{(i)}, X^{(j)}$ (respectively $Y^{(i)}, Y^{(j)}$), if the corresponding points are distinct.

If all determinants are nonzero, then the constraints (8.42-8.47) imply that all a_n's are zero. Things are slightly more complicated if some of the determinants are equal to 0.

We prove that if the matrices $\mathbf{G}^n$ are of rank 2, then no more than one of the three determinants of each of the two types can equal 0. We consider several cases.

The first case is when all points of one type are different. Suppose first that the three points represented by the three vectors $\mathbf{X}^{(n)}$ are not aligned. Then, having two of the determinants of type 2 equal to 0 implies that the point e_{21} is identical to one of the points $X^{(n)}$ since it is at the intersection of two of the lines they define. But, according to Equation 8.39, this situation implies that the corresponding matrix $\mathbf{G}^n$ is of rank 1, contradicting the hypothesis that this rank is 2. Similarly, if the three points $X^{(n)}$ are aligned, if one determinant is equal to 0, then the epipole e_{21} belongs to the line $\left(X^{(1)}, X^{(2)}, X^{(3)} \right)$ which means that the three epipolar lines $\mathcal{L}_2^1, \mathcal{L}_2^2, \mathcal{L}_2^3$ are identical, contradicting the hypothesis that they form a matrix of rank 2. Therefore, in this case, all three determinants are non-null.

The second case is when two of the points are equal, e.g. $\mathbf{X}^{(1)} \simeq \mathbf{X}^{(2)}$. The third point must then be different, otherwise we would only have one epipolar line contradicting the rank 2 assumption on those epipolar lines, and, if it is different, the epipole e_{21} must not be on the line defined by the two points for the same reason. Therefore in this case also at most one of the determinants is equal to 0.

Having at most one determinant of type 2 and one of type 3 equal to 0 implies that at least two of the a_n are 0. This remark is seen by inspecting the constraints

(8.42-8.47). If we now express the seventh constraint

$$a_1 a_2 a_3 \left| \mathbf{Y}^{(1)}, \mathbf{Y}^{(2)}, \mathbf{Y}^{(3)} \right| \left| \mathbf{X}^{(1)}, \mathbf{X}^{(2)}, \mathbf{X}^{(3)} \right| -$$

$$\left(\left| \mathbf{e}_{21}, \mathbf{X}^{(1)}, \mathbf{X}^{(2)} \right| \left| \mathbf{e}_{31}, \mathbf{Y}^{(1)}, \mathbf{Y}^{(3)} \right| + \left| \mathbf{e}_{31}, \mathbf{Y}^{(1)}, \mathbf{Y}^{(2)} \right| \left| \mathbf{e}_{21}, \mathbf{X}^{(1)}, \mathbf{X}^{(3)} \right| \right) a_1 +$$

$$\left(\left| \mathbf{e}_{31}, \mathbf{Y}^{(1)}, \mathbf{Y}^{(2)} \right| \left| \mathbf{e}_{21}, \mathbf{X}^{(2)}, \mathbf{X}^{(3)} \right| + \left| \mathbf{e}_{31}, \mathbf{Y}^{(2)}, \mathbf{Y}^{(3)}, \right| \left| \mathbf{e}_{21}, \mathbf{X}^{(1)}, \mathbf{X}^{(2)} \right| \right) a_2 -$$

$$\left(\left| \mathbf{e}_{21}, \mathbf{X}^{(2)}, \mathbf{X}^{(3)} \right| \left| \mathbf{e}_{31}, \mathbf{Y}^{(1)}, \mathbf{Y}^{(3)} \right| + \left| \mathbf{e}_{31}, \mathbf{Y}^{(2)}, \mathbf{Y}^{(3)} \right| \left| \mathbf{e}_{21}, \mathbf{X}^{(1)}, \mathbf{X}^{(3)} \right| \right) a_3 +$$

$$\left(\left| \mathbf{e}_{21}, \mathbf{X}^{(1)}, \mathbf{X}^{(2)} \right| \left| \mathbf{Y}^{(1)}, \mathbf{Y}^{(2)}, \mathbf{Y}^{(3)} \right| + \left| \mathbf{e}_{31}, \mathbf{Y}^{(1)}, \mathbf{Y}^{(2)} \right| \left| \mathbf{X}^{(1)}, \mathbf{X}^{(2)}, \mathbf{X}^{(3)} \right| \right) a_1 a_2 +$$

$$\left(\left| \mathbf{e}_{31}, \mathbf{Y}^{(2)}, \mathbf{Y}^{(3)} \right| \left| \mathbf{X}^{(1)}, \mathbf{X}^{(2)}, \mathbf{X}^{(3)} \right| + \left| \mathbf{e}_{21}, \mathbf{X}^{(2)}, \mathbf{X}^{(3)} \right| \left| \mathbf{Y}^{(1)}, \mathbf{Y}^{(2)}, \mathbf{Y}^{(3)} \right| \right) a_2 a_3 -$$

$$\left(\left| \mathbf{e}_{21}, \mathbf{X}^{(1)}, \mathbf{X}^{(3)} \right| \left| \mathbf{Y}^{(1)}, \mathbf{Y}^{(2)}, \mathbf{Y}^{(3)} \right| + \left| \mathbf{X}^{(1)}, \mathbf{X}^{(2)}, \mathbf{X}^{(3)} \right| \left| \mathbf{e}_{31}, \mathbf{Y}^{(1)}, \mathbf{Y}^{(3)} \right| \right) a_1 a_3,$$

we find that it is equal to the third a_n multiplied by two of the nonzero determinants, implying that the third a_n is null and completing the proof.

Let us give a few examples of the various cases. Let us assume first that $\left| \mathbf{e}_{21}, \mathbf{X}^{(1)}, \mathbf{X}^{(2)} \right| = \left| \mathbf{e}_{31}, \mathbf{Y}^{(1)}, \mathbf{Y}^{(2)} \right| = 0$. We find that the constraints (8.46), (8.47) and (8.45) imply $a_1 = a_2 = a_3 = 0$. The second situation occurs if we assume for example $\left| \mathbf{e}_{21}, \mathbf{X}^{(1)}, \mathbf{X}^{(2)} \right| = \left| \mathbf{e}_{31}, \mathbf{Y}^{(1)}, \mathbf{Y}^{(3)} \right| = 0$. We find that the constraints (8.47) and (8.45) imply $a_2 = a_3 = 0$. The constraint (8.38) takes then the form

$$- \left| \mathbf{e}_{21}, \mathbf{X}^{(1)}, \mathbf{X}^{(3)} \right| \left| \mathbf{e}_{31}, \mathbf{Y}^{(1)}, \mathbf{Y}^{(2)} \right| a_1$$

and implies $a_1 = 0$. □

Note that from a practical standpoint, Theorem 8.6 provides a simpler set of sufficient constraints than Theorem 8.5: The ten extended constraints are of degree 3 in the elements of $\mathcal{T}$ whereas the nine vertical constraints are of degree 6 as are the two epipolar constraints.

This situation is more or less similar to the one with the E-matrix (Longuet-Higgins, 1981). It has been shown in several places, for example in (Faugeras, 1993), propositions 7.2 and 7.3, that the set of real E-matrices is characterized either by the two equations

$$\det(\mathbf{E}) = 0, \qquad \frac{1}{2} \mathrm{Tr}^2 \left(\mathbf{E} \mathbf{E}^T \right) - \mathrm{Tr} \left(\left(\mathbf{E} \mathbf{E}^T \right)^2 \right) = 0,$$

or by the nine equations

$$\frac{1}{2} \mathrm{Tr} \left(\mathbf{E} \mathbf{E}^T \right) \mathbf{E} - \mathbf{E} \mathbf{E}^T \mathbf{E} = \mathbf{0}.$$

In a somewhat analogous way, the set of Trifocal tensors is characterized either by the fourteen, rank, epipolar and vertical constraints (Theorem 8.5) or by the twelve extended rank and epipolar constraints (Theorem 8.6).

8.6   The Affine case

The affine situation is characterized by the fact that the homographies induced by the plane at infinity Π_∞ between the retinal planes are known. We thus have a natural specialization of Proposition 8.16 to this case:

Proposition 8.27 *Let* $\mathbf{H}_{\infty ij}$, $i, j = 1, 2, 3, i \neq j$, *be the matrices of the homographies induced by* Π_∞ *between the retinal planes* i *and* j. *The matrices* $\mathbf{G}_i^n$, $n = 1, 2, 3$ *can be written*

$$\mathbf{G}_i^n = \mathbf{e}_{ji}\mathbf{H}_{\infty ik}^{(n)T} + \mathbf{H}_{\infty ij}^{(n)}\mathbf{e}_{ki}^T.$$

8.7   The Euclidean case

The Euclidean case is characterized by the fact that the internal parameters of the cameras are known. Let $\mathbf{A}_i$, $i = 1, 2, 3$, be the matrices of those internal parameters (see Chapter 4) Let also $\mathbf{R}_{ij}$, $\mathbf{t}_{ij}, i, j = 1, 2, 3, i \neq j$, be the rotation matrices and the translation vectors from view i to view j. We know from Chapter 5 that the infinity homographies and epipoles can be written as

$$\mathbf{H}_{\infty ij} \simeq \mathbf{A}_j\mathbf{R}_{ij}\mathbf{A}_i^{-1}, \quad \mathbf{e}_{ji} \simeq \mathbf{A}_j\mathbf{t}_{ij}.$$

If we change coordinates in the three retinal planes to adopt the intrinsic coordinates, those expressions become

$$\mathbf{H}_{\infty ij} = \mathbf{R}_{ij}, \quad \mathbf{e}_{ji} \simeq \mathbf{t}_{ij}.$$

Note that we have an equality for the infinity homographies, which is because we can normalize them so that their determinant is equal to 1, as for example in Chapter 11. This statement is not true for the epipoles which define the translation vectors between the optical centers only up to scale. As we will see in the following, there is only one such scale factor, i.e. the ratio $\|\mathbf{t}_{ij}\| : \|\mathbf{t}_{ik}\|$ can be recovered from the Trifocal tensor.

The expression of the Trifocal tensors in this case are a natural extension of Proposition 8.27:

Proposition 8.28 *Let* $\mathbf{R}_{ij}$, $\mathbf{t}_{ij}, i, j = 1, 2, 3, i \neq j$, *be the rotation matrices and the translation vectors from view* i *to view* j. *The matrices* $\mathbf{G}_i^n$, $n = 1, 2, 3$, *can be written*

$$\mathbf{G}_i^n = \mathbf{t}_{ij}\mathbf{R}_{ik}^{(n)T} + \mathbf{R}_{ij}^{(n)}\mathbf{t}_{ik}^T. \tag{8.48}$$

8.7.1   Computing the directions of the translation vectors and the rotation matrices

It is natural to ask how to recover the two rotation matrices and the two translation vectors, given a Euclidean Trifocal tensor $\mathcal{T}_i$. As several times before, we choose $i =$

1 and write $\mathcal{T}_1$, $\mathcal{T}$. Similarly, we write $\mathbf{R}_2$ (respectively $\mathbf{R}_3$) for $\mathbf{R}_{12}$ (respectively for $\mathbf{R}_{13}$). Similar notations apply to the translation vectors.

We assume that $\mathcal{T}$ is of the form given in Equation 8.16, i.e. that its coefficients satisfy the sufficient constraints that we studied at great length in Section 8.5 and start with the easiest, i.e. the determination of the direction of the translations:

Proposition 8.29 *The direction $\mathbf{u}_3$ (respectively $\mathbf{u}_2$) of the translation vector $\mathbf{t}_3$ (respectively $\mathbf{t}_2$), i.e. a unit vector parallel to $\mathbf{t}_3$ (respectively $\mathbf{t}_2$) is obtained by intersecting the lines represented by the right kernels $\mathcal{R}_3^n$, $n = 1, 2, 3$, (respectively the left kernels $\mathcal{L}_2^n$, $n = 1, 2, 3$) of the matrices $\mathbf{G}^n$.*

Proof : This proposition is a direct consequence of the fact that each tensor of the form (8.16) is such that the intersection of the lines represented by the right kernels (respectively the left kernels) of the matrices $\mathbf{G}^n$ is the epipole e_{31} (respectively e_{21}); see Proposition 8.7 (respectively 8.8). □

Let us proceed with the determination of the rotation matrices $\mathbf{R}_2$ and $\mathbf{R}_3$. We start by noticing that, if $\mathcal{T}$ is of the form given in Equation 8.48, then we have the relations

$$\mathbf{R}_k^{(n)} \cdot \mathcal{R}_k^n = 0, \quad n = 1, 2, 3, \quad k = 2, 3.$$

Geometrically, this statement means that the column vectors $\mathbf{R}_k^{(n)}$ of the rotation matrices $\mathbf{R}_k$ are in the planes defined by the pairs of orthogonal vectors $\mathbf{u}_k$ and $\mathbf{u}_k \times \mathcal{R}_k^n$; see Figure 8.21. Therefore we can write the equations

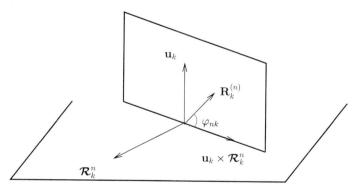

Figure 8.21: The vector $\mathbf{R}_k^{(n)}$ is in the plane defined by the orthogonal vectors $\mathbf{u}_k$ and $\mathbf{u}_k \times \mathcal{R}_k^n$.

$$\mathbf{R}_k^{(n)} = a_{nk}\mathbf{u}_k \times \mathcal{R}_k^n + s_{nk}\mathbf{u}_k, \quad k = 2, 3, \quad n = 1, 2, 3. \tag{8.49}$$

The orthogonality of the matrices $\mathbf{R}_k$, $k = 2, 3$, imposes

$$a_{nk}^2 \|\mathbf{u}_k \times \mathcal{R}_k^n\|^2 + s_{nk}^2 = 1 \quad a_{nk}a_{mk}(\mathbf{u}_k \times \mathcal{R}_k^n) \cdot (\mathbf{u}_k \times \mathcal{R}_k^m) + s_{nk}s_{mk} = 0 \quad n \neq m \tag{8.50}$$

We have taken into account the fact that $\|\mathbf{u}_k\| = 1$, $k = 2, 3$. We then define the quantities

$$c_{nk} = a_{nk}\|\mathbf{u}_k \times \mathcal{R}_k^n\|. \tag{8.51}$$

Equations (8.50) can be rewritten

$$c_{nk}^2 + s_{nk}^2 = 1, \quad c_{nk}c_{mk}\cos\theta_{nmk} + s_{nk}s_{mk} = 0, \quad n \neq m, \tag{8.52}$$

where θ_{nmk} is the angle between the vectors $\mathcal{R}_k^n$ and $\mathcal{R}_k^m$. Note that, since the three vectors $\mathcal{R}_k^n$, $n = 1, 2, 3$, are coplanar for each $k = 2, 3$, there is a relation between the angles:

$$\theta_{12k} + \theta_{23k} + \theta_{31k} = 0, \quad k = 2, 3.$$

The first of the two equations (8.52) allows us to interpret c_{nk} as a cosine and s_{nk} as a sine, in effect as the sine and the cosine of the angle φ_{nk} of the vector $\mathbf{R}_k^{(n)}$ with the vector $\mathbf{t}_k \times \mathcal{R}_k^n$ (see Figure 8.21).

This interpretation provides us with two interesting constraints on the tensor $\mathcal{T}$:

Proposition 8.30 *If the tensor $\mathcal{T}$ is a Euclidean tensor, then the angles θ_{nmk} must satisfy the two conditions*

$$\cos\theta_{12k}\cos\theta_{23k}\cos\theta_{31k} \leq 0, \quad k = 2, 3. \tag{8.53}$$

Proof :   For a given value of $k = 2, 3$, if none of the cosines c_{nk}, $n = 1, 2, 3$, is zero, then we can divide the two sides of the second of the two equations (8.52) by the product $c_{nk}c_{mk}$:

$$\tan\varphi_{nk}\tan\varphi_{mk} = -\cos\theta_{nmk}, \quad m \neq n, \quad k = 2, 3. \tag{8.54}$$

We multiply together the three equations obtained for the various values of m and n and obtain

$$\tan^2\varphi_{1k}\tan^2\varphi_{2k}\tan^2\varphi_{3k} = -\cos\theta_{12k}\cos\theta_{23k}\cos\theta_{31k}, \quad k = 2, 3.$$

Hence the statement in the proposition. □

Let us assume that the conditions (8.53) are satisfied. We have the following proposition that allows us to compute the two rotation matrices $\mathbf{R}_k$, $k = 2, 3$, from the left and right kernels of the tensor $\mathcal{T}$.

Proposition 8.31 *If conditions (8.53) are satisfied, then the rotation matrices $\mathbf{R}_2$ and $\mathbf{R}_3$ are given by equations (8.49), where the coefficients a_{nk} are related to the coefficients c_{nk} by equations (8.51) and the coefficients c_{nk} and s_{nk} are given by*

$$c_{nk}^2 = \cos^2\varphi_{nk} = \frac{(\mathcal{R}_k^n \cdot \mathcal{R}_k^n)(\mathcal{R}_k^l \cdot \mathcal{R}_k^m)}{(\mathcal{R}_k^n \times \mathcal{R}_k^l) \cdot (\mathcal{R}_k^n \times \mathcal{R}_k^m)} \tag{8.55}$$

and

$$s_{nk}^2 = \sin^2 \varphi_{nk} = -\frac{(\mathcal{R}_k^n \cdot \mathcal{R}_k^l)(\mathcal{R}_k^n \cdot \mathcal{R}_k^m)}{(\mathcal{R}_k^n \times \mathcal{R}_k^l) \cdot (\mathcal{R}_k^n \times \mathcal{R}_k^m)}, \tag{8.56}$$

where $k = 2, 3$ and $l \neq m \neq n = 1, 2, 3$.

Proof : Expressing the cosines $\cos \theta_{nmk}$ as functions of the vectors $\mathcal{R}_k^n$, we obtain

$$\tan \varphi_{1k} \tan \varphi_{2k} \tan \varphi_{3k} = \pm \frac{\sqrt{-(\mathcal{R}_k^1 \cdot \mathcal{R}_k^2)(\mathcal{R}_k^2 \cdot \mathcal{R}_k^3)(\mathcal{R}_k^3 \cdot \mathcal{R}_k^1)}}{\|\mathcal{R}_k^1\|\|\mathcal{R}_k^2\|\|\mathcal{R}_k^3\|}. \tag{8.57}$$

Let $b = \pm \dfrac{\sqrt{-(\mathcal{R}_k^1 \cdot \mathcal{R}_k^2)(\mathcal{R}_k^2 \cdot \mathcal{R}_k^3)(\mathcal{R}_k^3 \cdot \mathcal{R}_k^1)}}{\|\mathcal{R}_k^1\|\|\mathcal{R}_k^2\|\|\mathcal{R}_k^3\|}$, so we can now solve for the $\tan \varphi_{nk}$ by using Equations 8.54 and 8.57:

$$\tan \varphi_{nk} = \frac{b}{\cos \theta_{lmk}}, \quad l \neq m, \neq n = 1, 2, 3, \ k = 2, 3. \tag{8.58}$$

We then use the trigonometric identity

$$\frac{1}{\cos^2 \varphi_{nk}} = 1 + \tan^2 \varphi_{nk} = 1 + b^2 \frac{\|\mathcal{R}_k^l\|^2 \|\mathcal{R}_k^m\|^2}{(\mathcal{R}_k^l \cdot \mathcal{R}_k^m)^2}.$$

After some massaging, we obtain Equations 8.55 and 8.56. □

Conversely, given a projective Trifocal tensor $\mathcal{T}$, one may wonder what are the relations on its coefficients which are implied by equations (8.52) given the expressions (8.55) and (8.56).

The following proposition answers this question.

Proposition 8.32 *Given the expression (8.55) and (8.56) that give the values of c_{nk}^2 and s_{nk}^2 as functions of the left and right kernels of $\mathcal{T}$, the six constraints $c_{nk}^2 + s_{nk}^2 = 1$ and the six constraints $c_{nk}^2 c_{mk}^2 \cos^2 \theta_{nmk} - s_{nk}^2 s_{mk}^2 = 0$ are satisfied.*

Proof : The first six constraints yield the six equations

$$(\mathcal{R}_k^n \cdot \mathcal{R}_k^n)(\mathcal{R}_k^l \cdot \mathcal{R}_k^m) - (\mathcal{R}_k^n \cdot \mathcal{R}_k^l)(\mathcal{R}_k^n \cdot \mathcal{R}_k^m) - (\mathcal{R}_k^n \times \mathcal{R}_k^l \cdot \mathcal{R}_k^n \times \mathcal{R}_k^m) = 0,$$
$$k = 2, 3, \ l \neq m \neq n = 1, 2, 3,$$

which are seen to hold true for example by writing $\mathcal{R}_k^n = \alpha_k \mathcal{R}_k^l + \beta_k \mathcal{R}_k^m \ n \neq l \neq m$. The last six constraints need more massaging. □

8.7.2   Computing the ratio of the norms of the translation vectors

Let us now approach the problem of determining the scale of the translation vectors $\mathbf{t}_2$ and $\mathbf{t}_3$. Thus, we look for λ_2 and λ_3 such that

$$\mathbf{G}^n \simeq \lambda_2 \mathbf{u}_2 \mathbf{R}_3^{(n)T} + \lambda_3 \mathbf{R}_2^{(n)} \mathbf{u}_3^T, \quad n = 1, 2, 3. \tag{8.59}$$

The result is given in the following proposition.

Proposition 8.33 *The ratio $\lambda_2 : \lambda_3$ of the norms of the two translation vectors is obtained from any one of the equations*

$$\lambda_2 : \lambda_3 = u_1 s_{23} - u_2 s_{13} : u_2 s_{12} - u_1 s_{22} = u_2 s_{33} - u_3 s_{23} : u_3 s_{22} - u_2 s_{32} =$$
$$u_3 s_{13} - u_1 s_{33} : u_1 s_{32} - u_3 s_{12}. \tag{8.60}$$

Proof :   Equation 8.59 implies

$$\mathbf{u}_2^T \mathbf{G}^n \mathbf{u}_3 \simeq \lambda_2 \left(\mathbf{R}_3^{(n)} \cdot \mathbf{u}_3 \right) + \lambda_3 \left(\mathbf{R}_2^{(n)} \cdot \mathbf{u}_2 \right).$$

Following the previous discussion, $\mathbf{R}_k^{(n)} \cdot \mathbf{u}_k = s_{nk}$ and we have the relations

$$\mathbf{u}_2^T \mathbf{G}^1 \mathbf{u}_3 : \mathbf{u}_2^T \mathbf{G}^2 \mathbf{u}_3 : \mathbf{u}_2^T \mathbf{G}^3 \mathbf{u}_3 =$$
$$\lambda_2 s_{12} + \lambda_3 s_{13} : \lambda_2 s_{22} + \lambda_3 s_{23} : \lambda_2 s_{32} + \lambda_3 s_{33}.$$

Let $S_n = [s_{n2}, s_{n3}]^T$, $\boldsymbol{V} = [\lambda_2, \lambda_3]^T$ and $v_n = \mathbf{u}_2^T \mathbf{G}^n \mathbf{u}_3$, $n = 1, 2, 3$. The previous system of equations is equivalent to the three linear equations (among which only 2 are independent)

$$(v_2 \mathbf{S}_1 - v_1 \mathbf{S}_2) \cdot \boldsymbol{V} = 0,$$
$$(v_3 \mathbf{S}_2 - v_2 \mathbf{S}_3) \cdot \boldsymbol{V} = 0,$$
$$(v_1 \mathbf{S}_3 - v_3 \mathbf{S}_1) \cdot \boldsymbol{V} = 0.$$

The condition for this system to have a nonzero solution in $\boldsymbol{V}$ is easily found to be

$$v_3 \mathbf{S}_1 \times \mathbf{S}_2 + v_1 \mathbf{S}_2 \times \mathbf{S}_3 + v_2 \mathbf{S}_3 \times \mathbf{S}_1 = 0, \tag{8.61}$$

where the cross-product of two two-dimensional vectors is their determinant. If we denote by $\mathbf{V}$ the three-dimensional vector $[v_1, v_2, v_3]^T$ and by $\mathbf{V}_k$, $k = 2, 3$, the two three-dimensional vectors $[s_{1k}, s_{2k}, s_{3k}]^T$, Equation 8.61 is equivalent to

$$\mid \mathbf{V}, \mathbf{V}_2, \mathbf{V}_3 \mid = 0. \tag{8.62}$$

If this condition is satisfied then one has equations (8.60).

If we look a little closer, it turns out that this constraint is satisfied as soon as the tensor is a projective Trifocal tensor, because of Lemma 8.1. Because of Equations 8.49 and 8.51, the vector $\mathbf{V}_k$ is collinear to $[\mathbf{R}_k^{(1)} \cdot \mathbf{u}_k, \mathbf{R}_k^{(2)} \cdot \mathbf{u}_k, \mathbf{R}_k^{(3)} \cdot \mathbf{u}_k]^T$ which is equal to $\mathbf{R}_k^T \mathbf{u}_k$. Since $\mathbf{u}_k \simeq \mathbf{e}_{k1}$, $\mathbf{R}_k^T \mathbf{u}_k$ is the image in the first picture by the homography dual of $\mathbf{R}_k$ of the line represented in the kth retinal plane by $\mathbf{u}_k$. $\mathbf{R}_k$ is the homography induced by the plane at infinity between the retinal planes 1 and k. The nullity of the determinant (8.62) expresses nothing but the fact that the three lines $\boldsymbol{\mathcal{T}}(\mathbf{u}_2, \mathbf{u}_3)$, $\mathbf{R}_k^T \mathbf{u}_k$ intersect at a point. But this statement is exactly that of Lemma 8.1. $\square$

8.8 Affine cameras

We briefly describe some of the interesting special situations that arise when the three cameras perform parallel projections rather than the general perspective projections. We start with the projective case and finish the discussion, started in Section 5.4.3, of the recovery of the Euclidean parameters.

8.8.1 Projective setting

In the case where the three cameras are affine, the Trifocal tensors take a special form which we consider now. According to Section 4.4.2, the third rows of the projection matrices are such that

$$\boldsymbol{W}_i \simeq \boldsymbol{W}_j \simeq \boldsymbol{W}_k \simeq \varepsilon_4 = [0, 0, 0, 1]^T.$$

Considering Proposition 8.4, we can reformulate it as follows.

Proposition 8.34 *Given the three affine projection matrices*

$$\mathcal{P}_i \simeq \begin{bmatrix} \boldsymbol{U}_i^T \\ \boldsymbol{V}_i^T \\ \varepsilon_4^T \end{bmatrix}, \quad \mathcal{P}_j \simeq \begin{bmatrix} \boldsymbol{U}_j^T \\ \boldsymbol{V}_j^T \\ \varepsilon_4^T \end{bmatrix}, \quad \mathcal{P}_k \simeq \begin{bmatrix} \boldsymbol{U}_k^T \\ \boldsymbol{V}_k^T \\ \varepsilon_4^T \end{bmatrix},$$

the three Trifocal matrices that define the Trifocal tensor $\boldsymbol{\mathcal{T}}_i$ are given by the formulae

$$\mathbf{G}_i^1 = \begin{bmatrix} \mid \boldsymbol{V}_i, \varepsilon_4, \boldsymbol{U}_j, \boldsymbol{U}_k \mid & \mid \boldsymbol{V}_i, \varepsilon_4, \boldsymbol{U}_j, \boldsymbol{V}_k \mid & 0 \\ \mid \boldsymbol{V}_i, \varepsilon_4, \boldsymbol{V}_j, \boldsymbol{U}_k \mid & \mid \boldsymbol{V}_i, \varepsilon_4, \boldsymbol{V}_j, \boldsymbol{V}_k \mid & 0 \\ 0 & 0 & 0 \end{bmatrix} \equiv \begin{bmatrix} a_1 & b_1 & 0 \\ c_1 & d_1 & 0 \\ 0 & 0 & 0 \end{bmatrix}, \quad (8.63)$$

$$\mathbf{G}_i^2 = \begin{bmatrix} \mid \varepsilon_4, \boldsymbol{U}_i, \boldsymbol{U}_j, \boldsymbol{U}_k \mid & \mid \varepsilon_4, \boldsymbol{U}_i, \boldsymbol{U}_j, \boldsymbol{V}_k \mid & 0 \\ \mid \varepsilon_4, \boldsymbol{U}_i, \boldsymbol{V}_j, \boldsymbol{U}_k \mid & \mid \varepsilon_4, \boldsymbol{U}_i, \boldsymbol{V}_j, \boldsymbol{V}_k \mid & 0 \\ 0 & 0 & 0 \end{bmatrix} \equiv \begin{bmatrix} a_2 & b_2 & 0 \\ c_2 & d_2 & 0 \\ 0 & 0 & 0 \end{bmatrix}, \quad (8.64)$$

$$\mathbf{G}_i^3 = \begin{bmatrix} | \, \boldsymbol{U}_i, \boldsymbol{V}_i, \boldsymbol{U}_j, \boldsymbol{U}_k \, | & | \, \boldsymbol{U}_i, \boldsymbol{V}_i, \boldsymbol{U}_j, \boldsymbol{V}_k \, | & | \, \boldsymbol{U}_i, \boldsymbol{V}_i, \boldsymbol{U}_j, \boldsymbol{\varepsilon}_4 \, | \\ | \, \boldsymbol{U}_i, \boldsymbol{V}_i, \boldsymbol{V}_j, \boldsymbol{U}_k \, | & | \, \boldsymbol{U}_i, \boldsymbol{V}_i, \boldsymbol{V}_j, \boldsymbol{V}_k \, | & | \, \boldsymbol{U}_i, \boldsymbol{V}_i, \boldsymbol{V}_j, \boldsymbol{\varepsilon}_4 \, | \\ | \, \boldsymbol{U}_i, \boldsymbol{V}_i, \boldsymbol{\varepsilon}_4, \boldsymbol{U}_k \, | & | \, \boldsymbol{U}_i, \boldsymbol{V}_i, \boldsymbol{\varepsilon}_4, \boldsymbol{V}_k \, | & 0 \end{bmatrix} \equiv$$

$$\begin{bmatrix} a_3 & b_3 & c_3 \\ d_3 & e_3 & f_3 \\ g_3 & h_3 & 0 \end{bmatrix}. \quad (8.65)$$

Let us show that in this case we obtain transfer equations which are affine in the affine coordinates of the pixels. To simplify notations, we consider the case $j = 2$, $k = 3$ and $i = 1$. We write $\mathcal{T}$ instead of $\mathcal{T}_1$.

The general idea is the following. Given a triplet of corresponding pixels in the three views (m_1, m_2, m_3), if we consider a line l_2 (respectively a line l_3) going through m_2 (respectively through m_3), then the line $\mathcal{T}(l_2, l_3)$, if well-defined, has to go through m_1. Algebraically,

$$\mathbf{m}_1^T \mathcal{T}(\mathbf{l}_2, \mathbf{l}_3) = 0.$$

When we vary l_2 and l_3 through m_2 and m_3, we obtain a number of polynomial equations, in general of degree 3, between the coordinates of the three points. These equations are studied in detail in Chapter 9. In the case of affine cameras, it is easy to show that, because of the special form of $\mathcal{T}$, some of these relations are linear. This situation is similar to what happens with the epipolar constraint in the affine situation (see Section 5.4.1).

That is, let us consider the lines l_2, l_2', l_3, l_3' represented by $\boldsymbol{\varepsilon}_1 \times \mathbf{m}_2$, $\boldsymbol{\varepsilon}_2 \times \mathbf{m}_2$, $\boldsymbol{\varepsilon}_1 \times \mathbf{m}_3$, $\boldsymbol{\varepsilon}_2 \times \mathbf{m}_3$. The first two lines go through m_2, the last two through m_3. Let us denote by (u_i, v_i), $i = 1, 2, 3$, the affine coordinates of the point m_i, $i = 1, 2, 3$. Its projective coordinates are $u_i : v_i : 1$, $i = 1, 2, 3$. It is then easy to verify that we have the relations

$$\mathcal{T}(\mathbf{l}_2, \mathbf{l}_3) = [d_1, d_2, e_3 - f_3 v_3 - h_3 v_2]^T, \qquad \mathcal{T}(\mathbf{l}_2', \mathbf{l}_3) = [-b_1, -b_2, -b_3 + c_3 v_3 + h_3 u_2]^T,$$

$$\mathcal{T}(\mathbf{l}_2, \mathbf{l}_3') = [-c_1, -c_2, -d_3 + f_3 u_3 + g_3 v_2]^T, \mathcal{T}(\mathbf{l}_2', \mathbf{l}_3') = [a_1, a_2, a_3 - c_3 u_3 - g_3 u_2]^T.$$

We express that these three lines go through m_1 and obtain four *affine* equations relating the affine coordinates of the three points m_1, m_2, m_3:

$$e_3 + d_1 u_1 + d_2 v_1 - f_3 v_3 - h_3 v_2 = 0,$$

$$-b_3 - b_1 u_1 - b_2 v_1 + c_3 v_3 + h_3 u_2 = 0,$$

$$-d_3 - c_1 u_1 - c_2 v_1 + f_3 u_3 + g_3 v_2 = 0,$$

$$a_3 + a_1 u_1 + a_2 v_1 - c_3 u_3 - g_3 u_2 = 0.$$

8.8.2   Euclidean setting

We have seen in Section 5.4.3 how to recover some of the relative pose parameters of the second view with respect to the first. Those parameters that can be recovered are the relative scale s and two of the angles, denoted ϕ and θ, that define the relative rotation (see equations (5.43)). The remaining unknown angle, ρ, can be recovered using the Trifocal tensor in a very simple manner. We assume that the intrinsic parameters of the three views are known. The three projection matrices denoted here $\mathcal{P}$, $\mathcal{P}'$ and $\mathcal{P}''$, can therefore be written as

$$
\mathcal{P} = \begin{bmatrix} \varepsilon_1^T \\ \varepsilon_2^T \\ \varepsilon_4^T \end{bmatrix}, \quad
\mathcal{P}' = s \begin{bmatrix} r_{11} & r_{12} & r_{13} & t_1 \\ r_{21} & r_{22} & r_{23} & t_2 \\ & & \varepsilon_4^T & \end{bmatrix}, \quad
\mathcal{P}'' = s' \begin{bmatrix} r_{11}' & r_{12}' & r_{13}' & t_1' \\ r_{21}' & r_{22}' & r_{23}' & t_2' \\ & & \varepsilon_4^T & \end{bmatrix}.
$$

Using the notations of the previous section, it is easy to verify that, for example,

$$
a_1 : a_2 : \mathbf{G}_{31}^3 : \mathbf{G}_{13}^3 = -ss'(r_{11}r_{13}' - r_{11}'r_{13}) : -ss'(r_{12}r_{13}' - r_{13}r_{12}') - s'r_{13}' : sr_{13}.
$$

We now use the KvD representation of the rotation matrices $\mathbf{R}$ and $\mathbf{R}'$ that was used in Section 5.4.3 and note that we can write

$$
\mathbf{R} = \begin{bmatrix} \mathbf{L} + \mathbf{M}\cos\rho & \mathbf{N}\sin\rho \\ \mathbf{P}^T\sin\rho & \cos\rho \end{bmatrix}, \quad
\mathbf{R}' = \begin{bmatrix} \mathbf{L}' + \mathbf{M}'\cos\rho' & \mathbf{N}'\sin\rho' \\ \mathbf{P}'^T\sin\rho' & \cos\rho' \end{bmatrix},
$$

where $\mathbf{L}$, $\mathbf{M}$, $\mathbf{L}'$, $\mathbf{M}'$ are known 2×2 matrices and $\mathbf{N}$, $\mathbf{P}$, $\mathbf{N}'$, $\mathbf{P}'$ are known 2×1 vectors. Therefore we have

$$
r_{11}r_{13}' - r_{11}'r_{13} = (l_{11} + m_{11}\cos\rho)n_1'\sin\rho' - (l_{11}' + m_{11}'\cos\rho')n_1\sin\rho,
$$
$$
r_{12}r_{13}' - r_{13}r_{12}' = (l_{12} + m_{12}\cos\rho)n_1'\sin\rho' - (l_{12}' + m_{12}'\cos\rho')n_1\sin\rho,
$$
$$
r_{13}' = n_1'\sin\rho',
$$
$$
r_{13} = n_1\sin\rho.
$$

Hence we obtain

$$
\frac{a_1}{\mathbf{G}_{31}^3} = a\cos\rho + b\cos\rho',
$$
$$
\frac{a_2}{\mathbf{G}_{31}^3} = a'\cos\rho + b'\cos\rho',
$$

where a, b, a', b' are known quantities. These two equations yield in general the values of $\cos\rho$ and $\cos\rho'$.

8.9 Summary and Conclusion

We have studied in great detail the structure of the three Trifocal tensors generated by three views. The reader may be a bit overwhelmed by the richness and the complexity of the results. To provide the reader with quick access to those results which are the most useful in practice we now summarize them and give pointers to the parts in the chapter where they are proved.

8.9.1   Perspective projection matrices, Fundamental matrices and Trifocal tensors

Given three views, let $\mathcal{P}_1$, $\mathcal{P}_2$ and $\mathcal{P}_3$ be their perspective projection matrices. We have seen in Proposition 8.4 how to compute the Trifocal tensor $\mathcal{T}_1$. This tensor is useful for the following. Given a line l_2 in the second image and a line l_3 in the third image, they are in general the images of a 3D line L (see Theorem 8.1 for when it is not the case). The image in the first image of L is also in general a line l_1 which can be computed from l_2 and l_3 with the Trifocal tensor $\mathcal{T}_1$:

$$l_1 \simeq \mathcal{T}_1(l_2, l_3).$$

The tensor $\mathcal{T}_1$ can be seen as a 3×3 cube resulting from the stacking of three 3×3 matrices, the Trifocal matrices (see Figure 8.8), $\mathbf{G}_1^1$, $\mathbf{G}_1^2$, $\mathbf{G}_1^3$. The matrices corresponding to $\mathcal{T}_1$ are obtained from the (see also Proposition 8.4)

$$\mathbf{G}_1^1 = \begin{bmatrix} |\boldsymbol{V}_1, \boldsymbol{W}_1, \boldsymbol{U}_2, \boldsymbol{U}_3| & |\boldsymbol{V}_1, \boldsymbol{W}_1, \boldsymbol{U}_2, \boldsymbol{V}_3| & |\boldsymbol{V}_1, \boldsymbol{W}_1, \boldsymbol{U}_2, \boldsymbol{W}_3| \\ |\boldsymbol{V}_1, \boldsymbol{W}_1, \boldsymbol{V}_2, \boldsymbol{U}_3| & |\boldsymbol{V}_1, \boldsymbol{W}_1, \boldsymbol{V}_2, \boldsymbol{V}_3| & |\boldsymbol{V}_1, \boldsymbol{W}_1, \boldsymbol{V}_2, \boldsymbol{W}_3| \\ |\boldsymbol{V}_1, \boldsymbol{W}_1, \boldsymbol{W}_2, \boldsymbol{U}_3| & |\boldsymbol{V}_1, \boldsymbol{W}_1, \boldsymbol{W}_2, \boldsymbol{V}_3| & |\boldsymbol{V}_1, \boldsymbol{W}_1, \boldsymbol{W}_2, \boldsymbol{W}_3| \end{bmatrix},$$

$$\mathbf{G}_1^2 = \begin{bmatrix} |\boldsymbol{W}_1, \boldsymbol{U}_1, \boldsymbol{U}_2, \boldsymbol{U}_3| & |\boldsymbol{W}_1, \boldsymbol{U}_1, \boldsymbol{U}_2, \boldsymbol{V}_3| & |\boldsymbol{W}_1, \boldsymbol{U}_1, \boldsymbol{U}_2, \boldsymbol{W}_3| \\ |\boldsymbol{W}_1, \boldsymbol{U}_1, \boldsymbol{V}_2, \boldsymbol{U}_3| & |\boldsymbol{W}_1, \boldsymbol{U}_1, \boldsymbol{V}_2, \boldsymbol{V}_3| & |\boldsymbol{W}_1, \boldsymbol{U}_1, \boldsymbol{V}_2, \boldsymbol{W}_3| \\ |\boldsymbol{W}_1, \boldsymbol{U}_1, \boldsymbol{W}_2, \boldsymbol{U}_3| & |\boldsymbol{W}_1, \boldsymbol{U}_1, \boldsymbol{W}_2, \boldsymbol{V}_3| & |\boldsymbol{W}_1, \boldsymbol{U}_1, \boldsymbol{W}_2, \boldsymbol{W}_3| \end{bmatrix},$$

$$\mathbf{G}_1^3 = \begin{bmatrix} |\boldsymbol{U}_1, \boldsymbol{V}_1, \boldsymbol{U}_2, \boldsymbol{U}_3| & |\boldsymbol{U}_1, \boldsymbol{V}_1, \boldsymbol{U}_2, \boldsymbol{V}_3| & |\boldsymbol{U}_1, \boldsymbol{V}_1, \boldsymbol{U}_2, \boldsymbol{W}_3| \\ |\boldsymbol{U}_1, \boldsymbol{V}_1, \boldsymbol{V}_2, \boldsymbol{U}_3| & |\boldsymbol{U}_1, \boldsymbol{V}_1, \boldsymbol{V}_2, \boldsymbol{V}_3| & |\boldsymbol{U}_1, \boldsymbol{V}_1, \boldsymbol{V}_2, \boldsymbol{W}_3| \\ |\boldsymbol{U}_1, \boldsymbol{V}_1, \boldsymbol{W}_2, \boldsymbol{U}_3| & |\boldsymbol{U}_1, \boldsymbol{V}_1, \boldsymbol{W}_2, \boldsymbol{V}_3| & |\boldsymbol{U}_1, \boldsymbol{V}_1, \boldsymbol{W}_2, \boldsymbol{W}_3| \end{bmatrix}.$$

An important property of these matrices is that their rank is 2 and that their nullspaces yield the two epipoles e_{21} and e_{31}. Let us denote by $\mathcal{R}_3^n$, $n = 1, 2, 3$, the right nullspace of $\mathbf{G}_1^n$ and by $\mathcal{L}_2^n$, $n = 1, 2, 3$, its left nullspace. The three vectors $\mathcal{R}_3^n$, $n = 1, 2, 3$, and the three vectors $\mathcal{L}_2^n$, $n = 1, 2, 3$, are of rank 2 and the epipoles can be recovered as the cross-product of any two of them, when they are nonzero:

$$\mathbf{e}_{21} \simeq \mathcal{L}_2^1 \times \mathcal{L}_2^2 \simeq \mathcal{L}_2^2 \times \mathcal{L}_2^3 \simeq \mathcal{L}_2^3 \times \mathcal{L}_2^1$$

and

$$\mathbf{e}_{31} \simeq \mathcal{R}_3^1 \times \mathcal{R}_3^2 \simeq \mathcal{R}_3^2 \times \mathcal{R}_3^3 \simeq \mathcal{R}_3^3 \times \mathcal{R}_3^1.$$

More details can be found in Propositions 8.7 and 8.8.

The epipoles e_{12} and e_{13} can also be recovered fairly simply from $\mathcal{T}_1$ as explained in Proposition 8.9. For e_{12}, the procedure is as follows. Pick any line l_2 of the second image not going through e_{21}; the three lines $\mathcal{T}_1\left(l_2, \mathcal{R}_3^n\right)$, $n = 1, 2, 3$ intersect at e_{12} which can thus be recovered as the cross-product of any two of the corresponding vectors, when they are nonzero:

$$\mathbf{e}_{12} \simeq \mathcal{T}_1\left(l_2, \mathcal{R}_3^1\right) \times \mathcal{T}_1\left(l_2, \mathcal{R}_3^2\right) \simeq$$
$$\mathcal{T}_1\left(l_2, \mathcal{R}_3^2\right) \times \mathcal{T}_1\left(l_2, \mathcal{R}_3^3\right) \simeq \mathcal{T}_1\left(l_2, \mathcal{R}_3^3\right) \times \mathcal{T}_1\left(l_2, \mathcal{R}_3^1\right).$$

A similar process applies to e_{31}: Pick any line l_3 of the third image not going through e_{31}; the three lines $\mathcal{T}_1\left(\mathcal{L}_2^n, l_3\right)$, $n = 1, 2, 3$ intersect at e_{13} which can thus be recovered as the cross-product of any two of the corresponding vectors, when they are nonzero:

$$\mathbf{e}_{13} \simeq \mathcal{T}_1\left(\mathcal{L}_2^1, l_3\right) \times \mathcal{T}_1\left(\mathcal{L}_2^2, l_3\right) \simeq$$
$$\mathcal{T}_1\left(\mathcal{L}_2^2, l_3\right) \times \mathcal{T}_1\left(\mathcal{L}_2^3, l_3\right) \simeq \mathcal{T}_1\left(\mathcal{L}_2^3, l_3\right) \times \mathcal{T}_1\left(\mathcal{L}_2^1, l_3\right).$$

$\mathcal{T}_1$ can also be considered in two ways as the result of stacking three other 3×3 matrices along the two horizontal orthogonal axes of the cube in Figure 8.8. The first set defines in general three homographies, denoted $\mathbf{H}_{21}^v$, $v = 1, 2, 3$, from the second retinal plane to the first (see Figure 8.11 in which $i = 1$ and $j = 2$). The second set defines also in general three homographies, denoted $\mathbf{H}_{31}^u$, $u = 1, 2, 3$, from the second retinal plane to the first (see Figure 8.12 in which $i = 1$ and $k = 3$).

Once $\mathcal{T}_1$ has been computed (see Chapter 9), e.g. from correspondences, the tensors $\mathcal{T}_2$ and $\mathcal{T}_3$ can be obtained from the results of Theorem 8.2.

Another question is how to recover the Fundamental matrices, given the Trifocal tensor $\mathcal{T}_1$. The simplest answer to this question is given in Proposition 8.11 which shows that $\mathbf{F}_{21}$ and $\mathbf{F}_{31}$ are readily computed from the intrinsic homographies $\mathbf{H}_{21}^v$, $v = 1, 2, 3$, $\mathbf{H}_{31}^u$, $u = 1, 2, 3$, and the epipoles e_{12} and e_{13}:

$$\mathbf{F}_{21} = [\mathbf{e}_{12}]_\times \mathbf{H}_{21}^v, \quad v = 1, 2, 3,$$

and

$$\mathbf{F}_{31} = [\mathbf{e}_{13}]_\times \mathbf{H}_{31}^u, \quad u = 1, 2, 3.$$

8.9.2 Transfer

The question of transferring geometric primitives from two images to a third is important in practice and has been discussed several times in this chapter where we have shown that the Trifocal tensor allowed us to transfer each pair (p_2, p_3) of geometric primitives in the second and third image, respectively, to a primitive p_1 in the first, where p_i, $i = 1, 2$, is either a point or a line.

In the case of two lines (l_2, l_3), the transferred primitive is in general a line l_1 which can be computed as shown in the first row of Table 8.1 and in Equation 8.9. The geometric intuition can be gained from Figure 8.7, setting $i = 1$, $j = 2$ and $k = 3$. Cases where the transfer does not work are explained in Theorem 8.1.

In the case of a point and a line, i.e. (m_2, l_3) or (l_2, m_3), the transferred primitive is in general a point m_1, image of the point of intersection of the optical ray defined by the point and the corresponding optical center and the plane defined by the line and the corresponding optical center. The point can be considered in infinitely many ways as the intersection of two lines l_2 and l_2' (see Figure 8.22) in the case (m_2, l_3) and l_3 and l_3' in the case (l_2, m_3) (see Figure 8.23). The computation of the transferred point is given by the second row of Table 8.1 for the first case and by the third row in the third case.

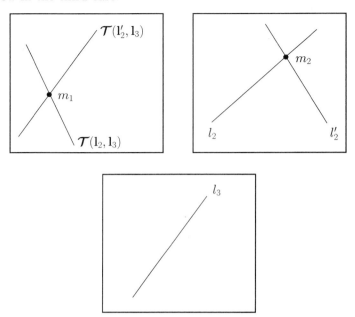

Figure 8.22: The Trifocal tensor can be used to transfer the pair (m_2, l_3) to the first image plane (see text).

In the case of two points, (m_2, m_3), the problem is in general impossible unless these two points satisfy the epipolar constraint between views 2 and 3. But we can always consider these two points in infinitely many ways as the intersections of two lines (l_2, l'_2) and (l_3, l'_3). The transferred point m_1 is therefore at the intersection of the four transferred lines $\mathcal{T}_1(l_2, l_3)$, $\mathcal{T}_1(l'_2, l_3)$, $\mathcal{T}_1(l_2, l'_3)$ and $\mathcal{T}_1(l'_2, l'_3)$; see Figure 8.24. If these four lines do not intersect at a point, then the two points m_2 and m_3 do not satisfy the epipolar constraint. The computation is shown in the fourth row of Table 8.1.

Note that it is often convenient, when transferring points, to choose the lines through these points and the points ε_1, ε_2 and ε_3. For example, if m is a point, one uses the lines represented by the cross-products $\mathbf{m} \times \varepsilon_i$, $i = 1, 2, 3$.

8.10   References and further reading

The idea that a point correspondence in two views determines the position of the point in a third view and can therefore be used to constrain admissible matches

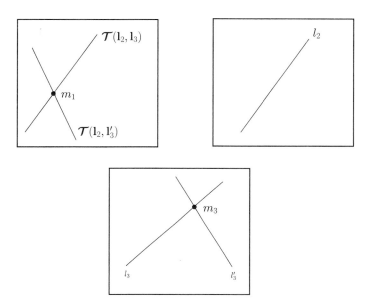

Figure 8.23: The Trifocal tensor can be used to transfer the pair (l_2, m_3) to the first image plane (see text).

(trinocular stereo) was explored in the 80's (Yachida et al., 1986; Ayache and Lustman, 1987), and extended by Faugeras and Robert (Faugeras and Robert, 1996) to the predition of orientations and curvatures. Schmid and Zisserman (Schmid and Zisserman, 1998) show how the Trifocal tensor can be used for transferring a conic or the curvature from two views to a third. It was noticed in (Faugeras and Robert, 1996; Luong and Viéville, 1996; Viéville et al., 1996a) that the three Fundamental matrices are not independant.

Although Barrett *et al.* (Barrett et al., 1992) applied this idea to image transfer, the idea that this could also be used to generate novel views from existing ones is due to Faugeras and Laveau (Faugeras and Laveau, 1994). Seitz and Dyer (Seitz and Dyer, 1996) propose a method for interpolating between two images (*image morphing*) by remarking that if an adequate homography is first applied to the two images, then the intermediate image can be obtained by linear interpolation. This has been extended to dynamic scenes (Manning and Dyer, 1999).

Avidan and Shashua (Avidan and Shashua, 1997) propose a method for generating a sequence of novel views from two *calibrated* images using the Trifocal tensor.

As far as we can trace it back, the Trifocal tensor first appeared as a collection of three matrices **G**, in independent work by Spetsakis and Aloimonos (Spetsakis and Aloimonos, 1990a) and Weng *et al.* (Weng et al., 1992b) on reconstruction of lines with calibrated cameras. The tensorial properties were used (through a

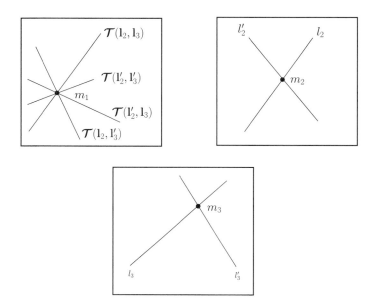

Figure 8.24: The Trifocal tensor can be used to transfer the pair (m_2, m_3) to the first image plane (see text).

concatenation of the three matrices) in (Spetsakis and Aloimonos, 1990b), where an unified algorithm for points and line was given, including a derivation of the trilinearities in the calibrated case. However, these authors stated that a point match between three views provided only three independant equations, while we now know that this number is four. The work on lines was latter extended to the uncalibrated case by Hartley (Hartley, 1994b), and Viéville et al. (Viéville and Luong, 1993; Viéville et al., 1996a). The latter reference identifies specifically the entity as a tensor, uses the tensorial notation for the first time, and lists the nine necessery constraints satisfied by the tensor (but does not prove that they are sufficient). Meanwhile, Shashua (Shashua, 1995) introduced a set of 27 coefficients (organized in entries of nine vectors of dimension 3) for a set of four trilinearity relations between coordinates of corresponding points in three uncalibrated views. Subsequently, Hartley (Hartley, 1995; Hartley, 1997d) made the link between the three matrices appearing in the motion of lines, and Shashua's coefficients, using the tensor notation to express a unified algorithm, while Shashua and Werman (Shashua and Werman, 1995) studied the homographies generated by permutations of the coefficients of the tensor. More properties of the tensor were uncovered by Faugeras and Mourrain (Faugeras and Mourrain, 1995a) using the Grassman-Cayley algebra. The first complete algebraic characterization of the Trifocal tensors is due to Papadopoulo and Faugeras (Papadopoulo and Faugeras, 1998).

$(\mathbf{l}_2, \mathbf{l}_3)$	$\mathbf{l}_1 \simeq \mathcal{T}_1(\mathbf{l}_2, \mathbf{l}_3)$
$(\mathbf{m}_2, \mathbf{l}_3)$	$\mathbf{m}_1 \simeq \mathcal{T}_1(\mathbf{l}_2, \mathbf{l}_3) \times \mathcal{T}_1(\mathbf{l}'_2, \mathbf{l}_3)$ $\mathbf{l}_2 \times \mathbf{l}'_2 \simeq \mathbf{m}_2$
$(\mathbf{l}_2, \mathbf{m}_3)$	$\mathbf{m}_1 \simeq \mathcal{T}_1(\mathbf{l}_2, \mathbf{l}_3) \times \mathcal{T}_1(\mathbf{l}_2, \mathbf{l}'_3)$ $\mathbf{l}_3 \times \mathbf{l}'_3 \simeq \mathbf{m}_3$
$(\mathbf{m}_2, \mathbf{m}_3)$	$\mathbf{m}_1 \simeq \mathcal{T}_1(\mathbf{l}_2, \mathbf{l}_3) \times \mathcal{T}_1(\mathbf{l}_2, \mathbf{l}'_3) \simeq$ $\mathcal{T}_1(\mathbf{l}_2, \mathbf{l}'_3) \times \mathcal{T}_1(\mathbf{l}'_2, \mathbf{l}_3) \simeq$ etc...

Table 8.1: The transfer of primitives from views 2 and 3 to view 1.

A different method to extract the rotations from the Trifocal tensor in the Euclidean case was developed by Rousso *et al.* (Rousso et al., 1996). Shashua and Anandan (Shashua and Anandan, 1996) generalize the trilinear constraints to take into account the uncertainties of the points. Since the framework includes the aperture problem, they can also derive a "brightness constraint" on the tensor based on image spatio-temporal derivatives which is used for actual structure from motion recovery in (Stein and Shashua, 1997).

As in the case of two views, particular motions yield further constraints on the Trifocal tensor, which in turn can be used to simplify tasks such as self-calibration. An important example of particular motion, planar motion, is studied in (Armstrong et al., 1996) and (Faugeras et al., 1998a).

In the parallel case, Ulman and Basri (Ullman and Basri, 1991) first used the linear tranfer of equation of points over three views for recognition. Quan and Kanade (Quan and Kanade, 1997), in the context of reconstruction from lines, introduce a one-dimensional form of the Trifocal tensor, based on the 2×3 inhomogeneous reduced affine projection matrix. They showed that the motion of lines can be reduced to the motion of points for one-dimensional cameras. Astrom *et al.* (Astrom et al., 1999b) revisit the problem of motion of lines from minimal data. They find that instead of seven lines in three views (generating two solutions), the minimal data is six lines in three views which generate four solutions. Furthermore, with seven lines in three views, they propose a linear algorithm which yields a unique solution.

Thorhallsson and Murray (Thorhallsson and Murray, 1999) specialize the projective formalism of (Heyden, 1998a) to the case of affine cameras. They obtain an affine specialization of the relations between points and lines, as well as necessary and sufficient constraints on the components of the tensor, which turn out to be considerably simpler than in the general case.

Euclidean structure from motion from weak perspective views has been studied for a while (Ullman, 1979). Shapiro *et al.* (Shapiro et al., 1995) provide a discussion of earlier algorithms for Euclidean reconstruction from three weak perspective affine views, including (Lee and Huang, 1990; Koenderink and van Doorn, 1991). A new closed-form solution using Euler angles is proposed by Xu and Sugimoto (Xu and Sugimoto, 1999). By reducing the problem to finding triangles, with known angles, on a sphere, Shimshoni *et al.* (Shimshoni et al., 1999) obtain a comparable result. All these algorithms first solve for the two-view geometry, then try to combine the two-view parameters to obtain the reconstruction, but they don't take into acount the specific relationship between two-view geometry and three-view geometry. This has been fixed in by Quan and Ohta (Quan and Ohta, 1998).

Critical configurations for three views are not as well known as those for two views. The case of reconstruction from lines in the Euclidean case is studied by Buchanan (Buchanan, 1992), Maybank (Maybank, 1995), and Navab and Faugeras (Navab and Faugeras, 1997). Stein and Shashua (Stein and Shashua, 1999) show that the case when the set of lines in space intersect at a common line causes linear reconstruction to be degenerate because of rank deficiency. However this is not a critical configuration since the nonlinear methods (taking into account the constraints satisfied by the tensor) still yield an unique solution. Considering points, much less is known. Maybank and Shashua show that the three way ambiguity found by Quan (Quan, 1995) for six points seen in three views persists even if more views are added when the optical centre of the camera remains on a certain quadratic surface. The simpler case of 2-D reconstruction from three 1-D images (arising for instance from the affine projection of lines) is studied by Quan (Quan, 1999). There always exists two possible reconstructions which are related by a quadratic transformation with the camera centers as the fundamental points.

9 Determining the Trifocal tensor

We have seen in Chapter 8 that the Trifocal tensor was the basic descriptor of the projective geometry of three views. We will also see in the next chapter that it is central to methods for recovering the 3D projective geometry of the observed scene. Just as in the case of the Fundamental matrix, it is therefore important to have robust and reliable methods for estimating the Trifocal tensors of three views from image measurements, i.e. from line and point correspondences.

We will follow pretty much the same path as in Chapter 6, starting in Section 9.1 with the linear methods that ignore the algebraic constraints satisfied by the coefficients of the Trifocal tensor. In order to enforce these constraints, we need ways of parameterizing the set of admissible Trifocal tensors. This task turns out to be much more challenging than for the Fundamental matrices because of the increase in the complexity of the constraints. Section 9.2 describes a number of possible parameterizations.

In the next section, Section 9.3, we show how to impose the constraints on a tensor that does not satisfy them, e.g. a tensor resulting from the linear estimation procedure. After some brief comments, made in Section 9.4, on the problem of changing views, i.e. of recovering the other two tensors[1] when one is known, we discuss in Section 9.5 the nonlinear methods of estimation which guarantee that the resulting tensor is an admissible Trifocal tensor.

In this chapter, we work with triples of images from which triplets of corresponding features — points or lines — have been extracted. As with the two-view case 6.1, these features allow for the estimation of Trifocal geometry. The various methods to do so and their properties are discussed hereafter. Note that estimating the Trifocal tensor is still quite a hot research topic at the time of this writing and some problems are still waiting for a satisfactory solution. The material presented in this chapter is thus more a snapshot of the current state of the art than a definitive treaty on the problem.

Throughout this chapter, tensorial notation is adopted. Points and lines will be denoted by the letters $\mathbf{m}$ and $\mathbf{l}$ respectively. An element will be denoted as $\mathbf{f}$, $\mathbf{f}'$ or $\mathbf{f}''$ whenever it is associated with the first, the second or the third image respectively. The shorthand notation $\boldsymbol{\mathcal{T}}$ will be used for $\boldsymbol{\mathcal{T}}_1$ and the 27 coefficients of $\boldsymbol{\mathcal{T}}$ will be denoted by $\mathcal{T}_w^{uv}$, with reference to Figure 8.8. Let the projective coordinates of a point $\mathbf{m}$ be denoted by $\left[m^1, m^2, m^3\right]^T$ (i.e. we use contravariant indices, see Chapter 1) and those of a line $\mathbf{l}$ by $[l_1, l_2, l_3]^T$ (i.e. we use covariant indices). We use the Levi-Civita tensor defined in Chapter 3, Proposition 3.29, to express cross-products as

$$l_i = \epsilon_{ijk} m'^j m''^k \equiv \sum_{j,k} \epsilon_{ijk} m'^j m''^k \qquad \mathbf{l} = \mathbf{m}' \times \mathbf{m}''. \qquad (9.1)$$

---

[1] Remember that three views are defining three Trifocal tensors that are related only throught a complex algebraical operation.

9.1   The linear algorithm

As in Section 6.1 for Fundamental matrices, the simplest method to obtain the Trifocal tensor is to solve a linear system of equations. The basic idea (Hartley, 1997d; Shashua, 1995) is to neglect all of the various Trifocal constraints and take all of the 27 coefficients of the Trifocal tensor as unknowns. This yields a method which is very fast and easy to implement, but which gives tensors that do not satisfy the constraints of Trifocal tensors (see (Faugeras and Papadopoulo, 1998) and Sections 8.4 and 8.5).

In this section, this algorithm and the refinements that are practically needed to make it effective are presented. Some typical results obtained with this method will be shown and used to illustrate its shortcomings.

9.1.1   Normalization again!

As with the estimation of the Fundamental matrix, the Trifocal tensor deals with projective coordinates whose orders of magnitude are very different (as seen in Section 6.1.1) and results in poor numerical conditioning of the matrices that are involved in the linear algorithm. As will be seen in the forthcoming sections, the entries of the matrices are products of three coordinates. Thus, a single order of magnitude discrepancy is transformed into a three order of magnitude discrepancy in the estimation matrix. For this reason, the problem is even worse for the Trifocal tensor than for Fundamental matrices, and normalizing the input data is mandatory.

The normalization of each image feature is the same as the one described for the Fundamental matrix. However, with the Trifocal tensor estimations, we have to take account not only of points but also of lines. Defining a normalization for data containing lines and points is not straightforward since the coordinates of points and lines are of a different nature but a single normalization is wanted. The way this difficulty has been dealt with here is to consider that, even though the Trifocal tensor deals with lines, the image measurements are always line segments. One way to make those line segments participate to the computation of the normalization transformation is to take account only of their endpoints. With this assumption, the normalization computation can be done for each image exactly as described in Section 6.1.1 and gives three affine transformations $\mathbf{H}$, $\mathbf{H}'$, and $\mathbf{H}''$ for the three images respectively. These define a new system of coordinates for each image[2]:

$$\widehat{\mathbf{l}} = \mathbf{H}\mathbf{l} \ , \quad \widehat{\mathbf{l}'} = \mathbf{H}'\mathbf{l}' \ , \quad \widehat{\mathbf{l}''} = \mathbf{H}''\mathbf{l}'' \ .$$

Assuming that $\widehat{\mathcal{T}}$ is the Trifocal tensor estimated using the normalized coordinate system for each image, we are interested in recovering the Trifocal tensor $\mathcal{T}$

---

[2]The Trifocal tensor being an object that deals essentially with lines (see Chapter 8), the affine transformations that are considered here operate on lines rather than on points.

relating the images equipped with their original coordinate systems.

$$\begin{aligned}
\widehat{\mathbf{l}} = \mathbf{H}\mathbf{l} &= \mathbf{H}\mathcal{T}(\mathbf{l'}, \mathbf{l''}) \\
&= \widehat{\mathcal{T}}(\widehat{\mathbf{l'}}, \widehat{\mathbf{l''}}) \\
&= \widehat{\mathcal{T}}(\mathbf{H'}\mathbf{l'}, \mathbf{H''}\mathbf{l''}) \\
&= \overline{\mathcal{T}}(\mathbf{l'}, \mathbf{l''}) \ .
\end{aligned}$$

Introducing the Trifocal matrices $\mathbf{G}$ as in Equation 8.10, the last two lines of the previous formula give

$$\overline{\mathbf{G}^i} = \mathbf{H'}^T \widehat{\mathbf{G}^i} \mathbf{H''} \ .$$

Denoting by k_i^j the coefficients of the matrix $\mathbf{H}^{-1}$ and identifying $\mathcal{T}(\mathbf{l'}, \mathbf{l''})$ with $\mathbf{H}^{-1}\overline{\mathcal{T}}(\mathbf{l'}, \mathbf{l''})$ for all $\mathbf{l'}$ and $\mathbf{l''}$ leads to the following formulae:

$$\mathbf{G}^i = k_i^1 \overline{\mathbf{G}^1} + k_i^2 \overline{\mathbf{G}^2} + k_i^3 \overline{\mathbf{G}^3}$$

or

$$\mathbf{G}^i = k_i^1 \mathbf{H'}^T \widehat{\mathbf{G}^1} \mathbf{H''} + k_i^2 \mathbf{H'}^T \widehat{\mathbf{G}^2} \mathbf{H''} + k_i^3 \mathbf{H'}^T \widehat{\mathbf{G}^3} \mathbf{H''}. \tag{9.2}$$

9.1.2   The basic algorithm

Assume that there is a match $\mathbf{M}$ between features (for now, let us assume that this match can be any combination of points or lines). In each of the cases studied here, the Trifocal constraint can be expressed as a linear system $C(\mathbf{M}) = \mathbf{0}$. These systems, which will be detailed in further sections, can be arranged to be of the form

$$\mathbf{U}^T \mathbf{t} = 0 \ , \tag{9.3}$$

where $\mathbf{U}$ is a $27 \times N$ matrix that is specified below for each case and where $\mathbf{t}$ is a vector whose entries are the components of the Trifocal tensor. For the rest of the discussion, we adopt the convention that $\mathcal{T}_i^{jk}$ is the $(9i + 3j + k - 12)$-th component of $\mathbf{t}$, i.e.

$$\begin{aligned}
\mathbf{t} = [&\mathcal{T}_1^{11} \ \mathcal{T}_1^{12} \ \mathcal{T}_1^{13} \ \mathcal{T}_1^{21} \ \mathcal{T}_1^{22} \ \mathcal{T}_1^{23} \ \mathcal{T}_1^{31} \ \mathcal{T}_1^{32} \ \mathcal{T}_1^{33} \\
&\mathcal{T}_2^{11} \ \mathcal{T}_2^{12} \ \mathcal{T}_2^{13} \ \mathcal{T}_2^{21} \ \mathcal{T}_2^{22} \ \mathcal{T}_2^{23} \ \mathcal{T}_2^{31} \ \mathcal{T}_2^{32} \ \mathcal{T}_2^{33} \\
&\mathcal{T}_3^{11} \ \mathcal{T}_3^{12} \ \mathcal{T}_3^{13} \ \mathcal{T}_3^{21} \ \mathcal{T}_3^{22} \ \mathcal{T}_3^{23} \ \mathcal{T}_3^{31} \ \mathcal{T}_3^{32} \ \mathcal{T}_3^{33}]^T \ .
\end{aligned}$$

The mapping that associates $\mathbf{t}$ with $\mathcal{T}$ will be called $\mathcal{S}$ hereafter. Equation 9.3 is linear and homogeneous in the 27 coefficients of the tensor $\mathcal{T}$. Thus, if we are given 26 such equations, we will be able, in general, to determine a unique solution for $\mathcal{T}$, defined up to a scale factor. As usual, minimal configurations where only 26 equations are available are quite sensitive to noise. More equations are used in practice to get a more robust estimation of the Trifocal tensor by looking at the least-squares solution of the linear system, which can be formulated as

$$\min_{\mathcal{T}} \sum_i C(\mathbf{M}_i)^2. \tag{9.4}$$

This can be rewritten as

$$\min_{\mathbf{t}} \|\tilde{\mathbf{U}}\mathbf{t}\|^2 \,,$$

where $\tilde{\mathbf{U}}$ is a matrix obtained by concatenation of matrices of type $\mathbf{U}$, i.e. $\tilde{\mathbf{U}} = \left[\mathbf{U}_1^T, \dots, \mathbf{U}_n^T\right]^T$.

As in the case of the Fundamental matrix, and since $\mathcal{T}$ is only defined up to a global scale factor, one way to solve this system is to normalize one of the 27 coefficients to be 1, which yields a parameterization of the tensor by 26 values, and then to solve the normal equations associated with the least-squares problem. However, the preferred way is to solve the equivalent problem

$$\min_{\mathbf{t}} \|\tilde{\mathbf{U}}\mathbf{t}\| \quad \text{with} \quad \|\mathbf{t}\| = 1 \,, \tag{9.5}$$

whose solution is the eigenvector associated with the smallest eigenvalue of $\tilde{\mathbf{U}}^T\tilde{\mathbf{U}}$. As explained in Appendix A.1, this can be easily done by computing a singular value decomposition of the matrix $\tilde{\mathbf{U}}$. As in the Fundamental matrix case, the main advantages of this second method are that it has better stability and that the 27 coefficients of $\mathcal{T}$ play identical roles.

The following paragraphs detail the $\mathbf{U}$ matrix and the criterion C that is minimized in each of the possible configurations of point and line matches, starting with the two most common types of matches: Matches of three lines and matches of three points. Other configurations that give rise to linear equations are described as well even though they are much less useful in practice. The table below summarizes the main results of these sections, so that the reader not interested in the details can go directly to Section 9.1.3. For each admissible type of match, the number of linear equations and their rank are given (columns N and R), as well as the description of the $\mathbf{U}$ matrix corresponding to it (column Matrix). The entry C describes the symbol used to represent the number of matches of this type.

Type	N	R	Matrix	C
$(\mathbf{l}, \mathbf{l}', \mathbf{l}'')$	3	2	$\mathbf{U_{lll}} = \mathcal{S}(\epsilon^{qir} l_r l_j' l_k'')_{q \in \{1,2,3\}}$	n_{lll}
$(\mathbf{m}, \mathbf{m}', \mathbf{m}'')$	9	4	$\mathbf{U_{ppp}} = \mathcal{S}(\epsilon_{jrp}\epsilon_{ksq} m^i m'^r m''^s)_{(p,q) \in \{1,2,3\}^2}$	n_{ppp}
$(\mathbf{m}, \mathbf{l}', \mathbf{l}'')$	1	1	$\mathbf{U_{pll}} = \mathcal{S}(m^i l_j' l_k'')$	n_{pll}
$(\mathbf{m}, \mathbf{m}', \mathbf{l}'')$	3	2	$\mathbf{U_{ppl}} = \mathcal{S}(\epsilon_{jrp} m^i m'^r l_k'')_{p \in \{1,2,3\}}$	n_{ppl}
$(\mathbf{m}, \mathbf{l}', \mathbf{m}'')$	3	2	$\mathbf{U_{plp}} = \mathcal{S}(\epsilon_{ksq} m^i l_j' m''^s)_{q \in \{1,2,3\}}$	n_{plp}

9.1.2.1   The line-line-line configuration

Given the match $(\mathbf{l}, \mathbf{l}', \mathbf{l}'')$, by definition of the Trifocal tensor, the equation $\mathbf{l} \simeq \mathcal{T}(\mathbf{l}', \mathbf{l}'')$ is satisfied. Consequently, a system of 3 linear equations in the coefficients of $\mathcal{T}$ can be written: $\mathcal{T}(\mathbf{l}', \mathbf{l}'') \times \mathbf{l} = 0$. Because of the cross-product, this system is of rank 2:

$$C_{lll}(\mathbf{l}, \mathbf{l}', \mathbf{l}'') = \mathcal{T}(\mathbf{l}', \mathbf{l}'') \times \mathbf{l} = \epsilon^{qir} l_r l'_j l''_k \mathcal{T}_i^{jk} \ .$$

The corresponding $\mathbf{U}_{lll}$ matrix is:

$$
\begin{aligned}
\mathbf{U}_{lll}(\mathbf{l}, \mathbf{l}', \mathbf{l}'') &= \mathcal{S}(\epsilon^{qir} l_r l'_j l''_k)_{q \in \{1,2,3\}} \\[2mm]
&= \begin{bmatrix}
\mathbf{0}_{1 \times 9} & -l_3 \mathbf{K}_{ll}(\mathbf{l}', \mathbf{l}'') & l_2 \mathbf{K}_{ll}(\mathbf{l}', \mathbf{l}'') \\
l_3 \mathbf{K}_{ll}(\mathbf{l}', \mathbf{l}'') & \mathbf{0}_{1 \times 9} & -l_1 \mathbf{K}_{ll}(\mathbf{l}', \mathbf{l}'') \\
-l_2 \mathbf{K}_{ll}(\mathbf{l}', \mathbf{l}'') & l_1 \mathbf{K}_{ll}(\mathbf{l}', \mathbf{l}'') & \mathbf{0}_{1 \times 9}
\end{bmatrix} ,
\end{aligned}
\tag{9.6}
$$

where $\mathbf{K}_{ll}(\mathbf{l}', \mathbf{l}'') = \begin{bmatrix} l'_1 l''_1 & l'_1 l''_2 & l'_1 l''_3 & l'_2 l''_1 & l'_2 l''_2 & l'_2 l''_3 & l'_3 l''_1 & l'_3 l''_2 & l'_3 l''_3 \end{bmatrix}$.
The number of such line-line-line configurations is called n_{lll} hereafter.

9.1.2.2   The point-point-point configuration

Given a point match $(\mathbf{m}, \mathbf{m}', \mathbf{m}'')$, the criterion C_{ppp} is obtained by considering all pairs of lines such that the first belongs to the pencil of lines centered at $\mathbf{m}'$ and the second belongs to the pencil of lines centered at $\mathbf{m}''$. This is equivalent to considering two arbitrary points $\mathbf{x}'$ and $\mathbf{x}''$ in images 2 and 3 respectively. Then, $\mathbf{m}' \times \mathbf{x}'$ represents an arbitrary line of image 2 passing through the point $\mathbf{m}'$ and similarly $\mathbf{m}'' \times \mathbf{x}''$ represents an arbitrary line of image 3 passing through the point $\mathbf{m}''$. Consequently, $\mathcal{T}(\mathbf{m}' \times \mathbf{x}', \mathbf{m}'' \times \mathbf{x}'')$ is a line of image 1 containing the point $\mathbf{m}$ and $\mathcal{T}$ obeys the linear equation

$$Eq_{ppp}(\mathbf{x}', \mathbf{x}'') = \mathbf{m}^T \mathcal{T}(\mathbf{m}' \times \mathbf{x}', \mathbf{m}'' \times \mathbf{x}'') = m^i \mathcal{T}_i^{jk} \epsilon_{jrp} m'^r x'^p \epsilon_{ksq} m''^s x''^q = 0 \ .$$

Since this equation is true for all points $\mathbf{x}'$ and $\mathbf{x}''$ and since the equation is linear in the coordinates of each of these two points, it is sufficient, in theory, to choose the points in the projective bases of their respective images.

$$
\begin{aligned}
C_{ppp}(\mathbf{m}, \mathbf{m}', \mathbf{m}'') &= \epsilon_{jrp} \epsilon_{ksq} \mathcal{T}_i^{jk} m^i m'^r m''^s \\
&= Eq_{ppp}(\varepsilon^p, \varepsilon^q)
\end{aligned}
\qquad (p, q) \in \{1, 2, 3\}^2 \ ,
$$

where ε^i, $i = 1 \ldots 3$ is the canonical projective basis of images 2 and 3 (for simplicity the two bases have been identified here). $C_{ppp}(\mathbf{m}, \mathbf{m}', \mathbf{m}'')$ is thus a system of 9 linear equations. Since each pencil of lines is of linear dimension 2, the system is of rank[3] 4, and its matrix $\mathbf{U}_{ppp}$ is defined by

---

[3] All of the 9 equations are necessary though, in order to obtain a rank 4 system for all choices of $\mathbf{m}'$ and $\mathbf{m}''$.

$$
\begin{aligned}
\mathbf{U_{ppp}}(\mathbf{m}, \mathbf{m}', \mathbf{m}'') &= \mathcal{S}(\epsilon_{jrp}\epsilon_{ksq}m^i m'^r m''^s)_{(p,q)\in\{1,2,3\}^2} \\
&= \begin{bmatrix} m^1\mathbf{K_{pp}}(\mathbf{m}', \mathbf{m}'') & m^2\mathbf{K_{pp}}(\mathbf{m}', \mathbf{m}'') & m^3\mathbf{K_{pp}}(\mathbf{m}', \mathbf{m}'') \end{bmatrix} \;,
\end{aligned}
$$

with

$$
\mathbf{K_{pp}}(\mathbf{m}', \mathbf{m}'') = \begin{bmatrix}
\mathbf{0}_{3\times3} & m'^3[\mathbf{m}'']_{\times} & -m'^2[\mathbf{m}'']_{\times} \\
-m'^3[\mathbf{m}'']_{\times} & \mathbf{0}_{3\times3} & m'^1[\mathbf{m}'']_{\times} \\
m'^2[\mathbf{m}'']_{\times} & -m'^1[\mathbf{m}'']_{\times} & \mathbf{0}_{3\times3}
\end{bmatrix} \;.
$$

These 9 equations are often referred to as the trilinearities associated with the match

$(\mathbf{m}, \mathbf{m}', \mathbf{m}'')$. In the remainder of this section, n_{ppp} will represent the number of such point-point-point configurations.

9.1.2.3   The point-line-line configuration

Given the match $(\mathbf{m}, \mathbf{l}', \mathbf{l}'')$, by definition of the Trifocal tensor, $\mathcal{T}(\mathbf{l}', \mathbf{l}'')$ is a line of image 1 passing through the point $\mathbf{m}$. The criterion C_{pll} is thus restricted to a single linear equation:

$$
C_{pll} = \mathbf{m}^T \mathcal{T}(\mathbf{l}', \mathbf{l}'') = m^i \mathcal{T}_i^{jk} l'_j l''_k \;, \tag{9.7}
$$

with the corresponding $\mathbf{U_{pll}}$ matrix

$$
\begin{aligned}
\mathbf{U_{pll}}(\mathbf{m}, \mathbf{l}', \mathbf{l}'') &= \mathcal{S}(m^i l'_j l''_k) \\
&= \begin{bmatrix} m^1\mathbf{K_{ll}}(\mathbf{l}', \mathbf{l}'') & m^2\mathbf{K_{ll}}(\mathbf{l}', \mathbf{l}'') & m^3\mathbf{K_{ll}}(\mathbf{l}', \mathbf{l}'') \end{bmatrix} \;,
\end{aligned}
$$

and with $\mathbf{K_{ll}}(\mathbf{l}', \mathbf{l}'')$ defined as in Section 9.1.2.1.
The number of such point-line-line configurations is called n_{pll} hereafter.

9.1.2.4   The point-point-line configuration

Given the match $(\mathbf{m}, \mathbf{m}', \mathbf{l}'')$, the criterion C_{ppl} is obtained as in Section 9.1.2.2 by considering all of the lines belonging to the pencil centered at $\mathbf{m}'$. This is again equivalent to considering one arbitrary point $\mathbf{x}'$ in image 2. Then, $\mathbf{m}' \times \mathbf{x}'$ represents an arbitrary line of image 2 passing through the point $\mathbf{m}'$. Consequently, $\mathcal{T}(\mathbf{m}' \times \mathbf{x}', \mathbf{l}'')$ is a line of image 1 containing the point $\mathbf{m}$, and $\mathcal{T}$ obeys the linear equation

$$
Eq_{ppl}(\mathbf{x}') = \mathbf{m}^T \mathcal{T}(\mathbf{m}' \times \mathbf{x}', \mathbf{l}'') = m^i \mathcal{T}_i^{jk} \epsilon_{jrp} m'^r x'^p l''_k = 0 \;.
$$

This equation being linear and true for all points $\mathbf{x}'$, it is sufficient to choose this point in the projective basis of image 2:

$$
\begin{aligned}
C_{ppl}(\mathbf{m}, \mathbf{m}', \mathbf{l}'') &= m^i \mathcal{T}_i^{jk} \epsilon_{jrp} m'^r l_k'' \ , \quad p \in \{1,2,3\} \ , \\
&= Eq_{ppl}(\varepsilon^p)
\end{aligned}
$$

where ε^p, $p = 1 \dots 3$ is the canonical projective basis of image 2. $C_{ppl}(\mathbf{m}, \mathbf{m}', \mathbf{l}'')$ is thus a system of 3 linear equations. Since a pencil of lines is of dimension 2, this system is of rank 2, and its matrix $\mathbf{U_{ppl}}$ is defined by

$$
\begin{aligned}
\mathbf{U_{ppl}}(\mathbf{m}, \mathbf{m}', \mathbf{l}'') &= \mathcal{S}(\epsilon_{jrp} m^i m'^r l_k'')_{p \in \{1,2,3\}} \\
&= \left[m^1 \mathbf{K_{pl}}(\mathbf{m}', \mathbf{l}'') \quad m^2 \mathbf{K_{pl}}(\mathbf{m}', \mathbf{l}'') \quad m^3 \mathbf{K_{pl}}(\mathbf{m}', \mathbf{l}'') \right] \ ,
\end{aligned}
$$

with

$$
\mathbf{K_{pl}}(\mathbf{m}', \mathbf{l}'') = \begin{bmatrix} \mathbf{0}_{1\times 3} & m'^3 \mathbf{l}''^T & -m'^2 \mathbf{l}''^T \\ -m'^3 \mathbf{l}''^T & \mathbf{0}_{1\times 3} & m'^1 \mathbf{l}''^T \\ m'^2 \mathbf{l}''^T & -m'^1 \mathbf{l}''^T & \mathbf{0}_{1\times 3} \end{bmatrix} \ ,
$$

The number of such configurations is called n_{ppl}.

9.1.2.5   The point-line-point configuration

Given the match $(\mathbf{m}, \mathbf{l}', \mathbf{m}'')$, the reasoning to obtain the criterion C_{ppl} is very similar to the point-point-line case described in the previous section and it is left to the reader as an exercise to verify that

$$
\begin{aligned}
\mathbf{U_{plp}}(\mathbf{m}, \mathbf{l}', \mathbf{m}'') &= \mathcal{S}(\epsilon_{ksq} m^i l_j' m''^s)_{q \in \{1,2,3\}} \\
&= \left[m^1 \mathbf{K_{lp}}(\mathbf{l}', \mathbf{m}'') \quad m^2 \mathbf{K_{lp}}(\mathbf{l}', \mathbf{m}'') \quad m^3 \mathbf{K_{lp}}(\mathbf{l}', \mathbf{m}'') \right] \ .
\end{aligned}
$$

with

$$
\mathbf{K_{lp}}(\mathbf{l}', \mathbf{m}'') = \left[\ l_1' \mathbf{L_p}(\mathbf{m}'') \quad l_2' \mathbf{L_p}(\mathbf{m}'') \quad l_3' \mathbf{L_p}(\mathbf{m}'') \ \right] \ ,
$$

The number of such configurations is called n_{plp}.

9.1.3   Discussion

Combining the elements of the previous sections, it is easy to implement a linear algorithm for the estimation of the Trifocal tensor using standard linear algebra tools. The same algorithm can deal with matches made out of various combinations of points and lines. However, the careful reader may have noticed that three types of matches have not been considered in the previous list: Indeed the line-point-line or line-line-point or line-point-point type of match *do not* contribute to any linear equation. This is because the primitive observed in image 1 in those three cases is a line $\mathbf{l}$ and the one predicted from the data in images 2 and 3 is a point. We saw in the previous sections that a point's information must first be converted into information about a pencil of lines before it can be handled by the Trifocal tensor in a simple algebraic manner. Thus, the question that has to be answered in image 1 is "Is l a line belonging to some given pencil of lines?". Unfortunately, the algebraic test corresponding to this question is of degree 2 in the components of $\mathcal{T}$; thus no linear equations are available.

Another question that can be raised is "Must all the linear equations be incorporated in the linear system or can we just select a subset of them of maximal rank for each type of match?". Indeed, it is possible for each of the cases given in the previous sections to extract a minimal system from the one described. (This can be achieved for example by using a SVD of the **K** matrix.) However, extensive tests have shown that this gives essentially the same result as solving the full system. Moreover, the full process of building such a minimal system and solving it is always slower than just solving the full system. Consequently, doing equation selection seems to be have little value.

We have seen that the Trifocal tensor is defined by 26 coefficients. Given the ranks of the elementary matrices described in the previous sections, it is thus determined by the linear algorithm as soon as $n_{pll} + 2n_{lll} + 2n_{ppl} + 2n_{plp} + 4n_{ppp} \geq 26$. In the extreme situations where only one type of primitive is used, the minimal number of features required for the linear algorithm is either 7 points or 13 lines matched across the three images.

9.1.4   Some results

We present results to help the reader evaluate the quality of the methods used to estimate the Trifocal tensor. We use two different types of input.

9.1.4.1   Synthetic experiments

First, we use a set of ideal data points for which the result is known. These data are used to gather statistical results about the linear estimation process. For each noise level (Gaussian noise), noise is added to the ideal points 1000 times and the linear estimation procedure is run. Statistics are gathered from all of these samples. Figure 9.1 shows the three sets of points that are used as input. Notice that, even though the data are perfect, the geometrical situation of the cameras is realistic as it stems from a trinocular stereo setup.

To characterize the quality of the results, we first plot the statistics related to the smallest singular values. Figure 9.2 shows two plots. The upper plot shows the evolution of the smallest singular value with respect to the (Gaussian) noise level. As can be expected, the minimum singular value (which reflects the average error of the linear criterion) grows with the noise, as does its standard deviation. The bottom plot is more interesting: the displayed curves are related to the ratio of the two smallest singular values. As can be seen, this ratio first increases linearly

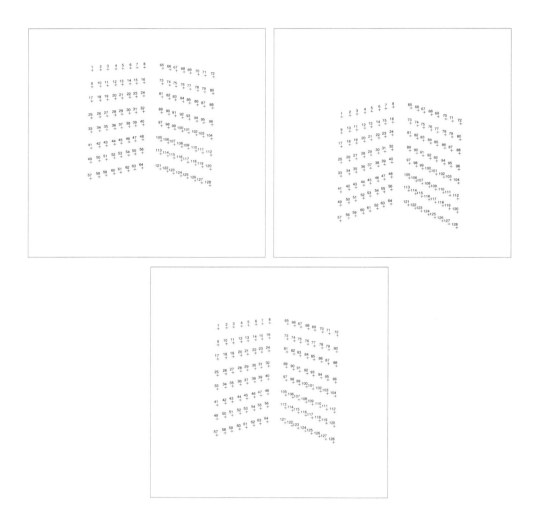

Figure 9.1: The data points used for the experiments on synthetic data.

as well as its standard deviation, but starting at the 0.3 standard deviation noise, the behavior of the curve clearly changes: It starts decreasing and the standard deviation stays roughly constant. What seems to be happening here is that the noise starts to hide completely the structural properties of the scene as seen from the images. Thus, the actual Trifocal tensor can no longer be recovered from the input data. In other words, what is measured in the smaller singular values is not only the Trifocal tensor but also part of the scene structure. Thus, the above algorithm is likely to produce very bad estimates in some situations. This result should be interpreted with care, as our data set comes from a very simple scene structure (the 3D points are scattered over two orthogonal planes) and a very particular viewing geometry (small baseline used for trinocular stereo). On the other hand, with many scenes (and particularly with urban scenes), these conditions might be a problem.

The next set of results is related to the geometric errors between the measured points in the first image and their predictions obtained by applying the Trifocal tensor to the data gathered from the other images. In Figure 9.3, we show the evolution of the average geometric errors, with the noise for the solution estimated by the linear algorithm on the upper plot and the theoretical solution on the bottom one. That is, we apply the estimated and theoretical tensors to the noisy primitives and compute the geometric errors (more on those in Section 9.5.2). Comparing those two plots, it can be seen that the linear method starts to show an unexpected behavior at noise levels of about 0.3–0.4 standard deviations. This is in agreement with the previous results. One more interesting piece of information is the fact that the curve showing the value of the maximum average error over the 1000 trials has values (that are not shown in the plot) in the range 12–440. Comparing those with the maximum average residual of the linear method (given by the maximum value of the smallest singular values), we can see that there are some noisy situations for which the linear and the geometrical criteria behave very differently.

Fortunately, all the situations are not as difficult as the one shown in this example as we will see next with some real situations. Nonetheless, the main lessons to be learned from this case are:

- Linear methods for estimating the Trifocal tensor can behave very badly in some situations.

- Even if they might work on average, linear methods can fail for special noise distributions.

- Checking the quality of the obtained result is mandatory. One such test is to verify that the ratio between the two smallest singular values is small enough (roughly less than 0.25 seems a reasonable choice).

- The linear and the geometric criteria can have very different behaviors.

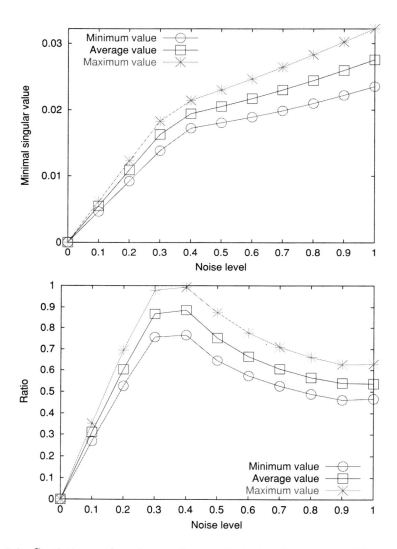

Figure 9.2: Statistics gathered over the smallest singular values. The upper plot shows the value of the smallest singular value whereas the bottom plot shows the ratio between the two smallest singular values. In each case, the minimum, average and maximum values over the 1000 trials are shown for each noise level.

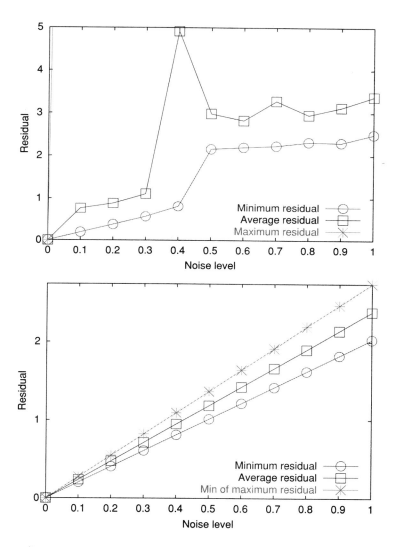

Figure 9.3: Statistics gathered over the geometric residuals. The upper plot shows the values of the mean of the geometric errors obtained using the tensor obtained by the linear algorithm whereas the bottom plot shows the geometric errors obtained using the exact theoretical tensor. In each case, the minimum, average and maximum values of the mean residual over the 1000 trials are shown for each noise level.

9.1.4.2   Real data experiments

We also use some real sets of images to see, for practical situations, the errors that we obtain from data corrupted by typical noise. The point matches were obtained manually (clicking the points in the images without subpixel accuracy) so that points exhibit a standard level of noise and no outliers are corrupting the input. Figures 9.4, 9.5 and 9.6 show the images and the points used for these experiments. These three experiments are referred to by the names **Office**, **Library** and **Arcades**, respectively. In addition, the points of experiments **Office** and **Library** have been refined to obtain sub-pixel accuracy and have also been used; these variants are called **Office'** and **Library'**, respectively.

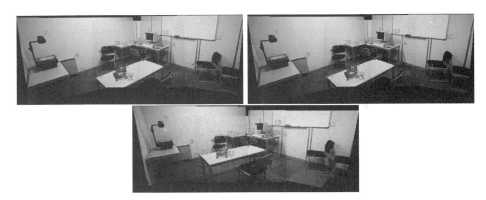

Figure 9.4: An indoor input scene, each image is a mosaic of smaller images (Courtesy **Luc Robert**, INRIA). These data correspond to the **Office** and **Office'** experiments.

Table 9.1 gives the results obtained using the linear algorithm. From these results, one can notice various things:

- The ratio of the two smallest singular values is usually small (less than 0.3) which shows that we can have some confidence in the results.

- While the average error remains relatively low, the maximum error can be significantly higher. The experiments **Library** and **Library'** show that rounding the point coordinates can increase the residuals (geometrical or linear) significantly.

It is important to note that the tensors that have been obtained in each of these cases *do not* satisfy the Trifocal tensor constraints. This means that the tensors that have been computed cannot be used in a change of view operation (the system being solved in a least-squares fashion) and give satisfactory results. Table 9.2 gives

Figure 9.5: Three views of the INRIA library (Courtesy **Sylvain Bougnoux**, INRIA). These data correspond to the **Library** and **Library'** experiments.

an example of the typical poor quality of doing such a computation. These data are obtained from the **Library'** experiment, which was the most accurate case (see table 9.1). Of course, for each experiment, three Trifocal tensors can be computed but these cannot be related to each other easily.

9.2 Parameterizing the Trifocal tensor

A central tool to estimate a consistent Trifocal tensor (i.e. a tensor satisfying the Trifocal constraints described in Sections 8.4 and 8.5 of Chapter 8) is to have a parameterization that allows a description of the admissible Trifocal tensors. Because of the great number of constraints that have to be satisfied, parameterization of the Trifocal tensor is not as straightforward as in the Fundamental matrix case. A consequence of this is that a variety of very different parameterizations have been proposed:

- Historically, the first parameterization was proposed by Hartley (Hartley, 1997d). This parameterization uses 2 standard projection matrices to represent a Trifocal tensor. It is extremely elegant and quite natural but has the major drawback of not being minimal since it uses a total of 22 degrees

Figure 9.6: Three views of the Arcades square in Valbonne (Courtesy **Sylvain Bougnoux**, INRIA). These data correspond to the **Arcades** experiment.

	Office	Office'	Library	Library'	Arcades
Avg. geometric error	1.6	1.4	2.3	0.5	0.77
Max geometric error	4.3	3.7	9.3	2.5	2.0
Smallest singular value	$6.6e^{-3}$	$6.0e^{-3}$	$2.6e^{-3}$	$3.6e^{-4}$	$4.8e^{-3}$
Ratio	0.19	0.17	$4.4e^{-2}$	$6.3e^{-3}$	0.24

Table 9.1: Quality of the linear estimation of the Trifocal tensor with real data. For each experiment, the average and maximum error is given as well as the smallest singular value and the ratio of the two smallest singular values.

	Average error	Maximum Error
Image 1	0.5	2.5
Image 2	1.8	4.9
Image 3	21.1	84.9

Table 9.2: The geometric errors for the **Library'** experiment. The Trifocal tensor computed using the linear method (that gives predictions in image 1) has been used in a "change of view" operation to compute the two other Trifocal tensor associated to the three images. These tensors have then been used for prediction. The average and maximum errors between the input data points and the predicted points are shown for each image.

of freedom. Thus to make the representation really effective some additional constraints which are not so natural have to be added.

- Torr and Zisserman proposed a minimal parameterization based on six point correspondences (Torr and Zisserman, 1997b). In this method, four of the points are used to define a canonical basis in each image, the projective coordinates of the two remaining points in those bases provide the 18 parameters that are needed. Unfortunately, a vector of 18 such parameters can represent up to three Trifocal tensors which cannot be discriminated without the use of a seventh point.

- Faugeras and Papadopoulo proposed another parameterization that is very close to the tensorial representation of the tensor and that relies directly on geometrical interpretations of the constraints that Trifocal tensors must satisfy (Faugeras and Papadopoulo, 1998). Unfortunately, similarly to what happens with the six-point correspondences parameterization, this parameterization is not one-to-one and a vector of 18 parameters represents two Trifocal tensors. Only the data can discriminate between the two candidates.

- Finally, the same authors proposed another minimal representation which is based on even less obvious geometrical properties of the Trifocal tensor that overcome the problem raised in the two previous ones (Papadopoulo and Faugeras, 1998). At the time of this writing, this parameterization is the only one that is both minimal and one-to-one.

We now review each of these parameterizations.

9.2.1 The parameterization by projection matrices

Since the Trifocal tensor represents configurations of three cameras, it is natural to try to parameterize it by means of projection matrices. In Chapter 8, the general formula linking the Trifocal tensor to a set of three projection matrices is given by Formula 8.12. However, since the Trifocal tensor is defined only up to a global collineation of the 3D space, this transform can be chosen in such a way that the first of these 3 cameras takes the standard form

$$\mathcal{P}_1 = \mathcal{P}_0.$$

In this same basis, the other two projection matrices take the form $\mathcal{P}_2 = \left[\alpha_j^i\right]$ and $\mathcal{P}_3 = \left[\beta_j^i\right]$. With this notation, the Trifocal tensor elements are given by the formula

$$\mathcal{T}_i^{jk} = \alpha_i^j \beta_4^k - \alpha_4^j \beta_i^k \ . \tag{9.8}$$

As such this gives a parameterization of the tensor in terms of 22 parameters (as each projection matrix is defined only up to a scale factor). As stated in (Hartley, 1997d), this means that the Jacobian of the nonlinear constraints cannot have full rank (since there is a three-dimensional set of solutions). Depending on the nonlinear minimization methods this may or may not be a problem, but it is likely to have poor convergence properties, to create instability problems, or just to increase the cost of the computation. One method to remove the superfluous degrees of freedom is to remark that with the previous formulae the coefficients G_{jk}^i do not change if we replace α_j^i and β_j^i by $\alpha_j^i + \lambda_j \alpha_4^i$ and $\beta_j^i + \lambda_j \beta_4^i$, respectively. Consequently, it is possible to impose an additional constraint, e.g. on the α_j^i. The method that has been proposed is to impose the three linear constraints $\sum_i \alpha_j^i \alpha_4^i = 0$, $j = 1, 2, 3$, which means that the fourth column of $\mathcal{P}_2$ is orthogonal to all of the other columns.[4] Imposing these 3 constraints results in a parameterization of the Trifocal tensor with 18 parameters. A slight drawback of this method is that the parameterization is not symmetric with respect to the 3 cameras.

9.2.2 The six-point parameterization

The six point parameterization finds its root in the study of the invariant quantities that can be defined by the observation of six points in three cameras (Quan, 1995). The algorithm uses six points $\mathbf{M}_i, i = 1 \ldots 6$, in general position in space to parameterize the Trifocal tensor. Five of those points are assigned to a 3D projective basis so that their projective coordinates can be set as follows: $\mathbf{M}_1 = [1, 0, 0, 0]^T$, $\mathbf{M}_2 = [0, 1, 0, 0]^T$, $\mathbf{M}_3 = [0, 0, 1, 0]^T$, $\mathbf{M}_4 = [0, 0, 0, 1]^T$ and $\mathbf{M}_5 = [1, 1, 1, 1]^T$. The remaining 3D point is given the coordinates $\mathbf{M}_6 = [X, Y, Z, W]$. Similarly, the images of the first four points in each image (the image of the point $\mathbf{M}_i$ in camera j is denoted by $\mathbf{m}_i^j$) are used to define a projective basis of each image plane, i.e. $\mathbf{m}_1^j = [1, 0, 0]^T$, $\mathbf{m}_2^j = [0, 0, 1]^T$, $\mathbf{m}_3^j = [0, 0, 1]^T$ and $\mathbf{m}_4^j = [1, 1, 1]^T$. For each

---

[4]This also means that these columns are linearly dependent.

image, given the basis defined by the first 4 points, it is possible to compute the co-ordinates in this basis of the fifth and sixth points (it is just a matter of computing and applying a homography). Given this basis for each image, it is easy to compute the projective coordinates of the fifth and sixth image points: $\mathbf{m}_5^j = [x_5^j, y_5^j, w_5^j]^T$ and $\mathbf{m}_6^j = [x_6^j, y_6^j, w_6^j]^T$.

This particular choice of coordinates mandates a very special form of the projection matrices. Using the first four points, it can be shown that they must be of the form

$$\mathcal{P}_i = \begin{bmatrix} \alpha^i & 0 & 0 & \delta^i \\ 0 & \beta^i & 0 & \delta^i \\ 0 & 0 & \gamma^i & \delta^i \end{bmatrix}.$$

Denoting by $\boldsymbol{\kappa}^i$ the vector $[\alpha^i, \beta^i, \gamma^i]^T$, the fifth point gives (because $\mathcal{P}_i$ is defined only up to a scale factor, we can take the following equation as an algebraic equality instead of a purely projective one)

$$\boldsymbol{\kappa}^i = \mathbf{m}_5^i - \delta^i[1, 1, 1]^T.$$

We write the projection equation for the sixth point:

$$\mathbf{m}_6^i \times \left(\begin{bmatrix} X & 0 & 0 \\ 0 & Y & 0 \\ 0 & 0 & Z \end{bmatrix} \boldsymbol{\kappa}^i + \delta^i \begin{bmatrix} W \\ W \\ W \end{bmatrix} \right) = \mathbf{m}_6^i \times \begin{bmatrix} Xx_5^i \\ Yy_5^i \\ Zw_5^i \end{bmatrix} + \delta^i \mathbf{m}_6^i \times \begin{bmatrix} W - X \\ W - Y \\ W - Z \end{bmatrix} = \mathbf{0}.$$

Because of the cross-product, this system has rank 2. In order to have a solution in δ^i, the two vectors of the sum must be proportional:

$$\left(\mathbf{m}_6^i \times \begin{bmatrix} Xx_5^i \\ Yy_5^i \\ Zw_5^i \end{bmatrix} \right) \times \left(\mathbf{m}_6^i \times \begin{bmatrix} W - X \\ W - Y \\ W - Z \end{bmatrix} \right) = \mathbf{0}.$$

Expanding the cross-product yields

$$\begin{vmatrix} x_6^i & Xx_5^i & W - X \\ y_6^i & Yy_5^i & W - Y \\ w_6^i & Zw_5^i & W - Z \end{vmatrix} \mathbf{m}_6^i = \mathbf{0}, \text{ which implies } \begin{vmatrix} x_6^i & Xx_5^i & W - X \\ y_6^i & Yy_5^i & W - Y \\ w_6^i & Zw_5^i & W - Z \end{vmatrix} = 0.$$

Expanding this determinant yields

$$x_5^i(y_6^i - w_6^i)XW + y_5^i(w_6^i - x_6^i)YW + w_5^i(x_6^i - y_6^i)ZW +$$
$$x_6^i(y_5^i - w_5^i)YZ + y_6^i(w_5^i - x_5^i)XZ + w_6^i(x_5^i - y_5^i)XY = 0.$$

This equation holds for each image, so that we get 3 linear constraints on the vector $\mathbf{u} = [XY, XZ, XW, YZ, YW, ZW]^T$. Moreover, it can be easily checked that the

sum of the coefficients of the previous equation is always zero so that this system
has a solution of the form

$$\mathbf{u} = \boldsymbol{\tau} + \lambda_1 \boldsymbol{\mu} + \lambda_2 [1,1,1,1,1,1]^T \, ,$$

where the vectors $\boldsymbol{\tau}$, $\boldsymbol{\mu}$ and $[1,1,1,1,1,1]^T$ represent a basis of the null-space of
the system. Looking at $\mathbf{u}$, it is clear that its components obey the constraints
$u_1 u_6 = u_2 u_5 = u_3 u_4$. Substituting the previous formula into these constraints
yields two linear equations in λ_2:

$$\begin{aligned}
&((\mu_1 - \mu_2 - \mu_5 + \mu_6)\lambda_1 + \tau_1 - \tau_2 - \tau_5 + \tau_6)\lambda_2 + \\
&\quad (\mu_1 \mu_6 - \mu_2 \mu_5)\lambda_1^2 + (\tau_1 \mu_6 + \tau_6 \mu_1 - \tau_2 \mu_5 - \tau_5 \mu_2)\lambda_1 + (\tau_1 \tau_6 - \tau_2 \tau_5) = 0, \\
&((\mu_1 - \mu_3 - \mu_4 + \mu_6)\lambda_1 + \tau_1 - \tau_3 - \tau_4 + \tau_6)\lambda_2 + \\
&\quad (\mu_1 \mu_6 - \mu_3 \mu_4)\lambda_1^2 + (\tau_1 \mu_6 + \tau_6 \mu_1 - \tau_3 \mu_4 - \tau_4 \mu_3)\lambda_1 + (\tau_1 \tau_6 - \tau_3 \tau_4) = 0.
\end{aligned}$$

Eliminating λ_2 yields one polynomial equation of degree 3 in λ_1:

$$\begin{aligned}
&((\mu_1 - \mu_2 - \mu_5 + \mu_6)\lambda_1 + \tau_1 - \tau_2 - \tau_5 + \tau_6) \\
&\quad ((\mu_1 \mu_6 - \mu_3 \mu_4)\lambda_1^2 + (\tau_1 \mu_6 + \tau_6 \mu_1 - \tau_3 \mu_4 - \tau_4 \mu_3)\lambda_1 + (\tau_1 \tau_6 - \tau_3 \tau_4)) - \\
&((\mu_1 - \mu_3 - \mu_4 + \mu_6)\lambda_1 + \tau_1 - \tau_3 - \tau_4 + \tau_6) \\
&\quad ((\mu_1 \mu_6 - \mu_2 \mu_5)\lambda_1^2 + (\tau_1 \mu_6 + \tau_6 \mu_1 - \tau_2 \mu_5 - \tau_5 \mu_2)\lambda_1 + (\tau_1 \tau_6 - \tau_2 \tau_5)) = 0.
\end{aligned} \tag{9.9}$$

Solving this equation yields one or three real solutions for λ_1, each of those providing
unique values for λ_2; $\mathbf{M}_6$; $\delta^i, i = 1 \ldots 3$; and $\mathcal{P}_i, i = 2,3$; and thus to 3 different
Trifocal tensors using Formula 8.12. The main advantage of this parameterization is
that it provides a consistent Trifocal tensor while requiring one point less than the
linear method. For this reason, it is a perfect candidate for being the underlying
parameterization for a robust algorithm based on, e.g.,least-median squares (the
original work is based on RANSAC). To remove the ambiguity arising from the
potentially multiple solutions, the robustness criterion is evaluated for all three
tensors and the one providing the smallest result is selected.

9.2.3   The tensorial parameterization

The constraints described by the 9 equations (8.28) can also be used to parameterize
the Trifocal tensors with 18 parameters. This parameterization is basically an
augmented subset of the Trifocal tensor coefficients, hence the name of tensorial
parameterization.

To obtain it, two of the constraints of (8.28) are chosen, for example $k_2 = l_2 =
1$, $k_3 = l_3 = 2$ and $k_2 = l_2 = 2$, $k_3 = l_3 = 3$. Notice that $\mathcal{T}^{22}$ is the only
vector that appears in both constraints. In general, the three vectors $\mathcal{T}^{23}$, $\mathcal{T}^{32}$ and
$\mathcal{T}^{33}$ are linearly independent, so that $\mathcal{T}^{22}$ can be expressed in the basis they form:
$\mathcal{T}^{22} = \alpha_1 \mathcal{T}^{23} + \alpha_2 \mathcal{T}^{32} + \alpha_3 \mathcal{T}^{33}$ Equation 8.28 then implies that $\alpha_1 + \alpha_2 \alpha_3 = 0$.

It is then easy to parameterize the set of vectors $\boldsymbol{\mathcal{T}}^{22}_{\cdot}$ that satisfy the constraint given by $k_2 = l_2 = 2$, $k_3 = l_3 = 3$: $\boldsymbol{\mathcal{T}}^{22}_{\cdot} = \mathbf{K} \left[-pq \; p \; q \right]^T$, where $\mathbf{K}$ is the matrix $\left[\boldsymbol{\mathcal{T}}^{23}_{\cdot} \; \boldsymbol{\mathcal{T}}^{32}_{\cdot} \; \boldsymbol{\mathcal{T}}^{33}_{\cdot} \right]$. Reporting this value of $\boldsymbol{\mathcal{T}}^{22}_{\cdot}$ in the constraint given by $k_2 = l_2 = 1$, $k_3 = l_3 = 2$, we obtain a polynomial equation P of total degree 4, and of degree 2 in p and q.

The Trifocal tensor can thus be parameterized by 18 parameters. Since there is a global scale factor, one coordinate, e.g. the first coordinate of $\boldsymbol{\mathcal{T}}^{11}_{\cdot}$, can be fixed to be 1. All the vectors $\boldsymbol{\mathcal{T}}^{11}_{\cdot}$, $\boldsymbol{\mathcal{T}}^{12}_{\cdot}$, $\boldsymbol{\mathcal{T}}^{21}_{\cdot}$, $\boldsymbol{\mathcal{T}}^{23}_{\cdot}$, $\boldsymbol{\mathcal{T}}^{32}_{\cdot}$ and $\boldsymbol{\mathcal{T}}^{33}_{\cdot}$ are thus described by 17 parameters. Adding p as the 18th parameter gives a parameterization of the Trifocal tensor. Indeed, then $\boldsymbol{\mathcal{T}}^{22}_{\cdot}$ can be recovered using the polynomial P. Then, as shown in (Faugeras and Mourrain, 1995b), $\boldsymbol{\mathcal{T}}^{13}_{\cdot}$ and $\boldsymbol{\mathcal{T}}^{31}_{\cdot}$ can be recovered up to a scale factor by the formulae

$$\left(\boldsymbol{\mathcal{T}}^{12}_{\cdot} \times \left(\left(\boldsymbol{\mathcal{T}}^{22}_{\cdot} \times \boldsymbol{\mathcal{T}}^{23}_{\cdot} \right) \times \left(\boldsymbol{\mathcal{T}}^{33}_{\cdot} \times \boldsymbol{\mathcal{T}}^{32}_{\cdot} \right) \right) \right) \times \left(\boldsymbol{\mathcal{T}}^{23}_{\cdot} \times \left(\left(\boldsymbol{\mathcal{T}}^{22}_{\cdot} \times \boldsymbol{\mathcal{T}}^{12}_{\cdot} \right) \times \left(\boldsymbol{\mathcal{T}}^{21}_{\cdot} \times \boldsymbol{\mathcal{T}}^{11}_{\cdot} \right) \right) \right) \; ,$$

and

$$\left(\boldsymbol{\mathcal{T}}^{21}_{\cdot} \times \left(\left(\boldsymbol{\mathcal{T}}^{22}_{\cdot} \times \boldsymbol{\mathcal{T}}^{32}_{\cdot} \right) \times \left(\boldsymbol{\mathcal{T}}^{33}_{\cdot} \times \boldsymbol{\mathcal{T}}^{23}_{\cdot} \right) \right) \right) \times \left(\boldsymbol{\mathcal{T}}^{32}_{\cdot} \times \left(\left(\boldsymbol{\mathcal{T}}^{22}_{\cdot} \times \boldsymbol{\mathcal{T}}^{21}_{\cdot} \right) \times \left(\boldsymbol{\mathcal{T}}^{12}_{\cdot} \times \boldsymbol{\mathcal{T}}^{11}_{\cdot} \right) \right) \right) \; ,$$

respectively. Each of the remaining scale factors can be recovered using the constraints given by $k_2 = 2$, $k_3 = 1$, $l_2 = 3$, $l_3 = 2$ and $k_2 = 1$, $k_3 = 2$, $l_2 = 2$, $l_3 = 3$, respectively.

It is important to note that, since the polynomial P has to be solved in order to recover the Trifocal tensor, each vector of 18 parameters yields in fact two Trifocal tensors (corresponding to each of the roots of the polynomial). Both tensors are valid; i.e. they satisfy all of the constraints of Trifocal tensors. Thus there is in general no way to distinguish between the two tensors and both have to be considered. However, some extra information may be of some help. This information can be either the image measurements or a boolean describing which of the two roots corresponds to the tensor that has been parameterized. More annoying is the fact that the polynomial P may have no real roots. This shows that the 18 parameters are not totally free but must satisfy an inequality constraint given by the discriminant of P with respect to q. These two drawbacks are particularly annoying if the parameterization is used in a nonlinear refinement step.

9.2.4   The minimal one-to-one parameterization

The final parameterization that is proposed in this section is both minimal and one-to-one. It is based upon a parameterization of rank-2 matrices similar to the one used for Fundamental matrices that represent the matrix by its left and right kernels and by a 1-D homography. As shown in the appendix A.2, the space of 3×3 matrices of rank ≤ 2 having given left and right kernels, denoted $\mathcal{L}$ and $\mathcal{R}$, respectively, is a vector space of dimension 4. We denote this vector space $\mathcal{M}(\mathcal{L}, \mathcal{R})$. We now reformulate the extended rank constraints within this framework.

The three Trifocal matrices $\mathbf{G}^i = \mathcal{T}_i^{\,\cdot\,\cdot}, i = 1\ldots 3$, are rank-2. We denote their left and right kernels as $\mathcal{L}^i$ and $\mathcal{R}^i$ respectively. Each $\mathbf{G}^i$ can thus be represented by its coordinates a_1^i, a_2^i, a_3^i and a_4^i in a basis of $\mathcal{M}(\mathcal{L}^i, \mathcal{R}^i)$. For simplicity, we assume hereafter, without loss of generality, that the first coordinates of $\mathcal{L}^i$ and $\mathcal{R}^i$ are those of highest magnitude, so that we work in the basis described by Equation A.3.

Since $\mathcal{L}^i, i = 1\ldots 3$, and $\mathcal{R}^i, i = 1\ldots 3$, are orthogonal to $\mathbf{e}_{21}$ and $\mathbf{e}_{31}$ respectively, we can write $\mathcal{L}^i = \mathbf{e}_{21} \times \mathbf{X}^{(i)}, i = 1\ldots 3$, and $\mathcal{R}^i = \mathbf{e}_{31} \times \mathbf{Y}^{(i)}, i = 1\ldots 3$, where $\mathbf{X}^{(i)}$ and $\mathbf{Y}^{(i)}$ are the vectors of Formula 8.41.

Plugging these values into the extended rank constraints (8.32)–(8.38) and using computer algebra to factorize the results leads to the following result which is an algebraic translation of Proposition 8.15.

Theorem 9.1 *Assuming that the first coordinates of $\mathcal{L}^i$ and $\mathcal{R}^i$ are those of highest magnitude, the four coefficients $a_j^i, j = 1\ldots 4$, representing $\mathbf{G}^i$ in $\mathcal{M}(\mathcal{L}^i, \mathcal{R}^i)$ satisfy the* linear *relation*

$$e_{21}^2 e_{31}^2 a_1^i + e_{21}^2 e_{31}^3 a_2^i + e_{21}^3 e_{31}^2 a_3^i + e_{21}^3 e_{31}^3 a_4^i = 0 , \quad i = 1\ldots 3 \qquad (9.10)$$

where $\mathbf{e}_{21} = \left[e_{21}^1, e_{21}^2, e_{21}^3\right]^T$ and $\mathbf{e}_{31} = \left[e_{31}^1, e_{31}^2, e_{31}^3\right]^T$.

Remark 9.1

- *The extended rank constraints contain other factors, not shown in Equations 9.10. It can be shown that these factors are irrelevant.*

- *In the general situation, the first coordinates of $\mathcal{L}^i$ and $\mathcal{R}^i$ are not those of highest magnitude. It is remarkable to note that Equations 9.10 remain essentially the same with the substitution of e_{21}^j and e_{31}^k by $e_{21}^{\lambda^i(j)}$ and $e_{31}^{\rho^i(k)}$, where λ^i and ρ^i are the circular permutations that bring respectively the coordinates of highest magnitude of $\mathcal{L}^i$ and $\mathcal{R}^i$ into first position. This is quite remarkable as the original constraints all depend on at least two of the three $\mathbf{G}^i, i = 1\ldots 3$.*

- *It is not difficult to show that Equations 9.10 are never degenerate provided that the proper permutations λ^i and ρ^i have been made.*

Assuming first that the six vectors $\mathcal{L}^i, i = 1\ldots 3$, and $\mathcal{R}^i, i = 1\ldots 3$, are given, the three matrices $\mathbf{G}^i, i = 1\ldots 3$, can be parameterized by 8 coefficients. To do so, consider the 12 coordinates $a_j^i, i = 1\ldots 3, j = 1\ldots 4$. Since for each i, the $a_j^i, j = 1\ldots 4$, satisfy Equation 9.10, it is possible to drop one of those four coordinates. For numerical stability, the best choice is to drop the coordinate which has the highest magnitude coefficient in Equation 9.10. Moreover, since the $\mathbf{G}^i$ are only defined up to a global scale factor, we can drop one more of the 9 remaining coordinates by normalizing this coordinate to 1. This leaves us with 8 coefficients that completely describe the $\mathbf{G}^i, i = 1 \ldots 3$, given the $\mathcal{L}^i, i = 1 \ldots 3$, and $\mathcal{R}^i, i = 1 \ldots 3$.

Since 8 parameters have been used, only 10 parameters remain to parameterize the $\mathcal{L}^i, i = 1 \ldots 3$, and $\mathcal{R}^i, i = 1 \ldots 3$. We next show that 5 parameters are enough to parameterize, e.g., the $\mathcal{L}^i, i = 1 \ldots 3$ (since a similar parameterization can be obtained for the $\mathcal{R}^i, i = 1 \ldots 3$, a minimal parameterization of the Trifocal tensor is thus obtained). $\mathbf{e}_{21}$ can be parameterized by 2 coordinates by normalizing its biggest coordinate to 1 (there are thus 3 maps). Assuming without loss of generality that $\|\mathcal{L}^i\| = 1, i = 1 \ldots 3$, and remembering that all these 3 vectors are orthogonal to the epipole $\mathbf{e}_{21}$, the 3 vectors $\mathcal{L}^i$ are conveniently represented by 3 angles in a canonical basis of the plane orthogonal to the direction defined by $\mathbf{e}_{21}$. Thus, all the $\mathcal{L}^i$ can be represented by 5 parameters.

As a consequence, we have obtained a minimal parameterization of the Trifocal tensor, i.e. by 18 parameters. As the reader may have noticed, the number of maps of this parameterization is very large ($9 \times 3^2 \times 3^6$) but it is nevertheless easy to define a general routine that chooses the best map and computes the parameterization.

9.3   Imposing the constraints

Since a Trifocal tensor $\widehat{\mathcal{T}}$ obtained from the linear method is not consistent (i.e. does not satisfy the Trifocal constraints), parameterizing such a tensor involves first a procedure that enforces the consistency. As in the Fundamental matrix case, this is usually (if not always) done considering only the obtained Trifocal tensor (ignoring the primitive matches that led to its computation). Consequently, this crucial step to most Trifocal tensor estimation methods can introduce a significant decrease in the quality of the solution with respect to the data. The operation is nonetheless mandatory. To impose the constraints, two routes can be taken:

- Define a robust version of the procedure that computes one of the parameterizations of the previous section from a tensor. Then, re-synthesize the Trifocal tensor from this parameterization. The tensor obtained in this way will be consistent.

- Use the formulae of the Trifocal constraints to define a projection method that takes a point in a 27 dimensional space (the space of all $3 \times 3 \times 3$ tensors) onto the variety of dimension 18 defined by those constraints (the variety of the admissible tensors).

The next two sections illustrate these basic approaches. A third section compares the results obtained with those.

9.3.1 Projecting by parameterizing

Some of the parameterizations defined in the previous section can lead to very simple procedures that can be used to impose the constraints. This is particularly the case with the parameterization by projection matrices (see Section 9.2.1) and with the minimal one (see Section 9.2.4)[5], which are taken here as examples.

Both parameterizations are based on the knowledge of the epipoles, so the first step is to estimate these out of a non-consistent tensor. This can be done very easily by considering the 3 Trifocal matrices $\widehat{\mathbf{G}}^i = \widehat{T}_i^{jk}, i = 1 \ldots 3$. Since these should be of rank 2, the first step is to enforce this constraint, which can easily be done using the closest rank method described in Section 6.1.3. Equipped with the new rank-2 versions $\widehat{\mathbf{G}}'$ of these matrices, it is now possible to extract their left and right kernels $\widehat{\mathcal{L}'}^i, i = 1 \ldots 3$, and $\widehat{\mathcal{R}'}^i, i = 1 \ldots 3$, as in Section 9.2.4. Because of Proposition 8.19, we also know that the matrices $\widehat{\mathcal{L}'}$ and $\widehat{\mathcal{R}'}$, whose columns are respectively the $\widehat{\mathcal{L}'}^i$ and the $\widehat{R'}^i$ should also be of rank 2 and that their kernels correspond to $\mathbf{e}_{21}$ and $\mathbf{e}_{31}$ respectively. Using a least-squares method to get these kernels gives estimations $\widehat{\mathbf{e}_{21}}$ and $\widehat{\mathbf{e}_{31}}$ of the epipoles.

Once estimations of the epipoles have been recovered, the methods for the two kinds of parameterizations follow different paths:

- For the parameterization by projection matrices, it is sufficient to solve the system 9.8 using least-squares to find values for the α_j^i and β_j^i coefficients ($i = 1 \ldots 3, j = 1 \ldots 3$). It is possible to make this estimation while enforcing the constraint $\sum_i \alpha_j^i \alpha_4^i = 0$.

- For the minimal parameterization, it is sufficient to solve the equation $\widehat{\mathbf{G}}^i = a_1^i \mathbf{M}_1^i + a_2^i \mathbf{M}_2^i + a_3^i \mathbf{M}_3^i + a_4^i \mathbf{M}_4^i$ ($\mathbf{M}_j^i, i = 1 \ldots 3, j = 1 \ldots 4$, is the basis taken for $\mathcal{M}(\widehat{\mathcal{L}'}^i, \widehat{\mathcal{R}'}^i)$) imposing the constraint (9.10).

In both cases, taking the image information during this last step is possible. The method for the parameterization by projection matrices case can be found as a by-product of Hartley's method (Hartley, 1998c).

9.3.2 Projecting using the algebraic constraints

Alternatively, it is also possible to develop a minimization scheme directly based on the Trifocal constraints. To do so, one just minimizes the residual of the algebraic constraints over the coefficients of the Trifocal tensor. The main advantage of this

---

[5]Being based on a very different kind of input, the six point parameterization is more difficult to use in this context. Given a non-consistent Trifocal tensor, it should be possible, in theory, to use it to define a set of six-point matches for the three images, and to excerpt a consistent tensor out of this description. The choice of the six points is, however, non-obvious.

method is that potentially all constraints are treated on the same level. Looking back at what has been described in the previous section, we see that the various constraints are enforced in a hierarchical way: first the rank constraints of the matrices $\mathbf{G}^i$ are enforced; then the Trifocal epipolar constraints are taken into account; and the final step (whatever the parameterization) enforces the remaining constraints.

One advantage of the scheme based directly on the Trifocal constraints is that it is possible in theory to handle all of the constraints at the same level. Thus, potentially, the magnitude of the changes of the coefficients of the Trifocal tensor required to impose the constraints is smaller. However, the high degree of some formulations of the constraints (e.g. those of Equation 8.28) imposes some modifications to this simple scheme in order to obtain convergence of the minimization procedure (i.e. to avoid staying trapped in some local minimum). In (Faugeras and Papadopoulo, 1998), this is obtained by dealing with the rank constraints of the matrices $\mathbf{G}^i$ separately. This still represents one level of hierarchy less than the methods using parameterization, but reduces nonetheless the main interest of such methods. There is hope, however, as the extended rank constraints (see Proposition 8.20) are of much lower degree and are thus much less prone to induce local minima. Initial results show that the convergence is much better when using the method described in (Faugeras and Papadopoulo, 1998) with these constraints, so that suppressing the hierarchy has a very good chance of working.

One fact remains: In all cases, the image data are ignored when applying these methods and this is undesirable since these data are the only relevant metric that can be used to measure the quality of the computed Trifocal tensor (i.e. its accuracy in describing the image data). Conceptually, it is possible to design a constrained least-squares minimization that will deal with this problem. We have to remember, however, that imposing constraints is just one step needed for a full nonlinear algorithm that will handle this problem in a much better way.

9.3.3 Some results

We now examine the effect of imposing the Trifocal constraints on the results obtained in the experiments of Section 9.1.4.2. For each of these experiments, the result of the linear estimation has been used as the input of the following projection methods:

P1 The projection by parameterization method using the parameterization by projection matrices.

P2 The projection by parameterization method using the minimal parameterization.

P3 The algebraic projection method sketched in Section 9.3.2 based on the extended rank constraint.

		Office		Office'		Library		Library'		Arcades	
		Avg.	Max	Avg.	Max	Avg.	Max	Avg.	Max	Avg.	Max
	1	1.6	4.3	1.4	3.7	2.3	9.3	0.5	2.5	0.8	2.0
P0	2	4461	29711	7795	100626	32.0	81.7	1.8	4.9	260	546
	3	876.6	5209.4	842.4	1436	334.0	1964.1	21.1	84.9	215	720
	1	2.2	8.4	2.7	11.7	3.0	10.6	1.0	5.4	2.9	10.1
P1	2	4.9	18.9	5.4	21.9	1.6	3.8	0.6	1.7	1.1	3.6
	3	5.6	32.5	5.4	28.7	0.9	3.0	0.4	1.6	2.7	8.3
	1	2.3	9.3	2.9	14.9	4.4	24.7	1.5	7.4	3.4	10.7
P2	2	5.7	24.2	6.5	29.0	1.5	4.0	0.6	1.6	1.3	3.5
	3	6.7	38.8	6.9	36.8	1.1	2.8	0.4	1.7	2.7	6.6
	1	3.3	17.8	3.1	18.8	2.7	10.6	1.0	4.6	1.5	4.3
P3	2	3.0	8.7	2.9	10.5	1.3	4.6	0.5	1.4	0.6	1.2
	3	4.5	21.3	4.6	18.8	0.8	2.6	0.4	1.7	1.6	3.4

Table 9.3: Quality of the various projection methods with real data. For each experiment, the average and maximum error is given. The number in the second column identifies the view of the triplet. For reference, the experiment P0 corresponds to the initial results provided to the projection method: These are the results of the linear method. Because the Trifocal constraints are not satisfied, a robust version of the change view operation has been used.

In each case, the geometric errors between the data points and the predicted ones are shown in table 9.3. For reference, the results obtained with the linear estimation of the Trifocal tensor (which is the initial input provided to the various projection methods) is shown as the experiment **P0**. In this case, the change of view operation leads to a non-coherent over-determined linear system which is solved using a least-squares technique. As can be seen, even though the geometric residuals remain small in image 1, those obtained in such a way in images 2 and 3 can be very large.

From these results, several observations can be made:

- For all the projection methods, the geometric errors in image 1 somewhat increase during the projection operation. On the other hand, the residual geometric errors in images 2 and 3 are considerably decreased.

- The methods P1 and P2 basically behave in the same manner, with P1 consistently giving slightly better results than P2.

- The method P3 does a better job in homogenizing the error patterns over the 3 cameras. This is sometimes at the cost of increasing the geometric errors in image 1 more than in methods P1 or P2.

- All of the methods presented here tend to work much better when applied to the tensor written in normalized coordinates (see Section 9.1.1).

In all of these cases, the resulting geometric errors – particularly the maximum errors – remain unacceptably large considering that the initial matching has been done manually on images of good quality (so that the maximum error should not exceed 3–5 pixels).

9.4   A note about the "change of view" operation

The change of view operation is important as it is the procedure that will allow for a symmetrical estimation of all three tensors associated with three views. This operation can be achieved in three ways.

- Use Theorem 8.2. However, as given the theorem is not explicit as no expressions are given for the values λ_m, $m = 1, 2, 3$. This lack of values actually corresponds to the fact that no expression that is always valid has been found yet. For this reason, it seems unsafe to use this approach.

- Directly use the equation $\mathbf{l}_j \simeq \mathcal{T}_j(\mathbf{l}_k, \mathcal{T}_i(\mathbf{l}_j, \mathbf{l}_k))$ that is true for all possible values of $\mathbf{l}_j$ and $\mathbf{l}_k$. When developed and organized as a polynomial in the coordinates of $\mathbf{l}_j$ and $\mathbf{l}_k$, this equation has 90 terms each of which has a coefficient which is linear in the coefficients of $\mathcal{T}_j$ and in the coefficients of $\mathcal{T}_i$ and must be zero. Removing the equations that appear multiple times, this gives a linear system of 54 equations in the 27 unknowns relating $\mathcal{T}_j$ to $\mathcal{T}_i$. With consistent tensors, this system is of rank 26 and has a non-trivial solution. With non-consistent tensors, a least-squares solution of the system can be used.

- Using the parameterization by projection matrices described in Section 9.2.1, it is possible to re-synthesize all three Trifocal tensors corresponding to the three views using Formula 8.12. If the initial tensor is not consistent, then the method sketched in Section 9.3.1 can be used to get the parameterization.

The last two methods are both valid and give the same results in the case of a consistent tensor. In the case of a non-consistent tensor, however, the least-squares implementations of these methods will give different solutions. For example, the method using the projection by projection matrices will always yield a consistent tensor as a result; this is not the case with the method based on the linear system. On the other hand, this last method should provide a solution that minimizes the algebraic error of the system characterizing the change of view operation, which cannot be claimed with the parameterization based method. This is strongly related to the topic discussed in Section 9.3.

9.5   Nonlinear methods

The linear method described in Section 9.1 has the main advantage of being easy to implement and of defining the Trifocal tensor as the unique minimum of a convex criterion. However, it suffers also from some structural and numerical limitations:

- It is based on an algebraic criterion, which is only loosely related to the more natural geometric criterion that defines the error between the measures and the predicted primitives (from the other views) in terms of image distances.

- It minimizes a criterion that is biased: The Trifocal tensor $\mathcal{T} = \mathcal{T}_1$ gives a special role to image 1. Consequently, the criteria that have been defined in Section 9.1 are not symmetric with respect to the primitives of the three images (contrary to what happens in the Fundamental matrix case). In particular, we have seen that the linear method cannot use the information available from the matches of type line-point-line or line-line-point or line-point-point.

- The Trifocal constraints are not satisfied by the solution obtained using the linear estimation since it assumes that all 27 parameters of the tensor are independent. With perfect data this is not a problem as the computed tensor will be very close to the real solution and hence the constraints will be satisfied. With noisy data, this is no longer the case.

Nonlinear methods can take care of these limitations at the cost of introducing local minima. On the other hand, there is usually no explicit way of finding the global minimum and nonlinear methods use iterative schemes that are highly sensitive to the initialization. Thus, as for the Fundamental matrix computation, the usual strategy is to initialize a nonlinear method with the result of the linear one (assuming that this result is close to the nonlinear optimum).

9.5.1   The nonlinear scheme

To achieve the nonlinear minimization, the main ingredients are:

- **A geometric criterion**, that will characterize the quality of the estimation and that will be minimized in order to refine the estimated Trifocal tensor.

- **A method for projecting** an initial tensor not satisfying the Trifocal constraints onto a "feasible" tensor.

- **A parameterization** of the Trifocal tensor: This is needed to ensure that the nonlinear optimization method "explores" only the feasible situations, i.e. those that are satisfying the Trifocal constraints.

- **The "change of view" operation**: This tool is needed to make the estimation procedure symmetric with respect to all of the images.

The general scheme is the following:

1. Compute an initialization $\widehat{\mathcal{T}}$ of the Trifocal tensor using the linear method (see Section 9.1).

2. Project this tensor $\widehat{\mathcal{T}}$ to obtain a consistent tensor $\overline{\mathcal{T}}$ (see Section 9.3) and parameterize the tensor using one of the parameterizations of Section 9.2. As seen in Section 9.3 these two steps can sometimes be combined. This gives an 18 parameter vector $\mathbf{p} = \mathbf{p}_0$ describing $\overline{\mathcal{T}}$.

3. Use an iterative algorithm to refine $\mathbf{p}$ so as to minimize a geometric criterion defined as:

   - Recover $\overline{\mathcal{T}} = \overline{\mathcal{T}_1}$ from $\mathbf{p}$ (see Section 9.2).
   - From $\overline{\mathcal{T}_1}$, compute $\overline{\mathcal{T}_2}$ and $\overline{\mathcal{T}_3}$ using the "change view" operation (see Section 9.4).
   - Sum up the geometric errors arising from $\overline{\mathcal{T}_1}$, $\overline{\mathcal{T}_2}$ and $\overline{\mathcal{T}_3}$ to obtain a criterion that is symmetric over the three views.

Note that overall this method is very similar to what is done by a bundle adjustment procedure. Some variants of this basic algorithm have been explored:

- The six-point parameterization can be used as a replacement of steps 1 and 2. Six initial point matches are randomly chosen from the input data to obtain an initial consistent Trifocal tensor. A robust criterion is then used to estimate the quality of the tensor with respect to all the primitives. By iterating over the choice of the initial points this leads to a method that deals with outliers. The main drawback of this method is its restriction to using only point matches for the initial parameterization, which is somewhat restrictive if the input consists essentially of line matches. See (Torr and Zisserman, 1997b) for more details.

- Dropping the symmetry over the three views (i.e. minimizing only the errors arising from e.g. $\mathcal{T}_1$), replacing the geometric criterion by the algebraic one (the one minimized by the linear method) and using the parameterization by projection matrices, it is possible to design a simpler estimation procedure in which the nonlinear optimization is used to refine only the epipole positions, the remaining parameters being estimated linearly using Equation 9.8. See (Hartley, 1997d) for more details.

9.5.2   A note about the geometric criterion

Up to now, we have omitted the details of the geometric criterion. Basically, the geometric criterion is very similar to the one used for the Fundamental matrix. The only difference here is that we have to deal with both lines and points. The situation is the following:

- In each image, the inputs are points and line-segments.

- The prediction obtained by the Trifocal tensor in one view given the primitives in the two other views is either a point or an infinite line.

Thus, if we want to deal with all of these types of primitives, we need to define and combine all of the geometric distances from an image feature to a predicted feature. The point-point and point-line distances are well known, but the distances from a line-segment to a point or a line require some attention. Let us call $\mathbf{s}$ the line-segment and $\mathbf{a}$ and $\mathbf{b}$ its endpoints.

The distance of a point m to the line segment s is very similar to the point-line distance. Denoting by $\mathbf{l}$, the support line of $\mathbf{s}$, one just has to pay attention to the endpoints of the segment. Two cases are possible:

- If the projection of $\mathbf{m}$ onto $\mathbf{l}$ lies on $\mathbf{s}$, then the distance between $\mathbf{m}$ and $\mathbf{s}$ is simply the distance between $\mathbf{m}$ and $\mathbf{l}$.

- If the projection of $\mathbf{m}$ onto $\mathbf{l}$ does not lie on $\mathbf{s}$, then the distance between $\mathbf{m}$ and $\mathbf{s}$ is the smaller of the two distances between $\mathbf{m}$ and $\mathbf{a}$ and $\mathbf{b}$ respectively.

The distance of a line-segment to a line l is slightly more complicated to define. Many definitions can be adopted. One solution very often taken is to sum up the distances from the two endpoints to the line. This is indeed a proper distance in mathematical terms. However, since we are combining very different error terms, it is also desirable that the various distances that we are summing up are weighted homogeneously over the various primitives (i.e. in a discrete image, a segment of length l has the importance of roughly l points). Thus, the only way to properly define this distance is to sum up the infinitesimal contributions of all of the points of the line-segment to the distance to the line $\mathbf{l}$. This is done by integrating the squared distance of $\mathbf{m}$ to $\mathbf{l}$ for every point $\mathbf{m}$ of $\mathbf{s}$, and taking the square root of this value. This computation can be done algebraically and the result is

$$d(\mathbf{s},\mathbf{l}) = \rho d(\mathbf{a},\mathbf{b}) \sqrt{\left(\frac{(\mathbf{u}^T\mathbf{a} - \mathbf{u}^T\mathbf{b})^2}{3} + d(\mathbf{a},\mathbf{l})d(\mathbf{b},\mathbf{l}) \right)} \ ,$$

where $\mathbf{u}$ is the normalized vector describing the normal to the line $\mathbf{l}$. ρ is a weighting factor used to balance the contributions of point distances and segment distances. This factor can be seen as a weight per unit length and this makes $d(\mathbf{s},\mathbf{l})$ homogeneous to a distance.

9.5.3   Results

We now examine the behavior of the nonlinear methods on the results obtained in the experiments of Section 9.1.4.2. For each of these experiments, the result of the linear estimation has been used. Then the algebraic projection method has been applied to obtain an initial tensor satisfying the Trifocal constraints. This tensor is parameterized and used as the initial solution in the nonlinear estimation techniques. Basically, two types of parameterizations have been used:

  P: The parameterization by projection matrices.

  M: The minimal parameterization.

  However, it should not be forgotten that the Trifocal tensor is a non-symmetric object across the three views. This property is also true of the two types of parameterizations above, since each of these attributes a special role to one of the cameras. Thus by changing views, each of these parameterization types actually gives three parameterizations for a single Trifocal tensor. Numerically, one indeed notices that, for a given type of parameterization, the three possible parameterizations do not give the same results. This is all the more important as it seems that the local minimum of the minimized criterion is highly dependent on the parameterization. Consequently, in order to avoid remaining trapped in those local minima, the nonlinear optimization procedure is applied using in sequence each of the three parameterizations. This has also the nice effect of making the nonlinear procedure as symmetric as possible over the three views.

  In each case, the geometric errors between the data points and the predicted ones are shown in table 9.4. For reference, the results obtained with the initial Trifocal tensor used as input to the nonlinear methods is shown as the experiment **P3**.

  As can be seen from the results, the nonlinear estimations substantially improve the quality of the estimates of the Trifocal tensors, decreasing dramatically the maximum errors. Still, these results are not yet perfect as the maximum errors are still too high. Indeed, it seems that these solutions often correspond to situations close to a local minimum with a narrow and flat valley leading to a better solution at a very slow speed.

  Another interesting fact is that for the projection methods, it seems that the parameterization by projection matrices performs better than the minimal parameterization. Although no real explanation can be given at the time of this writing, it seems to be related to the fact that the parameterization by projection matrices is "more linear" than the minimal parameterization which involves trigonometric functions.

		Office		Office'		Library		Library'		Arcades	
		Avg.	Max	Avg.	Max	Avg.	Max	Avg.	Max	Avg.	Max
P3	1	3.3	17.8	3.1	18.8	2.7	10.6	1.0	4.6	1.5	4.3
	2	3.0	8.7	2.9	10.5	1.3	4.6	0.5	1.4	0.6	1.2
	3	4.5	21.3	4.6	18.8	0.8	2.6	0.4	1.7	1.6	3.4
P	1	1.5	3.8	1.4	4.1	1.5	4.3	0.3	0.6	0.9	1.8
	2	2.2	5.2	2.1	5.2	1.2	4.1	0.2	0.4	0.5	1.1
	3	2.3	7.8	1.9	5.8	0.9	2.1	0.2	0.8	0.9	2.4
M	1	1.7	5.4	1.6	4.4	1.5	4.7	0.3	0.6	0.9	2.8
	2	2.3	5.6	2.2	5.2	1.2	3.7	0.2	0.4	0.5	1.0
	3	2.7	9.0	2.3	7.6	0.8	2.0	0.1	0.8	1.0	2.4

Table 9.4: Quality of the nonlinear estimation of the Trifocal tensor with real data. For each experiment, the average and maximum errors are given. The number in the second column identifies the view of the triplet. For comparison purposes, the results obtained before nonlinear refinement are shown: These are the results obtained in the P3 experiment given in Section 9.3.3.

9.6   References and further reading

There is actually very little material published on the topic of the estimation of the Trifocal tensor in the general case from image features beyond that already quoted in this chapter. There has been work done for some specific cases . In (Armstrong et al., 1996), the particularly important case of planar motion (the cameras are all in a plane and the rotations relating their respective positions have axes orthogonal to that plane). Stein and Shashua (Stein and Shashua, 1999) deal with the problem of estimating the Trifocal tensor in some geometrical situations where the linear algorithm is degenerate. The same authors also deal with the direct estimation of the three view geometry from intensity data (Stein and Shashua, 1997). Estimation of the Trifocal tensor from a plane plus parallax has also been studied in (Irani et al., 1998; Crimisini et al., 1998).

10
Stratification of $n \geq 3$ views and applications

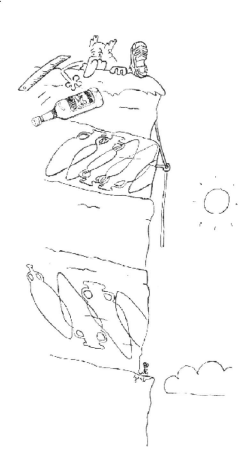

This chapter extends Chapter 7 to deal with an arbitrary number of cameras. The goal, to which the reader should now be accustomed, is to provide a stratified description of the geometry of the cameras and the structure of the scene according to the information that is available. As in the previous chapters we identify three main levels of description: Projective, affine and Euclidean, and we describe how to compute a canonical representation of the cameras' projection matrices. Many applications are presented along the way to illustrate the theoretical ideas and to show how they can be used to solve real problems.

Section 10.1 extends Section 7.1 to the case of an arbitrary number of cameras and defines the notion of the canonical representation of n views, for arbitrary n.

Section 10.2 is a thorough study of the projective setting. We begin by showing that the kind of description that started with two views and the Fundamental matrix and continued with three views and the Trifocal tensors ends with four views. Even though there is such a thing as the Quadrifocal tensor, it is algebraically dependent upon the Fundamental matrices and the Trifocal tensors and therefore probably not worth studying. Moreover, beyond four views there are no further tensors and we find that the simplest way to describe the geometry of $n \geq 4$ cameras is through their projection matrices. We thus return to the case of three cameras which will be the building block in the more general case of an arbitrary number of views. We show how to compute a canonical representation of the triplet of projection matrices given either a triplet of Fundamental matrices or a Trifocal tensor. We then discuss the general case ($n \geq 4$) and present two main classes of solutions for computing a canonical representation of the n-tuple of projection matrices. The first method, called the incremental method, starts from a canonical representation of an $n - 1$-tuple of projection matrices and incorporates an nth view, yielding the desired result. In order to do this, it is only required that the new view share correspondences with two others. The second method, called the global method, is more restrictive in that it requires that all image features used in the estimation of the canonical representation are seen in all n views. The method is first described in the case of affine cameras and then extended to the general case. Before we leave the subject of the projective stratum, we describe a method for refining the canonical representation that is quite useful not only in this setting but also in the affine and Euclidean frameworks. The method, called bundle adjustment, is a minimization method that has been developed by photogrammeters and requires a good initialization such as the one produced by the incremental or global methods.

Section 10.3 is an analysis of the computation of the affine and Euclidean canonical representations of $n \geq 3$ views from the projective and affine canonical representations, respectively. In the affine case, the only extra information required to upgrade the representation from projective to affine is the infinity morphism between any of the n views. In the Euclidean case the only extra information required to upgrade the representation from affine to Euclidean is the intrinsic parameters of one of the views.

Section 10.4 deals with the case of a sequence of images that are taken by a stereo rig, rather than by a single moving camera. The fact that the geometry of the rig is kept fixed opens the door to new possibilities, including that of upgrading from a projective representation to an affine one with a single rigid displacement.

10.1   Canonical representations of n views

We now extend the remarks of Section 7.1 to the case of an arbitrary number of cameras. Let them be represented by the n-tuple of perspective projection matrices $(\boldsymbol{\mathcal{P}}_1, \cdots, \boldsymbol{\mathcal{P}}_n)$ in some image and space coordinate systems. A change of coordinates defined by an homography $\boldsymbol{\mathcal{H}}$ changes the perspective projection matrices into $(\boldsymbol{\mathcal{P}}_1\boldsymbol{\mathcal{H}}, \cdots, \boldsymbol{\mathcal{P}}_n\boldsymbol{\mathcal{H}})$. In practice, the homography belongs to one of the three groups $\mathcal{PLG}$, $\mathcal{AG}$ and $\mathcal{E}$, respectively (see Chapter 2). For a given n-tuple of projection matrices, we consider its orbit, i.e. all n-tuples obtained by multiplying each projection matrix on the right by an element of the group. All n-tuples in the same orbit are equivalent in the intuitive sense that they all correspond to the same images. Mathematically, each of these three groups acts on n-tuples of projection matrices by multiplication to the right and we are led again to the definition of the following equivalence relation:

$$(\boldsymbol{\mathcal{P}}_1, \cdots, \boldsymbol{\mathcal{P}}_n) \equiv (\boldsymbol{\mathcal{P}}'_1, \cdots, \boldsymbol{\mathcal{P}}'_n) \Longleftrightarrow \exists \boldsymbol{\mathcal{H}} \in \mathcal{G} \quad \text{such that}$$
$$\boldsymbol{\mathcal{P}}_1 = \boldsymbol{\mathcal{P}}'_1\boldsymbol{\mathcal{H}} \quad \cdots \quad \boldsymbol{\mathcal{P}}_n = \boldsymbol{\mathcal{H}}\boldsymbol{\mathcal{P}}'_n,$$

where $\mathcal{G}$ is one of the previous three groups. The equivalence classes are the orbits.

As in the case of two cameras, the next step consists of identifying within each orbit an n-tuple which is simple and using it to represent the orbit. We use the same convention as in Section 7.1 and choose $\boldsymbol{\mathcal{P}}_1 \simeq \boldsymbol{\mathcal{P}}_0$ when $\mathcal{G} = \mathcal{PLG}$ or $\mathcal{AG}$ and $\boldsymbol{\mathcal{P}}_1 \simeq \mathbf{A}_1\boldsymbol{\mathcal{P}}_0$ when $\mathcal{G} = \mathcal{E}$, where $\mathbf{A}_1$ is the matrix of the internal parameters of the first view, representing a five-parameter affine transformation of $\mathbb{P}^2$. An element of a given orbit of the form $(\boldsymbol{\mathcal{P}}_0, \cdots, \boldsymbol{\mathcal{P}}_n)$ for $\mathcal{G} = \mathcal{PLG}$ or $\mathcal{G} = \mathcal{AG}$ or of the form $(\mathbf{A}_1\boldsymbol{\mathcal{P}}_0, \cdots, \boldsymbol{\mathcal{P}}_n)$ for $\mathcal{G} = \mathcal{E}$ is called a *canonical* element of the orbit. Similarly to the two views case, there exists a four-parameter set of canonical elements in each orbit when $\mathcal{G} = \mathcal{PLG}$, a one-parameter set when $\mathcal{G} = \mathcal{AG}$ and a unique element when $\mathcal{G} = \mathcal{E}$.

10.2   Projective stratum

We show that the analysis that started with two views and the concept of the Fundamental matrix and continued with three views and the concept of the Trifocal tensor, ends with four views and the Quadrifocal tensor which is completely determined by the Fundamental matrices and the Trifocal tensors.

10.2.1 Beyond the Fundamental matrix and the Trifocal tensor

Let us consider n cameras and their projection matrices $\boldsymbol{\mathcal{P}}_1, \ldots, \boldsymbol{\mathcal{P}}_n$. A 3D point M projects as $m_1, \ldots, m_n$ in the n views. Let $[x_i, y_i, z_i]^T$ be the projective coordinates of pixel m_i. For each camera, we have the Equations 4.6

$$x_i \boldsymbol{V}_i^T \mathbf{M} - y_i \boldsymbol{U}_i^T \mathbf{M} = 0,$$
$$y_i \boldsymbol{W}_i^T \mathbf{M} - z_i \boldsymbol{V}_i^T \mathbf{M} = 0,$$
$$z_i \boldsymbol{U}_i^T \mathbf{M} - x_i \boldsymbol{W}_i^T \mathbf{M} = 0.$$

If we concatenate these $3 \times n$ equations and write them in matrix form, we obtain

$$\boldsymbol{\mathcal{A}}\mathbf{M} = \mathbf{0}, \tag{10.1}$$

where the matrix $\boldsymbol{\mathcal{A}}$ is $3 \times n$.

If we consider (10.1) to be a system of linear equations in the unknown vector $\mathbf{M}$, i.e. we assume that we are given the n projection matrices $\boldsymbol{\mathcal{P}}_i$ and the n views m_i of the 3D point M, we see that the nullspace of $\boldsymbol{\mathcal{A}}$ has to be greater than or equal to 1, and therefore its rank has to be less than or equal to 3. Indeed, if the rank were equal to 4, the only solution would be $\mathbf{M} = \mathbf{0}$ which does not represent a projective point.

A consequence of this observation is that all 4×4 minors of $\boldsymbol{\mathcal{A}}$ must be equal to 0. Let us classify those minors. They fall into three categories, those that involve two cameras, those that involve three, and those that involve four. We consider them in turn.

Proposition 10.1 *The 4×4 minors of $\boldsymbol{\mathcal{A}}$ that involve two of the n cameras express the epipolar constraint between the corresponding pixels.*

Proof : Without loss of generality, we consider the minor

$$\begin{vmatrix} x_1 \boldsymbol{V}_1^T - y_1 \boldsymbol{U}_1^T \\ y_1 \boldsymbol{W}_1^T - z_1 \boldsymbol{V}_1^T \\ y_2 \boldsymbol{W}_2^T - z_2 \boldsymbol{V}_2^T \\ z_2 \boldsymbol{U}_2^T - x_2 \boldsymbol{W}_2^T \end{vmatrix}.$$

Because of Proposition 3.25 and Theorem 3.2 it is equal to the meet

$$(x_1 \boldsymbol{V}_1 - y_1 \boldsymbol{U}_1) \vartriangle (y_1 \boldsymbol{W}_1 - z_1 \boldsymbol{V}_1) \vartriangle (y_2 \boldsymbol{W}_2 - z_2 \boldsymbol{V}_2) \vartriangle (z_2 \boldsymbol{U}_2 - x_2 \boldsymbol{W}_2).$$

We expand the first and the last two meets and obtain

$$y_1 z_2 (x_1 \boldsymbol{V}_1 \vartriangle \boldsymbol{W}_1 + y_1 \boldsymbol{W}_1 \vartriangle \boldsymbol{U}_1 + z_1 \boldsymbol{U}_1 \vartriangle \boldsymbol{V}_1) \vartriangle$$
$$(x_2 \boldsymbol{V}_2 \vartriangle \boldsymbol{W}_2 + y_2 \boldsymbol{W}_2 \vartriangle \boldsymbol{U}_2 + z_2 \boldsymbol{U}_2 \vartriangle \boldsymbol{V}_2).$$

Except for the scale factor $y_1 z_2$, each of the terms in parentheses is, according to Proposition 4.4, the optical ray of the pixels m_1 and m_2, respectively. Therefore, the nullity of the minor is equivalent to the fact that these two optical rays intersect (Proposition 3.33), and that is the way we derived the Fundamental matrix in Proposition 5.9. $\square$

If we now consider the minors involving three of the cameras, two of the rows must arise from one camera and the other two rows from two others. We have the following proposition:

Proposition 10.2 *The 4×4 minors of $\boldsymbol{A}$ that involve three of the n cameras express Trifocal constraints between the corresponding three pixels.*

Proof : Without loss of generality, we consider the minor

$$\begin{vmatrix} x_1 \boldsymbol{V}_1^T - y_1 \boldsymbol{U}_1^T \\ y_1 \boldsymbol{W}_1^T - z_1 \boldsymbol{V}_1^T \\ y_2 \boldsymbol{W}_2^T - z_2 \boldsymbol{V}_2^T \\ z_3 \boldsymbol{U}_3^T - x_3 \boldsymbol{W}_2^T \end{vmatrix}.$$

Because of Proposition 3.25 and Theorem 3.2 it is equal to the meet

$$(x_1 \boldsymbol{V}_1 - y_1 \boldsymbol{U}_1) \triangle (y_1 \boldsymbol{W}_1 - z_1 \boldsymbol{V}_1) \triangle (y_2 \boldsymbol{W}_2 - z_2 \boldsymbol{V}_2) \triangle (z_3 \boldsymbol{U}_3 - x_3 \boldsymbol{W}_3).$$

We expand the first two meets and obtain

$$y_1 (x_1 \boldsymbol{V}_1 \triangle \boldsymbol{W}_1 + y_1 \boldsymbol{W}_1 \triangle \boldsymbol{U}_1 + z_1 \boldsymbol{U}_1 \triangle \boldsymbol{V}_1) \triangle (y_2 \boldsymbol{W}_2 - z_2 \boldsymbol{V}_2) \triangle (z_3 \boldsymbol{U}_3 - x_3 \boldsymbol{W}_3),$$

and it can be verified that this is equal to

$$y_1 \mathbf{m}_1^T \boldsymbol{\mathcal{T}}_1 (\mathbf{m}_2 \times \varepsilon_1, \mathbf{m}_3 \times \varepsilon_2).$$

Except for the scale factor y_1, this is one of the trilinearities described in Section 9.1.2.2 based on the Trifocal tensor. $\square$

If we now consider the minors involving four of the cameras, each row has to arise from one different camera, and we have the following proposition:

Proposition 10.3 *The 4×4 minors of $\boldsymbol{A}$ that involve four of the n cameras express the Quadrifocal constraints between the corresponding four pixels. These constraints can be simply expressed as functions of the Trifocal and epipolar constraints.*

Proof : Without loss of generality, we consider the minor

$$Q = \begin{vmatrix} x_1 \boldsymbol{V}_1^T - y_1 \boldsymbol{U}_1^T \\ x_2 \boldsymbol{V}_2^T - y_2 \boldsymbol{U}_2^T \\ x_3 \boldsymbol{V}_3^T - y_3 \boldsymbol{U}_3^T \\ x_4 \boldsymbol{V}_4^T - y_4 \boldsymbol{U}_4^T \end{vmatrix}.$$

Because of Proposition 3.25 and Theorem 3.2 it is equal to the meet

$$(x_1 \boldsymbol{V}_1 - y_1 \boldsymbol{U}_1) \, \triangle \, (x_2 \boldsymbol{V}_2 - y_2 \boldsymbol{U}_2) \, \triangle \, (x_3 \boldsymbol{V}_3 - y_3 \boldsymbol{U}_3) \, \triangle \, (x_4 \boldsymbol{V}_4 - y_4 \boldsymbol{U}_4).$$

In order to show that this is algebraically dependent on quantities involving Fundamental matrices and Trifocal tensors, we use the Cramer relation (Proposition 3.23). We denote as $\boldsymbol{\Pi}_i$, $i = 1, 2, 3, 4$, the vectors $x_i \boldsymbol{V}_i - y_i \boldsymbol{U}_i$, and we denote as $\boldsymbol{\Pi}$ the vector $y_1 \boldsymbol{W}_1 - z_1 \boldsymbol{V}_1$. These five vectors are related by the Cramer relation

$$| \, \boldsymbol{\Pi}, \boldsymbol{\Pi}_2, \boldsymbol{\Pi}_3, \boldsymbol{\Pi}_4 \, | \, \boldsymbol{\Pi}_1 - | \, \boldsymbol{\Pi}_1, \boldsymbol{\Pi}_2, \boldsymbol{\Pi}_3, \boldsymbol{\Pi}_4 \, | \, \boldsymbol{\Pi} +$$
$$| \, \boldsymbol{\Pi}_1, \boldsymbol{\Pi}, \boldsymbol{\Pi}_3, \boldsymbol{\Pi}_4 \, | \, \boldsymbol{\Pi}_2 - | \, \boldsymbol{\Pi}_1, \boldsymbol{\Pi}, \boldsymbol{\Pi}_2, \boldsymbol{\Pi}_4 \, | \, \boldsymbol{\Pi}_3 +$$
$$| \, \boldsymbol{\Pi}_1, \boldsymbol{\Pi}, \boldsymbol{\Pi}_2, \boldsymbol{\Pi}_3 \, | \, \boldsymbol{\Pi}_4 = \boldsymbol{0}.$$

We take the meet of both sides of this equation on the right with $\boldsymbol{\Pi}_1 \, \triangle \, \boldsymbol{U}_2 \, \triangle \, \boldsymbol{V}_2$. This eliminates the first and third term of the previous sum. We obtain

$$Q \, | \, \boldsymbol{\Pi}_1, \boldsymbol{\Pi}, \boldsymbol{U}_2, \boldsymbol{V}_2 \, | + | \, \boldsymbol{\Pi}_1, \boldsymbol{\Pi}, \boldsymbol{\Pi}_2, \boldsymbol{\Pi}_4 \, | \, | \, \boldsymbol{\Pi}_1, \boldsymbol{\Pi}_3, \boldsymbol{U}_2, \boldsymbol{V}_2 \, | -$$
$$| \, \boldsymbol{\Pi}_1, \boldsymbol{\Pi}, \boldsymbol{\Pi}_2, \boldsymbol{\Pi}_3 \, | \, | \, \boldsymbol{\Pi}_1, \boldsymbol{\Pi}_4, \boldsymbol{U}_2, \boldsymbol{V}_2 \, | = 0.$$

The coefficient of Q is equal to $y_1 (\mathbf{F}_{12} \mathbf{m}_1)_3$ (Proposition 5.9). The other two terms involve only the Trifocal tensors. In detail $| \, \boldsymbol{\Pi}_1, \boldsymbol{\Pi}, \boldsymbol{\Pi}_2, \boldsymbol{\Pi}_4 \, |$ and $| \, \boldsymbol{\Pi}_1, \boldsymbol{\Pi}_4, \boldsymbol{U}_2, \boldsymbol{V}_2 \, |$ involve two of the Trifocal tensors between views 1, 2 and 4. $| \, \boldsymbol{\Pi}_1, \boldsymbol{\Pi}_3, \boldsymbol{U}_2, \boldsymbol{V}_2 \, |$ and $| \, \boldsymbol{\Pi}_1, \boldsymbol{\Pi}, \boldsymbol{\Pi}_2, \boldsymbol{\Pi}_3 \, |$ involve two of the Trifocal tensors between views 1, 2 and 3. $\square$

Proposition 10.3 shows that Quadrifocal tensors do exist but do not add more information than the Fundamental matrices and the Trifocal tensors. Therefore, when we consider more than three views it is unnecessary to attempt to generalize the ideas of the Fundamental matrices and Trifocal tensors: There is such a generalization for four views but it is completely determined by the the lower order tensors and there is no such thing for more than four views.

10.2.2 The projection matrices: Three views

According to the previous section, it is unnecessary to worry about higher order relations between views than those provided by the binocular and trinocular constraints that have been studied in Chapters 5 and 8. Therefore, in the case of four and more views we will use only the binocular and trinocular constraints to compute the projection matrices of the views.

We start with the case of three views which we will then generalize to an arbitrary number of views. Suppose that we have estimated all three Fundamental matrices and that they are compatible in the sense of Chapter 8, definition 8.1. The question that we address again is what kind of 3D information can we extract about the world.

As in the case of three views analyzed in Chapter 7, the answer turns out to be that only projective information can be recovered from the Fundamental matrices. We show this explicitly by computing the canonical representation of the triple $(\mathcal{P}_1, \mathcal{P}_2, \mathcal{P}_3)$. Similarly to the two views case, there is a four-parameter family of matrices $(\mathcal{P}_2, \mathcal{P}_3)$ such that that $\mathcal{P}_1 \simeq \mathcal{P}_0$ and the three Fundamental matrices obtained from those three perspective projection matrices are proportional to the given Fundamental matrices.

Proposition 10.4 *For a given triple of compatible Fundamental matrices* $(\mathbf{F}_{12}, \mathbf{F}_{23}, \mathbf{F}_{31})$ *(see definition 8.1), the condition* $\mathcal{P} \simeq \mathcal{P}_0$ *implies that* $\mathcal{P}_2$ *and* $\mathcal{P}_3$ *take the simple forms*

$$\mathcal{P}_2 = \left[\mathbf{S}_{12} + \mathbf{e}_{21} \mathbf{r}_2^T \; \mu_2 \mathbf{e}_{21} \right] = \left[\mathbf{S}_{12}, \mathbf{e}_{21} \right] \begin{bmatrix} \mathbf{I}_3 & \mathbf{0}_3 \\ \mathbf{r}_2^T & \mu_2 \end{bmatrix} \tag{10.2}$$

and

$$\mathcal{P}_3 = \left[\mathbf{S}_{13} + \mathbf{e}_{31} \mathbf{r}_3^T \; \mu_3 \mathbf{e}_{31} \right] = \left[\mathbf{S}_{13}, \mathbf{e}_{31} \right] \begin{bmatrix} \mathbf{I}_3 & \mathbf{0}_3 \\ \mathbf{r}_3^T & \mu_3 \end{bmatrix}. \tag{10.3}$$

The values of μ_2 *and* μ_3 *satisfy the relation*

$$\mu_2 \; : \; \mu_3 = -\mathbf{S}_{12}^T \mathbf{F}_{23}^T \mathbf{e}_{31} \; : \; \mathbf{S}_{13}^T \mathbf{F}_{23} \mathbf{e}_{21}.$$

The vectors appearing on the right-hand side are parallel, representing the Trifocal line t_1 *in the first image. The vectors* $\mathbf{r}_2$ *and* $\mathbf{r}_3$ *can be related by*

$$\mathbf{r}_2 + \alpha \mathbf{r}_3 = \mathbf{r},$$

where $\alpha = -\mu_2/\mu_3$ *and* $\mathbf{r}$ *is a vector which can be computed from the three Fundamental matrices and the epipoles, as explained in the proof.*

Proof : Equations 10.2 and 10.3 are immediate consequences of Proposition 10.4. $\mathbf{r}_2$ (respectively $\mathbf{r}_3$) is the image in view 1 of the line of intersection of an arbitrary plane Π_1 (respectively Π_2) not going through the optical center C_1 with the intrinsic plane of the second camera with respect to the first view, i.e. determined by the line represented by $\mathbf{e}_{21}$ (respectively with the intrinsic plane of the third camera with respect to the first view, i.e. determined by the line represented by $\mathbf{e}_{31}$). We have so far only taken into account the Fundamental matrices $\mathbf{F}_{12}$ and $\mathbf{F}_{13}$. The consideration of $\mathbf{F}_{23}$ allows us to show that if $\mathbf{r}_2$ and μ_2 are given, $\mathbf{r}_3$ and μ_3 are fixed.

Consider a projective point P represented by the vector $[\mathbf{p}^T, q]$ in the current projective frame. Its image p_2 in view 2 is represented by

$$\mathbf{p}_2 \simeq \mathcal{P}_2 \mathbf{P} \simeq \mathbf{S}_{12} \mathbf{p} + (\mathbf{r}_2^T \mathbf{p} + \mu_2 q) \mathbf{e}_{21}.$$

Similarly, its image p_3 in view 3 is represented by

$$\mathbf{p}_3 \simeq \mathcal{P}_3 \mathbf{P} \simeq \mathbf{S}_{13} \mathbf{p} + (\mathbf{r}_3^T \mathbf{p} + \mu_3 q) \mathbf{e}_{31}.$$

We now express the fact that $\mathbf{p}_3^T \mathbf{F}_{23} \mathbf{p}_2$ must be 0 for all points P. We use the fact that since the three Fundamental matrices are compatible, $\mathbf{e}_{31}^T \mathbf{F}_{23} \mathbf{e}_{21} = 0$, and obtain $\mathbf{p}_3^T \mathbf{F}_{23} \mathbf{p}_2 = \mathbf{P}^T \mathcal{A} \mathbf{P}$.

The 4×4 matrix $\mathcal{A}$ is given by

$$\mathcal{A} \simeq \left[\begin{array}{cc} \mathbf{B} + \mathbf{r}_2 \mathbf{u}^T + \mathbf{r}_3 \mathbf{v}^T & \mathbf{0}_3 \\ \mu_2 \mathbf{u}^T + \mu_3 \mathbf{v}^T & 0 \end{array} \right],$$

where the matrix $\mathbf{B} = \mathbf{S}_{13}^T \mathbf{F}_{23} \mathbf{S}_{12}$, the vector $\mathbf{u}^T = \mathbf{e}_{21}^T \mathbf{F}_{23}^T \mathbf{S}_{13}$ and the vector $\mathbf{v}^T = \mathbf{e}_{31}^T \mathbf{F}_{23} \mathbf{S}_{12}$. The condition $\mathbf{P}^T \mathcal{A} \mathbf{P} = 0$ for all $\mathbf{P}$ is therefore equivalent to the two conditions

$$\mu_2 \mathbf{u} + \mu_3 \mathbf{v} = \mathbf{0},$$

and the matrix $\mathbf{C} = \mathbf{B} + \mathbf{r}_2 \mathbf{u}^T + \mathbf{r}_3 \mathbf{v}^T$ being antisymmetric.

The reader will easily convince himself that the two vectors $\mathbf{u}$ and $\mathbf{v}$ are two representations of the Trifocal line t_1 in the first image. Let us verify this for $\mathbf{u}$. From Chapter 8, Section 8.1.1, we know that the vector $\mathbf{F}_{23} \mathbf{e}_{21}$ represents the Trifocal line t_3. The matrix $\mathbf{S}_{13}^T \simeq \mathbf{F}_{13}^T [\mathbf{e}_{31}]_\times = \mathbf{F}_{31} [\mathbf{e}_{31}]_\times$ represents a planar morphism from the set of lines in image 3 to the set of lines in image 1. Applying it to the Trifocal line t_3 is therefore equivalent to applying $\mathbf{F}_{31}$ to the point of intersection of t_3 and the line represented by the vector $\mathbf{e}_{31}$. Since this is a point of t_3, when we apply $\mathbf{F}_{31}$ to it we obtain its epipolar line in the first image, i.e. t_1. The first of the two conditions therefore determines $\mu_2 : \mu_3$ as stated in the proposition.

Let us now write $\mathbf{v} = \alpha \mathbf{u}$, where $\alpha = -\mu_2 / \mu_3$ is known. Using the definitions $\mathbf{S}_{ij} = [\mathbf{e}_{ji}]_\times \mathbf{F}_{ij}$ (we can scale the three Fundamental matrices so that this is true), the second condition $\mathbf{C} + \mathbf{C}^T = \mathbf{0}$ can be rewritten as

$$(\mathbf{r}_2 + \alpha \mathbf{r}_3) \mathbf{u}^T + \mathbf{u} (\mathbf{r}_2 + \alpha \mathbf{r}_3)^T =$$
$$\mathbf{F}_{13}^T [\mathbf{e}_{31}]_\times \mathbf{F}_{23} [\mathbf{e}_{21}]_\times \mathbf{F}_{12} + \mathbf{F}_{12}^T [\mathbf{e}_{21}]_\times \mathbf{F}_{23}^T [\mathbf{e}_{31}]_\times \mathbf{F}_{13} \equiv \mathbf{D}.$$

We note that the left-hand side is a matrix of rank 2, and that its nullspace is generated by the vector $(\mathbf{r}_2 + \alpha \mathbf{r}_3) \times \mathbf{u}$. Similarly, the right-hand side is also of rank two since $\mathbf{D}\mathbf{e}_{12} \simeq \mathbf{D}\mathbf{e}_{13}$, each vector being a representation of the Trifocal line t_1. Let us verify it for example for $\mathbf{D}\mathbf{e}_{12}$. Up to the sign, it is the sum of $\mathbf{B}\mathbf{e}_{12}$, which is equal to $\mathbf{0}$ since $\mathbf{S}_{12}\mathbf{e}_{12} = \mathbf{0}$ and, $\mathbf{B}^T \mathbf{e}_{12} = \mathbf{S}_{12}^T \mathbf{F}_{23}^T \mathbf{S}_{13} \mathbf{e}_{12}$. According to the previous discussion, $\mathbf{S}_{13} \mathbf{e}_{12} = [\mathbf{e}_{31}]_\times \mathbf{F}_{13} \mathbf{e}_{12}$ represents a point on the Trifocal line t_3 which is mapped by $\mathbf{F}_{23}^T = \mathbf{F}_{32}$ to the Trifocal line t_2, which in turn is mapped by $\mathbf{S}_{12}^T$ to the Trifocal line t_1. We have verified that $\mathbf{D}\mathbf{e}_{12}$ is a representation of t_1. We can therefore compute two numbers β and γ such that $\mathbf{D}(\beta \mathbf{e}_{12} + \gamma \mathbf{e}_{13}) = \mathbf{0}$.

There is a slight difficulty here with respect to the choice of scale for the two vectors $\mathbf{e}_{12}$ and $\mathbf{e}_{13}$. We know from our discussions in Chapter 7 that in order to write $\mathcal{P}_2$ and $\mathcal{P}_3$ as in Equations 10.2 and 10.3, we fixed the scale of the vectors $\mathbf{e}_{21}$ and $\mathbf{e}_{31}$ but *not* of $\mathbf{e}_{12}$ and $\mathbf{e}_{13}$. In order to compute β and γ, we need to fix their scale. The simplest way to do this is to assume that they have unit norm. The final result does not, of course, depend on this choice.

Therefore we must have $\beta \mathbf{e}_{12} + \gamma \mathbf{e}_{13} \simeq (\mathbf{r}_2 + \alpha \mathbf{r}_3) \times \mathbf{u}$. Let us denote $\mathbf{s}$ the known vector $\beta \mathbf{e}_{12} + \gamma \mathbf{e}_{13}$; it is orthogonal to $\mathbf{u}$ since the epipoles $\mathbf{e}_{12}$ and $\mathbf{e}_{13}$ are on the Trifocal line t_1 represented by $\mathbf{u}$. This implies that the vector $\mathbf{r} = \mathbf{r}_2 + \alpha \mathbf{r}_3$ is a linear combination of $\mathbf{u}$ and $\mathbf{u} \times \mathbf{s}$:

$$\mathbf{r} = a\mathbf{u} + b\mathbf{u} \times \mathbf{s}.$$

Rewriting the constraint $\mathbf{C} + \mathbf{C}^T = \mathbf{0}$ as a function of the unknowns a and b, the known vectors $\mathbf{u}$ and $\mathbf{s}$ and the known matrix $\mathbf{D}$, we obtain

$$2a\mathbf{u}\mathbf{u}^T + b\left[(\mathbf{u} \times \mathbf{s})\mathbf{u}^T + \mathbf{u}(\mathbf{u} \times \mathbf{s})^T\right] = \mathbf{D}.$$

Applying both sides of the equation to the known vector $\mathbf{u}$, we obtain a vector equation that yields the values of a and b:

$$(2a\mathbf{u} + b(\mathbf{u} \times \mathbf{s}))\|\mathbf{u}\|^2 = \mathbf{D}\mathbf{u}.$$

The explicit values are

$$a = \frac{1}{2}\frac{\mathbf{u}^T\mathbf{D}\mathbf{u}}{\|\mathbf{u}\|^4},$$

$$b = \frac{(\mathbf{u} \times \mathbf{s})^T\mathbf{D}\mathbf{u}}{\|\mathbf{u} \times \mathbf{s}\|^2\|\mathbf{u}\|^2}.$$

From the values of a and b and the relation $\mathbf{r}_2 + \alpha \mathbf{r}_3 = \mathbf{r} = a\mathbf{u} + b\mathbf{u} \times \mathbf{s}$ we conclude that, given $\mathbf{r}_2$, we can compute $\mathbf{r}_3$.

Note that the proof gives an explicit way of computing the quantities $(\mathbf{r}_3, \mu_3)$ as functions of $(\mathbf{r}_2, \mu_2)$ from the three Fundamental matrices, the two epipoles (e_{12}, e_{13}) in the first image, the epipole e_{21} in the second image and the epipole e_{31} in the third image. $\square$

Unfortunately, the previous method for computing $\mathcal{P}_2$ and $\mathcal{P}_3$ fails if, for example, the three optical centers are aligned since in that case the Trifocal lines are not defined. Therefore we need another method for that case. Moreover, if we have estimated the Trifocal tensor between the three views using the methods described in Chapter 9, we would like to use it directly to compute the perspective projection matrices without going through the Fundamental matrices. We are going to show that if we use the Trifocal tensor which, as seen in Chapter 8, does not induce degeneracies in the case of aligned optical centers, we do not run into any problems. The method developed will also provide a direct way of computing the perspective projection matrices from the Trifocal tensor.

Proposition 10.5 *For a given Trifocal tensor $\mathcal{T}$, the condition $\mathcal{P}_1 \simeq \mathcal{P}_0$ implies that $\mathcal{P}_2$ and $\mathcal{P}_3$ take the simple forms (10.2) and (10.3). The ratio of μ_2 and μ_3 satisfies the relation*

$$\mu_2 : \mu_3 = \mid \mathcal{T}(l_2, l_3), \mathcal{T}(e_{21}, e_{31}), S_{12}^T l_2 \mid \cdot (l_3^T e_{31}) :$$

$$\mid \mathcal{T}(l_2, l_3), \mathcal{T}(e_{21}, e_{31}), S_{13}^T l_3 \mid \cdot (l_2^T e_{21}) \quad (10.4)$$

for "almost all" pairs (l_2, l_3) of lines in images 2 and 3, respectively. What we mean by "almost all" is detailed in the proof. The vectors r_2 and r_3 are related by

$$\alpha r_3 - r_2 = r, \quad (10.5)$$

where $\alpha = \frac{\mu_2}{\mu_3}$, and r is given by

$$r = \beta \frac{\mathcal{T}(e_{21}, e_{31})}{\|e_{21}\|^2 \cdot \|e_{31}\|^2}, \quad (10.6)$$

with

$$\beta = \frac{\mid S_{12}^T l_2, S_{13}^T l_3, \mathcal{T}(e_{21}, e_{31}) \mid \cdot (l_3^T e_{31})}{\mid S_{13}^T l_3, \mathcal{T}(l_2, l_3), \mathcal{T}(e_{21}, e_{31}) \mid}. \quad (10.7)$$

It is always possible to find two lines l_2 and l_3 such that Equations 10.4 and 10.7 are well-defined and β is nonzero.

*When the three projection matrices take this form, we say that they are in **projective canonical form**.*

Proof :   We know from Chapter 8 that the two Fundamental matrices F_{12} and F_{13} are easily computed from $\mathcal{T}$, thus explaining Equations 10.2 and 10.3. Instead of using F_{23} as in the proof of Proposition 10.4, we use the Trifocal tensor. From Equations 10.2 and 10.3, using Equations 8.12, 8.13 and 8.14, we can write the matrices G^n of $\mathcal{T}$ as functions of the matrices S_{12}, S_{13}, the vectors r_2 and r_3 and the two numbers μ_2 and μ_3:

$$G^n \simeq \mu_2 e_{21} S_{13}^{(n) T} - \mu_3 S_{12}^{(n)} e_{31}^T + (\mu_2 r_3^n - \mu_3 r_2^n) e_{21} e_{31}^T, \ n = 1, 2, 3,$$

where r_2^n and r_3^n are the nth coordinates of the vectors r_2 and r_3. It is important to note that we have written "$\simeq$" and not "$=$". This is because the given Trifocal tensor $\mathcal{T}$ is only proportional, not equal, to the one computed from the three perspective projection matrices. Note that the scale factor is global, i.e. it is the same for the three matrices G^n. Since the right-hand side of the previous equation is homogeneous in (μ_2, μ_3), the scale factor can be written $1/(a\mu_2 + b\mu_3)$, where a and b are unknown:

$$G^n = \frac{1}{a\mu_2 + b\mu_3} \left(\mu_2 e_{21} S_{13}^{(n) T} - \mu_3 S_{12}^{(n)} e_{31}^T + (\mu_2 r_3^n - \mu_3 r_2^n) e_{21} e_{31}^T \right),$$

$$n = 1, 2, 3. \quad (10.8)$$

Note that we have necessarily $a\mu_2 + b\mu_3 \neq 0$.

Let us now compute $\mathcal{T}(\mathbf{e}_{21}, \mathbf{e}_{31})$ using those expressions. Since ${\mathbf{S}_{13}^{(n)}}^T \mathbf{e}_{31} = {\mathbf{S}_{12}^{(n)}}^T \mathbf{e}_{21} = 0 \; n = 1, 2, 3$, we have

$$\frac{\mathcal{T}(\mathbf{e}_{21}, \mathbf{e}_{31})}{\|\mathbf{e}_{21}\|^2 \cdot \|\mathbf{e}_{31}\|^2} = \frac{\mu_2 \mathbf{r}_3 - \mu_3 \mathbf{r}_2}{a\mu_2 + b\mu_3}.$$

Therefore

$$\frac{\mu_2}{\mu_3}\mathbf{r}_3 - \mathbf{r}_2 = \left(b + a\frac{\mu_2}{\mu_3}\right)\frac{\mathcal{T}(\mathbf{e}_{21}, \mathbf{e}_{31})}{\|\mathbf{e}_{21}\|^2 \cdot \|\mathbf{e}_{31}\|^2}.$$

Let $\alpha = \frac{\mu_2}{\mu_3}$ and $\beta = a\alpha + b$, and rewrite the previous equation

$$\alpha \mathbf{r}_3 - \mathbf{r}_2 = \beta \frac{\mathcal{T}(\mathbf{e}_{21}, \mathbf{e}_{31})}{\|\mathbf{e}_{21}\|^2 \cdot \|\mathbf{e}_{31}\|^2}.$$

Let us now consider an arbitrary pair (l_2, l_3) of lines in images 2 and 3, respectively. Using the previous equation, we can eliminate the term $\frac{\mu_2 \mathbf{r}_3 - \mu_3 \mathbf{r}_2}{a\mu_2 + b\mu_3}$ from Equation 10.8 and write

$$\mathcal{T}(\mathbf{l}_2, \mathbf{l}_3) = \frac{\mathcal{T}(\mathbf{e}_{21}, \mathbf{e}_{31})}{\|\mathbf{e}_{21}\|^2 \cdot \|\mathbf{e}_{31}\|^2}(\mathbf{e}_{21}^T \mathbf{l}_2)(\mathbf{e}_{31}^T \mathbf{l}_3) +$$
$$\frac{1}{a\mu_2 + b\mu_3}\left(\mu_2(\mathbf{e}_{21}^T \mathbf{l}_2)\mathbf{S}_{13}^T \mathbf{l}_3 - \mu_3(\mathbf{e}_{31}^T \mathbf{l}_3)\mathbf{S}_{12}^T \mathbf{l}_2\right).$$

We then note that for each point m of the line l_{23} represented by $\mathcal{T}(\mathbf{e}_{21}, \mathbf{e}_{31})$ we have

$$\mathbf{m}^T \mathcal{T}(\mathbf{l}_2, \mathbf{l}_3) = \frac{1}{a\mu_2 + b\mu_3}\left(\mu_2(\mathbf{e}_{21}^T \mathbf{l}_2)(\mathbf{m}^T \mathbf{S}_{13}^T \mathbf{l}_3) - \mu_3(\mathbf{e}_{31}^T \mathbf{l}_3)(\mathbf{m}^T \mathbf{S}_{12}^T \mathbf{l}_2)\right). \quad (10.9)$$

Choosing two arbitrary points on l_{23} yields α. Let us for example choose the following two points: m_3 represented by $\mathbf{S}_{13}^T \mathbf{l}_3 \times \mathbf{l}_{23}$ and m_2 by $\mathbf{S}_{12}^T \mathbf{l}_2 \times \mathbf{l}_{23}$. Taking $m = m_2$, $m = m_3$ in Equation 10.9, and taking the ratio to eliminate $a\mu_2 + b\mu_3$, we obtain the ratio $\mu_2 : \mu_3$

$$\frac{\mathbf{m}_2^T \mathcal{T}(\mathbf{l}_2, \mathbf{l}_3)}{\mathbf{m}_3^T \mathcal{T}(\mathbf{l}_2, \mathbf{l}_3)} = -\frac{\mu_2}{\mu_3}\frac{(\mathbf{l}_2^T \mathbf{e}_{21})(\mathbf{m}_2^T \mathbf{S}_{13}^T \mathbf{l}_3)}{(\mathbf{l}_3^T \mathbf{e}_{31})(\mathbf{m}_3^T \mathbf{S}_{12}^T \mathbf{l}_2)}.$$

We notice that $\mathbf{m}_3^T \mathbf{S}_{12}^T \mathbf{l}_2 = -\mathbf{m}_2^T \mathbf{S}_{13}^T \mathbf{l}_3$ and obtain Equation 10.4. Having obtained $\alpha = \mu_2/\mu_3$, it is easy to obtain $\beta = a\alpha + b$ from Equation 10.9: Choosing $m = m_3$ we obtain Equation 10.7.

Since both μ_2 and μ_3 are nonzero, the method fails when any of the factors in Equations 10.4 and 10.7 become zero. The question thus is, can we choose the two lines l_2 and l_3 so that this does not happen?

The factor $\mathbf{l}_2^T \mathbf{e}_{21}$ (respectively $\mathbf{l}_3^T \mathbf{e}_{31}$) becomes zero if and only if l_2 (respectively l_3) is an epipolar line for the pair $(1, 2)$ (respectively $(1, 3)$). The factor $\mathbf{S}_{12}^T \mathbf{l}_2$ (respectively $\mathbf{S}_{13}^T \mathbf{l}_3$) is zero if and only if $l_2 = e_{21}$ (respectively $l_3 = e_{31}$). The vector $\mathcal{T}(\mathbf{e}_{21}, \mathbf{e}_{31})$ is never zero. Otherwise it would imply that the line of intersection of the two planes (C_2, e_{21}) and (C_3, e_{31}) would go through C_1 and therefore that those two planes would be epipolar planes for the pairs $(1, 2)$ and $(1, 3)$, respectively. But this is impossible since the two lines e_{21} and e_{31} do not, by construction, go through the epipoles e_{21} and e_{31}. Similarly, the line l_{23} does not go through either of the epipoles e_{12} or e_{13}. To summarize, we have so far eliminated the following possibilities:

- l_2 (respectively l_3) is not an epipolar line for the pair $(1, 2)$ (respectively $(1, 3)$) of views;

- l_2 (respectively l_3) is different from the line e_{21} (respectively e_{31}).

According to Theorem 8.1, the term $\mathcal{T}(\mathbf{l}_2, \mathbf{l}_3)$ is equal to $\mathbf{0}$ if and only if the pair (l_2, l_3) is a pair of corresponding epipolar lines for the pair $(2, 3)$ of views, or a pair of non-corresponding epipolar lines if the three optical centers are aligned. Therefore we must also eliminate those possibilities.

Having done this, the only remaining requirements are that both determinants in the numerator and denominator of (10.4) are nonzero. Geometrically this is equivalent to choosing l_2 and l_3 in such a way that $\mathcal{T}(\mathbf{l}_2, \mathbf{l}_3)$ does not go through either m_2 or m_3 and this is always possible. A feeling for this can be obtained by looking at Figure 10.1. $\square$

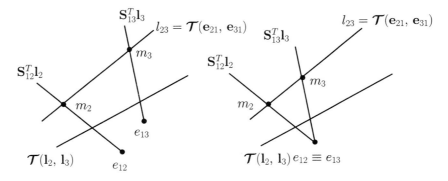

Figure 10.1: The choice of the point m on the line l_{23} (see text).

10.2.3 The projection matrices: An arbitrary number of views

We now deal with the general problem of computing the projective canonical representations of an arbitrary number n of views from a set of Fundamental matrices and Trifocal tensors. We present two techniques for achieving this. The first method is sequential and does not require all feature points to be seen in all views. The second method is global and requires that all feature points are seen in all views.

10.2.3.1 The incremental method

We have seen in the previous section how to compute a four-parameter family of perspective projection matrices for three cameras given their three Fundamental matrices or one of their Trifocal tensors. This can be extended to an arbitrary number n, $n > 3$.

Suppose we have a canonical representation of $n - 1$ views. What this means is that we have chosen one of the $n - 1$ views as the reference (we will assume without loss of generality that it is view 1) and a plane of reference Π not going through C_1, so that we can write

$$\mathcal{P}_1 \simeq \mathcal{P}_0,$$

and

$$\mathcal{P}_i = \left[\mathbf{S}_{1i} + \mathbf{e}_{i1} \mathbf{r}_i^T \, \mu_i \mathbf{e}_{i1} \right] \quad i = 2, \dots, n - 1.$$

As we have written it, each perspective projection matrix $\mathcal{P}_i$, $i = 2, \dots, n - 1$, is defined by the special matrix $\mathbf{S}_{1i}$ and the epipole e_{i1} with view 1, the vector $\mathbf{r}_i$ representing the image of the line of intersection of the reference plane Π with the intrinsic plane of view i with respect to view 1 and the scalar μ_i. It will be sufficient for the rest of the discussion to assume that $\mathcal{P}_i$ is given as

$$\mathcal{P}_i = \left[\mathbf{H}_{1i,\Pi} \, \mu_i \mathbf{e}_{i1} \right],$$

where $\mathbf{H}_{1i,\Pi} = \mathbf{S}_{1i} + \mathbf{e}_{i1} \mathbf{r}_i^T$ represents the homography induced by Π between view 1 and i. Let us also note that, because of Proposition 7.2, in the canonical frame of the first $n - 1$ views, the plane Π is represented by the vector $\mathbf{\Pi} = [0, 0, 0, 1]^T$.

We now acquire an nth view. Given the three Fundamental matrices or the Trifocal tensor of two previous views i and j ($1 \le i, j \le n - 1$) and the new view, we can construct a canonical representation for the triplet (i, j, n). In this representation, the perspective projection matrices $(\mathcal{P}_i', \mathcal{P}_j', \mathcal{P}_n')$ are such that $\mathcal{P}_i' \simeq \mathcal{P}_0$ and $\mathcal{P}_n'$ and $\mathcal{P}_j'$ are given by Equations 10.2 and 10.3. In detail, we have

$$\mathcal{P}_j' = \left[\mathbf{S}_{ij} + \mathbf{e}_{ji} \mathbf{r}_j'^T \, \mu_j' \mathbf{e}_{ji} \right]$$

and

$$\mathcal{P}_n' = \left[\mathbf{S}_{in} + \mathbf{e}_{ni} \mathbf{r}_n'^T \, \mu_n' \mathbf{e}_{ni} \right].$$

This is shown in Figure 10.2. The vectors $\mathbf{r}_j'$ and $\mathbf{r}_n'$ on the one hand, the two scalars μ_j' and μ_n' on the other, are related as explained in Propositions 10.4 and 10.5.

The problem is that the canonical representation of the first $n - 1$ views provides two different expressions for the perspective projection matrices of the views i and

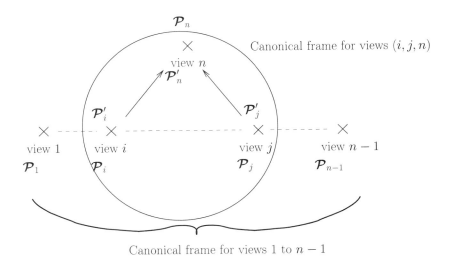

Figure 10.2: Stitching view n to views 1 to $n-1$.

j since the reference view is view 1, corresponding to two different projective bases. In order to "integrate" view n among the first $n-1$ views we need to choose the reference plane Π' that defines $\mathbf{r}'_j$ and $\mathbf{r}'_n$ to be the same, i.e. Π, as the one defined by $\mathbf{r}_i$ and $\mathbf{r}_j$. The difficulty is that $\mathbf{r}_j$ and $\mathbf{r}'_j$ are defined with respect to the first and the nth cameras, respectively, i.e. with respect to two different projective bases. Therefore, given $\mathbf{r}_j$, it is not completely obvious how to choose $\mathbf{r}'_j$. Note that since Π' does not go through C_i by definition, the same must be true of Π. This can be easily checked by considering the rank of $\mathbf{H}_{1i,\Pi}$. If necessary, the reference plane should be changed and the canonical representation of the first $n-1$ views upgraded accordingly.

We denote by $H_{ij,\Pi'}$ the homography induced between the image planes i and j by the plane Π' defined by the vector $\mathbf{r}'_j$ or the vector $\mathbf{r}'_n$. We show how to compute $\mathbf{r}'_j$ and μ'_j, i.e. how to choose the canonical frame of the triplet (i, j, n), so that when we return to the canonical frame of the first $n-1$ views we obtain the correct perspective projection matrices for views i and j. Let $\mathbf{H}_i$ be a matrix representing the change of projective coordinates from the canonical frame of the triplet (i, j, n) to the canonical frame of the first $n-1$ views. Such a matrix is given by

$$\mathbf{H}_i = \left[\begin{array}{c} \boldsymbol{\mathcal{P}}_i \\ \boldsymbol{\Pi}^T \end{array} \right].$$

We verify that $\boldsymbol{\mathcal{P}}_i \simeq \boldsymbol{\mathcal{P}}'_i \mathbf{H}_i \simeq \boldsymbol{\mathcal{P}}_0 \mathbf{H}_i$ and the condition we seek is

$$\boldsymbol{\mathcal{P}}_j \simeq \boldsymbol{\mathcal{P}}'_j \mathbf{H}_i$$

The main result is summarized in the following proposition:

Proposition 10.6 *The nth view can be stitched to the first $n-1$ views linearly from the canonical representation of any three views (i, j, n), $i, j = 1, \ldots, n - 1$. This means that the perspective projection matrix $\mathcal{P}_n$ of the nth view in the canonical frame of the first $n-1$ views can be computed linearly from the canonical representations of the first $n-1$ views and of the views (i, j, n).*

Proof :   Remember that, from Proposition 5.16, the vector $\mathbf{r}'_j$ is the image in view i of the line of intersection of the intrinsic plane of camera j and the plane Π. Therefore we have

$$\mathbf{r}'_j \simeq \tilde{\mathcal{P}}_i \left(\Pi \bigtriangleup \mathcal{P}_j^T \mathbf{e}_{ji} \right).$$

In detail, let $\boldsymbol{U}_i, \boldsymbol{V}_i, \boldsymbol{W}_i$ be the three row vectors of matrix $\mathcal{P}_i$ and let us denote Π_{ji} the vector $\mathcal{P}_j^T \mathbf{e}_{ji}$. Because of Proposition 4.11, we have

$$\mathbf{r}'_j \simeq [\,|\,\boldsymbol{V}_i, \boldsymbol{W}_i, \Pi, \Pi_{ji}\,|, \,|\,\boldsymbol{W}_i, \boldsymbol{U}_i, \Pi, \Pi_{ji}\,|, \,|\,\boldsymbol{U}_i, \boldsymbol{V}_i, \Pi, \Pi_{ji}\,|\,].$$

Since all quantities on the right-hand side are known, this yields the direction of $\mathbf{r}'_j$, a unit vector that we denote $\mathbf{r}'_{jN}$. We have therefore $\mathbf{r}'_j = \alpha'_j \mathbf{r}'_{jN}$. The scalar α'_j is computed by enforcing

$$\left(\mathbf{S}_{ij} + \alpha'_j \mathbf{e}_{ji} \mathbf{r}'^{T}_{jN} \right) \mathbf{H}_{1i,\Pi} \simeq \mathbf{H}_{1j,\Pi}, \qquad (10.10)$$

which ensures that the diagram of Figure 10.3 is commutative and yields α'_j linearly.

Note that the assumption that Π does not go through C_i is essential here because, were it not the case, the determinant of $\mathbf{H}_{1i,\Pi}$ would be 0 and, if the determinant of $\mathbf{H}_{1j,\Pi}$ were nonzero, Equation 10.10 would be impossible.

We have therefore determined $\mathbf{r}'_j$ and, because of Proposition 10.4 or 10.5, this also determines $\mathbf{r}'_n$. Since, because of the same propositions, the ratio $\mu'_n : \mu'_j$ is also known, there remains to fix one of the ratios $\mu'_j : \mu_k$, $k = 2, \cdots, n - 1$. We compute the ratio $\mu'_j : \mu_i$.

This is achieved by going back to the canonical system of the first $n-1$ views and multiplying $\mathcal{P}'_i, \mathcal{P}'_j$ (and of course $\mathcal{P}'_n$) on the right by the 4×4 matrix

$$\mathbf{H}_i = \left[\begin{array}{c} \mathcal{P}_i \\ \Pi^T \end{array} \right],$$

to obtain the original matrices $\mathcal{P}_i$ and $\mathcal{P}_j$. This is obviously true for view i. Taking into account the fact that $\Pi = [0, 0, 0, 1]^T$, we find

$$\mathcal{P}'_j \mathbf{H}_i = \left[\left(\mathbf{S}_{ij} + \mathbf{e}_{ji} \mathbf{r}'^{T}_j \right) \mathbf{H}_{1i,\Pi}, \; \mu_i \left(\mathbf{S}_{ij} + \mathbf{e}_{ji} \mathbf{r}'^{T}_j \right) \mathbf{e}_{i1} + \mu'_j \mathbf{e}_{ji} \right].$$

Our choice of $\mathbf{r}'_j$ guarantees the existence of an α (and we can compute it from

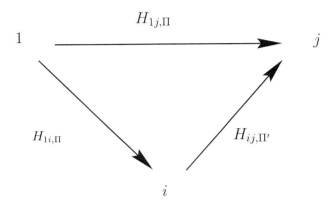

Figure 10.3: We choose $\mathbf{r}'_j$ in such a way that $H_{ij,\Pi'} \circ H_{1i,\Pi} = H_{1j,\Pi}$.

Equation 10.10) such that

$$\left(\mathbf{S}_{ij} + \mathbf{e}_{ji}\mathbf{r}'^{T}_{j}\right)\mathbf{H}_{1i,\Pi} = \alpha\mathbf{H}_{1j,\Pi}.$$

The ratio $\mu'_j : \mu_i$ is therefore obtained from the equation

$$\mu_i\left(\mathbf{S}_{ij} + \mathbf{e}_{ji}\mathbf{r}'^{T}_{j}\right)\mathbf{e}_{i1} + \mu'_j\mathbf{e}_{ji} = \alpha\mu_j\mathbf{e}_{j1}.$$

□

10.2.3.2   The global method

The case of affine cameras   What we call the global method is a generalization of a method developed for affine cameras by Tomasi and Kanade (Tomasi and Kanade, 1992) to the case of perspective cameras. We first describe their method and then show how it can be extended to deal with the full perspective projection case. This extension is due to Triggs and Sturm (Sturm and Triggs, 1996).

We therefore consider n affine cameras (see Chapter 4, Section 4.4.2) and p 3D points M_j. Each perspective projection matrix $\mathcal{P}_i$ takes the simpler form

$$\mathcal{P}_i = \left[\begin{array}{cc} \mathbf{P}_i & \mathbf{p}_i \\ \mathbf{0}^T_3 & 1 \end{array}\right],$$

where $\mathbf{P}_i$ is the 2×3 reduced projection matrix (see Proposition 4.23) of rank 2 and $\mathbf{p}_i$ is a vector of size 2. Let $\mathbf{M}_j$ be the vector of size 3 representing the affine coordinates of the jth 3D point in some affine coordinate system and $\mathbf{m}_{ij}$ be the vector of size 2 representing the affine coordinates of its image in the ith view. The projection equation can be written

$$\begin{bmatrix} \mathbf{m}_{ij} \\ 1 \end{bmatrix} = \begin{bmatrix} \mathbf{P}_i & \mathbf{p}_i \\ \mathbf{0}_3^T & 1 \end{bmatrix} \begin{bmatrix} \mathbf{M}_j \\ 1 \end{bmatrix}. \qquad (10.11)$$

We can further simplify the problem by taking the origin of the coordinates in each image plane at the centroid of the observed points. Because the cameras are affine, those centers of gravity are the images of the center of gravity of the 3D points which we can assume to be the origin of the 3D affine coordinate system (see Chapter 4, Section 4.4.2). This implies that the vectors $\mathbf{p}_i$ are all equal to zero.

The next thing we do is group all of the projection equations into a single large matrix equation:

$$\mathbf{W}_a = \begin{bmatrix} \mathbf{m}_{11} & \mathbf{m}_{12} & \dots & \mathbf{m}_{1p} \\ \mathbf{m}_{21} & \mathbf{m}_{22} & \dots & \mathbf{m}_{2p} \\ \vdots & \vdots & \ddots & \vdots \\ \mathbf{m}_{n1} & \mathbf{m}_{n2} & \dots & \mathbf{m}_{np} \end{bmatrix} = \begin{bmatrix} \mathbf{P}_1 \\ \mathbf{P}_2 \\ \vdots \\ \mathbf{P}_n \end{bmatrix} [\mathbf{M}_1, \mathbf{M}_2, \dots, \mathbf{M}_p]. \qquad (10.12)$$

The known $2n \times p$ matrix $\mathbf{W}_a$ appears as the product of a $2n \times 3$ matrix describing the unknown projection matrices and a $3 \times p$ matrix describing the unknown affine coordinates of the observed 3D points. Therefore, the rank of $\mathbf{W}_a$ is less than or equal to 3. Let $q = min(2n, p)$.

We compute the SVD of $\mathbf{W}_a$:

$$\mathbf{W}_a = \mathbf{U}_a \boldsymbol{\Sigma}_a \mathbf{V}_a^T.$$

$\mathbf{U}_a$ is the $2n \times q$ matrix of the first q orthogonal eigenvectors of the symmetric matrix $\mathbf{W}_a \mathbf{W}_a^T$, $\mathbf{V}_a$ the $p \times q$ orthogonal matrix of the first q orthogonal eigenvectors of the symmetric matrix $\mathbf{W}_a^T \mathbf{W}_a$ and $\boldsymbol{\Sigma}_a$ is the $q \times q$ diagonal matrix whose diagonal elements are the singular values of the matrix $\mathbf{W}_a$. Since we have seen that $\mathbf{W}_a$ was of rank less than or equal to 3, there are at most three nonzero such diagonal elements, denoted σ_1^2, σ_2^2 and σ_3^2 which we can assume to be the first three elements on the diagonal of $\boldsymbol{\Sigma}_a$.

Because of this, only the first three columns of the matrix $\mathbf{U}_a$ and the first three rows of $\mathbf{V}_a^T$ are relevant in the decomposition (we assume that $3 \le q$). Let us denote as $\mathbf{U}_a'$ and $\mathbf{V}_a'^T$ the corresponding $2n \times 3$ and $3 \times p$ matrices. The SVD of $\mathbf{W}_a$ can be rewritten

$$\mathbf{W}_a = \mathbf{U}_a' \boldsymbol{\Sigma}_a' \mathbf{V}_a'^T,$$

where $\boldsymbol{\Sigma}_a' = diag(\sigma_1^2, \sigma_2^2, \sigma_3^2)$. Let us write for example $\mathbf{U}_a'' = \mathbf{U}_a' \boldsymbol{\Sigma}_a'$. The SVD of $\mathbf{W}_a$ is now

$$\mathbf{W}_a = \mathbf{U}_a'' \mathbf{V}_a'^T.$$

The $2n \times 3$ matrix $\mathbf{U}_a^{''}$ can be interpreted as describing a set of n affine projection matrices and the $3 \times p$ matrix $\mathbf{V}_a^{'T}$ as describing the affine coordinates of p 3D points.

Both the projection matrices and the 3D points are defined only up to an arbitrary affine transformation that leaves the origin of coordinates fixed. Indeed, such a transformation is defined by an invertible 3×3 matrix $\boldsymbol{\mathcal{A}}$ such that the points $\mathbf{M}_j$ are transformed to $\boldsymbol{\mathcal{A}}\mathbf{M}_j$ and the matrices $\mathbf{P}_j$ are transformed to $\mathbf{P}_j\boldsymbol{\mathcal{A}}^{-1}$. One verifies that $\mathbf{W}_a = \left(\mathbf{U}_a^{''}\boldsymbol{\mathcal{A}}^{-1}\right)\left(\boldsymbol{\mathcal{A}}\mathbf{V}_a^{'T}\right)$.

The reconstruction that has been obtained is defined up to an arbitrary affine transformation that preserves the origin of coordinates.

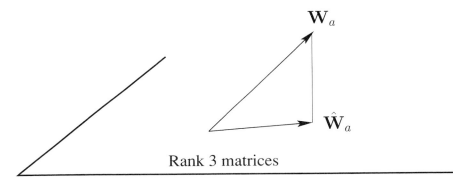

Figure 10.4: Among all rank-3 $2n \times p$ matrices $\mathbf{W}$, $\hat{\mathbf{W}}_a$ is the one that minimizes the Frobenius norm of the difference $\mathbf{W}_a - \mathbf{W}$.

In practice, because of the uncertainty in the measurement of the coordinates of the points m_{ij}, the rank of $\mathbf{W}_a$ is greater than 3, in effect $\mathbf{W}_a$ is usually full rank with 3 singular values that are significantly larger than the others. If one sets to 0 all but those 3 singular values and computes the product $\mathbf{U}_a^{''}\mathbf{V}_a^{'T}$, one obtains a matrix $\hat{\mathbf{W}}_a$ which is the best approximation of $\mathbf{W}_a$ by a matrix of rank 3 for the Frobenius norm (Golub and van Loan, 1989) (see Figure 10.4). Let $\hat{\mathbf{P}}_i$ be the n projection matrices and $\hat{\mathbf{M}}_j$ be the p 3D points obtained from $\hat{\mathbf{W}}_a$. Since the Frobenius norm of the difference $\mathbf{W}_a - \hat{\mathbf{W}}_a$ is equal to $\sum_{i,j} d^2\left(\mathbf{m}_{ij}, \hat{\mathbf{P}}_i\hat{\mathbf{M}}_j\right)$ (Equation 10.12), we conclude that the choice of $\hat{\mathbf{W}}_a$ is optimal in the sense that it minimizes the reprojection error.

Note that the method just described requires that all p points are visible in all n views. This assumption is often unrealistic in practice.

The case of perspective cameras   In the case of perspective cameras, affine geometry does not suffice anymore. Even if we choose a particular coordinate vector

$\mathbf{m}_{ij}$ for each of the np observed points m_{ij}, a particular projective basis of 3D space, we still have to cope with the problem that the perspective projection matrices $\boldsymbol{\mathcal{P}}_i$ can be multiplied independently by an arbitrary scale factor as is also the case for the coordinate vectors $\mathbf{M}_j$ of the 3D points M_j.

Therefore, if we assume that we have chosen in each image a particular projective basis, for example the one that defines the usual pixel coordinates, and for each pixel m_{ij}, we have chosen a particular coordinate vector, for example the one with the last coordinate equal to 1 as in Equation 10.11, we must introduce some extra degrees of freedom to make the projective equality $\mathbf{m}_{ij} \simeq \boldsymbol{\mathcal{P}}_i\mathbf{M}_j$ an equality. We denote by λ_{ij} the np scale factors such that

$$\lambda_{ij}\mathbf{m}_{ij} = \boldsymbol{\mathcal{P}}_i\mathbf{M}_j. \tag{10.13}$$

The reason we introduce those scale factors should be clear from the previous paragraph. In effect, they will allow us to write a projective analog of Equation 10.12:

$$\mathbf{W}_p = \begin{bmatrix} \lambda_{11}\mathbf{m}_{11} & \lambda_{12}\mathbf{m}_{12} & \dots & \lambda_{1p}\mathbf{m}_{1p} \\ \lambda_{21}\mathbf{m}_{21} & \lambda_{22}\mathbf{m}_{22} & \dots & \lambda_{2p}\mathbf{m}_{2p} \\ \vdots & \vdots & \ddots & \vdots \\ \lambda_{n1}\mathbf{m}_{n1} & \lambda_{n2}\mathbf{m}_{n2} & \dots & \lambda_{np}\mathbf{m}_{np} \end{bmatrix} = \begin{bmatrix} \boldsymbol{\mathcal{P}}_1 \\ \boldsymbol{\mathcal{P}}_2 \\ \vdots \\ \boldsymbol{\mathcal{P}}_n \end{bmatrix} [\mathbf{M}_1, \mathbf{M}_2, \dots, \mathbf{M}_p],$$

$$\tag{10.14}$$

with the appropriate changes in the dimensions of the matrices. Matrix $\mathbf{W}_p$ is now a $3n \times p$ matrix, and the two matrices on the right-hand side are of dimension $3n \times 4$ and $4 \times p$.

Let us assume for a moment that we have been able to compute a set of λ_{ij}'s such that the Equation 10.14 is true. The rest of the procedure that consists of computing a set of perspective projection matrices $\boldsymbol{\mathcal{P}}_i$, $i = 1, \dots, n$, and of coordinate vectors $\mathbf{M}_j$, $j = 1, \dots, p$, is very similar to the case of affine projection matrices described in the previous paragraph. Because of the decomposition of $\mathbf{W}_p$ as the product of a $3n \times 4$ matrix and a $4 \times p$ matrix, its rank has to be less than or equal to 4. We compute its SVD:

$$\mathbf{W}_p = \mathbf{U}_p\boldsymbol{\Sigma}_p\mathbf{V}_p^T.$$

As in the affine case, $\mathbf{U}_p$ is the $2n \times q$ matrix of the orthogonal first q eigenvectors of the symmetric matrix $\mathbf{W}_p\mathbf{W}_p^T$, $\mathbf{V}_p$ the $p \times q$ orthogonal matrix of the orthogonal first q eigenvectors of the symmetric matrix $\mathbf{W}_p^T\mathbf{W}_p$ and $\boldsymbol{\Sigma}_p$ is the $q \times q$ diagonal matrix whose diagonal elements are the singular values of the matrix $\mathbf{W}_p$. Since we have seen that $\mathbf{W}_p$ was of rank less than or equal to 4, there are at most four nonzero such diagonal elements, denoted σ_1^2, σ_2^2, σ_3^2 and σ_4^2 which we can assume to be the first four elements on the diagonal of $\boldsymbol{\Sigma}_p$.

We then introduce, as in the affine case, the $2n \times 4$ matrix $\mathbf{U}_p'$ and the $4 \times p$ matrix $\mathbf{V}_p'^T$ which are the first four columns and the first four rows, respectively, of the matrices $\mathbf{U}_p$ and $\mathbf{V}_p^T$. The SVD of $\mathbf{W}_p$ can be rewritten

$$\mathbf{W}_p = \mathbf{U}_p' \mathbf{\Sigma}_p' \mathbf{V}_p'^T,$$

where $\mathbf{\Sigma}_p' = diag(\sigma_1^2, \sigma_2^2, \sigma_3^2, \sigma_4^2)$. Let us write for example $\mathbf{U}_p'' = \mathbf{U}_p' \mathbf{\Sigma}_p'$. The SVD of $\mathbf{W}_p$ is now

$$\mathbf{W}_p = \mathbf{U}_p'' \mathbf{V}_p'^T.$$

The $2n \times 4$ matrix $\mathbf{U}_p''$ can be interpreted as describing a set of n perspective projection matrices and the $4 \times p$ matrix $\mathbf{V}_p'^T$ as describing the projective coordinates of p 3D points.

Both the projection matrices and the 3D points are defined only up to an arbitrary projective transformation. Indeed, such a transformation is defined by an invertible 4×4 matrix $\mathbf{H}$ such that the points $\mathbf{M}_j$ are transformed to $\mathbf{H}\mathbf{M}_j$ and the matrices $\mathcal{P}_j$ are transformed to $\mathcal{P}_j \mathbf{H}^{-1}$. One verifies that $\mathbf{W}_p = \left(\mathbf{U}_p'' \mathbf{H}^{-1} \right) \left(\mathbf{H} \mathbf{V}_p'^T \right)$.

The reconstruction that has been obtained is defined up to an arbitrary projective transformation.

The difficulty in order to make this work is to choose the scale factors λ_{ij}. It turns out to be itself a difficult problem. Let us see why. It should be clear that Equation 10.13 implies that

$$\lambda_{ij} \mathbf{F}_{ik} \mathbf{m}_{ij} = \lambda_{kj} \mathbf{e}_{ki} \times \mathbf{m}_{kj} \tag{10.15}$$

for all pairs of views (i, k) and for all points M_j as soon as we compute $\mathbf{F}_{ik}$ and $\mathbf{e}_{ki}$ according to the formulae (5.8) and (5.9). This equation yields the ratio $\lambda_{ij} : \lambda_{kj}$. Assume now that we have estimated the $n - 1$ Fundamental matrices $\mathbf{F}_{i\,i+1}$, $i = 1, \ldots, n - 1$. Then for a given 3D point, i.e. for a fixed value of j, we can linearly compute the ratios $\lambda_{1j} : \lambda_{2j} : \ldots : \lambda_{nj}$.

There are several problems with this simple approach. The first problem is that we have assumed that we had estimated the minimum number of Fundamental matrices, i.e. $n - 1$, to allow us to compute $\lambda_{1j} : \lambda_{2j} : \ldots : \lambda_{nj}$. But what happens if we have estimated more, perhaps even all of them, i.e. $\binom{n}{2}$? It is unclear that the corresponding system of linear equations in $\lambda_{1j}, \lambda_{2j}, \ldots, \lambda_{nj}$ will have a solution!

Let us take as a toy example the case $n = 3$. We know from Chapter 8 that the three Fundamental matrices $\mathbf{F}_{12}$, $\mathbf{F}_{23}$ and $\mathbf{F}_{31}$ must satisfy the three algebraic relations (8.3). If they do not, i.e. if our estimation procedure has not taken them into account, then the corresponding system of linear equations in $\lambda_{1j}, \lambda_{2j}, \ldots, \lambda_{nj}$ may not have a solution. In this case, we know how to avoid the problem, for example by computing the Fundamental matrix from one Trifocal tensor (see Chapter 8). But for larger values of n we do not know of any solution at the time of this writing.

Another closely related problem is that we have no way of computing the Fundamental matrices and the epipoles according to Equations 5.8 and 5.9 since this requires the knowledge of the perspective projection matrices which are among the

things we are trying to compute. This means that in Equation 10.15 there will be
unwanted and unknown scale factors on the Fundamental matrix and the epipole.
This is fine as long as we use only $n-1$ such equations, because the scale factors
are absorbed in the λ's. Problems arise if we use more equations. Returning to the
previous example with $n=3$, we see that even if the three Fundamental matrices
and the six epipoles do satisfy the three relations (8.3), we still have to adjust the
scale factors on those quantities in such a way that the six equations (8.4 and 8.5)
are satisfied. That problem is in itself difficult and becomes worse when we increase
the number of views and of Fundamental matrices.

Note in passing that in the case $n=3$, the results given in Proposition 10.5
allow us to solve the following problem: Given an estimated Trifocal tensor, recover
Fundamental matrices and epipoles that satisfy all nine equations (8.3, 8.4 and
8.5). This problem can be solved since we can compute three perspective projection
matrices.

10.2.3.3   The bundle adjustment method

We now describe a numerical method that can be applied in several contexts depending upon what information, projective, affine, or Euclidean, is known. We limit
ourselves to the computation of the projective canonical representation of n views
and to the case in which the observed primitives are points. We observe p points
$M_1,\ldots, M_p$. For simplicity in notation, we assume that all p points are visible in
all views, albeit this is not necessary for the method to work. The image of the jth
point in the ith view is denoted m_{ij}.

The problem that we want to solve is the following. The methods described in the
previous two sections provide us with estimates $(\mathcal{P}_0, \hat{\mathcal{P}}_1, \cdots, \hat{\mathcal{P}}_n)$ of the perspective
projection matrices and estimates $\hat{M}_j, j = 1, \cdots, p$, of the p 3-D points. In general
the reprojected points $\hat{m}_{ij}, i = 1, \cdots, n, j = 1, \cdots, p$, represented by $\hat{\mathcal{P}}_i\hat{\mathbf{M}}_j$ fail
to be identical to the measurements m_{ij}. The bundle adjustment method is a
numerical method for adjusting the projection matrices and the 3-D points *starting
from the initial estimate* provided by the results of Sections 10.2.3.1 or 10.2.3.2 in
such a way that the reprojected points become closer to the measured points.

Hence we consider the squared image distance $\varepsilon_{ij} = \frac{1}{2}d^2(m_{ij}, \hat{m}_{ij})$ between
the measured pixel m_{ij} and the reprojected pixel $\hat{m}_{ij}$ and attempt to minimize
simultaneously all the error measures ε_{ij} by adjusting the 3D points M_j and the
parameters of the perspective projection matrices $\mathcal{P}_i$.

If we stack the np numbers ε_{ij} into a large vector denoted ε, this vector is a
function of the p points M_j and the parameters of the $n-1$ perspective projection
matrices, i.e. a function of $N = 3p + 11(n-1)$ parameters.

The vector ε defines a function $\mathbf{f} : \mathbb{R}^N \longrightarrow \mathbb{R}^{np}$. A point in the space $\mathbb{R}^N$
represents p 3D points and $n-1$ perspective projection matrices. We have in
general estimates $\hat{\mathcal{P}}_i, i = 2, \cdots, n$, of the $n-1$ perspective projection matrices,
built for example as explained in Section 10.2.3.1 or 10.2.3.2. From those estimates

and the pixels m_{ij} we can compute estimates $\hat{M}_j$ of the 3D points. All those define a vector $\hat{\mathbf{x}}$ in $\mathbb{R}^N$ such that $\mathbf{f}(\hat{\mathbf{x}}) = \hat{\varepsilon}$. The central idea of the method is that it tries to change the vector $\hat{\mathbf{x}}$, i.e. to move the points $\hat{M}_j$ and to change the perspective projection matrices $\hat{\mathcal{P}}_i$ in such a way as to minimize the Euclidean norm of the resulting vector ε. In theory this norm should be zero; in practice only a local minimum for which not all coordinates of ε are equal to zero can be reached.

Technically, this is achieved as follows. Let $\mathbf{x}_0 = \hat{\mathbf{x}}$ and $\varepsilon_0 = \mathbf{f}(\mathbf{x}_0)$. At iteration k, $k = 1, \cdots$, we consider $\mathbf{f}(\mathbf{x}_{k-1} + \boldsymbol{\Delta})$ where the increment vector $\boldsymbol{\Delta}$ is small and we expand $\mathbf{f}$ up to first order at the point $\mathbf{x}_{k-1}$:

$$\mathbf{f}(\mathbf{x}_{k-1} + \boldsymbol{\Delta}) = \mathbf{f}(\mathbf{x}_{k-1}) + \mathbf{J}_{k-1}\boldsymbol{\Delta} + O(\|\boldsymbol{\Delta}\|).$$

$\mathbf{J}_{k-1}$ is the Jacobian matrix, i.e. the first-order derivative, of the function $\mathbf{f}$ evaluated at the point $\mathbf{x}_{k-1}$. Its exact form depends upon the parameterization of the perspective projection matrices $\mathcal{P}_i$ but it has a very particular structure that we will describe shortly. Before we do this, let us proceed with the determination of the increment vector $\boldsymbol{\Delta}$.

$\boldsymbol{\Delta}$ is chosen so as to minimize the norm of $\mathbf{f}(\mathbf{x}_{k-1} + \boldsymbol{\Delta})$ up to first order, i.e. it is chosen so that it minimizes the norm of $\mathbf{f}(\mathbf{x}_{k-1}) + \mathbf{J}_{k-1}\boldsymbol{\Delta}$. This is a standard linear least-squares problem whose solution is obtained by solving the linear system of equations

$$\mathbf{J}_{k-1}^T \mathbf{J}_{k-1} \boldsymbol{\Delta} + \mathbf{J}_{k-1}^T \varepsilon_{k-1} = \mathbf{0}. \tag{10.16}$$

These equations are called the *normal equations*. We have written ε_{k-1} for $\mathbf{f}(\mathbf{x}_{k-1})$. Let $\boldsymbol{\Delta}_{k-1}$ be a solution of that system. We then define

$$\mathbf{x}_k = \mathbf{x}_{k-1} + \boldsymbol{\Delta}_{k-1}$$

and iterate the procedure until convergence is reached.

In practice several problems can occur such as convergence to a local minimum where ε is not equal to $\mathbf{0}$, or even divergence if the first-order approximation is not good enough. It has been reported many times in the literature that the results are very sensitive to the initial point $\mathbf{x}_0$ and that it is very important that this point is close to a solution. Therefore the computation of a "good" initial estimate is essential.

Let us now study in slightly more detail the structure of the Jacobian matrix $\mathbf{J}$. It turns out that this matrix is very sparse. This can be seen as follows. Each coordinate of $\mathbf{f}(\mathbf{x})$ is one of the ε_{ij} and depends only upon the matrix $\mathcal{P}_i, i = 2, \cdots, n$, and the 3D point M_j. Each row of $\mathbf{J}$ contains the partial derivatives of the corresponding ε_{ij} with respect to all variables, the perspective projection matrices and the 3D points. But because of the previous remark, only the partial derivatives of ε_{ij} with respect to the parameters of $\mathcal{P}_i$ and the coordinates of M_j will be nonzero. We show as an example the case where we have three views ($n = 3$) of four points ($p = 4$) in Figure 10.5.

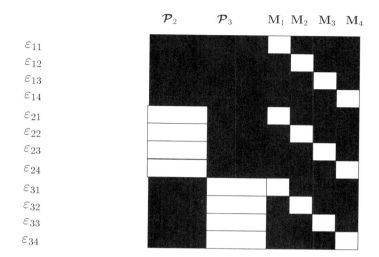

Figure 10.5: The $np \times N$ Jacobian matrix $\mathbf{J}$ is sparse. The nonzero parts are represented in white, the zero parts in black. For example, since ε_{11} is solely a function of M_1, only its partial derivatives with respect to the coordinates of M_1 are nonzero.

Having done this, we can make more precise the structure of the $N \times N$ matrix $\mathbf{J}^T\mathbf{J}$. We denote $\frac{\partial \varepsilon_{ij}}{\partial \boldsymbol{\mathcal{P}}_i}$ the partial derivative of ε_{ij} with respect to the parameters defining the projection matrix $\boldsymbol{\mathcal{P}}_i$. This is a 1×11 matrix in the case where we parameterize $\boldsymbol{\mathcal{P}}_i$ by its elements. Similarly, we denote $\frac{\partial \varepsilon_{ij}}{\partial \mathbf{M}_j}$ the partial derivative of ε_{ij} with respect to the coordinates of the 3D point $\mathbf{M}_j$. It is a 1×3 matrix. The structure of the symmetric matrix $\mathbf{J}^T\mathbf{J}$ is most easily described by introducing the following sets of matrices:

- The $n - 1$ 11×11 symmetric matrices $\mathbf{U}_i$ defined by

$$\mathbf{U}_i = \sum_{j=1}^{p} \left(\frac{\partial \hat{\mathbf{m}}_{ij}}{\partial \boldsymbol{\mathcal{P}}_i} \right)^T \mathbf{C}_{ij} \left(\frac{\partial \hat{\mathbf{m}}_{ij}}{\partial \boldsymbol{\mathcal{P}}_i} \right) \quad i = 2, \cdots, n,$$

- The p 3×3 symmetric matrices $\mathbf{V}_j$ defined by

$$\mathbf{V}_j = \sum_{i=1}^{n} \left(\frac{\partial \hat{\mathbf{m}}_{ij}}{\partial \mathbf{M}_j} \right)^T \mathbf{C}_{ij} \left(\frac{\partial \hat{\mathbf{m}}_{ij}}{\partial \mathbf{M}_j} \right),$$

- The $(n-1)p$ 11×3 matrices $\mathbf{W}_{ij}$ defined by

$$\mathbf{W}_{ij} = \left(\frac{\partial \hat{\mathbf{m}}_{ij}}{\partial \boldsymbol{\mathcal{P}}_i}\right)^T \mathbf{C}_{ij} \left(\frac{\partial \hat{\mathbf{m}}_{ij}}{\partial \mathbf{M}_j}\right) \quad i = 2, \cdots, n, \, j = 1, \cdots, p,$$

The matrix denoted $\mathbf{C}_{ij}$ above is the 2×2 matrix

$$\mathbf{C}_{ij} = (\hat{\mathbf{m}}_{ij} - \mathbf{m}_{ij})(\hat{\mathbf{m}}_{ij} - \mathbf{m}_{ij})^T.$$

The matrix $\mathbf{J}^T \mathbf{J}$ is built from those three classes of matrices as indicated in Figure 10.6.

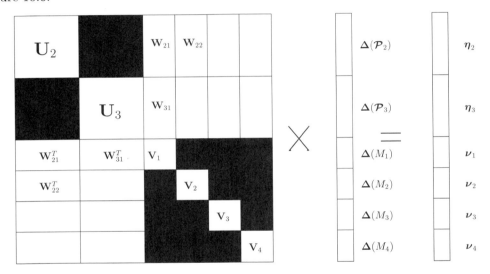

Figure 10.6: Normal equations.

In order to match the structure of $\mathbf{J}^T \boldsymbol{\varepsilon}_{k-1}$ to that of $\mathbf{J}^T \mathbf{J}$ it is useful to introduce the following two sets of matrices:

- The n vectors $\boldsymbol{\eta}_i$ of size 11 defined by

$$\boldsymbol{\eta}_i = \sum_{j=1}^{p} \left(\frac{\partial \hat{\mathbf{m}}_{ij}}{\partial \boldsymbol{\mathcal{P}}_i}\right)^T (\mathbf{m}_{ij} - \hat{\mathbf{m}}_{ij}) \varepsilon_{ij} \quad i = 2, \cdots, n,$$

- The p vectors $\boldsymbol{\nu}_j$ of size 3 defined by

$$\boldsymbol{\nu}_j = \sum_{i=1}^{n} \left(\frac{\partial \hat{\mathbf{m}}_{ij}}{\partial \mathbf{M}_j}\right)^T (\mathbf{m}_{ij} - \hat{\mathbf{m}}_{ij}) \varepsilon_{ij} \quad j = 1, \cdots, p.$$

The normal equations (10.16) can now be rewritten in a form that clearly shows the increments relative to the changes in the perspective projection matrices, denoted $\mathbf{\Delta}(\mathcal{P})$, and to the changes in the 3D points, denoted $\mathbf{\Delta}(\mathbf{M})$:

$$\begin{bmatrix} \mathbf{U} & \mathbf{W} \\ \mathbf{W}^T & \mathbf{V} \end{bmatrix} \begin{bmatrix} \mathbf{\Delta}(\mathcal{P}) \\ \mathbf{\Delta}(\mathbf{M}) \end{bmatrix} = \begin{bmatrix} \eta(\mathcal{P}) \\ \nu(\mathbf{M}) \end{bmatrix}. \tag{10.17}$$

Assume that the $3p \times 3p$ block-diagonal matrix $\mathbf{V}$ is invertible, and multiply both sides of (10.17) on the left by the matrix

$$\begin{bmatrix} \mathbf{I}_{11(n-1)} & -\mathbf{W}\mathbf{V}^{-1} \\ \mathbf{0}_{3p \times 11(n-1)} & \mathbf{I}_{3p} \end{bmatrix}.$$

We obtain

$$\begin{bmatrix} \mathbf{U} - \mathbf{W}\mathbf{V}^{-1}\mathbf{W}^T & \mathbf{0}_{3p} \\ \mathbf{W}^T & \mathbf{V} \end{bmatrix} \begin{bmatrix} \mathbf{\Delta}(\mathcal{P}) \\ \mathbf{\Delta}(\mathbf{M}) \end{bmatrix} = \begin{bmatrix} \eta(\mathcal{P}) - \mathbf{W}\mathbf{V}^{-1}\nu(\mathbf{M}) \\ \nu(\mathbf{M}) \end{bmatrix}.$$

This separates the block of variables $\mathbf{\Delta}(\mathcal{P})$ from $\mathbf{\Delta}(\mathbf{M})$:

$$(\mathbf{U} - \mathbf{W}\mathbf{V}^{-1}\mathbf{W}^T)\mathbf{\Delta}(\mathcal{P}) = \eta(\mathcal{P}) - \mathbf{W}\mathbf{V}^{-1}\nu(\mathbf{M}),$$

$$\mathbf{\Delta}(\mathbf{M}) = \mathbf{V}^{-1}(\nu(\mathbf{M}) - \mathbf{W}^T\mathbf{\Delta}(\mathcal{P})).$$

The first equation yields $\mathbf{\Delta}(\mathcal{P})$, the second $\mathbf{\Delta}(\mathbf{M})$.

10.2.3.4 An example of the recovery of the projective stratum

The 11 images of Figure 10.7 are part of a sequence of 45 images that were acquired with a Kodak DCS460 digital camera at various points of the INRIA campus in Sophia-Antipolis. The Fundamental matrices have been estimated between as many pairs of views as possible using the methods described in Chapter 6. The results for a subset of six images are shown in table 10.1. In its upper-diagonal part, this table shows the residuals, in pixels, i.e. the square root of the value of the expression 6.10 divided by the number of pixels used in the estimation of the Fundamental matrix. The number of pixels used in the estimation is shown in its lower-diagonal part. Similar results are shown in table 10.2 for the six views of a different scene shown in Figure 10.8.

10.3 Affine and Euclidean strata

We have seen in Chapter 7, section 7.3.4, how to recover the infinity homography between two views. Proposition 7.9 gives us the form of the one-parameter family of affine canonical forms for the two perspective projection matrices. The analysis that has been done in this chapter, section 10.2, shows that the projective canonical

	i.3	i.4	i.5	i.6	i.7	i.8
i.3		0.338	0.442	0.242	0.357	0.469
i.4	27		0.31	0.209	0.376	0.553
i.5	27	73		0.248	0.264	0.635
i.6	36	22	35		0.209	0.155
i.7	29	42	50	41		0.291
i.8	14	33	34	26	57	

Table 10.1: The Fundamental matrices between all $\binom{6}{2}$ pairs of views among the images 3 to 8 of Figure 10.7. The upper diagonal part of the matrix shows the residuals in pixels. The lower diagonal part shows the number of pairs of matched points that have been used in the estimation of the Fundamental matrices. Courtesy **Sylvain Bougnoux**, INRIA.

	i.0	i.1	i.2	i.3	i.4	i.5
i.0		0.91	0.73	0.59	0.74	0.62
i.1	40		0.45	0.4	0.5	0.67
i.2	41	70		0.36	0.45	0.38
i.3	40	66	71		0.41	0.31
i.4	40	67	72	71		0.34
i.5	45	61	66	64	81	

Table 10.2: The Fundamental matrices between all $\binom{6}{2}$ pairs of views among the images of Figure 10.8. The upper diagonal part of the matrix shows the residuals in pixels. The lower diagonal part shows the number of pairs of matched points that have been used in the estimation of the Fundamental matrices. Courtesy **Sylvain Bougnoux**, INRIA.

form of an arbitrary number, n, of views can be turned into an affine canonical form as soon as the infinity homography is known between any pair of the n views. We assume for simplicity but without loss of generality that this homography is known between the views 1 and 2. We obtain the following proposition:

Proposition 10.7 *Given the projective canonical form $(\mathcal{P}_0, \mathcal{P}_2, \ldots, \mathcal{P}_n)$ of n views and the infinity homography matrix $\mathbf{H}_{\infty 12}$ between the views 1 and 2, the affine canonical form of the n views is of the form*

$$\mathcal{P}_i^A = [\mathbf{H}_{\infty 1i} \, \mu_i \mathbf{e}_{i1}] \quad i = 2, \ldots, n.$$

$\mathbf{H}_{\infty 1i}$ *is a representation of the infinity homography between views 1 and i which can be computed from $\mathbf{H}_{\infty 12}$ for $i \geq 3$:*

$$\mathbf{H}_{\infty 1i} = \mathbf{S}_{1i} + \mathbf{e}_{i1} \mathbf{r}_{\infty i}^T.$$

Figure 10.7: 11 out of 45 views of the INRIA site in Sophia-Antipolis. Courtesy **Sylvain Bougnoux**, INRIA.

μ_i *is a scalar that can be computed from* μ_2 *for* $i \geq 3$.

Proof : The proof is exactly the same as in Propositions 10.4, 10.5 and 10.6. For example, in Propositions 10.4 and 10.5, the vector $\mathbf{r}_2$ corresponds in our context to the plane at infinity Π_∞ and is obtained from definition 5.6, Proposition 5.16 and the matrix $\mathbf{H}_{\infty 12}$ of the infinity homography between views 1 and 2. The Propositions 10.4, 10.5 and 10.6 explain how to compute $(\mathbf{r}_{\infty 3}, \mu_3), \ldots, (\mathbf{r}_{\infty n}, \mu_n)$. $\square$

We extend the previous result to the Euclidean setting as follows. We have seen in Chapter 11 several methods of recovering the intrinsic parameters of a camera. We will see more in sections 11.3 and 11.4. We now state and prove the general result

Figure 10.8: Six out of ten views of the Arcades square in Valbonne. Courtesy **Sylvain Bougnoux**, INRIA.

that if we are given an affine canonical representation of n cameras, the knowledge of the intrinsic parameters of one of them is sufficient to obtain the Euclidean canonical representation of those n views.

Proposition 10.8 *Given the affine canonical form* $(\boldsymbol{\mathcal{P}}_0, \boldsymbol{\mathcal{P}}_2^A, \ldots, \boldsymbol{\mathcal{P}}_n^A)$ *of n views and the matrix of the intrinsic parameters* $\mathbf{A}_i$, $1 \leq i \leq n$ *of any of the cameras, the Euclidean canonical form of the n views is of the form*

$$\boldsymbol{\mathcal{P}}_k = \left\{ \begin{array}{ll} \mathbf{A}_1 \boldsymbol{\mathcal{P}}_0 & if \quad k = 1, \\ \mathbf{A}_k \left[\mathbf{R}_k \, \mu_k \mathbf{t}_{k1} \right] & if \quad k = 2, \ldots, n. \end{array} \right.$$

$\mathbf{R}_k$ *is the matrix of the relative rotation between view 1 and view k.* $\mathbf{A}_k$ *is the matrix of the intrinsic parameters of camera k.* $\mathbf{t}_{k1}$ *is the vector* $\overrightarrow{C_k C_1}$ *expressed in the camera normalized coordinate system of the kth camera.*

Proof : We assume without loss of generality that $i = 1$. According to Proposition 10.7, $\boldsymbol{\mathcal{P}}_k^A = [\mathbf{H}_{\infty 1 k} \, \mu_k \mathbf{e}_{k1}]$. Let $\mathbf{K}$ be the Kruppa matrix of the kth view for $k = 1, \ldots, n$. Equation 11.1 of Chapter 11 yields

$$\mathbf{K}_k \simeq \mathbf{H}_{\infty 1 k} \mathbf{K}_1 \mathbf{H}_{\infty 1 k}$$

and $\mathbf{A}_k$ is obtained by Cholesky decomposition of $\mathbf{K}_k$. $\mathbf{R}_k$ is then obtained from Proposition 5.25 of Chapter 5:

$$\mathbf{R}_k = \alpha_k \mathbf{A}_k^{-1} \mathbf{H}_{\infty 1 k} \mathbf{A}_1,$$

where $\alpha_k = det(\mathbf{A}_k) \left(det(\mathbf{A}_1 \, det(\mathbf{H}_{\infty 1 k})) \right)^{-1}$.

Having computed the matrices $\mathbf{A}_k$ and $\mathbf{R}_k$, we can scale the perspective projection matrices $\boldsymbol{\mathcal{P}}_k^A$, $k = 2, \ldots, n$, so that they are equal to $\left[\mathbf{A}_k \mathbf{R}_k \mathbf{A}_1^{-1} \; \mu_k' \mathbf{e}_{k1}' \right]$. Let us further note that all the ratios $\mu_2' : \ldots : \mu_n'$ are known (Propositions 10.6 and 10.7). Therefore we have $\mathbf{e}_{k1}' = \mu \mathbf{A}_k \mathbf{t}_{k1}$. If we now apply the affine change of coordinate system defined by the matrix

$$\left[\begin{array}{cc} \mathbf{A}_1 & \mathbf{0}_3 \\ \mathbf{0}_3^T & 1 \end{array} \right],$$

we obtain the Euclidean canonical form with $\mu_k = \mu_k' \mu$. $\square$

10.4 Stereo rigs

In this section, we consider a moving stereo rig. We study the case when the two cameras which compose the rig are rigidly attached, and their intrinsic parameters are constant. When doing a rigid displacement of the rig, the four resulting views (the left and right view before and after the displacement) satisfy additional constraints, unlike the four views obtained from a single moving camera which in general are unconstrained. This makes it possible to recover the affine stratum, as described in Section 10.4.1 and using techniques described in the next chapter, the Euclidean stratum.

Using a stereo rig instead of a single moving camera also has the advantage that because the epipolar geometry between the left and right cameras is fixed, one can use all of the image pairs taken in a sequence to estimate the Fundamental matrix, therefore accumulating point matches for a better estimation. This is especially interesting when the scene is close to a critical configuration, because with generic motion, repetitions of critical configurations are no longer critical.

On the other hand, in some cases it might be easier to obtain monocular correspondences by tracking points over time in the left camera and in the right camera. In this situation, one can use the redundancy to recover the epipolar geometry of the stereo rig without using correspondences between the left and right cameras. This is described in the Euclidean case in Section 10.4.2.

10.4.1 Affine calibration

We consider in this section a moving stereo rig and suppose that the same set of points are observed before and after the rigid displacement. We first determine the epipolar geometry of the stereo rig between the left and right camera, and perform a projective reconstruction of this set of points before the displacement, let us say in $(\Pi, 1)$ (see Proposition 7.2 for an explanation of this notation), a projective canonical frame of the stereo rig that we denote $\mathcal{B}_1$ for simplicity. We do the same operation after the rigid displacement, in the *same* projective canonical frame, denoted $\mathcal{B}_2$ after the displacement. Since the ambiguity in reconstruction is at most projective, these two reconstructions are necessarily related by a homography $\mathcal{H}$ of $\mathbb{P}^3$, which can be determined from the two sets of reconstructed points. In this section, we will see that we can extract the affine calibration from $\mathcal{H}$, using a technique developed by (Horaud and Csurka, 1998).

Let us now consider $\mathcal{E}_1$ and $\mathcal{E}_2$ a Euclidean coordinate system attached to the stereo rig before and after the rigid displacement. Because we have used the same projective canonical frame before and after displacement, the form of the transformation from the projective coordinate system to the Euclidean coordinate system is known from (7.18):

$$\mathbf{Q}_{\mathcal{B}_1}^{\mathcal{E}_1} = \begin{bmatrix} \mathbf{A}^{-1} & \mathbf{0}_3 \\ -\mathbf{r}_\infty^T & 1 \end{bmatrix}, \tag{10.18}$$

where $\mathbf{A}$ is the matrix of intrinsic parameters of the left camera, and $\mathbf{r}_\infty$ is the intrinsic representation of the plane at infinity as defined by Equation 5.28. This expression depends only on the intrinsic and extrinsic parameters of the stereo rig. Since they are kept fixed, so is $\mathbf{Q}_{\mathcal{B}_1}^{\mathcal{E}_1} \equiv \mathbf{Q}_{\mathcal{B}_2}^{\mathcal{E}_2}$. Since $\mathcal{E}_1$ and $\mathcal{E}_2$ are Euclidean coordinate systems, the transformation between them is a rigid displacement. Therefore $\mathcal{H}$ is conjugate to the rigid displacement between the two cameras of the stereo rig, as illustrated by Figure 10.9:

$$\mathcal{H} = \mathbf{Q}_{\mathcal{E}_1}^{\mathcal{B}_1} \mathcal{D} \mathbf{Q}_{\mathcal{B}_1}^{\mathcal{E}_1}, \tag{10.19}$$

with

$$\mathcal{D} = \begin{bmatrix} \mathbf{R} & \mathbf{t} \\ \mathbf{0}_3^T & 1 \end{bmatrix}.$$

Note that we have used the symbol "equal" rather than "proportional" in this expression. This is because the scale factor can be recovered exactly by noting that two conjugate matrices have the same determinant and trace. The trace of a rigid displacement is always positive, therefore the scale of $\mathcal{H}$ is $\text{sign}(\text{trace}\mathcal{H})(\det\mathcal{H})^{1/4}$. After dividing $\mathcal{H}$ by this value the previous equality is exact.

Since the affine calibration of a camera undergoing a pure translation has already been studied in Section 7.3.4.2, in this section we concentrate on rigid displacements that have a non-null rotation. The following proposition makes it possible to extract the intrinsic representation of the plane at infinity $\mathbf{r}_\infty$ from a single general rigid displacement of the stereo rig:

Proposition 10.9 *Given a stereo rig of fixed geometry and intrinsic parameters, and $\mathcal{H}$, the homography of $\mathbb{P}^3$ between the projective representation in the canonical frame before and after a rigid displacement which is not a pure translation, the vector $\mathbf{\Pi}_\infty = \begin{bmatrix} -\mathbf{r}_\infty^T \\ 1 \end{bmatrix}$ is the intrinsic representation of the plane at infinity for the pair of cameras in the stereo rig. It is an eigenvector of the matrix $\mathcal{H}^{-T}$ associated with the eigenvalue 1. If the rigid displacement is not a planar motion, this eigenvector is unique, otherwise there is a second independent eigenvector associated with the*

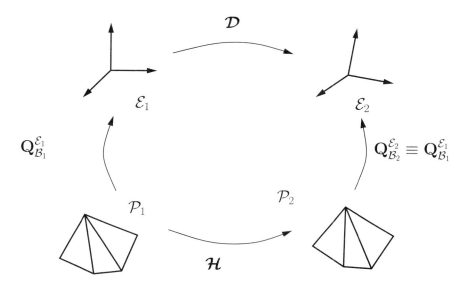

Figure 10.9: Motion of a stereo rig. The homography of $\mathbb{P}^3$ relating the projective reconstructions before and after the motion is conjugate to a rigid displacement: $\mathcal{H} = \mathbf{Q}_{\mathcal{E}_1}^{\mathcal{B}_1} \mathcal{D} \mathbf{Q}_{\mathcal{B}_1}^{\mathcal{E}_1}$.

eigenvalue 1, $\begin{bmatrix} \mathbf{A}^{-T} \mathbf{r} \\ 0 \end{bmatrix}$*, where* $\mathbf{A}$ *is the matrix of the intrinsic parameters of the left camera, and* $\mathbf{r}$ *is a unit vector parallel to the axis of rotation of the rigid displacement* $\mathcal{D}$ *of the rig.*

Proof :

The eigenvalues associated with a rigid displacement are $\lambda \in \{e^{i\theta}, e^{-i\theta}, 1, 1\}$ where θ is the angle of rotation. The geometric multiplicity of an eigenvalue is equal to the dimension of its associated eigenspace. Let $\mathbf{r}$ be the rotation axis and $\mathbf{t}$ be the translation. The geometric multiplicity of $\lambda = 1$ depends on the motion type: It is 1 for general motion ($\mathbf{r}^T \mathbf{t} \neq 0$), and 2 for planar motion ($\mathbf{r}^T \mathbf{t} = 0$).

The eigenvalues of $\mathcal{D}^{-T}$ are $1/\lambda$, and therefore among them is the value 1. Let's determine the eigenspace associated with this eigenvalue. Vectors $\mathbf{Y} = \begin{bmatrix} \mathbf{y} \\ \gamma \end{bmatrix}$ of this eigenspace satisfy $\mathcal{D}^{-T} \mathbf{Y} = \mathbf{Y}$, which splits into the two equations

$$\mathbf{R}\mathbf{y} = \mathbf{y},$$
$$\mathbf{t}^T \mathbf{R} \mathbf{y} = 0.$$

The first equation has two solutions, $\mathbf{y} = \mathbf{r}$ and $\mathbf{y} = 0$. For a general motion, only the second solution is possible for the system, and therefore the eigenspace is the

1-dimensional space spanned by $\mathbf{Y}_1 = [0,0,0,1]^T$, which represents the plane at infinity. For a planar motion, both solutions are possible for the system, and the eigenspace is the 2-dimensional space spanned by $\mathbf{Y}_1$ and $\mathbf{Y}_2 = \begin{bmatrix} \mathbf{r} \\ 0 \end{bmatrix}$, the plane orthogonal to the rotation axis and passing through the origin.

Transposing Equation 10.19 yields

$$\mathcal{H}^{-T} = \mathbf{Q}_{\mathcal{B}_1}^{\mathcal{E}_1\,T} \mathcal{D}^{-T} \mathbf{Q}_{\mathcal{B}_1}^{\mathcal{E}_1\,-T},$$

from which we obtain

$$\mathcal{H}^{-T}(\mathbf{Q}_{\mathcal{B}_1}^{\mathcal{E}_1\,T}\mathbf{Y}) = \mathbf{Q}_{\mathcal{B}_1}^{\mathcal{E}_1\,T} \mathcal{D}^{-T}\mathbf{Y}.$$

We conclude that the eigenvectors $\mathbf{X}$ of $\mathcal{H}^{-T}$ are obtained from the eigenvectors $\mathbf{Y}$ of $\mathcal{D}^{-T}$ by $\mathbf{X} = \mathbf{Q}_{\mathcal{B}_1}^{\mathcal{E}_1\,T}\mathbf{Y}$. Using the expression of $\mathbf{Q}_{\mathcal{B}_1}^{\mathcal{E}_1}$ in Equation 10.18 gives the announced result. □

We have studied a single rigid displacement of the stereo rig. We now extend our study to the case of multiple displacements. This has two interesting consequences. First, the advantage of using a stereo rig rather than a single camera is that not only it is possible to recover the plane at infinity, but also we can do so by combining any number of motions, the eigenvector being the common root of a set of linear equations, which in practice are solved by a linear least-squares procedure. Second, the previous proposition does not give us an affine calibration in the case of planar motion. However, by combining the constraints derived from two such planar motions with distinct rotation axes, we obtain a unique solution.

Proposition 10.10 *If $\mathcal{H}_1 \ldots \mathcal{H}_n$ are homographies of $\mathbb{P}^3$ arising from motions of a fixed stereo rig which include either one general motion or two planar motions with different rotation axes, then the unique non-trivial solution of the system*

$$\begin{bmatrix} \mathcal{H}_1^T - \mathbf{I}_4 \\ \vdots \\ \mathcal{H}_n^T - \mathbf{I}_4 \end{bmatrix} \mathbf{X} = 0$$

is the vector $\mathbf{\Pi}_\infty = \begin{bmatrix} -\mathbf{r}_\infty^T \\ 1 \end{bmatrix}$.

Proof : We notice that $\mathcal{H}^T$ and $\mathcal{H}^{-T}$ have the same eigenvector associated with $\lambda = 1$. The vector $\mathbf{r}_\infty$ depends only on the geometry of the stereo rig, not on its motion. Therefore it satisfies all of the equations of the system. The only thing left to prove is that if we have two planar motions with distinct rotation axes $\mathbf{r}_1$ and $\mathbf{r}_2$, the only common eigenvector for the eigenvalue 1 is $\mathbf{\Pi}_\infty$. Such a common eigenvector would satisfy

$$\lambda_1 \begin{bmatrix} -\mathbf{r}_\infty^T \\ 1 \end{bmatrix} + \mu_1 \begin{bmatrix} \mathbf{A}^{-T}\mathbf{r}_1 \\ 0 \end{bmatrix} = \lambda_2 \begin{bmatrix} -\mathbf{r}_\infty^T \\ 1 \end{bmatrix} + \mu_2 \begin{bmatrix} \mathbf{A}^{-T}\mathbf{r}_2 \\ 0 \end{bmatrix}.$$

After some simplifications, we find that this would imply $\mathbf{A}(\mu_1 \mathbf{r}_1 + \mu_2 \mathbf{r}_2) = 0$, and since $\mathbf{A}$ is invertible, $\mu_1 \mathbf{r}_1 + \mu_2 \mathbf{r}_2 = 0$. Since $\mathbf{r}_1$ and $\mathbf{r}_2$ are not proportional, $\mu_1 = \mu_2 = 0$, and therefore the common eigenvector has to be Π_s. $\square$

We have therefore seen that from the transformations $\mathcal{H}$ it is possible to extract the vector $\mathbf{r}_\infty$ which encodes the position of the plane at infinity in the chosen projective canonical frame of the two views of the stereo rig. This gives directly the infinity homography of the stereo rig from its Fundamental matrix using Equation 5.28.

We can go even further if we consider the two positions of the first camera of the rig (respectively, of the second camera of the rig). The plane at infinity induces a homography, denoted $\mathbf{H}_{1\infty}$ (respectively, $\mathbf{H}_{2\infty}$), between these two retinal planes. This homography can be readily recovered from the previous analysis as follows. The first three rows of the matrix Equation 10.19 are given by

$$\mathcal{H} = \left[\begin{array}{cc} \mathbf{H} & \mathbf{h} \\ \times & \times \end{array} \right] = \left[\begin{array}{cc} \mathbf{H}_{1\infty} - \mathbf{e}_1' \mathbf{r}_\infty^T & \mathbf{e}_1' \\ \times & \times \end{array} \right],$$

where $\mathbf{e}_1'$ is the epipole in the view corresponding to the second position of the first camera, with respect to the view corresponding to the first position of this camera (see Figure 10.10). Therefore $\mathbf{H}_{1\infty} = \mathbf{H} + \mathbf{h}\mathbf{r}_\infty^T$. If several such homographies can be estimated through a combination of motions of the rig, one can obtain the intrinsic parameters of the left camera using the techniques described in Section 11.1 and also the motion parameters, denoted $\mathbf{R}_1$ and $\mathbf{t}_1$.

10.4.2 Euclidean calibration

This section is complementary to the previous one where we showed how to compute the monocular homographies $\mathbf{H}_{1\infty}$ (respectively, $\mathbf{H}_{2\infty}$) from the epipolar geometry of the stereo rig. In this section, we show that from the rigid displacement $\mathcal{D}_1$ of the left camera and the rigid displacement $\mathcal{D}_2$ of the right camera, one can obtain the rigid displacement $\mathcal{D}$ between the cameras of the rig (Luong and Faugeras, 2000).

The difficulty arises from the fact that $\mathcal{D}_1$ and $\mathcal{D}_2$ are known in different coordinates systems. To cope with this problem, the idea is to use the commutativity of the following diagram which reflects Figure 10.10:

$$\begin{array}{ccc} \mathcal{E}_1^2 & \xrightarrow{\mathcal{D}} & \mathcal{E}_2^2 \\ \mathcal{D}_1 \uparrow & & \uparrow \mathcal{D}_2 \\ \mathcal{E}_1^1 & \xrightarrow{\mathcal{D}} & \mathcal{E}_2^1 \end{array}$$

In this diagram, the relative rigid displacement from the first to the second camera does not change between the initial and the final position of the stereo rig. We can thus write the matrix equation

$$\mathcal{D}\mathcal{D}_1 = \mathcal{D}_2 \mathcal{D}, \tag{10.20}$$

where $\mathcal{D}$ is the 4×4 unknown matrix of the rigid displacement from the first camera to the second camera, and $\mathcal{D}_1$ and $\mathcal{D}_2$ are the 4×4 rigid displacement matrices of the first and second cameras in their initial respective coordinate systems. Equation 10.20 can be decomposed into the following two matrix equations:

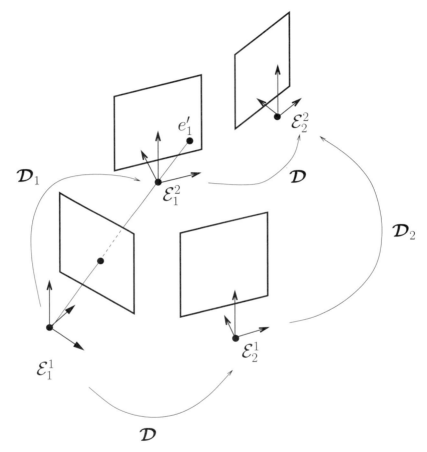

Figure 10.10: The stereo rig moves rigidly. The motion $\mathcal{D}_1$ of the first camera and $\mathcal{D}_2$ of the second camera, and the relative rigid displacement $\mathcal{D}$ between the two cameras of the rig, satisfy the constraint (10.20).

$$\mathbf{R}\mathbf{R}_1 = \mathbf{R}_2\mathbf{R}, \tag{10.21}$$

$$(\mathbf{I} - \mathbf{R}_2)\mathbf{t} = \mu_2 \mathbf{t}_2 - \mu_1 \mathbf{R}\mathbf{t}_1, \tag{10.22}$$

where μ_1 and μ_2 are unknown scale factors associated with $\mathcal{D}_1$ and $\mathcal{D}_2$ respectively. Equation 10.21 has been much studied in the framework of hand-eye calibration

(Chou and Kamel, 1988), (Shiu and Ahmad, 1989), (Tsai and Lenz, 1988), (Chen, 1991).

To solve it we use a quaternion representation of the rotations:

$$
\begin{aligned}
\mathbf{q_R} &= (s, \mathbf{v}), \\
\mathbf{q_{R_1}} &= (s_1, \mathbf{v}_1), \\
\mathbf{q_{R_2}} &= (s_2, \mathbf{v}_2).
\end{aligned}
$$

Writing Equation 10.21 in this representation yields

$$
\mathbf{q_R} * \mathbf{q_{R_1}} - \mathbf{q_{R_2}} * \mathbf{q_R} = 0, \tag{10.23}
$$

where $*$ indicates the quaternion product. There exists a 4×4 matrix $\mathbf{G}$, such that

$$
\mathbf{q_R} * \mathbf{q_{R_1}} - \mathbf{q_{R_2}} * \mathbf{q_R} = \mathbf{G}\mathbf{q_R}.
$$

A closed form solution can be obtained with two equations obtained by two rigid displacements of the stereo rig. If we use more displacements, we can improve the results by using a linear least-squares procedure.

We now suppose that we have computed $\mathbf{R}$, as previously described. A geometrical analysis shows that the matrix $\mathbf{I} - \mathbf{R}_2$ maps all vectors in the plane perpendicular to the axis $\mathbf{r}_2$ of the rotation $\mathbf{R}_2$. Thus, starting from relation (10.22), we can write

$$
\mathbf{r}_2.(\mu_2 \mathbf{t}_2 - \mu_1 \mathbf{R} \mathbf{t}_1) = 0.
$$

This allows us to determine the ratio $a = \mu_1 / \mu_2$. It is then possible to recover the direction $\mathbf{t}_\perp$ of the component of $\mathbf{t}$ orthogonal to $\mathbf{u}_2$, yielding the constraint

$$
\mathbf{t} \in \langle \mathbf{t}_\perp, \mathbf{r}_2 \rangle. \tag{10.24}
$$

If a second movement, *for which the axis $\mathbf{r}'_2$ of the rotation is different*, is performed, we can similarly compute a direction $\mathbf{t}'_\perp$. Combining the two constraints (10.24), and the same with primes, we obtain $\mathbf{t}$ up to a scale factor by

$$
\mathbf{t} = \lambda(\mathbf{t}_\perp \times \mathbf{u}_2) \times (\mathbf{t}'_\perp \times \mathbf{u}'_2). \tag{10.25}
$$

If we perform more than two rigid displacements, the direction of $\mathbf{t}$ can be recovered by a linear least-squares procedure.

This completes the computation of the relative position of the two cameras, up to a scale factor.

10.5   References and further reading

Multi-view constraints and representations The Quadrifocal tensor was discovered by Triggs (Triggs, 1995) and used for reconstruction by Heyden (Heyden, 1995a; Heyden, 1995b) who gave an algorithm for computation and extraction of projection matrices. This was improved by Hartley (Hartley, 1998b) by minimizing algebraic error.

Relations between different Trifocal tensors are described in (Shashua and Avidan, 1996), and between homographies in (Zelnik-Manor and Irani, 1999b). The relations between different multilinear constraints and the question of the minimal number of constraints necessary to generate all of them is investigated by Heyden and Astrom (Heyden and Astrom, 1996) using ideal theory. In particular, they give a precise answer to the question whether "the trilinear constraints follow from the bilinear one in the generic case".

The idea of using certain projection matrices as canonical representations for the geometries of multiple views in a stratified context is due to Luong and Vieville (Luong and Viéville, 1996). Heyden and Astrom (Heyden and Astrom, 1997b; Heyden, 1998b) have proposed a scheme in the same spirit, which differs in the fact that they choose four corresponding points for the canonical basis, which make relations much simpler, but dependent on the choice of these points.

Reconstruction from N views The first incremental method to build global representations (i.e. projection matrices) from local representations (i.e. Fundamental matrices and infinity homographies) in the projective and affine case is due to Luong and Vieville (Luong and Viéville, 1996). Avidan and Shashua (Avidan and Shashua, 1998) propose a similar approach where consecutive Fundamental matrices are connected through a property of the Trifocal tensor. So far the most general approach is that of Triggs (Triggs, 1997b) who points out that a set of linear constraints (called the closure constraints) make it possible to recover the projection matrices from the four categories of tensors, epipoles, Fundamental matrices, Trifocal tensors and Quadrifocal tensors.

Factorization methods were introduced by Tomasi and Kanade (Tomasi and Kanade, 1992) (Debrunner and Ahuja (Debrunner and Ahuja, 1990) presented a less general version which assumed fixed-axis rotation), originally as a batch approach for a single motion, and in the orthographic case. It has been extended to deal with weak perspective (Weinshall and Tomasi, 1995) in a recursive formulation; paraperspective (Poelman and Kanade, 1997); multiple motions (Costeira and Kanade, 1995); lines (Quan and Kanade, 1997); and points, lines, and planes simultaneously while taking into account uncertainty (Morris and Kanade, 1998). In order to apply the factorization method to the projective case, the main difficulty is to recover the projective depths. Sturm and Triggs (Sturm and Triggs, 1996; Triggs, 1996) first discovered a way to do this based on computation of the Fundamental matrices between pairs of views. In (Heyden et al., 1999), an iterative version is given. Ueshiba and Tomita (Ueshiba and Tomita, 1998) propose an approach which does not rely on the computation of the Fundamental matrices. Instead, the idea is to define a measure of "rank 4 proximity" of the measurement matrix and use it to estimate the projective depths by nonlinear minimization, using the affine camera model to initialize. They also derive metric constraints in case the intrinsic parameters are available.

The bundle adjustment method has been known in the Euclidean context for many years in the photogrammetry community (Brown, 1958; Brown, 1971; Faig, 1975; Sobel, 1974; Abdel-Aziz and Karara, 1971; Gruen, 1978; Slama, 1980; Gruen and Beyer, 1992). It has been more recently adapted to the projective framework (Mohr et al., 1993b; Hartley, 1993; Szeliski and Kang, 1994). Christy and Horaud (Christy and Horaud, 1996) provide an iterative method to solve the bundle adjustment equations in the calibrated case. The method uses the relation between perspective and weak perspective. It requires only a few affine iterations, which are linear. A comparison between the results obtained with Euclidean and projective bundle adjustment is due to Oliensis and Govindu. They find that while the Euclidean version is sometimes as accurate as the projective version even with uncertain intrinsic parameters, the projective version has less trouble with local minima.

Other recent work on projective reconstruction includes (Li and Brooks, 1999; Chen and Medioni, 1999a) (iterative methods), (Oliensis and Genc, 1999) (a quasilinear method, assuming motions are small), and (Garcia and Brunet, 1998; Saito and Kanade, 1999) (finding the point correspondences is part of the problem). Strategies to cope with degeneracies arising from non-parallax situations (fixed camera or planar structure) when recovering structure and motion in image sequences are studied in (Torr et al., 1999). Quan *et al.* (Quan et al., 1999) present a theoretical analysis of the minimal data necessary for reconstruction (Quan et al., 1999) when points are not seen in all views.

Cross and Zisserman (Cross and Zisserman, 1998) study the reconstruction of quadrics from their outlines. With two views, there is a one-parameter family of solutions, which is reduced to two given a point correspondence. The ambiguity is reduced for degenerate quadrics. Generally, with three views and more, there is no ambiguity. The reconstruction of curves is tackled by Berthilsoon *et al.* (Berthilsson et al., 1999).

Stereo rigs   The idea that with multiple views, between which there are Euclidean constraints such as those of a fixed stereo rig, can be used to recover Euclidean information, has been discovered in the context of object recognition by Forsyth *et al.* (Forsyth et al., 1994).

The possibility of self-calibrating a stereo rig based only on its rigidity and one general motion using Equation 10.19 was discovered independently by Zisserman *et al.* (Zisserman et al., 1995a) and Devernay and Faugeras (Devernay and Faugeras,

1996). The method in (Zisserman et al., 1995a) requires the computation of Fundamental matrices associated with the left and right camera, in addition to the one associated with the stereo rig, and is not easily extended to deal with multiple motions. The method in (Devernay and Faugeras, 1996) requires nonlinear minimization to find the Euclidean parameters in $\mathcal{H}_{PE}$. The method that we presented in this chapter was based on the work of Horaud et al. (Horaud and Csurka, 1998). The work of Csurka et al. (Csurka et al., 1998) differs from it by proposing a closed form solution. They give parameterizations of the matrix $\mathcal{H}_{12}$ using a real Jordan factorization in the case of general motion and planar motion, which make explicit the camera's intrinsic parameters. They find that four intrinsic parameters can be recovered from a single general motion (which was expected), and that three intrinsic parameters can be recovered from a single planar motion. All these methods require the estimation of a homography of $\mathbb{P}^3$ between two sets of 3-D points. Csurka et al. (Csurka et al., 1999) present linear, nonlinear, and robust methods to perform this task.

Zhang et al. (Zhang et al., 1996) assume that left-to-right correspondences, as well as temporal correspondences are available, so that the self-calibration problem is formulated as a Euclidean parameter minimization problem. Enciso and Vieville (Enciso and Vieville, 1997) generalize this approach. Updating camera calibration is much easier with a stereo rig (Zhang and Schenk, 1997). If the stereo rig is initially calibrated, and at least six left-to-right and temporal correspondences are available, then one just reconstructs the points at the first instant, and then uses them with the points observed at the second instant to obtain the new projection matrices.

Brooks et al. (Brooks et al., 1996) consider a particular kind of stereo head, with vergence and coplanar optical axes, undergoing a motion in which the baseline remains confined to a plane. Using a Euclidean parameterization, they derive a closed form solution for self-calibration. Planar motion of a stereo rig was used by Beardsley et al. (Beardsley et al., 1995). who showed that affine reconstruction can be obtained. Horaud, Czurka, Demirdjian, and Ruf have done a lot of work on uncalibrated stereo rigs, using a Jordan factorization of the homography $\mathcal{H}$ to find an appropriate parameterization. They study in great detail the pure rotation of a stereo rig (Ruf and Horaud, 1999a) on a pan-tilt head, and the pure translation of a stereo rig (Ruf et al., 1998). In the latter case, a closed form solution is given for the decomposition of $\mathcal{H}$ into the three parameters of the plane at infinity, and the translation parameters. The analysis is extended to rigid and articulated motions as seen by a stereo rig in (Ruf and Horaud, 1999b). In (Demirdjian and Horaud, 1992), they propose to segment rigid motions based on the homography $\mathcal{H}$ using a stereo rig, extending the idea of segmentation of rigid motions based on the Fundamental matrix using a single camera.

11
Self-calibration of a moving camera: From affine or projective calibration to full Euclidean calibration

We have described the three-dimensional geometry of the world as a stratification of projective, affine, and Euclidean layers. So far, we have seen in Chapters 7 and 10 that with some additional information about the world or the motion of the cameras, we could upgrade the representation from one layer to the next. In this chapter, we address the problem of upgrading the representation using constraints on the camera's intrinsic parameters. This problem can be alternatively formulated as the recovery of the internal parameters of a camera without the need for a calibration pattern, i.e. an object with known geometry in some three-dimensional Euclidean coordinate system.

We focus in the first two sections on the idea of directly relating the infinity morphism and the Fundamental matrix to the intrinsic parameters by elimination of the rigid motion. First, even though we have seen in Chapter 5 that the infinity morphism is an affine entity, we show here that it can also provide some Euclidean information, namely the intrinsic parameters of the camera. Second, even though we have also seen in the same chapter that the Fundamental matrix between two views is a projective entity, we show here that it can provide some Euclidean information, i.e. also the intrinsic parameters of the camera.

The situations where we can use the infinity morphism and those where we can use the Fundamental matrix are somewhat different. The infinity morphism can be most easily estimated from point correspondences when the camera's motion is restricted to keep the optical center fixed, i.e. the camera is purely rotating around an axis going through that optical center, whereas the Fundamental matrix is important as soon as there is enough translation in the motion of the camera that the distance between the positions of the optical centers is significant with respect to the distances of the 3D points in the scene.

The basic idea is that, once we have estimated the infinity morphism between two views if the optical centers are identical, or the Fundamental matrix if they are different, we can use their relations, described in Chapter 5, with the internal parameters of the camera to actually constrain those parameters and even, sometimes, to compute them. The computation of the internal parameters from the infinity morphism can be considered an upgrade from affine to Euclidean calibration while the computation of those parameters from the Fundamental matrix is an upgrade from projective to Euclidean calibration. A major role is played in this chapter by the Kruppa matrix introduced in Chapter 4. It is in fact this matrix that it is convenient to recover in both cases rather than the intrinsic parameters directly.

Section 11.1 introduces the relation between the Kruppa matrices of two views and the infinity morphism and shows that this relation provides in general four independent equations between the coefficients of the unknown Kruppa matrices. When those are identical, i.e. when the intrinsic parameters of the camera have not changed between the views, this set of equations is sufficient to recover four intrinsic parameters but insufficient to recover five. In the case where the skew is known, e.g. equal to 0, we show that two views provide a unique solution for the Kruppa matrix and hence for the calibration of the camera. In the case where the skew is not known, we show that, in general, three views are sufficient to uniquely recover the Kruppa matrix. To illustrate the theory, we give a real example and also show the application of the method to the construction of a mosaic.

Section 11.2 introduces various relations between the Fundamental matrix and the internal parameters of a pair of cameras. It starts with the idea, historically important, to relate the Fundamental and the Essential matrices. We show that, although conceptually simple, that relation yields one complicated algebraic equation between the intrinsic parameters of the two cameras. We then show that by taking the full-fledged projective viewpoint advocated in this book and introducing the absolute conic, we come up with a set of equations between the Kruppa matrices of the two views which are algebraically simpler than the one obtained with the previous approach. We have named these equations after Erwin Kruppa because of his pioneering contributions in the use of projective geometry to analyze perspective projection. There are three such equations of which only two are algebraically independent and we show that in general three views provide six independent equations that are sufficient to recover the five intrinsic parameters in the case where they are identical in the three views.

Section 11.3 investigates practical methods for self-calibration based on the Kruppa equations. These methods solve exclusively for the intrinsic parameters. Once these parameters are obtained, the motion and the structure can be determined. It is shown that the methods for estimating the uncertainty of these Fundamental matrices described in Chapter 6 play an important role in the accurate computation of the intrinsic parameters.

Section 11.4 is devoted to methods which solve not only for the intrinsic parameters (which are Euclidean entities), but also for the equation of the plane at infinity (an affine entity). We first pursue our investigation of the constant intrinsic parameter case for the simpler case of affine cameras, before turning to the case of perspective projection for which we describe several methods. The section ends with a method that does not assume that the intrinsic parameters are constant in all views but only that some of them are somewhat constrained, e.g. that the cameras are zero skew or that their aspect ratio is known. The method is based upon the estimation of the quadric dual to the absolute conic.

While motion was always eliminated in the approaches previously described, resulting in a relatively small number of unknowns, the methods described in Section 11.5 all involve the simultaneous determination of the intrinsic parameters and motion parameters. We first use the epipolar constraints, before describing an approach based directly on the projection equations, which in addition computes simultaneously the structure. The rest of the section is devoted to the description of the application of the previous techniques to the construction of 3D Euclidean models of a scene from photographs and to match moving, i.e. the insertion of synthetic objects in sequences of images of real scenes.

Section 11.6 ends the chapter with a discussion of the problem of degeneracy in self-calibration. Theoretically it is important to characterize the situations in which the equations that have been presented in the previous two sections become degenerate in the sense that they do not yield a unique solution for the Kruppa matrix or the intrinsic parameters, because it is part of our understanding of these equations. Practically it is also clearly important to know which camera motions should be avoided for our algorithms to estimate quickly and reliably the calibration parameters. We show that the problem of degeneracy is intrinsic (no pun intended) in the sense that it is algorithm independent: The degeneracy comes from the fact that we use a finite number of views to recover the equation of the image of the absolute conic. But we also show that, beside these intrinsic degeneracies, each particular method, e.g. the one based on the Kruppa equations, adds in general more degeneracies.

11.1   From affine to Euclidean

We start with the special case where the infinity homography $\mathbf{H}_\infty$ is known. This case is important because, as seen in Chapter 5, it corresponds to the situation where the camera is rotating with respect to an axis going through its optical center or to the situation where we have been able to recover the affine structure of the environment.

11.1.1   Theoretical analysis

We first show that the knowledge of $\mathbf{H}_\infty$ places some constraints on the internal parameters of the two views through the Kruppa matrix defined in Section 4.3.2:

Proposition 11.1 *Given the infinity homography* $\mathbf{H}_\infty$ *between two views, the relation between the Kruppa matrices is*

$$\mathbf{K}' \simeq \mathbf{H}_\infty \mathbf{K} \mathbf{H}_\infty^T. \tag{11.1}$$

Proof :   We know from Proposition 5.25 that $\mathbf{H}_\infty \simeq \mathbf{A}'\mathbf{R}\mathbf{A}^{-1}$; therefore, since $\mathbf{R}\mathbf{R}^T = \mathbf{I}_3$, $\mathbf{H}_\infty \mathbf{K} \mathbf{H}_\infty^T \simeq \mathbf{K}'$, where $\mathbf{K}$ and $\mathbf{K}'$ are the two Kruppa matrices. Another, more geometric, explanation is the remark that since Ω is by definition in the plane at infinity Π_∞, ω and ω' or rather ω^* and ω'^* are images of one another through the infinity homography H_∞: For any line l' belonging to ω'^*, i.e. such that $l'^T \mathbf{K}' l' = 0$, its image through the infinity homography is $\mathbf{H}_\infty^T l'$ and belongs to ω^*: $l'^T \mathbf{H}_\infty \mathbf{K} \mathbf{H}_\infty^T l' = 0$, which implies Equation 11.1. $\square$

This equation implies the equality, up to scale, of the two symmetric matrices $\mathbf{H}_\infty \mathbf{K} \mathbf{H}_\infty^T$ and $\mathbf{K}'$. In the case where the internal parameters are the same in the two views, i.e. when $\mathbf{K} = \mathbf{K}'$, this equality yields apparently five equations between those internal parameters. A natural question to ask is whether or not these constraints are sufficient to recover the intrinsic parameters of the camera. The answer to this question is unfortunately no, as shown in Proposition 11.2. We start with a lemma.

Lemma 11.1 *Let* $\mathbf{X}$ *be an unknown symmetric matrix and* $\mathbf{R}$ *be a rotation matrix,* $\mathbf{R} \neq \mathbf{I}_3$. *Let* $\mathbf{r}$ *be a unit vector parallel to the axis of rotation of* $\mathbf{R}$. *The solutions of the matrix equation*

$$\mathbf{R}\mathbf{X}\mathbf{R}^T - \mathbf{X} = \mathbf{0} \tag{11.2}$$

fall in the following two categories.

1. *If* $\mathbf{R}$ *is a rotation of 180 degrees, then*

$$\mathbf{X} = \lambda_1 \mathbf{u}_1 \mathbf{u}_1^T + \lambda_2 \mathbf{u}_2 \mathbf{u}_2^T + \mu \mathbf{r}\mathbf{r}^T, \tag{11.3}$$

   where $\mathbf{u}_1$ *and* $\mathbf{u}_2$ *are orthogonal unit vectors orthogonal to* $\mathbf{r}$, *and* λ_1, λ_2 *and* μ *are arbitrary real numbers.*

2. *If* $\mathbf{R}$ *is not a rotation of 180 degrees, then the solutions form a two-dimensional vector subspace* $\mathcal{V}_{\mathbf{r}} = span\left(\mathbf{I}_3, \mathbf{r}\mathbf{r}^T\right)$ *of the six-dimensional vector space of the symmetric matrices, i.e.*

$$\mathbf{X} = \lambda \mathbf{I}_3 + \mu \mathbf{r}\mathbf{r}^T, \tag{11.4}$$

   where λ *and* μ *are arbitrary real numbers.*

Proof : Let us rewrite Equation 11.2 as

$$\mathbf{R}\mathbf{X} = \mathbf{X}\mathbf{R}.$$

This equation shows that $\mathbf{r}$ is an eigenvector of $\mathbf{X}$ since $\mathbf{R}\mathbf{X}\mathbf{r} = \mathbf{X}\mathbf{R}\mathbf{r} = \mathbf{X}\mathbf{r}$ and that $\mathbf{R}$ must leave the other eigenspaces of $\mathbf{X}$ invariant since for each eigenvector $\mathbf{u}$ of $\mathbf{X}$, $\mathbf{R}\mathbf{X}\mathbf{u} = \lambda \mathbf{R}\mathbf{u} = \mathbf{X}\mathbf{R}\mathbf{u}$.

Consider the eigenspaces orthogonal to $\mathbf{r}$. Two cases can occur. The first case is that in which there are two orthogonal eigenspaces corresponding to the two distinct eigenvalues λ_1 and λ_2 and generated by the two unit norm orthogonal vectors $\mathbf{u}_1$ and $\mathbf{u}_2$. Since $\mathbf{R}\mathbf{u}_1$ is an eigenvector of $\mathbf{X}$ and is in the plane $span(\mathbf{u}_1, \mathbf{u}_2)$ (because $\mathbf{R}$'s axis is orthogonal to that plane), the only possibility is that $\mathbf{R}\mathbf{u}_1 = \pm\mathbf{u}_1$. In the first case, $\mathbf{R}$ is the identity; in the second it is a rotation of 180 degrees and $\mathbf{X}$ takes the form (11.3).

The second case to be considered is that in which there is an eigenplane orthogonal to $\mathbf{r}$ corresponding to the eigenvalue λ. The restriction of $\mathbf{X}$ to this eigenplane is $\lambda \mathbf{I}_3$ and $\mathbf{X}$ takes the form (11.4). $\square$

We are now ready to state a proposition:

Proposition 11.2 *The solutions in* $\mathbf{K}$, *a symmetric matrix, of the matrix equation*

$$\mathbf{H}_\infty \mathbf{K} \mathbf{H}_\infty^T = \mathbf{K}, \tag{11.5}$$

where $\mathbf{H}_\infty$ *is of rank 3, has all eigenvalues of unit magnitude, two of them complex conjugate, are given by*

$$\mathbf{K} = \lambda \mathbf{A} \mathbf{A}^T + \mu (\mathbf{A}\mathbf{r})(\mathbf{A}\mathbf{r})^T, \tag{11.6}$$

where λ *and* μ *are arbitrary constants and* $\mathbf{r}$ *is a unit vector satisfying* $\mathbf{R}\mathbf{r} = \mathbf{r}$.

Proof : From Proposition 5.26 we can assume that $\mathbf{H}_\infty = \mathbf{A}\mathbf{R}\mathbf{A}^{-1}$ and transform Equation 11.5 into

$$\mathbf{R} \left(\mathbf{A}^{-1} \mathbf{K} \mathbf{A}^{-T} \right) \mathbf{R}^T - \mathbf{A}^{-1} \mathbf{K} \mathbf{A}^{-T} = \mathbf{0},$$

which expresses the fact that $\mathbf{K}$ is a solution of the original equation if and only if $\mathbf{A}^{-1} \mathbf{K} \mathbf{A}^{-T}$ is a solution of

$$\mathbf{R}\mathbf{X}\mathbf{R}^T - \mathbf{X} = 0.$$

We then just have to apply Lemma 11.1 to complete the proof. □

Note that we have eliminated, as non-generic, the case where the rotation between the views is 180 degrees.

An interpretation of this proposition is that the knowledge of the infinity morphism between two views taken with the same camera imposes in general four constraints on the five intrinsic parameters. A special case of interest is the case in which the number of intrinsic parameters is reduced to four, e.g. when the skew is zero, a case of practical interest. We state the result in the following proposition.

Proposition 11.3 *When the camera is zero-skew, the knowledge of* $\mathbf{H}_\infty$ *yields in general a unique solution for the matrix* $\mathbf{K}$.

Proof : We know from Proposition 11.2 that the solutions of the system of linear equations $\mathbf{H}_\infty \mathbf{K} \mathbf{H}_\infty^T = \mathbf{K}$ form a vector space of dimension 2. Let $\mathbf{K}_1$, $\mathbf{K}_2$ be a basis of that vector subspace (in practice, it can be found for example by singular value decomposition (SVD), as seen in Section 11.1.2). Hence, all solutions are of the form

$$\mathbf{K} = \lambda_1 \mathbf{K}_1 + \lambda_2 \mathbf{K}_2. \tag{11.7}$$

Note that this basis is in general different from the basis $\left(\mathbf{A}\mathbf{A}^T, \mathbf{A}\mathbf{r}(\mathbf{A}\mathbf{r})^T \right)$, but when λ_1 and λ_2 vary, $\mathbf{K}$ takes all of the values given by Equation 11.6. This family of symmetric matrices contains one singular matrix, $\mathbf{A}\mathbf{r}(\mathbf{A}\mathbf{r})^T$, obtained for $\lambda = 0$ and, since $\mathbf{A}\mathbf{A}^T$ is non-singular, it is the only singular matrix in the family. Let us now use the fact that the camera is zero-skew. According to the analysis done in Section 4.3.2 and to Equation 4.37, $\mathbf{K}$ must satisfy the constraint

$$K_{13} K_{23} - K_{33} K_{12} = 0. \tag{11.8}$$

It can be verified that the matrix $\mathbf{Ar}(\mathbf{Ar})^T$ satisfies this equation.

The left-hand side of (11.8) is a second degree homogeneous polynomial in λ_1 and λ_2 which has in general two roots in $\frac{\lambda_1}{\lambda_2}$, yielding two solutions for $\mathbf{K}$. Among the two solutions, one of them must be proportional to $\mathbf{Ar}(\mathbf{Ar})^T$. The second solution must therefore be proportional to $\mathbf{AA}^T$. The scale factor can be accounted for by computing its Cholesky decomposition. $\square$

Let us now return to the general case of five intrinsic parameters. We can hope that if we perform two motions of the camera such that the corresponding rotation matrices are sufficiently different, in a sense to be made more precise, we should be able to recover the intrinsic parameters. We start with the following proposition.

Proposition 11.4 *Let* $\mathbf{R}_i, i = 1, 2$, *be two rotation matrices such that* $\mathbf{R}_1 \neq \mathbf{I}_3$, $\mathbf{R}_2 \neq \mathbf{I}_3$, *and furthermore none of them is a rotation of 180 degrees. Let* $\mathbf{X}$ *be an unknown symmetric matrix. The solutions in* $\mathbf{X}$ *of the system of two equations*

$$\mathbf{R}_i \mathbf{X} \mathbf{R}_i^T - \mathbf{X} = 0 \quad i = 1, 2,$$

are given by

$$\mathbf{X} \in \left\{ \begin{array}{ll} span(\mathbf{I}_3) & \textit{if the two rotations have different axes,} \\ span\left(\mathbf{I}_3, \mathbf{r}_1 \mathbf{r}_1^T\right) = span\left(\mathbf{I}_3, \mathbf{r}_2 \mathbf{r}_2^T\right) & \textit{otherwise.} \end{array} \right.$$

Proof : The solutions of the system of two linear matrix equations lie in the intersection of the two vector spaces $\mathcal{V}_{\mathbf{r}_i}$ $i = 1, 2$, of the solutions of each equation. It is easy to see that if the two rotations have different axes, then this intersection is reduced to the one-dimensional vector space generated by $\mathbf{I}_3$ whereas in the other case the two vector spaces are identical. $\square$

We are now in a position to prove our main result:

Theorem 11.1 *Let* $\mathbf{H}_{\infty i}, i = 1, 2$, *be two infinity homographies, i.e. such that there exist two rotation matrices (none of them of 180 degrees)* $\mathbf{R}_i, i = 1, 2$, *such that* $\mathbf{H}_{\infty i}, i = 1, 2$, *be congruent to* $\mathbf{R}_i, i = 1, 2$, *with the* same *matrix* $\mathbf{A}$. *Let* $\mathbf{K}$ *be an unknown symmetric matrix. The solutions* $\mathbf{K}$ *of the system of two equations*

$$\mathbf{H}_{\infty i} \mathbf{K} \mathbf{H}_{\infty i}^T - \mathbf{K} = 0 \quad i = 1, 2,$$

are given by:

$$\mathbf{K} \in \left\{ \begin{array}{ll} span\left(\mathbf{AA}^T\right) & \textit{if the two rotations have different axes,} \\ span\left(\mathbf{AA}^T, \mathbf{Ar}_1\left(\mathbf{Ar}_1^T\right)\right) = span\left(\mathbf{AA}^T, \mathbf{Ar}_2\left(\mathbf{Ar}_2^T\right)\right) & \textit{otherwise.} \end{array} \right.$$

Proof : The proof follows from Proposition 11.4 using the same argument as in Proposition 11.2. $\square$

This theorem tells us that unless we happen to rotate around the same axis the five intrinsic parameters are uniquely determined by two views, provided that we can estimate the two infinity morphisms.

11.1.2   Practical computation

Equation 11.5 can be rewritten as a system of six linear equations in the six unknown coefficients of the symmetric matrix $\mathbf{K}$:

$$\mathcal{M}\mathbf{k} = \mathbf{0}. \tag{11.9}$$

Because of the noise in $\mathcal{M}$, in practice one solves the minimization problem

$$\min_{\mathbf{k}} \|\mathcal{M}\mathbf{k}\|^2 \qquad \text{subject to} \qquad \|\mathbf{k}\| = 1. \tag{11.10}$$

Theoretically, according to Proposition 11.2, the rank of matrix $\mathcal{M}$ is four in general. Therefore, one expects two of the singular values of matrix $\mathcal{M}$ to be significantly smaller than the other four (see the next section for an example). The solutions of Problem 11.10 are therefore taken as being in the two-dimensional vector space generated by the two eigenvectors of the symmetric 6×6 matrix $\mathcal{M}^T\mathcal{M}$ corresponding to the two smallest eigenvalues.

If one has more than two views, as in Proposition 11.4, then one applies the same analysis and solves the system of linear equations

$$\mathcal{M}_n\mathbf{k} = \mathbf{0}. \tag{11.11}$$

$\mathcal{M}_n$ is an $6n \times 6$ matrix obtained by concatenating the n matrices provided by the knowledge of the infinity homography between n pairs of views. In practice one solves

$$\min_{\mathbf{k}} \|\mathcal{M}_n\mathbf{k}\|^2 \qquad \text{subject to} \qquad \|\mathbf{k}\| = 1. \tag{11.12}$$

Theoretically, according to Theorem 11.1, the rank of (11.11) is in general five as soon as n is larger than or equal to 2. The solution of (11.12) is therefore taken in the one-dimensional vector subspace generated by the eigenvector of the symmetric 6×6 matrix $\mathcal{M}_n^T\mathcal{M}_n$ corresponding to the smallest eigenvalue.

11.1.3   A numerical example

The knowledge of the infinity homography enables us to perform (partial) self-calibration from two views in the case of constant intrinsic parameters and also to deal with the case of variable intrinsic parameters, by propagating affine and then Euclidean information. However, it has been reported (Hartley, 1997b; Zisserman et al., 1995a) that the methods based on the infinity homography matrix are very sensitive to the precision of determination of the homography, and that in practice several views are necessary to obtain good results.

The following example may help to ground the previous propositions in reality. Three images of an indoor scene shown Figure 11.1 are used. The camera is zooming: The focal length has been changed from 8mm to 12mm (read on the lens barrel) between the second and the third view.

Figure 11.1: Three images taken by a camera, with epipolar lines shown. The camera has zoomed between the second and the third view, thereby changing the internal parameters.

Partial self-calibration of a camera from the infinity homography   The infinity homography matrix between the two first views has been determined using a calibration object with a good precision:

$$\mathbf{H}_{\infty 12} = \begin{bmatrix} 1.72134 & -0.172135 & -218.805 \\ 0.75804 & 1.59733 & -620.388 \\ 0.00109 & 0.00059 & 1.000 \end{bmatrix}.$$

The three eigenvalues of $\mathbf{H}_{\infty 12}$ have the same norm, 1.57575; thus we conclude that the intrinsic parameters remain constant between image 1 and image 2. We divide the entries of $\mathbf{H}_{\infty 12}$ by 1.57575 so that the determinant is now 1.

The singular values σ_i for the matrix $\boldsymbol{\mathcal{M}}$ in Equation 11.9 are

$$165495, \qquad 469, \qquad 2.02, \qquad 0.19, \qquad 1.6 10^{-9}, \qquad 9 10^{-13}.$$

We conclude that this matrix is of rank 4, as expected. Taking the last two columns of the orthogonal matrix $\mathbf{V}$ such that the SVD of $\boldsymbol{\mathcal{M}}$ is $\mathbf{U}\mathrm{diag}(\sigma_1, \ldots, \sigma_6)\mathbf{V}^T$ gives the space of solutions

$$
\begin{aligned}
K_{11} &= -.16481 - .75667t, & K_{12} &= -.38670 + .63966t, \\
K_{22} &= -.90735 - .13517t, & K_{23} &= -.00081 + .000855t, \\
K_{33} &= -.13351 - .80646t, & K_{13} &= -.23358 10^{-5} - .0009565t.
\end{aligned}
$$

The zero-skew constraint of Equation 4.37 leads to two solutions: $t_1 = .434624$, and $t_2 = 3.9219$. After substitution, we find that $\det(\mathbf{K}_1) = -.56 10^{-6}$ and $\det(\mathbf{K}_2) = -.46 10^{-17}$. Therefore, the solution to be kept is t_1, and by applying the formulae in Proposition 4.22, we recover

$$\alpha_u = 481, \ \alpha_v = 711, \ u_0 = 248, \ v_0 = 260.$$

Propagation of affine and Euclidean information   Having obtained some-
where in the image sequence Euclidean information, we show now how to propa-
gate it throughout the whole sequence, thus updating the calibration of a *zooming*
camera.

After determining the three Fundamental matrices between the images, we are
able to obtain, using Proposition 10.4 in Chapter 10, the other infinity homographies
from $\mathbf{H}_{\infty 12}$. In particular,

$$\mathbf{H}_{\infty 23} = \begin{bmatrix} 1.07992 & 0.30229 & -35.2662 \\ -0.90515 & 0.95915 & 413.5660 \\ -0.00004 & -0.00036 & 1.0000 \end{bmatrix}.$$

The norms of the eigenvalues are $1.21, 1.21,$and 1.0; thus we conclude that the
intrinsic parameters have changed between image 2 and image 3. The zooming thus
took place between these two images. Applying Formula 11.1 gives immediately the
new matrix $\mathbf{K}'$, from which the following parameters are computed:

$$\alpha_u = 642, \ \alpha_v = 950, \ u_0 = 248, \ v_0 = 263.$$

It can be verified that they correspond to the variation of focal length described
previously: We have $\frac{\alpha_u^{(3)}}{\alpha_u^{(1)}} \sim \frac{\alpha_v^{(3)}}{\alpha_v^{(1)}} \sim \frac{f^{(3)}}{f^{(1)}} = 1.5.$

We have thus updated the calibration of the intrinsic parameters. As explained
in Chapter 10, we can go even further and recover a set of Euclidean perspective
projection matrices which allow us to recover the structure of the scene up to a
similarity transformation.

11.1.4   Application to panoramic mosaicing

In Section 5.1.2 we explained how to build a planar mosaic using homographies.
There was no need for calibration, but, on the other hand, we had to reproject all
of the images onto a planar surface. If we wish to build a mosaic which encom-
passes a panoramic field of view (larger than 180 degrees), this reprojection is no
longer reasonable. By recovering the Euclidean parameters (intrinsic parameters
and rotations), we can reproject the images onto any surface, including a cylinder
or a sphere.

Figure 11.2 show a set of nine views which have been acquired on the site of
INRIA in Sophia-Antipolis with a Kodak DCS460 digital camera from an approximately constant viewpoint. They cover 360 degrees of field of view. The intrinsic
parameters have been computed using the technique described previously. The relative rotations have also been computed using techniques described in Chapter 10.
The images have then been mapped to a cylinder which is shown in Figure 11.3.
Note that the left and right sides of the resulting rectangular image match perfectly,
a demonstration of the quality of the calibration.

Figure 11.2: Nine images of INRIA at Sophia-Antipolis acquired from the same viewpoint.

If besides panning the camera, we take images by tilting it, with a sufficient number of images we can cover the whole sphere. This idea results in the spherical mosaics shown in Figure 11.4, where we show the two half-hemispheres. It can be noted that this representation makes it possible to synthesize any perspective view taken from the initial viewpoint in any direction, as illustrated in Figure 11.5.

11.2 From projective to Euclidean

In this section, we study the case of perspective projection. There is an important link between the Fundamental matrix and the intrinsic parameters, which comes from the fact that a general projection matrix can be decomposed into intrinsic parameters and a rigid displacement (see Chapter 4). Thus, the knowledge of the Fundamental matrix puts some constraints on the intrinsic parameters. This section studies these constraints in great detail and shows how they can be used for self-calibration.

We thus consider two pinhole cameras which perform perspective projection. We denote by C and C' the two optical centers (assumed to be different) and by $\mathbf{A}$

Figure 11.3: The mosaic built from the twelve images of Figure 11.2. Courtesy **Sylvain Bougnoux**, INRIA.

Figure 11.4: The two hemispheres of the spherical mosaic of the INRIA parking lot. Courtesy **Sylvain Bougnoux**, INRIA.

and $\mathbf{A}'$ the matrices of the internal parameters defined in Chapter 4.

11.2.1   The rigidity constraints: Algebraic formulations using the Essential matrix

The first natural idea is to use the relation described in Proposition 5.27 between the Fundamental matrix and the Essential matrix and the constraints (5.34) satisfied by the Essential matrix to come up with constraints between the internal parameters of two views.

Proposition 11.5 *The knowledge of the Fundamental matrix between the two views yields one algebraic polynomial relation of degree 8 between the coefficients of* $\mathbf{A}$ *and* $\mathbf{A}'$.

Figure 11.5: A semi-hemisphere of the mosaic of the Arcades square, and a synthesized perspective view. Courtesy **Sylvain Bougnoux**, INRIA.

Proof : We know from Proposition 5.27 that the relation

$$\mathbf{E} \simeq \mathbf{A}'^T \mathbf{F} \mathbf{A} \tag{11.13}$$

holds between the E-matrix, the F-matrix and the internal parameters. But we know from Chapter 5 that an E-matrix satisfies two algebraic constraints, the so-called Huang-Faugeras equations:

$$\det(\mathbf{E}) = 0, \qquad f(\mathbf{E}) = \frac{1}{2}\text{trace}^2\left(\mathbf{E}\mathbf{E}^T\right) - \text{trace}\left(\mathbf{E}\mathbf{E}^T\right)^2 = 0. \tag{11.14}$$

As we have $\det(\mathbf{F}) = 0$, the first condition is automatically satisfied and does not yield any valuable constraint in our framework; thus we are left with only one polynomial constraint, the second condition, which can be seen to be a polynomial of degree 8 on the coefficients of $\mathbf{A}$ and $\mathbf{A}'$. $\square$

A second expression of the rigidity constraints has been presented by Trivedi (Trivedi, 1988). If $\mathbf{E}$ is an essential matrix, then the symmetric matrix $\mathbf{S} = \mathbf{E}\mathbf{E}^T$, which *a priori* has six independent entries, depends only on the three components of $\mathbf{t}$:

$$\mathbf{S} \equiv \mathbf{E}\mathbf{E}^T = -[\mathbf{t}]_\times^2 = \begin{bmatrix} t_2^2 + t_3^2 & -t_1 t_2 & -t_1 t_3 \\ -t_2 t_1 & t_3^2 + t_1^2 & -t_2 t_3 \\ -t_3 t_1 & -t_3 t_2 & t_1^2 + t_2^2 \end{bmatrix}. \tag{11.15}$$

The matrix $\mathbf{S}$ has thus a special structure which is described in the following proposition.

Proposition 11.6 (Trivedi) *The elements of the matrix* $\mathbf{S}$ *are related by the three polynomial relations*

$$4 S_{ij} - \left(trace\left(\mathbf{S}\right) - 2 S_{ii} \right) \left(trace\left(\mathbf{S}\right) - 2 S_{jj} \right) = 0, \qquad 1 \le i < j \le 3, \qquad (11.16)$$

of which only two are independent.

The proof of this proposition can be found in (Trivedi, 1988) and (Luong, 1992).

It can be seen that the two Trivedi relations provide two polynomial relations of degree 8 between the coefficients of $\mathbf{A}$ and $\mathbf{A}'$ and a natural question is whether or not those conditions are the same as those obtained from the Huang-Faugeras equations. Fortunately, the answer to this question is positive:

Proposition 11.7 *The Huang-Faugeras and the Trivedi equations are equivalent.*

Proof : Let first suppose that we have (11.15). Then it follows immediately that $\det\left(\mathbf{E}\mathbf{E}^T\right) = 0$, and thus the first condition $\det(\mathbf{E}) = 0$ is satisfied. Adding the three equations in (11.16) yields

$$4 \left(S_{12}^2 + S_{13}^2 + S_{23}^2 \right) + S_{11}^2 + S_{22}^2 + S_{33}^2 - 2 \left(S_{11} S_{22} + S_{22} S_{33} + S_{33} S_{11} \right) = 0.$$

Since the matrix $\mathbf{S}$ is symmetric, the first term can be replaced by $4(S_{12} S_{21} + S_{13} S_{31} + S_{23} S_{32})$, and a simple computation shows that it is identical to the Huang-Faugeras condition:

$$trace^2\left(\mathbf{S}\right) - 2 trace\left(\mathbf{S}^2\right) = 0.$$

Conversely, let us then assume that the Huang-Faugeras conditions are satisfied. They are equivalent to the fact that the matrix $\mathbf{E}$ has one zero singular value and two equal nonzero singular values σ. By definition, there exists an orthogonal matrix $\mathbf{U}$ such that

$$\mathbf{S} = \mathbf{E}\mathbf{E}^T = \mathbf{U} \begin{bmatrix} 0 & 0 & 0 \\ 0 & \sigma^2 & 0 \\ 0 & 0 & \sigma^2 \end{bmatrix} \mathbf{U}^T.$$

This matrix equality can be expanded as

$$\mathbf{S} = \sigma^2 \left(U_{i2} U_{j2} + U_{i3} U_{j3} \right)_{1 \le i,j \le 3}.$$

Since $\mathbf{U}$ is orthogonal, its row vectors are orthonormal:

$$U_{i2} U_{j2} + U_{i3} U_{j3} = \begin{cases} -U_{i1} U_{j1} & \text{if } i \ne j, \\ 1 - U_{i1}^2 & \text{if } i = j. \end{cases}$$

The diagonal element $1 - U_{11}^2$ (respectively $1 - U_{21}^2$, $1 - U_{31}^2$) can be rewritten, because the column vectors of $\mathbf{U}$ are orthonormal, $U_{31}^2 + U_{21}^2$ (respectively $U_{11}^2 + U_{31}^2$, $U_{21}^2 + U_{11}^2$), which shows that $\mathbf{S}$ has exactly the form (11.15). $\square$

Unfortunately, the two independent Trivedi equations which are equivalent to the second Huang-Faugeras condition are not simpler than this one: they all yield algebraic constraints which are polynomials of degree 8 in the coefficients of $\mathbf{A}$ and $\mathbf{A}'$ (the intrinsic parameters) and thus are not quite suitable for practical computation, or even for theoretical study. This situation is why we are going to consider a *geometrical* interpretation of the rigidity constraint which yields low-order polynomial constraints.

11.2.2 The Kruppa equations: A geometric interpretation of the rigidity constraint

Geometric and algebraic derivation of the Kruppa equations   Let us consider an epipolar plane Π which is tangent to Ω. Then the corresponding epipolar lines l and l' are tangent to the images ω and ω' of Ω, respectively. It follows that the two tangents to ω drawn from the epipole $\mathbf{e}$ are in correspondence under the epipolar homography with the two tangents to ω' drawn from the epipole $\mathbf{e}'$, as illustrated by Figure 11.6.

Let $\mathbf{K}$ and $\mathbf{K}'$ be the Kruppa matrices, introduced in Chapter 5, in the first and second image (Equation 4.34). The fact that the camera is moving rigidly implies two polynomial constraints on the coefficients of $\mathbf{K}$ and $\mathbf{K}'$:

Proposition 11.8 *The two Kruppa matrices satisfy the relation*

$$\mathbf{F}\mathbf{K}\mathbf{F}^T \simeq [\mathbf{e}']_\times \mathbf{K}'[\mathbf{e}']_\times, \tag{11.17}$$

which is equivalent to two polynomial equations of degree 2 in the coefficients of $\mathbf{K}$ and $\mathbf{K}'$. These equations are called the **Kruppa** *equations.*

Proof :   The epipolar line $l' = (e', y')$ is tangent to ω' if and only if

$$\left(\mathbf{e}' \times \mathbf{y}'\right)^T \mathbf{K}' \left(\mathbf{e}' \times \mathbf{y}'\right) = -\mathbf{y}'^T [\mathbf{e}']_\times \mathbf{K}'[\mathbf{e}']_\times \mathbf{y}' = 0. \tag{11.18}$$

The epipolar line corresponding to the point $\mathbf{y}'$ is $\mathbf{F}^T\mathbf{y}'$ and is tangent to ω if and only if

$$\mathbf{y}'^T \mathbf{F}\mathbf{K}\mathbf{F}^T \mathbf{y}' = 0. \tag{11.19}$$

Writing that (11.18) and (11.19) are equivalent yields the so-called Kruppa equations.

Another, purely algebraic, way of obtaining those equations is to start with Equation 11.1,

$$\mathbf{K}' \simeq \mathbf{H}_\infty \mathbf{K} \mathbf{H}_\infty^T,$$

to multiply left and right by $[\mathbf{e}']_\times$,

$$[\mathbf{e}']_\times \mathbf{K}'[\mathbf{e}']_\times \simeq [\mathbf{e}']_\times \mathbf{H}_\infty \mathbf{K} \mathbf{H}_\infty^T [\mathbf{e}']_\times,$$

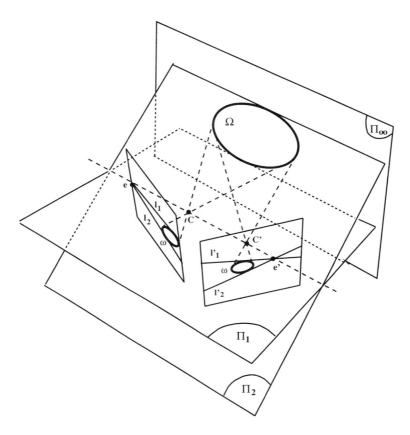

Figure 11.6: The absolute conic and the epipolar homography.

and to use Equation 5.16 to obtain

$$\mathbf{F} \simeq [\mathbf{e}']_\times \mathbf{H}_\infty$$

In order to obtain the two Kruppa equations, we assume for simplicity that the epipole e' is not at infinity, i.e. that its last coordinate is not zero. We can therefore parameterize the epipolar lines (e', y') by their point of intersection with the line at infinity: $\mathbf{y}'_\infty = [1, \tau, 0]^T$. The relations in (11.18) (respectively (11.19)) take the form $P(\tau) = k_0 + k_1\tau + k_2\tau^2 = 0$ (respectively $P'(\tau) = k'_0 + k'_1\tau + k'_2\tau^2 = 0$), and the Kruppa equations express the fact that the coefficients of those two polynomials in τ are proportional:

$$k_0 : k_1 : k_2 = k'_0 : k'_1 : k'_2. \tag{11.20}$$

We thus have two algebraically independent equations among the three equations

$$Eq_1 = k_1 k_2' - k_1' k_2 = 0, \qquad Eq_2 = k_2 k_0' - k_2' k_0 = 0, \qquad Eq_3 = k_0 k_1' - k_0' k_1 = 0.$$
(11.21)

$\square$

An advantage of the Kruppa equations is that since the coefficients k_i (respectively k_i') depend linearly on the entries of $\mathbf{K}$ (respectively $\mathbf{K}'$), they are only of degree *two* in these entries, and therefore of degree 4 in the entries of $\mathbf{A}$ and $\mathbf{A}'$, thus providing a much simpler expression of the rigidity constraint than the one obtained by the purely algebraic methods described at the beginning of this section.

In Section 11.4.2.3 we give another interpretation of the Kruppa equations in terms of the quadric dual to the absolute conic.

Equivalence between the Kruppa and the Huang-Faugeras equations   It would be reassuring to show that the two formulations, the algebraic and the geometric, are equivalent. This demonstration our next task. We have to show that the set of Kruppa equations (11.20) is equivalent to the constraint induced by the second equation (11.14). This equivalence is *a priori* not intuitive, since we just saw that there are *two* Kruppa equations.

Proposition 11.9 *The two Kruppa equations are equivalent to the constraint obtained from the second Huang-Faugeras equations.*

Proof :   Let us make a change of retinal coordinate system in each of the two retinal planes, so that the new Fundamental matrix is diagonalized. To achieve this, we use the SVD: there exists two orthogonal matrices $\mathbf{U}$ and $\mathbf{V}$ such that $\mathbf{F} = \mathbf{U}\mathrm{diag}(\lambda, \mu, 0)\mathbf{V}^T$, where $\lambda \neq 0$ and $\mu \neq 0$ since we know that a Fundamental matrix must be of rank two.

We use matrix $\mathbf{V}$ to change retinal coordinates in the first retina and matrix $\mathbf{U}$ to change retinal coordinates in the second retina, so the new matrices of intrinsic parameters are $\mathbf{A}_n = \mathbf{A}\mathbf{V}$ and $\mathbf{A}'_n = \mathbf{A}'\mathbf{U}$ in the first and second retina, respectively. Furthermore, in the new pixel coordinate systems we have $\mathbf{e} = \mathbf{e}' = (0,0,1)^T$.

The Kruppa equations are then easily shown to be given by

$$K_{22} : K_{11} : -K_{12} = \lambda^2 K_{11}' : \mu^2 K_{22}' : \lambda\mu K_{12}',$$

which yields

$$Eq_1 = \mu(\lambda K_{11} K_{12}' + \mu K_{12} K_{22}'), \qquad Eq_2 = \lambda(\lambda K_{12} K_{11}' + \mu K_{22} K_{12}'),$$
$$Eq_3 = \mu^2 K_{22} K_{22}' - \lambda^2 K_{11} K_{11}'.$$

Let us now express the condition $f(\mathbf{E}) = 0$. Since $\mathbf{E} \simeq \mathbf{A}'^T \mathbf{F} \mathbf{A}$, some algebra (done partially using the symbolic computation program MAPLE), leads to

$$f(\mathbf{E}) \simeq -\frac{1}{2}((\lambda^2 K_{11} K'_{11} - \mu^2 K_{22} K'_{22})^2 +$$
$$2\lambda\mu(\lambda K_{12} K'_{11} + \mu K_{22} K'_{12})(\lambda K_{11} K'_{12} + \mu K_{12} K'_{22})),$$

so that

$$f(\mathbf{E}) \simeq -\frac{1}{2}\left(Eq_3^2 + 2Eq_1 Eq_2\right).$$

It is clear that if the Kruppa equations are satisfied, then $f(\mathbf{E}) = 0$.

Let us now prove the converse.

We notice that

$$K_{22} Eq_1 - K_1 Eq_2 = K_{12} Eq_3. \tag{11.22}$$

In the case in which $K_{12} \neq 0$, the previous equation can be rewritten, using (11.22),

$$(K_{22} Eq_1 - K_{11} Eq_2)^2 + 2Eq_1 Eq_2 K_{12}^2 = 0. \tag{11.23}$$

Thus, expanding,

$$K_{22}^2 Eq_1^2 + K_{11}^2 Eq_2^2 = 2Eq_1 Eq_2 \left(K_{11} K_{22} - K_{12}^2\right)\left(K_{11} K_{22} - K_{12}^2\right). \tag{11.24}$$

Because $\mathbf{K} = \mathbf{A}_n \mathbf{A}_n^T$ and $\mathbf{K}' = \mathbf{A}'_n \mathbf{A}_n'^T$, if we denote by $\mathbf{l}_i$, $i = 1, 2, 3$, and $\mathbf{l}'_i$, $i = 1, 2, 3$, the row vectors of $\mathbf{A}_n$ and $\mathbf{A}'_n$, then

$$\begin{aligned} K_{12} &= \mathbf{l}_1^T \mathbf{l}_2, \\ K_{22} &= \|\mathbf{l}_2\|^2, \\ K_{11} &= \|\mathbf{l}_1\|^2. \end{aligned} \tag{11.25}$$

According to the definitions (11.26) of K_{12}, K_{11}, K_{22}, the Schwartz inequality implies that $K_{11} K_{22} - K_{12}^2$ is superior to or equal to zero. If it is zero, then one obtains from (11.24) $K_{11} E_1 = K_{22} E_2 = 0$. Since $K_{22} K_{11} = K_{12}^2 \neq 0$, it follows that $E_1 = E_2 = 0$. If it is strictly positive, then $E_1 E_2 \geq 0$. Equation 11.23 is the sum of two positive terms; thus they have to be simultaneously zero; thus $E_1 E_2 = 0$ and $E_3 = 0$.

The case which remains is $K_{12} = 0$. The Kruppa equations take then the simple form

$$\lambda\mu K_{11} K'_{12} = \lambda\mu K_{22} K'_{12} = \mu^2 K_{22} K'_{22} - \lambda^2 K_{11} K'_{11} = 0,$$

which is equivalent to

$$\begin{cases} K'_{12} &= 0 \\ \lambda^2 K_{11} K'_{11} - \mu^2 K_{22} K'_{22} &= 0 \end{cases} \quad \text{or} \quad \begin{cases} K'_{12} \neq 0 \\ K_{22} = K_{11} = 0 \end{cases}$$

and to

$$f(\mathbf{E}) \simeq 2\lambda^2\mu^2 K_{22}K_{11}K_{12}'^2 + \left(\lambda^2 K_{11}K_{11}' - \mu^2 K_{22}K_{22}'\right)^2 = 0.$$

□

As a consequence of this proof, we obtain the following formulae which give the Kruppa equations as a function of the singular value decomposition of the Fundamental matrix.

Proposition 11.10 *The Kruppa equations derived from the SVD of the Fundamental matrix* $\mathbf{F} = \mathbf{U}\,diag(\lambda,\mu,0)\mathbf{V}^T$, *where* $\mathbf{U} = [\mathbf{u}_1,\mathbf{u}_2,\mathbf{u}_3]$ *and* $\mathbf{V} = [\mathbf{v}_1,\mathbf{v}_2,\mathbf{v}_3]$ *are two orthogonal matrices, are*

$$\frac{\lambda^2\mathbf{v}_1^T\mathbf{K}\mathbf{v}_1}{\mathbf{u}_2^T\mathbf{K}\mathbf{u}_2} = \frac{\mu^2\mathbf{v}_2^T\mathbf{K}\mathbf{v}_2}{\mathbf{u}_1^T\mathbf{K}\mathbf{u}_1} = -\frac{\lambda\mu\mathbf{v}_1^T\mathbf{K}\mathbf{v}_2}{\mathbf{u}_1^T\mathbf{K}\mathbf{u}_2}.$$

It is interesting to note that in the calibrated case $\mathbf{K} = \mathbf{I}_3$, and therefore those equations reduce to $\lambda^2 = \mu^2$, in accordance with the condition on the Essential matrix in Equation 5.34.

11.2.3 Using two rigid displacements of a camera: A method for self-calibration

The idea behind the method is to use the Kruppa equations in the case of a single camera that we move in a static scene while keeping its intrinsic parameters fixed. In that case $\mathbf{A} = \mathbf{A}'$, $\mathbf{K} = \mathbf{K}'$, and each pair of views provides potentially two equations that constrain the intrinsic parameters. Intuitively, if sufficiently many different rigid displacements are made, then one might hope that one will be able to recover all intrinsic parameters.

How many rigid displacements or images are necessary? Each displacement yields two independent algebraic equations. We have in general five coefficients to estimate, and therefore three displacements are necessary. In the case in which some intrinsic parameters have known values, e.g. zero skew, a smaller number of rigid displacements may be sufficient. For example, in the case of zero skew, we have the additional constraint (4.37).

Given three views taken from three different viewpoints, there are three displacements, denoted D_{12}, D_{23}, and D_{13}. One could worry about the fact that since the third rigid displacement is a composition of the first two, $D_{13} = D_{23}D_{12}$, the two equations provided by D_{13} are algebraically dependent on the four equations provided by D_{12} and D_{23}, thus resulting in an under-constrained system. One way to see that this is not the case is to count unknowns. Two Fundamental matrices depend only upon 14 parameters (see Chapter 5). On the other hand, the Euclidean information which is recovered by self-calibration consists of the three rigid displacements, i.e. three rotations and three translations defined up to a common scale factor, and the 5 intrinsic parameters. The rigid displacements depend on 11 parameters: 3 for each of the rotations $\mathbf{R}_{21}$ and $\mathbf{R}_{32}$, 2 for each of the directions of translations $\mathbf{t}_{12}$ and $\mathbf{t}_{23}$, and one for the ratio of the norms of the translations. The total is 16 parameters; thus the information is not entirely contained in the first two Fundamental matrices. The two missing parameters are actually recovered thanks to the two additional Kruppa equations provided by the third Fundamental matrix.

We give now a simple numerical example to show that in the general case the equations are independent. The first two rigid displacements are

$$\mathbf{R}_{21} = \begin{bmatrix} 1 & 0 & 0 \\ 0 & 0 & -1 \\ 0 & 1 & 0 \end{bmatrix} \qquad \mathbf{t}_{21} = \begin{bmatrix} 1 \\ 2 \\ 1 \end{bmatrix},$$

$$\mathbf{R}_{32} = \begin{bmatrix} 0 & 1 & 0 \\ -1 & 0 & 0 \\ 0 & 0 & 1 \end{bmatrix} \qquad \mathbf{t}_{32} = \begin{bmatrix} 2 \\ 0 \\ -1 \end{bmatrix}.$$

The rigid displacement obtained by composition of D_1 and D_2, expressed in the coordinate system of the first camera, is

$$\mathbf{R}_{31} = \mathbf{R}_{21}\mathbf{R}_{32} = \begin{bmatrix} 0 & 1 & 0 \\ 0 & 0 & -1 \\ -1 & 0 & 0 \end{bmatrix} \qquad \mathbf{t}_{31} = \mathbf{R}_{21}\mathbf{t}_{32} + \mathbf{t}_{21} = \begin{bmatrix} 3 \\ 3 \\ 1 \end{bmatrix}.$$

If we take as intrinsic parameter matrix $\mathbf{A}$ the identity matrix, then the Fundamental matrices are identical to the Essential matrices. Setting $K_{33} = 1$, the six Kruppa equations are

$$
\begin{aligned}
Eq_1 \;=\; & 4\,K_{11} - 2\,K_{13}K_{11} - 4\,K_{23}K_{11} - 4\,K_{22}K_{11} + 6\,K_{12}K_{11} + 4\,K_{13}K_{22} - 2\,K_{23}K_{22} \\
& + 2\,K_{12}K_{22} - 4\,K_{12}^2 - 4\,K_{12} + 4\,K_{23}K_{12} - 4\,K_{13}^2 + 2\,K_{13} + 4\,K_{23}K_{13} - 2\,K_{23}, \\
Eq_1' \;=\; & 3\,K_{11} - 8\,K_{23}K_{11} - 3\,K_{22}K_{11} + K_{22}^2 + 8\,K_{13}K_{22} - 4\,K_{23}K_{22} - 2\,K_{12}K_{22} \\
& - 8\,K_{12} + 8\,K_{23}K_{12} + 2\,K_{13} + 8\,K_{23}K_{13} - 4\,K_{23} - 1, \\
Eq_2 \;=\; & 4\,K_{13}K_{11} + 2\,K_{12}K_{11} + 4\,K_{23}K_{22} + 2\,K_{12}K_{22} + 16\,K_{12} + 8\,K_{13}K_{12} + 8\,K_{23}K_{12} \\
& + 16\,K_{13}^2 + 16\,K_{13} + 16\,K_{23}^2 + 16\,K_{23}, \\
Eq_2' \;=\; & -K_{11}^2 - 4\,K_{11} - 4\,K_{13}K_{11} + K_{22}^2 + 4\,K_{22} + 4 \;,\, K_{23}K_{22}, \\
Eq_3 \;=\; & -18\,K_{11}^2 + 60\,K_{13}K_{11} - 52\,K_{23}K_{11} + 12\,K_{12}K_{11} + 18\,K_{22} - 6\,K_{13}K_{22} \\
& - 6\,K_{23}K_{22} + 2\,K_{12}K_{22} + 12\,K_{12}^2 + 54\,K_{12} - 36\,K_{23}K_{12} - 36\,K_{13}^2 + 54\,K_{13} \\
& - 12\,K_{23}K_{13} + 18\,K_{23}, \\
Eq_3' \;=\; & -9\,K_{11}^2 - K_{11} + 60\,K_{13}K_{11} - 54\,K_{23}K_{11} + 9\,K_{22}K_{11} + K_{22}^2 + 9\,K_{22} \\
& - 6\,K_{23}K_{22} + 6\,K_{12}K_{22} + 54\,K_{12} - 36\,K_{23}K_{12} - 36\,K_{13}^2 + 60\,K_{13} - 9.
\end{aligned}
$$

A solution of the system of equations Eq_1, Eq'_1, Eq_2, Eq'_2 obtained from the rigid displacements $\mathbf{D}_1$ and $\mathbf{D}_2$ is

$$K_{11} = 0, \quad K_{12} = -1, \quad K_{13} = \frac{1}{2}, \quad K_{22} = -4, \quad K_{23} = 0.$$

Substituting these values into the equations obtained from $\mathbf{D}_3$ yields $Eq_3 = -76$, $Eq'_3 = -38$; thus we have verified that these equations are independent from the previous ones, i.e. that they cannot be written as polynomials in Eq_1, Eq'_1, Eq_2, Eq'_2.

Degenerate cases   There are many cases in which the Kruppa equations are degenerate, i.e. do not provide enough information for recovering the internal parameters. In this section we discuss only a few of the simplest cases. Section 11.6 provides a more detailed analysis. There are situations when one rigid displacement is such that the Kruppa equations do not provide any constraint at all: They include pure translation, pure rotation, and affine viewing situation.

Pure translation   In the case in which the rigid displacement is a pure translation (the rotation is the identity $\mathbf{R} = \mathbf{I}_3$), it can be seen from Equation 11.13 that the Fundamental matrix is antisymmetric. Since $\mathbf{E} = [\mathbf{t}]_\times$ and $\mathbf{A} = \mathbf{A}'$, we have $\mathbf{F} \simeq \mathbf{A}^{-T}[\mathbf{t}]_\times \mathbf{A}$ which is an antisymmetric matrix. If $\mathbf{F}$ is antisymmetric, $\mathbf{e} \simeq \mathbf{e}'$. From (5.16), we conclude that

$$\forall \mathbf{y}, \mathbf{F}\mathbf{y} \simeq \mathbf{e} \times \mathbf{y}.$$

Equations 11.18 and 11.19 are equivalent, and thus the Kruppa equations reduce to tautologies. A geometric interpretation is that since the two tangents to ω in the first image *are* the tangents to ω in the second image, no further constraint is put on ω by considering a second image.

Pure rotation   In the case of zero translation, the Fundamental matrix is the null matrix and there are no epipolar constraints and thus no Kruppa equations. The rigid displacement is a pure rotation whose axis contains the optical center of the camera. Section 11.1 is dedicated to this case.

Affine viewing   If the viewing geometry can be described with the affine projection model, then it can be verified by substitution of the form of the affine Fundamental matrix given in Equation 5.39 into the Kruppa equations given in Equation 11.17 that they reduce to the form $K_{33}f(a, b, c, d)$, which is never or always zero. Let see what happens to the geometric constraint from which the Kruppa equations are derived.

- The plane at infinity Π_∞ is mapped into the line at infinity l_∞ by an affine projection. The absolute conic is mapped into two points I, J of l_∞ in the first image and two points I', J' of l_∞ in the second image.

- Since the epipolar lines are parallel, they intersect l_∞ at a single point d in the first image, d' in the second image.

- The tangency condition reduces to the fact that d is either I or J and d' is either I' or J'.

11.3 Computing the intrinsic parameters using the Kruppa equations

This section is devoted to a first family of techniques for solving the problem of recovering the Euclidean stratum from the projective stratum, represented by a collection of Fundamental matrices. These techniques solve the Kruppa equations in some way to recover the intrinsic parameters. They then exploit the relation (5.33) between the fundamental matrix and the essential matrix to recover the essential matrices from which the relative rotations and the directions of the translations can be recovered; see Section 5.3.3. Note that the ratio of the lengths of any of the translation vectors can be computed using Propositions 10.6, 10.7 and 10.8, or as explained in Section 11.5.1.

These methods entirely separate the estimation of the intrinsic parameters from the estimation of the motion parameters. Section 11.3.1 details formulae to recover the focal lengths of two cameras (certainly the most important intrinsic parameter) from a single Fundamental matrix. Section 11.3.2 discusses methods which take advantage of the polynomial structure of the equations to solve from three views with constant intrinsic parameters. Section 11.3.3 presents an optimization based approach to solve the same equations, which is efficient to integrate multiple views. It is an interesting application of the methods, described in Chapter 6, for estimating the uncertainty of the fundamental matrix.

11.3.1 Recovering the focal lengths for two views

One Fundamental matrix yields two Kruppa equations; therefore we should be able to recover two intrinsic parameters assuming that the rest of them is known. We consider cameras which have zero skew, unit aspect ratio (Section 4.3.1), and known principal points $\mathbf{c}$ and $\mathbf{c}'$:

Proposition 11.11 (Bougnoux) *For a pair of cameras with Fundamental matrix* **F**, *epipole* $\mathbf{e}'$, *and intrinsic parameters*

$$\mathbf{A} = \begin{bmatrix} f & 0 & u_0 \\ 0 & f & v_0 \\ 0 & 0 & 1 \end{bmatrix} \quad and \quad \mathbf{A}' = \begin{bmatrix} f' & 0 & u_0' \\ 0 & f' & v_0' \\ 0 & 0 & 1 \end{bmatrix},$$

the focal length of the first camera is given by

$$f = \sqrt{ -\frac{ \mathbf{c'}^T \left[\mathbf{e'}\right]_\times \tilde{\mathbf{I}} \mathbf{F} \mathbf{c} \left(\mathbf{c}^T \mathbf{F}^T \mathbf{c'} \right) }{ \mathbf{c'}^T \left[\mathbf{e'}\right]_\times \tilde{\mathbf{I}} \mathbf{F} \tilde{\mathbf{I}} \mathbf{F}^T \mathbf{c'} } }, \quad where \ \tilde{\mathbf{I}} = \begin{bmatrix} 1 & 0 & 0 \\ 0 & 1 & 0 \\ 0 & 0 & 0 \end{bmatrix}, \qquad (11.26)$$

and $\mathbf{c} = [u_0, v_0, 1]^T$ *and* $\mathbf{c'} = [u'_0, v'_0, 1]^T$ *are the principal points.*

Proof :   Under our assumptions, the Kruppa matrix of the first camera can be written

$$\mathbf{K} = \mathbf{A}\mathbf{A}^T = \begin{bmatrix} f^2 + u_0^2 & u_0 v_0 & u_0 \\ u_0 v_0 & f^2 + v_0^2 & v_0 \\ u_0 & v_0 & 1 \end{bmatrix} = f^2 \tilde{\mathbf{I}} + \mathbf{c}\mathbf{c}^T.$$

Let us note $\mathbf{l} = \mathbf{F}\mathbf{c}$, $\mathbf{m} = \left[\mathbf{e'}\right]_\times \mathbf{c'}$, $\tilde{\mathbf{F}} = \mathbf{F}\tilde{\mathbf{I}}\mathbf{F}^T$ and

$$\tilde{\mathbf{E}}' = \left[\mathbf{e'}\right]_\times \tilde{\mathbf{I}} \left[\mathbf{e'}\right]_\times^{\mathbf{T}} = \begin{bmatrix} e'^2_3 & 0 & -e'_1 e'_3 \\ 0 & e'^2_3 & -e'_2 e'_3 \\ -e'_1 e'_3 & -e'_2 e'_3 & e'^2_1 + e'^2_2 \end{bmatrix}. \qquad (11.27)$$

The Kruppa equations (11.17) can be rewritten with the proportionality factor x:

$$f^2 \tilde{\mathbf{F}} + \mathbf{l}\mathbf{l}^T = x \left(f'^2 \tilde{\mathbf{E}}' + \mathbf{m}\mathbf{m}^T \right). \qquad (11.28)$$

Using $\tilde{E}'_{12} = 0$, if $m_1 m_2 = 0$, then we conclude from that equation that

$$f^2 \tilde{F}_{12} + l_1 l_2 = 0;$$

otherwise, we obtain the scale factor $x = \frac{f^2 \tilde{F}_{12} + l_1 l_2}{m_1 m_2}$, which we substitute back into Equation 11.28:

$$f^2 f'^2 \tilde{F}_{12} \tilde{\mathbf{E}}' + f^2 \left(\tilde{F}_{12} \mathbf{m}\mathbf{m}^T - m_1 m_2 \tilde{\mathbf{F}} \right) + f'^2 l_1 l_2 \tilde{\mathbf{E}}' + l_1 l_2 \mathbf{m}\mathbf{m}^T - m_1 m_2 \mathbf{l}\mathbf{l}^T = 0.$$

This equation is polynomial of degree 2 in f^2 and f'^2 with matrix coefficients. We can rewrite it as $f^2 f'^2 \mathbf{A} + f^2 \mathbf{B} + f'^2 \mathbf{C} + \mathbf{D} = \mathbf{0}_{3\times 3}$ with $\mathbf{A}$, $\mathbf{B}$, $\mathbf{C}$ and $\mathbf{D}$ four 3×3 symmetric matrices which depend only on the epipolar geometry and principal points. Let us call EQ those 6 equations. EQ_{12} was already used for the parameter x.

Now from $\tilde{E}'_{11} = \tilde{E}'_{22}$, we conclude that we must have $EQ_{11} = EQ_{22}$, which means $A_{11} = A_{22}$, $C_{11} = C_{22}$ and

$$(B_{11} - B_{22})f^2 + D_{11} - D_{22} = 0. \qquad (11.29)$$

With some algebra, we obtain

$$
\begin{aligned}
B_{11} &= \tilde{F}_{12}m_1^2 - \tilde{F}_{11}m_1m_2 &&= -m_1 \begin{bmatrix} F_{11} & F_{12} & 0 \end{bmatrix} \mathbf{F}^T c' e_3', \\
D_{11} &= l_1l_2m_1^2 - m_1m_2l_1^2 &&= -l_1m_1 \left(\mathbf{c}^T \mathbf{F} \mathbf{c}' \right) e_3'
\end{aligned}
$$

and

$$
\begin{aligned}
B_{22} &= \tilde{F}_{12}m_2^2 - \tilde{F}_{22}m_1m_2 &&= m_2 \begin{bmatrix} F_{21} & F_{22} & 0 \end{bmatrix} \mathbf{F}^T c' e_3', \\
D_{22} &= l_1l_2m_2^2 - m_1m_2l_2^2 &&= D_{22} = -l_2m_2 \left(\mathbf{c}^T \mathbf{F} \mathbf{c}' \right) e_3'.
\end{aligned}
$$

We remark that $e_1' EQ_{11} = -e_3' EQ_{13}$ and $e_2' EQ_{21} = -e_3' EQ_{23}$. So, as EQ_{13} and EQ_{23} should be verified, we can always simplify by m_3 and write Equation 11.29 as

$$
\mathbf{m}^T \tilde{\mathbf{l}} \left(\tilde{\mathbf{F}} f^2 + \mathbf{F} \mathbf{c} \mathbf{c}^T \mathbf{F}^T \right) \mathbf{c}' = 0,
$$

from which the announced formula follows. □

It can be noted that this formula gives a null focal length (a degenerate value) if $\mathbf{c}^T \mathbf{F}^T \mathbf{c}' = 0$, or, in other words, the two principal points are in epipolar correspondence. This statement actually means that the two optical axes intersect at a common point, a situation which will be studied in more detail in Section 11.6. In the same spirit as the previous calculations, it is also possible to solve for the scale factors in each direction α_u and α_v if they are presumed constant in the two views. The Kruppa equations yield a system of two polynomials of degree two with two unknowns which has an analytical solution.

11.3.2   Solving the Kruppa equations for three views

We have seen that three rigid displacements yield six equations in the entries of the Kruppa matrix $\mathbf{K}$. The equations are homogeneous, so the solution is determined only up to a scale factor. In effect there are five unknowns. Trying to solve the over-determined problem with numerical methods usually fails, so five equations are chosen from the six and solved first. As the equations are each of degree two, the number of solutions in the general case is $32 = 2^5$. The remaining equation could just be used to discard the spurious solutions, but this strategy ignores the uncertainty on the coefficients, and it is better to exploit the redundancy of information to obtain a more robust algorithm as well as a gross estimate of the variance of the solutions.

How do we solve a system of 5 polynomial equations of degree 2 in 5 variables? Providing an initial guess and using an iterative numerical method will generally not find all of the solutions: Many of the starting points will yield trajectories that do not converge and many other trajectories will converge to the same solution. However it is not acceptable to miss solutions, since there is only one correct solution amongst the 32.

Recently developed methods in numerical continuation can reliably compute all solutions to polynomial systems. These methods have been improved over a decade to provide reliable solutions to kinematics problems. Some details of these improvements are explained in (Wampler et al., 1988), which is a detailed tutorial presentation. The solution of a system of nonlinear equations by numerical continuation is suggested by the idea that small changes in the parameters of the system usually produce small changes in the solutions. Suppose the solutions to problem A (the initial system) are known and solutions to problem B (the target system) are required. Solutions are tracked as the parameters of the system are slowly changed from those of A to those of B. Although for a general nonlinear system numerous difficulties can arise, such as divergence or bifurcation of a solution path, for a polynomial system all such difficulties can be avoided.

Details and experimental results can be found in (Luong and Faugeras, 1994a). The main advantage of the method is that no initialization is needed. If the points are measured with a good precision, the results can be sufficiently precise. Another advantage is that it is easy to assess the success or failure of the algorithm. However there are several drawbacks as follows.

- The method is suitable only for the case of the minimum number of rigid displacements, as it is difficult to use all the $\binom{n}{5}$ constraints provided by a sequence of n views without increasing considerably the amount of computations.

- It is difficult to take into account uncertainty for the input (Fundamental matrices) as well as to produce estimates of the uncertainty for the output (camera parameters).

- The computational cost of solving the polynomial system is relatively high.

- It is not possible to express the constraints of positivity of $\mathbf{K}$ when solving the systems, since continuation works in the complex plane. Thus, with noisy data, it can happen that no acceptable solution are found.

It is easy to enforce the zero-skew constraint $\gamma = 0$ within this framework, since it is also a polynomial of degree two in the entries of the Kruppa matrix (Equation 4.37). Two rigid displacements and this constraint generate a system of five equations and are therefore sufficient to find a solution.

11.3.3 Nonlinear optimization to accumulate the Kruppa equations for $n > 3$ views: The "Kruppa" method

Suppose we have n views with constant intrinsic parameters, and estimated $N \leq \binom{n}{2}$ fundamental matrices, denoted $\mathbf{F}_i$, between pairs of views. For each fundamental matrix, we consider two Kruppa equations (11.21). Those equations are polynomials of degree two in the entries of the Kruppa matrix $\mathbf{K}$ with coefficients that are functions of the entries of $\mathbf{F}_i$; we denote $Eq_1(\mathbf{F}_i, \mathbf{K})$ and $Eq_2(\mathbf{F}_i, \mathbf{K})$ those two equations (see Section 11.2.2).

For each matrix $\mathbf{K}$, we can compute, using the techniques described in Section 6.6, the variances $\sigma_{Eq_j}(\mathbf{F}_i, \mathbf{K})$, $j = 1, 2$, of the two Kruppa equations as

$$\sigma^2_{Eq_j} = \left(\frac{\partial Eq_j}{\partial \mathbf{F}_i} \right)^T \mathbf{\Lambda}_{\mathbf{F}_i} \frac{\partial Eq_j}{\partial \mathbf{F}_i}.$$

One then minimizes with respect to the five parameters of $\mathbf{K}$ the error criterion

$$\sum_{i=1}^{N} \frac{Eq_1(\mathbf{F}_i, \mathbf{K})^2}{\sigma_{Eq_1}(\mathbf{F}_i, \mathbf{K})} + \frac{Eq_2(\mathbf{F}_i, \mathbf{K})^2}{\sigma_{Eq_2}(\mathbf{F}_i, \mathbf{K})}. \qquad (11.30)$$

To enforce the fact that $\mathbf{K} = \mathbf{A}\mathbf{A}^T$ must be a positive matrix, the minimization is done with the parameters of the intrinsic parameters matrix $\mathbf{A}$ defined in Equation 4.30. Several variants are possible depending on the simplification on $\mathbf{A}$ chosen (see Section 4.3.1), satisfactory results being obtained with the three parameter model (zero-skew, unit aspect ratio).

There are several ways of finding a starting point for the minimization of (11.30). One way is to choose two (zero-skew) or three views among the n and to solve the corresponding Kruppa equations by the method described in the previous section. Another method, which does not require iterative computations and can be used robustly with several views, is described by Zeller (Zeller, 1996):

- For each fundamental matrix $\mathbf{F}_i$, take $\gamma = 0$, the principal point at the image center, and analytically solve the two Kruppa equations for α_i and β_i.

- The initial values for α and β are taken as the median values of the α_i and β_i.

An example of results obtained with three different synthetic sequences is shown in Figure 11.7. In each sequence, 100 points, which are confined to the inside of a cube, are observed from the ten viewpoints which are indicated by their camera coordinate system and the optical axis. The noise level is 1.0 pixels (in a 512×512 image).

In the first sequence, the viewpoints are well-distributed, roughly on a sphere centered at the middle of the cube, and the optical axes are roughly going through the center of the sphere: This situation is a good approximation to the critical sequence described in Section 11.6.2. In the second sequence, the views are almost coplanar: This situation is one of the intrinsic critical sequences described in Section 11.6.1. But they are also roughly on the same sphere as in the first sequence. The third sequence is a case of a critical sequence in which the rotation axes are identical.

The second row of Figure 11.7 shows the different values of α_i and β_i obtained by the analytical method described above. It can be seen that for all three sequences the pairs (α_i, β_i) roughly fall on a line whose slope is close to the correct aspect ratio. This observation confirms the analysis of Section 11.6.2. It has been found that the aspect ratio computed by this method is quite insensitive to the choice of (u_0, v_0).

11.4 Computing the Euclidean canonical form

All of the methods that are described in this section start from the projective stratum computed as explained in Section 10.2 and represented by the projection matrices. They upgrade the representation from projective to affine and Euclidean by directly computing the projection matrices. The main idea is to notice that, once the projective projection matrices have been obtained, there only remains to find one homography of space to turn them into affine or Euclidean projection matrices. We start in Section 11.4.1 with the affine camera case, where we start already from affine. In the perspective case, as explained in Section 11.4.2, the homography can very simply be parametrized by 8 parameters: 5 parameters for the intrinsic parameters and 3 for the plane at infinity. We then examine different families of methods. Each method in the first family produces an affine representation (Section 11.4.2.1), each method in the second family relies on an intermediate affine stage (Section 11.4.2.2), and each method in the third family treats the two stages uniformly (Section 11.4.2.3). A further advantage of these methods is that they extend naturally to the case of varying internal parameters, discussed in Section 11.4.2.4.

11.4.1 The affine camera case

If the camera performs a parallel projection (affine camera, see Chapter 4), then the ambiguity in reconstruction is already at most affine. We examine now how to recover the intrinsic parameters of the affine camera so that Euclidean information can be obtained. We have seen in Section 10.2.3.2 how to recover the 2×3 reduced projection matrices $\mathbf{P}_i^A, i = 1, \cdots, n$, of a set of affine cameras up to an arbitrary affine transformation of the space.

We have given in Chapter 4, Section 4.4.3, several definitions of the intrinsic parameters of an affine camera. They all come down to the decomposition of the Euclidean matrices $\mathbf{P}_i^E$ as

$$\mathbf{P}_i^E = \mathbf{A}_i \mathbf{R}_i,$$

where $\mathbf{A}_i$ is the 2×3 matrix of the intrinsic parameters and $\mathbf{R}_i$ is a 3×3 matrix of rotation. The self-calibration method consists of finding an invertible 3×3 matrix $\mathbf{Q}$ corresponding to an affine change of coordinates such that

$$\mathbf{P}_i^A \mathbf{Q} = \mathbf{P}_i^E = \mathbf{A}_i \mathbf{R}_i. \tag{11.31}$$

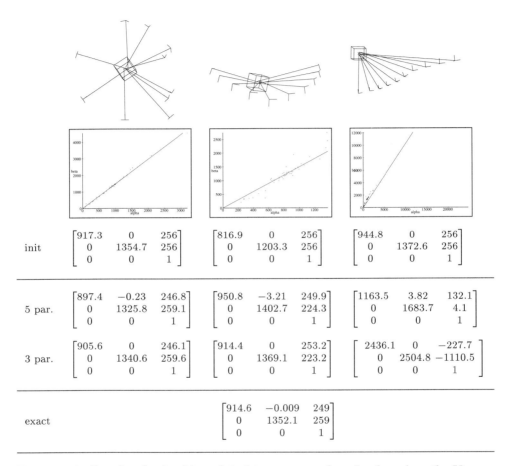

init	$\begin{bmatrix} 917.3 & 0 & 256 \\ 0 & 1354.7 & 256 \\ 0 & 0 & 1 \end{bmatrix}$	$\begin{bmatrix} 816.9 & 0 & 256 \\ 0 & 1203.3 & 256 \\ 0 & 0 & 1 \end{bmatrix}$	$\begin{bmatrix} 944.8 & 0 & 256 \\ 0 & 1372.6 & 256 \\ 0 & 0 & 1 \end{bmatrix}$
5 par.	$\begin{bmatrix} 897.4 & -0.23 & 246.8 \\ 0 & 1325.8 & 259.1 \\ 0 & 0 & 1 \end{bmatrix}$	$\begin{bmatrix} 950.8 & -3.21 & 249.9 \\ 0 & 1402.7 & 224.3 \\ 0 & 0 & 1 \end{bmatrix}$	$\begin{bmatrix} 1163.5 & 3.82 & 132.1 \\ 0 & 1683.7 & 4.1 \\ 0 & 0 & 1 \end{bmatrix}$
3 par.	$\begin{bmatrix} 905.6 & 0 & 246.1 \\ 0 & 1340.6 & 259.6 \\ 0 & 0 & 1 \end{bmatrix}$	$\begin{bmatrix} 914.4 & 0 & 253.2 \\ 0 & 1369.1 & 223.2 \\ 0 & 0 & 1 \end{bmatrix}$	$\begin{bmatrix} 2436.1 & 0 & -227.7 \\ 0 & 2504.8 & -1110.5 \\ 0 & 0 & 1 \end{bmatrix}$
exact		$\begin{bmatrix} 914.6 & -0.009 & 249 \\ 0 & 1352.1 & 259 \\ 0 & 0 & 1 \end{bmatrix}$	

Figure 11.7: Results obtained by minimizing an error function based on the Kruppa equations weighted by their uncertainty. The first row shows the configuration of the ten views. The second row shows the distribution of the pairs (α_i, β_i), see text. The third row shows the initial matrices $\mathbf{A}$. The next two rows show the values obtained after optimization respectively with respect to the five parameters of $\mathbf{A}$, or only with three parameters ($\gamma = 0$, $\beta = k_0 \alpha$).

The unknowns are $\mathbf{Q}$, $\mathbf{A}_i$ and $\mathbf{R}_i$. In order to succeed, one needs to make some extra assumptions. One reasonable such assumption is that the matrix of intrinsic parameters is "almost" constant:

$$\mathbf{A}_i = \lambda_i \mathbf{A},$$

where λ_i varies from one camera to the next. We can eliminate the rotation matrix $\mathbf{R}_i$ in (11.31) by transposing and multiplying:

$$\mathbf{P}_i^A \mathbf{Q} \mathbf{Q}^T \mathbf{P}_i^{AT} = \lambda_i^2 \mathbf{A} \mathbf{A}^T.$$

Let $\mathbf{X} = \mathbf{Q} \mathbf{Q}^T$, and let $\mathbf{q}_i$ and $\mathbf{s}_i$ be the two row vectors of $\mathbf{P}_i^A$. The previous equation can be rewritten as

$$\begin{bmatrix} \mathbf{q}_i^T \mathbf{X} \mathbf{q}_i & \mathbf{c}_i^T \mathbf{X} \mathbf{s}_i \\ \mathbf{q}_i^T \mathbf{X} \mathbf{s}_i & \mathbf{s}_i^T \mathbf{X} \mathbf{s}_i \end{bmatrix} = \lambda_i^2 \mathbf{A} \mathbf{A}^T. \tag{11.32}$$

Writing the two proportionality equations for each pair of consecutive views to eliminate the unknown scale factor gives $2(n-1)$ relations which are quadratic in the entries of $\mathbf{X}$. Since $\mathbf{X}$ is symmetric and defined up to a scale factor, it has five unknowns. Therefore, in the case of the general affine camera, four views are necessary. If we suppose further that the unknown scale factor λ_i is constant, then we can write three equalities, which are linear in the entries of $\mathbf{X}$, so that only three views are necessary.

11.4.2 The general formulation in the perspective case

Starting from a set of projective projection matrices $\boldsymbol{\mathcal{P}}_i$, the core of all those methods is to find a homography $\boldsymbol{\mathcal{H}}$ of $\mathbb{P}^3$ which transforms these matrices into their canonical Euclidean forms:

$$\boldsymbol{\mathcal{P}}_i \boldsymbol{\mathcal{H}} \simeq \mathbf{A}[\mathbf{R}_i \, \mathbf{t}_i], \qquad 1 \le i \le n, \tag{11.33}$$

where we can assume that $\mathbf{R}_1 = \mathbf{I}_3$ and $\mathbf{t}_1 = \mathbf{0}$ (see Section 10.3).

With the notations of Chapter 7, we have (Equation 7.18)

$$\boldsymbol{\mathcal{H}} \equiv \mathbf{Q}_{\mathcal{E}}^{\mathcal{B}_0} = \begin{bmatrix} \mathbf{A} & \mathbf{0}_3 \\ \mathbf{r}_\infty^T \mathbf{A} & \mu \end{bmatrix} \tag{11.34}$$

and write the projective projection matrices as

$$\boldsymbol{\mathcal{P}}_1 = [\mathbf{I}_3 \, \mathbf{0}], \qquad \boldsymbol{\mathcal{P}}_i = [\mathbf{P}_i \, \mathbf{p}_i], \, 2 \le i \le m.$$

The equations in (11.33) are equivalent to

$$(\mathbf{P}_i + \mathbf{p}_i \mathbf{r}_\infty^T) \mathbf{A} \simeq \mathbf{A} \mathbf{R}_i, \tag{11.35}$$

$$\mu \mathbf{p}_i \simeq \mathbf{A} \mathbf{t}_i.$$

These $2(n-1)$ equations form the basis for all of the self-calibration algorithms that we describe next.

11.4.2.1   From projective to affine

The method of Pollefeys and Van Gool (Pollefeys and Gool, 1999) relies on the assumption of constant intrinsic parameters to recover the affine stratum.

Let us start with Equation 11.35 and multiply both sides on the right with the matrix $\mathbf{A}^{-1}$:

$$\mathbf{P}_i + \mathbf{p}_i \mathbf{r}_\infty^T \simeq \mathbf{A} \mathbf{R}_i \mathbf{A}^{-1}.$$

The right-hand side is recognized as being the infinity morphism between views 1 and i (Proposition 5.25). This observation induces a constraint on the left-hand side: It is proportional to a matrix which is similar to a rotation matrix. Since the eigenvalues of a rotation matrix are of unit magnitude, the eigenvalues of the matrix $\mathbf{P}_i + \mathbf{p}_i \mathbf{r}_\infty^T$ must have the same magnitudes, as mentioned in Proposition 5.26. This situation can be written as a fourth degree polynomial in the coordinates of $\mathbf{r}_\infty$. If the characteristic polynomial is

$$\det \left(\mathbf{P}_i + \mathbf{p}_i \mathbf{r}_\infty^T - \lambda \mathbf{I}_3 \right) = a_3 \lambda^3 + a_2 \lambda^2 + a_1 \lambda + a_0,$$

then a necessary condition is $a_3 a_1^3 = a_2^3 a_0$. Each view except the first provides one such constraint on $\mathbf{r}_\infty$, and therefore four views are in general sufficient to obtain a finite number of solutions.

Once the affine stratum has been recovered, the Kruppa matrix can be recovered from the matrices $\mathbf{H}_{\infty 1 i}$ as described in Section 11.1.

11.4.2.2   Searching for the plane at infinity

As proposed for example by Hartley (Hartley, 1993; Hartley, 1997b), one can recover simultaneously the affine stratum (represented by the vector $\mathbf{r}_\infty$) and the Euclidean stratum (represented by the matrix of intrinsic parameters $\mathbf{A}$).

The main ideas are as follows. Given a value of $\mathbf{r}_\infty$, the infinity morphism from view 1 to view i can be computed for all i's:

$$\mathbf{H}_{\infty 1 i} = \mathbf{P}_i + \mathbf{p}_i r_\infty^T.$$

Next, the Kruppa matrix can be obtained from the set of $\mathbf{H}_{\infty 1 i}$ using the methods described in Section 11.1. If this matrix is definite, then the matrix $\mathbf{A}$ can be obtained by Cholesky decomposition.

Consider now the QR decomposition of the matrix in the left-hand side of Equation 11.35:

$$\left(\mathbf{P}_i + \mathbf{p}_i \mathbf{r}_\infty^T \right) \mathbf{A} = \mathbf{A}_i' \mathbf{R}_i',$$

and notice that if one has the correct values for $\mathbf{r}_\infty$ and $\mathbf{A}$, then one has $\mathbf{R}_i = \mathbf{R}_i'$ and $\mathbf{A}_i' \simeq \mathbf{A}$. It is therefore natural to minimize the error function

$$\sum_{i=2}^{n} \| \alpha_i \mathbf{A}^{-1} \mathbf{A}_i' - \mathbf{I}_3 \|^2$$

with respect to $\mathbf{A}$ and $\mathbf{r}_\infty$. The numbers α_i are equal to $3\,\mathrm{sgn}\left(\det\left(\mathbf{A}^{-1}\mathbf{A}'_i\right)\right)/\mathrm{tr}\left(\mathbf{A}^{-1}\mathbf{A}'_i\right)$ so that the sum of the squares of the three diagonal elements of the matrices $\mathbf{A}^{-1}\mathbf{A}'_i$ is equal to 3.

There is no closed-form solution to this minimization problem. To obtain initialization values for $\mathbf{A}$ and $\mathbf{r}_\infty$, the idea is to try different values of $\mathbf{r}_\infty$ until a value of $\mathbf{A}$ can be computed, i.e. until the Kruppa matrix is definite. If it is not definite, then another value of $\mathbf{r}_\infty$ is tried.

Hartley describes an interesting way to constrain the possible values of $\mathbf{r}_\infty$ by considering the so-called *Cheiral inequalities*, resulting from the fact that all of the reconstructed points have to lie in front of the cameras. To give a clear explanation of these inequalities would require a fair amount of details, so we refer the interested reader to (Hartley, 1998a; Hartley et al., 1999).

11.4.2.3 The absolute quadric

Heyden and Astrom's method Another possibility (Heyden and Astrom, 1996) for upgrading the representation from projective to Euclidean is to multiply each side of Equation 11.35 by its transpose. This step has the effect of eliminating the unknown rotation matrices $\mathbf{R}_i$. One obtains the equations (called the Kruppa constraints in (Heyden and Astrom, 1996))

$$\left(\mathbf{P}_i + \mathbf{p}_i\mathbf{r}_\infty^T\right)\mathbf{K}\left(\mathbf{P}_i + \mathbf{p}_i\mathbf{r}_\infty^T\right)^T \simeq \mathbf{K}, \qquad (11.36)$$

where $\mathbf{K}$ is the Kruppa matrix. This expression contains five equations since the matrices are symmetric and defined up to a scale factor. Three camera matrices yield ten equations, which is enough to recover the eight unknowns.

If one introduces the $n-1$ scale factors $\lambda_2,\ldots,\lambda_n$, then one is naturally led to the minimization of the error function

$$\sum_{i=2}^n \|\left(\mathbf{P}_i + \mathbf{p}_i\mathbf{r}_\infty^T\right)\mathbf{K}\left(\mathbf{P}_i + \mathbf{p}_i\mathbf{r}_\infty^T\right)^T - \lambda_i\mathbf{K}\|^2$$

with respect to the $n-1$ scalars λ_i, the vector $\mathbf{r}_\infty$, and the definite symmetric matrix $\mathbf{K}$. Let us give an interpretation of this method in terms of the absolute quadric dual to the absolute conic (see Chapter 2, Section 2.6.3).

Trigg's method Suppose, as usual, that we have recovered the projective stratum and that the projection matrices are given in a canonical projective coordinate frame $\mathcal{B}_0$ by the matrices $\mathcal{P}_i$, $i = 1,\ldots,n$. We now apply Proposition 2.23 and consider the quadric dual to the absolute conic Ω. In that projective coordinate frame, this quadric is represented by a 4×4 symmetric matrix $\mathcal{Q}^*_{\mathcal{B}_0}$ of rank 3, i.e. as a degenerate quadric. In effect it is a quadric cone, the set of all planes tangent to Ω.

The vertex of the cone is the plane at infinity. In a Euclidean frame, the absolute quadric is represented by the matrix (Equation 2.23)

$$\mathcal{Q}_{\mathcal{E}}^* = \begin{bmatrix} \mathbf{I}_3 & \mathbf{0}_3 \\ \mathbf{0}_3^T & 0 \end{bmatrix}.$$

The absolute quadric encodes Euclidean structure in a way similar to the absolute conic. It is invariant under Euclidean transformation. It also encodes affine structure since the plane at infinity is its vertex, determined as a null vector of its matrix.

Let us now consider one camera represented by its projection matrix $\mathcal{P}$. Let l be a line in the retinal plane of our camera and $\mathbf{l}$ one of its coordinate vectors. The plane Π defined by l and the optical center C of the camera is represented by the vector $\mathcal{P}^T\mathbf{l}$ (see Section 4.1.2). It is tangent to the absolute conic if and only if it belongs to the absolute quadric, i.e.

$$\mathbf{l}^T\mathcal{P}\mathcal{Q}_{\mathcal{B}_0}^*\mathcal{P}^T\mathbf{l} = 0.$$

The 3×3 symmetric matrix $\mathcal{P}\mathcal{Q}_{\mathcal{B}_0}^*\mathcal{P}^T$ defines a conic in the plane dual to the retinal plane of the camera which is of course nothing but our old friend ω^* the conic dual to the image ω of the absolute conic Ω (see Section 4.3.2). Therefore we must have

$$\mathcal{P}\mathcal{Q}_{\mathcal{B}_0}^*\mathcal{P}^T \simeq \mathbf{K}, \tag{11.37}$$

where $\mathbf{K}$ is the Kruppa matrix of the camera.

It is easy to relate $\mathcal{Q}_{\mathcal{B}_0}^*$ and $\mathcal{Q}_{\mathcal{E}}^*$ using for example Proposition 3.24. Using that proposition, $\mathcal{Q}_{\mathcal{B}_0}^* = \mathbf{Q}_{\mathcal{E}}^{\mathcal{B}_0}\mathcal{Q}_{\mathcal{E}}^*\mathbf{Q}_{\mathcal{E}}^{\mathcal{B}_0\ T}$. Using Equation 11.34, we find the expression of the matrix of the absolute quadric in the projective frame:

$$\mathcal{Q}_{\mathcal{B}_0}^* = \begin{bmatrix} \mathbf{A}\mathbf{A}^T & \mathbf{A}\mathbf{A}^T\mathbf{r}_\infty \\ \mathbf{r}_\infty^T\mathbf{A}\mathbf{A}^T & \mathbf{r}_\infty^T\mathbf{A}\mathbf{A}^T\mathbf{r}_\infty \end{bmatrix} = \begin{bmatrix} \mathbf{K} & \mathbf{K}\mathbf{r}_\infty \\ \mathbf{r}_\infty^T\mathbf{K} & \mathbf{r}_\infty^T\mathbf{K}\mathbf{r}_\infty \end{bmatrix}.$$

Plugging this expression into Equation 11.37, we obtain exactly the Kruppa constraints of Equation 11.36.

11.4.2.4   Dealing with non-constant intrinsic parameters

In practice the assumption that the internal parameters are constant is sometimes somewhat unrealistic. For example, in a sequence of twenty-four images of the INRIA library in Sophia-Antipolis of which we show four in Figure 11.8, the internal parameters have not been kept constant, but it is very reasonable to assume that the skew parameter is equal to 0 and that the aspect ratio $\frac{\alpha_u}{\alpha_v}$ is constant in all views. Is it possible in that case to self-calibrate the views?

The answer to this question is in general yes. Using Equation 11.37, it should be clear that any constraint on the coefficients of $\mathbf{K}$ can be translated into a constraint

Figure 11.8: Four out of twenty-four views of the INRIA library in Sophia-Antipolis with varying internal parameters. Courtesy **Sylvain Bougnoux**, INRIA.

on the matrix $\mathcal{Q}^*$. Since this matrix depends upon 8 parameters (a symmetric matrix of rank 3 defined up to scale), one would expect that, given enough views, one could recover its coefficients.

To be more specific, let us consider the zero skew constraint and the constant aspect ratio constraint. As shown in Chapter 4, Equation 4.37, the zero-skew constraint is equivalent to

$$K_{13}K_{23} - K_{33}K_{12} = 0,$$

whereas the aspect ratio $\frac{\alpha_u}{\alpha_v}$ is equal to $\sqrt{\dfrac{K_{11} - K_{13}^2}{K_{22} - K_{23}^2}}$. For each view i, let us denote by $\mathbf{K}_i$ the matrix $\mathcal{P}_i \mathcal{Q}^* \mathcal{P}_i^T$. The zero-skew constraint leads to the nonlinear minimization of the error function

$$\sum_{i=1}^{n} \left(K_{i13}K_{i23} - K_{i33}K_{i12} \right)^2$$

with respect to the 8 parameters of $\mathcal{Q}^*$. Once $\mathcal{Q}^*$ has been obtained, one can compute the coefficients of the matrices $\mathbf{K}_i$ and recover the intrinsic parameters of the cameras. The plane at infinity can be recovered in a variety of manners for example as the null space of $\mathcal{Q}^*$.

Bougnoux (Bougnoux, 1998) proposes to initialize the nonlinear minimization in an unconventional way. He first estimates the focal length using the formula in Section 11.3.1, then given the intrinsic parameters $\mathbf{A}$, obtains an estimate of $\mathbf{r}_\infty$ by solving a linear least-squares system in $\mathbf{A}\mathbf{r}_\infty$ obtained from manipulations of Equation 11.36.

To continue with the example of Figure 11.8, we show in Table 11.1 the internal parameters obtained with that method of six of the twenty-four views, . It is seen that if α_u, α_v, u_0 and v_0 vary from view to view, then the ratio α_u/α_v and the cosine of the skew $\cos(\gamma)$ remain pretty much constant. The focal lengths, in pixels,

α_u	α_v	u_0	v_0	α_u/α_v	$\cos(\gamma)$
616.8	616.8	384	256	1	0
722.1	719.7	361	259	1.003	0.0028
876.0	873.3	319	257	1.003	-0.0032
946.0	947.2	299	250	0.999	-0.0001
1190.5	1193.8	248	255	0.997	0.0010
1019.2	1016.8	318	248	1.002	-0.0017

Table 11.1: This table shows the internal parameters of six of the twenty-four views of the INRIA library in Sophia-Antipolis. Courtesy **Sylvain Bougnoux**, INRIA.

of the twenty-four views are shown in Figure 11.9. Three dimensional Euclidean reconstruction is then possible, as shown in Figure 11.10, as well as texture mapping (Figure 11.11).

11.5   Computing all the Euclidean parameters

The idea behind all of the previous approaches was to use the fact that rotation matrices are orthogonal in order to eliminate the motion parameters and to relate the projective or affine quantities to Euclidean quantities. By contrast, the methods in this section do so by parametrizing the projective quantities by Euclidean quantities, thus making it possible to compute them directly. This approach requires that at least the intrinsic parameters and the motion parameters be computed simultaneously, so these methods are based on large-scale nonlinear optimization and require a good starting point which can be obtained by one of the previous method. Section 11.5.1 presents a method based on the global minimization of the epipolar constraints with respect to Euclidean parameters. Section 11.5.2 is a global bundle adjustment which involves also the structure. Further results obtained with these methods are shown in Section 11.5.3.

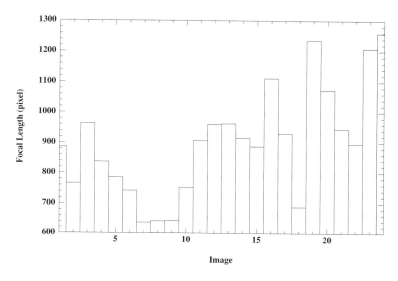

Figure 11.9: The focal lengths (in pixels) of the twenty-four views of the INRIA library in Sophia-Antipolis. Courtesy **Sylvain Bougnoux**, INRIA.

11.5.1   Simultaneous computation of motion and intrinsic parameters: The "Epipolar/Motion" method

The methods previously studied decoupled the estimation of the intrinsic parameters from the estimation of the motion parameters. In effect, the Kruppa equations allow us to do this since they *eliminate* the unknown motion parameters. This behavior is advantageous since, as we saw, the methods involve at most five unknowns, and allow semi-analytical, as well as efficient, iterative solutions. One disadvantage is that once the intrinsic parameters have been estimated, their values cannot be changed, for example as a consequence of a poor estimation of the motion parameters. This problem appears when trying to decompose the Essential matrices $\mathbf{E}_i$ estimated from $\mathbf{A}^T\mathbf{F}\mathbf{A}$, where $\mathbf{F}_i$ are the estimated Fundamental matrices and $\mathbf{A}$ the estimated intrinsic parameters: The constraints in (5.34) could possibly be poorly satisfied.

Contrary to this situation, the global method that we describe in this section simultaneously estimates all of the intrinsic and extrinsic parameters. The *form of the parameterization* ensures that the constraints in (5.34) on the essential matrices are satisfied. The basic idea is to consider the error function (6.10) where $\mathbf{F}_i$ is written as an explicit function of the unknowns $\mathbf{A}$, $\mathbf{R}_i$ and $\mathbf{u}_i$ using (5.33) and (5.32). We denote by (m_{ij}, m'_{ij}) the jth correspondence in the ith pair of views.

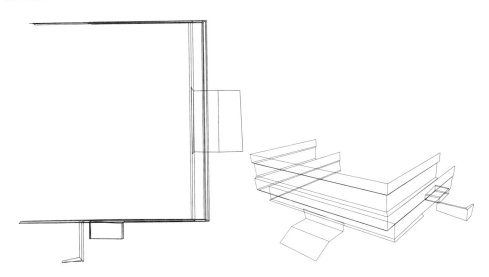

Figure 11.10: Top view and front view of the Euclidean reconstruction of the INRIA library in Sophia-Antipolis. The model has been obtained from a total of twenty-four views with varying internal parameters. Courtesy **Sylvain Bougnoux**, INRIA.

The error function C is therefore

$$C = \sum_{i=1}^{N} \sum_{j} d^2 \left(\mathbf{m}'_{ij}, \mathbf{A}^{-T} [\mathbf{u}_i]_\times \mathbf{R}_i \mathbf{A}^{-1} \mathbf{m}_{ij} \right) + d^2 \left(\mathbf{m}_{ij}, \mathbf{A}^{-T} \mathbf{R}_i^T [\mathbf{u}_i]_\times \mathbf{A}^{-1} \mathbf{m}'_{ij} \right),$$

(11.38)

where the vectors $\mathbf{u}_i$ are unit vectors parallel to the translation vectors $\mathbf{t}_i$ between the cameras, $\mathbf{u}_i = \mathbf{t}_i / \|\mathbf{t}_i\|$. The starting point of the minimization can, for example, be obtained by the methods described in the previous two sections.

The algorithm, which can accommodate N rigid displacements ($N \geq 2$) and, for each displacement i, a minimum of eight correspondences ($\mathbf{m}_{ij}, \mathbf{m}'_{ij}$), can be summarized as follows.

1. Estimate the N fundamental matrices $\mathbf{F}_i$ from the correspondences.

2. Compute an initial estimate of the intrinsic parameters by one of the methods described in Sections 11.3.2 and 11.3.3.

3. Compute the N initial motions ($\mathbf{R}_i, \mathbf{t}_i$) from $\mathbf{F}_i$ and the intrinsic parameters. This computation is done by computing the Essential matrices $\mathbf{E}_i = \mathbf{A}^T \mathbf{F}_i \mathbf{A}$. Those matrices do not usually satisfy the constraints in (5.34). They are then corrected by the SVD-based method described in Section 5.3.3.

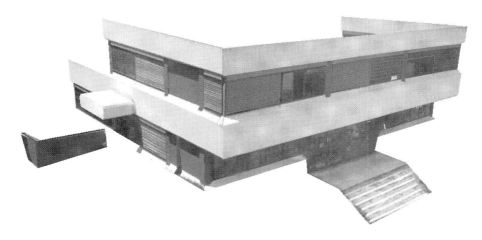

Figure 11.11: Textured front view of the Euclidean reconstruction of the INRIA library in Sophia-Antipolis. Courtesy **Sylvain Bougnoux**, INRIA.

4. Minimize, with respect to the $6N - 1 + int$ variables (we have $3N$ parameters for the N rotations, $3N - 1$ parameters for the translations which are globally defined up to scale, and int is the number of intrinsic parameters) the error function in (11.38).

An interesting feature of this method is that it allows us to take into account some of the constraints between multiple views. For example, in the case of three views, instead of minimizing over the 15 motion parameters $\mathbf{R}_{12}, \mathbf{u}_{12}$, $\mathbf{R}_{23}, \mathbf{u}_{23}$, and $\mathbf{R}_{13}, \mathbf{u}_{13}$, we can replace for example $\mathbf{R}_{13}$ by $\mathbf{R}_{23}\mathbf{R}_{12}$ and $\mathbf{u}_{13}$ by $\mu\mathbf{u}_{23} + \mathbf{R}_{23}\mathbf{u}_{12}/\|\mu\mathbf{u}_{23} + \mathbf{R}_{23}\mathbf{u}_{12}\|$, where μ is the ratio $\|\mathbf{t}_{23}\|/\|\mathbf{t}_{12}\|$. This ratio can be obtained as explained in Propositions 10.6, 10.7 and 10.8, or, more efficiently, by observing the images $\mathbf{m}_1$, $\mathbf{m}_2$, $\mathbf{m}_3$ of one point M in the three views.

Let Z_1, Z_2, Z_3 be the depths of M in the three cameras' normalized coordinate systems. If $\mathbf{m}_1$, $\mathbf{m}_2$, $\mathbf{m}_3$ are the normalized pixel coordinate vectors, then the Euclidean disparity equations can be written (Proposition 7.17)

$$Z_2\mathbf{m}_2 = Z_1\mathbf{R}_{12}\mathbf{m}_1 + \mathbf{t}_{12},$$
$$Z_3\mathbf{m}_3 = Z_2\mathbf{R}_{23}\mathbf{m}_2 + \mathbf{t}_{23}.$$

The first equation yields

$$\frac{Z_2}{\|\mathbf{t}_{12}\|} = \frac{\mathbf{u}_{12} \times \mathbf{R}_{12}\mathbf{m}_1}{\mathbf{m}_2 \times \mathbf{R}_{12}\mathbf{m}_1},$$

and the second yields

$$\frac{Z_2}{\|\mathbf{t}_{23}\|} = \frac{\mathbf{u}_{23} \times \mathbf{m}_3}{\mathbf{m}_3 \times \mathbf{R}_{23}\mathbf{m}_2}.$$

The elimination of Z_2 between those two equations yields μ.

The number of motion parameters is therefore reduced to 11, and trinocular constraints are enforced by the parameterization. Experiments in (Luong and Faugeras, 1994a) have shown that the results are generally better than those of the method based only on the Kruppa equations.

As an example of the kinds of results that can be obtained with this method, we have collected four times five views with a camera. For each set of five views, the intrinsic parameters were kept constant. Each set had a different focal length. To obtain ground truth, a calibration grid was present in one of the images of each of the four sequences. The results are shown in Table 11.2. It shows that the best results are obtained for short focal lengths, which yield large fields of view. Although the focal length is overestimated by the method for large values, we notice that the computed aspect ratio is quite consistent over the whole range of focal lengths. We also note that the principal point is not estimated very accurately. However, as shown by the 3D reconstruction errors discussed next, this lack of accuracy is not of primary importance. The intrinsic and extrinsic parameters estimated by this

focal	method	α_u	α_v	u_0	v_0	$\theta - \frac{\pi}{2}$	$\frac{\alpha_u}{\alpha_v}$
9	grid	481.31	711.54	248.57	260.97	10^{-7}	.6764
	selfcalib	503.49	760.71	250.24	282.67		.6618
12	grid	642.45	950.37	248.30	263.31	-5.10^{-7}	.6759
	selfcalib	636.12	921.36	201.52	338.89		.6904
20	grid	1036.38	1539.6	252.43	272.53	7.10^{-8}	.6731
	selfcalib	1208.83	1838.48	251.93	200.58		.6575
30	grid	1573.20	2330.953	207.98	210.35	4.10^{-7}	.6749
	selfcalib	2047.61	3063.94	249.678	198.463		.6682

Table 11.2: Parameters obtained with a zoom camera.

method have been used to reconstruct points of a known object. Three images have been used and three projection matrices computed from the extrinsic and intrinsic parameters using the formulae of Proposition 7.14

$$\mathcal{P}_1 = [\mathbf{A}\,\mathbf{0}_3], \qquad \mathcal{P}_2 = \mathbf{A}[\mathbf{R}_{12}\,\mathbf{t}_{12}], \qquad \mathcal{P}_3 = \mathbf{A}[\mathbf{R}_{23}\mathbf{R}_{12}\,\mathbf{R}_{23}\mathbf{t}_{12} + \mu_2\mathbf{t}_{23}].$$

We have then performed a 3D trinocular reconstruction from the matched points. The coordinates of the 3D points are obtained in the canonical coordinate system associated to the first camera. They are defined up to scale, since we can reconstruct only up a similarity with the self-calibration technique. In order to compare the reconstruction with the reference data, we have computed the best similarity which relates the two sets of 3D points. After applying this similarity to the initial reconstruction, the final average relative error in 3D space with this sequence is less than 2%.

Figure 11.12: Some views of a sequence of 15 images of the Valbonne church.

11.5.2   Global optimization on structure, motion, and calibration parameters

This method also comes as a complement to those described in Section 11.3. It uses them to initialize the minimization of an error function that is similar to (6.14):

$$\sum_{i=1}^{n} \sum_{j} d^2\left(\mathbf{m}_{ij}, \boldsymbol{\mathcal{P}}_i(\mathbf{q}_i)\mathbf{M}_j\right) \tag{11.39}$$

In this expression, the vectors $\mathbf{q}_i$ represent the parameters used to represent the ith projection matrix $\boldsymbol{\mathcal{P}}_i$. This function is the sum of the squares, ε_{ij}, of the reprojection errors of Section 10.2.3.3.

In effect, once relatively good estimates for the intrinsic parameters $\mathbf{A}$ and the extrinsic parameters $\mathbf{R}_i$, $\mathbf{t}_i$ have been obtained, the minimization of the function (11.39) with respect to those parameters and the coordinates of the points M_j can be carried out to refine the results. This approach is similar in spirit to the method described in Section 11.5.1. Compared with the minimization of the set of epipolar constraints described in that section, the minimization of the reprojection error has the advantage of providing two constraints per point, and can therefore be expected to yield better results when many images are available. However, it requires the computation of the 3-D coordinates of each point, and therefore is computationally more expensive. It has been found (Hartley, 1994a; Zeller, 1996) that this stage only slightly modifies the intrinsic and extrinsic parameters obtained by the Kruppa or the canonic transformation method.

Figure 11.13 shows an example of reconstruction obtained with this method, starting from a sequence of fifteen images. Four of them are shown in Figure 11.12. Since a 3D model of the scene is not available, to assess the precision of the results, a few angles and ratio of lengths are computed in Figure 11.14.

Figure 11.13: Some line segments, and the corresponding 3D Euclidean reconstruction.

11.5.3   More applications

We now show some more results obtained from the self-calibration methods that have been described.

Figure 11.15 shows an application to the construction of a 3D model of a complicated site. The models are obtained in several stages. First, images of the site are acquired from as many viewpoints as possible in order to guarantee full coverage. Next, the views are calibrated using one of the techniques that have been described in this chapter. This process is automatic. Third and last, the views and the calibration parameters are used in a modeling system to construct a 3D Euclidean representation of the scene. This operation is partially manual. The model shown in Figure 11.15 and have been obtained from forty-five images with constant intrinsic parameters. These parameters have been obtained by combining

Anglecomputed	real	Ratio	computed	real	
$\cos(1,3)$	1.000	1	2/4	0.993	1
$\cos(1,2)$	0.054	0	4/5	0.999	1
$\cos(3,5)$	0.032	0	10/12	1.050	1
$\cos(6,7)$	0.999	1	8/9	1.004	1
$\cos(15,16)$	1.000	1	17/18	0.966	1
$\cos(19,20)$	0.101	0	13/14	0.902	1

Figure 11.14: Some line segments, and the corresponding Euclidean measurements.

the methods described in Sections 11.3.3, 11.5.1 and 11.5.2. Note that, contrary to photogrammetric methods, no reference points with known coordinates have been used.

The images that have been used to build this three-dimensional model can be used to map textures on the polyhedral description using some standard computer graphics techniques. One result is shown in Figure 11.16.

The next example demonstrates the capacity of this class of methods to deal with continuous streams of images for applications to augmented reality. Given a number of images of a single scene, we add to the scene one or more artificial objects while respecting the geometry of the scene and/or the movements of the objects in the scene. A first example was shown in Figures 1.6, 1.7, and 1.8. The second sequence is a video sequence taken with a hand-held camera (Figure 11.17 shows three images extracted from that sequence). The scene is static and the only movement is that of the camera. The intrinsic parameters are changing over the sequence.

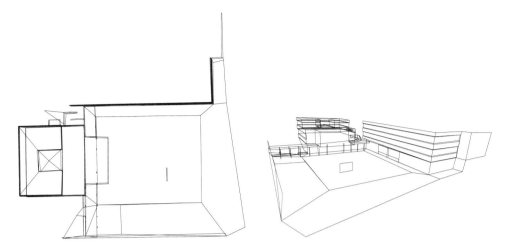

Figure 11.15: Top and front view of the Euclidean reconstruction of the INRIA site in Sophia-Antipolis. The model has been obtained from a total of forty-five views. Courtesy **Sylvain Bougnoux**, INRIA.

The sequences are then processed as follows. First, characteristic points are tracked automatically in the sequence with a technique based on image correlation. Then, a number of views of the sequence are manually selected to correspond to sufficiently different positions of the camera so that the estimation of the fundamental matrices between the pairs of views is robust. For the second sequence we first identify subsequences where the intrinsic parameters are roughly constant and then select the views. The next step is to estimate the fundamental matrices and to solve the system of the Kruppa equations by the methods described in Sections 11.3.3 and 11.5.1 to obtain an initial estimate of the intrinsic parameters of the camera. Thus we have access to a Euclidean reconstruction of the scene and consequently to the position and the relative orientation of the cameras in the space at the chosen instants. Those initial estimates are then refined by the technique described in Section 11.5.2.

After this step, we have a more precise estimate of the intrinsic parameters and the relative positions and orientations of the cameras at chosen times. Then we can obtain this position at any time of the sequence by simple interpolation of the intrinsic (for the second sequence) and extrinsic parameters. The interpolated quantities are the intrinsic parameters, the translation and the rotation. Only the rotation is problematic since the structure of the rotation group is a bit complicated, but the use of a parametrization with Euler angles or quaternions leads to a satisfactory solution.

Since the relative positions of the camera are known after the above computa-

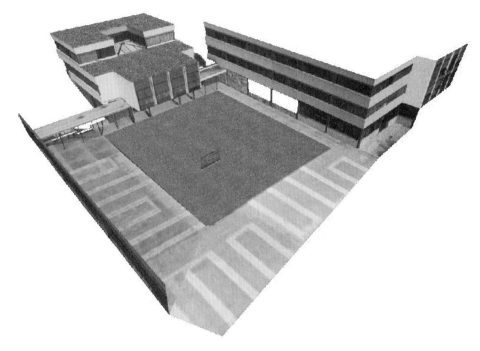

Figure 11.16: Textured front view of the Euclidean reconstruction of the INRIA site in Sophia-Antipolis. Courtesy **Sylvain Bougnoux**, INRIA.

tions, we can easily model by stereo the part of the scene we want to modify, a planar scene for the helicopter sequence, part of the table with a box sitting on top for the hand-held camera sequence. This three-dimensional model is then transfered into a CAD system which will "put on top" another virtual object like the power plant in Figure 1.7 or the lamp in Figure 11.18. A "reasonable" source of light can be positioned with respect to the set "ground+power plant" for the first sequence or "table+box+lamp" in order to compute shadows with the help of classical image synthesis techniques. The model is then reinserted into the initial sequence by combining the initial intensities of the ground, in the first example, of the table and the box in the second, with the shadows.

We show in Figures 1.8 and 11.19 three images of the modified sequences. These images correspond to those of Figures 1.6 and 11.17. The results are quite remarkable: The synthetic objects appear, as they should, to be static with respect to the environment. The impression is even stronger when looking at the modified sequences.

Figure 11.17: Three images of the sequence taken with a hand-held camera. Courtesy **Luc Robert**, INRIA.

11.6   Degeneracies in self-calibration

In this section we sketch out an analysis of the problem of degeneracies in self-calibration. We start with a description of the *intrinsic* degeneracies, i.e. of those which are present *independently* of the algorithm which is used for solving the calibration problem, e.g. solving the Kruppa equations. We then describe some particular degeneracies that are due to the particular type of algorithm used.

Let us therefore restate the calibration problem (i.e. the upgrade of the representation from projective to Euclidean) as that of recovering a plane in projective space and a conic Ω in that plane which is proper (i.e. non-degenerate) and imaginary and such that all of its images are also proper (they are also imaginary since the projection matrices are real).

We explore the possibility that there may be several solutions to this problem. Any such solution will be called a *spurious* solution to the calibration problem. In-

Figure 11.18: Model to insert in the sequence of Figure 11.17.

tuitively, the reason why there may exist such spurious solutions is that we usually perform a finite number of rigid displacements with the camera and only enforce that the images of the absolute conic are identical for those views, whereas the absolute conic satisfies this property for all possible rigid displacements. A particular sequence of displacements for which there exist spurious absolute conics will be called a *critical sequence*.

Our exposition follows that of Sturm (Sturm, 1997a). We consider only the simpler case where the spurious conics lie in the true plane at infinity. The case where they lie in a plane that is not the real plane at infinity is discussed in (Sturm, 1997a). We will nonetheless obtain a fairly complete description of the intrinsic critical sequences, i.e. of the sequences that are critical for self-calibration independently of the particular algorithm used for self-calibration. We will then describe some critical sequences that are specific to a given algorithm.

11.6.1 The spurious absolute conics lie in the real plane at infinity

Let us assume that we have n views and choose the world coordinate system as the normalized coordinate system of one of the cameras, e.g. the first, and the image coordinate systems as the intrinsic coordinate systems. All projection matrices are therefore of the form

$$\mathcal{P}_i \simeq [\mathbf{R}_i \, \mathbf{t}_i],$$

Figure 11.19: Results obtained from the images and model in Figures 11.17 and 11.18.

where the matrices $\mathbf{R}_i$ are rotation matrices.

A proper imaginary conic Ω in Π_∞ is represented by a definite symmetric 3×3 matrix $\mathbf{C}$ and the matrix $\mathbf{c}_i$ of the image ω_i of Ω in view i is

$$\mathbf{c}_i \simeq \mathbf{R}_i \mathbf{C} \mathbf{R}_i^T.$$

The images of Ω in two views will be identical if and only if their matrices are proportional ($\mathbf{c}_i \simeq \mathbf{c}_j$) and, since the $\mathbf{R}_i$'s are rotation matrices (therefore of determinants equal to 1), this is equivalent to

$$\mathbf{R}_i \mathbf{C} \mathbf{R}_i^T = \mathbf{R}_j \mathbf{C} \mathbf{R}_j^T \ \ i \neq j; \tag{11.40}$$

note the $=$ sign. The analysis of this equation yields a complete characterization of the critical sequences of rigid displacements and of the spurious absolute conics.

Proposition 11.12 (Sturm) *The critical sequences of displacements with respect* *to a proper imaginary conic in the plane at infinity are those for which the relative rotations between any two views of the sequence fall into one of three cases:*

1. *A rotation of angle 0 (pure translation case).*

2. *An arbitrary rotation around a fixed axis* **r**.

3. *A 180-degree rotation around an axis perpendicular to a fixed direction* **r**.

In case 1, the cameras are translated with respect to each other and all proper imaginary conics in the plane at infinity are spurious absolute conics. In cases 2 and 3, the spurious absolute conics form part of a one-parameter linear family of conics defined by the matrices

$$\mathbf{C} = \lambda \mathbf{I}_3 + \mu \mathbf{r} \mathbf{r}^T,$$

where λ *and* μ *are two arbitrary parameters.*

Proof : Rewrite Equation (11.40) as

$$\mathbf{R}\mathbf{C} = \mathbf{C}\mathbf{R}, \tag{11.41}$$

where $\mathbf{R} = \mathbf{R}_j^T \mathbf{R}_i$ is the relative rotation between the two views. This equation shows that the matrix $\mathbf{R}$ must leave the eigenspaces of the symmetric definite matrix $\mathbf{C}$ invariant. There are only three possible cases corresponding to the number of distinct eigenvalues.

Three equal eigenvalues Ω is the real absolute conic. The eigenspace of $\mathbf{C}$ is the whole space and therefore $\mathbf{R}$ must be the identity matrix.

Two equal eigenvalues The corresponding eigenspace is a plane Π. The eigenspace corresponding to the simple eigenvalue is of dimension 1; it is defined by a vector $\mathbf{r}$ orthogonal to the plane. The rotations which leave Π and $span(\mathbf{r})$ globally invariant are the identity, all of the rotations of axis $\mathbf{r}$ and the rotations of 180 degrees around an axis in Π, i.e. orthogonal to $\mathbf{r}$. They form a group.

Three different eigenvalues The three eigenspaces are orthogonal and of dimension 1. The rotations which leave those three eigenspaces globally invariant are the identity and all of the 180 degrees rotations around any of the three directions defined by the three eigenvectors. They form a subgroup of the previous group.

Conversely, if the relative rotation $\mathbf{R}$ is one of the above, let us show that there exist spurious absolute conics. If $\mathbf{R}$ is the identity, then Equation 11.41 is true for all definite symmetric matrices $\mathbf{C}$: All proper imaginary conics in the plane at infinity are spurious absolute conics in the case of camera translation. Otherwise, let $\mathbf{r}$ be the vector defining the axis of rotation, and define the family of symmetric matrices

$$\mathbf{C} = \lambda \mathbf{I}_3 + \mu \mathbf{r}\mathbf{r}^T, \qquad\qquad (11.42)$$

where λ and μ are arbitrary real numbers. Any rotation $\mathbf{R}$ around $\mathbf{r}$ satisfies the relations $\mathbf{R}\mathbf{r} = \mathbf{r}$ and $\mathbf{R}^T\mathbf{r} = \mathbf{r}$ and therefore (11.41) is satisfied. The matrix $\mathbf{C}$ is positive definite if and only if its eigenvalues are positive. The eigenvalue corresponding to the eigenspace of dimension 1 generated by $\mathbf{r}$ is readily seen to be equal to $\lambda + \mu\|\mathbf{r}\|^2$ and the double eigenvalue corresponding to the plane Π orthogonal to $\mathbf{r}$ is equal to λ. Therefore there are two infinite subfamilies of definite matrices of the linear family defined by (11.42). The first one is defined by the relations $\lambda > 0$ and $\lambda + \mu\|\mathbf{r}\|^2 > 0$, the second one by the relations $\lambda < 0$ and $\lambda + \mu\|\mathbf{r}\|^2 < 0$. $\quad\square$

The practical implications of this proposition are important since some of the critical sequences are often used for acquiring sequences of images. An example is the case where the camera is translating arbitrarily while rotating by an arbitrary angle around a fixed direction (pure translation is a special case that has been identified in the previous section as a degenerate case of the Kruppa equations); see Figure 11.20. Another special case is the case of planar motion, often encountered in mobile

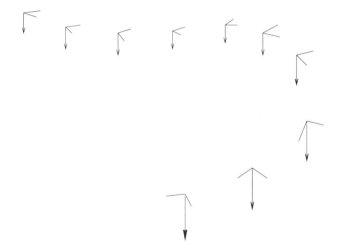

Figure 11.20: The motion of a camera translating arbitrarily while rotating around a fixed direction is critical with respect to self-calibration.

robotics, where the translations are limited to a fixed plane and the rotations are around the direction orthogonal to the plane; see Figure 11.21. Yet another special case is that of orbital motion in which the motion is planar and the camera is

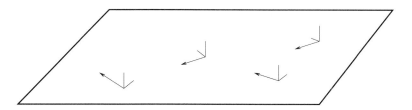

Figure 11.21: The motion of a camera translating in the plane and rotating around an axis perpendicular to the plane is critical with respect to self-calibration.

rotating around a point of the plane and pointing to that point. This kind of motion is often used when acquiring images of an object for 3D modeling; see Figure 11.22.

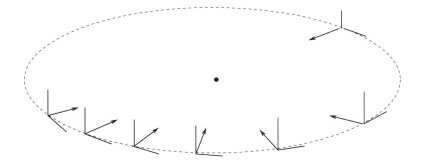

Figure 11.22: The motion of a camera rotating in the plane around a fixed point and pointing to that point is critical with respect to self-calibration.

11.6.2 Degeneracies of the Kruppa equations

In the last two sections, we have described intrinsic degeneracies of the self-calibration process. One might expect that a particular algorithm would suffer from those degeneracies and, perhaps, from others. This is the case for the class of algorithms that solve the Kruppa equations: There exist non-intrinsic critical sequences and spurious absolute conics. We describe such a degeneracy in the next proposition.

Proposition 11.13 *When the optical centers lie on a sphere and the optical axes go through the center of the sphere, there exists a one-parameter family of spurious solutions to the Kruppa equations. The ratio $\frac{\alpha_u}{\alpha_v}$ cannot be recovered from the sequence of views.*

Proof : Consider a sphere with a smaller radius than the one of the sphere on which the optical centers lie. The cones tangent to that sphere whose vertices are the optical centers intersect the retinal planes along identical circles centered at the principal points. In the pixel coordinate frames, those circles appear as ellipses. Consider now a pair of cameras: There are two epipolar planes that are tangent to the sphere and the corresponding epipolar lines are tangent to the two ellipses in the image planes. Therefore those ellipses satisfy the Kruppa equations.

Note that since the ellipses are real, they cannot be the images of a spurious absolute conic. But imagine that we increase the radius of the sphere so that the optical centers are inside the sphere. The tangent cones are now imaginary and intersect the image planes along imaginary circles which are still centered at the principal points. In the pixel coordinate frames those imaginary circles are proper imaginary ellipses. Similarly to the real case, if we consider a pair of optical centers, then the corresponding pair of proper imaginary ellipses satisfy the Kruppa equations.

When we vary the radius of the sphere, these ellipses only change by a scale factor: All of the internal parameters remain the same, except α_u and α_v that are scaled by the same factor. In particular, their ratio remains constant. $\square$

This degeneracy of the Kruppa equations is interesting in practice and in theory. It explains why the methods which start from the projection matrices (Section 11.4) have generally been found to be more stable than the methods which start from the Fundamental matrices (Section 11.3).

There does not exist a spurious absolute conic in this case. But there exists a spurious absolute *quadric*, i.e. the sphere. The reason is that the Kruppa equations do not enforce the planarity of the absolute conic.

11.7   Discussion

The methods described in Section 11.1 work fairly well if the infinity homography has been precisely estimated. This is the case in particular when the optical center of the camera remains fixed.

The methods based on the Kruppa equations described in Sections 11.2 and 11.3 rely on an initial estimation of the Fundamental matrices and work well if these matrices have been accurately estimated and/or if their uncertainty is taken into account. They are mostly useful for providing initial values of the internal parameters which can in turn be used as initial values for other algorithms. But they can also be pushed further to recover the motion parameters (through the Essential matrices) and the scale factors μ_i, as explained in Proposition 10.8. These parameters can also be used as initial values for other methods, such as the two described in Section 11.5 for which good initial values are required.

The methods described in Section 11.4 rely on an initial computation of the projective canonical form which is obtained by an estimation of the Fundamental matrices or Trifocal tensors, as explained in Chapter 10. They then estimate the infinity homography and the intrinsic parameters either sequentially (Section 11.4.2.1) or simultaneously (Sections 11.4.2.2 and 11.4.2.3). In all cases some reasonable initial values must be available. The methods mentioned so far all assume that the intrinsic parameters are constant. The one explained in Section 11.4.2.4 is different in this respect and elegantly exploits the relationship between the matrix of the absolute quadric and the intrinsic parameters.

All of the methods can be refined by a global optimization over all of the parameters of the problem, as described in Section 11.5.2, which is even more computationally expensive. This method does not have a projective stage, and requires a very good initialization.

Experiments in (Luong and Faugeras, 1994a; Zhang et al., 1996) show that the motion and the 3D reconstruction parameters are not affected much by large variations of the positions of the principal points. In fact, (Christy and Horaud, 1996) shows that the most important parameter is the aspect ratio, which turns out to be the parameter which is the most precisely estimated. The very reason why some parameters are not precisely estimated by the self-calibration methods is that their influence on the 3D reconstruction is small.

11.8   References and further reading

General methods   The Kruppa equations have been discovered by Faugeras and Maybank (Faugeras and Maybank, 1990a) and named after the Austrian mathematician Erwin Kruppa who had been working on problems of photogrammetry (Kruppa, 1913). They were used to develop the first theory of self-calibration (Maybank and Faugeras, 1992). The first working general self-calibration algorithms are based on those equations (Faugeras et al., 1992; Luong, 1992; Luong and Faugeras, 1994a). Zeller (Zeller, 1996; Zeller and Faugeras, 1996) proposes a method to initialize them, and to solve them accurately using the uncertainty of the Fundamental matrix. A detailed algebraic study of those equations is also done. The simplification of the Kruppa equations based on an SVD of the Fundamental matrix was first used in (Luong, 1992), then reformulated in (Hartley, 1997a) and more simply in (Lourakis and Deriche, 2000), where it is the basis for a self-calibration algorithm. In the same spirit, Mendonça and Cipolla (Mendonça and Cipolla, 1999) minimize the residual of the singular values constraints (Huang-Faugeras) on the essential matrix, which is expressed as a function of the Fundamental matrices and the unknown intrinsic parameters. All of those methods are based on reprojected constraints, and use the Fundamental matrix.

The first self-calibration method which operates in $\mathbb{P}^3$ and starts from the projective reconstruction was due to Hartley (Hartley, 1993; Hartley, 1997b). The method relies heavily on an intermediate localization of the plane at infinity which was eventually done by partitioning (Hartley et al., 1999). Later, Heyden and Astrom (Heyden and Astrom, 1996) introduced an easier way to express Euclidean constraints in the projective reconstruction, and Triggs (Triggs, 1997a) gave it a concise formulation in terms of the absolute quadric, which made it a popular method, able to naturally tackle the varying intrinsic parameters problem. Some numerical refinements were presented by Oliensis (Oliensis, 1999).

Self-calibration with varying intrinsic parameters was first theoretically investigated by Heyden and Astrom (Heyden and Astrom, 1997a), who showed that four zero-skew and unit aspect ratio cameras yield a Euclidean reconstruction. They subsequently obtained the very general theoretical result that it is sufficient that just one of the intrinsic parameters is known (Heyden and Astrom, 1998), or constant (Heyden and rAström, 1999). Pollefeys (Pollefey et al., 1996) addressed at the same time the less general case of varying focal length, and then (Pollefeys et al., 1999) showed that it is sufficient to know the skew. Before the theoretical proofs, practical solutions were proposed. Encisso *et al.* (Enciso and Vieville, 1997) relied on minimization of calibration and motion parameters. Bougnoux (Bougnoux, 1998) expressed the constraints of unit aspect ratio and zero-skew on the Euclidean projection matrices in order to constrain the canonical transformation parameters.

Particular cases   Self-calibration for an affine camera was proposed by Quan (Quan, 1996). Kahl and Heyden (Heyden and Kahl, 1998) first used an affine camera, which they self-calibrated. The resulting Euclidean parameters initialized a perspective bundle adjustment.

Several authors (Hartley, 1992; Ponce et al., 1994; Rousso and Shilat, 1998) have studied the problem of extracting the focal lengths from the fundamental matrix, assuming that the other intrinsic parameters are known. Brooks *et al.* (Brooks et al., 1996) pointed out degenerate cases which occur for a verging stereo system with coplanar optical axes. Of course, this is a particular case of a situation we described in this chapter. They found that self-calibration of the focal lengths is possible only if the focal lengths are assumed to be identical, and provided that the inward vergences are not identical. In (de Agapito et al., 1998), they performed an error analysis in the neighborhood of degenerate configurations and showed that this error can be considerable. Using the Kruppa equations, Bougnoux (Bougnoux, 1998) was able to obtain a closed-form solution which made it possible for him to study in (Bougnoux, 99) the degenerate configurations.

The possibility of recovering constant intrinsic parameters from the infinity homography was suggested by Luong and Viéville (Luong and Viéville, 1996) and studied in more detail by Hartley (Hartley, 1997b). The method was extended to variable intrinsic parameters by Seo and Hong. In (Seo and Hong, 1999), they proved that self-calibration of a stationary camera with varying intrinsic parameters and zero skew is unique, and they studied the effect of the error on the principal point and the recovered focal length. Agapito *et al.* (de Agapito et al., 1999) proposed a simpler algorithm by remarking that solving for the image of the absolute conic instead of its dual makes it possible to express certain constraints (such as zero-skew) linearly.

Viéville (Viéville, 1994) gave an algorithm for self-calibration of a camera undergoing a axis rotation. Armstrong *et al.* (Armstrong et al., 1996) reformulated the problem in terms of estimating fixed points and proposed a solution using the trifocal tensor. In a similar vein, Faugeras *et al.* (Faugeras et al., 1998a) described self-calibration of a 1D camera based on the trifocal tensor of three 1D images. They proved that a 2D camera undergoing a planar motion reduces to a 1D camera.

Planar scenes are typically degenerate cases, since the Fundamental matrix, as well as the projective reconstruction, cannot be estimated uniquely. Triggs (Triggs, 1998) showed that five views of a plane is sufficient to recover all of the intrinsics parameters of a camera, less if some parameters are fixed *a priori*. The basic constraint is that the projections of the two circular points of the 3D plane must lie on the image of the absolute conic.

Although a few critical cases were suggested before, the first systematic classification of critical sequences for self-calibration is due to Sturm (Sturm, 1997a). This classification was later extended to variable focal lengths. Assuming that focal lengths are the only unknowns, Bougnoux (Bougnoux, 99) obtained a classification and parameterization. In (Bougnoux, 1998) he gave an explanation for the instability of the recovered intrinsic parameters. Other work including more general hypotheses such as zero-skew and known aspect ratios is discussed in (Sturm, 1999; Kahl, 1999). In the case of constant intrinsic parameters, Ma *et al.* (Ma et al., 1999) explicitly characterized the ambiguities in calibration and reconstruction in the critical cases in terms of subgroups, and applied the analysis to derive the ambiguity in the synthesis of new views. Zisserman *et al.* (Zisserman et al., 1998) studied in great detail the one-parameter ambiguity which arises when the camera rotations are about axes with a common direction, investigating in particular the cases in which an additional constraint does not resolve this ambiguity.

A Appendix

A.1 Solution of $\min_{\mathbf{x}} \|\mathbf{Ax}\|^2$ subject to $\|\mathbf{x}\|^2 = 1$

The constrained minimization problem:

$$\min_{\mathbf{x}} \|\mathbf{Ax}\|^2 \quad \text{subject to} \quad \|\mathbf{x}\|^2 = 1 \; , \tag{A.1}$$

can be reformulated, using the Lagrange multiplier λ, as the unconstrained problem:

$$\min_{\mathbf{x}} C(\mathbf{x}, \lambda) \quad \text{where} \quad C(\mathbf{x}, \lambda) = \|\mathbf{Ax}\|^2 + \lambda(1 - \|\mathbf{x}\|^2) \; . \tag{A.2}$$

Since:

$$\frac{\partial C}{\partial \mathbf{x}} = 2\mathbf{A}^T \mathbf{Ax} - 2\lambda \mathbf{x} \; ,$$

the necessary condition $\frac{\partial C}{\partial \mathbf{x}} = 0$ leads to $\mathbf{A}^T \mathbf{Ax} = \lambda \mathbf{x}$, therefore $\mathbf{x}$ must be one of the unit eigenvectors of matrix $\mathbf{A}^T \mathbf{A}$, and λ the associated eigenvalue. For such values of $\mathbf{x}$ and λ, we have $C(\mathbf{x}, \lambda) = \lambda$. The solution is therefore obtained by choosing the eigenvector $\mathbf{x}$ of matrix $\mathbf{A}^T \mathbf{A}$ corresponding to the smallest eigenvalue.

Since matrix $\mathbf{A}^T \mathbf{A}$ is symmetric and positive, all the eigenvalues are real and positive. The problem of computing those eigenvalues is equivalent to that of computing a singular value decomposition (SVD) for matrix $\mathbf{A}$. Consider the SVD:

$$\mathbf{U}^T \mathbf{AV} = \text{diag}(\sigma_1, \ldots, \sigma_n) \; ,$$

with $\mathbf{U}$ and $\mathbf{V}$ orthogonal matrices. Easy algebra leads to:

$$\mathbf{A}^T \mathbf{A} = \mathbf{V} \text{diag}(\sigma_1^2, \ldots, \sigma_n^2) \mathbf{V}^T \; ,$$

which is the Schur decomposition of the symmetric matrix $\mathbf{A}^T \mathbf{A}$. The eigenvectors are the column vectors of $\mathbf{V}$ and the associated eigenvalues are the squared singular values.

A.2   A note about rank-2 matrices

There is a common point to the objects introduced to deal with multiple view geometry such as fundamental matrices or trifocal tensor: They all involve at some point matrices of rank 2. Furthermore, in most cases, the left and right kernels of these matrices are attached to geometrical properties of the system of cameras. This suggests that the set $\mathcal{M}(\mathbf{L}, \mathbf{R})$ of all the matrices that have a given left kernel $\mathbf{L} = [l_1, l_2, l_3]^T \neq \mathbf{0}$ and right kernel $\mathbf{R} = [r_1, r_2, r_3]^T \neq \mathbf{0}$ is of some importance, and it indeed received a lot of attention with the study and parameterization of the fundamental matrix. Most of this section is just a slightly different formulation of a well-known parameterization of the fundamental matrix, which uses the 2 epipoles and 4 coefficients (defined up to a scale factor) of the original matrix (that describe the homography relating the epipolar lines in the two images) (Luong and Faugeras, 1996).

Obviously, $\mathcal{M}(\mathbf{L}, \mathbf{R})$ is a linear space of dimension 4. Thinking in terms of linear spaces, a basis of this space can be found and the coordinates of a given matrix of $\mathcal{M}(\mathbf{L}, \mathbf{R})$ in that basis correspond (although may be not directly) to the 4 coefficients of the fundamental matrix parameterization. Thus, exactly as in this case, there is no systematic way to define a basis for $\mathcal{M}(\mathbf{L}, \mathbf{R})$ that would be valid for all choices of $\mathbf{L}$ and $\mathbf{R}$: Different maps cannot be avoided as long as we want a minimal basis. To simplify the presentation, we will assume that the highest components in magnitude of both $\mathbf{L}$ and $\mathbf{R}$ are in first position: In this case, the four matrices of rank 1 $\mathbf{M}_1$, $\mathbf{M}_2$, $\mathbf{M}_3$ and $\mathbf{M}_4$ constitute a basis of $\mathcal{M}(\mathbf{L}, \mathbf{R})$. are obtained similarly (just apply circular permutations to $\mathbf{L}$ and $\mathbf{R}$ to bring the situation to the one discussed above).

$$\mathbf{M}_1 = \begin{bmatrix} r_3 l_3 & 0 & -r_1 l_3 \\ 0 & 0 & 0 \\ -r_3 l_1 & 0 & r_1 l_1 \end{bmatrix}, \quad \mathbf{M}_2 = \begin{bmatrix} -r_2 l_3 & r_1 l_3 & 0 \\ 0 & 0 & 0 \\ r_2 l_1 & -r_1 l_1 & 0 \end{bmatrix},$$

$$\mathbf{M}_3 = \begin{bmatrix} -r_3 l_2 & 0 & r_1 l_2 \\ r_3 l_1 & 0 & -r_1 l_1 \\ 0 & 0 & 0 \end{bmatrix}, \quad \mathbf{M}_4 = \begin{bmatrix} r_2 l_2 & -r_1 l_2 & 0 \\ -r_2 l_1 & r_1 l_1 & 0 \\ 0 & 0 & 0 \end{bmatrix}. \quad (\text{A.3})$$

This basis is valid as long as $l_1 \neq 0$ and $r_1 \neq 0$. This explains our choice of having maximal magnitudes for those coefficients. The 8 other maps that correspond to different choices for the positions of the highest components are obtained similarly (just apply two circular permutations λ and ρ to $\mathbf{L}$ and $\mathbf{R}$ respectively to bring the situation to the one discussed above; the resulting base is obtained by permuting rows and columns of $\mathbf{M}_i, i = 1 \ldots 4$ by λ and ρ, respectively.

The coordinates of a matrix $\mathbf{M}$ of $\mathcal{M}(\mathbf{L}, \mathbf{R})$ in this basis will be called a_1, a_2, a_3 and a_4:

$$\mathbf{M} = a_1 \mathbf{M}_1 + a_2 \mathbf{M}_2 + a_3 \mathbf{M}_3 + a_4 \mathbf{M}_4 \ .$$

$\mathbf{M}$ is of rank 1 iff $a_2 a_3 - a_1 a_4 = 0$.

References

Abdel-Aziz, Y. and Karara, H. (1971). Direct linear transformation into object space coordinates in close-range photogrammetry. In *Proceedings of the Symposium on Close-Range Photogrammetry, University of Illinois at Urbana-Champaign, Urbana, Illinois*, pages 1–18.

Abhyankar, S. S. (1985). *Algebraic Geometry for Scientists and Engineers*. Number 35 in Mathematical Surveys and Monographs. American Mathematical Society.

Aloimonos, J. (1990). Perspective approximations. *Image and Vision Computing*, 8(3):179–192.

Anandan, P., Hanna, K., and Kumar, R. (1994). Shape Recovery from Multiple Views: A Parallax Based Approach. In *Proceedings of the International Conference on Pattern Recognition*, pages A:685–688, Jerusalem, Israel. Computer Society Press.

Armstrong, M., Zisserman, A., and Hartley, R. (1996). Self-calibration from image triplets. In *Fourth European Conference on Computer Vision*, pages 3–16.

Astrom, K. (1995). Fundamental Limitations on Projective Invariants of Planar Curves. *IEEE Transactions on Pattern Analysis and Machine Intelligence*, 17(1):77–81.

Astrom, K., Cipolla, R., and Giblin, P. (1999a). Generalised Epipolar Constraints. *The International Journal of Computer Vision*, 33(1):51–72.

Astrom, K. and Heyden, A. (1998). Continuous Time Matching Constraints for Image Streams. *The International Journal of Computer Vision*, 28(1):85–96.

Astrom, K., Heyden, A., Kahl, F., and Oskarsson, M. (1999b). Structure and Motion from Lines under Affine Projections. In *Proceedings of the 7th International Conference on Computer Vision*, pages 285–292, Kerkyra, Greece. IEEE Computer Society, IEEE Computer Society Press.

Atkinson, K. (1989). *An introduction to numerical analysis.* John Wiley and Sons, 2nd edition.

Avidan, S. and Shashua, A. (1997). Novel view synthesis in tensor space. In *Proceedings of the International Conference on Computer Vision and Pattern Recognition*, pages 1034–1040, San Juan, Puerto Rico. IEEE Computer Society, IEEE.

Avidan, S. and Shashua, A. (1998). Threading fundamental matrices. In Burkhardt, H. and Neumann, B., editors, *Proceedings of the 5th European Conference on Computer Vision*, volume 1 of *Lecture Notes in Computer Science*, pages 124–140, Freiburg, Germany. Springer-Verlag.

Ayache, N. and Lustman, F. (1987). Fast and reliable passive trinocular stereovision. In *Proceedings of the 1st International Conference on Computer Vision*, pages 422–427, London, England. IEEE Computer Society Press.

Bard, Y. (1974). *Nonlinear Parameter Estimation.* Academic Press.

Barnabei, M., Brini, A., and Rota, G.-C. (1985). On the exterior calculus of invariant theory. *Journal of Algebra*, 96:pp 120–160.

Barrett, E., Payton, P., Haag, N., and Brill, M. (1991). General Methods for Determining Projective Invariants in Imagery. *Computer Vision, Graphics, and Image Processing*, 53(1):46–65.

Barrett, E. B., Brill, M. H., Haag, N. N., and Payton, P. M. (1992). Invariant linear methods in photogrammetry and model-matching. In Mundy, J. L. and Zimmerman, A., editors, *Geometric Invariance in Computer Vision*, chapter 14. MIT Press.

Basri, R. (1996). Paraperspective ≡ Affine. *The International Journal of Computer Vision*, 19(2):169–179.

Basu, A. (1993). Active calibration: Alternative strategy and analysis. In *Proceedings of the International Conference on Computer Vision and Pattern Recognition*, pages 495–500, New-York, NY. IEEE Computer Society, IEEE.

Beardsley, P. (1992). *Applications of projective geometry to robot vision.* PhD thesis, University of Oxford.

Beardsley, P., Zisserman, A., and Murray, D. (1994). Navigation using affine structure from motion. In Eklundh, J.-O., editor, *Proceedings of the 3rd European Conference on Computer Vision*, volume 2 of *Lecture Notes in Computer Science*, pages 85–96, Stockholm, Sweden. Springer-Verlag.

Beardsley, P. A., Reid, I. D., Zisserman, A., and Murray, D. W. (1995). Active visual navigation using non-metric structure. In *Proceedings of the 5th International Conference on Computer Vision*, pages 58–64, Boston, MA. IEEE Computer Society Press.

Beardsley, P. A., Zisserman, A., and Murray, D. W. (1997). Sequential update of projective and affine structure from motion. *The International Journal of Computer Vision*, 23(3):235–259.

Belhumeur, P., Kriegman, D., and Yuille, A. (1997). The Bas-Relief Ambiguity. In *Proceedings of the International Conference on Computer Vision and Pattern Recognition*, pages 1040–1046, San Juan, Puerto Rico. IEEE Computer Society, IEEE.

Bergen, J., Anandan, P., Hanna, K., and Hingorani, R. (1992). Hierarchical Model-Based Motion Estimation. In Sandini, G., editor, *Proceedings of the 2nd European Conference on Computer Vision*, pages 237–252, Santa Margherita, Italy. Springer-Verlag.

Berger, M. (1987). *Geometry*. Springer-Verlag.

Berthilsson, R., Astrom, K., and Heyden, A. (1999). Reconstruction of Curves in r^3, using Factorization and Bundle Adjustment. In *Proceedings of the 7th International Conference on Computer Vision*, pages 674–679, Kerkyra, Greece. IEEE Computer Society, IEEE Computer Society Press.

Beyer, H. (1990). Linejitter and geometric calibration of CCD cameras. *ISPRS Journal of photometry and remote sensing*, 45:17–32.

Beyer, H. A. (1992). Accurate calibration of CCD-cameras. In *Proceedings of the International Conference on Computer Vision and Pattern Recognition*, Urbana Champaign, IL. IEEE.

Bjorkman, M. and Eklundh, J. (1999). Real-time epipolar geometry estimation and disparity. In *Proceedings of the 7th International Conference on Computer Vision*, pages 234–241, Kerkyra, Greece. IEEE Computer Society, IEEE Computer Society Press.

Bookstein, F. (1979). Fitting conic sections to scattered data. *Computer Vision, Graphics, and Image Processing*, 9:56–71.

Bosse, A. (1648). *Manière universelle de M. Desargues pour pratiquer la perspective.* Paris.

Bosse, A. (1664). *Traité des manières de dessiner les ordres de l'architecture.* Paris.

Boufama, B. and Mohr, R. (1995). Epipole and fundamental matrix estimation using the virtual parallax property. In *Proceedings of the 5th International Conference on Computer Vision*, pages 1030–1036, Boston, MA. IEEE Computer Society Press.

Boufama, B., Mohr, R., and Veillon, F. (1993). Euclidean constraints for uncalibrated reconstruction. In *Proceedings of the 4th International Conference on Computer Vision*, pages 466–470, Berlin, Germany. IEEE Computer Society Press.

Bougnoux, S. (1998). From projective to euclidean space under any practical situation, a criticism of self-calibration. In *IEEE International Conference on Computer Vision*, pages 790–796.

Bougnoux, S. (99). Paradigmes et paradoxes d'étalonnage en vision par ordinateur. Master's thesis, UNSA.

Brand, P., Mohr, R., and Bobet, P. (1993). Distorsions optiques : correction dans un modèle projectif. Technical Report 1933, LIFIA–INRIA Rhône-Alpes.

Brillault-O'Mahony, B. (1991). New Method for Vanishing Point Detection. *Computer Vision, Graphics, and Image Processing*, 54(2):289–300.

Brodsky, T., Fermuller, C., and Aloimonos, Y. (1998). Self-Calibration from Image Derivatives. In *Proceedings of the 6th International Conference on Computer Vision*, pages 83–89, Bombay, India. IEEE Computer Society, IEEE Computer Society Press.

Brooks, M., Chojnacki, W., and Baumela, L. (1997). Determining the Egomotion of an Uncalibrated Camera from Instantaneous Optical Flow. *Journal of the Optical Society of America A*, 14(10):2670–2677.

Brooks, M., Chojnacki, W., van den Hengel, A., and Baumela, L. (1998). Robust techniques fot the estimation of structure from motion in the uncalibrated case. In Burkhardt, H. and Neumann, B., editors, *ECCV'98*, volume 1 of *Lecture Notes in Computer Science*, pages 281–295, Freiburg, Germany. Springer, Berlin.

Brooks, M., de Agapito, L., Huynh, D., and Baumela, L. (1996). Direct Methods for Self-Calibration of a Moving Stereo Head. In Buxton, B., editor, *Proceedings of the 4th European Conference on Computer Vision*, pages II:415–426, Cambridge, UK.

Brown, D. (1966). Decentering distorsion of lenses. *Photogrammetric Engineering*, 32(3):444–462.

Brown, D. C. (1958). A solution to the general problem of multiple station analytical stereotriangulation. Technical Report 43, RCA Data Reduction Technical Report, Patrick Air Force base, Florida.

Brown, D. C. (1971). Close-range camera calibration. *Photogrammetric Engineering*, 37(8):855–866.

Buchanan, T. (1992). On the critical set for photogrammetric reconstruction using line tokens in $p_3(c)$. *Geometricae Dedicata*, (44):223–232.

Burns, J., Weiss, R., and Riseman, E. (1993). View Variation of Point Set and Line Segment Features. *IEEE Transactions on Pattern Analysis and Machine Intelligence*, 15(1):51–68.

Caprile, B. and Torre, V. (1990). Using Vanishing Points for Camera Calibration. *The International Journal of Computer Vision*, 4(2):127–140.

Carlsson, S. (1994). Multiple image invariance using the double algebra. In Mundy, J. L., Zissermann, A., and Forsyth, D., editors, *Applications of Invariance in Computer Vision*, volume 825 of *Lecture Notes in Computer Science*, pages 145–164. Springer-Verlag.

Carlsson, S. (1995). Duality of reconstruction and positioning from projective views. In *Worshop on Representations of Visual Scenes*, pages 85–92.

Carlsson, S. and Weinshall, D. (1998). Dual computation of projective shape and camera positions from multiple images. *The International Journal of Computer Vision*, 27(3):227–241.

Chai, J. and Ma, S. (1998). Robust epipolar geometry estimation using genetic algorithm. *Pattern Recognition Letters*, 19(9):829–838.

Champleboux, G., Lavallé, S., Sautot, P., and Cinquin, P. (1992). Accurate calibration of cameras and range imaging sensors: the NPBS method. In *Proc. International Conference on Robotics and Automation*, pages 1552–1557, Nice, France.

Chasles, M. (1855). Question No. 296. *Nouv. Ann. Math.*, 14:50.

Chen, H. (1991). Pose determination from line-to-plane correspondences: existence condition and the closed-form solutions. *IEEE Transactions on Pattern Analysis and Machine Intelligence*, 13(6):530–541.

Chen, Q. and Medioni, G. (1999a). Efficient iterative solutions to m-view projective reconstruction problem. In *Proceedings of the International Conference on Computer Vision and Pattern Recognition*, pages II:55–61, Fort Collins, Colorado. IEEE Computer Society.

Chen, Q. and Medioni, G. (1999b). A volumetric stereo matching method: Application to image-based modeling. In *Proceedings of the International Conference on Computer Vision and Pattern Recognition*, pages I:29–34, Fort Collins, Colorado. IEEE Computer Society.

Chen, S. (1995). Quicktime vr - an image-based approach to virtual environment navigation. In *Computer Graphics (SIGGRAPH'95)*, pages 29–38.

Chou, J. and Kamel, M. (1988). Quaternions approach to solve the kinematic equation of rotation, $A_a A_x = A_x A_a$, of a sensor-mounted robotic manipulator. In *Proc. International Conference on Robotics and Automation*, pages 656–662.

Christy, S. and Horaud, R. (1996). Euclidean shape and motion from multiple perspective views by affine iterations. *IEEE Transactions on Pattern Analysis and Machine Intelligence*, 18(11):1098–1104.

Cipolla, R., **r**Astrom, K. E., and Giblin, P. J. (1995). Motion from the frontier of curved surfaces. In *Proceedings of the 5th International Conference on Computer Vision*, pages 269–275, Boston, MA. IEEE Computer Society Press.

Clemens, D. T. and Jacobs, D. W. (1991). Model group indexing for recognition. In *Proceedings of the International Conference on Computer Vision and Pattern Recognition*, pages 4–9, Lahaina, Hawai. IEEE.

Collins, R. and Tsin, Y. (1999). Calibration of an outdoor active camera system. In *Proceedings of the International Conference on Computer Vision and Pattern Recognition*, pages I:528–534, Fort Collins, Colorado. IEEE Computer Society.

Collins, R. and Weiss, R. (1990). Vanishing point calculation as a statistical inference on the unit sphere. In *Proceedings of the 3rd International Conference on Computer Vision*, pages 400–403, Osaka, Japan. IEEE Computer Society Press.

Costeira, J. and Kanade, T. (1995). A multi-body factorization method for motion analysis. In *Proceedings of the 5th International Conference on Computer Vision*, pages 1071–1076, Boston, MA. IEEE Computer Society Press.

Criminisi, A., Reid, I., and Zisserman, A. (1998). Duality, rigidity and planar parallax. In Burkhardt, H. and Neumann, B., editors, *Proceedings of the 5th European Conference on Computer Vision*, volume 1406–1407 of *Lecture Notes in Computer Science*, Freiburg, Germany. Springer-Verlag.

Criminisi, A., Reid, I., and Zisserman, A. (1999a). A plane measuring device. *Image and Vision Computing*, 17(8):625–634.

Criminisi, A., Reid, I., and Zisserman, A. (1999b). Single view metrology. In *Proceedings of the 7th International Conference on Computer Vision*, pages 434–441, Kerkyra, Greece. IEEE Computer Society, IEEE Computer Society Press.

Crimisini, A., Reid, I., and Zisserman, A. (1998). Duality, rigidity and planar parallax. In Burkhardt, H. and Neumann, B., editors, *Proceedings of the 5th European Conference on Computer Vision*, volume 1406–1407 of *Lecture Notes in Computer Science*, pages 846–861, Freiburg, Germany. Springer-Verlag.

Cross, G., Fitzgibbon, A., and Zisserman, A. (1999). Parallax geometry of smooth surfaces in multiple views. In *Proceedings of the 7th International Conference on Computer Vision*, pages 323–329, Kerkyra, Greece. IEEE Computer Society, IEEE Computer Society Press.

Cross, G. and Zisserman, A. (1998). Quadric reconstruction from dual-space geometry. In *Proceedings of the 6th International Conference on Computer Vision*, pages 25–31, Bombay, India. IEEE Computer Society, IEEE Computer Society Press.

Csurka, G., Demirdjian, D., and Horaud, R. (1999). Finding the collineation between two projective reconstructions. *Computer Vision and Image Understanding*, 75(3):260–268.

Csurka, G., Demirdjian, D., Ruf, A., and Horaud, R. (1998). Closed-form solutions for the euclidean calibration of a stereo rig. In Burkhardt, H. and Neumann, B., editors, *Proceedings of the 5th European Conference on Computer Vision*, volume 1406–1407 of *Lecture Notes in Computer Science*, Freiburg, Germany. Springer-Verlag.

Csurka, G., Zeller, C., Zhang, Z., and Faugeras, O. (1997). Characterizing the uncertainty of the fundamental matrix. *CVGIP: Image Understanding*, 68(1):18–36.

Dahler, J. (1987). Problems with Digital Image Acquistion with CCD Cameras. In *Intercommission Conference on Fast Processing of Photogrammetric Data*.

Damisch, H. (1994). *The Origin of Perspective*. MIT Press. First appeared in 1987 as L'origine de la perspective, Flamarion.

Davis, J. (1998). Mosaics of scenes with moving objects. In *Proceedings of the International Conference on Computer Vision and Pattern Recognition*, pages 354–360, Santa Barbara, California. IEEE Computer Society.

de Agapito, L., Hartley, R., and Hayman, E. (1999). Linear Calibration of a Rotating and Zooming Camera. In *Proceedings of the International Conference on Computer Vision and Pattern Recognition*, pages I:15–21, Fort Collins, Colorado. IEEE Computer Society.

de Agapito, L., Huynh, D., and M.J.Brooks (1998). Self-calibrating a stereo head: An error analysis in the neighbourhood of degenerate configurations. In *Proceedings of the 6th International Conference on Computer Vision*, Bombay, India. IEEE Computer Society, IEEE Computer Society Press.

de Vinci, L. (recent edition, 1998). *The Notebooks*. Oxford World's classics, Oxford. written around 1500.

Debrunner, C. and Ahuja, N. (1990). A direct data approximation based motion estimation algorithm. In *Proceedings of the 10th International Conference on Pattern Recognition*, pages 384–389, Atlantic City, N.J. Computer Society Press.

della Francesca, P. (1942, new edition 1984). *De prospectiva pingendi*. G. Fasola, Florence. Original edition around 1465.

Dema, S. (1996). A self-calibration technique for active vision systems. *IEEE Transactions on Robotics and Automation*, 12(1):114–120.

Demazure, M. (1988). Sur Deux Problèmes de Reconstruction. Technical Report 882, INRIA.

Demirdjian, D. and Horaud, R. (1992). A projective framework for scene segmentation in the presence of moving objects. In *Proceedings of the International Conference on Computer Vision and Pattern Recognition*, pages I:2–8, Urbana Champaign, IL. IEEE.

Devernay, F. and Faugeras, O. (1995). Automatic calibration and removal of distortion from scenes of structured environments. In Rudin, L. I. and Bramble, S. K., editors, *Investigative and Trial Image Processing*, volume 2567 of *Proc. SPIE*, San Diego, CA. SPIE.

Devernay, F. and Faugeras, O. (1996). From projective to euclidean reconstruction. In *Proceedings of the International Conference on Computer Vision and Pattern Recognition*, pages 264–269, San Francisco, CA. IEEE.

Dron, L. (1993). Dynamic camera self-calibration for controlled motion sequences. In *Proceedings of the International Conference on Computer Vision and Pattern Recognition*, pages 501–506, New-York, NY. IEEE Computer Society, IEEE.

Du, F. and Brady, M. (1993). Self-calibration of the intrinsic parameters of cameras for active vision systems. In *Proceedings of the International Conference on Computer Vision and Pattern Recognition*, pages 477–482, New-York, NY. IEEE Computer Society, IEEE.

Dürer, A. (1977). *Underweysung der Messung*. Albaris Books, New York. Original edition 1525, Nuremberg.

Enciso, R. and Vieville, T. (1997). Self-calibration from four views with possibly varying intrinsic parameters. *Image and Vision Computing*, 15(4):293–305.

Enciso, R., Viéville, T., and Faugeras, O. (1994). Approximation du changement de focale et de mise au point par une transformation affine à trois paramètres. *Traitement du Signal*, 11(5):361–372.

Faig, W. (1975). Calibration of close-range photogrammetry systems: Mathematical formulation. *Photogrammetric Engineering and Remote Sensing*, 41(12):1479–1486.

Fang, J. and Huang, T. (1984). Some experiments on estimating the 3D motion parameters of a rigid body from two consecutive image frames. *IEEE Transactions on Pattern Analysis and Machine Intelligence*, 6:545–554.

Faugeras, O. (1992). What can be seen in three dimensions with an uncalibrated stereo rig? In Sandini, G., editor, *Proceedings of the 2nd European Conference on Computer Vision*, pages 563–578, Santa Margherita, Italy. Springer-Verlag.

Faugeras, O. (1993). *Three-Dimensional Computer Vision: a Geometric Viewpoint*. MIT Press.

Faugeras, O. (1995). Stratification of 3-D vision: projective, affine, and metric representations. *Journal of the Optical Society of America A*, 12(3):465–484.

Faugeras, O. and Laveau, S. (1994). Representing three-dimensional data as a collection of images and fundamental matrices for image synthesis. In *Proceedings of the International Conference on Pattern Recognition*, pages 689–691, Jerusalem, Israel. Computer Society Press.

Faugeras, O., Luong, T., and Maybank, S. (1992). Camera self-calibration: theory and experiments. In Sandini, G., editor, *Proceedings of the 2nd European Conference on Computer Vision*, pages 321–334, Santa Margherita, Italy. Springer-Verlag.

Faugeras, O. and Lustman, F. (1986). Let us suppose that the world is piecewise planar. In Faugeras, O. and Giralt, G., editors, *Robotics Research : The Third International Symposium*, pages 33–40. MIT Press.

Faugeras, O. and Lustman, F. (1988). Motion and structure from motion in a piecewise planar environment. *International Journal of Pattern Recognition and Artificial Intelligence*, 2(3):485–508.

Faugeras, O., Lustman, F., and Toscani, G. (1987). Motion and structure from point and line matches. In *Proceedings of the 1st International Conference on Computer Vision*, pages 25–34, London, England. IEEE Computer Society Press.

Faugeras, O. and Maybank, S. (1990a). Motion from point matches: multiplicity of solutions. *The International Journal of Computer Vision*, 4(3):225–246. also INRIA Tech. Report 1157.

Faugeras, O. and Mourrain, B. (1995a). On the geometry and algebra of the point and line correspondences between n images. Technical Report 2665, INRIA.

Faugeras, O. and Mourrain, B. (1995b). On the geometry and algebra of the point and line correspondences between n images. In *Proceedings of the 5th International Conference on Computer Vision*, pages 951–956, Boston, MA. IEEE Computer Society Press.

Faugeras, O. and Papadopoulo, T. (1998). A nonlinear method for estimating the projective geometry of three views. In *Proceedings of the 6th International Conference on Computer Vision*, pages 477–484, Bombay, India. IEEE Computer Society, IEEE Computer Society Press.

Faugeras, O., Quan, L., and Sturm, P. (1998a). Self-calibration of a 1d projective camera and its application to the self-calibration of a 2d projective camera. In Burkhardt, H. and Neumann, B., editors, *Proceedings of the 5th European Conference on Computer Vision*, volume 1406–1407 of *Lecture Notes in Computer Science*, pages 36–52, Freiburg, Germany. Springer-Verlag.

Faugeras, O. and Robert, L. (1996). What can two images tell us about a third one? *The International Journal of Computer Vision*, 18(1):5–20.

Faugeras, O., Robert, L., Laveau, S., Csurka, G., Zeller, C., Gauclin, C., and Zoghlami, I. (1998b). 3-D reconstruction of urban scenes from image sequences. *Computer Vision and Image Understanding*, 69(3):292–309.

Faugeras, O. and Toscani, G. (1986). The calibration problem for stereo. In *Proceedings of the International Conference on Computer Vision and Pattern Recognition*, pages 15–20, Miami Beach, FL. IEEE.

Faugeras, O. D. and Maybank, S. (1990b). Motion from point matches: multiplicity of solutions. *The International Journal of Computer Vision*, 4(3):225–246. also INRIA Tech. Report 1157.

Field, J. (1997). *The Invention of Infinity : Mathematics and Art in the Renaissance*. Oxford university press, Oxford.

Fischler, M. and Bolles, R. (1981). Random sample consensus: A paradigm for model fitting with applications to image analysis and automated cartography. *Communications of the ACM*, 24:381–385.

Forsyth, D., Mundy, J., Zisserman, A., and Brown, C. (1990). Projectively invariant representations using implicit algebraic curves. In Faugeras, O., editor, *Proceedings of the 1st European Conference on Computer Vision*, pages 427–436, Antibes, France. Springer-Verlag.

Forsyth, D. A., Mundy, J. L., Zisserman, A., and Rothwell, C. A. (1994). Using global consistency to recognise euclidean objects with an uncalibrated camera. In *Proceedings of the International Conference on Computer Vision and Pattern Recognition*, pages 502–507, Seattle, WA. IEEE.

Fraser, C. (1992). Photogrammetric camera component calibration: a review of analytical techniques. In *Workshop on calibration and orientation of cameras in computer vision. XVII Congress ISPRS*.

Ganapathy, S. (1984). Decomposition of transformation matrices for robot vision. *Pattern Recognition Letters*, 2:401–412.

Garcia, B. and Brunet, P. (1998). 3d reconstruction with projective octrees and epipolar geometry. In *Proceedings of the 6th International Conference on Computer Vision*, pages 1067–1072, Bombay, India. IEEE Computer Society, IEEE Computer Society Press.

Garding, J., Porrill, J., Frisby, J., and Mayhew, J. (1996). Uncalibrated relief reconstruction and model alignment from binocular disparities. In Buxton, B., editor, *Proceedings of the 4th European Conference on Computer Vision*, pages I:427–438, Cambridge, UK.

Gluckman, J. and Nayar, S. (1999). Planar catadioptric stereo: Geometry and calibration. In *Proceedings of the International Conference on Computer Vision and Pattern Recognition*, pages I:22–28, Fort Collins, Colorado. IEEE Computer Society.

Golub, G. and van Loan, C. (1989). *Matrix Computations*. The John Hopkins University Press.

Gracie, G. (1968). Analytical photogrammetry applied to single terrestrial photograph mensuration. In *XIth international conference on Photogrammetry*, Lausanne, Switzerland.

Gremban, K. D., Thorpe, C. E., and Kanade, T. (1988). Geometric Camera Calibration using Systems of Linear Equations. In *Image Understanding Workshop*, pages 820–825.

Grotsky, W. and Tamburino, L. (1990). A unified approach to the linear camera calibration problem. *IEEE Transactions on Pattern Analysis and Machine Intelligence*, 12:663–671.

Gruen, A. (1978). Accuracy, reliability and statistics in close-range photogrammetry. In *Proceedings of the Symposium of the ISP Commission V*, Stockholm.

Gruen, A. and Beyer, H. A. (1992). System calibration through self-calibration. In *Proceedings of the Workshop on Calibration and Orientation of Cameras in Computer Vision*, Washington D.C.

Gupta, R. and Hartley, R. (1997). Linear pushbroom cameras. *IEEE Transactions on Pattern Analysis and Machine Intelligence*, 19(9):963–975.

Haralick, R. (1986). Computer vision theory: The lack thereof. *Computer Vision, Graphics, and Image Processing*, 36:372–386.

Hartley, R. (1992). Estimation of relative camera positions for uncalibrated cameras. In Sandini, G., editor, *Proceedings of the 2nd European Conference on Computer Vision*, pages 579–587, Santa Margherita, Italy. Springer-Verlag.

Hartley, R. (1993). Euclidean reconstruction from uncalibrated views. In Mundy, J. L., Zissermann, A., and Forsyth, D., editors, *Applications of Invariance in Computer Vision*, volume 825 of *LNCS*, pages 187–202. Springer-Verlag.

Hartley, R. (1994a). Lines and points in three views-an integrated approach. In *Proceedings of the ARPA Image Understanding Workshop*. Defense Advanced Research Projects Agency, Morgan Kaufmann Publishers, Inc.

Hartley, R. (1994b). Self-calibration from multiple views with a rotating camera. In Eklundh, J.-O., editor, *Proceedings of the 3rd European Conference on Computer Vision*, volume 800-801 of *Lecture Notes in Computer Science*, pages 471–478, Stockholm, Sweden. Springer-Verlag.

Hartley, R. (1995). A linear method for reconstruction from lines and points. In *Proceedings of the 5th International Conference on Computer Vision*, pages 882–887, Boston, MA. IEEE Computer Society Press.

Hartley, R. (1997a). In defense on the 8-point algorithm. *PAMI*, 19(6):580–593.

Hartley, R. (1997b). Self-calibration of stationary cameras. *The International Journal of Computer Vision*, 22(1):5–23.

Hartley, R. (1997c). Self-calibration of stationary cameras. *The International Journal of Computer Vision*, 22(1):5–24.

Hartley, R. (1998a). Chirality. *The International Journal of Computer Vision*, 26(1):41–61.

Hartley, R. (1998b). Chirality. *The International Journal of Computer Vision*, 26(1):41–62.

Hartley, R. (1998c). Minimizing algebraic error in geometric estimation problems. In *Proceedings of the 6th International Conference on Computer Vision*, pages 469–476, Bombay, India. IEEE Computer Society, IEEE Computer Society Press.

Hartley, R. (1999). Theory and practice of projective rectification. *The International Journal of Computer Vision*, 35(2):1–16.

Hartley, R., de Agapito, L., Reid, I., and Hayman, E. (1999). Camera calibration and the search for infinity. In *Proceedings of the 7th International Conference on Computer Vision*, pages 510–515, Kerkyra, Greece. IEEE Computer Society, IEEE Computer Society Press.

Hartley, R., Gupta, R., and Chang, T. (1992). Stereo from uncalibrated cameras. In *Proceedings of the International Conference on Computer Vision and Pattern Recognition*, pages 761–764, Urbana Champaign, IL. IEEE.

Hartley, R. and Saxena, T. (1997). The cubic rational polynomial camera model. In *ARPA Image Understanding Workshop*, pages 649–654.

Hartley, R. and Sturm, P. (1997). Triangulation. *Computer Vision and Image Understanding*, 68(2):146–157.

Hartley, R. I. (1997d). Lines and points in three views and the trifocal tensor. *The International Journal of Computer Vision*, 22(2):125–140.

Hartley, R. I. and Gupta, R. (1993). Computing matched-epipolar projections. In *Proceedings of the International Conference on Computer Vision and Pattern Recognition*, pages 549–555, New-York, NY. IEEE Computer Society, IEEE.

Heeger, D. J. and Jepson, A. D. (1992). Subspace methods for recovering rigid motion i: Algorithm and implementation. *The International Journal of Computer Vision*, 7(2):95–117.

Hesse, O. (1863). Die cubische gleichung, von welcher die lösung des problems der homographie von m. chasles abhängt. *J. reine angew. Math.*, 62:188–192.

Heyden, A. (1995a). *Geometry and algebra of multiple projective transformations*. PhD thesis, Lund University, Dept of mathematics, Sweden.

Heyden, A. (1995b). *Geometry and Algebra of Multiple Projective Transformations*. PhD thesis, Lund University.

Heyden, A. (1998a). A common framework for multiple-view tensors. In Burkhardt, H. and Neumann, B., editors, *Proceedings of the 5th European Conference on Computer Vision*, volume 1406–1407 of *Lecture Notes in Computer Science*, Freiburg, Germany. Springer-Verlag.

Heyden, A. (1998b). Reduced multilinear constraints: Theory and experiments. *The International Journal of Computer Vision*, 30(1):5–26.

Heyden, A. and Astrom, K. (1996). Algebraic varieties in multiple view geometry. In Buxton, B., editor, *Proceedings of the 4th European Conference on Computer Vision*, pages II:671–682, Cambridge, UK.

Heyden, A. and Astrom, K. (1997a). Euclidean reconstruction from image sequences with varying and unknown focal length and principal point. In *Proceedings of the International Conference on Computer Vision and Pattern Recognition*, pages 438–443, San Juan, Puerto Rico. IEEE Computer Society, IEEE.

Heyden, A. and Astrom, K. (1997b). Simplifications of multilinear forms for sequences of images. *Image and Vision Computing*, 15(10):749–757.

Heyden, A. and Astrom, K. (1998). Euclidean reconstruction from image sequences with varying and unknown focal length and principal point. In *Proceedings of the 3rd Asian Conference on Computer Vision*, Hong Kong.

Heyden, A. and rAström, K. (1999). Flexible calibration: Minimal cases for autocalibration. In *Proceedings of the 7th International Conference on Computer Vision*, volume 1, pages 350–355, Kerkyra, Greece. IEEE Computer Society, IEEE Computer Society Press.

Heyden, A., Berthilsson, R., and Sparr, G. (1999). An iterative factorization method for projective structure and motion from image sequences. *Image and Vision Computing*, 17(13):981–991.

Heyden, A. and Kahl, F. (1998). Robust self-calibration and euclidean reconstruction via affine approximation. In *Proceedings of the International Conference on Pattern Recognition*, page CV12, Brisbane, Australia. Computer Society Press.

Hofmann, W. (1950). *Das Problem der Gefährlichen Flächen in Theorie und praxis*. PhD thesis, Fakultät für Bauwesen der technischen Hochschule München.

Horaud, R. and Csurka, G. (1998). Self-calibration and euclidean reconstruction using motions of a stereo rig. In *Proceedings of the 6th International Conference on Computer Vision*, Bombay, India. IEEE Computer Society, IEEE Computer Society Press.

Horaud, R., Dornaika, F., Lamiroy, B., and Christy, S. (97). Object pose: The link between weak perspective, paraperspective, and full perspective. *The International Journal of Computer Vision*, 22(2).

Horn, B. (1986). *Robot Vision*. MIT Press.

Horn, B. K. (1987). Closed-form Solution of Absolute Orientation using Unit Quaternions. *Journal of the Optical Society A*, 4(4):629–642.

Horn, B. K. (1990). Relative orientation. *The International Journal of Computer Vision*, 4(1):59–78.

Hu, X. and Ahuja, N. (1993). Sufficient conditions for double or unique solution of motion and structure. *CVGIP: Image Understanding*, 58:161–176.

Huang, T. and Lee, C. (1989). Motion and structure from orthographic projections. *IEEE Transactions on Pattern Analysis and Machine Intelligence*, 11:536–540.

Huang, T. S. and Faugeras, O. D. (1989). Some properties of the E matrix in two-view motion estimation. *IEEE Transactions on Pattern Analysis and Machine Intelligence*, 11(12):1310–1312.

Huber, P. (1981). *Robust Statistics*. John Wiley & Sons, New York.

Hung, Y. and Shieh, S. (1990). When should we consider lens distortion in camera calibration? In *Proc. IAPR worshop on machine vision applications*, pages 367–370, Tokyo.

Huynh, D. (1999). Affine reconstruction from monocular vision in the presence of a symmetry plane. In *Proceedings of the 7th International Conference on Computer Vision*, pages 476–482, Kerkyra, Greece. IEEE Computer Society, IEEE Computer Society Press.

Irani, M. and Anandan, P. (1996). Parallax Geometry of Pairs of Points for 3D Scene Analysis. In Buxton, B., editor, *Proceedings of the 4th European Conference on Computer Vision*, volume I, pages 17–30, Cambridge, UK.

Irani, M., Anandan, P., and Weinshall, D. (1998). From reference frames to referenceplanes:multi-view parallax geometry and applications. In Burkhardt, H. and Neumann, B., editors, *Proceedings of the 5th European Conference on Computer Vision*, volume 1406–1407 of *Lecture Notes in Computer Science*, pages 829–845, Freiburg, Germany. Springer-Verlag.

Irani, M., Hsu, S., and Anandan, P. (1995). Video compression using mosaic representations. *Signal Processing: Image Communications*, 7(4):529–552.

Irani, M., Rousso, B., and Peleg, S. (1997). Recovery of ego-motion using region alignment. *IEEE Transactions on Pattern Analysis and Machine Intelligence*, 19(3):268–272.

Isgro, F. and Trucco, E. (1999). Projective rectification without epipolar geometry. In *Proceedings of the International Conference on Computer Vision and Pattern Recognition*, pages I:94–99, Fort Collins, Colorado. IEEE Computer Society.

Jelinek, D. and Taylor, C. (1999). Reconstruction of linearly parameterized models from single images with a camera of unknown focal length. In *Proceedings of the International Conference on Computer Vision and Pattern Recognition*, pages II:346–352, Fort Collins, Colorado. IEEE Computer Society.

Kahl, F. (1999). Critical motions and ambiguous euclidean reconstructions in autocalibration. In *Proceedings of the 7th International Conference on Computer Vision*, pages 469–475, Kerkyra, Greece. IEEE Computer Society, IEEE Computer Society Press.

Kahl, F. and Heyden, A. (1998). Using conic correspondence in two images to estimate the epipolar geometry. In *Proceedings of the 6th International Conference on Computer Vision*, pages 761–766, Bombay, India. IEEE Computer Society, IEEE Computer Society Press.

Kahl, F. and Heyden, A. (1999). Affine structure and motion from points, lines and conics. *The International Journal of Computer Vision*, 33(3):1–18.

Kanade, T. (1981). Recovery of the three-dimensional shape of an object from a single view. *Artificial Intelligence Journal*, 17:409–460.

Kanatani, K. and Ohta, N. (1999). Accuracy bounds and optimal computation of homography for image mosaicing applications. In *Proceedings of the 7th International Conference on Computer Vision*, pages 73–79, Kerkyra, Greece. IEEE Computer Society, IEEE Computer Society Press.

Ke, Q., Xu, G., and Ma, S. (1998). Recovering epipolar geometry by reactive tabu search. In *Proceedings of the 6th International Conference on Computer Vision*, pages 767–771, Bombay, India. IEEE Computer Society, IEEE Computer Society Press.

Kemp, M. (1990). *The science of art: optical themes in western art from Brunelleschi to Seurat*. Yale University Press.

Kim, T., Seo, Y., and Hong, K. (1998). Physics-based 3d position analysis of a soccer ball from monocular image sequences. In *Proceedings of the 6th International Conference on Computer Vision*, pages 721–726, Bombay, India. IEEE Computer Society, IEEE Computer Society Press.

Kingslake, R. (1992). *Optics in photography.* Spie optical engineering press, Bellingham, WA.

Koenderink, J. and vanDoorn, A. (1997). The generic bilinear calibration-estimation problem. *The International Journal of Computer Vision*, 23(3):217–234.

Koenderink, J. J. and van Doorn, A. J. (1975). Invariant properties of the motion parallax field due to the movement of rigid bodies relative to an observer. *Optica Acta*, 22:717–723.

Koenderink, J. J. and van Doorn, A. J. (1991). Affine structure from motion. *Journal of the Optical Society of America*, A8:377–385.

Krames, J. (1940). Zur ermittlung eines objektes aus zwei perspektiven. (ein beitrag zur theorie der gefährlichen örter.). *Monatshefte für Mathematik und Physik*, 49:327–354.

Kriegman, D. and Belhumeur, P. (1998). What shadows reveal about object structure. In Burkhardt, H. and Neumann, B., editors, *Proceedings of the 5th European Conference on Computer Vision*, volume 1406–1407 of *Lecture Notes in Computer Science*, pages 399–414, Freiburg, Germany. Springer-Verlag.

Krotkov, E. P. (1989). *Active Computer Vision by Cooperative Focus and Stereo.* Springer-Verlag.

Kruppa, E. (1913). Zur Ermittlung eines Objektes aus zwei Perspektiven mit innerer Orientierung. *Sitz.-Ber. Akad. Wiss., Wien, math. naturw. Kl., Abt. IIa.*, 122:1939–1948.

Kumar, R., Anandan, P., Irani, M., Bergen, J., and Hanna, K. (1995). Representation of scenes from collections of images. In *IEEE Workshop on Representation of Visual Scenes*. IEEE.

Laveau, S. and Faugeras, O. (1996). Oriented projective geometry for computer vision. In Buxton, B., editor, *Proceedings of the 4th European Conference on Computer Vision*, pages 147–156, Cambridge, UK.

Lavest, J. (1992). *Stéréovision axiale par zoom pour la robotique.* PhD thesis, Université Blaise Pascal de Clermont-Ferrand, France.

Lavest, J., Rives, G., and Dhome, M. (1993). 3-D reconstruction by zooming. *IEEE Trans. on Robotics and Automation*, 9(2):196–207.

Lawn, J. and Cipolla, R. (1994). Robust egomotion estimation from affine motion parallax. In Eklundh, J.-O., editor, *Proceedings of the 3rd European Conference on Computer Vision*, volume 800-801 of *Lecture Notes in Computer Science*, pages A:205–210, Stockholm, Sweden. Springer-Verlag.

Lawn, J. and Cipolla, R. (1996). Reliable extraction of the camera motion using constraints on the epipole. In Buxton, B., editor, *Proceedings of the 4th European Conference on Computer Vision*, pages 161–173, Cambridge, UK.

Lee, C. and Huang, T. (1990). Finding point correspondences and determining motion of a rigid object from two weak perspective views. *Computer Vision, Graphics, and Image Processing*, (52):309–327.

Lee, C.-H. (1991). Time-varying images: The effect of finite resolution on uniqueness. *CVGIP: Image Understanding*, 54(3):325–332.

Leedan, Y. and Meer, P. (1998). Estimation with bilinear constraints in computer vision. In *Proceedings of the 6th International Conference on Computer Vision*, pages 733–738, Bombay, India. IEEE Computer Society, IEEE Computer Society Press.

Lenz, R. (1987). Lens distorsion corrected CCD camera calibration with coplanar calibration points for real-time 3D measurements. In *Proc. ISPRS Intercomission conference on fast processing of photogrammetric data*, pages 60–67, Interlaken.

Lenz, R. and Tsai, R. (1987). Techniques for calibrating of the scale factor and image center for high accuracy 3D machine vision metrology. In *International Conference on Robotics and Automation*, pages 68–75, Raleigh, NC.

Li, F., Brady, J., and Wiles, C. (1996). Fast computation of the fundamental matrix for an active stereo vision system. In Buxton, B., editor, *Proceedings of the 4th European Conference on Computer Vision*, pages I:157–166, Cambridge, UK.

Li, Y. and Brooks, M. (1999). An efficient recursive factorization method for determining structure from motion. In *Proceedings of the International Conference on Computer Vision and Pattern Recognition*, pages I:138–143, Fort Collins, Colorado. IEEE Computer Society.

Liebowitz, D., Criminisi, A., and Zisserman, A. (1999). Creating architectural models from images. In *Proc. EuroGraphics*, volume 18, pages 39–50.

Liebowitz, D. and Zisserman, A. (1998). Metric rectification for perspective images of planes. In *Proceedings of the International Conference on Computer Vision and Pattern Recognition*, pages 482–488, Santa Barbara, California. IEEE Computer Society.

Liebowitz, D. and Zisserman, A. (1999). Combining scene and auto-calibration constraints. In *Proceedings of the 7th International Conference on Computer Vision*, Kerkyra, Greece. IEEE Computer Society, IEEE Computer Society Press.

Longuet-Higgins, H. (1981). A computer algorithm for reconstructing a scene from two projections. *Nature*, 293:133–135.

Longuet-Higgins, H. (1988). Multiple interpretations of a pair of images of a surface. *Proc. Roy. Soc. Lond. A.*, 418:1–15.

Longuet-Higgins, H. C. (1984). The reconstruction of a scene from two projections - configurations that defeat the 8-point algorithm. In *Proceedings First Conference on Artificial Intelligence Applications*, pages 395–397, Denver, Colorado.

Longuet-Higgins, H. C. and Prazdny, K. (1980). The interpretation of moving retinal images. *Proceedings of the Royal Society of London*, B 208:385–387.

Loop, C. and Zhang, Z. (1999). Computing rectifying homographies for stereo vision. In *Proceedings of the International Conference on Computer Vision and Pattern Recognition*, Fort Collins, Colorado. IEEE Computer Society.

Lourakis, M. I. and Deriche, R. (2000). Camera self-calibration using the singular value decomposition of the fundamental matrix. In *Proc. of the 4th Asian Conference on Computer Vision*, volume I, pages 403–408.

Luong, Q. and Viéville, T. (1996). Canonical representations for the geometries of multiple projective views. *Computer Vision and Image Understanding*, 64(2):193–229.

Luong, Q.-T. (1992). *Matrice Fondamentale et Calibration Visuelle sur l'Environnement-Vers une plus grande autonomie des systèmes robotiques*. PhD thesis, Université de Paris-Sud, Centre d'Orsay.

Luong, Q.-T. and Faugeras, O. (1994a). The fundamental matrix: theory, algorithms, and stability analysis. *The International Journal of Computer Vision*.

Luong, Q.-T. and Faugeras, O. (1994b). A stability analysis of the fundamental matrix. In Eklundh, J.-O., editor, *Proceedings of the 3rd European Conference on Computer Vision*, volume 800-801 of *Lecture Notes in Computer Science*, pages 577–588, Stockholm, Sweden. Springer-Verlag.

Luong, Q.-T. and Faugeras, O. (2000). Self-calibration of a stereo rig from unknown camera motions and point correspondences. In Grun, A. and Huang, T., editors, *Calibration and orientation of cameras in computer vision*. Springer-Verlag. To appear. Also presented at XVII ISPRS, Washington, 1992 and INRIA Tech Report RR-2014.

Luong, Q.-T. and Faugeras, O. D. (1996). The fundamental matrix: Theory, algorithms and stability analysis. *The International Journal of Computer Vision*, 17(1):43–76.

Luong, Q.-T. and Viéville, T. (1993). Canonical representations for the geometries of multiple projective views. Technical Report UCB/CSD 93-772, Berkeley. Oct. 1993, revised July 1994.

Lutton, E., Maitre, H., and Lopez-Krahe, J. (1994). Contribution to the determination of vanishing points using hough transform. *IEEE Transactions on Pattern Analysis and Machine Intelligence*, 16(4):430–438.

Ma, Y., Soatto, S., Kosecka, J., and Sastry, S. (1999). Euclidean reconstruction and reprojection up to subgroups. In *Proceedings of the 7th International Conference on Computer Vision*, pages 773–780, Kerkyra, Greece. IEEE Computer Society, IEEE Computer Society Press.

Magee, M. and Aggarwal, J. (1984). Determining vanishing points from perspective images. *Computer Vision, Graphics, and Image Processing*, 26(2):256–267.

Mann, S. and Picard, R. (1997). Video orbits of the projective group: A simple approach to featureless estimation of parameters. *IEEE Transactions on Image Processing*, 6(9):1281–1295.

Mann, S. and Picard, R. W. (1994). Virtual bellows: Constructing high quality stills from video. In *International Conference on Image Processing*, pages 363–367.

Manning, R. and Dyer, C. (1999). Interpolating view and scene motion by dynamic view morphing. In *Proceedings of the International Conference on Computer Vision and Pattern Recognition*, pages I:388–394, Fort Collins, Colorado. IEEE Computer Society.

Martins, H., Birk, J., and Kelley, R. (1981). Camera models based on data from two calibration planes. *Computer Graphics and Image Processing*, 17:173–180.

Marugame, A., Katto, J., and Ohta, M. (1999). Structure recovery with multiple cameras from scaled orthographic and perspective views. *IEEE Transactions on Pattern Analysis and Machine Intelligence*, 21(7):628–633.

Maybank, S. (1985). The angular velocity associated with the optical flow field arising from motion through a rigid environment. *Philosophical Transactions of the Royal Society*, 401:317–326.

Maybank, S. (1987). *A theoretical study of optical flow*. PhD thesis, Birbeck College, University of London.

Maybank, S. (1990). Properties of essential matrices. *International Journal of Imaging Systems and technology*, 2:380–384.

Maybank, S. (1992). *Theory of reconstruction From Image Motion*. Springer-Verlag.

Maybank, S. (1995). The critical line congruence for reconstruction from three images. *Applicable algebra in engineering communication and computing*, 6:89–113.

Maybank, S. and Sturm, P. (1999). MDL, Collineations and the Fundamental matrix. In *Proceedings of the 10th British Machine Vision Conference*, The University of Nottingham. British Machine Vision Association, BMVA Press.

Maybank, S. J. and Faugeras, O. D. (1992). A theory of self-calibration of a moving camera. *The International Journal of Computer Vision*, 8(2):123–152.

Mclean, G. and Kotturi, D. (1995). Vanishing point detection by line clustering. *IEEE Transactions on Pattern Analysis and Machine Intelligence*, 17(11):1090–1095.

Meer, P., Mintz, D., Rosenfeld, A., and Kim, D. (1991). Robust regression methods for computer vision: A review. *The International Journal of Computer Vision*, 6(1):59–70.

Mendonçca. and Cipolla, R. (1999). Estimation of epipolar geometry from apparent contours: Affine and circular motion cases. In *Proceedings of the International Conference on Computer Vision and Pattern Recognition*, pages I:9–14, Fort Collins, Colorado. IEEE Computer Society.

Mendonçca, P. and Cipolla, R. (1999). A simple techinique for self-calibration. In *Proceedings of the International Conference on Computer Vision and Pattern Recognition*, pages I:500–505, Fort Collins, Colorado. IEEE Computer Society.

Mohr, R. and Arbogast, E. (1990). It can be done without camera calibration. *Pattern Recognition Letters*, 12:39–43.

Mohr, R., Boufama, B., and Brand, P. (1993a). Accurate projective reconstruction. In Mundy, J. and Zisserman, A., editors, *Applications of Invariance in Computer Vision*, volume 825 of *Lecture Notes in Computer Science*, pages 257–276, Berlin. Springer-Verlag.

Mohr, R., Boufama, B., and Brand, P. (1995). Understanding positioning from multiple images. *Artificial Intelligence*, 78:213–238.

Mohr, R. and Morin, L. (1991). Relative positioning from geometric invariants. In *Proceedings of the International Conference on Computer Vision and Pattern Recognition*, pages 139–144, Lahaina, Hawai. IEEE.

Mohr, R., Veillon, F., and Quan, L. (1993b). Relative 3d reconstruction using multiple uncalibrated images. In *Proceedings of the International Conference on Computer Vision and Pattern Recognition*, pages 543–548, New-York, NY. IEEE Computer Society, IEEE.

Moons, T., VanGool, L., Proesmans, M., and Pauwels, E. (1996). Affine reconstruction from perspective image pairs with a relative object-camera translation in between. *IEEE Transactions on Pattern Analysis and Machine Intelligence*, 18(1):77–83.

Morris, D. and Kanade, T. (1998). A unified factorization algorithm for points, line segments and planes with uncertainty models. In *Proceedings of the 6th International Conference on Computer Vision*, pages 696–702, Bombay, India. IEEE Computer Society, IEEE Computer Society Press.

Mukherjee, D. P., Zisserman, A., and Brady, J. M. (1995). Shape from symmetry—detecting and exploiting symmetry in affine images. In *Philosophical Transactions of the Royal Society of London, SERIES A*, volume 351, pages 77–106.

Mundy, J. L. and Zisserman, A., editors (1992). *Geometric Invariance in Computer Vision*. MIT Press.

Mundy, J. L., Zisserman, A., and Forsyth, D., editors (1994). *Applications of Invariance in Computer Vision*, volume 825 of *Lecture Notes in Computer Science*. Springer-Verlag.

Mundy, J. L. and Zissermann, A. (1994). Repeated structures: image correspondence constraints and 3d structure recovery. In Mundy, J. L., Zissermann, A., and Forsyth, D., editors, *Applications of Invariance in Computer Vision*, volume 825 of *LNCS*, pages 89–106. Springer-Verlag.

Nalwa, V. and Pauchon, E. (1987). Edgel aggregation and edge description. *Computer Vision, Graphics, and Image Processing*, 40(1):79–94.

Navab, N. and Faugeras, O. (1997). The critical sets of lines for camera displacement estimation: A mixed euclidean-projective and constructive approach. *The International Journal of Computer Vision*, 23(1):17–44.

Negahdaripour, S. (1989). Critical Surface Pairs and Triplets. *The International Journal of Computer Vision*, 3(4):293–312.

Ohta, Y.-i., Maenobu, K., and Sakai, T. (1981). Obtaining surface orientation from texels under perspective projection. In *Proceedings of the 7th International Joint Conference on Artificial Intelligence*, pages 746–751, Vancouver, Canada.

Oliensis, J. (1999). Fast and accurate self-calibration. In *Proceedings of the 7th International Conference on Computer Vision*, pages 745–752, Kerkyra, Greece. IEEE Computer Society, IEEE Computer Society Press.

Oliensis, J. and Genc, Y. (1999). Fast algorithms for projective multi-frame structure from motion. In *Proceedings of the 7th International Conference on Computer Vision*, pages 536–543, Kerkyra, Greece. IEEE Computer Society, IEEE Computer Society Press.

Olsen, S. (1992). Epipolar line estimation. In *Proceedings of the 2nd European Conference on Computer Vision*, pages 307–311, Santa Margherita Ligure, Italy.

Panofsky, E. (1991). *Perspective As Symbolic Form*. MIT Press. First appeared in 1927.

Papadopoulo, T. and Faugeras, O. (1998). A new characterization of the trifocal tensor. In Burkhardt, H. and Neumann, B., editors, *Proceedings of the 5th European Conference on Computer Vision*, volume 1406–1407 of *Lecture Notes in Computer Science*, Freiburg, Germany. Springer-Verlag.

Peleg, S. and Herman, J. (1997). Panoramic mosaics by manifold projection. In *Proceedings of the International Conference on Computer Vision and Pattern Recognition*, pages 338–343, San Juan, Puerto Rico. IEEE Computer Society, IEEE.

Peuchot, B. (1992). Camera virtual equivalent model - 0.01 pixel detectors. In *14th Annual International Conference IEEE EMBS. Satellite Symposium on 3D Advanced Image Processing in Medecine*, pages 41–45.

Poelman, C. and Kanade, T. (1997). A paraperspective factorization method for shape and motion recovery. *IEEE Transactions on Pattern Analysis and Machine Intelligence*, 19(3):206–218.

Pollefey, M., Van Gool, L., and Proesmans, M. (1996). Euclidean 3d reconstruction from image sequences with variable focal lenghts. In Buxton, B., editor, *Proceedings of the 4th European Conference on Computer Vision*, pages I:31–42, Cambridge, UK.

Pollefeys, M. and Gool, L. V. (1999). Stratified self-calibration with the modulus constraint. *IEEE Transactions on Pattern Analysis and Machine Intelligence*, 21(8):707–724.

Pollefeys, M., Koch, R., and Gool, L. V. (1999). Self-calibration and metric reconstruction in spite of varying and unknown internal camera parameters. *The International Journal of Computer Vision*, 32(1):7–25.

Ponce, J. and Genc, Y. (1998). Epipolar geometry and linear subspace methods: A new approach to weak calibration. *The International Journal of Computer Vision*, 28(3):223–243.

Ponce, J., Marimont, D., and Cass, T. (1994). Analytical methods for uncalibrated stereo and motion reconstruction. In Eklundh, J.-O., editor, *Proceedings of the 3rd European Conference on Computer Vision*, volume 800-801 of *Lecture Notes in Computer Science*, pages 463–470, Stockholm, Sweden. Springer-Verlag.

Porrill, J. and Pollard, S. (1991). Curve matching and stereo calibration. *Image and Vision Computing*, 9:45–50.

Press, W. H., Flannery, B. P., Teukolsky, S. A., and Vetterling, W. T. (1988). *Numerical Recipes in C*. Cambridge University Press.

Puget, P. and Skordas, T. (1990). An optimal solution for mobile camera calibration. In Faugeras, O., editor, *Proceedings of the 1st European Conference on Computer Vision*, pages 187–198, Antibes, France. Springer-Verlag.

Quan, L. (1995). Invariants of six points and projective reconstruction from three uncalibrated images. *IEEE Transactions on Pattern Analysis and Machine Intelligence*, 17(1).

Quan, L. (1996). Self-calibration of an affine camera from multiple views. *The International Journal of Computer Vision*, 19(1):93–105.

Quan, L. (1999). Inherent two-way ambiguity in 2d projective reconstruction from three uncalibrated 1d images. In *Proceedings of the 7th International Conference on Computer Vision*, pages 344–349, Kerkyra, Greece. IEEE Computer Society, IEEE Computer Society Press.

Quan, L., Heyden, A., and Kahl, F. (1999). Minimal projective reconstruction with missing data. In *Proceedings of the International Conference on Computer Vision and Pattern Recognition*, pages II:210–216, Fort Collins, Colorado. IEEE Computer Society.

Quan, L. and Kanade, T. (1996). A factorization method for affine structure from line correspondences. In *Proceedings of the International Conference on Computer Vision and Pattern Recognition*, pages 803–808, San Francisco, CA. IEEE.

Quan, L. and Kanade, T. (1997). Affine structure from line correspondences with uncalibrated affine cameras. *IEEE Transactions on Pattern Analysis and Machine Intelligence*, 19(8):834–845.

Quan, L. and Mohr, R. (1989). Determining perspective structures using hierarchical Hough transform. *Pattern Recognition Letters*, 9(4):279–286.

Quan, L. and Mohr, R. (1992). Affine shape representation from motion through reference points. *Journal of mathematical imaging and vision*, 1:145–151.

Quan, L. and Ohta, Y. (1998). A new linear method for euclidean motion/structure from three calibrated affine views. In *International Conference on Computer Vision and Pattern Recognition*, pages 172–177.

Reid, I. and Zisserman, A. (1996). Goal-directed video metrology. In Buxton, B.,
    editor, *Proceedings of the 4th European Conference on Computer Vision*, pages
    II:645–658, Cambridge, UK.

Rey, W. J. (1983). *Introduction to Robust and Quasi-Robust Statistical Methods*.
    Springer, Berlin, Heidelberg.

Robert, L. (1996). Camera calibration without feature extraction. *Computer Vision
    and Image Understanding*, 63(2):314–325.

Robert, L., Buffa, M., and Hebert, M. (1995). Weakly-calibrated stereo perception
    for rover navigation. In *Proceedings of the 5th International Conference on
    Computer Vision*, pages 46–51, Boston, MA. IEEE Computer Society Press.

Robert, L. and Faugeras, O. (1995). Relative 3-D positioning and 3-D convex hull
    computation from a weakly calibrated stereo pair. *Image and Vision Comput-
    ing*, 13(3):189–197. also INRIA Technical Report 2349.

Robert, L. and Hebert, M. (1994). Deriving orientation cues from stereo images. In
    Eklundh, J.-O., editor, *Proceedings of the 3rd European Conference on Com-
    puter Vision*, volume 800-801 of *Lecture Notes in Computer Science*, pages
    377–388, Stockholm, Sweden. Springer-Verlag.

Robert, L., Zeller, C., Faugeras, O., and Hébert, M. (1996). Applications of non-
    metric vision to some visually-guided robotics tasks. In Aloimonos, Y., editor,
    Visual Navigation: From Biological Systems to Unmanned Ground Vehicles,
    chapter ? Lawrence Erlbaum Associates. Use robert-zeller-etal:97 instead.

Roberts, L. (1965). Machine perception of three-dimensional solids. In Tippett, J.
    and Berkowitz, D. and Clapp, L. and Koester, C. and Vanderburgh, A., editor,
    Optical and Electrooptical Information processing, pages 159–197. MIT Press.

Rothwell, C., Faugeras, O., and Csurka, G. (1997). A comparison of projective
    reconstruction methods for pairs of views. *Computer Vision and Image Under-
    standing*, 68(1):37–58.

Rothwell, C. A., Forsyth, D. A., Zisserman, A., and Mundy, J. (1993). Extracting
    projective structure from single perspective views of 3D point sets. In *Proceed-
    ings of the 4th International Conference on Computer Vision*, pages 573–582,
    Berlin, Germany. IEEE Computer Society Press.

Rousseeuw, P. and Leroy, A. (1987). *Robust Regression and Outlier Detection*. John
    Wiley & Sons, New York.

Rousso, B., Avidan, S., and Peleg, S. (1996). Robust recovery of camera rotation
    from three frames. In *Proceedings of the International Conference on Computer
    Vision and Pattern Recognition*, San Francisco, CA. IEEE.

Rousso, B. and Shilat, E. (1998). Varying focal length self-calibration and pose estimation. In *Proceedings of the International Conference on Computer Vision and Pattern Recognition*, pages 469–474, Santa Barbara, California. IEEE Computer Society.

Ruf, A., Csurka, G., and Horaud, R. (1998). Projective translations and affine stereo calibration. In *Proceedings of the International Conference on Computer Vision and Pattern Recognition*, volume I, pages 475–481, Santa Barbara CA, USA. IEEE Computer Society.

Ruf, A. and Horaud, R. (1999a). Projective rotations applied to a pan-tilt stereo head. In *Proceedings of the International Conference on Computer Vision and Pattern Recognition*, pages I:144–150, Fort Collins, Colorado. IEEE Computer Society.

Ruf, A. and Horaud, R. (1999b). Rigid and articulated motion seen with an uncalibrated stereo rig. In *Proceedings of the 7th International Conference on Computer Vision*, pages 789–796, Kerkyra, Greece. IEEE Computer Society, IEEE Computer Society Press.

Saito, H. and Kanade, T. (1999). Shape reconstruction in projective voxel grid space from large number of images. In *Proceedings of the International Conference on Computer Vision and Pattern Recognition*, pages II:49–54, Fort Collins, Colorado. IEEE Computer Society.

Sampson, P. (1982). Fitting conic sections to "very scattered" data: An iterarive refinement of the bookstein algorithm. *Computer Graphics and Image Processing*, 18:97–108.

Sawhney, H., Hsu, S., and Kumar, R. (1998). Robust video mosaicing through topology inference and local to global alignment. In Burkhardt, H. and Neumann, B., editors, *Proceedings of the 5th European Conference on Computer Vision*, volume 1406–1407 of *Lecture Notes in Computer Science*, pages 103–119, Freiburg, Germany. Springer-Verlag.

Sawhney, H. and Kumar, R. (1999). True multi-image alignment and its application to mosaicing and lens distortion correction. *IEEE Transactions on Pattern Analysis and Machine Intelligence*, 21(3):245–243.

Sawhney, H. S. (1994). Simplifying motion and structure analysis using planar parallax and image warping. In *Proceedings of the International Conference on Pattern Recognition*, Jerusalem, Israel. Computer Society Press.

Schmid, C. and Zisserman, A. (1998). The geometry and matching of curves in multiple views. In Burkhardt, H. and Neumann, B., editors, *Proceedings of the 5th European Conference on Computer Vision*, volume 1406–1407 of *Lecture Notes in Computer Science*, pages 394–409, Freiburg, Germany. Springer-Verlag.

Seitz, S. and Dyer, C. (1996). View morphing. In *SIGGRAPH*, pages 21–30, New Orleans.

Semple, J. and Kneebone, G. (1952). *Algebraic Projective Geometry*. Oxford: Clarendon Press. Reprinted 1979.

Semple, J. and Roth, L. (1949). *Introduction to Algebraic Geometry*. Oxford: Clarendon Press. Reprinted 1987.

Seo, Y. and Hong, K. (1999). About the self-calibration of a rotating and zooming camera: Theory and practice. In *Proceedings of the 7th International Conference on Computer Vision*, pages 183–188, Kerkyra, Greece. IEEE Computer Society, IEEE Computer Society Press.

Shapiro, L. (1995). *Affine analysis of image sequences*. Cambridge University Press.

Shapiro, L. and Brady, M. (1995). Rejecting outliers and estimating errors in an orthogonal-regression framework. *Phil. Trans. Royal Soc. of Lon. A*, 350:407–439.

Shapiro, L. S., Zisserman, A., and Brady, M. (1995). 3d motion recovery via affine epipolar geometry. *The International Journal of Computer Vision*, 16(2):147–182.

Shashua, A. (1994). Projective structure from uncalibrated images: structure from motion and recognition. *IEEE Transactions on Pattern Analysis and Machine Intelligence*, 16(8):778–790.

Shashua, A. (1995). Algebraic functions for recognition. *IEEE Transactions on Pattern Analysis and Machine Intelligence*, 17(8):779–789.

Shashua, A. and Anandan, P. (1996). Trilinear constraints revisited: Generalized trilinear constraints and the tensor brightness constraint. In *ARPA96*, pages 815–820.

Shashua, A. and Avidan, S. (1996). The rank 4 constraint in multiple (over 3) view geometry. In Buxton, B., editor, *Proceedings of the 4th European Conference on Computer Vision*, pages II:196–206, Cambridge, UK.

Shashua, A. and Navab, N. (1996). Relative affine structure - canonical model for 3D from 2D geometry and applications. *IEEE Transactions on Pattern Analysis and Machine Intelligence*, 18:873–883.

Shashua, A. and Toelg, S. (1997). The quadric reference surface: Theory and applications. *The International Journal of Computer Vision*, 23(2):185–198.

Shashua, A. and Werman, M. (1995). Trilinearity of three perspective views and its associated tensor. In *Proceedings of the 5th International Conference on Computer Vision*, pages 920–925, Boston, MA. IEEE Computer Society Press.

Shimshoni, I., Basri, R., and Rivlin, E. (1999). A geometric interpretation of weak-perspective motion. *IEEE Transactions on Pattern Analysis and Machine Intelligence*, 21(3):252–257.

Shiu, Y. and Ahmad, S. (1989). Calibration of wrist-mounted robotic sensors by solving homogeneous transform equations of the form $AX = XB$. *IEEE Transactions on Robotics and Automation*, 5(1):16–29.

Shortis, M., Burner, A., Snow, W., and Goad, W. (1991). Calibration tests of industrial and scientific CCD cameras. In *Proc. 1st Australian Photogrammetry Conf.*, Sydney.

Shufelt, J. (1999). Performance evaluation and analysis of vanishing point detection techniques. *IEEE Transactions on Pattern Analysis and Machine Intelligence*, 21(3):282–288.

Shum, H.-Y. and Szeliski, R. (1999). Construction of panoramic image mosaics with global and local alignment. *The International Journal of Computer Vision*.

Sinclair, D. (1996). The euclidean hinge constraint in articulated motions. In *Proceedings of the International Conference on Pattern Recognition*, page A8E.2, Vienna, Austria. Computer Society Press.

Sinclair, D. and Blake, A. (1996). Quantitative planar region detection. *The International Journal of Computer Vision*, 18(1):77–91.

Sinclair, D., Blake, A., Smith, S., and Rothwell, C. (1993). Planar region detection and motion recovery. *Image and Vision Computing*, 11(4):229–234.

Sinclair, D., Paletta, L., and Pinz, A. (1997). Euclidean structure recovery through articulated motion. In *Proceedings of the 10th Scandinavian Conference on Image Analysis*, Lappeenranta, Finland.

Sinclair, D. and Zesar, K. (1996). Further constraints on visual articulated motions. In *Proceedings of the International Conference on Computer Vision and Pattern Recognition*, pages 94–99, San Francisco, CA. IEEE.

Slama, C. C., editor (1980). *Manual of Photogrammetry*. American Society of Photogrammetry, fourth edition.

Sobel, I. (1974). On Calibrating Computer Controlled Cameras for Perceiving 3-D Scenes. *Artificial Intelligence Journal*, 5:184–198.

Sparr, G. and Nielsen, L. (1990). Shape and mutual cross-ratios with applications to the interior, exterior and relative orientation. In Faugeras, O., editor, *Proceedings of the 1st European Conference on Computer Vision*, pages 607–609, Antibes, France. Springer-Verlag.

Spetsakis, M. E. and Aloimonos, J. (1990a). Structure from Motion Using Line Correspondences. *The International Journal of Computer Vision*, 4:171–183.

Spetsakis, M. E. and Aloimonos, Y. (1990b). A unified theory of structure from motion. In *Proc. DARPA IU Workshop*, pages 271–283.

Spivak, M. (1979). *A Comprehensive Introduction to Differential Geometry*, volume I–V. Publish or Perish, Berkeley, CA. Second edition.

Stein, G. (1997). Lens distortion calibration using point correspondences. In *Proceedings of the International Conference on Computer Vision and Pattern Recognition*, pages 602–608, San Juan, Puerto Rico. IEEE Computer Society, IEEE.

Stein, G. and Shashua, A. (1997). Model-based brightness constraints: on direct estimation of structure and motion. In *Proc. of CVPR'97*, pages 400–406, San Juan, Puerto Rico. IEEE CS Press.

Stein, G. and Shashua, A. (1999). On degeneracy of linear reconstruction from three views: Linear line complex and applications. *IEEE Transactions on Pattern Analysis and Machine Intelligence*, 21(3):244–251.

Stein, G. P. (1993). Internal camera calibration using rotation and geometric shapes. Master's thesis, Massachusetts Institute of Technology. AITR-1426.

Stolfi, J. (1991). *Oriented Projective Geometry, A Framework for Geometric Computations*. Academic Press, Inc., 1250 Sixth Avenue, San Diego, CA.

Straforini, M., Coelho, C., and Campani, M. (1993). Extraction of vanishing points from images of indoor and outdoor scenes. *Image and Vision Computing*, 11(2):91–99.

Stroebel, L. (1999). *View Camera Technique*. Focal Press, 7th edition.

Stroebel, L., Compton, J., Current, I., and Zakia, R. (1990). *Basic Photographic Materials and Processes*. Focal Press.

Sturm, P. (1997a). Critical motion sequences for monocular self-calibration and uncalibrated euclidean reconstruction. In *Proceedings of the Conference on Computer Vision and Pattern Recognition, Puerto Rico, USA*, pages 1100–1105.

Sturm, P. (1997b). *Vision 3D non calibrée. Contributions à la reconstruction projective et étude des mouvements critiques pour l'auto-calibrage*. PhD thesis, INPG, Grenoble, France.

Sturm, P. (1999). Critical motion sequences for the self-calibration of cameras and stereo systems with variable focal length. In *10th British Machine Vision Conference*, pages 63–72, Nottingham, England.

Sturm, P. and Triggs, B. (1996). A factorization based algorithm for multi-image projective structure and motion. In Buxton, B., editor, *Proceedings of the 4th European Conference on Computer Vision*, pages 709–720, Cambridge, UK.

Sturm, P. F. and Maybank, S. J. (1999). On plane-based camera calibration: A general algorithm, singularities, applications. In *Proceedings of the International Conference on Computer Vision and Pattern Recognition*, volume I, pages 432–437, Fort Collins, Colorado. IEEE Computer Society.

Sturm, R. (1869). Das problem der projektivität und seine anwendung auf die flächen zweiten grades. *Math. Ann.*, 1:533–574.

Sutherland, I. (1974). Three-dimensional data input by tablet. *Proceedings of the IEEE*, 62(4):453–461.

Szeliski, R. (1996). Video mosaics for virtual environments. *IEEE CGA*, 16(2):22–30.

Szeliski, R. and Coughland, J. (1994). Hierarchical spline-based image registration. In *International Conference on Computer Vision and Pattern Recognition*, pages 194–201, Seattle, WA.

Szeliski, R. and Kang, S. (1994). Recovering 3D shape and motion from image streams using nonlinear least squares. *Journal Vis. Commun. and Image Repr.*, 5(1):10–28.

Tai, A., Kittler, J., Petrou, M., and Windeatt, T. (1993). Vanishing point detection. *Image and Vision Computing*, 11:240–245.

Tang, C., Medioni, G., and Lee, M. (1999). Epipolar geometry estimation by tensor voting in 8d. In *Proceedings of the 7th International Conference on Computer Vision*, pages 502–509, Kerkyra, Greece. IEEE Computer Society, IEEE Computer Society Press.

Tarabanis, K. and Tsai, R. (1991). Computing viewpoints that satisfy optical constraints. In *Proceedings of the International Conference on Computer Vision and Pattern Recognition*, pages 152–158, Lahaina, Hawai. IEEE.

Tarabanis, K., Tsai, R., and Goodman, D. (1992). Modeling of a computer-controlled zoom lens. In *Proc. International Conference on Robotics and Automation*, pages 1545–1551, Nice.

Thompson, E. (1968). The projective geometry of relative orientation. *Photogrammetria*, 23(1):67–75.

Thorhallsson, T. and Murray, D. (1999). The tensors of three affine views. In *Proceedings of the International Conference on Computer Vision and Pattern Recognition*, pages I:450–456, Fort Collins, Colorado. IEEE Computer Society.

Tomasi, C. and Kanade, T. (1992). Shape and motion from image streams under orthography: a factorization method. *The International Journal of Computer Vision*, 9(2):137–154.

Torr, P. (1995). *Motion segmentation and outlier detection*. PhD thesis, University of Oxford.

Torr, P., Fitzgibbon, A., and Zisserman, A. (1999). The problem of degeneracy in structure and motion recovery from uncalibrated image sequences. *The International Journal of Computer Vision*, 32(1):27–44.

Torr, P. and Murray, D. (1994). Stochastic motion clustering. In Eklundh, J.-O., editor, *Proceedings of the 3rd European Conference on Computer Vision*, pages 328–337, Vol.II, Stockholm, Sweden.

Torr, P. and Zisserman, A. (1997a). Robust parameterization and computation of the trifocal tensor. *Image and Vision Computing*, 15:591–605.

Torr, P. and Zisserman, A. (1997b). Robust parameterization and computation of the trifocal tensor. *Image and Vision Computing*, 15:591–605.

Torr, P. and Zisserman, A. (1998). Robust computation and parametrization of multiple view relations. In *Proceedings of the 6th International Conference on Computer Vision*, pages 733–739, Bombay, India. IEEE Computer Society, IEEE Computer Society Press.

Torr, P., Zisserman, A., and Maybank, S. (1998). Robust detection of degenerate configurations while estimating the fundamental matrix. *Computer Vision and Image Understanding*, 71(3):312–333.

Torr, P. H. S. (1998). Geometric motion segmentation and model selection. *Philosophical Transactions of the Royal Society A*, pages 1321–1340.

Torr, P. H. S. and Murray, D. W. (1997). The development and comparison of robust methods for estimating the fundamental matrix. *IJCV*, 24(3):271–300.

Toscani, G. (1987). *Système de Calibration optique et perception du mouvement en vision artificielle*. PhD thesis, Paris-Orsay.

Toscani, G. and Faugeras, O. (1987). Structure and motion from two perspective views. In *Proc. International Conference on Robotics and Automation*, pages 221–227, Raleigh.

Triggs, B. (1995). Matching constraints and the joint image. In *Proceedings of the 5th International Conference on Computer Vision*, pages 338–343, Boston, MA. IEEE Computer Society Press.

Triggs, B. (1996). Factorization methods for projective structure and motion. In *Proceedings of the International Conference on Computer Vision and Pattern Recognition*, pages 845–851, San Francisco, CA. IEEE.

Triggs, B. (1997a). Autocalibration and the absolute quadric. In *Proceedings of the International Conference on Computer Vision and Pattern Recognition*, pages 609–614, San Juan, Puerto Rico. IEEE Computer Society, IEEE.

Triggs, B. (1997b). Linear projective reconstruction from matching tensors. *Image and Vision Computing*, 15.

Triggs, B. (1998). Autocalibration from planar scenes. In Burkhardt, H. and Neumann, B., editors, *Proceedings of the 5th European Conference on Computer Vision*, volume I of *Lecture Notes in Computer Science*, pages 89–105, Freiburg, Germany. Springer-Verlag.

Triggs, B. (1999a). Differential matching constraints. In *Proceedings of the 7th International Conference on Computer Vision*, Kerkyra, Greece. IEEE Computer Society, IEEE Computer Society Press.

Triggs, B. (1999b). Shape representation and recovery camera pose and calibration from 4 or 5 known 3d points. In *Proceedings of the 7th International Conference on Computer Vision*, pages 278–284, Kerkyra, Greece. IEEE Computer Society, IEEE Computer Society Press.

Trivedi, H. P. (1988). Can multiple views make up for lack of camera registration. *Image and Vision Computing*, 6(1):29–32.

Tsai, R. (1986). Multiframe image point matching and 3d surface reconstruction. *IEEE Transactions on Pattern Analysis and Machine Intelligence*, 5:159–174.

Tsai, R. (1989). Synopsis of recent progress on camera calibration for 3D machine vision. In Khatib, O., Craig, J. J., and Lozano-Pérez, T., editors, *The Robotics Review*, pages 147–159. MIT Press.

Tsai, R. and Huang, T. (1982). Estimating Three-dimensional motion parameters of a rigid planar patch, II: singular value decomposition. *IEEE Transactions on Acoustic, Speech and Signal Processing*, 30.

Tsai, R. and Huang, T. (1984). Uniqueness and estimation of three-dimensional motion parameters of rigid objects with curved surfaces. *IEEE Transactions on Pattern Analysis and Machine Intelligence*, 6(1):13–26.

Tsai, R. and Lenz, R. (1988). Real time versatile robotics hamd/eye calibration using 3D machine vision. In *Proc. International Conference on Robotics and Automation*, pages 554–561.

Tsai, R. Y. (1987). A versatile camera calibration technique for high-accuracy 3D machine vision metrology using off-the-shelf TV cameras and lenses. *IEEE Journal of Robotics and Automation*, 3(4):323–344.

Ueshiba, T. and Tomita, F. (1998). A factorization method for projective and euclidean reconstruction from multiple perspective views via iterative depth estimation. In Burkhardt, H. and Neumann, B., editors, *Proceedings of the 5th European Conference on Computer Vision*, volume 1406–1407 of *Lecture Notes in Computer Science*, Freiburg, Germany. Springer-Verlag.

Ullman, S. (1979). *The Interpretation of Visual Motion*. MIT Press.

Ullman, S. and Basri, R. (1991). Recognition by linear combinations of models. *IEEE Transactions on Pattern Analysis and Machine Intelligence*, 13(10):992–1006.

Vaillant, R. (1990). *Géométrie différentielle et vision par ordinateur: détection et reconstruction de contours d'occultation de la surface d'un objet non-polyhédrique*. PhD thesis, University of Paris XI, Orsay. in french.

Van Gool, L., Proesmans, M., and Zisserman, A. (1998). Planar homologies as a basis for grouping and recognition. *Image and Vision Computing*, 16:21–26.

Verri, A. and Trucco, E. (1999). Finding the epipole from uncalibrated optical flow. *Image and Vision Computing*, 17(8):605–609.

Viéville, T. (1994). Autocalibration of visual sensor parameters on a robotic head. *Image and Vision Computing*, 12.

Viéville, T. and Faugeras, O. (1996). The first order expansion of motion equations in the uncalibrated case. *CVGIP: Image Understanding*, 64(1):128–146.

Viéville, T., Faugeras, O. D., and Luong, Q.-T. (1996a). Motion of points and lines in the uncalibrated case. *The International Journal of Computer Vision*, 17(1):7–42.

Viéville, T. and Lingrand, D. (1999). Using specific displacements to analyze motion without calibration. *The International Journal of Computer Vision*, 31(1):5–29.

Viéville, T. and Luong, Q.-T. (1993). Motion of points and lines in the uncalibrated case. Technical Report RR 2054, INRIA.

Viéville, T., Zeller, C., and Robert, L. (1996b). Using collineations to compute motion and structure in an uncalibrated image sequence. *The International Journal of Computer Vision*, 20(3):213–242.

Vredeman de Vries, H. (1604). *Perspective*. Den Hag and Leiden.

Wampler, C., Morgan, A., and Sommese, A. (1988). Numerical continuation methods for solving polynomial systems arising in kinematics. Technical Report GMR-6372, General Motors Research Labs.

Weber, J. and Malik, J. (1997). Rigid-body segmentation and shape-description from dense optical-flow under weak perspective. *IEEE Transactions on Pattern Analysis and Machine Intelligence*, 19(2):139–143.

Wei, G. and Ma, S. (1991). Two plane camera calibration: A unified model. In *Proceedings of the International Conference on Computer Vision and Pattern Recognition*, pages 133–138, Hawaii.

Wei, G. and Ma, S. (1993). A complete two-plane camera calibration method and experimental comparisons. In *Proc. Fourth International Conference on Computer Vision*, pages 439–446, Berlin.

Weinshall, D., Anandan, P., and Irani, M. (1998). From ordinal to euclidean reconstruction with partial scene calibration. In *SMILE98, 3D Structure from Multiple Images of Large-Scale Environments*, pages 208–223. Springer, LNCS.

Weinshall, D. and Tomasi, C. (1995). Linear and incremental acquisition of invariant shape models from images sequences. *IEEE Transactions on Pattern Analysis and Machine Intelligence*, 17(5):512–517.

Weinshall, D., Werman, M., and Shashua, A. (1996). Duality of multi-point and multi-frame geometry: Fundamental shape matrices and tensors. In Buxton, B., editor, *Proceedings of the 4th European Conference on Computer Vision*, pages II:217–227, Cambridge, UK.

Weng, J., Ahuja, N., and Huang, T. (1993). Optimal motion and structure estimation. *IEEE Transactions on Pattern Analysis and Machine Intelligence*, 15(9):864–884.

Weng, J., Cohen, P., and Rebibo, N. (1992a). Motion and structure estimation from stereo image sequences. *IEEE Transactions on Robotics and Automation*, 8(3):362–382.

Weng, J., Huang, T., and Ahuja, N. (1989). Motion and structure from two perspective views: algorithms, error analysis and error estimation. *IEEE Transactions on Pattern Analysis and Machine Intelligence*, 11(5):451–476.

Weng, J., Huang, T., and Ahuja, N. (1992b). Motion and structure from line correspondences: Closed-form solution, uniqueness and optimization. *IEEE Transactions on Pattern Analysis and Machine Intelligence*, 14(3).

Wexler, Y. and Shashua, A. (1999). Q-warping: Direct computation of quadratic reference surfaces. In *Proceedings of the International Conference on Computer Vision and Pattern Recognition*, pages I:333–338, Fort Collins, Colorado. IEEE Computer Society.

Wiles, C. and Brady, M. (1996a). Ground plane motion camera models. In Buxton, B., editor, *Proceedings of the 4th European Conference on Computer Vision*, pages II:238–247, Cambridge, UK.

Wiles, C. and Brady, M. (1996b). On the appropriatness of camera models. In Buxton, B., editor, *Proceedings of the 4th European Conference on Computer Vision*, pages II:228–237, Cambridge, UK.

Willson, R. and Shafer, S. (1993). What is the center of the image? In *Proceedings of the International Conference on Computer Vision and Pattern Recognition*, pages 670–671, New-York, NY. IEEE Computer Society, IEEE.

Willson, R. G. (1994). *Modeling and Calibration of Automated Zoom Lenses*. PhD thesis, Department of Electrical and Computer Engineering, Carnegie Mellon University. CMU-RI-TR-94-03.

Wunderlich, W. (1941). Zur Eindeutigkeitsfrage der hauptaufgabe der Photogrammetrie. *Monatshefte für Mathematik und Physik*, 50:151–164.

Xu, G. and Sugimoto, N. (1999). Linear algorithm for motion from three weak perspective images using euler angles. *IEEE Transactions on Pattern Analysis and Machine Intelligence*, 21(1):54–57.

Xu, G. and Tsuji, S. (1996). Correspondence and segmentation of multiple rigid motions via epipolar geometry. In *Proceedings of the International Conference on Pattern Recognition*, pages A:213–217, Vienna, Austria. Computer Society Press.

Xu, G. and Zhang, Z. (1996). *Epipolar Geometry in Stereo, Motion and Object Recognition*. Kluwer Academic Publishers.

Yachida, M., Kitamura, Y., and Kimachi, M. (1986). Trinocular vision: New approach for correspondence problem. In *International Conference on Pattern Recognition*, pages 1041–1044. IEEE. Paris, France.

Yakimovsky, Y. and Cunningham, R. (1978). A system for extracting three-dimensional measurements from a stereo pair of tv cameras. *Computer Graphics and Image Processing*, 7:323–344.

Zeller, C. (1996). *Calibration Projective Affine et Euclidienne en Vision par Ordinateur*. PhD thesis, École Polytechnique.

Zeller, C. and Faugeras, O. (1996). Camera self-calibration from video sequences: the Kruppa equations revisited. Research Report 2793, INRIA.

Zelnik-Manor, L. and Irani, M. (1999a). Multi-frame alignment of planes. In *Proceedings of the International Conference on Computer Vision and Pattern Recognition*, pages I:151–156, Fort Collins, Colorado. IEEE Computer Society.

Zelnik-Manor, L. and Irani, M. (1999b). Multi-view subspace constraints on homographies. In *Proceedings of the 7th International Conference on Computer Vision*, pages 710–715, Kerkyra, Greece. IEEE Computer Society, IEEE Computer Society Press.

Zhang, Z. (1995). Estimating motion and structure from correspondences of line segments between two perspective images. In *Proceedings of the 5th International Conference on Computer Vision*, pages 257–262, Boston, MA. IEEE Computer Society Press.

Zhang, Z. (1996). On the epipolar geometry between two images with lens distortion. In *International Conference on Pattern Recognition*, volume I, pages 407–411, Vienna, Austria.

Zhang, Z. (1998a). Determining the epipolar geometry and its uncertainty: a review. *The International Journal of Computer Vision*, 27(2):161–195.

Zhang, Z. (1998b). Understanding the relationship between the optimization criteria in two-view motion analysis. In The Institute of Electrical ans Electronics Engineers, I., editor, *International Conference on Computer Vision*, pages 772–777, Bombay, India. IEEE Computer Society, Narosa Publishing HOUSE.

Zhang, Z. (1999). Flexible camera calibration by viewing a plane from unknown orientations. In *Proceedings of the 7th International Conference on Computer Vision*, pages 666–673, Kerkyra, Greece. IEEE Computer Society, IEEE Computer Society Press.

Zhang, Z., Anandan, P., and Shum, H.-Y. (1999). What can be determined from a full and a weak perspective image? In *Proceedings of the 7th International Conference on Computer Vision*, pages 680–687, Kerkyra, Greece. IEEE Computer Society, IEEE Computer Society Press.

Zhang, Z., Deriche, R., Faugeras, O., and Luong, Q.-T. (1995). A robust technique for matching two uncalibrated images through the recovery of the unknown epipolar geometry. *Artificial Intelligence Journal*, 78:87–119.

Zhang, Z., Faugeras, O., and Deriche, R. (1997). An effective technique for calibrating a binocular stereo through projective reconstruction using both a calibration object and the environment. *Journal of Computer Vision Research - VIDERE*, 1(1).

Zhang, Z., Isono, K., and Akamatsu, S. (1998). Euclidean structure from uncalibrated images using fuzzy domain knowledge: Application to facial images synthesis. In *Proceedings of the 6th International Conference on Computer Vision*, pages 784–789, Bombay, India. IEEE Computer Society, IEEE Computer Society Press.

Zhang, Z., Luong, Q.-T., and Faugeras, O. (1996). Motion of an uncalibrated stereo rig: self-calibration and metric reconstruction. *IEEE Transactions on Robotics and Automation*, 12(1):103–113.

Zhang, Z. and Schenk, V. (1997). Self-maintaining camera calibration over time. In *Proceedings of the International Conference on Computer Vision and Pattern Recognition*, pages 231–236, San Juan, Puerto Rico. IEEE Computer Society, IEEE.

Zhang, Z. and Xu, G. (1998). Unified theory of uncalibrated stereo for both perspective and affine cameras. *JMIV*, 9(3):213–229.

Zhuang, X., Wang, T., and Zhang, P. (1992). A highly robust estimator through partially likelihood function modeling and its application in computer vision. *IEEE Transactions on Pattern Analysis and Machine Intelligence*, 14(1):19–34.

Zisserman, A., Beardsley, P. A., and Reid, I. D. (1995a). Metric calibration of a stereo rig. In *Proc. Workshop on Visual Scene Representation*, Boston, MA.

Zisserman, A., Forsyth, D., Mundy, J., Rothwell, C., Liu, J., and Pillow, N. (1995b). 3D object recognition using invariance. *Artificial Intelligence Journal*, 78:239–288.

Zisserman, A., Liebowitz, D., and Armstrong, M. (1998). Resolving ambiguities in auto-calibration. *Philosophical Transactions of the Royal Society of London, SERIES A*, 356(1740):1193–1211.

Zoglami, I., Faugeras, O., and Deriche, R. (1997). Using geometric corners to build a 2d mosaic from a set of images. In *Proceedings of the International Conference on Computer Vision and Pattern Recognition*, pages 420–425, San Juan, Puerto Rico. IEEE Computer Society, IEEE.

Index

self-calibration, 31, 56, 57, 60, 65, 310,
            313, 380, 467, 531, 537, 540–
            591
        degeneracies, 582–588
similarity, *see* vector or affine similar-
            ity
similarity invariant, *see* Euclidean in-
            variant
Singular Value Decomposition, 213, 284,
            372, 517, 546, 555, 574, 589
skew, 14, 41, 55, **210**, 211, 215, 216,
            228, 229, 238, 398, 544, 547,
            563, 571, 590
special matrix, 30, 33, 38, **276**, 278,
            362, 403, 404, 507, 510, 527
standard deviation, 331, 334, 477
        robust, 332
stereo, xv, 20, 106, 260, 267, 335, 336,
            346, 348, 352, 372, 376, 377,
            379, 465
        rig, 30, 270, 289, 312, 337, 361,
            376, 391, 393, 503, 529–535,
            537
SVD, *see* Singular Value Decomposi-
            tion

transfer, 35, 44, 48, 50, 59, 413–415,
            439, 440, 460, 463–467
transposition, 103, 129
Trifocal
        axes constraint, 442, **444**
        constraint, 45, 47, 50, 482, 485,
            486, 488, 491, 492, 494, 496,
            505
        epipolar constraint, **442**, 446, 450,
            493
        extended rank constraint, **445**, 446,
            450, 489
        horizontal constraint, **444**
        line, **416**, 418, 424, 439, 507
        matrix, 49, **420**, 429, 431, 435,
            446, 448, 454, 459, 462, 472,
            490, 492, 510

plane, 44, 45, 379, **413**, 422, 439
rank constraint, **442**, 446, 450,
            451
tensor, xxiv, 45, 51, 419–425, 441,
            446, 471, 496, 510
        Euclidean, 411, 454–459, 467
        parametrization, 483–491
vertical constraint, **442**, 446, 450
trilinearity, 44, 466, 475
Tukey function, 331, 337

umbilic, 117, 119

vanishing
        line, 38, 175, **202**, 206, 291, 292,
            310
        point, 5, 10, 13, 19, 20, 175, **202**,
            205, 222, 288, 377, 388, 389,
            391, 397, 399
variance, 327, 564
vector
        basis
            canonical, xx, 87, 95, 131, 158,
                159, 162, 164, 168, 187, 191,
                200, 442
            dual, 159, 162, 181
            orthonormal, 74
        norm, 74
        similarity, 75, 77
        space, xix, 130, 132, 134, 139, 143,
            146, 168
            complex, 76
            dual, 146, 147, 150
            Euclidean, 74

weak calibration, **261**, 285, 310
weak perspective, 220, 222, 224, 229,
            468, 536

zoom, 2, 56, 222, 233, 548, 576